National Party Platforms

This compilation is based on Kirk H. Porter's **National Party Platforms,** first published in 1924.

Revised Edition

National Party Platforms

Volume I 1840-1956

Compiled by Donald Bruce Johnson

UNIVERSITY OF ILLINOIS PRESS Urbana Chicago London

Library of Congress Cataloging in Publication Data

Johnson, Donald Bruce, 1921-   comp.
  National party platforms.

  Edition for 1973 by D. B. Johnson and K. H. Porter
published under title: National party platforms, 1840-1972.
  Includes indexes.
  CONTENTS: v. 1. 1840-1956.—v. 2. 1960-1976.
  1. Political parties—United States—History.
I. Porter, Kirk Harold, 1891-   II. Title.
JK2255.J64 1978   329′.0213′0973   78-17373
ISBN 0-252-00692-5 (set)
ISBN 0-252-00687-9 (vol. 1)
ISBN 0-252-00688-7 (vol. 2)

Preface

One can never be certain that he or she has collected all of the national party platforms. There are two very good reasons for this: it has not always been possible to determine exactly what a political party is, and at times it has been difficult to identify what constitutes the platform of an organization claiming to be a national party. Individuals form groups which they call national parties though they offer candidates in only one or two states and then go out of existence after the election. Other minor parties persist year after year with very small organizations and few supporters at the polls. Thus, the criteria for determining which parties or organizations shall have their platforms included in what might purport to be a complete collection must, of necessity, be somewhat arbitrary. We have taken some account of the size of the group which professed to be a national party, the relative permanence of the organization, and its historical significance. We have included the platforms of those parties which have seemed to be of consequence by these standards.

Occasionally, as in the period before 1860, in 1912, and again in 1948, a segment of a major party has withdrawn from a party convention, assembled in a convention of its own, nominated candidates, and adopted a platform. For cases in which these defections have proved to be of real importance, the platforms have been included. Historically, such factional parties have in some years had a substantial influence upon party development and in other years had virtually no effect at all. Similarly, ideological or primarily single-issue parties have had varying impacts on American political history.

This collection does not pretend to be a history of political parties, and it does not contain the platform of every group that has chosen to call itself a political party. Nevertheless, we have assembled here authenticated copies of all the platforms of the major parties and of those of the principal minor parties.

In the statements of the parties in the nineteenth century, it was often difficult to know what comprised the actual platform, and decisions had to be made concerning the inclusion or exclusion of resolutions added after conventions had adjourned, resolutions thanking committee members, and other statements of appreciation. For example, Thomas V. Cooper and Hector T. Fenton, in a huge history entitled *American Politics (Non-Partisan) from the Beginning to Date* (1882), included, in a chapter titled "Political Platforms," the Virginia Resolutions of 1789, several other state resolutions, Washington's Farewell Address, the Republican platform adopted in a congressional caucus in 1800, the Clintonian platform of 1812, and the resolutions passed by the Hartford convention in 1815. In addition, although the Democratic convention was held in Baltimore on May 21, 1832, they also identified the following "National Democratic Platform" adopted at Washington City, May 11, 1832, as well as the "Locofoco Platform" of 1836:

1832.—National Democratic Platform,
adopted at a ratification Meeting
at Washington City; May 11.

Resolved, That an adequate protection to American industry is indispensable to the prosperity of the country; and that an abandonment of the policy at this period would be attended with consequences ruinous to the best interests of the nation.

Resolved, That a uniform system of internal improvements, sustained and supported by the general government, is calculated to secure, in the highest degree, the harmony, the strength and permanency of the republic.

Resolved, That the indiscriminate removal of public officers for a mere difference of political opinion, is a gross abuse of power; and that the doctrine lately boldly preached in the United States Senate, that "to the victors belong the spoils of the vanquished," is detrimental to the interests, corrupting to the morals, and dangerous to the liberties of the country.

1836.—"Locofoco" Platform,
New York, January.

We hold these truths to be self-evident, that all men are created free and equal; that they are endowed by their Creator with certain inalienable rights, among which are life, liberty, and the pursuit of happiness; that the true foundation of republican government is the equal rights of every citizen in his person and property, and in their management; that the idea is quite unfounded that on entering into society we give up any natural right; that the rightful power of all legislation is to declare and enforce only our nat-

ural rights and duties, and to take none of them from us; that no man has the natural right to commit aggressions on the equal rights of another, and this is all from which the law ought to restrain him; that every man is under the natural duty of contributing to the necessities of society, and this is all the law should enforce on him; that when the laws have declared and enforced all this, they have fulfilled their functions.

We declare unqualified hostility to bank notes and paper money as a circulating medium, because gold and silver is the only safe and constitutional currency; hostility to any and all monopolies by legislation, because they are violations of equal rights of the people; hostility to the dangerous and unconstitutional creation of vested rights or prerogatives by legislation, because they are usurpations of the people's sovereign rights; no legislative or other authority in the body politic can rightfully, by charter or otherwise, exempt any man or body of men, in any case whatever, from trial by jury and the jurisdiction or operation of the laws which govern the community.

We hold that each and every law or act of incorporation, passed by preceding legislatures, can be rightfully altered and repealed by their successors; and that they should be altered or repealed, when necessary for the public good, or when required by a majority of the people.

The Locofocos, some of whom identified themselves as members of the "Equal Rights Party," were radical Democrats active in New York from 1835 to 1837. Although they reunited with the regular Democrats during the administration of President Martin Van Buren (1836–1840) the name Locos was used by Whigs and Republicans to identify opponents as late as the campaign of 1860.

Earlier in that same period, the *Proceedings of the United States Anti-Masonic Convention,* published in Boston after the party convention was held in Philadelphia on September 11, 1830, contained (on page 84) eight paragraphs representing "resolutions expressive of the sentiments of this Convention on the subject of freemasonry." They are as follows:

RESOLUTIONS.

Resolved, That in the judgment of this Convention, the revelations which have been made and published of the secret obligations, rites, and ceremonies of the society of freemasons, are true.

Resolved, That in the opinion of this Convention, founded upon the most thorough investigation, not only of historical facts, but also of masonic tradition, the institution of freemasonry originated in the city of

London, in the early part of the last century.

Resolved, That the oaths of freemasonry are neither legally, morally, nor religiously obligatory.

Resolved, That in the judgment of this Convention, an actual adherence by freemasons to the principles contained in the obligations of the order, is inconsistent with the higher and paramount duties which they owe to the state, and is a disqualification for offices of public trust.

Resolved, That the organization and principles of the society of freemasons, are inconsistent with the genius of our republican institutions.

Resolved, That it is the right and duty of the people, to abate the evils of freemasonry, in the same manner as under our free institutions all other great moral and political evils are abated; by the exercise of the right of suffrage.

Resolved, That the political character of freemasonry is established in the clearest manner, by the direct testimony of numerous freemasons of the highest respectability, who have seceded from the institution, and by their publication of a masonic appeal, made to the fraternity of Massachusetts by the grand master of the grand lodge of that state, in favour of a candidate for governor of that state who was a freemason, in preference to the opposing candidate, who was not a freemason; and that such political character is in entire accordance with the letter and spirit of several of the degrees of the order.

Resolved, That the whole history of freemasonry, and that of the United States for the last thirty-five years, and more especially for the last four years, demonstrate that the institution of freemasonry has rendered the press in the United States, subservient to its will; that it is a plain principle of politics, that no society of men ought to exist among us, which can directly or indirectly, abridge the freedom of the press; and that when such abridgment does take place, there is no remedy for the evil, but the appeal to the people, in the exercise of the elective franchise.

Another significant example of such resolutions was a document drawn up by a national gathering of young men in Washington, D.C., on May 11, 1832. Both Thomas Hudson McKee, in his volume *The National Conventions and Platforms of All Political Parties*, published in 1906, and Edward Stanwood, in his *History of the Presidency*, published in 1898, identify these resolutions as the first *platform* ever issued by a national convention. Actually, the assembly of young men was a meeting called in response to a recommendation made at the National Republican Convention that nominated Henry Clay for president and was held in Baltimore on December 12, 1831. The resolutions,

of some historical interest, were published as follows:

1. *Resolved,* That, in the opinion of this convention, although the fundamental principles adopted by our fathers, as a basis upon which to raise a superstructure of American independence, can never be annihilated, yet the time has come when nothing short of the united energies of all the friends of the American republic can be relied on to sustain and perpetuate that hallowed work.

2. *Resolved,* That an adequate protection to American industry is indispensable to the prosperity of the country; and that an abandonment of the policy at this period would be attended with consequences ruinous to the best interests of the nation.

3. *Resolved,* That a uniform system of internal improvements, sustained and supported by the general government, is calculated to secure, in the highest degree, the harmony, the strength, and the permanency of the republic.

4. *Resolved,* That the Supreme Court of the United States is the only tribunal recognized by the Constitution for deciding in the last resort all questions arising under the Constitution and laws of the United States, and that upon the preservation of the authority and jurisdiction of that court inviolate depends the existence of the nation.

5. *Resolved,* That the Senate of the United States is pre-eminently a conservative branch of the federal government; that upon a fearless and independent exercise of its constitutional functions depends the existence of the nicely balanced powers of that government; and that all attempts to overawe its deliberations by the public press or by the national executive deserve the indignant reprobation of every American citizen.

6. *Resolved,* That the political course of the present executive has given us no pledge that he will defend and support these great principles of American policy and the Constitution; but, on the contrary, has convinced us that he will abandon them whenever the purposes of party require it.

7. *Resolved,* That the indiscriminate removal of public officers, for the mere difference of political opinion, is a gross abuse of power; and that the doctrine lately "boldly preached" in the Senate of the United States, that "to the victor belong the spoils of the enemy," is detrimental to the interests, corrupting to the morals, and dangerous to the liberties of this country.

8. *Resolved,* That we hold the disposition shown by the present national administration to accept the advice of the King of Holland, touching the northeastern boundary of the United States, and thus to transfer a portion of the territory and citizens of a state of this

Union to a foreign power, to manifest a total destitution of patriotic American feeling, inasmuch as we consider the life, liberty, property, and citizenship of every inhabitant of every state as entitled to the national protection.

9. *Resolved*, That the arrangement between the United States and Great Britain relative to the colonial trade, made in pursuance of the instructions of the late Secretary of State, was procured in a manner derogatory to the national character, and is injurious to this country in its practical results.

10. *Resolved*, That it is the duty of every citizen of this republic, who regards the honor, the prosperity, and the preservation of our Union, to oppose by every honorable measure the re-election of Andrew Jackson, and to promote the election of Henry Clay, of Kentucky, and John Sergeant, of Pennsylvania, as President and Vice-President of the United States.

An extensive search for additional platforms has been unrewarding. Members of the Government and General Research Division of the Library of Congress and I have been unable to discover the existence of any heretofore unreported platforms of the Whigs in 1836 or 1840. In their *History of American Presidential Elections, 1789–1968*, Arthur M. Schlesinger, Jr., and Fred L. Israel include a twenty-three page "Statement by the Democratic Republicans of the United States, Washington, July 31, 1835," but they also note that the Democratic Republicans did not issue a formal platform in 1836.

Therefore, under the circumstances, it is fair to assert that platform-making in national representative conventions did not begin until 1840. The Democratic Party platform published that year is presented in this volume as the first national party platform.

The problem of authenticating more recent platforms was not as great, and the material included in these documents contains few belated resolutions or dubious apparent revisions.

The sources from which these platforms have been obtained have varied. Political party platforms are not government documents, and no public official is responsible for collecting or preserving them. Indeed, in many of the minor parties party officers themselves have assumed no responsibility for preserving official copies of the platforms. Occasionally, they cannot be had even from party headquarters, if in fact headquarters still exist. In the case of the major parties, official proceedings of the conventions have been pub-

lished and used in some years; more recently, the platforms have been published in the *Congressional Record*. However, even these may have been surreptitiously edited in minor ways. For the less prominent parties, the platforms have been obtained through correspondence with party leaders during the campaigns and from campaign literature issued by party headquarters. It should be noted that sometimes there is variation in copies of a platform obtained from the same party headquarters. Platforms in some instances obviously have been altered, edited, or corrected before being published in party literature or pamphlets, and official records may be literally nonexistent. In the platforms presented here, no revisions whatever have been attempted. We have followed literally the punctuation and capitalization found in the official proceedings, or, in the case of minor parties, in the campaign literature. No endeavor has been made to edit, correct, or reparagraph the material in this volume, and the platforms are unabridged. Where headings appear to have been part of the official proceedings, they have been retained; where they seem to have been inserted by those who prepared the literature, they usually have been omitted. The use of newspapers, almanacs, and contemporaneous secondary sources has been avoided as much as possible to preserve the authenticity of original sources, but in a few instances such media have seemed to be the most reliable.

Perhaps a word should be said about the significance of American party platforms. It has been asserted that the platforms of our major parties are unnecessarily long, repetitious, evasive, equivocal, and couched in phrases that mean many things to various publics. They are often silent on matters of vital concern to the nation, not binding on the candidates, and forgotten by the party leaders. It has been charged that there is little significant difference between the platforms of the Republican and Democratic parties, and that the resolutions included are mere "catch-alls" to obtain the widest possible support. From time to time, certain presidential candidates have repudiated specific planks in the party platforms, and nearly all candidates have been forced to ignore some portions of the platforms which were made before the nominees were chosen.

All of these statements have been true at one time or another in our history. In some years, portions of the platforms have been meaningless tirades designed to create temporary enthusiasm among already partisan delegates at the national conventions. In reality, party platforms are much more than this, and anyone who has observed meetings of the resolutions committee at a national nominating convention can attest that many individuals representing diverse ideas and interests become greatly concerned indeed over what does or does not go into a party platform. Platforms are drafted very carefully and months of work often go into their preparation. If this is true, then what functions does the party platform fulfill on the American political scene in any particular year?

In the first place, unsatisfactory as they may be, party platforms are the principal official statements of party principles and policies. To be sure, there are other important statements, but the platforms are evidence of what those party leaders who draft the declarations believe to be the important issues of the year. Furthermore, the platforms, in a sense, pay homage to those who have been able to incorporate their ideas into certain planks. In this way, platforms often reflect political trends. Developments of new economic, social, and political movements may be observed, particularly when declarations contained in previous minor party platforms are adopted by the major parties after sufficient public opinion has been generated to support the change. Second, platforms invariably cite weaknesses in the program of the opposition parties and thus foreshadow issues that become significant in the campaigns or on the social or economic scene during a particular era.

Platforms also serve as a criterion by which to judge party success or failure during an administration, and they provide the voters with information with which to evaluate the organization. This function points to the fact that there is usually a distinction between the platform of the party in power and the platforms of other parties attempting to gain control of the government. The platform of the president's party invariably illustrates the desires, achievements, and thoughts of the chief executive in office. Recent presidents have demanded that platform drafts be cleared with them before submission to the conventions. The planks reflect the interests important to the administration and the ambitions of the incumbent.

On the other hand, the platforms of the major "out" party, or parties, are usually formulated as a result of a more turbulent struggle of interest groups, and the product may be a greater conglomeration of invective and promise. All parties utilize the platforms as propaganda by which to attract attention to party activities. Moreover, this function is emphasized for the major parties by the testimony of those group representatives appearing before resolutions committees and by the relative effects of such testimony that are reflected in the planks of the final document.

Most important, the platforms usually assert certain party principles and objectives that, stated generally, serve as a catalyst for the factions within the party and the voters represented by these factions. This is the overriding purpose of the platforms which has been implicit in all of these criticisms and explanations. The platforms are instruments of parties attempting to gain control of the government. They become part of the election strategy. In a democracy, where majority votes are necessary to achieve this control, a degree of consensus is demanded. The platforms represent an endeavor to unite the party and amalgamate as many interest groups as possible to obtain a workable consensus. Given the confederate nature of our parties and the economic, social, sectional, racial, and other interests abroad in the nation, the platforms represent an accommodation of these interests in any one election year and an illustration of the emphasis these forces place upon particular issues. Of necessity, some platform pronouncements must be vague to encompass the party regulars and to attract new adherents. They must be designed to offend as few people as possible, but at the same time they are significant reflections of interest group strengths within the party organization. The very equivocations used are meaningful because they emphasize the issues on which the party factions must hedge to maintain or obtain support. In short, platforms are one indication of the predominant forces in operation during any election year and a statement of the issues which individuals representing these forces believe to have the greatest popular appeal. In this sense, they are one barometer of opinion in American political history.

Finally, recent research has revealed that very significant numbers of party pledges have achieved reality in legislation and public administration and that promises made frequently *are* carried out. This is particularly true when both major parties advocate a policy or when platforms have been explicit on important issues. (See Paul T. David, "Party Platforms as National Plans," *Public Administration Review*, XXXI, May/June, 1971, 305–15, and Gerald M. Pomper, *Elections in America*, New York: Dodd, Mead, 1968, chs. 7 and 8, and other sources cited by these authors.) In a way, this is a refutation of those who cite the most conspicuous examples of candidates and party leaders who have ignored platform declarations, and it lends credence to the belief that those who possess the power to forge winning combinations do endeavor to carry out the platforms that were formulated by the same coalescing process.

I should like to thank the many party officials and other persons who have cooperated in the compilation, typing, and correspondence involved in the assembly of this volume. The popular election returns and the electoral college votes have been obtained from *A History of the Presidency*, by Edward Stanwood (Boston: Houghton Mifflin Co., 1898) and *Presidential Elections since 1789*, published by Congressional Quarterly, Inc., (Washington, D.C.: 1975). CQ acquired most of its returns from the Historical Archive of the Inter-University Consortium for Political Research at the University of Michigan.

D.B.J.
Department of Political Science
University of Iowa

Kirk H. Porter, who assembled the first book of National Party Platforms, 1840–1924 (New York: Macmillan, 1924), which is included in this volume, died in May of 1972. His lifelong interest in political parties and politics made this collection possible. We are all indebted to him for his political research.

Contents

CAMPAIGN OF 1840

The presidential campaign of 1840, famous for its "log cabin" and "hard cider" slogans, was conducted by General William Henry Harrison of Ohio for the Whig Party and the incumbent, Martin Van Buren, running on the Democratic Party ticket. John Tyler was the Whig's vice-presidential candidate, but the Democratic convention adopted a resolution which allowed the state electors to vote as they pleased for vice-president, "trusting that, before the election shall take place, their opinions shall become so concentrated as to secure the choice of a Vice-President by the electoral colleges." The electors split their ballots among Richard Johnson, Littleton Tazewell, and James K. Polk.

The Liberty Party ran James Gillespie Birney of New York for president and Thomas Earle of Pennsylvania for vice-president.

In the November election, Harrison polled 1,275,016 popular votes to 1,129,102 for Van Buren and 7,069 for Birney. The Whig ticket received 234 electoral votes to 60 for the Democrats.

No platform was adopted by the Whigs, but the Democrats, on the second day of their convention, adopted the principles presented here.

Democratic Platform of 1840

1. *Resolved,* That the federal government is one of limited powers, derived solely from the constitution, and the grants of power shown therein, ought to be strictly construed by all the departments and agents of the government, and that it is inexpedient and dangerous to exercise doubtful constitutional powers.

2. *Resolved,* That the constitution does not confer upon the general government the power to commence and carry on, a general system of internal improvements.

3. *Resolved,* That the constitution does not confer authority upon the federal government, directly or indirectly, to assume the debts of the several states, contracted for local internal improvements, or other state purposes; nor would such assumption be just or expedient.

4. *Resolved,* That justice and sound policy forbid the federal government to foster one branch of industry to the detriment of another, or to cherish the interests of one portion to the injury of another portion of our common country —that every citizen and every section of the country, has a right to demand and insist upon an equality of rights and privileges, and to complete and ample protection of person and property from domestic violence, or foreign aggression.

5. *Resolved,* That it is the duty of every branch of the government, to enforce and practice the most rigid economy, in conducting our public affairs, and that no more revenue ought to be raised, than is required to defray the necessary expenses of the government.

6. *Resolved,* That congress has no power to charter a national bank; that we believe such an institution one of deadly hostility to the best interests of the country, dangerous to our republican institutions and the liberties of the people, and calculated to place the business of the country within the control of a concentrated money power, and above the laws and the will of the people.

7. *Resolved,* That congress has no power, under the constitution, to interfere with or control the domestic institutions of the several states, and that such states are the sole and proper judges of everything appertaining to their own affairs, not prohibited by the constitution; that all efforts by abolitionists or others, made to induce congress to interfere with questions of slavery, or to take incipient steps in relation thereto, are calculated to lead to the most alarming and dangerous consequences, and that all such efforts have an inevitable tendency to diminish the happiness of the people, and endanger the stability and permanency of the union, and ought not to be countenanced by any friend to our political institutions.

8. *Resolved,* That the separation of the moneys of the government from banking institutions, is indispensable for the safety of the funds of the government, and the rights of the people.

9. *Resolved,* That the liberal principles em-

bodied by Jefferson in the Declaration of Independence, and sanctioned in the constitution, which makes ours the land of liberty, and the asylum of the oppressed of every nation, have ever been cardinal principles in the democratic faith; and every attempt to abridge the present privilege of becoming citizens, and the owners of soil among us, ought to be resisted with the same spirit which swept the alien and sedition laws from our statute-book.

CAMPAIGN OF 1844

In May of 1844, acting under the "two-thirds" rule, a seriously divided Democratic Party nominated, on the ninth ballot, the first "dark horse," James K. Polk of Tennessee. He was selected in preference to Martin Van Buren and Lewis Cass of Michigan. Silas Wright, a senator from New York, was nominated for vice-president, but he declined the nomination after it had been made. George M. Dallas of Pennsylvania was subsequently chosen as Polk's running mate.

The united Whig Party enthusiastically and unanimously nominated Henry Clay for president on the first ballot. He ran with Theodore Frelinghuysen of New Jersey.

President Tyler, ignored by the delegates to both the Whig and the Democratic conventions, was nominated by a mass convention in Baltimore on the same day that the Democrats held their gathering. The movement for him did not attract public support, and Tyler withdrew his candidacy in August.

The Abolitionists, who wanted a separate party, met in Buffalo in August, 1843, and established the Liberty Party under the leadership of James Gillespie Birney of New York, their presidential candidate, and Thomas Morris of Ohio, the vice-presidential candidate. The party platform was more than three thousand words—the longest platform written by any party in the nineteenth century.

In the November election, Polk received 1,339,494 popular votes to Clay's 1,300,004. Birney attracted 62,103 votes. Polk won the electoral votes 170 to 105 in the twenty-six states voting.

Democratic Platform of 1844

1. *Resolved*, That the American Democracy place their trust, not in factitious symbols, not in displays and appeals insulting to the judgment and subversive of the intellect of the people, but in a clear reliance upon the intelligence, patriotism, and the discriminating justice of the American masses.

Resolved, That we regard this as a distinctive feature of our political creed, which we are proud to maintain before the world, as the great moral element in a form of government springing from and upheld by the popular will; and we contrast it with the creed and practice of Federalism, under whatever name or form, which seeks to palsy the will of the constituent, and which conceives no imposture too monstrous for the popular credulity.

Resolved, therefore, That, entertaining these views, the Democratic party of this Union, through their delegates assembled in general convention of the States, coming together in a spirit of concord, of devotion to the doctrines and faith of a free representative government, and appealing to their fellow-citizens for the rectitude of their intentions, renew and reassert before the American people the declaration of principles avowed by them on a former occasion, when, in general convention, they presented their candidates for the popular suffrages.

1. That the Federal Government is one of limited powers, derived solely from the Constitution, and the grants of power shown therein ought to be strictly construed by all the departments and agents of the government, and that it is inexpedient and dangerous to exercise doubtful constitutional powers.

2. That the Constitution does not confer upon the General Government the power to commence or carry on a general system of internal improvements.

3. That the Constitution does not confer authority upon the Federal Government, directly or indirectly, to assume the debts of the several States, contracted for local internal improvements or other State purposes; nor would such assumption be just or expedient.

4. That justice and sound policy forbid the Federal Government to foster one branch of industry to the detriment of another, or to cherish the interests of one portion to the injury of another portion of our common country—that every citizen and every section of the country has a right to demand and insist upon an equality of rights and privileges, and to complete and ample

protection of person and property from domestic violence or foreign aggression.

5. That it is the duty of every branch of the government to enforce and practice the most rigid economy in conducting our public affairs, and that no more revenue ought to be raised than is required to defray the necessary expenses of the government.

6. That Congress has no power to charter a United States Bank, that we believe such an institution one of deadly hostility to the best interests of the country, dangerous to our republican institutions and the liberties of the people, and calculated to place the business of the country within the control of a concentrated money power, and above the laws and the will of the people.

7. That Congress has no power, under the Constitution, to interfere with or control the domestic institutions of the several States; and that such States are the sole and proper judges of everything pertaining to their own affairs, not prohibited by the Constitution; that all efforts, by abolitionists or others, made to induce Congress to interfere with questions of slavery, or to take incipient steps in relation thereto, are calculated to lead to the most alarming and dangerous consequences, and that all such efforts have an inevitable tendency to diminish the happiness of the people and endanger the stability and permanency of the Union, and ought not to be countenanced by any friend to our Political Institutions.

8. That the separation of the money of the government from banking institutions is indispensable for the safety of the funds of the government and the rights of the people.

9. That the liberal principles embodied by Jefferson in the Declaration of Independence, and sanctioned in the Constitution, which makes ours the land of liberty and the asylum of the oppressed of every nation, have ever been cardinal principles in the Democratic faith; and every attempt to abridge the present privilege of becoming citizens, and the owners of soil among us, ought to be resisted with the same spirit which swept the alien and sedition laws from our statute-book.

Resolved, That the proceeds of the Public Lands ought to be sacredly applied to the national objects specified in the Constitution, and that we are opposed to the laws lately adopted, and to any law for the Distribution of such proceeds among the States, as alike inexpedient in policy and repugnant to the Constitution.

Resolved, That we are decidedly opposed to taking from the President the qualified veto power by which he is enabled, under restrictions and responsibilities amply sufficient to guard the public interest, to suspend the passage of a bill, whose merits cannot secure the approval of two-thirds of the Senate and House of Representatives, until the judgment of the people can be obtained thereon, and which has thrice saved the American People from the corrupt and tyrannical domination of the Bank of the United States.

Resolved, That our title to the whole of the Territory of Oregon is clear and unquestionable; that no portion of the same ought to be ceded to England or any other power, and that the re-occupation of Oregon and the re-annexation of Texas at the earliest practicable period are great American measures, which this Convention recommends to the cordial support of the Democracy of the Union.

Liberty Platform of 1844

PREAMBLE

Being assembled in general Convention, as the representatives of the Liberty party in the United States, and feeling it incumbent on us to set forth, clearly and fully, the principles which govern us, and the purposes which we seek to accomplish, and this, the rather because these principles and purposes have been much misunderstood, and either ignorantly or maliciously much misrepresented: be it therefore

1. *Resolved,* That human brotherhood is a cardinal doctrine of true Democracy, as well as of pure Christianity, which spurns all inconsistent limitations; and neither the political party which repudiates it, nor the political system which is not based upon it, nor controlled in its practical workings, by it, can be truly Democratic or permanent.

2. *Resolved,* That the Liberty party, placing itself upon this broad principle, will demand the absolute and unqualified divorce of the General Government from Slavery, and also the restoration of equality of rights, among men, in every State where the party exists, or may exist.

3. *Resolved,* That the Liberty party has not

been organized for any temporary purpose, by interested politicians, but has arisen from among the people, in consequence of a conviction, hourly gaining ground, that no other party in the country represents the true principles of American Liberty, or the true spirit of the Constitution of the United States.

4. *Resolved,* That the Liberty party has not been organized merely for the overthrow of Slavery. Its first decided effort must indeed be directed against slaveholding, as the grossest form and most revolting manifestation of Despotism; but it will also carry out the principles of Equal Rights, into all their practical consequences and applications, and support every just measure conducive to individual and social freedom.

5. *Resolved,* That the Liberty party is not a Sectional party, but a National party—has not originated in a desire to accomplish a single object, but in a comprehensive regard to the great interests of the whole country—is not a new party, or a third party, but is the party of 1776, reviving the principles of that memorable era, and striving to carry them into practical application.

6. *Resolved,* That it was understood in the time of the Declaration and the Constitution, that the existence of slavery in some of the States, was in derogation of the principles of American Liberty, and a deep stain upon the character of the country, and the implied faith of the States and the Nation was pledged, that slavery should never be extended beyond its then existing limits; but should be gradually, and, yet, at no distant day, wholly abolished by State authority.

7. *Resolved,* That the faith of the States, and the nation they pledged, was most nobly redeemed by the voluntary abolition of slavery in several of the States, and by the adoption of the ordinance of 1787, for the government of the Territory North West of the river Ohio, then the only Territory in the United States, and consequently the only Territory subject in this respect to the control of Congress, by which ordinance slavery was forever excluded from the vast regions which now compose the States of Ohio, Indiana, Illinois, Michigan, and the Territory of Wiskonsan, and an incapacity to bear up any other than freemen, was impressed on the soil itself.

8. *Resolved,* That the faith of the States and Nation thus pledged, has been shamefully violated by the omission, on the part of many of the States, to take any measures whatever for the abolition of slavery within their respective limits; by the continuance of slavery in the District of Columbia, and in the Territories of Louisiana and Florida; by the legislation of Congress; by the protection afforded by national legislation and negotiation to slaveholding in American vessels, on the high seas, employed in the coastwise slave traffic; and by the extension of slavery far beyond its original limits, by acts of Congress, admitting new slave States into the Union.

9. *Resolved,* That the fundamental truths of the Declaration of Independence, that all men are endowed by their Creator with certain inalienable rights, among which are life, liberty, and the pursuit of happiness, was made the fundamental law of our National Government, by that amendment of the constitution which declares that no person shall be deprived of life, liberty or property, without due process of law.

10. *Resolved,* That we recognize as sound, the doctrine maintained by slaveholding Jurists, that slavery is against natural rights, and strictly local, and that its existence and continuance rest on no other support than State legislation, and not on any Authority of Congress.

11. *Resolved,* That the General Government has, under the Constitution, no power to establish or continue slavery any where, and therefore that all treaties and acts of Congress establishing, continuing or favoring slavery in the District of Columbia, in the Territory of Florida, or on the high seas, are unconstitutional, and all attempts to hold men as property within the limits of exclusive national jurisdiction, ought to be prohibited by law.

12. *Resolved,* That the plea sometimes urged, in behalf of the constitutionality of slaveholding under the sanction of national legislation, that the continuance of slavery was secured in the District of Columbia, by stipulations in the Deeds of cession by Virginia and Maryland, and in Florida by the provisions of the Treaty with Spain is false in fact; and the other plea, sometimes urged to the same purpose, that Congress might constitutionally authorize slaveholding in the District, under the power to legislate for the same in all cases whatsoever, and in Florida under the power to make needful rules and regulations for the government of national territories, and in American vessels on the seas under the power to regulate

commerce, cannot be sound in law, so long as the great Interdict of the People against depriving *any person* of life, liberty, or property, without due process of law, remains unaltered.

13. *Resolved,* That the provision of the Constitution of the United States, which confers extraordinary political powers on the owners of slaves, and thereby constituting the two hundred and fifty thousand slaveholders in the slave States a privileged aristocracy; and the provision for the reclamation of fugitive slaves from service, are anti-republican in their character, dangerous to the liberties of the people, and ought to be abrogated.

14. *Resolved,* That the operation of the first of these provisions is seen in the growth of a power in the country, hostile to free institutions, to free labor, and to freedom itself, which is appropriately denominated the slave power; this power has maintained slavery in the original States, has secured its continuance in the District and in the Territories, has created seven new slave States, has caused disastrous fluctuations in our national policy, foreign and domestic, has gradually usurped the control of our home legislation, has waged unrelenting war against the most sacred rights of freedom, has violated and set at naught the right of petition, has dictated the action of political parties, has filled almost all the offices of the National Government with slaveholders, and the abettors of slaveholders, and threatens, if not arrested in its career, the total overthrow of popular freedom.

15. *Resolved,* That the practical operation of the second of these provisions, is seen in the enactment of the act of Congress respecting persons escaped from their masters, which act, if the construction given to it by the Supreme Court of the United States in the case of Prigg *vs.* Pennsylvania be correct, nullifies the habeas corpus acts of all the States, takes away the whole legal security of personal freedom, and ought therefore to be immediately repealed.

16. *Resolved,* That the peculiar patronage and support hitherto extended to slavery and slaveholding, by the General Government, ought to be immediately withdrawn, and the example and influence of national authority ought to be arrayed on the side of Liberty and free labor.

17. *Resolved,* That we cherish no harsh or unkind feelings towards any of our brethren of the slave States, while we express unmitigated abhorrence of that system of slaveholding which has stripped a large portion of their population of every right, and which has established an aristocracy worse than feudal in the midst of Republican States, and which denies to the poor non-slaveholder and his children the benefits of education, and crushes them in the dust, or drives them out as exiles from the land of their birth.

18. *Resolved,* That the impoverished and embarrassed condition of the slave States, so much deplored by their own statesmen, may be clearly traced to the fact that the coerced, reluctant, and ill-directed labor of slaves will not supply their own scanty subsistence, and also support their masters in the habits of wasteful extravagance which slavery generates.

19. *Resolved,* That the withering and impoverishing effect of slavery on the free States, is seen in the fact, among many others, that these States are taxed to the amount of about half a million of dollars a year, to pay the deficits of the slave States, and that the slave States have received, for years past, to the amount, as it is estimated, of more than ten millions of dollars a year, for which no payment has ever been, or ever will be made.

20. *Resolved,* That we behold with sorrow and shame, and indignation, the dishonor brought upon the name of the country by the influence of the slave power upon our National Government —corrupting its administration at home—paralyzing all generous action and utterance in behalf of right and freedom abroad, and exhibiting the American people to the world in the ridiculous and contemptible character of patrons of the slave trade.

21. *Resolved,* That we are inflexibly opposed to that policy of the General Government, which plies every art, and strains every effort of negotiation, to secure the markets of the world for the products of slave labor, while the products of free labor are to a great extent, confined to the non-paying market of the slave States; and we insist that it is the duty of the Government, in its intercourse with foreign nations, to employ all its influence, and to exert its utmost energies to extend the markets for the products of free labor, and we do not doubt that if this duty be performed in good faith, the result will be most auspicious to the general and permanent prosperity of the country.

22. *Resolved,* That we are fully persuaded that it is indispensably necessary to the salvation of the union of the States, to the preservation of the liberties of the people, and to the permanent restoration of prosperity in every department of business, that the National Government be rescued from the grasp of the slave power; that the spirit and practice of slaveholding be expelled from our National Legislature, and that the administration of the Government be conducted henceforth in conformity with the principles of the Constitution, and for the benefit of the whole population.

23. *Resolved,* That the practice of the General Government, which prevails in the slave States, of employing slaves upon the public works, instead of free laborers, and paying aristocratic masters, with a view to secure or reward political services, is utterly indefensible, and ought to be abandoned.

24. *Resolved,* That we believe intelligence, religion, and morality, to be the indispensable supports of good government, and are therefore in favor of general education; we believe, also, that good government itself is necessary to the welfare of society, and are therefore in favor of rigid public economy, and strict adherence to the principles of justice in every department of its administration.

25. *Resolved,* That freedom of speech and of the press, and the right of petition, and the right of trial by jury, are sacred and inviolable; and that all rules, regulations and laws, in derogation of either are oppressive, unconstitutional, and not to be endured by a free people.

26. *Resolved,* That we regard voting in an eminent degree, as a moral and religious duty, which when exercised, should be by voting for those who will do all in their power for immediate emancipation.

27. *Resolved,* That we can never lose our vote, although in ever so small a minority, when cast for the slave's redemption; as each vote for the slave, whether in minority or majority, is a part of that great mass of means which will work out his final deliverance.

28. *Resolved,* That the Whig and Democratic parties always throw away their votes, whether in a majority or minority, and do worse than throw them away, as long as they cast them for binding the slave with fetters, and loading him with chains, and for depriving him of himself, his wife and his children, which these parties always have

done, in bowing down to the slaveholding portions of said parties.

29. *Resolved,* That we especially entreat the friends of Liberty in the slave States to reflect on the vast importance of voting openly for Liberty, and Liberty men; and to remember and adopt the words of the illustrious Washington, who said, "There is but one proper and effectual mode by which the abolition of slavery can be accomplished, and that is by legislative authority; and this, as far as my suffrage will go, shall not be wanting."

30. *Resolved,* That we earnestly exhort the Liberty men everywhere, to organize for efficient action in their respective States, counties, cities, towns, and districts, and not to turn to the right side or to the left, until despotism shall have been driven from its last entrenchment, and thanksgivings for victory in the second great struggle for Liberty and Independence shall be heard throughout the land.

31. *Resolved,* That we most earnestly recommend that the Liberty party make efforts to secure the control of the town power, so that every officer shall be a Liberty party man; and that our friends should not fail to nominate a Liberty ticket annually in their towns, and sustain the same, never yielding to a compromise with the other parties.

32. *Resolved,* That a county and State organization of the Liberty party should be faithfully maintained; and we also recommend that our friends employ some proper person to lecture, organize, and distribute tracts in each Congressional district, in the several States, for the space of at least three months in a year.

33. *Resolved,* That the friends of Liberty in each town form tract organizations, of men and women, to distribute tracts in every family in such towns, by directing the labors of said tract distribution, so that no neighborhood or family be overlooked or unsupplied.

34. *Resolved,* That it be recommended that said tract distributors circulate petitions through the several towns, praying Congress to abolish the abominable act of Congress, of the 12th of February, 1793, so that we may be delivered from the unconstitutional obligation to become kidnappers on our own soil.

35. *Resolved,* That this Convention recommend to the friends of Liberty in all those free States where any inequality of rights and privi-

leges exists on account of color, to employ their utmost energies to remove all such remnants and effects of the slave system.

36. *Resolved,* That we cordially welcome our colored fellow citizens to fraternity with us in the *Liberty party,* in its great contest to secure the rights of mankind, and the religion of our common country.

37. *Whereas,* The Constitution of these United States is a series of agreements, covenants, or contracts between the people of the United States, each with all, and all with each; and

Whereas, It is a principle of universal morality, that the moral laws of the Creator are paramount to all human laws; or, in the language of an apostle, that "we ought to obey God, rather than men;"—and

Whereas, The principle of Common Law—that any contract, covenant, or agreement, to do an act derogatory to natural right, is vitiated and annulled by its inherent immorality—has been recognized by one of the Justices of the Supreme Court of the United States, who, in a recent case, expressly holds that *"any* contract that rests upon such a basis, is *void"*;—and

Whereas, The third clause of the second section of the fourth article of the Constitution of the United States—when construed as providing for the surrender of a fugitive slave—*does* "rest upon such a basis," in that it is a contract to rob a man of a natural right—namely, his natural right to his own liberty; and is, therefore, absolutely *void.*

Therefore, Resolved, That we hereby give it to be distinctly understood, by this nation and the world, that, as abolitionists, considering that the strength of our cause lies in its righteousness—and our hope for it in our conformity to the LAWS OF GOD, and our respect for the RIGHTS OF MAN, we owe it to the Sovereign Ruler of the Universe, as a proof of our allegiance to Him, in all our civil relations and offices, whether as private citizens, or as public functionaries sworn to support the Constitution of the United States, to regard and to treat the third clause of the second section of the fourth article of that instrument, whenever applied to the case of a fugitive slave, as utterly null and void, and consequently as forming no part of the Constitution of the United States, whenever we are called upon, or sworn, to support it.

38. *Resolved,* That the power given to Congress by the Constitution, to provide for calling out the militia to suppress insurrection, does not make it the duty of the Government to maintain slavery, by military force, much less does it make it the duty of the citizens to form a part of such military force. When freemen unsheath the sword it should be to strike for *Liberty,* not for Despotism.

39. *Resolved,* That to preserve the peace of the citizens, and secure the blessings of freedom, the Legislature of each of the free States, ought to keep in force suitable statutes rendering it penal for any of its inhabitants to transport, or aid in transporting from such State, any person sought, to be thus transported, merely because subject to the slave laws of any other States; this remnant of independence being accorded to the free States, by the decision of the Supreme Court, in the case of Prigg, *vs.* the State of Pennsylvania.

40. *Resolved,* That we recognize in Daniel O'Connell, a true Patriot of the Liberty school, and admire his consistent devotion to freedom throughout the world. We thank him and the Irish people whom he represents, for their sympathy with us in our great struggle.

41. *Resolved,* That the thanks of this Convention are hereby tendered to Professor Taylor, for his kindness in furnishing the spacious tent, belonging to the Oberlin Collegiate Institute, which has been occupied by the Convention during its sittings.

42. *Resolved,* That the doings of the Convention be published, under the direction of the Secretaries.

43. *Resolved,* That the thanks of this Convention be tendered to the authorities of the County of Erie, and of the city of Buffalo, for the use of the Court House and the Park for its sittings.

44. *Resolved,* That the thanks of this Convention be presented to the President, Vice-Presidents, and Secretaries, for their services during its session.

Whig Platform of 1844

Resolved, That, in presenting to the country the names of Henry Clay for president, and of Theodore Frelinghuysen for vice-president of the United States, this Convention is actuated by the conviction that all the great principles of the

Whig party—principles inseparable from the public honor and prosperity—will be maintained and advanced by these candidates.

Resolved, That these principles may be summed as comprising: a well-regulated currency; a tariff for revenue to defray the necessary expenses of the government, and discriminating with special reference to the protection of the domestic labor of the country; the distribution of the proceeds of the sales of the public lands; a single term for the presidency; a reform of executive usurpations; —and, generally—such an administration of the affairs of the country as shall impart to every branch of the public service the greatest practicable efficiency, controlled by a well regulated and wise economy.

Resolved, That the name of Henry Clay needs no eulogy; the history of the country since his first appearance in public life is his history; its brightest pages of prosperity and success are identified with the principles which he has upheld, as its darkest and more disastrous pages are with every material departure in our public policy from those principles.

Resolved, That in Theodore Frelinghuysen we present a man pledged alike by his revolutionary ancestry and his own public course to every measure calculated to sustain the honor and interest of the country. Inheriting the principles as well as the name of a father who, with Washington, on the fields of Trenton and of Monmouth, perilled life in the contest for liberty, and afterwards, as a senator of the United States, acted with Washington in establishing and perpetuating that liberty, Theodore Frelinghuysen, by his course as Attorney-General of the State of New Jersey for twelve years, and subsequently as a senator of the United States for several years, was always strenuous on the side of law, order, and the constitution, while as a private man, his head, his hand, and his heart have been given without stint to the cause of morals, education, philanthropy, and religion.

CAMPAIGN OF 1848

As the conventions of 1848 were being assembled, the issue of slavery threatened to split the parties. The liberal antislavery Democrats were called the "Barnburners" and the conservatives, the "Hunkers," because they merely "hunkered" for office. The Whigs were divided between the "Conscience" Whigs of the North and the "Cotton" Whigs of the South. Splinter groups from both the New York Barnburners and the Conscience Whigs, together with members of the Liberty Party of 1844, met in convention in Buffalo, New York, and formed a new third party, the Free Soilers, dedicated not only to the opposition of any extension of slavery into the territories but also to free land for settlers, "free speech, free labor, free men," and other internal policy reforms.

Actually, compromises were effected in each party and the platforms were slightly more moderate than in 1844. The Democrats' presidential nominee was Lewis Cass of Michigan, a northern senator who believed that states and territories could determine their own policies in regard to slavery. General William O. Butler of Kentucky was nominated for vice-president.

The Whigs, meeting in Philadelphia, nominated General Zachary Taylor of Virginia and Millard Fillmore of New York. The Free Soil delegates chose former President Martin Van Buren as their standard-bearer. Charles Francis Adams of Massachusetts was their candidate for vice-president.

In the election that followed, the Whigs obtained 1,361,393 votes—47.28 percent of the total. The Democrats received 1,223,460 votes—42.49 percent. Van Buren and the Free Soilers captured 291,501 votes—10.12 percent of the total. The Van Buren candidacy divided the Democratic vote and denied the election to Cass—as the abolitionists had intended. Thirty states participated in the election, and in all but two a plurality produced the winner. Taylor received 163 electoral votes to 127 for Cass.

Democratic Platform of 1848

Resolved, That the American Democracy place their trust in the intelligence, the patriotism, and the discriminating justice of the American people.

Resolved, That we regard this as a distinctive feature of our political creed, which we are proud to maintain before the world as the great moral element in a form of government springing from and upheld by the popular will; and we contrast it with the creed and practice of Federalism, under whatever name or form, which seeks to palsy the will of the constituent, and which conceives no imposture too monstrous for the popular credulity.

Resolved, therefore, That, entertaining these views, the Democratic party of this Union, through their Delegates assembled in general convention of the States, coming together in a spirit of concord, of devotion to the doctrines and faith of a free representative government, and appealing to their fellow-citizens for the rectitude of their intentions, renew and reassert before the American people the declaration of principles avowed by them when, on a former occasion, in general convention, they presented their candidates for the popular suffrage.

1. That the Federal Government is one of limited powers, derived solely from the Constitution; and the grants of power shown therein ought to be strictly construed by all the departments and agents of the Government; and that it is inexpedient and dangerous to exercise doubtful constitutional powers.

2. That the Constitution does not confer upon the General Government the power to commence and carry on a general system of internal improvements.

3. That the Constitution does not confer authority upon the Federal Government, directly or indirectly, to assume the debts of the several States, contracted for local internal improvements, or other State purposes; nor would such assumption be just and expedient.

4. That justice and sound policy forbid the Federal Government to foster one branch of industry to the detriment of another, or to cherish the interests of one portion to the injury of another

portion of our common country; that every citizen, and every section of the country, has a right to demand and insist upon an equality of rights and privileges, and to complete and ample protection of persons and property from domestic violence or foreign aggression.

5. That it is the duty of every branch of the Government to enforce and practice the most rigid economy in conducting our public affairs, and that no more revenue ought to be raised than is required to defray the necessary expenses of the Government, and for the gradual but certain extinction of the debt created by the prosecution of a just and necessary war, after peaceful relations shall have been restored.

6. That Congress has no power to charter a national bank; that we believe such an institution one of deadly hostility to the best interests of the country, dangerous to our republican institutions and the liberties of the people, and calculated to place the business of the country within the control of a concentrated money power, and above the laws and the will of the people; and that the results of Democratic legislation, in this and all other financial measures upon which issues have been made between the two political parties of the country, have demonstrated to candid and practical men of all parties, their soundness, safety, and utility in all business pursuits.

7. That Congress has no power under the Constitution to interfere with or control the domestic institutions of the several States, and that such States are the sole and proper judges of everything appertaining to their own affairs, not prohibited by the Constitution; that all efforts of the Abolitionists or others made to induce Congress to interfere with questions of slavery, or to take incipient steps in relation thereto, are calculated to lead to the most alarming and dangerous consequences; and that all such efforts have an inevitable tendency to diminish the happiness of the people, and endanger the stability and permanence of the Union, and ought not to be countenanced by any friend to our political institutions.

8. That the separation of the moneys of the Government from banking institutions is indispensable for the safety of the funds of the Government and the rights of the people.

9. That the liberal principles embodied by Jefferson in the Declaration of Independence, and sanctioned in the Constitution, which makes ours the land of liberty, and the asylum of the oppressed of every nation, have ever been cardinal principles in the Democratic faith, and every attempt to abridge the present privilege of becoming citizens and the owners of soil among us, ought to be resisted with the same spirit which swept the alien and sedition laws from our statute-book.

Resolved, That the proceeds of the public lands ought to be sacredly applied to the national object specified in the Constitution; and that we are opposed to any law for the distribution of such proceeds among the States, as alike inexpedient in policy and repugnant to the Constitution.

Resolved, That we are decidedly opposed to taking from the President the qualified veto power, by which he is enabled, under restrictions and responsibilities amply sufficient to guard the public interests, to suspend the passage of a bill whose merits cannot secure the approval of two-thirds of the Senate and House of Representatives, until the judgment of the people can be obtained thereon, and which has saved the American people from the corrupt and tyrannical domination of the Bank of the United States, and from a corrupting system of general internal improvements.

Resolved, That the war with Mexico, provoked on her part by years of insult and injury, was commenced by her army crossing the Rio Grande, attacking the American troops, and invading our sister State of Texas; and that, upon all the principles of patriotism and laws of nations, it is a just and necessary war on our part, in which every American citizen should have shown himself on the side of his country, and neither morally nor physically, by word or by deed, have given "aid and comfort to the enemy."

Resolved, That we would be rejoiced at the assurance of peace with Mexico founded on the just principles of indemnity for the past and security for the future; but that, while the ratification of the liberal treaty offered to Mexico remains in doubt, it is the duty of the country to sustain the administration in every measure necessary to provide for the vigorous prosecution of the war, should that treaty be rejected.

Resolved, That the officers and soldiers who have carried the arms of their country into Mexico, have crowned it with imperishable glory. Their unconquerable courage, their daring enterprise, their unfaltering perseverance and fortitude when assailed on all sides by innumerable foes, and that more formidable enemy, the diseases of the climate, exalt their devoted patriotism into the highest heroism, and give them a right to the profound gratitude of their country, and the admiration of the world.

Resolved, That the Democratic National Convention of the thirty States composing the American Republic, tender their fraternal congratulations to the National Convention of the Republic of France, now assembled as the free-suffrage representatives of the sovereignty of thirty-five millions of republicans, to establish government on those eternal principles of equal rights for which *their* Lafayette and *our* Washington fought side by side in the struggle for our own national independence; and we would especially convey to them, and to the whole people of France, our earnest wishes for the consolidation of their liberties, through the wisdom that shall guide their counsels, on the basis of a democratic constitution, not derived from grants or concessions of kings or parliaments, but originating from the only true source of political power recognized in the States of this Union—the inherent and inalienable right of the people, in their sovereign capacity, to make and to amend their forms of government in such manner as the welfare of the community may require.

Resolved, That in view of the recent development of the grand political truth, of the sovereignty of the people, and their capacity and power for self-government, which is prostrating thrones and erecting republics on the ruins of despotism in the Old World, we feel that a high and sacred duty is devolved, with increased responsibility, upon the Democratic party of this country, as the party of the *people,* to sustain and advance among us constitutional "liberty, equality, and fraternity," by continuing to resist all monopolies and exclusive legislation for the benefit of the few at the expense of the many, and by a vigilant and constant adherence to those principles and compromises of the Constitution which are broad enough and strong enough to embrace and uphold the Union as it was, the Union as it is, and the Union as it shall be, in the full expansion of the energies and capacity of this great and progressive people.

Voted, That a copy of these resolutions be forwarded, through the American Minister at Paris, to the National Convention of the Republic of France.

Resolved, That the fruits of the great political triumph of 1844, which elected James K. Polk and George M. Dallas President and Vice-President of the United States, have fulfilled the hopes of the Democracy of the Union—in defeating the declared purposes of their opponents to create a national bank; in preventing the corrupt and unconstitutional distribution of the land proceeds, from the common treasury of the Union, for local purposes; in protecting the currency and the labor of the country from ruinous fluctuations, and guarding the money of the people for the use of the people, by the establishment of the constitutional treasury; in the noble impulse given to the cause of free trade, by the repeal of the tariff in 1842 and the creation of the more equal, honest, and productive tariff of 1846; and that, in our opinion, it would be a fatal error to weaken the bands of political organization by which these great reforms have been achieved, and risk them in the hands of their known adversaries, with whatever delusive appeals they may solicit our surrender of that vigilance, which is the only safeguard of liberty.

Resolved, That the confidence of the Democracy of the Union in the principles, capacity, firmness, and integrity of James K. Polk, manifested by his nomination and election in 1844, has been signally justified by the strictness of his adherence to sound Democratic doctrines, by the purity of purpose, the energy and ability which have characterized his administration in all our affairs at home and abroad; that we tender to him our cordial congratulations upon the brilliant success which has hitherto crowned his patriotic efforts, and assure him, that at the expiration of his Presidential term, he will carry with him to his retirement the esteem, respect, and admiration of a grateful country.

Resolved, That this Convention hereby present to the people of the United States, Lewis Cass, of Michigan, as the candidate of the Democratic party for the office of President, and William O. Butler, of Kentucky, as the candidate of the Democratic party for the office of Vice-President of the United States.

Free Soil Platform of 1848

Whereas, We have assembled in Convention, as a union of *Freemen,* for the sake of Freedom, forgetting all past political differences in a common resolve to maintain the rights of Free Labor against the aggressions of the Slave Power, and to secure Free Soil for a Free People:

And whereas, The political Conventions recently assembled at Baltimore and Philadelphia, the one stifling the voice of a great constituency entitled to be heard in its deliberations, and the other abandoning its distinctive principles for mere availability, have dissolved the national party organizations heretofore existing, by nominating for the Chief Magistracy of the United States, under Slaveholding dictation, candidates, *neither of whom* can be supported by the opponents of Slavery-extension, without a *sacrifice of consistency, duty,* and *self-respect.*

And whereas, These nominations, so made, furnish the occasion and demonstrate the necessity of the union of the People under the banners of Free Democracy, in a solemn and formal *declaration* of their *independence* of the *Slave Power,* and of their fixed determination to rescue the Federal Government from its control:

Resolved, therefore, that we, the people here assembled, remembering the example of our *fathers* in the days of the first Declaration of Independence, putting our trust in God for the triumph of our cause, and invoking his guidance in our endeavors to advance it, do now plant ourselves upon the NATIONAL PLATFORM OF FREEDOM, in opposition to the Sectional Platform of Slavery.

Resolved, That Slavery in the several States of this Union which recognize its existence, depends upon the State laws alone, which cannot be repealed or modified by the Federal Government, and for which laws that Government is not responsible. We therefore propose no interference by Congress with Slavery within the limits of any State.

Resolved, That the PROVISO of Jefferson, to prohibit the existence of Slavery, after 1800 in all the Territories of the United States, Southern and Northern; the votes of six States, and sixteen delegates, in the Congress of 1784, for the Proviso, to three States and seven delegates against it; the actual exclusion of Slavery from the North-western Territory by the ORDINANCE OF 1787, *unanimously* adopted by the States in Congress, and the entire history of that period, clearly show that it was the settled policy of the nation, *not* to *extend, nationalize,* or *encourage,* but to limit, localize, and discourage, Slavery; and to *this policy* which should never have been departed from, the Government ought to *return.*

Resolved, That our fathers ordained the Constitution of the United States, in order, among other great national objects, to establish justice, promote the general welfare, and secure the blessings of Liberty; but expressly *denied* to the Federal Government, which they created, all constitutional power to *deprive any person* of life, *liberty,* or property, without due legal process.

Resolved, That in the judgment of this Convention, Congress has no more power to make a SLAVE than to make a KING; no more power to institute or establish SLAVERY, than to institute or establish a MONARCHY. No such power can be found among those specifically conferred by the Constitution, or derived by just implication from them.

Resolved, THAT IT IS THE DUTY OF THE FEDERAL GOVERNMENT TO RELIEVE ITSELF FROM ALL RESPONSIBILITY FOR THE EXISTENCE OR CONTINUANCE OF SLAVERY WHEREVER THAT GOVERNMENT POSSESS CONSTITUTIONAL POWER TO LEGISLATE ON THAT SUBJECT, AND IS THUS RESPONSIBLE FOR ITS EXISTENCE.

Resolved, That the true, and, in the judgment of this Convention, the *only* safe means of preventing the extension of Slavery into territory now free, is to prohibit its existence in all such territory by *an act of Congress.*

Resolved, That we accept the issue which the Slave Power has forced upon us, and to their demand for more Slave States and more Slave Territory, our calm but final answer is: No more Slave States and no more Slave Territory. Let the soil of our extensive domains be kept free, for the hardy pioneers of our own land, and the oppressed and banished of other lands seeking homes of comfort and fields of enterprise in the New World.

Resolved, That the bill lately reported by the Committee of Eight in the Senate of the United States, was no compromise, but an absolute surrender of the rights of the non-slaveholders of the States; and while we rejoice to know that a measure which, while opening the door for the introduction of Slavery into Territories now free, would also have opened the door to litigation and strife among the future inhabitants thereof, to the ruin of their peace and prosperity, was defeated in the House of Representatives,—its passage, in hot haste, by a majority, embracing several Senators who voted in open violation of the known will of their constituents, should warn the People to see to it, that their representatives be not suffered to betray them. There must be no more compromises with Slavery: if made, they must be repealed.

Resolved, That we demand Freedom and established institutions for our brethren in Oregon, now exposed to hardships, peril, and massacre, by the reckless hostility of the Slave Power to the establishment of Free Government for Free Territories—and not only for them, but for our new brethren in California and New Mexico.

And whereas, It is due not only to this occasion, but to the whole people of the United States, that we should also declare ourselves on certain other questions of national policy, therefore,

Resolved, That we demand CHEAP POSTAGE for the people; a retrenchment of the expenses and patronage of the Federal Government; the *abolition* of all *unnecessary* offices and salaries; and the election by the People of all civil officers in the service of the Government, so far as the same may be practicable.

Resolved, That *river* and *harbor improvements,* when demanded by the safety and convenience of commerce with foreign nations, or among the several States, are objects of *national concern;* and that it is the duty of Congress, in the exercise of its constitutional powers, to provide therefor.

Resolved, That the FREE GRANT TO ACTUAL SETTLERS, in consideration of the expenses they incur in making settlements in the wilderness, which are usually fully equal to their actual cost, and of the public benefits resulting therefrom, of reasonable portions of the public lands, under suitable limitations, is a wise and just measure of public policy, which will promote, in various ways, the interest of all the States of this Union; and we therefore recommend it to the favorable consideration of the American People.

Resolved, That the obligations of honor and patriotism require the earliest practical payment of the national debt, and we are therefore in favor of such a tariff of duties as will raise revenue adequate to defray the necessary expenses of the Federal Government, and to pay annual instalments of our debt and the interest thereon.

Resolved, That we inscribe on our banner, "FREE SOIL, FREE SPEECH, FREE LABOR, and FREE MEN," and under it we will fight on, and fight ever, until a triumphant victory shall reward our exertions.

Whig Platform of 1848

1. *Resolved,* That the Whigs of the United States, here assembled by their Representatives, heartily ratify the nominations of General Zachary Taylor as President and Millard Fillmore as Vice-President of the United States, and pledge themselves to their support.

2. *Resolved,* That the choice of General Taylor as the Whig candidate for President we are glad to discover sympathy with a great popular sentiment throughout the nation—a sentiment which, having its origin in admiration of great military success, has been strengthened by the development, in every action and every word, of sound conservative opinions, and of true fidelity to the great example of former days, and to the principles of the Constitution as administered by its founders.

3. *Resolved,* That General Taylor, in saying that, had he voted in 1844, he would have voted the Whig ticket, gives us the assurance—and no better is needed from a consistent and truth-speaking man—that his heart was with us at the crisis of our political destiny, when Henry Clay was our candidate and when not only Whig principles were well defined and clearly asserted, but Whig measures depended on success. The heart that was with us then is with us now, and we have a soldier's word of honor, and a life of public and private virtue, as the security.

4. *Resolved,* That we look on General Taylor's administration of the Government as one conducive of Peace, Prosperity, and Union. Of Peace —because no one better knows, or has greater reason to deplore, what he has seen sadly on the field of victory, the horrors of war, and especially of a foreign and aggressive war. Of Prosperity— now more than ever needed to relieve the nation from a burden of debt, and restore industry— agricultural, manufacturing and commercial—to

its accustomed and peaceful functions and influences. Of Union—because we have a candidate whose very position as a Southwestern man, reared on the banks of the great stream whose tributaries, natural and artificial, embrace the whole Union, renders the protection of the interests of the whole country his first trust, and whose various duties in past life have been rendered, not on the soil or under the flag of any State or section, but over the wide frontier, and under the broad banner of the Nation.

5. *Resolved,* That standing, as the Whig Party does, on the broad and firm platform of the Constitution, braced up by all its inviolable and sacred guarantees and compromises, and cherished in the affections because protective of the interests of the people, we are proud to have, as the exponent of our opinions, one who is pledged to construe it by the wise and generous rules which Washington applied to it, and who has said, (and no Whig desires any other assurance) that he will make Washington's Administration the model of his own.

6. *Resolved,* That as Whigs and Americans, we are proud to acknowledge our gratitude for the great military services which, beginning at Palo Alto, and ending at Buena Vista, first awakened the American people to a just estimate of him who is now our Whig Candidate. In the discharge of a painful duty—for his march into the enemy's country was a reluctant one; in the

command of regulars at one time and volunteers at another, and of both combined; in the decisive though punctual discipline of his camp, where all respected and beloved him; in the negotiations of terms for a dejected and desperate enemy; in the exigency of actual conflict, when the balance was perilously doubtful—we have found him the same —brave, distinguished and considerate, no heartless spectator of bloodshed, no trifler with human life or human happiness, and we do not know which to admire most, his heroism in withstanding the assaults of the enemy in the most hopeless fields of Buena Vista—mourning in generous sorrow over the graves of Ringgold, of Clay, or of Hardin—or in giving in the heat of battle, terms of merciful capitulation to a vanquished foe at Monterey, and not being ashamed to avow that he did it to spare women and children, helpless infancy, and more helpless age, against whom no American soldier ever wars. Such a military man, whose triumphs are neither remote nor doubtful, whose virtues these trials have tested, we are proud to make our Candidate.

7. *Resolved,* That in support of this nomination we ask our Whig friends throughout the nation to unite, to co-operate zealously, resolutely, with earnestness in behalf of our candidate, whom calumny cannot reach, and with respectful demeanor to our adversaries, whose Candidates have yet to prove their claims on the gratitude of the nation.

NOTE:

A Whig National Convention, at which General Zachary Taylor was nominated for the presidency, was assembled for three days beginning June 7, 1848, in Philadelphia, Pennsylvania. The Convention adopted no Platform of Principles at that time. On the evening of the final day of the sessions, however, a ratification meeting was held in Philadelphia, at which Governor William F. Johnston of Pennsylvania presided. Speeches were given by Governor John Morehead of North Carolina, who had presided over the nominating convention, by General Leslie Coombs of Kentucky, and by several other persons. Participants in this meeting adopted the platform printed here. It evidently was

drawn up by the Pennsylvania Whig State Ratifying Convention, but it is noteworthy that the first resolution is made in the name of "the Whigs of the United States, here assembled by their Representatives. . . ."

We insert this cautionary footnote because the platform, to our knowledge, was neither adopted nationally nor regarded as the official party platform by all of the ideologically divided Whigs that year. See *A Political Text-book for 1860: Comprising a Brief View of Presidential Nominations and Elections Including All the National Platforms Ever Yet Adopted*: . . . , compiled by Horace Greeley and John F. Cleveland and published by the Tribune Association in New York (1860) pages 15 and 16; also *Niles Register,* vol. 74, pages 349, 354-358.

CAMPAIGN OF 1852

In June of 1852, when the issue of slavery was again dividing both the nation and the political parties, the Democrats, meeting in Baltimore, selected a compromise candidate, Franklin Pierce of New Hampshire, on the forty-ninth ballot, after the convention had deadlocked over six other aspirants for thirty-five ballots. A southern senator, William R. King of Alabama, was chosen as the vice-presidential nominee.

Later in the month, at a convention marked by intense conflicts, the thoroughly divided Whigs shelved President Fillmore and nominated Mexican War hero Winfield Scott, a Virginian with northern support, on the fifty-third ballot. Seven men nominated for the vice-presidency refused it, but William Graham of North Carolina was chosen.

The Free Democratic Party, composed of former members of the Free Soil and Liberty parties as well as antislavery Whigs, chosen John P. Hale of New Hampshire and George W. Julian of Indiana as their 1852 candidates.

After a low-key campaign, the Democrats defeated the Whigs 1,607,510 votes to 1,386,942; the Free Democrats had 155,210. The electors voted 254 to 42 for Pierce and King over Scott and Graham.

Democratic Platform of 1852

Resolved, That the American democracy place their trust in the intelligence, the patriotism, and the discriminating justice of the American people.

Resolved, That we regard this as a distinctive feature of our political creed, which we are proud to maintain before the world as the great moral element in a form of government springing from and upheld by the popular will; and we contrast it with the creed and practice of federalism, under whatever name or form, which seeks to palsy the will of the constituent, and which conceives no imposture too mónstrous for the popular credulity.

Resolved, therefore, That, entertaining these views, the democratic party of this Union, through their delegates assembled in a general convention, coming together in a spirit of concord, of devotion to the doctrines and faith of a free representative government, and appealing to their fellow-citizens for the rectitude of their intentions, renew and reassert before the American people the declaration of principles avowed by them when on former occasions, in general convention, they have presented their candidates for the popular suffrages.

1. That the federal government is one of limited powers, derived solely from the constitution, and the grants of power made therein ought to be strictly construed by all the departments and agents of the government; and that it is inexpedient and dangerous to exercise doubtful constitutional powers.

2. That the constitution does not confer upon the general government the power to commence and carry on a general system of internal improvements.

3. That the constitution does not confer authority upon the federal government, directly or indirectly, to assume the debts of the several States, contracted for local and internal improvements or other State purposes; nor would such assumption be just or expedient.

4. That justice and sound policy forbid the federal government to foster one branch of industry to the detriment of any other, or to cherish the

interests of one portion to the injury of another portion of our common country; that every citizen, and every section of the country, has a right to demand and insist upon an equality of rights and privileges, and to complete an ample protection of person and property from domestic violence or foreign aggression.

5. That it is the duty of every branch of the government to enforce and practice the most rigid economy in conducting our public affairs, and that no more revenue ought to be raised than is required to defray the necessary expenses of the government, and for the gradual but certain extinction of the public debt.

6. That Congress has no power to charter a national bank; that we believe such an institution one of deadly hostility to the best interests of the country, dangerous to our republican institutions and the liberties of the people, and calculated to place the business of the country within the control of a concentrated money power, and above the laws and the will of the people; and that the results of democratic legislation in this and all other financial measures upon which issues have been made between the two political parties of the country, have demonstrated, to candid and practical men of all parties, their soundness, safety, and utility in all business pursuits.

7. That the separation of the moneys of the government from banking institutions is indispensable for the safety of the funds of the government and the rights of the people.

8. That the liberal principles embodied by Jefferson in the Declaration of Independence, and sanctioned in the constitution, which make ours the land of liberty and the asylum of the oppressed of every nation, have ever been cardinal principles in the democratic faith; and every attempt to abridge the privilege of becoming citizens and the owners of the soil among us ought to be resisted with the same spirit that swept the alien and sedition laws from our statute-books.

9. That Congress has no power under the constitution to interfere with or control the domestic institutions of the several States, and that such States are the sole and proper judges of everything appertaining to their own affairs not prohibited by the constitution; that all efforts of the abolitionists or others made to induce Congress to interfere with questions of slavery, or to take incipient steps in relation thereto, are calculated

to lead to the most alarming and dangerous consequences; and that all such efforts have an inevitable tendency to diminish the happiness of the people and endanger the stability and permanency of the Union, and ought not to be countenanced by any friend of our political institutions.

Resolved, That the foregoing proposition covers, and was intended to embrace, the whole subject of slavery agitation in Congress; and therefore the democratic party of the Union, standing on this national platform, will abide by and adhere to a faithful execution of the acts known as the compromise measures settled by the last Congress —"the act for reclaiming fugitives from service or labor" included; which act, being designed to carry out an express provision of the constitution, cannot, with fidelity thereto be repealed nor so changed as to destroy or impair its efficiency.

Resolved, That the democratic party will resist all attempts at renewing, in congress or out of it, the agitation of the slavery question, under whatever shape or color the attempt may be made.

Resolved, That the proceeds of the public lands ought to be sacredly applied to the national object specified in the Constitution; and that we are opposed to any law for the distribution of such proceeds among the states as, alike inexpedient in policy and repugnant to the constitution.

Resolved, That we are decidedly opposed to taking from the President the qualified veto power, by which he is enabled, under restrictions and responsibilities amply sufficient to guard the public interests, to suspend the passage of a bill whose merits cannot secure the approval of two-thirds of the Senate and House of Representatives, until the judgment of the people can be obtained thereon, and which has saved the American people from the corrupt and tyrannical domination of the Bank of the United States, and from a corrupting system of general internal improvements.

Resolved, That the democratic party will faithfully abide by and uphold the principles laid down in the Kentucky and Virginia resolutions of 1798, and in the report of Mr. Madison to the Virginia legislature in 1799; that it adopts those principles as constituting one of the main foundations of its political creed, and is resolved to carry them out in their obvious meaning and import.

Resolved, That the war with Mexico, upon all the principles of patriotism and the laws of nations, was a just and necessary war on our part, in which every American citizen should have shown himself on the side of his country, and neither morally nor physically, by word or deed, have given "aid and comfort to the enemy."

Resolved, That we rejoice at the restoration of friendly relations with our sister republic of Mexico, and earnestly desire for her all the blessings and prosperity which we enjoy under republican institutions; and we congratulate the American people on the results of that war, which have so manifestly justified the policy and conduct of the democratic party, and insured to the United States, "indemnity for the past and security for the future."

Resolved, That, in view of the condition of popular institutions in the Old World, a high and sacred duty is devolved, with increased responsibility upon the democratic party of this country, as the party of the people, to uphold and maintain the rights of every State, and thereby the Union of the States, and to sustain and advance among us constitutional liberty, by continuing to resist all monopolies and exclusive legislation for the benefit of the few at the expense of the many, and by a vigilant and constant adherence to those principles and compromises of the constitution, which are broad enough and strong enough to embrace and uphold the Union as it was, the Union as it is, and the Union as it shall be, in the full expansion of the energies and capacity of this great and progressive people.

Free Democratic Platform of 1852

Having assembled in National Convention as the delegates of the Free Democracy of the United States, united by a common resolve to maintain right against wrongs, and freedom against slavery; confiding in the intelligence, patriotism, and the discriminating justice of the American people, putting our trust in God for the triumph of our cause, and invoking his guidance in our endeavors to advance it, we now submit to the candid judgment of all men the following declaration of principles and measures:

I. That Governments, deriving their just powers from the consent of the governed, are instituted among men to secure to all, those inalienable rights of life, liberty, and the pursuit of happiness, with which they are endowed by their Creator, and of which none can be deprived by valid legislation, except for crime.

II. That the true mission of American Democracy is to maintain the liberties of the people the sovereignty of the States, and the perpetuity of the Union, by the impartial application to public affairs, without sectional discriminations, of the fundamental principles of equal rights, strict justice, and economical administration.

III. That the Federal Government is one of limited powers, derived solely from the Constitution, and the grants of power therein ought to be strictly construed by all the departments and agents of the Government, and it is inexpedient and dangerous to exercise doubtful constitutional powers.

IV. That the Constitution of the United States, ordained to form a more perfect union, to establish justice, and secure the blessings of liberty, expressly denies to the General Government all power to deprive any person of life, liberty, or property, without due process of law; and therefore the Government, having no more power to make a slave than to make a king, and no more power to establish slavery than to establish monarchy, should at once proceed to relieve itself from all responsibility for the existence of slavery wherever it possesses constitutional power to legislate for its extinction.

V. That, to the persevering and importunate demands of the slave power for more slave States, new slave Territories, and the nationalization of slavery, our distinct and final answer is—no more slave States, no slave Territory, no nationalized slavery, and no national legislation for the extradition of slaves.

VI. That slavery is a sin against God and a crime against man, which no human enactment nor usage can make right; and that Christianity, humanity, and patriotism, alike demand its abolition.

VII. That the Fugitive Slave Act of 1850 is repugnant to the Constitution, to the principles of the common law, to the spirit of Christianity, and to the sentiments of the civilized world. We therefore deny its binding force upon the American People, and demand its immediate and total repeal.

VIII. That the doctrine that any human law is a finality, and not subject to modification or repeal, is not in accordance with the creed of the founders of our Government, and is dangerous to the liberties of the people.

IX. That the acts of Congress known as the Compromise measures of 1850, by making the admission of a sovereign State contingent upon the adoption of other measures demanded by the special interest of slavery; by their omission to guarantee freedom in free Territories; by their attempt to impose unconstitutional limitations on the power of Congress and the people to admit new States; by their provisions for the assumption of five millions of the State debt of Texas, and for the payment of five millions more and the cession of a large territory to the same State under menace, as an inducement to the relinquishment of a groundless claim, and by their invasion of the sovereignty of the States and the liberties of the people through the enactment of an unjust, oppressive, and unconstitutional Fugitive Slave Law, are proved to be inconsistent with all the principles and maxims of Democracy, and wholly inadequate to the settlement of the questions of which they are claimed to be an adjustment.

X. That no permanent settlement of the slavery question can be looked for, except in the practical recognition of the truth, that slavery is sectional, and freedom national; by the total separation of the General Government from slavery, and the exercise of its legitimate and constitutional influence on the side of freedom; and by leaving to the States the whole subject of slavery and the extradition of fugitives from service.

XI. That all men have a natural right to a portion of the soil; and that, as the use of the soil is indispensable to life, the right of all men to the soil is as sacred as their right to life itself.

XII. That the public lands of the United States belong to the people, and should not be sold to individuals nor granted to corporations, but should be held as a sacred trust for the benefit of the people, and should be granted in limited quantities, free of cost, to landless settlers.

XIII. That a due regard for the Federal Constitution, and sound administrative policy, demand that the funds of the General Government be kept separate from banking institutions; that inland and ocean postage should be reduced to the lowest possible point; that no more revenue should be raised than is required to defray the strictly necessary expenses of the public service,

and to pay off the public debt; and that the power and patronage of the Government should be diminished by the abolition of all unnecessary offices, salaries, and privileges, and by the election by the people of all civil officers in the service of the United States, so far as may be consistent with the prompt and efficient transaction of the public business.

XIV. That river and harbor improvements, when necessary to the safety and convenience of commerce with foreign nations or among the several States, are objects of national concern, and it is the duty of Congress in the exercise of its constitutional powers to provide for the same.

XV. That emigrants and exiles from the Old World should find a cordial welcome to homes of comfort and fields of enterprise in the New; and every attempt to abridge their privilege of becoming citizens and owners of the soil among us ought to be resisted with inflexible determination.

XVI. That every nation has a clear right to alter or change its own Government, and to administer its own concerns in such manner as may best secure the rights and promote the happiness of the people; and foreign interference with that right is a dangerous violation of the law of nations, against which all independent Governments should protest, and endeavor by all proper means to prevent; and especially is it the duty of the American Government, representing the chief republic of the world, to protest against and by all proper means to prevent the intervention of Kings and Emperors against nations seeking to establish for themselves republican or constitutional Governments.

XVII. That the independence of Hayti ought to be recognised by our Government, and our commercial relations with it placed on the footing of the most favored nations.

XVIII. That as, by the Constitution, "the citizens of each State shall be entitled to all privileges and immunities of citizens of the several States," the practice of imprisoning colored seamen of other States, while the vessels to which they belong lie in port, and refusing to exercise the right to bring such cases before the Supreme Court of the United States, to test the legality of such proceedings, is a flagrant violation of the Constitution, and an invasion of the rights of the citizens of other States, utterly inconsistent with the professions made by the slaveholders, that they wish the provisions of the Constitution faithfully observed by every State in the Union.

XIX. That we recommend the introduction into all treaties, hereafter to be negotiated between the United States and foreign nations, of some provision for the amicable settlement of difficulties by a resort to decisive arbitration.

XX. That the Free Democratic party is not organized to aid either the Whig or Democratic wing of the great Slave Compromise party of the nation, but to defeat them both; and that repudiating and renouncing both, as hopelessly corrupt, and utterly unworthy of confidence, the purpose of the Free Democracy is to take possession of the Federal Government, and administer it for the better protection of the rights and interests of the whole people.

XXI. That we inscribe on our banner, FREE SOIL, FREE SPEECH, FREE LABOR, and FREE MEN, and under it will fight on and fight ever, until a triumphant victory shall reward our exertions.

XXII. That upon this Platform the Convention presents to the American People, as a candidate for the office of President of the United States, JOHN P. HALE, of New Hampshire, and as a candidate for the office of Vice-President of the United States, George W. Julian, of Indiana, and earnestly commends them to the support of all freemen and parties.

Whig Platform of 1852

The Whigs of the United States, in Convention assembled, firmly adhering to the great conservative principles by which they are controlled and governed, and now as ever relying upon the intelligence of the American people, with an abiding confidence in their capacity for self-government, and their devotion to the Constitution and the Union, do proclaim the following as the political sentiments and determination for the establishment and maintenance of which their national organization as a party was effected:

First: The Government of the United States is of a limited character, and it is confined to the exercise of powers expressly granted by the Constitution, and such as may be necessary and proper for carrying the granted powers into full execution, and that all powers not granted or necessarily implied are expressly reserved to the States respectively and to the people.

Second: The State Governments should be held secure in their reserved rights, and the General Government sustained on its constitutional powers, and that the Union should be revered and watched over as the palladium of our liberties.

Third: That while struggling freedom everywhere enlists the warmest sympathy of the Whig party, we still adhere to the doctrines of the Father of his Country, as announced in his Farewell Address, of keeping ourselves free from all entangling alliances with foreign countries, and of never quitting our own to stand upon foreign ground, that our mission as a republic is not to propagate our opinions, or impose on other countries our form of government by artifice or force; but to teach, by example, and show by our success, moderation and justice, the blessings of self-government, and the advantages of free institutions.

Fourth: That, as the people make and control the Government, they should obey its constitution, laws and treaties, as they would retain their self-respect, and the respect which they claim and will enforce from foreign powers.

Fifth: Revenue sufficient for the expenses of an economical administration of the Government in time of peace ought to be derived from a duty on imports, and not from direct taxation; and in laying such duties, sound policy requires a just discrimination, whereby suitable encouragement may be afforded to American industry, equally to all classes, and to all parts of the country.

Sixth: The Constitution vests in Congress the power to open and repair harbors, and remove obstructions from navigable rivers, whenever such improvements are necessary for the common defence, and for the protection and facility of commerce with foreign nations, or among the States, said improvements being, in every instance, national and general in their character.

Seventh: The Federal and State Governments are parts of one system, alike necessary for the common prosperity, peace and security, and ought to be regarded alike with a cordial, habitual and immovable attachment. Respect for the authority of each and acquiescence in the just constitutional measures of each, are duties required by the plainest considerations of national, state, and individual welfare.

Eighth: That the series of acts of the Thirty-first Congress,—the act known as the Fugitive Slave Law, included—are received and acquiesced in by the Whig Party of the United States as a settlement in principle and substance, of the dangerous and exciting question which they embrace; and, so far as they are concerned, we will maintain them, and insist upon their strict enforcement, until time and experience shall demonstrate the necessity of further legislation to guard against the evasion of the law on one hand, and the abuse of their powers on the other, not impairing their present efficiency; and we deprecate all further agitation of the question thus settled, as dangerous to our peace; and will discountenance all efforts to continue or renew such agitation whenever, wherever, or however the attempt may be made; and we will maintain this system as essential to the nationality of the Whig party and of the Union.

CAMPAIGN OF 1856

In 1856, the Whig Party virtually disappeared from the political scene, the Democrats shelved an incumbent president, and a new party, the Republicans, which opposed the expansion of slavery in the territories, was born. In addition, another new American party nominated a former president for the office.

The Democrats chose James Buchanan of Pennsylvania over President Franklin Pierce on the seventeenth ballot; the party was deeply divided over slavery, and strategy called for a northern candidate who would accept a platform pledging the nation to "non-interference by Congress with slavery in state and territory. . . ." Congressman John Breckinridge of Kentucky was nominated for vice-president.

The new Republican Party, composed of Conscience Whigs, abolitionists, free soilers, and others opposed to the expansion of slavery and to the Pierce administration, nominated a former explorer and United States senator, John C. Frémont. William Dayton of New Jersey was nomi-

nated as his running mate. The American Party, or "Know Nothing" Party, whose members sometimes disavowed knowledge of their movement, was dedicated to the restriction of immigration, opposition to the Roman Catholic Church, and the promotion of nativistic public policies. It absorbed much of the Whig support in the South. Delegates to its convention in 1856 nominated former President Millard Fillmore for president and Andrew Jackson Donelson of Tennessee for vice-president. The almost defunct Whigs endorsed the Know-Nothing slate of Fillmore and Donelson, but adopted the platform presented here.

In the election, Buchanan, with solid southern support, polled 1,836,072 popular votes to 1,342,345 for Frémont and 873,053 for Fillmore running on a combined American and Whig ticket. Buchanan was elected president with 174 electoral votes to 114 for Frémont and 8 for Fillmore.

American (Know Nothing) Platform of 1856

I. An humble acknowledgment to the Supreme Being who rules one universe, for His protecting care vouchsafed to our fathers in their revolutionary struggle, and hitherto manifested to us, their descendants, in the preservation of the liberties, the independence and the union of these states.

II. The perpetuation of the Federal Union, as the palladium of our civil and religious liberties, and the only sure bulwark of American independence.

III. *Americans must rule America;* and to this end, *native*-born citizens should be selected for all state, federal, or municipal offices of government employment, in preference to naturalized citizens—*nevertheless,*

IV. Persons born of American parents residing

temporarily abroad, shall be entitled to all the rights of native-born citizens; but

V. No person should be selected for political station (whether of native or foreign birth), who recognizes any alliance or obligation of any description to any foreign prince, potentate or power, who refuses to recognize the federal and state constitutions (each within its own sphere), as paramount to all other laws, as rules of particular [political] action.

VI. The unequalled recognition and maintenance of the reserved rights of the several states, and the cultivation of harmony and fraternal goodwill between the citizens of the several states, and to this end, non-interference by Congress with questions appertaining solely to the individual states, and non-intervention by each state with the affairs of any other state.

VII. The recognition of the right of the native-born and naturalized citizens of the United States, permanently residing in any territory thereof, to frame their constitutions and laws, and to regulate their domestic and social affairs in their own mode, subject only to the provisions of the federal Constitution, with the right of admission into the Union whenever they have the requisite population for one representative in Congress. *Provided, always,* That none but those who are citizens of the United States, under the Constitution and laws thereof, and who have a fixed residence in any such territory, are to participate in the formation of the constitution, or in the enactment of laws for said territory or state.

VIII. An enforcement of the principles that no state or territory can admit other than native-born citizens to the right of suffrage, or of holding political office unless such persons shall have been naturalized according to the laws of the United States.

IX. A change in the laws of naturalization, making a continued residence of twenty-one years, of all not heretofore provided for, an indispensable requisite for citizenship hereafter, and excluding all paupers or persons convicted of crime from landing upon our shores; but no interference with the vested rights of foreigners.

X. Opposition to any union between Church and State; no interference with religious faith or worship, and no test oaths for office, except those indicated in the 5th section of this platform.

XI. Free and thorough investigation into any and all alleged abuses of public functionaries, and a strict economy in public expenditures.

XII. The maintenance and enforcement of all laws until said laws shall be repealed, or shall be declared null and void by competent judicial authority.

XIII. Opposition to the reckless and unwise policy of the present administration in the general management of our national affairs, and more especially as shown in removing "Americans" (by designation) and conservatives in principle, from office, and placing foreigners and ultraists in their places, as shown in a truckling subserviency to the stronger, and an insolent and cowardly bravado toward the weaker powers; as shown in reopening sectional agitation, by the repeal of the Missouri Compromise; as shown in granting to unnaturalized foreigners the right of suffrage in Kansas and Nebraska, as shown in its vacillating course on the Kansas and Nebraska question; as shown in the removal of Judge Bronson from the collectorship of New York upon false and untenable grounds; as shown in the corruptions which pervade some of the departments of the government; as shown in disgracing meritorious naval officers through prejudice or caprice; as shown in the blundering mismanagement of our foreign relations.

XIV. Therefore, to remedy existing evils, and prevent the disastrous consequences otherwise resulting therefrom, we would build up the "American Party" upon the principles hereinbefore stated eschewing all sectional questions, and uniting upon those purely national, and admitting into said party all American citizens (referred to in the 3rd, 4th, and 5th sections) who openly avow the principles and opinions heretofore expressed, and who will subscribe their names to this platform.—*Provided nevertheless,* that a majority of those members present at any meeting of a local council where an applicant applies for membership in the American party, may, for any reason by them deemed sufficient, deny admission to such applicant.

XV. A free and open discussion of all political principles embraced in our platform.

Democratic Platform of 1856

Resolved, That the American Democracy place their trust in the intelligence, the patriotism, and the discriminating justice of the American people.

Resolved, That we regard this as a distinctive feature of our political creed, which we are proud to maintain before the world, as the great moral element in a form of government springing from and upheld by the popular will; and we contrast it with the creed and practice of Federalism, under whatever name or form, which seeks to palsy the will of the constituent, and which conceives no imposture too monstrous for the popular credulity.

Resolved, therefore, That, entertaining these views, the Democratic party of this Union, through their Delegates assembled in a general Convention, coming together in a spirit of concord, of devotion to the doctrines and faith of a free representative government, and appealing to their fellow-citizens for the rectitude of their intentions, renew and re-assert before the American people, the declarations of principles avowed by them when, on former occasions in general Convention, they have presented their candidates for the popular suffrage.

1. That the Federal Government is one of limited power, derived solely from the Constitution; and the grants of power made therein ought to be strictly construed by all the departments and agents of the government; and that it is inexpedient and dangerous to exercise doubtful constitutional powers.

2. That the Constitution does not confer upon the General Government the power to commence and carry on a general system of internal improvements.

3. That the Constitution does not confer authority upon the Federal Government, directly or indirectly, to assume the debts of the several States, contracted for local and internal improvements, or other State purposes; nor would such assumption be just or expedient.

4. That justice and sound policy forbid the Federal Government to foster one branch of industry to the detriment of any other, or to cherish the interests of one portion to the injury of another portion of our common country; that every citizen and every section of the country has a right to demand and insist upon an equality of rights and privileges, and to complete and ample protection of persons and property from domestic violence or foreign aggression.

5. That it is the duty of every branch of the Government to enforce and practice the most rigid economy in conducting our public affairs, and that no more revenue ought to be raised than is required to defray the necessary expenses of the Government, and for the gradual but certain extinction of the public debt.

6. That the proceeds of the public lands ought to be sacredly applied to the national objects specified in the Constitution; and that we are opposed to any law for the distribution of such proceeds among the States, as alike inexpedient in policy and repugnant to the Constitution.

7. That Congress has no power to charter a national bank; that we believe such an institution one of deadly hostility to the best interests of the country, dangerous to our republican institutions and the liberties of the people, and calcu-

lated to place the business of the country within the control of a concentrated money power, and above the laws and the will of the people; and that the results of Democratic legislation in this and all other financial measures upon which issues have been made between the two political parties of the country, have demonstrated to candid and practical men of all parties, their soundness, safety, and utility, in all business pursuits.

8. That the separation of the moneys of the Government from banking institutions is indispensable for the safety of the funds of the Government and the rights of the people.

9. That we are decidedly opposed to taking from the President the qualified veto power, by which he is enabled, under restrictions and responsibilities amply sufficient to guard the public interests, to suspend the passage of a bill whose merits cannot secure the approval of two-thirds of the Senate and House of Representatives, until the judgment of the people can be obtained thereon, and which has saved the American people from the corrupt and tyrannical domination of the Bank of the United States, and from a corrupting system of general internal improvements.

10. That the liberal principles embodied by Jefferson in the Declaration of Independence, and sanctioned by the Constitution, which makes ours the land of liberty and the asylum of the oppressed of every nation, have ever been cardinal principles in the Democratic faith, and every attempt to abridge the privilege of becoming citizens and the owners of soil among us, ought to be resisted with the same spirit which swept the alien and sedition laws from our statute-books.

And Whereas, Since the foregoing declaration was uniformly adopted by our predecessors in National Conventions, an adverse political and religious test has been secretly organized by a party claiming to be exclusively American, it is proper that the American Democracy should clearly define its relation thereto, and declare its determined opposition to all secret political societies, by whatever name they may be called.

Resolved, That the foundation of this union of States having been laid in, and its prosperity, expansion, and pre-eminent example in free government, built upon entire freedom in matters of religious concernment, and no respect of person in regard to rank or place of birth; no party can justly be deemed national, constitutional, or in accordance with American principles, which bases its exclusive organization upon religious opinions and accidental birth-place. And hence a political crusade in the nineteenth century, and in the United States of America, against Catholic and foreign-born is neither justified by the past history or the future prospects of the country, nor in unison with the spirit of toleration and enlarged freedom which peculiarly distinguishes the American system of popular government.

Resolved, That we reiterate with renewed energy of purpose the well considered declarations of former Conventions upon the sectional issue of Domestic slavery, and concerning the reserved rights of the States.

1. That Congress has no power under the Constitution, to interfere with or control the domestic institutions of the several States, and that such States are the sole and proper judges of everything appertaining to their own affairs, not prohibited by the Constitution; that all efforts of the abolitionists, or others, made to induce Congress to interfere with questions of slavery, or to take incipient steps in relation thereto, are calculated to lead to the most alarming and dangerous consequences; and that all such efforts have an inevitable tendency to diminish the happiness of the people and endanger the stability and permanency of the Union, and ought not to be countenanced by any friend of our political institutions.

2. That the foregoing proposition covers, and was intended to embrace the whole subject of slavery agitation in Congress; and therefore, the Democratic party of the Union, standing on this national platform, will abide by and adhere to a faithful execution of the acts known as the compromise measures, settled by the Congress of 1850; "the act for reclaiming fugitives from service or labor," included; which act being designed to carry out an express provision of the Constitution, cannot, with fidelity thereto, be repealed, or so changed as to destroy or impair its efficiency.

3. That the Democratic party will resist all attempts at renewing, in Congress or out of it, the agitation of the slavery question under whatever shape or color the attempt may be made.

4. That the Democratic party will faithfully abide by and uphold, the principles laid down in the Kentucky and Virginia resolutions of 1798, and in the report of Mr. Madison to the Virginia Legislature in 1799; that it adopts those principles as constituting one of the main foundations of its political creed, and is resolved to carry them out in their obvious meaning and import.

And that we may more distinctly meet the issue on which a sectional party, subsisting exclusively on slavery agitation, now relies to test the fidelity of the people, North and South, to the Constitution and the Union—

1. *Resolved,* That claiming fellowship with, and desiring the co-operation of all who regard the preservation of the Union under the Constitution as the paramount issue—and repudiating all sectional parties and platforms concerning domestic slavery, which seek to embroil the States and incite to treason and armed resistance to law in the Territories; and whose avowed purposes, if consummated, must end in civil war and disunion, the American Democracy recognize and adopt the principles contained in the organic laws establishing the Territories of Kansas and Nebraska as embodying the only sound and safe solution of the "slavery question" upon which the great national idea of the people of this whole country can repose in its determined conservatism of the Union—NON-INTERFERENCE BY CONGRESS WITH SLAVERY IN STATE AND TERRITORY, OR IN THE DISTRICT OF COLUMBIA.

2. That this was the basis of the compromises of 1850—confirmed by both the Democratic and Whig parties in national Conventions—ratified by the people in the election of 1852, and rightly applied to the organization of Territories in 1854.

3. That by the uniform application of this Democratic principle to the organization of territories, and to the admission of new States, with or without domestic slavery, as they may elect—the equal rights, of all the States will be preserved intact—the original compacts of the Constitution maintained inviolate—and the perpetuity and expansion of this Union insured to its utmost capacity of embracing, in peace and harmony, every future American State that may be constituted or annexed, with a republican form of government.

Resolved, That we recognize the right of the people of all the Territories, including Kansas and Nebraska, acting through the legally and fairly expressed will of a majority of actual residents, and whenever the number of their inhabitants justifies it, to form a Constitution, with or without domestic slavery, and be admitted into the Union upon terms of perfect equality with the other States.

Resolved, Finally, That in view of the condition of popular institutions in the Old World (and the dangerous tendencies of sectional agitation, combined with the attempt to enforce civil and religious disabilities against the rights of acquiring and enjoying citizenship, in our own land)—a high and sacred duty is devolved with increased responsibility upon the Democratic party of this country, as the party of the Union, to uphold and maintain the rights of every State, and thereby the Union of the States; and to sustain and advance among us constitutional liberty, by continuing to resist all monopolies and exclusive legislation for the benefit of the few, at the expense of the many, and by a vigilant and constant adherence to those principles and compromises of the Constitution, which are broad enough and strong enough to embrace and uphold the Union as it was, the Union as it is, and the Union as it shall be, in the full expansion of the energies and capacity of this great and progressive people.

1. *Resolved,* That there are questions connected with the foreign policy of this country, which are inferior to no domestic question whatever. The time has come for the people of the United States to declare themselves in favor of free seas and progressive free trade throughout the world, and, by solemn manifestations, to place their moral influence at the side of their successful example.

2. *Resolved,* That our geographical and political position with reference to the other States of this continent, no less than the interest of our commerce and the development of our growing power, requires that we should hold as sacred the principles involved in the Monroe Doctrine: their bearing and import admit of no misconstruction; they should be applied with unbending rigidity.

3. *Resolved,* That the great highway which nature, as well as the assent of the States most immediately interested in its maintenance, has marked out for a free communication between the Atlantic and the Pacific oceans, constitutes one of the most important achievements realized by the spirit of modern times and the unconquer-able energy of our people. That result should be secured by a timely and efficient exertion of the control which we have the right to claim over it, and no power on earth should be suffered to impede or clog its progress by any interference with the relations it may suit our policy to establish between our government and the Governments of the States within whose dominions it lies. We can, under no circumstances, surrender our preponderance in the adjustment of all questions arising out of it.

4. *Resolved,* That, in view of so commanding an interest, the people of the United States cannot but sympathize with the efforts which are being made by the people of Central America to regenerate that portion of the continent which covers the passage across the Interoceanic Isthmus.

5. *Resolved,* That the Democratic party will expect of the next Administration that every proper effort be made to insure our ascendency in the Gulf of Mexico, and to maintain a permanent protection to the great outlets through which are emptied into its waters the products raised out of the soil and the commodities created by the industry of the people of our Western valleys and the Union at large.

Resolved, That the Democratic party recognizes the great importance, in a political and commercial point of view, of a safe and speedy communication, by military and postal roads, through our own territory, between the Atlantic and Pacific coasts of this Union, and that it is the duty of the Federal Government to exercise promptly all its constitutional power to the attainment of that object, thereby binding the Union of these States in indissoluble bonds, and opening to the rich commerce of Asia an overland transit from the Pacific to the Mississippi River, and the great lakes of the North.

Resolved, That the administration of Franklin Pierce has been true to the great interests of the country. In the face of the most determined opposition it has maintained the laws, enforced economy, fostered progress, and infused integrity and vigor into every department of the government at home. It has signally improved our treaty relations, extended the field of commercial enterprise, and vindicated the rights of American citizens abroad. It has asserted with eminent impartiality the just claims of every section, and has at all times been faithful to the Constitution. We therefore proclaim our unqualified approbation of its measures and its policy.

Republican Platform of 1856

This Convention of Delegates, assembled in pursuance of a call addressed to the people of the United States, without regard to past political differences or divisions, who are opposed to the repeal of the Missouri Compromise; to the policy of the present Administration; to the extension of Slavery into Free Territory; in favor of the admission of Kansas as a Free State; of restoring the action of the Federal Government to the principles of Washington and Jefferson; and for the purpose of presenting candidates for the offices of President and Vice-President, do

Resolved: That the maintenance of the principles promulgated in the Declaration of Independence, and embodied in the Federal Constitution are essential to the preservation of our Republican institutions, and that the Federal Constitution, the rights of the States, and the union of the States, must and shall be preserved.

Resolved: That, with our Republican fathers, we hold it to be a self-evident truth, that all men are endowed with the inalienable right to life, liberty, and the pursuit of happiness, and that the primary object and ulterior design of our Federal Government were to secure these rights to all persons under its exclusive jurisdiction; that, as our Republican fathers, when they had abolished Slavery in all our National Territory, ordained that no person shall be deprived of life, liberty, or property, without due process of law, it becomes our duty to maintain this provision of the Constitution against all attempts to violate it for the purpose of establishing Slavery in the Territories of the United States by positive legislation, prohibiting its existence or extension therein. That we deny the authority of Congress, of a Territorial Legislation, of any individual, or association of individuals, to give legal existence to Slavery in any Territory of the United States, while the present Constitution shall be maintained.

Resolved: That the Constitution confers upon Congress sovereign powers over the Territories of the United States for their government; and that in the exercise of this power, it is both the right and the imperative duty of Congress to prohibit in the Territories those twin relics of barbarism—Polygamy, and Slavery.

Resolved: That while the Constitution of the United States was ordained and established by the people, in order to "form a more perfect union, establish justice, insure domestic tranquility, provide for the common defense, promote the general welfare, and secure the blessings of liberty," and contain ample provision for the protection of the life, liberty, and property of every citizen, the dearest Constitutional rights of the people of Kansas have been fraudulently and violently taken from them.

Their Territory has been invaded by an armed force;

Spurious and pretended legislative, judicial, and executive officers have been set over them, by whose usurped authority, sustained by the military power of the government, tyrannical and unconstitutional laws have been enacted and enforced;

The right of the people to keep and bear arms has been infringed.

Test oaths of an extraordinary and entangling nature have been imposed as a condition of exercising the right of suffrage and holding office.

The right of an accused person to a speedy and public trial by an impartial jury has been denied;

The right of the people to be secure in their persons, houses, papers, and effects, against unreasonable searches and seizures, has been violated;

They have been deprived of life, liberty, and property without due process of law;

That the freedom of speech and of the press has been abridged;

The right to choose their representatives has been made of no effect;

Murders, robberies, and arsons have been instigated and encouraged, and the offenders have been allowed to go unpunished;

That all these things have been done with the knowledge, sanction, and procurement of the present National Administration; and that for this high crime against the Constitution, the Union, and humanity, we arraign that Administration, the President, his advisers, agents, supporters, apologists, and accessories, either *before* or *after* the fact, before the country and before the world; and that it is our fixed purpose to bring the actual perpetrators of these atrocious outrages and their accomplices to a sure and condign punishment thereafter.

Resolved, That Kansas should be immediately admitted as a state of this Union, with her present Free Constitution, as at once the most effectual way of securing to her citizens the enjoyment of the rights and privileges to which they are entitled, and of ending the civil strife now raging in her territory.

Resolved, That the highwayman's plea, that "might makes right," embodied in the Ostend Circular, was in every respect unworthy of American diplomacy, and would bring shame and dishonor upon any Government or people that gave it their sanction.

Resolved, That a railroad to the Pacific Ocean by the most central and practicable route is imperatively demanded by the interests of the whole country, and that the Federal Government ought to render immediate and efficient aid in its construction, and as an auxiliary thereto, to the immediate construction of an emigrant road on the line of the railroad.

Resolved, That appropriations by Congress for the improvement of rivers and harbors, of a national character, required for the accommodation and security of our existing commerce, are authorized by the Constitution, and justified by the obligation of the Government to protect the lives and property of its citizens.

Resolved, That we invite the affiliation and cooperation of the men of all parties, however differing from us in other respects, in support of the principles herein declared; and believing that the spirit of our institutions as well as the Constitution of our country, guarantees liberty of conscience and equality of rights among citizens, we oppose all legislation impairing their security.

Whig Platform of 1856

Resolved, That the Whigs of the United States are assembled here by reverence for the Constitution, and unalterable attachment to the National Union, and a fixed determination to do all in their power to preserve it for themselves and posterity. They have no new principles to announce—no new platform to establish, but are content broadly to rest where their fathers have rested upon the Constitution of the United States, wishing no safer guide, no higher law.

Resolved, That we regard with the deepest anxiety the present disordered condition of our national affairs. A portion of the country being ravaged by civil war and large sections of our population embittered by mutual recriminations, and we distinctly trace these calamities to the culpable neglect of duty by the present National Administration.

Resolved, That the Government of these United States was formed by the conjunction in political unity of widespread geographical sections, materially differing not only in climate and products, but in their social and domestic institutions, and that any cause that shall permanently array these sections in political hostility and organized parties, founded only on geographical distinctions must inevitably prove fatal to the continuance of the National Union.

Resolved, That the Whigs of the United States have declared as a fundamental article of their political faith, the absolute necessity for avoiding geographical parties; that the danger so clearly discerned by the "Father of his Country," founded on geographical distinction, has now become fearfully apparent in the agitation convulsing the nation, which must be arrested at once if we would preserve our Constitutional Union from dismemberment, and the name of America from being blotted out from the family of civilized nations.

Resolved, That all who revere the Constitution and Union, must look with alarm at the parties in the field in the present Presidential campaign— one claiming only to represent sixteen Northern States, and the other appealing to the passions and prejudices of the Southern States—that the success of either faction must add fuel to the flame which now threatens to wrap our dearest interest in a common ruin.

Resolved, That the only remedy for an evil so appalling is to support the candidate pledged to neither geographical section nor arrayed in political antagonism, but holding both in just and equal regard; that we congratulate the friends of the Union that such a candidate exists in Millard Fillmore.

Resolved, That, without adopting or referring

to the peculiar principles of the party which has already selected Millard Fillmore as their candidate, we look to him as a well-tried and faithful friend of the Constitution and the Union, eminent alike for his wisdom and firmness, for his justice and moderation in foreign relations, for his calm and pacific temperament, well becoming a great and enlightened Government. For his devotion to the Constitution in its true spirit, and his inflexibility in executing the laws; but, beyond all these attributes, of being representative of neither of the two sectional parties now struggling for political supremacy.

Resolved, That in the present exigency of political affairs, we are not called upon to discuss subordinate questions of administration in exercising the Constitutional powers of government. It is enough to know that civil war is raging, and the Union is in peril; and proclaim a conviction that the restoration of the Fillmore Presidency will furnish the best if not the only means of restoring peace.

CAMPAIGN OF 1860

As the nation headed toward civil war, divided bitterly over the issues of slavery and the rights of citizens, the parties chose candidates in 1860. The Democrats, split sectionally and over procedural as well as policy matters, nominated Stephen A. Douglas, but only after the convention had adjourned in April and reconvened in June. Two groups of delegates bolted the respective sessions, and the vice-presidential candidate selected by the convention refused to accept the nomination. A former governor of Georgia, Herschel V. Johnson, ultimately was chosen by the national committee to complete the slate.

Many of the delegates who had bolted the April convention, together with other dissident southern Democrats and Buchanan administrators who walked out of the final convention in June, subsequently nominated Vice-President John C. Breckinridge of Kentucky for president and Senator Joseph Lane of Oregon for vice-president. These delegates, from nineteen states, were dedicated to noninterference with slavery in the territories—by either congressional or territorial legislation.

The sectional Republican Party, opposed to any extension of slavery in the territories, met in Chicago and nominated Abraham Lincoln of Illinois on the third ballot. Senator Hannibal Hamlin of Maine was chosen as the vice-presidential candidate. The Know Nothing–American Party members, together with some conservative Whigs, also formed a new party, the Constitutional Union Party, to ignore the slavery issue and to try to maintain a united nation. This group nominated John Bell of Tennessee for president and Edward Everett of Massachusetts as his running mate.

In a highly sectional election, Lincoln carried the North with 1,865,908 votes—less than 40 percent of the total. The deep South went to Breckinridge, who polled 848,019 votes—18 percent of the total. Douglas (1,380,202 popular votes—30 percent of the total) and Bell, with 590,901 votes, divided the border states. The defection of the Breckinridge faction in the South cost Douglas and the Democrats the election.

Lincoln was a majority choice in the electoral college: he had 180 to 72 for Breckinridge, 39 for Bell, and 12 for Douglas. Within two months of Lincoln's inauguration, the war between the states began.

Constitutional Union Platform of 1860

Whereas, Experience has demonstrated that Platforms adopted by the partisan Conventions of the country have had the effect to mislead and deceive the people, and at the same time to widen the political divisions of the country, by the creation and encouragement of geographical and sectional parties; therefore

Resolved, that it is both the part of patriotism and of duty to *recognize* no political principle other than THE CONSTITUTION OF THE COUNTRY, THE UNION OF THE STATES, AND THE ENFORCEMENT OF THE LAWS, and that, as representatives of the Constitutional Union men of the country, in National Convention assembled, we hereby pledge ourselves to maintain, protect, and defend, separately and unitedly, these great principles of public liberty and national safety, against all enemies, at home and abroad; believing that thereby peace may once more be restored to the country; the rights of the People and of the States re-established, and the Government again placed in that condition of justice, fraternity and equality, which, under the example and Constitution of our fathers, has solemnly bound every citizen of the United States to maintain a more perfect union, establish justice, insure domestic tranquillity, provide for the common defense, promote the general welfare, and secure the blessings of liberty to ourselves and our posterity.

Democratic Platform of 1860

1. *Resolved,* That we, the Democracy of the Union in Convention assembled, hereby declare our affirmance of the resolutions unanimously adopted and declared as a platform of principles by the Democratic Convention at Cincinnati, in the year 1856, believing that Democratic principles are unchangeable in their nature, when applied to the same subject matters; and we recommend, as the only further resolutions, the following:

2. Inasmuch as difference of opinion exists in the Democratic party as to the nature and extent of the powers of a Territorial Legislature, and as

to the powers and duties of Congress, under the Constitution of the United States, over the institution of slavery within the Territories,

Resolved, That the Democratic party will abide by the decision of the Supreme Court of the United States upon these questions of Constitutional law.

3. *Resolved,* That it is the duty of the United States to afford ample and complete protection to all its citizens, whether at home or abroad, and whether native or foreign born.

4. *Resolved,* That one of the necessities of the age, in a military, commercial, and postal point of view, is speedy communication between the Atlantic and Pacific States; and the Democratic party pledge such Constitutional Government aid as will insure the construction of a Railroad to the Pacific coast, at the earliest practicable period.

5. *Resolved,* That the Democratic party are in favor of the acquisition of the Island of Cuba on such terms as shall be honorable to ourselves and just to Spain.

6. *Resolved,* That the enactments of the State Legislatures to defeat the faithful execution of the Fugitive Slave Law, are hostile in character, subversive of the Constitution, and revolutionary in their effect.

7. *Resolved,* That it is in accordance with the interpretation of the Cincinnati platform, that during the existence of the Territorial Governments the measure of restriction, whatever it may be, imposed by the Federal Constitution on the power of the Territorial Legislature over the subject of the domestic relations, as the same has been, or shall hereafter be finally determined by the Supreme Court of the United States, should be respected by all good citizens, and enforced with promptness and fidelity by every branch of the general government.

Democratic (Breckenridge Faction) Platform of 1860

Resolved, That the platform adopted by the Democratic party at Cincinnati be affirmed, with the following explanatory resolutions:

1. That the Government of a Territory organized by an act of Congress is provisional and temporary, and during its existence all citizens of the United States have an equal right to settle with their property in the Territory, without their rights, either of person or property, being destroyed or impaired by Congressional or Territorial legislation.

2. That it is the duty of the Federal Government, in all its departments, to protect, when necessary, the rights of persons and property in the Territories, and wherever else its constitutional authority extends.

3. That when the settlers in a Territory, having an adequate population, form a State Constitution, the right of sovereignty commences, and being consummated by admission into the Union, they stand on an equal footing with the people of other States, and the State thus organized ought to be admitted into the Federal Union, whether its Constitution prohibits or recognizes the institution of slavery.

Resolved, That the Democratic party are in favor of the acquisition of the Island of Cuba, on such terms as shall be honorable to ourselves and just to Spain, at the earliest practicable moment.

Resolved, That the enactments of State Legislatures to defeat the faithful execution of the Fugitive Slave Law are hostile in character, subversive of the Constitution, and revolutionary in their effect.

Resolved, That the Democracy of the United States recognize it as the imperative duty of this Government to protect the naturalized citizen in all his rights, whether at home or in foreign lands, to the same extent as its native-born citizens.

WHEREAS, One of the greatest necessities of the age, in a political, commercial, postal and military point of view, is a speedy communication between the Pacific and Atlantic coasts. Therefore be it

Resolved, That the National Democratic party do hereby pledge themselves to use every means in their power to secure the passage of some bill, to the extent of the constitutional authority of Congress, for the construction of a Pacific Railroad from the Mississippi River to the Pacific Ocean, at the earliest practicable moment.

Republican Platform of 1860

Resolved, That we, the delegated representatives of the Republican electors of the United States, in Convention assembled, in discharge of the duty we owe to our constituents and our country, unite in the following declarations:

1. That the history of the nation during the last four years, has fully established the propriety and necessity of the organization and perpetuation of the Republican party, and that the causes which called it into existence are permanent in their nature, and now, more than ever before, demand its peaceful and constitutional triumph.

2. That the maintenance of the principles promulgated in the Declaration of Independence and embodied in the Federal Constitution, "That all men are created equal; that they are endowed by their Creator with certain inalienable rights; that among these are life, liberty and the pursuit of happiness; that to secure these rights, governments are instituted among men, deriving their just powers from the consent of the governed," is essential to the preservation of our Republican institutions; and that the Federal Constitution, the Rights of the States, and the Union of the States must and shall be preserved.

3. That to the Union of the States this nation owes its unprecedented increase in population, its surprising development of material resources, its rapid augmentation of wealth, its happiness at home and its honor abroad; and we hold in abhorrence all schemes for disunion, come from whatever source they may. And we congratulate the country that no Republican member of Congress has uttered or countenanced the threats of disunion so often made by Democratic members, without rebuke and with applause from their political associates; and we denounce those threats of disunion, in case of a popular overthrow of their ascendency as denying the vital principles of a free government, and as an avowal of contemplated treason, which it is the imperative duty of an indignant people sternly to rebuke and forever silence.

4. That the maintenance inviolate of the rights of the states, and especially the right of each state to order and control its own domestic institutions according to its own judgment exclusively, is essential to that balance of powers on which the perfection and endurance of our political fabric depends; and we denounce the lawless invasion by armed force of the soil of any state or territory, no matter under what pretext, as among the gravest of crimes.

5. That the present Democratic Administration has far exceeded our worst apprehensions, in its measureless subserviency to the exactions of a sectional interest, as especially evinced in its desperate exertions to force the infamous Lecompton Constitution upon the protesting people of Kansas; in construing the personal relations between master and servant to involve an unqualified property in persons; in its attempted enforcement everywhere, on land and sea, through the intervention of Congress and of the Federal Courts of the extreme pretensions of a purely local interest; and in its general and unvarying abuse of the power intrusted to it by a confiding people.

6. That the people justly view with alarm the reckless extravagance which pervades every department of the Federal Government; that a return to rigid economy and accountability is indispensable to arrest the systematic plunder of the public treasury by favored partisans; while the recent startling developments of frauds and corruptions at the Federal metropolis, show that an entire change of administration is imperatively demanded.

7. That the new dogma that the Constitution, of its own force, carries slavery into any or all of the territories of the United States, is a dangerous political heresy, at variance with the explicit provisions of that instrument itself, with contemporaneous exposition, and with legislative and judicial precedent; is revolutionary in its tendency, and subversive of the peace and harmony of the country.

8. That the normal condition of all the territory of the United States is that of freedom: That, as our Republican fathers, when they had abolished slavery in all our national territory, ordained that "no persons should be deprived of life, liberty or property without due process of law," it becomes our duty, by legislation, whenever such legislation is necessary, to maintain this provision of the Constitution against all attempts to violate it; and we deny the authority of Congress, of a territorial legislature, or of any individuals, to give legal existence to slavery in any territory of the United States.

9. That we brand the recent reopening of the African slave trade, under the cover of our national flag, aided by perversions of judicial power, as a crime against humanity and a burning shame to our country and age; and we call upon Congress to take prompt and efficient measures for

the total and final suppression of that execrable traffic.

10. That in the recent vetoes, by their Federal Governors, of the acts of the legislatures of Kansas and Nebraska, prohibiting slavery in those territories, we find a practical illustration of the boasted Democratic principle of Non-Intervention and Popular Sovereignty, embodied in the Kansas-Nebraska Bill, and a demonstration of the deception and fraud involved therein.

11. That Kansas should, of right, be immediately admitted as a state under the Constitution recently formed and adopted by her people, and accepted by the House of Representatives.

12. That, while providing revenue for the support of the general government by duties upon imports, sound policy requires such an adjustment of these imports as to encourage the development of the industrial interests of the whole country; and we commend that policy of national exchanges, which secures to the workingmen liberal wages, to agriculture remunerative prices, to mechanics and manufacturers an adequate reward for their skill, labor, and enterprise, and to the nation commercial prosperity and independence.

13. That we protest against any sale or alienation to others of the public lands held by actual settlers, and against any view of the free-homestead policy which regards the settlers as paupers or suppliants for public bounty; and we demand

the passage by Congress of the complete and satisfactory homestead measure which has already passed the House.

14. That the Republican party is opposed to any change in our naturalization laws or any state legislation by which the rights of citizens hitherto accorded to immigrants from foreign lands shall be abridged or impaired; and in favor of giving a full and efficient protection to the rights of all classes of citizens, whether native or naturalized, both at home and abroad.

15. That appropriations by Congress for river and harbor improvements of a national character, required for the accommodation and security of an existing commerce, are authorized by the Constitution, and justified by the obligation of Government to protect the lives and property of its citizens.

16. That a railroad to the Pacific Ocean is imperatively demanded by the interests of the whole country; that the federal government ought to render immediate and efficient aid in its construction; and that, as preliminary thereto, a daily overland mail should be promptly established.

17. Finally, having thus set forth our distinctive principles and views, we invite the co-operation of all citizens, however differing on other questions, who substantially agree with us in their affirmance and support.

CAMPAIGN OF 1864

In 1864, President Abraham Lincoln was nominated by the Republicans on the first ballot at their national convention in Baltimore. Lincoln left the selection of his running mate to the delegates, and they chose a Democrat, the former senator and military governor of Tennessee, Andrew Johnson. This strategy fit the "union" theme which had been emphasized in the call to the convention. The president's war policies were not without criticism within his party, however, and a group of radical Republicans held a separate convention in Cleveland shortly before the Baltimore gathering. They adopted a platform and nominated General John C. Frémont for president and General John Cochrane of New York for vice-president. The movement failed to attract support, and both men withdrew from the race late in September.

The Democrats, meeting in Chicago, split over war policies. The "Copperheads" wanted a negotiated peace with the South; other groups supported the war but criticized the administration's unconstitutional disregard for personal liberties. Nevertheless, they united to nominate General George B. McClellan of New Jersey for president on the first ballot and Representative George H. Pendleton of Ohio for vice-president on the second.

In the election, counting the votes of soldiers in the field, Lincoln and Johnson received 2,213,665 popular votes and 212 electoral votes to 1,802,237 popular votes and 21 electoral votes for McClellan and Pendleton.

Democratic Platform of 1864

Resolved, That in the future, as in the past, we will adhere with unswerving fidelity to the Union under the Constitution as the only solid foundation of our strength, security, and happiness as a people, and as a framework of government equally conducive to the welfare and prosperity of all the States, both Northern and Southern.

Resolved, That this convention does explicitly declare, as the sense of the American people, that after four years of failure to restore the Union by the experiment of war, during which, under the pretense of a military necessity of war-power higher than the Constitution, the Constitution itself has been disregarded in every part, and public liberty and private right alike trodden down, and the material prosperity of the country essentially impaired, justice, humanity, liberty, and the public welfare demand that immediate efforts be made for a cessation of hostilities, with a view of an ultimate convention of the States, or other peaceable means, to the end that, at the earliest practicable moment, peace may be restored on the basis of the Federal Union of the States.

Resolved, That the direct interference of the military authorities of the United States in the recent elections held in Kentucky, Maryland, Missouri, and Delaware was a shameful violation of the Constitution, and a repetition of such acts in the approaching election will be held as revolutionary, and resisted with all the means and power under our control.

Resolved, That the aim and object of the Democratic party is to preserve the Federal Union and the rights of the States unimpaired, and they hereby declare that they consider that the administrative usurpation of extraordinary and dangerous powers not granted by the Constitution—the subversion of the civil by military law in States not in insurrection; the arbitrary military arrest, imprisonment, trial, and sentence of American citizens in States where civil law exists in full force; the suppression of freedom of speech and of the press; the denial of the right of asylum; the open and avowed disregard of State rights; the employment of unusual test-oaths; and the interference with and denial of the right of the people to bear arms in their defense is calculated to prevent a restoration of the Union and the perpetuation of a Government deriving its just powers from the consent of the governed.

Resolved, That the shameful disregard of the Administration to its duty in respect to our fellow-citizens who now are and long have been prisoners of war and in a suffering condition, deserves the severest reprobation on the score alike of public policy and common humanity.

Resolved, That the sympathy of the Democratic party is heartily and earnestly extended to the soldiery of our army and sailors of our navy, who are and have been in the field and on the sea under the flag of our country, and, in the events of its attaining power, they will receive all the care, protection, and regard that the brave soldiers and sailors of the republic have so nobly earned.

Republican Platform of 1864

1. *Resolved,* That it is the highest duty of every American citizen to maintain against all their enemies the integrity of the Union and the paramount authority of the Constitution and laws of the United States; and that, laying aside all differences of political opinion, we pledge ourselves, as Union men, animated by a common sentiment and aiming at a common object, to do everything in our power to aid the Government in quelling by force of arms the Rebellion now raging against its authority, and in bringing to the punishment due to their crimes the Rebels and traitors arrayed against it.

2. *Resolved,* That we approve the determination of the Government of the United States not to compromise with Rebels, or to offer them any terms of peace, except such as may be based upon an unconditional surrender of their hostility and a return to their just allegiance to the Constitution and laws of the United States, and that we call upon the Government to maintain this position and to prosecute the war with the utmost possible vigor to the complete suppression of the Rebellion, in full reliance upon the self-sacrificing patriotism, the heroic valor and the undying devotion of the American people to the country and its free institutions.

3. *Resolved,* That as slavery was the cause, and now constitutes the strength of this Rebellion, and as it must be, always and everywhere, hostile to the principles of Republican Government, justice and the National safety demand its utter and complete extirpation from the soil of the Republic; and that, while we uphold and maintain the acts and proclamations by which the Government, in its own defense, has aimed a deathblow at this gigantic evil, we are in favor, furthermore, of such an amendment to the Constitution, to be made by the people in conformity with its provisions, as shall terminate and forever prohibit the existence of Slavery within the limits of the jurisdiction of the United States.

4. *Resolved,* That the thanks of the American people are due to the soldiers and sailors of the Army and Navy, who have periled their lives in defense of the country and in vindication of the honor of its flag; that the nation owes to them some permanent recognition of their patriotism and their valor, and ample and permanent provision for those of their survivors who have received disabling and honorable wounds in the service of the country; and that the memories of those who have fallen in its defense shall be held in grateful and everlasting remembrance.

5. *Resolved,* That we approve and applaud the practical wisdom, the unselfish patriotism and the unswerving fidelity to the Constitution and the principles of American liberty, with which ABRAHAM LINCOLN has discharged, under circumstances of unparalleled difficulty, the great duties and responsibilities of the Presidential office; that we approve and indorse, as demanded by the emergency and essential to the preservation of the nation and as within the provisions of the Constitution, the measures and acts which he has adopted to defend the nation against its open and secret foes; that we approve, especially, the Proclamation of Emancipation, and the employment as Union soldiers of men heretofore held in slavery; and that we have full confidence in his determination to carry these and all other Constitutional measures essential to the salvation of the country into full and complete effect.

6. *Resolved,* That we deem it essential to the general welfare that harmony should prevail in the National Councils, and we regard as worthy of public confidence and official trust those only who cordially indorse the principles proclaimed in these resolutions, and which should characterize the administration of the government.

7. *Resolved,* That the Government owes to all men employed in its armies, without regard to distinction of color, the full protection of the laws of war—and that any violation of these laws, or of the usages of civilized nations in time of war, by the Rebels now in arms, should be made the subject of prompt and full redress.

8. *Resolved,* That foreign immigration, which in the past has added so much to the wealth, development of resources and increase of power to the nation, the asylum of the oppressed of all na-

tions, should be fostered and encouraged by a liberal and just policy.

9. *Resolved,* That we are in favor of the speedy construction of the railroad to the Pacific coast.

10. *Resolved,* That the National faith, pledged for the redemption of the public debt, must be kept inviolate, and that for this purpose we recommend economy and rigid responsibility in the public expenditures, and a vigorous and just system of taxation; and that it is the duty of every loyal state to sustain the credit and promote the use of the National currency.

11. *Resolved,* That we approve the position taken by the Government that the people of the United States can never regard with indifference the attempt of any European Power to overthrow by force or to supplant by fraud the institutions of any Republican Government on the Western Continent and that they will view with extreme jealousy, as menacing to the peace and independence of their own country, the efforts of any such power to obtain new footholds for Monarchical Government, sustained by foreign military force, in near proximity to the United States.

CAMPAIGN OF 1868

In the aftermath of the Civil War, the "National Union Republican Party," as the platform writers termed the organization, convened in Chicago in 1868. All of the states that had seceded were represented by delegates. General Ulysses S. Grant was the only candidate nominated for president and he received a unanimous vote on the first ballot. After a spirited contest among eleven aspirants for the vice-presidential nomination, Speaker of the House Schuyler Colfax of Indiana was chosen on the fifth ballot.

The Democratic Party met on July 4, 1868, in Tammany Hall in New York City. A former governor of New York, Horatio Seymour, a compromise choice who had originally declined to be a candidate, was selected as the presidential standard-bearer on the twenty-second ballot. General Francis P. Blair of Missouri was chosen as the vice-presidential candidate.

Although not all of the southern states were given the right to choose electors, thirty-seven states participated in the election. Grant received 3,013,650 popular votes and 214 electoral votes to Seymour's 2,708,744 popular votes and 80 electoral votes.

Democratic Platform of 1868

The Democratic party in National Convention assembled, reposing its trust in the intelligence, patriotism, and discriminating justice of the people; standing upon the Constitution as the foundation and limitation of the powers of the government, and the guarantee of the liberties of the citizen; and recognizing the questions of slavery and secession as having been settled for all time to come by the war, or the voluntary action of the Southern States in Constitutional Conventions assembled, and never to be renewed or reagitated; does, with the return of peace, demand,

First. Immediate restoration of all the States to their rights in the Union, under the Constitution, and of civil government to the American people.

Second. Amnesty for all past political offenses, and the regulation of the elective franchise in the States, by their citizens.

Third. Payment of the public debt of the United States as rapidly as practicable. All moneys drawn from the people by taxation, except so much as is requisite for the necessities of the government, economically administered, being honestly applied to such payment, and where the obligations of the government do not expressly state upon their face, or the law under which they were issued does not provide, that they shall be paid in coin, they ought, in right and in justice, to be paid in the lawful money of the United States.

Fourth. Equal taxation of every species of property, according to its real value, including government bonds and other public securities.

Fifth. One currency for the government and the people, the laborer and the office-holder, the pensioner and the soldier, the producer and the bond-holder.

Sixth. Economy in the administration of the government, the reduction of the standing army and navy; the abolition of the Freedmen's Bureau; and all political instrumentalities designed to secure negro supremacy; simplification of the system and discontinuance of inquisitorial modes of assessing and collecting internal revenue, so that the burden of taxation may be equalized and lessened, the credit of the government and the currency made good; the repeal of all enactments for enrolling the State militia into national forces in time of peace; and a tariff for revenue upon foreign imports, such as will afford incidental protection to domestic manufactures, and as will, without impairing the revenue, impose the least burden upon, and best promote and encourage the great industrial interests of the country.

Seventh. Reform of abuses in the administration; the expulsion of corrupt men from office; the abrogation of useless offices; the restoration of rightful authority to, and the independence of the executive and judicial departments of the government; the subordination of the military to the civil power, to the end that the usurpations of Congress and the despotism of the sword may cease.

Eighth. Equal rights and protection for naturalized and native-born citizens at home and abroad; the assertion of American nationality, which shall command the respect of foreign powers, and furnish an example and encouragement to people struggling for national integrity, constitutional liberty, and individual rights, and the maintenance of the rights of naturalized citizens against the absolute doctrine of immutable allegiance and the claims of foreign powers to punish them for alleged crimes committed beyond their jurisdiction.

In demanding these measures and reforms we arraign the Radical party for its disregard of right, and the unparalleled oppression and tyranny which have marked its career.

After the most solemn and unanimous pledge of both Houses of Congress to prosecute the war exclusively for the maintenance of the government and the preservation of the Union under the Constitution, it has repeatedly violated that most sacred pledge, under which alone was rallied that noble volunteer army which carried our flag to victory.

Instead of restoring the Union, it has, so far as in its power, dissolved it, and subjected ten States, in time of profound peace, to military despotism and negro supremacy.

It has nullified there the right of trial by jury; it has abolished the *habeas corpus,* that most sacred writ of liberty; it has overthrown the freedom of speech and of the press; it has substituted arbitrary seizures and arrests, and military trials and secret star-chamber inquisitions, for the constitutional tribunals; it has disregarded in time of peace the right of the people to be free from searches and seizures; it has entered the post and telegraph offices, and even the private rooms of individuals, and seized their private papers and letters without any specific charge or notice of affidavit, as required by the organic law; it has converted the American capitol into a Bastile; it has established a system of spies and official espionage to which no constitutional monarchy of Europe would now dare to resort; it has abolished the right of appeal, on important constitutional

questions, to the Supreme Judicial tribunal, and threatens to curtail, or destroy, its original jurisdiction, which is irrevocably vested by the Constitution; while the learned Chief Justice has been subjected to the most atrocious calumnies, merely because he would not prostitute his high office to the support of the false and partisan charges preferred against the President. Its corruption and extravagance have exceeded anything known in history, and by its frauds and monopolies it has nearly doubled the burden of the debt created by the war; it has stripped the President of his constitutional power of appointment, even of his own Cabinet. Under its repeated assaults the pillars of the government are rocking on their base, and should it succeed in November next and inaugurate its President, we will meet, as a subjected and conquered people, amid the ruins of liberty and the scattered fragments of the Constitution.

And we do declare and resolve, That ever since the people of the United States threw off all subjection to the British crown, the privilege and trust of suffrage have belonged to the several States, and have been granted, regulated, and controlled exclusively by the political power of each State respectively, and that any attempt by congress, on any pretext whatever, to deprive any State of this right, or interfere with its exercise, is a flagrant usurpation of power, which can find no warrant in the Constitution; and if sanctioned by the people will subvert our form of government, and can only end in a single centralized and consolidated government, in which the separate existence of the States will be entirely absorbed, and an unqualified despotism be established in place of a federal union of co-equal States; and that we regard the reconstruction acts so-called, of Congress, as such an usurpation, and unconstitutional, revolutionary, and void.

That our soldiers and sailors, who carried the flag of our country to victory against a most gallant and determined foe, must ever be gratefully remembered, and all the guarantees given in their favor must be faithfully carried into execution.

That the public lands should be distributed as widely as possible among the people, and should be disposed of either under the pre-emption or homestead laws, or sold in reasonable quantities, and to none but actual occupants, at the minimum price established by the government. When grants of the public lands may be deemed necessary for the encouragement of important public improvements, the proceeds of the sale of such lands, and not the lands themselves, should be so applied.

That the President of the United States, Andrew Johnson, in exercising the power of his high office in resisting the aggressions of Congress upon the Constitutional rights of the States and the people, is entitled to the gratitude of the whole American people; and in behalf of the Democratic party, we tender him our thanks for his patriotic efforts in that regard.

Upon this platform the Democratic party appeals to every patriot, including all the Conservative element, and all who desire to support the Constitution and restore the Union, forgetting all past differences of opinion, to unite with us in the present great struggle for the liberties of the people; and that to all such, to whatever party they may have heretofore belonged, we extend the right hand of fellowship, and hail all such co-operating with us as friends and brethren.

Resolved, That this convention sympathize cordially with the workingmen of the United States in their efforts to protect the rights and interests of the laboring classes of the country.

Resolved, That the thanks of the convention are tendered to Chief Justice Salmon P. Chase for the justice, dignity, and impartiality with which he presided over the court of impeachment on the trial of President Andrew Johnson.

Republican Platform of 1868

The National Union Republican Party of the United States, assembled in National Convention, in the city of Chicago, on the 20th day of May, 1868, make the following declaration of principles:

First—We congratulate the country on the assured success of the reconstruction policy of Congress, as evinced by the adoption, in the majority of the States lately in rebellion, of constitutions securing equal civil and political rights to all, and regard it as the duty of the Government to sustain those constitutions, and to prevent the people of such States from being remitted to a state of anarchy or military rule.

Second—The guaranty by Congress of equal suffrage to all loyal men at the South was demanded by every consideration of public safety, of gratitude, and of justice, and must be maintained; while the question of suffrage in all the loyal States properly belongs to the people of those States.

Third—We denounce all forms of repudiation as a national crime; and national honor requires the payment of the public indebtedness in the utmost good faith to all creditors at home and abroad, not only according to the letter, but the spirit of the laws under which it was contracted.

Fourth—It is due to the labor of the nation, that taxation should be equalized and reduced as rapidly as the national faith will permit.

Fifth—The National Debt, contracted as it has been for the preservation of the Union for all time to come, should be extended over a fair period of redemption, and it is the duty of Congress to reduce the rate of interest thereon whenever it can be done honestly.

Sixth—That the best policy to diminish our burden of debt, is to so improve our credit that capitalists will seek to loan us money at lower rates of interest than we now pay and must continue to pay so long as repudiation, partial or total, open or covert, is threatened or suspected.

Seventh—The Government of the United States should be administered with the strictest economy; and the corruptions which have been so shamefully nursed and fostered by Andrew Johnson call loudly for radical reform.

Eighth—We profoundly deplore the untimely and tragic death of Abraham Lincoln, and regret the accession of Andrew Johnson to the Presidency, who has acted treacherously to the people who elected him and the cause he was pledged to support; has usurped high legislative and judicial functions; has refused to execute the laws; has used his high office to induce other officers to ignore and violate the laws; has employed his executive powers to render insecure the property, the peace, the liberty, and life of the citizen; has abused the pardoning power; has denounced the National Legislature as unconstitutional; has persistently and corruptly resisted, by every means in his power, every proper attempt at the reconstruction of the States lately in rebellion; has perverted the public patronage into an engine of wholesale corruption; and has been justly impeached for high crimes and misdemeanors, and properly pronounced guilty thereof by the vote of thirty-five senators.

Ninth—The doctrine of Great Britain and other European powers, that because a man is once a subject, he is always so, must be resisted, at every hazard, by the United States, as a relic of the feudal times, not authorized by the law of nations, and at war with our national honor and independence. Naturalized citizens are entitled to be protected in all their rights of citizenship, as though they were native-born; and no citizen of the United States, native or naturalized, must be liable to arrest and imprisonment by any foreign power, for acts done or words spoken in this country; and, if so arrested and imprisoned, it is the duty of the Government to interfere in his behalf.

Tenth—Of all who were faithful in the trials of the late war, there were none entitled to more especial honor than the brave soldiers and seamen who endured the hardships of campaign and cruise, and imperilled their lives in the service of the country. The bounties and pensions provided by law for these brave defenders of the nation, are obligations never to be forgotten. The widows and orphans of the gallant dead are the wards of the people—a sacred legacy bequeathed to the nation's protecting care.

Eleventh—Foreign immigration, which in the past, has added so much to the wealth, development of resources, and increase of power to this nation—the asylum of the oppressed of all nations—should be fostered and encouraged by a liberal and just policy.

Twelfth—This Convention declares its sympathy with all the oppressed people which are struggling for their rights.

Thirteenth—We highly commend the spirit of magnanimity and forgiveness with which men who have served in the rebellion, but now frankly and honestly co-operate with us in restoring the peace of the country, and reconstructing the Southern State Governments upon the basis of impartial justice and equal rights, are received back into the communion of the loyal people; and we favor the removal of the disqualifications and restrictions imposed upon the late rebels, in the same measure as the spirit of disloyalty will die out, and as may be consistent with the safety of the loyal people.

Fourteenth—We recognize the great principles laid down in the immortal Declaration of Independence as the true foundation of Democratic Government; and we hail with gladness every effort toward making these principles a living reality on every inch of American soil.

CAMPAIGN OF 1872

In a period of postwar ferment over policies in the South and the administration of the government in Washington, six parties nominated candidates and adopted platforms in 1872.

The Labor Reform Party members met in Columbus, Ohio, in February and nominated Justice David Davis of Illinois and Joel Parker of New Jersey, but both candidates declined the nominations in June. Later, Charles O'Conor of New York was nominated for president and no one was chosen for the vice-presidential position. The Prohibition Party first appeared in this campaign and also held its convention in February in Columbus. James Black of Pennsylvania and John Russell of Michigan were nominated by acclamation for president and vice-president.

The Liberal Republicans, opposed to Grant and his administration, included many distinguished leaders who met in a mass meeting in Cincinnati and nominated Horace Greeley of New York for president on the sixth ballot and B. Gratz Brown of Missouri for vice-president on the second. Interestingly, the Democratic Party convention, meeting subsequently in Baltimore for only six hours, illustrated its flexible state of mind by adopting both the candidates and the platform of the Liberal Republicans.

The Republican convention unanimously renominated the incumbent, Ulysses S. Grant, but chose Henry Wilson of Massachusetts over Vice-President Schuyler Colfax to be Grant's running mate. "Straight-Out" Democrats, who could not accept Greeley, convened in Louisville, Kentucky, in September and also nominated Charles O'Conor for president and John Quincy Adams of Massachusetts for vice-president.

In November of 1872, for the first time, all thirty-seven states of the Union chose their electors by popular vote. Grant received 3,598,235 popular votes to 2,834,761 for Greeley, 18,602 for O'Conor, and 5,608 for Black. Although electoral votes from Arkansas and Louisiana were rejected by Congress, Grant and Wilson received 286 electoral votes. Greeley died before the electoral votes were cast, so the sixty-three electors pledged to him scattered their votes among four other persons.

Democratic Platform of 1872

We, the Democratic Electors of the United States in Convention assembled, do present the following principles, already adopted at Cincinnati, as essential to just government.

1. We recognize the equality of all men before the law, and hold that it is the duty of the Government in its dealings with the people to mete out equal and exact justice to all, of whatever nativity, race, color or persuasion, religion or politics.

2. We pledge ourselves to maintain the union of these States, emancipation and enfranchisement; and to oppose any reopening of the questions settled by the thirteenth, fourteenth and fifteenth amendments of the Constitution.

3. We demand the immediate and absolute removal of all disabilities imposed on account of the rebellion which was finally subdued seven years ago, believing that universal amnesty will result in complete pacification in all sections of the country.

4. Local self-government, with impartial suffrage, will guard the rights of all citizens more securely than any centralized power. The public welfare requires the supremacy of the civil over the military authority, and the freedom of person under the protection of the *habeas corpus*. We demand for the individual the largest liberty consistent with public order; for the State, self-government, and for the Nation a return to the methods of peace and the constitutional limitations of power.

5. The Civil Service of the Government has become a mere instrument of partisan tyranny and personal ambition, and an object of selfish greed. It is a scandal and reproach upon free

institutions, and it breeds a demoralization danger-ous to the perpetuity of Republican Government.

6. We therefore regard a thorough reform of the Civil Service as one of the most pressing necessities of the hour; that honesty, capacity, and fidelity constitute the only valid claim to public employment; that the offices of the Government cease to be a matter of arbitrary favorit-ism and patronage, and that public station shall become again a place of honor. To this end it is imperatively required that no President shall be a candidate for re-election.

7. We demand a system of Federal taxation which shall not unnecessarily interfere with the industry of the people and which shall provide the means necessary to pay the expenses of the Government, economically administered, the pensions, the interest on the public debt, and a moderate annual reduction of the principal thereof; and recognizing that there are in our midst honest but irreconcilable differences of opinion with regard to the respective systems of protection and free trade, we remit the discussion of the subject to the people in their Congressional Districts, and the decision of the Congress thereon, wholly free from Executive interference or dictation.

8. The public credit must be sacredly main-tained, and we denounce repudiation in every form and guise.

9. A speedy return to specie payment is de-manded alike by the highest considerations of commercial morality and honest government.

10. We remember with gratitude the heroism and sacrifices of the soldiers and sailors of the Republic, and no act of ours shall ever detract from their justly earned fame for the full reward of their patriotism.

11. We are opposed to all further grants of lands to railroads or other corporations. The pub-lic domain should be held sacred to actual settlers.

12. We hold that it is the duty of the Govern-ment, in its intercourse with foreign nations, to cultivate the friendships of peace by treating with all on fair and equal terms, regarding it alike dishonorable either to demand what is not right or to submit to what is wrong.

13. For the promotion and success of these vital principles, and the support of the candidates nominated by this Convention, we invite and cordially welcome the co-operation of all patriotic citizens without regard to previous political affilia-tions.

Democratic (Straight-Out) Platform of 1872

Whereas, A frequent recurrence to first princi-ples and eternal vigilance against abuses are the wisest provisions for liberty, which is the source of progress, and fidelity to our constitutional sys-tem is the only protection for either; therefore

Resolved, That the original basis of our whole political structure is consent in every part thereof. The people of each State voluntarily created their State, and the States voluntarily formed the Union; and each State provided by its written Constitution for everything a State could do for the protection of life, liberty, and property within it, and each State, jointly with the others, pro-vided a Federal Union for foreign and interstate relations.

Resolved, That all Governmental powers, whether State or Federal, are trust powers coming from the people of each State, and that they are limited to the written letter of the Constitution and the laws passed in pursuance of it; which powers must be exercised in the utmost good faith, the Constitution itself proving in what manner they may be altered and amended.

Resolved, That the interests of labor and capital should not be permitted to conflict, but should be harmonized by judicious legislation. While such a conflict continues, labor, which is the parent of wealth, is entitled to paramount con-sideration.

Resolved, That we proclaim to the world that principle is to be preferred to power; that the Democratic party is held together by the cohesion of time-honored principles, which they will never surrender in exchange for all the offices which Presidents can confer. The pangs of the minori-ties are doubtless excruciating; but we welcome an eternal minority under the banner inscribed with our principles, rather than an almighty and everlasting majority purchased by their abandon-ment.

Resolved, That having been betrayed at Balti-more into a false creed and a false leadership by the Convention, we repudiate both, and appeal to the people to approve our platform and to rally to the polls and support the true platform and the candidates who embody it.

Labor Reform Platform of 1872

1. We hold that all political power is inherent in the people, and free government founded on their authority and established for their benefit; that all citizens are equal in political rights, entitled to the largest religious and political liberty compatible with the good order of society, as also the use and enjoyment of the fruits of their labor and talents; and no man, or set of men, is entitled to exclusive separate emoluments and privileges from the Government, but in consideration of public services; and any laws destructive of these fundamental principles are without moral binding force, and should be repealed; and believing that all evils resulting from unjust legislation now affecting the industrial classes can be removed by the adoption of the principles contained in the following declaration: Therefore,

2. *Resolved*, That it is the duty of the Government to establish a just standard of distribution of capital and labor by providing a purely national circulating medium based on the faith and resources of the nation, issued directly to the people without the intervention of any system of banking corporations, which money shall be a legal tender in the payment of all debts, public and private, and interchangeable, at the option of the holder, for Government bonds bearing a rate of interest not to exceed 3.75 per cent, subject to future legislation by Congress.

3. *Resolved*, That the national debt should be paid in good faith, according to the original contract, at the earliest option of the Government, without mortgaging the property of the people and the future earnings of labor, to enrich a few capitalists at home and abroad.

4. *Resolved*, That justice demands that the burdens of government should be so adjusted as to bear equally on all classes and interests; and that the exemption from taxation of Government bonds bearing extortionate rates of interest is a violation of all just principles of revenue laws.

5. *Resolved*, That the public lands of the United States belong to the people, and should not be sold to individuals nor granted to corporations, but should be held as a sacred trust for the benefit of the people, and should be granted free of cost to landless settlers only, in amounts not exceeding 160 acres of land.

6. *Resolved*, That Congress should modify the tariff so as to admit free such articles of common use as we can neither produce nor grow, and lay duties for revenue mainly upon articles of luxury, and upon such articles of manufacture as we, having the raw materials in abundance, will assist in further developing the resources of the country.

7. *Resolved*, That the presence in our country of Chinese laborers imported by capitalists in large numbers for servile use, is an evil entailing want and its consequent train of misery and crime on all classes of the American people, and should be prohibited by legislation.

8. *Resolved*, That we ask for the enactment of a law by which all mechanics and day laborers employed by or on behalf of the Government, whether directly or indirectly, through persons, firms, or corporations, contracting with the State, shall conform to the reduced standard of eight hours a day recently adopted by Congress for the national employes, and also for an amendment to the act of incorporation for cities and towns, by which all laborers and mechanics employed at their expense shall conform to the same number of hours.

9. *Resolved*, That the enlightened spirit of the age demands the abolition of the system of contract labor in our prisons and other reformatory institutions.

10. *Resolved*, That the protection of life, liberty, and property are the three cardinal principles of government, and the first two more sacred than the latter; therefore, money for prosecuting wars should, as it is required, be assessed and collected from the wealth of the country, and not entailed as a burden on posterity.

11. *Resolved*, That it is the duty of the government to so exercise its power over railroads and telegraph corporations that they shall not in any case be privileged to exact such rates of freight, transportation or charges by whatever name, as may bear unduly or inequitably upon either producer or consumer.

12. *Resolved*, That there should be such a reform in the Civil Service of the National Government as will remove it beyond all partisan influ-

ence, and place it in the charge and under the direction of intelligent and competent business men.

13. *Resolved,* That as both history and experience teach us that power ever seeks to perpetuate itself by any and all means at its command, and that its prolonged possession in the hands of one person is always dangerous to the liberty of free people, and believing, too, that the spirit of our organic laws and the stability and safety of our free institutions are best obeyed on the one hand and secured on the other, by a regular constitutional change in the chief of the country at each quadrennial election, therefore, we are in favor of limiting the occupancy of the Presidential chair to one term.

14. *Resolved,* That we are in favor of granting general amnesty and restoring the Union at once on the basis of equality of rights and privileges to all; the impartial administration of justice being the only true bond of the union to bind the States together and restore the Government of the people.

Liberal Republican Platform of 1872

We, the Liberal Republicans of the United States in National Convention assembled at Cincinnati, proclaim the following principles as essential to just government.

First: We recognize the equality of all men before the law, and hold that it is the duty of Government in its dealings with the people to mete out equal and exact justice to all of whatever nativity, race, color, or persuasion, religious or political.

Second: We pledge ourselves to maintain the union of these States, emancipation, and enfranchisement, and to oppose any re-opening of the questions settled by the Thirteenth, Fourteenth, and Fifteenth Amendments to the Constitution.

Third: We demand the immediate and absolute removal of all disabilities imposed on account of the Rebellion, which was finally subdued seven years ago, believing that universal amnesty will result in complete pacification in all sections of the country.

Fourth: Local self-government, with impartial suffrage, will guard the rights of all citizens more securely than any centralized power. The public welfare requires the supremacy of the civil over the military authority, and freedom of person under the protection of the *habeas corpus.* We demand for the individual the largest liberty consistent with public order; for the State, self-government, and for the nation a return to the methods of peace and the constitutional limitations of power.

Fifth: The Civil Service of the Government has become a mere instrument of partisan tyranny and personal ambition and an object of selfish greed. It is a scandal and reproach upon free institutions and breeds a demoralization dangerous to the perpetuity of republican government. We therefore regard such thorough reforms of the Civil Service as one of the most pressing necessities of the hour; that honesty, capacity, and fidelity constitute the only valid claim to public employment; that the offices of the Government cease to be a matter of arbitrary favoritism and patronage, and that public station become again a post of honor. To this end it is imperatively required that no President shall be a candidate for re-election.

Sixth: We demand a system of Federal taxation which shall not unnecessarily interfere with the industry of the people, and which shall provide the means necessary to pay the expenses of the Government economically administered, the pensions, the interest on the public debt, and a moderate reduction annually of the principal thereof; and, recognizing that there are in our midst honest but irreconcilable differences of opinion with regard to the respective systems of Protection and Free Trade, we remit the discussion of the subject to the people in their Congress Districts, and to the decision of Congress thereon, wholly free of Executive interference or dictation.

Seventh: The public credit must be sacredly maintained, and we denounce repudiation in every form and guise.

Eighth: A speedy return to specie payment is demanded alike by the highest considerations of commercial morality and honest government.

Ninth: We remember with gratitude the heroism and sacrifices of the soldiers and sailors of the Republic, and no act of ours shall ever detract from their justly-earned fame or the full reward of their patriotism.

Tenth: We are opposed to all further grants

of lands to railroads or other corporations. The public domain should be held sacred to actual settlers.

Eleventh: We hold that it is the duty of the Government, in its intercourse with foreign nations to cultivate the friendship of peace, by treating with all on fair and equal terms, regarding it alike dishonorable either to demand what is not right, or to submit to what is wrong.

Twelfth: For the promotion and success of these vital principles and the support of the candidates nominated by this Convention, we invite and cordially welcome the co-operation of all patriotic citizens, without regard to previous affiliations.

Prohibition Platform of 1872

Resolved, That we reaffirm the following resolutions adopted by the National Prohibition Convention, held at Chicago, Sept. 2, 1869:

"*Whereas,* Protection and allegiance are reciprocal duties, and every citizen who yields obedience to the just demands of the Government is entitled to the full, free and perfect protection of that Government in the enjoyment of personal security, personal liberty and private property; and

"*Whereas,* The traffic in intoxicating drinks greatly impairs the personal security and personal liberty of a large mass of citizens, and renders private property insecure; and

"*Whereas,* All other political parties are hopelessly unwilling to adopt an adequate policy on this question; therefore

"We, in National Convention assembled, as citizens of this free Republic, sharing the duties and responsibilities of its Government, in discharge of a solemn duty we owe to our country and our race, unite in the following declaration of principles:

"1. That while we acknowledge the pure patriotism and profound statesmanship of those patriots who laid the foundations of this Government, securing at once the rights of the States severally, and their inseparable union by the Federal Constitution, we would not merely garnish the sepulchers of our republican fathers, but we do hereby renew our solemn pledges of fealty to the imperishable principles of civil and re-

ligious liberty embodied in the Declaration of American Independence and our Federal Constitution.

"2. That the traffic in intoxicating beverages is a dishonor to Christian civilization, inimical to the best interests of society, a political wrong of unequalled enormity, subversive of the ordinary objects of government, not capable of being regulated or restrained by any system of license whatever, but imperatively demanding for its suppression effective legal Prohibition by both State and National legislation."

3. That while we recognize the good providence of Almighty God in supervising the interests of this nation from its establishment to the present time, having organized our party for the legal Prohibition of the liquor traffic, our reliance for success is upon the same omnipotent arm.

4. That there can be no greater peril to the nation than the existing party competition for the liquor vote; that any party not openly opposed to the traffic, experience shows, will engage in this competition, will court the favor of the criminal classes, will barter away the public morals, the purity of the ballot, and every object of good government, for party success.

5. That while adopting national political measures for the Prohibition of the liquor traffic, we will continue the use of all moral means in our power to persuade men away from the injurious practice of using intoxicating beverages.

6. That we invite all persons, whether total abstainers or not, who recognize the terrible injuries inflicted by the liquor traffic, to unite with us for its overthrow, and to secure thereby peace, order and the protection of persons and property.

7. That competency, honesty and sobriety are indispensable qualifications for holding public office.

8. That removals from public service for mere difference of political opinion is a practice opposed to sound policy and just principles.

9. That fixed and moderate salaries should take the place of official fees and perquisites; the franking privilege, sinecures, and all unnecessary offices and expenses should be abolished, and every possible means be employed to prevent corruption and venality in office; and by a rigid system of accountability from all its officers, and guards over the public treasury, the utmost econ-

omy should be practiced and enforced in every department of the Government.

10. That we favor the election of President, Vice-President and United States Senators by direct vote of the people.

11. That we are in favor of a sound national currency, adequate to the demands of business and convertible into gold and silver at the will of the holder, and the adoption of every measure compatible with justice and the public safety, to appreciate our present currency to the gold standard.

12. That the rates of inland and ocean postage, of telegraphic communication, of railroad and water transportation and travel, should be reduced to the lowest practicable point, by force of laws wisely and justly framed, with reference not only to the interest of capital employed but to the higher claim of the general good.

13. That an adequate public revenue being necessary, it may properly be raised by impost duties and by an equitable assessment upon the property and legitimate business of the country; nevertheless we are opposed to any discrimination of capital against labor, as well as to all monopoly and class legislation.

14. That the removal of the burdens, moral, physical, pecuniary and social, imposed by the traffic in intoxicating drinks will, in our judgment, emancipate labor and practically thus promote labor reform.

15. That the fostering and extension of common schools under the care and support of the State, to supply the want of a general and liberal education, is a primary duty of a good government.

16. That the right of suffrage rests on no mere circumstance of color, race, former social condition, sex or nationality, but inheres in the nature of man; and when from any cause it has been withheld from citizens of our country who are of suitable age and mentally and morally qualified for the discharge of its duties, it should be speedily restored by the people in their sovereign capacity.

17. That a liberal and just policy should be pursued to promote foreign immigration to our shores, always allowing to the naturalized citizens equal rights, privileges and protection under the Constitution with those who are native-born.

Republican Platform of 1872

The Republican party of the United States, assembled in National Convention in the city of Philadelphia, on the 5th and 6th days of June, 1872, again declares its faith, appeals to its history, and announces its position upon the questions before the country.

First. During eleven years of supremacy it has accepted with grand courage the solemn duties of the time. It suppressed a gigantic rebellion, emancipated four millions of slaves, decreed the equal citizenship of all, and established universal suffrage. Exhibiting unparalleled magnanimity, it criminally punished no man for political offenses, and warmly welcomed all who proved loyalty by obeying the laws and dealing justly with their neighbors. It has steadily decreased with firm hand the resultant disorders of a great war, and initiated a wise and humane policy toward the Indians. The Pacific railroad and similar vast enterprises have been generously aided and successfully conducted, the public lands freely given to actual settlers, immigration protected and encouraged, and a full acknowledgment of the naturalized citizens' rights secured from European Powers. A uniform national currency has been provided, repudiation frowned down, the national credit sustained under the most extraordinary burdens, and new bonds negotiated at lower rates. The revenues have been carefully collected and honestly applied. Despite large annual reductions of the rates of taxation, the public debt has been reduced during General Grant's Presidency at the rate of a hundred millions a year, great financial crises have been avoided, and peace and plenty prevail throughout the land. Menacing foreign difficulties have been peacefully and honorably composed, and the honor and power of the nation kept in high respect throughout the world. This glorious record of the past is the party's best pledge for the future. We believe the people will not intrust the Government to any party or combination of men composed chiefly of those who have resisted every step of this beneficent progress.

Second. The recent amendments to the national Constitution should be cordially sustained because they are right, not merely tolerated because they are law, and should be carried out according to their spirit by appropriate legislation, the enforcement of which can safely be entrusted only to the party that secured those amendments.

Third. Complete liberty and exact equality in the enjoyment of all civil, political, and public rights should be established and effectually maintained throughout the Union, by efficient and appropriate State and Federal legislation. Neither the law nor its administration should admit any discrimination in respect of citizens by reason of race, creed, color, or previous condition of servitude.

Fourth. The National Government should seek to maintain honorable peace with all nations, protecting its citizens everywhere, and sympathizing with all people who strive for greater liberty.

Fifth. Any system of the civil service under which the subordinate positions of the government are considered rewards for mere party zeal is fatally demoralizing, and we therefore favor a reform of the system by laws which shall abolish the evils of patronage, and make honesty, efficiency, and fidelity the essential qualifications for public positions, without practically creating a life-tenure of office.

Sixth. We are opposed to further grants of the public lands to corporations and monopolies, and demand that the national domain be set apart for free homes for the people.

Seventh. The annual revenue, after paying current expenditures, pensions, and the interest on the public debt, should furnish a moderate balance for the reduction of the principal and that revenue, except so much as may be derived from a tax upon tobacco and liquors, should be raised by duties upon importations, the details of which should be so adjusted as to aid in securing remunerative wages to labor, and to promote the industries, prosperity, and growth of the whole country.

Eighth. We hold in undying honor the soldiers and sailors whose valor saved the Union. Their pensions are a sacred debt of the nation, and the widows and orphans of those who died for their country are entitled to the care of a generous and grateful people. We favor such additional legislation as will extend the bounty of the Government to all our soldiers and sailors who were honorably discharged, and who, in the line of duty, became disabled, without regard to the length of service or the cause of such discharge.

Ninth. The doctrine of Great Britain and other European powers concerning allegiance—"Once a subject always a subject"—having at last, through the efforts of the Republican party, been abandoned, and the American idea of the individual's right to transfer allegiance having been accepted by European nations, it is the duty of our Government to guard with jealous care the rights of adopted citizens against the assumption of unauthorized claims by their former governments; and we urge continued careful encouragement and protection of voluntary immigration.

Tenth. The franking privilege ought to be abolished, and the way prepared for a speedy reduction in the rates of postage.

Eleventh. Among the questions which press for attention is that which concerns the relations of capital and labor, and the Republican party recognizes the duty of so shaping legislation as to secure full protection and the amplest field for capital, and for labor—the creator of capital—the largest opportunities and a just share of the mutual profits of these two great servants of civilization.

Twelfth. We hold that Congress and the President have only fulfilled an imperative duty in their measures for the suppression of violent and treasonable organizations in certain lately rebellious regions, and for the protection of the ballot-box, and therefore they are entitled to the thanks of the nation.

Thirteenth. We denounce repudiation of the public debt, in any form or disguise, as a national crime. We witness with pride the reduction of the principal of the debt, and of the rates of interest upon the balance, and confidently expect that our excellent national currency will be perfected by a speedy resumption of specie payment.

Fourteenth. The Republican party is mindful of its obligations to the loyal women of America for their noble devotion to the cause of freedom. Their admission to wider fields of usefulness is viewed with satisfaction, and the honest demand of any class of citizens for additional rights should be treated with respectful consideration.

Fifteenth. We heartily approve the action of Congress in extending amnesty to those lately in rebellion, and rejoice in the growth of peace and fraternal feeling throughout the land.

Sixteenth. The Republican party proposes to respect the rights reserved by the people to themselves as carefully as the powers delegated by them to the State and to the Federal Government. It disapproves of the resort to unconstitutional laws for the purpose of removing evils, by interference with rights not surrendered by the people to either the State or National Government.

Seventeenth. It is the duty of the general Government to adopt such measures as may tend to encourage and restore American commerce and ship-building.

Eighteenth. We believe that the modest patriotism, the earnest purpose, the sound judgment, the practical wisdom, the incorruptible integrity, and the illustrious services of Ulysses S. Grant have commended him to the heart of the American people, and with him at our head we start to-day upon a new march to victory.

Nineteenth. Henry Wilson, nominated for the Vice-Presidency, known to the whole land from the early days of the great struggle for liberty as an indefatigable laborer in all campaigns, an incorruptible legislator and representative man of American institutions, is worthy to associate with our great leader and share the honors which we pledge our best efforts to bestow upon them.

CAMPAIGN OF 1876

When the Republicans met in convention in Cincinnati in June, Rutherford B. Hayes, the governor of Ohio, was chosen as the presidential nominee on the seventh ballot over House Speaker James G. Blaine of Maine and six other aspirants. Representative William A. Wheeler of New York was nominated for vice-president.

The Democrats, in St. Louis, nominated Governor Samuel J. Tilden of New York, over the opposition of the leaders of Tammany Hall, on the second ballot. Thomas A. Hendricks of Indiana was nominated for vice-president.

The Prohibitionists again nominated candidates —Green Clay Smith of Kentucky for president and G. T. Stewart of Ohio for vice-president. In addition, the first convention of a new party, the Independent National Party, or Greenback Party, was held in Indianapolis in May of 1876. Peter Cooper of New York was nominated for president and General Samuel F. Cary of Ohio was selected for the vice-presidential candidacy.

In the famous disputed election, Tilden received more popular votes than Hayes, Cooper, and Smith combined—the only time this has happened in which the victor has not become president. Four states turned in double returns and their electoral votes were contested. An electoral commission was established by law in 1877 to decide the validity of the disputed votes. Consisting of eight Republicans and seven Democrats, the commission voted on each state separately but in each case awarded the electoral vote to Hayes. The dispute eventually landed in the Congress, where many votes were taken to determine whether both houses would accept the decisions. A threatened filibuster did not materialize because of a compromise between southern Democrats and Republicans over Reconstruction policy, and a final vote was reached on March 2, 1877. The electoral count accepted was 185 votes for Hayes and Wheeler to 184 for Tilden and Hendricks.

Democratic Platform of 1876

We, the delegates of the Democratic party of the United States, in National Convention assembled, do hereby declare the administration of the Federal Government to be in great need of immediate reform; do hereby enjoin upon the nominees of this Convention, and of the Democratic party in each State, a zealous effort and co-operation to this end, and do here appeal to our fellow-citizens of every former political connection to undertake with us this first and most pressing patriotic duty for the Democracy of the whole country. We do here reaffirm our faith in the permanence of the Federal Union, our devotion to the Constitution of the United States, with its amendments universally accepted as a final settlement of the controversies that engendered civil war, and do here record our steadfast confidence in the perpetuity of republican self-government; in absolute acquiescence in the will of the majority, the vital principle of republics; in the supremacy of the civil over the military; in the two-fold separation of church and state, for the sake alike of civil and religious freedom; in the equality of all citizens before just laws of their own enactment; in the liberty of individual conduct unvexed by sumptuary laws; in the faith-

ful education of the rising generation, that they may preserve, enjoy and transmit these best conditions of human happiness and hope. We behold the noblest products of a hundred years of changeful history. But while upholding the bond of our Union and great charter of these our rights, it behooves a free people to practice also that eternal vigilance which is the price of liberty.

Reform is necessary to rebuild and establish in the hearts of the whole people the Union eleven years ago happily rescued from the danger of the secession of States, but now to be saved from a corrupt centralism which, after inflicting upon ten States the rapacity of carpet-bag tyrannies, has honeycombed the offices of the Federal Government itself with incapacity, waste and fraud; infected States and municipalities with the contagion of misrule, and locked fast the prosperity of an industrious people in the paralysis of hard times. Reform is necessary to establish a sound currency, restore the public credit and maintain the national honor.

We denounce the failure for all these eleven years to make good the promise of the legal tender notes, which are a changing standard of value in the hands of the people, and the non-payment of which is a disregard of the plighted faith of the nation.

We denounce the improvidence which, in eleven years of peace, has taken from the people in Federal taxes thirteen times the whole amount of the legal-tender notes and squandered four times their sum in useless expense, without accumulating any reserve for their redemption. We denounce the financial imbecility and immorality of that party, which, during eleven years of peace, has made no advance toward resumption, no preparation for resumption, but instead has obstructed resumption by wasting our resources and exhausting all our surplus income, and while annually professing to intend a speedy return to specie payments, has annually enacted fresh hindrances thereto. As such hindrance we denounce the resumption clause of the act of 1875 and we here demand its repeal. We demand a judicious system of preparation by public economies, by official retrenchments, and by wise finance, which shall enable the nation soon to assure the whole world of its perfect ability and its perfect readiness to meet any of its promises at the call of the creditor entitled to payment.

We believe such a system, well-advised, and, above all, intrusted to competent hands for execution, creating at no time an artificial scarcity of currency, and at no time alarming the public mind into a withdrawal of that vast machinery of credit by which ninety-five per cent of our business transactions are performed—a system open and public and inspiring general confidence—would from the day of its adoption bring healing on its wings to all our harassed industries, set in motion the wheels of commerce, manufactures and the mechanic arts, restore employment to labor, and renew in all its natural sources the prosperity of the people.

Reform is necessary in the sum and mould of Federal taxation, to the end that capital may be set free from distrust, and labor lightly burdened. We denounce the present tariff levied upon nearly four thousand articles as a masterpiece of injustice, inequality and false pretense, which yields a dwindling and not a yearly rising revenue, has impoverished many industries to subsidize a few. It prohibits imports that might purchase the products of American labor; it has degraded American commerce from the first to an inferior rank upon the high seas; it has cut down the values of American manufactures at home and abroad; it has depleted the returns of American agriculture, an industry followed by half our people; it costs the people five times more than it produces to the treasury, obstructs the process of production and wastes the fruits of labor; it promotes fraud, fosters smuggling, enriches dishonest officials, and bankrupts honest merchants. We demand that all custom-house taxation shall be only for revenue. Reform is necessary in the scale of public expense, Federal, State and municipal. Our Federal taxation has swollen from sixty millions gold in 1860 to four hundred and fifty millions currency in 1870; our aggregate taxation from one hundred and fifty-four millions gold in 1860 to seven hundred and thirty millions currency, in 1870, all in one decade; from less than five dollars per head to more than eighteen dollars per head. Since the peace the people have paid to their tax-gatherers more than thrice the sum of the national debt, and more than twice the sum for the Federal Government alone. We demand a rigorous frugality in every department and from every officer of the Government.

Reform is necessary to put a stop to the profligate waste of public lands and their diversion from actual settlers by the party in power, which has squandered two hundred millions of acres upon railroads alone, and out of more than thrice that aggregate has disposed of less than a sixth directly to the tillers of the soil.

Reform is necessary to correct the omissions of a Republican Congress and the errors of our treaties and our diplomacy, which has stripped our fellow-citizens of foreign birth and kindred race, re-erasing [re-crossing] the Atlantic from the shield of American citizenship, and has exposed our brethren of the Pacific coast to the incursions of a race not sprung from the same great parent stock, and in fact now by law denied citizenship through naturalization as being unaccustomed to the traditions of a progressive civilization, one exercised in liberty under equal laws; and we denounce the policy which thus discards the liberty-loving German and tolerates the revival of the coolie-trade in Mongolian women for immoral purposes, and Mongolian men held to perform servile labor contracts, and demand such modification of the treaty with the Chinese Empire, or such legislation within constitutional limitations, as shall prevent further importation or immigration of the Mongolian race.

Reform is necessary and can never be effected

but by making it the controlling issue of the election and lifting it above the two issues with which the office-holding classes and the party in power seek to smother it:—

First—The false issue with which they would enkindle sectarian strife in respect to the public schools, of which the establishment and support belong exclusively to the several States, and which the Democratic party has cherished from their foundation, and is resolved to maintain without partiality or preference for any class, sect or creed, and without contributions from the treasury to any.

Second—The false issue by which they seek to light anew the dying embers of sectional hate between kindred peoples once unnaturally estranged but now reunited in one indivisible republic, and a common destiny.

Reform is necessary in the civil service. Experience proves that efficient economical conduct of the government is not possible if its civil service be subject to change at every election, be a prize fought for at the ballot-box, be an approved reward of party zeal instead of posts of honor assigned for proved competency and held for fidelity in the public employ; that the dispensing of patronage should neither be a tax upon the time of our public men nor an instrument of their ambition. Here again, profession falsified in the performance attest that the party in power can work out no practical or salutary reform. Reform is necessary even more in the higher grades of the public service. President, Vice-President, judges, senators, representatives, cabinet officers —these and all others in authority are the people's servants. Their offices are not a private perquisite; they are a public trust. When the annals of this Republic show disgrace and censure of a Vice-President; a late Speaker of the House of Representatives marketing his rulings as a presiding officer; three Senators profiting secretly by their votes as law-makers; five chairmen of the leading committees of the late House of Representatives exposed in jobbery; a late Secretary of the Treasury forcing balances in the public accounts; a late Attorney-General misappropriating public funds; a Secretary of the Navy enriched and enriching friends by a percentage levied off the profits of contractors with his department; an Ambassador to England censured in a dishonorable speculation; the President's Private Secretary barely es-

caping conviction upon trial for guilty complicity in frauds upon the revenue; a Secretary of War impeached for high crimes and misdemeanors— the demonstration is complete, that the first step in reform must be the people's choice of honest men from another party, lest the disease of one political organization infect the body politic, and lest by making no change of men or parties, we get no change of measures and no real reform.

All these abuses, wrongs, and crimes, the product of sixteen years' ascendency of the Republican party, create a necessity for reform, confessed by Republicans themselves; but their reformers are voted down in Convention and displaced from the cabinet. The party's mass of honest voters is powerless to resist the eighty thousand office-holders, its leaders and guides. Reform can only be had by a peaceful civic revolution. We demand a change of system, a change of administration, a change of parties, that we may have a change of measures and of men.

Resolved, That this Convention, representing the Democratic party of the States, do cordially indorse the action of the present House of Representatives in reducing and curtailing the expenses of the Federal Government, in cutting down enormous salaries, extravagant appropriations, and in abolishing useless offices and places not required by the public necessities, and we shall trust to the firmness of the Democratic members of the House that no committee of conference and no misinterpretation of rules will be allowed to defeat these wholesome measures of economy demanded by the country.

Resolved, That the soldiers and sailors of the Republic, and the widows and orphans of those who have fallen in battle, have a just claim upon the care, protection and gratitude of their fellow-citizens.

Independent (Greenback) Platform of 1876

The Independent party is called into existence by the necessities of the people whose industries are prostrated, whose labor is deprived of its just reward by a ruinous policy which the Republican and Democratic parties refuse to change, and in view of the failure of these parties to furnish relief to the depressed industries of the country, thereby disappointing just hopes and expectations of the suffering people, we declare our principles and invite all independent and patriotic men to join our ranks in this movement for financial reform and industrial emancipation:

First. We demand the immediate and unconditional repeal of the Specie-Resumption act of January 14, 1875, and the rescue of our industries from ruin and disaster resulting from its enforcement; and we call upon all patriotic men to organize in every Congressional district of the country with a view of electing representatives to Congress who will carry out the wishes of the people in this regard, and stop the present suicidal and destructive policy of contraction.

Second. We believe that a United States note, issued directly by the Government, and convertible on demand into United States obligations bearing a rate of interest not exceeding one cent a day on each $100, and exchangeable for United States notes at par, will afford the best circulating medium ever devised; such United States notes should be full legal-tender for all purposes except for payment of such obligations as are by existing contracts expressly made payable in coin; and we hold that it is the duty of the Government to provide such circulating medium, and insist in the language of Thomas Jefferson, that "bank paper must be suppressed and the circulation restored to the nation, to whom it belongs."

Third. It is the paramount duty of the Government in all its legislation to keep in view the full development of all legitimate business,—agricultural, mining, manufacturing and commercial.

Fourth. We most earnestly protest against any further issue of gold bonds for sale in foreign markets, by which we would be made for a long period "hewers of wood and drawers of water" to foreigners, especially as the American people would gladly and promptly take at par all bonds the Government may need to sell, provided they are made payable at the option of the holder, and bearing interest at 3.65 per cent per annum, or even a lower rate.

Fifth. We further protest against the sale of Government bonds for the purpose of purchasing silver to be used as a substitute for our more convenient and less fluctuating fractional currency, which, although well calculated to enrich owners of silver mines, yet in operation it will still further

oppress in taxation an already overburdened people.

Prohibition Reform Platform of 1876

The Prohibition Reform party of the United States, organized in the name of the people to revive, enforce and perpetuate in the Government the doctrines of the Declaration of Independence, submit in this Centennial year of the Republic for the suffrages of all good citizens the following platform of national reforms and measures:

1. The legal Prohibition in the District of Columbia, the Territories and in every other place subject to the laws of Congress, of the importation, exportation, manufacture and traffic of all alcoholic beverages, as high crimes against society; an Amendment of the National Constitution to render these Prohibitory measures universal and permanent, and the adoption of treaty stipulations with foreign Powers to prevent the importation and exportation of all alcoholic beverages.

2. The abolition of class legislation and of special privileges in the Government, and the adoption of equal suffrage and eligibility to office without distinction of race, religious creed, property or sex.

3. The appropriation of the public lands in limited quantities to actual settlers only; the reduction of the rates of inland and ocean postage, of telegraphic communication, of railroad and water transportation and travel to the lowest practical point by force of laws, wisely and justly framed, with reference not only to the interests of capital employed but to the higher claims of the general good.

4. The suppression, by law, of lotteries and gambling in gold, stocks, produce and every form of money and property, and the penal inhibition of the use of the public mails for advertising schemes of gambling and lotteries.

5. The abolition of those foul enormities, polygamy and the social evil, and the protection of purity, peace and happiness of homes by ample and efficient legislation.

6. The national observance of the Christian Sabbath, established by laws prohibiting ordinary labor and business in all departments of public service and private employments (works of neces-

sity, charity and religion excepted) on that day.

7. The establishment by mandatory provisions in National and State Constitutions, and by all necessary legislation, of a system of free public schools for the universal and forced education of all the youth of the land.

8. The free use of the Bible, not as a ground of religious creeds, but as a text-book of purest morality, the best liberty and the noblest literature, in our public schools, that our children may grow up in its light and that its spirit and principles may pervade our nation.

9. The separation of the Government in all its departments and institutions, including the public schools and all funds for their maintenance, from the control of every religious sect or other association, and the protection alike of all sects by equal laws, with entire freedom of religious faith and worship.

10. The introduction into all treaties, hereafter negotiated with foreign Governments, of a provision for the amicable settlement of international difficulties by arbitration.

11. The abolition of all barbarous modes and instruments of punishment; the recognition of the laws of God and the claims of humanity in the discipline of jails and prisons, and of that higher and wiser civilization worthy of our age and nation, which regards the reform of criminals as a means for the prevention of crime.

12. The abolition of executive and legislative patronage, and the election of President, Vice-President, United States Senators, and of civil officers, so far as practicable, by the direct vote of the people.

13. The practice of a friendly and liberal policy to immigrants from all nations, the guaranty to them of ample protection and of equal rights and privileges.

14. The separation of the money of Government from all banking institutions. The National Government only should exercise the high prerogative of issuing paper money, and that should be subject to prompt redemption on demand, in gold and silver, the only equal standards of value recognized by the civilized world.

15. The reduction of the salaries of public officers in a just ratio with the decline of wages and market prices, the abolition of sinecures, unnecessary offices and official fees and perquisites;

the practice of strict economy in Government expenses, and a free and thorough investigation into any and all alleged abuses of public trusts.

Republican Platform of 1876

When, in the economy of Providence, this land was to be purged of human slavery, and when the strength of government of the people by the people and for the people was to be demonstrated, the Republican party came into power. Its deeds have passed into history, and we look back to them with pride. Incited by their memories, and with high aims for the good of our country and mankind, and looking to the future with unfaltering courage, hope, and purpose, we, the representatives of the party, in national convention assembled, make the following declaration of principles:—

1. The United States of America is a nation, not a league. By the combined workings of the national and state governments, under their respective constitutions, the rights of every citizen are secured at home and abroad, and the common welfare promoted.

2. The Republican party has preserved these governments to the hundredth anniversary of the nation's birth, and they are now embodiments of the great truth spoken at its cradle, that all men are created equal; that they are endowed by their Creator with certain inalienable rights, among which are life, liberty, and the pursuit of happiness; that for the attainment of these ends governments have been instituted among men, deriving their just powers from the consent of the governed. Until these truths are cheerfully obeyed, and if need be, vigorously enforced, the work of the Republican party is unfinished.

3. The permanent pacification of the Southern section of the Union and the complete protection of all its citizens in the free enjoyment of all their rights, are duties to which the Republican party is sacredly pledged. The power to provide for the enforcement of the principles embodied in the recent constitutional amendments is vested by those amendments in the Congress of the United States; and we declare it to be the solemn obligation of the legislative and executive departments of the government to put into immediate

and vigorous exercise all their constitutional powers for removing any just causes of discontent on the part of any class, and securing to every American citizen complete liberty and exact equality in the exercise of all civil, political, and public rights. To this end we imperatively demand a congress and a chief executive whose courage and fidelity to these duties shall not falter until these results are placed beyond dispute or recall.

4. In the first act of congress, signed by President Grant, the national government assumed to remove any doubt of its purpose to discharge all just obligations to the public creditors, and solemnly pledged its faith "to make provisions at the earliest practicable period, for the redemption of the United States notes in coin." Commercial prosperity, public morals, and the national credit demand that this promise be fulfilled by a continuous and steady progress to specie payment.

5. Under the constitution, the President and heads of departments are to make nominations for office, the senate is to advise and consent to appointments, and the house of representatives is to accuse and prosecute faithless officers. The best interest of the public service demands that these distinctions be respected; that senators and representatives who may be judges and accusers should not dictate appointments to office. The invariable rule for appointments should have reference to the honesty, fidelity, and capacity of the appointees, giving to the party in power those places where harmony and vigor of administration require its policy to be represented, but permitting all others to be filled by persons selected with sole reference to the efficiency of the public service and the right of citizens to share in the honor of rendering faithful service to their country.

6. We rejoice in the quickened conscience of the people concerning political affairs. We will hold all public officers to a rigid responsibility, and engage that the prosecution and punishment of all who betray official trusts shall be speedy, thorough, and unsparing.

7. The public school system of the several states is the bulwark of the American republic; and, with a view to its security and permanence, we recommend an amendment to the constitution of the United States, forbidding the application of any public funds or property for the benefit of any school or institution under sectarian control.

8. The revenue necessary for current expenditures and the obligations of the public debt must be largely derived from duties upon importations, which, so far as possible, should be so adjusted as to promote the interests of American labor and advance the prosperity of the whole country.

9. We reaffirm our opposition to further grants of the public lands to corporations and monopolies, and demand that the national domain be devoted to free homes for the people.

10. It is the imperative duty of the government so to modify existing treaties with European governments, that the same protection shall be afforded to the adopted American citizen that is given to native-born, and all necessary laws be passed to protect emigrants, in the absence of power in the states for that purpose.

11. It is the immediate duty of congress fully to investigate the effects of the immigration and importation of Mongolians on the moral and material interests of the country.

12. The Republican party recognizes with approval the substantial advances recently made toward the establishment of equal rights for women, by the many important amendments effected by Republican legislatures in the laws which concern the personal and property relations of wives, mothers, and widows, and by the appointment and election of women to the superintendence of education, charities, and other public trusts. The honest demands of this class of citizens for additional rights, privileges, and immunities should be treated with respectful consideration.

13. The constitution confers upon congress sovereign power over the territories of the United States for their government. And in the exercise of this power it is the right and duty of congress to prohibit and extirpate in the territories that relic of barbarism, polygamy; and we demand such legislation as will secure this end and the supremacy of American institutions in all the territories.

14. The pledges which our nation has given to our soldiers and sailors must be fulfilled. The grateful people will always hold those who imperilled their lives for the country's preservation in the kindest remembrance.

15. We sincerely deprecate all sectional feel-

ing and tendencies. We therefore note with deep solicitude that the Democratic party counts, as its chief hope of success, upon the electoral vote of a united South, secured through the efforts of those who were recently arrayed against the nation; and we invoke the earnest attention of the country to the grave truth, that a success thus achieved would reopen sectional strife and imperil national honor and human rights.

16. We charge the Democratic party with being the same in character and spirit as when it sympathized with treason; with making its control of the house of representatives the triumph and opportunity of the nation's recent foes; with reasserting and applauding in the national capitol the sentiments of unrepentant rebellion; with sending Union soldiers to the rear, and promoting Confederate soldiers to the front; with deliberately proposing to repudiate the plighted faith of the government; with being equally false and imbecile upon the over-shadowing financial question; with thwarting the ends of justice, by its partisan mis-managements and obstruction of investigation; with proving itself, through the period of its ascendency in the lower house of congress, utterly incompetent to administer the government;—and we warn the country against trusting a party thus alike unworthy, recreant, and incapable.

17. The national administration merits commendation for its honorable work in the management of domestic and foreign affairs, and President Grant deserves the continued hearty gratitude of the American people, for his patriotism and his eminent services in war and in peace.

18. We present as our candidates for President and Vice-President of the United States two distinguished statesmen, of eminent ability and character, and conspicuously fitted for those high offices, and we confidently appeal to the American people to intrust the administration of their public affairs to Rutherford B. Hayes and William A. Wheeler.

CAMPAIGN OF 1880

In 1880, President Hayes was not a candidate for reelection. Thus, when the Republicans met in Chicago in June, the principal candidates were former President Ulysses S. Grant, James G. Blaine of Maine, and Secretary of the Treasury John Sherman of Ohio, who was nominated by Representative James A. Garfield. When none of the favorites could obtain a majority after thirty-four ballots, the delegates began shifting to Garfield over his protests. The Ohio congressman was the first delegate to see himself chosen from the floor. Chester A. Arthur, of New York, was selected as Garfield's running mate on the first ballot.

The Democrats met in Cincinnati and quickly (on the second ballot) nominated General Winfield Scott Hancock of Pennsylvania over nine other aspirants after Samuel Tilden, the 1876 winner, declared that he was not seeking another nomination. Former Representative William English of Indiana was proposed for the vice-presidency by acclamation.

The members of the Greenback Party also met in Chicago in June to nominate Representative James B. Weaver of Iowa for president and B. J. Chambers of Texas for vice-president. The Prohibitionists held their convention in Cleveland, and General Neal Dow of Maine was nominated for president and H. A. Thompson of Ohio was selected for vice-president.

The election in November was extremely close. The Republicans received 4,446,158 popular votes (48.27 percent) to 4,444,260 (48.25 percent) for the Democrats! The Greenbackers, a coalition of farmers and laborers, cast 305,997 votes for Weaver. The Prohibition Party received 10,305 votes. The electoral vote count was 214 for Garfield and 155 for Hancock.

Democratic Platform of 1880

The Democrats of the United States, in Convention assembled, declare:

1. We pledge ourselves anew to the constitutional doctrines and traditions of the Democratic party as illustrated by the teachings and example of a long line of Democratic statesmen and patriots, and embodied in the platform of the last National Convention of the party.

2. Opposition to centralization and to that dangerous spirit of encroachment which tends to consolidate the powers of all the departments in one, and thus to create whatever be the form of government, a real despotism. No sumptuary laws; separation of Church and State, for the good of each; common schools fostered and protected.

3. Home rule; honest money, consisting of gold and silver, and paper convertible into coin on demand; the strict maintenance of the public faith, State and National, and a tariff for revenue only.

4. The subordination of the military to the civil power, and a general and thorough reform of the civil service.

5. The right to a free ballot is the right preservative of all rights, and must and shall be maintained in every part of the United States.

6. The existing administration is the representative of conspiracy only, and its claim of right to surround the ballot-boxes with troops and deputy marshals, to intimidate and obstruct the election, and the unprecedented use of the veto to maintain its corrupt and despotic powers, insult the people and imperil their institutions.

7. We execrate the course of this administration in making places in the civil service a reward for political crime, and demand a reform by statute which shall make it forever impossible for a defeated candidate to bribe his way to the seat of the usurper by billeting villains upon the people.

8. The great fraud of 1876-77, by which, upon a false count of the electoral votes of two States, the candidate defeated at the polls was declared to be President, and for the first time in American history, the will of the people was set aside under a threat of military violence, struck a deadly blow at our system of representative government. The Democratic party, to preserve the country from the horrors of a civil war, submitted for the time in firm and patriotic faith that the people would punish this crime in 1880. This issue precedes and dwarfs every other. It imposes a more sacred duty upon the people of the Union than ever addressed the conscience of a nation of free men.

9. The resolution of Samuel J. Tilden not again to be a candidate for the exalted place to which he was elected by a majority of his countrymen, and from which he was excluded by the

leaders of the Republican party, is received by the Democrats of the United States with deep sensibility, and they declare their confidence in his wisdom, patriotism, and integrity, unshaken by the assaults of a common enemy, and they further assure him that he is followed into the retirement he has chosen for himself by the sympathy and respect of his fellow-citizens, who regard him as one who, by elevating the standards of public morality, merits the lasting gratitude of his country and his party.

10. Free ships and a living chance for American commerce on the seas, and on the land no discrimination in favor of transportation lines, corporations, or monopolies.

11. Amendment of the Burlingame Treaty. No more Chinese immigration, except for travel, education, and foreign commerce, and that even carefully guarded.

12. Public money and public credit for public purposes solely, and public land for actual settlers.

13. The Democratic party is the friend of labor and the laboring man, and pledges itself to protect him alike against the cormorant and the commune.

14. We congratulate the country upon the honesty and thrift of a Democratic Congress which has reduced the public expenditure $40,-000,000 a year; upon the continuation of prosperity at home, and the national honor abroad, and, above all, upon the promise of such a change in the administration of the government as shall insure us genuine and lasting reform in every department of the public service.

Greenback Platform of 1880

Civil government should guarantee the divine right of every laborer to the results of his toil, thus enabling the producers of wealth to provide themselves with the means for physical comfort, and the facilities for mental, social and moral culture; and we condemn as unworthy of our civilization the barbarism which imposes upon the wealth-producers a state of perpetual drudgery as the price of bare animal existence. Notwithstanding the enormous increase of productive power, and the universal introduction of labor-saving machinery, and the discovery of new agents for the increase of wealth, the task of the laborer is scarcely lightened, the hours of toil are but little shortened; and few producers are lifted from poverty into comfort and pecuniary independence. The associated monopolies, the international syndicate and other income classes demand dear money and cheap labor: a "strong government," and hence a weak people.

Corporate control of the volume of money has been the means of dividing society into hostile classes, of the unjust distribution of the products of labor, and of building up monopolies of associated capital endowed with power to confiscate private property. It has kept money scarce, and scarcity of money enforces debt, trade and public and corporate loans. Debt engenders usury, and usury ends in the bankruptcy of the borrower. Other results are deranged markets, uncertainty in manufacturing enterprise and agriculture, precarious and intermittent employment for the laborers, industrial war, increasing pauperism and crime, and the consequent intimidation and disfranchisement of the producer and a rapid declension into corporate feudalism; therefore, we declare:

First—That the right to make and issue money is a sovereign power to be maintained by the people for the common benefit. The delegation of this right to corporations is a surrender of the central attribute of sovereignty, (void) of constitutional sanction, conferring upon a subordinate and irresponsible power absolute dominion over industry and commerce. All money, whether metallic or paper, should be issued and its volume controlled by the Government, and not by or through banking corporations, and when so issued should be a full legal-tender for all debts, public and private.

Second—That the bonds of the United States should not be refunded, but paid as rapidly as practicable, according to contract. To enable the Government to meet these obligations, legal-tender currency should be substituted for the notes of the National banks, the National banking system abolished, and the unlimited coinage of silver, as well as gold, established by law.

Third—That labor should be so protected by National and State authority as to equalize the burdens and insure a just distribution of its results; the eight-hour law of Congress should be enforced, the sanitary condition of industrial establishments placed under rigid control; the competition of contract labor abolished, a bureau of labor statistics established, factories, mines, and workshops inspected, the employment of children under fourteen years of age forbidden, and wages paid in cash.

Fourth—Slavery being simply cheap labor, and cheap labor being simple slavery, the importation and presence of Chinese serfs necessarily tends to brutalize and degrade American labor, therefore immediate steps should be taken to abrogate the Burlingame Treaty.

Fifth—Railroad land grants forfeited by reason of non-fulfillment of contract should be immediately reclaimed by the Government, and henceforth the public domain reserved exclusively as homes for actual settlers.

Sixth—It is the duty of Congress to regulate inter-State commerce. All lines of communication and transportation should be brought under such legislative control as shall secure moderate, fair and uniform rates for passenger and freight traffic.

Seventh—We denounce as destructive to prosperity and dangerous to liberty, the action of the old parties in fostering and sustaining gigantic land, railroad, and money corporations and monopolies, invested with, and exercising powers belonging to the Government, and yet not responsible to it for the manner of their exercise.

Eighth—That the Constitution, in giving Congress the power to borrow money, to declare war, to raise and support armies, to provide and maintain a navy, never intended that the men who loaned their money for an interest consideration should be preferred to the soldier and sailor who perilled their lives and shed their blood on land and sea in defense of their country, and we condemn the cruel class legislation of the Republican party, which, while professing great gratitude to the soldier, has most unjustly discriminated against him and in favor of the bondholder.

Ninth—All property should bear its just proportion of taxation, and we demand a graduated income tax.

Tenth—We denounce as most dangerous the efforts everywhere manifested to restrict the right of suffrage.

Eleventh—We are opposed to an increase of the standing army in times of peace, and the insidious scheme to establish an enormous military power under the guise of militia laws.

Twelfth—We demand absolute democratic rules for the government of Congress, placing all representatives of the people upon an equal footing, and taking away from committees a veto power greater than that of the President.

Thirteenth—We demand a government of the people, by the people, and for the people, instead of a government of the bondholder, by the bondholder, and for the bondholder; and we denounce every attempt to stir up sectional strife as an effort to conceal monstrous crimes against the people.

Fourteenth—In the furtherance of these ends we ask the co-operation of all fair-minded people. We have no quarrel with individuals, wage no war upon classes, but only against vicious institutions. We are not content to endure further discipline from our present actual rulers, who, having dominion over money, over transportation, over land and labor, and largely over the press and machinery of Government, wield unwarrantable power over our institutions, and over our life and property.

Resolved: That every citizen of due age, sound mind, and not a felon, be fully enfranchised, and that this resolution be referred to the States, with recommendation for their favorable consideration.

Prohibition Reform Platform of 1880

The Prohibition Reform party of the United States, organized in the name of the people to revive, enforce and perpetuate in the Government the doctrines of the Declaration of Independence, submit for the suffrages of all good citizens the following platform of national reforms and measures:

1. In the examination and discussion of the temperance question it has been proven, and is an accepted truth, that alcoholic drinks, whether fermented, brewed or distilled, are poisonous to the healthy human body, the drinking of which is not only needless but hurtful, necessarily tending to form intemperate habits, increasing greatly the number, severity and fatal termination of diseases, weakening and deranging the intellect, polluting the affections, hardening the heart and corrupting the morals, depriving many of reason and still more of its healthful exercise, and annually bringing down large numbers to untimely

graves, producing in the children of many who drink a predisposition to intemperance, insanity and various bodily and mental diseases, causing a diminution of strength, feebleness of vision, fickleness of purpose and premature old age, and producing to all future generations a deterioration of moral and physical character. The legalized importation, manufacture and sale of intoxicating drinks minister to their uses and teach the erroneous and destructive sentiment that such use is right, thus tending to produce and perpetuate the above-mentioned evils. Alcoholic drinks are thus the implacable enemy of man as an individual.

2. That the liquor traffic is to the home equally an enemy, proving a disturber and a destroyer of its peace, prosperity and happiness, taking from it the earnings of the husband, depriving the dependent wife and children of essential food, clothing and education, bringing into it profanity and abuse, setting at naught the vows of the marriage altar, breaking up the family and sundering children from parents, and thus destroying one of the most beneficent institutions of our Creator, and removing the sure foundation for good government, national prosperity and welfare.

3. That to the community it is equally an enemy, producing demoralization, vice and wickedness; its places of sale being often resorts for gambling, lewdness and debauchery, and the hiding places of those who prey upon society, counteracting the efficacy of religious effort and of all means for the intellectual elevation, moral purity, social happiness and the eternal good of mankind, without rendering any counteracting or compensating benefits, being in its influence and effect evil and only evil, and that continually.

4. That to the State it is equally an enemy, legislative inquiry, judicial investigation and the official reports of all penal, reformatory and dependent institutions showing that the manufacture and sale of such beverages is the promoting cause of intemperance, crime and pauperism, of demands upon public and private charity; imposing the larger part of taxation, thus paralyzing thrift, industry, manufacture and commercial life, which but for it would be unnecessary; disturbing the peace of the streets and highways; filling prisons and poorhouses; corrupting politics, legislation and the execution of the laws; shortening

lives, diminishing health, industry and productive power in manufacture and art; and is manifestly unjust as well as injurious to the community upon which it is imposed, and contrary to all just views of civil liberty, as well as a violation of a fundamental maxim of our common law to use your own property or liberty so as not to injure others.

5. That it is neither right nor politic for the State to afford legal protection to any traffic or system which tends to waste the resources, to corrupt the social habits and to destroy the health and lives of the people; that the importation, manufacture and sale of intoxicating beverages is proven to be inimical to the true interests of the individual, the home, the community, the State, and destructive to the order and welfare of society, and ought, therefore, to be classed among crimes to be prohibited.

6. That in this time of profound peace at home and abroad the entire separation of the general Government from the drink traffic, and its Prohibition in the District of Columbia, the Territories and in all places and ways over which (under the Constitution) Congress has control or power, is a political issue of first importance to the peace and prosperity of the nation. There can be no stable peace and protection to personal liberty, life or property until secured by National and State Constitutional Prohibition enforced by adequate laws.

7. That all legitimate industries require deliverance from taxation and loss which the liquor traffic imposes upon them, and financial or other legislation cannot accomplish so much to increase production and cause demand for labor, and as a result, for the comfort of living, as the suppression of this traffic would bring to thousands of homes as one of its blessings.

8. That the administration of Government and the execution of the laws being by and through political parties, we arraign the Republican party, which has been in continuous power in the nation for 20 years, as being false to its duty, as false to its loudly-proclaimed principles of "equal justice to all and special favors to none," and of protection to the weak and dependent; and that through moral cowardice it has been and is unable to correct the mischief which the trade in liquor has constantly inflicted upon the industrial interests, commerce and social happiness of the people. On the contrary, its subjection to and

complicity with the liquor interest appears: (1) By the facts that 5,652 distilleries, 2,830 breweries, and 175,266 places of sale of the poisonous liquors, involving an annual waste, direct and indirect, to the nation of $1,500,000,000, and a sacrifice of 100,000 lives, have under its legislation grown up and been fostered as a legitimate source of revenue; (2) That during its history six Territories have been organized and five States admitted into the Union with Constitutions provided and approved by Congress, but the Prohibition of this debasing and destructive traffic has not been provided for, nor even the people given at the time of admission the power to forbid it in any one of them; (3) That its history further shows that not in a single instance has an original Prohibitory law been enacted in any State controlled by it, while in four States so governed the laws found on its advent to power have been repealed; (4) That at its National Convention of 1872 it declared as a part of its party faith that "it disapproves of a resort to unconstitutional laws for the purpose of removing evils by interference with the right not surrendered by the people to either State or National Government," which the author of this plank says "was adopted by the Platform Committee with the full and explicit understanding that its purpose was the discountenancing of all so-called temperance (Prohibitory) and Sunday laws"; (5) That notwithstanding the deep interest felt by the people during the last quadrennium in the legal suppression of the drink curse, shown by many forms of public expression, this party at its last National Convention, held in Chicago during the present month, in making new promises by its platform, says not one word on this question, nor holds out any hope of relief.

9. That we arraign also the Democratic party as unfaithful and unworthy of reliance on this question; for although not clothed with power, but occupying the relation of the opposition party during 20 years past, strong in number and organization, it has allied itself with the liquor-traffickers and has become in all the States of the Union their special political defenders. In its National Convention of 1876, as an article of its political faith, it declared against Prohibition and just laws in restraint of the trade in drink by saying it was opposed to what it was pleased to call "all sumptuary laws." The National party has been dumb on the question.

10. That the drink-traffickers, realizing that history and experience, in all ages, climes and conditions of men declare their business destructive to all good, and finding no support from the Bible, morals or reason, appeal to misapplied law for their justification, and entrench themselves behind the evil elements of political party for defense, party tactics and party inertia having become the battling forces protecting this evil.

11. That in view of the foregoing facts and history, we cordially invite all voters, without regard to former party affiliation, to unite with us in the use of the ballot for the abolition of the drink system now existing under the authority of our National and State Governments. We also demand as a right that women, having in other respects the privileges of citizens, shall be clothed with the ballot for their protection, and as a rightful means for a proper settlement of the liquor question.

12. That to remove the apprehensions of some who allege that loss of public revenue would follow the suppression of the drink trade, we confidently point to the experience of government abroad and at home, which shows that thrift and revenue from consumption of legitimate manufactures and commerce have so largely followed the abolition of the drink as to fully supply all loss of liquor taxes.

13. That we recognize the good providence of Almighty God, who has preserved and prospered us as a nation, and, asking for his spirit to guide us to ultimate success, we will look for it, relying upon his omnipotent arm.

Republican Platform of 1880

The Republican party, in National Convention assembled, at the end of twenty years since the Federal Government was first committed to its charge, submits to the people of the United States this brief report of its administration:

It suppressed a rebellion which had armed nearly a million of men to subvert the national authority. It reconstructed the Union of the States, with freedom instead of slavery as its corner-stone. It transformed 4,000,000 human beings from the likeness of things to the rank of citizens. It relieved Congress from the infamous work of hunting fugitive slaves, and charged it to see that slavery does not exist. It has raised the value of our paper currency from 38 per cent to the par of gold. It has restored upon a solid basis payment in coin of all national obligations, and has given us a currency absolutely good and equal in every part of our extended country. It has lifted the credit of the Nation from the point where six per cent bonds sold at eighty-six to that where four per cent bonds are eagerly sought at a premium.

Under its administration, railways have increased from 31,000 miles in 1860, to more than 82,000 miles in 1879.

Our foreign trade increased from $700,000,000 to $1,115,000,000 in the same time, and our exports, which were $20,000,000 less than our imports in 1860, were $265,000,000 more than our imports in 1879.

Without resorting to loans, it has, since the war closed, defrayed the ordinary expenses of Government besides the accruing interest of the public debt, and has disbursed annually more than $30,000,000 for soldiers' and sailors' pensions. It has paid $880,000,000 of the public debt, and, by refunding the balance at lower rates, has reduced the annual interest-charge from nearly $150,000,000 to less than $89,000,000. All the industries of the country have revived; labor is in demand; wages have increased, and throughout the entire country there is evidence of a coming prosperity greater than we have ever enjoyed.

Upon this record the Republican party asks for the continued confidence and support of the people, and this Convention submits for their approval the following statement of the principles and purposes which will continue to guide and inspire its efforts.

1. We affirm that the work of the Republican party for the last twenty-one years has been such as to commend it to the favor of the Nation; that the fruits of the costly victories which we have achieved through immense difficulties should be preserved; that the peace regained should be cherished; that the Union should be perpetuated, and that the liberty secured to this generation should be transmitted undiminished to other generations; that the order established and the

credit acquired should never be impaired; that the pensions promised should be paid; that the debt so much reduced should be extinguished by the full payment of every dollar thereof; that the reviving industries should be further promoted, and that the commerce already increasing should be steadily encouraged.

2. The Constitution of the United States is a supreme law, and not a mere contract. Out of confederated States it made a sovereign nation. Some powers are denied to the Nation, while others are denied to the States; but the boundary between the powers delegated and those reserved is to be determined by the National and not by the State tribunal.

3. The work of popular education is one left to the care of the several States, but it is the duty of the National Government to aid that work to the extent of its constitutional power. The intelligence of the Nation is but the aggregate of the intelligence in the several States, and the destiny of the Nation must be guided, not by the genius of any one State, but by the aggregate genius of all.

4. The Constitution wisely forbids Congress to make any law respecting the establishment of religion, but it is idle to hope that the Nation can be protected against the influence of secret sectarianism while each State is exposed to its domination. We, therefore, recommend that the Constitution be so amended as to lay the same prohibition upon the Legislature of each State, and to forbid the appropriation of public funds to the support of sectarian schools.

5. We affirm the belief, avowed in 1876, that the duties levied for the purpose of revenue should so discriminate as to favor American labor; that no further grants of the public domain should be made to any railway or other corporation; that slavery having perished in the States, its twin barbarity, polygamy, must die in the Territories; that everywhere the protection accorded to a citizen of American birth must be secured to citizens by American adoption; that we deem it the duty of Congress to develop and improve our seacoast and harbors, but insist that further subsidies to private persons or corporations must cease; that the obligations of the Republic to the men who preserved its integrity in the day of battle are undiminished by the lapse of fifteen years since

their final victory. To do them honor is, and shall forever be, the grateful privilege and sacred duty of the American people.

6. Since the authority to regulate immigration and intercourse between the United States and foreign nations rests with the Congress of the United States and the treaty-making power, the Republican party, regarding the unrestricted immigration of the Chinese as a matter of grave concernment under the exercise of both these powers, would limit and restrict that immigration by the enactment of such just, humane and reasonable laws and treaties as will produce that result.

7. That the purity and patriotism which characterized the earlier career of Rutherford B. Hayes in peace and war, and which guided the thoughts of our immediate predecessors to him for a presidential candidate, have continued to inspire him in his career as Chief Executive; and that history will accord to his administration the honors which are due to an efficient, just and courteous discharge of the public business, and will honor his vetoes interposed between the people and attempted partisan laws.

8. We charge upon the Democratic party the habitual sacrifice of patriotism and justice to a supreme and insatiable lust for office and patronage; that to obtain possession of the National Government, and control of the place, they have obstructed all efforts to promote the purity and to conserve the freedom of the suffrage, and have devised fraudulent ballots and invented fraudulent certification of returns; have labored to unseat lawfully elected members of Congress, to secure at all hazards the vote of a majority of the States in the House of Representatives; have endeavored to occupy by force and fraud the places of trust given to others by the people of Maine, rescued by the courage and action of Maine's patriotic sons; have, by methods vicious in principle and tyrannical in practice, attached partisan legislation to appropriation bills, upon whose passage the very movement of the Government depended; have crushed the rights of the individual; have advocated the principles and sought the favor of the Rebellion against the Nation, and have endeavored to obliterate the sacred memories of the war, and to overcome its inestimably valuable results of nationality, personal freedom and individual equality.

The equal, steady and complete enforcement of the law, and the protection of all our citizens in the enjoyment of all privileges and immunities guaranteed by the Constitution, are the first duties of the Nation. The dangers of a solid south can only be averted by a faithful performance of every promise which the Nation has made to the citizen. The execution of the laws, and the punishment of all those who violate them, are the only safe methods by which an enduring peace can be secured and genuine prosperity established through the South. Whatever promises the Nation makes the Nation must perform. A Nation cannot safely relegate this duty to the States. The solid south must be divided by the peaceful agencies of the ballot, and all honest opinions must there find free expression. To this end honest voters must be protected against terrorism, violence or fraud. And we affirm it to be the duty and the purpose of the Republican party to use all legitimate means to restore all the States of this Union to the most perfect harmony that may be possible, and we submit to the practical, sensible people of these United States to say whether it would not be dangerous to the dearest interests of our country at this time to surrender the administration of the National Government to a party which seeks to overthrow the existing policy, under which we are so prosperous, and thus bring distrust and confusion where there is now order, confidence and hope.

9. The Republican party, adhering to the principle affirmed by its last National Convention, of respect for the constitutional rules governing appointments to office, adopts the declaration of President Hayes that the reform of the civil service should be thorough, radical and complete. To this end it demands the co-operation of the Legislative with the Executive Departments of the Government, and that Congress shall so legislate that fitness, ascertained by proper practical tests, shall admit to the public service.

CAMPAIGN OF 1884

In 1884, party lines were indistinct; the major parties were divided into factions, and several minor parties also split over specific issues. The first convention, held by the short-lived Anti-Monopoly Party in May, nominated General Benjamin Butler of Massachusetts for president. The party's national committee later chose General Absolom West of Mississippi as his running mate. The Greenback National Party met later in the month and also nominated Butler and West.

The Republicans, who gathered in Chicago on June 3, were sharply divided between the supporters of President Arthur and those of James G. Blaine of Maine, who was nominated on the fourth ballot. They chose John Logan of Illinois for vice-president. However, these nominations produced such a schism within the party that many party members publicly stated that they would not support the ticket.

The Democrats nominated New York Governor Grover Cleveland, over the objections of Tammany Hall, on the second ballot. Thomas A. Hendricks of Indiana was nominated as his vice-presidential candidate.

The Prohibitionists also divided in 1884. They held two conventions and nominated different candidates. In Chicago, the American Prohibition National Party nominated Samuel Pomeroy of Kansas for president and John A. Conant of Connecticut for vice-president. Although the party adopted the platform presented here, it apparently was not on the ballot in any state. The National Prohibition Party held its convention in Pittsburgh in July. John P. St. John of Kansas was chosen as the presidential candidate, and William Daniel of Maryland was unanimously chosen for vice-president.

In the campaign, one faction of the Republican Party, the Mugwumps, supported Cleveland, as did the members of Tammany Hall in New York. The election was very close. By a margin of less than 2,000 votes in New York and less than 30,000 votes nationally, Cleveland became the first Democrat in the White House in a quarter of a century. He received 4,874,621 popular votes to 4,848,936 for Blaine. Butler received 175,096 and St. John 147,482. It was widely believed by political observers at the time that the Prohibitionist candidates detracted many more votes from the Republicans than from the Democrats. The final electoral vote was 219 for Cleveland to 182 for Blaine.

American Prohibition National Platform of 1884

We hold: 1. That ours is a Christian and not a heathen Nation, and that the God of the Christian Scriptures is the author of civil government.

2. That the Bible should be associated with books of science and literature in all our educational institutions.

3. That God requires and man needs a Sabbath.

4. That we demand the prohibition of the importation, manufacture, and sale of intoxicating drinks.

5. That the charters of all secret lodges granted by our Federal and State Legislatures should be withdrawn and their oaths prohibited by law.

6. We are opposed to putting prison labor or depreciated contract labor from foreign countries in competition with free labor to benefit manufacturers, corporations, and speculators.

7. We are in favor of a thorough revision and enforcement of the law concerning patents and inventions for the prevention and punishment of frauds either upon inventors or the general public.

8. We hold to and will vote for woman suffrage.

9. We hold that the civil equality secured to all American citizens by Arts. 13, 14, and 15 of our amended National Constitution should be preserved inviolate, and the same equality should be extended to Indians and Chinamen.

10. That international differences should be settled by arbitration.

11. That land and other monopolies should be discouraged.

12. That the General Government should furnish the people with an ample and sound currency.

13. That it should be the settled policy of the Government to reduce the tariffs and taxes as rapidly as the necessities of revenue and vested business interest will allow.

14. That polygamy should be immediately suppressed by law and that the Republican party is censurable for its long neglect of its duty in respect to this evil.

15. And, finally, we demand for the American people the abolition of Electoral Colleges and a direct vote for President and Vice-President of the United States.

Anti-Monopoly Platform of 1884

The Anti-Monopoly organization of the United States in convention assembled, declares:

1. That labor and capital should be allies and we demand justice for both by protecting the rights of all against privileges for the few.

2. That corporations, the creatures of law, should be controlled by law.

3. That we propose the greatest reduction practicable in public expenses.

4. That in the enactment and vigorous execution of just laws, equality of rights, equality of burdens, equality of privileges, and equality of powers in all citizens will be secured.

To this end, we further declare:

5. That it is the duty of the Government to immediately exercise its constitutional prerogative to regulate commerce among the States. The great instruments by which this commerce is carried on are transportation, money, and the transmission of intelligence. They are now mercilessly controlled by giant monopolies, to the impoverishment of labor, and the crushing out of healthful competition, and the destruction of business security. We hold it, therefore, to be the imperative and immediate duty of Congress to pass all needful laws for the control and regulation of those great agents of commerce in accordance with the oft-repeated decisions of the Supreme Court of the United States.

6. That these monopolies, which have exacted from enterprise such heavy tribute, have also inflicted countless wrongs upon the toiling millions of the United States, and no system of reform should commend itself to the support of the people which does not protect the man who earns his bread by the sweat of his face. Bureaus of labor statistics must be established, both State and National; arbitration take the place of brute force in the settlement of disputes between employer and employed; the National eight-hour law be honestly enforced; the importation of foreign labor *under contract* be made illegal; and whatever practical reforms may be necessary for the protection of united labor must be granted, to the end that unto the toiler shall be given that proportion of the profits of the thing or value created which his labor bears to the cost of production.

7. That we approve and favor the passage of an Inter-State Commerce bill. Navigable waters should be improved by the Government and be free.

8. We demand the payment of the bonded debt as it falls due; the election of the United States Senators by the direct vote of the people of their respective States; a graduated income tax; and a tariff, which is a tax upon the people, that shall be so levied as to bear as lightly as possible upon necessaries. We denounce the present tariff as being largely in the interest of monopoly, and demand that it be speedily and radically reformed in the interest of labor instead of capital.

9. That no further grants of public lands shall be made to corporations. All enactments granting land to corporations should be strictly construed; and all land-grants should be forfeited where the terms upon which the grants were made have not been strictly complied with. The public lands must be held for homes for actual settlers, and must not be subject to purchase or control by non-resident foreigners or other speculators.

10. That we deprecate the discrimination of American legislation against the greatest of American industries—agriculture, by which it has been deprived of nearly all beneficial legislation while forced to bear the brunt of taxation. And we demand for it the fostering care of Government and the just recognition of its importance in the development and advancement of our land. And we appeal to the American farmer to co-operate with us in our endeavors to advance the National interests of the country, and the over-

throw of monopoly in every shape when and wherever found.

Democratic Platform of 1884

The Democratic party of the Union, through its representatives in National Convention assembled, recognizes that, as the nation grows older, new issues are born of time and progress, and old issues perish. But the fundamental principles of the Democracy, approved by the united voice of the people, remain, and will ever remain, as the best and only security for the continuance of free government. The preservation of personal rights; the equality of all citizens before the law; the reserved rights of the States; and the supremacy of the Federal Government within the limits of the Constitution, will ever form the true basis of our liberties, and can never be surrendered without destroying that balance of rights and powers which enables a continent to be developed in peace, and social order to be maintained by means of local self-government.

But it is indispensable for the practical application and enforcement of these fundamental principles, that the Government should not always be controlled by one political party. Frequent change of administration is as necessary as constant recurrence to the popular will. Otherwise abuses grow, and the Government, instead of being carried on for the general welfare, becomes an instrumentality for imposing heavy burdens on the many who are governed, for the benefit of the few who govern. Public servants thus become arbitrary rulers.

This is now the condition of the country. Hence a change is demanded. The Republican party, so far as principle is concerned, is a reminiscence; in practice, it is an organization for enriching those who control its machinery. The frauds and jobbery which have been brought to light in every department of the Government, are sufficient to have called for reform within the Republican party; yet those in authority, made reckless by the long possession of power, have succumbed to its corrupting influence, and have placed in nomination a ticket against which the independent portion of the party are in open revolt.

Therefore a change is demanded. Such a change was alike necessary in 1876, but the will

of the people was then defeated by a fraud which can never be forgotten, nor condoned. Again, in 1880, the change demanded by the people was defeated by the lavish use of money contributed by unscrupulous contractors and shameless jobbers who had bargained for unlawful profits, or for high office.

The Republican party during its legal, its stolen, and its bought tenure of power, has steadily decayed in moral character and political capacity.

Its platform promises are now a list of its past failures.

It demands the restoration of our Navy. It has squandered hundreds of millions to create a navy that does not exist.

It calls upon Congress to remove the burdens under which American shipping has been depressed. It imposed and has continued those burdens.

It professes a policy of reserving the public lands for small holdings by actual settlers. It has given away the people's heritage till now a few railroads, and non-resident aliens, individual and corporate, possess a larger area than that of all our farms between the two seas.

It professes a preference for free institutions. It organized and tried to legalize a control of State elections by Federal troops.

It professes a desire to elevate labor. It has subjected American workingmen to the competition of convict and imported contract labor.

It professes gratitude to all who were disabled, or died in the war, leaving widows and orphans. It left to a Democratic House of Representatives the first effort to equalize both bounties and pensions.

It proffers a pledge to correct the irregularities of our tariff. It created and has continued them. Its own Tariff Commission confessed the need of more than twenty per cent reduction. Its Congress gave a reduction of less than four per cent.

It professes the protection of American manufactures. It has subjected them to an increasing flood of manufactured goods, and a hopeless competition with manufacturing nations, not one of which taxes raw materials.

It professes to protect all American industries. It has impoverished many to subsidize a few.

It professes the protection of American labor. It has depleted the returns of American agriculture—an industry followed by half of our people.

It professes the equality of all men before the law. Attempting to fix the status of colored citizens, the acts of its Congress were overset by the decision of its Courts.

It "accepts anew the duty of leading in the work of progress and reform." Its caught criminals are permitted to escape through contrived delays or actual connivance in the prosecution. Honeycombed with corruption, outbreaking exposures no longer shock its moral sense. Its honest members, its independent journals, no longer maintain a successful contest for authority in its councils or a veto upon bad nominations.

That change is necessary is proved by an existing surplus of more than $100,000,000, which has yearly been collected from a suffering people. Unnecessary taxation is unjust taxation. We denounce the Republican party for having failed to relieve the people from crushing war taxes which have paralyzed business, crippled industry, and deprived labor of employment and of just reward.

The Democracy pledges itself to purify the Administration from corruption, to restore economy, to revive respect for law, and to reduce taxation to the lowest limit consistent with due regard to the preservation of the faith of the Nation to its creditors and pensioners.

Knowing full well, however, that legislation affecting the operations of the people should be cautious and conservative in method, not in advance of public opinion, but responsive to its demands, the Democratic party is pledged to revise the tariff in a spirit of fairness to all interests.

But in making reduction in taxes, it is not proposed to injure any domestic industries, but rather to promote their healthy growth. From the foundation of this Government, taxes collected at the Custom House have been the chief source of Federal Revenue. Such they must continue to be. Moreover, many industries have come to rely upon legislation for successful continuance, so that any change of law must be at every step regardful of the labor and capital thus involved. The process of reform must be subject in the execution to this plain dictate of justice.

All taxation shall be limited to the requirements of economical government. The necessary reduction and taxation can and must be effected without depriving American labor of the ability to compete successfully with foreign labor, and without imposing lower rates of duty than will be ample to cover any increased cost of production which may exist in consequence of the higher rate of wages prevailing in this country.

Sufficient revenue to pay all the expenses of the Federal Government, economically administered, including pensions, interest, and principal on the public debt, can be got, under our present system of taxation, from the custom house taxes on fewer imported articles, bearing heaviest on articles of luxury, and bearing lightest on articles of necessity.

We, therefore, denounce the abuses of the existing tariff; and, subject to the preceding limitations, we demand that Federal taxation shall be exclusively for public purposes and shall not exceed the needs of the Government economically administered.

The system of direct taxation known as the "Internal Revenue," is a war tax, and so long as the law continues, the money derived therefrom should be sacredly devoted to the relief of the people from the remaining burdens of the war, and be made a fund to defray the expenses of the care and comfort of worthy soldiers disabled in line of duty in the wars of the Republic and for the payment of such pensions as Congress may from time to time grant to such soldiers, a like fund for the sailors having been already provided; and any surplus should be paid into the Treasury.

We favor an American continental policy based upon more intimate commercial and political relations with the fifteen sister Republics of North, Central, and South America, but entangling alliances with none.

We believe in honest money, the gold and silver coinage of the Constitution, and a circulating medium convertible into such money without loss.

Asserting the equality of all men before the law, we hold that it is the duty of the Government, in its dealings with the people, to mete out equal and exact justice to all citizens of whatever nativity, race, color, or persuasion—religious or political.

We believe in a free ballot and a fair count; and we recall to the memory of the people the noble struggle of the Democrats in the Forty-fifth and Forty-sixth Congresses, by which a reluctant Republican opposition was compelled to assent to legislation making everywhere illegal the presence of troops at the polls, as the conclusive proof that a Democratic administration will preserve liberty with order.

The selection of Federal officers for the Territories should be restricted to citizens previously resident therein.

We oppose sumptuary laws which vex the citizen and interfere with individual liberty; we favor honest Civil Service Reform, and the compensation of all United States officers by fixed salaries; the separation of Church and State; and the diffusion of free education by common schools, so that every child in the land may be taught the rights and duties of citizenship.

While we favor all legislation which will tend to the equitable distribution of property, to the prevention of monopoly, and to the strict enforcement of individual rights against corporate abuses, we hold that the welfare of society depends upon a scrupulous regard for the rights of property as defined by law.

We believe that labor is best rewarded where it is freest and most enlightened. It should therefore be fostered and cherished. We favor the repeal of all laws restricting the free action of labor, and the enactment of laws by which labor organizations may be incorporated, and of all such legislation as will tend to enlighten the people as to the true relations of capital and labor.

We believe that the public lands ought, as far as possible, to be kept as homesteads for actual settlers; that all unearned lands heretofore improvidently granted to railroad corporations by the action of the Republican party should be restored to the public domain; and that no more grants of land shall be made to corporations, or be allowed to fall into the ownership of alien absentees.

We are opposed to all propositions which upon any pretext would convert the General Government into a machine for collecting taxes to be distributed among the States, or the citizens thereof.

In reaffirming the declaration of the Democratic platform of 1856, that, "the liberal principles embodied by Jefferson in the Declaration of Independence, and sanctioned in the Constitution, which make ours the land of liberty and the asylum of the oppressed of every Nation, have ever been cardinal principles in the Democratic

faith," we nevertheless do not sanction the importation of foreign labor, or the admission of servile races, unfitted by habits, training, religion, or kindred, for absorption into the great body of our people, or for the citizenship which our laws confer. American civilization demands that against the immigration or importation of Mongolians to these shores our gates be closed.

The Democratic party insists that it is the duty of the Government to protect, with equal fidelity and vigilance, the rights of its citizens, native and naturalized, at home and abroad, and to the end that this protection may be assured, United States papers of naturalization, issued by courts of competent jurisdiction, must be respected by the Executive and Legislative departments of our own Government, and by all foreign powers.

It is an imperative duty of this Government to efficiently protect all the rights of persons and property of every American citizen in foreign lands, and demand and enforce full reparation for any invasion thereof.

An American citizen is only responsible to his own Government for any act done in his own country, or under her flag, and can only be tried therefor on her own soil and according to her laws; and no power exists in this Government to expatriate an American citizen to be tried in any foreign land for any such act.

This country has never had a well-defined and executed foreign policy save under Democratic administration; that policy has ever been, in regard to foreign nations, so long as they do not act detrimental to the interests of the country or hurtful to our citizens, to let them alone; that as a result of this policy we call the acquisition of Louisiana, Florida, California, and of the adjacent Mexican territory by purchase alone, and contrast these grand acquisitions of Democratic statesmanship with the purchase of Alaska, the sole fruit of a Republican administration of nearly a quarter of a century.

The Federal Government should care for and improve the Mississippi River and other great waterways of the Republic, so as to secure for the interior States easy and cheap transportation to tide water.

Under a long period of Democratic rule and policy, our merchant marine was fast overtaking and on the point of outstripping that of Great Britain.

Under twenty years of Republican rule and policy, our commerce has been left to British bottoms, and almost has the American flag been swept off the high seas.

Instead of the Republican party's British policy, we demand for the people of the United States an American policy.

Under Democratic rule and policy our merchants and sailors, flying the stars and stripes in every port, successfully searched out a market for the varied products of American industry.

Under a quarter of a century of Republican rule and policy, despite our manifest advantage of all other nations in high-paid labor, favorable climate and teeming soils; despite freedom of trade among all these United States; despite their population by the foremost races of men and an annual immigration of the young, thrifty and adventurous of all nations; despite our freedom here from the inherited burdens of life and industry in the old-world monarchies—their costly war navies, their vast tax-consuming, non-producing standing armies; despite twenty years of peace—that Republican rule and policy have managed to surrender to Great Britain, along with our commerce, the control of the markets of the world.

Instead of the Republican party's British policy, we demand on behalf of the American Democracy, an American policy.

Instead of the Republican party's discredited scheme and false pretense of friendship for American labor, expressed by imposing taxes, we demand in behalf of the Democracy, freedom for American labor by reducing taxes, to the end that these United States may compete with unhindered powers for the primacy among nations in all the arts of peace and fruits of liberty.

With profound regret we have been apprised by the venerable statesman through whose person was struck that blow at the vital principle of republics (acquiescence in the will of the majority), that he cannot permit us again to place in his hands the leadership of the Democratic hosts, for the reason that the achievement of reform in the administration of the Federal Government is an undertaking now too heavy for his age and failing strength.

Rejoicing that his life has been prolonged until the general judgment of our fellow-countrymen is united in the wish that that wrong were righted in his person, for the Democracy of the United States we offer to him in his withdrawal from public cares not only our respectful sympathy and esteem, but also that best homage of freemen, the pledge of our devotion to the principles and the cause now inseparable in the history of this Republic from the labors and the name of Samuel J. Tilden.

With this statement of the hopes, principles and purposes of the Democratic party, the great issue of Reform and change in Administration is submitted to the people in calm confidence that the popular voice will pronounce in favor of new men, and new and more favorable conditions for the growth of industry, the extension of trade, the employment and the due reward of labor and of capital, and the general welfare of the whole country.

Greenback National Platform of 1884

Eight years ago our young party met in this city for the first time, and proclaimed to the world its immortal principles, and placed before the American people as a presidential candidate that great philanthropist and spotless statesman, Peter Cooper. Since that convention our party has organized all over the Union, and through discussion and agitation has been educating the people to a sense of their rights and duties to themselves and their country. These labors have accomplished wonders. We now have a great, harmonious party, and thousands who believe in our principles in the ranks of other parties.

"We point with pride to our history." We forced the remonetization of the silver dollar; prevented the refunding of the public debt into long-time bonds; secured the payment of the bonds, until the "best banking system the world ever saw" for robbing the producer now totters because of its contracting foundation; we have stopped the squandering of our public domain upon corporations; we have stopped the wholesale destruction of the greenback currency, and secured a decision of the Supreme Court of the United States establishing forever the right of the people to issue their own money.

Notwithstanding all this, never in our history have the banks, land-grant railroads, and other monopolies, been more insolent in their demands for further privileges—still more class legislation.

In this emergency the dominant parties are arrayed against the people, and are the abject tools of the corporate monopolies.

In the last Congress they repealed over $12,-000,000 of annual taxes for the banks, throwing the burden upon the people to pay or pay interest thereon.

Both old parties in the present Congress vie with each other in their efforts to further repeal taxes in order to stop the payment of the public debt, and save the banks whose charters they have renewed for twenty years. Notwithstanding the distress of business, the shrinkage of wages and panic, they persist in locking up, on various pretexts, $400,000,000 of money, every dollar of which the people pay interest upon, and need, and most of which should be promptly applied to pay bonds now payable.

The old parties are united—as they cannot agree what taxes to repeal—in efforts to squander the income of the Government upon every pretext rather than pay the debt.

A bill has already passed the United States Senate making the banks a present of over $50,-000,000 more of the people's money in order to enable them to levy a still greater burden of interest-taxes.

A joint effort is being made by the old party leaders to overthrow the sovereign constitutional power of the people to control their own financial affairs and issue their own money, in order to forever enslave the masses to bankers and other business. The House of Representatives has passed bills reclaiming nearly 100,000,000 acres of lands granted to and forfeited by railroad companies. These bills have gone to the Senate, a body composed largely of aristocratic millionaires, who, according to their own party papers, generally purchased their elections in order to protect great monopolies which they represent. This body has thus far defied the people and the House, and refused to act upon these bills in the interest of the people.

Therefore, we, the National party of the United States, in national convention assembled, this 29th day of May A. D. 1884, declare:

1. That we hold the late decision of the Supreme Court on the legal-tender question to be a full vindication of the theory which our party has always advocated on the right and authority of Congress over the issue of legal-tender notes, and we hereby pledge ourselves to uphold said decision, and to defend the Constitution against alterations or amendments intended to deprive the people of any rights or privileges conferred by that instrument. We demand the issue of such money in sufficient quantities to supply the actual demand of trade and commerce, in accordance with the increase of population and the development of our industries. We demand the substitution of greenbacks for national bank notes and the prompt payment of the public debt. We want that money which saved our country in time of war and which has given it prosperity and happiness in peace. We condemn the retirement of the fractional currency and the small denominations of greenbacks, and demand their restoration. We demand the issue of the hoards of money now locked up in the United States Treasury, by applying them to the payment of the public debt now due.

2. We denounce, as dangerous to our republican institutions, those methods and policies of the Democratic and Republican parties which have sanctioned or permitted the establishment of land, railroad, money and other gigantic corporate monopolies; and we demand such governmental action as may be necessary to take from such monopolies the powers they have so corruptly and unjustly usurped, and restore them to the people, to whom they belong.

3. The public lands, being the natural inheritance of the people, we denounce that policy which has granted to corporations vast tracts of land, and we demand that immediate and vigorous measures be taken to reclaim from such corporations, for the people's use and benefit, all such land grants as have been forfeited by reason of non-fulfillment of contract, or that may have been wrongfully acquired by corrupt legislation, and that such reclaimed lands and other public domain be henceforth held as a sacred trust, to be granted only to actual settlers in limited quantities; and we also demand that the alien ownership of land, individual or corporate, shall be prohibited.

4. We demand Congressional regulation of inter-State commerce. We denounce "pooling," stock watering and discrimination in rates and charges, and demand that Congress shall correct these abuses, even, if necessary, by the construction of national railroads. We also demand the

establishment of a government postal telegraph system.

5. All private property, all forms of money and obligations to pay money, should bear their just proportion of the public taxes. We demand a graduated income tax.

6. We demand the amelioration of the condition of labor by enforcing the sanitary laws in industrial establishments, by the abolition of the convict labor system, by a rigid inspection of mines and factories, by a reduction of the hours of labor in industrial establishments, by fostering educational institutions, and by abolishing child labor.

7. We condemn all importations of contract labor, made with a view of reducing to starvation wages the workingmen of this country, and demand laws for its prevention.

8. We insist upon a constitutional amendment reducing the terms of United States Senators.

9. We demand such rules for the government of Congress as shall place all Representatives of the people upon an equal footing, and take away from committees a veto power greater than that of the President.

10. The question as to the amount of duties to be levied upon various articles of import has been agitated and quarreled over and has divided communities for nearly a hundred years. It is not now and never will be settled unless by the abolition of indirect taxation. It is a convenient issue—always raised when the people are excited over abuses in their midst. While we favor a wise revision of the tariff laws, with a view to raising a revenue from luxuries rather than necessaries, we insist that as an economic question its importance is insignificant as compared with financial issues; for whereas we have suffered our worst panics under low and also under high tariff, we have never suffered from a panic nor seen our factories and workshops closed while the volume of money in circulation was adequate to the needs of commerce. Give our farmers and manufacturers money as cheap as you now give it to our bankers, and they can pay high wages to labor, and compete with all the world.

11. For the purpose of testing the sense of the people upon the subject, we are in favor of submitting to a vote of the people an amendment to the Constitution in favor of suffrage regardless of sex, and also on the subject of the liquor traffic.

12. All disabled soldiers of the late war should be equitably pensioned, and we denounce the policy of keeping a small army of office-holders whose only business is to prevent, on technical grounds, deserving soldiers from obtaining justice from the government they helped to save.

13. As our name indicates, we are a National party, knowing no East, no West, no North, no South. Having no sectional prejudices, we can properly place in nomination for the high offices of State as candidates, men from any section of the Union.

14. We appeal to all people who believe in our principles to aid us by voice, pen and votes.

Prohibition Platform of 1884

1. The Prohibition party, in National Convention assembled, acknowledge Almighty God as the rightful sovereign of all men, from whom the just powers of government are derived and to whose laws human enactments should conform as an absolute condition of peace, prosperity and happiness.

2. That the importation, manufacture, supply and sale of alcoholic beverages, created and maintained by the laws of the National and State Governments during the entire history of such laws, are everywhere shown to be the promoting cause of intemperance, with resulting crime and pauperism, making large demands upon public and private charity; imposing large and unjust taxation for the support of penal and sheltering institutions, upon thrift, industry, manufactures and commerce; endangering the public peace; desecrating the Sabbath; corrupting our politics, legislation and administration of the laws; shortening lives, impairing health and diminishing productive industry; causing education to be neglected and despised; nullifying the teachings of the Bible, the church and the school, the standards and guides of our fathers and their children in the founding and growth of our widely-extended country; and which, imperilling the perpetuity of our civil and religious liberties, are baleful fruits by which we know that these laws are contrary to God's laws and contravene our happiness. We therefore call upon our fellow-citizens to aid in the repeal of these laws and in the legal suppression of this baneful liquor traffic.

3. During the 24 years in which the Republican party has controlled the general Government and many of the States, no effort has been made to change this policy. Territories have been created, Governments for them established, States admitted to the Union, and in no instance in either case has this traffic been forbidden or the people been permitted to prohibit it. That there are now over 200,000 distilleries, breweries, wholesale and retail dealers in their products, holding certificates and claiming the authority of Government for the continuation of the business so destructive to the moral and material welfare of the people, together with the fact that they have turned a deaf ear to remonstrance and petition for the correction of this abuse of civil government, is conclusive that the Republican party is insensible to or impotent for the redress of these wrongs, and should no longer be entrusted with the powers and responsibilities of Government. Although this party in its late National Convention was silent on the liquor question, not so its candidates, Messrs. Blaine and Logan. Within the year past Mr. Blaine has recommended that the revenue derived from the liquor traffic be distributed among the States; and Senator Logan has, by bill, proposed to devote these revenues to the support of the public schools. Thus both virtually recommend the perpetuation of the traffic, and that the States and their citizens become partners in the liquor crime.

4. That the Democratic party has in its national deliverances of party policy arrayed itself on the side of the drink-makers and sellers by declaring against the policy of Prohibition under the false name of "sumptuary laws"; that when in power in many of the States it has refused remedial legislation, and that in Congress it has obstructed the creation of a Commission of Inquiry into the effects of this traffic, proving that it should not be entrusted with power and place.

5. That there can be no greater peril to the nation than the existing competition of the Republican and Democratic parties for the liquor vote. Experience shows that any party not openly opposed to the traffic will engage in this competition, will court the favor of the criminal classes, will barter the public morals, the purity of the ballot and every trust and object of good government for party success. Patriots and good citizens should therefore, immediately withdraw from all connection with these parties.

6. That we favor reforms in the abolition of all sinecures with useless offices and officers, and in elections by the people instead of appointments by the President; that as competency, honesty and sobriety are essential qualifications for office, we oppose removals except when absolutely necessary to secure effectiveness in vital issues; that the collection of revenues from alcoholic liquors and tobacco should be abolished, since the vices of men are not proper subjects of taxation; that revenue from customs duties should be levied for the support of the Government economically administered, and in such manner as will foster American industries and labor; that the public lands should be held for homes for the people, and not bestowed as gifts to corporations, or sold in large tracts for speculation upon the needs of actual settlers; that grateful care and support should be given to our soldiers and sailors disabled in the service of their country, and to their dependent widows and orphans; that we repudiate as un-American and contrary to and subversive to the principles of the Declaration of Independence, that any person or people should be excluded from residence or citizenship who may desire the benefits which our institutions confer upon the oppressed of all nations; that while these are important reforms, and are demanded for purity of administration and the welfare of the people, their importance sinks into insignificance when compared with the drink traffic, which now annually wastes $800,000,000 of the wealth created by toil and thrift, dragging down thousands of families from comfort to poverty, filling jails, penitentiaries, insane asylums, hospitals and institutions for dependency, impairing the health and destroying the lives of thousands, lowering intellectual vigor and dulling the cunning hand of the artisan, causing bankruptcy, insolvency and loss in trade, and by its corrupting power endangering the perpetuity of free institutions; that Congress should exercise its undoubted power by prohibiting the manufacture and sale of intoxicating beverages in the District of Columbia, the Territories of the United States and all places over which the Government has exclusive jurisdiction; that hereafter no State should be admitted to the Union until its Constitution shall expressly and forever prohibit polygamy and the manufacture and sale of intoxicating beverages, and that Congress shall submit to

the States an Amendment to the Constitution forever prohibiting the importation, exportation, manufacture and sale of alcoholic drinks.

7. We earnestly call the attention of the mechanic, the miner and manufacturer to the investigation of the baneful effects upon labor and industry of the needless liquor business. It will be found the robber who lessens wages and profits, foments discontent and strikes, and the destroyer of family welfare. Labor and all legitimate industries demand deliverance from the taxation and loss which this traffic imposes; and no tariff or other legislation can so healthily stimulate production, or increase the demand for capital and labor, or insure so much of comfort and content to the laborer, mechanic and capitalist as would the suppression of this traffic.

8. That the activity and co-operation of the women of America for the promotion of temperance has in all the history of the past been a strength and encouragement which we gratefully acknowledge and record. In the later and present phase of the movement for the Prohibition of the traffic, the purity of purpose and method, the earnestness, zeal, intelligence and devotion of the mothers and daughters of the Woman's Christian Temperance Union have been eminently blessed of God. Kansas and Iowa have been given them as "sheaves" of rejoicing, and the education and arousing of the public mind, and the now prevailing demand for the Constitutional Amendment, are largely the fruit of their prayers and labors. Sharing in the efforts that shall bring the question of the abolition of this traffic to the polls, they shall join in the grand "Praise God, from whom all blessings flow," when by law victory shall be achieved.

9. That, believing in the civil and the political equality of the sexes, and that the ballot in the hands of woman is her right for protection and would prove a powerful ally for the abolition of the liquor traffic, the execution of the law, the promotion of reform in civil affairs, the removal of corruption in public life, we enunciate the principle and relegate the practical outworking of this reform to the discretion of the Prohibition party in the several States according to the condition of public sentiment in those States.

10. That we gratefully acknowledge the presence of the divine spirit guiding the counsels and granting the success which has been vouchsafed in the progress of the temperance reform; and we earnestly ask the voters of these United States to make the principles of the above declaration dominant in the Government of the nation.

Republican Platform of 1884

The Republicans of the United States in National Convention assembled renew their allegiance to the principles upon which they have triumphed in six successive Presidential elections; and congratulate the American people on the attainment of so many results in legislation and administration, by which the Republican party has, after saving the Union, done so much to render its institutions just, equal and beneficent, the safeguard of liberty and the embodiment of the best thought and highest purpose of our citizens.

The Republican party has gained its strength by quick and faithful response to the demands of the people for the freedom and equality of all men; for a united nation, assuring the rights of all citizens; for the elevation of labor; for an honest currency; for purity in legislation, and for integrity and accountability in all departments of the government, and it accepts anew the duty of leading in the work of progress and reform.

We lament the death of President Garfield, whose sound statesmanship, long conspicuous in Congress, gave promise of a strong and successful administration; a promise fully realized during the short period of his office as President of the United States. His distinguished services in war and peace have endeared him to the hearts of the American people.

In the administration of President Arthur, we recognize a wise, conservative and patriotic policy, under which the country has been blessed with remarkable prosperity; and we believe his eminent services are entitled to and will receive the hearty approval of every citizen.

It is the first duty of a good government to protect the rights and promote the interests of its own people.

The largest diversity of industry is most productive of general prosperity, and of the comfort and independence of the people.

We, therefore, demand that the imposition of duties on foreign imports shall be made, not "for revenue only," but that in raising the requisite revenues for the government, such duties shall be so levied as to afford security to our diversified industries and protection to the rights and wages of the laborer; to the end that active and intelligent labor, as well as capital, may have its just reward, and the laboring man his full share in the national prosperity.

Against the so-called economic system of the Democratic party, which would degrade our labor to the foreign standard, we enter our earnest protest.

The Democratic party has failed completely to relieve the people of the burden of unnecessary taxation by a wise reduction of the surplus.

The Republican party pledges itself to correct the inequalities of the tariff, and to reduce the surplus, not by the vicious and indiscriminate process of horizontal reduction, but by such methods as will relieve the tax-payer without injuring the laborer or the great productive interests of the country.

We recognize the importance of sheep husbandry in the United States, the serious depression which it is now experiencing, and the danger threatening its future prosperity; and we, therefore, respect the demands of the representatives of this important agricultural interest for a readjustment of duties upon foreign wool, in order that such industry shall have full and adequate protection.

We have always recommended the best money known to the civilized world; and we urge that efforts should be made to unite all commercial nations in the establishment of an international standard which shall fix for all the relative value of gold and silver coinage.

The regulation of commerce with foreign nations and between the States, is one of the most important prerogatives of the general government; and the Republican party distinctly announces its purpose to support such legislation as will fully and efficiently carry out the constitutional power of Congress over inter-State commerce.

The principle of public regulation of railway corporations is a wise and salutary one for the protection of all classes of the people; and we favor legislation that shall prevent unjust discrimination and excessive charges for transportation, and that shall secure to the people, and the railways alike, the fair and equal protection of the laws.

We favor the establishment of a national bureau of labor; the enforcement of the eight hour law, a wise and judicious system of general education by adequate appropriation from the national revenues, wherever the same is needed. We believe that everywhere the protection to a citizen of American birth must be secured to citizens by American adoption; and we favor the settlement of national differences by international arbitration.

The Republican party, having its birth in a hatred of slave labor and a desire that all men may be truly free and equal, is unalterably opposed to placing our workingmen in competition with any form of servile labor, whether at home or abroad. In this spirit, we denounce the importation of contract labor, whether from Europe or Asia, as an offense against the spirit of American institutions; and we pledge ourselves to sustain the present law restricting Chinese immigration, and to provide such further legislation as is necessary to carry out its purposes.

Reform of the civil service, auspiciously begun under Republican administration, should be completed by the further extension of the reform system already established by law, to all the grades of the service to which it is applicable. The spirit and purpose of the reform should be observed in all executive appointments; and all laws at variance with the objects of existing reform legislation should be repealed, to the end that the dangers to free institutions, which lurk in the power of official patronage, may be wisely and effectively avoided.

The public lands are a heritage of the people of the United States, and should be reserved as far as possible for small holdings by actual settlers. We are opposed to the acquisition of large tracts of these lands by corporations or individuals, especially where such holdings are in the hands of non-resident or aliens. And we will endeavor to obtain such legislation as will tend to correct this evil. We demand of Congress the speedy forfeiture of all land grants which have lapsed by reason of non-compliance with acts of incorporation, in all cases where there has been no attempt in good faith to perform the conditions of such grants.

The grateful thanks of the American people are due to the Union soldiers and sailors of the late war; and the Republican party stands pledged to suitable pensions for all who were disabled, and for the widows and orphans of those who died in the war. The Republican party also pledges itself to the repeal of the limitations contained in the arrears act of 1879. So that all invalid soldiers shall share alike, and their pensions begin with the date of disability or discharge, and not with the date of application.

The Republican party favors a policy which shall keep us from entangling alliances with foreign nations, and which gives us the right to expect that foreign nations shall refrain from meddling in American affairs; a policy which seeks peace and trade with all powers, but especially with those of the Western Hemisphere.

We demand the restoration of our navy to its old-time strength and efficiency, that it may in any sea protect the rights of American citizens and the interests of American commerce; and we call upon Congress to remove the burdens under which American shipping has been depressed, so that it may again be true that we have a commerce which leaves no sea unexplored, and a navy which takes no law from superior force.

Resolved, That appointments by the President to offices in the Territories should be made from the *bona-fide* citizens and residents of the Territories wherein they are to serve.

Resolved, That it is the duty of Congress to enact such laws as shall promptly and effectually suppress the system of polygamy within our Territories; and divorce the political from the ecclesiastical power of the so-called Mormon church; and that the laws so enacted should be rigidly enforced by the civil authorities, if possible, and by the military, if need be.

The people of the United States, in their organized capacity, constitute a Nation and not a mere confederacy of States; the National Government is supreme within the sphere of its national duties; but the States have reserved rights which should be faithfully maintained. Each should be guarded with jealous care, so that the harmony of our system of government may be preserved and the Union kept inviolate.

The perpetuity of our institutions rests upon the maintenance of a free ballot, an honest count, and correct returns. We denounce the fraud and violence practised by the Democracy in Southern States, by which the will of a voter is defeated, as dangerous to the preservation of free institutions; and we solemnly arraign the Democratic party as being the guilty recipient of fruits of such fraud and violence.

We extend to the Republicans of the South, regardless of their former party affiliations, our cordial sympathy; and we pledge to them our most earnest efforts to promote the passage of such legislation as will secure to every citizen, of whatever race and color, the full and complete recognition, possession and exercise of all civil and political rights.

CAMPAIGN OF 1888

In 1888, it was assumed that the same candidates who had participated in the 1884 election would again be the contestants, but James G. Blaine withdrew from the campaign, thus creating a wide-open Republican convention in which fourteen candidates divided the votes on the first ballot. After six days and eight ballots, General Benjamin Harrison of Indiana was nominated for president and Levi P. Morton was nominated for vice-president. The Democrats nominated the incumbent president, Grover Cleveland, by acclamation, and chose former Senator Allen G. Thurman of Ohio as his running mate.

In addition to the major parties, the Prohibition Party, at its fifth national convention, nominated Clinton B. Fisk of New Jersey for president and John A. Brooks of Missouri as his running mate. Two factions of parties supporting labor also offered candidates in 1888. The Union Labor Party selected Alson J. Streeter of Illinois for president and Samuel Evans of Texas for vice-president. The United Labor Party chose Robert H. Cowdrey of Illinois for president and W. H. T. Wakefield of Kansas for vice-president. A group of citizens devoted to protecting the United States from foreigners, who called themselves the American Party, held a convention at which they chose James Langdon Curtis of New York for president and James Greer of Tennessee for vice-president.

In the famous election that followed, Cleveland polled nearly 100 thousand more popular votes than Harrison, but lost in the electoral college, 233 to 168. There were more than 11 million votes cast and the minor parties were well supported. Fisk received 249,813; Streeter garnered 146,602; Curtis 1,591; Cowdrey 2,818; and all others 7,006. These figures are from the *Congressional Quarterly* compilations from the Inter-University Consortium for Political Research at the University of Michigan and from Stanwood's *History of the Presidency*. Other sources indicate different totals, but all reports confirm the results above.

American Platform of 1888

Believing that the time has arrived when a due regard for the present and future prosperity of our country makes it imperative that the people of the United States of America should take full and entire control of their government, to the exclusion of revolutionary and incendiary foreigners, now seeking our shores from every quarter of the globe, and recognizing that the first and most important duty of an American citizen is to maintain the Government in all attainable purity and strength, we make the following declaration of principles:

Resolved, That all law-abiding citizens of the United States of America, whether native or foreign born, are political equals (except as provided by the Constitution), and all are entitled to and should receive the full protection of the laws.

Whereas, There are seventeen states in this Union wherein persons are allowed to vote at all elections without being citizens of the United States; and,

Whereas, Such a system tends to place the management of the Government in the hands of those who owe no allegiance to our political institutions; therefore,

Resolved, That the Constitution of the United States should be so amended as to prohibit the Federal and State governments from conferring upon any person the right to vote unless such person be a citizen of the United States.

Resolved, That we are in favor of fostering and encouraging American industries of every class and kind, and declare that the assumed issue "Protection" *vs.* "Free Trade" is a fraud and a snare. The best "protection" is that which protects the labor and life blood of the republic from the degrading competition with and contaminations by imported foreigners; and the most dangerous "free trade" is that in paupers, criminals, communists, and anarchists, in which the balance has always been against the United States.

Whereas, One of the greatest evils of unrestricted foreign immigration is the reduction of the wages of the American workingman and workingwoman to the level of the underfed and underpaid labor of foreign countries: therefore,

Resolved, That we demand that no immigrant shall be admitted into the United States without a passport obtained from the American Consul at the port from which he sails; that no passport shall be issued to any pauper, criminal, or insane person, or to any person who, in the judgment of the consul, is not likely to become a desirable citizen of the United States; and that for each immigrant passport there shall be collected by the Consul issuing the same the sum of one hundred dollars ($100), to be by him paid into the Treasury of the United States.

Resolved, That the present naturalization laws of the United States should be unconditionally repealed.

Resolved, That the soil of America should belong to Americans; That no alien non-resident should be permitted to own real estate in the United States, and that the realty possessions of the resident alien should be limited in value and area.

Resolved, That we favor educating the boys and girls of American citizens as mechanics and artisans, thus fitting them for the places now filled by foreigners, who supply the greater part of our skilled labor, and thereby almost entirely control the great industries of our country, save, perhaps, that of agriculture alone; and that our boys and girls may be taught trades, we demand the establishment and maintenance of free technical schools.

Resolved, That universal education is a necessity of our Government, and that our American free school system should be preserved and maintained as the safeguard of American liberty.

Resolved, That no language except the English shall be taught in the common schools supported at the public expense.

Whereas, an unemployed population is the greatest evil that can befall any nation, and in this country it cannot be eliminated by European methods, such as extra police and standing armies, therefore,

Resolved, That the surplus in the Treasury should be devoted to the material improvement of our coast and frontier defences, and the construction of an American navy in American workshops, by American labor.

Resolved, That we demand the enactment of a law which shall require all persons having charge in any way of any department, bureau, or division of the Government to forthwith dismiss from the public service all persons employed in or about any such department, bureau, or division in any way or manner who are not citizens of the United States; that no person shall be appointed to or hold office or place in the service of the United States who is not a citizen of the United States either by nativity or by full naturalization, according to law.

Resolved, That after the year 1898 it shall be required of every voter before he exercises the right of suffrage to be able to read the written or printed Constitution of the United States, in the English language, and to write his own name upon the register, to show that he is fitted to share in the administration of the government of the republic.

Resolved, That we recognize the right of labor to organize for its protection, by all lawful and peaceful means to secure to itself the greatest reward for its thrift and industry; and we believe in governmental arbitration in the settlement of industrial differences.

Resolved, That we are in favor of such legislation by Congress as will re-establish the American marine.

Resolved, That no flag shall float on any public buildings, municipal, State, or National, in the United States, except the Municipal, State, or National flag of the United States—the flag of the Stars and Stripes.

Resolved, That we reassert the American principles of absolute freedom of religious worship and belief, the permanent separation of Church and State; and we oppose the appropriation of public money or property to any church or institution administered by a church.

We maintain that all church property should be subject to taxation.

Resolved, That the Presidential term shall be extended to six years, and the President shall be ineligible to re-election.

Resolved, That the American Party declares that it recognizes no North, no South, no East, no West in these United States, but one people, pledged to the general welfare and to liberty and independence.

Democratic Platform of 1888

The Democratic party of the United States, in National Convention assembled, renews the pledge of its fidelity to Democratic faith and reaffirms the platform adopted by its representatives in the Convention of 1884, and indorses the views expressed by President Cleveland in his last annual message to Congress as the correct interpretation of that platform upon the question of Tariff reduction; and also indorses the efforts of our Democratic Representatives in Congress to secure a reduction of excessive taxation.

Chief among its principles of party faith are the maintenance of an indissoluble Union of free and indestructible States, now about to enter upon its second century of unexampled progress and renown; devotion to a plan of government regulated by a written Constitution, strictly specifying every granted power and expressly reserving to the States or people the entire ungranted residue of power; the encouragement of a jealous popular vigilance directed to all who have been chosen for brief terms to enact and execute the laws, and are charged with the duty of preserving peace, insuring equality and establishing justice.

The Democratic party welcomes an exacting scrutiny of the administration of the Executive power which four years ago was committed to its trust in the selection of Grover Cleveland as President of the United States; and it challenges the most searching inquiry concerning its fidelity and devotion to the pledges which then invited the suffrages of the people.

During a most critical period of our financial affairs, resulting from over taxation, the anomalous condition of our currency, and a public debt unmatured, it has by the adoption of a wise and conservative course, not only averted disaster, but greatly promoted the prosperity of the people.

It has reversed the improvident and unwise policy of the Republican party touching the public domain, and has reclaimed from corporations and syndicates, alien and domestic, and restored to the people, nearly one hundred millions of acres of valuable land to be sacredly held as homesteads for our citizens.

While carefully guarding the interests of the taxpayers and conforming strictly to the principles of justice and equity, it has paid out more for pensions and bounties to the soldiers and sailors of the Republic than was ever paid before during an equal period.

By intelligent management and a judicious and economical expenditure of the public money it has set on foot the reconstruction of the American Navy upon a system which forbids the recurrence of scandal and insures successful results.

It has adopted and consistently pursued a firm and prudent foreign policy, preserving peace with all nations while scrupulously maintaining all the rights and interests of our Government and people at home and abroad.

The exclusion from our shores of Chinese laborers has been effectually secured under the provisions of a treaty, the operation of which has been postponed by the action of a Republican majority in the Senate.

Honest reform in the Civil Service has been inaugurated and maintained by President Cleveland, and he has brought the public service to the highest standard of efficiency, not only by rule and precept, but by the example of his own untiring and unselfish administration of public affairs.

In every branch and department of the Government under Democratic control, the rights and welfare of all the people have been guarded and defended; every public interest has been protected, and the equality of all our citizens before the law, without regard to race or section, has been steadfastly maintained.

Upon its record, thus exhibited, and upon the pledge of a continuance to the people of these benefits of good government, the National Democracy invokes a renewal of popular trust by the reelection of a Chief Magistrate who has been faithful, able and prudent.

They invoke in addition to that trust, the transfer also to the Democracy of the entire legislative power.

The Republican party, controlling the Senate and resisting in both Houses of Congress a reformation of unjust and unequal tax laws, which have outlasted the necessities of war and are now undermining the abundance of a long peace, deny to the people equality before the law and the fairness and the justice which are their right.

Thus the cry of American labor for a better share in the rewards of industry is stifled with false pretenses, enterprise is fettered and bound down to home markets; capital is discouraged with doubt, and unequal, unjust laws can neither be properly amended nor repealed.

The Democratic party will continue, with all the power confided to it, the struggle to reform these laws in accordance with the pledges of its last platform indorsed at the ballot-box by the suffrages of the people.

Of all the industrious freemen of our land, an immense majority, including every tiller of the soil, gain no advantage from excessive tax laws; but the price of nearly everything they buy is increased by the favoritism of an unequal system of tax legislation.

All unnecessary taxation is unjust taxation.

It is repugnant to the creed of Democracy, that by such taxation the costs of the necessaries of life should be unjustifiably increased to all our people.

Judged by Democratic principles, the interests of the people are betrayed, when, by unnecessary taxation, trusts and combinations are permitted and fostered, which, while unduly enriching the few that combine, rob the body of our citizens by depriving them of the benefits of natural competition. Every Democratic rule of governmental action is violated when through unnecessary taxation a vast sum of money, far beyond the needs of an economical administration, is drawn from the people and the channels of trade, and accumulated as a demoralizing surplus in the National Treasury.

The money now lying idle in the Federal Treasury, resulting from superfluous taxation amounts to more than $125,000,000, and the surplus collected is reaching the sum of more than $60,000,-000 annually.

Debauched by this immense temptation the remedy of the Republican party is to meet and exhaust by extravagant appropriations and expenses, whether constitutional or not, the accumulation of extravagant taxation.

The Democratic remedy is to enforce frugality in public expense and abolish needless taxation.

Our established domestic industries and enterprises should not, and need not, be endangered by a reduction and correction of the burdens of taxation. On the contrary, a fair and careful revision of our tax laws, with due allowance for the difference between the wages of American and foreign labor, must promote and encourage every branch of such industries and enterprises by giving them assurance of an extended market and steady and continuous operations.

In the interest of American labor, which should in no event be neglected, the revision of our tax laws contemplated by the Democratic party would promote the advantage of such labor by cheapening the cost of necessaries of life in the home of every workingman and at the same time securing to him steady and remunerative employment.

Upon this great issue of tariff reform, so closely concerning every phase of our national life, and upon every question involved in the problem of good government, the Democratic party submits its principles and professions to the intelligent suffrages of the American people.

Resolution Presented by Mr. Scott, of Pennsylvania:

Resolved, That this convention hereby indorses and recommends the early passage of the bill for the reduction of the revenue now pending in the House of Representatives.

Resolution Presented by Mr. Lehmann, of Iowa:

Resolved, That a just and liberal policy should be pursued in reference to the Territories; that the right of self-government is inherent in the people and guaranteed under the Constitution; that the Territories of Washington, Dakota, Montana and New Mexico are, by virtue of population and development, entitled to admission into the Union as States, and we unqualifiedly condemn the course of the Republican party in refusing Statehood and self-government to their people.

Resolution Presented by ex-Governor Leon Abbett, of New Jersey:

Resolved, That we express our cordial sympathy with the struggling people of all nations in their effort to secure for themselves the inestimable blessings of self-government and civil and religious liberty. And we especially declare our sympathy with the efforts of those noble patriots who, led by Gladstone and Parnell, have conducted their grand and peaceful contest for home rule in Ireland.

Prohibition Platform of 1888

The Prohibition party, in National Convention assembled, acknowledging Almighty God as the source of all power in government, do hereby declare:

1. That the manufacture, importation, exportation, transportation and sale of alcoholic beverages should be made public crimes, and prohibited as such.

2. That such Prohibition must be secured through Amendments to our National and State

Constitutions, enforced by adequate laws adequately supported by administrative authority; and to this end the organization of the Prohibition party is imperatively demanded in State and Nation.

3. That any form of license, taxation or regulation of the liquor traffic is contrary to good government; that any party which supports regulation, license or taxation enters into alliance with such traffic and becomes the actual foe of the State's welfare, and that we arraign the Republican and Democratic parties for their persistent attitude in favor of the license iniquity, whereby they oppose the demand of the people for Prohibition, and, through open complicity with the liquor crime, defeat the enforcement of law.

4. For the immediate abolition of the Internal Revenue system, whereby our National Government is deriving support from our greatest national vice.

5. That an adequate public revenue being necessary, it may properly be raised by import duties; but import duties should be so reduced that no surplus shall be accumulated in the Treasury, and that the burdens of taxation shall be removed from foods, clothing and other comforts and necessaries of life, and imposed on such articles of import as will give protection both to the manufacturing employer and producing laborer against the competition of the world.

6. That the right of suffrage rests on no mere circumstances of race, color, sex or nationality, and that where, from any cause, it has been withheld from citizens who are of suitable age, and mentally and morally qualified for the exercise of an intelligent ballot, it should be restored by the people through the Legislatures of the several States, on such educational basis as they may deem wise.

7. That civil service appointments for all civil offices, chiefly clerical in their duties, should be based upon moral, intellectual and physical qualifications, and not upon party service or party necessity.

8. For the abolition of polygamy and the establishment of uniform laws governing marriage and divorce.

9. For prohibiting all combinations of capital to control and to increase the cost of products for popular consumption.

10. For the preservation and defense of the Sabbath as a civil institution, without oppressing any who religiously observe the same on any other than the first day of the week.

11. That arbitration is the Christian, wise and economical method of settling national differences, and the same method should, by judicious legislation, be applied to the settlement of disputes between large bodies of employes and their employers; that the abolition of the saloon would remove the burdens, moral, physical, pecuniary and social, which now oppress labor and rob it of its earnings, and would prove to be a wise and successful way of promoting labor reform, and we invite labor and capital to unite with us for the accomplishment thereof; that monopoly in land is a wrong to the people, and the public lands should be reserved to the actual settlers; and that men and women should receive equal wages for equal work.

12. That our immigration laws should be so enforced as to prevent the introduction into our country of all convicts, inmates of other dependent institutions, and others physically incapacitated for self-support, and that no person should have the ballot in any State who is not a citizen of the United States.

13. Recognizing and declaring that Prohibition of the liquor traffic has become the dominant issue in national politics, we invite to full party fellowship all those who, on this one dominant issue, are with us agreed, in the full belief that this party can and will remove sectional differences, promote national unity, and insure the best welfare of our entire land.

Resolved, That we hold that men are born free and equal, and should be made secure in all their civil and political rights.

Resolved, That we condemn the Democratic and Republican parties for persistently denying the right of self-government to the 600,000 people of Dakota.

Republican Platform of 1888

The Republicans of the United States assembled by their delegates in National Convention, pause on the threshold of their proceedings to honor the memory of their first great leader—the immortal champion of liberty and the rights of the people—Abraham Lincoln; and to cover also with wreaths of imperishable remembrance and gratitude the heroic names of our later leaders who have been more recently called away from our councils—Grant, Garfield, Arthur, Logan, Conkling. May their memories be faithfully cherished!

We also recall with our greetings, and with prayer for his recovery, the name of one of our living heroes, whose memory will be treasured in the history of both Republicans and of the Republic—the name of that noble soldier and favorite child of victory, Philip H. Sheridan. In the spirit of those great leaders and of our own devotion to human liberty, and with that hostility to all forms of despotism and oppression which is the fundamental idea of the Republican party, we send fraternal congratulations to our fellow Americans of Brazil upon their great act of emancipation, which completed the abolition of slavery throughout the two American continents. We earnestly hope that we may soon congratulate our fellow-citizens of Irish birth upon the peaceful recovery of home rule for Ireland.

We reaffirm our unswerving devotion to the National Constitution and the indissoluble Union of the States; to the autonomy reserved to the States under the Constitution; to the personal rights and liberties of citizens in all the States and Territories of the Union, and especially to the supreme and sovereign right of every lawful citizen, rich or poor, native or foreign born, white or black, to cast one free ballot in public elections, and to have that ballot duly counted. We hold the free and honest popular ballot and the just and equal representation of all the people to be the foundation of our Republican government and demand effective legislation to secure the integrity and purity of elections, which are the fountains of all public authority. We charge that the present Administration and the Democratic majority in Congress owe their existence to the suppression of the ballot by a criminal nullification of the Constitution and laws of the United States.

We are uncompromisingly in favor of the American system of protection; we protest against its destruction as proposed by the President and his party. They serve the interests of Europe; we will support the interests of America. We accept the issue, and confidently appeal to the people for their judgment. The protective system must be maintained. Its abandonment has always been followed by general disaster to all interests, except those of the usurer and the sheriff. We denounce the Mills bill as destructive to the general business, the labor and the farming interests of the country, and we heartily indorse the consistent and patriotic action of the Republican Representatives in Congress in opposing its passage.

We condemn the proposition of the Democratic party to place wool on the free list, and we insist that the duties thereon shall be adjusted and maintained so as to furnish full and adequate protection to that industry throughout the United States.

The Republican party would effect all needed reduction of the National revenue by repealing the taxes upon tobacco, which are an annoyance and burden to agriculture, and the tax upon spirits used in the arts, and for mechanical purposes, and by such revision of the tariff laws as will tend to check imports of such articles as are produced by our people, the production of which gives employment to our labor, and releases from import duties those articles of foreign production (except luxuries), the like of which cannot be produced at home. If there shall remain a larger revenue than is requisite for the wants of the government we favor the entire repeal of internal taxes rather than the surrender of any part of our protective system at the joint behests of the whiskey trusts and the agents of foreign manufacturers.

We declare our hostility to the introduction into this country of foreign contract labor and of Chinese labor, alien to our civilization and constitution; and we demand the rigid enforcement of the existing laws against it, and favor such immediate legislation as will exclude such labor from our shores.

We declare our opposition to all combinations of capital organized in trusts or otherwise to control arbitrarily the condition of trade among our citizens; and we recommend to Congress and the State Legislatures in their respective jurisdictions such legislation as will prevent the execution of all schemes to oppress the people by undue charges on their supplies, or by unjust rates for the transportation of their products to market. We approve the legislation by Congress to prevent alike unjust burdens and unfair discriminations between the States.

We reaffirm the policy of appropriating the public lands of the United States to be homesteads for American citizens and settlers—not aliens—which the Republican party established in 1862 against the persistent opposition of the Democrats in Congress, and which has brought our great Western domain into such magnificent development. The restoration of unearned railroad land grants to the public domain for the use of actual settlers, which was begun under the Administration of President Arthur, should be continued. We deny that the Democratic party has ever restored one acre to the people, but declare that by the joint action of the Republicans and Democrats in Congress about 60,000,000 acres of unearned lands originally granted for the construction of railroads have been restored to the public domain, in pursuance of the conditions inserted by the Republican party in the original grants. We charge the Democratic Administration with failure to execute the laws securing to settlers the title to their homesteads, and with using appropriations made for that purpose to harass innocent settlers with spies and prosecutions under the false pretense of exposing frauds and vindicating the law.

The government by Congress of the Territories is based upon necessity only to the end that they may become States in the Union; therefore, whenever the conditions of population, material resources, public intelligence and morality are such as to insure a stable local government therein, the people of such Territories should be permitted as a right inherent in them to form for themselves constitutions and State government, and be admitted into the Union. Pending the preparation for Statehood, all officers thereof should be selected from the *bona-fide* residents and citizens of the Territory wherein they are to serve. South Dakota should of right be immediately admitted as a State in the Union under the constitution framed and adopted by her people, and we heartily indorse the action of the Republican Senate in twice passing bills for her admission. The refusal of the Democratic House of Representatives, for partisan purposes, to favorably consider these bills is a willful violation of the sacred American principle of local self-government, and merits the condemnation of all just men. The pending bills in the Senate to enable the people of Washington, North Dakota and Montana Territories to form constitutions and establish State governments, should be passed without unnecessary delay. The Republican party pledges itself to do all in its power to facilitate the admission of the Territories of New Mexico, Wyoming, Idaho and Arizona to the enjoyment of self-government as States, such of them as are now qualified, as soon as possible, and the others as soon as they may become so.

The political power of the Mormon Church in the Territories as exercised in the past is a menace to free institutions too dangerous to be longer suffered. Therefore we pledge the Republican party to appropriate legislation asserting the sovereignty of the Nation in all Territories where the same is questioned, and in furtherance of that end to place upon the statute books legislation stringent enough to divorce the political from the ecclesiastical power, and thus stamp out the attendant wickedness of polygamy.

The Republican party is in favor of the use of both gold and silver as money, and condemns the policy of the Democratic Administration in its efforts to demonetize silver.

We demand the reduction of letter postage to one cent per ounce.

In a Republic like ours, where the citizen is the sovereign, and the official the servant, where no power is exercised except by the will of the people, it is important that the sovereign—the people—should possess intelligence. The free school is the promoter of that intelligence which is to preserve us a free Nation; therefore, the State or Nation, or both combined, should support free institutions of learning sufficient to afford every child growing up in the land the opportunity of a good common school education.

We earnestly recommend that prompt action be taken by Congress in the enactment of such legislation as will best secure the rehabilitation of our American merchant marine, and we protest against the passage by Congress of a free ship bill as calculated to work injustice to labor by lessening the wages of those engaged in preparing materials as well as those directly employed in our shipyards. We demand appropriations for the early rebuilding of our navy; for the construction of coast fortifications and modern ordnance and other approved modern means of defense for the protection of our defenseless harbors and cities; for the payment of just pensions to our soldiers; for necessary works of National importance in the improvement of harbors and the channels of internal, coastwise, and foreign commerce; for the encouragement of the shipping interests of the Atlantic, Gulf and Pacific States, as well as for the payment of the maturing public debt. This policy will give employment to our labor, activity to our various industries, increase the security of our country, promote trade, open new and direct markets for our produce, and cheapen the cost of transportation. We affirm this to be far better for our country than the Democratic policy of loaning the government's money, without interest, to "pet banks."

The conduct of foreign affairs by the present Administration has been distinguished by its inefficiency and its cowardice. Having withdrawn from the Senate all pending treaties effected by Republican Administrations for the removal of foreign burdens and restrictions upon our commerce, and for its extension into better markets, it has neither effected nor proposed any others in their stead. Professing adherence to the Monroe doctrine it has seen with idle complacency the extension of foreign influence in Central America and of foreign trade everywhere among our neighbors. It has refused to charter, sanction or encourage any American organization for construction of the Nicaragua Canal, a work of vital importance to the maintenance of the Monroe doctrine and of our National influence in Central and South America, and necessary for the development of trade with our Pacific territory, with South America, and with the islands and further coasts of the Pacific Ocean.

We arraign the present Democratic Administration for its weak and unpatriotic treatment of the fisheries question, and its pusillanimous surrender of the essential privileges to which our fishing vessels are entitled in Canadian ports under the treaty of 1818, the reciprocal maritime legislation of 1830, and the comity of nations, and which Canadian fishing vessels receive in the ports of the United States. We condemn the policy of the present Administration and the Democratic majority in Congress toward our fisheries as unfriendly and conspicuously unpatriotic, and as tending to destroy a valuable National industry, and an indispensable resource of defense against a foreign enemy. "The name American applies alike to all citizens of the Republic and imposes upon all alike the same obligation of obedience to the laws. At the same time that citizenship is and must be the panoply and safeguard of him

who wears it, and protect him, whether high or low, rich or poor, in all his civil rights. It should and must afford him protection at home and follow and protect him abroad in whatever land he may be on a lawful errand."

The men who abandoned the Republican party in 1884 and continue to adhere to the Democratic party have deserted not only the cause of honest government, of sound finance, of freedom and purity of the ballot, but especially have deserted the cause of reform in the civil service. We will not fail to keep our pledges because they have broken theirs, or because their candidate has broken his. We therefore repeat our declaration of 1884, to wit: "The reform of the civil service, auspiciously begun under the Republican Administration, should be completed by the further extension of the reform system already established by law, to all the grades of the service to which it is applicable. The spirit and purpose of the reform should be observed in all executive appointments, and all laws at variance with the object of existing reform legislation should be repealed, to the end that the dangers to free institutions which lurk in the power of official patronage may be wisely and effectively avoided."

The gratitude of the Nation to the defenders of the Union cannot be measured by laws. The legislation of Congress should conform to the pledges made by a loyal people and be so enlarged and extended as to provide against the possibility that any man who honorably wore the Federal uniform shall become the inmate of an almshouse, or dependent upon private charity. In the presence of an overflowing treasury it would be a public scandal to do less for those whose valorous service preserved the government. We denounce the hostile spirit shown by President Cleveland in his numerous vetoes of measures for pension relief, and the action of the Democratic House of Representatives in refusing even a consideration of general pension legislation.

In support of the principles herewith enunciated we invite the co-operation of patriotic men of all parties, and especially of all workingmen, whose prosperity is seriously threatened by the free-trade policy of the present Administration.

Resolution Relating to Prohibition

Offered by Mr. Boutelle, of Maine:

The first concern of all good government is the

virtue and sobriety of the people and the purity of their homes. The Republican party cordially sympathizes with all wise and well-directed efforts for the promotion of temperance and morality.

Union Labor Platform of 1888

PREAMBLE

General discontent prevails on the part of the wealth-producer. Farmers are suffering from a poverty which has forced most of them to mortgage their estates, and the prices of products are so low as to offer no relief except through bankruptcy. Laborers are sinking into greater dependence. Strikes are resorted to without bringing relief, because of the inability of employers in many cases to pay living wages, while more and more are driven into the street. Business men find collections almost impossible, and meantime hundreds of millions of idle public money which is needed for relief is locked up in the United States Treasury or placed without interest in favored banks, in grim mockery of distress. Land monopoly flourishes as never before, and more owners of the soil are daily becoming tenants. Great transportation corporations still succeed in extorting their profits on watered stock through unjust charges. The United States Senate has become an open scandal, its membership being purchased by the rich in open defiance of the popular will. Various efforts are made to squander the public money, which are designed to empty the Treasury without paying the public debt. Under these and other alarming conditions, we appeal to the people of our country to come out of old party organizations, whose indifference to the public welfare is responsible for this distress, and aid the Union Labor Party to repeal existing class legislation and relieve the distress of our industries by establishing the following:

PLATFORM

While we believe that the proper solution of the financial distress will greatly relieve those now in danger of losing their homes by mortgage foreclosures, and enable all industrious persons to secure a home as the highest result of civilization, we oppose land monopoly in every form, demand the forfeiture of unearned grants, the limitation of land ownership, and such other legislation as will stop speculation in lands and holding it unused from those whose necessities require it. We believe the earth was made for the people and not to make an idle aristocracy to subsist through rents upon the toils of the industrious, and that corners in land are as bad as corners in food, and that those who are not residents or citizens should not be allowed to own lands in the United States. A homestead should be exempt to a limited extent from execution or taxation.

The means of communication and transportation shall be owned by the people, as is the United States postal system.

The establishment of a national monetary system in the interest of the producer, instead of the speculator and usurer, by which the circulating medium, in necessary quantity and full legal tender, shall be issued directly to the people without the intervention of banks and loaned to citizens upon land security at a low rate of interest so as to relieve them from the extortion of usury and enable them to control the money supply. Postal savings banks should be established, and while we have free coinage of gold we should have free coinage of silver. We demand the immediate application of all the money in the United States Treasury to the payment of the bonded debt, and condemn the further issue of interest-bearing bonds, either by the National Government or by States, Territories or municipalities.

Arbitration should take the place of strikes and other injurious methods of settling labor disputes. The letting of convict labor to contractors should be prohibited, the contract system be abolished on public works, the hours of labor in industrial establishments be reduced commensurate with the increased production by labor-saving machinery, employees protected from bodily injury, equal pay for equal work for both sexes, and labor, agricultural, and co-operative associations be fostered and encouraged by law. The foundation of a republic is in the intelligence of its citizens, and children who are driven into workshops, mines, and factories are deprived of the education which should be secured to all by proper legislation.

We demand the passage of a service pension bill to every honorably discharged soldier and sailor of the United States.

A graduated income tax is the most equitable system of taxation, placing the burden of government on those who can best afford to pay, instead of laying it on the farmers and producers, and exempting millionaires, bond-holders and corporations.

We demand a constitutional amendment making United States senators elective by a direct vote of the people.

We demand the strict enforcement of laws prohibiting the importation of subjects of foreign countries under contract.

We demand the passage and enforcement of such legislation as will absolutely exclude the Chinese from the United States.

The right to vote is inherent in citizenship irrespective of sex, and is properly within the province of state legislation.

The paramount issues to be solved in the interests of humanity are the abolition of usury, monopoly, and trusts, and we denounce the Democratic and Republican parties for creating and perpetuating these monstrous evils.

United Labor Platform of 1888

We, the delegates of the United Labor Party of the United States, in National Convention assembled, hold that the corruptions of government and the impoverishment of the masses result from neglect of the self-evident truths proclaimed by the founders of this republic, that all men are created equal and are endowed with inalienable rights. We aim at the abolition of the system which compels men to pay their fellow-creatures for the use of the common bounties of nature, and permits monopolizers to deprive labor of natural opportunities for employment.

We see access to farming land denied to labor, except on payment of exorbitant rent or the acceptance of mortgage burdens, and labor, thus forbidden to employ itself, driven into the cities. We see the wage-workers of the cities subjected to this unnatural competition, and forced to pay an exorbitant share of their scanty earnings for cramped and unhealthful lodgings. We see the same intense competition condemning the great majority of business and professional men to a bitter and often unavailing struggle to avoid bankruptcy, and that while the price of all that labor produces ever falls, the price of land ever rises.

We trace these evils to a fundamental wrong —the making of the land on which all must live the exclusive property of but a portion of the community. To this denial of natural rights are due want of employment, low wages, business depressions, that intense competition which makes it so difficult for the majority of men to get a comfortable living, and that wrongful distribution of wealth which is producing the millionaire on one side and the tramp on the other.

To give all men an interest in the land of their country; to enable all to share in the benefits of social growth and improvement; to prevent the shutting out of labor from employment by the monopolization of natural opportunities; to do away with the one-sided competition which cuts down wages to starvation rates; to restore life to business and prevent periodical depressions; to do away with that monstrous injustice which deprives producers of the fruits of their toil, while idlers grow rich; to prevent the conflicts which are arraying class against class, and which are fraught with menacing dangers to society—we propose so to change the existing system of taxation that no one shall be taxed on the wealth he produces, nor any one suffered to appropriate wealth he does not produce by taking to himself the increasing values which the growth of society adds to land.

What we propose is not the disturbing of any man in his holding or title, but, by taxation of land according to its value and not according to its area, to devote to common use and benefit those values which arise not from the exertion of the individual, but from the growth of society, and to abolish all taxes on industry and its products. This increased taxation of land values must, while relieving the working farmer and small homestead owner of the undue burdens now imposed upon them, make it unprofitable to hold land for speculation, and thus throw open abundant opportunities for the employment of labor and the building up of homes.

We would do away with the present unjust and wasteful system of finance, which piles up hundreds of millions of dollars in treasury vaults while we are paying interest on an enormous debt; and we would establish in its stead a monetary system in which a legal-tender circulating medium should be issued by the Government without the intervention of banks.

We wish to abolish the present unjust and wasteful system of ownership of railroads and telegraphs by private corporations—a system which, while failing to supply adequately public needs, impoverishes the farmer, oppresses the manufacturer, hampers the merchant, impedes travel and communication, and builds up enormous fortunes and corrupting monopolies that are becoming more powerful than the Government itself. For this system we would substitute Government ownership and control for the benefit of the whole people instead of private profit.

While declaring the foregoing to be the fundamental principles and aims of the United Labor Party, and while conscious that no reform can give effectual and permanent relief to labor that does not involve the legal recognition of equal rights to natural opportunities, we, nevertheless, as measures of relief from some of the evil effects of ignoring those rights, favor such legislation as may tend to reduce the hours of labor, to prevent the employment of children of tender years, to avoid the competition of convict labor with honest industry, to secure the sanitary inspection of tenements, factories, and mines, and to put an end to the abuse of conspiracy laws.

We desire also to so simplify the procedure of our courts, and diminish the expense of legal proceedings, that the poor may therein be placed on an equality with the rich, and the long delays which now result in scandalous miscarriages of justice may be prevented.

Since the ballot is the only means by which, in our republic the redress of political and social grievances is to be sought, we especially and emphatically declare for the adoption of what is known as the Australian system of voting, in order that the effectual secrecy of the ballot, and the relief of candidates for public office from the heavy expenses now imposed upon them, may prevent bribery and intimidation, do away with practical discriminations in favor of the rich and unscrupulous, and lessen the pernicious influence of money in politics.

We denounce the Democratic and Republican parties as hopelessly and shamelessly corrupt, and, by reason of their affiliation with monopolies, equally unworthy of the suffrages of those who do not live upon public plunder; we therefore require of those who would act with us that they sever all connection with both.

In support of these aims, we solicit the co-operation of all patriotic citizens who, sick of the degradation of politics, desire by constitutional methods to establish justice, to preserve liberty, to extend the spirit of fraternity, and to elevate humanity.

CAMPAIGN OF 1892

In 1892, President Harrison was nominated on the first ballot of the Republican convention that met in Minneapolis. Whitelaw Reid of New York was nominated for vice-president by acclamation. At the Democratic convention in Chicago, former President Grover Cleveland was nominated on the first ballot over ten other candidates and over the objection of his own New York delegation, which was pledged to Governor David Hill of the Empire State. Adlai E. Stevenson of Illinois was chosen vice-presidential candidate on the first ballot, defeating seven other candidates.

The National Prohibition Party, meeting in Cincinnati, selected John Bidwell of California for president and J. B. Cranfill of Texas for vice-president. The first national convention of the People's Party was also held in 1892. This party, known as the Populists, was a coalition of farmers in the West and South. In five states, the Democrats nominated no electors and voted for the Populist candidates instead; in others, fusion between Democrats and Populists was not uncommon. General James B. Weaver of Iowa was nominated for president. For vice-president, James G. Field of Virginia was chosen.

The two labor parties of 1888 disappeared, but at a Socialist Labor Party convention held in New York Simon Wing of Massachusetts was nominated for president and Charles H. Matchett of New York for vice-president.

Forty-four states participated in the election. Cleveland, with 5,551,883 popular votes—46 percent of the total—was elected over Harrison, who acquired 5,179,244—43 percent. The Populist, James Weaver, received 1,024,280 votes and 8.5 percent of the popular vote. Prohibition candidate John Bidwell received 270,770 votes; Simon Wing and some other minor candidates obtained 29,920 votes. The electoral vote was 277 for Cleveland, 145 for Harrison, and 22 for Weaver.

Democratic Platform of 1892

The representatives of the Democratic party of the United States, in National Convention assembled, do reaffirm their allegiance to the principles of the party, as formulated by Jefferson and exemplified by the long and illustrious line of his successors in Democratic leadership, from Madison to Cleveland; we believe the public welfare demands that these principles be applied to the conduct of the Federal Government, through the accession to power of the party that advocates them; and we solemnly declare that the need of a return to these fundamental principles of free popular government, based on home rule and individual liberty, was never more urgent than now, when the tendency to centralize all power at the Federal capital has become a menace to the reserved rights of the States that strikes at the very roots of our Government under the Constitution as framed by the fathers of the Republic.

We warn the people of our common country, jealous for the preservation of their free institutions, that the policy of Federal control of elections, to which the Republican party has committed itself, is fraught with the gravest dangers, scarcely less momentous than would result from a revolution practically establishing monarchy on the ruins of the Republic. It strikes at the North as well as at the South, and injures the colored citizen even more than the white; it means a horde of deputy marshals at every polling place, armed with Federal power; returning boards appointed and controlled by Federal authority, the outrage of the electoral rights of the people in the several States, the subjugation of the colored people to the control of the party in power, and the reviving of race antagonisms, now happily abated, of the utmost peril to the safety and happiness of all; a measure deliberately and justly described by a leading Republican Senator as "the most infamous bill that ever crossed the threshold of the Senate." Such a policy, if sanctioned by law, would mean the dominance of a self-perpetuating oligarchy of office-holders, and the party first intrusted with its machinery could be dislodged from power only by an appeal to the reserved right of the people to resist oppression, which is inherent in all self-governing communities. Two years ago this revolutionary policy was emphatically condemned by the people at the polls, but in contempt of that verdict the Republican party has defiantly declared in its latest authoritative utterance that its success in the coming elections will mean the enactment of the Force Bill and the usurpation of despotic control over elections in all the States.

Believing that the preservation of Republican government in the United States is dependent upon the defeat of this policy of legalized force and fraud, we invite the support of all citizens who desire to see the Constitution maintained in its integrity with the laws pursuant thereto, which have given our country a hundred years of unexampled prosperity; and we pledge the Democratic party, if it be intrusted with power, not only to the defeat of the Force Bill, but also to relentless opposition to the Republican policy of profligate expenditure, which, in the short space of two years, has squandered an enormous surplus and emptied an overflowing Treasury, after piling new burdens of taxation upon the already overtaxed labor of the country.

We denounce Republican protection as a fraud, a robbery of the great majority of the American people for the benefit of the few. We declare it to be a fundamental principle of the Democratic party that the Federal Government has no constitutional power to impose and collect tariff duties, except for the purpose of revenue only, and we demand that the collection of such taxes shall be limited to the necessities of the Government when honestly and economically administered.

We denounce the McKinley tariff law enacted by the Fifty-first Congress as the culminating atrocity of class legislation; we indorse the efforts made by the Democrats of the present Congress to modify its most oppressive features in the direction of free raw materials and cheaper manufactured goods that enter into general consumption; and we promise its repeal as one of the beneficent results that will follow the action of the people in intrusting power to the Democratic party. Since the McKinley tariff went into operation there have been ten reductions of the wages of the laboring man to one increase. We deny that there has been any increase of prosperity to the country since that tariff went into operation, and we point to the fullness and distress, the wage reductions and strikes in the iron trade, as the best possible evidence that no such prosperity has resulted from the McKinley Act.

We call the attention of thoughtful Americans to the fact that after thirty years of restrictive taxes against the importation of foreign wealth, in exchange for our agricultural surplus, the homes and farms of the country have become burdened with a real estate mortgage debt of over $2,500,-000,000, exclusive of all other forms of indebtedness; that in one of the chief agricultural States of the West there appears a real estate mortgage debt averaging $165 per capita of the total population, and that similar conditions and tendencies are shown to exist in other agricultural-exporting States. We denounce a policy which fosters no industry so much as it does that of the Sheriff.

Trade interchange, on the basis of reciprocal advantages to the countries participating, is a time-honored doctrine of the Democratic faith, but we denounce the sham reciprocity which juggles with the people's desire for enlarged foreign markets and freer exchanges by pretending to establish closer trade relations for a country whose articles of export are almost exclusively agricultural products with other countries that are also agricultural, while erecting a custom-house barrier of prohibitive tariff taxes against the richest countries of the world, that stand ready to take our entire surplus of products, and to exchange therefor commodities which are necessaries and comforts of life among our own people.

We recognize in the Trusts and Combinations, which are designed to enable capital to secure more than its just share of the joint product of Capital and Labor, a natural consequence of the prohibitive taxes, which prevent the free competition, which is the life of honest trade, but believe their worst evils can be abated by law, and we demand the rigid enforcement of the laws made to prevent and control them, together with such further legislation in restraint of their abuses as experience may show to be necessary.

The Republican party, while professing a policy of reserving the public land for small holdings by actual settlers, has given away the people's heritage, till now a few railroads and non-resident aliens, individual and corporate, possess a larger area than that of all our farms between the two seas. The last Democratic administration reversed the improvident and unwise policy of the Republican party touching the public domain, and reclaimed from corporations and syndicates, alien and domestic, and restored to the people nearly one hundred million (100,000,000) acres of valuable land, to be sacredly held as homesteads for our citizens, and we pledge ourselves to continue this policy until every acre of land so unlawfully held shall be reclaimed and restored to the people.

We denounce the Republican legislation known as the Sherman Act of 1890 as a cowardly make-shift, fraught with possibilities of danger in the future, which should make all of its supporters, as well as its author, anxious for its speedy repeal. We hold to the use of both gold and silver as the standard money of the country, and to the coinage of both gold and silver without discriminating against either metal or charge for mintage, but the dollar unit of coinage of both metals must be of equal intrinsic and exchangeable value, or be adjusted through international agreement or by such safeguards of legislation as shall insure the maintenance of the parity of the two metals and the equal power of every dollar at all times in the markets and in the payment of debts; and we demand that all paper currency shall be kept at par with and redeemable in such coin. We insist upon this policy as especially necessary for the protection of the farmers and laboring classes, the first and most defenseless victims of unstable money and a fluctuating currency.

We recommend that the prohibitory 10 per cent tax on State bank issues be repealed.

Public office is a public trust. We reaffirm the declaration of the Democratic National Convention of 1876 for the reform of the civil service, and we call for the honest enforcement of all laws regulating the same. The nomination of a President, as in the recent Republican Convention, by delegations composed largely of his appointees, holding office at his pleasure, is a scandalous satire upon free popular institutions and a startling illustration of the methods by which a President may gratify his ambition. We denounce a policy under which the Federal office-holders usurp control of party conventions in the States, and we pledge the Democratic party to reform these and all other abuses which threaten individual liberty and local self-government.

The Democratic party is the only party that has ever given the country a foreign policy consistent and vigorous, compelling respect abroad and inspiring confidence at home. While avoiding entangling alliances, it has aimed to cultivate friendly relations with other nations, and especially with our neighbors on the American Continent, whose destiny is closely linked with our own, and we view with alarm the tendency to a policy of irritation and bluster which is liable at any time to confront us with the alternative of humiliation or war. We favor the maintenance of a navy strong enough for all purposes of national defense, and to properly maintain the honor and dignity of the country abroad.

This country has always been the refuge of the oppressed from every land—exiles for conscience sake—and in the spirit of the founders of our Government we condemn the oppression practised by the Russian Government upon its Lutheran and Jewish subjects, and we call upon our National Government, in the interest of justice and humanity, by all just and proper means, to use its prompt and best efforts to bring about a cessation of these cruel persecutions in the dominions of the Czar and to secure to the oppressed equal rights.

We tender our profound and earnest sympathy to those lovers of freedom who are struggling for home rule and the great cause of local self-government in Ireland.

We heartily approve all legitimate efforts to prevent the United States from being used as the dumping ground for the known criminals and professional paupers of Europe; and we demand the rigid enforcement of the laws against Chinese immigration and the importation of foreign workmen under contract, to degrade American labor and lessen its wages; but we condemn and denounce any and all attempts to restrict the immigration of the industrious and worthy of foreign lands.

This Convention hereby renews the expression of appreciation of the patriotism of the soldiers and sailors of the Union in the war for its preservation, and we favor just and liberal pensions for all disabled Union soldiers, their widows and dependents, but we demand that the work of the Pension Office shall be done industriously, impartially and honestly. We denounce the present administration of that office as incompetent, corrupt, disgraceful and dishonest.

The Federal Government should care for and improve the Mississippi River and other great waterways of the Republic, so as to secure for the interior States easy and cheap transportation to tide water. When any waterway of the Republic is of sufficient importance to demand the aid of the Government, such aid should be extended upon a definite plan of continuous work, until permanent improvement is secured.

For purposes of national defense and the promotion of commerce between the States, we recognize the early construction of the Nicaragua Canal and its protection against foreign control as of great importance to the United States.

Recognizing the World's Columbian Exposition as a national undertaking of vast importance, in which the General Government has invited the co-operation of all the powers of the world, and appreciating the acceptance by many of such powers of the invitation so extended, and the broad and liberal efforts being made by them to contribute to the grandeur of the undertaking, we are of opinion that Congress should make such necessary financial provision as shall be requisite to the maintenance of the national honor and public faith.

Popular education being the only safe basis of popular suffrage, we recommend to the several States most liberal appropriations for the public schools. Free common schools are the nursery of good government, and they have always received the fostering care of the Democratic party, which favors every means of increasing intelligence. Freedom of education, being an essential of civil and religious liberty, as well as a necessity for the development of intelligence, must not be interfered with under any pretext whatever. We are opposed to State interference with parental rights and rights of conscience in the education of children as an infringement of the fundamental Democratic doctrine that the largest individual liberty consistent with the rights of others insures the highest type of American citizenship and the best government.

We approve the action of the present House of Representatives in passing bills for admitting into the Union as States of the Territories of New Mexico and Arizona, and we favor the early admission of all the Territories having the necessary population and resources to entitle them to Statehood, and while they remain Territories we hold that the officials appointed to administer the government of any Territory, together with the Districts of Columbia and Alaska, should be *bona-fide* residents of the Territory or district in which their duties are to be performed. The Democratic party believes in home rule and the control of their own affairs by the people of the vicinage.

We favor legislation by Congress and State Legislatures to protect the lives and limbs of railway employees and those of other hazardous transportation companies, and denounce the inactivity of the Republican party, and particularly the Republican Senate, for causing the defeat of measures beneficial and protective to this class of wage workers.

We are in favor of the enactment by the States of laws for abolishing the notorious sweating system, for abolishing contract convict labor, and for prohibiting the employment in factories of children under 15 years of age.

We are opposed to all sumptuary laws, as an interference with the individual rights of the citizen.

Upon this statement of principles and policies, the Democratic party asks the intelligent judgment of the American people. It asks a change of administration and a change of party, in order that there may be a change of system and a change of methods, thus assuring the maintenance unimpaired of institutions under which the Republic has grown great and powerful.

People's Platform of 1892

Assembled upon the 116th anniversary of the Declaration of Independence, the People's Party of America in their first national convention, invoking upon their action the blessing of Almighty God, put forth in the name and on behalf of the people of this country, the following preamble and declaration of principles:

Preamble

The conditions which surround us best justify our co-operation; we meet in the midst of a nation brought to the verge of moral, political, and material ruin. Corruption dominates the ballot-box, the Legislatures, the Congress, and touches even the ermine of the bench. The people are demoralized; most of the States have been compelled to isolate the voters at the polling places to prevent universal intimidation and bribery. The newspapers are largely subsidized or muzzled, public opinion silenced, business prostrated, homes covered with mortgages, labor impoverished, and the land concentrating in the hands of capitalists. The urban workmen are denied the right to organize for self-protection; imported pauperized labor beats down their wages, a hireling standing army, unrecognized by our laws, is established to shoot them down, and they are rapidly degenerating into European conditions. The fruits of the toil of millions are boldly stolen to build up colossal fortunes for a few, unprecedented in the history of mankind; and the possessors of these, in turn despise the Republic and endanger liberty. From the same prolific womb of governmental injustice we breed the two great classes—tramps and millionaires.

The national power to create money is appropriated to enrich bond-holders; a vast public debt payable in legal tender currency has been funded into gold-bearing bonds, thereby adding millions to the burdens of the people.

Silver, which has been accepted as coin since the dawn of history, has been demonetized to add to the purchasing power of gold by decreasing the value of all forms of property as well as human labor, and the supply of currency is purposely abridged to fatten usurers, bankrupt enterprise, and enslave industry. A vast conspiracy against mankind has been organized on two continents, and it is rapidly taking possession of the world. If not met and overthrown at once, it forebodes terrible social convulsions, the destruction of civilization, or the establishment of an absolute despotism.

We have witnessed for more than a quarter of a century the struggles of the two great political parties for power and plunder, while grievous wrongs have been inflicted upon the suffering people. We charge that the controlling influence dominating both these parties have permitted the existing dreadful conditions to develop without serious effort to prevent or restrain them. Neither do they now promise us any substantial reform. They have agreed together to ignore, in the coming campaign, every issue but one. They propose to drown the outcries of a plundered people with the uproar of a sham battle over the tariff, so that capitalists, corporations, national banks, rings, trusts, watered stock, the demonetization of silver and the oppressions of the usurers may all be lost sight of. They propose to sacrifice our homes, lives, and children on the altar of mammon; to destroy the multitude in order to secure corruption funds from the millionaires.

Assembled on the anniversary of the birthday of the nation, and filled with the spirit of the grand general and chief who established our independence, we seek to restore the government of the Republic to the hands of "the plain people," with which class it originated. We assert our purposes to be identical with the purposes of the National Constitution, to form a more perfect union and establish justice, insure domestic tranquillity, provide for the common defense, promote the general welfare, and secure the blessings of liberty for ourselves and our posterity.

We declare that this Republic can only endure as a free government while built upon the love of the whole people for each other and for the nation; that it cannot be pinned together by bayonets; that the civil war is over and that every passion and resentment which grew out of it must die with it, and that we must be in fact, as we are in name, one united brotherhood of freemen.

Our country finds itself confronted by conditions for which there is no precedent in the history of the world; our annual agricultural productions amount to billions of dollars in value, which must, within a few weeks or months be exchanged for billions of dollars' worth of commodities consumed in their production; the existing currency supply is wholly inadequate to make this exchange; the results are falling prices, the formation of combines and rings, the impoverishment of the producing class. We pledge ourselves that, if given power, we will labor to correct these evils by wise and reasonable legislation, in accordance with the terms of our platform.

We believe that the power of government—in other words, of the people—should be expanded (as in the case of the postal service) as rapidly and as far as the good sense of an intelligent people and the teachings of experience shall justify, to the end that oppression, injustice and poverty, shall eventually cease in the land.

While our sympathies as a party of reform are naturally upon the side of every proposition which will tend to make men intelligent, virtuous and temperate, we nevertheless regard these questions, important as they are, as secondary to the great issues now pressing for solution, and upon which not only our individual prosperity, but the very existence of free institutions depend; and we ask all men to first help us to determine whether we are to have a republic to administer, before we differ as to the conditions upon which it is to be administered, believing that the forces of reform this day organized will never cease to move forward, until every wrong is remedied, and equal rights and equal privileges securely established for all the men and women of this country.

PLATFORM

We declare, therefore,

First—That the union of the labor forces of the United States this day consummated shall be permanent and perpetual; may its spirit enter into all hearts for the salvation of the Republic and the uplifting of mankind.

Second—Wealth belongs to him who creates it, and every dollar taken from industry without an equivalent is robbery. "If any will not work, neither shall he eat." The interests of rural and civic labor are the same; their enemies are identical.

Third—We believe that the time has come when the railroad corporations will either own the people or the people must own the railroads, and should the government enter upon the work of owning and managing all railroads, we should favor an amendment to the Constitution by which all persons engaged in the government service shall be placed under a civil service regulation of the most rigid character, so as to prevent the increase of the power of the national administration by the use of such additional government employees.

Finance—We demand a national currency, safe, sound, and flexible, issued by the general government only, a full legal tender for all debts, public and private, and that without the use of banking corporations, a just, equitable and efficient means of distribution direct to the people, at a tax not to exceed 2 per cent per annum, to be provided as set forth by the sub-treasury plan of the Farmers' Alliance, or a better system; also by payments in discharge of its obligations for public improvements.

1. We demand free and unlimited coinage of silver and gold at the present legal ratio of 16 to 1.

2. We demand that the amount of circulating medium be speedily increased to not less than $50 per capita.

3. We demand a graduated income tax.

4. We believe that the money of the country should be kept as much as possible in the hands of the people, and hence we demand that all State and national revenues shall be limited to the necessary expenses of the government, economically and honestly administered.

5. We demand that postal savings banks be established by the government for the safe deposit of the earnings of the people and to facilitate exchange.

Transportation—Transportation being a means of exchange and a public necessity, the government should own and operate the railroads in the interest of the people. The telegraph and telephone, like the post office system, being a necessity for the transmission of news, should be owned and operated by the government in the interest of the people.

Land—The land, including all the natural sources of wealth, is the heritage of the people, and should not be monopolized for speculative purposes, and alien ownership of land should be prohibited. All land now held by railroads and other corporations in excess of their actual needs, and all lands now owned by aliens, should be reclaimed by the government and held for actual settlers only.

Prohibition Platform of 1892

The Prohibition Party, in National Convention assembled, acknowledging Almighty God as the source of all true government, and His law as the standard to which human enactments must conform to secure the blessings of peace and prosperity, presents the following declaration of principles:

The liquor traffic is a foe to civilization, the arch enemy of popular government, and a public nuisance. It is the citadel of the forces that corrupt politics, promote poverty and crime, degrade the nation's home life, thwart the will of the people, and deliver our country into the hands of rapacious class interests. All laws that under the guise of regulation legalize and protect this traffic or make the Government share its ill-gotten gains, are "vicious in principle and powerless as a remedy." We declare anew for the entire suppression of the manufacture, sale, importation, exportation and transportation of alcoholic liquors as a beverage by Federal and State legislation, and the full powers of Government should be exerted to secure this result. Any party that fails to recognize the dominant nature of this issue in American politics is undeserving of the support of the people.

No citizen should be denied the right to vote on account of sex, and equal labor should receive equal wages, without regard to sex.

The money of the country should consist of gold, silver, and paper, and be issued by the General Government only, and in sufficient quantity to meet the demands of business and give full opportunity for the employment of labor. To this end an increase in the volume of money is demanded, and no individual or corporation should be allowed to make any profit through its issue. It should be made a legal tender for the payment of all debts, public and private. Its volume should be fixed at a definite sum per capita and made to increase with our increase in population.

Tariff should be levied only as a defense against foreign governments which levy tariff upon or bar out our products from their markets, revenue being incidental. The residue of means necessary to an economical administration of the Government should be raised by levying a burden on what the people possess, instead of upon what they consume.

Railroad, telegraph, and other public corporations should be controlled by the Government in the interest of the people, and no higher charges allowed than necessary to give fair interest on the capital actually invested.

Foreign immigration has become a burden upon industry, one of the factors in depressing wages and causing discontent; therefore our immigration laws should be revised and strictly enforced. The time of residence for naturalization should be extended, and no naturalized person should be allowed to vote until one year after he becomes a citizen.

Non-resident aliens should not be allowed to acquire land in this country, and we favor the limitation of individual and corporate ownership of land. All unearned grants of land to railroad companies or other corporations should be reclaimed.

Years of inaction and treachery on the part of the Republican and Democratic parties have resulted in the present reign of mob law, and we demand that every citizen be protected in the right of trial by constitutional tribunals.

All men should be protected by law in their right to one day's rest in seven.

Arbitration is the wisest and most economical and humane method of settling national differences.

Speculations in margins, the cornering of grain, money and products, and the formation of pools, trusts, and combinations for the arbitrary advancement of prices should be suppressed.

We pledge that the Prohibition Party, if elected to power, will ever grant just pensions to disabled veterans of the Union army and navy, their widows and orphans.

We stand unequivocally for the American Public School, and opposed to any appropriation of any public moneys for sectarian schools. We declare that only by united support of such common schools, taught in the English language, can we hope to become and remain a homogeneous and harmonious people.

We arraign the Republican and Democratic Parties as false to the standards reared by their founders; as faithless to the principles of the illustrious leaders of the past to whom they do homage with the lips; as recreant to the "higher law," which is as inflexible in political affairs as in personal life; and as no longer embodying the aspirations of the American people, or inviting the confidence of enlightened, progressive patriotism. Their protest against the admission of "moral issues" into politics is a confession of their own moral degeneracy. The declaration of an eminent authority that municipal misrule is "the one conspicuous failure of American politics" follows as a natural consequence of such degeneracy, and it is true alike of cities under Republican and Democratic control. Each accuses the other of extravagance in congressional appropriations, and both are alike guilty; each protests when out of power against the infraction of the civil-service laws, and each when in power violates those laws in letter and spirit; each professes fealty to the interests of the toiling masses, but both covertly truckle to the money power in their administration of public affairs. Even the tariff issue, as represented in the Democratic Mills bill and the Republican McKinley bill, is no longer treated by them as an issue upon great and divergent principles of government, but is a mere catering to different sectional and class interests. The attempt in many States to wrest the Australian ballot system from its true purpose, and to so de-form it as to render it extremely difficult for new parties to exercise the right of suffrage, is an outrage upon popular government. The competition of both the parties for the vote of the slums, and their assiduous courting of the liquor power and subserviency to the money power, has resulted in placing those powers in the position of practical arbiters of the destinies of the nation. We renew our protest against these perilous tendencies, and invite all citizens to join us in the upbuilding of a party that has shown in five national campaigns that it prefers temporary defeat to an abandonment of the claims of justice, sobriety, personal rights and the protection of American homes.

Recognizing and declaring that prohibition of the liquor traffic has become the dominant issue in national politics, we invite to full party fellowship all those who on this one dominant issue are with us agreed, in the full belief that this party can and will remove sectional differences, promote national unity, and insure the best welfare of our entire land.

Resolved, That we favor a liberal appropriation by the Federal Government for the World's Columbian Exposition, but only on the condition that the sale of intoxicating drinks upon the Exposition grounds is prohibited, and that the Exposition be kept closed on Sunday.

Republican Platform of 1892

The representatives of the Republicans of the United States, assembled in general convention on the shores of the Mississippi River, the everlasting bond of an indestructible Republic, whose most glorious chapter of history is the record of the Republican party, congratulate their countrymen on the majestic march of the nation under the banners inscribed with the principles of our platform of 1888, vindicated by victory at the polls and prosperity in our fields, workshops and mines, and make the following declaration of principles:

We reaffirm the American doctrine of protection. We call attention to its growth abroad. We maintain that the prosperous condition of our country is largely due to the wise revenue legislation of the Republican congress.

We believe that all articles which cannot be produced in the United States, except luxuries, should be admitted free of duty, and that on all imports coming into competition with the products of American labor, there should be levied duties equal to the difference between wages abroad and at home. We assert that the prices of manufactured articles of general consumption have been reduced under the operations of the tariff act of 1890.

We denounce the efforts of the Democratic majority of the House of Representatives to destroy our tariff laws by piecemeal, as manifested by their attacks upon wool, lead and lead ores, the chief products of a number of States, and we ask the people for their judgment thereon.

We point to the success of the Republican policy of reciprocity, under which our export trade has vastly increased and new and enlarged markets have been opened for the products of our farms and workshops. We remind the people of the bitter opposition of the Democratic party to this practical business measure, and claim that, executed by a Republican administration, our present laws will eventually give us control of the trade of the world.

The American people, from tradition and interest, favor bi-metallism, and the Republican party demands the use of both gold and silver as standard money, with such restrictions and under such provisions, to be determined by legislation, as will secure the maintenance of the parity of values of the two metals so that the purchasing and debt-paying power of the dollar, whether of silver, gold, or paper, shall be at all times equal. The interests of the producers of the country, its farmers and its workingmen, demand that every dollar, paper or coin, issued by the government, shall be as good as any other.

We commend the wise and patriotic steps already taken by our government to secure an international conference, to adopt such measures as will insure a parity of value between gold and silver for use as money throughout the world.

We demand that every citizen of the United States shall be allowed to cast one free and unrestricted ballot in all public elections, and that such ballot shall be counted and returned as cast; that such laws shall be enacted and enforced as will secure to every citizen, be he rich or poor, native or foreign-born, white or black, this sovereign right, guaranteed by the Constitution. The free and honest popular ballot, the just and equal representation of all the people, as well as their just and equal protection under the laws, are the foundation of our Republican institutions, and the party will never relax its efforts until the integrity of the ballot and the purity of elections shall be fully guaranteed and protected in every State.

SOUTHERN OUTRAGES

We denounce the continued inhuman outrages perpetrated upon American citizens for political reasons in certain Southern States of the Union.

FOREIGN RELATIONS

We favor the extension of our foreign commerce, the restoration of our mercantile marine by home-built ships, and the creation of a navy for the protection of our National interests and the honor of our flag; the maintenance of the most friendly relations with all foreign powers; entangling alliances with none; and the protection of the rights of our fishermen.

We reaffirm our approval of the Monroe doctrine and believe in the achievement of the manifest destiny of the Republic in its broadest sense.

We favor the enactment of more stringent laws and regulations for the restriction of criminal, pauper and contract immigration.

MISCELLANEOUS

We favor efficient legislation by Congress to protect the life and limbs of employees of transportation companies engaged in carrying on inter-State commerce, and recommend legislation by the respective States that will protect employees engaged in State commerce, in mining and manufacturing.

The Republican party has always been the champion of the oppressed and recognizes the dignity of manhood, irrespective of faith, color, or nationality; it sympathizes with the cause of home rule in Ireland, and protests against the persecution of the Jews in Russia.

The ultimate reliance of free popular government is the intelligence of the people, and the maintenance of freedom among men. We therefore declare anew our devotion to liberty of thought and conscience, of speech and press, and approve all agencies and instrumentalities which contribute to the education of the children of the land, but while insisting upon the fullest measure of religious liberty, we are opposed to any union of Church and State.

We reaffirm our opposition, declared in the Republican platform of 1888, to all combinations of capital organized in trusts or otherwise, to control arbitrarily the condition of trade among our citizens.

We heartily indorse the action already taken upon this subject, and ask for such further legislation as may be required to remedy any defects in existing laws, and to render their enforcement more complete and effective.

We approve the policy of extending to towns, villages and rural communities the advantages of the free delivery service, now enjoyed by the larger cities of the country, and reaffirm the declaration contained in the Republican platform of 1888, pledging the reduction of letter postage to 1 cent at the earliest possible moment consistent with the maintenance of the Post Office Department, and the highest class of postal service.

We commend the spirit and evidence of reform in the civil service, and the wise and consistent enforcement by the Republican party of the laws regulating the same.

NICARAGUA CANAL

The construction of the Nicaragua Canal is of the highest importance to the American people, both as a measure of National defense and to build up and maintain American commerce, and it should be controlled by the United States Government.

TERRITORIES

We favor the admission of the remaining Territories at the earliest practicable date, having due regard to the interests of the people of the Territories and of the United States. All the Federal officers appointed for the Territories should be selected from *bona-fide* residents thereof, and the right of self-government should be accorded as far as practicable.

ARID LANDS

We favor the cession, subject to the homestead laws, of the arid public lands, to the States and Territories in which they lie, under such Congressional restrictions as to disposition, reclamation and occupancy by settlers as will secure the maximum benefits to the people.

THE COLUMBIAN EXPOSITION

The World's Columbian Exposition is a great national undertaking, and Congress should promptly enact such reasonable legislation in aid thereof as will insure a discharge of the expenses and obligations incident thereto, and the attainment of results commensurate with the dignity and progress of the Nation.

INTEMPERANCE

We sympathize with all wise and legitimate efforts to lessen and prevent the evils of intemperance and promote morality.

PENSIONS

Ever mindful of the services and sacrifices of the men who saved the life of the Nation, we pledge anew to the veteran soldiers of the Republic a watchful care and recognition of their just claims upon a grateful people.

HARRISON'S ADMINISTRATION

We commend the able, patriotic and thoroughly American administration of President Harrison. Under it the country has enjoyed remarkable prosperity and the dignity and honor of the Nation, at home and abroad, have been faithfully maintained, and we offer the record of pledges kept as a guarantee of faithful performance in the future.

Socialist Labor Platform of 1892

The Socialist Labor Party of the United States, in convention assembled, reasserts the inalienable right of all men to life, liberty, and the pursuit of happiness.

With the founders of the American republic we hold that the purpose of government is to secure every citizen in the enjoyment of this right; but in the light of our social conditions we hold, furthermore, that no such right can be exercised under a system of economic inequality, essentially destructive of life, of liberty, and of happiness.

With the founders of this republic we hold that the true theory of politics is that the machinery of government must be owned and controlled by the whole people; but in the light of our industrial development we hold, furthermore, that the true theory of economics is that the machinery of production must likewise belong to the people in common.

To the obvious fact that our despotic system of

economics is the direct opposite of our democratic system of politics, can plainly be traced the existence of a privileged class, the corruption of government by that class, the alienation of public property, public franchises and public functions to that class, and the abject dependence of the mightiest of nations upon that class. Again, through the perversion of democracy to the ends of plutocracy, labor is robbed of the wealth which it alone produces, is denied the means of self-employment, and, by compulsory idleness in wage-slavery, is even deprived of the necessaries of life. Human power and natural forces are thus wasted, that the plutocracy may rule. Ignorance and misery, with all their concomitant evils, are perpetuated, that the people may be kept in bondage. Science and invention are diverted from their humane purpose to the enslavement of women and children.

Against such a system the Socialistic Labor Party once more enters its protest. Once more it reiterates its fundamental declaration, that private property in the natural sources of production and in the instruments of labor is the obvious cause of all economic servitude and political dependence; and

WHEREAS, the time is fast coming when, in the natural course of social evolution, this system, through the destructive action of its failures and crises, on the one hand, and the constructive tendencies of its trusts and other capitalistic combinations, on the other hand, shall have worked out its own downfall; therefore, be it

RESOLVED, That we call upon the people to organize with a view to the substitution of the co-operative commonwealth for the present state of planless production, industrial war, and social disorder—a commonwealth in which every worker shall have the free exercise and full benefit of his faculties, multiplied by all the modern factors of civilization. We call upon them to unite with us in a mighty effort to gain by all practicable means the political power.

In the meantime, and with a view to immediate improvement in the condition of labor, we present the following "Demands":

SOCIAL DEMANDS

1. Reduction of the hours of labor in proportion to the progress of production.

2. The United States shall obtain possession of the railroads, canals, telegraphs, telephones,

and all other means of public transportation and communication.

3. The municipalities to obtain possession of the local railroads, ferries, water-works, gas-works, electric plants, and all industries requiring municipal franchises.

4. The public lands to be declared inalienable. Revocation of all land grants to corporations or individuals, the conditions of which have not been complied with.

5. Legal incorporation by the States of local Trade Unions which have no national organization.

6. The United States to have the exclusive right to issue money.

7. Congressional legislation providing for the scientific management of forests and waterways, and prohibiting the waste of the natural resources of the country.

8. Inventions to be free to all; the inventors to be remunerated by the nation.

9. Progressive income tax and tax on inheritances; the smaller incomes to be exempt.

10. School education of all children under fourteen years of age to be compulsory, gratuitous, and accessible to all by public assistance in meals, clothing, books, etc., where necessary.

11. Repeal of all pauper, tramp, conspiracy, and sumptuary laws. Unabridged right of combination.

12. Official statistics concerning the condition of labor. Prohibition of the employment of children of school age and of the employment of female labor in occupations detrimental to health or morality. Abolition of the convict labor contract system.

13. All wages to be paid in lawful money of the United States. Equalization of women's wages with those of men where equal service is performed.

14. Laws for the protection of life and limb in all occupations, and an efficient employer's liability law.

POLITICAL DEMANDS

1. The people to have the right to propose laws and to vote upon all measures of importance, according to the Referendum principle.

2. Abolition of the Presidency, Vice-Presidency, and Senate of the United States. An Executive Board to be established, whose members are to be elected, and may at any time be recalled by the House of Representatives as the only legislative body. The States and Municipalities to adopt corresponding amendment to their constitutions and statutes.

3. Municipal self-government.

4. Direct vote and secret ballots in all elections. Universal and equal right of suffrage, without regard to color, creed, or sex. Election days to be legal holidays. The principle of minority representation to be introduced.

5. All public officers to be subject to recall by their respective constituencies.

6. Uniform civil and criminal law throughout the United States. Administration of justice to be free of charge. Abolition of capital punishment.

CAMPAIGN OF 1896

Factionalism, primarily over the issue of currency, dominated the political parties of 1896. Even the Prohibitionists were divided between the "narrow gaugers" who wanted to focus more exclusively on the issue of the control of alcoholic beverages and the "broad gaugers" who wanted the party to take positions on the currency and other topics of concern to "humanity." The former selected Joshua Levering of Maryland as a candidate for president and Hale Johnson of Illinois as the vice-presidential candidate. The "broad gaugers," who bolted the convention, organized the National Party and nominated the Reverend Charles E. Bentley of Nebraska by acclamation for president and James Southgate of North Carolina for vice-president.

The Republicans nominated William McKinley of Ohio for president, on the first ballot, and Garret A. Hobart of New Jersey for vice-president. Thirty-four delegates, including four United States senators and two House members, walked out of the convention to protest the currency plank in the platform. They and their followers later banded together as the National Silver Party and nominated, by acclamation, the same men as the Democrats.

The Democratic convention in July was dominated by the advocates of the free coinage of silver and gold in the ratio of sixteen to one. After his famous "Cross of Gold" speech and five ballots, William Jennings Bryan of Nebraska was nominated for president. Arthur Sewall of Maine was nominated for vice-president. Again there was a bolt against a major party; gold standard advocates seceded from the convention and held their own convention at Indianapolis in September. They called themselves the National Democrats and nominated John M. Palmer of Illinois for president and General Simon B. Buckner of Kentucky for vice-president.

The Socialist Labor Party, meeting in New York City, nominated Charles H. Matchett of New York for president and Matthew Maguire of New Jersey for vice-president.

The People's Party (Populists) was weakened in 1896 by the defection of many of its members to the Democrats. Nevertheless, at their convention in St. Louis they first nominated Thomas E. Watson of Georgia for vice-president and then selected the Democratic candidate, William Jennings Bryan, for president.

After an exciting campaign, McKinley and Hobart received 7,108,480 votes (51 percent of the total) to 6,511,495 for Bryan and Sewall. Bryan and Watson, on the Populist ticket, polled another 200,000. Palmer received 133,435 votes; Levering, 125,072 votes; Bentley acquired 19,363; and Matchett garnered 36,356. McKinley, in a sectional result, carried the North, East, California, and Oregon. He acquired 271 electoral votes to 176 for Bryan.

Democratic Platform of 1896

We, the Democrats of the United States in National Convention assembled, do reaffirm our allegiance to those great essential principles of justice and liberty, upon which our institutions are founded, and which the Democratic Party has advocated from Jefferson's time to our own—freedom of speech, freedom of the press, freedom of conscience, the preservation of personal rights, the equality of all citizens before the law, and the faithful observance of constitutional limitations.

During all these years the Democratic Party has resisted the tendency of selfish interests to the centralization of governmental power, and steadfastly maintained the integrity of the dual scheme of government established by the founders of this Republic of republics. Under its guidance and teachings the great principle of local self-government has found its best expression in the maintenance of the rights of the States and in its assertion of the necessity of confining the general government to the exercise of the powers granted by the Constitution of the United States.

The Constitution of the United States guarantees to every citizen the rights of civil and religious liberty. The Democratic Party has always been the exponent of political liberty and religious freedom, and it renews its obligations and reaffirms its devotion to these fundamental principles of the Constitution.

THE MONEY PLANK

Recognizing that the money question is paramount to all others at this time, we invite attention to the fact that the Federal Constitution named silver and gold together as the money metals of the United States, and that the first coinage law passed by Congress under the Constitution made the silver dollar the monetary unit and admitted gold to free coinage at a ratio based upon the silver-dollar unit.

We declare that the act of 1873 demonetizing silver without the knowledge or approval of the American people has resulted in the appreciation of gold and a corresponding fall in the prices of commodities produced by the people; a heavy increase in the burdens of taxation and of all debts, public and private; the enrichment of the money-lending class at home and abroad; the prostration of industry and impoverishment of the people.

We are unalterably opposed to monometallism which has locked fast the prosperity of an industrial people in the paralysis of hard times. Gold monometallism is a British policy, and its adoption has brought other nations into financial servitude to London. It is not only un-American but anti-American, and it can be fastened on the United States only by the stifling of that spirit and love of liberty which proclaimed our political independence in 1776 and won it in the War of the Revolution.

We demand the free and unlimited coinage of both silver and gold at the present legal ratio of 16 to 1 without waiting for the aid or consent of any other nation. We demand that the standard silver dollar shall be a full legal tender, equally with gold, for all debts, public and private, and we favor such legislation as will prevent for the future the demonetization of any kind of legal-tender money by private contract.

We are opposed to the policy and practice of surrendering to the holders of the obligations of the United States the option reserved by law to the Government of redeeming such obligations in either silver coin or gold coin.

Interest-Bearing Bonds

We are opposed to the issuing of interest-bearing bonds of the United States in time of peace and condemn the trafficking with banking syndicates, which, in exchange for bonds and at an enormous profit to themselves, supply the Federal Treasury with gold to maintain the policy of gold monometallism.

Against National Banks

Congress alone has the power to coin and issue money, and President Jackson declared that this power could not be delegated to corporations or individuals. We therefore denounce the issuance of notes intended to circulate as money by National banks as in derogation of the Constitution, and we demand that all paper which is made a legal tender for public and private debts, or which is receivable for dues to the United States, shall be issued by the Government of the United States and shall be redeemable in coin.

Tariff Resolution

We hold that tariff duties should be levied for purposes of revenue, such duties to be so adjusted as to operate equally throughout the country, and not discriminate between class or section, and that taxation should be limited by the needs of the Government, honestly and economically administered. We denounce as disturbing to business the Republican threat to restore the McKinley law, which has twice been condemned by the people in National elections and which, enacted under the false plea of protection to home industry, proved a prolific breeder of trusts and monopolies, enriched the few at the expense of the many, restricted trade and deprived the producers of the great American staples of access to their natural markets.

Until the money question is settled we are opposed to any agitation for further changes in our tariff laws, except such as are necessary to meet the deficit in revenue caused by the adverse decision of the Supreme Court on the income tax. But for this decision by the Supreme Court, there would be no deficit in the revenue under the law passed by the Democratic Congress in strict pursuance of the uniform decisions of that court for nearly 100 years, that court having in that decision sustained Constitutional objections to its enactment which had previously been over-ruled by the ablest Judges who have ever sat on that bench. We declare that it is the duty of Congress to use all the Constitutional power which remains after that decision, or which may come from its reversal by the court as it may hereafter be constituted, so that the burdens of taxation may be equally and impartially laid, to the end that wealth may bear its due proportion of the expense of the Government.

IMMIGRATION AND ARBITRATION

We hold that the most efficient way of protecting American labor is to prevent the importation of foreign pauper labor to compete with it in the home market, and that the value of the home market to our American farmers and artisans is greatly reduced by a vicious monetary system which depresses the prices of their products below the cost of production, and thus deprives them of the means of purchasing the products of our home manufactories; and as labor creates the wealth of the country, we demand the passage of such laws as may be necessary to protect it in all its rights.

We are in favor of the arbitration of differences between employers engaged in interstate commerce and their employees, and recommend such legislation as is necessary to carry out this principle.

TRUSTS AND POOLS

The absorption of wealth by the few, the consolidation of our leading railroad systems, and the formation of trusts and pools require a stricter control by the Federal Government of those arteries of commerce. We demand the enlargement of the powers of the Interstate Commerce Commission and such restriction and guarantees in the control of railroads as will protect the people from robbery and oppression.

DECLARE FOR ECONOMY

We denounce the profligate waste of the money wrung from the people by oppressive taxation and the lavish appropriations of recent Republican Congresses, which have kept taxes high, while the labor that pays them is unemployed and the products of the people's toil are depressed in price till they no longer repay the cost of production. We demand a return to that simplicity and economy which befits a Democratic Government, and a reduction in the number of useless offices, the salaries of which drain the substance of the people.

FEDERAL INTERFERENCE IN LOCAL AFFAIRS

We denounce arbitrary interference by Federal authorities in local affairs as a violation of the Constitution of the United States, and a crime against free institutions, and we especially object to government by injunction as a new and highly dangerous form of oppression by which Federal Judges, in contempt of the laws of the States and rights of citizens, become at once legislators, judges and executioners; and we approve the bill passed at the last session of the United States Senate, and now pending in the House of Representatives, relative to contempts in Federal courts and providing for trials by jury in certain cases of contempt.

PACIFIC RAILROAD

No discrimination should be indulged in by the Government of the United States in favor of any of its debtors. We approve of the refusal of the Fifty-third Congress to pass the Pacific Railroad Funding bill and denounce the effort of the present Republican Congress to enact a similar measure.

PENSIONS

Recognizing the just claims of deserving Union soldiers, we heartily indorse the rule of the present Commissioner of Pensions, that no names shall be arbitrarily dropped from the pension roll; and the fact of enlistment and service should be deemed conclusive evidence against disease and disability before enlistment.

ADMISSION OF TERRITORIES

We favor the admission of the Territories of New Mexico, Arizona and Oklahoma into the Union as States, and we favor the early admission of all the Territories, having the necessary population and resources to entitle them to Statehood, and, while they remain Territories, we hold that the officials appointed to administer the government of any Territory, together with the District of Columbia and Alaska, should be *bona-fide* residents of the Territory or District in which their duties are to be performed. The Democratic party believes in home rule and that all public lands of the United States should be appropriated to the establishment of free homes for American citizens.

We recommend that the Territory of Alaska be granted a delegate in Congress and that the general land and timber laws of the United States be extended to said Territory.

SYMPATHY FOR CUBA

The Monroe doctrine, as originally declared, and as interpreted by succeeding Presidents, is a permanent part of the foreign policy of the United States, and must at all times be maintained.

We extend our sympathy to the people of Cuba in their heroic struggle for liberty and independence.

CIVIL-SERVICE LAWS

We are opposed to life tenure in the public service, except as provided in the Constitution. We favor appointments based on merit, fixed terms of office, and such an administration of the civil-service laws as will afford equal opportunities to all citizens of ascertained fitness.

THIRD-TERM RESOLUTION

We declare it to be the unwritten law of this Republic, established by custom and usage of 100 years, and sanctioned by the examples of the greatest and wisest of those who founded and have maintained our Government that no man should be eligible for a third term of the Presidential office.

IMPROVEMENT OF WATERWAYS

The Federal Government should care for and improve the Mississippi River and other great waterways of the Republic, so as to secure for the interior States easy and cheap transportation to tidewater. When any waterway of the Republic is of sufficient importance to demand aid of the Government such aid should be extended upon a definite plan of continuous work until permanent improvement is secured.

CONCLUSION

Confiding in the justice of our cause and the necessity of its success at the polls, we submit the foregoing declaration of principles and purposes to the considerate judgment of the American people. We invite the support of all citizens who approve them and who desire to have them made effective through legislation, for the relief of the people and the restoration of the country's prosperity.

National Platform of 1896

The National party, recognizing God as the Author of All just power in government, presents the following declaration of principles, which it pledges itself to enact into effective legislation when given the power to do so.

1. The suppression of the manufacture and sale, importation, exportation, and transportation of intoxicating liquors for beverage purposes. We utterly reject all plans for regulating or compromising with this traffic, whether such plans be called local option, taxation, license, or public control. The sale of liquors for medicinal and other legitimate uses should be conducted by the State, without profit, and with such regulations as will prevent fraud or evasion.

2. No citizen should be denied the right to vote on account of sex.

3. All money should be issued by the General Government only, and without the intervention of any private citizen, corporation, or banking institution. It should be based upon the wealth, stability, and integrity of the nation. It should be a full legal tender for all debts, public and private, and should be of full volume to meet the demands of the legitimate business interests of the country. For the purpose of honestly liquidating our outstanding coin obligations, we favor the free and unlimited coinage of both silver and gold, at the ratio 16 to 1, without consulting any other nation.

4. Land is the common heritage of the people and should be preserved from monopoly and speculation. All unearned grants of land, subject to forfeiture should be reclaimed by the Government, and no portion of the public domain should hereafter be granted except to actual settlers, continuous use being essential to tenure.

5. Railroads, telegraphs, and other natural monopolies should be owned and operated by the Government, giving to the people the benefit of the service at actual cost.

6. The National Constitution should be so amended as to allow the National revenue to be raised by equitable adjustment of taxation on the properties and incomes of the people, and import duties should be levied as a means of securing equitable commercial relations with other nations.

7. The contract convict labor system, through which speculators are enriched at the expense of the State, should be abolished.

8. All citizens should be protected by law in their right to one day of rest in seven, without oppressing any who conscientiously observe any other than the first day of the week.

9. The American public schools, taught in the English language, should be maintained, and no public funds should be appropriated for sectarian institutions.

10. The President, Vice-President, and United States Senators should be elected by direct vote of the people.

11. Ex-soldiers and sailors of the United States Army and Navy, their widows and minor children, should receive liberal pensions, granted on disability and term of service, not merely as a debt of gratitude, but for service rendered in the preservation of the Union.

12. Our immigration laws should be so revised as to exclude paupers and criminals. None but citizens of the United States should be allowed to vote in any State, and naturalized citizens should not vote until one year after naturalization papers have been issued.

13. The initiative and referendum, and proportional representation, should be adopted.

14. Having herein presented our principles and purposes, we invite the co-operation and support of all citizens who are with us substantially agreed.

National Democratic Platform of 1896

This convention has assembled to uphold the principles upon which depend the honor and welfare of the American people in order that Democrats throughout the Union may unite their patriotic efforts to avert disaster from their country and ruin from their party.

The Democratic party is pledged to equal and exact justice to all men of every creed and condition; to the largest freedom of the individual consistent with good government; to the preservation of the Federal government in its constitutional vigor, and to the support of the States in all their just rights; to economy in the public expenditures; to the maintenance of the public faith and sound money; and it is opposed to paternalism and all class legislation.

Chicago Platform Condemned

The declarations of the Chicago convention attack individual freedom, the right of private contract, the independence of the judiciary and the authority of the President to enforce Federal laws. They advocate a reckless attempt to increase the price of silver by legislation to the debasement of our monetary standard, and threaten unlimited issues of paper money by the government. They abandon for Republican allies the Democratic cause of tariff reform to court the favor of protectionists to their fiscal heresy.

In view of these and other grave departures from Democratic principles, we cannot support the candidates of that convention nor be bound by its acts. The Democratic party has survived defeats, but could not survive a victory won in behalf of the doctrine and policy proclaimed in its name at Chicago.

The conditions, however, which made possible such utterances from a national convention are the direct result of class-legislation by the Republican party. It still proclaims, as it has for years, the power and duty of government to raise and maintain prices by law; and it proposes no remedy for existing evils except oppressive and unjust taxation.

Democratic Principles

The National Democracy here reconvened, therefore renews its declaration of faith in Democratic principles, especially as applicable to the conditions of the times.

Taxation, tariff, excise or direct, is rightfully imposed only for public purposes, and not for private gain. Its amount is justly measured by public expenditures, which should be limited by scrupulous economy. The sum derived by the treasury from tariff and excise levies is affected by the state of trade and volume of consumption. The amount required by the treasury is determined by the appropriations made by Congress. The demand of the Republican party for an increase in tariff taxation has its pretext in the deficiency of the revenue, which has its causes in the stagnation of trade and reduced consumption, due entirely to the loss of confidence that has followed the Populist threat of free coinage and depreciation of our money and the Republican practice of extravagant appropriations beyond the needs of good government. We arraign and condemn the Populistic conventions of Chicago and St. Louis for their co-operation with the Republican party in creating these conditions, which are pleaded in justification of a heavy increase of the burdens of the people by a further resort to protection. We, therefore, denounce protection and its ally, free coinage of silver, as schemes for the personal profit of a few at the expense of the masses, and oppose the two parties which stand for these schemes as hostile to the people of the Republic, whose food and shelter, comfort and prosperity are attacked by higher taxes and depreciated money.

TARIFF

In fine, we reaffirm the historic Democratic doctrine of tariff for revenue only.

We demand that henceforth modern and liberal policies toward American shipping shall take the place of our imitation of the restricted statutes of the eighteenth century, which were long ago abandoned by every maritime power but the United States, and which, to the nation's humiliation, has driven American capital and enterprise to the use of alien flags and alien crews, have made the stars and stripes an almost unknown emblem in foreign ports, and have virtually extinguished the race of American seamen. We oppose the pretense that discriminating duties will promote shipping; that scheme is an invitation to commercial warfare upon the United States, un-American in the light of our great commercial treaties, offering no gain whatever to American shipping, while greatly increasing ocean freights on our agricultural and manufactured products.

FOR A GOLD STANDARD

The experience of mankind has shown that by reason of their natural qualities gold is the necessary money of the large affairs of commerce and business, while silver is conveniently adapted to minor transactions, and the most beneficial use of both together can be insured only by the adoption of the former as a standard of monetary measure, and the maintenance of silver at a parity with gold by its limited coinage under suitable safeguards of law. Thus the largest possible enjoyment of both metals is gained with a value universally accepted throughout the world, which constitutes the only practical bimetallic currency, assuring the most stable standard, and especially the best and safest money for all who earn their livelihood by labor or the produce of husbandry. They cannot suffer when paid in the best money known to man, but are the peculiar and most defenseless victims of a debased and fluctuating currency, which offers continual profits to the money-changer at their cost.

Realizing these truths, demonstrated by long public inconvenience and loss, the Democratic party, in the interests of the masses and of equal justice to all, practically established by the legisla-

tion of 1834 and 1853 the gold standard of monetary measurement, and likewise entirely divorced the government from banking and currency issues. To this long-established Democratic policy we adhere, and insist upon the maintenance of the gold standard and of the parity therewith of every dollar issued by the government, and are firmly opposed to the free and unlimited coinage of silver and to the compulsory purchase of silver bullion. But we denounce also the further maintenance of the present costly patchwork system of national paper currency as a constant source of injury and peril.

We assert the necessity of such intelligent currency reform as will confine the government to its legitimate functions, completely separated from the banking business, and afford to all sections of our country a uniform, safe and elastic bank currency under governmental supervision, measured in volume by the needs of business.

THE ADMINISTRATION

The fidelity, patriotism and courage with which President Cleveland has fulfilled his great public trust, the high character of his administration, its wisdom and energy in the maintenance of civil order and the enforcement of the laws, its equal regard for the rights of every class and every section, its firm and dignified conduct of foreign affairs, and its sturdy persistence in upholding the credit and honor of the nation, are fully recognized by the Democratic party, and will secure to him a place in history beside the Fathers of the Republic.

We also commend the administration for the great progress made in the reform of the public service, and we indorse its efforts to extend the merit system still further. We demand that no backward step be taken, but that the reform be supported and advanced until the un-Democratic spoils system of appointments shall be eradicated.

OTHER AFFAIRS

We demand strict economy in the appropriations and in the administration of the government.

We favor arbitration for the settlement of international disputes.

We favor a liberal policy of pensions to deserving soldiers and sailors of the United States.

The Supreme Court of the United States was

wisely established by the framers of our Constitution as one of the three co-ordinate branches of the government. Its independence and authority to interpret the law of the land, without fear or favor, must be maintained. We condemn all efforts to degrade that tribunal, or impair the confidence and respect which it has deservedly held.

The Democratic party ever has maintained, and ever will maintain, the supremacy of law, the independence of its judicial administration, the inviolability of contracts, and the obligations of all good citizens to resist every illegal trust, combination or attempt against the just rights of property and the good order of society, in which are bound up the peace and happiness of our people.

Believing these principles to be essential to the well-being of the Republic, we submit them to the consideration of the American people.

National Silver Platform of 1896

We, the national silver party, in convention assembled, hereby adopt the following declaration of principles:

First. The paramount issue at this time in the United States is indisputably the money question. It is between the gold standard, gold bonds, and bank currency on the one side, and the bimetallic standard, no bonds, and government currency on the other.

On this issue we declare ourselves to be in favor of a distinctively American financial system.

We are unalterably opposed to single gold standard, and demand an immediate return to the constitutional standard of gold and silver, by restoration by this government, independently of any foreign power, of the unrestricted coinage of both gold and silver into standard money at a ratio of 16 to 1, and upon terms of exact equality as they existed prior to 1873; the silver coin to be a full legal tender equally with gold, for all debts and dues, public and private.

We favor such legislation as will prevent for the future the demonetization of any kind of legal-tender by private contract. We hold the power to control and regulate paper currency is inseparable from the power to coin money, and hence all currency intended to circulate as money should be issued and its volume controlled by the general government only and should be legal tender.

We are unalterably opposed to the issue by the United States of interest-bearing bonds in time of peace, and we denounce as a blunder worse than a crime, the present treasury policy, concurred in by a republican house, of plunging the country in debt by hundreds of millions in a vain attempt to maintain the gold standard by borrowing gold.

We demand the payment of all coin obligations of the United States as provided by existing laws, in either gold or silver coin, at the option of the government, and not at the option of the creditor.

The demonetization of silver of 1873 enormously increased the demand for gold, enhancing its purchasing power and lowering all prices measured by that standard, and since that unjust indefensible act, the prices of American products have fallen, upon an average of nearly 50 per cent., carrying down with them, proportionately, the money value of all other forms of property.

Such a fall of prices destroyed the profits of legitimate industry, injuring the producer for the benefit of the non-producer, increasing the burden of the debtor, swelling the gains of creditors, paralyzing the productive energies of the American people, relegating to idleness vast numbers of willing workers, sending shadows of despair into the home of the honest toiler, filling the land with tramps and paupers, and building up colossal fortunes at the money centers to maintain the gold standard. The country has within the last two years, in a time of profound peace and plenty been loaded down with $262,000,000 additional interest-bearing debt, under such circumstances as to allow a syndicate of native and foreign bankers to realize a net profit of millions on a single deal.

It stands confessed that a gold standard can only be upheld by so depleting our paper currency as to force the prices of our products below the European and even below the Asiatic level, to enable us to sell in foreign markets, thus aggravating the very evils of which our people so bitterly complain, degrading American labor and striking at the foundations of our civilization itself.

Advocates of gold standard persistently claim that the cause of our distress is overproduction— that we have produced so much that it made us poor—which implies that the true remedy is to close the factory, abandon the farm and throw a multitude of people out of employment, a doctrine that leaves us unnerved and disheartened, and absolutely without hope for the future. We affirm it to be unquestioned that there can be no such economic paradox as overproduction and at the same time tens of thousands of our fellow citizens remain half clothed and half fed, and who are piteously clamoring for the common necessities of life.

Second. That over and above all other questions of policy, we are in favor of restoring to the people of the United States the time-honored money of the Constitution—gold and silver, not one, but both—the money of Washington, Hamilton, Jefferson, Monroe, Jackson, and Lincoln, to the end that the American people may receive honest pay for an honest product; that an American debtor may pay his just obligations in honest standard, and not in a standard that has appreciated one hundred per cent above all the great staples of the country, and to the end, further, that silver standard countries may be deprived of the unjust advantage they now enjoy in the difference in exchange between gold and silver—an advantage which tariff legislation alone cannot overcome.

We, therefore, confidently appeal to the people of the United States to leave in abeyance for the moment all other questions, however important and even momentous though they may be, to sunder, if need be, all former party ties and affiliations, and unite in one supreme effort to free themselves and their children from the domination of the money power—a power more destructive than any which has ever been fastened upon the civilized men of any race or in any age, and upon the consummation of our desires and efforts we invoke the aid of all patriotic American citizens, and the gracious favor of Divine Providence.

Inasmuch as the patriotic majority of the Chicago convention embodied in the financial plank of its platform the principles enunciated in the platform of the American bimetallic party, promulgated at Washington, D. C., January 22, 1896, and herein reiterated, which is not only the paramount, but the only real issue in the pending campaign, therefore, recognizing that their nominees embody these patriotic principles, we recommend that this Convention nominate William J. Bryan, of Nebraska, for President, and Arthur Sewall, of Maine, for Vice-President.

People's Platform of 1896

The People's Party, assembled in National Convention, reaffirms its allegiance to the principles declared by the founders of the Republic, and also to the fundamental principles of just government as enunciated in the platform of the party in 1892.

We recognize that through the connivance of the present and preceding Administrations the country has reached a crisis in its National life, as predicted in our declaration four years ago, and that prompt and patriotic action is the supreme duty of the hour.

We realize that, while we have political independence, our financial and industrial independence is yet to be attained by restoring to our country the Constitutional control and exercise of the functions necessary to a people's government, which functions have been basely surrendered by our public servants to corporate monopolies. The influence of European moneychangers has been more potent in shaping legislation than the voice of the American people. Executive power and patronage have been used to corrupt our legislatures and defeat the will of the people, and plutocracy has thereby been enthroned upon the ruins of democracy. To restore the Government intended by the fathers, and for the welfare and prosperity of this and future generations, we demand the establishment of an economic and financial system which shall make us masters of our own affairs and independent of European control, by the adoption of the following declaration of principles:

THE FINANCES

1. We demand a National money, safe and sound, issued by the General Government only, without the intervention of banks of issue, to be a full legal tender for all debts, public and private; a just, equitable, and efficient means of distribution, direct to the people, and through the lawful disbursements of the Government.

2. We demand the free and unrestricted coinage of silver and gold at the present legal ratio of 16 to 1, without waiting for the consent of foreign nations.

3. We demand that the volume of circulating medium be speedily increased to an amount sufficient to meet the demand of the business and

population, and to restore the just level of prices of labor and production.

4. We denounce the sale of bonds and the increase of the public interest-bearing debt made by the present Administration as unnecessary and without authority of law, and demand that no more bonds be issued, except by specific act of Congress.

5. We demand such legislation as will prevent the demonetization of the lawful money of the United States by private contract.

6. We demand that the Government, in payment of its obligation, shall use its option as to the kind of lawful money in which they are to be paid, and we denounce the present and preceding Administrations for surrendering this option to the holders of Government obligations.

7. We demand a graduated income tax, to the end that aggregated wealth shall bear its just proportion of taxation, and we regard the recent decision of the Supreme Court relative to the income-tax law as a misinterpretation of the Constitution and an invasion of the rightful powers of Congress over the subject of taxation.

8. We demand that postal savings-banks be established by the Government for the safe deposit of the savings of the people and to facilitate exchange.

RAILROADS AND TELEGRAPHS

1. Transportation being a means of exchange and a public necessity, the Government should own and operate the railroads in the interest of the people and on a non-partisan basis, to the end that all may be accorded the same treatment in transportation, and that the tyranny and political power now exercised by the great railroad corporations, which result in the impairment, if not the destruction of the political rights and personal liberties of the citizens, may be destroyed. Such ownership is to be accomplished gradually, in a manner consistent with sound public policy.

2. The interest of the United States in the public highways built with public moneys, and the proceeds of grants of land to the Pacific railroads, should never be alienated, mortgaged, or sold, but guarded and protected for the general welfare, as provided by the laws organizing such railroads. The foreclosure of existing liens of the United States on these roads should at once follow default in the payment thereof by the debtor

companies; and at the foreclosure sales of said roads the Government shall purchase the same, if it becomes necessary to protect its interests therein, or if they can be purchased at a reasonable price; and the Government shall operate said railroads as public highways for the benefit of the whole people, and not in the interest of the few, under suitable provisions for protection of life and property, giving to all transportation interests equal privileges and equal rates for fares and freight.

3. We denounce the present infamous schemes for refunding these debts, and demand that the laws now applicable thereto be executed and administered according to their intent and spirit.

4. The telegraph, like the Post Office system, being a necessity for the transmission of news, should be owned and operated by the Government in the interest of the people.

THE PUBLIC LANDS

1. True policy demands that the National and State legislation shall be such as will ultimately enable every prudent and industrious citizen to secure a home, and therefore the land should not be monopolized for speculative purposes. All lands now held by railroads and other corporations in excess of their actual needs should by lawful means be reclaimed by the Government and held for actual settlers only, and private land monopoly, as well as alien ownership, should be prohibited.

2. We condemn the land grant frauds by which the Pacific railroad companies have, through the connivance of the Interior Department, robbed multitudes of *bona-fide* settlers of their homes and miners of their claims, and we demand legislation by Congress which will enforce the exemption of mineral land from such grants after as well as before the patent.

3. We demand that *bona-fide* settlers on all public lands be granted free homes, as provided in the National Homestead Law, and that no exception be made in the case of Indian reservations when opened for settlement, and that all lands not now patented come under this demand.

THE REFERENDUM

We favor a system of direct legislation through the initiative and referendum, under proper Constitutional safeguards.

DIRECT ELECTION OF PRESIDENT AND SENATORS BY THE PEOPLE

We demand the election of President, Vice-President, and United States Senators by a direct vote of the people.

SYMPATHY FOR CUBA

We tender to the patriotic people of Cuba our deepest sympathy for their heroic struggle for political freedom and independence, and we believe the time has come when the United States, the great Republic of the world, should recognize that Cuba is, and of right ought to be, a free and independent state.

THE TERRITORIES

We favor home rule in the Territories and the District of Columbia, and the early admission of the Territories as States.

PUBLIC SALARIES

All public salaries should be made to correspond to the price of labor and its products.

EMPLOYMENT TO BE FURNISHED BY GOVERNMENT

In times of great industrial depression, idle labor should be employed on public works as far as practicable.

ARBITRARY JUDICIAL ACTION

The arbitrary course of the courts in assuming to imprison citizens for indirect contempt and ruling by injunction should be prevented by proper legislation.

PENSIONS

We favor just pensions for our disabled Union soldiers.

A FAIR BALLOT

Believing that the elective franchise and an untrammeled ballot are essential to a government of, for, and by the people, the People's party condemns the wholesale system of disfranchisement adopted in some States as unrepublican and undemocratic, and we declare it to be the duty of the several State legislatures to take such action as will secure a full, free and fair ballot and an honest count.

THE FINANCIAL QUESTION "THE PRESSING ISSUE"

While the foregoing propositions constitute the platform upon which our party stands, and for the vindication of which its organization will be maintained, we recognize that the great and pressing issue of the pending campaign, upon which the present election will turn, is the financial question, and upon this great and specific issue between the parties we cordially invite the aid and co-operation of all organizations and citizens agreeing with us upon this vital question.

Prohibition Platform of 1896

We the members of the Prohibition party, in National Convention assembled, renewing our acknowledgment of allegiance to Almighty God as the Rightful Ruler of the Universe, lay down the following as our declaration of political purpose:

PLATFORM

The Prohibition party, in National Convention assembled, declares its firm conviction that the manufacture, exportation, importation and sale of alcoholic beverages has produced such social, commercial, industrial, and political wrongs, and is now so threatening the perpetuity of all our social and political institutions that the suppression of the same by a National party organized therefor, is the greatest object to be accomplished by the voters of our country, and is of such importance that it, of right, ought to control the political actions of all our patriotic citizens until such suppression is accomplished.

The urgency of this cause demands the union without further delay of all citizens who desire the prohibition of the liquor traffic; therefore,

Resolved, That we favor the legal prohibition by State and National legislation of the manufacture, importation, exportation, and interstate transportation and sale of alcoholic beverages; that we declare our purpose to organize and unite all the friends of prohibition into one party, and in order to accomplish this end we deem it but right to leave every Prohibitionist the freedom of his own convictions upon all other political questions, and trust our representatives to take such action upon other political questions as the change occasioned by prohibition and the welfare of the whole people shall demand.

Republican Platform of 1896

The Republicans of the United States, assembled by their representatives in National Convention, appealing for the popular and historical justification of their claims to the matchless achievements of thirty years of Republican rule, earnestly and confidently address themselves to the awakened intelligence, experience and conscience of their countrymen in the following declaration of facts and principles:

For the first time since the civil war the American people have witnessed the calamitous consequence of full and unrestricted Democratic control of the government. It has been a record of unparalleled incapacity, dishonor and disaster. In administrative management it has ruthlessly sacrificed indispensable revenue, entailed an unceasing deficit, eked out ordinary current expenses with borrowed money, piled up the public debt by $262,000,000 in time of peace, forced an adverse balance of trade, kept a perpetual menace hanging over the redemption fund, pawned American credit to alien syndicates and reversed all the measures and results of successful Republican rule. In the broad effect of its policy it has precipitated panic, blighted industry and trade with prolonged depression, closed factories, reduced work and wages, halted enterprise and crippled American production, while stimulating foreign production for the American market. Every consideration of public safety and individual interest demands that the government shall be wrested from the hands of those who have shown themselves incapable of conducting it without disaster at home and dishonor abroad and shall be restored to the party which for thirty years administered it with unequaled success and prosperity. And in this connection, we heartily endorse the wisdom, patriotism and success of the administration of Benjamin Harrison. We renew and emphasize our allegiance to the policy of protection, as the bulwark of American industrial independence, and the foundation of American development and prosperity. This true American policy taxes foreign products and encourages home industry. It puts the burden of revenue on foreign goods; it secures the American market for the American producer. It upholds the American standard of wages for the American workingman; it puts the factory by the side of the farm and makes the American farmer less dependent on foreign demand and price; it diffuses general thrift, and founds the strength of all on the strength of each. In its reasonable application it is just, fair and impartial, equally opposed to foreign control and domestic monopoly to sectional discrimination and individual favoritism.

We denounce the present tariff as sectional, injurious to the public credit and destructive to business enterprise. We demand such an equitable tariff on foreign imports which come into competition with the American products as will not only furnish adequate revenue for the necessary expenses of the Government, but will protect American labor from degradation and the wage level of other lands. We are not pledged to any particular schedules. The question of rates is a practical question, to be governed by the conditions of time and of production. The ruling and uncompromising principle is the protection and development of American labor and industries. The country demands a right settlement, and then it wants rest.

We believe the repeal of the reciprocity arrangements negotiated by the last Republican Administration was a National calamity, and demand their renewal and extension on such terms as will equalize our trade with other nations, remove the restrictions which now obstruct the sale of American products in the ports of other countries, and secure enlarged markets for the products of our farms, forests, and factories.

Protection and Reciprocity are twin measures of American policy and go hand in hand. Democratic rule has recklessly struck down both, and both must be re-established. Protection for what we produce; free admission for the necessaries of life which we do not produce; recriprocal agreement of mutual interests, which gain open markets for us in return for our open markets for others. Protection builds up domestic industry and trade and secures our own market for ourselves; reciprocity builds up foreign trade and finds an outlet for our surplus. We condemn the present administration for not keeping pace [faith] with the sugar producers of this country. The Republican party favors such protection as will lead to the production on American soil of all the sugar which the American people use, and for which they pay other countries more than one hundred million dollars annually. To all our products; to those of the mine and the fields, as well as to those of the shop and the factory, to hemp and wool, the product of the great industry sheep husbandry; as well as to the foundry, as to the mills, we promise the most ample protection. We favor the early American policy of discriminating duties for the upbuilding of our merchant marine. To the protection of our shipping in the foreign-carrying trade, so that American ships, the product of American labor, employed in American ship-yards, sailing under the stars and stripes, and manned, officered and owned by Americans, may regain the carrying of our foreign commerce.

The Republican party is unreservedly for sound money. It caused the enactment of a law providing for the redemption [resumption] of specie payments in 1879. Since then every dollar has been as good as gold. We are unalterably opposed to every measure calculated to debase our currency or impair the credit of our country. We are therefore opposed to the free coinage of silver, except by international agreement with the leading commercial nations of the earth, which agreement we pledge ourselves to promote, and until such agreement can be obtained the existing gold standard must be maintained. All of our silver and paper currency must be maintained at parity with gold, and we favor all measures designated to maintain inviolable the obligations of the United States, of all our money, whether coin or paper, at the present standard, the standard of most enlightened nations of the earth.

The veterans of the Union Armies deserve and should receive fair treatment and generous recognition. Whenever practicable they should be given the preference in the matter of employment. And they are entitled to the enactment of such laws as are best calculated to secure the fulfillment of the pledges made to them in the dark days of the country's peril.

We denounce the practice in the pension bureau so recklessly and unjustly carried on by the present Administration of reducing pensions and arbitrarily dropping names from the rolls, as deserving the severest condemnation of the American people.

Our foreign policy should be at all times firm, vigorous and dignified, and all our interests in the western hemisphere should be carefully watched and guarded.

The Hawaiian Islands should be controlled by the United States, and no foreign power should be permitted to interfere with them. The Nicaragua Canal should be built, owned and operated by the United States. And, by the purchase of the Danish Islands we should secure a much needed Naval station in the West Indies.

The massacres in Armenia have aroused the deep sympathy and just indignation of the American people, and we believe that the United States should exercise all the influence it can properly exert to bring these atrocities to an end. In Turkey, American residents have been exposed to gravest [grievous] dangers and American property destroyed. There, and everywhere, American citizens and American property must be absolutely protected at all hazards and at any cost.

We reassert the Monroe Doctrine in its full extent, and we reaffirm the rights of the United States to give the Doctrine effect by responding to the appeal of any American State for friendly intervention in case of European encroachment.

We have not interfered and shall not interfere, with the existing possession of any European power in this hemisphere, and to the ultimate union of all the English speaking parts of the continent by the free consent of its inhabitants; from the hour of achieving their own independence the people of the United States have regarded with sympathy the struggles of other American peoples to free themselves from European domination. We watch with deep and abiding interest the heroic battles of the Cuban patriots against cruelty and oppression, and best hopes go out for the full success of their determined contest for liberty. The government of Spain, having lost control of Cuba, and being unable to protect the property or lives of resident American citizens, or to comply with its Treaty obligations, we believe that the government of the United States should actively use its influence and good offices to restore peace and give independence to the Island.

The peace and security of the Republic and the maintenance of its rightful influence among the nations of the earth demand a naval power commensurate with its position and responsibilities. We, therefore, favor the continued enlargement of the navy, and a complete system of harbor and sea-coast defenses.

For the protection of the equality of our American citizenship and of the wages of our workingmen, against the fatal competition of low priced labor, we demand that the immigration laws be thoroughly enforced, and so extended as to exclude from entrance to the United States those who can neither read nor write.

The civil service law was placed on the statute book by the Republican party which has always sustained it, and we renew our repeated declarations that it shall be thoroughly and heartily, and honestly enforced, and extended wherever practicable.

We demand that every citizen of the United States shall be allowed to cast one free and unrestricted ballot, and that such ballot shall be counted and returned as cast.

We proclaim our unqualified condemnation of the uncivilized and preposterous [barbarous] practice well known as lynching, and the killing of human beings suspected or charged with crime without process of law.

We favor the creation of a National Board of Arbitration to settle and adjust differences which may arise between employers and employed engaged in inter-State commerce.

We believe in an immediate return to the free homestead policy of the Republican party, and urge the passage by Congress of a satisfactory free homestead measure which has already passed the House, and is now pending in the senate.

We favor the admission of the remaining Territories at the earliest practicable date having due regard to the interests of the people of the Territories and of the United States. And the Federal officers appointed for the Territories should be selected from the *bona-fide* residents thereof, and the right of self-government should be accorded them as far as practicable.

We believe that the citizens of Alaska should have representation in the Congress of the United States, to the end that needful legislation may be intelligently enacted.

We sympathize fully with all legitimate efforts to lessen and prevent the evils of intemperance and promote morality. The Republican party is mindful of the rights and interests of women, and believes that they should be accorded equal opportunities, equal pay for equal work, and protection to the home. We favor the admission of women to wider spheres of usefulness and welcome their co-operation in rescuing the country from Democratic and Populist mismanagement and misrule.

Such are the principles and policies of the Republican party. By these principles we will apply it to those policies and put them into execution. We rely on the faithful and considerate judgment of the American people, confident alike of the history of our great party and in the justice of our cause, and we present our platform and our candidates in the full assurance that their selection will bring victory to the Republican party, and prosperity to the people of the United States.

Socialist Labor Platform of 1896

The Socialist Labor Party of the United States, in Convention assembled, re-asserts the inalienable right of all men to life, liberty, and the pursuit of happiness.

With the founders of the American Republic, we hold that the purpose of government is to secure every citizen in the enjoyment of this right; but in the light of our social conditions, we hold furthermore, that no such right can be exercised under a system of economic inequality, essentially destructive of life, of liberty, and of happiness.

With the founders of this Republic, we hold that the true theory of politics is that the machinery of government must be owned and controlled by the whole people; but in the light of our industrial development we hold, furthermore, that the true theory of economics is that the machinery of production must likewise belong to the people in common.

To the obvious fact that our despotic system of economics is the direct opposite of our democratic system of politics, can plainly be traced the existence of a privileged class, the corruption of government by that class, the alienation of public property, public franchises and public functions to that class, and the abject dependence of the mightiest of nations upon that class.

Again, through the perversion of democracy to the ends of plutocracy, labor is robbed of the wealth which it alone produces, is denied the means of self-employment, and, by compulsory idleness in wage slavery, is even deprived of the necessaries of life.

Human power and natural forces are thus wasted, that the plutocracy may rule.

Ignorance and misery, with all their concomitant evils, are perpetuated, that the people may be kept in bondage.

Science and invention are diverted from their humane purpose, to the enslavement of women and children.

Against such a system the Socialist Labor Party once more enters its protest. Once more it reiterates its fundamental declaration that private property in the natural sources of production and in the instruments of labor is the obvious cause of all economic servitude and political dependence.

The time is fast coming, when, in the natural course of social evolution, this system, through the destructive action of its failures and crises on one hand, and the constructive tendencies of its trusts and other capitalistic combinations on the other hand, shall have worked out its own downfall.

We, therefore, call upon the wage-workers of the United States, and upon all other honest citizens, to organize under the banner of the Socialist Labor Party into a class-conscious body, aware of its rights and determined to conquer them by taking possession of the public powers, so that, held together by an indomitable spirit of solidarity under the most trying conditions of the present class struggle, we may put a summary end to that barbarous struggle by the abolition of classes, the restoration of the land and of all the means of production, transportation and distribution to the people as a collective body, and the substitution of the Co-operative Commonwealth for the present state of planless production, industrial war, and social disorder; a commonwealth in which every worker shall have the free exercise and full benefit of his faculties, multiplied by all modern factors of civilization.

RESOLUTIONS

With a view to immediate improvement in the condition of labor we present the following demands:

1. Reduction of the hours of labor in proportion to the progress of production.

2. The United States to obtain possession of the mines, railroads, canals, telegraphs, telephones, and all other means of public transportation and communication; the employees to operate the same co-operatively under control of the Federal Government and to elect their own superior officers, but no employee shall be discharged for political reasons.

3. The municipalities to obtain possession of the local railroads, ferries, water-works, gas-works, electric plants, and all industries requiring municipal franchises; the employees to operate the same co-operatively under control of the municipal administration and to elect their own superior officers, but no employees shall be discharged for political reasons.

4. The public land to be declared inalienable. Revocation of all land grants to corporations or individuals, the conditions of which have not been complied with.

5. The United States to have the exclusive right to issue money.

6. Congressional legislation providing for the scientific management of forests and waterways, and prohibiting the waste of the natural resources of the country.

7. Inventions to be free to all; the inventors to be remunerated by the nation.

8. Progressive income tax and tax on inheritances; the smaller incomes to be exempt.

9. School education of all children under fourteen years of age to be compulsory, gratuitous and accessible to all by public assistance in meals, clothing, books, etc., where necessary.

10. Repeal of all pauper, tramp, conspiracy, and sumptuary laws. Unabridged right of combination.

11. Prohibition of the employment of children of school age and the employment of female labor in occupations detrimental to health or morality. Abolition of the convict labor contract system.

12. Employment of the unemployed by the public authorities (county, city, State and Nation).

13. All wages to be paid in lawful money of the United States. Equalization of women's wages to those of men where equal service is performed.

14. Laws for the protection of life and limb in

all occupations, and an efficient employer's liability law.

15. The people to have the right to propose laws and to vote upon all measures of importance, according to the referendum principle.

16. Abolition of the veto power of the Executive (National, State, or Municipal), wherever it exists.

17. Abolition of the United States Senate and all upper legislative chambers.

18. Municipal self-government.

19. Direct vote and secret ballots in all elections. Universal and equal right of suffrage without regard to color, creed, or sex. Election days to be legal holidays. The principle of proportional representative [sic] to be introduced.

20. All public officers to be subject to recall by their respective constituencies.

21. Uniform civil and criminal law throughout the United States. Administration of justice to be free of charge. Abolition of capital punishment.

CAMPAIGN OF 1900

In 1900, the Republicans unanimously renominated President McKinley on the first ballot and chose Theodore Roosevelt, governor of New York, to be the vice-presidential candidate (Vice-President Hobart had died in 1899). The Democrats, more united than in 1896, again nominated William Jennings Bryan, this time without opposition. Adlai Stevenson of Illinois, who had been vice-president under Grover Cleveland, was renominated for that office. The currency, imperialism, and the place of corporations in American society were the principal issues of the year.

The minor parties were divided. The Populist Party, its issues largely preempted by the Democrats, was declining in appeal. One of its wings, the Fusionists, endorsed Bryan and Stevenson. The Anti-Fusionist faction (middle-of-the-road) selected Wharton Barker of Pennsylvania for president and Ignatius Donnelly of Minnesota for vice-president. The Socialist Labor Party, following Marxist Daniel DeLeon, continued its campaign, nominating Joseph F. Malloney of Massa-chusetts to head its ticket and Valentine Remmel of Pennsylvania as his running mate. Dissenting Socialist Laborites created the Social Democratic Party and nominated Eugene V. Debs of Indiana and Job Harriman of California as their ticket. Some dissident Republicans who supported the coinage of free silver established a party called the Silver Republican Party and also endorsed Bryan and Stevenson. The Prohibitionists nominated John Granville Woolley of Illinois for president and Henry Brewer Metcalf of Rhode Island for vice-president.

After a spirited campaign, McKinley again was elected over Bryan—this time by nearly a million popular votes. McKinley had 7,218,039 to 6,358,345 for Bryan (150,000 less than in 1896). Woolley polled 209,004 votes; Wharton received 50,000 from Populists who refused to support the Democratic ticket; the Socialist Labor Party ran about as well as it had in 1896; and Eugene Debs attracted 86,935 ballots. McKinley received 292 electoral votes to 155 for Bryan.

Democratic Platform of 1900

We, the representatives of the Democratic party of the United States assembled in National Convention, on the Anniversary of the adoption of the Declaration of Independence, do reaffirm our faith in that immortal proclamation of the inalienable rights of man, and our allegiance to the Constitution framed in harmony therewith by the fathers of the Republic. We hold with the United States Supreme Court that the Declaration of Independence is the spirit of our government, of which the Constitution is the form and letter.

We declare again that all governments instituted among men derive their just powers from the consent of the governed; that any government not based upon the consent of the governed is a tyranny; and that to impose upon any people a government of force is to substitute the methods of imperialism for those of a republic. We hold that the Constitution follows the flag, and denounce the doctrine that an Executive or Congress deriving their existence and their powers from the Constitution can exercise lawful authority beyond it or in violation of it. We assert that no nation can long endure half republic and half empire, and we warn the American people that imperialism abroad will lead quickly and inevitably to despotism at home.

Believing in these fundamental principles, we denounce the Porto Rican law, enacted by a Republican Congress against the protest and opposition of the Democratic minority, as a bold and open violation of the nation's organic law and a flagrant breach of the national good faith. It imposes upon the people of Porto Rico a government without their consent and taxation without representation. It dishonors the American people by repudiating a solemn pledge made in their behalf by the Commanding General of our Army, which the Porto Ricans welcomed to a peaceful and unresisted occupation of their land. It dooms to poverty and distress a people whose helplessness appeals with peculiar force to our justice and magnanimity. In this, the first act of its imperialistic programme, the Republican party seeks to commit the United States to a colonial policy, inconsistent with republican institutions and condemned by the Supreme Court in numerous decisions.

We demand the prompt and honest fulfillment of our pledge to the Cuban people and the world that the United States has no disposition nor intention to exercise sovereignty jurisdiction, or control over the Island of Cuba, except for its pacification. The war ended nearly two years ago, profound peace reigns over all the island, and still the administration keeps the government of the island from its people, while Republican carpet-bag officials plunder its revenues and exploit the colonial theory, to the disgrace of the American people.

We condemn and denounce the Philippine policy of the present administration. It has involved the Republic in an unnecessary war, sacrificed the lives of many of our noblest sons, and placed the United States, previously known and applauded throughout the world as the champion of freedom, in the false and un-American position of crushing with military force the efforts of our former allies to achieve liberty and self-government. The Filipinos cannot be citizens without endangering our civilization; they cannot be subjects without imperiling our form of government; and as we are not willing to surrender our civilization nor to convert the Republic into an empire, we favor an immediate declaration of the nation's purpose to give the Filipinos, first, a stable form of government; second, independence; and third, protection from outside interference, such as has been given for nearly a century to the republics of Central and South America.

The greedy commercialism which dictated the Philippine policy of the Republican administration attempts to justify it with the plea that it will pay; but even this sordid and unworthy plea fails when brought to the test of facts. The war of "criminal aggression" against the Filipinos, entailing an annual expense of many millions, has already cost more than any possible profit that could accrue from the entire Philippine trade for years to come. Furthermore, when trade is extended at the expense of liberty, the price is always too high.

We are not opposed to territorial expansion when it takes in desirable territory which can be erected into States in the Union, and whose people are willing and fit to become American citizens. We favor trade expansion by every peaceful and legitimate means. But we are unalterably opposed to seizing or purchasing distant islands to be governed outside the Constitution, and whose people can never become citizens.

We are in favor of extending the Republic's influence among the nations, but we believe that that influence should be extended not by force and violence, but through the persuasive power of a high and honorable example.

The importance of other questions, now pending before the American people is no wise diminished and the Democratic party takes no backward step from its position on them, but the burning issue of imperialism growing out of the Spanish war involves the very existence of the Republic and the destruction of our free institutions. We regard it as the paramount issue of the campaign.

The declaration in the Republican platform adopted at the Philadelphia Convention, held in June, 1900, that the Republican party "steadfastly adheres to the policy announced in the Monroe Doctrine" is manifestly insincere and deceptive. This profession is contradicted by the avowed policy of that party in opposition to the spirit of the Monroe Doctrine to acquire and hold sovereignty over large areas of territory and large numbers of people in the Eastern Hemisphere. We insist on the strict maintenance of the Monroe Doctrine in all its integrity, both in letter and in spirit, as necessary to prevent the extension of European authority on this Continent and as essential to our supremacy in American affairs. At the same time we declare that no American people shall ever be held by force in unwilling subjection to European authority.

We oppose militarism. It means conquest abroad and intimidation and oppression at home. It means the strong arm which has ever been fatal to free institutions. It is what millions of our citizens have fled from in Europe. It will impose upon our peace loving people a large standing army and unnecessary burden of taxation, and will be a constant menace to their liberties. A small standing army and a well-disciplined state militia are amply sufficient in time of peace. This republic has no place for a vast military establishment, a sure forerunner of compulsory military service and conscription. When the nation is in danger the volunteer soldier is his country's best defender. The National Guard of the United States should ever be cherished in the patriotic hearts of a free people. Such organizations are ever an element of strength and safety. For the first time in our history, and coeval with the Philippine conquest, has there been a wholesale departure from our time honored and approved system of volunteer organization. We denounce it as un-American, un-Democratic, and un-Republican, and as a subversion of the ancient and fixed principles of a free people.

Private monopolies are indefensible and intolerable. They destroy competition, control the price of all material, and of the finished product, thus robbing both producer and consumer. They lessen the employment of labor, and arbitrarily fix the terms and conditions thereof; and deprive individual energy and small capital of their opportunity of betterment.

They are the most efficient means yet devised for appropriating the fruits of industry to the benefit of the few at the expense of the many, and unless their insatiate greed is checked, all wealth will be aggregated in a few hands and the Republic destroyed. The dishonest paltering with the trust evil by the Republican party in State and national platforms is conclusive proof of the truth of the charge that trusts are the legitimate product of Republican policies, that they are fostered by Republican laws, and that they are protected by the Republican administration, in return for campaign subscriptions and political support.

We pledge the Democratic party to an unceasing warfare in nation, State and city against private monopoly in every form. Existing laws against trusts must be enforced and more stringent ones must be enacted providing for publicity as to the affairs of corporations engaged in inter-State commerce requiring all corporations to show, before doing business outside the State of their origin, that they have no water in their stock, and that they have not attempted, and are not attempting, to monopolize any branch of business or the production of any articles of merchandise;

and the whole constitutional power of Congress over inter-State commerce, the mails and all modes of inter-State communication, shall be exercised by the enactment of comprehensive laws upon the subject of trusts. Tariff laws should be amended by putting the products of trusts upon the free list, to prevent monopoly under the plea of protection. The failure of the present Republican administration, with an absolute control over all the branches of the national government, to enact any legislation designed to prevent or even curtail the absorbing power of trusts and illegal combinations, or to enforce the anti-trust laws already on the statute-books proves that insincerity of the high-sounding phrases of the Republican platform.

Corporations should be protected in all their rights and their legitimate interests should be respected, but any attempt by corporations to interfere with the public affairs of the people or to control the sovereignty which creates them, should be forbidden under such penalties as will make such attempts impossible.

We condemn the Dingley tariff law as a trust breeding measure, skillfully devised to give the few favors which they do not deserve, and to place upon the many burdens which they should not bear.

We favor such an enlargement of the scope of the inter-State commerce law as will enable the commission to protect individuals and communities from discrimination, and the public from unjust and unfair transportation rates.

We reaffirm and indorse the principles of the National Democratic Platform adopted at Chicago in 1896, and we reiterate the demand of that platform for an American financial system made by the American people for themselves, and which shall restore and maintain a bi-metallic price-level, and as part of such system the immediate restoration of the free and unlimited coinage of silver and gold at the present legal ratio of 16 to 1, without waiting for the aid or consent of any other nation.

We denounce the currency bill enacted at the last session of Congress as a step forward in the Republican policy which aims to discredit the sovereign right of the National Government to issue all money, whether coin or paper, and to bestow upon national banks the power to issue and control the volume of paper money for their own benefit. A permanent national bank currency, secured by government bonds, must have a permanent debt to rest upon, and, if the bank currency is to increase with population and business, the debt must also increase. The Republican currency scheme is, therefore, a scheme for fastening upon the taxpayers a perpetual and growing debt for the benefit of the banks. We are opposed to this private corporation paper circulated as money, but without legal tender qualities, and demand the retirement of national bank notes as fast as government paper or silver certificates can be substituted for them.

We favor an amendment to the Federal Constitution, providing for the election of United States Senators by direct vote of the people, and we favor direct legislation wherever practicable.

We are opposed to government by injunction; we denounce the blacklist, and favor arbitration as a means of settling disputes between corporations and their employees.

In the interest of American labor and the uplifting of the workingman, as the cornerstone of the prosperity of our country, we recommend that Congress create a Department of Labor, in charge of a secretary, with a seat in the Cabinet, believing that the elevation of the American laborer will bring with it increased production and increased prosperity to our country at home and to our commerce abroad.

We are proud of the courage and fidelity of the American soldiers and sailors in all our wars; we favor liberal pensions to them and their dependents, and we reiterate the position taken in the Chicago platform of 1896, that the fact of enlistment and service shall be deemed conclusive evidence against disease and disability before enlistment.

We favor the immediate construction, ownership and control of the Nicaraguan Canal by the United States, and we denounce the insincerity of the plank in the Republican National Platform for an Isthmian Canal in face of the failure of the Republican majority to pass the bill pending in Congress.

We condemn the Hay-Pauncefote treaty as a surrender of American rights and interests not to be tolerated by the American people.

We denounce the failure of the Republican party to carry out its pledges to grant statehood to the territories of Arizona, New Mexico and Oklahoma, and we promise the people of those territories immediate statehood and home rule during their condition as territories, and we favor home rule and a territorial form of government for Alaska and Porto Rico.

We favor an intelligent system of improving the arid lands of the West, storing the waters for the purpose of irrigation, and the holding of such lands for actual settlers.

We favor the continuance and strict enforcement of the Chinese exclusion law, and its application to the same classes of all Asiatic races.

Jefferson said: "Peace, commerce and honest friendship with all nations; entangling alliance with none." We approve this wholesome doctrine, and earnestly protest against the Republican departure which has involved us in so-called world politics, including the diplomacy of Europe and the intrigue and land-grabbing of Asia, and we especially condemn the ill-concealed Republican alliance with England, which must mean discrimination against other friendly nations, and which has already stifled the nation's voice while liberty is being strangled in Africa.

Believing in the principles of self-government and rejecting, as did our forefathers, the claim of monarchy, we view with indignation the purpose of England to overwhelm with force the South African Republics. Speaking, as we believe, for the entire American nation, except its Republican office-holders and for all freemen everywhere, we extend our sympathies to the heroic burghers in their unequal struggle to maintain their liberty and independence.

We denounce the lavish appropriations of recent Republican Congresses, which have kept taxes high and which threaten the perpetuation of the oppressive war levies. We oppose the accumulation of a surplus to be squandered in such barefaced frauds upon the taxpayers as the shipping subsidy bill, which, under the false pretense of prospering American shipbuilding, would put unearned millions into the pockets of favorite contributors to the Republican campaign fund. We favor the reduction and speedy repeal of the war taxes, and a return to the time-honored Democratic policy of strict economy in governmental expenditures.

Believing that our most cherished institutions are in great peril, that the very existence of our constitutional republic is at stake, and that the decision now to be rendered will determine whether or not our children are to enjoy these blessed privileges of free government, which have made the United States great, prosperous and honored, we earnestly ask for the foregoing declaration of principles, the hearty support of the liberty-loving American people, regardless of previous party affiliations.

People's (Fusion Faction) Platform of 1900

The People's party of the United States, in convention assembled, congratulating its supporters on the wide extension of its principles in all directions, does hereby reaffirm its adherence to the fundamental principles proclaimed in its two prior platforms and calls upon all who desire to avert the subversion of free institutions by corporate and imperialistic power to unite with it in bringing the Government back to the ideals of Washington, Jefferson, Jackson, and Lincoln.

It extends to its allies in the struggle for financial and economic freedom, assurances of its loyalty to the principles which animate the allied forces and the promise of honest and hearty cooperation in every effort for their success.

To the people of the United States we offer the following platform as the expression of our unalterable convictions:

That we denounce the act of March 14, 1900, as the culmination of a long series of conspiracies to deprive the people of their constitutional rights over the money of the nation and relegate to a gigantic money trust the control of the purse and hence of the people.

We denounce this act, first, for making all money obligations, domestic and foreign, payable in gold coin or its equivalent, thus enormously increasing the burdens of the debtors and enriching the creditors.

For refunding "coin bonds" not to mature for years into long-time gold bonds, so as to make their payment improbable and our debt perpetual.

For taking from the Treasury over $50,000,000 in a time of war and presenting it, at a premium, to bond-holders, to accomplish the refunding of bonds not due.

For doubling the capital of bankers by returning to them the face value of their bonds in current money notes so that they may draw one interest from the Government and another from the people.

For allowing banks to expand and contract their circulation at pleasure, thus controlling prices of all products.

For authorizing the Secretary of the Treasury to issue new gold bonds to an unlimited amount whenever he deems it necessary to replenish the gold hoard, thus enabling usurers to secure more bonds and more bank currency by drawing gold from the Treasury, thereby creating an "endless chain" for perpetually adding to a perpetual debt.

For striking down the greenback in order to force the people to borrow $346,000,000 more from the banks at an annual cost of over $20,000,000.

While barring out the money of the Constitution this law opens the printing mints of the Treasury to the free coinage of bank paper money, to enrich the few and impoverish the many.

We pledge anew the People's party never to cease the agitation until this great financial conspiracy is blotted from the statute-books, the Lincoln greenback restored, the bonds all paid, and all corporation money forever retired.

We affirm the demand for the reopening of the mints of the United States to the free and unlimited coinage of silver and gold at the present legal ratio of 16 to 1, the immediate increase in the volume of silver coins and certificates thus created to be substituted, dollar for dollar, for the bank notes issued by private corporations under special privilege granted by law of March 14, 1900, and prior National banking laws, the remaining portion of the bank notes to be replaced with full legal-tender Government paper money, and its volume so controlled as to maintain at all times a stable money market and a stable price-level.

We demand a graduated income and inheritance tax, to the end that aggregated wealth shall bear its just proportion of taxation.

We demand that postal savings banks be established by the Government for the safe deposit of the savings of the people and to facilitate exchange.

With Thomas Jefferson we declare the land, including all natural sources of wealth, the inalienable heritage of the people. Government should so act as to secure homes for the people and prevent land monopoly. The original homestead policy should be enforced, and future settlers upon the public domain should be entitled to a free homestead, while all who have paid an acreage price to the Government under existing laws should have their homestead rights restored.

Transportation being a means of exchange and a public necessity, the Government should own and operate the railroads in the interest of the people and on a non-partisan basis, to the end that all may be accorded the same treatment in transportation, and that the extortion, tyranny, and political power now exercised by the great railroad corporations, which result in the impairment, if not the destruction, of the political rights and personal liberties of the citizen, may be destroyed. Such ownership is to be accomplished in a manner consistent with sound public policy.

Trusts, the overshadowing evil of the age, are the result and culmination of the private ownership and control of the three great instruments of commerce—money, transportation, and the means of transmission of information—which instruments of commerce are public functions, and which our forefathers declared in the Constitution should be controlled by the people through their Congress for the public welfare. The one remedy for the trusts is that the ownership and control be assumed and exercised by the people.

We further demand that all tariffs on goods controlled by a trust shall be abolished.

To cope with the trust evil, the people must act directly, without the intervention of representatives, who may be controlled or influenced. We therefore demand direct legislation, giving the people the law-making and veto power under the initiative and referendum. A majority of the people can never be corruptly influenced.

Applauding the valor of our army and navy in the Spanish war, we denounce the conduct of the Administration in changing a war for humanity into a war of conquest. The action of the Administration in the Philippines is in conflict with all the precedents of our National life; at war with the Declaration of Independence, the Constitution, and the plain precepts of humanity. Murder and arson have been our response to the appeals of the people who asked only to establish a free government in their own land. We demand a stoppage of this war of extermination by the assurance to the Philippines of independence and protection under a stable government of their own creation.

The Declaration of Independence, the Constitution, and the American flag are one and inseparable. The island of Porto Rico is a part of the territory of the United States, and by levying special and extraordinary customs duties on the commerce of that island the Administration has violated the Constitution, abandoned the fundamental principles of American liberty, and has striven to give the lie to the contention of our forefathers that there should be no taxation without representation.

Out of the Imperialism which would force an undesired domination on the people of the Philippines springs the un-American cry for a large standing army. Nothing in the character or purposes of our people justifies us in ignoring the plain lesson of history and putting our liberties in jeopardy by assuming the burden of militarism, which is crushing the people of the Old World. We denounce the Administration for its sinister efforts to substitute a standing army for the citizen soldiery, which is the best safeguard of the Republic.

We extend to the brave Boers of South Africa our sympathy and moral support in their patriotic struggle for the right of self-government, and we are unalterably opposed to any alliance, open or covert, between the United States and any other nation that will tend to the destruction of human liberty.

And a further manifestation of imperialism is to be found in the mining districts of Idaho. In the Cœur d'Alene soldiers have been used to overawe miners striving for a greater measure of industrial independence. And we denounce the State Government of Idaho and the Federal Government for employing the military arm of the Government to abridge the civil rights of the people, and to enforce an infamous permit system which denies to laborers their inherent liberty and compels them to forswear their manhood and their right before being permitted to seek employment.

The importation of Japanese and other laborers under contract to serve monopolistic corporations is a notorious and flagrant violation of the immigration laws. We demand that the Federal Government shall take cognizance of this menacing evil and repress it under existing laws. We further pledge ourselves to strive for the enactment of more stringent laws for the exclusion of Mongolian and Malayan immigration.

We indorse municipal ownership of public utilities, and declare that the advantages which have accrued to the public under that system would be multiplied a hundredfold by its extension to natural inter-State monopolies.

We denounce the practice of issuing injunctions in the cases of dispute between employers and employees, making criminal acts by organizations which are not criminal when performed by individuals, and demand legislation to restrain the evil.

We demand that United States Senators and all other officials as far as practicable be elected by direct vote of the people, believing that the elective franchise and untrammeled ballot are essential to a government for and by the people.

The People's party condemns the wholesale system of disfranchisement by coercion and intimidation, adopted in some States, as un-republican and un-democratic. And we declare it to be the duty of the several State Legislatures to take such action as will secure a full, free, and fair ballot, and an honest count.

We favor home rule in the Territories and the District of Columbia, and the early admission of the Territories as States.

We denounce the expensive red-tape system, political favoritism, cruel and unnecessary delay and criminal evasion of the statutes in the management of the Pension Office, and demand the simple and honest execution of the law, and the fulfillment by the nation of its pledges of service pension to all its honorably discharged veterans.

People's (Middle-of-the-Road Faction) Platform of 1900

The People's party of the United States, assembled in National Convention this 10th day of May, 1900, affirming our unshaken belief in the cardinal tenets of the People's party as set forth in the Omaha platform, and pledging ourselves anew to continue advocacy of those grand principles of human liberty, until right shall triumph over might and love over greed, do adopt and proclaim this declaration of faith:

We demand the initiative and referendum, and the imperative mandate for such changes of existing fundamental and statute law as will enable the people in their sovereign capacity to propose and compel the enactment of such laws as they desire, to reject such as they deem injurious to their interests, and to recall unfaithful public servants.

We demand the public ownership and operation of those means of communication, transportation, and production which the people may elect, such as railroads, telegraph and telephone lines, coal mines, etc.

The land, including all natural sources of wealth, is a heritage of the people and should not be monopolized for speculative purposes, and alien ownership of land should be prohibited. All lands now held by railroads and other corporations in excess of their actual needs, and all lands now owned by aliens, should be reclaimed by the Government and held for actual settlers only.

A scientific and absolute paper money, based upon the entire wealth and population of the nation, not redeemable in any specific commodity, but made a full legal tender for all debts, and receivable for all taxes and public dues, and issued by the Government only without the intervention of banks, and in sufficient quantity to meet the demands of commerce, is the best currency that can be devised, but until such a financial system is secured, which we shall press for adoption, we favor the free and unlimited coinage of both silver and gold at the legal ratio of 16 to 1.

We demand the levy and collection of a graduated tax on incomes and inheritances, and a constitutional amendment to secure the same, if necessary.

We demand the election of President, Vice-President, Federal Judges, and United States Senators by direct vote of the people.

We are opposed to trusts, and declare the contention between the old parties on the monopoly question is a sham battle, and that no solution of this mighty problem is possible without the adoption of the principles of public ownership of public utilities.

Prohibition Platform of 1900

Preamble

The National Prohibition party, in convention represented, at Chicago, June 27 and 28, 1900, acknowledge Almighty God as the Supreme Source of all just government. Realizing that this Republic was founded upon Christian principles and can endure only as it embodies justice and righteousness, and asserting that all authority should seek the best good of all the governed, to this end wisely prohibiting what is wrong and permitting only what is right, hereby records and proclaims:

First—We accept and assert the definition given by Edmund Burke, that "a party is a body of men joined together for the purpose of promoting, by their joint endeavor, the national interest upon some particular principle upon which they are all agreed."

We declare that there is no principle now advocated, by any other party, which could be made a fact in government with such beneficent moral and material results as the principle of prohibition, applied to the beverage liquor traffic; that the national interest could be promoted in no other way so surely and widely as by its adoption and assertion through a National policy, and the cooperation therein by every State, forbidding the manufacture, sale, exportation, importation, and transportation of intoxicating liquors for beverage purposes; that we stand for this as the only principle, proposed by any party anywhere, for the settlement of a question greater and graver than any other before the American people, and involving more profoundly than any other their moral future, and financial welfare; and that all the patriotic citizenship of this country, agreed upon this principle, however much disagreement there may be as to minor considerations and issues, should stand together at the ballot-box, from this time forward, until prohibition is the established policy of the United States, with a party in power to enforce it and to insure its moral and material benefits.

We insist that such a party, agreed upon this principle and policy, having sober leadership, without any obligation for success to the saloon vote and to those demoralizing political combinations of men and money now allied therewith and suppliant thereto, can successfully cope with all other and lesser problems of government, in legislative halls and in the executive chair, and that it is useless for any party to make declarations in its platforms as to any questions concerning which there may be serious differences of opinion

in its own membership, and as to which, because of such differences, the party could legislate only on a basis of mutual concessions when coming into power.

We submit that the Democratic and Republican parties are alike insincere in their assumed hostility to trusts and monopolies. They dare not and do not attack the most dangerous of them all, the liquor power. So long as the saloon debauches the citizens and breeds the purchasable voter, money will continue to buy its way to power. Break down this traffic, elevate manhood, and a sober citizenship will find a way to control dangerous combinations of capital.

We propose as a first step in the financial problems of the nation to save more than a billion of dollars every year, now annually expended to support the liquor traffic and to demoralize our people. When that is accomplished, conditions will have so improved that, with a clearer atmosphere, the country can address itself to the questions as to the kind and quantity of currency needed.

Second—We reaffirm as true indisputably the declaration of William Windom when Secretary of the Treasury in the cabinet of President Arthur, that "Considered socially, financially, politically, or morally, the licensed liquor traffic is or ought to be the overwhelming issue in American politics," and that "the destruction of this iniquity stands next on the calendar of the world's progress." We hold that the existence of our party presents this issue squarely to the American people, and lays upon them the responsibility of choice between liquor parties, dominated by distillers and brewers, with their policy of saloon-perpetuation, breeding waste, wickedness, woe, pauperism, taxation, corruption and crime, and our one party of patriotic and moral principle, with a policy which defends it from domination by corrupt bosses and which insures it forever against the blighting control of saloon politics.

We face with sorrow, shame, and fear the awful fact that this liquor traffic has a grip on our Government, municipal, State, and National, through the revenue system and saloon sovereignty, which no other party dares to dispute; a grip which dominates the party now in power, from caucus to Congress, from policeman to President, from the rumshop to the White House; a grip which compels the executive to consent that law shall be nullified in behalf of the brewer, that the canteen shall curse our army and spread intemperance across the seas, and that our flag shall wave as the symbol of partnership, at home and abroad, between this Government and the men who defy and defile it for their unholy gain.

Third—We charge upon President McKinley, who was elected to his high office by appeal to Christian sentiment and patriotism almost unprecedented and by a combination of moral influences never before seen in this country, that, by his conspicuous example as a wine-drinker at public banquets and a wine-serving host in the White House, he has done more to encourage the liquor business, to demoralize the temperance habits of young men, and to bring Christian practices and requirements into disrepute, than any other President this republic has had. We further charge upon President McKinley responsibility for the army canteen, with all its dire brood of disease, immorality, sin, and death, in this country, in Cuba, in Porto Rico, and the Philippines; and we insist that by his attitude concerning the canteen, and his apparent contempt for the vast number of petitions and petitioners protesting against it, he has outraged and insulted the moral sentiment of this country in such a manner and to such a degree as calls for its righteous uprising and his indignant and effective rebuke.

We challenge denial of the fact that our Chief Executive, as commander in chief of the military forces of the United States, at any time prior to or since March 2, 1899, could have closed every army saloon, called a canteen, by executive order, as President Hayes in effect did before him, and should have closed them, for the same reasons which actuated President Hayes; we assert that the act of Congress passed March 2, 1899, forbidding the sale of liquor "in any post-exchange or canteen," by any "officer or private soldier" or by "any other person on any premises used for military purposes in the United States," was and is as explicit an act of prohibition as the English language can frame.

We declare our solemn belief that the Attorney-General of the United States in his interpretation of that law, and the Secretary of War in his acceptance of that interpretation and his refusal to enforce the law, were and are guilty of treasonable nullification thereof, and that President McKinley, through his assent to and indorsement of such interpretation and refusal, on the part of officials appointed by and responsible to him, shares responsibility in their guilt; and we record our conviction that a new and serious peril confronts our country, in the fact that its President, at the behest of the beer power, dares and does abrogate a law of Congress, through subordinates removable at will by him and whose acts become his, and thus virtually confesses that laws are to be administered or to be nullified in the interest of a law-defying business, by an Administration under mortgage to such business for support.

Fourth—We deplore the fact that an Administration of this Republic claiming the right and power to carry our flag across seas, and to conquer and annex new territory, should admit its lack of power to prohibit the American saloon on subjugated soil, or should openly confess itself subject to liquor sovereignty under that flag. We are humiliated, exasperated and grieved, by the evidence painfully abundant, that this Administration's policy of expansion is bearing so rapidly its first fruits of drunkenness, insanity, and crime under the hot-house sun of the tropics; and when the president of the first Philippine commission said: "It was unfortunate that we introduced and established the saloon there, to corrupt the natives and to exhibit the vices of our race," we charge the inhumanity and unchristianity of this act upon the Administration of William McKinley and upon the party which elected and would perpetuate the same.

Fifth—We declare that the only policy which the government of the United States can of right uphold as to the liquor traffic, under the national Constitution, upon any territory under the military or civic control of that Government, is the policy of prohibition; that "to establish justice, insure domestic tranquillity, provide for the common defense, promote the general welfare, and secure the blessings of liberty to ourselves and our posterity," as the Constitution provides, the liquor traffic must neither be sanctioned nor tolerated, and that the revenue policy, which makes our Government a partner with distillers and brewers and barkeepers, is a disgrace to our civilization, an outrage upon humanity, and a crime against God.

We condemn the present Administration at Washington because it has repealed the prohibitory laws in Alaska, and has given over the partly civilized tribes there to be the prey of the American grog-shop; and because it has entered upon a license policy in our new possessions by incorporating the same in the recent act of Congress in the code of laws for the government of the Hawaiian Islands.

We call general attention to the fearful fact that exportation of liquors from the United States to the Philippine Islands increased from $337 in 1898 to $467,198 in the first ten months of the fiscal year ending June 30, 1900; and that while our exportation of liquors to Cuba never reached $30,000 a year previous to American occupation of that island, our exports of such liquors to Cuba during the fiscal year of 1899 reached the sum of $629,855.

Sixth—One great religious body (the Baptist) having truly declared of the liquor traffic "that it has no defensible right to exist, that it can never be reformed, and that it stands condemned by its unrighteous fruits as a thing un-Christian, un-American, and perilous utterly to every interest in life"; another great religious body (the Methodist) having as truly asserted, and reiterated that "no political party has a right to expect, nor should receive, the votes of Christian men so long as it stands committed to the license system, or refuses to put itself on record in an attitude of open hostility to the saloon"; other great religious bodies having made similar deliverances, in language plain and unequivocal, as to the liquor traffic and the duty of Christian citizenship in opposition thereto; and the fact being plain and undeniable that the Democratic party stands for license, the saloon, and the canteen, while the Republican party, in policy and administration, stands for the canteen, the saloon and revenue therefrom, we declare ourselves justified in expecting that Christian voters everywhere shall cease their complicity with the liquor curse by refusing to uphold a liquor party, and shall unite themselves with the only party which upholds the prohibition policy, and which for nearly thirty years has been the faithful defender of the church, the State, the home, and the school, against the saloon, its expanders and perpetrators, their actual and persistent foes.

We insist that no differences of belief as to any other question or concern of government should stand in the way of such a union of moral and Christian citizenship as we hereby invite, for the speedy settlement of this paramount moral, industrial, financial and political issue, which our party presents; and we refrain from declaring ourselves upon all minor matters, as to which differences of opinion may exist, that hereby we may offer to the American people a platform so broad that all can stand upon it who desire to see sober citizenship actually sovereign over the allied hosts of evil, sin, and crime, in a government of the people, by the people, and for the people.

We declare that there are but two real parties to-day concerning the liquor traffic—Perpetuationists and Prohibitionists—and that patriotism, Christianity, and every interest of genuine republicanism and of pure democracy, besides the loyal demands of our common humanity, require the speedy union, in one solid phalanx at the ballot-box, of all who oppose the liquor traffic's perpetuation, and who covet endurance for this Republic.

Republican Platform of 1900

The Republicans of the United States, through their chosen representatives, met in National Convention, looking back upon an unsurpassed record of achievement and looking forward into a great field of duty and opportunity, and appealing to the judgment of their countrymen, make these declarations:

The expectation in which the American people, turning from the Democratic party, intrusted power four years ago to a Republican Chief Magistrate and a Republican Congress, has been met and satisfied. When the people then assembled at the polls, after a term of Democratic legislation and administration, business was dead, industry paralyzed and the National credit disastrously impaired. The country's capital was hidden away and its labor distressed and unemployed. The Democrats had no other plan with which to improve the ruinous conditions which they had themselves produced than to coin silver at the ratio of sixteen to one. The Republican party, denouncing this plan as sure to produce conditions even worse than those from which relief was sought, promised to restore prosperity by means of two legislative measures—a protective tariff and a law making gold the standard of value. The people by great majorities issued to the Republican party a commission to enact these laws. This commission has been executed, and the Republican promise is redeemed. Prosperity more general and more abundant than we have ever known has followed these enactments. There is no longer controversy as to the value of any Government obligations. Every American dollar is a gold dollar or its assured equivalent, and American credit stands higher than that of any other nation. Capital is fully employed and labor everywhere is profitably occupied. No single fact can more strikingly tell the story of what Republican Government means to the country than this— That while during the whole period of one hundred and seven years from 1790 to 1897 there was an excess of exports over imports of only $383,028,497, there has been in the short three years of the present Republican administration an excess of exports over imports in the enormous sum of $1,483,537,094.

And while the American people, sustained by this Republican legislation, have been achieving these splendid triumphs in their business and commerce, they have conducted and in victory concluded a war for liberty and human rights. No thought of National aggrandizement tarnished the high purpose with which American standards were unfurled. It was a war unsought and patiently resisted, but when it came the American Government was ready. Its fleets were cleared for action. Its armies were in the field, and the quick and signal triumph of its forces on land and sea bore equal tribute to the courage of American soldiers and sailors, and to the skill and foresight of Republican statesmanship. To ten millions of the human race there was given "a new birth of freedom," and to the American people a new and noble responsibility.

We indorse the administration of William McKinley. Its acts have been established in wisdom and in patriotism, and at home and abroad it has distinctly elevated and extended the influence of the American nation. Walking untried paths and facing unforeseen responsibilities, President McKinley has been in every situation the true American patriot and the upright statesman, clear in vision, strong in judgment, firm in action, always inspiring and deserving the confidence of his countrymen.

In asking the American people to indorse this Republican record and to renew their commission to the Republican party, we remind them of the fact that the menace to their prosperity has always resided in Democratic principles, and no less in the general incapacity of the Democratic party to conduct public affairs. The prime essential of business prosperity is public confidence in the good sense of the Government and in its ability to deal intelligently with each new problem of administration and legislation. That confidence the Democratic party has never earned. It is hopelessly inadequate, and the country's prosperity, when Democratic success at the polls is announced, halts and ceases in mere anticipation of Democratic blunders and failures.

We renew our allegiance to the principle of the gold standard and declare our confidence in the wisdom of the legislation of the Fifty-sixth Congress, by which the parity of all our money and the stability of our currency upon a gold basis has been secured. We recognize that interest rates are a potent factor in production and business activity, and for the purpose of further equalizing and of further lowering the rates of interest, we favor such monetary legislation as will enable the varying needs of the season and of all sections to be promptly met in order that trade may be evenly sustained, labor steadily employed and commerce enlarged. The volume of money in circulation was never so great per capita as it is to-day. We declare our steadfast opposition to the free and unlimited coinage of silver. No measure to that end could be considered which was without the support of the leading commercial countries of the world. However firmly Republican legislation may seem to have secured the country against the peril of base and discredited currency, the election of a Democratic President could not fail to impair the country's credit and to bring once more into question the intention of the American people to maintain upon the gold standard the parity of their money circulation. The Democratic party must be convinced that the American people will never tolerate the Chicago platform.

We recognize the necessity and propriety of the honest co-operation of capital to meet new business conditions and especially to extend our rapidly increasing foreign trade, but we condemn all conspiracies and combinations intended to restrict business, to create monopolies, to limit production, or to control prices; and favor such legislation as will effectively restrain and prevent all such abuses, protect and promote competition and secure the rights of producers, laborers, and all who are engaged in industry and commerce.

We renew our faith in the policy of Protection to American labor. In that policy our industries have been established, diversified and maintained. By protecting the home market competition has been stimulated and production cheapened. Opportunity to the inventive genius of our people has been secured and wages in every department of labor maintained at high rates, higher now than ever before, and always distinguishing our working people in their better conditions of life from those of any competing country. Enjoying the blessings of the American common school, secure in the right of self-government and protected in the occupancy of their own markets, their constantly increasing knowledge and skill have enabled them to finally enter the markets of the world. We favor the associated policy of reciprocity so directed as to open our markets on favorable terms for what we do not ourselves produce in return for free foreign markets.

In the further interest of American workmen we favor a more effective restriction of the immigration of cheap labor from foreign lands, the extension of opportunities of education for working children, the raising of the age limit for child labor, the protection of free labor as against contract convict labor, and an effective system of labor insurance.

Our present dependence upon foreign shipping for nine-tenths of our foreign carrying is a great loss to the industry of this country. It is also a serious danger to our trade, for its sudden withdrawal in the event of European war would seriously cripple our expanding foreign commerce. The National defense and naval efficiency of this country, moreover, supply a compelling reason for legislation which will enable us to recover our former place among the trade-carrying fleets of the world.

The Nation owes a debt of profound gratitude to the soldiers and sailors who have fought its battles, and it is the Government's duty to provide for the survivors and for the widows and orphans of those who have fallen in the country's wars. The pension laws, founded in this just sentiment, should be liberally administered, and preference should be given wherever practicable with respect to employment in the public service, to soldiers and sailors and to their widows and orphans.

We commend the policy of the Republican party in maintaining the efficiency of the civil service. The Administration has acted wisely in its efforts to secure for public service in Cuba, Puerto Rico, Hawaii, and the Philippine Islands, only those whose fitness has been determined by training and experience. We believe that employment in the public service in these territories should be confined as far as practicable to their inhabitants.

It was the plain purpose of the fifteenth amendment to the Constitution, to prevent discrimination on account of race or color in regulating the elective franchise. Devices of State governments, whether by statutory or constitutional enactment, to avoid the purpose of this amendment are revolutionary, and should be condemned.

Public movements looking to a permanent improvement of the roads and highways of the country meet with our cordial approval, and we recommend this subject to the earnest consideration of the people and of the Legislatures of the several states.

We favor the extension of the Rural Free Delivery service wherever its extension may be justified.

In further pursuance of the constant policy of the Republican party to provide free homes on the public domain, we recommend adequate national legislation to reclaim the arid lands of the United States, reserving control of the distribution of water for irrigation to the respective States and territories.

We favor home rule for, and the early admission to statehood of the Territories of New Mexico, Arizona, and Oklahoma.

The Dingley Act, amended to provide sufficient revenue for the conduct of the war, has so well performed its work that it has been possible to reduce the war debt in the sum of $40,000,000. So ample are the Government's revenues and so great is the public confidence in the integrity of its obligations that its newly-funded two per cent bonds sell at a premium. The country is now justified in expecting, and it will be the policy of the Republican party to bring about, a reduction of the war taxes.

We favor the construction, ownership, control and protection of an Isthmian Canal by the Government of the United States. New markets are necessary for the increasing surplus of our farm products. Every effort should be made to open and obtain new markets, especially in the Orient, and the Administration is warmly to be commended for its successful efforts to commit all trading and colonizing nations to the policy of the open door in China.

In the interest of our expanding commerce we recommend that Congress create a Department of Commerce and Industries, in the charge of a Secretary with a seat in the Cabinet. The United States Consular system should be reorganized under the supervision of this new Department upon such a basis of appointment and tenure as will render it still more serviceable to the Nation's increasing trade.

The American Government must protect the person and property of every citizen wherever they are wrongfully violated or placed in peril.

We congratulate the women of America upon their splendid record of public service in the volunteer aid association and as nurses in camp and hospital during the recent campaigns of our armies in the East and West Indies, and we appreciate their faithful co-operation in all works of education and industry.

President McKinley has conducted the foreign affairs of the United States with distinguished credit to the American people. In releasing us from the vexatious conditions of a European alliance for the government of Samoa, his course is especially to be commended. By securing to our undivided control the most important island of the Samoan group and the best harbor in the Southern Pacific, every American interest has been safeguarded.

We approve the annexation of the Hawaiian Islands to the United States.

We commend the part taken by our Government in the Peace Conference at The Hague. We assert our steadfast adherence to the policy announced in the Monroe Doctrine. The provisions of The Hague Convention were wisely regarded when President McKinley tendered his friendly offices in the interest of peace between Great Britain and the South African Republic. While the American Government must continue the policy prescribed by Washington, affirmed by every succeeding President and imposed upon us by The Hague treaty, of non-intervention in

European controversies, the American people earnestly hope that a way may soon be found, honorable alike to both contending parties, to terminate the strife between them.

In accepting by the Treaty of Paris the just responsibility of our victories in the Spanish war, the President and the Senate won the undoubted approval of the American people. No other course was possible than to destroy Spain's sovereignty throughout the West Indies and in the Philippine Islands. That course created our responsibility before the world, and with the unorganized population whom our intervention had freed from Spain, to provide for the maintenance of law and order, and for the establishment of good government and for the performance of international obligations. Our authority could not be less than our responsibility; and wherever sovereign rights were extended it became the high duty of the Government to maintain its authority, to put down armed insurrection and to confer the blessings of liberty and civilization upon all the rescued peoples.

The largest measure of self-government consistent with their welfare and our duties shall be secured to them by law.

To Cuba independence and self-government were assured in the same voice by which war was declared, and to the latter this pledge shall be performed.

The Republican party, upon its history, and upon this declaration of its principles and policies confidently invokes the considerate and approving judgment of the American people.

Silver Republican Platform of 1900

We, the Silver Republican party, in National Convention assembled, declare these as our principles and invite the co-operation of all who agree therewith:

We recognize that the principles set forth in the Declaration of Independence are fundamental and everlastingly true in their application to governments among men. We believe the patriotic words of Washington's farewell to be the words of soberness and wisdom, inspired by the spirit of right and truth. We treasure the words of Jefferson as priceless gems of American statesmanship.

We hold in sacred remembrance the broad philanthropy and patriotism of Lincoln, who was the great interpreter of American history and the great apostle of human rights and of industrial freedom; and we declare, as was declared by the convention that nominated the great emancipator, that the maintenance of the principles promulgated in the Declaration of Independence and embodied in the Federal Constitution, "that all men are created equal; that they are endowed by their Creator with certain inalienable rights; that among these are life, liberty, and the pursuit of happiness; that to secure these rights governments are instituted among men, deriving their just powers from the consent of the governed," is essential to the preservation of our republican institutions.

We declare our adherence to the principle of bimetallism as the right basis of a monetary system under our National Constitution, a principle that found place repeatedly in Republican platforms, from the demonetization of silver in 1873 to the St. Louis Republican Convention in 1896.

Since that convention a Republican Congress and a Republican President, at the dictation of the trusts and money power, have passed and approved a currency bill which in itself is a repudiation of the doctrine of bimetallism advocated theretofore by the President and every great leader of his party.

This currency law destroys the full money power of the silver dollar, provides for the payment of all government obligations and the redemption of all forms of paper money in gold alone; retires the time-honored and patriotic greenbacks, constituting one-sixth of the money in circulation, and surrenders to banking corporations a sovereign function of issuing all paper money, thus enabling these corporations to control the prices of labor and property by increasing or diminishing the volume of money in circulation, thus giving the banks power to create panics and bring disaster upon business enterprises.

The provisions of this currency law making the bonded debt of the Republic payable in gold alone, change the contract between the Government and the bond-holders to the advantage of the latter, and is in direct opposition to the declaration of the Matthews resolution passed by Congress in 1878, for which resolution the present Republican President, then a member of Congress, voted, as did also all leading Republicans, both in the House and Senate.

We declare it to be our intention to lend our efforts to the repeal of this currency law, which not only repudiates ancient and time-honored principles of the American people before the Constitution was adopted, but is violative of the principles of the Constitution itself, and we shall not cease our efforts until there has been established in its place a monetary system based upon the free and unlimited coinage of silver and gold into money at the present legal ratio of 16 to 1 by the independent action of the United States, under which system all paper money shall be issued by the Government and all such money coined or issued shall be a full legal tender in payment of all debts, public and private, without exception.

We are in favor of a graduated tax upon incomes, and if necessary to accomplish this we favor an amendment to the Constitution.

We believe that United States Senators ought to be elected by a direct vote of the people, and we favor such amendment of the Constitution and such legislation as may be necessary to that end.

We favor the maintenance and the extension wherever practicable of the merit system in the public service, appointments to be made according to fitness, competitively ascertained, and public servants to be retained in office only so long as shall be compatible with the efficiency of the service.

Combinations, trusts, and monopolies contrived and arranged for the purpose of controlling the prices and quantity of articles supplied to the public are unjust, unlawful, and oppressive.

Not only do these unlawful conspiracies fix the prices of commodities in many cases, but they invade every branch of the State and National Government with their polluting influence and control the actions of their employees and dependents in private life until their influence actually imperils society and the liberty of the citizen.

We declare against them. We demand the most stringent laws for their destruction and the most severe punishment of their promoters and maintainers and the energetic enforcement of such laws by the courts.

We believe the Monroe doctrine to be sound in principle and a wise National policy, and we demand a firm adherence thereto. We condemn acts inconsistent with it and that tend to make us parties to the interest and to involve us in the controversies of European nations and to recognition by pending treaty, of the right of England to be considered in the construction of an interoceanic canal. We declare that such a canal when constructed ought to be controlled by the United States in the interests of American nations.

We observe with anxiety and regard with disapproval the increasing ownership of American lands by aliens, and their growing control over international transportation, natural resources, and public utilities. We demand legislation to protect our public domain, our natural resources, our franchises, and our internal commerce and to keep them free and maintain their independence of all foreign monopolies, institutions, and influences, and we declare our opposition to the leasing of the public lands of the United States whereby corporations and syndicates will be able to secure control thereof and thus monopolize the public domain, the heritage of the people.

We are in favor of the principles of direct legislation. In view of the great sacrifice made and patriotic services rendered, we are in favor of liberal pensions to deserving soldiers, their widows, orphans, and other dependents. We believe that enlistment and service should be accepted as conclusive proof that the soldier was free from disease and disability at the time of his enlistment. We condemn the present administration of the pension laws.

We tender to the patriotic people of the South African Republic our sympathy and express our admiration for them in their heroic attempts to preserve their political freedom and maintain their national independence. We declare the destruction of those republics and the subjugation of their people to be a crime against civilization.

We believe this sympathy should have been voiced by the American Congress, as was done in the case of the French, the Greeks, the Hungarians, the Polanders, the Armenians, and the Cubans, and as the traditions of this country would have dictated. We declare the Porto Rican Tariff law to be not only a serious but a dangerous departure from the principles of our form of government. We believe in a republican form of government and are opposed to monarchy and to the whole theory of imperialistic control.

We believe in self-government—a government by the consent of the governed—and are unaltera-

bly opposed to a government based upon force. It is clear and certain that the inhabitants of the Philippine archipelago cannot be made citizens of the United States without endangering our civilization. We are, therefore, in favor of applying to the Philippine archipelago the principle we are solemnly and publicly pledged to observe in the case of Cuba.

There no longer being any necessity for collecting war taxes, we demand the repeal of the war taxes levied to carry on the war with Spain.

We favor the immediate admission into the Union of States the Territories of Arizona, New Mexico, and Oklahoma.

We demand that our nation's promises to Cuba shall be fulfilled in every particular.

We believe the National Government should lend every aid, encouragement, and assistance toward the reclamation of the arid lands of the United States, and to that end we are in favor of a comprehensive survey thereof and an immediate ascertainment of the water supply available for such reclamation, and we believe it to be the duty of the General Government to provide for the construction of storage reservoirs and irrigation works so that the water supply of the arid region may be utilized to the greatest possible extent in the interests of the people, while preserving all rights of the State.

Transportation is a public necessity and the means and methods of it are matters of public concern. Railway companies exercise a power over industries, business, and commerce which they ought not to do, and should be made to serve the public interests without making unreasonable charges of unjust discrimination.

We observe with satisfaction the growing sentiment among the people in favor of the public ownership and operation of public utilities.

We are in favor of expanding our commerce in the interests of American labor and for the benefit of all our people, by every honest and peaceful means. Our creed and our history justify the nations of the earth in expecting that wherever the American flag is unfurled in authority human liberty and political freedom will be found. We protest against the adoption of any policy that will change in the thought of the world, the meaning of our flag.

We are opposed to the importation of Asiatic laborers in competition with American labor, and favor a more rigid enforcement of the laws relating thereto.

The Silver Republican party of the United States, in the foregoing principles, seeks to perpetuate the spirit and to adhere to the teachings of Abraham Lincoln.

Social Democratic Platform of 1900

The Social Democratic Party of the United States, in convention assembled, reaffirms its allegiance to the revolutionary principles of International Socialism and declares the supreme political issue in America to-day to be the contest between the working class and the capitalist class for the possession of the powers of government. The party affirms its steadfast purpose to use those powers, once achieved, to destroy wage slavery, abolish the institution of private property in the means of production, and establish the Co-operative Commonwealth.

In the United States, as in all other civilized countries, the natural order of economic development has separated society into two antagonistic classes—the capitalists, a comparatively small class, the possessors of all the means of production and distribution (land, mines, machinery, and means of transportation and communication), and the large and ever-increasing class of wage workers, possessing no means of production.

This economic supremacy has secured to the dominant class the full control of the government, the pulpit, the schools, and the public press; it has thus made the capitalist class the arbiters of the fate of the workers, whom it is reducing to a condition of dependence, economically exploited and oppressed, intellectually and physically crippled and degraded, and their political equality rendered a bitter mockery.

The contest between these two classes grows ever sharper. Hand in hand with the growth of monopolies goes the annihilation of small industries and of the middle class depending upon them; ever larger grows the multitude of destitute wage workers and of the unemployed, and ever fiercer the struggle between the class of the exploiter and the exploited, the capitalists and the wage workers.

The evil effects of capitalist production are intensified by the recurring industrial crises which render the existence of the greater part of the population still more precarious and uncertain.

These facts amply prove that the modern means of production have outgrown the existing social order based on production for profit.

Human energy and natural resources are wasted for individual gain.

Ignorance is fostered that wage slavery may be perpetuated. Science and invention are perverted to the exploitation of men, women, and children.

The lives and liberties of the working class are recklessly sacrificed for profit.

Wars are fomented between nations; indiscriminate slaughter is encouraged; the destruction of whole races is sanctioned, in order that the capitalist class may extend its commercial dominion abroad and enhance its supremacy at home.

The introduction of a new and higher order of society is the historic mission of the working class. All other classes, despite their apparent or actual conflicts, are interested in upholding the system of private ownership in the means of production. The Democratic, Republican, and all other parties which do not stand for the complete overthrow of the capitalist system of production, are alike the tools of the capitalist class.

The workers can most effectively act as a class in their struggle against the collective power of the capitalist class only by constituting themselves into a political party, distinct and opposed to all parties formed by the propertied classes.

We, therefore, call upon the wage-workers of the United States, without distinction of color, race, sex, or creed, and upon all citizens in sympathy with the historic mission of the working class, to organize under the banner of the Social Democratic Party as a party truly representing the interests of the toiling masses and uncompromisingly waging war upon the exploiting class, until the system of wage slavery shall be abolished and the Co-operative Commonwealth established. Pending the accomplishment of this our ultimate purpose, we pledge every effort of the Social Democratic Party for the immediate improvement of the condition of labor and for the securing of its progressive demands.

IMMEDIATE DEMANDS

As steps in that direction, we make the following demands:

First—Revision of our federal constitution, in order to remove the obstacles to complete control of Government by the people irrespective of sex.

Second—The public ownership of all industries controlled by monopolies, trusts, and combines.

Third—The public ownership of all railroads, telegraphs, and telephones; all means of transportation and communication; all water-works, gas and electric plants, and other public utilities.

Fourth—The public ownership of all gold, silver, copper, lead, iron, coal, and other mines, and all oil and gas wells.

Fifth—The reduction of the hours of labor in proportion to increasing facilities of production.

Sixth—The inauguration of a system of public works and improvements for the employment of the unemployed, the public credit to be utilized for that purpose.

Seventh—Useful inventions to be free, the inventors to be remunerated by the public.

Eighth—Labor legislation to be national, instead of local, and international when possible.

Ninth—National insurance of working people against accidents, lack of employment, and want in old age.

Tenth—Equal civic and political rights for men and women, and the abolition of all laws discriminating against women.

Eleventh—The adoption of the initiative and referendum, proportional representation, and the right of recall of representatives by the voters.

Twelfth—Abolition of war and the introduction of international arbitration.

Socialist Labor Platform of 1900

The Socialist Labor Party of the United States in Convention assembled, reasserts the inalienable right of all men to life, liberty, and the pursuit of happiness.

With the founders of the American Republic we hold that the purpose of government is to secure every citizen in the enjoyment of this right; but in the light of our social conditions we hold, furthermore, that no such right can be exercised under a system of economic inequality, essentially destructive of life, of liberty, and of happiness.

With the founders of this Republic, we hold that the true theory of politics is that the machinery of government must be owned and con-trolled by the whole people; but in the light of our industrial development we hold, furthermore, that the true theory of economics is that the machinery of production must likewise belong to the people in common.

To the obvious fact that our despotic system of economics is the direct opposite of our democratic system of politics, can plainly be traced the existence of a privileged class, the corruption of government by that class, the alienation of public property, public franchises and public functions to that class, and the abject dependence of the mightiest of nations upon that class.

Again, through the perversion of democracy to the ends of plutocracy, labor is robbed of the wealth which it alone produces, is denied the means of self-employment, and, by compulsory idleness in wage slavery, is even deprived of the necessaries of life.

Human power and natural forces are thus wasted, that the plutocracy may rule.

Ignorance and misery, with all their concomitant evils, are perpetuated, that the people may be kept in bondage.

Science and invention are diverted from their humane purpose to the enslavement of women and children.

Against such a system the Socialist Labor Party once more enters its protest. Once more it reiterates its fundamental declaration that private property in the natural sources of production and in the instruments of labor is the obvious cause of all economic servitude and political dependence.

The time is fast coming when, in the natural course of social evolution, this system, through the destructive action of its failures and crises on the one hand, and the constructive tendencies of its trusts and other capitalistic combinations on the other hand, shall have worked out its own downfall.

We, therefore, call upon the wage workers of the United States, and upon all other honest citizens, to organize under the banner of the Socialist Labor Party into a class-conscious body, aware of its rights and determined to conquer them by taking possession of the public powers; so that, held together by an indomitable spirit of solidarity under the most trying conditions of the present class struggle, we may put a summary end to that barbarous struggle by the abolition of classes, the restoration of the land and of all the means of production, transportation and distribution to the people as a collective body, and the substitution of the Co-operative Commonwealth for the present state of planless production, industrial war and social disorder; a commonwealth in which every worker shall have the free exercise and full benefit of his faculties, multiplied by all the modern factors of civilization.

CAMPAIGN OF 1904

In 1904 the Republicans unanimously chose President Theodore Roosevelt as their candidate on the first ballot. For his running mate, the delegates nominated Senator Charles W. Fairbanks of Indiana by acclamation. The platform was adopted without opposition. The Democrats, in contrast to their two previous conventions, turned to a conservative, Alton B. Parker, chief justice of the New York Court of Appeals, over the objection of William Jennings Bryan. For vice-president, the convention selected Henry G. Davis, a former senator from West Virginia, who was eighty years of age. At its first national convention, the Socialist Party (the former Social Democratic Party) nominated Eugene V. Debs of Indiana for president and Benjamin Hanford of New York for vice-president. The Populists nominated Thomas E. Watson of Georgia for president and Thomas Tibbles of Nebraska for vice-president.

Silas C. Swallow of Pennsylvania was the presidential candidate of the Prohibition Party, and George W. Carroll of Texas was his running mate. The Socialist Labor Party chose Charles Hunter Corregan of New York for president and William W. Cox of Illinois for vice-president. A moderate faction of the Socialist Labor Party supported Debs.

In the November election, Roosevelt easily defeated Parker, 7,626,593 to 5,082,898 popular votes. Debs received 402,489 votes; Swallow, 258,596; and Watson, representing the former middle-of-the-road Populists, attracted 114,051 votes. Corregan got 33,156 votes. Roosevelt carried all of the northern states for 336 electoral votes. Parker won the solid South, plus Texas, Kentucky, and 7 of the 8 votes in Maryland for a total of 140 electoral ballots.

Democratic Platform of 1904

The Democratic party of the United States, in National Convention assembled, declares its devotion to the essential principles of the Democratic faith which bring us together in party communion.

Under these principles local self-government and National unity and prosperity were alike established. They underlaid our independence, the structure of our free Republic, and every Democratic expansion from Louisiana to California, and Texas to Oregon, which preserved faithfully in all the States the tie between taxation and representation. They yet inspirit the masses of our people, guarding jealously their rights and liberties, and cherishing their fraternity, peace and orderly development. They remind us of our duties and responsibilities as citizens and impress upon us, particularly at this time, the necessity of reform and the rescue of the administration of Government from the headstrong, arbitrary and spasmodic methods which distract business by uncertainty, and pervade the public mind with dread, distrust and perturbation.

FUNDAMENTAL PRINCIPLES

The application of these fundamental principles to the living issues of the day constitutes the first step toward the assured peace, safety and progress of our nation. Freedom of the press, of conscience, and of speech; equality before the law of all citizens; right of trial by jury; freedom of the person defended by the Writ of Habeas Corpus; liberty of personal contract untrammeled by sumptuary laws; supremacy of the civil over military authority; a well-disciplined militia; separation of Church and State; economy in expenditures; low taxes, that labor may be lightly burdened; prompt and sacred fulfillment of public and private obligations; fidelity to treaties; peace and friendship with all nations, entangling alliances with none; absolute acquiescence in the will of the majority, the vital principle of Republics — these are doctrines which Democracy has established as proverbs of the Nation, and they should be constantly invoked, and enforced.

ECONOMY OF ADMINISTRATION

Large reductions can easily be made in the annual expenditures of the Government without impairing the efficiency of any branch of the public service, and we shall insist upon the strictest economy and frugality compatible with vigorous and efficient civil, military and naval administration as a right of the people, too clear to be denied or withheld.

HONESTY IN THE PUBLIC SERVICE

We favor the enforcement of honesty in the public service, and to that end a thorough legislative investigation of those executive departments of the Government already known to teem with corruption, as well as other departments suspected of harboring corruption, and the punishment of ascertained corruptionists without fear or favor or regard to persons. The persistent and deliberate refusal of both the Senate and House of Representatives to permit such investigation to be made demonstrates that only by a change in the executive and in the legislative departments can complete exposure, punishment and correction be obtained.

FEDERAL GOVERNMENT CONTRACTS WITH TRUSTS

We condemn the action of the Republican party in Congress in refusing to prohibit an executive department from entering into contracts with convicted trusts or unlawful combinations in restraint of inter-State trade. We believe that one of the best methods of procuring economy and honesty in the public service is to have public officials, from the occupant of the White House down to the lowest of them, return, as nearly as may be, to Jeffersonian simplicity of living.

EXECUTIVE USURPATION

We favor the nomination and election of a President imbued with the principles of the Constitution, who will set his face sternly against executive usurpation of legislative and judicial functions, whether that usurpation be veiled under the guise of executive construction of existing laws, or whether it take refuge in the tyrant's plea of necessity or superior wisdom.

IMPERIALISM

We favor the preservation, so far as we can, of an open door for the world's commerce in the Orient without unnecessary entanglement in Oriental and European affairs, and without arbitrary, unlimited, irresponsible and absolute government anywhere within our jurisdiction. We oppose, as fervently as did George Washington, an indefinite, irresponsible, discretionary and vague absolutism and a policy of colonial exploitation, no matter where or by whom invoked or exercised. We believe with Thomas Jefferson and John Adams, that no Government has a right to make one set of laws for those "at home" and another and a different set of laws, absolute in their character, for those "in the colonies." All men under the American flag are entitled to the protection of the institutions whose emblem the flag is; if they are inherently unfit for those institutions, then they are inherently unfit to be members of the American body politic. Wherever there may exist a people incapable of being governed under American laws, in consonance with the American Constitution, the territory of that people ought not to be part of the American domain.

We insist that we ought to do for the Filipinos what we have done already for the Cubans, and it is our duty to make that promise now, and upon suitable guarantees of protection to citizens of our own and other countries resident there at the time of our withdrawal to set the Filipino people upon their feet, free and independent, to work out their own destiny.

The endeavor of the Secretary of War, by pledging the Government's endorsement for "promoters" in the Philippine Islands to make the United States a partner in speculative exploitation of the archipelago, which was only temporarily held up by the opposition of Democratic Senators in the last session, will, if successful, lead to entanglements from which it will be difficult to escape.

TARIFF

The Democratic party has been, and will continue to be, the consistent opponent of that class of tariff legislation by which certain interests have been permitted, through Congressional favor, to draw a heavy tribute from the American people. This monstrous perversion of those equal opportunities which our political institutions were established to secure, has caused what may once have been infant industries to become the greatest combinations of capital that the world has ever known. These special favorites of the Government have, through trust methods, been converted into monopolies, thus bringing to an end domestic competition, which was the only alleged check upon the extravagant profits made possible by the protective system. These industrial combinations, by the financial assistance they can give, now control the policy of the Republican party.

We denounce protectionism as a robbery of

the many to enrich the few, and we favor a tariff limited to the needs of the Government economically, effectively and constitutionally administered and so levied as not to discriminate against any industry, class or section, to the end that the burdens of taxation shall be distributed as equally as possible.

We favor a revision and a gradual reduction of the tariff by the friends of the masses and for the common weal, and not by the friend of its abuses, its extortions and its discriminations, keeping in view the ultimate end of "equality of burdens and equality of opportunities," and the constitutional purpose of raising a revenue by taxation, to wit: the support of the Federal Government in all its integrity and virility, but in simplicity.

TRUSTS AND UNLAWFUL COMBINATIONS

We recognize that the gigantic trusts and combinations designed to enable capital to secure more than its just share of the joint product of capital and labor, and which have been fostered and promoted under Republican rule, are a menace to beneficial competition and an obstacle to permanent business prosperity.

A private monopoly is indefensible and intolerable.

Individual equality of opportunity and free competition are essential to a healthy and permanent commercial prosperity; and any trust, combination or monopoly tending to destroy these by controlling production, restricting competition or fixing prices and wages, should be prohibited and punished by law. We especially denounce rebates and discriminations by transportation companies as the most potent agency in promoting and strengthening these unlawful conspiracies against trade.

We demand an enlargement of the powers of the Interstate Commerce Commission, to the end that the traveling public and shippers of this country may have prompt and adequate relief from the abuses to which they are subjected in the matter of transportation. We demand a strict enforcement of existing civil and criminal statutes against all such trusts, combinations and monopolies; and we demand the enactment of such further legislation as may be necessary effectually to suppress them.

Any trust or unlawful combination engaged in inter-State commerce which is monopolizing any branch of business or production, should not be permitted to transact business outside of the State of its origin, whenever it shall be established in any court of competent jurisdiction that such monopolization exists. Such prohibition should be enforced through comprehensive laws to be enacted on the subject.

CAPITAL AND LABOR

We favor the enactment and administration of laws giving labor and capital impartially their just rights. Capital and labor ought not to be enemies. Each is necessary to the other. Each has its rights, but the rights of labor are certainly no less "vested," no less "sacred" and no less "inalienable" than the rights of capital.

We favor arbitration of differences between corporate employers and their employees and a strict enforcement of the eight hour law on all Government work.

We approve the measure which passed the United States Senate in 1896, but which a Republican Congress has ever since refused to enact, relating to contempts in Federal courts and providing for trial by jury in cases of indirect contempt.

CONSTITUTIONAL GUARANTIES

Constitutional guaranties are violated whenever any citizen is denied the right to labor, acquire and enjoy property or reside where interest or inclination may determine. Any denial thereof by individuals, organizations or governments should be summarily rebuked and punished.

We deny the right of any executive to disregard or suspend any constitutional privilege or limitation. Obedience to the laws and respect for their requirements are alike the supreme duty of the citizen and the official.

The military should be used only to support and maintain the law. We unqualifiedly condemn its employment for the summary banishment of citizens without trial, or for the control of elections.

WATERWAYS

We favor liberal appropriations for the care and improvement of the waterways of the country. When any waterway like the Mississippi River is of sufficient importance to demand the special aid of the Government, such aid should be extended with a definite plan of continuous work until permanent improvement is secured.

We oppose the Republican policy of starving home development in order to feed the greed for conquest and the appetite for national "prestige" and display of strength.

RECLAMATION OF ARID LANDS AND DOMESTIC DEVELOPMENT

We congratulate our Western citizens upon the passage of the measure known as the Newlands Irrigation Act for the irrigation and reclamation of the arid lands of the West—a measure framed by a Democrat, passed in the Senate by a non-partisan vote, and passed in the House against the opposition of almost all the Republican leaders by a vote the majority of which was Democratic. We call attention to this great Democratic measure, broad and comprehensive as it is, working automatically throughout all time without further action of Congress, until the reclamation of all the lands in the arid West capable of reclamation, is accomplished, reserving the lands reclaimed for homeseekers in small tracts and rigidly guarding against land monopoly, as an evidence of the policy of domestic development contemplated by the Democratic party, should it be placed in power.

THE ISTHMIAN CANAL

The Democracy when entrusted with power will construct the Panama Canal speedily, honestly and economically, thereby giving to our people what Democrats have always contended for—a great inter-oceanic canal, furnishing shorter and cheaper lines of transportation, and broader and less trammeled trade relations with the other peoples of the world.

AMERICAN CITIZENSHIP

We pledge ourselves to insist upon the just and lawful protection of our citizens at home and abroad, and to use all proper measures to secure for them, whether native born or naturalized, and without distinction of race or creed, the equal protection of laws and the enjoyment of all rights and privileges open to them under the covenants of our treaties of friendship and commerce; and if under existing treaties the right of travel and sojourn is denied to American citizens or recognition is withheld from American passports by any countries on the ground of race or creed, we favor the beginning of negotiations with the governments of such countries to secure by new treaties the removal of these unjust discriminations.

We demand that all over the world a duly authenticated passport issued by the Government of the United States to an American citizen shall be proof of the fact that he is an American citizen and shall entitle him to the treatment due him as such.

ELECTION OF SENATORS BY THE PEOPLE

We favor the election of United States Senators by direct vote of the people.

STATEHOOD FOR TERRITORIES

We favor the admission of the Territory of Oklahoma and the Indian Territory. We also favor the immediate admission of Arizona and New Mexico, as separate States, and territorial governments for Alaska and Porto Rico.

We hold that the officials appointed to administer the government of any Territory, as well as the District of Alaska, should be *bona-fide* residents at the time of their appointment of the Territory or district in which their duties are to be performed.

CONDEMNATION OF POLYGAMY

We demand the extermination of polygamy within the jurisdiction of the United States, and the complete separation of Church and State in political affairs.

MERCHANT MARINE

We denounce the ship subsidy bill recently passed by the United States Senate as an iniquitous appropriation of public funds for private purposes and a wasteful, illogical and useless attempt to overcome by subsidy the obstructions raised by Republican legislation to the growth and development of American commerce on the sea.

We favor the upbuilding of a merchant marine without new or additional burdens upon the people and without bounties from the public treasury.

RECIPROCITY

We favor liberal trade arrangements with Canada, and with peoples of other countries where they can be entered into with benefit to American agriculture, manufactures, mining or commerce.

MONROE DOCTRINE

We favor the maintenance of the Monroe Doctrine in its full integrity.

ARMY

We favor the reduction of the Army and of Army expenditures to the point historically demonstrated to be safe and sufficient.

PENSIONS. OUR SOLDIERS AND SAILORS

The Democracy would secure to the surviving soldiers and sailors and their dependents generous pensions, not by an arbitrary executive order, but by legislation which a grateful people stand ready to enact.

Our soldiers and sailors who defend with their lives the Constitution and the laws have a sacred interest in their just administration. They must, therefore, share with us the humiliation with which we have witnessed the exaltation of court favorites, without distinguished service, over the scarred heroes of many battles, or aggrandizement by executive appropriations out of the treasuries of prostrate peoples in violation of the act of Congress which fixes the compensation of allowance of the military officers.

CIVIL SERVICE

The Democratic party stands committed to the principles of civil service reform, and we demand their honest, just and impartial enforcement.

We denounce the Republican party for its continuous and sinister encroachments upon the spirit and operation of civil service rules, whereby it has arbitrarily dispensed with examinations for office in the interest of favorites, and employed all manner of devices to overreach and set aside the principles upon which the Civil Service is based.

SECTIONAL AND RACE AGITATION

The race question has brought countless woes to this country. The calm wisdom of the American people should see to it that it brings no more.

To revive the dead and hateful race and sectional animosities in any part of our common country means confusion, distraction of business, and the reopening of wounds now happily healed. North, South, East and West have but recently stood together in line of battle from the walls of Pekin to the hills of Santiago, and as sharers of a common glory and a common destiny, we should share fraternally the common burdens.

We therefore deprecate and condemn the Bourbon-like selfish, and narrow spirit of the recent Republican Convention at Chicago which sought to kindle anew the embers of racial and sectional strife, and we appeal from it to the sober common sense and patriotic spirit of the American people.

THE REPUBLICAN ADMINISTRATION

The existing Republican administration has been spasmodic, erratic, sensational, spectacular and arbitrary. It has made itself a satire upon the Congress, courts, and upon the settled practices and usages of national and international law.

It summoned the Congress in hasty and futile extra session and virtually adjourned it, leaving behind in its flight from Washington uncalled calendars and unaccomplished tasks.

It made war, which is the sole power of Congress, without its authority, thereby usurping one of its fundamental prerogatives. It violated a plain statute of the United States as well as plain treaty obligations, international usages and constitutional law; and has done so under pretense of executing a great public policy which could have been more easily effected lawfully, constitutionally and with honor.

It forced strained and unnatural constructions upon statutes, usurping judicial interpretation, and substituting for congressional enactment executive decree.

It withdrew from the Congress its customary duties of investigation which have heretofore made the representatives of the people and the States the terror of evildoers.

It conducted a secretive investigation of its own, and boasting of a few sample convicts, it threw a broad coverlet over the bureaus which had been their chosen field of operative abuses, and kept in power the superior officers under whose administration the crimes had been committed.

It ordered assault upon some monopolies, but paralyzed by a first victory, it flung out the flag of truce and cried out that it would not "run amuck"; leaving its future purposes beclouded by its vacillations.

APPEAL TO THE PEOPLE

Conducting the campaign upon this declaration of our principles and purposes, we invoke for our candidates the support not only of our great and time-honored organization, but also the active assistance of all of our fellow citizens who, disregarding past differences, desire the perpetuation of our constitutional Government as framed and established by the fathers of the Republic.

People's Platform of 1904

The People's party reaffirms its adherence to the basic truths of the Omaha platform of 1892, and of the subsequent platforms of 1896 and 1900. In session in its fourth national convention on July 4, 1904, in the city of Springfield, Ill., it draws inspiration from the day that saw the birth of the nation as well as its own birth as a party, and also from the soul of him who lives at its present place of meeting. We renew our allegiance to the old-fashioned American spirit that gave this nation existence, and made it distinctive among the peoples of the earth. We again sound the key-note of the Declaration of Independence that all men are created equal in a political sense, which was the sense in which that instrument, being a political document, intended that the utterance should be understood. We assert that the departure from this fundamental truth is responsible for the ills from which we suffer as a nation, that the giving of special privileges to the few has enabled them to dominate the many, thereby tending to destroy the political equality which is the corner-stone of democratic government.

Holding fast to the truths of the fathers we vigorously protest against the spirit of mammonism and of thinly veiled monarchy that is invading certain sections of our national life, and of the very administration itself. This is a nation of peace, and we deplore the appeal to the spirit of force and militarism which is shown in ill-advised and vainglorious boasting and in more harmful ways in the denial of the rights of man under martial law.

A political democracy and an industrial despotism cannot exist side by side; and nowhere is this truth more plainly shown than in the gigantic transportation monopolies which have bred all sorts of kindred trusts, subverted the governments of many of the States, or established their official agents in the National Government. We submit that it is better for the Government to own the railroads than for the railroads to own the Government, and that one or the other alternative seems inevitable.

We call the attention of our fellow-citizens to the fact that the surrender of both of the old parties to corporative influences leaves the People's party the only party of reform in the nation.

Therefore we submit the following platform of principles to the American people:—

The issuing of money is a function of government, and should never be delegated to corporations or individuals. The Constitution gives to Congress alone power to issue money and regulate its value.

We therefore demand that all money shall be issued by the Government in such quantity as shall maintain a stability in prices, every dollar to be full legal tender, none of which shall be a debt redeemable in other money.

We demand that postal-savings banks be established by the Government for the safe deposit of the savings of the people.

We believe in the right of labor to organize for the benefit and protection of those who toil; and pledge the efforts of the People's party to preserve this right inviolate. Capital is organized and has no right to deny to labor the privilege which it claims for itself. We feel that intelligent organization of labor is essential; that it raises the standard of workmanship; promotes the efficiency, intelligence, independence and character of the wage earner. We believe with Abraham Lincoln that labor is prior to capital, and is not its slave, but its companion, and we plead for that broad spirit of toleration and justice which will promote industrial peace through the observance of the principles of voluntary arbitration.

We favor the enactment of legislation looking to the improvement of conditions for wage earners, the abolition of child labor, the suppression of sweat shops, and of convict labor in competition with free labor, and the exclusion from American shores of foreign pauper labor.

We favor the shorter work day, and declare that if eight hours constitute a day's labor in Government service, that eight hours should constitute a day's labor in factories, workshops and mines.

As a means of placing all public questions directly under the control of the people, we demand that legal provision be made under which the people may exercise the initiative, referendum and proportional representation and direct vote for all public officers with the right of recall.

Land, including all the natural sources of wealth, is a heritage of all the people, and should not be monopolized for speculative purposes, and alien ownership of land should be prohibited.

We demand a return to the original interpretation of the Constitution and a fair and impartial enforcement of laws under it, and denounce government by injunction and imprisonment without the right of trial by jury.

To prevent unjust discrimination and monopoly the Government should own and control the railroads, and those public utilities which in their nature are monopolies. To perfect the postal service, the Government should own and operate the general telegraph and telephone systems and provide a parcels post.

As to these trusts and monopolies which are not public utilities or natural monopolies, we demand that those special privileges which they now enjoy, and which alone enables them to exist, should be immediately withdrawn. Corporations being the creatures of government should be subjected to such governmental regulations and control as will adequately protect the public. We demand the taxation of monopoly privileges, while they remain in private hands, to the extent of the value of the privileges granted.

We demand that Congress shall enact a general law uniformly regulating the power and duties of all incorporated companies doing interstate business.

Prohibition Platform of 1904

The Prohibition party, in national convention assembled, at Indianapolis, June 30, 1904, recognizing that the chief end of all government is the establishment of those principles of righteousness and justice which have been revealed to men as the will of the ever-living God, desiring His blessing upon our national life, and believing in the perpetuation of the high ideals of government of the people, by the people and for the people, established by our fathers, makes the following declaration of principles and purposes:

The widely prevailing system of the licensed and legalized sale of alcoholic beverages is so ruinous to individual interests, so inimical to public welfare, so destructive of national wealth and so subversive of the rights of great masses of our citizenship, that the destruction of the traffic is, and for years has been, the most important question in American politics.

We denounce the lack of statesmanship exhibited by the leaders of the Democratic and Republican parties in their refusal to recognize the paramount importance of this question, and the cowardice with which the leaders of these parties have courted the favor of those whose selfish interests are advanced by the continuation and augmentation of the traffic, until to-day the influence of the liquor traffic practically dominates national, State and local government throughout the nation.

We declare the truth, demonstrated by the experience of half a century, that all methods of dealing with the liquor traffic which recognize its right to exist, in any form, under any system of license or tax or regulation, have proved powerless to remove its evils, and useless as checks upon its growth, while the insignificant public revenues which have accrued therefrom have seared the public conscience against a recognition of its iniquity.

We call public attention to the fact, proved by the experience of more than fifty years, that to secure the enactment and enforcement of prohibitory legislation, in which alone lies the hope of the protection of the people from the liquor traffic, it is necessary that the legislative, executive and judicial branches of government should be in the hands of a political party in harmony with the prohibition principle, and pledged to its embodiment in law, and to the execution of those laws.

We pledge the Prohibition party, wherever given power by the suffrages of the people, to the enactment and enforcement of laws prohibiting and abolishing the manufacture, importation, transportation and sale of alcoholic beverages.

We declare that there is not only no other issue of equal importance before the American people to-day, but that the so-called issues upon which the Democratic and Republican parties seek to divide the electorate of the country are, in large part, subterfuges under the cover of which they wrangle for the spoils of office.

Recognizing that the intelligent voters of the country may properly ask our attitude upon other questions of public concern, we declare ourselves in favor of:

The impartial enforcement of all law.

The safeguarding of the people's rights by a rigid application of the principles of justice to all combinations and organizations of capital and labor.

The recognition of the fact that the right of suffrage should depend upon the mental and moral qualifications of the citizen.

A more intimate relation between the people and government, by a wise application of the principle of the initiative and referendum.

Such changes in our laws as will place tariff schedules in the hands of an omnipartisan commission.

The application of uniform laws to all our country and dependencies.

The election of United States Senators by vote of the people.

The extension and honest administration of the civil service laws.

The safeguarding of every citizen in every place under the government of the people of the United States, in all the rights guaranteed by the laws and the Constitution.

International arbitration, and we declare that our nation should contribute, in every manner consistent with national dignity, to the permanent establishment of peace between all nations.

The reform of our divorce laws, the final extirpation of polygamy, and the total overthrow of the present shameful system of the illegal sanction of the social evil, with its unspeakable traffic in girls, by the municipal authorities of almost all our cities.

Republican Platform of 1904

Fifty years ago the Republican party came into existence dedicated among other purposes to the great task of arresting the extension of human slavery. In 1860 it elected its first President. During twenty-four years of the forty-four which have elapsed since the election of Lincoln the Republican party has held complete control of the government. For eighteen more of the forty-four years it has held partial control through the possession of one or two branches of the government, while the Democratic party during the same period has had complete control for only two years. This long tenure of power by the Republican party is not due to chance. It is a demonstration that the Republican party has commanded the confidence of the American people for nearly two generations to a degree never equalled in our history, and has displayed a high capacity for rule and government which has been made even more conspicuous by the incapacity and infirmity of purpose shown by its opponents.

The Republican party entered upon its present period of complete supremacy in 1897. We have every right to congratulate ourselves upon the work since then accomplished, for it has added lustre even to the traditions of the party which carried the government through the storms of civil war.

We then found the country after four years of Democratic rule in evil plight, oppressed with misfortune, and doubtful of the future. Public credit had been lowered, the revenues were declining, the debt was growing, the administration's attitude toward Spain was feeble and mortifying, the standard of values was threatened and uncertain, labor was unemployed, business was sunk in the depression which had succeeded the panic of 1893, hope was faint and confidence was gone.

We met these unhappy conditions vigorously, effectively, and at once. We replaced a Democratic tariff law based on free trade principles and garnished with sectional protection by a consistent protective tariff, and industry, freed from oppression and stimulated by the encouragement of wise laws, has expanded to a degree never before known, has conquered new markets, and has created a volume of exports which has surpassed imagination. Under the Dingley tariff labor has been fully employed, wages have risen, and all industries have revived and prospered.

We firmly established the gold standard which was then menaced with destruction. Confidence returned to business, and with confidence an unexampled prosperity.

For deficient revenues, supplemented by improvident issues of bonds, we gave the country an income which produced a large surplus and which enabled us only four years after the Spanish War had closed to remove over one hundred millions of annual war taxes, reduce the public debt, and lower the interest charges of the Government.

The public credit which had been so lowered that in time of peace a Democratic administration made large loans at extravagant rates of interest in order to pay current expenditures, rose under Republican administration to its highest point and enabled us to borrow at 2 per cent even in time of war.

We refuse to palter longer with the miseries of Cuba. We fought a quick and victorious war with Spain. We set Cuba free, governed the island for three years, and then gave it to the Cuban people with order restored, with ample revenues, with education and public health established, free from debt, and connected with the United States by wise provisions for our mutual interests.

We have organized the government of Porto Rico, and its people now enjoy peace, freedom, order, and prosperity.

In the Philippines we have suppressed insurrection, established order, and given to life and property a security never known there before. We have organized civil government, made it effective and strong in administration, and have conferred upon the people of those islands the largest civil liberty they have ever enjoyed.

By our possession of the Philippines we were enabled to take prompt and effective action in the relief of the legations at Peking and a decisive part in preventing the partition and preserving the integrity of China.

The possession of a route for an Isthmian canal, so long the dream of American statesmanship, is now an accomplished fact. The great work of connecting the Pacific and Atlantic by a canal is at last begun, and it is due to the Republican party.

We have passed laws which will bring the arid lands of the United States within the area of cultivation.

We have reorganized the army and put it in the highest state of efficiency.

We have passed laws for the improvement and support of the militia.

We have pushed forward the building of the navy, the defence and protection of our honor and our interests.

Our administration of the great departments of the Government has been honest and efficient, and wherever wrongdoing has been discovered, the Republican administration has not hesitated to probe the evil and bring offenders to justice without regard to party or political ties.

Laws enacted by the Republican party which the Democratic party failed to enforce and which were intended for the protection of the public against the united discrimination or the illegal encroachment of vast aggregations of capital, have been fearlessly enforced by a Republican President, and new laws insuring reasonable publicity as to the operations of great corporations, and providing additional remedies for the prevention of discrimination in freight rates, have been passed by a Republican Congress.

In this record of achievement during the past eight years may be read the pledges which the Republican party has fulfilled. We promise to continue these policies, and we declare our constant adherence to the following principles:

Protection, which guards and develops our industries, is a cardinal policy of the Republican party. The measure of protection should always at least equal the difference in the cost of production at home and abroad. We insist upon the maintenance of the principle of protection, and therefore rates of duty should be readjusted only when conditions have so changed that the public interest demands their alteration, but this work cannot safely be committed to any other hands than those of the Republican party. To intrust it to the Democratic party is to invite disaster. Whether, as in 1892, the Democratic party declares the protective tariff unconstitutional, or whether it demands tariff reform or tariff revision, its real object is always the destruction of the protective system. However specious the name, the purpose is ever the same. A Democratic tariff has always been followed by business adversity: a Republican tariff by business prosperity. To a Republican Congress and a Republican President this great question can be safely intrusted. When the only free trade country among the great nations agitates a return to protection, the chief protective country should not falter in maintaining it.

We have extended widely our foreign markets, and we believe in the adoption of all practicable methods for their further extension, including commercial reciprocity wherever reciprocal arrangements can be effected consistent with the principles of protection and without injury to

American agriculture, American labor, or any American industry.

We believe it to be the duty of the Republican party to uphold the gold standard and the integrity and value of our national currency. The maintenance of the gold standard, established by the Republican party, cannot safely be committed to the Democratic party which resisted its adoption and has never given any proof since that time of belief in it or fidelity to it.

While every other industry has prospered under the fostering aid of Republican legislation, American shipping engaged in foreign trade in competition with the low cost of construction, low wages and heavy subsidies of foreign governments, has not for many years received from the Government of the United States adequate encouragement of any kind. We therefore favor legislation which will encourage and build up the American merchant marine, and we cordially approve the legislation of the last Congress which created the Merchant Marine Commission to investigate and report upon this subject.

A navy powerful enough to defend the United States against any attack, to uphold the Monroe Doctrine, and watch over our commerce, is essential to the safety and the welfare of the American people. To maintain such a navy is the fixed policy of the Republican party.

We cordially approve the attitude of President Roosevelt and Congress in regard to the exclusion of Chinese labor, and promise a continuance of the Republican policy in that direction.

The Civil Service Law was placed on the statute books by the Republican party, which has always sustained it, and we renew our former declarations that it shall be thoroughly and honestly enforced.

We are always mindful of the country's debt to the soldiers and sailors of the United States, and we believe in making ample provision for them, and in the liberal administration of the pension laws.

We favor the peaceful settlement of international differences by arbitration.

We commend the vigorous efforts made by the Administration to protect American citizens in foreign lands, and pledge ourselves to insist upon the just and equal protection of all of our citizens abroad. It is the unquestioned duty of the government to procure for all our citizens, without

distinction, the rights of travel and sojourn in friendly countries, and we declare ourselves in favor of all proper efforts tending to that end.

Our great interests and our growing commerce in the Orient render the condition of China of high importance to the United States. We cordially commend the policy pursued in that direction by the administrations of President McKinley and President Roosevelt.

We favor such Congressional action as shall determine whether by special discrimination the elective franchise in any State has been unconstitutionally limited, and, if such is the case, we demand that representation in Congress and in the electoral college shall be proportionately reduced as directed by the Constitution of the United States.

Combinations of capital and of labor are the results of the economic movement of the age, but neither must be permitted to infringe upon the rights and interests of the people. Such combinations, when lawfully formed for lawful purposes, are alike entitled to the protection of the laws, but both are subject to the laws and neither can be permitted to break them.

The great statesman and patriotic American, William McKinley, who was re-elected by the Republican party to the Presidency four years ago, was assassinated just at the threshold of his second term. The entire nation mourned his untimely death and did that justice to his great qualities of mind and character which history will confirm and repeat.

The American people were fortunate in his successor, to whom they turned with a trust and confidence which have been fully justified. President Roosevelt brought to the great responsibilities thus sadly forced upon him a clear hand, a brave heart, and earnest patriotism, and high ideals of public duty and public service. True to the principles of the Republican party and to the policies which that party had declared, he has also shown himself ready for every emergency and has met new and vital questions with ability and with success.

The confidence of the people in his justice, inspired by his public career, enabled him to render personally an inestimable service to the country by bringing about a settlement of the coal strike, which threatened such disastrous results at the opening of Winter in 1902.

Our foreign policy under his administration has not only been able, vigorous, and dignified, but in the highest degree successful.

The complicated questions which arose in Venezuela were settled in such a way by President Roosevelt that the Monroe doctrine was signally vindicated, and the cause of peace and arbitration greatly advanced.

His prompt and vigorous action in Panama, which we commend in the highest terms, not only secured to us the canal route, but avoided foreign complications which might have been of a very serious character.

He has continued the policy of President McKinley in the Orient, and our position in China, signalized by our recent commercial treaty with that empire, has never been so high.

He secured the tribunal by which the vexed and perilous question of the Alaskan boundary was finally settled.

Whenever crimes against humanity have been perpetrated which have shocked our people, his protest has been made, and our good offices have been tendered, but always with due regard to international obligations.

Under his guidance we find ourselves at peace with all the world, and never were we more respected or our wishes more regarded by foreign nations.

Pre-eminently successful in regard to our foreign relations, he has been equally fortunate in dealing with domestic questions. The country has known that the public credit and the national currency were absolutely safe in the hands of his administration. In the enforcement of the laws he has shown not only courage, but the wisdom which understands that to permit laws to be violated or disregarded opens the door to anarchy, while the just enforcement of the law is the soundest conservatism. He has held firmly to the fundamental American doctrine that all men must obey the law; that there must be no distinction between rich and poor, between strong and weak, but that justice and equal protection under the law must be secured to every citizen without regard to race, creed, or condition.

His administration has been throughout vigorous and honorable, high minded and patriotic. We commend it without reservation to the considerate judgment of the American people.

Socialist Platform of 1904

1. The Socialist Party, in convention assembled, makes its appeal to the American people as the defender and preserver of the idea of liberty and self-government, in which the nation was born; as the only political movement standing for the program and principles by which the liberty of the individual may become a fact; as the only political organization that is democratic, and that has for its purpose the democratizing of the whole of society.

To this idea of liberty the Republican and Democratic parties are equally false. They alike struggle for power to maintain and profit by an industrial system which can be preserved only by the complete overthrow of such liberties as we already have, and by the still further enslavement and degradation of labor.

Our American institutions came into the world in the name of freedom. They have been seized upon by the capitalist class as the means of rooting out the idea of freedom from among the people. Our state and national legislatures have become the mere agencies of great propertied interests. These interests control the appointments and decisions of the judges of our courts. They have come into what is practically a private ownership of all the functions and forces of government. They are using these to betray and conquer foreign and weaker peoples, in order to establish new markets for the surplus goods which the people make, but are too poor to buy. They are gradually so invading and restricting the right of suffrage as to take away unawares the right of the worker to a vote or voice in public affairs. By enacting new and misinterpreting old laws, they are preparing to attack the liberty of the individual even to speak or think for himself, or for the common good.

By controlling all the sources of social revenue, the possessing class is able to silence what might be the voice of protest against the passing of liberty and the coming of tyranny. It completely controls the university and public school, the pulpit and the press, and the arts and literatures. By making these economically dependent upon itself, it has brought all the forms of public teaching into servile submission to its own interests.

Our political institutions are also being used as

the destroyers of that individual property upon which all liberty and opportunity depend. The promise of economic independence to each man was one of the faiths upon which our institutions were founded. But, under the guise of defending private property, capitalism is using our political institutions to make it impossible for the vast majority of human beings ever to become possessors of private property in the means of life.

Capitalism is the enemy and destroyer of essential private property. Its development is through the legalized confiscation of all that the labor of the working class produces, above its subsistence-wage. The private ownership of the means of employment grounds society in an economic slavery which renders intellectual and political tyranny inevitable.

Socialism comes so to organize industry and society that every individual shall be secure in that private property in the means of life upon which his liberty of being, thought and action depend. It comes to rescue the people from the fast increasing and successful assault of capitalism upon the liberty of the individual.

2. As an American socialist party, we pledge our fidelity to the principles of international socialism, as embodied in the united thought and action of the socialists of all nations. In the industrial development already accomplished, the interests of the world's workers are separated by no national boundaries. The condition of the most exploited and oppressed workers, in the most remote places of the earth, inevitably tends to drag down all the workers of the world to the same level. The tendency of the competitive wage system is to make labor's lowest condition the measure or rule of its universal condition. Industry and finance are no longer national but international, in both organization and results. The chief significance of national boundaries, and of the so-called patriotisms which the ruling class of each nation is seeking to revive, is the power which these give to capitalism to keep the workers of the world from uniting, and to throw them against each other in the struggles of contending capitalist interests for the control of the yet unexploited markets of the world, or the remaining sources of profit.

The socialist movement, therefore, is a world-movement. It knows of no conflicts of interests between the workers of one nation and the workers of another. It stands for the freedom of the workers of all nations; and, in so standing, it makes for the full freedom of all humanity.

3. The socialist movement owes its birth and growth to that economic development or world-process which is rapidly separating a working or producing class from a possessing or capitalist class. The class that produces nothing possesses labor's fruits, and the opportunities and enjoyments these fruits afford, while the class that does the world's real work has increasing economic uncertainty, and physical and intellectual misery, for its portion.

The fact that these two classes have not yet become fully conscious of their distinctions from each other, the fact that the lines of division and interest may not yet be clearly drawn, does not change the fact of the class conflict.

This class struggle is due to the private ownership of the means of employment, or the tools of production. Wherever and whenever man owned his own land and tools, and by them produced only the things which he used, economic independence was possible. But production, or the making of goods, has long ceased to be individual. The labor of scores, or even thousands, enters into almost every article produced. Production is now social or collective. Practically everything is made or done by many men—sometimes separated by seas or continents—working together for the same end. But this co-operation in production is not for the direct use of the things made by the workers who make them, but for the profit of the owners of the tools and means of production; and to this is due the present division of society into two classes; and from it have sprung all the miseries, inharmonies and contradictions of our civilization.

Between these two classes there can be no possible compromise or identity of interest, any more than there can be peace in the midst of war, or light in the midst of darkness. A society based upon this class division carries in itself the seeds of its own destruction. Such a society is founded in fundamental injustice. There can be no possible basis for social peace, for individual freedom, for mental and moral harmony, except in the conscious and complete triumph of the working class as the only class that has the right or power to be.

4. The socialist program is not a theory imposed upon society for its acceptance or rejection. It is but the interpretation of what is, sooner or later, inevitable. Capitalism is already struggling to its destruction. It is no longer competent to organize or administer the work of the world, or even to preserve itself. The captains of industry are appalled at their own inability to control or direct the rapidly socializing forces of industry. The so-called trust is but a sign and form of the developing socialization of the world's work. The universal increase of the uncertainty of employment, the universal capitalist determination to break down the unity of labor in the trades unions, the widespread apprehensions of impending change, reveal that the institutions of capitalist society are passing under the power of inhering forces that will soon destroy them.

Into the midst of the strain and crisis of civilization, the socialist movement comes as the only conservative force. If the world is to be saved from chaos, from universal disorder and misery, it must be by the union of the workers of all nations in the socialist movement. The socialist party comes with the only proposition or program for intelligently and deliberately organizing the nation for the common good of all its citizens. It is the first time that the mind of man has ever been directed toward the conscious organization of society.

Socialism means that all those things upon which the people in common depend shall by the people in common be owned and administered. It means that the tools of employment shall belong to their creators and users; that all production shall be for the direct use of the producers; that the making of goods for profit shall come to an end; that we shall all be workers together; and that all opportunities shall be open and equal to all men.

5. To the end that the workers may seize every possible advantage that may strengthen them to gain complete control of the powers of government, and thereby the sooner establish the co-operative commonwealth, the Socialist Party pledges itself to watch and work, in both the economic and the political struggle, for each successive immediate interest of the working class; for shortened days of labor and increases of wages; for the insurance of the workers against accident, sickness and lack of employment; for pensions for aged and exhausted workers; for the public ownership of the means of transportation, communication and exchange; for the graduated taxation of incomes, inheritances, franchises and land values, the proceeds to be applied to the public employment and improvement of the conditions of the workers; for the complete education of children, and their freedom from the workshop; for the prevention of the use of the military against labor in the settlement of strikes; for the free administration of justice; for popular government, including initiative, referendum, proportional representation, equal suffrage of men and women, municipal home rule, and the recall of officers by their constituents; and for every gain or advantage for the workers that may be wrested from the capitalist system, and that may relieve the suffering and strengthen the hands of labor. We lay upon every man elected to any executive or legislative office the first duty of striving to procure whatever is for the workers' most immediate interest, and for whatever will lessen the economic and political powers of the capitalist, and increase the like powers of the worker.

But, in so doing, we are using these remedial measures as means to the one great end of the co-operative commonwealth. Such measures of relief as we may be able to force from capitalism are but a preparation of the workers to seize the whole powers of government, in order that they may thereby lay hold of the whole system of industry, and thus come into their rightful inheritance.

To this end we pledge ourselves, as the party of the working class, to use all political power, as fast as it shall be entrusted to us by our fellow-workers, both for their immediate interests and for their ultimate and complete emancipation. To this end we appeal to all the workers of America, and to all who will lend their lives to the service of the workers in their struggle to gain their own, and to all who will nobly and disinterestedly give their days and energies unto the workers' cause, to cast in their lot and faith with the socialist party. Our appeal for the trust and suffrages of our fellow-workers is at once an appeal for their common good and freedom, and for the freedom and blossoming of our common humanity. In pledging ourselves, and those we represent, to be faithful to the appeal which we make, we believe that we are but preparing the soil of that economic freedom from which will spring the freedom of the whole man.

Socialist Labor Platform of 1904

The Socialist Labor Party of America, in convention assembled, reasserts the inalienable right of man to life, liberty and the pursuit of happiness.

We hold that the purpose of government is to secure to every citizen the enjoyment of this right: but taught by experience we hold furthermore that such right is illusory to the majority of the people, to wit, the working class, under the present system of economic inequality that is essentially destructive to *their* life, *their* liberty and *their* happiness.

We hold that the true theory of politics is that the machinery of government must be controlled by the whole people; but again taught by experience we hold furthermore that the true theory of economics is that the means of production must likewise be owned, operated and controlled by the people in common. Man cannot exercise his right of life, liberty and the pursuit of happiness without the ownership of the land on and the tool with which to work. Deprived of these, his life, his liberty and his fate fall into the hands of the class that owns those essentials for work and production.

We hold that the existing contradiction between the theory of democratic government and the fact of a despotic economic system—the private ownership of the natural and social opportunities—divides the people into two classes, the capitalist class and the working class; throws society into the convulsions of the Class Struggle, and perverts government to the exclusive benefit of the Capitalist Class.

Thus labor is robbed of the wealth which it alone produces, is denied the means of self-employment, and, by compulsory idleness in wage slavery, is even deprived of the necessaries of life.

Against such a system the Socialist Labor Party raises the banner of revolt, and demands the unconditional surrender of the Capitalist Class.

The time is fast coming when, in the natural course of social evolution, this system, through the destructive action of its failures and crises on the one hand, and the constructive tendencies of its trusts and other capitalist combinations on the other hand, will have worked out its own downfall.

We, therefore, call upon the wage workers of America to organize under the banner of the Socialist Labor Party into a class-conscious body, aware of its rights and determined to conquer them.

And we also call upon all other intelligent citizens to place themselves squarely upon the ground of Working Class interests, and join us in this mighty and noble work of human emancipation, so that we may put summary end to the existing barbarous class conflict by placing the land and all the means of production, transportation and distribution into the hands of the people as a collective body, and substituting the co-operative commonwealth for the present state of planless production, industrial war and social disorder—a commonwealth in which every worker shall have the free exercise and full benefit of his faculties, multiplied by all the modern factors of civilization.

CAMPAIGN OF 1908

In 1908, Theodore Roosevelt was not a candidate for reelection, but his choice for his successor, William Howard Taft, easily defeated six other aspirants on the first ballot. Representative James S. Sherman of New York was nominated for the vice-presidency. On the first ballot, the Democrats nominated William Jennings Bryan of Nebraska for the third time. Then the delegates chose John W. Kern of Indiana as his running mate.

The Socialists nominated Eugene V. Debs of Indiana for president and Benjamin Hanford of New York for vice-president. The other minor parties offering candidates included the Prohibitionists, who nominated Eugene W. Chafin of Illinois and Aaron Watkins of Ohio; the Populists (People's Party), who again selected Thomas E. Watson of Georgia for president and Samuel Williams of Indiana for his vice-presidential candidate; and the Socialist Labor Party, headed by August Gillhaus of New York, with Donald L. Munro of Virginia for the second position. A new party, the Independence Party—formed by a group of followers of William Randolph Hearst of New York—appeared on some state ballots for the first and only time. It nominated Thomas Hisgen of Massachusetts for president and John Temple Graves of Georgia for vice-president.

In the election, the Republicans again defeated the Democrats headed by Bryan, 7,676,258 popular votes to 6,406,801. Debs received 420,380; Chafin 252,821; Watson, 28,376; Gillhaus, 14,018; and Hisgen for the Independence Party, 82,537 votes in thirty-eight states. In the electoral college Bryan carried the same states as Parker had in 1904, plus Oklahoma, Nebraska, Colorado, and Nevada. He received 162 electoral votes to 321 for Taft.

Democratic Platform of 1908

We, the representatives of the Democracy of the United States, in National Convention assembled, reaffirm our belief in, and pledge our loyalty to, the principles of the party.

We rejoice at the increasing signs of an awakening throughout the country. The various investigations have traced graft and political corruption to the representatives of the predatory wealth, and laid bare the unscrupulous methods by which they have debauched elections and preyed upon a defenseless public through the subservient officials whom they have raised to place and power.

The conscience of the nation is now aroused to free the Government from the grip of those who have made it a business asset of the favor-seeking corporations. It must become again a people's government, and be administered in all its departments according to the Jeffersonian maxim, "equal rights to all; special privileges to none."

"Shall the people rule?" is the overshadowing issue which manifests itself in all the questions now under discussion.

INCREASE OF OFFICE-HOLDERS

Coincident with the enormous increase in expenditures is a like addition to the number of office-holders. During the past year 23,784 were added, costing $16,156,000, and in the past six years of Republican administration the total number of new offices created, aside from many commissions, has been 99,319, entailing an additional expenditure of nearly $70,000,000 as against only 10,279 new offices created under the Cleveland and McKinley administrations, which involved an expenditure of only $6,000,000. We denounce this great and growing increase in the number of office-holders as not only unnecessary and wasteful, but also as clearly indicating a deliberate purpose on the part of the Administration to keep the Republican party in power at public expense by thus increasing the number of its retainers and dependents. Such procedure we declare to be no less dangerous and corrupt than the open purchase of votes at the polls.

ECONOMY IN ADMINISTRATION

The Republican Congress in the session just ended made appropriations amounting to $1,008,-000,000, exceeding the total expenditures of the past fiscal year by $90,000,000 and leaving a deficit of more than $60,000,000 for the fiscal year just ended. We denounce the heedless waste of the people's money which has resulted in this appalling increase as a shameful violation of all prudent considerations of government and as no less than a crime against the millions of working men and women, from whose earnings the great proportion of these colossal sums must be extorted through excessive tariff exactions and other indirect methods. It is not surprising that in the face of this shocking record the Republican platform contains no reference to economical administration or promise thereof in the future. We demand that a stop be put to this frightful extravagance, and insist upon the strictest economy in every department compatible with frugal and efficient administration.

ARBITRARY POWER—THE SPEAKER

The House of Representatives was designed by the fathers of the Constitution to be the popular branch of our Government, responsive to the public will.

The House of Representatives, as controlled in recent years by the Republican party, has ceased to be a deliberative and legislative body, responsive to the will of a majority of its members, but has come under the absolute domination of the Speaker, who has entire control of its deliberations and powers of legislation.

We have observed with amazement the popular branch of our Federal Government helpless to obtain either the consideration or enactment of measures desired by a majority of its members.

Legislative control becomes a failure when one member in the person of the Speaker is more powerful than the entire body.

We demand that the House of Representatives shall again become a deliberative body, controlled by a majority of the people's representatives, and not by the Speaker; and we pledge ourselves to adopt such rules and regulations to govern the House of Representatives as will enable a majority of its members to direct its deliberations and control legislation.

MISUSE OF PATRONAGE

We condemn as a violation of the spirit of our institutions the action of the present Chief Executive in using the patronage of his high office to secure the nomination for the Presidency of one of his Cabinet officers. A forced succession to the Presidency is scarcely less repugnant to public sentiment than is life tenure in that office. No good intention on the part of the Executive, and no virtue in the one selected, can justify the establishment of a dynasty. The right of the people freely to select their officials is inalienable and cannot be delegated.

PUBLICITY OF CAMPAIGN CONTRIBUTIONS

We demand Federal legislation forever terminating the partnership which has existed between corporations of the country and the Republican party under the expressed or implied agreement that in return for the contribution of great sums of money wherewith to purchase elections, they should be allowed to continue substantially unmolested in their efforts to encroach upon the rights of the people.

Any reasonable doubt as to the existence of this relation has been forever dispelled by the sworn testimony of witnesses examined in the insurance investigation in New York, and the open admission of a single individual—unchallenged by the Republican National Committee—that he himself at the personal request of the Republican candidate for the Presidency raised over a quarter of a million dollars to be used in a single State during the closing hours of the last campaign. In order that this practice shall be stopped for all time, we demand the passage of a statute punishing by imprisonment any officer of a corporation who shall either contribute on behalf of, or consent to the contribution by, a corporation, of any money or thing of value to be used in furthering the election of a President or Vice-President of the United States or of any member of the Congress thereof.

We denounce the Republican party, having complete control of the Federal Government, for their failure to pass the bill, introduced in the last Congress, to compel the publication of the names of contributors and the amounts contributed toward campaign funds, and point to the evidence of their insincerity when they sought by an absolutely irrelevant and impossible amendment to defeat the passage of the bill. As a further evidence of their intention to conduct their campaign in the coming contest with vast sums of money wrested from favor-seeking corporations, we call attention to the fact that the recent Republican National Convention at Chicago refused, when the issue was presented to it, to declare against such practices.

We pledge the Democratic party to the enactment of a law prohibiting any corporation from contributing to a campaign fund and any individual from contributing an amount above a reasonable maximum, and providing for the publication before election of all such contributions.

The Rights of the States

Believing, with Jefferson, in "the support of the State governments in all their rights as the most competent administrations for our domestic concerns, and the surest bulwarks against anti-republican tendencies," and in "the preservation of the General Government in its whole constitutional vigor, as the sheet anchor of our peace at home and safety abroad," we are opposed to the centralization implied in the suggestion, now frequently made, that the powers of the General Government should be extended by judicial construction. There is no twilight zone between the Nation and the State in which exploiting interests can take refuge from both; and it is as necessary that the Federal Government shall exercise the powers delegated to it as it is that the State governments shall use the authority reserved to them; but we insist that Federal remedies for the regulation of interstate commerce and for the prevention of private monopoly shall be added to, not substituted for, State remedies.

Tariff

We welcome the belated promise of tariff reform now offered by the Republican party in tardy recognition of the righteousness of the Democratic position on this question; but the people cannot safely entrust the execution of this important work to a party which is so deeply obligated to the highly protected interests as is the Republican party. We call attention to the significant fact that the promised relief is postponed until after the coming election—an election to succeed in which the Republican party must have that same support from the beneficiaries of the high protective tariff as it has always heretofore received from them; and to the further fact that during years of uninterrupted power no action whatever has been taken by the Republican Congress to correct the admittedly existing tariff iniquities.

We favor immediate revision of the tariff by the reduction of import duties. Articles entering into competition with trust-controlled products should be placed upon the free list, and material reductions should be made in the tariff upon the necessaries of life, especially upon articles competing with such American manufactures as are sold abroad more cheaply than at home; and gradual reductions should be made in such other schedules as may be necessary to restore the tariff to a revenue basis.

Existing duties have given to the manufacturers of paper a shelter behind which they have organized combinations to raise the price of pulp and of paper, thus imposing a tax upon the spread of knowledge. We demand the immediate repeal of the tariff on wood pulp, print paper, lumber, timber and logs, and that these articles be placed upon the free list.

Trusts

A private monopoly is indefensible and intolerable. We therefore favor the vigorous enforcement of the criminal law against guilty trust magnates and officials, and demand the enactment of such additional legislation as may be necessary to make it impossible for a private monopoly to exist in the United States. Among the additional remedies we specify three: First, a law preventing a duplication of directors among competing corporations; second, a license system which will, without abridging the right of each State to create corporations, or its right to regulate as it will foreign corporations doing business within its limits, make it necessary for a manufacturing or trading corporation engaged in interstate commerce to take out a Federal license before it shall be permitted to control as much as twenty-five per cent of the product in which it deals, the license to protect the public from watered stock and to prohibit the control by such corporation of more than fifty per cent of the total amount of any product consumed in the United States; and, third, a law compelling such licensed corporations to sell to all purchasers in all parts of the country on the same terms, after making due allowance for cost of transportation.

Railroad Regulation

We assert the right of Congress to exercise complete control over interstate commerce and the right of each State to exercise like control over commerce within its borders.

We demand such enlargement of the powers of the Interstate Commerce Commission as may be necessary to enable it to compel railroads to perform their duties as common carriers and prevent discrimination and extortion.

We favor the efficient supervision and rate regulation of railroads engaged in interstate commerce. To this end we recommend the valuation of railroads by the Interstate Commerce Commission, such valuation to take into consideration the physical value of the property, the original cost of production, and all elements of value that will render the valuation fair and just.

We favor such legislation as will prohibit the railroads from engaging in business which brings them into competition with their shippers; also legislation which will assure such reduction in transportation rates as conditions will permit, care being taken to avoid reduction that would compel a reduction of wages, prevent adequate service, or do injustice to legitimate investments.

We heartily approve the laws prohibiting the pass and the rebate, and we favor any further necessary legislation to restrain, correct and prevent such abuses.

We favor such legislation as will increase the power of the Interstate Commerce Commission, giving to it the initiative with reference to rates and transportation charges put into effect by the railroad companies, and permitting the Interstate Commerce Commission, on its own initiative, to declare a rate illegal and as being more than should be charged for such service. The present law relating thereto is inadequate, by reason of the fact that the Interstate Commerce Commission is without power to fix or investigate a rate until complaint has been made to it by the shipper.

We further declare in favor of a law providing that all agreements of traffic or other associations of railway agents affecting interstate rates, service or classification, shall be unlawful, unless filed with and approved by the Interstate Commerce Commission.

We favor the enactment of a law giving to the Interstate Commerce Commission the power to inspect proposed railroad tariff rates or schedules before they shall take effect, and, if they be found to be unreasonable, to initiate an adjustment thereof.

Banking

The panic of 1907, coming without any legitimate excuse, when the Republican party had for a decade been in complete control of the Federal government, furnishes additional proof that it is either unwilling or incompetent to protect the interests of the general public. It has so linked the country to Wall street that the sins of the speculators are visited upon the whole people. While refusing to rescue the wealth producers from spoliation at the hands of the stock gamblers and speculators in farm products, it has deposited Treasury funds, without interest and without competition, in favorite banks. It has used an emergency for which it is largely responsible to force through Congress a bill changing the basis of bank currency and inviting market manipulation, and has failed to give to the 15,000,000 depositors of the country protection in their savings.

We believe that in so far as the needs of commerce require an emergency currency, such currency should be issued and controlled by the Federal Government, and loaned on adequate security to National and State banks. We pledge ourselves to legislation under which the national banks shall be required to establish a guarantee fund for the prompt payment of the depositors of any insolvent national bank, under an equitable system which shall be available to all State banking institutions wishing to use it.

We favor a postal savings bank if the guaranteed bank can not be secured, and that it be constituted so as to keep the deposited money in the communities where it is established. But we condemn the policy of the Republican party in providing postal savings banks under a plan of conduct by which they will aggregate the deposits of the rural communities and redeposit the same while under Government charge in the banks of Wall street, thus depleting the circulating medium of the producing regions and unjustly favoring the speculative markets.

Income Tax

We favor an income tax as part of our revenue system, and we urge the submission of a constitutional amendment specifically authorizing Congress to levy and collect a tax upon individual and corporate incomes, to the end that wealth may bear its proportionate share of the burdens of the Federal Government.

Labor and Injunctions

The courts of justice are the bulwark of our liberties, and we yield to none in our purpose to maintain their dignity. Our party has given to the bench a long line of distinguished judges, who have added to the respect and confidence in which this department must be jealously maintained. We resent the attempt of the Republican party to raise a false issue respecting the judiciary. It is an unjust reflection upon a great body of our citizens to assume that they lack respect for the courts.

It is the function of the courts to interpret the laws which the people create, and if the laws appear to work economic, social or political injustice, it is our duty to change them. The only basis upon which the integrity of our courts can stand is that of unswerving justice and protection of life, personal liberty and property. If judicial processes may be abused, we should guard them against abuse.

Experience has proved the necessity of a modification of the present law relating to injunctions, and we reiterate the pledge of our national platforms of 1896 and 1904 in favor of the measure which passed the United States Senate in 1896, but which a Republican Congress has ever since refused to enact, relating to contempts in Federal courts and providing for trial by jury in cases of indirect contempt.

Questions of judicial practice have arisen especially in connection with industrial disputes. We deem that the parties to all judicial proceedings should be treated with rigid impartiality, and that injunctions should not be issued in any cases in which injunctions would not issue if no industrial dispute were involved.

The expanding organization of industry makes it essential that there should be no abridgment of the right of wage earners and producers to organize for the protection of wages and the improvement of labor conditions, to the end that such labor organizations and their members should not be regarded as illegal combinations in restraint of trade.

We favor the eight hour day on all Government work.

We pledge the Democratic party to the enactment of a law by Congress, as far as the Federal jurisdiction extends, for a general employer's liability act covering injury to body or loss of life of employes.

We pledge the Democratic party to the enactment of a law creating a Department of Labor, represented separately in the President's Cabinet, in which Department shall be included the subject of mines and mining.

MERCHANT MARINE

We believe in the upbuilding of the American merchant marine without new or additional burdens upon the people and without bounties from the public treasury.

THE NAVY

The constitutional provision that a navy shall be provided and maintained means an adequate navy, and we believe that the interests of this country would be best served by having a navy sufficient to defend the coasts of this country and protect American citizens wherever their rights may be in jeopardy.

PROTECTION OF AMERICAN CITIZENS

We pledge ourselves to insist upon the just and lawful protection of our citizens at home and abroad, and to use all proper methods to secure for them, whether native born or naturalized, and without distinction of race or creed, the equal protection of the law and the enjoyment of all rights and privileges open to them under our treaties; and if, under existing treaties, the right of travel and sojourn is denied to American citizens, or recognition is withheld from American passports by any countries on the ground of race or creed, we favor prompt negotiations with the governments of such countries to secure the removal of these unjust discriminations.

We demand that all over the world a duly authenticated passport issued by the Government of the United States to an American citizen, shall be proof of the fact that he is an American citizen and shall entitle him to the treatment due him as such.

CIVIL SERVICE

The laws pertaining to the civil service should be honestly and rigidly enforced, to the end that merit and ability shall be the standard of appointment and promotion rather than services rendered to a political party.

PENSIONS

We favor a generous pension policy, both as a matter of justice to the surviving veterans and their dependents, and because it tends to relieve the country of the necessity of maintaining a large standing army.

HEALTH BUREAU

We advocate the organization of all existing national public health agencies into a national bureau of public health with such power over sanitary conditions connected with factories, mines, tenements, child labor and other such subjects as are properly within the jurisdiction of the Federal government and do not interfere with the power of the States controlling public health agencies.

AGRICULTURAL AND MECHANICAL EDUCATION

The Democratic party favors the extension of agricultural, mechanical and industrial education. We therefore favor the establishment of district agricultural experiment stations and secondary agricultural and mechanical colleges in the several States.

POPULAR ELECTION OF SENATORS

We favor the election of United States Senators by direct vote of the people, and regard this reform as the gateway to other national reforms.

OKLAHOMA

We welcome Oklahoma to the sisterhood of States and heartily congratulate her upon the auspicious beginning of a great career.

PANAMA CANAL

We believe that the Panama Canal will prove of great value to our country, and favor its speedy completion.

ARIZONA AND NEW MEXICO

The National Democratic party has for the last sixteen years labored for the admission of Arizona and New Mexico as separate States of the Federal Union, and recognizing that each possesses every qualification successfully to maintain separate State governments, we favor the immediate admission of these Territories as separate States.

GRAZING LANDS

The establishment of rules and regulations, if any such are necessary, in relation to free grazing upon the public lands outside of forest or other reservations, until the same shall eventually be disposed of, should be left to the people of the States respectively in which such lands may be situated.

WATERWAYS

Water furnishes the cheaper means of transportation, and the National Government, having the control of navigable waters, should improve them to their fullest capacity. We earnestly favor the immediate adoption of a liberal and comprehensive plan for improving every water course in the Union which is justified by the needs of commerce; and, to secure that end, we favor, when practicable, the connection of the Great Lakes with the navigable rivers and with the Gulf through the Mississippi River, and the navigable rivers with each other, and the rivers, bays and sounds of our coasts with each other, by artificial canals, with a view of perfecting a system of inland waterways to be navigated by vessels of standard draught.

We favor the co-ordination of the various services of the Government connected with waterways in one service, for the purpose of aiding in the completion of such a system of inland waterways; and we favor the creation of a fund ample for continuous work, which shall be conducted under the direction of a commission of experts to be authorized by law.

POST ROADS

We favor Federal aid to State and local authorities in the construction and maintenance of post roads.

TELEGRAPH AND TELEPHONE

We pledge the Democratic party to the enactment of a law to regulate, under the jurisdiction of the Interstate Commerce Commission, the rates and services of telegraph and telephone companies engaged in the transmission of messages between the States.

NATURAL RESOURCES

We repeat the demand for internal development and for the conservation of our natural resources contained in previous platforms, the enforcement of which Mr. Roosevelt has vainly sought from a reluctant party; and to that end we insist upon the preservation, protection and replacement of needed forests, the preservation of the public domain for home seekers, the protection of the national resources in timber, coal, iron and oil against monopolistic control, the development of our waterways for navigation and every other useful purpose, including the irrigation of arid lands, the reclamation of swamp lands, the clarification of streams, the development of water power, and the preservation of electric power, generated by this natural force, from the control of monopoly; and to such end we urge the exercise of all powers, national, State and municipal, both separately and in co-operation.

We insist upon a policy of administration of our forest reserves which shall relieve it of the abuses which have arisen thereunder, and which shall, as far as practicable, conform to the police regulations of the several States wherein the reserves are located, which shall enable homesteaders as of right to occupy and acquire title to all portions thereof which are especially adapted to agriculture, and which shall furnish a system of timber sales available as well to the private citizen as to the larger manufacturer and consumer.

Hawaii

We favor the application of the principles of the land laws of the United States to our newly acquired territory, Hawaii, to the end that the public lands of that territory may be held and utilized for the benefit of *bona-fide* homesteaders.

The Philippines

We condemn the experiment in imperialism as an inexcusable blunder which has involved us in enormous expense, brought us weakness instead of strength, and laid our nation open to the charge of abandoning a fundamental doctrine of self-government. We favor an immediate declaration of the nation's purpose to recognize the indedendence of the Philippine Islands as soon as a stable government can be established, such independence to be guaranteed by us as we guarantee the independence of Cuba, until the neutralization of the islands can be secured by treaty with other powers. In recognizing the independence of the Philippines our Government should retain such land as may be necessary for coaling stations and naval bases.

Alaska and Porto Rico

We demand for the people of Alaska and Porto Rico the full enjoyment of the rights and privileges of a territorial form of government, and that the officials appointed to administer the government of all our territories and the District of Columbia should be thoroughly qualified by previous *bona-fide* residence.

Pan-American Relations

The Democratic party recognizes the importance and advantage of developing closer ties of Pan-American friendship and commerce between the United States and her sister nations of Latin America, and favors the taking of such steps, consistent with Democratic policies, for better acquaintance, greater mutual confidence, and larger exchange of trade as will bring lasting benefit not only to the United States, but to this group of American Republics, having constitutions, forms of government, ambitions and interests akin to our own.

Asiatic Immigration

We favor full protection, by both National and State governments within their respective spheres, of all foreigners residing in the United States under treaty, but we are opposed to the admission of Asiatic immigrants who can not be amalgamated with our population, or whose presence among us would raise a race issue and involve us in diplomatic controversies with Oriental powers.

Foreign Patents

We believe that where an American citizen holding a patent in a foreign country is compelled to manufacture under his patent within a certain time, similar restrictions should be applied in this country to the citizens or subjects of such a country.

Conclusion

The Democratic party stands for Democracy; the Republican party has drawn to itself all that is aristocratic and plutocratic.

The Democratic party is the champion of equal rights and opportunities to all; the Republican party is the party of privilege and private monopoly. The Democratic party listens to the voice of the whole people and gauges progress by the prosperity and advancement of the average man; the Republican party is subservient to the comparatively few who are the beneficiaries of governmental favoritism. We invite the co-operation of all, regardless of previous political affiliation or past differences, who desire to preserve a government of the people, by the people and for the people and who favor such an administration of the government as will insure, as far as human wisdom can, that each citizen shall draw from society a reward commensurate with his contribution to the welfare of society.

Independence Platform of 1908

We, independent American citizens, representing the Independence party in forty-four States and two Territories, have met in national convention to nominate, absolutely independent of all other political parties, candidates for President and Vice-President of the United States.

Our action is based upon a determination to wrest the conduct of public affairs from the hands of selfish interests, political tricksters and corrupt bosses, and make the Government, as the founders intended, an agency for the common good.

At a period of unexampled national prosperity and promise a staggering blow was dealt to legitimate business by the unmolested practice of stock watering and dishonest financiering. Multitudes of defenceless investors, thousands of honest business men, and an army of idle workingmen are paying the penalty. Year by year, fostered by wasteful and reckless governmental extravagance, by the manipulation of trusts and by a privilege creating tariff, the cost of living mounts higher and higher. Day by day the control of the Government drifts further away from the people and more firmly into the grip of machine politicians and party bosses.

The Republican and Democratic parties are not only responsible for these conditions, but are committed to their indefinite continuance. Prodigal of promises, they are so barren of performance that to a new party of independent voters the country must look for the establishment of a new policy and a return to genuine popular government.

Our object is not to introduce violent innovations or startlingly new features. We of the Independence party look back as Lincoln did, to the Declaration of Independence as the fountain-head of all political inspiration. It is not our purpose to attempt to revolutionize the American system of government, but to restore the action of the Government to the principles of Washington and

Jefferson and Lincoln. It is not our purpose, either, to effect a radical change in the American system of government, but to conserve for the citizens of the United States their privileges and liberties won for them by the founders of this Government and to perpetuate the principles and policies upon which the nation's greatness has been built.

The Independence party is, therefore, a conservative force in American politics, devoted to the preservation of American liberty and independence, to honesty in elections, to opportunity in business and to equality before the law.

Those who believe in the Independence party and work with it are convinced that a genuine democracy should exist; that a true republican form of government should continue; that the power of government should rest with the majority of the people, and that the Government should be conducted for the benefit of the whole citizenship, rather than for the special advantage of any particular class.

As of first importance in order to restore the power of government to the people, to make their will supreme in the primaries, in the elections and in the control of public officials after they have been elected, we declare for direct nominations, the initiative and referendum and the right of recall.

It is idle to cry out against the evil of bossism while we perpetuate a system under which the boss is inevitable. The destruction of the individual boss is of little value. The people in their politics must establish a system which will eliminate not only an objectionable boss but the system of bossism. Representative government is made a mockery by the system of modern party conventions dominated by the bosses and controlled by cliques. We demand the natural remedy of direct nominations by which the people not only elect, but which is far more important, select their representatives.

We believe in the principle of the initiative and referendum, and we particularly demand that no franchise grant go into operation until the terms and conditions have been approved by popular vote in the locality interested.

We demand for the people the right to recall public officials from the public service. The power to make officials reside in the people, and in them also should reside the power to unmake and remove from office any official who demonstrates his unfitness or betrays the public trust.

Of next importance in destroying the power of selfish special interests and the corrupt political bosses whom they control is to wrest from their hands their main weapon—the corruption fund. We demand severe and effective legislation against all forms of corrupt practices at elections, and advocate prohibiting the use of any money at elections except for meetings, literature and the necessary travelling expenses of the candidates. Bidding for votes the Republican and Democratic candidates are making an outcry about publicity of contributions, although both the Republican and Democratic parties have for years consistently blocked every effort to pass a corrupt practices act. Publicity of contributions is desirable and should be required, but the main matter of importance is the use to which contributions are put. We believe that the dishonest use of money in the past, whether contributed by individuals or by corporations, has been chiefly responsible for the corruption which has undermined our system of popular government.

We demand honest conduct of public office and business alike and an economical administration of public affairs, and we condemn the gross extravagance of Federal administration and its appalling annual increase in appropriations. Unnecessary appropriations mean unnecessary taxes, and unnecessary taxes, whether direct or indirect, are paid by the people, and add to the ever increasing cost of living.

We condemn the evil of overcapitalization. Modern industrial conditions make the corporation and stock company a necessity, but overcapitalization in corporations is as harmful and criminal as is personal dishonesty in an individual. Compelling the payment of dividends upon great sums that have never been invested, upon masses of watered stock not justified by the property, overcapitalization prevents the better wages, the better public service and the lower cost that should result from American inventive genius and that wide organization which is replacing costly individual competition. The collapse of dishonestly inflated enterprises robs investors, closes banks, destroys confidence and engenders panics. The Independence party advocates as a primary necessity for sounder business conditions and improved public service the enactment of laws,

State and national, to prevent watering of stock, dishonest issues of bonds and other forms of corporation frauds.

We denounce the so-called labor planks of the Republican and Democratic platforms as political buncombe and contemptible claptrap, unworthy of national parties claiming to be serious and sincere.

The Republican declaration that "no injunction or temporary or restraining order should not be issued without notice, except where irreparable injury would result from delay," is empty verbiage, for a showing of irreparable injury can always be made and is always made in ex parte affidavits.

The Democratic declaration that "injunctions should not be issued in any case in which injunctions should not issue if no industrial dispute were involved" is meaningless and worthless.

Such insincere and meaningless declarations place a low estimate upon the intelligence of the average American workingman and exhibit either ignorance of or indifference to the real interest of labor.

The Independence party condemns the arbitrary use of the writ of injunction and contempt proceedings as a violation of the fundamental American right of trial by jury.

From the foundation of our Government down to 1872 the Federal Judiciary act prohibited the issue of any injunction without reasonable notice until after a hearing. We assert that in all actions growing out of a dispute between employers and employés concerning terms or conditions of employment no injunction should issue until after a trial upon the merits, that such trial should be held before a jury, and that in no case of alleged contempt should any person be deprived of liberty without a trial by jury.

The Independence party believes that the distribution of wealth is as important as the creation of wealth, and indorses these organizations among farmers and workers which tend to bring about a just distribution of wealth through good wages for workers and good prices for farmers, and which protect the employer and the consumer through equality of price for labor and for product, and we favor such legislation as will remove them from the operation of the Sherman anti-trust law.

We indorse the eight hour work day, favor its application to all Government employés, and demand the enactment of laws requiring that all work done for the Government, whether Federal or State, and whether done directly or indirectly through contractors or sub-contractors shall be done on an eight hour basis.

We favor the enactment of a law defining as illegal any combination or conspiracy to blacklist employés.

We demand protection for workmen through enforced use of standard safety appliances and provisions of hygienic conditions in the operation of factories, railways, mills, mines and all industrial undertakings.

We advocate State and Federal inspection of railways to secure a greater safety for railway employés and for the travelling public. We call for the enactment of stringent laws fixing employers' liabilities, and a rigid prohibition of child labor through co-operation between the State governments and the National Government.

We condemn the manufacture and sale of prison-made goods in the open market in competition with free labor manufactured goods. We demand that convicts shall be employed direct by the different States in the manufacture of products for use in State institutions and in making good roads and in no case shall convicts be hired out to contractors or sub-contractors.

We favor the creation of a Department of Labor, including mines and mining, the head of which shall be a member of the President's Cabinet.

The great abuses of grain inspection, by which the producers are plundered, demand immediate and vigorous correction. To that end we favor Federal inspection under a strict civil service law.

The Independence party declares the right to issue money is inherent in the Government, and it favors the establishment of a central governmental bank, through which the money so issued shall be put into general circulation.

We demand a revision of the tariff, not by the friends of the tariff, but by the friends of the people, and declare for a gradual reduction of tariff duties, with just consideration for the rights of the consuming public and of established industry. There should be no protection for oppressive trusts which sell cheaply abroad and take advantage of the tariff at home to crush competition, raise prices, control production and limit work and wages.

The railroads must be kept open to all upon exactly equal terms. Every form of rebate and discrimination in railroad rates is a crime against business and must be stamped out. We demand adequate railroad facilities and advocate a bill empowering shippers in time of need to compel railroads to provide sufficient cars for freight and passenger traffic and other railroad facilities through summary appeal to the courts. We favor the creation of an Interstate Commerce Court, whose sole function it shall be to review speedily and enforce summarily the orders of the Interstate Commerce Commission. The Interstate Commerce Commission has the power to initiate investigation into the reasonableness of rates and practices and no increase in rates should be put into effect until opportunity for such investigation is afforded. The Interstate Commerce Commission should proceed at once with a physical valuation of railroads engaged in interstate commerce.

We believe that legitimate organizations in business designed to secure an economy of operation and increased production are beneficial wherever the public participates in the advantages which result. We denounce all combinations for restraint of trade and for the establishment of monopoly in all products of labor, and declare that such combinations are not combinations for production, but for extortion, and that activity in this direction is not industry, but robbery.

In case of infractions of the Anti-Trust law or of the Interstate Commerce act, we believe in the enforcement of a prison penalty against the guilty and responsible individuals controlling the management of the offending corporations, rather than a fine imposed upon stockholders.

We advocate the extension of the principle of public ownership of public utilities, including railroads, as rapidly as municipal, State, or National Government shall demonstrate ability to conduct public utilities for the public benefit. We favor specifically government ownership of the telegraphs, such as prevails in every other civilized country in the world, and demand as an immediate measure that the Government shall purchase and operate the telegraphs in connection with the postal service.

The parcels post system should be rapidly and widely extended and Government postal savings banks should be established where the people's deposits will be secure, the money to be loaned to the people in the locality of the several banks at a rate of interest to be fixed by the Government.

We favor the immediate development of a national system of good roads connecting all States, and national aid to States in the construction and maintenance of post roads.

We favor a court of review of the censorship and arbitrary rulings of the Post-Office Department.

We favor the admission of Arizona and New Mexico to separate Statehood.

We advocate such legislation, both State and national, as will suppress the bucket shop and prohibit the fictitious selling of farm products for future delivery.

We favor the creation of a national department of public health, to be presided over by a member of the medical profession, this department to exercise such authority over matters of public health, hygiene, and sanitation which come properly within the jurisdiction of the National Government and does not interfere with the rights of states or municipalities.

We oppose Asiatic immigration which does not amalgamate with our population, creates race issues and un-American conditions, and which reduces wages and tends to lower the high standard of living and the high standard of morality which American civilization has established.

We demand the passage of an exclusion act which shall protect American workingmen from competition with Asiatic cheap labor and which shall protect American civilization from the contamination of Asiatic conditions.

The Independence party declares for peace and against aggression, and will promote the movement for the settlement of international disputes by arbitration.

We believe, however, that a small navy is poor economy and that a strong navy is the best protection in time of war and the best preventive of war. We, therefore, favor the speedy building of a navy sufficiently strong to protect at the same time both the Atlantic and Pacific Coasts of the United States.

We rejoice in the adoption by both the Democratic and Republican platforms of the demand of the Independence party for improved national waterways and the Mississippi inland deep-waters project, to complete a ship canal from the Gulf to the Great Lakes. We favor the extension of this system to the tributaries of the Mississippi by means of which thirty States shall be served and 20,000 miles added to the coast line of the United States. The reclamation of arid land should be continued and the irrigation programme now contemplated by the Government extended and steps taken for the conservation of the country's natural resources, which should be guarded not only against devastation and waste, but against falling into the control of the monopoly. The abuses growing out of the administration of our forest preserves must be corrected and provisions should be made for free grazing from public lands outside of forest or other reservations. In behalf of the people residing in arid portions of our Western States we protest vigorously against the policy of the Federal Government in selling the exclusive use of water and electric power derived from public works to private corporations, thus creating a monopoly and subjecting citizens living in those sections to exorbitant charges for light and power, and diverting enterprises originally started for public benefit into channels for corporate greed and oppression, and we demand that no more exclusive contracts be made.

American citizens abroad, whether native born or naturalized, and of whatever race or creed, must be secured in the enjoyment of all rights and privileges under our treaties, and wherever such rights are withheld by any country on the ground of race or religious faith, steps should be taken to secure the removal of such unjust discrimination.

We advocate the popular election of United States Senators and of judges, both State and Federal, and favor a graduated income tax and any constitutional amendment necessary to these ends.

Equality of opportunity, the largest measure of individual liberty consistent with equal rights, the overthrow of the rule of special interest and the restoration of government by the majority exercised for the benefit of the whole community; these are the purposes to which the Independence party is pledged, and we invite the co-operation of all patriots and progressive citizens, irrespective of party, who are in sympathy with these principles and in favor of their practical enforcement.

People's Platform of 1908

The People's Party of the United States, in convention assembled, at St. Louis, Mo., this 2d day of April, 1908, with increased confidence in its contentions, reaffirms the declarations made by its first national convention at Omaha, in 1892.

The admonitions of Washington's farewell address; the state papers of Jefferson, and the words of Lincoln, are the teachings of our greatest apostles of human rights and political liberty. There has been a departure from the teaching of these great patriots during recent administrations. The Government has been controlled so as to place the rights of property above the rights of humanity, and has brought the country to a condition that is full of danger to our national wellbeing. Financial combinations have had too much power over Congress, and too much influence with the administrative departments of the Government.

Prerogatives of government have been unwisely and often corruptly surrendered to corporate monopoly and aggregations of predatory wealth. The supreme duty of the hour is for the people to insist that these functions of government be exercised in their own interest. Not the giver of the "thirty pieces of silver" has been condemned, but the "Judas" who received them, has been execrated through the ages. The sycophants of monopoly deserve no better fate.

The issuance of money is a function of government and should not be delegated to corporation or individual. The Constitution gives Congress alone the power to issue money and regulate the value thereof; we, therefore, demand that all money shall be issued by the Government direct to the people without the intervention of banks, and shall be a full legal tender for all debts, public and private, and in quantity sufficient to supply the needs of the country.

The issuance and distribution of full legal tender money from the Treasury, shall not be through private banks, preferred or otherwise, but direct to the people without interest, for the construction and purchase of Federal and internal improvements and utilities, and for the employment of labor.

We demand that postal savings banks be established by the Government for the safe deposit of the savings of the people.

The public domain is a sacred heritage of all the people and should be held for homesteads for actual settlers only. Alien ownership should be forbidden, and lands now held by aliens or by corporations, who have violated the conditions of their grants, should be restored to the public domain.

To prevent unjust discrimination and monopoly, the Government should own and control the railroads and those public utilities, which in their nature are monopolies. To perfect the postal service, the Government should own and operate the general telegraph and telephone systems and provide a parcels post.

As to those trusts and monopolies which are not public utilities or national monopolies, we demand that those special privileges which they now enjoy, and which alone enable them to exist, shall be immediately withdrawn.

Corporations being the creatures of government, should be subjected to such governmental regulation and control as will adequately protect the public.

We demand the taxation of monopoly privileges while they remain in private hands, to the extent of the value of the privilege granted.

We demand that Congress shall enact a general law uniformly regulating the powers and duties of all incorporated companies doing interstate business.

As a means of placing all public questions directly under the control of the people, we demand that legal provision be made under which the people may exercise the initiative and referendum, proportional representation, and direct vote for all public officers, with the right of recall.

We recommend a Federal statute that will recognize the principle of the initiative and referendum, and thereby restore to the voters the right to instruct their national representatives.

We believe in the right of those who labor, to organize for their mutual protection and benefit, and pledge the efforts of the People's Party to preserve this right inviolate.

We condemn the recent attempt to destroy the power of trades union through the unjust use of the Federal injunction, substituting government by injunction for free government.

We favor the enactment of legislation looking to the improvement of conditions for wage earners.

We demand the abolition of child labor in factories and mines, and the suppression of sweatshops.

We oppose the use of convict labor in competition with free labor.

We demand the exclusion from American shores of foreign pauper labor, imported to beat down the wages of intelligent American workingmen.

We favor the eight hour work day, and legislation protecting the lives and limbs of workmen through the use of safety appliances.

We demand the enactment of an employer's liability act within constitutional bounds.

We declare against the continuation of the criminal carelessness in the operation of mines, through which thousands of miners have lost their lives to increase the dividends of stockholders, and demand the immediate adoption of precautionary measures to prevent a repetition of such horrible catastrophes.

We declare that in times of depression, when workingmen are thrown into enforced idleness, that works of public improvement should be at once inaugurated and work provided for those who cannot otherwise secure employment.

We especially emphasize the declaration of the Omaha platform, that "Wealth belongs to him who creates it and every dollar taken from industry without a just equivalent is robbery."

We congratulate the farmers of the country upon the enormous growth of their splendid organizations, and the good already accomplished through them, securing higher prices for farm products and better conditions generally, for those engaged in agricultural pursuits. We urge the importance of maintaining these organizations and extending their power and influence.

We condemn all unwarranted assumption of authority by inferior Federal courts, in annulling, by injunction, the laws of the States, and demand legislative action by Congress, which will prohibit such usurpation, and will restrict to the Supreme Court of the United States, the exercise of power in cases involving State legislation.

We are opposed to gambling in futures.

We present to all people the foregoing declaration of principles and policies as our deep, earnest and abiding convictions; and now, before the country and in the name of the great moral, but eternal power in the universe, that makes for right thinking and right living and determines the destiny of nations, this convention pledges that the People's Party will stand by these principles and policies in success and in defeat; that never again will the party by the siren songs and false promises of designing politicians, be tempted to change its course, or be drawn again upon the treacherous rocks of fusion.

Prohibition Platform of 1908

The Prohibition Party of the United States, assembled in convention at Columbus, Ohio, July 15 16, 1908, expressing gratitude to Almighty God for the victories of our principles in the past, for encouragement at present, and for confidence in early and triumphant success in the future, makes the following declaration of principles, and pledges their enactment into law when placed in power:—

1. The submission by Congress to the several States, of an amendment to the Federal constitution prohibiting the manufacture, sale, importation, exportation, or transportation of alcoholic liquors for beverage purposes.

2. The immediate prohibition of the liquor traffic for beverage purposes in the District of Columbia, in the Territories, and all places over which the National Government has jurisdiction; the repeal of the internal revenue tax on alcoholic liquors and the prohibition of interstate traffic therein.

3. The election of United States Senators by direct vote of the people.

4. Equitable graduated income and inheritance taxes.

5. The establishment of postal savings banks and the guaranty of deposits in banks.

6. The regulation of all corporations doing an interstate commerce business.

7. The creation of a permanent tariff commission.

8. The strict enforcement of law instead of official tolerance and practical license of the social evil which prevails in many of our cities, with its unspeakable traffic in girls.

9. Uniform marriage and divorce laws.

10. An equitable and constitutional employers liability act.

11. Court review of Post-Office Department decisions.

12. The prohibition of child labor in mines, workshops, and factories.

13. Legislation basing suffrage only upon intelligence and ability to read and write the English language.

14. The preservation of the mineral and forest resources of the country, and the improvement of the highways and waterways.

Believing in the righteousness of our cause and the final triumph of our principles, and convinced of the unwillingness of the Republican and Democratic parties to deal with these issues, we invite to full party fellowship all citizens who are with us agreed.

Republican Platform of 1908

Once more the Republican Party, in National Convention assembled, submits its cause to the people. This great historic organization, that destroyed slavery, preserved the Union, restored credit, expanded the national domain, established a sound financial system, developed the industries and resources of the country, and gave to the nation her seat of honor in the councils of the world, now meets the new problems of government with the same courage and capacity with which it solved the old.

REPUBLICANISM UNDER ROOSEVELT

In this greatest era of American advancement the Republican party has reached its highest service under the leadership of Theodore Roosevelt. His administration is an epoch in American history. In no other period since national sovereignty was won under Washington, or preserved under Lincoln, has there been such mighty progress in those ideals of government which make for justice, equality and fair dealing among men. The highest aspirations of the American people have found a voice. Their most exalted servant represents the best aims and worthiest purposes of all his countrymen. American manhood has been lifted to a nobler sense of duty and obligation. Conscience and courage in public station and higher standards of right and wrong in private life have become cardinal principles of political faith; capital and labor have been brought into closer relations of confidence and interdependence, and the abuse of wealth, the tyranny of power, and all the evils of privilege and favoritism have been put to scorn by the simple, manly virtues of justice and fair play.

The great accomplishments of President Roosevelt have been, first and foremost, a brave and impartial enforcement of the law, the prosecution of illegal trusts and monopolies, the exposure and punishment of evil-doers in the public service; the more effective regulation of the rates and service of the great transportation lines; the complete overthrow of preferences, rebates and discriminations; the arbitration of labor disputes; the amelioration of the condition of wage-workers everywhere; the conservation of the natural resources of the country; the forward step in the improvement of the inland waterways; and always the earnest support and defence of every wholesome safeguard which has made more secure the guarantees of life, liberty and property.

These are the achievements that will make for Theodore Roosevelt his place in history, but more than all else the great things he has done will be an inspiration to those who have yet greater things to do. We declare our unfaltering adherence to the policies thus inaugurated, and pledge their continuance under a Republican administration of the Government.

EQUALITY OF OPPORTUNITY

Under the guidance of Republican principles the American people have become the richest nation in the world. Our wealth to-day exceeds that of England and all her colonies, and that of France and Germany combined. When the Republican Party was born the total wealth of the country was $16,000,000,000. It has leaped to $110,000,000,000 in a generation, while Great Britain has gathered but $60,000,000,000 in five hundred years. The United States now owns one-fourth of the world's wealth and makes one-third of all modern manufactured products. In the great necessities of civilization, such as coal, the motive power of all activity; iron, the chief basis of all industry; cotton, the staple foundation of all fabrics; wheat, corn and all the agricultural products that feed mankind, America's supremacy is undisputed. And yet her great natural wealth has been scarcely touched. We have a vast domain of 3,000,000 square miles, literally bursting with latent treasure, still waiting the magic of capital and industry to be converted to the practical uses of mankind; a country rich in soil and climate, in the unharnessed energy of its rivers and in all the varied products of the field, the forest and the factory. With gratitude for God's bounty, with pride in the splendid productiveness of the past and with confidence in the plenty and prosperity of the future, the Republican party declares for the principle that in the development and enjoyment of wealth so great and blessings so benign there shall be equal opportunity for all.

THE REVIVAL OF BUSINESS

Nothing so clearly demonstrates the sound basis upon which our commercial, industrial and agricultural interests are founded, and the necessity of promoting their continued welfare through the operation of Republican policies, as the recent safe passage of the American people through a financial disturbance which, if appearing in the midst of Democratic rule or the menace of it, might have equalled the familiar Democratic panics of the past. We congratulate the people upon this renewed evidence of American supremacy and hail with confidence the signs now manifest of a complete restoration of business prosperity in all lines of trade, commerce and manufacturing.

RECENT REPUBLICAN LEGISLATION

Since the election of William McKinley in 1896, the people of this country have felt anew the wisdom of intrusting to the Republican party, through decisive majorities, the control and direction of national legislation.

The many wise and progressive measures adopted at recent sessions of Congress have demonstrated the patriotic resolve of Republican leadership in the legislative department to keep step in the forward march toward better government.

Notwithstanding the indefensible filibustering of a Democratic minority in the House of Representatives during the last session, many wholesome and progressive laws were enacted, and we especially commend the passage of the emergency currency bill; the appointment of the national monetary commission; the employer's and Government liability laws, the measures for the greater efficiency of the Army and Navy; the widow's

pension bill; the child labor law for the District of Columbia; the new statutes for the safety of railroad engineers and firemen, and many other acts conserving the public welfare.

REPUBLICAN PLEDGES FOR THE FUTURE

Tariff

The Republican party declares unequivocally for a revision of the tariff by a special session of Congress immediately following the inauguration of the next President, and commends the steps already taken to this end in the work assigned to the appropriate committees of Congress, which are now investigating the operation and effect of existing schedules.

In all tariff legislation the true principle of protection is best maintained by the imposition of such duties as will equal the difference between the cost of production at home and abroad, together with a reasonable profit to American industries. We favor the establishment of maximum and minimum rates to be administered by the President under limitations fixed in the law, the maximum to be available to meet discriminations by foreign countries against American goods entering their markets, and the minimum to represent the normal measure of protection at home; the aim and purpose of the Republican policy being not only to preserve, without excessive duties, that security against foreign competition to which American manufacturers, farmers and producers are entitled, but also to maintain the high standard of living of the wage-earners of this country, who are the most direct beneficiaries of the protective system. Between the United States and the Philippines we believe in a free interchange of products with such limitations as to sugar and tobacco as will afford adequate protection to domestic interests.

Currency

We approve the emergency measures adopted by the Government during the recent financial disturbance, and especially commend the passage by Congress, at the last session of the law designed to protect the country from a repetition of such stringency. The Republican party is committed to the development of a permanent currency system, responding to our greater needs; and the appointment of the National Monetary

Commission by the present Congress, which will impartially investigate all proposed methods, insures the early realization of this purpose. The present currency laws have fully justified their adoption, but an expanding commerce, a marvellous growth in wealth and population, multiplying the centres of distribution, increasing the demand for the movement of crops in the West and South, and entailing periodic changes in monetary conditions, disclose the need of a more elastic and adaptable system. Such a system must meet the requirements of agriculturists, manufacturers, merchants and business men generally, must be automatic in operation, minimizing the fluctuations of interest rates, and above all, must be in harmony with that Republican doctrine, which insists that every dollar shall be based upon, and as good as, gold.

Postal Savings

We favor the establishment of a postal savings bank system for the convenience of the people and the encouragement of thrift.

Trusts

The Republican party passed the Sherman Antitrust law over Democratic opposition, and enforced it after Democratic dereliction. It has been a wholesome instrument for good in the hands of a wise and fearless administration. But experience has shown that its effectiveness can be strengthened and its real objects better attained by such amendments as will give to the Federal Government greater supervision and control over, and secure greater publicity in, the management of that class of corporations engaged in interstate commerce having power and opportunity to effect monopolies.

Railroads

We approve the enactment of the railroad rate law and the vigorous enforcement by the present administration of the statutes against rebates and discriminations, as a result of which the advantages formerly possessed by the large shipper over the small shipper have substantially disappeared; and in this connection we commend the appropriation by the present Congress to enable the Interstate Commerce Commission to thoroughly investigate, and give publicity to, the accounts of interstate railroads. We believe, however, that the interstate commerce law should be further amended so as to give railroads the right to make and publish tariff agreements, subject to the approval of the Commission, but maintaining always the principle of competition between naturally competing lines and avoiding the common control of such lines by any means whatsoever. We favor such national legislation and supervision as will prevent the future over-issue of stocks and bonds by interstate carriers.

Railroad and Government Employees

The enactment in constitutional form at the present session of Congress of the employer's liability law; the passage and enforcement of the safety appliance statutes, as well as the additional protection secured for engineers and firemen; the reduction in the hours of labor of trainmen and railroad telegraphers; the successful exercise of the powers of mediation and arbitration between interstate railroads and their employes, and the law making a beginning in the policy of compensation for injured employes of the Government, are among the most commendable accomplishments of the present administration. But there is further work in this direction yet to be done, and the Republican party pledges its continued devotion to every cause that makes for safety and the betterment of conditions among those whose labor contributes so much to the progress and welfare of the country.

Wage-Earners Generally

The same wise policy which has induced the Republican party to maintain protection to American labor; to establish an eight hour day in the construction of all public works; to increase the list of employes who shall have preferred claims for wages under the bankruptcy laws; to adopt a child labor statute for the District of Columbia; to direct an investigation into the condition of working women and children, and later, of employes of telephone and telegraph companies engaged in interstate business; to appropriate $150,000 at the recent session of Congress in order to secure a thorough inquiry into the causes of catastrophes and loss of life in the mines; and to amend and strengthen the laws prohibiting the importation of contract labor, will be pursued in every legitimate direction within Federal authority to lighten the burdens and increase the opportunity for happiness and advancement of all who toil. The Republican party recognizes the special needs of wage-workers generally, for their well-being means the well-being of all. But more important than all other considerations is that of good citizenship and we especially stand for the needs of every American, whatever his occupation, in his capacity as a self-respecting citizen.

Court Procedure

The Republican party will uphold at all times the authority and integrity of the courts, State and Federal, and will ever insist that their powers to enforce their process and to protect life, liberty and property shall be preserved inviolate. We believe, however, that the rules of procedure in the Federal Courts with respect to the issuance of the writ of injunction should be more accurately defined by statute, and that no injunction or temporary restraining order should be issued without notice, except where irreparable injury would result from delay, in which case a speedy hearing thereafter should be granted.

The American Farmer

Among those whose welfare is as vital to the welfare of the whole country as is that of the wage-earner, is the American farmer. The prosperity of the country rests peculiarly upon the prosperity of agriculture. The Republican party during the last twelve years has accomplished extraordinary work in bringing the resources of the National Government to the aid of the farmer, not only in advancing agriculture itself, but in increasing the conveniences of rural life. Free rural mail delivery has been established; it now reaches millions of our citizens, and we favor its extension until every community in the land receives the full benefits of the postal service. We recognize the social and economical advantages of good country roads, maintained more and more largely at public expense, and less and less at the expense of the abutting owner. In this work we commend the growing practice of State aid, and we approve the efforts of the National Agricultural Department by experiments and otherwise to make clear to the public the best methods of road construction.

Rights of the Negro

The Republican party has been for more than

fifty years the consistent friend of the American Negro. It gave him freedom and citizenship. It wrote into the organic law the declarations that proclaim his civil and political rights, and it believes to-day that his noteworthy progress in intelligence, industry and good citizenship has earned the respect and encouragement of the nation. We demand equal justice for all men, without regard to race or color; we declare once more, and without reservation, for the enforcement in letter and spirit of the Thirteenth, Fourteenth and Fifteenth amendments to the Constitution which were designed for the protection and advancement of the negro, and we condemn all devices that have for their real aim his disfranchisement for reasons of color alone, as unfair, un-American and repugnant to the Supreme law of the land.

Natural Resources and Waterways

We indorse the movement inaugurated by the administration for the conservation of natural resources; we approve all measures to prevent the waste of timber; we commend the work now going on for the reclamation of arid lands, and reaffirm the Republican policy of the free distribution of the available areas of the public domain to the landless settler. No obligation of the future is more insistent and none will result in greater blessings to posterity. In line with this splendid undertaking is the further duty, equally imperative, to enter upon a systematic improvement upon a large and comprehensive plan, just to all portions of the country, of the waterways, harbors, and Great Lakes, whose natural adaptability to the increasing traffic of the land is one of the greatest gifts of a benign Providence.

The Army and Navy

The 60th Congress passed many commendable acts increasing the efficiency of the Army and Navy; making the militia of the States an integral part of the national establishment; authorizing joint manœuvres of army and militia; fortifying new naval bases and completing the construction of coaling stations; instituting a female nurse corps for naval hospitals and ships, and adding two new battleships, ten torpedo boat destroyers, three steam colliers, and eight submarines to the strength of the Navy. Although at peace with all the world, and secure in the consciousness that the American people do not desire and will not provoke a war with any other country, we nevertheless declare our unalterable devotion to a policy that will keep this Republic ready at all times to defend her traditional doctrines, and assure her appropriate part in promoting permanent tranquillity among the nations.

Protection of American Citizens Abroad

We commend the vigorous efforts made by the administration to protect American citizens in foreign lands, and pledge ourselves to insist upon the just and equal protection of all our citizens abroad. It is the unquestioned duty of the Government to procure for all our citizens, without distinction, the rights of travel and sojourn in friendly countries, and we declare ourselves in favor of all proper efforts tending to that end.

Extension of Foreign Commerce

Under the administration of the Republican party, the foreign commerce of the United States has experienced a remarkable growth, until it has a present annual valuation of approximately $3,000,000,000, and gives employment to a vast amount of labor and capital which would otherwise be idle. It has inaugurated, through the recent visit of the Secretary of State to South America and Mexico a new era of Pan-American commerce and comity, which is bringing us into closer touch with our twenty sister American republics, having a common historical heritage, a republican form of government, and offering us a limitless field of legitimate commercial expansion.

Arbitration and The Hague Treaties

The conspicuous contributions of American statesmanship to the great cause of international peace so signally advanced in the Hague conferences, are an occasion for just pride and gratification. At the last session of the Senate of the United States eleven Hague conventions were ratified, establishing the rights of neutrals, laws of war on land, restriction of submarine mines, limiting the use of force for the collection of contractual debts, governing the opening of hostilities, extending the application of Geneva principles and, in many ways, lessening the evils of war and promoting the peaceful settlement of international controversies. At the same session twelve arbitration conventions with great nations were confirmed, and extradition, boundary and neutralization

treaties of supreme importance were ratified. We indorse such achievements as the highest duty a people can perform and proclaim the obligation of further strengthening the bonds of friendship and good-will with all the nations of the world.

Merchant Marine

We adhere to the Republican doctrine of encouragement to American shipping and urge such legislation as will revive the merchant marine prestige of the country, so essential to national defence, the enlargement of foreign trade and the industrial prosperity of our own people.

Veterans of the Wars

Another Republican policy which must ever be maintained is that of generous provision for those who have fought the country's battles, and for the widows and orphans of those who have fallen. We commend the increase in the widows' pensions, made by the present Congress, and declare for a liberal administration of all pension laws, to the end that the people's gratitude may grow deeper as the memories of heroic sacrifice grow more sacred with the passing years.

Civil Service

We reaffirm our former declarations that the civil service laws, enacted, extended, and enforced by the Republican party, shall continue to be maintained and obeyed.

Public Health

We commend the efforts designed to secure greater efficiency in National Public Health agencies and favor such legislation as will effect this purpose.

Bureau of Mines and Mining

In the interest of the great mineral industries of our country, we earnestly favor the establishment of a Bureau of Mines and Mining.

Cuba, Porto Rico, Philippines, and Panama

The American Government, in Republican hands, has freed Cuba, given peace and protection to Porto Rico and the Philippines under our flag, and begun the construction of the Panama Canal. The present conditions in Cuba vindicate the wisdom of maintaining, between that Republic and this, imperishable bonds of mutual interest, and the hope is now expressed that the Cuban people will soon again be ready to assume complete sovereignty over their land.

In Porto Rico the Government of the United States is meeting loyal and patriotic support; order and prosperity prevail, and the well-being of the people is in every respect promoted and conserved.

We believe that the native inhabitants of Porto Rico should be at once collectively made citizens of the United States, and that all others properly qualified under existing laws residing in said island should have the privilege of becoming naturalized.

In the Philippines insurrection has been suppressed, law is established and life and property made secure. Education and practical experience are there advancing the capacity of the people for government, and the policies of McKinley and Roosevelt are leading the inhabitants step by step to an ever-increasing measure of home rule.

Time has justified the selection of the Panama route for the great Isthmian Canal, and events have shown the wisdom of securing authority over the zone through which it is to be built. The work is now progressing with a rapidity far beyond expectation, and already the realization of the hopes of centuries has come within the vision of the near future.

New Mexico and Arizona

We favor the immediate admission of the Territories of New Mexico and Arizona as separate States in the Union.

Centenary of the Birth of Lincoln

February 12, 1909, will be the 100th anniversary of the birth of Abraham Lincoln, an immortal spirit whose fame has brightened with the receding years, and whose name stands among the first of those given to the world by the great Republic. We recommend that this centennial anniversary be celebrated throughout the confines of the nation, by all the people thereof, and especially by the public schools, as an exercise to stir the patriotism of the youth of the land.

Democratic Incapacity for Government

We call the attention of the American people to the fact that none of the great measures here advocated by the Republican party could be enacted, and none of the steps forward here proposed could be taken under a Democratic administration or under one in which party responsibility is divided. The continuance of present policies, therefore, absolutely requires the continuance in power of that party which believes in them and which possesses the capacity to put them into operation.

Fundamental Differences Between Democracy and Republicanism

Beyond all platform declarations there are fundamental differences between the Republican party and its chief opponent which make the one worthy and the other unworthy of public trust.

In history, the difference between Democracy and Republicanism is that the one stood for debased currency, the other for honest currency; the one for free silver, the other for sound money; the one for free trade, the other for protection; the one for the contraction of American influence, the other for its expansion; the one has been forced to abandon every position taken on the great issues before the people, the other has held and vindicated all.

In experience, the difference between Democracy and Republicanism is that one means adversity, while the other means prosperity; one means low wages, the other means high; one means doubt and debt, the other means confidence and thrift.

In principle, the difference between Democracy and Republicanism is that one stands for vacillation and timidity in government, the other for strength and purpose; one stands for obstruction, the other for construction; one promises, the other performs, one finds fault, the other finds work.

The present tendencies of the two parties are even more marked by inherent differences. The trend of Democracy is toward socialism, while the Republican party stands for a wise and regulated individualism. Socialism would destroy wealth, Republicanism would prevent its abuse. Socialism would give to each an equal right to take; Republicanism would give to each an equal right to earn. Socialism would offer an equality of possession which would soon leave no one anything to possess, Republicanism would give equality of opportunity which would assure to each his share of a constantly increasing sum of possessions. In line with this tendency the Democratic party of to-day believes in Government ownership, while the Republican party believes in Government regulation. Ultimately Democracy would have the nation own the people, while Republicanism would have the people own the nation.

Upon this platform of principles and purposes, reaffirming our adherence to every Republican doctrine proclaimed since the birth of the party, we go before the country, asking the support not only of those who have acted with us heretofore, but of all our fellow citizens who, regardless of past political differences, unite in the desire to maintain the policies, perpetuate the blessings and make secure the achievements of a greater America.

Socialist Platform of 1908

PRINCIPLES

Human life depends upon food, clothing and shelter. Only with these assured are freedom, culture and higher human development possible. To produce food, clothing or shelter, land and machinery are needed. Land alone does not satisfy human needs. Human labor creates machinery and applies it to the land for the production of raw materials and food. Whoever has control of land and machinery controls human labor, and with it human life and liberty.

To-day the machinery and the land used for industrial purposes are owned by a rapidly decreasing minority. So long as machinery is simple and easily handled by one man, its owner cannot dominate the sources of life of others. But when machinery becomes more complex and expensive, and requires for its effective operation the organized effort of many workers, its influence reaches over wide circles of life. The owners of such machinery become the dominant class.

In proportion as the number of such machine owners compared to all other classes decreases, their power in the nation and in the world increases. They bring ever larger masses of working people under their control, reducing them to the point where muscle and brain are their only productive property. Millions of formerly self-employing workers thus become the helpless wage slaves of the industrial masters.

As the economic power of the ruling class grows it becomes less useful in the life of the nation. All the useful work of the nation falls upon the shoulders of the class whose only property is its manual and mental labor power — the wage worker—or of the class who have but little land and little effective machinery outside of their labor power — the small traders and small farmers. The ruling minority is steadily becoming useless and parasitic.

A bitter struggle over the division of the products of labor is waged between the exploiting propertied classes on the one hand and the exploited, propertyless class on the other. In this struggle the wage-working class cannot expect adequate relief from any reform of the present order at the hands of the dominant class.

The wage-workers are therefore the most determined and irreconcilable antagonists of the ruling class. They suffer most from the curse of class rule. The fact that a few capitalists are permitted to control all the country's industrial resources and social tools for their individual profit, and to make the production of the necessaries of life the object of competitive private enterprise and speculation is at the bottom of all the social evils of our time.

In spite of the organization of trusts, pools and combinations, the capitalists are powerless to regulate production for social ends. Industries are largely conducted in a planless manner. Through periods of feverish activity the strength and health of the workers are mercilessly used up, and during periods of enforced idleness the workers are frequently reduced to starvation.

The climaxes of this system of production are the regularly recurring industrial depressions and crises which paralyze the nation every fifteen or twenty years.

The capitalist class, in its mad race for profits, is bound to exploit the workers to the very limit of their endurance and to sacrifice their physical, moral and mental welfare to its own insatiable greed. Capitalism keeps the masses of workingmen in poverty, destitution, physical exhaustion and ignorance. It drags their wives from their homes to the mill and factory. It snatches their children from the playgrounds and schools and grinds their slender bodies and unformed minds into cold dollars. It disfigures, maims and kills hundreds of thousands of workingmen annually in mines, on railroads and in factories. It drives millions of workers into the ranks of the unemployed, and forces large numbers of them into beggary, vagrancy and all forms of crime and vice.

To maintain their rule over their fellow men the capitalists must keep in their pay all organs of the public powers, public mind and public conscience. They control the dominant parties and, through them, the elected public officials. They select the executives, bribe the legislatures and corrupt the courts of justice. They own and censor the press. They dominate the educational institutions. They own the nation politically and intellectually just as they own it industrially.

The struggle between wage-workers and capitalists grows ever fiercer, and has now become the only vital issue before the American people. The wage-working class, therefore, has the most direct interest in abolishing the capitalist system. But in abolishing the present system, the workingmen will free not only their own class, but also all other classes of modern society. The small farmer, who is to-day exploited by large capital more indirectly but not less effectively than is the wage laborer; the small manufacturer and trader, who is engaged in a desperate and losing struggle for economic independence in the face of the all-conquering power of concentrated capital; and even the capitalist himself, who is the slave of his wealth rather than its master. The struggle of the working class against the capitalist class, while it is a class struggle, is thus at the same time a struggle for the abolition of all classes and class privileges.

The private ownership of the land and means of production used for exploitation, is the rock upon which class rule is built; political government is its indispensable instrument. The wage-workers cannot be freed from exploitation without conquering the political power and substituting collective for private ownership of the land and means of production used for exploitation.

The basis for such transformation is rapidly developing within present capitalist society. The factory system, with its complex machinery and minute division of labor, is rapidly destroying all vestiges of individual production in manufacture. Modern production is already very largely a collective and social process. The great trusts and monopolies which have sprung up in recent years have organized the work and management of the principal industries on a national scale, and have fitted them for collective use and operation.

The Socialist Party is primarily an economic and political movement. It is not concerned with matters of religious belief.

In the struggle for freedom the interests of the modern workers are identical. The struggle is not only national, but international. It embraces the world and will be carried to ultimate victory by the united workers of the world.

To unite the workers of the nation and their allies and sympathizers of all other classes to this end, is the mission of the Socialist party. In this battle for freedom the Socialist party does not strive to substitute working class rule for capitalist class rule, but by working class victory, to free all humanity from class rule and to realize the international brotherhood of man.

PLATFORM FOR 1908

The Socialist party, in national convention assembled, again declares itself as the party of the working class, and appeals for the support of all workers of the United States and of all citizens who sympathize with the great and just cause of labor.

We are at this moment in the midst of one of those industrial breakdowns that periodically paralyze the life of the nation. The much-boasted era of our national prosperity has been followed by one of general misery. Factories, mills and mines are closed. Millions of men, ready, willing and able to provide the nation with all the necessaries and comforts of life are forced into idleness and starvation.

Within recent years the trusts and monopolies have attained an enormous and menacing development. They have acquired the power to dictate the terms upon which we shall be allowed to live. The trusts fix the prices of our bread, meat and sugar, of our coal, oil and clothing, of our raw material and machinery, of all the necessities of life.

The present desperate condition of the workers has been made the opportunity for a renewed onslaught on organized labor. The highest courts of the country have within the last year rendered decision after decision depriving the workers of rights which they had won by generations of struggle.

The attempt to destroy the Western Federation of Miners, although defeated by the solidarity of organized labor and the Socialist movement, revealed the existence of a far-reaching and unscrupulous conspiracy by the ruling class against the organization of labor.

In their efforts to take the lives of the leaders of the miners the conspirators violated state laws and the federal constitution in a manner seldom equaled even in a country so completely dominated by the profit-seeking class as is the United States.

The Congress of the United States has shown its contempt for the interests of labor as plainly and unmistakably as have the other branches of government. The laws for which the labor organizations have continually petitioned have failed to pass. Laws ostensibly enacted for the benefit of labor have been distorted against labor.

The working class of the United States cannot expect any remedy for its wrongs from the present ruling class or from the dominant parties. So long as a small number of individuals are permitted to control the sources of the nation's wealth for their private profit in competition with each other and for the exploitation of their fellowmen, industrial depressions are bound to occur at certain intervals. No currency reforms or other legislative measures proposed by capitalist reformers can avail against these fatal results of utter anarchy in production.

Individually competition leads inevitably to combinations and trusts. No amount of government regulation, or of publicity, or of restrictive legislation will arrest the natural course of modern industrial development.

While our courts, legislatures and executive officers remain in the hands of the ruling classes and their agents, the government will be used in the interests of these classes as against the toilers.

Political parties are but the expression of economic class interests. The Republican, the Democratic, and the so-called "Independence" parties and all parties other than the Socialist party, are financed, directed and controlled by the representatives of different groups of the ruling class.

In the maintenance of class government both the Democratic and Republican parties have been equally guilty. The Republican party has had control of the national government and has been directly and actively responsible for these wrongs. The Democratic party, while saved from direct responsibility by its political impotence, has shown itself equally subservient to the aims of the capitalist class whenever and wherever it has been in power. The old chattel slave-owning aristocracy of the south, which was the backbone of the Democratic party, has been supplanted by a child slave plutocracy. In the great cities of our country the Democratic party is allied with the criminal element of the slums as the Republican party is allied with the predatory criminals of the palace in maintaining the interests of the possessing class.

The various "reform" movements and parties which have sprung up within recent years are but the clumsy expression of widespread popular discontent. They are not based on an intelligent understanding of the historical development of civilization and of the economic and political needs of our time. They are bound to perish as the numerous middle class reform movements of the past have perished.

PROGRAM

As measures calculated to strengthen the working class in its fight for the realization of this ultimate aim, and to increase its power of resistance against capitalist oppression, we advocate and pledge ourselves and our elected officers to the following program:

GENERAL DEMANDS

1—The immediate government relief for the unemployed workers by building schools, by reforesting of cutover and waste lands, by reclamation of arid tracts, and the building of canals, and by extending all other useful public works. All persons employed on such works shall be employed directly by the government under an eight hour work day and at the prevailing union wages. The government shall also loan money to states and municipalities without interest for the purpose of carrying on public works. It shall contribute to the funds of labor organizations for the purpose of assisting their unemployed members, and shall take such other measures within its power as will lessen the widespread misery of the workers caused by the misrule of the capitalist class.

2—The collective ownership of railroads, telegraphs, telephones, steamship lines and all other means of social transportation and communication, and all land.

3—The collective ownership of all industries which are organized on a national scale and in which competition has virtually ceased to exist.

4—The extension of the public domain to include mines, quarries, oil wells, forests and water-power.

5—The scientific reforestation of timber lands, and the reclamation of swamp lands. The land so reforested or reclaimed to be permanently retained as a part of the public domain.

6—The absolute freedom of press, speech and assemblage.

INDUSTRIAL DEMANDS

7—The improvement of the industrial condition of the workers,

(a) By shortening the workday in keeping with the increased productiveness of machinery.

(b) By securing to every worker a rest period of not less than a day and a half in each week.

(c) By securing a more effective inspection of workshops and factories.

(d) By forbidding the employment of children under sixteen years of age.

(e) By forbidding the interstate transportation of the products of child labor, of convict labor and of all uninspected factories.

(f) By abolishing official charity and substituting in its place compulsory insurance against unemployment, illness, accident, invalidism, old age and death.

POLITICAL DEMANDS

8—The extension of inheritance taxes, graduated in proportion to the amount of the bequests and the nearness of kin.

9—A graduated income tax.

10—Unrestricted and equal suffrage for men and women, and we pledge ourselves to engage in an active campaign in that direction.

11—The initiative and referendum, proportional representation and the right of recall.

12—The abolition of the senate.

13—The abolition of the power usurped by the supreme court of the United States to pass upon the constitutionality of legislation enacted by Congress. National laws to be repealed or abrogated only by act of Congress or by a referendum of the whole people.

14—That the constitution be made amendable by majority vote.

15—The enactment of further measures for general education and for the conservation of health. The bureau of education to be made a department. The creation of a department of public health.

16—The separation of the present bureau of labor from the department of commerce and labor, and the establishment of a department of labor.

17—That all judges be elected by the people for short terms, and that the power to issue injunctions shall be curbed by immediate legislation.

18—The free administration of justice.

Such measures of relief as we may be able to force from capitalism are but a preparation of the workers to seize the whole power of government, in order that they may thereby lay hold of the whole system of industry and thus come to their rightful inheritance.

Socialist Labor Platform of 1908

The Socialist Labor Party of America, in convention assembled, reasserts the inalienable right of man to life, liberty and the pursuit of happiness.

We hold that the purpose of government is to secure to every citizen the enjoyment of this right: but taught by experience we hold furthermore that such right is illusory to the majority of the people, to wit, the working class, under the present system of economic inequality that is essentially destructive of *their* life, *their* liberty, and *their* happiness.

We hold that the true theory of politics is that the machinery of government must be controlled by the whole people; but again taught by experience we hold furthermore that the true theory of economics is that the means of production must likewise be owned, operated and controlled by the people in common. Man cannot exercise his right of life, liberty and the pursuit of happiness without the ownership of the land on and the tool with which to work. Deprived of these, his life, his liberty and his fate fall into the hands of the class that owns those essentials for work and production.

We hold that the existing contradiction between the theory of democratic government and the fact of a despotic economic system—the private ownership of the natural and social opportunities—divides the people into two classes, the Capitalist Class and the Working Class; throws society into the convulsions of the Class Struggle, and perverts Government to the exclusive benefit of the Capitalist Class.

Thus labor is robbed of the wealth which it

alone produces, is denied the means of self-employment, and, by compulsory idleness in wage slavery, is even deprived of the necessaries of life.

Against such a system the Socialist Labor party raises the banner of revolt, and demands the unconditional surrender of the Capitalist Class.

The time is fast coming when, in the natural course of social evolution, this system, through the destructive action of its failures and crises on the one hand, and the constructive tendencies of its trusts and other capitalist combinations on the other hand, will have worked out its own downfall.

We, therefore, call upon the wage workers of America to organize under the banner of the Socialist Labor Party into a class-conscious body, aware of its rights and determined to conquer them.

And we also call upon all other intelligent citizens to place themselves squarely upon the ground of Working Class interests, and join us in this mighty and noble work of human emancipation, so that we may put summary end to the existing barbarous class conflict by placing the land and all the means of production, transportation and distribution into the hands of the people as a collective body, and substituting the co-operative commonwealth for the present state of planless production, industrial war and social disorder—a commonwealth in which every worker shall have the free exercise and full benefit of his faculties, multiplied by all the modern factors of civilization.

CAMPAIGN OF 1912

The Republican Party met in June of 1912 and renominated President William Howard Taft and Vice-President James S. Sherman. The convention, one of the most acrimonious in American history, was bitterly divided between conservatives supporting Taft and progressives endorsing former President Theodore Roosevelt. Taft controlled the delegates, however, and easily won the nomination on the first ballot. The progressives reassembled in August and nominated Roosevelt for president and Governor Hiram W. Johnson of California for vice-president.

The Democrats cast forty-six ballots before Governor Woodrow Wilson of New Jersey was selected over House Speaker Champ Clark of Missouri. From among nine candidates for the vice-presidential nomination, Indiana Governor Thomas R. Marshall was chosen.

The Socialists again nominated Eugene V. Debs, who made his fourth bid for the presidency. Emil Seidel of Wisconsin was selected as the vice-presidential candidate. The Populists went out of existence, but the Prohibition Party again nominated Eugene Chafin and Aaron Watkins as their candidates and the Socialist Labor Party chose Arthur E. Reimer of Massachusetts as its presidential candidate and former candidate August Gillhaus of New York as his running mate.

In the November election, the division within the Republican Party enabled the Democrats to elect their first president in the twentieth century. Wilson polled 6,293,152 popular votes—42 percent—to 3,486,333 for Taft and 4,119,207 for Roosevelt. Roosevelt's percentage of the vote—27.39—was the largest ever obtained by a minor-party candidate. Debs received 900,369 votes—many from ex-Populists—in this remarkable election. Chafin polled 207,972 popular votes and Reimer obtained 29,374.

In the electoral vote, the dramatic effect of the G.O.P. split was most evident. Wilson carried forty-two states for 531 votes. Roosevelt, victorious in six states, received 88 electoral votes. President Taft won only in Utah and Vermont, with eight electors casting ballots for him.

Democratic Platform of 1912

We, the representatives of the Democratic party of the United States, in national convention assembled, reaffirm our devotion to the principles of Democratic government formulated by Thomas Jefferson and enforced by a long and illustrious line of Democratic Presidents.

TARIFF REFORM

We declare it to be a fundamental principle of the Democratic party that the Federal government, under the Constitution, has no right or power to impose or collect tariff duties, except for the purpose of revenue, and we demand that the collection of such taxes shall be limited to the necessities of government honestly and economically administered.

The high Republican tariff is the principal cause of the unequal distribution of wealth; it is a system of taxation which makes the rich richer and the poor poorer; under its operations the American farmer and laboring man are the chief sufferers; it raises the cost of the necessaries of life to them, but does not protect their product or wages. The farmer sells largely in free markets and buys almost entirely in the protected markets. In the most highly protected industries, such as cotton and wool, steel and iron, the wages of the laborers are the lowest paid in any of our industries. We denounce the Republican pretence on that subject and assert that American wages are established by competitive conditions, and not by the tariff.

We favor the immediate downward revision of the existing high and in many cases prohibitive tariff duties, insisting that material reductions be speedily made upon the necessaries of life. Articles entering into competition with trust-controlled products and articles of American manufacture which are sold abroad more cheaply than at home should be put upon the free list.

We recognize that our system of tariff taxation is intimately connected with the business of the country, and we favor the ultimate attainment of the principles we advocate by legislation that will not injure or destroy legitimate industry.

We denounce the action of President Taft in vetoing the bills to reduce the tariff in the cotton, woolen, metals, and chemical schedules and the Farmers' free bill, all of which were designed to give immediate relief to the masses from the exactions of the trusts.

The Republican party, while promising tariff revision, has shown by its tariff legislation that such revision is not to be in the people's interest, and having been faithless to its pledges of 1908, it should not longer enjoy the confidence of the nation. We appeal to the American people to support us in our demand for a tariff for revenue only.

HIGH COST OF LIVING

The high cost of living is a serious problem in every American home. The Republican party, in its platform, attempts to escape from responsibility for present conditions by denying that they are due to a protective tariff. We take issue with them on this subject, and charge that excessive prices result in a large measure from the high tariff laws enacted and maintained by the Republican party and from trusts and commercial conspiracies fostered and encouraged by such laws, and we assert that no substantial relief can be secured for the people until import duties on the necessaries of life are materially reduced and these criminal conspiracies broken up.

ANTI-TRUST LAW

A private monopoly is indefensible and intolerable. We therefore favor the vigorous enforcement of the criminal as well as the civil law against trusts and trust officials, and demand the enactment of such additional legislation as may be necessary to make it impossible for a private monopoly to exist in the United States.

We favor the declaration by law of the conditions upon which corporations shall be permitted to engage in interstate trade, including, among others, the prevention of holding companies, of interlocking directors, of stock watering, of discrimination in price, and the control by any one corporation of so large a proportion of any industry as to make it a menace to competitive conditions.

We condemn the action of the Republican administration in compromising with the Standard Oil Company and the tobacco trust and its failure to invoke the criminal provisions of the anti-trust law against the officers of those corporations after the court had declared that from the undisputed facts in the record they had violated the criminal

provisions of the law.

We regret that the Sherman anti-trust law has received a judicial construction depriving it of much of its efficiency and we favor the enactment of legislation which will restore to the statute the strength of which it has been deprived by such interpretation.

RIGHTS OF THE STATES

We believe in the preservation and maintenance in their full strength and integrity of the three co-ordinate branches of the Federal government— the executive, the legislative, and the judicial— each keeping within its own bounds and not encroaching upon the just powers of either of the others.

Believing that the most efficient results under our system of government are to be attained by the full exercise by the States of their reserved sovereign powers, we denounce as usurpation the efforts of our opponents to deprive the States of any of the rights reserved to them, and to enlarge and magnify by indirection the powers of the Federal government.

We insist upon the full exercise of all the powers of the Government, both State and national, to protect the people from injustice at the hands of those who seek to make the government a private asset in business. There is no twilight zone between the nation and the State in which exploiting interests can take refuge from both. It is as necessary that the Federal government shall exercise the powers delegated to it as it is that the States shall exercise the powers reserved to them, but we insist that Federal remedies for the regulation of interstate commerce and for the prevention of private monopoly, shall be added to, and not substituted for State remedies.

INCOME TAX AND POPULAR ELECTION OF SENATORS

We congratulate the country upon the triumph of two important reforms demanded in the last national platform, namely, the amendment of the Federal Constitution authorizing an income tax, and the amendment providing for the popular election of senators, and we call upon the people of all the States to rally to the support of the pending propositions and secure their ratification.

We note with gratification the unanimous sentiment in favor of publicity, before the election, of campaign contributions—a measure demanded in our national platform of 1908, and at that time opposed by the Republican party—and we commend the Democratic House of Representatives for extending the doctrine of publicity to recommendations, verbal and written, upon which presidential appointments are made, to the ownership and control of newspapers, and to the expenditures made by and in behalf of those who aspire to presidential nominations, and we point for additional justification for this legislation to the enormous expenditures of money in behalf of the President and his predecessor in the recent contest for the Republican nomination for President.

Presidential Primary

The movement toward more popular government should be promoted through legislation in each State which will permit the expression of the preference of the electors for national candidates at presidential primaries.

We direct that the National Committee incorporate in the call for the next nominating convention a requirement that all expressions of preference for Presidential candidates shall be given and the selection of delegates and alternates made through a primary election conducted by the party organization in each State where such expression and election are not provided for by State law. Committeemen who are hereafter to constitute the membership of the Democratic National Committee, and whose election is not provided for by law, shall be chosen in each State at such primary elections, and the service and authority of committeemen, however chosen, shall begin immediately upon the receipt of their credentials, respectively.

Campaign Contributions

We pledge the Democratic party to the enactment of a law prohibiting any corporation from contributing to a campaign fund and any individual from contributing any amount above a reasonable maximum.

Term of President

We favor a single Presidential term, and to that end urge the adoption of an amendment to the Constitution making the President of the United States ineligible to reëlection, and we pledge the candidates of this Convention to this principle.

Democratic Congress

At this time, when the Republican party, after a generation of unlimited power in its control of the Federal Government, is rent into factions, it is opportune to point to the record of accomplishment of the Democratic House of Representatives in the Sixty-second Congress. We indorse its action and we challenge comparison of its record with that of any Congress which has been controlled by our opponents.

We call the attention of the patriotic citizens of our country to its record of efficiency, economy and constructive legislation.

It has, among other achievements, revised the rules of the House of Representatives so as to give to the Representatives of the American people freedom of speech and of action in advocating, proposing and perfecting remedial legislation.

It has passed bills for the relief of the people and the development of our country; it has endeavored to revise the tariff taxes downward in the interest of the consuming masses and thus to reduce the high cost of living.

It has proposed an amendment to the Federal Constitution providing for the election of United States Senators by the direct vote of the people.

It has secured the admission of Arizona and New Mexico as two sovereign States.

It has required the publicity of campaign expenses both before and after election and fixed a limit upon the election expenses of United States Senators and Representatives.

It has passed a bill to prevent the abuse of the writ of injunction.

It has passed a law establishing an eight hour day for workmen on all national public work.

It has passed a resolution which forced the President to take immediate steps to abrogate the Russian treaty.

And it has passed the great supply bills which lessen waste and extravagance, and which reduce the annual expenses of the government by many millions of dollars.

We approve the measure reported by the Democratic leaders in the House of Representatives for the creation of a council of national defence, which will determine a definite naval program with a view to increased efficiency and economy.

The party that proclaimed and has always enforced the Monroe Doctrine, and was sponsor for the new navy, will continue faithfully to observe the constitutional requirements to provide and maintain an adequate and well-proportioned navy sufficient to defend American policies, protect our citizens and uphold the honor and dignity of the nation.

REPUBLICAN EXTRAVAGANCE

We denounce the profligate waste of the money wrung from the people by oppressive taxation through the lavish appropriations of recent Republican Congresses, which have kept taxes high and reduced the purchasing power of the people's toil. We demand a return to that simplicity and economy which befits a Democratic government and a reduction in the number of useless offices, the salaries of which drain the substance of the people.

RAILROADS, EXPRESS COMPANIES, TELEGRAPH AND TELEPHONE LINES

We favor the efficient supervision and rate regulation of railroads, express companies, telegraph and telephone lines engaged in interstate commerce. To this end we recommend the valuation of railroads, express companies, telegraph and telephone lines by the Interstate Commerce Commission, such valuation to take into consideration the physical value of the property, the original cost, the cost of reproduction, and any element of value that will render the valuation fair and just.

We favor such legislation as will effectually prohibit the railroads, express, telegraph and telephone companies from engaging in business which brings them into competition with their shippers or patrons; also legislation preventing the overissue of stocks and bonds by interstate railroads, express companies, telegraph and telephone lines, and legislation which will assure such reduction in transportation rates as conditions will permit, care being taken to avoid reduction that would compel a reduction of wages, prevent adequate service, or do injustice to legitimate investments.

BANKING LEGISLATION

We oppose the so-called Aldrich bill or the establishment of a central bank; and we believe our country will be largely freed from panics and consequent unemployment and business depression by such a systematic revision of our banking laws as will render temporary relief in localities where such relief is needed, with protection from control of dominion by what is known as the money trust.

Banks exist for the accommodation of the public, and not for the control of business. All legislation on the subject of banking and currency should have for its purpose the securing of these accommodations on terms of absolute security to the public and of complete protection from the misuse of the power that wealth gives to those who possess it.

We condemn the present methods of depositing government funds in a few favored banks, largely situated in or controlled by Wall Street, in return for political favors, and we pledge our party to provide by law for their deposit by competitive bidding in the banking institutions of the country, national and State, without discrimination as to locality, upon approved securities and subject to call by the Government.

RURAL CREDITS

Of equal importance with the question of currency reform is the question of rural credits or agricultural finance. Therefore, we recommend that an investigation of agricultural credit societies in foreign countries be made, so that it may be ascertained whether a system of rural credits may be devised suitable to conditions in the United States; and we also favor legislation permitting national banks to loan a reasonable proportion of their funds on real estate security.

We recognize the value of vocational education, and urge Federal appropriations for such training and extension teaching in agriculture in co-operation with the several States.

WATERWAYS

We renew the declaration in our last platform relating to the conservation of our natural resources and the development of our waterways. The present devastation of the Lower Mississippi Valley accentuates the movement for the regulation of river flow by additional bank and levee protection below, and the diversion, storage and control of the flood waters above, their utilization for beneficial purposes in the reclamation of arid and swamp lands and the development of water power, instead of permitting the floods to continue, as heretofore, agents of destruction.

We hold that the control of the Mississippi River is a national problem. The preservation of the depth of its waters for the purpose of navigation, the building of levees to maintain the integrity of its channel and the prevention of the overflow of the land and its consequent devastation, resulting in the interruption of interstate commerce, the disorganization of the mail service, and the enormous loss of life and property impose an obligation which alone can be discharged by the general government.

To maintain an adequate depth of water the entire year, and thereby encourage water transportation, is a consummation worthy of legislative attention, and presents an issue national in its character. It calls for prompt action on the part of Congress, and the Democratic party pledges itself to the enactment of legislation leading to that end.

We favor the co-operation of the United States and the respective States in plans for the comprehensive treatment of all waterways with a view of co-ordinating plans for channel improvement, with plans for drainage of swamp and overflowed lands, and to this end we favor the appropriation by the Federal Government of sufficient funds to make surveys of such lands, to develop plans for draining of the same, and to supervise the work of construction.

We favor the adoption of a liberal and comprehensive plan for the development and improvement of our inland waterways, with economy and efficiency, so as to permit their navigation by vessels of standard draft.

Post Roads

We favor national aid to State and local authorities in the construction and maintenance of post roads.

Rights of Labor

We repeat our declarations of the platform of 1908, as follows:

"The courts of justice are the bulwarks of our liberties, and we yield to none in our purpose to maintain their dignity. Our party has given to the bench a long line of distinguished justices who have added to the respect and confidence in which this department must be jealously maintained. We resent the attempt of the Republican party to raise a false issue respecting the judiciary. It is

an unjust reflection upon a great body of our citizens to assume that they lack respect for the courts.

"It is the function of the courts to interpret the laws which the people enact, and if the laws appear to work economic, social or political injustice, it is our duty to change them. The only basis upon which the integrity of our courts can stand is that of unswerving justice and protection of life, personal liberty, and property. As judicial processes may be abused, we should guard them against abuse.

"Experience has proved the necessity of a modification of the present law relating to injunction, and we reiterate the pledges of our platforms of 1896 and 1904 in favor of a measure which passed the United States Senate in 1898, relating to contempt in Federal Courts, and providing for trial by jury in cases of indirect contempt.

"Questions of judicial practice have arisen especially in connection with industrial disputes. We believe that the parties to all judicial proceedings should be treated with rigid impartiality, and that injunctions should not be issued in any case in which an injunction would not issue if no industrial dispute were involved.

"The expanding organization of industry makes it essential that there should be no abridgement of the right of the wage earners and producers to organize for the protection of wages and the improvement of labor conditions, to the end that such labor organizations and their members should not be regarded as illegal combinations in restraint of trade.

"We pledge the Democratic party to the enactment of a law creating a department of labor, represented separately in the President's cabinet in which department shall be included the subject of mines and mining."

We pledge the Democratic party, so far as the Federal jurisdiction extends, to an employés' compensation law providing adequate indemnity for injury to body or loss of life.

Conservation

We believe in the conservation and the development, for the use of all the people, of the natural resources of the country. Our forests, our sources of water supply, our arable and our mineral lands, our navigable streams, and all the other material resources with which our country has been so lavishly endowed, constitute the foundation of our national wealth. Such additional legislation as may be necessary to prevent their being wasted or absorbed by special or privileged interests, should be enacted and the policy of their conservation should be rigidly adhered to.

The public domain should be administered and disposed of with due regard to the general welfare. Reservations should be limited to the purposes which they purport to serve and not extended to include land wholly unsuited therefor. The unnecessary withdrawal from sale and settlement of enormous tracts of public land, upon which tree growth never existed and cannot be promoted, tends only to retard development, create discontent, and bring reproach upon the policy of conservation.

The public land laws should be administered in a spirit of the broadest liberality toward the settler exhibiting a *bona-fide* purpose to comply therewith, to the end that the invitation of this government to the landless should be as attractive as possible, and the plain provisions of the forest reserve act permitting homestead entries to be made within the national forests should not be nullified by administrative regulations which amount to a withdrawal of great areas of the same from settlement.

Immediate action should be taken by Congress to make available the vast and valuable coal deposits of Alaska under conditions that will be a perfect guarantee against their falling into the hands of monopolizing corporations, associations or interests.

We rejoice in the inheritance of mineral resources unequalled in extent, variety, or value, and in the development of a mining industry unequalled in its magnitude and importance. We honor the men who, in their hazardous toil underground, daily risk their lives in extracting and preparing for our use the products of the mine, so essential to the industries, the commerce, and the comfort of the people of this country. And we pledge ourselves to the extension of the work of the bureau of mines in every way appropriate for national legislation with a view to safeguarding the lives of the miners, lessening the waste of essential resources, and promoting the economic development of mining, which, along with agriculture, must in the future, even more than in the past, serve as the very foundation of our national prosperity and welfare, and our international commerce.

AGRICULTURE

We believe in encouraging the development of a modern system of agriculture and a systematic effort to improve the conditions of trade in farm products so as to benefit both consumer and producer. And as an efficient means to this end we favor the enactment by Congress of legislation that will suppress the pernicious practice of gambling in agricultural products by organized exchanges or others.

MERCHANT MARINE

We believe in fostering, by constitutional regulation of commerce, the growth of a merchant marine, which shall develop and strengthen the commercial ties which bind us to our sister republics of the south, but without imposing additional burdens upon the people and without bounties or subsidies from the public treasury.

We urge upon Congress the speedy enactment of laws for the greater security of life and property at sea; and we favor the repeal of all laws, and the abrogation of so much of our treaties with other nations, as provide for the arrest and imprisonment of seamen charged with desertion, or with violation of their contract of service.

Such laws and treaties are un-American, and violate the spirit, if not the letter, of the Constitution of the United States.

We favor the exemption from tolls of American ships engaged in coastwise trade passing through the Panama canal.

We also favor legislation forbidding the use of the Panama Canal by ships owned or controlled by railroad carriers engaged in transportation competitive with the canal.

PURE FOOD AND PUBLIC HEALTH

We reaffirm our previous declarations advocating the union and strengthening of the various governmental agencies relating to pure foods, quarantine, vital statistics and human health. Thus united, and administered without partiality to or discrimination against any school of medicine or system of healing, they would constitute a single health service, not subordinated to any commercial or financial interests, but devoted exclusively to the conservation of human life and efficiency. Moreover, this health service should co-operate with the health agencies of our various States and cities, without interference with their prerogatives, or with the freedom of individuals to employ such medical or hygienic aid as they may see fit.

CIVIL SERVICE LAW

The law pertaining to the civil service should be honestly and rigidly enforced, to the end that merit and ability shall be the standard of appointment and promotion, rather than service rendered to a political party; and we favor a reorganization of the civil service, with adequate compensation commensurate with the class of work performed for all officers and employés; and also favor the extension to all classes of civil service employés of the benefits of the provisions of the employers' liability law. We also recognize the right of direct petition to Congress by employés for the redress of grievances.

LAW REFORM

We recognize the urgent need of reform in the administration of civil and criminal law in the United States, and we recommend the enactment of such legislation and the promotion of such measures as will rid the present legal system of the delays, expense, and uncertainties incident to the system as now administered.

THE PHILIPPINES

We reaffirm the position thrice announced by the Democracy in national convention assembled against a policy of imperialism and colonial exploitation in the Philippines or elsewhere. We condemn the experiment in imperialism as an inexcusable blunder, which has involved us in enormous expense, brought us weakness instead of strength, and laid our nation open to the charge of abandonment of the fundamental doctrine of self-government. We favor an immediate declaration of the nation's purpose to recognize the independence of the Philippine Islands as soon as a stable government can be established, such independence to be guaranteed by us until the neutralization of the islands can be secured by treaty with other Powers.

In recognizing the independence of the Philippines, our government should retain such land as may be necessary for coaling stations and naval bases.

ARIZONA AND NEW MEXICO

We welcome Arizona and New Mexico to the sisterhood of States, and heartily congratulate them upon their auspicious beginnings of great and glorious careers.

ALASKA

We demand for the people of Alaska the full enjoyment of the rights and privileges of a Territorial form of government, and we believe that the officials appointed to administer the government of all our Territories and the District of Columbia should be qualified by previous *bona-fide* residence.

THE RUSSIAN TREATY

We commend the patriotism of the Democratic members of the Senate and House of Representatives which compelled the termination of the Russian treaty of 1832, and we pledge ourselves anew to preserve the sacred rights of American citizenship at home and abroad. No treaty should receive the sanction of our government which does not recognize the equality of all of our citizens, irrespective of race or creed, and which does not expressly guarantee the fundamental right of expatriation.

The constitutional rights of American citizens should protect them on our borders and go with them throughout the world, and every American citizen residing or having property in any foreign country is entitled to and must be given the full protection of the United States government, both for himself and his property.

PARCELS POST AND RURAL DELIVERY

We favor the establishment of a parcels post or postal express, and also the extension of the rural delivery system as rapidly as practicable.

PANAMA CANAL EXPOSITION

We hereby express our deep interest in the great Panama Canal Exposition to be held in San Francisco in 1915, and favor such encouragement as can be properly given.

PROTECTION OF NATIONAL UNIFORM

We commend to the several States the adoption of a law making it an offence for the proprietors of places of public amusement and entertainment to discriminate against the uniform of the United States, similar to the law passed by Congress applicable to the District of Columbia and the Territories in 1911.

PENSIONS

We renew the declaration of our last platform relating to a generous pension policy.

RULE OF THE PEOPLE

We direct attention to the fact that the Democratic party's demand for a return to the rule of the people expressed in the national platform four years ago, has now become the accepted doctrine of a large majority of the electors. We again remind the country that only by a larger exercise of the reserved power of the people can they protect themselves from the misuse of delegated power and the usurpation of government instrumentalities by special interests. For this reason the National Convention insisted on the overthrow of Cannonism and the inauguration of a system by which United States Senators could be elected by direct vote. The Democratic party offers itself to the country as an agency through which the complete overthrow and extirpation of corruption, fraud, and machine rule in American politics can be effected.

CONCLUSION

Our platform is one of principles which we believe to be essential to our national welfare. Our pledges are made to be kept when in office, as well as relied upon during the campaign, and we invite the co-operation of all citizens, regardless of party, who believe in maintaining unimpaired the institutions and traditions of our country.

Progressive Platform of 1912

The conscience of the people, in a time of grave national problems, has called into being a new party, born of the nation's sense of justice. We of the Progressive party here dedicate ourselves to the fulfillment of the duty laid upon us by our fathers to maintain the government of the people, by the people and for the people whose foundations they laid.

We hold with Thomas Jefferson and Abraham Lincoln that the people are the masters of their Constitution, to fulfill its purposes and to safeguard it from those who, by perversion of its intent, would convert it into an instrument of injustice. In accordance with the needs of each generation the people must use their sovereign powers to establish and maintain equal opportunity and industrial justice, to secure which this Government was founded and without which no republic can endure.

This country belongs to the people who inhabit it. Its resources, its business, its institutions and its laws should be utilized, maintained or altered in whatever manner will best promote the general interest.

It is time to set the public welfare in the first place.

THE OLD PARTIES

Political parties exist to secure responsible government and to execute the will of the people.

From these great tasks both of the old parties have turned aside. Instead of instruments to promote the general welfare, they have become the tools of corrupt interests which use them impartially to serve their selfish purposes. Behind the ostensible government sits enthroned an invisible government owing no allegiance and acknowledging no responsibility to the people.

To destroy this invisible government, to dissolve the unholy alliance between corrupt business and corrupt politics is the first task of the statesmanship of the day.

The deliberate betrayal of its trust by the Republican party, the fatal incapacity of the Democratic party to deal with the new issues of the new time, have compelled the people to forge a new instrument of government through which to give effect to their will in laws and institutions.

Unhampered by tradition, uncorrupted by power, undismayed by the magnitude of the task, the new party offers itself as the instrument of the people to sweep away old abuses, to build a new and nobler commonwealth.

A COVENANT WITH THE PEOPLE

This declaration is our covenant with the people, and we hereby bind the party and its candidates in State and Nation to the pledges made herein.

THE RULE OF THE PEOPLE

The National Progressive party, committed to the principles of government by a self-controlled democracy expressing its will through representatives of the people, pledges itself to secure such alterations in the fundamental law of the several States and of the United States as shall insure the representative character of the government.

In particular, the party declares for direct primaries for the nomination of State and National officers, for nation-wide preferential primaries for candidates for the presidency; for the direct election of United States Senators by the people; and we urge on the States the policy of the short ballot, with responsibility to the people secured by the initiative, referendum and recall.

AMENDMENT OF CONSTITUTION

The Progressive party, believing that a free people should have the power from time to time to amend their fundamental law so as to adapt it progressively to the changing needs of the people, pledges itself to provide a more easy and expeditious method of amending the Federal Constitution.

NATION AND STATE

Up to the limit of the Constitution, and later by amendment of the Constitution, it found necessary, we advocate bringing under effective national jurisdiction those problems which have expanded beyond reach of the individual States.

It is as grotesque as it is intolerable that the several States should by unequal laws in matter of common concern become competing commercial agencies, barter the lives of their children, the health of their women and the safety and well being of their working people for the benefit of their financial interests.

The extreme insistence on States' rights by the Democratic party in the Baltimore platform demonstrates anew its inability to understand the world into which it has survived or to administer the affairs of a union of States which have in all essential respects become one people.

EQUAL SUFFRAGE

The Progressive party, believing that no people can justly claim to be a true democracy which denies political rights on account of sex, pledges itself to the task of securing equal suffrage to men and women alike.

CORRUPT PRACTICES

We pledge our party to legislation that will compel strict limitation of all campaign contributions and expenditures, and detailed publicity of both before as well as after primaries and elections.

PUBLICITY AND PUBLIC SERVICE

We pledge our party to legislation compelling the registration of lobbyists; publicity of committee hearings except on foreign affairs, and recording of all votes in committee; and forbidding federal appointees from holding office in State or National political organizations, or taking part as officers or delegates in political conventions for the nomination of elective State or National officials.

THE COURTS

The Progressive party demands such restriction of the power of the courts as shall leave to the people the ultimate authority to determine fundamental questions of social welfare and public policy. To secure this end, it pledges itself to provide:

1. That when an Act, passed under the police power of the State, is held unconstitutional under the State Constitution, by the courts, the people, after an ample interval for deliberation, shall have an opportunity to vote on the question whether they desire the Act to become law, notwithstanding such decision.

2. That every decision of the highest appellate court of a State declaring an Act of the Legislature unconstitutional on the ground of its violation of the Federal Constitution shall be subject to the same review by the Supreme Court of the United States as is now accorded to decisions sustaining such legislation.

ADMINISTRATION OF JUSTICE

The Progressive party, in order to secure to the people a better administration of justice and by that means to bring about a more general respect for the law and the courts, pledges itself to work unceasingly for the reform of legal procedure and judicial methods.

We believe that the issuance of injunctions in cases arising out of labor disputes should be prohibited when such injunctions would not apply when no labor disputes existed.

We also believe that a person cited for contempt in labor disputes, except when such contempt was committed in the actual presence of the court or so near thereto as to interfere with the proper administration of justice, should have a right to trial by jury.

SOCIAL AND INDUSTRIAL JUSTICE

The supreme duty of the Nation is the conservation of human resources through an enlightened measure of social and industrial justice. We pledge ourselves to work unceasingly in State and Nation for:

Effective legislation looking to the prevention of industrial accidents, occupational diseases, overwork, involuntary unemployment, and other injurious effects incident to modern industry;

The fixing of minimum safety and health standards for the various occupations, and the exercise of the public authority of State and Nation, including the Federal Control over interstate commerce, and the taxing power, to maintain such standards;

The prohibition of child labor;

Minimum wage standards for working women, to provide a "living wage" in all industrial occupations;

The general prohibition of night work for women and the establishment of an eight hour day for women and young persons;

One day's rest in seven for all wage workers;

The eight hour day in continuous twenty-four-hour industries;

The abolition of the convict contract labor system; substituting a system of prison production for governmental consumption only; and the application of prisoners' earnings to the support of their dependent families;

Publicity as to wages, hours and conditions of labor; full reports upon industrial accidents and diseases, and the opening to public inspection of all tallies, weights, measures and check systems on labor products;

Standards of compensation for death by industrial accident and injury and trade disease which will transfer the burden of lost earnings from the families of working people to the industry, and thus to the community;

The protection of home life against the hazards of sickness, irregular employment and old age through the adoption of a system of social insurance adapted to American use;

The development of the creative labor power of America by lifting the last load of illiteracy from American youth and establishing continuation schools for industrial education under public control and encouraging agricultural education and demonstration in rural schools;

The establishment of industrial research laboratories to put the methods and discoveries of science at the service of American producers;

We favor the organization of the workers, men and women, as a means of protecting their interests and of promoting their progress.

DEPARTMENT OF LABOR

We pledge our party to establish a department of labor with a seat in the cabinet, and with wide jurisdiction over matters affecting the conditions of labor and living.

COUNTRY LIFE

The development and prosperity of country life are as important to the people who live in the cities as they are to the farmers. Increase of prosperity on the farm will favorably affect the cost of living, and promote the interests of all who dwell in the country, and all who depend upon its products for clothing, shelter and food.

We pledge our party to foster the development of agricultural credit and co-operation, the teaching of agriculture in schools, agricultural college extension, the use of mechanical power on the farm, and to re-establish the Country Life Commission, thus directly promoting the welfare of the farmers, and bringing the benefits of better farming, better business and better living within their reach.

HIGH COST OF LIVING

The high cost of living is due partly to worldwide and partly to local causes; partly to natural and partly to artificial causes. The measures proposed in this platform on various subjects such as the tariff, the trusts and conservation, will of themselves remove the artificial causes.

There will remain other elements such as the tendency to leave the country for the city, waste, extravagance, bad system of taxation, poor methods of raising crops and bad business methods in marketing crops.

To remedy these conditions requires the fullest information and based on this information, effective government supervision and control to remove all the artificial causes. We pledge ourselves to such full and immediate inquiry and to immediate action to deal with every need such inquiry discloses.

HEALTH

We favor the union of all the existing agencies of the Federal Government dealing with the public health into a single national health service without discrimination against or for any one set of therapeutic methods, school of medicine, or school of healing with such additional powers as may be necessary to enable it to perform efficiently such duties in the protection of the public from preventable diseases as may be properly undertaken by the Federal authorities, including the executing of existing laws regarding pure food, quarantine and cognate subjects, the promotion of vital statistics and the extension of the registration area of such statistics, and co-operation with the health activities of the various States and cities of the Nation.

BUSINESS

We believe that true popular government, justice and prosperity go hand in hand, and, so believing, it is our purpose to secure that large measure of general prosperity which is the fruit of legitimate and honest business, fostered by equal justice and by sound progressive laws.

We demand that the test of true prosperity shall be the benefits conferred thereby on all the citizens, not confined to individuals or classes, and that the test of corporate efficiency shall be the ability better to serve the public; that those who profit by control of business affairs shall justify that profit and that control by sharing with the public the fruits thereof.

We therefore demand a strong National regulation of inter-State corporations. The corporation is an essential part of modern business. The concentration of modern business, in some degree, is both inevitable and necessary for national and international business efficiency. But the existing concentration of vast wealth under a corporate system, unguarded and uncontrolled by the Nation, has placed in the hands of a few men enormous, secret, irresponsible power over the daily life of the citizen—a power insufferable in a free Government and certain of abuse.

This power has been abused, in monopoly of National resources, in stock watering, in unfair competition and unfair privileges, and finally in sinister influences on the public agencies of State and Nation. We do not fear commercial power, but we insist that it shall be exercised openly, under publicity, supervision and regulation of the most efficient sort, which will preserve its good while eradicating and preventing its ill.

To that end we urge the establishment of a strong Federal administrative commission of high standing, which shall maintain permanent active supervision over industrial corporations engaged in inter-State commerce, or such of them as are of public importance, doing for them what the Government now does for the National banks, and what is now done for the railroads by the Inter-State Commerce Commission.

Such a commission must enforce the complete publicity of those corporation transactions which are of public interest; must attack unfair competition, false capitalization and special privilege, and by continuous trained watchfulness guard and keep open equally all the highways of American commerce.

Thus the business man will have certain knowledge of the law, and will be able to conduct his business easily in conformity therewith; the investor will find security for his capital; dividends will be rendered more certain, and the savings of the people will be drawn naturally and safely into the channels of trade.

Under such a system of constructive regulation, legitimate business, freed from confusion, uncertainty and fruitless litigation, will develop normally in response to the energy and enterprise of the American business man.

We favor strengthening the Sherman Law by prohibiting agreement to divide territory or limit output; refusing to sell to customers who buy from business rivals; to sell below cost in certain areas while maintaining higher prices in other places; using the power of transportation to aid or injure special business concerns; and other unfair trade practices.

PATENTS

We pledge ourselves to the enactment of a patent law which will make it impossible for patents to be suppressed or used against the public welfare in the interests of injurious monopolies.

INTER-STATE COMMERCE COMMISSION

We pledge our party to secure to the Inter-State Commerce Commission the power to value the physical property of railroads. In order that the power of the commission to protect the people may not be impaired or destroyed, we demand the abolition of the Commerce Court.

CURRENCY

We believe there exists imperative need for prompt legislation for the improvement of our National currency system. We believe the present method of issuing notes through private agencies is harmful and unscientific.

The issue of currency is fundamentally a Government function and the system should have as basic principles soundness and elasticity. The control should be lodged with the Government and should be protected from domination or manipulation by Wall Street or any special interests.

We are opposed to the so-called Aldrich currency bill, because its provisions would place our currency and credit system in private hands, not subject to effective public control.

COMMERCIAL DEVELOPMENT

The time has come when the Federal Government should co-operate with manufacturers and producers in extending our foreign commerce. To this end we demand adequate appropriations by Congress, and the appointment of diplomatic and consular officers solely with a view to their special fitness and worth, and not in consideration of political expediency.

It is imperative to the welfare of our people that we enlarge and extend our foreign commerce.

In every way possible our Federal Government should co-operate in this important matter. Germany's policy of co-operation between government and business has, in comparatively few years, made that nation a leading competitor for the commerce of the world.

CONSERVATION

The natural resources of the Nation must be promptly developed and generously used to supply the people's needs, but we cannot safely allow them to be wasted, exploited, monopolized or controlled against the general good. We heartily favor the policy of conservation, and we pledge our party to protect the National forests without hindering their legitimate use for the benefit of all the people.

Agricultural lands in the National forests are, and should remain, open to the genuine settler. Conservation will not retard legitimate development. The honest settler must receive his patent promptly, without hindrance, rules or delays.

We believe that the remaining forests, coal and oil lands, water powers and other natural resources still in State or National control (except agricultural lands) are more likely to be wisely conserved and utilized for the general welfare if held in the public hands.

In order that consumers and producers, managers and workmen, now and hereafter, need not pay toll to private monopolies of power and raw material, we demand that such resources shall be retained by the State or Nation, and opened to immediate use under laws which will encourage development and make to the people a moderate return for benefits conferred.

In particular we pledge our party to require reasonable compensation to the public for water power rights hereafter granted by the public.

We pledge legislation to lease the public grazing lands under equitable provisions now pending which will increase the production of food for the people and thoroughly safeguard the rights of the actual homemaker. Natural resources, whose conservation is necessary for the National welfare, should be owned or controlled by the Nation.

GOOD ROADS

We recognize the vital importance of good roads and we pledge our party to foster their extension in every proper way, and we favor the early construction of National highways. We also favor the extension of the rural free delivery service.

ALASKA

The coal and other natural resources of Alaska should be opened to development at once. They are owned by the people of the United States, and are safe from monopoly, waste or destruction only while so owned.

We demand that they shall neither be sold nor

given away, except under the Homestead Law, but while held in Government ownership shall be opened to use promptly upon liberal terms requiring immediate development.

Thus the benefit of cheap fuel will accrue to the Government of the United States and to the people of Alaska and the Pacific Coast; the settlement of extensive agricultural lands will be hastened; the extermination of the salmon will be prevented and the just and wise development of Alaskan resources will take the place of private extortion or monopoly.

We demand also that extortion or monopoly in transportation shall be prevented by the prompt acquisition, construction or improvement by the Government of such railroads, harbor and other facilities for transportation as the welfare of the people may demand.

We promise the people of the Territory of Alaska the same measure of legal self-government that was given to other American territories, and that Federal officials appointed there shall be qualified by previous *bona-fide* residence in the Territory.

WATERWAYS

The rivers of the United States are the natural arteries of this continent. We demand that they shall be opened to traffic as indispensable parts of a great Nation-wide system of transportation, in which the Panama Canal will be the central link, thus enabling the whole interior of the United States to share with the Atlantic and Pacific seaboards in the benefit derived from the canal.

It is a National obligation to develop our rivers, and especially the Mississippi and its tributaries, without delay, under a comprehensive general plan covering each river system from its source to its mouth, designed to secure its highest usefulness for navigation, irrigation, domestic supply, water power and the prevention of floods.

We pledge our party to the immediate preparation of such a plan, which should be made and carried out in close and friendly co-operation between the Nation, the States and the cities affected.

Under such a plan, the destructive floods of the Mississippi and other streams, which represent a vast and needless loss to the Nation, would be controlled by forest conservation and water stor-

age at the headwaters, and by levees below; land sufficient to support millions of people would be reclaimed from the deserts and the swamps, water power enough to transform the industrial standings of whole States would be developed, adequate water terminals would be provided, transportation by river would revive, and the railroads would be compelled to co-operate as freely with the boat lines as with each other.

The equipment, organization and experience acquired in constructing the Panama Canal soon will be available for the Lakes-to-the-Gulf deep waterway and other portions of this great work, and should be utilized by the Nation in co-operation with the various States, at the lowest net cost to the people.

PANAMA CANAL

The Panama Canal, built and paid for by the American people, must be used primarily for their benefit.

We demand that the canal shall be so operated as to break the transportation monopoly now held and misused by the transcontinental railroads by maintaining sea competition with them; that ships directly or indirectly owned or controlled by American railroad corporations shall not be permitted to use the canal, and that American ships engaged in coastwise trade shall pay no tolls.

The Progressive party will favor legislation having for its aim the development of friendship and commerce between the United States and Latin-American nations.

TARIFF

We believe in a protective tariff which shall equalize conditions of competition between the United States and foreign countries, both for the farmer and the manufacturer, and which shall maintain for labor an adequate standard of living.

Primarily the benefit of any tariff should be disclosed in the pay envelope of the laborer. We declare that no industry deserves protection which is unfair to labor or which is operating in violation of Federal law. We believe that the presumption is always in favor of the consuming public.

We demand tariff revision because the present tariff is unjust to the people of the United States. Fair dealing toward the people requires an immediate downward revision of those schedules wherein duties are shown to be unjust or excessive.

We pledge ourselves to the establishment of a non-partisan scientific tariff commission, reporting both to the President and to either branch of Congress, which shall report, first, as to the costs of production, efficiency of labor, capitalization, industrial organization and efficiency and the general competitive position in this country and abroad of industries seeking protection from Congress; second, as to the revenue producing power of the tariff and its relation to the resources of Government; and, third, as to the effect of the tariff on prices, operations of middlemen, and on the purchasing power of the consumer.

We believe that this commission should have plenary power to elicit information, and for this purpose to prescribe a uniform system of accounting for the great protected industries. The work of the commission should not prevent the immediate adoption of acts reducing these schedules generally recognized as excessive.

We condemn the Payne-Aldrich bill as unjust to the people. The Republican organization is in the hands of those who have broken, and cannot again be trusted to keep, the promise of necessary downward revision.

The Democratic party is committed to the destruction of the protective system through a tariff for revenue only—a policy which would inevitably produce widespread industrial and commercial disaster.

We demand the immediate repeal of the Canadian Reciprocity Act.

INHERITANCE AND INCOME TAX

We believe in a graduated inheritance tax as a National means of equalizing the obligations of holders of property to Government, and we hereby pledge our party to enact such a Federal law as will tax large inheritances, returning to the States an equitable percentage of all amounts collected.

We favor the ratification of the pending amendment to the Constitution giving the Government power to levy an income tax.

PEACE AND NATIONAL DEFENSE

The Progressive party deplores the survival in our civilization of the barbaric system of warfare among nations with its enormous waste of resources even in time of peace, and the consequent impoverishment of the life of the toiling masses. We pledge the party to use its best endeavors to substitute judicial and other peaceful means of settling international differences.

We favor an international agreement for the limitation of naval forces. Pending such an agreement, and as the best means of preserving peace, we pledge ourselves to maintain for the present the policy of building two battleships a year.

TREATY RIGHTS

We pledge our party to protect the rights of American citizenship at home and abroad. No treaty should receive the sanction of our Government which discriminates between American citizens because of birthplace, race, or religion, or that does not recognize the absolute right of expatriation.

THE IMMIGRANT

Through the establishment of industrial standards we propose to secure to the able-bodied immigrant and to his native fellow workers a larger share of American opportunity.

We denounce the fatal policy of indifference and neglect which has left our enormous immigrant population to become the prey of chance and cupidity.

We favor Governmental action to encourage the distribution of immigrants away from the congested cities, to rigidly supervise all private agencies dealing with them and to promote their assimilation, education and advancement.

PENSIONS

We pledge ourselves to a wise and just policy of pensioning American soldiers and sailors and their widows and children by the Federal Government. And we approve the policy of the southern States in granting pensions to the ex-Confederate soldiers and sailors and their widows and children.

PARCEL POST

We pledge our party to the immediate creation of a parcel post, with rates proportionate to distance and service.

CIVIL SERVICE

We condemn the violations of the Civil Service Law under the present administration, including the coercion and assessment of subordinate employés, and the President's refusal to punish such violation after a finding of guilty by his own commission; his distribution of patronage among subservient congressmen, while withholding it from those who refuse support of administration measures; his withdrawal of nominations from the Senate until political support for himself was secured, and his open use of the offices to reward those who voted for his renomination.

To eradicate these abuses, we demand not only the enforcement of the civil service act in letter and spirit, but also legislation which will bring under the competitive system postmasters, collectors, marshals, and all other non-political officers, as well as the enactment of an equitable retirement law, and we also insist upon continuous service during good behavior and efficiency.

GOVERNMENT BUSINESS ORGANIZATION

We pledge our party to readjustment of the business methods of the National Government and a proper co-ordination of the Federal bureaus, which will increase the economy and efficiency of the Government service, prevent duplications, and secure better results to the taxpayers for every dollar expended.

GOVERNMENT SUPERVISION OVER INVESTMENTS

The people of the United States are swindled out of many millions of dollars every year, through worthless investments. The plain people, the wage earner and the men and women with small savings, have no way of knowing the merit of concerns sending out highly colored prospectuses offering stock for sale, prospectuses that make big returns seem certain and fortunes easily within grasp.

We hold it to be the duty of the Government to protect its people from this kind of piracy. We, therefore, demand wise, carefully thought out legislation that will give us such Governmental supervision over this matter as will furnish to the people of the United States this much-needed protection, and we pledge ourselves thereto.

CONCLUSION

On these principles and on the recognized desirability of uniting the Progressive forces of the Nation into an organization which shall unequivocally represent the Progressive spirit and policy we appeal for the support of all American citizens, without regard to previous political affiliations.

Prohibition Platform of 1912

The Prohibition Party in National Convention at Atlantic City, N. J., July 10, 1912, recognizing God as the source of all governmental authority, makes the following declarations of principles and policies:

1. The alcoholic drink traffic is wrong; is the most serious drain on the wealth and resources of the nation; is detrimental to the general welfare and destructive of the inalienable rights of life, liberty and the pursuit of happiness. All laws taxing or licensing a traffic which produces crime, poverty and political corruption, and spreads disease and death should be repealed. To destroy such a traffic there must be elected to power a political party which will administer the government from the standpoint that the alcoholic drink traffic is a crime and not a business, and we pledge that the manufacture, importation, exportation, transportation and sale of alcoholic beverages shall be prohibited.

We favor:

2. Suffrage for women on the same terms as for men.

3. A uniform marriage and divorce law. The extermination of polygamy. And the complete suppression of the traffic in girls.

4. Absolute protection of the rights of labor, without impairment of the rights of capital.

5. The settlement of all international disputes by arbitration.

6. The abolition of child labor in mines, workshops and factories, with the rigid enforcement of the laws now flagrantly violated.

7. The election of United States Senators by direct vote of the people.

8. A Presidential term of six years, and one term only.

9. Court review of Post Office and other departmental decisions and orders; the extension of the Postal Savings Bank system, and of Rural Delivery, and the establishment of an efficient parcels post.

10. The initiative, referendum and recall.

11. As the tariff is a commercial question it should be fixed on the scientific basis of accurate knowledge, secured by means of a permanent, omni-partisan tariff commission, with ample powers.

12. Equitable graduated income and inheritance taxes.

13. Conservation of our forest and mineral reserves, and the reclamation of waste lands. All mineral and timber lands, and water powers, now owned by the government, should be held perpetually, and leased for revenue purposes.

14. Clearly defined laws for the regulation and control of corporations transacting an inter-State business.

15. Efficiency and economy in governmental administration.

16. The protection of one day in seven as a day of rest.

To these fundamental principles, the National Prohibition Party renews its long allegiance, and on these issues invites the co-operation of all good citizens, to the end that the true object of government may be attained, namely, equal and exact justice for all.

Republican Platform of 1912

The Republican party, assembled by its representatives in National Convention, declares its unchanging faith in government of the people, by the people, for the people. We renew our allegiance to the principles of the Republican party and our devotion to the cause of Republican institutions established by the fathers.

It is appropriate that we should now recall with a sense of veneration and gratitude the name of our first great leader, who was nominated in this city, and whose lofty principles and superb devotion to his country are an inspiration to the party he honored—Abraham Lincoln.

In the present state of public affairs we should be inspired by his broad statesmanship and by his tolerant spirit toward men.

The Republican party looks back upon its record with pride and satisfaction, and forward to its new responsibilities with hope and confidence. Its achievements in government constitute the most luminous pages in our history. Our greatest national advance has been made during the years of its ascendancy in public affairs. It has been genuinely and always a party of progress; it has never been either stationary or reactionary. It has gone from the fulfilment of one great pledge to the fulfilment of another in response to the public need and to the popular will.

We believe in our self-controlled representative democracy which is a government of laws, not of men, and in which order is the prerequisite of progress.

The principles of constitutional government, which make provisions for orderly and effective expression of the popular will, for the protection of civil liberty and the rights of man, and for the interpretation of the law by an untrammelled and independent judiciary, have proved themselves capable of sustaining the structure of a government which, after more than a century of development, embraces one hundred millions of people, scattered over a wide and diverse territory, but bound by common purpose, common ideals and common affection to the Constitution of the United States. Under the Constitution and the principles asserted and vitalized by it, the United States has grown to be one of the great civilized and civilizing powers of the earth. It offers a home and an opportunity to the ambitious and the industrious from other lands. Resting upon the broad basis of a people's confidence and a people's support, and managed by the people themselves, the government of the United States will meet the problems of the future as satisfactorily as it has solved those of the past.

The Republican party is now, as always, a party of advanced and constructive statemanship. It is prepared to go forward with the solution of those new questions, which social, economic and political development have brought into the forefront of the nation's interest. It will strive, not only in the nation but in the several States, to enact the necessary legislation to safeguard the public health; to limit effectively the labor of women and children, and to protect wage earners engaged in dangerous occupations; to enact comprehensive and generous workman's compensation laws in place of the present wasteful and unjust system of employers' liability; and in all possible ways to satisfy the just demand of the people for the study and solution of the complex and constantly changing problems of social welfare.

In dealing with these questions, it is important that the rights of every individual to the freest possible development of his own powers and resources and to the control of his own justly acquired property, so far as those are compatible with the rights of others, shall not be interfered with or destroyed. The social and political structure of the United States rests upon the civil liberty of the individual; and for the protection of that liberty the people have wisely, in the National and State Constitutions, put definite limitations upon themselves and upon their governmental officers and agencies. To enforce these limitations, to secure the orderly and coherent exercise of governmental powers, and to protect the rights of even the humblest and least favored individual are the function of independent Courts of Justice.

The Republican party reaffirms its intention to uphold at all times the authority and integrity of the Courts, both State and Federal, and it will ever insist that their powers to enforce their process and to protect life, liberty and property shall be preserved inviolate. An orderly method is provided under our system of government by which the people may, when they choose, alter or amend the constitutional provisions which underlie that government. Until these constitutional provisions are so altered or amended, in orderly fashion, it is the duty of the courts to see to it that when challenged they are enforced.

That the Courts, both Federal and State, may bear the heavy burden laid upon them to the complete satisfaction of public opinion, we favor legislation to prevent long delays and the tedious and costly appeals which have so often amounted to a denial of justice in civil cases and to a failure to protect the public at large in criminal cases.

Since the responsibility of the Judiciary is so great, the standards of judicial action must be always and everywhere above suspicion and reproach. While we regard the recall of judges as unnecessary and unwise, we favor such action as may be necessary to simplify the process by which any judge who is found to be derelict in his duty may be removed from office.

Together with peaceful and orderly development at home, the Republican party earnestly favors all measures for the establishment and protection of the peace of the world and for the development of closer relations between the various nations of the earth. It believes most earnestly in the peaceful settlement of international disputes and in the reference of all justiciable controversies between nations to an International Court of Justice.

Monopoly and Privilege

The Republican party is opposed to special privilege and to monopoly. It placed upon the statute-book the interstate commerce act of 1887, and the important amendments thereto, and the

anti-trust act of 1890, and it has consistently and successfully enforced the provisions of these laws. It will take no backward step to permit the reestablishment in any degree of conditions which were intolerable.

Experience makes it plain that the business of the country may be carried on without fear or without disturbance and at the same time without resort to practices which are abhorrent to the common sense of justice. The Republican party favors the enactment of legislation supplementary to the existing anti-trust act which will define as criminal offences those specific acts that uniformly mark attempts to restrain and to monopolize trade, to the end that those who honestly intend to obey the law may have a guide for their action and those who aim to violate the law may the more surely be punished. The same certainty should be given to the law prohibiting combinations and monopolies that characterize other provisions of commercial law; in order that no part of the field of business opportunity may be restricted by monopoly or combination, that business success honorably achieved may not be converted into crime, and that the right of every man to acquire commodities, and particularly the necessaries of life, in an open market uninfluenced by the manipulation of trust or combination, may be preserved.

Federal Trade Commission

In the enforcement and administration of Federal Laws governing interstate commerce and enterprises impressed with a public use engaged therein, there is much that may be committed to a Federal trade commission, thus placing in the hands of an administrative board many of the functions now necessarily exercised by the courts. This will promote promptness in the administration of the law and avoid delays and technicalities incident to court procedure.

The Tariff

We reaffirm our belief in a protective tariff. The Republican tariff policy has been of the greatest benefit to the country, developing our resources, diversifying our industries, and protecting our workmen against competition with cheaper labor abroad, thus establishing for our wage-earners the American standard of living. The protective tariff is so woven into the fabric of our industrial and agricultural life that to substitute for it a tariff for revenue only would destroy many industries and throw millions of our people out of employment. The products of the farm and of the mine should receive the same measure of protection as other products of American labor.

We hold that the import duties should be high enough, while yielding a sufficient revenue, to protect adequately American industries and wages. Some of the existing import duties are too high, and should be reduced. Readjustment should be made from time to time to conform to changing conditions and to reduce excessive rates, but without injury to any American industry. To accomplish this correct information is indispensable. This information can best be obtained by an expert commission, as the large volume of useful facts contained in the recent reports of the Tariff Board has demonstrated.

The pronounced feature of modern industrial life is its enormous diversification. To apply tariff rates justly to these changing conditions requires closer study and more scientific methods than ever before. The Republican party has shown by its creation of a Tariff Board its recognition of this situation, and its determination to be equal to it. We condemn the Democratic party for its failure either to provide funds for the continuance of this board or to make some other provision for securing the information requisite for intelligent tariff legislation. We protest against the Democratic method of legislating on these vitally important subjects without careful investigation.

We condemn the Democratic tariff bills passed by the House of Representatives of the Sixty-second Congress as sectional, as injurious to the public credit, and as destructive to business enterprise.

Cost of Living

The steadily increasing cost of living has become a matter not only of national but of world-wide concern. The fact that it is not due to the protective tariff system is evidenced by the existence of similar conditions in countries which have a tariff policy different from our own, as well as by the fact that the cost of living has increased while rates of duty have remained stationary or been reduced.

The Republican party will support a prompt scientific inquiry into the causes which are operative, both in the United States and elsewhere, to increase the cost of living. When the exact facts are known, it will take the necessary steps to remove any abuses that may be found to exist, in order that the cost of the food, clothing and shelter of the people may in no way be unduly or artificially increased.

Banking and Currency

The Republican party has always stood for a sound currency and for safe banking methods. It is responsible for the resumption of specie payments and for the establishment of the gold standard. It is committed to the progressive development of our banking and currency systems. Our banking arrangements to-day need further revision to meet the requirements of current conditions. We need measures which will prevent the recurrence of money panics and financial disturbances and which will promote the prosperity of business and the welfare of labor by producing constant employment. We need better currency facilities for the movement of crops in the West and South. We need banking arrangements under American auspices for the encouragement and better conduct of our foreign trade. In attaining these ends, the independence of individual banks, whether organized under national or State charters, must be carefully protected, and our banking and currency system must be safeguarded from any possibility of domination by sectional, financial, or political interests.

It is of great importance to the social and economic welfare of this country that its farmers have facilities for borrowing easily and cheaply the money they need to increase the productivity of their land. It is as important that financial machinery be provided to supply the demand of farmers for credit as it is that the banking and currency systems be reformed in the interest of general business. Therefore, we recommend and urge an authoritative investigation of agricultural credit societies and corporations in other countries and the passage of State and Federal laws for the establishment and capable supervision of organizations having for their purpose the loaning of funds to farmers.

The Civil Service

We reaffirm our adherence to the principle of appointment to public office based on proved fitness, and tenure during good behavior and efficiency. The Republican party stands committed to the maintenance, extension and enforcement of the Civil Service Law, and it favors the passage of legislation empowering the President to extend the competitive service as far as practicable. We favor legislation to make possible the equitable retirement of disabled and superannuated members of the Civil Service in order that a higher standard of efficiency may be maintained.

We favor the amendment of the Federal Employers' Liability Law so as to extend its provisions to all government employés, as well as to provide a more liberal scale of compensation for injury and death.

CAMPAIGN CONTRIBUTIONS

We favor such additional legislation as may be necessary more effectually to prohibit corporations from contributing funds, directly or indirectly, to campaigns for the nomination or election of the President, the Vice-President, Senators, and Representatives in Congress.

We heartily approve the recent Act of Congress requiring the fullest publicity in regard to all campaign contributions, whether made in connection with primaries, conventions, or elections.

CONSERVATION POLICY

We rejoice in the success of the distinctive Republican policy of the conservation of our National resources, for their use by the people without waste and without monopoly. We pledge ourselves to a continuance of such a policy.

We favor such fair and reasonable rules and regulations as will not discourage or interfere with actual *bona-fide* homeseekers, prospectors and miners in the acquisition of public lands under existing laws.

PARCELS POST

In the interest of the general public, and particularly of the agricultural or rural communities, we favor legislation looking to the establishment, under proper regulations, of a parcels post, the postal rates to be graduated under a zone system in proportion to the length of carriage.

PROTECTION OF AMERICAN CITIZENSHIP

We approve the action taken by the President and the Congress to secure with Russia as with other countries, a treaty that will recognize the absolute right of expatriation and that will prevent all discrimination of whatever kind between American citizens, whether native-born or aliens, and regardless of race, religion or previous political allegiance. The right of asylum is a precious possession of the people of the United States, and it is to be neither surrendered nor restricted.

THE NAVY

We believe in the maintenance of an adequate navy for the National defence, and we condemn the action of the Democratic House of Representatives in refusing to authorize the construction of additional ships.

MERCHANT MARINE

We believe that one of the country's most urgent needs is a revived merchant marine. There should be American ships, and plenty of them, to make use of the great American Inter-Oceanic canal now nearing completion.

FLOOD PREVENTION IN THE MISSISSIPPI VALLEY

The Mississippi River is the nation's drainage ditch. Its flood waters, gathered from thirty-one States and the Dominion of Canada, constitute an overpowering force which breaks the levees and pours its torrents over many millions of acres of the richest land in the Union, stopping mails, impeding commerce, and causing great loss of life and property. These floods are national in scope, and the disasters they produce seriously affect the general welfare. The States unaided cannot cope with this giant problem; hence, we believe the Federal Government should assume a fair proportion of the burden of its control, so as to prevent the disasters from recurring floods.

RECLAMATION

We favor the continuance of the policy of the government with regard to the reclamation of arid lands; and for the encouragement of the speedy settlement and improvement of such lands we favor an amendment to the law that will reasonably extend the time within which the cost of any reclamation project may be repaid by the landowners under it.

RIVERS AND HARBORS

We favor a liberal and systematic policy for the improvement of our rivers and harbors. Such improvements should be made upon expert information and after a careful comparison of cost and prospective benefits.

ALASKA

We favor a liberal policy toward Alaska to promote the development of the great resources of that district, with such safeguards as will prevent waste and monopoly.

We favor the opening of the coal lands to development through a law leasing the lands on such terms as will invite development and provide fuel for the navy and the commerce of the Pacific Ocean, while retaining title in the United States to prevent monopoly.

PHILIPPINE POLICY

The Philippine policy of the Republican party has been and is inspired by the belief that our duty toward the Filipino people is a national obligation which should remain entirely free from partisan politics.

IMMIGRATION

We pledge the Republican party to the enactment of appropriate laws to give relief from the constantly growing evil of induced or undesirable immigration, which is inimical to the progress and welfare of the people of the United States.

SAFETY AT SEA

We favor the speedy enactment of laws to provide that seamen shall not be compelled to endure involuntary servitude, and that life and property at sea shall be safeguarded by the ample equipment of vessels with lifesaving appliances and with full complements of skilled, able-bodied seamen to operate them.

REPUBLICAN ACCOMPLISHMENT

The approaching completion of the Panama Canal, the establishment of a Bureau of Mines, the institution of postal savings banks, the increased provision made in 1912 for the aged and infirm soldiers and sailors of the Republic and for their widows, and the vigorous administration of laws relating to Pure Foods and Drugs, all mark the successful progress of Republican administration, and are additional evidences of its effectiveness.

ECONOMY AND EFFICIENCY IN GOVERNMENT

We commend the earnest effort of the Republican administration to secure greater economy and increased efficiency in the conduct of government business; extravagant appropriations and the creation of unnecessary offices are an injustice to the taxpayer and a bad example to the citizen.

CIVIC DUTY

We call upon the people to quicken their interest in public affairs, to condemn and punish lynchings and other forms of lawlessness, and to strengthen in all possible ways a respect for law and the observance of it. Indifferent citizenship is an evil against which the law affords no adequate protection and for which legislation can provide no remedy.

ARIZONA AND NEW MEXICO

We congratulate the people of Arizona and New Mexico upon the admission of those States, thus merging in the Union in final and enduring form the last remaining portion of our continental territory.

We retify [ratify] in all its parts the platform of 1908 respecting citizenship for the people of Porto Rico.

REPUBLICAN ADMINISTRATION

We challenge successful criticism of the sixteen years of Republican administration under Presidents McKinley, Roosevelt, and Taft. We heartily reaffirm the indorsement of President McKinley contained in the platforms of 1900 and of 1904, and that of President Roosevelt contained in the Platforms of 1904 and 1908.

We invite the intelligent judgment of the American people upon the administration of William H. Taft. The country has prospered and been at peace under his Presidency. During the years in which he had the co-operation of a Republican Congress an unexampled amount of constructive legislation was framed and passed in the interest of the people and in obedience to their wish. That legislation is a record on which any administration might appeal with confidence to the favorable judgment of history.

We appeal to the American Electorate upon the record of the Republican party, and upon this declaration of its principles and purposes. We are confident that under the leadership of the candidates here to be nominated our appeal will not be in vain; that the Republican party will meet every just expectation of the people whose servant it is; that under its administration and its laws our nation will continue to advance; that peace and prosperity will abide with the people;

and that new glory will be added to the great Republic.

Socialist Platform of 1912

The Socialist party declares that the capitalist system has outgrown its historical function, and has become utterly incapable of meeting the problems now confronting society. We denounce this outgrown system as incompetent and corrupt and the source of unspeakable misery and suffering to the whole working class.

Under this system the industrial equipment of the nation has passed into the absolute control of a plutocracy which exacts an annual tribute of hundreds of millions of dollars from the producers. Unafraid of any organized resistance, it stretches out its greedy hands over the still undeveloped resources of the nation—the land, the mines, the forests and the water-powers of every State in the Union.

In spite of the multiplication of labor-saving machines and improved methods in industry which cheapen the cost of production, the share of the producers grows ever less, and the prices of all the necessities of life steadily increase. The boasted prosperity of this nation is for the owning class alone. To the rest it means only greater hardship and misery. The high cost of living is felt in every home. Millions of wage-workers have seen the purchasing power of their wages decrease until life has become a desperate battle for mere existence.

Multitudes of unemployed walk the streets of our cities or trudge from State to State awaiting the will of the masters to move the wheels of industry.

The farmers in every state are plundered by the increasing prices exacted for tools and machinery and by extortionate rents, freight rates and storage charges.

Capitalist concentration is mercilessly crushing the class of small business men and driving its members into the ranks of propertyless wage-workers. The overwhelming majority of the people of America are being forced under a yoke of bondage by this soulless industrial despotism.

It is this capitalist system that is responsible for the increasing burden of armaments, the poverty, slums, child labor, most of the insanity, crime and prostitution, and much of the disease that afflicts mankind.

Under this system the working class is exposed to poisonous conditions, to frightful and needless perils to life and limb, is walled around with court decisions, injunctions and unjust laws, and is preyed upon incessantly for the benefit of the controlling oligarchy of wealth. Under it also, the children of the working class are doomed to ignorance, drudging toil and darkened lives.

In the face of these evils, so manifest that all thoughtful observers are appalled at them, the legislative representatives of the Republican and Democratic parties remain the faithful servants of the oppressors. Measures designed to secure to the wage-earners of this Nation as humane and just treatment as is already enjoyed by the wage-earners of all other civilized nations have been smothered in committee without debate, and laws ostensibly designed to bring relief to the farmers and general consumers are juggled and transformed into instruments for the exaction of further tribute. The growing unrest under oppression has driven these two old parties to the enactment of a variety of regulative measures, none of which has limited in any appreciable degree the power of the plutocracy, and some of which have been perverted into means for increasing that power. Anti-trust laws, railroad restrictions and regulations, with the prosecutions, indictments and investigations based upon such legislation, have proved to be utterly futile and ridiculous.

Nor has this plutocracy been seriously restrained or even threatened by any Republican or Democratic executive. It has continued to grow in power and insolence alike under the administration of Cleveland, McKinley, Roosevelt and Taft.

In addition to this legislative juggling and this executive connivance, the courts of America have sanctioned and strengthened the hold of this plutocracy as the Dred Scott and other decisions strengthened the slave-power before the civil war. They have been used as instruments for the oppression of the working class and for the suppression of free speech and free assembly.

We declare, therefore, that the longer sufferance of these conditions is impossible, and we purpose to end them all. We declare them to be the product of the present system in which industry is carried on for private greed, instead of for the welfare of society. We declare, furthermore, that for these evils there will be and can be no remedy and no substantial relief except through Socialism under which industry will be carried on for the common good and every worker receive the full social value of the wealth he creates.

Society is divided into warring groups and classes, based upon material interests. Fundamentally, this struggle is a conflict between the two main classes, one of which, the capitalist class, owns the means of production, and the other, the working class, must use these means of production on terms dictated by the owners.

The capitalist class, though few in numbers, absolutely controls the government—legislative, executive and judicial. This class owns the machinery of gathering and disseminating news through its organized press. It subsidizes seats of learning—the colleges and schools—and even religious and moral agencies. It has also the added prestige which established customs give to any order of society, right or wrong.

The working class, which includes all those who are forced to work for a living, whether by hand or brain, in shop, mine or on the soil, vastly outnumbers the capitalist class. Lacking effective organization and class solidarity, this class is unable to enforce its will. Given such a class solidarity and effective organization, the workers will have the power to make all laws and control all industry in their own interest.

All political parties are the expression of economic class interests. All other parties than the Socialist party represent one or another group of the ruling capitalist class. Their political conflicts reflect merely superficial rivalries between competing capitalist groups. However they result, these conflicts have no issue of real value to the workers. Whether the Democrats or Republicans win politically, it is the capitalist class that is victorious economically.

The Socialist party is the political expression of the economic interests of the workers. Its defeats have been their defeats and its victories their victories. It is a party founded on the science and laws of social development. It proposes that, since all social necessities to-day are socially produced, the means of their production and distribution shall be socially owned and democratically controlled.

In the face of the economic and political aggressions of the capitalist class the only reliance left the workers is that of their economic organizations and their political power. By the intelligent and class-conscious use of these, they may resist successfully the capitalist class, break the fetters of wage-slavery, and fit themselves for the future society, which is to displace the capitalist system. The Socialist party appreciates the full significance of class organization and urges the wage-earners, the working farmers and all other useful workers to organize for economic and political action, and we pledge ourselves to support the toilers of the fields as well as those in the shops, factories and mines of the nation in their struggles for economic justice.

In the defeat or victory of the working class party in this new struggle for freedom lies the defeat or triumph of the common people of all economic groups, as well as the failure or triumph of popular government. Thus the Socialist party is the party of the present-day revolution which marks the transition from economic individualism to socialism, from wage slavery to free co-operation, from capitalist oligarchy to industrial democracy.

WORKING PROGRAM

As measures calculated to strengthen the working class in its fight for the realization of its ultimate aim, the co-operative commonwealth, and to increase its power of resistance against capitalist oppression, we advocate and pledge ourselves and our elected officers to the following programme:

Collective Ownership

1. The collective ownership and democratic management of railroads, wire and wireless telegraphs and telephones, express service, steamboat lines, and all other social means of transportation and communication and of all large-scale industries.

2. The immediate acquirement by the municipalities, the states or the federal government of all grain elevators, stock yards, storage warehouses, and other distributing agencies, in order to reduce the present extortionate cost of living.

3. The extension of the public domain to include mines, quarries, oil wells, forests and water power.

4. The further conservation and development

of natural resources for the use and benefit of all the people:

(a) By scientific forestation and timber protection.

(b) By the reclamation of arid and swamp tracts.

(c) By the storage of flood waters and the utilization of water power.

(d) By the stoppage of the present extravagant waste of the soil and of the products of mines and oil wells.

(e) By the development of highway and waterway systems.

5. The collective ownership of land wherever practicable, and in cases where such ownership is impracticable, the appropriation by taxation of the annual rental value of all land held for speculation or exploitation.

6. The collective ownership and democratic management of the banking and currency system.

Unemployment

The immediate government relief of the unemployed by the extension of all useful public works. All persons employed on such works to be engaged directly by the government under a work day of not more than eight hours and at not less than the prevailing union wages. The government also to establish employment bureaus; to lend money to states and municipalities without interest for the purpose of carrying on public works, and to take such other measures within its power as will lessen the widespread misery of the workers caused by the misrule of the capitalist class.

Industrial Demands

The conservation of human resources, particularly of the lives and well-being of the workers and their families:

1. By shortening the work day in keeping with the increased productiveness of machinery.

2. By securing to every worker a rest period of not less than a day and a half in each week.

3. By securing a more effective inspection of workshops, factories and mines.

4. By forbidding the employment of children under sixteen years of age.

5. By the co-operative organization of the industries in the federal penitentiaries for the benefit of the convicts and their dependents.

6. By forbidding the interstate transportation of the products of child labor, of convict labor and of all uninspected factories and mines.

7. By abolishing the profit system in government work and substituting either the direct hire of labor or the awarding of contracts to cooperative groups of workers.

8. By establishing minimum wage scales.

9. By abolishing official charity and substituting a non-contributory system of old age pensions, a general system of insurance by the State of all its members against unemployment and invalidism and a system of compulsory insurance by employers of their workers, without cost to the latter, against industrial diseases, accidents and death.

Political Demands

1. The absolute freedom of press, speech and assemblage.

2. The adoption of a graduated income tax, the increase of the rates of the present corporation tax and the extension of inheritance taxes, graduated in proportion to the value of the estate and to nearness of kin—the proceeds of these taxes to be employed in the socialization of industry.

3. The abolition of the monopoly ownership of patents and the substitution of collective ownership, with direct rewards to inventors by premiums or royalties.

4. Unrestricted and equal suffrage for men and women.

5. The adoption of the initiative, referendum and recall and of proportional representation, nationally as well as locally.

6. The abolition of the Senate and of the veto power of the President.

7. The election of the President and Vice-President by direct vote of the people.

8. The abolition of the power usurped by the Supreme Court of the United States to pass upon the constitutionality of the legislation enacted by Congress. National laws to be repealed only by act of Congress or by a referendum vote of the whole people.

9. Abolition of the present restrictions upon the amendment of the constitution, so that instrument may be made amendable by a majority of the voters in a majority of the States.

10. The granting of the right of suffrage in the District of Columbia with representation in Congress and a democratic form of municipal government for purely local affairs.

11. The extension of democratic government to all United States territory.

12. The enactment of further measures for general education and particularly for vocational education in useful pursuits. The Bureau of Education to be made a Department.

13. The enactment of further measures for the conservation of health. The creation of an independent bureau of health, with such restrictions as will secure full liberty to all schools of practice.

14. The separation of the present Bureau of Labor from the Department of Commerce and Labor and its elevation to the rank of a department.

15. Abolition of all federal district courts and the United States circuit courts of appeals. State courts to have jurisdiction in all cases arising between citizens of the several states and foreign corporations. The election of all judges for short terms.

16. The immediate curbing of the power of the courts to issue injunctions.

17. The free administration of the law.

18. The calling of a convention for the revision of the constitution of the United States.

Such measures of relief as we may be able to force from capitalism are but a preparation of the workers to seize the whole powers of government, in order that they may thereby lay hold of the whole system of socialized industry and thus come to their rightful inheritance.

Socialist Labor Platform of 1912

The Socialist Labor Party of the United States of America in National Convention assembled in New York on April 10th, 1912, re-affirming its previous platform pronouncements, and in accord with the International Socialist Movement, declares:—

Social conditions, as illustrated by the events that crowded into the last four years, have ripened so fast that each and all the principles, hitherto proclaimed by the Socialist Labor Party, and all and each of the methods that the Socialist Labor Party has hitherto advocated, stand to-day most conspicuously demonstrated.

The Capitalist Social System has wrought its own destruction. Its leading exponents, the present incumbent in the presidential chair, and his "illustrious predecessor," however, seemingly at war with each other on principles, cannot conceal the identity of their political views. The oligarchy proclaimed by the tenets of the one, the monarchy proclaimed by the tenets of the other, jointly proclaim the conviction of the foremost men of the Ruling Class that the Republic of Capital is at the end of its tether.

True to the economic laws from which Socialism proceeds, dominant wealth has to such an extent concentrated into the hands of a select few, the Plutocracy, that the lower layers of the Capitalist Class feel driven to the ragged edge, while the large majority of the people, the Working Class, are being submerged.

True to the sociologic laws, by the light of which Socialism reads its forecasts, the Plutocracy is breaking through its republic-democratic shell and is stretching out its hands towards Absolutism in government; the property-holding layers below it are turning at bay; the proletariat is awakening to its consciousness of class, and thereby to the perception of its historic mission.

In the midst of this hurly, all the colors of the rainbow are being projected upon the social mists from the prevalent confusion of thought.

From the lower layers of the Capitalist Class the bolder, yet foolhardy, portion bluntly demands that "the Trust be smashed."

Even if the Trust could, it should not be smashed; even if it should, it cannot. The law of social progress pushes toward a system of production that shall crown the efforts of man, without arduous toil, with an abundance of the necessaries for material existence, to the end of allowing leisure for mental and spiritual expansion. The Trust is a mechanical contrivance wherewith to solve the problem. To smash the contrivance were to re-introduce the days of small-fry competition, and set back the hands of the dial of time. The mere thought is foolhardy. He who undertakes the feat might as well brace himself against the cascade of Niagara. The cascade of Social Evolution would whelm him.

The less bold among the smaller property-holding element proposes to "curb" the Trust with a variety of schemes. The very forces of social evolution that propel the development of the Trust stamp the "curbing" schemes, whether political or economic, as childish. They are attempts to hold back a runaway horse by the tail. The laws by which the attempt has been tried strew the path of the runaway. They are splintered to pieces with its kicks, and serve only to furnish a livelihood for the Corporation and the Anti-Corporation lawyer.

From still lower layers of the same property-holding class, social layers that have sniffed the breath of Socialism and imagine themselves Socialists, comes the iridescent theory of capturing the Trust for the people by the ballot only. The "capture of the Trust for the people" implies the Social Revolution. To imply the Social Revolution with the ballot only, without the means to enforce the ballot's fiat, in case of Reaction's attempt to override it, is to fire blank cartridges at a foe. It is worse. It is to threaten his existence without the means to carry out the threat. Threats of revolution, without provisions to carry them out, result in one of two things only—either the leaders are bought out, or the revolutionary class, to which the leaders appeal and which they succeed in drawing after themselves, are led like cattle to the shambles. The Commune disaster of France stands a monumental warning against the blunder.

An equally iridescent hue of the rainbow is projected from a still lower layer, a layer that lies almost wholly within the submerged class—the theory of capturing the Trust for the Working Class with the fist only. The capture of the Trust for the people implies something else besides revolution. It implies revolution carried on by the masses. For reasons parallel to those that decree the day of small-fry competition gone by, mass-revolutionary conspiracy is, to-day, an impossibility. The Trust-holding Plutocracy may successfully put through a conspiracy of physical force. The smallness of its numbers makes a successful conspiracy possible on its part. The hugeness of the numbers requisite for a revolution against the Trust-holding Plutocracy excludes Conspiracy from the arsenal of the Revolution. The idea of capturing the Trust with physical force only is a wild chimera.

Only two programs—the program of the Plutocracy and the programme of the Socialist Labor Party—grasp the situation.

The Political State, another name for the Class State, is worn out in this, the leading capitalist nation of the world, most prominently. The Industrial or Socialist State is throbbing for birth. The Political State, being a Class State, is govern-ment separate and apart from the productive energies of the people; it is government mainly for holding the ruled class in subjection. The Industrial or Socialist State, being the denial of the Class State, is government that is part and parcel of the productive energies of the people.

As their functions are different, so are the structures of the two States different.

The structure of the Political State contemplates territorial "representation" only; the structure of the Industrial State contemplates representation of industries, of useful occupations only.

The economic or industrial evolution has reached that point where the Political State no longer can maintain itself under the forms of democracy. While the Plutocracy has relatively shrunk, the enemies it has raised against itself have become too numerous to be dallied with. What is still worse, obedient to the law of its own existence the Political State has been forced not merely to multiply enemies against itself; it has been forced to recruit and group the bulk of these enemies, the revolutionary bulk, at that.

The Working Class of the land, the historically revolutionary element, is grouped by the leading occupations, agricultural as well as industrial, in such manner that the "autonomous craft union" one time the palladium of the workers, has become a harmless scarecrow upon which the capitalist birds roost at ease, while the Industrial Unions cast ahead of them the constituencies of the government of the future, and, jointly, point to the Industrial State.

Nor yet is this all. Not only has the Political State raised its own enemies; not only has itself multiplied them; not only has itself recruited and drilled them; not only has itself grouped them into shape and form to succeed it; it is, furthermore, driven by its inherent necessities, prodding on the Revolutionary Class by digging ever more fiercely into its flanks the harpoon of exploitation.

With the purchasing power of wages sinking to ever lower depths; with certainty of work hanging on ever slenderer threads; with an ever more gigantically swelling army of the unemployed; with the needs of profits pressing the Plutocracy harder and harder recklessly to squander the workers' limbs and life; what with all this and the parallel process of merging the workers of all industries into one interdependent solid mass, the final break-up is rendered inevitable and at hand.

No wild schemes and no rainbow-chasing will stead in the approaching emergency. The Plutocracy knows this—and so does the Socialist Labor Party—and logical is the programme of each.

The programme of the Plutocracy is feudalic Autocracy, translated into Capitalism. Where a Social Revolution is pending, and, for whatever reason, is not enforced, *reaction* is the alternative.

The programme of the Socialist Labor Party is *revolution*—the Industrial or Socialist Republic, the Social Order where the Political State is overthrown; where the Congress of the land consists of the representatives of the useful occupations of the land; where, accordingly, a government is an essential factor in production; where the blessings to man that the Trust is instinct with, are freed from the trammels of the private ownership that now turn the potential blessings into a curse; where, accordingly, abundance can be the patrimony of all who work; and the shackles of wage slavery are no more.

In keeping with the goals of the different programmes are the means of their execution.

The means in contemplation by *reaction* is the bayonet. To this end *reaction* is seeking, by means of the police spy and other agencies, to lash the proletariat into acts of violence that may give a color to the resort to the bayonet. By its manœuvres, it is egging the Working Class on to deeds of fury. The capitalist press echoes the policy, while the pure and simple political Socialist Party press, generally, is snared into the trap.

On the contrary, the means firmly adhered to by the Socialist Labor Party is the constitutional method of political action, backed by the industrially and class-consciously organized proletariat, to the exclusion of Anarchy, and all that thereby hangs.

At such a critical period in the Nation's existence the Socialist Labor Party calls upon the Working Class of America, more deliberately serious than ever before to rally at the polls under the Party's banner. And the Party also calls upon all intelligent citizens to place themselves squarely upon the ground of Working Class interests, and join us in this mighty and noble work of human emancipation, so that we may put summary end to the existing barbarous class conflict by placing the land and all the means of production, transportation and distribution into the hands of the people as a collective body, and substituting for the present state of planless production, industrial war, and social disorder, the Social or Industrial Commonwealth—a commonwealth in which every worker shall have the free exercise and full benefit of his faculties, multiplied by all the modern factors of civilization.

CAMPAIGN OF 1916

In 1916, the Democrats renominated President Wilson and Vice-President Marshall at their convention in St. Louis. The Republicans, meeting in Chicago, selected Charles Evans Hughes, former governor of New York and a Supreme Court justice, as their standard-bearer. Charles W. Fairbanks of Indiana, the former vice-president, was chosen as his running mate.

The Progressives also held a convention in Chicago, nominating Theodore Roosevelt and John M. Parker, of Louisiana, for their candidates. However, Roosevelt refused to accept the nomination and asked his supporters to vote for Hughes. The party polled slightly more than 35,000 votes —less than 1 percent of the total—in November. The other minor parties were those that had previously waged campaigns. The Socialists chose Allan Benson of New York for president by a mail ballot after their previous candidate, Eugene V. Debs, declined the nomination. George R. Kirkpatrick of New Jersey was selected for the vice-presidential candidacy. The Prohibition Party members chose James F. Hanly of Indiana and Ira Landrith of Tennessee as their ticket. The Socialist Labor Party was represented by Arthur E. Reimer of Massachusetts and Caleb Harrison of Illinois.

In November, the election was close. The outcome was undecided until the votes from the West Coast were reported. Wilson received 9,126,300 popular votes to 8,546,789 for Hughes. Benson obtained 589,924 votes; Hanly, 221,030; and 15,284 persons reportedly voted for Reimer. In the electoral college, Wilson received 277 votes to 254 for Hughes. A shift of 4,000 votes in California would have given the election to the Republicans.

Democratic Platform of 1916

The Democratic Party, in National Convention assembled, adopts the following declaration to the end that the people of the United States may both realize the achievements wrought by four years of Democratic administration and be apprised of the policies to which the party is committed for the further conduct of National affairs.

I. RECORD OF ACHIEVEMENT

We endorse the administration of Woodrow Wilson. It speaks for itself. It is the best exposition of sound Democratic policy at home and abroad.

We challenge comparison of our record, our keeping of pledges and our constructive legislation, with those of any party of any time.

We found our country hampered by special privilege, a vicious tariff, obsolete banking laws and an inelastic currency. Our foreign affairs were dominated by commercial interests for their selfish ends. The Republican Party, despite repeated pledges, was impotent to correct abuses which it had fostered. Under our Administration, under a leadership which has never faltered, these abuses have been corrected, and our people have been freed therefrom.

Our archaic banking and currency system, prolific of panic and disaster under Republican administrations,—long the refuge of the money trust, —has been supplanted by the Federal Reserve Act, a true democracy of credit under government control, already proved a financial bulwark in a world crisis, mobilizing our resources, placing abundant credit at the disposal of legitimate industry and making a currency panic impossible.

We have created a Federal Trade Commission to accommodate perplexing questions arising under the anti-trust laws, so that monopoly may be strangled at its birth and legitimate industry encouraged. Fair competition in business is now assured.

We have effected an adjustment of the tariff, adequate for revenue under peace conditions, and fair to the consumer and to the producer. We have adjusted the burdens of taxation so that swollen incomes bear their equitable share. Our revenues have been sufficient in times of world stress, and will largely exceed the expenditures for the current fiscal year.

We have lifted human labor from the category of commodities and have secured to the workingman the right of voluntary association for his protection and welfare. We have protected the rights of the laborer against the unwarranted issuance of writs of injunction, and have guaranteed to him the right of trial by jury in cases of alleged contempt committed outside the presence of the court.

We have advanced the parcel post to genuine efficiency, enlarged the postal savings system, added ten thousand rural delivery routes and extensions, thus reaching two and one-half millions additional people, improved the postal service in every branch, and for the first time in our history, placed the post-office system on a self-supporting basis, with actual surplus in 1913, 1914 and 1916.

II. ECONOMIC FREEDOM

The reforms which were most obviously needed to clear away special privilege, prevent unfair discrimination and release the energies of men of all ranks and advantages, have been effected by recent legislation. We must now remove, as far as possible, every remaining element of unrest and uncertainty from the path of the business men of America, and secure for them a continued period of quiet, assured and confident prosperity.

III. TARIFF

We reaffirm our belief in the doctrine of a tariff for the purpose of providing sufficient revenue for the operation of the government economically administered, and unreservedly endorse the Underwood tariff law as truly exemplifying that doctrine. We recognize that tariff rates are necessarily subject to change to meet changing conditions in the world's productions and trade. The events of the last two years have brought about many momentous changes. In some respects their effects are yet conjectural and wait to be disclosed, particularly in regard to our foreign trade. Two years of a war which has directly involved most of the chief industrial nations in the world, and which has indirectly affected the life and industry of all nations are bringing about economic changes more varied and far-reaching than the world has ever before experienced. In order to ascertain just what those changes may be, the Democratic Congress is providing for a non-partisan tariff commission to make impartial and thorough study of every economic fact that may throw light either upon our past or upon our future fiscal policy with regard to the imposition of taxes on imports or with regard to the changed and changing conditions under which our trade is carried on. We

cordially endorse this timely proposal and declare ourselves in sympathy with the principle and purpose of shaping legislation within that field in accordance with clearly established facts rather than in accordance with the demands of selfish interests or upon information provided largely, if not exclusively, by them.

IV. AMERICANISM

The part that the United States will play in the new day of international relationships that is now upon us will depend upon our preparation and our character. The Democratic party, therefore, recognizes the assertion and triumphant demonstration of the indivisibility and coherent strength of the nation as the supreme issue of this day in which the whole world faces the crisis of manifold change. It summons all men of whatever origin or creed who would count themselves Americans, to join in making clear to all the world the unity and consequent power of America. This is an issue of patriotism. To taint it with partisanship would be to defile it. In this day of test, America must show itself not a nation of partisans but a nation of patriots. There is gathered here in America the best of the blood, the industry and the genius of the whole world, the elements of a great race and a magnificent society to be welded into a mighty and splendid Nation. Whoever, actuated by the purpose to promote the interest of a foreign power, in disregard of our own country's welfare or to injure this government in its foreign relations or cripple or destroy its industries at home, and whoever by arousing prejudices of a racial, religious or other nature creates discord and strife among our people so as to obstruct the wholesome process of unification, is faithless to the trust which the privileges of citizenship repose in him and is disloyal to his country. We therefore condemn as subversive to this Nation's unity and integrity, and as destructive of its welfare, the activities and designs of every group or organization, political or otherwise, that has for its object the advancement of the interest of a foreign power, whether such object is promoted by intimidating the government, a political party, or representatives of the people, or which is calculated and tends to divide our people into antagonistic groups and thus to destroy that complete agreement and solidarity of the people and that unity of sentiment and purpose so essential to the perpetuity of the Nation and its free institutions. We condemn all alliances and combinations of individuals in this country, of whatever nationality or descent, who agree and conspire together for the purpose of embarrassing or weakening our government or of improperly influencing or coercing our public representatives in dealing or negotiating with any foreign power. We charge that such conspiracies among a limited number exist and have been instigated for the purpose of advancing the interests of foreign countries to the prejudice and detriment of our own country. We condemn any political party which, in view of the activity of such conspirators, surrenders its integrity or modifies its policy.

V. PREPAREDNESS

Along with the proof of our character as a Nation must go the proof of our power to play the part that legitimately belongs to us. The people of the United States love peace. They respect the rights and covet the friendship of all other nations. They desire neither any additional territory nor any advantage which cannot be peacefully gained by their skill, their industry, or their enterprise; but they insist upon having absolute freedom of National life and policy, and feel that they owe it to themselves and to the rôle of spirited independence which it is their sole ambition to play that they should render themselves secure against the hazard of interference from any quarter, and should be able to protect their rights upon the seas or in any part of the world. We therefore favor the maintenance of an army fully adequate to the requirements of order, of safety, and of the protection of the nation's rights, the fullest development of modern methods of seacoast defence and the maintenance of an adequate reserve of citizens trained to arms and prepared to safeguard the people and territory of the United States against any danger of hostile action which may unexpectedly arise; and a fixed policy for the continuous development of a navy, worthy to support the great naval traditions of the United States and fully equal to the international tasks which this Nation hopes and expects to take a part in performing. The plans and enactments of the present Congress afford substantial proof of our purpose in this exigent matter.

VI. INTERNATIONAL RELATION

The Democratic administration has throughout the present war scrupulously and successfully held to the old paths of neutrality and to the peaceful pursuit of the legitimate objects of our National life which statesmen of all parties and creeds have prescribed for themselves in America since the beginning of our history. But the circumstances of the last two years have revealed necessities of international action which no former generation can have foreseen. We hold that it is the duty of the United States to use its power, not only to make itself safe at home, but also to make secure its just interests throughout the world, and, both for this end and in the interest of humanity, to assist the world in securing settled peace and justice. We believe that every people has the right to choose the sovereignty under which it shall live; that the small states of the world have a right to enjoy from other nations the same respect for their sovereignty and for their territorial integrity that great and powerful nations expect and insist upon; and that the world has a right to be free from every disturbance of its peace that has its origin in aggression or disregard of the rights of people and nations; and we believe that the time has come when it is the duty of the United States to join the other nations of the world in any feasible association that will effectively serve those principles, to maintain inviolate the complete security of the highway of the seas for the common and unhindered use of all nations.

The present Administration has consistently sought to act upon and realize in its conduct of the foreign affairs of the Nation the principle that should be the object of any association of the nations formed to secure the peace of the world and the maintenance of national and individual rights. It has followed the highest American traditions. It has preferred respect for the fundamental rights of smaller states even to property interests, and has secured the friendship of the people of these States for the United States by refusing to make a more material interest an excuse for the assertion of our superior power against the dignity of their sovereign independence. It has regarded the lives of its citizens and the claims of humanity as of greater moment than material rights, and peace as the best basis for the just settlement of commercial claims. It has made the honor and ideals of the United States its standard alike in negotiation and action.

VII. PAN-AMERICAN CONCORD

We recognize now, as we have always recognized, a definite and common interest between the United States and the other peoples and republics of the Western Hemisphere in all matters of National independence and free political development. We favor the establishment and maintenance of the closest relations of amity and mutual helpfulness between the United States and the other republics of the American continents for the support of peace and the promotion of a common prosperity. To that end we favor all measures which may be necessary to facilitate intimate intercourse and promote commerce between the United States and her neighbors to the south of us, and such international understandings as may be practicable and suitable to accomplish these ends.

We commend the action of the Democratic administration in holding the Pan-American Financial Conference at Washington in May, 1915, and organizing the International High Commission, which represented the United States in the recent meeting of representatives of the Latin-American Republics at Buenos Aires, April, 1916, which have so greatly promoted the friendly relations between the people of the Western Hemisphere.

VIII. MEXICO

The Monroe Doctrine is reasserted as a principle of Democratic faith. That doctrine guarantees the independent republics of the two Americas against aggression from another continent. It implies, as well, the most scrupulous regard upon our part for the sovereignty of each of them. We court their good will. We seek not to despoil them. The want of a stable, responsible government in Mexico, capable of repressing and punishing marauders and bandit bands, who have not only taken the lives and seized and destroyed the property of American citizens in that country, but have insolently invaded our soil, made war upon and murdered our people thereon, has rendered it necessary temporarily to occupy, by our armed forces, a portion of the territory of that friendly state. Until, by the restoration of law and order therein, a repetition of such incursions is improbable, the necessity for their remaining will continue. Intervention, implying as it does, military subjugation, is revolting to the people of the United States, notwithstanding the provocation to that course has been great and should be resorted to, if at all, only as a last recourse. The stubborn resistance of the President and his advisers to every demand and suggestion to enter upon it, is creditable alike to them and to the people in whose name he speaks.

IX. MERCHANT MARINE

Immediate provision should be made for the development of the carrying trade of the United States. Our foreign commerce has in the past been subject to many unnecessary and vexatious obstacles in the way of legislation of Republican Congresses. Until the recent Democratic tariff legislation, it was hampered by unreasonable burdens of taxation. Until the recent banking legislation, it had at its disposal few of the necessary instrumentalities of international credit and exchange. Until the formulation of the pending act to promote the construction of a merchant marine, it lacked even the prospect of adequate carriage by sea. We heartily endorse the purposes and policy of the pending shipping bill and favor all such additional measures of constructive or remedial legislation as may be necessary to restore our flag to the seas and to provide further facilities for our foreign commerce, particularly such laws as may be requisite to remove unfair conditions of competition in the dealings of American merchants and producers with competitors in foreign markets.

X. CONSERVATION

For the safeguarding and quickening of the life of our own people, we favor the conservation and development of the natural resources of the country through a policy which shall be positive rather than negative, a policy which shall not withhold such resources from development but which, while permitting and encouraging their use, shall prevent both waste and monopoly in their exploitation, and we earnestly favor the passage of acts which will accomplish these objects, reaffirming the declaration of the platform of 1912 on this subject.

The policy of reclaiming our arid lands should be steadily adhered to.

XI. THE ADMINISTRATION AND THE FARMER

We favor the vigorous prosecution of investigations and plans to render agriculture more profitable and country life more healthful, comfortable and attractive, and we believe that this should be a dominant aim of the nation as well as of the States. With all its recent improvement, farming still lags behind other occupations in development as a business, and the advantages of an advancing civilization have not accrued to rural communities in a fair proportion. Much has been accomplished in this field under the present administration, far more than under any previous administration. In the Federal Reserve Act of the last Congress, and the Rural Credits Act of the present Congress, the machinery has been created which will make credit available to the farmer constantly and readily, placing him at last upon a footing of equality with the merchant and the manufacturer in securing the capital necessary to carry on his enterprises. Grades and standards necessary to the intelligent and successful conduct of the business of agriculture have also been established or are in the course of establishment by law. The long-needed Cotton Futures Act, passed by the Sixty-Third Congress, has now been in successful operation for nearly two years. A Grain Grades Bill, long needed, and a permissive Warehouse Bill, intended to provide better storage facilities and to enable the farmer to obtain certificates upon which he may secure advances of money have been passed by the House of Representatives, have been favorably reported to the Senate, and will probably become law during the present session of the Congress. Both Houses have passed a good-roads measure, which will be of far reaching benefit to all agricultural communities. Above all, the most extraordinary and significant progress has been made, under the direction of the Department of Agriculture, in extending and perfecting practical farm demonstration work which is so rapidly substituting scientific for empirical farming. But it is also necessary that rural activities should be better directed through co-operation and organization, that unfair methods of competition should be eliminated and the conditions requisite for the just, orderly and economical marketing of farm products created. We approve the Democratic administration for having emphatically directed attention for the first time to the essential interests of agriculture involved in farm marketing and finance, for creating the Office of Markets and Rural Organization in connection with the Department of Agriculture, and for extending the co-operative machinery necessary for conveying information to farmers by means of demonstration. We favor continued liberal provision, not only for the benefit of production, but also for the study and solution of problems of farm marketing and finance and for the extension of existing agencies for improving country life.

XII. GOOD ROADS

The happiness, comfort and prosperity of rural life, and the development of the city, are alike conserved by the construction of public highways. We, therefore, favor national aid in the construction of post roads and roads for like purposes.

XIII. GOVERNMENT EMPLOYMENT

We hold that the life, health and strength of the men, women and children of the Nation are its greatest asset and that in the conservation of these the Federal Government, wherever it acts as the employer of labor, should both on its own account and as an example, put into effect the following principles of just employment:

1. A living wage for all employees.

2. A working day not to exceed eight hours, with one day of rest in seven.

3. The adoption of safety appliances and the establishment of thoroughly sanitary conditions of labor.

4. Adequate compensation for industrial accidents.

5. The standards of the "Uniform Child Labor Law," wherever minors are employed.

6. Such provisions for decency, comfort and health in the employment of women as should be accorded the mothers of the race.

7. An equitable retirement law providing for the retirement of superannuated and disabled employees of the civil service, to the end that a higher standard of efficiency may be maintained.

We believe also that the adoption of similar principles should be urged and applied in the legislation of the States with regard to labor within their borders and that through every possible agency the life and health of the people of the nation should be conserved.

XIV. LABOR

We declare our faith in the Seamen's Act, passed by the Democratic Congress, and we promise our earnest continuance of its enforcement.

We favor the speedy enactment of an effective Federal Child Labor Law and the regulation of the shipment of prison-made goods in interstate commerce.

We favor the creation of a Federal Bureau of Safety in the Department of Labor, to gather facts concerning industrial hazards, and to recommend legislation to prevent the maiming and killing of human beings.

We favor the extension of the powers and functions of the Federal Bureau of Mines.

We favor the development upon a systematic scale of the means already begun under the present administration, to assist laborers throughout the Nation to seek and obtain employment, and the extension of the Federal Government of the same assistance and encouragement as is now given to agricultural training.

We heartily commend our newly established Department of Labor for its fine record in settling strikes by personal advice and through conciliating agents.

XV. Public Health

We favor a thorough reconsideration of the means and methods by which the Federal Government handles questions of public health to the end that human life may be conserved by the elimination of loathsome disease, the improvement of sanitation and the diffusion of a knowledge of disease prevention.

We favor the establishment by the Federal Government of tuberculosis sanitariums for needy tubercular patients.

XVI. Senate Rules

We favor such alteration of the rules of procedure of the Senate of the United States as will permit the prompt transaction of the Nation's legislative business.

XVII. Economy and the Budget

We demand careful economy in all expenditures for the support of the government, and to that end favor a return by the House of Representatives to its former practice of initiating and preparing all appropriation bills through a single committee chosen from its membership, in order that responsibility may be central, expenditures

standardized and made uniform, and waste and duplication in the public service as much as possible avoided. We favor this as a practicable first step towards a budget system.

XVIII. Civil Service

We reaffirm our declarations for the rigid enforcement of the civil service laws.

XIX. Philippine Islands

We heartily endorse the provisions of the bill, recently passed by the House of Representatives, further promoting self-government in the Philippine Islands as being in fulfillment of the policy declared by the Democratic Party in its last national platform, and we reiterate our endorsement of the purpose of ultimate independence for the Philippine Islands, expressed in the preamble of that measure.

XX. Woman Suffrage

We recommend the extension of the franchise to the women of the country by the States upon the same terms as to men.

XXI. Protection of Citizens

We again declare the policy that the sacred rights of American citizenship must be preserved at home and abroad, and that no treaty shall receive the sanction of our Government which does not expressly recognize the absolute equality of all our citizens irrespective of race, creed or previous nationality, and which does not recognize the right of expatriation. The American Government should protect American citizens in their rights, not only at home but abroad, and any country having a government should be held to strict accountability for any wrongs done them, either to person or property. At the earliest practical opportunity our country should strive earnestly for peace among the warring nations of Europe and seek to bring about the adoption of the fundamental principle of justice and humanity, that all men shall enjoy equality of right and freedom from discrimination in the lands wherein they dwell.

XXII. Prison Reform

We demand that the modern principles of prison reform be applied in our Federal Penal System. We favor such work for prisoners as shall give them training in remunerative occupations so that they may make an honest living when released from prison; the setting apart of the net wages of the prisoner to be paid to his dependent family or to be reserved for his own use upon his release; the liberal extension of the principles of the Federal Parole Law, with due regard both to the welfare of the prisoner and the interests of society; the adoption of the Probation System especially in the case of first offenders not convicted of serious crimes.

XXIII. PENSIONS

We renew the declarations of recent Democratic platforms relating to generous pensions for soldiers and their widows, and call attention to our record of performance in this particular.

XXIV. WATERWAYS AND FLOOD CONTROL

We renew the declaration in our last two platforms relating to the development of our waterways. The recent devastation of the lower Mississippi Valley and several other sections by floods accentuates the movement for the regulation of river flow by additional bank and levee protection below, and diversion, storage and control of the flood waters above, and their utilization for beneficial purposes in the reclamation of arid and swamp lands and development of waterpower, instead of permitting the floods to continue as heretofore agents of destruction. We hold that the control of the Mississippi River is a National problem. The preservation of the depth of its waters for purposes of navigation, the building of levees and works of bank protection to maintain the integrity of its channel and prevent the overflow of its valley resulting in the interruption of interstate commerce, the disorganization of the mail service, and the enormous loss of life and property, impose an obligation which alone can be discharged by the National Government.

We favor the adoption of a liberal and comprehensive plan for the development and improvement of our harbors and inland waterways with economy and efficiency so as to permit their navigation by vessels of standard draft.

XXV. ALASKA

It has been and will be the policy of the Democratic party to enact all laws necessary for the speedy development of Alaska and its great natural resources.

XXVI. TERRITORIES

We favor granting to the people of Alaska, Hawaii and Porto Rico the traditional territorial government accorded to the territories of the United States since the beginning of our government, and we believe that the officials appointed to administer the government of those several territories should be qualified by previous *bonafide* residence.

XXVII. CANDIDATES

We unreservedly endorse our President and Vice-President, Woodrow Wilson, of New Jersey, and Thomas Riley Marshall of Indiana, who have performed the functions of their great offices faithfully and impartially and with distinguished ability.

In particular, we commend to the American people the splendid diplomatic victories of our great President, who has preserved the vital interests of our Government and its citizens, and kept us out of war.

Woodrow Wilson stands to-day the greatest American of his generation.

XXVIII. CONCLUSION

This is a critical hour in the history of America, a critical hour in the history of the world. Upon the record above set forth, which shows great constructive achievement in following out a consistent policy for our domestic and internal development; upon the record of the Democratic administration, which has maintained the honor, the dignity and the interests of the United States, and, at the same time, retained the respect and friendship of all the nations of the world; and upon the great policies for the future strengthening of the life of our country, the enlargement of our National vision and the ennobling of our international relations, as set forth above, we appeal with confidence to the voters of the country.

Prohibition Platform of 1916

The Prohibition Party, assembled in its Twelfth National Convention in the city of St. Paul, Minnesota, on this Twentieth day of July, 1916, grateful to Almighty God for the blessings of liberty, for our institutions and the multiplying signs of early victory for the cause for which the Party stands in order that the people may know the source of its faith and the basis of its action, should it be clothed with governmental power, challenges the attention of the Nation and asks the votes of the people on this Declaration of principles.

We denounce the traffic in intoxicating liquors. We believe in its abolition. It is a crime—not a business—and should not have governmental sanction.

We demand—and if given power, we will effectuate the demand—that the manufacture, importation, exportation, transportation and sale of alcoholic beverage purposes shall be prohibited.

To the accomplishment of that end, we pledge the exercise of all governmental power and amendment of statutes and the amendment of constitutions, State and National. Only by a political party committed to this purpose can such policy be made effective. We call upon all voters, so believing, to place the Prohibition Party in power upon this issue as a necessary step in the solution of the liquor problem.

The right of citizens of the United States to vote should not be denied or abridged by the United States or by any State on account of sex. We declare in favor of the enfranchisement of women by amendments to State and Federal Constitutions.

We condemn the Republican and Democratic parties for their failure to submit an equal suffrage amendment to the National Constitution. We remind the four million women voters that our Party was the first to declare for their political rights, which it did in 1872. We invite their co-operation in electing the Prohibition Party to power.

We are committed to the policy of peace and friendliness with all nations. We are unalterably opposed to the wasteful military programme of the Democratic Republican Parties. Militarism protects no worthy institution. It endangers them all. It violates the high principles which have brought us as a Nation to the present hour. We are for a constructive programme in preparedness for peace. We declare for and will promote a

world court, to which national differences shall be submitted, so maintained as to give its decrees binding force.

We will support a compact among nations to dismantle navies and disband armies, but until such court and compact are established we pledge ourselves to maintain an effective army and navy and to provide coast defenses entirely adequate for national protection.

We are opposed to universal military service, and to participation in the rivalry that has brought Europe to the shambles and now imperils the civilization of the race.

Private profit, so far as constitutionally possible, should be taken out of the manufacture of war munitions and all war equipment.

In normal times we favor the employment of the army in vast reclamation plans, in reforesting hills and mountains, in building State and National highways, in the construction of an inland waterway from Florida to Maine, in the opening of Alaska and in unnumbered other projects which will make. our soldiers constructive builders of peace. For such service there should be paid an adequate individual wage.

Those units of our navy which are capable of being converted into merchantmen and passenger vessels should be constructed with that purpose in view, and chiefly so utilized in times of peace.

We condemn the political parties, which for more than thirty years have allowed munition and war equipment manufacturers to plunder the people and to jeopardize the highest interest of the Nation by furnishing honey-combed armour plate and second rate battleships which the Navy League now declares are wholly inadequate.

We will not allow the country to forget that the first step toward physical, economic, moral and political preparedness is the enactment of National Prohibition.

The countries at war are preparing for a fierce industrial struggle to follow the cessation of hostilities. As a matter of commercial economy, international friendliness, business efficiency, and as a help to peace, we demand that reciprocal trade treaties be negotiated with all nations with which we have trade relations. A Commission of specialists, free from the control of any party, should be appointed with power to gather full information of all phases of the questions of tariff and reciprocity, and to recommend such legislation as it deems necessary for the welfare of American business and labor.

The necessity of legislation to enable American ship builders or owners to meet foreign competition, on the most favorable terms, is obvious.

Materials for construction should be admitted free of duty.

The purchase of ships abroad, when low prices invite, should be allowed and, when so purchased, should be admitted to American registry.

Harbor rules and charges and navigation laws should not be onerous, but favorable to the highest degree.

Liberal payment should be made by the Government for the carrying of mails or for transport services.

All shipping from the United States to any of our possessions should be reserved to ships of American registry.

The people should not overlook the fact that the effect of Nationwide Prohibition, on labor and industry generally, will be such as to lower the cost of ship building per unit, and at the same time permit the payment of higher wages. The increased volume of trade and commerce, which will result, when the wastage of the liquor traffic is stopped, will quicken our shipping on every sea and send our flag on peaceful missions into every port. This is urged as an incidental effect of wise action on the liquor question, but is none the less to be desired and will aid in the solution of the problem of our merchant marine.

Mexico needs not a conqueror, but a good Samaritan. We are opposed to the violation of the sovereignty of the Mexican people, and we will countenance no war of aggression against them. We pledge the help of this country in the suppression of lawless bands of marauders and murderers, who have taken the lives of American citizens, on both sides of the border, as well as of Mexicans in their own country.

The lives and property of our citizens, when about their lawful pursuits, either in the United States or in Mexico, must and will be protected. In the event of a break-down of government across the border, we would use, in the interests of civilization, the force necessary for the establishment of law and order.

In this connection we affirm our faith in the Monroe Doctrine, proclaimed in the early days of the Nation's life and unswervingly maintained for nearly a hundred years.

We cannot claim the benefits of the Doctrine and refuse to assume or discharge the responsibility and the duties which inhere therein and flow therefrom.

Those duties have long been unmet in Mexico. We should meet them now, acting, not for territory, not for conquest or for ourselves alone, but for and with all the nations of North and South America.

The Democratic party has blundered, and four years ago the Republican party evaded and passed on the problem it now asks the opportunity to solve.

The abandonment of the Philippines at this time would be an injustice to them and a violation of our plain duty. As soon as they are prepared for self-government, by education and training, they should be granted their independence on terms just to themselves and us.

We reaffirm our declaration in favor of conservation of forests, water power and other natural resources.

Departmental decisions ought not to be final, but the rights of the people should be protected by provision for court review.

In order that the public service may be of the highest standard, the government should be a model employer in all respects. To enforce the civil service law in spirit as well as in letter, all promotions should be non-political, based only upon proven fitness; all recommendations for demotions or removals from the service should be subjected to the review of a non-partisan board or commission.

The merit system should be extended to cover all postmasters, collectors of revenue, marshals and other such public officials whose duties are purely administrative.

We reaffirm our allegiance to the principle of secure tenure of office, during good behavior and capable effort, as the means of obtaining expert service. We declare for the enactment of an equitable retirement law for disabled and superannuated employees, in return for faithful service rendered, to maintain a high degree of efficiency in public office.

We stand for Americanism. We believe this country was created for a great mission among the nations of the earth. We rejoice in the fact that it has offered asylum to the oppressed of other lands and for those, more fortunately situated, who yet wished to improve their condition. It is the land of all peoples and belongs not to any one—it is the heritage of all. It should come first in the affections of every citizen, and he who loves another land more than this is not fit for citizenship here, but he is a better citizen who, loving his country, has reverence for the land of his fathers and gains from its history and traditions that which inspires him to nobler service to the one in which he lives.

The Federal Government should interest itself in helping the newcomer into that vocation and locality where he shall most quickly become an American. Those fitted by experience and training for agricultural pursuits should be encouraged to develop the millions of acres of rich and idle land.

We favor uniform marriage and divorce laws, the extermination of polygamy and the complete suppression of the traffic in women and girls.

Differences between capital and labor should be settled through arbitration, by which the rights of the public are conserved as well as those of the disputants. We declare for the prohibition of child labor in factories, mines and workshops; an eight hour maximum day, with one day of rest in seven; for more rigid sanitary requirements and such working conditions as shall foster the physical and moral well-being of the unborn; for the protection of all who toil, by the extension of Employers' Liability Acts; for the adoption of safety appliances for the safeguarding of labor; and for laws that will promote the just division of the wealth which labor and capital jointly produce. Provision should be made for those who suffer from industrial accidents and occupational diseases.

We pledge a business-like administration of the Nation's affairs; the abolition of useless offices, bureaus and commissions; economy in the expenditure of public funds; efficiency in governmental service; and the adoption of the budget system. The president should have power to veto any single item or items of an appropriation bill.

We condemn, and agree when in power to remedy, that which is known as "pork barrel" legislation, by which millions of dollars have been appropriated for rivers where there is no commerce, harbors where there are no ships and public buildings where there is no need.

We are in favor of a single presidential term of six years.

Public utilities and other resources that are natural monopolies are at the present time exploited for personal gain under a monopolistic system. We demand the public ownership or control of all such utilities by the people and their operation and administration in the interests of all the people.

We stand for the preservation and development of our free institutions and for absolute separation of church and state with the guaranty of full religious and civil liberty.

We stand for the rights, safety, justice and development of humanity; we believe in the equality of all before the law; in old-age pensions and insurance against unemployment and in help for needy mothers, all of which could be provided from what is now wasted for drink.

We favor the initiative, referendum and recall.

While it is admitted that grain and cotton are fundamental factors in our national life, it cannot be denied that proper assistance and protection are not given these commodities at terminal markets, in the course of inter-state commerce.

We favor and pledge our efforts to obtain grain elevators at necessary terminal markets, such elevators to be owned and operated by the Federal Government; also to secure Federal grain inspection under a system of civil service and to secure the abolition of any Board of Trade, Chamber of Commerce, or other place of gambling in grain or trading in "options" or "futures" or "short-selling," or any other form of so-called speculation wherein products are not received or delivered, but wherein so-called contracts are settled by the payment of "margins" or "differences" through clearing houses or otherwise.

This Party stands committed to free and open markets based upon legitimate supply and demand, absolutely free from questionable practices of market manipulation. We also favor government warehouses for cotton at proper terminals where the interests of producers require the same; and the absolute divorce of all railroad elevators or warehouses owned by railroad companies, either public or private, from operation and control of private individuals in competition with the public in merchandising grain, cotton or other farm products.

We furthermore endorse all proper methods among producers of those means of co-operative mutual enterprise, which tend toward broader and better markets for both producer and consumer.

This is the day of opportunity for the American

people. The triumph of neither old political party is essential to our safety or progress. The defeat of either will be no public misfortune. They are one party. By age and wealth, by membership and traditions, by platforms and in the character of their candidates, they are the Conservative Party of the United States. The Prohibition Party as the promoter of every important measure of social justice presented to the American people in the last two generations, and as the originator of nearly all such legislation, remains now the only great Progressive Party.

The patriotic voters, who compose the Republican and Democratic parties, can, by voting the Prohibition ticket this year, elect the issue of National Prohibition.

To those, in whatever party, who have the vision of a land redeemed from drink, we extend a cordial invitation to join with us in carrying the banner of Prohibition to Nationwide victory.

Republican Platform of 1916

In 1861 the Republican party stood for the Union. As it stood for the Union of States, it now stands for a united people, true to American ideals, loyal to American traditions, knowing no allegiance except to the Constitution, to the Government, and to the Flag of the United States. We believe in American policies at home and abroad.

PROTECTION OF AMERICAN RIGHTS

We declare that we believe in and will enforce the protection of every American citizen in all the rights secured to him by the Constitution, by treaties and the laws of nations, at home and abroad, by land and by sea. These rights, which in violation of the specific promise of their party made at Baltimore in 1912, the Democratic President and the Democratic Congress have failed to defend, we will unflinchingly maintain.

FOREIGN RELATIONS

We desire peace, the peace of justice and right, and believe in maintaining a strict and honest neutrality between the belligerents in the great war in Europe. We must perform all our duties and insist upon all our rights as neutrals without fear and without favor. We believe that peace and neutrality, as well as the dignity and influence of the United States, cannot be preserved by shifty expedients, by phrase-making, by performances in language, or by attitudes ever changing in an effort to secure votes or voters. The present Administration has destroyed our influence abroad and humiliated us in our own eyes. The Republican party believes that a firm, consistent, and courageous foreign policy, always maintained by Republican Presidents in accordance with American traditions, is the best, as it is the only true way, to preserve our peace and restore us to our rightful place among the nations.

We believe in the pacific settlement of international disputes, and favor the establishment of a world court for that purpose.

MEXICO

We deeply sympathize with the fifteen million people of Mexico who, for three years have seen their country devastated, their homes destroyed, their fellow citizens murdered and their women outraged, by armed bands of desperadoes led by self-seeking, conscienceless agitators who when temporarily successful in any locality have neither sought nor been able to restore order or establish and maintain peace.

We express our horror and indignation at the outrages which have been and are being perpetrated by these bandits upon American men and women who were or are in Mexico by invitation of the laws and of the government of that country and whose rights to security of person and property are guaranteed by solemn treaty obligations. We denounce the indefensible methods of interference employed by this Administration in the internal affairs of Mexico and refer with shame to its failure to discharge the duty of this country as next friend to Mexico, its duty to other powers who have relied upon us as such friend, and its duty to our citizens in Mexico, in permitting the continuance of such conditions, first by failure to act promptly and firmly, and second, by lending its influence to the continuation of such conditions through recognition of one of the factions responsible for these outrages.

We pledge our aid in restoring order and maintaining peace in Mexico. We promise to our citizens on and near our border, and to those in Mexico, wherever they may be found, adequate and absolute protection in their lives, liberty, and property.

MONROE DOCTRINE

We reaffirm our approval of the Monroe Doctrine, and declare its maintenance to be a policy of this country essential to its present and future peace and safety and to the achievement of its manifest destiny.

LATIN AMERICA

We favor the continuance of Republican policies which will result in drawing more and more closely the commercial, financial and social relations between this country and the countries of Latin America.

PHILIPPINES

We renew our allegiance to the Philippine policy inaugurated by McKinley, approved by Congress, and consistently carried out by Roosevelt and Taft. Even in this short time it has enormously improved the material and social conditions of the Islands, given the Philippine people a constantly increasing participation in their government, and if persisted in will bring still greater benefits in the future.

We accepted the responsibility of the Islands as a duty to civilization and the Filipino people. To leave with our task half done would break our pledges, injure our prestige among nations, and imperil what has already been accomplished.

We condemn the Democratic administration for its attempt to abandon the Philippines, which was prevented only by the vigorous opposition of Republican members of Congress, aided by a few patriotic Democrats.

RIGHT OF EXPATRIATION

We reiterate the unqualified approval of the action taken in December, 1911, by the President and Congress to secure with Russia, as with other countries, a treaty that will recognize the absolute right of expatriation and prevent all discrimination of whatever kind between American citizens whether native-born or alien, and regardless of race, religion or previous political allegiance. We renew the pledge to observe this principle and to maintain the right of asylum, which is neither to be surrendered nor restricted, and we unite in the cherished hope that the war which is now desolating the world may speedily end, with a complete and lasting restoration of brotherhood among the nations of the earth and the assurance of full equal rights, civil and religious, to all men in every land.

PROTECTION OF THE COUNTRY

In order to maintain our peace and make certain the security of our people within our own borders the country must have not only adequate but thorough and complete national defence ready for any emergency. We must have a sufficient and effective Regular Army and a provision for ample reserves, already drilled and disciplined, who can be called at once to the colors when the hour of danger comes.

We must have a Navy so strong and so well proportioned and equipped, so thoroughly ready and prepared, that no enemy can gain command of the sea and effect a landing in force on either our Western or our Eastern coast. To secure these results we must have a coherent continuous policy of national defence, which even in these perilous days the Democratic party has utterly failed to develop, but which we promise to give to the country.

TARIFF

The Republican party stands now, as always, in the fullest sense for the policy of tariff protection to American industries and American labor and does not regard an anti-dumping provision as an adequate substitute.

Such protection should be reasonable in amount but sufficient to protect adequately American industries and American labor and so adjusted as to prevent undue exactions by monopolies or trusts. It should, moreover, give special attention to securing the industrial independence of the United States as in the case of dye-stuffs.

Through wise tariff and industrial legislation our industries can be so organized that they will become not only a commercial bulwark but a powerful aid to national defence.

The Underwood tariff act is a complete failure in every respect. Under its administration imports have enormously increased in spite of the fact that intercourse with foreign countries has been largely cut off by reason of the war, while the revenues of which we stand in such dire need have been greatly reduced.

Under the normal conditions which prevailed prior to the war it was clearly demonstrated that this Act deprived the American producer and the

American wage earner of that protection which enabled them to meet their foreign competitors, and but for the adventitious conditions created by the war, would long since have paralyzed all forms of American industry and deprived American labor of its just reward.

It has not in the least degree reduced the cost of living, which has constantly advanced from the date of its enactment. The welfare of our people demands its repeal and its substitution of a measure which in peace as well as in war will produce ample revenue and give reasonable protection to all forms of American production in mine, forest, field and factory.

We favor the creation of a tariff commission with complete power to gather and compile information for the use of Congress in all matters relating to the tariff.

Business

The Republican party has long believed in the rigid supervision and strict regulation of the transportation and of the great corporations of the country. It has put its creed into its deeds, and all really effective laws regulating the railroads and the great industrial corporations are the work of Republican Congresses and Presidents. For this policy of regulation and supervision the Democrats, in a stumbling and piecemeal way, are within the sphere of private enterprise and in direct competition with its own citizens, a policy which is sure to result in waste, great expense to the taxpayer and in an inferior product.

The Republican party firmly believes that all who violate the laws in regulation of business, should be individually punished. But prosecution is very different from persecution, and business success, no matter how honestly attained, is apparently regarded by the Democratic party as in itself a crime. Such doctrines and beliefs choke enterprise and stifle prosperity. The Republican party believes in encouraging American business as it believes in and will seek to advance all American interests.

Rural Credits

We favor an effective system of Rural Credits as opposed to the ineffective law proposed by the present Democratic Administration.

Rural Free Delivery

We favor the extension of the Rural Free De-livery system and condemn the Democratic administration for curtailing and crippling it.

Merchant Marine

In view of the policies adopted by all the maritime nations to encourage their shipping interest, and in order to enable us to compete with them for the ocean-carrying trade, we favor the payment to ships engaged in the foreign trade of liberal compensation for services actually rendered in carrying the mails, and such further legislation as will build up an adequate American Merchant Marine and give us ships which may be requisitioned by the Government in time of national emergency.

We are utterly opposed to the Government ownership of vessels as proposed by the Democratic party, because Government-owned ships, while effectively preventing the development of the American Merchant Marine by private capital, will be entirely unable to provide for the vast volume of American freights and will leave us more helpless than ever in the hard grip of foreign syndicates.

Transportation

Interstate and intrastate transportation have become so interwoven that the attempt to apply two and often several sets of laws to its regulation has produced conflicts of authority, embarrassment in operation and inconvenience and expense to the public.

The entire transportation system of the country has become essentially national. We, therefore, favor such action by legislation, or, if necessary, through an amendment to the Constitution of the United States, as will result in placing it under complete Federal control.

Economy and a National Budget

The increasing cost of the national government and the need for the greatest economy of its resources in order to meet the growing demands of the people for government service call for the severest condemnation of the wasteful appropriations of this democratic administration, of its shameless raids on the treasury, and of its opposition to and rejection of President Taft's oft-repeated proposals and earnest efforts to secure economy and efficiency through the establishment of a simple businesslike budget system to which we pledge our support and which we hold to be necessary to effect a real reform in the administration of national finance.

CONSERVATION

We believe in a careful husbandry of all the natural resources of the nation—a husbandry which means development without waste; use without abuse.

CIVIL SERVICE REFORM

The Civil Service Law has always been sustained by the Republican party, and we renew our repeated declarations that it shall be thoroughly and honestly enforced and extended wherever practicable. The Democratic party has created since March 4, 1913, thirty thousand offices outside of the Civil Service Law at an annual cost of forty-four million dollars to the taxpayers of the country.

We condemn the gross abuse and the misuse of the law by the present Democratic Administration and pledge ourselves to a reorganization of this service along lines of efficiency and economy.

TERRITORIAL OFFICIALS

Reaffirming the attitude long maintained by the Republican party, we hold that officials appointed to administer the government of any territory should be *bona-fide* residents of the territory in which their duties are to be performed.

LABOR LAWS

We pledge the Republican party to the faithful enforcement of all Federal laws passed for the protection of labor. We favor vocational education, the enactment and rigid enforcement of a Federal child labor law; the enactment of a generous and comprehensive workmen's compensation law, within the commerce power of Congress, and an accident compensation law covering all Government employees. We favor the collection and collation, under the direction of the Department of Labor, of complete data relating to industrial hazards for the information of Congress, to the end that such legislation may be adopted as may be calculated to secure the safety, conservation and protection of labor from the dangers incident to industry and transportation.

SUFFRAGE

The Republican party, reaffirming its faith in government of the people, by the people, for the people, as a measure of justice to one-half the adult people of this country, favors the extension of the suffrage to women, but recognizes the right of each state to settle this question for itself.

CONCLUSION

Such are our principles, such are our "purposes and policies." We close as we began. The times are dangerous and the future is fraught with peril. The great issues of the day have been confused by words and phrases. The American spirit, which made the country and saved the union, has been forgotten by those charged with the responsibility of power. We appeal to all Americans, whether naturalized or native-born, to prove to the world that we are Americans in thought and in deed, with one loyalty, one hope, one aspiration. We call on all Americans to be true to the spirit of America, to the great traditions of their common country, and above all things, to keep the faith.

Socialist Platform of 1916

In the midst of the greatest crisis and bloodiest struggle of all history the socialist party of America re-affirms its steadfast adherence to the principles of international brotherhood, world peace and industrial democracy.

The great war which has engulfed so much of civilization and destroyed millions of lives is one of the natural results of the capitalist system of production.

The socialist party, as the political expression of the economic interests of the working class, calls upon them to take a determined stand on the question of militarism and war, and to recognize the opportunity which the great war has given them of forcing disarmament and furthering the cause of industrial freedom.

An armed force in the hands of the ruling class serves two purposes: to protect and further the policy of imperialism abroad and to silence by force the protest of the workers against industrial despotism at home. Imperialism and militarism plunged Europe into this world war. America's geographical and industrial situation has kept her out of the cataclysm. But Europe's extremity has been the opportunity of America's ruling class to amass enormous profits. As a result there is a surfeit of capital which demands the policy of imperialism to protect and further investments abroad. Hence the frenzy of militarism into which the ruling class has made every attempt to force the United States.

The workers in Europe were helpless to avert the war because they were already saddled with the burden of militarism. The workers of the United States are yet free from this burden and have the opportunity of establishing a working class policy and program against war. They can compel the government of the United States to lead the way in an international movement for disarmament and to abandon the policy of imperialism which is forcing the conquest of Mexico and must, if carried out, eventually plunge the United States into a world war.

The working class must recognize the cry of preparedness against foreign invasion as a mere cloak for the sinister purpose of imperialism abroad and industrial tyranny at home. The class struggle, like capitalism, is international. The proletariat of the world has but one enemy, the capitalist class, whether at home or abroad. We must refuse to put into the hands of this enemy an armed force even under the guise of a "democratic army," as the workers of Australia and Switzerland have done.

Therefore the socialist party stands opposed to military preparedness, to any appropriations of men or money for war or militarism, while control of such forces through the political state rests in the hands of the capitalist class. The socialist party stands committed to the class war, and urges upon the workers in the mines and forests, on the railways and ships, in factories and fields, the use of their economic and industrial power, by refusing to mine the coal, to transport soldiers, to furnish food or other supplies for military purposes, and thus keep out of the hands of the ruling class the control of armed forces and economic power, necessary for aggression abroad and industrial despotism at home.

The working class must recognize militarism as the greatest menace to all efforts toward industrial freedom, and regardless of political or industrial affiliations must present a united front in the fight against preparedness and militarism.

Hideous as they are, the horrors of the far-stretched battle field of the old world are dwarfed by the evil results of the capitalist system, even in normal times. Instead of being organized to provide all members of society with an abundance of food, clothing and shelter, and the highest attainable freedom and culture, industry is at present organized and conducted for the benefit of a parasite class. All the powers of government and all our industrial genius are directed to the end of securing to the relatively small class of capital investors the largest amount of profits which can be wrung from the labor of the ever-increasing class whose only property is muscle and brain, manual and mental labor power.

The dire consequences of this system are everywhere apparent. The workers are oppressed and deprived of much that makes for physical, mental and moral well-being. Year by year poverty and industrial accidents destroy more lives than all the armies and navies in the world.

To preserve their privilege and power is the most vital interest of the possessing class, while it is the most vital interest of the working class to resist oppression, improve its position and struggle to obtain security of life and liberty. Hence there exists a conflict of interests, a social war within the nation, which can know neither truce nor compromise. So long as the few own and control the economic life of the nation the many must be enslaved, poverty must coexist with riotous luxury and civil strife prevail.

The socialist party would end these conditions by reorganizing the life of the nation upon the basis of socialism. Socialism would not abolish private property, but greatly extend it. We believe that every human being should have and own all the things which he can use to advantage, for the enrichment of his own life, without imposing disadvantage or burden upon any other human being. Socialism admits the private ownership and individual direction of all things, tools, economic processes and functions which are individualistic in character, and requires the collective ownership and democratic control and direction of those which are social or collectivistic in character.

We hold that this country cannot enjoy happiness and prosperity at home and maintain lasting peace with other nations so long as its industrial wealth is monopolized by a capitalist oligarchy. In this, as in every other campaign, all special issues arising from temporary situations, whether domestic or foreign, must be subordinated to the major issue—the need of such a reorganization of our economic life as will remove the land, the mines, forests, railroads, mill and factories, all the things required for our physical existence, from the clutches of industrial and financial freebooters and place them securely and permanently in the hands of the people.

If men were free to labor to satisfy their desires there could be in this country neither poverty nor involuntary unemployment. But the men in this country are not free to labor to satisfy their desires. The great industrial population can labor only when the capitalist class who own the industries believe they can market their product at a profit. The needs of millions are subordinated to the greeds of a few. The situation is not unlike that of a pyramid balanced upon its apex. Oftentimes this pyramid tumbles and industrial depression comes. There was such a crash in 1907. If the capitalist owners had been willing to get out of the way, industry could have been revived in a day. But the capitalist owners are never willing to get out of the way. Their greeds come first—the people's needs, if at all, afterwards. Therefore, business did not quickly revive after the industrial depression in 1907. Mr. Taft was elected to bring good times, but in four years failed to bring them. Mr. Wilson was elected to bring good times, but not all of the measures he advocated had the slightest effect upon industry. The European war has brought to this country tremendous orders for military supplies and has created a period of prosperity for the few. For the masses of the people there is but an opportunity to work hard for a bare living, which is not prosperity, but slavery. As against the boast of the present national administration that its political program, now fully in force, had brought prosperity to the masses, we call attention to the statement of the federal public health service that $800 is required a year to enable a family to avoid physical deterioration through lack of decent living conditions, that more than half of the families of working men receive less than that amount, that nearly a third receive less than $500 a year, and that one family in twelve received less than $300 a year.

The capitalist class for a great many years has been trying to saddle upon this country a great army and a greater navy. A greater army is desired to keep the working class of the United States in subjection. A greater navy is desired to safeguard the foreign investments of American capitalists and to "back-up" American diplomacy in its efforts to gain foreign markets for American capitalists. The war in Europe, which diminished and is still diminishing the remote possibility of European attack upon the United States, was nevertheless seized upon by capitalists and by unscrupulous politicians as a means of spreading fear throughout the country, to the end that, by false pretenses, great military establishments might be obtained. We denounce such "preparedness" as both false in principle, unnecessary in character and dangerous in its plain tendencies toward militarism. We advocate that sort of social preparedness which expresses itself in better homes, better bodies and better minds, which are alike the products of plenty and the necessity of effective defense in war.

The socialist party maintains its attitude of unalterable opposition to war.

We reiterate the statement that the competitive nature of capitalism is the cause of modern war and that the co-operative nature of socialism is alone adapted to the task of ending war by removing its causes. We assert, however, that, even under the present capitalist order, additional measures can be taken to safeguard peace, and to this end we demand:

Measures to Insure Peace

1. That all laws and appropriations for the increase of the military and naval forces of the United States shall be immediately repealed.

2. That the power be taken from the president to lead the nation into a position which leaves no escape from war. No one man, however exalted in official station, should have the power to decide the question of peace or war for a nation of a hundred millions. To give one man such power is neither democratic nor safe. Yet the president exercises such power when he determines what shall be the nation's foreign policies and what shall be the nature and tone of its diplomatic intercourse with other nations. We, therefore, demand that the power to fix foreign policies and conduct diplomatic negotiations shall be lodged in congress and shall be exercised publicly, the people reserving the right to order congress, at any time, to change its foreign policy.

3. That no war shall be declared or waged by the United States without a referendum vote of

the entire people, except for the purpose of repelling invasion.

4. That the Monroe doctrine shall be immediately abandoned as a danger so great that even its advocates are agreed that it constitutes perhaps our greatest single danger of war. The Monroe doctrine was originally intended to safeguard the peace of the United States. Though the doctrine has changed from a safeguard to a menace, the capitalist class still defends it for the reason that our great Capitalists desire to retain South and Central America as their private trade preserve. We favor the cultivation of social, industrial and political friendship with all other nations in the western hemisphere, as an approach to a world confederation of nations, but we oppose the Monroe doctrine because it takes from our hands the peace of America and places it in the custody of any nation, that would attack the sovereignty of any state in the western world.

5. That the independence of the Philippine Islands be immediately recognized as a measure of justice both to the Philippines and to ourselves. The Filipinos are entitled to self-government, we are entitled to be freed from the necessity of building and maintaining enough dreadnoughts to defend them in the event of war.

6. The government of the United States shall call a congress of all neutral nations to mediate between the belligerent powers in an effort to establish an immediate and lasting peace without indemnities or forcible annexation of territory and based on a binding and enforcible international treaty, which shall provide for concerted disarmament on land and at sea and for an international congress with power to adjust all disputes between nations and which shall guarantee freedom and equal rights to all oppressed nations and races.

WORKING PROGRAM

As general measures calculated to strengthen the working class in its fight for the realization of its ultimate aim the co-operative commonwealth, and to increase its power of resistance against capital oppression, we advocate and pledge ourselves and our elected officers to the following program.

Political Demands

1. Unrestricted and equal suffrage for men and women.
2. The immediate adoption of the so-called "Susan B. Anthony amendment" to the constitution of the United States granting the suffrage to women on equal terms with men.
3. The adoption of the initiative, referendum and recall and of proportional representation, nationally as well as locally.
4. The abolition of the senate and of the veto power of the president.
5. The election of the president and the vice-president by direct vote of the people.
6. The abolition of the present restriction upon the amendment of the constitution so that that instrument may be made amendable by a majority of the voters in the country.
7. The calling of a convention for the revision of the constitution of the United States.
8. The abolition of the power usurped by the Supreme Court of the United States to pass upon the constitutionality of legislation enacted by congress. National laws to be repealed only by act of congress or by a referendum vote of the whole people.
9. The immediate curbing of the power of the courts to issue injunctions.
10. The election of all judges of the United States courts for short terms.
11. The free administration of the law.
12. The granting of the right of suffrage in the District of Columbia with representation in congress and a democratic form of municipal government for purely local affairs.
13. The extension of democratic government to all United States territory.
14. The freedom of press, speech and assemblage.
15. The increase of the rates of the present income tax and corporation tax and the extension of inheritance taxes, graduated in proportion to the value of the estate and to nearness of kin— the proceeds of these taxes to be employed in the socialization of industry.
16. The enactment of further measures for general education in useful pursuits. The bureau of education to be made a department.
17. The enactment of further measures for the conservation of health and the creation of an independent department of health.
18. The abolition of the monopoly ownership of patents and the substitution of collective ownership, with direct rewards to inventors by premiums or royalties.

Collective Ownership

1. The collective ownership and democratic management of railroads, telegraphs and telephones, express service, steamboat lines and all other social means of transportation and communication and of all large-scale industries.

2. The immediate acquirement by the municipalities, and the states of the federal government of all grain elevators, stock yards, storage warehouses and other distributing agencies, in order to relieve the farmer from the extortionate charges of the middlemen and to reduce the present high cost of living.

3. The extension of the public domain to include mines, quarries, oil wells, forests and water power.

4. The further conservation and development of natural resources for the use and benefit of all the people:

(a) By scientific afforestation and timber protection.

(b) By the reclamation of arid and swamp tracts.

(c) By the storage of flood waters and the utilization of water power.

(d) By the stoppage of the present extravagant waste of the soil and the products of mines and oil wells.

(e) By the development of highway and waterway systems.

5. The collective ownership of land wherever practicable, and, in cases where such ownership is impracticable, the appropriation by taxation of the annual rental value of all lands held for speculation or exploitation.

6. All currency shall be issued by the government of the United States and shall be legal tender for the payment of taxes and impost duties and for the discharge of public and private debts. The government shall lend money on bonds to counties and municipalities at a nominal rate of interest for the purpose of taking over or establishing public utilities and for building or maintaining public roads or highways and public schools —up to 25 per cent of the assessed valuation of such counties or municipalities. Said bonds are to be repaid in twenty equal and annual installments, and the currency issued for that purpose by the government is to be canceled and destroyed seriatim as the debt is paid. All banks and banking institutions shall be owned by the government of the United States or by the states.

7. Government relief of the unemployed by the extension of all useful public works. All persons employed on such work to be engaged directly by the government under a work day of not more than eight hours and at not less than the prevailing union wages. The government also to establish employment bureaus; to lend money to states and municipalities without interest for the purpose of carrying on public works; to contribute money to unemployment funds of labor unions and other organizations of workers, and to take such other measures within its power as will lessen the widespread misery of the workers caused by the misrule of the capitalist class.

Industrial Demands

The conservation of human resources, particularly of the lives and well-being of the workers and their families:

1. By shortening the work-day in keeping with the increased productiveness of machinery.

2. By securing to every worker a rest period of not less than a day and a half in each week.

3. By securing the freedom of political and economic organization and activities.

4. By securing a more effective inspection of workshops, factories and mines.

5. By forbidding the employment of children under eighteen years of age.

6. By forbidding the interstate transportation of the products of child labor and of all uninspected factories and mines.

7. By establishing minimum wage scales.

8. By abolishing official charity and substituting a non-contributory system of old age pensions, a general system of insurance by the state against invalidism, and a system of compulsory insurance by employers of their workers, without cost to the latter, against industrial diseases, accidents and death.

9. By establishing mothers' pensions.

Socialist Labor Platform of 1916

The Socialist Labor Party, in national convention assembled, reaffirming its previous platform declarations, reasserts the right of man to life, liberty, and the pursuit of happiness.

We hold that the purpose of government is to secure to every citizen the enjoyment of this right; but taught by experience we hold furthermore that such right is illusory to the majority of the people, to wit, the working class, under the present system of economic inequality that is essentially destructive of *their* life, *their* liberty, and *their* happiness.

We hold that the true theory of economics is that the means of production must be owned, operated, and controlled by the people in common. Man cannot exercise his right of life, liberty, and the pursuit of happiness without the ownership of the land on, and the tool with which to work. Deprived of these, his life, his liberty, and his fate fall into the hands of that class which owns these essentials for work and production.

We hold that the existing contradiction between social production and capitalist appropriation—the latter resulting from the private ownership of the natural and social opportunities—divides the people into two classes: the Capitalist Class and the Working Class; throws society into the convulsions of the Class Struggle; and perverts government in the interests of the Capitalist Class.

Thus Labor is robbed of the wealth it alone produces, is denied the means of self-employment, and by compulsory idleness in wage-slavery, is even deprived of the necessaries of life.

Against such a system the Socialist Labor Party raises the banner of revolt, and demands the unconditional surrender of the Capitalist Class.

In place of such a system the Socialist Labor Party aims to substitute a system of social ownership of the means of production, industrially administered by the Working Class—the workers to assume control and direction as well as operation of their industrial affairs.

This solution of necessity requires the organization of the Working Class as a class upon revolutionary political and industrial lines.

We therefore call upon the wage workers to organize themselves into a revolutionary political organization under the banner of the Socialist Labor Party; and to organize themselves likewise upon the industrial field into a revolutionary industrial union in keeping with their political aims.

And we also call upon all other intelligent citizens to place themselves squarely upon the ground of Working Class interests, and join us in this mighty and noble work of human emancipation, so that we may put summary end to the existing barbarous class conflict by placing the land and all the means of production, transportation, and distribution into the hands of the people as a collective body, and substituting the Co-operative Commonwealth for the present state of planless production, industrial war, and social disorder—a Commonwealth in which every worker shall have the free exercise and full benefit of his faculties, multiplied by all the factors of modern civilization.

CAMPAIGN OF 1920

In 1920 the Democrats, who had no acknowledged leader after President Wilson became ill, nominated twenty-four candidates on the first ballot and struggled through forty-four ballots before James M. Cox, the governor of Ohio, was chosen as their presidential candidate. Franklin D. Roosevelt of New York was nominated by acclamation for the vice-presidency.

The Republicans also had an open convention with eleven men nominated for the presidency. Warren G. Harding, a senator from Ohio, who was sixth on the first ballot, was finally selected on the tenth ballot. Calvin Coolidge, the governor of Massachusetts, was chosen as his running mate on the first ballot.

The Socialists again nominated Eugene V. Debs, who was serving a prison term for opposing the war, for president. Seymour Stedman of Illinois was nominated as the vice-presidential candidate. A new entry into the presidential contest, the Farmer-Labor Party, nominated Parley Christensen of Utah and Maximilian S. Hayes of Ohio as its ticket. The Prohibitionists selected Aaron Watkins of Ohio and David L. Colvin of New York as their candidates. William Wesley Cox of Missouri was the presidential candidate of the Socialist Labor Party; August Gillhaus of New York was again nominated for the vice-presidency.

The Republicans easily defeated the Democrats, 16,133,314 popular votes to 9,140,884. The Socialists polled 913,664 and the Farmer-Laborites 264,540. The Prohibition Party polled 188,391 votes, and the Socialist Labor Party received 30,418. Harding carried the entire North plus Tennessee. He received 404 electoral votes to 127 for James Cox.

Democratic Platform of 1920

The Democratic Party, in its National Convention now assembled, sends greetings to the President of the United States, Woodrow Wilson, and hails with patriotic pride the great achievements for country and the world wrought by a Democratic administration under his leadership.

It salutes the mighty people of this great republic, emerging with imperishable honor from the severe tests and grievous strains of the most tragic war in history, having earned the plaudits and the gratitude of all free nations.

It declares its adherence to the fundamental progressive principles of social, economic and industrial justice and advance, and purposes to resume the great work of translating these principles into effective laws, begun and carried far by the Democratic administration and interrupted only when the war claimed all the national energies for the single task of victory.

LEAGUE OF NATIONS

The Democratic Party favors the League of Nations as the surest, if not the only, practicable means of maintaining the permanent peace of the world and terminating the insufferable burden of great military and naval establishments. It was for this that America broke away from traditional isolation and spent her blood and treasure to crush a colossal scheme of conquest. It was upon this basis that the President of the United States, in prearrangement with our allies, consented to a suspension of hostilities against the Imperial German Government; the Armistice was granted and a Treaty of Peace negotiated upon the definite assurance to Germany, as well as to the powers pitted against Germany, that "a general association of nations must be formed, under specific covenants, for the purpose of affording mutual guarantees of political independence and territorial integrity to great and small states alike." Hence, we not only congratulate the President on the vision manifested and the vigor exhibited in the prosecution of the war; but we felicitate him and his associates on the exceptional achievement at Paris involved in the adoption of a league and treaty so near akin to previously expressed American ideals and so intimately related to the aspirations of civilized peoples everywhere.

We commend the President for his courage and his high conception of good faith in steadfastly standing for the covenant agreed to by all the associated and allied nations at war with Germany, and we condemn the Republican Senate for its refusal to ratify the treaty merely because it was the product of Democratic statesmanship, thus interposing partisan envy and personal hatred in the way of the peace and renewed prosperity of the world.

By every accepted standard of international morality the President is justified in asserting that the honor of the country is involved in this business; and we point to the accusing fact that, before it was determined to initiate political antagonism to the treaty, the now Republican chairman of the Senate Foreign Relations Committee himself publicly proclaimed that any proposition for a separate peace with Germany, such as he and his party associates thereafter reported to the Senate, would make us "guilty of the blackest crime."

On May 15 last the Knox substitute for the Versailles Treaty was passed by the Republican Senate; and this Convention can contrive no more fitting characterization of its obloquy than that made in the *Forum* magazine of December, 1918, by Henry Cabot Lodge, when he said:

"If we send our armies and young men abroad to be killed and wounded in northern France and Flanders with no result but this, our entrance into war with such an intention was a crime which nothing can justify. The intent of Congress and the intent of the President was that there could be no peace until we could create a situation where no such war as this could recur.

"We cannot make peace except in company with our allies.

"It would brand us with everlasting dishonor and bring ruin to us also if we undertook to make a separate peace."

Thus, to that which Mr. Lodge, in saner moments, considered "the blackest crime" he and his party in madness sought to give the sanctity of law; that which eighteen months ago was of "everlasting dishonor," the Republican Party and its candidates to-day accept as the essence of faith.

We endorse the President's view of our international obligations and his firm stand against reservations designed to cut to pieces the vital provisions of the Versailles Treaty and we commend the Democrats in Congress for voting against resolutions for separate peace which would disgrace the nation.

We advocate the immediate ratification of the treaty without reservations which would impair its essential integrity; but do not oppose the acceptance of any reservations making clearer or more specific the obligations of the United States to the league associates. Only by doing this may we retrieve the reputation of this nation among the powers of the earth and recover the moral leadership which President Wilson won and which Republican politicians at Washington sacrificed. Only by doing this may we hope to aid effectively

in the restoration of order throughout the world and to take the place which we should assume in the front rank of spiritual, commercial and industrial advancement.

We reject as utterly vain, if not vicious, the Republican assumption that ratification of the treaty and membership in the League of Nations would in any wise impair the integrity or independence of our country. The fact that the covenant has been entered into by twenty-nine nations, all as jealous of their independence as we of ours, is a sufficient refutation of such a charge. The President repeatedly has declared, and this Convention reaffirms, that all our duties and obligations as a member of the league must be fulfilled in strict conformity with the Constitution of the United States, embodied in which is the fundamental requirement of declaratory action by the Congress before this nation may become a participant in any war.

SENATE RULES

We favor such alteration of the rules of procedure of the Senate of the United States as will permit the prompt transaction of the nation's legislative business.

CONDUCT OF THE WAR

During the war President Wilson exhibited the very broadest conception of liberal Americanism. In his conduct of the war, as in the general administration of his high office, there was no semblance of partisan bias. He invited to Washington as his councilors and coadjutors hundreds of the most prominent and pronounced Republicans in the country. To these he committed responsibilities of the gravest import and most confidential nature. Many of them had charge of vital activities of the government.

And yet, with the war successfully prosecuted and gloriously ended, the Republican Party in Congress, far from applauding the masterly leadership of the President and felicitating the country on the amazing achievements of the American government, has meanly requited the considerate course of the chief magistrate by savagely defaming the Commander-in-Chief of the Army and Navy and by assailing nearly every public officer of every branch of the service intimately concerned in winning the war abroad and preserving the security of the government at home.

We express something that the Republican Convention omitted to express—we express to the soldiers and sailors of America the admiration of their fellow countrymen. Guided by the genius of such commanders as General John J. Pershing, the armed forces of America constituted a decisive factor in the victory and brought new lustre to the flag.

We commend the patriotic men and women, who sustained the efforts of their government in the crucial hours of the war, and contributed to the brilliant administrative success, achieved under the broad-visioned leadership of the President.

FINANCIAL ACHIEVEMENTS

A review of the record of the Democratic Party during the administration of Woodrow Wilson presents a chapter of substantial achievements unsurpassed in the history of the republic. For fifty years before the advent of this administration periodical convulsions had impeded the industrial progress of the American people and caused unestimable loss and distress. By the enactment of the Federal Reserve Act the old system, which bred panics, was replaced by a new system, which insured confidence. It was an indispensable factor in winning the war, and to-day it is the hope and inspiration of business. Indeed, one vital danger against which the American people should keep constantly on guard, is the commitment of this system to partisan enemies who struggled against its adoption and vainly attempted to retain in the hands of speculative bankers a monopoly of the currency and credits of the nation. Already there are well defined indications of an assault upon the vital principles of the system in the event of Republican success at the elections in November.

Under Democratic leadership the American people successfully financed their stupendous part in the greatest war of all time. The Treasury wisely insisted during the war upon meeting an adequate portion of the war expenditure from current taxes and the bulk of the balance from popular loans, and, during the first full fiscal year after fighting stopped, upon meeting current expenditures from current receipts notwithstanding the new and unnecessary burdens thrown upon the Treasury by the delay, obstruction and extravagance of a Republican Congress.

The non-partisan Federal Reserve authorities have been wholly free of political interference or motive; and, in their own time and their own way,

have used courageously, though cautiously, the instruments at their disposal to prevent undue expansion of credit in the country. As a result of these sound Treasury and Federal Reserve policies, the inevitable war inflation has been held down to a minimum, and the cost of living has been prevented from increasing in this country in proportion to the increase in other belligerent countries and in neutral countries which are in close contact with the world's commerce and exchanges.

After a year and a half of fighting in Europe, and despite another year and a half of Republican obstruction at home, the credit of the Government of the United States stands unimpaired, the Federal Reserve note is the unit of value throughout all the world; and the United States is the one great country in the world which maintains a free gold market.

We condemn the attempt of the Republican party to deprive the American people of their legitimate pride in the financing of the war—an achievement without parallel in the financial history of this or any other country, in this or any other war. And in particular we condemn the pernicious attempt of the Republican Party to create discontent among the holders of the bonds of the Government of the United States and to drag our public finance and our banking and currency system back into the arena of party politics.

TAX REVISION

We condemn the failure of the present Congress to respond to the oft-repeated demand of the President and the Secretaries of the Treasury to revise the existing tax laws. The continuance in force in peace times of taxes devised under pressure of imperative necessity to produce a revenue for war purposes is indefensible and can only result in lasting injury to the people. The Republican Congress persistently failed, through sheer political cowardice, to make a single move toward a readjustment of tax laws which it denounced before the last election and was afraid to revise before the next election.

We advocate reform and a searching revision of the War Revenue Acts to fit peace conditions so that the wealth of the nation may not be withdrawn from productive enterprise and diverted to wasteful or non-productive expenditure.

We demand prompt action by the next Congress for a complete survey of existing taxes and their modification and simplification with a view to secure greater equity and justice in the tax burden and improvement in administration.

PUBLIC ECONOMY

Claiming to have effected great economies in Government expenditures, the Republican Party cannot show the reduction of one dollar in taxation as a corollary of this false pretense. In contrast, the last Democratic Congress enacted legislation reducing taxes from eight billions, designed to be raised, to six billions for the first year after the Armistice, and to four billions thereafter; and there the total is left undiminished by our political adversaries. Two years after Armistice Day a Republican Congress provides for expending the stupendous sum of $5,403,390,327.30, and wouldn't even lop off the thirty cents.

Affecting great paper economies by reducing departmental estimates of sums which would not have been spent in any event, and by reducing formal appropriations, the Republican statement of expenditures omits the pregnant fact that the Congress authorized the use of one and a half billion dollars in the hands of various departments and bureaus, which otherwise would have been covered back into the Treasury, and which should be added to the Republican total of expenditures.

HIGH COST OF LIVING

The high cost of living and the depreciation of bond values in this country are primarily due to the war itself, to the necessary governmental expenditures for the destructive purposes of war, to private extravagance, to the world shortage of capital, to the inflation of foreign currencies and credits, and, in large degree, to conscienceless profiteering.

The Republican Party is responsible for the failure to restore peace and peace conditions in Europe, which is a principal cause of post-armistice inflation the world over. It has denied the demand of the President for necessary legislation to deal with secondary and local causes. The sound policies pursued by the Treasury and the Federal Reserve system have limited in this country, though they could not prevent, the inflation which was worldwide. Elected upon specific promises to curtail public expenditures and to bring the country back to a status of ef-

fective economy, the Republican Party in Congress wasted time and energy for more than a year in vain and extravagant investigations, costing the tax-payers great sums of money, while revealing nothing beyond the incapacity of Republican politicians to cope with the problems. Demanding that the President, from his place at the Peace Table, call the Congress into extraordinary session for imperative purposes of readjustment, the Congress when convened spent thirteen months in partisan pursuits, failing to repeal a single war statute which harassed business or to initiate a single constructive measure to help business. It busied itself making a pre-election record of pretended thrift, having not one particle of substantial existence in fact. It raged against profiteers and the high cost of living without enacting a single statute to make the former afraid or doing a single act to bring the latter within limitations.

The simple truth is that the high cost of living can only be remedied by increased production, strict governmental economy and a relentless pursuit of those who take advantage of post-war conditions and are demanding and receiving outrageous profits.

We pledge the Democratic Party to a policy of strict economy in government expenditures, and to the enactment and enforcement of such legislation as may be required to bring profiteers before the bar of criminal justice.

THE TARIFF

We reaffirm the traditional policy of the Democratic Party in favor of a tariff for revenue only and confirm the policy of basing tariff revisions upon the intelligent research of a non-partisan commission, rather than upon the demands of selfish interests, temporarily held in abeyance.

BUDGET

In the interest of economy and good administration, we favor the creation of an effective budget system, that will function in accord with the principles of the Constitution. The reform should reach both the executive and legislative aspects of the question. The supervision and preparation of the budget should be vested in the Secretary of the Treasury as the representative of the President. The budget, as such, should not be increased by the Congress except by a two-thirds vote, each House, however, being free to exercise its constitutional privilege of making appropriations through independent bills. The appropriation bills should be considered by single Committees of the House and Senate. The audit system should be consolidated and its powers expanded so as to pass upon the wisdom of, as well as the authority for, expenditures.

A budget bill was passed in the closing days of the second session of the Sixty-sixth Congress which, invalidated by plain constitutional defects and defaced by considerations of patronage, the President was obliged to veto. The House amended the bill to meet the Executive objection. We condemn the Republican Senate for adjourning without passing the amended measure, when by devoting an hour or two more to this urgent public business a budget system could have been provided.

AGRICULTURAL INTERESTS

To the great agricultural interests of the country, the Democratic Party does not find it necessary to make promises. It already is rich in its record of things actually accomplished. For nearly half a century of Republican rule not a sentence was written into the Federal Statutes affording one dollar of bank credits to the farming interests of America. In the first term of this Democratic administration the National Bank Act was so altered as to authorize loans of five years' maturity on improved farm lands. Later was established a system of farm loan banks, from which the borrowings already exceed three hundred millions of dollars; and under which the interest rate to farmers has been so materially reduced as to drive out of business the farm loan sharks who formerly subsisted by extortion upon the great agricultural interests of the country.

Thus it was a Democratic Congress in the administration of a Democratic President which enabled the farmers of America for the first time to obtain credit upon reasonable terms and insured their opportunity for the future development of the nation's agricultural resources. Tied up in Supreme Court proceedings, in a suit by hostile interests, the Federal Farm Loan System, originally opposed by the Republican candidate for the Presidency, appealed in vain to a Republican Congress for adequate financial assistance to tide over the interim between the beginning and the ending of the current year, awaiting a final decision of the highest court on the validity of the contested act. We pledge prompt consistent support of sound and effective measures to sustain, to amplify and to perfect the rural Credits Statutes and thus to check and reduce the growth and course of farm tenancy.

Not only did the Democratic Party put into effect a great Farm Loan system of land mortgage banks, but it passed the Smith-Lever agricultural extension act, carrying to every farmer in every section of the country, through the medium of trained experts and by demonstration farms, the practical knowledge acquired by the Federal Agricultural Department in all things relating to agriculture, horticulture and animal life; it established the Bureau of Markets, the Bureau of Farm Management, and passed the Cotton Futures Act, the Grain Grades Bill, the Co-operative Farm Administration Act, and the Federal Warehouse Act.

The Democratic Party has vastly improved the rural mail system and has built up the parcel post system to such an extent as to render its activities and its practical service indispensable to the farming community. It was this wise encouragement and this effective concern of the Democratic Party for the farmers of the United States that enabled this great interest to render such essential service in feeding the armies of America and the allied nations of the war and succoring starving populations since Armistice Day.

Meanwhile the Republican leaders at Washington have failed utterly to propose one single measure to make rural life more tolerable. They have signalized their fifteen months of Congressional power by urging schemes which would strip the farms of labor; by assailing the principles of the Farm Loan system and seeking to impair its efficiency; by covertly attempting to destroy the great nitrogen plant at Mussel Shoals upon which the government has expended $70,-000,000 to supply American farmers with fertilizers at reasonable cost; by ruthlessly crippling nearly every branch of agricultural endeavor, literally starving the productive mediums through which the people must be fed.

We favor such legislation as will confirm to the primary producers of the nation the right of collective bargaining, and the right of co-operative handling and marketing of the products of the workshop and the farm and such legislation as will facilitate the exportation of our farm products.

We favor comprehensive studies of farm production costs and the uncensored publication of facts found in such studies.

LABOR AND INDUSTRY

The Democratic Party is now, as ever, the firm friend of honest labor and the promoter of progressive industry. It established the Department of Labor at Washington and a Democratic President called to his official council board the first practical workingman who ever held a cabinet portfolio. Under this administration have been established employment bureaus to bring the man and the job together; have been peaceably determined many bitter disputes between capital and labor; were passed the Child-Labor Act, the Workingman's Compensation Act (the extension of which we advocate so as to include laborers engaged in loading and unloading ships and in interstate commerce), the Eight-Hour Law, the act for Vocational Training, and a code of other wholesome laws affecting the liberties and bettering the conditions of the laboring classes. In the Department of Labor the Democratic administration established a Woman's Bureau, which a Republican Congress destroyed by withholding appropriations.

Labor is not a commodity; it is human. Those who labor have rights, and the national security and safety depend upon a just recognition of those rights and the conservation of the strength of the workers and their families in the interest of sound-hearted and sound-headed men, women and children. Laws regulating hours of labor and conditions under which labor is performed, when passed in recognition of the conditions under which life must be lived to attain the highest development and happiness, are just assertions of the national interest in the welfare of the people.

At the same time, the nation depends upon the products of labor; a cessation of production means loss and, if long continued, means disaster. The whole people, therefore, have a right to insist that justice shall be done to those who work, and in turn that those whose labor creates the necessities upon which the life of the nation depends must recognize the reciprocal obligation between the worker and the state.

They should participate in the formulation of sound laws and regulations governing the conditions under which labor is performed, recognize and obey the laws so formulated, and seek their amendment when necessary by the processes ordinarily addressed to the laws and regulations affecting the other relations of life.

Labor, as well as capital, is entitled to adequate compensation. Each has the indefeasible right of organization, of collective bargaining and of speaking through representatives of their own selection. Neither class, however, should at any time nor in any circumstances take action that will put in jeopardy the public welfare. Resort to strikes and lockouts which endanger the health or lives of the people is an unsatisfactory device for determining disputes, and the Democratic Party pledges itself to contrive, if possible, and put into effective operation a fair and comprehensive method of composing differences of this nature.

In private industrial disputes, we are opposed to compulsory arbitration as a method plausible in theory, but a failure in fact. With respect to government service, we hold distinctly that the rights of the people are paramount to the right to strike. However, we profess scrupulous regard for the conditions of public employment and pledge the Democratic Party to instant inquiry into the pay of government employees and equally speedy regulations designed to bring salaries to a just and proper level.

WOMAN'S SUFFRAGE

We endorse the proposed 19th Amendment of the Constitution of the United States granting equal suffrage to women. We congratulate the legislatures of thirty-five states which have already ratified said amendment and we urge the Democratic Governors and Legislatures of Tennessee, North Carolina and Florida and such states as have not yet ratified the Federal Suffrage Amendment to unite in an effort to complete the process of ratification and secure the thirty-sixth state in time for all the women of the United States to participate in the fall election.

We commend the effective advocacy of the measure by President Wilson.

WELFARE OF WOMEN AND CHILDREN

We urge co-operation with the states for the protection of child life through infancy and maternity care; in the prohibition of child labor and by adequate appropriations for the Children's

Bureau and the Woman's Bureau in the Department of Labor.

EDUCATION

Co-operative Federal assistance to the states is immediately required for the removal of illiteracy, for the increase of teachers' salaries and instruction in citizenship for both native and foreign-born; increased appropriation for vocational training in home economics; re-establishment of joint Federal and state employment service with women's departments under the direction of technically qualified women.

WOMEN IN INDUSTRY

We advocate full representation of women on all commissions dealing with women's work or women's interests and a reclassification of the Federal Civil Service free from discrimination on the ground of sex; a continuance of appropriations for education in sex hygiene; Federal legislation which shall insure that American women resident in the United States, but married to aliens, shall retain their American citizenship, and that the same process of naturalization shall be required for women as for men.

DISABLED SOLDIERS

The Federal government should treat with the utmost consideration every disabled soldier, sailor, and marine of the world war, whether his disability be due to wounds received in line of action or to health impaired in service; and for the dependents of the brave men who died in line of duty the government's tenderest concern and richest bounty should be their requital. The fine patriotism exhibited, the heroic conduct displayed, by American soldiers, sailors and marines at home and abroad, constitute a sacred heritage of posterity, the worth of which can never be recompensed from the Treasury and the glory of which must not be diminished by any such expedients.

The Democratic administration wisely established a War Risk Insurance Bureau, giving four and a half millions of enlisted men insurance at unprecedentedly low rates and through the medium of which compensation of men and women injured in service is readily adjusted, and hospital facilities for those whose health is impaired are abundantly afforded.

The Federal Board for Vocational Education should be made a part of the War Risk Insurance Bureau, in order that the task may be treated as a whole, and this machinery of protection and assistance must receive every aid of law and appropriation necessary to full and effective operation.

We believe that no higher or more valued privilege can be afforded to an American citizen than to become a freeholder in the soil of the United States, and to that end we pledge our party to the enactment of soldier settlements and home aid legislation which will afford to the men who fought for America the opportunity to become land and home owners under conditions affording genuine government assistance unencumbered by needless difficulties of red tape or advance financial investment.

THE RAILROADS

The railroads were subjected to Federal control as a war measure, without other idea than the swift transport of troops, munitions and supplies. When human life and national hopes were at stake profits could not be considered and were not. Federal operation, however, was marked by an intelligence and efficiency that minimized loss and resulted in many and marked reforms. The equipment taken over was not only grossly inadequate but shamefully outworn. Unification practices overcame these initial handicaps and provided additions, betterments and improvements. Economies enabled operation without the rate raises that private control would have found necessary, and labor was treated with an exact justice that secured the enthusiastic co-operation that victory demanded. The fundamental purpose of Federal control was achieved fully and splendidly, and at far less cost to the taxpayer than would have been the case under private operation. Investments in railroad properties were not only saved by government operation, but government management returned these properties vastly improved in every physical and executive detail. A great task was greatly discharged.

The President's recommendation of return to private ownership gave the Republican majority a full year in which to enact the necessary legislation. The House took six months to formulate its ideas, and another six months was consumed by the Republican Senate in equally vague debate. As a consequence, the Esch-Cummins Bill went to the President in the closing hours of Congress, and he was forced to a choice between the chaos of a veto and acquiescence in the measure submitted, however grave may have been his objections to it.

There should be a fair and complete test of the law until careful and mature action by Congress may cure its defects and insure a thoroughly effective transportation system under private ownership without government subsidy at the expense of the taxpayers of the country.

IMPROVED HIGHWAYS

Improved roads are of vital importance not only to commerce and industry but also to agriculture and rural life. The Federal Road Act of 1916, enacted by a Democratic Congress, represented the first systematic effort of the government to insure the building of an adequate system of roads in this country. The act, as amended, has resulted in placing the movement for improved highways on a progressive and substantial basis in every State in the Union and in bringing under actual construction more than 13,000 miles of roads suited to the traffic needs of the communities in which they are located.

We favor a continuance of the present Federal aid plan under existing Federal and State agencies, amended so as to include as one of the elements in determining the ratio in which the several states shall be entitled to share in the fund, the area of any public lands therein.

Inasmuch as the postal service has been extended by the Democratic Party to the door of practically every producer and every consumer in the country (rural free delivery alone having been provided for 6,000,000 additional patrons within the past eight years without materially added cost), we declare that this instrumentality can and will be used to the maximum of its capacity to improve the efficiency of distribution and reduce the cost of living to consumers while increasing the profitable operations of producers.

We strongly favor the increased use of the motor vehicle in the transportation of the mails and urge the removal of the restrictions imposed by the Republican Congress on the use of motor devices in mail transportation in rural territories.

THE POSTAL SERVICE

The efficiency of the Post Office Department has been vindicated against a malicious and designing assault, by the efficiency of its operation. Its record refutes its assailants. Their voices are silenced and their charges have collapsed.

We recommend the work of the Joint Commission on the reclassification of salaries of postal employes, recently concluded, which commission was created by a Democratic administration. The Democratic Party has always favored and will continue to favor the fair and just treatment of all government employes.

FREE SPEECH AND PRESS

We resent the unfounded reproaches directed against the Democratic administration for alleged interference with the freedom of the press and freedom of speech.

No utterance from any quarter has been assailed, and no publication has been repressed, which has not been animated by treasonable purposes, and directed against the nation's peace, order and security in time of war.

We reaffirm our respect for the great principles of free speech and a free press, but assert as an indisputable proposition that they afford no toleration of enemy propaganda or the advocacy of the overthrow of the government of the state or nation by force or violence.

INLAND WATERWAYS

We call attention to the failure of the Republican National Convention to recognize in any way the rapid development of barge transportation on our inland waterways, which development is the result of the constructive policies of the Democratic administration. And we pledge ourselves to the further development of adequate transportation facilities on our rivers and to the further improvement of our inland waterways, and we recognize the importance of connecting the Great Lakes with the sea by way of the Mississippi River and its tributaries, as well as by the St. Lawrence River. We favor an enterprising Foreign Trade policy with all nations, and in this connection we favor the full utilization of all Atlantic, Pacific, and Gulf ports, and an equitable distribution of shipping facilities between the various ports.

Transportation remains an increasingly vital problem in the continued development and prosperity of the nation.

Our present facilities for distribution by rail are inadequate and the promotion of transportation by water is imperative.

We therefore favor a liberal and comprehensive

policy for the development and utilization of our harbors and interior waterways.

Merchant Marine

We desire to congratulate the American people upon the rebirth of our Merchant Marine which once more maintains its former place in the world. It was under a Democratic administration that this was accomplished after seventy years of indifference and neglect, thirteen million tons having been constructed since the act was passed in 1916. We pledge the policy of our party to the continued growth of our Merchant Marine under proper legislation so that American products will be carried to all ports of the world by vessels built in American yards, flying the American flag.

Reclamation of Arid Lands

By wise legislation and progressive administration, we have transformed the government reclamation projects, representing an investment of $100,000,000, from a condition of impending failure and loss of confidence in the ability of the government to carry through such large enterprises, to a condition of demonstrated success, whereby formerly arid and wholly unproductive lands now sustain 40,000 prosperous families and have an annual crop production of over $70,000,000, not including the crops grown on a million acres outside the projects supplied with storage water from government works.

We favor ample appropriations for the continuation and extension of this great work of home-building and internal improvement along the same general lines, to the end that all practical projects shall be built, and waters now running to waste shall be made to provide homes and add to the food supply, power resources, and taxable property, with the government ultimately reimbursed for the entire outlay.

Flood Control

We commend the Democratic Congress for the redemption of the pledge contained in our last platform by the passage of the Flood Control Act of March 1st, 1917, and point to the successful control of the floods of the Mississippi River and the Sacramento River, California, under the policy of that law, for its complete justification. We favor the extension of this policy to other flood control problems wherever the Federal

interest involved justified the expenditure required.

The Trade Commission

The Democratic Party heartily endorses the creation and work of the Federal Trade Commission in establishing a fair field for competitive business, free from restraints of trade and monopoly and recommends amplification of the statutes governing its activities so as to grant it authority to prevent the unfair use of patents in restraint of trade.

Live Stock Markets

For the purpose of insuring just and fair treatment in the great interstate live stock market, and thus instilling confidence in growers through which production will be stimulated and the price of meats to consumers be ultimately reduced, we favor the enactment of legislation for the supervision of such markets by the national government.

Port Facilities

The urgent demands of the war for adequate transportation of war material as well as for domestic need, revealed the fact that our port facilities and rate adjustments were such as to seriously affect the whole country in times of peace as well as war.

We pledge our party to stand for equality of rates, both import and export, for the ports of the country, to the end that there may be adequate and fair facilities and rates for the mobilization of the products of the country offered for shipment.

Petroleum

The Democratic Party recognizes the importance of the acquisition by Americans of additional sources of supply of petroleum and other minerals and declares that such acquisition both at home and abroad should be fostered and encouraged. We urge such action, legislative and executive, as may secure to American citizens the same rights in the acquirement of mining rights in foreign countries as are enjoyed by the citizens or subjects of any other nation.

Mexico

The United States is the neighbor and friend

of the nations of the three Americas. In a very special sense, our international relations in this hemisphere should be characterized by good will and free from any possible suspicion as to our national purpose.

The administration, remembering always that Mexico is an independent nation and that permanent stability in her government and her institutions could come only from the consent of her own people to a government of their own making, has been unwilling either to profit by the misfortunes of the people of Mexico or to enfeeble their future by imposing from the outside a rule upon their temporarily distracted councils. (a) As a consequence, order is gradually reappearing in Mexico; at no time in many years have American lives and interests been so safe as they are now; peace reigns along the border and industry is resuming.

When the new government of Mexico shall have given ample proof of its ability permanently to maintain law and order, signified its willingness to meet its international obligations and written upon its statute books just laws under which foreign investors shall have rights as well as duties, that government should receive our recognition and sympathetic assistance. Until these proper expectations have been met, Mexico must realize the propriety of a policy that asserts the right of the United States to demand full protection for its citizens.

Ireland

The great principle of national self-determination has received constant reiteration as one of the chief objectives for which this country entered the war and victory established this principle.

Within the limitations of international comity and usage, this Convention repeats the several previous expressions of the sympathy of the Democratic Party of the United States for the aspirations of Ireland for self-government.

Armenia

We express our deep and earnest sympathy for the unfortunate people of Armenia, and we believe that our government, consistent with its Constitution and principles, should render every possible and proper aid to them in their efforts to establish and maintain a government of their own.

Porto Rico

We favor granting to the people of Porto Rico the traditional territorial form of government, with a view to ultimate statehood, accorded to all territories of the United States since the beginning of our government, and we believe that the officials appointed to administer the government of such territories should be qualified by previous *bona-fide* residence therein.

Alaska

We commend the Democratic administration for inaugurating a new policy as to Alaska, as evidenced by the construction of the Alaska railroad and opening of the coal and oil fields.

We declare for the modification of the existing coal land law, to promote development without disturbing the features intended to prevent monopoly.

For such changes in the policy of forestry control as will permit the immediate initiation of the paper pulp industry.

For relieving the territory from the evils of long-distance government by arbitrary and interlocking bureaucratic regulation, and to that end we urge the speedy passage of a law containing the essential features of the Land-Curry Bill now pending, co-ordinating and consolidating all Federal control of natural resources under one department to be administered by a non-partisan board permanently resident in the territory.

For the fullest measure of territorial self-government with the view of ultimate statehood, with jurisdiction over all matters not of purely Federal concern, including fisheries and game, and for an intelligent administration of Federal control we believe that all officials appointed should be qualified by previous *bona-fide* residence in the territory.

For a comprehensive system of road construction with increased appropriations and the full extension of the Federal Road Aid Act to Alaska.

For the extension to Alaska of the Federal Farm Loan Act.

The Philippines

We favor the granting of independence without unnecessary delay to the 10,500,000 inhabitants of the Philippine Islands.

HAWAII

We favor a liberal policy of homesteading public lands in Hawaii to promote a larger middle-class citizen population, with equal rights to all citizens.

The importance of Hawaii as an outpost on the western frontier of the United States, demands adequate appropriations by Congress for the development of our harbors and highways there.

NEW NATIONS

The Democratic Party expresses its active sympathy with the people of China, Czecho-Slovakia, Finland, Poland, Persia, Jugo-Slavia and others who have recently established representative governments and who are striving to develop the institutions of true Democracy.

ASIATIC IMMIGRANTS

The policy of the United States with reference to the non-admission of Asiatic immigrants is a true expression of the judgment of our people, and to the several states, whose geographical situation or internal conditions make this policy, and the enforcement of the laws enacted pursuant thereto, of particular concern, we pledge our support.

REPUBLICAN CORRUPTION

The shocking disclosure of the lavish use of money by aspirants for the Republican nomination for the highest office in the gift of the people, has created a painful impression throughout the country. Viewed in connection with the recent conviction of a Republican Senator from the State of Michigan for the criminal transgression of the law limiting expenditures on behalf of a candidate for the United States Senate, it indicates the re-entry, under Republican auspices, of money as an influential factor in elections, thus nullifying the letter and flaunting the spirit of numerous laws, enacted by the people, to protect the ballot from the contamination of corrupt practices. We deplore these delinquencies and invoke their stern popular rebuke, pledging our earnest efforts to a strengthening of the present statutes against corrupt practices, and their rigorous enforcement.

We remind the people that it was only by the return of a Republican Senator in Michigan, who is now under conviction and sentence for the criminal misuse of money in his election, that the present organization of the Senate with a Republican majority was made possible.

CONCLUSION

Believing that we have kept the Democratic faith, and resting our claims to the confidence of the people not upon grandiose promises, but upon the solid performances of our party, we submit our record to the nation's consideration and ask that the pledges of this platform be appraised in the light of that record.

Farmer-Labor Platform of 1920

PREAMBLE

The American Declaration of Independence, adopted July 4, 1776, states that governments are instituted to secure to the people the rights of life, liberty and pursuit of happiness and that governments derive their just powers from the consent of the governed.

Democracy cannot exist unless all power is preserved to the people. The only excuse for the existence of government is to serve, not to rule, the people.

In the United States of America, the power of government, the priceless and inalienable heritage of the people, has been stolen from the people—has been seized by a few men who control the wealth of the nation and by the tools of these men, maintained by them in public office to do their bidding.

The administrative offices of the government and congress are controlled by the financial barons —even the courts have been prostituted—and the people as a result of this usurpation have been reduced to economic and industrial servitude.

Under the prevailing order in the United States, wealth is monopolized by a few and the people are kept in poverty, while costs of living mount until the burden of providing the necessaries of life is well-nigh intolerable.

Having thus robbed the people first of their power and then of their wealth, the wielders of financial power, seeking new fields of exploitation, have committed the government of the United States, against the will of the people, to imperialistic policies and seek to extend these enterprises to such lengths that our nation to-day stands in danger of becoming an empire instead of a republic.

Just emerging from a war which we said we fought to extend democracy to the ends of the earth, we find ourselves helpless while the masters of our government, who are also the masters of industry and commerce, league themselves with the masters of other nations to prevent self-determination by helpless people and to exploit and rob them, notwithstanding that we committed ourselves to guaranty of self-government for all such peoples.

Following the greedy spectacle of the peace conference, the money-masters feared an awakening of the people which threatened to exact for mankind those benefits for which the war was said to have been fought. Thereupon these masters, in the United States, through their puppets in public office, in an effort to stifle free discussion, stripped from the inhabitants of this land, rights and liberties guaranteed under American doctrines on which this country was founded and guaranteed also by the federal constitution.

These rights and liberties must be restored to the people.

More than this must be done. All power to govern this nation must be restored to the people. This involved industrial freedom, for political democracy is only an empty phrase without industrial democracy. This can not be done by superficial, palliative measures such as are, from time to time, thrown as sops to the voters by the Republican and Democratic parties. Patchwork cannot repair the destruction of democracy wrought by these two old parties. Reconstruction is necessary.

The invisible government of the United States maintains the two old parties to confuse the voters with false issues. These parties, therefore, can not seriously attempt reconstruction, which, to be effective, must smash to atoms the money power of the proprietors of the two old parties.

Into this breach step the amalgamated groups of forward looking men and women who perform useful work with hand and brain, united in the FARMER-LABOR Party of the United States by a spontaneous and irresistible impulse to do righteous battle for democracy against its despoilers, and more especially determined to function together because of the exceptionally brazen defiance shown by the two old parties in the selection of their candidates and the writing of their platforms in this campaign. This party, financed by its rank and file and not by big business, sets about the task of fundamental reconstruction of democracy in the United States, to restore all power to the people and to set up a governmental structure that will prevent seizure, henceforth, of that power by a few unscrupulous men.

The reconstruction proposed is set forth in the following platform of national issues, to which all candidates of the Farmer-Labor Party are pledged:

1. 100 PER CENT AMERICANISM

Restoration of civil liberties and American doctrines and their preservation inviolate, including free speech, free press, free assemblage, right of asylum, equal opportunity, and trial by jury; return of the Department of Justice to the functions for which it was created, to the end that laws may be enforced without favor and without discrimination; amnesty for all persons imprisoned because of their patriotic insistence upon their constitutional guaranties, industrial activities or religious beliefs; repeal of all so-called "espionage," "sedition," and "criminal syndicalist," laws; protection of the right of all workers to strike, and stripping from the courts of powers unlawfully usurped by them and used to defeat the people and foster big business, especially the power to issue anti-labor injunctions and to declare unconstitutional laws passed by Congress.

To Americanize the federal courts, we demand that federal judges be elected for terms not to exceed four years, subject to recall.

As Americanism means democracy, suffrage should be universal. We demand immediate ratification of the nineteenth amendment and full, unrestricted political rights for all citizens, regardless of sex, race, color or creed, and for civil service employes.

Democracy demands also that the people be equipped with the instruments of the initiative, referendum and recall, with the special provision that war may not be declared except in cases of actual military invasion, before referring the question to a direct vote of the people.

2. ABOLISH IMPERIALISM AT HOME AND ABROAD

Withdrawal of the United States from further participation (under the treaty of Versailles) in the reduction of conquered peoples to economic or political subjection to the small groups of men who manipulate the bulk of the world's wealth; refusal to permit our government to aid in the exploitation of the weaker people of the earth by these men; refusal to permit use of the agencies of our government (through dollar diplomacy or other means) by the financial interests of our country to exploit other peoples, including emphatic refusal to go to war with Mexico at the behest of Wall Street; recognition of the elected government of the Republic of Ireland and of the government established by the Russian people; denial of assistance financial, military, or otherwise, for foreign armies invading these countries, and an embargo on the shipment of arms and ammunition to be used against the Russian or Irish people; instant lifting of the blockade against Russia; recognition of every government set up by people who wrest their sovereignty from oppressors, in accordance with the right of self-determination for all peoples; abolition of secret treaties and prompt publication of all diplomatic documents received by the State Department; withdrawal from imperialistic enterprises upon which we already have embarked (including the dictatorship we exercise in varying degrees over the Philippines, Hawaii, Haiti, the Dominican Republic, Porto Rico, Cuba, Samoa and Guam); and prevention of the imposition upon the people of the United States of any form whatever of conscription, military or industrial, or of military training.

We stand committed to a league of free peoples, organized and pledged to destruction of autocracy, militarism and economic imperialism throughout the world and to bring about a world-wide disarmament and open diplomacy, to the end that there shall be no more kings and no more wars.

3. Democratic Control of Industry

The right of labor to an increasing share in the responsibilities and management of industry; application of this principle to be developed in accordance with the experience of actual operation.

4. Public Ownership and Operation

Immediate repeal of the Esch-Cummins Law; public ownership and operation, with democratic operation of the railroads, mines and natural resources, including stock-yards, large abattoirs, grain-elevators, water-power, and coal-storage and terminal warehouses; government ownership and democratic operation of the railroads, mines and of such natural resources as are in whole or in part bases of control by special interests of basic industries and monopolies such as lands containing coal, iron, copper, oil, large water-power and commercial timber tracts; pipe lines and oil tanks; telegraph and telephone lines; and establishment of a public policy that no land (including natural resources) and no patents shall be held out of use for speculation or to aid monopoly; establishment of national and state owned banks where the money of the government must, and that of individuals may, be deposited; granting of credit to individuals or groups according to regulations laid down by Congress which will safe-guard deposits.

We denounce the attempt to scuttle our great government-owned merchant marine and favor bringing ocean-going commerce to our inland ports.

5. Promotion of Agricultural Prosperity

Legislation that will effectively check and reduce the growth and evils of farm tenancy; establishment of public markets; extension of the federal farm loan system, making personal credit readily available and cheap to farmers; maintenance of dependable transportation for farm products; organization of a state and national service that will furnish adequate advice and guidance to applicants for farms and to farmers already on the land; legislation to promote and protect farmers' and consumers' co-operative organizations conducted for mutual benefit; comprehensive studies of costs of production of farm and staple manufactured products and uncensored publication of facts found in such studies.

6. Government Finance

We demand that economy in governmental expenditures shall replace the extravagance that has run riot under the present administration. The governmental expenditures of the present year of peace, as already disclosed, exceed $6,000,-000—or six times the annual expenditures of the pre-war period. We condemn and denounce the system that has created one war-millionaire for every three American soldiers killed in the war in France, and we demand that this war-acquired wealth shall be taxed in such a manner as to prevent the shifting of the burden of taxation to the shoulders of the poor in the shape of higher prices and of increased living costs.

We are opposed, therefore, to consumption taxes and to all indirect taxation for support of current operations of the government. For support of such current operations, we favor steeply graduated income taxes, exempting individual incomes amounting to less than $3,000 a year, with a further exemption allowance of $300 for every child under 18 and also for every child over 18 who may be pursuing an education to fit himself for life. In the case of state governments and of local governments we favor taxation of land value, but not of improvements or of equipment, and also sharply graduated taxes on inheritance.

7. REDUCE THE COST OF LIVING

Stabilization of currency so that it may not fluctuate as at present, carrying the standard of living of all the people down with it when it depreciates; federal control of the meat packing industry; extension and perfection of the Parcel Post system to bring producer and consumer closer together; enforcing existing laws against profiteers, especially the big and powerful ones.

8. JUSTICE TO THE SOLDIERS

We favor paying the soldiers of the late war as a matter of right and not as charity, a sufficient sum to make their war-pay not less than civilian earnings. We denounce the delays in payment, and the inadequate compensation to disabled soldiers and sailors and their dependents, and we pledge such changes as will promptly and adequately give sympathetic recognition of their services and sacrifices.

9. LABOR'S BILL OF RIGHTS

During the years that Labor has tried in vain to obtain recognition of the rights of the workers at the hands of the government through the agencies of the Republican and Democrat parties, the principal demands of Labor have been catalogued and presented by the representatives of Labor, who have gone to convention after convention of the old parties—to Congress after Congress of old-party office-holders. Those conventions and sessions of Congress have, from time to time, included in platforms and laws a few fragments of Labor's program, carefully rewritten, however,

to interpose no interference with the oppression of Labor by private wielders of the power of capital. It remains for the Farmer-Labor Party, the people's own party, financed by the people themselves, to pledge itself to the entire Bill of Rights of Labor, the conditions enumerated therein to be written into the laws of the land to be enjoyed by the workers, organized or unorganized, without the amelioration of a single word in the program. Abraham Lincoln said: "Labor is the superior of Capital, and deserves the highest consideration."

We pledge the application of this fundamental principle in the enactment and administration of legislation.

(a) The unqualified right of all workers, including civil service employes, to organize and bargain collectively with employers through such representatives of their unions as they choose.

(b) Freedom from compulsory arbitration and all other attempts to coerce workers.

(c) A maximum standard 8-hour day and 44-hour week.

(d) Old age and unemployment payments and workmen's compensation to insure workers and their dependents against accident and disease.

(e) Establishment and operation, through periods of depression, of governmental work on housing, road-building, reforestation, reclamation of cut-over timber, desert and swamp lands and development of ports, waterways and water-power plants.

(f) Re-education of the cripples of industry as well as the victims of war.

(g) Abolition of employment of children under sixteen years of age.

(h) Complete and effective protection for women in industry, with equal pay for equal work.

(i) Abolition of private employment, detective and strike-breaking agencies and extension of the federal free employment service.

(j) Prevention of exploitation of immigration and immigrants by employers.

(k) Vigorous enforcement of the Seamen's Act, and the most liberal interpretation of its provisions. The present provisions for the protection of seamen and for the safety of the traveling public, must not be minimized.

(l) Exclusion from interstate commerce of the products of convict labor.

(m) A federal department of education to advance democracy and effectiveness in all public school systems throughout the country, to the end that the children of workers in industrial and rural communities may have maximum opportunity of training to become unafraid, well-informed citizens of a free country.

Prohibition Platform of 1920

The Prohibition Party assembled in National Convention in the city of Lincoln, Nebraska, on this twenty-second day of July, 1920, expresses its thanks to Almighty God for the victory over the beverage liquor traffic which crowns fifty years of consecrated effort. The principles which we have advocated throughout our history have been so far recognized that the manufacture and traffic in intoxicating drink have been forever prohibited in the fundamental law of the land; Congress has rightly interpreted the Eighteenth Amendment in laws enacted for its enforcement; and the Supreme Court has upheld both the Amendment and the law.

Asking that it be clothed with governmental power, the Prohibition Party challenges the attention of the Nation and requests the votes of the people on this Declaration of Principles.

NULLIFICATION CONDEMNED

The organized liquor traffic is engaged in a treasonable attempt to nullify the Amendment by such modification of the enforcement act as will increase the alcoholic content in beer and wine and thus thwart the will of the people as constitutionally expressed.

In the face of this open threat the Republican and Democratic parties refused to make platform declarations in favor of law enforcement, though petitioned so to do by multitudes of people. Thus the Prohibition Party remains the sole political champion of National Prohibition.

The Prohibition Party in its platform in 1872 declared. "There can be no greater peril to the nation than the existing party competition for the liquor vote; any party not openly opposed to the traffic, experience shows, will engage in this competition, will court the favor of the criminal classes, will barter away the public morals, the purity of the ballot, and every object of good government for party success." Notwithstanding

the liquor traffic is now outlawed by the Constitution this fitly describes the present political attitude of the old parties.

The issue is not only the ENFORCEMENT but also the MAINTENANCE of the law to make the Amendment effective.

The proposed increase in the alcoholic content of beverages would be fraught with grave danger in that it would mean the return of the open saloon with all its attendant evils.

THE LEAGUE OF NATIONS

The League of Nations is now in existence and is functioning in world affairs. We favor the entrance of the United States into the League by the immediate ratification of the treaty of peace, not objecting to reasonable reservations interpreting American understanding of the covenant. The time is past when the United States can hold aloof from the affairs of the world. Such course is short-sighted and only invites disaster.

PEACE

We stand for a constitutional amendment providing that treaties of peace shall be ratified by a majority of both Houses of Congress.

We stand by our declaration of 1916 against militarism and universal military training. Without it our boys were in a short time trained to whip the greatest army ever assembled and with national prohibition to make sure the most virile manhood in the world we should encourage universal disarmament and devotion to the acts of peace.

EDUCATION

We stand for compulsory education with instruction in the English language, which, if given in private or parochial schools, must be equivalent to that afforded by the public schools, and be under state supervision.

SUFFRAGE

The Prohibition Party has long advocated the enfranchisement of women. Suffrage should not be conditioned upon sex. We congratulate the women upon the freedom which the Party has helped them to achieve.

WOMAN AND THE HOME

We approve and adopt the program of the

National League of Women Voters providing for:

The prohibition of child labor;

Adequate appropriation for the Children's Bureau;

Protection for infant life through a federal program for maternity and infancy care;

A Federal department of education, Federal aid for the removal of illiteracy and the increase of teachers' salaries;

Instruction of the youth and the newcomer to our shores in the duties and ideals of citizenship;

Vocational training in home economics;

Federal supervision of the marketing and distribution of food, the enactment and enforcement of such measures as will open the channels of trade, prevent excess profits, and eliminate unfair competition and control of the necessities of life;

The establishment of a Woman's Bureau in the Department of Labor to determine standards and policies which will improve working conditions for women and increase their efficiency;

The appointment of women in the mediation and conciliation service and on any industrial commissions and tribunals which may be created;

The establishment of a joint Federal and State employment service with women's departments under the direction of qualified women;

The merit system in the Civil Service free from discrimination on account of sex with a wage scale determined by skill demanded for the work and in no wise below the cost of living as established by official investigation;

Appropriation to carry on a campaign against venereal diseases and for public education in sex hygiene;

Federal legislation permitting an American born woman to retain her citizenship while resident in the United States, though married to an alien;

And further, that an alien woman who marries an American citizen must take the obligation of citizenship before she can become a citizen.

Economy in Administration

We believe in the Budget system and we stand for economy in governmental administration. There should be a reduction in boards, committees, commissions and offices which consume taxes and increase expenses.

Labor and Industry

We stand for Industrial Peace. We believe the time has come for the government to assume responsibility for the protection of the public against the waste and terror of industrial warfare, and to that end we demand legislation defining the rights of labor and the creation of industrial courts, which will guarantee to labor and employing capital equal and exact justice, and to the general public protection against the paralysis of industry due to this warfare.

Profiteering

The prohibition Party pledges the nation to rid it of the profiteer and to close the door against his return. It will endeavor to eliminate all unnecessary middlemen by the encouragement of organizations among producers that will bring those who sell and those who use nearer together. It will enact and enforce laws needful to effectively prevent excessive charges by such middlemen. To this end it will demand legislation subjecting to the penalties of the criminal law all corporate officers and employees who give or carry out instructions that result in extortion; it will make it unlawful for anyone engaged in Interstate Commerce to make the sale of one article dependent upon the purchase of another article and it will require such corporation to disclose to customers the difference between cost price and selling price or limit the profit that can be legally charged as the rate of interest is now limited.

Agriculture

We pledge our aid to the farmer in working out a plan to equalize prices, to secure labor, and to organize a system of co-operative marketing, including public terminals, mills and storage for the purpose of encouraging agriculture and securing for the farmer such return as will tend to increase production.

We favor such extension of the parcel post as will further facilitate the direct traffic between the producer and consumer.

Presidential Qualifications

The qualifications for President stated in the Constitution have to do with age and citizenship. We call attention to the fact that of greater importance are those not so stated referring to moral, intellectual and spiritual endowments. The President of the United States in his daily life, his home and family relationships and in his official career is expected to typify the finest and best the country can produce. He is the leader of the nation. The moral force and power of his example are immeasurable. No man or woman should ever be elected to the high office who is out of harmony with the purposes of the people or who lacks sympathy with their highest and holiest ideals, and with the Christian principles upon which the nation was founded.

Law and Order

A crying evil of the day is the general lax enforcement of law. Without obedience to law and maintenance of order our American institutions must perish.

The Prohibition Party now, as ever, pledges impartial enforcement of all law.

Conclusion

In this national and world crisis the Prohibition Party reminds the people of its long time faithfulness and its wisdom, proved by the many reforms which it was the first to advocate; and on its record as the oldest minority party—one which has never sold its birthright for a mess of pottage but throughout the years has stood for the best interests of the country—it asks the favorable consideration of the voters, believing that by its support they can make it necessary for all political organizations to come up to a higher level and to render a finer quality of service.

It pledges itself resolutely to stand for the right and oppose the wrong and dauntlessly to lead in the advocacy of righteous and patriotic principles. On its record and on this Declaration of Principles it submits its case to the American people.

Republican Platform of 1920

The Republican party, assembled in representative national convention, reaffirms its unyielding devotion to the Constitution of the United States, and to the guaranties of civil, political and religious liberty therein contained. It will resist all attempts to overthrow the foundations of the government or to weaken the force of its controlling principles and ideals, whether these attempts be made in the form of international policy or domestic agitation.

For seven years the national government has been controlled by the Democratic party. During that period a war of unparalleled magnitude has shaken the foundations of civilization, decimated the population of Europe, and left in its train economic misery and suffering second only to the war itself.

The outstanding features of the Democratic administration have been complete unpreparedness for war and complete unpreparedness for peace.

Unpreparedness for War

Inexcusable failure to make timely preparations is the chief indictment against the Democratic administration in the conduct of the war. Had not our associates protected us, both on land and sea, during the first twelve months of our participation and furnished us to the very day of the armistice with munitions, planes, and artillery, this failure would have been punished with disaster. It directly resulted in unnecessary losses to our gallant troops, in the imperilment of victory itself, and in an enormous waste of public funds, literally poured into the breach created by gross neglect. To-day it is reflected in our huge tax burdens and in the high cost of living.

Unpreparedness for Peace

Peace found the administration as unprepared for peace as war found it unprepared for war. The vital need of the country demanded the early and systematic return of a peace time basis.

This called for vision, leadership, and intelligent planning. All three have been lacking. While the country has been left to shift for itself, the government has continued on a wartime basis. The administration has not demobilized the army of place holders. It continued a method of financing which was indefensible during the period of reconstruction. It has used legislation passed to meet the emergency of war to continue its arbitrary and inquisitorial control over the life of the people in the time of peace, and to carry confusion into industrial life. Under the despot's plea of necessity or superior wisdom, executive usurpation of legislative and judicial function still undermines our institutions. Eighteen months after the armistice, with its wartime powers unabridged, its wartime departments undischarged, its wartime army of place holders still mobilized, the administration still continues to flounder helplessly.

The demonstrated incapacity of the Democratic party has destroyed public confidence, weakened the authority of the government, and produced a feeling of distrust and hesitation so universal as to increase enormously the difficulty of readjustment and to delay the return to normal conditions.

Never has our nation been confronted with graver problems. The people are entitled to know in definite terms how the parties purpose solving these problems. To that end, the Republican party declares its policy and programme to be as follows:

CONSTITUTIONAL GOVERNMENT

We undertake to end executive autocracy and restore to the people their constitutional government.

The policies herein declared will be carried out by the Federal and State governments, each acting within its constitutional powers.

FOREIGN RELATIONS

The foreign policy of the Administration has been founded upon no principle and directed by no definite conception of our nation's rights and obligations. It has been humiliating to America and irritating to other nations, with the result that after a period of unexampled sacrifice, our motives are suspected, our moral influence impaired, and our Government stands discredited and friendless among the nations of the world.

We favor a liberal and generous foreign policy founded upon definite moral and political principle, characterized by a clear understanding of and a firm adherence to our own rights, and unfailing respect for the rights of others. We should afford full and adequate protection to the life, liberty, property and all international rights of every American citizen, and should require a proper respect for the American flag; but we should be equally careful to manifest a just regard for the rights of other nations. A scrupulous observance of our international engagements when lawfully assumed is essential to our own honor and self-respect, and the respect of other nations. Subject to a due regard for our international obligations, we should leave our country free to develop its civilization along lines most conducive to the happiness and welfare of its people, and to cast its influence on the side of justice and right should occasion require.

(a) Mexico

The ineffective policy of the present Administration in Mexican matters has been largely responsible for the continued loss of American lives in that country and upon our border; for the enormous loss of American and foreign property; for the lowering of American standards of morality and social relations with Mexicans, and for the bringing of American ideals of justice, national honor and political integrity into contempt and ridicule in Mexico and throughout the world.

The policy of wordy, futile written protests against the acts of Mexican officials, explained the following day by the President himself as being meaningless and not intended to be considered seriously, or enforced, has but added in degree to that contempt, and has earned for us the sneers and jeers of Mexican bandits, and added insult upon insult against our national honor and dignity.

We should not recognize any Mexican government, unless it be a responsible government willing and able to give sufficient guarantees that the lives and property of American citizens are respected and protected; that wrongs will be promptly corrected and just compensation will be made for injury sustained. The Republican party pledges itself to a consistent, firm and effective policy towards Mexico that shall enforce respect for the American flag and that shall protect the rights of American citizens lawfully in Mexico to security of life and enjoyment of property, in accordance with established principles of international law and our treaty rights.

The Republican party is a sincere friend of the Mexican people. In its insistence upon the maintenance of order for the protection of American citizens within its borders a great service will be rendered the Mexican people themselves; for a continuation of present conditions means disaster to their interests and patriotic aspirations.

(b) Mandate for Armenia

We condemn President Wilson for asking Congress to empower him to accept a mandate for Armenia. We commend the Republican Senate for refusing the President's request to empower him to accept the mandate for Armenia. The acceptance of such mandate would throw the United States into the very maelstrom of European quarrels. According to the estimate of the Harbord Commission, organized by authority of President Wilson, we would be called upon to send 59,000 American boys to police Armenia and to expend $276,000,000 in the first year and $756,000,000 in five years. This estimate is made upon the basis that we would have only roving bands to fight; but in case of serious trouble with the Turks or with Russia, a force exceeding 200,000 would be necessary.

No more striking illustration can be found of President Wilson's disregard of the lives of American boys or of American interests.

We deeply sympathize with the people of Armenia and stand ready to help them in all proper ways, but the Republican party will oppose now and hereafter the acceptance of a mandate for any country in Europe or Asia.

(c) League of Nations

The Republican party stands for agreement among the nations to preserve the peace of the world. We believe that such an international association must be based upon international justice, and must provide methods which shall maintain the rule of public right by the development of law and the decision of impartial courts, and which shall secure instant and general international conference whenever peace shall be threatened by political action, so that the nations pledged to do and insist upon what is just and fair may exercise their influence and power for the prevention of war.

We believe that all this can be done without the compromise of national independence, without depriving the people of the United States in advance of the right to determine for themselves what is just and fair when the occasion arises, and without involving them as participants and not as peacemakers in a multitude of quarrels, the merits of which they are unable to judge.

The covenant signed by the President at Paris failed signally to accomplish this great purpose, and contains stipulations, not only intolerable for an independent people, but certain to produce the injustice, hostility and controversy among nations which it proposed to prevent.

That covenant repudiated, to a degree wholly unnecessary and unjustifiable, the time-honored policies in favor of peace declared by Washington, Jefferson, and Monroe, and pursued by all American administrations for more than a century, and it ignored the universal sentiment of America for generations past in favor of international law and arbitration, and it rested the hope of the future upon mere expediency and negotiation.

The unfortunate insistence of the President upon having his own way, without any change and without any regard to the opinions of a majority of the Senate, which shares with him in the treaty-making power, and the President's demand that the Treaty should be ratified without any modification, created a situation in which Senators were required to vote upon their consciences and their oaths according to their judgment against the Treaty as it was presented, or submit to the commands of a dictator in a matter where the authority and the responsibility under the Constitution were theirs, and not his.

The Senators performed their duty faithfully. We approve their conduct and honor their courage and fidelity. And we pledge the coming Republican administration to such agreements with the other nations of the world as shall meet the full duty of America to civilization and humanity, in accordance with American ideals, and without surrendering the right of the American people to exercise its judgment and its power in favor of justice and peace.

CONGRESS AND RECONSTRUCTION

Despite the unconstitutional and dictatorial course of the President and the partisan obstruction of the Democratic congressional minority, the Republican majority has enacted a program of constructive legislation which in great part, however, has been nullified by the vindictive vetoes of the President.

The Republican Congress has met the problems presented by the administration's unpreparedness for peace. It has repealed the greater part of the vexatious war legislation. It has enacted a transportation act making possible the rehabilitation of the railroad systems of the country, the operation of which, under the present Democratic administration, has been wasteful, extravagant, and inefficient in the highest degree. The transportation act made provision for the peaceful settlement of wage disputes, partially nullified, however, by the President's delay in appointing the wage board created by the Act. This delay precipitated the outlaw railroad strike.

We stopped the flood of public treasure, recklessly poured into the lap of an inept shipping board, and laid the foundations for the creation of a great merchant marine; we took from the incompetent Democratic administration the administration of the telegraph and telephone lines of the country and returned them to private ownership; we reduced the cost of postage and increased the pay of the postal employes—the poorest paid of all public servants; we provided pensions for superannuated and retired civil servants; and for an increase in pay of soldiers and sailors we reorganized the Army on a peace footing and provided for the maintenance of a powerful and efficient navy.

The Republican Congress established by law a permanent woman's bureau in the Department of Labor; we submitted to the country the constitutional amendment for woman suffrage, and furnished twenty-nine of the thirty-five legislatures which have ratified it to date.

Legislation for the relief of the consumers of print paper, for the extension of the powers of the government under the Food Control Act, for broadening the scope of the War Risk Insurance Act, better provision for the dwindling number of aged veterans of the Civil War and for the better support of the maimed and injured of the great war, and for making practical the vocational rehabilitation act, has been enacted by the Republican Congress.

We passed an oil leasing and water power bill to unlock for the public good the great pent-up resources of the country; we have sought to check the profligacy of the administration, to realize upon the assets of the government and to husband the revenues derived from taxation. The Republicans in Congress have been responsible for cuts in the estimates for government expenditure of nearly $3,000,000,000 since the signing of the armistice.

We enacted a national executive budget law; we strengthened the Federal Reserve Act to permit banks to lend needed assistance to farmers; we authorized financial incorporations to develop export trade; and finally, amended the rules of the Senate and House, which will reform evils in procedure and guarantee more efficient and responsible government.

Agriculture

The farmer is the backbone of the nation. National greatness and economic independence demand a population distributed between industry and the farm, and sharing on equal terms the prosperity which it holds is wholly dependent upon the efforts of both. Neither can prosper at the expense of the other without inviting joint disaster.

The crux of the present agricultural condition lies in prices, labor and credit.

The Republican party believes that this condition can be improved by: practical and adequate farm representation in the appointment of governmental officials and commissions; the right to form co-operative associations for marketing their products, and protection against discrimination; the scientific study of agricultural prices and farm production costs, at home and abroad, with a view to reducing the frequency of abnormal fluctuation; the uncensored publication of such reports; the authorization of associations for the extension of personal credit; a national inquiry on the co-ordination of rail, water and motor transportation with adequate facilities for receiving, handling and marketing food; the encouragement of our export trade; and end to unnecessary price-fixing and ill-considered efforts arbitrarily to reduce prices of farm products which invariably result to the disadvantage both of producer and consumer; and the encouragement of the production and importation of fertilizing material and of its extensive use.

The Federal Farm Loan Acts should be so administered as to facilitate the acquisition of farm land by those desiring to become owners and proprietors and thus minimize the evils of farm tenantry, and to furnish such long time credits as farmers may need to finance adequately their larger and long time production operations.

Industrial Relations

There are two different conceptions of the relations of capital and labor. The one is contractual and emphasizes the diversity of interest of employer and employé. The other is that of co-partnership in a common task.

We recognize the justice of collective bargaining as a means of promoting good will, establishing closer and more harmonious relations between employers and employés and realizing the true ends of industrial justice.

The strike or the lockout, as a means of settling industrial disputes, inflicts such loss and suffering on the community as to justify government initiative to reduce its frequency and limit its consequences. We denied the right to strike against the government; but the rights and interests of all government employés must be safeguarded by impartial laws and tribunals.

In public utilities we favor the establishment of an impartial tribunal to make an investigation of the facts and to render decision to the end that there may be no organized interruption of service necessary to the lives and health and welfare of the people. The decisions of the tribunal to be morally but not legally binding, and an informed public sentiment be relied on to secure their acceptance. The tribunals, however, should refuse to accept jurisdiction except for the purpose of investigation as long as the public service be interrupted. For public utilities we favor the type of tribunal provided for in the Transportation Act of 1920.

In private industries we do not advocate the principle of compulsory arbitration, but we favor impartial commissions and better facilities for voluntary mediation, conciliation and arbitration supplemented by the full publicity which will enlist the influence of an aroused public opinion. The government should take the initiative in inviting the establishment of tribunals or commissions for the purpose of voluntary arbitration and of investigation of disputed issues.

We demand the exclusion from interstate commerce of the products of convict labor.

NATIONAL ECONOMY

A Republican Congress reduced the estimates submitted by the Administration almost three billion dollars. Greater economies could have been effected had it not been for the stubborn refusal of the Administration to co-operate with Congress in an economy program. The universal demand for an executive budget is a recognition of the incontrovertible fact that leadership and sincere assistance on the part of the executive departments are essential to effective economy and constructive retrenchment.

The Overman Act invested the President of the United States with all the authority and power necessary to restore the Federal Government to a normal peace basis and to reorganize, retrench and demobilize. The dominant fact is that eight-

een months after the armistice, the United States Government is still on a war time basis, and the expenditure program of the Executive reflects war time extravagance rather than rigid peace time economy.

As an example of the failure to retrench which has characterized the post war time administration we cite the fact that not including the war and navy departments, the executive departments and other establishments at Washington actually record an increase subsequent to the armistice of 2,184 employés. The net decrease in pay roll costs contained in the 1921 demands submitted by the Administration is only one per cent below that of 1920. The annual expenses of Federal operations can be reduced hundreds of millions of dollars without impairing the efficiency of the public service.

We pledge ourselves to a carefully planned readjustment on a peace time basis and to a policy of rigid economy, to the better co-ordination of departmental activities, to the elimination of unnecessary officials and employés, and to the raising of the standard of individual efficiency.

THE EXECUTIVE BUDGET

We congratulate the Republican Congress on the enactment of a law providing for the establishment of an Executive Budget as a necessary instrument for a sound and business-like administration of the national finances; and we condemn the veto of the President which defeated this great financial reform.

REORGANIZATION OF FEDERAL DEPARTMENTS AND BUREAUS

We advocate a thorough investigation of the present organization of the Federal departments and bureaus, with a view to securing consolidation, a more business-like distribution of functions, the elimination of duplication, delays and overlapping of work and the establishment of an up-to-date and efficient administrative organization.

WAR POWERS OF THE PRESIDENT

The President clings tenaciously to his autocratic war time powers. His veto of the resolution declaring peace and his refusal to sign the bill repealing war time legislation, no longer necessary, evidenced his determination not to restore to the Nation and to the State the form of government provided for by the Constitution. This usurpation is intolerable and deserves the severest condemnation.

Taxation

The burden of taxation imposed upon the American people is staggering; but in presenting a true statement of the situation we must face the fact that, while the character of the taxes can and should be changed, an early reduction of the amount of revenue to be raised is not to be expected. The next Republican Administration will inherit from its Democratic predecessor a floating indebtedness of over three billion dollars—the prompt liquidation of which is demanded by sound financial consideration. Moreover, the whole fiscal policy of the Government must be deeply influenced by the necessity of meeting obligations in excess of five billion dollars which mature in 1923. But sound policy equally demands the early accomplishment of that real reduction of the tax burden which may be achieved by substituting simple for complex tax laws and procedure, prompt and certain determination of the tax liability for delay and uncertainty, tax laws which do not, for tax laws which do, excessively mulct the consumer or needlessly repress enterprise and thrift.

We advocate the issuance of a simplified form of income return; authorizing the Treasury Department to make changes in regulations effective only from the date of their approval empowering the Commissioner of Internal Revenue, with the consent of the taxpayers, to make final and conclusive settlements of tax claims and assessments barring fraud, the creation of a Tax Board consisting of at least three representatives of the tax-paying public and the heads of the principal divisions of the Bureau of Internal Revenue to act as a standing committee on the simplification of forms, procedure and law and to make recommendations to the Congress.

Banking and Currency

The fact is that the war to a great extent, was financed by a policy of inflation, through certificate borrowings from the banks, and bonds issued at artificial rates sustained by the low discount rates established by the Federal Reserve Board. The continuance of this policy since the armistice lays the administration open to severe criticism. Almost up to the present time the practices of the Federal Reserve Board as to credit control have been frankly dominated by the convenience of the Treasury.

The results have been a greatly increased war cost, a serious loss to the millions of people who, in good faith, bought liberty bonds and victory notes at par, and extensive post war speculation followed to-day by a restricted credit for legitimate industrial expansion and as a matter of public policy, we urge all banks to give credit preference to essential industry.

The Federal Reserve System should be free from political influence, which is quite as important as its independence of domination by financial combinations.

The High Cost of Living

The prime cause of the "High Cost of Living" has been first and foremost, a fifty per cent depreciation in the purchasing power of the dollar, due to a gross expansion of our currency and credit. Reduced production, burdensome taxation, swollen profits, and the increased demand for goods arising from a fictitious but enlarged buying power, have been contributing forces in a greater or less degree. We condemn the unsound fiscal policies of the Democratic Administration which have brought these things to pass, and their attempts to impute the consequences to minor and secondary causes. Much of the injury wrought is irreparable. There is no short way out, and we decline to deceive the people with vain promises or quack remedies. But as the political party that throughout its history has stood for honest money and sound finance, we pledge ourselves to earnest and consistent attack upon the high cost of living, by rigorous avoidance of further inflation in war government borrowing, by courageous and intelligent deflation of over-expanded credit and currency, by encouragement of heightened production of goods and services, by prevention of unreasonable profits, by exercise of public economy and stimulation of private thrift and by revision of war imposed taxes unsuited to peace time economy.

Profiteering

We condemn the Democratic Administration for failure impartially to enforce the Anti-Profiteering Laws enacted by the Republican Congress.

RAILROADS

We are opposed to government ownership and operation or employé operation of the Railroads. In view of the conditions prevailing in this country, the experience of the last two years, and the conclusion which may fairly be drawn from an observation of the transportation systems of other countries it is clear that adequate transportation service both for the present and future can be furnished more certainly, economically and efficiently through private ownership and operation under proper regulation and control.

There should be no speculative profit in rendering the service of transportation; but in order to do justice to the capital already invested in railway enterprise, to restore railway credit, to induce future investment at a reasonable rate, and to furnish a large facility to meet the requirements of the constantly increasing development and distribution a fair return upon actual value of the railway property used in transportation should be made reasonably sure, and at the same time to provide constant employment to those engaged in transportation service, with fair hours and favorable working conditions, at wages or compensation at least equal to those prevailing in similar lines of industry.

We endorse the transportation act of 1920 enacted by the Republican Congress as a most constructive legislative achievement.

WATERWAYS

We declare it to be our policy to encourage and develop water transportation service and facilities in connection with the commerce of the United States.

REGULATION OF INDUSTRY AND COMMERCE

We approve in general the existing Federal Legislation against monopoly and combinations in restraint of trade, but since the known certainty of a law is the safety of all, we advocate such amendment as will provide American business men with better means of determining in advance whether a proposed combination is or is not unlawful. The Federal Trade Commission, under a Democratic Administration, has not accomplished the purpose for which it was created. This commission properly organized and its duties efficiently administered should afford protection to the public and legitimate business interests. There

should be no persecution of honest business; but to the extent that circumstances warrant we pledge ourselves to strengthen the law against unfair practices.

We pledge the party to an immediate resumption of trade relations with every nation with which we are at peace.

INTERNATIONAL TRADE AND TARIFF

The uncertain and unsettled condition of international balances, the abnormal economic and trade situation of the world, and the impossibility of forecasting accurately even the near future, preclude the formulation of a definite program to meet conditions a year hence. But the Republican party reaffirms its belief in the protective principles and pledges itself to a revision of the tariff as soon as conditions shall make it necessary for the preservation of the home market for American labor, agriculture and industry.

MERCHANT MARINE

The National defense and our foreign commerce require a merchant marine of the best type of modern ship, flying the American flag, and manned by American seamen, owned by private capital, and operated by private energy. We endorse the sound legislation recently enacted by the Republican Congress that will insure the promotion and maintenance of the American Merchant Marine.

We favor the application of the workmen's compensation act to the Merchant Marine.

We recommend that all ships engaged in coastwise trade and all vessels of the American Merchant Marine shall pass through the Panama Canal without payment of tolls.

IMMIGRATION

The standard of living and the standard of citizenship of a nation are its most precious possessions, and the preservation and the elevation of those standards is the first duty of our government. The immigration policy of the U. S. should be such as to insure that the number of foreigners in the country at any one time shall not exceed that which can be assimilated with reasonable rapidity, and to favor immigrants whose standards are similar to ours.

The selective tests that are at present applied should be improved by requiring a higher physical standard, a more complete exclusion of mental defectives and of criminals, and a more effective inspection applied as near the source of immigration as possible, as well as at the port of entry. Justice to the foreigner and to ourselves demands provision for the guidance, protection and better economic distribution of our alien population. To facilitate government supervision, all aliens should be required to register annually until they become naturalized.

The existing policy of the United States for the practical exclusion of Asiatic immigrants is sound, and should be maintained.

NATURALIZATION

There is urgent need of improvement in our naturalization law. No alien should become a citizen until he has become genuinely American, and adequate tests for determining the alien's fitness for American citizenship should be provided for by law.

We advocate, in addition, the independent naturalization of married women. An American woman, resident in the United States, should not lose her citizenship by marriage to an alien.

FREE SPEECH AND ALIEN AGITATION

We demand that every American citizen shall enjoy the ancient and constitutional right of free speech, free press and free assembly and the no less sacred right of the qualified voted [sic] to be represented by his duly chosen representatives; but no man may advocate resistance to the law, and no man may advocate violent overthrow of the government.

Aliens within the jurisdiction of the United States are not entitled of right to liberty of agitation directed against the government of American institutions.

Every government has the power to exclude and deport those aliens who constitute a real menace to its peaceful existence. But in view of the large numbers of people affected by the immigration acts and in view of the vigorous malpractice of the Departments of Justice and Labor, an adequate public hearing before a competent administrative tribunal should be assured to all.

LYNCHING

We urge Congress to consider the most effective means to end lynching in this country which con-

tinues to be a terrible blot on our American civilization.

PUBLIC ROADS AND HIGHWAYS

We favor liberal appropriations in co-operation with the States for the construction of highways, which will bring about a reduction in transportation costs, better marketing of farm products, improvement in rural postal delivery, as well as meet the needs of military defense.

In determining the proportion of Federal aid for road construction among the States, the sums lost in taxation to the respective States by the setting apart of large portions of their area as forest reservations should be considered as a controlling factor.

CONSERVATION

Conservation is a Republican policy. It began with the passage of the Reclamation Act signed by President Roosevelt. The recent passage of the coal, oil and phosphate leasing act by a Republican Congress and the enactment of the water-power bill fashioned in accordance with the same principle, are consistent landmarks in the development of the conservation of our national resources. We denounce the refusal of the President to sign the waterpower bill, passed after ten years of controversy. The Republican party has taken an especially honorable part in saving our national forests and in the effort to establish a national forest policy. Our most pressing conservation question relates to our forests. We are using our forest resources faster than they are being renewed. The result is to raise unduly the cost of forest products to consumers and especially farmers, who use more than half the lumber produced in America, and in the end to create a timber famine. The Federal Government, the States and private interests must unite in devising means to meet the menace.

RECLAMATION

We favor a fixed and comprehensive policy of reclamation to increase national wealth and production.

We recognize in the development of reclamation through Federal action with its increase of production and taxable wealth a safeguard for the nation.

We commend to Congress a policy to reclaim

lands and the establishment of a fixed national policy of development of natural resources in relation to reclamation through the now designated government agencies.

ARMY AND NAVY

We feel the deepest pride in the fine courage, the resolute endurance, the gallant spirit of the officers and men of our army and navy in the World War. They were in all ways worthy of the best traditions of the nation's defenders, and we pledge ourselves to proper maintenance of the military and naval establishments upon which our national security and dignity depend.

THE SERVICE MEN

We hold in imperishable remembrance the valor and the patriotism of the soldiers and sailors of America who fought in the great war for human liberty, and we pledge ourselves to discharge to the fullest the obligations which a grateful nation justly should fulfill, in appreciation of the services rendered by its defenders on sea and on land.

Republicans are not ungrateful. Throughout their history they have shown their gratitude toward the nation's defenders. Liberal legislation for the care of the disabled and infirm and their dependents has ever marked Republican policy toward the soldier and sailor of all the wars in which our country has participated. The present Congress has appropriated generously for the disabled of the World War.

The amounts already applied and authorized for the fiscal year 1920-21 for this purpose reached the stupendous sum of $1,180,571,893. The legislation is significant of the party's purpose in generously caring for the maimed and disabled men of the recent war.

CIVIL SERVICE

We renew our repeated declaration that the civil service law shall be thoroughly and honestly enforced and extended wherever practicable. The recent action of Congress in enacting a comprehensive civil service retirement law and in working out a comprehensive employment and wage policy that will guarantee equal and just treatment to the army of government workers, and in centralizing the administration of the new and progressive employment policy in the hands of the Civil Service Commission is worthy of all praise.

POSTAL SERVICE

We condemn the present administration for its destruction of the efficiency of the postal service, and the telegraph and telephone service when controlled by the government and for its failure to properly compensate employés whose expert knowledge is essential to the proper conduct of the affairs of the postal system. We commend the Republican Congress for the enactment of legislation increasing the pay of postal employés, who up to that time were the poorest paid in the government service.

WOMAN SUFFRAGE

We welcome women into full participation in the affairs of government and the activities of the Republican Party. We earnestly hope that Republican legislatures in states which have not yet acted on the Suffrage Amendment will ratify the amendment, to the end that all of the women of the nation of voting age may participate in the election of 1920 which is so important to the welfare of our country.

SOCIAL PROGRESS

The supreme duty of the nation is the conservation of human resources through an enlightened measure of social and industrial justice. Although the federal jurisdiction over social problems is limited, they affect the welfare and interest of the nation as a whole. We pledge the Republican party to the solution of these problems through national and state legislation in accordance with the best progressive thought of the country.

EDUCATION AND HEALTH

We endorse the principle of Federal aid to the States for the purpose of vocational and agricultural training.

Wherever Federal money is devoted to education, such education must be so directed as to awaken in the youth the spirit of America and a sense of patriotic duty to the United States.

A thorough system of physical education for all children up to the age of 19, including adequate health supervision and instruction, would remedy conditions revealed by the draft and would add to the economic and industrial strength of the nation. National leadership and stimulation will be necessary to induce the States to adopt a wise system of physical training.

The public health activities of the Federal government are scattered through numerous departments and bureaus, resulting in inefficiency, duplication and extravagance. We advocate a greater centralization of the Federal functions, and in addition urge the better co-ordination of the work of the Federal, State and local health agencies.

CHILD LABOR

The Republican party stands for a Federal child labor law and for its rigid enforcement. If the present law be found unconstitutional or ineffective, we shall seek other means to enable Congress to prevent the evils of child labor.

WOMEN IN INDUSTRY

Women have special problems of employment which make necessary special study. We recommend Congress for the permanent establishment of the Women's Bureau in the United States Department of Labor to serve as a source of information to the States and to Congress.

The principle of equal pay for equal service should be applied throughout all branches of the Federal government in which women are employed.

Federal aid for vocational training should take into consideration the special aptitudes and needs of women workers.

We demand Federal legislation to limit the hours of employment of women engaged in intensive industry, the product of which enters into interstate commerce.

HOUSING

The housing shortage has not only compelled careful study of ways of stimulating building, but it has brought into relief the unsatisfactory character of the housing accommodations of large numbers of the inhabitants of our cities. A nation of home owners is the best guaranty of the maintenance of those principles of liberty, law and order upon which our government is founded. Both National and State governments should encourage in all proper ways the acquiring of homes by our citizens. The United States Government should make available the valuable information on housing and town planning collected during the war. This information should be kept up to date and made currently available.

HAWAII

For Hawaii we recommend Federal assistance in Americanizing and educating their greatly disproportionate foreign population; home rule; and the rehabilitation of the Hawaiian race.

Pointing to its history and relying on its fundamental principles, we declare that the Republican party has the genius, courage and constructive ability to end executive usurpation and restore constitutional government; to fulfill our world obligations without sacrificing our national independence; to raise the national standards of education, health and general welfare; to re-establish a peace time administration and to substitute economy and efficiency for extravagance and chaos; to restore and maintain the national credit; to reform unequal and burdensome taxes; to free business from arbitrary and unnecessary official control; to suppress disloyalty without the denial of justice; to repel the arrogant challenge of any class and to maintain a government of all the people as contrasted with government for some of the people, and finally, to allay unrest, suspicion and strife, and to secure the co-operation and unity of all citizens in the solution of the complex problems of the day; to the end that our country, happy and prosperous, proud of its past, sure of itself and of its institutions, may look forward with confidence to the future.

Socialist Platform of 1920

In the national campaign of 1920 the Socialist Party calls upon all American workers of hand and brain, and upon all citizens who believe in political liberty and social justice, to free the country from the oppressive misrule of the old political parties, and to take the government into their own hands under the banner and upon the program of the Socialist Party.

The outgoing administration, like Democratic and Republican administrations of the past, leave behind it a disgraceful record of solemn pledges unscrupulously broken and public confidence ruthlessly betrayed.

It obtained the suffrage of the people on a

platform of peace, liberalism and social betterment, but drew the country into a devastating war, and inaugurated a régime of despotism, reaction and oppression unsurpassed in the annals of the republic.

It promised to the American people a treaty which would assure to the world a reign of international right and true democracy. It gave its sanction and support to an infamous pact formulated behind closed doors by predatory elder statesmen of European and Asiatic imperialism. Under this pact territories have been annexed against the will of their populations and cut off from their sources of sustenance; nations seeking their freedom in the exercise of much heralded right of self-determination have been brutally fought with armed force, intrigue and starvation blockades.

To the millions of young men, who staked their lives on the field of battle, to the people of the country who gave unstintingly of their toil and property to support the war, the Democratic administration held out the sublime ideal of a union of the peoples of the world organized to maintain perpetual peace among nations on the basis of justice and freedom. It helped create a reactionary alliance of imperialistic governments, banded together to bully weak nations, crush working-class governments and perpetuate strife and warfare.

While thus furthering the ends of reaction, violence and oppression abroad, our administration suppressed the cherished and fundamental rights and civil liberties at home.

Upon the pretext of war-time necessity, the Chief Executive of the republic and the appointed heads of his administration were clothed with dictatorial powers (which were often exercised arbitrarily), and Congress enacted laws in open and direct violation of the constitutional safeguards of freedom of expression.

Hundreds of citizens who raised their voices for the maintenance of political and industrial rights during the war were indicted under the Espionage Law, tried in an atmosphere of prejudice and hysteria and are now serving inhumanly long jail sentences for daring to uphold the traditions of liberty which once were sacred in this country.

Agents of the Federal government unlawfully raided homes and meeting places and prevented or broke up peaceable gatherings of citizens.

The postmaster-general established a censorship of the press more autocratic than that ever tolerated in a régime of absolutism, and has harassed and destroyed publications on account of their advanced political and economic views, by excluding them from the mails.

And after the war was in fact long over, the administration has not scrupled to continue a policy of repression and terrorism under the shadow and hypocritical guise of war-time measures.

It has practically imposed involuntary servitude and peonage on a large class of American workers by denying them the right to quit work and coercing them into acceptance of inadequate wages and onerous conditions of labor. It has dealt a foul blow to the traditional American right of asylum by deporting hundreds of foreign born workers by administrative order, on the mere suspicion of harboring radical views, and often for the sinister purpose of breaking labor strikes.

In the short span of three years our self-styled liberal administration has succeeded in undermining the very foundation of political liberty and economic rights which this republic has built up in more than a century of struggle and progress.

Under the cloak of a false and hypocritical patriotism and under the protection of governmental terror the Democratic administration has given the ruling classes unrestrained license to plunder the people by intensive exploitation of labor, by the extortion of enormous profits and by increasing the cost of all necessities of life. Profiteering has become reckless and rampant, billions have been coined by the capitalists out of the suffering and misery of their fellow men. The American financial oligarchy has become a dominant factor in the world, while the condition of the American workers has grown more precarious.

The responsibility does not rest upon the Democratic party alone. The Republican party, through its representatives in Congress and otherwise, has not only openly condoned the political misdeeds of the last three years, but has sought to outdo its Democratic rival in the orgy of political reaction and repression. Its criticism of the Democratic administrative policy is that it is not reactionary and drastic enough.

America is now at the parting of the roads. If the outraging of political liberty and concentration of economic power into the hands of the few is permitted to go on, it can have only one consequence, the reduction of the country to a state of absolute capitalist despotism.

We particularly denounce the militaristic policy of both old parties, of investing countless hundreds of millions of dollars in armaments after the victorious completion of what was to have been the "last war." We call attention to the fatal results of such a program in Europe, carried on prior to 1914, and culminating in the Great War; we declare that such a policy, adding unbearable burdens to the working class and to all the people, can lead only to the complete Prussianization of the nation, and ultimately to war; and we demand immediate and complete abandonment of this fatal program.

The Socialist Party sounds the warning. It calls upon the people to defeat both parties at the polls, and to elect the candidates of the Socialist Party to the end of restoring political democracy and bringing about complete industrial freedom.

The Socialist Party of the United States therefore summons all who believe in this fundamental doctrine to prepare for a complete reorganization of our social system, based upon public ownership of public necessities; upon government by representatives chosen from occupational as well as from geographical groups in harmony with our industrial development, and with citizenship based on service; that we may end forever the exploitation of class by class.

To achieve this end the Socialist Party pledges itself to the following program:

1. SOCIAL

1. All business vitally essential for the existence and welfare of the people, such as railroads, express service, steamship lines, telegraphs, mines, oil wells, power plants, elevators, packing houses, cold storage plants and all industries operating on a national scale, should be taken over by the nation.

2. All publicly owned industries should be administered jointly by the government and representatives of the workers, not for revenue or profit, but with the sole object of securing just compensation and humane conditions of employment to the workers and efficient and reasonable service to the public.

3. All banks should be acquired by the government, and incorporated in a unified public banking system.

4. The business of insurance should be taken over by the government, and should be extended to include insurance against accident, sickness, invalidity, old age and unemployment, without contribution on the part of the worker.

5. Congress should enforce the provisions of the Thirteenth, Fourteenth and Fifteenth Amendments with reference to the Negroes, and effective federal legislation should be enacted to secure to the Negroes full civil, political, industrial and educational rights.

2. INDUSTRIAL

1. Congress should enact effective laws to abolish child labor, to fix minimum wages, based on an ascertained cost of a decent standard of life, to protect migratory and unemployed workers from oppression, to abolish detective and strike-breaking agencies and to establish a shorter work-day in keeping with increased industrial productivity.

3. POLITICAL

1. The constitutional freedom of speech, press and assembly should be restored by repealing the Espionage Law and all other repressive legislation, and by prohibiting the executive usurpation of authority.

2. All prosecutions under the Espionage Law should be discontinued, and all persons serving prison sentences for alleged offenses growing out of religious beliefs, political views or industrial activities should be fully pardoned and immediately released.

3. No alien should be deported from the United States on account of his political views or participation in labor struggles, nor in any event without proper trial on specific charges. The arbitrary power to deport aliens by administrative order should be repealed.

4. The power of the courts to restrain workers in their struggles against employers by the Writ of Injunction or otherwise, and their power to nullify congressional legislation, should be abrogated.

5. Federal judges should be elected by the people and be subject to recall.

6. The President and the Vice-President of the United States should be elected by direct

popular election, and be subject to recall. All members of the Cabinet should be elected by Congress and be responsible at all times to the vote thereof.

7. Suffrage should be equal and unrestricted in fact as well as in law for all men and women throughout the nation.

8. Because of the strict residential qualification of suffrage in this country, millions of citizens are disfranchised in every election; adequate provision should be made for the registration and voting of migratory workers.

9. The Constitution of the United States should be amended to strengthen the safeguards of civil and political liberty, and to remove all obstacles to industrial and social reform and reconstruction, including the changes enumerated in this program, in keeping with the will and interest of the people. It should be made amendable by a majority of the voters of the nation upon their own initiative, or upon the initiative of Congress.

4. FOREIGN RELATIONS

1. All claims of the United States against allied countries for loans made during the war should be canceled upon the understanding that all war debts among such countries shall likewise be canceled. The largest possible credit in food, raw materials and machinery should be extended to the stricken nations of Europe in order to help them rebuild the ruined world.

2. The Government of the United States should initiate a movement to dissolve the mischievous organization called the "League of Nations" and to create an international parliament, composed of democratically elected representatives of all nations of the world based upon the recognition of their equal rights, the principles of self-determination, the right to national existence of colonies and other dependencies, freedom of international trade and trade routes by land and sea, and universal disarmament, and be charged with revising the Treaty of Peace on the principles of justice and conciliation.

3. The United States should immediately make peace with the Central Powers and open commercial and diplomatic relations with Russia under the Soviet Government. It should promptly recognize the independence of the Irish Republic.

4. The United States should make and proclaim it a fixed principal in its foreign policy that American capitalists who acquire concessions or make investments in foreign countries do so at their own risk, and under no circumstances should our government enter into diplomatic negotiations or controversies or resort to armed conflicts on account of foreign property-claims of American capitalists.

5. FISCAL

1. All war debts and other debts of the Federal Government should immediately be paid in full, the funds for such payment to be raised by means of a progressive property tax, whose burden should fall upon the rich and particularly upon great fortunes made during the war.

2. A standing progressive income tax and a graduated inheritance tax should be levied to provide for all needs of the government, including the cost of its increasing social and industrial functions.

3. The unearned increment of land should be taxed; all land held out of use should be taxed at full rental value.

Socialist Labor Platform of 1920

The world stands upon the threshold of a new social order. The capitalist system of production and distribution is doomed; capitalist appropriation of labor's produce forces the bulk of mankind into wage slavery, throws society into the convulsions of the class struggle, and momentarily threatens to engulf humanity in chaos and disaster. At this crucial period in history the Socialist Labor Party of America, in 15th National Convention assembled, reaffirming its former platform declarations, calls upon the workers to rally around the banner of the Socialist Labor Party, the only party in this country that blazes the trail to the Workers' Industrial Republic.

Since the advent of civilization human society has been divided into classes. Each new form of society has come into being with a definite purpose to fulfill in the progress of the human race. Each has been born, has grown, developed, prospered, become old, outworn, and has finally been overthrown. Each society has developed within itself the germs of its own destruction as well as the germs which went to make up the society of the future.

The capitalist system rose during the seventeenth, eighteenth, and nineteenth centuries, by the overthrow of feudalism. Its great and all-important mission in the development of man was to improve, develop, and concentrate the means of production and distribution, thus creating a system of co-operative production. This work was completed in advanced capitalist countries about the beginning of the 20th century. That moment capitalism had fulfilled its historic mission, and from that moment the capitalist class became a class of parasites.

In the course of human progress mankind has passed through class rule, private property, and individualism in production and exchange, from the enforced and inevitable want, misery, poverty, and ignorance of savagery and barbarism to the affluence and high productive capacity of civilization. For all practical purposes, co-operative production has now superseded individual production.

Capitalism no longer promotes the greatest good of the greatest number. Private production carries with it private ownership of the products. Production is carried on, not to supply the needs of humanity, but for the profit of the individual owner, the company, or the trust. The worker, not receiving the full product of his labor, can not buy back all he produces. The capitalist wastes part in riotous living; the rest must find a foreign market. By the opening of the twentieth century the capitalist world—England, America, Germany, France, Japan, China, etc.—was producing at a mad rate for the world market. A capitalist deadlock of market brought on in 1914 the capitalist collapse popularly known as the World War. The capitalist world can not extricate itself out of the débris. America to-day is choking under the weight of her own gold and products.

This situation has brought on the present stage of human misery—starvation, want, cold, disease, pestilence, and war. This state is brought about in the midst of plenty, when the earth can be made to yield hundred-fold, when the machinery of production is made to multiply human energy and ingenuity by the hundred. The present state of misery exists solely because the mode of production rebels against the mode of exchange.

Private property in the means of life has become a social crime. The land was made by no man; the modern machines are the result of the combined ingenuity of the human race from time immemorial; the land can be made to yield and the machines can be set in motion only by the collective effort of the workers. Progress demands the collective ownership of the land on and the tools with which to produce the necessities of life. The owner of the means of life to-day partakes of the nature of a highwayman; he stands with his gun before society's temple; it depends upon him whether the million mass may work, earn, eat, and live. The capitalist system of production and exchange must be supplanted if progress is to continue.

In place of the capitalist system the Socialist Labor Party aims to substitute a system of social ownership of the means of production, industrially administered by the workers, who assume control and direction as well as operation of their industrial affairs.

We therefore call upon the wage workers to organize themselves into a revolutionary political organization under the banner of the Socialist Labor Party; and to organize themselves likewise upon the industrial field into a Socialist industrial union, as now exemplified by the Workers' International Industrial Union, in keeping with their political aims.

And we also call upon all other intelligent citizens to place themselves squarely upon the ground of working class interests, and join us in this mighty and noble work of human emancipation, so that we may put summary end to the existing barbarous class conflict by placing the land and all the means of production, transportation, and distribution into the hands of the people as a collective body, and substituting Industrial Self-Government for the present state of planless production, industrial war and social disorder—a government in which every worker shall have the free exercise and full benefit of his faculties, multiplied by all the modern factors of civilization.

CAMPAIGN OF 1924

In June, 1924, Calvin Coolidge, who had become the chief executive on the death of President Harding, was easily nominated on the first ballot at the Republican convention. Eight candidates for the vice-presidency were nominated, and Charles G. Dawes of Illinois was chosen on the third ballot. Two weeks later, at the longest national convention in American history, the Democrats nominated sixteen candidates and, operating under the two-thirds rule, took 103 ballots and nine days of balloting to select John W. Davis of West Virginia as their compromise nominee. Governor Charles W. Bryan of Nebraska was chosen as the vice-presidential candidate.

Senator Robert M. La Follette of Wisconsin was nominated for the presidency by the Conference for Progressive Political Action which met in Cleveland, Ohio, in July, but he also ran as an independent in several states. Senator Burton K. Wheeler of Montana was his personally chosen running mate. The Conference adopted a platform, and at a later date Senator La Follette published a platform of his own. Both platforms are included in this volume. The Socialist Party published only a Declaration of Principles instead of a platform and supported La Follette in the election.

Herman P. Faris of Missouri and Marie Caroline Brehm of California were the candidates of the Prohibition Party. The Socialist Labor Party members nominated Frank T. Johns of Oregon and Verne L. Reynolds of New York as their ticket. The Workers (Communist) Party published a platform and nominated William Z. Foster of Illinois for president and Benjamin Gitlow of New York for vice-president.

In November, the Republicans overwhelmed the Democrats and the Progressives, 15,717,553 popular votes to 8,386,169 for Davis and 4,814,050 for La Follette. Faris and the Prohibitionists polled 54,833 votes; the Socialist Labor Party received 28,368; Foster, for the Workers Party, attracted 38,080 votes. Coolidge received 382 electoral votes; Davis won the solid South and 136 votes. Wisconsin cast its 13 electoral votes for its favorite son, Robert La Follette.

Democratic Platform of 1924

We, the representatives of the democratic party, in national convention assembled, pay our profound homage to the memory of Woodrow Wilson. Our hearts are filled with gratitude that American democracy should have produced this man, whose spirit and influence will live on through the ages; and that it was our privilege to have co-operated with him in the advancement of ideals of government which will serve as an example and inspiration for this and future generations. We affirm our abiding faith in those ideals and pledge ourselves to take up the standard which he bore and to strive for the full triumph of the principles of democracy to which he dedicated his life.

DEMOCRATIC PRINCIPLES

The democratic party believes in equal rights to all and special privilege to none. The republican party holds that special privileges are essential to national prosperity. It believes that national prosperity must originate with the special interests and seep down through the channels of trade to the less favored industries to the wage earners and small salaried employes. It has accordingly enthroned privilege and nurtured selfishness.

The republican party is concerned chiefly with material things; the democratic party is concerned chiefly with human rights. The masses, burdened by discriminating laws and unjust administration, are demanding relief. The favored special interests, represented by the republican party, contented with their unjust privileges, are demanding that no change be made. The democratic party stands for remedial legislation and progress. The republican party stands still.

COMPARISON OF PARTIES

We urge the American people to compare the record of eight unsullied years of democratic administration with that of the republican administration. In the former there was no corruption. The party pledges were faithfully fulfilled and a democratic congress enacted an extraordinary number of constructive and remedial laws. The economic life of the nation was quickened.

Tariff taxes were reduced. A federal trade commission was created. A federal farm loan system was established. Child labor legislation was enacted. A good roads bill was passed. Eight hour laws were adopted. A secretary of labor was given a seat in the cabinet of the president. The Clayton amendment to the Sherman anti-trust act was passed, freeing American labor and taking it from the category of commodities. By the Smith-Lever bill improvement of agricultural conditions was effected. A corrupt practice act was adopted. A well-considered warehouse act was passed. Federal employment bureaus were created, farm loan banks were organized and the federal reserve system was established. Privilege was uprooted. A corrupt lobby was driven from the national capital. A higher sense of individual and national duty was aroused. America enjoyed an unprecedented period of social and material progress.

During the time which intervened between the inauguration of a democratic administration on March 4, 1913, and our entrance into the world war, we placed upon the statute-books of our country more effective constructive and remedial legislation than the republican party had placed there in a generation.

During the great struggle which followed we had a leadership that carried America to greater heights of honor and power and glory than she had ever known before in her entire history.

Transition from this period of exalted democratic leadership to the sordid record of the last three and a half years makes the nation ashamed. It marks the contrast between a high conception of public service and an avid purpose to distribute spoils.

G. O. P. CORRUPTION

Never before in our history has the government been so tainted by corruption and never has an administration so utterly failed. The nation has been appalled by the revelations of political de-

pravity which have characterized the conduct of public affairs. We arraign the republican party for attempting to limit inquiry into official delinquencies and to impede if not to frustrate the investigations to which in the beginning the republican party leaders assented, but which later they regarded with dismay.

These investigations sent the former secretary of the interior to Three Rivers in disgrace and dishonor. These investigations revealed the incapacity and indifference to public obligation of the secretary of the navy, compelling him by force of public opinion to quit the cabinet. These investigations confirmed the general impression as to the unfitness of the attorney general by exposing an official situation and personal contacts which shocked the conscience of the nation and compelled his dismissal from the cabinet.

These investigations disclosed the appalling conditions of the veterans bureau with its fraud upon the government and its cruel neglect of the sick and disabled soldiers of the world war. These investigations revealed the criminal and fraudulent nature of the oil leases which caused the congress, despite the indifference of the executive, to direct recovery of the public domain and the prosecution of the criminal.

Such are the exigencies of partisan politics that republican leaders are teaching the strange doctrine that public censure should be directed against those who expose crime rather than against criminals who have committed the offenses. If only three cabinet officers out of ten are disgraced, the country is asked to marvel at how many are free from taint. Long boastful that it was the only party "fit to govern," the republican party has proven its inability to govern even itself. It is at war with itself. As an agency of government it has ceased to function.

This nation cannot afford to entrust its welfare to a political organization that cannot master itself, or to an executive whose policies have been rejected by his own party. To retain in power an administration of this character would inevitably result in four years more of continued disorder, internal dissension and governmental inefficiency. A vote for Coolidge is a vote for chaos.

ISSUES

The dominant issues of the campaign are created by existing conditions. Dishonesty, discrimination, extravagances and inefficiency exist in government. The burdens of taxation have become unbearable. Distress and bankruptcy in agriculture, the basic industry of our country, is affecting the happiness and prosperity of the whole people. The cost of living is causing hardship and unrest.

The slowing down of industry is adding to the general distress. The tariff, the destruction of our foreign markets and the high cost of transportation are taking the profit out of agriculture, mining and other raw material industries. Large standing armies and the cost of preparing for war still cast their burdens upon humanity. These conditions the existing republican administration has proven itself unwilling or unable to redress.

The democratic party pledges itself to the following program:

Honest government.

We pledge the democratic party to drive from public places all which make barter of our national power, its resources or the administration of its laws; to punish those guilty of these offenses.

To put none but the honest in public office; to practice economy in the expenditure of public money; to reverence and respect the rights of all under the constitution.

To condemn and destroy government by the spy and blackmailer which was by this republican administration both encouraged and practiced.

Tariff and Taxation

The Fordney-McCumber tariff act is the most unjust, unscientific and dishonest tariff tax measure ever enacted in our history. It is class legislation which defrauds the people for the benefit of a few, it heavily increases the cost of living, penalizes agriculture, corrupts the government, fosters paternalism and, in the long run, does not benefit the very interests for which it was intended.

We denounce the republican tariff laws which are written, in great part, in aid of monopolies and thus prevent that reasonable exchange of commodities which would enable foreign countries to buy our surplus agricultural and manufactured products with resultant profit to the toilers and producers of America.

Trade interchange, on the basis of reciprocal advantages to the countries participating is a time-honored doctrine of democratic faith. We declare our party's position to be in favor of a tax on commodities entering the customs house that will promote effective competition, protect against monopoly and at the same time produce a fair revenue to support the government.

The greatest contributing factor in the increase and unbalancing of prices is unscientific taxation. After having increased taxation and the cost of living by $2,000,000,000 under the Fordney-Mc-Cumber tariff, all that the republican party could suggest in the way of relief was a cut of $300,-000,000 in direct taxes; and that was to be given principally to those with the largest incomes.

Although there was no evidence of a lack of capital for investment to meet the present requirements of all legitimate industrial enterprises and although the farmers and general consumers were bearing the brunt of tariff favors already granted to special interests, the administration was unable to devise any plan except one to grant further aid to the few. Fortunately this plan of the administration failed and under democratic leadership, aided by progressive republicans, a more equitable one was adopted, which reduces direct taxes by about $450,000,000.

The issue between the president and the democratic party is not one of tax reduction or of the conservation of capital. It is an issue of relative burden of taxation and of the distribution of capital as affected by the taxation of income. The president still stands on the so-called Mellon plan, which his party has just refused to indorse or mention in its platform.

The income tax was intended as a tax upon wealth. It was not intended to take from the poor any part of the necessities of life. We hold that the fairest tax with which to raise revenue for the federal government is the income tax. We favor a graduated tax upon incomes, so adjusted as to lay the burdens of government upon the taxpayers in proportion to the benefits they enjoy and their ability to pay.

We oppose the so-called nuisance taxes, sales taxes and all other forms of taxation that unfairly shift to the consumer the burdens of taxation. We refer to the democratic revenue measure passed by the last congress as distinguished from the Mellon tax plan as an illustration of the policy of the democratic party. We first made a flat reduction of 25 per cent upon the tax of all incomes payable this year and then we so changed the proposed Mellon plan as to eliminate taxes upon the poor, reducing them upon moderate incomes and, in a lesser degree, upon the incomes of multi-millionaires. We hold that all taxes are unnecessarily high and pledge ourselves to further reductions.

We denounce the Mellon plan as a device to relieve multi-millionaires at the expense of other taxpayers, and we accept the issue of taxation tendered by President Coolidge.

AGRICULTURE

During the four years of republican government the economic condition of the American farmer has changed from comfort to bankruptcy, with all its attendant miseries. The chief causes for this are:

(a) The republican party policy of isolation in international affairs has prevented Europe from getting back to its normal balance, and, by leaving unsolved the economic problems abroad, has driven the European city population from industrial activities to the soil in large numbers in order to earn the mere necessaries of life. This has deprived the American farmer of his normal export trade.

(b) The republican policy of a prohibitive tariff, exemplified in the Fordney-McCumber law, which has forced the American farmer, with his export market debilitated, to buy manufactured goods at sustained high domestic levels, thereby making him the victim of the profiteer.

(c) The republican policy of high transportation rates, both rail and water, which has made it impossible for the farmer to ship his produce to market at even a living profit.

To offset these policies and their disastrous results, and to restore the farmer again to economic equality with other industrialists, we pledge ourselves:

(a) To adopt an international policy of such co-operation by direct official, instead of indirect and evasive unofficial means, as will re-establish the farmers' export market by restoring the industrial balance in Europe and the normal flow of international trade with the settlement of Europe's economic problems.

(b) To adjust the tariff so that the farmer and all other classes can buy again in a competitive manufacturers' market.

(c) To readjust and lower rail and water rates which will make our markets, both for the buyer and the seller, national and international instead of regional and local.

(d) To bring about the early completion of international waterway systems for transportation and to develop our water powers for cheaper fertilizer and use on our farms.

(e) To stimulate by every proper governmental activity the progress of the co-operative marketing movement and the establishment of an export marketing corporation or commission in order that the exportable surplus may not establish the price of the whole crop.

(f) To secure for the farmer credits suitable for his needs.

(g) By the establishment of these policies and others naturally supplementary thereto, to reduce the margin between what the producer receives for his products and the consumer has to pay for his supplies, to the end that we secure an equality for agriculture.

RAILROADS

The sponsors for the Esch-Cummins transportation act of 1920, at the time of its presentation to congress, stated that it had for its purposes the reduction of the cost of transportation, the improvement of service, the bettering of labor conditions, the promotion of peaceful co-operation between employer and employe, and at the same time the assurance of a fair and just return to the railroads upon their investment.

We are in accord with these announced purposes, but contend that the act has failed to accomplish them. It has failed to reduce the cost of transportation. The promised improvement in service has not been realized. The labor provisions of the act have proven unsatisfactory in settling differences between employer and employes. The so-called recapture clause has worked out to the advantage of the strong and has been of no benefit to the weak. The pronouncement in the act for the development of both rail and water transportation has proved futile. Water transportation upon our inland waterways has not been encouraged, the limitation of our coastwise trade is threatened by the administration of the act. It has unnecessarily interfered with the power of the states to regulate purely intrastate transportation. It must therefore be so rewritten that the high purpose which the public welfare demands may be accomplished.

Railroad freight rates should be so readjusted as to give the bulky basic, low-priced raw commodities, such as agricultural products, coal and ores the lowest rates, placing the higher rates upon more valuable and less bulky manufactured products.

MUSCLE SHOALS

We reaffirm and pledge the fulfillment of the policy, with reference to Muscle Shoals, as declared and passed by the democratic majority of the sixty-fourth congress in the national defense act of 1916, "for the production of nitrates or other products needed for munitions of war and useful in the manufacture of fertilizers."

We hold that the production of cheaper and high grade fertilizers is essential to agricultural prosperity. We demand prompt action by congress for the operation of the Muscle Shoals plants to maximum capacity in the production, distribution and sale of commercial fertilizers to the farmers of the country and we oppose any legislation that limits the production of fertilizers at Muscle Shoals by limiting the amount of power to be used in their manufacture.

CREDIT AND CURRENCY

We denounce the recent cruel and unjust contraction of legitimate and necessary credit and currency, which was directly due to the so-called deflation policy of the republican party, as declared in its national platform of June, 1920, and in the speech of acceptance of its candidate for the presidency. Within eighteen months after the election of 1920 this policy resulted in withdrawing bank loans by over $5,000,000,000 and in contracting our currency by over $1,500,000,000.

The contraction bankrupted hundreds of thousands of farmers and stock growers in America and resulted in widespread industrial depression and unemployment. We demand that the federal reserve system be so administered as to give stability to industry, commerce and finance, as was intended by the democratic party, which gave the federal reserve system to the nation.

RECLAMATION

The democratic party was foremost in urging reclamation for the immediate arid and semiarid lands of the west. The lands are located in the public land states, and, therefore, it is due to the government to utilize their resources by reclamation. Homestead entrymen under reclamation projects have suffered from the extravagant inefficiencies and mistakes of the federal government.

The reclamation act of 1924, recommended by the fact finding commission and added as an amendment to the second deficiency appropriation bill at the last session of congress, was eliminated from that bill by the republican conferees in the report they presented to congress one hour before adjournment. The democratic party pledges itself actively, efficiently and economically to carry on the reclamation projects, and to make equitable adjustment for the mistakes the government has made.

CONSERVATION

We pledge recovery of the navy's oil reserves, and all other parts of the public domain which have been fraudulently or illegally leased or otherwise wrongfully transferred to the control of private interests; vigorous prosecution of all public officials, private citizens and corporations that participated in these transactions; revision of the water power act, the general leasing act and all other legislation relating to public domain, that may be essential to its conservation and honest and efficient use on behalf of the people of the country.

We believe that the nation should retain title to its water power and we favor the expeditious creation and development of our water power. We favor strict public control and conservation of all the nation's natural resources, such as coal, iron, oil and timber, and their use in such manner as may be to the best interest of our citizens.

The conservation of migratory birds, the establishment of game preserves, and the protection and conservation of wild life is of importance to agriculturists as well as sportsmen. Our disappearing national natural resources of timber calls for a national policy of reforestation.

IMPROVED HIGHWAYS

Improved roads are of vital importance, not only to commerce and industry, but also to agriculture and natural life. We call attention to the record of the democratic party in this matter and favor continuance of federal aid under existing federal and state agencies.

MINING

Mining is one of the basic industries of this country. We produce more coal, iron, copper and silver than any other country. The value of our mineral production is second only to agriculture.

Mining has suffered like agriculture and from the same causes. It is the duty of our government to foster this industry and to remove the restrictions that destroy its prosperity.

MERCHANT MARINE

The democratic party condemns the vacillating policy of the republican administration in the failure to develop an American flag shipping policy. There has been a marked decrease in the volume of American commerce carried in American vessels as compared to the record under a democratic administration.

We oppose as illogical and unsound all efforts to overcome by subsidy the handicap to American shipping and commerce imposed by republican policies.

We condemn the practice of certain American railroads in favoring foreign ships, and pledge ourselves to correct such discriminations. We declare for an American owned merchant marine, American built and manned by American crews, which is essential for naval security in war and is a protection to the American farmer and manufacturer against excessive ocean freight charges on products of farm and factory.

We declare that the government should own and operate such merchant ships as will insure the accomplishment of these purposes and to continue such operation so long as it may be necessary without obstructing the development and growth of a privately owned American flag shipping.

NECESSITIES OF LIFE

We pledge the democratic party to regulate by governmental agencies the anthracite coal industry and all other corporations controlling the necessaries of life where public welfare has been subordinated to private interests.

EDUCATION

We believe with Thomas Jefferson and founders of the republic that ignorance is the enemy of freedom and that each state, being responsible for the intellectual and moral qualifications of its citizens and for the expenditure of the moneys collected by taxation for the support of its schools, shall use its sovereign right in all matters pertaining to education. The federal government should offer to the states such counsel, advice and aid as may be made available through the federal agencies for the general improvement of our schools in view of our national needs.

CIVIL SERVICE

We denounce the action of the republican administration in its violations of the principles of civil service by its partisan removals and manipulation of the eligible lists in the postoffice department and other governmental departments; by its packing the civil service commission so that commission became the servile instrument of the administration in its wish to deny to the former service men their preferential rights under the law and the evasion of the requirements of the law with reference to appointments in the department.

We pledge the democratic party faithfully to comply with the spirit as well as the regulation of civil service; to extend its provisions to internal revenue officers and to other employes of the government not in executive positions, and to secure to former service men preference in such appointments.

POSTAL EMPLOYES

We declare in favor of adequate salaries to provide decent living conditions for postal employes.

POPULAR ELECTIONS

We pledge the democratic party to a policy which will prevent members of either house who fail of re-election from participating in the subsequent sessions of congress. This can be accomplished by fixing the days for convening the congress immediately after the biennial national election; and to this end we favor granting the right to the people of the several states to vote on proposed constitutional amendments on this subject.

PROBATION

We favor the extension of the probation principle to the courts of the United States.

ACTIVITIES OF WOMEN

We welcome the women of the nation to their rightful place by the side of men in the control of the government whose burdens they have always shared.

The democratic party congratulates them upon the essential part which they have taken in the progress of our country, and the zeal with which they are using their political power to aid the enactment of beneficial laws and the exaction of fidelity in the public service.

Veterans of Wars

We favor generous appropriations, honest management and sympathetic care and assistance in the hospitalization, rehabilitation and compensation of the veterans of all wars and their dependents. The humanizing of the veterans' bureau is imperatively required.

Contributions

The nation now knows that the predatory interests have, by supplying republican campaign funds, systematically purchased legislative favors and administrative immunity. The practice must stop; our nation must return to honesty and decency in politics.

Elections are public affairs conducted for the sole purpose of ascertaining the will of the sovereign voters. Therefore, we demand that national elections shall hereafter be kept free from the poison of excessive private contributions. To this end, we favor reasonable means of publicity, at public expense, so that candidates, properly before the people for federal offices, may present their claims at a minimum of cost. Such publicity should precede the primary and the election.

We favor the prohibition of individual contributions, direct and indirect, to the campaign funds of congressmen, senators or presidential candidates, beyond a reasonable sum to be fixed in the law, for both individual contributions and total expenditures, with requirements for full publicity. We advocate a complete revision of the corrupt practice act to prevent Newberryism and the election evils disclosed by recent investigations.

Narcotics

Recognizing in narcotic addiction, especially the spreading of heroin addiction among the youth, a grave peril to America and to the human race, we pledge ourselves vigorously to take against it all legitimate and proper measures for education, for control and for suppression at home and abroad.

Prohibition Law

The republican administration has failed to enforce the prohibition law; is guilty of trafficking in liquor permits, and has become the protector of violators of this law.

The democratic party pledges itself to respect and enforce the constitution and all laws.

Rights of States

We demand that the states of the union shall be preserved in all their vigor and power. They constitute a bulwark against the centralizing and destructive tendencies of the republican party.

We condemn the efforts of the republican party to nationalize the functions and duties of the states.

We oppose the extension of bureaucracy, the creation of unnecessary bureaus and federal agencies and the multiplication of offices and office-holders.

We demand a revival of the spirit of local self-government essential to the preservation of the free institutions of our republic.

Asiatic Immigration

We pledge ourselves to maintain our established position in favor of the exclusion of Asiatic immigration.

Philippines

The Filipino peoples have succeeded in maintaining a stable government and have thus fulfilled the only condition laid down by congress as a prerequisite to the granting of independence. We declare that it is now our liberty and our duty to keep our promise to these people by granting them immediately the independence which they so honorably covet.

Alaska

The maladministration of affairs in Alaska is a matter of concern to all our people. Under the republican administration, development has ceased and the fishing industry has been seriously impaired. We pledge ourselves to correct the evils which have grown up in the administration of that rich domain.

An adequate form of local self-government for Alaska must be provided and to that end we favor the establishment of a full territorial form of government for that territory similar to that enjoyed by all the territories except Alaska during the last century of American history.

HAWAII

We believe in a policy for continuing the improvements of the national parks, the harbors and breakwaters, and the federal roads of the territory of Hawaii.

VIRGIN ISLANDS

We recommend legislation for the welfare of the inhabitants of the Virgin islands.

LAUSANNE TREATY

We condemn the Lausanne treaty. It barters legitimate American rights and betrays Armenia, for the Chester oil concessions.

We favor the protection of American rights in Turkey and the fulfillment of President Wilson's arbitral award respecting Armenia.

DISARMAMENT

We demand a strict and sweeping reduction of armaments by land and sea, so that there shall be no competitive military program or naval building. Until international agreements to this end have been made we advocate an army and navy adequate for our national safety.

Our government should secure a joint agreement with all nations for world disarmament and also for a referendum of war, except in case of actual or threatened attack.

Those who must furnish the blood and bear the burdens imposed by war should, whenever possible, be consulted before this supreme sacrifice is required of them.

GREECE

We welcome to the sisterhood of republics the ancient land of Greece which gave to our party its priceless name. We extend to her government and people our cordial good wishes.

WAR

War is a relic of barbarism and it is justifiable only as a measure of defense.

In the event of war in which the man power of the nation is drafted, all other resources should likewise be drafted. This will tend to discourage war by depriving it of its profits.

PERSONAL FREEDOM

The democratic party reaffirms its adherence and devotion to those cardinal principles contained in the constitution and the precepts upon which our government is founded, that congress shall make no laws respecting the establishment of religion, or prohibiting the free exercises thereof, or abridging the freedom of speech or of the press or of the right of the people peaceably to assemble and to petition the government for a redress of grievances, that the church and the state shall be and remain separate, and that no religious test shall ever be required as a qualification to any office of public trust under the United States. These principles, we pledge ourselves ever to defend and maintain. We insist at all times upon obedience to the orderly processes of the law and deplore and condemn any effort to arouse religious or racial dissension.

LEAGUE OF NATIONS

The democratic party pledges all its energies to the outlawing of the whole war system. We refuse to believe that the wholesale slaughter of human beings on the battlefield is any more necessary to man's highest development than is killing by individuals.

The only hope for world peace and for economic recovery lies in the organized efforts of sovereign nations co-operating to remove the causes of war and to substitute law and order for violence.

Under democratic leadership a practical plan was devised under which fifty-four nations are now operating, and which has for its fundamental purpose the free co-operation of all nations in the work of peace.

The government of the United States for the last four years has had no foreign policy, and consequently it has delayed the restoration of the political and economic agencies of the world. It has impaired our self-respect at home and injured our prestige abroad. It has curtailed our foreign markets and ruined our agricultural prices.

It is of supreme importance to civilization and to mankind that America be placed and kept on the right side of the greatest moral question of all time, and therefore the democratic party renews its declarations of confidence in the idea of world peace, the league of nations and the world court of justice as together constituting the supreme effort of the statesmanship and religious conviction of our time to organize the world for peace.

Further, the democratic party declared that it will be the purpose of the next administration to do all in its power to secure for our country that moral leadership in the family of nations which, in the providence of God, has been so clearly marked out for it. There is no substitute for the league of nations as an agency working for peace, therefore, we believe, that, in the interest of permanent peace, and in the lifting of the great burdens of war from the backs of the people, and in order to establish a permanent foreign policy on these supreme questions, not subject to change with change of party administration, it is desirable, wise and necessary to lift this question out of party politics and to that end to take the sense of the American people at a referendum election, advisory to the government, to be held officially, under act of congress, free from all other questions and candidacies, after ample time for full consideration and discussion throughout the country, upon the question, in substance, as follows:

"Shall the United States become a member of the league of nations upon such reservations or amendments to the covenant of the league as the president and the senate of the United States may agree upon."

Immediately upon an affirmative vote we will carry out such mandate.

Waterways

We favor and will promote deep waterways from the great lakes to the gulf and to the Atlantic ocean.

Flood Control

We favor a policy for the fostering and building of inland waterways and the removal of discrimination against water transportation. Flood control and the lowering of flood levels is essential to the safety of life and property, the productivity of our lands, the navigability of our streams and the reclaiming of our wet and overflowed lands and the creation of hydro-electric power. We favor the expeditious construction of flood relief works on the Mississippi and Colorado rivers and also such reclamation and irrigation projects upon the Colorado river as may be found to be feasible and practical.

We favor liberal appropriations for prompt coordinated surveys by the United States to determine the possibilities of general navigation improvements and water power development on navigable streams and their tributaries, to secure reliable information as to the most economical navigation improvement, in combination with the most efficient and complete development of water power.

We favor suspension of the granting of federal water power licenses by the federal water power committee until congress has received reports from the water power commission with regard to applications for such licenses.

Private Monopolies

The federal trade commission has submitted to the republican administration numerous reports showing the existence of monopolies and combinations in restraint of trade, and has recommended proceedings against these violators of the law. The few prosecutions which have resulted from this abundant evidence furnished by this agency created by the democratic party, while proving the indifference of the administration to the violations of law by trusts and monopolies and its friendship for them, nevertheless demonstrate the value of the federal trade commission.

We declare that a private monopoly is indefensible and intolerable, and pledge the democratic party to vigorous enforcement of existing laws against monopoly and illegal combinations, and to the enactment of such further measures as may be necessary.

Fraudulent Stock Sale

We favor the immediate passage of such legislation as may be necessary to enable the states efficiently to enforce their laws relating to the gradual financial strangling of innocent investors, workers and consumers, caused by the indiscriminate promotion, refinancing and reorganizing of corporations on an inflated and over-capitalized basis, resulting already in the undermining and collapse of many railroads, public service and industrial corporations, manifesting itself in unemployment, irreparable loss and waste and which constitute a serious menace to the stability of our economic system.

AVIATION

We favor a sustained development of aviation by both the government and commercially.

LABOR, CHILD WELFARE

Labor is not a commodity. It is human. We favor collective bargaining and laws regulating hours of labor and conditions under which labor is performed. We favor the enactment of legislation providing that the product of convict labor shipped from one state to another shall be subject to the laws of the latter state exactly as though they had been produced therein. In order to mitigate unemployment attending business depression, we urge the enactment of legislation authorizing the construction and repair of public works be initiated in periods of acute unemployment.

We pledge the party to co-operate with the state governments for the welfare, education and protection of child life and all necessary safeguards against exhaustive debilitating employment conditions for women.

Without the votes of democratic members of congress the child labor amendment would not have been submitted for ratification.

LATIN-AMERICA

From the day of their birth, friendly relations have existed between the Latin-American republics and the United States. That friendship grows stronger as our relations become more intimate. The democratic party sends to these republics its cordial greeting; God has made us neighbors— justice shall keep us friends.

La Follette's Platform of 1924

The great issue before the American people today is the control of government and industry by private monopoly.

For a generation the people have struggled patiently, in the face of repeated betrayals by successive administrations, to free themselves from this intolerable power which has been undermining representative government.

Through control of government, monopoly has steadily extended its absolute dominion to every basic industry.

In violation of law, monopoly has crushed competition, stifled private initiative and independent enterprise, and without fear of punishment now exacts extortionate profits upon every necessity of life consumed by the public.

The equality of opportunity proclaimed by the Declaration of Independence and asserted and defended by Jefferson and Lincoln as the heritage of every American citizen has been displaced by special privilege for the few, wrested from the government of the many.

FUNDAMENTAL RIGHTS IN DANGER

That tyrannical power which the American people denied to a king, they will no longer endure from the monopoly system. The people know they cannot yield to any group the control of the economic life of the nation and preserve their political liberties. They know monopoly has its representatives in the halls of Congress, on the Federal bench, and in the executive departments; that these servile agents barter away the nation's natural resources, nullify acts of Congress by judicial veto and administrative favor, invade the people's rights by unlawful arrests and unconstitutional searches and seizures, direct our foreign policy in the interests of predatory wealth, and make wars and conscript the sons of the common people to fight them.

The usurpation in recent years by the federal courts of the power to nullify laws duly enacted by the legislative branch of the government is a plain violation of the Constitution. Abraham Lincoln, in his first inaugural address, said: "The candid citizen must confess that if the policy of the government, upon vital questions affecting the whole people, is to be irrevocably fixed by decisions of the Supreme Court, the people will have ceased to be their own rulers, having to that extent practically resigned their government into the hands of that eminent tribunal." The Constitution specifically vests all legislative power in the Congress, giving that body power and authority to override the veto of the president. The federal courts are given no authority under the Constitution to veto acts of Congress. Since the federal courts have assumed to exercise such veto power, it is essential that the Constitution shall give the Congress the right to override such judicial veto, otherwise the Court will make itself master over the other coordinate branches of the government. The people themselves must approve or disapprove the present exercise of legislative power by the federal courts.

DISTRESS OF AMERICAN FARMERS

The present condition of American agriculture constitutes an emergency of the gravest character. The Department of Commerce report shows that during 1923 there was a steady and marked increase in dividends paid by the great industrial corporations. The same is true of the steam and electric railways and practically all other large corporations. On the other hand, the Secretary of Agriculture reports that in the fifteen principal wheat growing states more than 108,000 farmers since 1920 have lost their farms through foreclosure or bankruptcy; that more than 122,000 have surrendered their property without legal proceedings, and that nearly 375,000 have retained possession of their property only through the leniency of their creditors, making a total of more than 600,000 or 26 per cent of all farmers who have virtually been bankrupted since 1920 in these fifteen states alone.

Almost unlimited prosperity for the great corporations and ruin and bankruptcy for agriculture is the direct and logical result of the policies and legislation which deflated the farmer while extending almost unlimited credit to the great corporations; which protected with exorbitant tariffs the industrial magnates, but depressed the prices of the farmers' products by financial juggling while greatly increasing the cost of what he must buy; which guaranteed excessive freight rates to the railroads and put a premium on wasteful management while saddling an unwarranted burden on to the backs of the American farmer; which permitted gambling in the products of the farm by grain speculators to the great detriment of the farmer and to the great profit of the grain gambler.

A COVENANT WITH THE PEOPLE

Awakened by the dangers which menace their freedom and prosperity the American people still retain the right and courage to exercise their sovereign control over their government. In order to destroy the economic and political power of monopoly, which has come between the people and their government, we pledge ourselves to the following principles and policies:

THE HOUSE CLEANING

1. We pledge a complete housecleaning in the Department of Justice, the Department of the Interior, and the other executive departments. We demand that the power of the Federal Government be used to crush private monopoly, not to foster it.

NATURAL RESOURCES

2. We pledge recovery of the navy's oil reserves and all other parts of the public domain which have been fraudulently or illegally leased, or otherwise wrongfully transferred, to the control of private interests; vigorous prosecution of all public officials, private citizens and corporations that participated in these transactions; complete revision of the water-power act, the general leasing act, and all other legislation relating to the public domain. We favor public ownership of the nation's water power and the creation and development of a national super-water-power system, including Muscle Shoals, to supply at actual cost light and power for the people and nitrate for the farmers, and strict public control and permanent conservation of all the nation's resources, including coal, iron and other ores, oil and timber lands, in the interest of the people.

RAILROADS

3. We favor repeal of the Esch-Cummins railroad law and the fixing of railroad rates upon the basis of actual, prudent investment and cost of service. We pledge speedy enactment of the Howell-Barkley Bill for the adjustment of controversies between railroads and their employees, which was held up in the last Congress by joint action of reactionary leaders of the Democratic and Republican parties. We declare for public ownership of railroads with definite safeguards against bureaucratic control, as the only final solution of the transportation problem.

TAX REDUCTION

4. We favor reduction of Federal taxes upon individual incomes and legitimate business, limiting tax exactions strictly to the requirements of the government administered with rigid economy,

particularly by curtailment of the eight hundred million dollars now annually expended for the army and navy in preparation for future wars; by the recovery of the hundreds of millions of dollars stolen from the Treasury through fraudulent war contracts and the corrupt leasing of the public resources; and by diligent action to collect the accumulated interest upon the eleven billion dollars owing us by foreign governments.

We denounce the Mellon tax plan as a device to relieve multi-millionaires at the expense of other tax payers, and favor a taxation policy providing for immediate reductions upon moderate incomes, large increases in the inheritance tax rates upon large estates to prevent the indefinite accumulation by inheritance of great fortunes in a few hands; taxes upon excess profits to penalize profiteering, and complete publicity, under proper safeguards, of all Federal tax returns.

The Courts

5. We favor submitting to the people, for their considerate judgment, a constitutional amendment providing that Congress may by enacting a statute make it effective over a judicial veto.

We favor such amendment to the constitution as may be necessary to provide for the election of all Federal Judges, without party designation, for fixed terms not exceeding ten years, by direct vote of the people.

The Farmers

6. We favor drastic reduction of the exhorbitant duties on manufactures provided in the Fordney-McCumber tariff legislation, the prohibiting of gambling by speculators and profiteers in agricultural products; the reconstruction of the Federal Reserve and Federal Farm Loan Systems, so as to eliminate control by usurers, speculators and international financiers, and to make the credit of the nation available upon fair terms to all and without discrimination to business men, farmers and home-builders. We advocate the calling of a special session of Congress to pass legislation for the relief of American agriculture. We favor such further legislation as may be needful or helpful in promoting and protecting cooperative enterprises. We demand that the Interstate Commerce Commission proceed forthwith to reduce by an approximation to pre-war levels the present freight rates on agricultural products, including live stock, and upon the materials required upon American farms for agricultural purposes.

Labor

7. We favor abolition of the use of injunctions in labor disputes and declare for complete protection of the right of farmers and industrial workers to organize, bargain collectively through representatives of their own choosing, and conduct without hindrance cooperative enterprises.

We favor prompt ratification of the Child Labor amendment, and subsequent enactment of a Federal law to protect children in industry.

Postal Service

8. We believe that a prompt and dependable postal service is essential to the social and economic welfare of the nation; and that as one of the most important steps toward establishing and maintaining such a service, it is necessary to fix wage standards that will secure and retain employees of character, energy and ability.

We favor the enactment of the postal salary adjustment measure (S. 1898) for the employees of the postal service, passed by the first session of the 68th Congress, vetoed by the President and now awaiting further consideration by the next session of Congress.

We endorse liberalizing the Civil Service Retirement Law along the lines of S. 3011 now pending in Congress.

War Veterans

9. We favor adjusted compensation for the veterans of the late war, not as charity, but as a matter of right, and we demand that the money necessary to meet this obligation of the government be raised by taxes laid upon wealth in proportion to the ability to pay, and declare our opposition to the sales tax or any other device to shift this obligation onto the backs of the poor in higher prices and increased cost of living. We do not regard the payment at the end of a long period of a small insurance as provided by the law recently passed as in any just sense a discharge of the nation's obligations to the veterans of the late war.

Great Lakes to Sea

10. We favor a deep waterway from the Great Lakes to the sea. The government should, in conjunction with Canada, take immediate action to

give the northwestern states an outlet to the ocean for cargoes, without change in bulk, thus making the primary markets on the Great Lakes equal to those of New York.

POPULAR SOVEREIGNTY

11. Over and above constitutions and statutes and greater than all, is the supreme sovereignty of the people, and with them should rest the final decision of all great questions of national policy. We favor such amendments to the Federal Constitution as may be necessary to provide for the direct nomination and election of the President, to extend the initiative and referendum to the federal government, and to insure a popular referendum for or against war except in cases of actual invasion.

PEACE ON EARTH

12. We denounce the mercenary system of foreign policy under recent administrations in the interests of financial imperialists, oil monopolists and international bankers, which has at times degraded our State Department from its high service as a strong and kindly intermediary of defenseless governments to a trading outpost for those interests and concession-seekers engaged in the exploitations of weaker nations, as contrary to the will of the American people, destructive of domestic development and provocative of war. We favor an active foreign policy to bring about a revision of the Versailles treaty in accordance with the terms of the armistice, and to promote firm treaty agreements with all nations to outlaw wars, abolish conscription, drastically reduce land, air and naval armaments, and guarantee public referendum on peace and war.

Conference for
Progressive Political Action Platform, 1924

For 148 years the American people have been seeking to establish a government for the service of all and to prevent the establishment of a government for the mastery of the few. Free men of every generation must combat renewed efforts of organized force and greed to destroy liberty. Every generation must wage a new war for freedom against new forces that seek through new devices to enslave mankind.

Under our representative democracy the people protect their liberties through their public agents.

The test of public officials and public polities alike must be: Will they serve or will they exploit the common need?

The reactionary continues to put his faith in mastery for the solution of all problems. He seeks to have what he calls the strong men and best minds rule and impose their decisions upon the masses of their weaker brethren.

The progressive, on the contrary, contends for less autocracy and more democracy in government, for less power of privilege and greater obligations of service.

Under the principle of ruthless individualism and competition, that government is deemed best which offers to the few the greatest chance of individual gain.

Under the progressive principle of cooperation, that government is deemed best which offers to the many the highest level of average happiness and well being.

It is our faith that we all go up or down together—that class gains are temporary delusions and that eternal laws of compensation make every man his brother's keeper.

PROGRAM OF PUBLIC SERVICE

In that faith we present our program of public service:

(1) The use of the power of the federal government to crush private monopoly, not to foster it.

(2) Unqualified enforcement of the constitutional guarantees of freedom of speech, press, and assemblage.

(3) Public ownership of the nation's water power and creation of a public super-power system. Strict public control and permanent conservation of all natural resources, including coal, iron, and other ores, oil, and timber lands in the interest of the people. Promotion of public works in times of business depression.

(4) Retention of surtax on swollen incomes, restoration of the tax on excess profits, taxation of stock dividends, profits undistributed to evade taxes, rapidly progressive taxes on large estates and inheritances, and repeal of excessive tariff duties, especially on trust-controlled necessities of life and of nuisance taxes on consumption, to relieve the people of the present unjust burden of taxation and compel those who profited by the war to pay their share of the war's cost, and to provide the funds for adjusted compensation

solemnly pledged to the veterans of the World War.

(5) Reconstruction of the federal reserve and federal farm loan systems to provide for direct public control of the nation's money and credit to make it available on fair terms to all, and national and state legislation to permit and promote co-operative banking.

(6) Adequate laws to guarantee to farmers and industrial workers the right to organize and bargain collectively through representatives of their own choosing for the maintenance or improvement of their standard of life.

(7) Creation of a government marketing corporation to provide a direct route between farm producer and city consumer and to assure farmers fair prices for their products, and protect consumers from the profiteers in foodstuffs and other necessaries of life. Legislation to control the meat-packing industry.

(8) Protection and aid of cooperative enterprises by national and state legislation.

(9) Common international action to effect the economic recovery of the world from the effects of the World War.

(10) Repeal of the Cummins-Esch law. Public ownership of railroads, with democratic operation, and with definite safeguards against bureaucratic control.

(11) Abolition of the tyranny and usurpation of the courts, including the practice of nullifying legislation in conflict with the political, social or economic theories of the judges. Abolition of injunctions in labor disputes and of the power to punish for contempt without trial by jury. Election of all federal judges without party designation for limited terms.

(12) Prompt ratification of the child labor amendment and subsequent enactment of a federal law to protect children in industry. Removal of legal discriminations against women by measures not prejudicial to legislation necessary for the protection of women and for the advancement of social welfare.

(13) A deep waterway from the great lakes to the sea.

(14) We denounce the mercenary system of degraded foreign policy under recent administrations in the interests of financial imperialists, oil monopolists, and international bankers, which has at times degraded our State Department from its high service as a strong and kindly intermediary of defenseless governments to a trading outpost for those interests and concession seekers engaged in the exploitation of weaker nations, as contrary to the will of the American people, destructive of domestic development and provocative of war. We favor an active foreign policy to bring about a revision of the Versailles treaty in accordance with the terms of the armistice, and to promote firm treaty agreements with all nations to outlaw wars, abolish conscription, drastically reduce land, air and naval armaments and guarantee public referendum on peace and war.

In supporting this program we are applying to the needs of today the fundamental principles of American democracy, opposing equally the dictatorship of plutocracy and the dictatorship of the proletariat.

We appeal to all Americans without regard to partisan affiliation and we raise the standards of our faith so that all of like purpose may rally and march in this campaign under the banners of progressive union.

The nation may grow rich in the vision of greed. The nation will grow great in the vision of service.

Prohibition Platform of 1924

The Prohibition Party in National Convention at Columbus, Ohio, this sixth day of June, 1924, recognizing Almighty God as the source of all governmental authority and that the principles enunciated by His Son, Jesus Christ, should guide in all matters pertaining to government, makes the following declaration of principles:

Our Party and Its Philosophy

Four years of nullification of the Eighteenth Amendment by the Democratic and Republican officials have demonstrated the soundness of the philosophy of the Prohibition party that a law conferring a right will enforce itself, but a law prohibiting a wrong, financially and politically entrenched, requires a party thoroughly committed to its maintenance and enforcement. Little or no improvement can be expected so long as the friends of the prohibitory law divide themselves among political parties seeking the votes of the law violators and the nullificationists, which votes are regarded to be as necessary to the success of those political parties as are the votes of the law-abiders.

The astounding revelations of corruption and maladministration in government, extending to the Cabinet itself, are but the inevitable consequences of the moral bankruptcy of a political party which, perpetuating the old liquor régime, is dependent upon the wet vote for its margin of plurality.

INTERNATIONAL RELATIONS

The time is past when the United States can hold aloof from the affairs of the World. We support the proposal for the entry of this Country into the Court of International Justice, as an important step for substituting law for force in the settlement of international disputes.

LABOR, CAPITAL AND THE GENERAL PUBLIC

While adhering to our time honored position of demanding justice for both Labor and Capital, we declare that the interests of the general public are paramount to both. Therefore, we favor the speedy enactment by Congress and the several state Legislatures, each in its respective jurisdiction, of such legislation as shall impartially protect all three of these classes.

AGRICULTURE

In the constantly increasing trend of population from the country into the towns and cities, with the constant abandonment of the farms, this country faces a grave peril. It is self-evident that the farmer, with his investment in his lands, buildings, live-stock, machinery, tools, and labor, ought to receive more than one-half of the dollar paid by the consumer for the products of the farm, where no process of manufacture intervenes. If given power, we will by appropriate legislation endeavor to secure to the farmer his just share of the proceeds of his toil.

CONSERVATION

All natural resources, including mineral, oil, and timber lands, water powers and other wealth still remaining to the United States after the wasteful and profligate administration of corrupt old party officials, should be held perpetually and operated to produce revenue for the use of the Government. They must not be ruthlessly squandered by men or corporations for their own enrichment, nor

must they become the collateral of political parties for promissory notes issued for value received.

UNJUST BALLOT LAWS

We denounce the enactment by the Republican and Democratic parties in many states of unjust and discriminatory election laws, that make it almost, and in some states entirely impossible for minor parties to retain their place on the official ballot, or for new parties to be formed, and we demand their repeal.

THE BIBLE IN THE SCHOOLS

The Bible is the Magna Charta of human liberty and national safety and is of highest educational value. Therefore it should have a large place in our public schools.

AMERICANIZATION OF ALIENS

Recognizing the fact that there are large numbers of unassimilated aliens now in this country who, in their present condition and environment, are incapable of assimilation, and are therefore a menace to our institutions, we declare for an immediate, scientific investigation, looking forward to a constructive program for Americanizing these aliens.

SEPARATION OF DEPARTMENTS OF GOVERNMENT

We deplore the prevailing disregard of the parties in power of the Constitutional division of governmental powers into Legislative, Executive, and Judicial branches, and when placed in authority we pledge strict observance of such division.

WOMAN AND THE HOME

We approve and adopt the program of the National League of Women Voters for public welfare in government in so far as a strict regard for the division of powers under our dual form of government will permit.

CIVIL SERVICE

We favor the extension of the merit system to all the agencies of the Executive branch of our government.

FREE INSTITUTIONS

We favor freedom of speech, a free press, our free public school system, and compulsory attendance in our public schools. We are unalterably opposed to public monies being used for sectarian purposes. We favor keeping open to public inspection all places where public wards are cared for.

CONCLUSION

On this record of principles, and on its record of long-time faithfulness and vision, proved by the many reforms which it was the first to advocate, the National Prohibition Party summons all those who favor suppression of the liquor traffic, the enforcement of law, the maintenance of constitutional government, the purification of our politics, honesty and efficiency in administration, and the building of a better citizenship, to join with us in a new alignment in a political party to achieve these transcendent objectives.

Republican Platform of 1924

We the delegates of the republican party in national convention assembled, bow our heads in reverent memory of Warren G. Harding.

We nominated him four years ago to be our candidate; the people of the nation elected him their president. His human qualities gripped the affections of the American people. He was a public servant unswerving in his devotion to duty.

A staunch republican, he was first of all a true patriot, who gave unstintingly of himself during a trying and critical period of our national life.

His conception and successful direction of the limitation of armaments conference in Washington was an accomplishment which advanced the world along the path toward peace.

As delegates of the republican party, we share in the national thanksgiving that in the great emergency created by the death of our great leader there stood forth fully equipped to be his successor one whom we had nominated as vice-president—Calvin Coolidge, who as vice-president and president by his every act has justified the faith and confidence which he has won from the nation.

He has put the public welfare above personal considerations. He has given to the people practical idealism in office. In his every act, he has won without seeking the applause of the people of the country. The constantly accumulating evidence of his integrity, vision and single minded devotion to the needs of the people of this nation strengthens and inspires our confident faith in his continued leadership.

SITUATION IN 1921

When the republican administration took control of the government in 1921, there were four and a half million unemployed; industry and commerce were stagnant; agriculture was prostrate; business was depressed; securities of the government were selling below their par values.

Peace was delayed; misunderstanding and friction characterized our relations abroad. There was a lack of faith in the administration of government resulting in a growing feeling of distrust in the very principles upon which our institutions are founded.

To-day industry and commerce are active; public and private credits are sound; we have made peace; we have taken the first step toward disarmament and strengthened our friendship with the world powers, our relations with the rest of the world are on a firmer basis, our position was never better understood, our foreign policy never more definite and consistent. The tasks to which we have put our hands are completed. Time has been too short for the correction of all the ills we received as a heritage from the last democratic administration, and the notable accomplishments under republican rule warrant us in appealing to the country with entire confidence.

PUBLIC ECONOMY

We demand and the people of the United States have a right to demand rigid economy in government. A policy of strict economy enforced by the republican administration since 1921 has made possible a reduction in taxation and has enabled the government to reduce the public debt by $2,500,000,000. This policy vigorously enforced has resulted in a progressive reduction of public expenditures until they are now two billions dollars per annum less than in 1921. The tax burdens of the people have been relieved to the extent of $1,250,000,000 per annum. Government securities have been increased in value more than $3,000,000,000. Deficits have been converted in surpluses. The budget system has been firmly established and the number of federal employes has been reduced more than one hundred thousand. We commend the firm insistence of President Coolidge upon rigid government economy and pledge him our earnest support to this end.

FINANCE AND TAXATION

We believe that the achievement of the republican administration in reducing taxation by $1,250,000,000 per annum; reducing of the public debt by $2,432,000,000; installing a budget system; reducing the public expenditures from $5,500,000,000 per annum to approximately $3,400,000,000 per annum, thus reducing the ordinary expenditures of the government to substantially a pre-war basis, and the complete restoration of public credit; the payment or refunding of $7,500,000,000 of public obligations without disturbance of credit or industry—all during the short period of three years—presents a record unsurpassed in the history of public finance.

The assessment of taxes wisely and scientifically collected and the efficient and economical expenditure of the money received by the government are essential to the prosperity of our nation.

Carelessness in levying taxes inevitably breeds extravagance in expenditures. The wisest of taxation rests most rightly on the individual and economic life of the country. The public demand for a sound tax policy is insistent.

Progressive tax reduction should be accomplished through tax reorganization. It should not be confined to less than 4,000,000 of our citizens who pay direct taxes, but is the right of more than 100,000,000 who are daily paying their taxes through their living expenses. Congress has in the main confined its work to tax reduction. The matter of tax reform is still unsettled and is equally essential.

We pledge ourselves to the progressive reduction of taxes of all the people as rapidly as may be done with due regard for the essential expenditures for the government administered with rigid economy and to place our tax system on a sound peace time basis.

We endorse the plan of President Coolidge to call in November a national conference of federal and state officials for the development of the effective methods of lightening the tax burden of our citizens and adjusting questions of taxation as between national and state governments.

We favor the creation by appropriate legislation of a non-partisan federal commission to make a comprehensive study and report upon the tax system of the states and federal government with a view to an intelligent reformation of our systems of taxation to a more equitable basis and a proper adjustment of the subjects of taxation as between the national and state governments with justice to the taxpayer and in conformity with the sound economic principles.

REORGANIZATION

We favor a comprehensive reorganization of the executive departments and bureaus along the line of the plan recently submitted by a joint committee of the congress which has the unqualified support of President Coolidge.

CIVIL SERVICE

Improvement in the enforcement of the merit system both by legislative enactment and executive action since March 4, 1921, has been marked and effective. By executive order the appointment of presidential postmasters has been placed on the merit basis similar to that applying to the classified service.

We favor the classification of postmasters in first, second and third class postoffices and the placing of the prohibition enforcement field forces within the classified civil service without necessarily incorporating the present personnel.

FOREIGN DEBTS

In fulfillment of our solemn pledge in the national platform of 1920 we have steadfastly refused to consider the cancellation of foreign debts. Our attitude has not been that of an oppressive creditor seeking immediate return and ignoring existing financial conditions, but has been based on the conviction that a moral obligation such as was incurred should not be disregarded.

We stand for settlements with all debtor countries, similar in character to our debt agreement with Great Britain. That settlement achieved under a republican administration, was the greatest international financial transaction in the history of the world. Under the terms of the agreement the United States now receives an annual return upon four billion six hundred million dollars owing to us by Great Britain with a definite obligation of ultimate payment in full.

The justness of the basis employed has been formally recognized by other debtor nations.

Great nations cannot recognize or admit the principle of repudiation. To do so would undermine the integrity essential for international trade, commerce and credit. Thirty-five per cent of the total foreign debt is now in process of liquidation.

The Tariff

We reaffirm our belief in the protective tariff to extend needed protection to our productive industries. We believe in protection as a national policy, with due and equal regard to all sections and to all classes. It is only by adherence to such a policy that the well being of the consumers can be safeguarded that there can be assured to American agriculture, to American labor and to American manufacturers a return to perpetuate American standards of life. A protective tariff is designed to support the high American economic level of life for the average family and to prevent a lowering to the levels of economic life prevailing in other lands.

In the history of the nation the protective tariff system has ever justified itself by restoring confidence, promoting industrial activity and employment, enormously increasing our purchasing power and bringing increased prosperity to all our people.

The tariff protection to our industry works for increased consumption of domestic agricultural products by an employed population instead of one unable to purchase the necessities of life. Without the strict maintenance of the tariff principle our farmers will need always to compete with cheap lands and cheap labor abroad and with lower standards of living.

The enormous value of the protective principle has once more been demonstrated by the emergency tariff act of 1921 and the tariff act of 1922.

We assert our belief in the elastic provision adopted by congress in the tariff act of 1922 providing for a method of readjusting the tariff rates and the classifications in order to meet changing economic conditions when such changed conditions are brought to the attention of the president by complaint or application.

We believe that the power to increase or decrease any rate of duty provided in the tariff furnishes a safeguard on the one hand against excessive taxes and on the other hand against too high customs charges.

The wise provisions of this section of the tariff act afford ample opportunity for tariff duties to be adjusted after a hearing in order that they may cover the actual differences in the cost of production in the United States and the principal competing countries of the world.

We also believe that the application of this provision of the tariff act will contribute to business stability by making unnecessary general disturbances which are usually incident to general tariff revisions.

Foreign Relations

The republican party reaffirmed its stand for agreement among the nations to prevent war and preserve peace. As an immediate step in this direction we endorse the permanent court of international justice and favor the adherence of the United States to this tribunal as recommended by President Coolidge. This government has definitely refused membership in the league of nations or to assume any obligations under the covenant of the league. On this we stand.

While we are unwilling to enter into political commitments which would involve us in the conflict of European politics, it should be the purpose and high privilege of the United States to continue to co-operate with other nations in humanitarian efforts in accordance with our cherished traditions. The basic principles of our foreign policy must be independence without indifference to the rights and necessities of others and co-operation without entangling alliances. The policy overwhelmingly approved by the people has been vindicated since the end of the great war.

America's participation in world affairs under the administration of President Harding and President Coolidge has demonstrated the wisdom and prudence of the national judgment. A most impressive example of the capacity of the United States to serve the cause of the world peace without political affiliations was shown in the effective and beneficent work of the Dawes commission toward the solution of the perplexing question of German reparations.

The first conference of great powers in Washington called by President Harding accomplished the limitation of armaments and the readjustment of the relations of the powers interested in the far east. The conference resulted in an agreement to reduce armaments, relieved the competitive nations involved from the great burdens of taxation arising from the construction and maintenance of capital battleships; assured a new, broader and better understanding in the far east; brought the assurance of peace in the region of the Pacific and formally adopted the policy of the open door for trade and commerce in the great markets of the far east.

This historic conference paved the way to avert the danger of renewed hostilities in Europe, and to restore the necessary economic stability. While the military forces of America have been restored to a peace footing, there has been an increase in the land and air forces abroad which constitutes a continual menace to the peace of the world and a bar to the return of prosperity.

We firmly advocate the calling of a conference on the limitation of land forces, the use of submarines and poison gas, as proposed by President Coolidge, when, through the adoption of a permanent reparations plan the conditions in Europe will make negotiations and co-operation opportune and possible.

By treaties of peace, safeguarding our rights and without derogating those of our former associates in arms, the republican administration ended the war between this country and Germany and Austria. We have concluded and signed with other nations during the past three years more than fifty treaties and international agreements in the furtherance of peace and good will.

New sanctions and new proofs of permanent accord have marked our relations with all Latin-America. The long standing controversy between Chile and Peru has been advanced toward settlement by its submission to the president of the United States as arbitrator and with the helpful co-operation of this country a treaty has been signed by the representatives of sixteen American republics which will stabilize conditions on the American continent and minimize the opportunities for war.

Our difficulties with Mexico have happily yielded to a most friendly adjustment. Mutual confidence has been restored and a pathway for that friendliness and helpfulness which should exist between this government and the government of our neighboring republic has been marked. Agreements have been entered into for the determination by judicial commissions of the claims of the citizens of each country against the respective governments. We can confidently look forward to more permanent and more stable relations with this republic that joins for so many miles our southern border.

Our policy, now well defined, of giving practical aid to other peoples without assuming political obligations has been conspicuously demonstrated. The ready and generous response of America to the needs of the starving in Russia and the suddenly stricken people of Japan gave evidence of our helpful interest in the welfare of the distressed in other lands.

The work of our representatives in dealing with subjects of such universal concern as the traffic in women and children, the production and distribution of narcotic drugs, the sale of arms and in matters affecting public health and morals, demonstrates that we can effectively do our part for humanity and civilization without forfeiting, limiting or restricting our national freedom of action.

The American people do cherish their independence, but their sense of duty to all mankind will ever prompt them to give their support, service and leadership to every cause which makes for peace and amity among the nations of the world.

AGRICULTURE

In dealing with agriculture the republican party recognizes that we are faced with a fundamental national problem, and that the prosperity and welfare of the nation as a whole is dependent upon the prosperity and welfare of our agricultural population.

We recognize our agricultural activities are still struggling with adverse conditions that have brought about distress. We pledge the party to take whatever steps are necessary to bring back a balanced condition between agriculture, industry and labor, which was destroyed by the democratic party through an unfortunate administration of legislation passed as war-time measures.

We affirm that under the republican administration the problems of the farm have received more serious consideration than ever before both by definite executive action and by congressional action not only in the field of general legislation but also in the enactment of laws to meet emergency situations.

The restoration of general prosperity and the purchasing power of our people through tariff protection has resulted in an increased domestic consumption of food products while the price of many agricultural commodities are above the war price level by reason of direct tariff protection.

Under the leadership of the president at the most critical time, a corporation was organized by private capital making available $100,000,000 to assist the farmers of the northwest.

In realization of the disturbance in the agricultural export market, the result of the financial depression in Europe, and appreciating that the export field would be enormously improved by economic rehabilitation and the resulting increased consuming power, a sympathetic support and direction was given to the work of the American representatives on the European reparations commission.

The revival in 1921 of the war finance corporation with loans of over $300,000,000 averted in 1921 a complete collapse in the agricultural industry.

We have established new intermediate credit banks for agriculture and increased the capital of the federal farm loan system. Emergency loans have been granted to drought stricken areas. We have enacted into law the co-operative marketing act, the grain futures and packer control acts; given to agriculture direct representation on the federal reserve board and on the federal aid commission. We have greatly strengthened our foreign marketing service for the disposal of our agricultural products.

The crux of the problem from the standpoint of the farmer is the net profit he receives after his outlay. The process of bringing the average prices of what he buys and what he sells closer together can be promptly expedited by reduction in taxes, steady employment in industry and stability in business.

This process can be expedited directly by lower freight rates, by better marketing through co-operative efforts and a more scientific organization of the physical human machinery of distribution and by a greater diversification of farm products.

We promise every assistance in the reorganization of the market system on sounder and more economical lines and where diversification is needed government assistance during the period of transition. Vigorous efforts of this administration toward broadening our exports market will be continued. The republican party pledges itself to the development and enactment of measures which will place the agricultural interests of America on a basis of economic equality with other industries to assure its prosperity and success. We favor adequate tariff protection to such of our agriculture products as are threatened by competition. We favor, without putting the government into business, the establishment of a federal system of organization for co-operative marketing of farm products.

HIGHWAYS

The federal aid road act, adopted by the republican congress in 1921 has been of inestimable value to the development of the highway systems of the several states and of the nation. We pledge a continuation of this policy of federal co-operation with the states in highway building.

We favor the construction of roads and trails in our national forests necessary to their protection and utilization. In appropriations, therefore, the taxes which these lands would pay if taxable, should be considered as a controlling factor.

LABOR

The increasing stress of industrial life, the constant and necessary efforts because of world competition to increase production and decrease costs has made it specially incumbent on those in authority to protect labor from undue exactions.

We commend congress for having recognized this possibility in its prompt adoption of the recommendation of President Coolidge for a constitutional amendment authorizing congress to legislate on the subject of child labor, and we urge the prompt consideration of that amendment by the legislatures of the various states.

There is no success great enough to justify the employment of women in labor under conditions which will impair their natural functions.

We favor high standards for wage, working and living conditions among the women employed in industry. We pledge a continuance of the successful efforts of the republican administration to eliminate the seven-day, twelve-hour day industry.

We regard with satisfaction the elimination of the twelve-hour day in the steel industry and the agreement eliminating the seven-day work week of alternate thirteen and eleven hours accomplished through the efforts of Presidents Harding and Coolidge.

We declare our faith in the principle of the eight-hour day.

We pledge a continuation of the work of rehabilitating workers in industry as conducted by the federal board for vocational education, and favor adequate appropriations for this purpose.

We favor a broader and better system of vocational education, a more adequate system of federal free employment agencies with facilities for assisting the movements of seasonal and migratory labor, including farm labor, with ample organization for bringing the man and his job together.

RAILROADS

We believe that the demand of the American people for improved railroad service at cheaper rates is justified and that it can be fulfilled by the consolidation of the railroads into a lesser number of connecting systems with the resultant operating economy. The labor board provision should be amended to meet the requirements made evident by experience gained from its actual creation.

Collective bargaining, voluntary mediation and arbitration are the most important steps in maintaining peaceful labor relations. We do not believe in compulsory action at any time. Public opinion must be the final arbiter in any crisis which so vitally affects public welfare as the suspension of transportation. Therefore, the interests of the public require the maintenance of an impartial tribunal which can in any emergency make an investigation of the fact and publish its conclusions. This is accepted as a basis of popular judgment.

GOVERNMENT CONTROL

The prosperity of the American nation rests on the vigor of private initiative which has bred a spirit of independence and self-reliance. The republican party stands now, as always, against all attempts to put the government into business.

American industry should not be compelled to struggle against government competition. The right of the government to regulate, supervise and control public utilities and public interests, we believe, should be strengthened, but we are firmly opposed to the nationalization or government ownership of public utilities.

COAL

The price and a constant supply of this essential commodity are of vital interest to the public. The government has no constitutional power to regulate prices, but can bring its influence to bear by the powerful instrument afforded by full publicity. When through industrial conflict, its supply is threatened, the president should have authority to appoint a commission to act as mediators and as a medium for voluntary arbitration. In the event of a strike, the control of distribution must be invoked to prevent profiteering.

MERCHANT MARINE

The republican party stands for a strong and permanent merchant marine built by Americans, owned by Americans and manned by Americans to secure the necessary contact with world markets for our surplus agricultural products and manufactures; to protect our shippers and importers from exorbitant ocean freight rates, and to become a powerful arm of our national defense.

That part of the merchant marine now owned by the government should continue to be improved in its economic and efficient management, with reduction of the losses now paid by the government through taxation until it is finally placed on so sound a basis that, with ocean freight rates becoming normal, due to improvement in international affairs, it can be sold to American citizens.

WATERWAYS

Fully realizing the vital importance of transportation in both cost and service to all of our people, we favor the construction of the most feasible waterways from the Great Lakes to the Atlantic seaboard and the Gulf of Mexico, and the improvement and development of rivers, harbors and waterways, inland and coastwise, to the fullest extent justified by the present and potential tonnage available.

We favor a comprehensive survey of the conditions under which the flood waters of the Colorado river may be controlled and utilized for the benefit of the people of the states which border thereon.

The federal water power act establishes a national water power policy and the way has thereby been opened for the greatest water power development in history under conditions which preserve initiative of our people, yet protect the public interest.

WORLD WAR VETERANS

The republican party pledges a continual and increasing solicitude for all those suffering any disability as a result of service to the United States in time of war. No country and no administration has ever shown a more generous disposition in the care of its disabled, or more thoughtful consideration in providing a sound administration for the solution of the many problems involved in making intended benefits fully, directly and promptly available to the veterans.

The confusion, inefficiency and maladministration existing heretofore since the establishment of this government agency has been cured, and plans are being actively made looking to a further improvement in the operation of the bureau by the passage of new legislation. The basic statute has been so liberalized as to bring within its terms 100,000 additional beneficiaries. The privilege of hospitalization in government hospitals, as recommended by President Coolidge, has been granted to all veterans irrespective of the origin of disability, and over $50,000,000 has been appropriated for hospital construction which will provide sufficient beds to care for all. Appropriations totalling over $1,100,000,000, made by the republican congress for the care of the disabled, evidence the unmistakable purpose of the government not to consider costs when the welfare of these men is at stake. No legislation for the benefit of the disabled soldiers proposed during the last four years by veterans' organizations has failed to receive consideration.

We pledge ourselves to meet the problems of the future affecting the care of our wounded and disabled in a spirit of liberality, and with that thoughtful consideration which will enable the government to give to the individual veteran that full measure of care guaranteed by an effective administrative machinery.

CONSERVATION

We believe in the development, effective and efficient, whether of oil, timber, coal or water power resources of this government only as needed and only after the public needs have become a matter of public record, controlled with a scrupulous regard and ever-vigilant safeguards against waste, speculation and monopoly.

The natural resources of the country belong to all the people and are a part of an estate belonging to generations yet unborn. The government policy should be to safeguard, develop and utilize these possessions. The conservation policy of the nation originated with the republican party under the inspiration of Theodore Roosevelt.

We hold it a privilege of the republican party to build as a memorial to him on the foundation which he laid.

EDUCATION AND RELIEF

The conservation of human resources is one of the most solemn responsibilities of government. This is an obligation which cannot be ignored and which demands that the federal government shall, as far as lies in its power, give to the people and the states the benefit of its counsel.

The welfare activities of the government connected with the various departments are already numerous and important, but lack the co-ordination which is essential to effective action. To meet these needs we approve the suggestion for the creation of a cabinet post of education and relief.

WAR-TIME MOBILIZATION

We believe that in time of war the nation should draft for its defense not only its citizens but also every resource which may contribute to success. The country demands that should the United States ever again be called upon to defend itself by arms the president be empowered to draft such material resources and such service as may be required, and to stabilize the prices of services and essential commodities, whether used in actual warfare or private activities.

COMMERCIAL AVIATION

We advocate the early enactment of such legislation and the taking of such steps by the government as will tend to promote commercial aviation.

ARMY AND NAVY

There must be no further weakening of our regular army and we advocate appropriations sufficient to provide for the training of all members of the national guard, the citizens' military training camps, the reserve officers' training camps and the reserves who may offer themselves for service. We pledge ourselves for service. We pledge ourselves to round out and maintain the navy to the full strength provided the United States by the letter and spirit of the limitation of armament conference.

The Negro

We urge the congress to enact at the earliest possible date a federal anti-lynching law so that the full influence of the federal government may be wielded to exterminate this hideous crime. We believe that much of the misunderstanding which now exists can be eliminated by humane and sympathetic study of its causes. The president has recommended the creation of a commission for the investigation of social and economic conditions and the promotion of mutual understanding and confidence.

Orderly Government

The republican party reaffirms its devotion to orderly government under the guarantees embodied in the constitution of the United States. We recognize the duty of constant vigilance to preserve at all times a clean and honest government and to bring to the bar of justice every defiler of the public service in or out of office.

Dishonesty and corruption are not political attributes. The recent congressional investigations have exposed instances in both parties of men in public office who are willing to sell official favors and men out of office who are willing to buy them in some cases with money and others with influence.

The sale of influence resulting from the holding of public position or from association while in public office or the use of such influence for private gain or advantage is a perversion of public trust and prejudicial to good government. It should be condemned by public opinion and forbidden by law.

We demand the speedy, fearless and impartial prosecution of all wrong doers, without regard for political affiliations; but we declare no greater wrong can be committed against the people than the attempt to destroy their trust in the great body of their public servants. Admitting the deep humiliation which all good citizens share that our public life should have harbored some dishonest men, we assert that these undesirables do not represent the standard of our national integrity.

The government at Washington is served to-day by thousands of earnest, conscientious and faithful officials and employés in every department.

It is a grave wrong against these patriotic men and women to strive indiscriminately to besmirch the names of the innocent and undermine the confidence of the people in the government under which they live. It is even a greater wrong when this is done for partisan purposes or for selfish exploitation.

Immigration

The unprecedented living conditions in Europe following the world war created a condition by which we were threatened with mass immigration that would have seriously disturbed our economic life. The law recently enacted is designed to protect the inhabitants of our country, not only the American citizen, but also the alien already with us who is seeking to secure an economic foothold for himself and family from the competition that would come from unrestricted immigration. The administrative features of the law represent a great constructive advance, and eliminate the hardships suffered by immigrants under emergency statute.

We favor the adoption of methods which will exercise a helpful influence among the foreign born population and provide for the education of the alien in our language, customs, ideals and standards of life. We favor the improvement of naturalization laws.

Socialist Labor Platform of 1924

The world stands upon the threshold of a new social order. The capitalist system of production and distribution is doomed; capitalist appropriation of labor's product forces the bulk of mankind into wage slavery, throws society into the convulsions of the class struggle, and momentarily threatens to engulf humanity in chaos and disaster. At this crucial period in history the Socialist Labor Party of America, in 16th National Convention assembled, reaffirming its former platform declarations, calls upon the workers to rally around the banner of the Socialist Labor Party, the only party in this country that blazes the trail to the Worker's Industrial Republic.

Since the advent of civilization human society has been divided into classes. Each new form of society has come into being with a definite purpose to fulfill in the progress of the human race. Each has been born, has grown, developed, prospered, become old, outworn, and has finally been overthrown. Each society has developed within itself the germs of its own destruction as well as the germs which went to make up the society of the future.

The capitalist system rose during the seventeenth, eighteenth, and nineteenth centuries by the overthrow of feudalism. Its great and all-important mission in the development of man was to improve, develop, and concentrate the means of production and distribution, thus creating a system of co-operative production. This work was completed in advanced capitalist countries about the beginning of the 20th century. That moment capitalism had fulfilled its historic mission, and from that moment the capitalist class became a class of parasites.

In the course of human progress mankind has passed, through class rule, private property, and individualism in production and exchange, from the enforced and inevitable want, misery, poverty, and ignorance of savagery and barbarism to the affluence and high productive capacity of civilization. For all practical purposes, co-operative production has now superseded individual production.

Capitalism no longer promotes the greatest good of the greatest number. It no longer spells progress, but reaction. Private production carries with it private ownership of the products. Production is carried on, not to supply the needs of humanity, but for the profit of the individual owner, the company, or the trust. The worker, not receiving the full product of his labor, cannot buy back all he produces. The capitalist wastes part in riotous living; the rest must find a foreign market. By the opening of the twentieth century the capitalist world—England, America, Germany, France, Japan, China, etc.—was producing at a mad rate for the world market. A capitalist deadlock of markets brought on in 1914 the capitalist collapse popularly known as the World War. The capitalist world can not extricate itself out of the débris. America to-day is choking under the weight of her own gold and products.

This situation has brought on the present stage of human misery—starvation, want, cold, disease, pestilence, and war. This state is brought about in the midst of plenty, when the earth can be made to yield hundred-fold, when the machinery of production is made to multiply human energy and ingenuity by the hundred. The present state of misery exists solely because the mode of production rebels against the mode of exchange. Private property in the means of life has become a social crime. The land was made by no man; the modern machines are the result of the combined ingenuity of the human race from time immemorial; the land can be made to yield and the machines can be set in motion only by the collective effort of the workers. Progress demands the collective ownership of the land on and the tools with which to produce the necessities of life. The owner of the means of life to-day partakes of the nature of a highwayman; he stands with his gun before society's temple; it depends upon him whether the million mass may work, earn, eat, and live. The capitalist system of production and exchange must be supplanted if progress is to continue.

In place of the capitalist system the Socialist Labor Party aims to substitute a system of social ownership of the means of production, industrially administered by the workers, who assume control and direction as well as operation of their industrial affairs.

We therefore call upon the wage workers to organize themselves into a revolutionary political organization under the banner of the Socialist Labor Party; and to organize themselves likewise upon the industrial field into a Socialist industrial union, in order to consolidate the material power necessary for the establishment of the Socialist Industrial Republic.

We also call upon all intelligent citizens to place themselves squarely upon the ground of working class interest, and join us in this mighty and noble work of human emancipation, so that we may put summary end to the existing barbarous class conflict by placing the land and all the means of production, transportation, and distribution into the hands of the people as a collective body, and substituting Industrial Self-Government for the present state of planless production, industrial war and social disorder—a government in which every worker shall have the free exercise and full benefit of his faculties, multiplied by all the modern factors of civilization.

Workers' Party Platform, 1924

The workers and exploited farmers of the United States face the question of how to organize and use their political power in the coming election. Before deciding this question every industrial worker, agricultural worker and exploited farmer should give fundamental consideration to the situation which exists in this country.

IN THE GRIP OF THE EXPLOITERS

The United States is the wealthiest country in the world. We have natural resources which supply us with raw materials and a great industrial organization which can turn these raw materials into the finished products which satisfy human needs. With the raw materials available and the tremendous machinery of production we have the means of giving a high standard of life —good food, good clothing, good homes, the opportunity for education and recreation—to every person in this country. This high standard of life is denied the workers and exploited farmers of the United States. Millions of these producers of wealth are able to secure for their labor only the means for a bare existence. Millions of workers must work long hours, under bad working conditions, for low wages. Millions are periodically unemployed, as at present, with all the consequent misery and suffering for themselves and their families. In order to keep these conditions from growing worse, millions of industrial workers are periodically compelled to go on strike to fight back the greedy employers. Millions of farmers have been driven into bankruptcy and from the land because of inability to earn enough for a living.

These conditions prevail in a country in which we have the means of supplying a high standard of life to every person because a relatively small class has fastened its grip upon the raw materials and industries and uses these to enrich itself at the expense of the producers. Through theft, fraud, corruption, bribery, and the capitalist system of profit taking, this capitalist class has become the owner of the land, raw material and machinery of production upon which the workers and farmers are dependent for a livelihood.

The raw materials and industries of the United States are owned by the Garys, Morgans, Rockefellers, Fords, McCormicks, and other great capitalists. The workers and farmers alike pay tribute to these capitalists. They are compelled to accept a low standard of living in order that the capitalists may amass even greater fortunes for themselves.

It is this system of capitalist ownership of industry which gives the wealth produced to the few, that denies the millions of industrial workers, agricultural workers and exploited farmers the enjoyment of that high standard of life which their labor and the wealth they produce make possible in this country.

It is this system of capitalist ownership of industry which is the basis of the class struggle between the workers, fighting for more of what they produce, and the capitalists, ever bent on securing greater and greater profits for themselves.

HOW THE CAPITALISTS USE THE GOVERNMENT

The government of the United States is and has been a government of, by, and for the capitalists. It is through the government and use of the governmental power that the capitalists maintain their grip on the industries and their power to rob the industrial workers, agricultural workers, and farmers.

During the war, with the connivance of government officials, the capitalists looted the country of billions of wealth. Since the war the shipping board deals, the war veterans' board corruption, the Teapot Dome exposures, have shown how the capitalists fill their pockets at the expense of the working and farming masses.

Governmental legislation is framed so as to yield the capitalists more and more profits. Tariff laws, taxation laws, agrarian bank laws, are all framed so as to enable the bankers and industrial magnates to take more and more of what the workers produce.

To prevent the workers from securing better wages and working conditions through strikes, the capitalists use the government to destroy these strikes. The disgraceful Daugherty injunction against the railway shopmen, the use of troops against miners in their strike in 1922, the use of the Railway Labor Board against the railroad workers, are only outstanding examples of the continual use of the governmental power by the capitalists to protect themselves in taking greater and greater profits out of the labor of the workers.

The government is a dictatorship of the capitalists and their instrument for the oppression and exploitation of the workers. Although the workers are permitted to vote, the capitalists are able, through their control of the means of information and through their economic power, to completely dominate the government, national, state and local.

THE ELECTION THIS YEAR

It is these conditions which the workers and exploited farmers must consider in using their political power in the election this year.

The capitalist dictatorship has named two candidates, the Republican, strikebreaker Coolidge, and the Morgan-Rockefeller lawyer Davis. Both are agents of the capitalist class. They, and the other candidates of the two old parties, will loyally serve the capitalists if returned to power—as they have done in the past.

La Follette, who is running as an independent, progressive Republican, is equally a supporter of the capitalist system of exploitation. The only difference between La Follette and Coolidge and Davis is that La Follette represents the independent manufacturers, bankers and merchants, who are seeking greater power and profit for themselves and are trying to use the workers and farmers to attain that end.

La Follette is the representative of little business against big business, but not the representative of the workers and exploited farmers in their struggle against the capitalists. La Follette's platform is not a workers' and farmers' platform, but a little business men's platform with some bait thrown in for sections of the skilled workers.

Against these three candidates of the capitalist system of exploitation, big and little, the Workers' (Communist) Party presents working class candidates—Foster and Gitlow—and a working class platform.

THE WORKERS MUST RULE

There is only one way in which the exploitation of the workers and farmers of this country can be ended. That is through the workers organizing their mass power, ending the capitalist dictatorship and establishing the Workers' and Farmers' Government.

In place of the capitalist dictatorship there must be established the rule of the workers. The governmental power must be used in the interest of the workers and farmers as it is now used by the capitalist dictatorship in the interest of the capitalist class.

The Russian workers and peasants have established their rule in the form of the Soviet government and are using their power against the capitalists and for themselves—to build a Communist social system which will give the workers and farmers the fruits of their toil.

The Workers' party is fighting for the rule of the 30,000,000 workers and their families in the United States. This rule will be established through a proletarian revolution which will create a Soviet government and the dictatorship of the proletariat.

This Workers' and Farmers' Government will wrest out of the hands of the capitalists the raw material and great industries and operate them for the happiness and well-being of the producers. It will build in place of the capitalist system of production a Communist system of production.

The Workers' Party calls upon workers and exploited farmers to join it in the struggle to establish the Workers' and Farmers' Government in the United States. It urges them to demonstrate their support of the program of the Workers' Party by voting against the three capitalist candidates and for the Communist candidates—Foster and Gitlow.

IMMEDIATE PROGRAM

1. For a Mass Farmer-Labor Party

The Workers' Party has for two years carried on a consistent campaign for the formation of a mass Farmer-Labor Party to unite the industrial workers and exploited farmers for independent political action. The betrayal of the Conference for Progressive Political Action in accepting the independent candidacy of La Follette, the betrayal of the Farmer-Labor Party by the Socialist Party and the La Follette supporters among the workers and farmers, the attack upon the Farmer-Labor Party by La Follette, who does not want a party of workers and farmers, made the achievement of this goal impossible in this election campaign. The Workers' party declares its purpose to continue the struggle to mobilize the workers and exploited farmers for independent political action through a mass Farmer-Labor Party.

2. Nationalization of Industry and Workers' Control

The Workers' Party declares itself in favor of the immediate nationalization of all large-scale industries, such as railroads, mines, super-power plants, and means of communication and transportation, and for the organization of the workers in these industries for participation in the management and direction of the industries nationalized, thus developing industrial democracy, until industry comes under the control of those who produce the wealth of the nation, subject only to such general control as will protect the interest of the producers as a whole.

3. Compel Industry and the Government to Pay Wages to the Unemployed

Industry in the United States is slowing down and the workers face another period of industrial crisis with millions of unemployed unable to earn a living. The Workers' Party declares that industry must support the unemployed to whom it cannot give work. The government must take the accumulated profits of industry. It must levy excess profit and inheritance taxes to create an unemployment fund, to be administered by the workers, for payment of union wages to workers without jobs. The Workers' Party will initiate the organization of unemployment councils to fight for these demands.

4. Down with Injunctions and the Use of Police and Soldiers Against Workers

The Workers' Party calls upon the workers and exploited farmers to fight with it against the use of injunctions in labor disputes, intimidation of strikers through police and soldiers, and the use of criminal syndicalist laws to suppress the demands of the revolutionary workers, as well as other infringements of the rights of the workers.

5. Release All Political and Class War Prisoners

The Workers' Party will fight for the immediate and unconditional release of all workers imprisoned because of their political or economic views and for participation in the class struggle.

6. Land for the Users—Nationalize the Farmers' Marketing Industries

Land was created for all the people and we demand a system of land tenure which will eliminate landlordism and tenantry and will secure the land to the users thereof. We demand the nationalization of all means of transportation and industries engaged in the preparation and distribution of farm products, with participation of the farmers in the management of these industries.

7. Down with Militarism and Imperialist Wars

The World War and its slaughter of millions and destruction of billions of wealth was the product of capitalist imperialism. The capitalist government of the United States is already preparing for a new war. It is using its power to oppress weaker nations in the interest of the capitalists, as in Haiti, Santo Domingo, and Central America. It is holding the Philippine Islands in subjection. It is aiding to force the Dawes plan upon Germany in order to enslave the workers of that country. The Workers' Party will fight against militarism and imperialist wars and the use of the governmental power for the exploitation of weaker nations. It demands freedom for the Philippines and the right of self-determination for all colonies and territories of the United States.

8. Recognize the Workers' and Peasants' Government of Russia

The Union of Soviet Socialist Republics is the only workers' and farmers' government in the world. The capitalist government of the United States refuses it recognition and the restoration of full trade relations. The Workers' Party will rally the workers for immediate, unconditional recognition of the Union of Soviet Socialist Republics.

The measures outlined here are measures for immediate struggle and mobilization of the workers against the capitalist class and the capitalist dictatorship in the United States. The end of the glaring evils of capitalist society can only come with the victory of the workers and the establishment of the Workers' and Peasants' government through which capitalism will be abolished and the Communist society created. The Workers' Party will carry on the struggle until this goal is achieved.

CAMPAIGN OF 1928

In 1928, Herbert C. Hoover of California, the secretary of commerce under the retiring president, Calvin Coolidge, was nominated as the Republican candidate for president on the first ballot of the G.O.P. convention. Senator Charles Curtis of Kansas easily won the vice-presidential nomination. The Democrats, in a more compromising mood than in 1924, quickly nominated Governor Alfred E. Smith of New York, after only one ballot. Senator Joseph T. Robinson of Arkansas was chosen, also on the first ballot, to be Smith's running mate.

Five minor parties nominated presidential candidates. The Socialists nominated Norman Thomas of New York for president and James Maurer of Pennsylvania for vice-president. The Socialist Labor Party members chose Verne Reynolds of Michigan and Jeremiah Crowley of New York as

their ticket. The Workers (Communist) Party was again headed by William Z. Foster of Illinois and Benjamin Gitlow of New York. The Prohibition Party selected William F. Varney of New York and James A. Edgerton of Virginia as their candidates, and the Farmer-Labor Party named Frank E. Webb of California as its presidential candidate and Will Vereen of Georgia as its vice-presidential candidate.

The two major parties received nearly 99 percent of the votes. The Republicans carried forty-two states and received 21,411,991 popular votes. The Democrats obtained 15,000,185 votes. The Socialists attracted 266,453 votes; the Communists, 48,170; the Socialist Labor Party, 21,608; the Prohibitionists, 34,489; and the Farmer-Labor Party, 6,390. In the electoral count, Hoover was elected with 444 votes to 87 for Smith.

Democratic Platform for 1928

We, the Democratic Party in convention assembled, pause to pay our tribute of love and respect to the memory of him who in his life and in his official actions voiced the hopes and aspirations of all good men and women of every race and clime, the former President of the United States, Woodrow Wilson. His spirit moves on and his example and deeds will exalt those who come after us as they have inspired us.

We are grateful that we were privileged to work with him and again pay tribute to his high ideals and accomplishments.

We reaffirm our devotion to the principles of Democratic government formulated by Jefferson and enforced by a long and illustrious line of Democratic Presidents.

We hold that government must function not to centralize our wealth but to preserve equal opportunity so that all may share in our priceless resources; and not confine prosperity to a favored few. We, therefore, pledge the Democratic Party to encourage business, small and great alike; to conserve human happiness and liberty; to break the shackles of monopoly and free business of the nation; to respond to the popular will.

The function of a national platform is to declare general principles and party policies. We do not, therefore, assume to bind our party respecting local issues or details of legislation.

We, therefore, declare the policy of the Democratic Party with regard to the following dominant national issues:

THE RIGHTS OF THE STATES

We demand that the constitutional rights and powers of the states shall be preserved in their full vigor and virtue. These constitute a bulwark against centralization and the destructive tendencies of the Republican Party.

We oppose bureaucracy and the multiplication of offices and officeholders.

We demand a revival of the spirit of local self-government, without which free institutions cannot be preserved.

REPUBLICAN CORRUPTION

Unblushingly the Republican Party offers as its record agriculture prostrate, industry depressed, American shipping destroyed, workmen without employment; everywhere disgust and suspicion, and corruption unpunished and unafraid.

Never in the entire history of the country has there occurred in any given period of time or, indeed, in all time put together, such a spectacle of sordid corruption and unabashed rascality as that which has characterized the administration of federal affairs under eight blighting years of Republican rule. Not the revels of reconstruction, nor all the compounded frauds succeeding that evil era, have approached in sheer audacity the shocking thieveries and startling depravities of officials high and low in the public service at Washington. From cabinet ministers, with their treasonable crimes, to the cheap vendors of official patronage, from the purchasers of seats in the United States Senate to the vulgar grafters upon alien trust funds, and upon the hospital resources of the disabled veterans of the World War; from the givers and receivors of stolen funds for Republican campaign purposes to the public men who sat by silently consenting and never revealing a fact or uttering a word in condemnation, the whole official organization under Republican rule has become saturated with dishonesty defiant of public opinion and actuated only by a partisan desire to perpetuate its control of the government.

As in the time of Samuel J. Tilden, from whom the presidency was stolen, the watchword of the day should be: "Turn the rascals out." This is the appeal of the Democratic Party to the people of the country. To this fixed purpose should be devoted every effort and applied every resource of the party; to this end every minor difference on non-essential issues should be put aside and a determined and a united fight be made to rescue the government from those who have betrayed their trust by disgracing it.

ECONOMY AND REORGANIZATION

The Democratic Party stands for efficiency and economy in the administration of public affairs and we pledge:

(a) Business-like reorganization of all the departments of the government.

(b) Elimination of duplication, waste and overlapping.

(c) Substitution of modern business-like methods for existing obsolete and antiquated conditions.

No economy resulted from the Republican Party rule. The savings they claim take no account of the elimination of expenditures following the end of the World War, the large sums realized from the sale of war materials, nor its failure to supply sufficient funds for the efficient conduct of many important governmental activities.

FINANCING AND TAXATION

(a) The Federal Reserve system, created and inaugurated under Democratic auspices, is the greatest legislative contribution to constructive business ever adopted. The administration of the system for the advantage of stock market speculators should cease. It must be administered for the benefit of farmers, wage earners, merchants, manufacturers and others engaged in constructive business.

(b) The taxing function of governments, free or despotic, has for centuries been regarded as the power above all others which requires vigilant scrutiny to the end that it be not exercised for purposes of favor or oppression.

Three times since the World War the Democrats in Congress have favored a reduction of the tax burdens of the people in face of stubborn opposition from a Republican administration; and each time these reductions have largely been made for the relief of those least able to endure the exactions of a Republican fiscal policy. The tax bill of the session recently ended was delayed by Republican tactics and juggled by partisan considerations so as to make impossible a full measure of relief to the greater body of taxpayers. The moderate reductions afforded were grudgingly conceded and the whole proceeding in Congress, dictated as far as possible from the White House and the treasury, denoted the proverbial desire of the Republican Party always to discriminate against the masses in favor of privileged classes.

The Democratic Party avows its belief in the fiscal policy inaugurated by the last Democratic Administration, which provided a sinking fund sufficient to extinguish the nation's indebtedness within a reasonable period of time, without harassing the present and next succeeding generations with tax burdens which, if not unendurable, do in fact check initiative in enterprise and progress in business. Taxes levied beyond the actual requirements of the legally established sinking fund are but an added burden upon the American people, and the surplus thus accumulated in the federal treasury is an incentive to the increasingly extravagant expenditures which have characterized Republican administrations. We, therefore, favor a further reduction of the internal taxes of the people.

TARIFF

The Democratic tariff legislation will be based on the following policies:

(a) The maintenance of legitimate business

and a high standard of wages for American labor.

(b) Increasing the purchasing power of wages and income by the reduction of those monopolistic and extortionate tariff rates bestowed in payment of political debts.

(c) Abolition of log-rolling and restoration of the Wilson conception of a fact-finding tariff commission, quasi-judicial and free from the executive domination which has destroyed the usefulness of the present commission.

(d) Duties that will permit effective competition, insure against monopoly and at the same time produce a fair revenue for the support of government. Actual difference between the cost of production at home and abroad, with adequate safeguard for the wage of the American laborer must be the extreme measure of every tariff rate.

(e) Safeguarding the public against monopoly created by special tariff favors.

(f) Equitable distribution of the benefits and burdens of the tariff among all.

Wage-earner, farmer, stockman, producer and legitimate business in general have everything to gain from a Democratic tariff based on justice to all.

CIVIL SERVICE

Grover Cleveland made the extension of the merit system a tenet of our political faith. We shall preserve and maintain the civil service.

AGRICULTURE

Deception upon the farmer and stock raiser has been practiced by the Republican Party through false and delusive promises for more than fifty years. Specially favored industries have been artificially aided by Republican legislation. Comparatively little has been done for agriculture and stock raising, upon which national prosperity rests. Unsympathetic inaction with regard to this problem must cease. Virulent hostility of the Republican administration to the advocates of farm relief and denial of the right of farm organizations to lead in the development of farm policy must yield to Democratic sympathy and friendliness.

Four years ago the Republican Party, forced to acknowledge the critical situation, pledged itself to take all steps necessary to bring back a balanced condition between agriculture and other industries and labor. Today it faces the country not only with that pledge unredeemed but broken by the acts of a Republican President, who is primarily responsible for the failure to offer a constructive program to restore equality to agriculture.

While he has had no constructive and adequate program to offer in its stead, he has twice vetoed farm relief legislation and has sought to justify his disapproval of agricultural legislation partly on grounds wholly inconsistent with his acts, making industrial monopolies the beneficiaries of government favor; and in endorsing the agricultural policy of the present administration the Republican Party, in its recent convention, served notice upon the farmer that the so-called protective system is not meant for him; that while it offers protection to the privileged few, it promises continued world prices to the producers of the chief cash crops of agriculture.

We condemn the policy of the Republican Party which promises relief to agriculture only through a reduction of American farm production to the needs of the domestic market. Such a program means the continued deflation of agriculture, the forcing of additional millions from the farms, and the perpetuation of agricultural distress for years to come, with continued bad effects on business and labor throughout the United States.

The Democratic Party recognizes that the problems of production differ as between agriculture and industry. Industrial production is largely under human control, while agricultural production, because of lack of co-ordination among the 6,500,000 individual farm units, and because of the influence of weather, pests and other causes, is largely beyond human control. The result is that a large crop frequently is produced on a small acreage and a small crop on a large acreage; and, measured in money value, it frequently happens that a large crop brings less than a small crop.

Producers of crops whose total volume exceeds the needs of the domestic market must continue at a disadvantage until the government shall intervene as seriously and as effectively in behalf of the farmer as it has intervened in behalf of labor and industry. There is a need of supplemental legislation for the control and orderly handling of agricultural surpluses, in order that the price of the surplus may not determine the price of the whole crop. Labor has benefited by collective bargaining and some industries by tariff. Agriculture must be as effectively aided.

The Democratic Party in its 1924 platform pledged its support to such legislation. It now reaffirms that stand and pledges the united efforts of the legislative and executive branches of government, as far as may be controlled by the party, to the immediate enactment of such legislation, and to such other steps as are necessary to establish and maintain the purchasing power of farm products and the complete economic equality of agriculture.

The Democratic Party has always stood against special privilege and for common equality under the law. It is a fundamental principle of the party that such tariffs as are levied must not discriminate against any industry, class or section. Therefore, we pledge that in its tariff policy the Democratic Party will insist upon equality of treatment between agriculture and other industries.

Farm relief must rest on the basis of an economic equality of agriculture with other industries. To give this equality a remedy must be found which will include among other things:

(a) Credit aid by loans to co-operatives on at least as favorable a basis as the government aid to the merchant marine.

(b) Creation of a federal farm board to assist the farmer and stock raiser in the marketing of their products, as the Federal Reserve Board has done for the banker and business man. When our archaic banking and currency system was revised after its record of disaster and panic under Republican administrations, it was a Democratic Congress in the administration of a Democratic President that accomplished its stabilization through the Federal Reserve Act creating the Federal Reserve Board, with powers adequate to its purpose. Now, in the hour of agriculture's need, the Democratic Party pledges the establishment of a new agricultural policy fitted to present conditions, under the direction of a farm board vested with all the powers necessary to accomplish for agriculture what the Federal Reserve Board has been able to accomplish for finance, in full recognition of the fact that the banks of the country, through voluntary co-operation, were never able to stabilize the financial system of the country until the government powers were invoked to help them.

(c) Reduction through proper government agencies of the spread between what the farmer and stock raiser gets and the ultimate consumer pays, with consequent benefits to both.

(d) Consideration of the condition of agriculture in the formulation of government financial and tax measures.

We pledge the party to foster and develop co-operative marketing associations through appropriate governmental aid. We recognize that experience has demonstrated that members of such associations alone can not successfully assume the full responsibility for a program that benefits all producers alike. We pledge the party to an earnest endeavor to solve this problem of the distribution of the cost of dealing with crop surpluses over the marketed units of the crop whose producers are benefited by such assistance. The solution of this problem would avoid government subsidy, to which the Democratic Party has always been opposed. The solution of this problem will be a prime and immediate concern of a Democratic administration.

We direct attention to the fact that it was a Democratic Congress, in the administration of a Democratic President, which established the federal loan system and laid the foundation for the entire rural credits structure, which has aided agriculture to sustain in part the shock of the policies of two Republican administrations; and we promise thorough-going administration of our rural credits laws, so that the farmers in all sections may secure the maximum benefits intended under these acts.

MINING

Mining is one of the basic industries of this country. We produce more coal, iron and copper than any other country. The value of our mineral production is second only to agriculture. Mining has suffered like agriculture, and from similar causes. It is the duty of our government to foster this industry and to remove the restrictions that destroy its prosperity.

FOREIGN POLICY

The Republican administration has no foreign policy; it has drifted without plan. This great nation can not afford to play a minor role in world politics. It must have a sound and positive foreign policy, not a negative one. We declare for a constructive foreign policy based on these principles:

(a) Outlawry of war and an abhorrence of militarism, conquest and imperialism.

(b) Freedom from entangling political alliances with foreign nations.

(c) Protection of American lives and rights.

(d) Non-interference with the elections or other internal political affairs of any foreign nation. This principle of non-interference extends to Mexico, Nicaragua and all other Latin-American nations. Interference in the purely internal affairs of Latin-American countries must cease.

(e) Rescue of our country from its present impaired world standing and restoration to its former position as a leader in the movement for international arbitration, conciliation, conference and limitation of armament by international agreement.

(f) International agreements for reduction of all armaments and the end of competitive war preparations, and, in the meantime, the maintenance of an army and navy adequate for national defense.

(g) Full, free and open co-operation with all other nations for the promotion of peace and justice throughout the world.

(h) In our foreign relations this country should stand as a unit, and, to be successful, foreign policies must have the approval and the support of the American people.

(i) Abolition of the practice of the President of entering into and carrying out agreements with a foreign government, either de facto or de jure, for the protection of such government against revolution or foreign attack, or for the supervision of its internal affairs, when such agreements have not been advised and consented to by the Senate, as provided in the Constitution of the United States, and we condemn the administration for carrying out such an unratified agreement that requires us to use our armed forces in Nicaragua.

(j) Recognition that the Monroe Doctrine is a cardinal principle of this government promulgated for the protection of ourselves and our Latin-American neighbors. We shall seek their friendly co-operation in the maintenance of this doctrine.

(k) We condemn the Republican administration for lack of statesmanship and efficiency in negotiating the 1921 treaty for the limitation of armaments, which limited only the construction of battleships and ships of over ten thousand tons. Merely a gesture towards peace, it accomplished

no limitation of armament, because it simply substituted one weapon of destruction for another. While it resulted in the destruction of our battleships and the blueprints of battleships of other nations, it placed no limitation upon construction of aircraft, submarines, cruisers, warships under ten thousand tons, poisonous gases or other weapons of destruction. No agreement was ratified with regard to submarines and poisonous gases. The attempt of the President to remedy the failure of 1921 by the Geneva Conference of 1928 was characterized by the same lack of statesmanship and efficiency and resulted in entire failure.

In consequence, the race between nations in the building of unlimited weapons of destruction still goes on and the peoples of the world are still threatened with war and burdened with taxation for additional armament.

WATERPOWER, WATERWAYS AND FLOOD CONTROL

The federal government and state governments, respectively, now have absolute and exclusive sovereignty and control over enormous waterpowers, which constitute one of the greatest assets of the nation. This sovereign title and control must be preserved respectively in the state and federal governments, to the end that the people may be protected against exploitation of this great resource and that water powers may be expeditiously developed under such regulations as will insure to the people reasonable rates and equitable distribution.

We favor and will promote deep waterways from the Great Lakes to the Gulf and to the Atlantic Ocean.

We favor the fostering and building up of water transportation through improvement of inland waterways and removal of discrimination against water transportation. Flood control and the lowering of flood levels are essential to the safety of life and property, and the productivity of our lands, the navigability of our streams, the reclaiming of our wet and overflowed lands. We favor expeditious construction of flood relief works on the Mississippi and Colorado rivers and such reclamation and irrigation projects upon the Colorado River as may be found feasible.

We favor appropriations for prompt co-ordinated surveys by the United States to determine the possibilities of general navigation improvements and waterpower development on navigable streams and their tributaries and to secure reliable information as to the most economical navigation improvement, in combination with the most efficient and complete development of waterpower.

We favor the strict enforcement of the Federal Waterpower Act, a Democratic act, and insist that the public interest in waterpower sites, ignored by two Republican administrations, be protected.

Being deeply impressed by the terrible disasters from floods in the Mississippi Valley during 1927, we heartily endorse the Flood Control Act of last May, which recognizes that the flood waters of the Mississippi River and its tributaries constitute a national problem of the gravest character and makes provision for their speedy and effective control. This measure is a continuation and expansion of the policy established by a Democratic Congress in 1917 in the act of that year for controlling floods on the Mississippi and Sacramento rivers. It is a great piece of constructive legislation, and we pledge our party to its vigorous and early enforcement.

Conservation and Reclamation

We shall conserve the natural resources of our country for the benefit of the people and to protect them against waste and monopolization. Our disappearing resources of timber call for a national policy of reforestation. The federal government should improve and develop its public lands so that they may go into private ownership and become subjected to taxation for the support of the states wherein they exist. The Democratic administration will actively, efficiently and economically carry on reclamation projects and make equitable adjustments with the homestead entrymen for the mistakes the government has made, and extend all practical aid to refinance reclamation and drainage projects.

Transportation

Efficient and economical transportation is essential to the prosperity of every industry. Cost of transportation controls the income of every human being and materially affects the cost of living. We must, therefore, promote every form of transportation to a state of highest efficiency. Recognizing the prime importance of air transportation, we shall encourage its development by every possible means. Improved roads are of vital importance not only to commerce and industry, but also to agriculture and rural life. The federal government should construct and maintain at its own expense roads upon its public lands. We reaffirm our approval of the Federal Roads Law, enacted by a Democratic administration. Common carriers, whether by land, water or rail, must be protected in an equal opportunity to compete, so that governmental regulations against exorbitant rates and inefficiency will be aided by competition.

Labor

(a) We favor the principle of collective bargaining, and the Democratic principle that organized labor should choose its own representatives without coercion or interference.

(b) Labor is not a commodity. Human rights must be safeguarded. Labor should be exempt from the operation of anti-trust laws.

(c) We recognize that legislative and other investigations have shown the existence of grave abuse in the issuance of injunctions in labor disputes. No injunctions should be granted in labor disputes except upon proof of threatened irreparable injury and after notice and hearing and the injunction should be confined to those acts which do directly threaten irreparable injury. The expressed purpose of representatives of capital, labor and the bar to devise a plan for the elimination of the present evils with respect to injunctions must be supported and legislation designed to accomplish these ends formulated and passed.

(d) We favor legislation providing that products of convict labor shipped from one state to another shall be subject to laws of the latter state, as though they had been produced therein.

Unemployment

Unemployment is present, widespread and increasing. Unemployment is almost as destructive to the happiness, comfort, and well-being of human beings as war. We expend vast sums of money to protect our people against the evils of war, but no governmental program is anticipated to prevent the awful suffering and economic losses of unemployment. It threatens the well-being of millions of our people and endangers the prosperity of the nation. We favor the adoption by the government, after a study of this subject, of a scientific plan whereby during periods of unemployment appropriations shall be made available for the construction of necessary public works and the lessening, as far as consistent with public interests, of government construction work when labor is generally and satisfactorily employed in private enterprise.

Study should also be made of modern methods of industry and a constructive solution found to absorb and utilize the surplus human labor released by the increasing use of machinery.

ACCIDENT COMPENSATION TO GOVERNMENT EMPLOYEES

We favor legislation making fair and liberal compensation to government employees who are injured in accident or by occupational disease and to the dependents of such workers as may die as a result thereof.

FEDERAL EMPLOYEES

Federal employees should receive a living wage based upon American standards of decent living. Present wages are, in many instances, far below that standard. We favor a fair and liberal retirement law for government employees in the classified service.

VETERANS

Through Democratic votes, and in spite of two Republican Presidents' opposition, the Congress has maintained America's traditional policy to generously care for the veterans of the World War. In extending them free hospitalization, a statutory award for tuberculosis, a program of progressive hospital construction, and provisions for compensation for the disabled, the widows and orphans, America has surpassed the record of any nation in the history of the world. We pledge the veterans that none of the benefits heretofore accorded by the Wilson administration and the votes of Democrat members of Congress shall be withdrawn; that these will be added to more in accordance with the veterans' and their dependents' actual needs. Generous appropriations, honest management, the removal of vexatious administration delays, and sympathetic assistance for the veterans of all wars, is what the Democratic Party demands and promises.

WOMEN AND CHILDREN

We declare for equality of women with men in all political and governmental matters.

Children are the chief asset of the nation. Therefore their protection through infancy and childhood against exploitation is an important national duty.

The Democratic Party has always opposed the exploitation of women in industry and has stood for such conditions of work as will preserve their health and safety.

We favor an equal wage for equal service; and likewise favor adequate appropriations for the women's and children's bureau.

IMMIGRATION

Laws which limit immigration must be preserved in full force and effect, but the provisions contained in these laws that separate husbands from wives and parents from infant children are inhuman and not essential to the purpose or the efficacy of such laws.

RADIO

Government supervision must secure to all the people the advantage of radio communication and likewise guarantee the right of free speech. Official control in contravention of this guarantee should not be tolerated. Governmental control must prevent monopolistic use of radio communication and guarantee equitable distribution and enjoyment thereof.

COAL

Bituminous coal is not only the common base of manufacture, but it is a vital agency in our interstate transportation. The demoralization of this industry, its labor conflicts and distress, its waste of a national resource and disordered public service, demand constructive legislation that will allow capital and labor a fair share of prosperity, with adequate protection to the consuming public.

CONGRESSIONAL ELECTION REFORM

We favor legislation to prevent defeated members of both houses of Congress from participating in the sessions of Congress by fixing the date for convening the Congress immediately after the biennial national election.

LAW ENFORCEMENT

The Republican Party, for eight years in complete control of the government at Washington, presents the remarkable spectacle of feeling compelled in its national platform to promise obedience to a provision of the federal Constitution, which it has flagrantly disregarded and to apologize to the country for its failure to enforce laws enacted by the Congress of the United States. Speaking for the national Democracy, this convention pledges the party and its nominees to an honest effort to enforce the eighteenth amendment and all other provisions of the federal Constitution and all laws enacted pursuant thereto.

Campaign Expenditures

We condemn the improper and excessive use of money in elections as a danger threatening the very existence of democratic institutions. Republican expenditures in senatorial primaries and elections have been so exorbitant as to constitute a national scandal. We favor publicity in all matters affecting campaign contributions and expenditures. We shall, beginning not later than August 1, 1928, and every thirty days thereafter, the last publication and filing being not later than five days before the election, publish in the press and file with the appropriate committees of the House and Senate a complete account of all contributions, the names of the contributors, the amounts expended and the purposes for which the expenditures are made, and will, at all times, hold open for public inspection the books and records relating to such matters. In the event that any financial obligations are contracted and not paid, our National Committee will similarly report and publish, at least five days before the election, all details respecting such obligations.

We agree to keep and maintain a permanent record of all campaign contributions and expenditures and to insist that contributions by the citizens of one state to the campaign committees of other states shall have immediate publicity.

Merchant Marine

We reaffirm our support of an efficient, dependable American merchant marine for the carriage of the greater portion of our commerce and for the national defense.

The Democratic Party has consistently and vigorously supported the shipping services maintained by the regional United States Shipping Board in the interest of all ports and all sections of our country, and has successfully opposed the discontinuance of any of these lines. We favor the transfer of these lines gradually to the local private American companies, when such com-

panies can show their ability to take over and permanently maintain the lines. Lines that can not now be transferred to private enterprise should continue to be operated as at present and should be kept in an efficient state by remodeling of some vessels and replacement of others.

We are unalterably opposed to a monopoly in American shipping and are opposed to the operation of any of our services in a manner that would retard the development of any ports or section of our country.

We oppose such sacrifices and favoritism as exhibited in the past in the matter of alleged sales, and insist that the primary purpose of legislation upon this subject be the establishment and maintenance of an adequate American merchant marine.

Armenia

We favor the most earnest efforts on the part of the United States to secure the fulfillment of the promises and engagements made during and following the World War by the United States and the allied powers to Armenia and her people.

Education

We believe with Jefferson and other founders of the Republic that ignorance is the enemy of freedom and that each state, being responsible for the intellectual and moral qualifications of its citizens and for the expenditure of the moneys collected by taxation for the support of its schools, shall use its sovereign right in all matters pertaining to education.

The federal government should offer to the states such counsel, advice, results of research and aid as may be made available through the federal agencies for the general improvement of our schools in view of our national needs.

Monopolies and Anti-Trust Laws

During the last seven years, under Republican rule, the anti-trust laws have been thwarted, ignored and violated so that the country is rapidly becoming controlled by trusts and sinister monopolies formed for the purpose of wringing from the necessaries of life an unrighteous profit. These combinations are formed and conducted in violation of law, encouraged, aided and abetted in their activities by the Republican administration and are driving all small tradespeople and small industrialists out of business. Competition is one of the most sacred, cherished and economic rights of the American people. We demand the strict enforcement of the anti-trust laws and the enactment of other laws, if necessary, to control this great menace to trade and commerce, and thus to preserve the right of the small merchant and manufacturer to earn a legitimate profit from his business.

Dishonest business should be treated without influence at the national capitol. Honest business, no matter its size, need have no fears of a Democratic administration. The Democratic Party will ever oppose illegitimate and dishonest business. It will foster, promote, and encourage all legitimate enterprises.

Canal Zone

We favor the employment of American citizens in the operation and maintenance of the Panama Canal in all positions above the grade of messenger and favor as liberal wages and conditions of employment as prevailed under previous Democratic administrations.

Alaska—Hawaii

We favor the development of Alaska and Hawaii in the traditional American way, through self-government. We favor the appointment of only bona fide residents to office in the territories. We favor the extension and improvement of the mail, air mail, telegraph and radio, agricultural experimenting, highway construction, and other necessary federal activities in the territories.

Porto Rico

We favor granting to Porto Rico such territorial form of government as would meet the present economic conditions of the island, and provide for the aspirations of her people, with the view to ultimate statehood accorded to all territories of the United States since the beginning of our government, and we believe any officials appointed to administer the government of such territories should be qualified by previous bona fide residence therein.

Philippines

The Filipino people have succeeded in maintaining a stable government and have thus fulfilled the only condition laid down by the Congress as a prerequisite to the granting of independence. We declare that it is now our duty to keep our promise to these people by granting them immediately the independence which they so honorably covet.

Public Health

The Democratic Party recognizes that not only the productive wealth of the nation but its contentment and happiness depends upon the health of its citizens. It, therefore, pledges itself to enlarge the existing Bureau of Public Health and to do all things possible to stamp out communicable and contagious diseases, and to ascertain preventive means and remedies for these diseases, such as cancer, infantile paralysis and others which heretofore have largely defied the skill of physicians.

We pledge our party to spare no means to lift the apprehension of diseases from the minds of our people, and to appropriate all moneys necessary to carry out this pledge.

Conclusion

Affirming our faith in these principles, we submit our cause to the people.

Farmer-Labor Platform of 1928

1. We believe in using governmental powers to utilize the labor-saving features of our trusts and corporations in the interests of the people instead of for the profit of the few.

2. Unqualified enforcement of the constitutional guaranties of freedom of speech, press and assemblage.

3. Public ownership and permanent conservation under democratic public management of all natural resources, including coal, iron and other ores, oil, timber lands and all means of production and distribution, including railroads, super-power such as Muscle Shoals and Boulder Dam, or any industry that may become a monopoly.

4. Direct government issue of money paid into circulation and government operation of banking and exchange in the common interest.

5. Guaranteed public employment for all whom private industry does not employ, and unemployment insurance.

6. We believe in the enforcement of all laws.

7. Adequate farm relief by applying the prin-

ciple of an equalization fee and the acquisition by genuine co-operative societies as well as government ownership of grain elevators, storage and distributing agencies on a nonprofit basis, in the equitable interest of the farmer, city worker and consumer.

8. We favor abolition of the use of injunctions in labor disputes and declare for complete protection of the right of farmers' facilities.

9. We favor the ratification of the passed child labor amendment.

10. We favor a deep waterway from the great lakes to the sea. The government should, in conjunction with Canada, take immediate action to give the northwestern states an outlet to the ocean for cargoes without changing bulk, thus making the primary markets on the great lakes equal to those of New York.

11. We are opposed to exploitation and imperialism in all forms, and we favor the scrapping of all implements of warfare and the withdrawal of military forces from Nicaragua, and in non-interference in the local affairs of Mexico, Latin America, China or any other country.

12. We favor recognizing the Soviet Russian government and the establishment of trade relations.

13. Abolition of bureaus, commissions, committees or other like organizations exercising legislative or judicial powers.

14. We favor adequate pensions to the aged, to victims of war and industry, to widows and all indigents.

15. We demand that all men and women who served as welfare workers overseas be federalized, thereby making them eligible to pensions and hospitalization, and also they and the veterans choose their own method of treatment and choice of practitioner.

16. We believe in the calling of a constitutional convention to consider a throrough revision of our organic law in line with modern principles of human welfare.

17. We favor independence of the Philippines, autonomy for Porto Rico and civil government for the Virgin Islands.

18. We favor revision of tax laws so that large incomes and inheritances may be made to carry the burden of the cost of government and social insurance.

19. We favor proper legislation to assure economic reforestation, reclamation and irrigation, with particular consideration of the southern farmers' problems, also flood prevention and flood relief.

20. We favor the restoration of the franchise and complete self-government to citizens of the District of Columbia. We also favor legislation that will provide means for every adult citizen regardless of race or nationality to vote for national officers regardless of where one may be in the nation on election day, also to abolish the electoral college and "lame duck" sessions of congress, and election of president and vice-president by direct vote of the people.

Prohibition Platform for 1928 [1]

The Prohibition party contemplates with gratitude and solemn joy the triumphs of the great cause, of which, in partisan matters it has been the champion for threescore years, yet for the common victory we would not withhold recognition due the many thousands in times past and the unnumbered millions now, though not affiliated with our party, who firmly stood and now stand ardently for national prohibition.

We note in review that among political parties the Prohibition party is the only one in the last fifty years whose majority issue has triumphed. For half a century it was the lone sponsor of two policies now imbedded in the Constitution, viz: Prohibition and Woman Suffrage. Both are parts of our basic law and believed in by an overwhelming majority of the people. Forty-six of the forty-eight states have ratified Prohibition. The government is no longer a partner in the liquor traffic and no more takes tribute from the iniquitous trade in return for legal protection.

THE MAJOR PARTIES

We are glad to believe and declare that nullifi-

[1] A lengthy Prohibition Party Platform for 1928 was submitted by the party's Platform Committee to the party's national convention.

The convention was hopelessly split over whether or not to offer Prohibition Party candidates or to endorse the Republican candidate, Herbert Hoover. The delegates finally adopted this short platform together with a set of resolutions which provided that the Prohibition candidates would withdraw from the campaign if such a request were made by the party's Executive Committee.

cation of Federal provisions for enforcement of prohibition is not a tenet of the Democratic or Republican parties, but that all nullification is the act of liquor sympathizers whose disregard of all laws in conflict with their desires is common knowledge confirmed by heaped up precedents. Nullification was blasted by Andrew Jackson, the Democrat, in his day, and resisted to the death by Abraham Lincoln, the Republican. We deprecate the custom of political parties in their platforms charging all sins and shortcomings to each other. Oft-repeated folly does not thereby become wisdom, and falsehood frequently stated does not become the truth. We appeal to their sense of shame and intellectual pride for reform in this regard. A greater circumspection in putting officials in office will lessen the necessity of a call to turn the rascals out.

RESOLUTIONS ADOPTED BY THE PROHIBITION NATIONAL CONVENTION, CHICAGO, ILLINOIS, JULY 12, 1928

First: That the supreme objective of all good citizens of America in this campaign is to annihilate the beverage liquor traffic and maintain our Constitution which objective is opposed by the wet Tammany candidate;

Second: That the activities of the Prohibition party in this campaign shall be dominated by the purpose to promote the above objective;

Third: That we carry on a vigorous and effective campaign in behalf of the principle of National Prohibition of which our party was the pioneer champion;

Fourth: That we join with the good citizens of all parties in a union of forces to prevent the threatened calamity of the election of the wet Tammany candidate;

Fifth: That no separate presidential electors be placed upon the ballot in any state where the nomination of such electors will contribute to the election of said candidate;

Sixth: That in all states where we are an official party we nominate state and local candidates and carry on an aggressive campaign;

Seventh: That the Nominees of this Convention shall withdraw on request of the Executive Committee, at any time prior to September first next, and the said Committee is authorized and empowered to substitute other candidates supporting the objective named above.

Republican Platform of 1928

The Republican Party in national convention assembled presents to the people of the Nation this platform of its principles, based on a record of its accomplishments, and asks and awaits a new vote of confidence. We reaffirm our devotion to the Constitution of the United States and the principles and institution of the American system of representative government.

THE NATIONAL ADMINISTRATION

We endorse without qualification the record of the Coolidge administration.

The record of the Republican Party is a record of advancement of the nation. Nominees of Republican National conventions have for 52 of the 72 years since the creation of our party been the chief executives of the United States. Under Republican inspiration and largely under Republican executive direction the continent has been bound with steel rails, the oceans and great rivers have been joined by canals, waterways have been deepened and widened for ocean commerce, and with all a high American standard of wage and living has been established.

By unwavering adherence to sound principles, through the wisdom of Republican policies, and the capacity of Republican administrations, the foundations have been laid and the greatness and prosperity of the country firmly established.

Never has the soundness of Republican policies been more amply demonstrated and the Republican genius for administration been better exemplified than during the last five years under the leadership of President Coolidge.

No better guaranty of prosperity and contentment among all our people at home, no more reliable warranty of protection and promotion of American interests abroad can be given than the pledge to maintain and continue the Coolidge policies. This promise we give and will faithfully perform.

Under this Administration the country has been lifted from the depths of a great depression to a level of prosperity. Economy has been raised to the dignity of a principle of government. A standard of character in public service has been established under the chief Executive, which has given to the people of the country a feeling of stability and confidence so all have felt encouraged to proceed on new undertakings in trade and commerce. A foreign policy based on the traditional American position and carried on with wisdom and steadfastness has extended American influence throughout the world and everywhere promoted and protected American interests.

The mighty contribution to general well-being which can be made by a government controlled by men of character and courage, whose abilities are equal to their responsibilities, is self-evident, and should not blind us to the consequences which its loss would entail. Under this administration a high level of wages and living has been established and maintained. The door of opportunity has been opened wide to all. It has given to our people greater comfort and leisure, and the mutual profit has been evident in the increasingly harmonious relations between employers and employees, and the steady rise by promotion of the men in the shops to places at the council tables of the industries. It has also been made evident by the increasing enrollments of our youth in the technical schools and colleges, the increase in savings and life insurance accounts, and by our ability, as a people, to lend the hand of succor not only to those overcome by disasters in our own country but in foreign lands. With all there has been a steady decrease in the burden of Federal taxation, releasing to the people the greatest possible portion of the results of their labor from Government exactions.

For the Republican Party we are justified in claiming a major share of the credit for the position which the United States occupies today as the most favored nation on the globe, but it is well to remember that the confidence and prosperity which we enjoy can be shattered, if not destroyed, if this belief in the honesty and sincerity of our government is in any way affected. A continuation of this great public peace of mind now existing, which makes for our material well being, is only possible by holding fast to the plans and principles which have marked Republican control.

The record of the present Administration is a guaranty of what may be expected of the next. Our words have been made deeds. We offer not promises but accomplishments.

PUBLIC ECONOMY

The citizen and taxpayer has a natural right to be protected from unnecessary and wasteful expenditures. This is a rich but also a growing nation with constantly increasing legitimate demands for public funds. If we are able to spend wisely and meet these requirements, it is first necessary that we save wisely. Spending extravagantly not only deprives men through taxation of the fruits of their labor, but oftentimes means the postponement of vitally important public works. We commend President Coolidge for his establishment of this fundamental principle of sound administration and pledge ourselves to live up to the high standard he has set.

FINANCE AND TAXATION

The record of the United States Treasury under Secretary Mellon stands unrivalled and unsurpassed. The finances of the nation have been managed with sound judgment. The financial policies have yielded immediate and substantial results.

In 1921 the credit of our government was at a low ebb. We were burdened with a huge public debt, a load of war taxes, which in variety and weight exceeded anything in our national life, while vast unfunded intergovernmental debts disorganized the economic life of the debtor nations and seriously affected our own by reason of the serious obstacles which they presented to commercial intercourse. This critical situation was evidenced by a serious disturbance in our own life which made for unemployment.

Today all these major financial problems have been solved.

THE PUBLIC DEBT

In seven years the public debt has been reduced by $6,411,000,000. From March 1921 to September 1928 over eleven billion dollars of securities, bearing high rates of interest, will have been retired or refunded into securities bearing a low rate of interest, while Liberty Bonds, which were selling below par, now command a premium. These operations have resulted in an annual saving in interest charges of not less than $275,000,000, without which the most recent tax reduction measure would not have been made possible. The Republican Party will continue to reduce our National debt as rapidly as possible and in accordance with the provision of existing laws and the present program.

TAX REDUCTION

Wise administrative management under Republican control and direction has made possible a reduction of over a billion eight hundred million dollars a year in the tax bill of the American people. Four separate tax reduction measures have been enacted, and millions of those least able to pay have been taken from the tax rolls.

Excessive and uneconomic rates have been radically modified, releasing for industrial and payroll expansion and development great sums of money which formerly were paid in taxes to the Federal government.

Practically all the war taxes have been eliminated and our tax system has been definitely restored to a peace time basis.

We pledge our party to a continuation of these sound policies and to such further reduction of the tax burden as the condition of the Treasury may from time to time permit.

TARIFF

We reaffirm our belief in the protective tariff as a fundamental and essential principle of the economic life of this nation. While certain provisions of the present law require revision in the light of changes in the world competitive situation since its enactment, the record of the United States since 1922 clearly shows that the fundamental protective principle of the law has been fully justified. It has stimulated the development of our natural resources, provided fuller employment at higher wages through the promotion of industrial activity, assured thereby the continuance of the farmer's major market, and further raised the standards of living and general comfort and well-being of our people. The great expansion in the wealth of our nation during the past fifty years, and particularly in the past decade, could not have been accomplished without a protective tariff system designed to promote the vital interests of all classes.

Nor have these manifest benefits been restricted to any particular section of the country. They are enjoyed throughout the land either directly or indirectly. Their stimulus has been felt in industries, farming sections, trade circles, and communities in every quarter. However, we realize that there are certain industries which cannot now successfully compete with foreign producers because of lower foreign wages and a lower cost of living abroad, and we pledge the next Republican Congress to an examination and where necessary a revision of these schedules to the end that American labor in these industries may again command the home market, may maintain its standard of living, and may count upon steady employment in its accustomed field.

Adherence to that policy is essential for the continued prosperity of the country. Under it the standard of living of the American people has been raised to the highest levels ever known. Its example has been eagerly followed by the rest of the world whose experts have repeatedly reported with approval the relationship of this policy to our prosperity, with the resultant emulation of that example by other nations.

A protective tariff is as vital to American agriculture as it is to American manufacturing. The Republican Party believes that the home market, built up under the protective policy, belongs to the American farmer, and it pledges its support of legislation which will give this market to him to the full extent of his ability to supply it. Agriculture derives large benefits not only directly from the protective duties levied on competitive farm products of foreign origin, but also, indirectly, from the increase in the purchasing power of American workmen employed in industries similarly protected. These benefits extend also to persons engaged in trade, transportation, and other activities.

The Tariff Act of 1922 has justified itself in the expansion of our foreign trade during the past five years. Our domestic exports have increased from 3.8 billions of dollars in 1922 to 4.8 billions in 1927. During the same period imports have increased from 3.1 billions to 4.4 billions. Contrary to the prophesies of its critics, the present tariff law has not hampered the natural growth in the exportation of the products of American agriculture, industry, and mining, nor has it restricted the importation of foreign commodities which this country can utilize without jeopardizing its economic structure.

The United States is the largest customer in the world today. If we were not prosperous and able to buy, the rest of the world also would suffer. It is inconceivable that American labor will ever consent to the abolition of protection which would bring the American standard of living down to the level of that in Europe, or that the American farmer could survive if the enormous consuming power of the people in this country were curtailed and its market at home, if not destroyed, at least seriously impaired.

Foreign Debts

In accordance with our settled policy and platform pledges, debt settlement agreements have been negotiated with all of our foreign debtors with the exception of Armenia and Russia. That with France remains as yet unratified. Those with Greece and Austria are before the Congress for necessary authority. If the French Debt Settlement be included, the total amount funded is eleven billion five hundred twenty-two million three hundred fifty-four thousand dollars. We have steadfastly opposed and will continue to oppose cancellation of foreign debts.

We have no desire to be oppressive or grasping, but we hold that obligations justly incurred should be honorably discharged. We know of no authority which would permit public officials, acting as trustees, to shift the burden of the War from the shoulders of foreign taxpayers to those of our own people. We believe that the settlements agreed to are fair to both the debtor nation and to the American taxpayer. Our Debt Commission took into full consideration the economic condition and resources of the debtor nations, and were ever mindful that they must be permitted to preserve and improve their economic position, to bring their budgets into balance, to place their currencies and finances on a sound basis, and to improve the standard of living of their people. Giving full weight to these considerations, we know of no fairer test than ability to pay, justly estimated.

The people can rely on the Republican Party to adhere to a foreign debt policy now definitely established and clearly understood both at home and abroad.

Settlement of War Claims

A satisfactory solution has been found for the question of War Claims. Under the Act, approved by the President on March 10, 1928, a provision was made for the settlement of War Claims of the United States and its citizens against the German, Austrian and Hungarian Governments, and of the claims of the nationals of these governments against the United States; and for the return to its owners of the property seized by the Alien Property Custodian during the War, in accordance with our traditional policy of respect for private property.

Foreign Policies

We approve the foreign policies of the Administration of President Coolidge. We believe they express the will of the American people in working actively to build up cordial international understanding that will make world peace a permanent reality. We endorse the proposal of the Secretary of State for a multilateral treaty proposed to the principal powers of the world and open to the signatures of all nations, to renounce war as an instrument of national policy and declaring in favor of pacific settlement of international disputes, the first step in outlawing war. The idea has stirred the conscience of mankind and gained widespread approval, both of governments and of the people, and the conclusion of the treaty will be acclaimed as the greatest single step in history toward the conservation of peace.

In the same endeavor to substitute for war the peaceful settlement of international disputes the administration has concluded arbitration treaties in a form more definite and more inclusive than ever before and plans to negotiate similar treaties with all countries willing in this manner to define their policy peacefully to settle justiciable disputes. In connection with these, we endorse the Resolution of the Sixth Pan American Conference held at Havana, Cuba, in 1928, which called a conference on arbitration and conciliation to meet in Washington during the year and express our earnest hope that such conference will greatly further the principles of international arbitration. We shall continue to demand the same respect and protection for the persons and property of American citizens in foreign countries that we cheerfully accord in this country to the persons and property of aliens.

The commercial treaties which we have negotiated and those still in the process of negotiation are based on strict justice among nations, equal opportunity for trade and commerce on the most-favored-nation principle and are simplified so as to eliminate the danger of misunderstanding. The object and the aim of the United States is to further the cause of peace, of strict justice between nations with due regard for the rights of others in all international dealings. Out of justice grows peace. Justice and consideration have been and will continue to be the inspiration of our nation.

The record of the Administration toward Mexico has been consistently friendly and with equal consistency have we upheld American rights. This firm and at the same time friendly policy has brought recognition of the inviolability of legally acquired rights. This condition has been reached without threat or without bluster, through a calm support of the recognized principles of international law with due regard to the rights of a sister sovereign state. The Republican Party will continue to support American rights in Mexico, as elsewhere in the world, and at the same time to promote and strengthen friendship and confidence.

There has always been, as there always will be, a firm friendship with Canada. American and Canadian interests are in a large measure identical. Our relationship is one of fine mutual understanding and the recent exchange of diplomatic officers between the two countries is worthy of commendation.

The United States has an especial interest in the advancement and progress of all the Latin American countries. The policy of the Republican Party will always be a policy of thorough friendship and co-operation. In the case of Nicaragua, we are engaged in co-operation with the government of that country upon the task of assisting to restore and maintain peace, order and stability, and in no way to infringe upon her sovereign rights. The Marines, now in Nicaragua, are there to protect American lives and property and to aid in carrying out an agreement whereby we have undertaken to do what we can to restore and maintain order and to insure a fair and free election. Our policy absolutely repudiates any idea of conquest or exploitation, and is actuated solely by an earnest and sincere desire to assist a friendly and neighboring state which has appealed for aid in a great emergency. It is the same policy the United States has pursued in other cases in Central America.

The Administration has looked with keen sympathy on the tragic events in China. We have avoided interference in the internal affairs of that unhappy nation merely keeping sufficient naval and military forces in China to protect the lives of the Americans who are there on legitimate business and in still larger numbers for nobly humanitarian reasons. America has not been stampeded into making reprisals but, on the other hand, has consistently taken the position of leadership among the nations in a policy of wise moderation. We shall always be glad to be of assistance to China when our duty is clear.

The Republican Party maintains the traditional American policy of non-interference in the political affairs of other nations. This government has definitely refused membership in the League of Nations and to assume any obligations under the covenant of the League.

On this we stand.

In accordance, however, with the long established American practice of giving aid and assistance to other peoples, we have most usefully assisted by co-operation in the humanitarian and technical work undertaken by the League, without involving ourselves in European politics by accepting membership.

The Republican Party has always given and will continue to give its support to the development of American foreign trade, which makes for domestic prosperity. During this administration extraordinary strides have been made in opening up new markets for American produce and manufacture. Through these foreign contacts a mutually better international understanding has been reached which aids in the maintenance of world peace.

The Republican Party promises a firm and consistent support of American persons and legitimate American interests in all parts of the world. This support will never contravene the rights of other nations. It will always have in mind and support in every way the progressive development of international law, since it is through the operation of just laws, as well as through the growth of friendly understanding, that world peace will be made permanent. To that end the Republican Party pledges itself to aid and assist in the perfection of principles of international law and the settlement of international disputes.

CIVIL SERVICE

The merit system in government service originated with and has been developed by the Republican Party. The great majority of our public service employees are now secured through and maintained in the government service rules. Steps have already been taken by the Republican Congress to make the service more attractive as to wages and retirement privileges, and we commend what has been done, as a step in the right direction.

AGRICULTURE

The agricultural problem is national in scope and, as such, is recognized by the Republican Party which pledges its strength and energy to the solution of the same. Realizing that many farmers are facing problems more difficult than those which are the portion of many other basic industries, the party is anxious to aid in every way possible. Many of our farmers are still going through readjustments, a relic of the years directly following the great war. All the farmers are being called on to meet new and perplexing conditions created by foreign competition, the complexities of domestic marketing, labor problems, and a steady increase in local and state taxes.

The general depression in a great basic industry inevitably reacts upon the conditions in the country as a whole and cannot be ignored. It is a matter of satisfaction that the desire to help in the correction of agricultural wrongs and conditions is not confined to any one section of our country or any particular group.

The Republican Party and the Republican Administration, particularly during the last five years, have settled many of the most distressing problems as they have arisen, and the achievements in aid of agriculture are properly a part of this record. The Republican Congresses have been most responsive in the matter of agricultural appropriations, not only to meet crop emergencies, but for the extension and development of the activities of the Department of Agriculture.

The protection of the American farmer against foreign farm competition and foreign trade practices has been vigorously carried on by the Department of State. The right of the farmers to engage in collective buying and co-operative selling as provided for by the Capper-Volstead Act of 1922 has been promulgated through the Department of Agriculture and the Department of Justice, which have given most valuable aid and assistance to the heads of the farm organizations. The Treasury Department and the proper committees of Congress have lightened the tax burden on farming communities, and through the Federal Farm Loan System there has been made available to the farmers of the nation one billion eight hundred fifty millions of dollars for loaning purposes at a low rate of interest, and through the Intermediate Credit Banks six hundred fifty-five million dollars of short term credits have been made available to the farmers. The Post Office Department has systematically and generously extended the Rural Free Delivery routes into even the most sparsely settled communities.

When a shortage of transportation facilities threatened to deprive the farmers of their opportunity to reach waiting markets overseas, the President, appreciative and sensitive of the condition and the possible loss to the communities, ordered the reconditioning of Shipping Board vessels, thus relieving a great emergency.

Last, but not least, the Federal Tariff Commission has at all times shown a willingness under the provisions of the Flexible Tariff Act to aid the farmers when foreign competition, made possible by low wage scales abroad, threatened to deprive our farmers of their domestic markets. Under this Act the President has increased duties on wheat, flour, mill feed, and dairy products. Numerous other farm products are now being investigated by the Tariff Commission.

We promise every assistance in the reorganization of the marketing system on sounder and more economical lines and, where diversification is needed, Government financial assistance during the period of transition.

The Republican Party pledges itself to the enactment of legislation creating a Federal Farm Board clothed with the necessary powers to promote the establishment of a farm marketing system of farmer-owned-and-controlled stabilization corporations or associations to prevent and control surpluses through orderly distribution.

We favor adequate tariff protection to such of our agricultural products as are affected by foreign competition.

We favor, without putting the Government into business, the establishment of a Federal system of organization for co-operative and orderly marketing of farm products.

The vigorous efforts of this Administration towards broadening our exports market will be continued.

The Republican Party pledges itself to the development and enactment of measures which will place the agricultural interests of America on a basis of economic equality with other industries to insure its prosperity and success.

MINING

The money value of the mineral products of the country is second only to agriculture. We lead the countries of the world in the production of coal, iron, copper and silver. The nation suffers as a whole from any disturbance in the securing of any one of these minerals, and particularly when the coal supply is affected. The mining industry has always been self-sustaining, but we believe that the Government should make every effort to aid the industry by protection by removing any restrictions which may be hampering its development, and by increased technical and economic research investigations which are necessary for its welfare and normal development. The Party is anxious, hopeful, and willing to assist in any feasible plan for the stabilization of the coal mining industry, which will work with justice to the miners, consumers and producers.

HIGHWAYS

Under the Federal Aid Road Act, adopted by the Republican Congress in 1921, and supplemented by generous appropriations each year, road construction has made greater advancement than for many decades previous. Improved highway conditions is a gauge of our rural developments and our commercial activity. We pledge our support to continued appropriations for this work commensurate with our needs and resources.

We favor the construction of roads and trails in our national forests necessary to their protection and utilization. In appropriations therefor the taxes which these lands would pay if taxable should be considered as a controlling factor.

LABOR

The Labor record of the Republican Party stands unchallenged. For 52 of the 72 years of our national existence Republican Administrations have prevailed. Today American labor enjoys the highest wage and the highest standard of living throughout the world. Through the saneness and soundness of Republican rule the American workman is paid a "real wage" which allows comfort for himself and his dependents, and an opportunity and leisure for advancement. It is not surprising that the foreign workman, whose greatest ambition still is to achieve a "living wage," should look with longing towards America as the goal of his desires.

The ability to pay such wages and maintain such a standard comes from the wisdom of the protective legislation which the Republican Party has placed upon the national statute books, the tariff which bars cheap foreign-made goods from the American market and provides continuity of employment for our workmen and fair profits for the manufacturers, the restriction of immigration which not only prevents the glutting of our labor market, but allows to our newer immigrants a greater opportunity to secure a footing in their upward struggle.

The Party favors freedom in wage contracts, the right of collective bargaining by free and responsible agents of their own choosing, which develops and maintains that purposeful co-operation which gains its chief incentive through voluntary agreement.

We believe that injunctions in labor disputes have in some instances been abused and have given rise to a serious question for legislation.

The Republican Party pledges itself to continue its efforts to maintain this present standard of living and high wage scale.

RAILROADS

Prompt and effective railroad service at the lowest rates which will provide for its maintenance and allow a reasonable return to the investor so they may be encouraged to advance new capital for acquired developments, has long been recognized by the Republican Party as a necessity of national existence.

We believe that the present laws under which our railroads are regulated are soundly based on correct principles, the spirit of which must always be preserved. Because, however, of changes in the public demands, trade conditions and of the character of the competition, which even the greatest railroads are now being called upon to meet, we feel that in the light of this new experience possible modifications or amendments, the need of which is proved, should be considered.

The Republican Party initiated and set in operation the Interstate Commerce Commission. This body has developed a system of railroad control and regulation which has given to the transportation public an opportunity not only to make suggestions for the improvement of railroad service, but to protest against discriminatory rates or schedules. We commend the work which that body is accomplishing under mandate of law in considering these matters and seeking to distribute equitably the burden of transportation between commodities based on their ability to bear the same.

MERCHANT MARINE

The Republican Party stands for the American-built, American-owned, and American-operated merchant marine. The enactment of the White-Jones Bill is in line with a policy which the party has long advocated.

Under this measure, substantial aid and encouragement are offered for the building in American yards of new and modern ships which will carry the American flag.

The Republican Party does not believe in government ownership or operation, and stands specifically for the sale of the present government vessels to private owners when appropriate arrangements can be made. Pending such a sale, and because private owners are not ready as yet to operate on certain of the essential trade routes, the bill enacted allows the maintenance of these necessary lines under government control till such transfer can be made.

MISSISSIPPI FLOOD RELIEF AND CONTROL

The Mississippi Valley flood in which seven hundred thousand of our fellow citizens were placed in peril of life, and which destroyed hundreds of million of dollars' worth of property, was met with energetic action by the Republican Administration.

During this disaster the President mobilized every public and private agency under the direction of Secretary Hoover of the Department of Commerce and Dwight Davis, the Secretary of War. Thanks to their joint efforts, a great loss of life was prevented and everything possible was done to rehabilitate the people in their homes and to relieve suffering and distress.

Congress promptly passed legislation authorizing the expenditure of $325,000,000 for the construction of flood control works, which it is believed will prevent the recurrence of such a disaster.

RADIO

We stand for the administration of the radio facilities of the United States under wise and expert government supervision which will

(1) Secure to every home in the nation, whether city or country, the great educational and inspirational values of broadcast programs, adequate in number and varied in character, and

(2) Assign the radio communication channels, regional, continental, and transoceanic,—in the best interest of the American business man, the American farmer, and the American public generally.

WATERWAYS

Cheaper transportation for bulk goods from the midwest agricultural sections to the sea is recognized by the Republican Party as a vital factor for the relief of agriculture. To that end we favor the continued development in inland and in intra-coastal waterways as an essential part of our transportation system.

The Republican Administration during the last four years initiated the systematic development of the Mississippi system of inland transportation lanes, and it proposes to carry on this modernization of transportation to speedy completion. Great improvements have been made during this administration in our harbors, and the party pledges itself to continue these activities for the modernization of our national equipment.

VETERANS

Our country is honored whenever it bestows relief on those who have faithfully served its flag. The Republican Party, appreciative of this solemn obligation and honor, has made its sentiments evident in Congress. Our expenditures for the benefit of all our veterans now aggregate 750 million dollars annually. Increased hospital facilities have been provided, payments in compensation have more than doubled, and in the matter of rehabilitations, pensions, and insurance, generous provision has been made. The administration of laws dealing with the relief of veterans and their dependents has been a difficult task, but every effort has been made to carry service to the veteran and bring about not only a better and generous interpretation of the law, but a sympathetic consideration of the many problems of the veteran. Full and adequate relief for our disabled veterans is our aim, and we commend the action of Congress in further liberalizing the laws applicable to veterans' relief.

PUBLIC UTILITIES

Republican Congresses and Administrations have steadily strengthened the Interstate Commerce Commission. The protection of the public from exactions or burdens in rates for service by reason of monopoly control, and the protection of the smaller organizations from suppression in their own field, has been a fundamental idea in all regulatory enactments. While recognizing that at times Federal regulations might be more effective than State regulations in controlling intrastate utilities, the Party favors and has sustained State regulations, believing that such responsibility in the end will create a force of State public opinion which will be more effective in preventing discriminations and injustices.

CONSERVATION

We believe in the practical application of the conservation principle by the wise development of our natural resources. The measure of development is our national requirement, and avoidance of waste so that future generations may share in this natural wealth. The Republican policy is to prevent monopolies in the control and utilization of natural resources. Under the General Leasing Law, enacted by a Republican Congress, the ownership of the mineral estate remains in the Government, but development occurs through private capital and energy. Important for the operation of this law is the classification and appraisement of public lands according to their mineral content and value. Over five hundred million acres of public land have been thus classified.

To prevent wasteful exploitation of our oil products, President Coolidge appointed an Oil Conservation Board, which is now conducting an inquiry into all phases of petroleum production, in the effort to devise a national policy for the conservation and proper utilization of our oil resources.

The Republican Party has been forehanded in assuring the development of water power in accordance with public interest. A policy of permanent public retention of the power sites on public land and power privileges in domestic and international navigable streams, and one-third of the potential water power resources in the United States on public domain, has been assured by the Federal Water Powers Act, passed by a Republican Congress.

LAW ENFORCEMENT

We reaffirm the American Constitutional Doctrine as announced by George Washington in his "Farewell Address," to-wit:

"The Constitution which at any time exists until changed by the explicit and authentic act by the whole people is sacredly obligatory upon all."

We also reaffirm the attitude of the American people toward the Federal Constitution as declared by Abraham Lincoln:

"We are by both duty and inclination bound to stick by that Constitution in all its letter and spirit from beginning to end. I am for the honest enforcement of the Constitution. Our safety, our liberty, depends upon preserving the Constitution of the United States, as our forefathers made it inviolate."

The people through the method provided by the Constitution have written the Eighteenth Amendment into the Constitution. The Republican Party pledges itself and its nominees to the observance and vigorous enforcement of this provision of the Constitution.

HONESTY IN GOVERNMENT

We stand for honesty in government, for the appointment of officials whose integrity cannot be questioned. We deplore the fact that any official has ever fallen from this high standard and that certain American citizens of both parties have so far forgotten their duty as citizens as to traffic in national interests for private gain. We have prosecuted and shall always prosecute any official who subordinates his public duty to his personal interest.

The Government today is made up of thousands of conscientious, earnest, self-sacrificing men and women, whose single thought is service to the nation.

We pledge ourselves to maintain and, if possible, to improve the quality of this great company of Federal employees.

CAMPAIGN EXPENDITURES

Economy, honesty, and decency in the conduct of political campaigns are a necessity if representative government is to be preserved to the people and political parties are to hold the respect of the citizens at large.

The Campaign of 1924 complied with all these requirements. It was a campaign, the expenses of which were carefully budgeted in advance, and, which, at the close, presented a surplus and not a deficit.

There will not be any relaxing of resolute endeavor to keep our elections clean, honest and free from taint of any kind. The improper use of money in governmental and political affairs is a great national evil. One of the most effective remedies for this abuse is publicity in all matters touching campaign contributions and expenditures. The Republican Party, beginning not later than August 1, 1928, and every 30 days thereafter,—the last publication being not later than five days before the election—will file with the Committees of the House and Senate a complete account of all contributions, the names of the contributors, the amounts expended, and for what purposes, and will at all times hold its records and books touching such matters open for inspection.

The party further pledges that it will not create, or permit to be created, any deficit which shall exist at the close of the campaign.

RECLAMATION

Federal reclamation of arid lands is a Republican policy, adopted under President Roosevelt, carried forward by succeeding Republican Presidents, and put upon a still higher plane of efficiency and production by President Coolidge. It has increased the wealth of the nation and made the West more prosperous.

An intensive study of the methods and practices of reclamation has been going on for the past four years under the direction of the Department of the Interior in an endeavor to create broader human opportunities and their financial and economic success. The money value of the crops raised on reclamation projects is showing a steady and gratifying increase as well as the number of farms and people who have settled on the lands.

The continuation of a surplus of agricultural products in the selling markets of the world has influenced the Department to a revaluation of plans and projects. It has adopted a ten-year program for the completion of older projects and will hold other suggestions in abeyance until the surveys now under way as to the entire scope of the work are completed.

COMMERCIAL AVIATION

Without governmental grants or subsidies and entirely by private initiative, the nation has made extraordinary advances in the field of commercial aviation. Over 20,000 miles of air mail service privately operated are now being flown daily, and the broadening of this service is an almost weekly event. Because of our close relations with our sister republics on the south and our neighbor on the north, it is fitting our first efforts should be to establish an air communication with Latin-America and Canada.

The achievements of the aviation branches of the Army and Navy are all to the advantage of commercial aviation, and in the Mississippi flood disaster the work performed by civil and military aviators was of inestimable value.

The development of a system of aircraft registration, inspection and control is a credit to the Republican Administration, which, quick to appreciate the importance of this new transportation development, created machinery for its safeguarding.

IMMIGRATION

The Republican Party believes that in the interest of both native and foreign-born wage-earners, it is necessary to restrict immigration. Unrestricted immigration would result in widespread unemployment and in the breakdown of the American standard of living. Where, however, the law works undue hardships by depriving the immigrant of the comfort and society of those bound by close family ties, such modification should be adopted as will afford relief.

We commend Congress for correcting defects for humanitarian reasons and for providing an effective system of examining prospective immigrants in their home countries.

NATURALIZATION

The priceless heritage of American citizenship is our greatest gift to our friends of foreign birth.

Only those who will be loyal to our institutions, who are here in conformity with our laws, and who are in sympathy with our national traditions, ideals, and principles, should be naturalized.

NAVY

We pledge ourselves to round out and maintain the Navy in all types of combatant ships to the full ratio provided for the United States by the Washington Treaty for the Limitation of Naval Armament and any amendment thereto.

HAWAII-ALASKA

We favor a continuance for the Territory of Hawaii of Federal assistance in harbor improvements, the appropriation of its share of federal funds and the systematic extension of the settlement of public lands by the Hawaiian race.

We indorse the policy of the present administration with reference to Alaska and favor a continuance of the constructive development of the territory.

WOMEN AND PUBLIC SERVICE

Four years ago at the Republican National Convention in Cleveland women members of the National Committee were welcomed into full association and responsibility in party management. During the four years which have passed they have carried with their men associates an equal share of all responsibilities and their contribution to the success of the 1924 campaign is well recognized.

The Republican Party, which from the first has sought to bring this development about, accepts wholeheartedly equality on the part of women, and in the public service it can present a record of appointments of women in the legal, diplomatic, judicial, treasury and other governmental departments. We earnestly urge on the women that they participate even more generally than now in party management and activity.

NATIONAL DEFENSE

We believe that in time of war the nation should draft for its defense not only its citizens but also every resource which may contribute to success. The country demands that should the United States ever again be called upon to defend itself by arms, the President be empowered to draft such material resources and such services as may

be required, and to stabilize the prices of services and essential commodities, whether utilized in actual warfare or private activity.

OUR INDIAN CITIZENS

National citizenship was conferred upon all native born Indians in the United States by the General Indian Enfranchisement Act of 1924. We favor the creation of a Commission to be appointed by the President including one or more Indian citizens to investigate and report to Congress upon the existing system of the administration of Indian affairs and to report any inconsistencies that may be found to exist between that system and the rights of the Indian citizens of the United States. We also favor the repeal of any law and the termination of any administrative practice which may be inconsistent with Indian citizenship, to the end that the Federal guardianship existing over the persons and properties of Indian tribal communities may not work a prejudice to the personal and property rights of Indian citizens of the United States. The treaty and property rights of the Indians of the United States must be guaranteed to them.

THE NEGRO

We renew our recommendation that the Congress enact at the earliest possible date a Federal Anti-Lynching Law so that the full influence of the Federal Government may be wielded to exterminate this hideous crime.

HOME RULE

We believe in the essential unity of the American people. Sectionalism in any form is destructive of national life. The Federal Government should zealously protect the national and international rights of its citizens. It should be equally zealous to respect and maintain the rights of the States and territories and to uphold the vigor and balance of our dual system of government. The Republican party has always given its energies to supporting the Government in this direction when any question has arisen.

There are certain other well-defined Federal obligations such as interstate commerce, the development of rivers and harbors, and the guarding and conservation of national resources. The effort, which, however, is being continually made to have the Federal Government move into the field of state activities, has never had, and never will have the support of the Republican Party. In the majority of the cases state citizens and officers are most pressing in their desire to have the Federal Government take over these state functions. This is to be deplored for it weakens the sense of initiative and creates a feeling of dependence which is unhealthy and unfortunate for the whole body politic.

There is a real need of restoring the individual and local sense principles; there is a real need of restoring the individual and local sense of responsibility and self-reliance; there is a real need for the people once more to grasp the fundamental fact that under our system of government they are expected to solve many problems themselves through their municipal and State governments, and to combat the tendency that is all too common to turn to the Federal Government as the easiest and least burdensome method of lightening their own responsibilities.

Socialist Party National Platform, 1928

PREAMBLE

We Americans are told that we live in the most prosperous country in the world. Certainly, our natural resources, our mechanical equipment, our physical power, the technical capacity of our engineers and the skill of our workers in farm and factory make it possible for us to attain a level of well-being of which our fathers never dared to dream.

Yet poverty abounds. The owners of our natural resources and industrial equipment and the government which they have made virtually their tool have not given us plenty, freedom or peace in any such degree as we have the right and duty to demand.

Men are hungry while farmers go bankrupt for lack of effective demand for food. Tenant farming has reached a proportion of almost 40 per cent; more than 40 per cent of the value of farm lands is covered by mortgages. Industrial workers are scarcely better off. In good years there are at least 1,000,000 unemployed. By a conservative estimate in these times of stock market prosperity the number has arisen to 4,000,000. About ⅓ of those of our population 65 years of age and upward are at least partially dependent upon some form of charity. While real wages have risen for

certain groups they have risen scarcely more than half the increase of productive power of the workers. And what gains have been made are far from universal as the misery of textile workers and the tragedy of the coal fields—to cite only two examples—abundantly prove. In fact, at the present time a majority of workers obtain a wage insufficient to maintain themselves and families in health and decency. Furthermore the rapid increase in the use of machinery and the growing intensity of work are leading to quicker exhaustion and greater insecurity.

UNIONS BEREFT OF RIGHTS BY CLASS JUSTICE

Meanwhile the owning class has been using the government to curtail the power of the workers whose organized might, especially through their unions, has been chiefly responsible for whatever material gains they have made. To curb the workers, civil liberties are denied, injunctions are invoked against union activities and the courts are made the instruments of that class justice of which the Mooney case and the legalized murder of Sacco and Vanzetti were conspicuous examples.

Not only plenty and freedom but peace is endangered by this system under which the many are exploited for the profit of the few. Sons of the workers now die in President Coolidge's infamous little imperialist war in Nicaragua, as they died in President Wilson's similar wars in Haiti, Santo Domingo and Mexico, and above all in that great imperialistic war born of the trade and financial rivalries of the nations which cost our country forty billion dollars and hundreds of thousands of lives.

From the wars, waste and cruelty of a system where the rightful heritage of the workers is the private property of the few only the united efforts of farmers and workers of hand and brain, through their cooperatives, unions and political party, can save us. We must make government in cities, states and nation the servant of the people. That requires our own political party. We cannot place our trust in "good men" or political Messiahs. Bitter experience has proved that we cannot trust the alternate rule of the Republican and Democratic parties. They belong to the landlords, bankers, oil speculators, coal and power barons, in short to the capitalist class which finances them. Under their control the government by what it does and leaves undone, by its calculated inefficiency as well as its repression and corruption, makes our alleged democracy largely an illusion. Corruption is natural under parties which are the tools of the forces of privilege. It has become accepted even by the men who are victims of it.

Labor's Weapon in the Class Struggle

These things need not be. The Socialist Party offers itself as the political party of the producing classes, the workers in farm, factory, mine or office. It is our political weapon in the class struggle and in its triumph lies our hope of ending that struggle. Our record proves our good faith. As the only democratic labor party in the United States, we stand now as always, in America and in all lands, for the collective ownership of natural resources and basic industries and their democratic management for the use and benefit of all instead of the private profit of the privileged few.

With this ultimate aim in view, the Socialist Party enters the presidential campaign of 1928 with the following program:

Public Ownership and Conservation

To recover the rightful heritage of the people we propose:

1. Nationalization of our natural resources, beginning with the coal mines and water sites, particularly at Boulder Dam and Muscle Shoals.

2. A publicly owned giant power system under which the federal government shall cooperate with the states and municipalities in the distribution of electrical energy to the people at cost. Only when public agencies have full control over the generation, transmission and distribution of electrical power can the consumers be guaranteed against exploitation by the great electrical interests of the country. Public ownership of these and other industries must include employee representation in the management and the principle of collective bargaining must be recognized.

3. National ownership and democratic management of railroads and other means of transportation and communication.

4. An adequate national program for flood control, flood relief, reforestation, irrigation and reclamation.

Unemployment Relief

To relieve the tragic misery of millions of unemployed workers and their families we propose:

1. Immediate governmental relief of the unemployed by the extension of all public works and a program of long range planning of public works following the present depression. All persons thus employed to be engaged at hours and wages fixed by bona-fide labor unions.

2. Loans to states and municipalities without interest for the purpose of carrying on public works and the taking of such other measures as will lessen widespread misery.

3. A system of unemployment insurance.

4. The nation-wide extension of public employment agencies in cooperation with city federations of labor.

Labor Legislation

The lives and well-being of the producers and their families should be the first charge on society. We therefore urge:

1. A system of health and accident insurance and of old age pension as well as unemployment insurance. As long as workers are dependent primarily upon their employers rather than on the community for protection against the exigencies of old age, sickness, accident and unemployment, employers hostile or indifferent to the labor movement will be able to use their private insurance schemes as powerful weapons against organized labor.

2. Shortening the workday in keeping with the steadily increasing productivity of labor due to improvements in machinery and methods.

3. Securing to every worker a rest period of no less than two days in each week.

4. Enacting of an adequate federal anti-child labor amendment.

5. Abolition of the brutal exploitation of convicts under the contract system and substitution of a cooperative organization of industries in penitentiaries and workshops for the benefit of convicts and their dependents, the products to be used in public institutions, and the convict workers to be employed at wages current in the industry.

Taxation

For the proper support of government and as a step toward social justice we propose:

1. Increase of taxation on high income levels, of corporation taxes and inheritance taxes, the proceeds to be used for old age pensions and other forms of social insurance.

2. Appropriation by taxation of the annual rental value of all land held for speculation.

CIVIL LIBERTIES

To secure to the people the civil rights without which democracy is impossible, we demand:

1. Federal legislation to enforce the first amendment to the constitution so as to guarantee effectually freedom of speech, press and assembly, and to penalize any official who interferes with the civil rights of any citizen.

2. Abolition of injunctions in labor disputes.

3. Repeal of the espionage law and of other repressive legislation and restoration of civil and political rights to those unjustly convicted under war time laws with reimbursement for time served.

4. Legislation protecting foreign born workers from deportation and refusal of citizenship on account of political opinions.

5. Modification of immigration laws to permit the reuniting of families and to offer a refuge for those fleeing from political or religious persecution.

6. Abolition of detective agencies engaged in interstate business.

ANTI-LYNCHING

As a measure of protection for the oppressed, especially for our Negro fellow citizens, we propose:

Enactment of the Berger anti-lynching bill making participation in lynching a felony.

POLITICAL DEMOCRACY

The constitution of the United States was drafted in 1787 and was designed to meet conditions utterly different from those prevailing today. In order to make our form of government better suited to exigencies of the times, we propose the immediate calling of a constitutional convention. A modernized constitution should provide, among other things, for the election of the President and Vice-President by direct popular vote of the people, for reduction of the representation in Congress of those states where large sections of the citizens are disfranchised by force or fraud, and proportional representation, and for the abolition of the usurped power of the Supreme Court to pass upon the constitutionality of legislation enacted by Congress.

CREDIT AND BANKING

For our emancipation from the money trust, we propose:

Nationalization of the banking and currency system, beginning with extension of the service of the postal savings banks to cover every department of the banking business.

FARM RELIEF

The Socialist Party believes that the farmer is entitled to special consideration because of the importance of agriculture, because of the farmers' present economic plight and because the farmer is unable to control the prices of what he buys and what he sells. Many of the party's demands, including public development of electrical energy, nationalization of coal and railroads, and reform of the credit system will be of distinct benefit to the farmer.

As a further means of agricultural relief, we propose:

1. Acquisition by bona fide cooperative societies and by federal, state and municipal governments of grain elevators, stockyards, storage warehouses and other distributing agencies and the conduct of these services on a non-profit basis.

2. Encouragement of farmers' cooperative purchasing and marketing societies and of credit agencies.

3. Social insurance against losses due to adverse weather conditions, such as hail, drought, cyclone and flood.

INTERNATIONAL RELATIONS

We are unalterably opposed to imperialism and militarism. Therefore we propose:

1. Immediate withdrawal of American forces from Nicaragua and abandonment of the policy of military intervention in Central America and other countries.

2. That all private loans and investments of American citizens in foreign countries shall be made at the sole risk of the bondholders and investors. The United States government shall not resort to any military or other coercive intervention with foreign governments for the protection of such loans and investments.

3. Cancellation of all war debts due the United States from its former associated powers on condition of a simultaneous cancellation of all inter-allied debts and a corresponding remission of the

reparation obligations of the Central Powers and on the further condition that our debtors reduce their military expenditures below pre-war level. The Socialist Party especially denounces the debt settling policy of our government in favoring the Fascist dictatorship of Italy and thereby helping to perpetuate the political enslavement of the Italian nation.

4. Recognizing both the services and the limitations of the League of Nations, the need of revision of its convenant and the Treaty of Versailles, we unite with the workers of Europe in demanding that the League be made all inclusive and democratic, and that the machinery for the revision of the peace treaty under article 19 of the covenant be elaborated and made effective. We favor the entry of the United States at the time and under conditions which will further these clauses and promote the peace of the world.

5. The recognition of the Russian government.

6. Aggressive activity against militarism, against the large navy and army program of our present administration, and in behalf of international disarmament.

7. Treaties outlawing war and the substitution of peaceful methods for the settlement of international disputes.

8. Independence of the Philippines on terms agreed upon in negotiations with the Filipinos; autonomy for Porto Rico and civil government for the Virgin Islands.

Platform of the Socialist Labor Party

The Socialist Labor Party of the United States of America in National Convention assembled in New York on May 13, 1928, reaffirming its previous platform pronouncements, and in accord with international Socialist principles, declares:

Social conditions, as illustrated by events crowded into the last few years, have ripened so fast that the principles, hitherto proclaimed by the Socialist Labor Party, as well as the methods that the Socialist Labor Party has hitherto advocated, stands conspiciously demonstrated.

The Capitalist Social System has wrought its own destruction. Its leading exponents, even when seemingly at war on principles, cannot conceal the identity of their political views. The absence of dividing lines between the two leading political clearing houses of capitalism—the Republican and Democratic parties; the supineness, almost exultant readiness with which the leading politicians—aspirants for the presidency and other important posts in the Political State—yield themselves to the needs of ultra-capitalism, to the exclusion of the needs of the producing masses, proclaim the inner conviction of the foremost men of the Ruling Class that the Republic of Capital is at the end of its tether.

True to economic laws, from which Socialism proceeds, dominant wealth has to such an extent concentrated into the hands of a select few, the modern industrial autocracy, that the lower layers of the capitalist class feel driven to the ragged edge, while the large majority of the people, the working class, are being submerged.

True to sociologic laws, by the light of which Socialism reads its forecasts, the industrial autocracy is breaking through its republican-democratic shell and is stretching out its hands towards abolutism in government; the property-holding layers below it are turning at bay; the proletariat is awakening to its consciousness of class, and thereby to the perception of its historic mission.

In the midst of this hurly-burly, and the resulting confusion of thought, all the colors of the rainbow are being projected upon the social mists.

From the lower layers of the capitalist class issue demands for reforms designed to check the logical tendencies of capitalism, demands covering the entire range of social visionariness. Overwhelmed by gigantic combinations in industry and finance, the middle and lower sections of the capitalist class clamor for a return of the age of competition. But even if such a return were possible it should not be effected; even if it should it cannot. To the thinker it is self-evident that the system neither can nor will return to what the Industrial Revolution has been gradually sloughing off during a century of progress.

The law of social progress pushes toward a system of production that shall crown the efforts of man—a system which without arduous toil, with an abundance of necessaries for material existence, will allow leisure for mental and spiritual expansion. The gigantic machine of modern production is a mechanical contrivance which is solving the problem of material needs which has confronted mankind from its infancy. To smash this contrivance and to reintroduce the days of small-fry competition would set back the hands of the dial of time. The mere thought is foolhardy.

He who undertakes the feat might as well brace himself against the cascade of Niagara. The cascade of Social Evolution would overwhelm him.

From the lowest layers of the property-holding class—layers that have sniffed the breath of Socialism and imagine themselves Socialists—comes the iridescent theory of capturing the machinery of production for the people by the ballot only, with a vague idea of government ownership and operation as the aim. But the "capture of the machinery of production for the people" implies the Social Revolution. To imply the Social Revolution with the ballot, without the means of enforcing the fiat of the ballot in case the Reaction attempts to override it, is to fire blank cartridges at a foe. It is worse. It is to threaten his existence without the means to carry out the threat, which can result in only one of two things—either the leaders are bought out, or the revolutionary class, to which they appeal and which they succeed in drawing along, are led like cattle to the shambles.

An equally iridescent hue of the rainbow is projected from a layer that lies almost wholly within the submerged class—the theory of capturing the machinery of production for the working class with physical force only and through underground conspiracies. The capture of the machinery of production for the people implies something strikingly different from all previous revolutions. It implies revolution carried on by the masses. For sociologic reasons mass-revolutionary conspiracy is, today, an impossibility, even an absurdity. The trust-holding autocracy may successfully put through a conspiracy of physical force. The smallness of its numbers make conspiracy possible. The hugeness of the numbers, requisite for a revolution against the trustholding autocracy, excludes conspiracy from the arsenal of the Revolution, and just as that autocracy at one point of the social circle boldly aims for absolutism and dictatorship in government, so this all but submerged layer at the merging point proclaims its aim to be dictatorship, thus closing the circle.

All these groups have one thing in common: they plant themselves upon the presumption of a continuation of the Political State—a presumption that is at war with logic and social evolution.

Only two programs—the program of Industrial Top-Capitalism and the program of the Socialist Labor Party grasp the situation.

The Political State, the instrument of class rule and oppression, is worn out in this, the leading capitalist nation of the world. The Socialist or Industrial Government is throbbing for birth. The Political State, being a class state, is government separate and apart from the productive energies of the people; it is government mainly for holding the ruled class in subjection. The Socialist or Industrial Government, being the denial of the class state, is government that is an integral part of the productive energies of the people.

As their functions differ, so are the structures of the two "States" different.

The structure of the Political State is based on territorial representation; the structure of the Industrial Government demands representation by industries and useful occupations.

The economic or industrial evolution has reached that point where the Political State no longer can maintain itself under the forms of democracy. While the Industrial Autocracy has relatively shrunk, the enemies it is raising against itself are becoming numerous. Moreover, obedient to the law of its existence, the Political State not only multiplies its enemies; it has been forced to recruit and group the bulk of these enemies, and the revolutionary bulk at that.

The working class of the land, the historically revolutionary element, is grouped by occupations, agricultural as well as industrial, in such manner that—while the "autonomous craft union," at one time the palladium of workers, has become a harmless scarecrow upon which the capitalist birds roost at ease—the Revolutionary Industrial Unions will spring logically from the modern organization of industry itself and, casting ahead of them the constituencies of the government of the future, point to the Industrial Governmental Organization.

Nor is this all. Not only has the Political State raised its own enemies; not only has it multiplied them; not only has it recruited and drilled them; not only has it grouped them into shape to succeed it; it is, furthermore, driven by its inherent necessities to prodding on the revolutionary class by digging ever more fiercely into its flanks the harpoon of exploitation.

With the purchasing power of wages sinking to ever lower depths; with certainty of work hanging on ever slenderer threads; with an ever more gigantically swelling army of the unemployed; with the need of profits pressing the Industrial Autocracy harder and harder to squander recklessly the workers' limbs and lives; what with all this and the parallel process of merging the workers of all industries into one interdependent solid mass, the final break-up is rendered inevitable.

No wild schemes and no rainbow-chasing will stead in the approaching emergency. The Industrial Autocracy knows this—and so does the Socialist Labor Party—and logical is the program of each.

The program of the Industrial Autocracy is Industrial Feudalism. Where a Social Revolution is pending and for whatever reason is not accomplished, REACTION is the alternative.

The program of the Socialist Labor Party is REVOLUTION—the Industrial or Socialist Republic, the social order where the Political State is overthrown; where the "Congress" of the land, the legislative and executive central directing authority, consists of representatives of the useful occupations; where, accordingly, the government will be an essential factor in production; where the gigantic machines are freed from the trammels of the private ownership that now turn into a curse the blessings which these machines are instinct with; where, accordingly, abundance can be the patrimony of all who work; where the shackles of wage slavery are no more.

In keeping with the goals of the different programs are the means of their execution.

The means in contemplation by REACTION is forcible repression. To this end REACTION is seeking, by means of industrial spies and other agencies, to lash the proletariat into acts of violence that may give color to a resort to physical force. By its maneuvers, it is egging the working class on to deeds of fury. The capitalist press echoes the policy, while the pure and simple reformers, pure and simple trade unionists, and "revolutionary" visionaries generally, are snared into the trap.

To the contrary, the means firmly adhered to by the Socialist Labor Party is the constitutional method of political action, backed by the industrially and classconsciously organized proletariat, to the exclusion of anarchy, underground conspiracies, and all that thereby hangs.

At such a critical period in the nation's existence the Socialist Labor Party calls upon the working class of America, more deliberately serious than ever before, to rally at the polls under the Party's banner. And the Party also calls upon all intelligent citizens to place themselves squarely upon the ground of working class interests, and join us in this mighty and noble work of human emancipation, so that we may put summary end to the existing barbarous class conflict by placing the land and all the means of production, transportation and distribution into the hands of the people as a collective body, and substituting for the present state of planless production, industrial war and social disorder, the Socialist or Industrial Commonwealth—a commonwealth in which every worker shall have the free exercise and full benefit of his faculties, multiplied by all the modern factors of civilization.

National Platform of the Workers (Communist) Party, 1928

I. AMERICA TODAY

President Coolidge said to the big bankers and manufacturers in Philadelphia: "We hold a great treasure which must be protected." In the name of the working class and the exploited farmers of this country the Workers (Communist) Party raises the question: *Who owns the "great treasure," in whose interests must it be protected, and who bears the burden of its protection?* And our answer is: The "great treasure" is owned by a handful of powerful bankers, manufacturers, and railroad magnates. The only share of it the workers and working farmers receive is exploitation and poverty, and all the burden of defense of the "great treasure" of American imperialism rests on the shoulders of the industrial and agricultural workers.

America is today the most powerful country in the world. America's wealth, the "great treasure," mounts up to 400 billion dollars. Half of the gold of the world is now in the possession of the United States. With but seven per cent of the world's total population America controls the bulk of the world's resources: 44 per cent of the world's coal, 70 per cent of the oil produced, 52 out of every 100 tons of steel, 60 per cent of the cotton and corn, and half of the world's railways, copper and pig iron.

A gigantic accumulation and concentration of capital is going on. The total amount of bank deposits is now over 56 billion dollars. There are over 1,000 factories in America employing more than 1,000 workers each, with a total of about 2½ million workers. Of all wage-earners in manufacturing over 56 per cent work in those 10,000 factories each of which turns out annually products to the amount of a million dollars or over.

Trustification is asserting itself with irresistible power. Consolidations of railways, big combines and mergers in all industries are the order of the day. The United States Steel Corporation has a capital of 1.4 billion dollars. A food trust is attempting to combine 2 billion dollars into one powerful corporation. The recent consolidation of the Brooklyn Edison Company and the Consolidated Gas Company of New York resulted in a merger of over one billion dollars. Five powerful companies control almost half of the whole national output of water power, and eleven groups control 80 per cent. Eight companies control three-fourths of the anthracite coal. Two companies exercise control over half of the copper resources of the country.

A process of centralization similar to that in *production* is going on in the field of *distribution.* There are today 3,893 chain store organizations controlling 101,536 retail outlets in thirty merchandise fields. These chains realized in 1927 a volume of business estimated at almost six billion dollars or 16 per cent of the total retail business of the country. The anti-trust laws function today not as instruments of "trust-busting" but as a means of trustification.

The United States is the leading country in respect to capitalist rationalization. The productive power of American industries has increased tremendously. In a decade productivity per employee in American manufacturing has increased 33 per cent, cost of management has decreased 12 per cent, but wages per unit of production have increased only 2 per cent. Overdevelopment of industrial productive capacity is one of the basic features of American imperialism.

Finance capital is almighty today. *Banks and industries are merged.* The climax of this development was marked by the fact that J. P. Morgan, head of American finance capital, became the head of the United States Steel Corporation, the country's biggest industrial company. Hand in hand with the trustification of industry goes the trustification of State power. *The Government of the United States is today an administration of finance capital.* The identity of the dominating personnel in finance capital and government administration is complete. Finance capital sends its direct representatives to the Cabinet as well as ambassadors to foreign countries.

Trustification, high tariff, monopoly, merger of trusts and State power, growing export of capital —this is the picture of American imperialism today.

The stabilization of European industries and the decline of British imperialism have increased competition on a world scale. United States imperialism is in a growing measure dependent on the world market, and it struggles for world hegemony in every corner of the world—from Latin America to China. It is engaged in murderous competition for the Russian market as well as for the markets of the British Empire.

Increased competition, increased struggle for the resources of raw material and for the export of capital, high tariff walls, and ever-larger armies and navies create a growing menace of war. *A second world war is inevitable.* Wars on a smaller scale are going on today in a period which the spokesmen of imperialism call the era of "world peace." American imperialism is conducting a war of extermination against Nicaragua, is participating in interventions in China, and is an active accomplice of the capitalist conspiracy against Soviet Russia.

Two main antagonisms lead today towards a world conflagration. One is the chief capitalist antagonism between British and American imperialism, which has taken the place of the pre-war British-German rivalry. The other one is the general capitalist conspiracy against the Union of Socialist Soviet Republics.

Although British imperialism is today the most reactionary force in world politics, American imperialism is the leading power and represents the most dangerous, most aggressive force of world capitalism. There is an ever-clearer crystallization of the *two poles:* on the one hand, *the counter-revolutionary pole* under the leadership of the United States to defend capitalism against the growing revolt of the colonial peoples and the working masses of the capitalist countries; on the other hand, *the revolutionary pole* under the leadership of Soviet Russia, around which all the oppressed peoples of the colonies and all the exploited workers of the world rally.

Wealth and Poverty

The United States is the richest country in the world. "Uncle Shylock" is the creditor of all countries. The world owes the United States today not less than 23½ billion dollars. The yearly income of the United States from foreign investments amounts today to the huge sum of one billion dollars. The number of millionaires is growing fast. In 1919 there were only 65 incomes over a million; in 1926 there were 228. In 1919 there were only 189 incomes between $500,000 and $1,000,000; in 1926 the number was 465.

In his 1926 address to Congress President Coolidge said: "The wealth of our country is not public wealth but private wealth. It does not belong to the Government; it belongs to the people." The prodigious wealth of the country is private wealth, but the "people" who own it are not the workers and exploited farmers. They are the few millionaires. The country is growing richer, but the share of the millions of working people in the wealth of the country is decreasing and the share of the few powerful millionaires is increasing with amazing speed. One per cent of all recipients of any income in this country receive not less than 20 per cent of the whole national income and get not less than 86.2 per cent of all corporate dividends. *One per cent of the population possesses today not less than 33 per cent of all wealth; 10 per cent own 64 per cent; and the poorest 25 per cent possess only 3½ per cent.* The overwhelming majority of the "people" to whom President Coolidge refers are born poor and die poor. The Federal Trade Commission states that "about one per cent of the estimated number of decedents owned about 59 per cent of the estimated wealth, and more than 90 per cent was owned by about 13 per cent of the decedents."

The accumulated wealth is not distributed equally. *Hand in hand with the growing fortunes of the few millionaires goes the growing exploitation and poverty of the unskilled workers, Negroes, and exploited farmers.* Even President Coolidge was forced to admit in his Hammond dedication speech that there is a *"considerable class of unskilled workers who have not come into full participation in the wealth of the nation."* The share of the wage-earners in the national income has decreased. The manufacturing wage-earners received only 40.1 per cent of the "value product" in 1925 as against 44.8 per cent in 1921. The wages of the shamelessly exploited four million agricultural workers amounted in 1920 to 2.3 per cent of the national income and in 1926 to only 1.4 per cent. *The "democratization" of wealth is only a capitalist myth.* Bankers and industrial magnates own the big corporations. The workers do not possess more than one per cent of all stocks and bonds. "High American wages" is today the most popular publicity stunt of American and international capitalism, but high wages embrace only a thin aristocratic stratum of the working class. The overwhelming majority of wage-earners is not able to earn even sufficient to fulfill the most elementary needs of a decent life. In the middle of the most advertised prosperity, in the summer of 1926, the Federal Bureau of Labor Statistics estimated that the average wages for "common labor" were 42.6 cents an hour. The United States Department of Labor was forced to admit that huge sections of the working class are receiving wages of only $10.34 a week.

President Coolidge made the bold declaration that *"the people are prosperous,"* but reality shows that the overwhelming majority of the people work on starvation wages, that nearly 60 per cent of the workers still work more than 48 hours a week, that women and children, Negro and foreign-born unskilled workers are exploited at least as mercilessly as the most exploited strata of the European working class. *The prosperity of the "people" is best illustrated by the miserable shacks of the Southern cotton fields and the poverty-stricken slums of the Eastern cities.* In his 1926 address to Congress President Coolidge said: "The power of the purse is the power over liberty." A handful of millionaires exercise power over the purse, and they exercise power over the liberty of the overwhelming majority of the people of the United States. A handful of powerful millionaires own all the means of production—the factories, machinery, mines, railroads, water power—of this country, and are thus in a position to force the overwhelming majority of the people into wage slavery. *The wealth of the few is the poverty of the many; the liberty of the few is the bondage of the masses.*

Indictment of American Capitalism

Overproduction and starvation, overtime and unemployment, accumulation of wealth and accumulation of poverty—these are the features of capitalist prosperity for the workers and working farmers. The very fact that there can be such a thing as overproduction as long as the needs of every member of society are still unsatisfied is the most terrible indictment against capitalist society. Cyclones of periodic crises sweep over the whole capitalist economy. Capitalist society is unable to control its own forces of production. As the President of the United States Chamber of Commerce put it in his speech of May 10, 1928, there has been an *"economic thunderbolt of increasing production unloosed by industry."*

Unemployment is a permanent phenomenon in capitalist society. There is at any time 1½ million unemployed. The constant industrial reserve army is one of the props of capitalist society. The present depression with its 4 to 5 million unemployed workers brings untold misery. The labor of hundreds of thousands of children is one of the basic institutions of capitalism. Peonage, no better than chattel slavery, Jim Crowism and lynching are regular accompaniments of present-day capitalist prosperity. The shameless exploitation of the unskilled foreign-born workers and the oppression of whole races are parts of the capitalist system. The modern industrial serfdom of company towns is in existence to the glory of the "freest" constitution in the world. Capitalist industry conducts in the form of industrial accidents a bloody war of extermination against the working class. The infamous speed-up system causes the workers to age prematurely. Old workers are thrown away like slack, like useless by-products. Not less than 1,800,000 old people are forced to live the life of "dependents." Sickness and early death are the punishment for poverty. The United States Public Health Service states: "Both sickness and death are much more frequent among those with low incomes than among those with incomes adequate to comfortable living."

Capitalist decency and morality is symbolized by almshouses, brothels, slums, and bootleg saloons. Prostitution of science, literature, and art is on the same level as prostitution of women. Capitalist "justice" is equivalent to frame-ups, third degree, filling the penitentiaries with political prisoners, execution of working-class fighters like Sacco and Vanzetti. There is a crusade against the "crime wave," against petty larceny by the poor, conducted by those who are guilty of large-scale corruption and lobbying. With the exception of backward and impoverished China and India the powerful and rich and civilized United States is the only country which does not have any social legislation. The latest "achievement" of American imperialist civilization is the appearance of a *rentier* class completely divorced from the process of production and foisting its parasitic existence upon the toiling masses. Jingoism, militarism, robber wars against Nicaragua and China—these are the results of American capitalism.

President Coolidge summed up in the following way his picture of American capitalism: *"Those are some of the economic results which have accrued from the American principles of reliance upon the initiative and the freedom of the individual. It is the very antithesis of Communism."* And President Coolidge is right. American capitalism as it is—with all its economic, political, and moral results—is the very antithesis of Communism. There is no other altenative. *The issue is capitalism or Communism.* The Workers (Communist) Party of America declares itself the deadly enemy of capitalism. It has as its aim the overthrow of capitalism, the establishment of a workers' and farmers' government, the establishment of a Communist society in which the means of production will not be the private property of the few, a society which will not be based on profit but on labor, which will not be founded on class divisions, which will eradicate both imperialist wars and class wars, which will be able to eliminate poverty.

The Parties of Big and Small Business

With the exception of the Workers (Communist) Party all political parties and groups are defenders of the present capitalist society.

The two old capitalist parties, the Republican and Democratic, are twin brothers in the expression of the interests of the bosses.

The *Republican Party,* which in the interests of

the then revolutionary capitalism conducted a war against chattel slavery, is today working in the interests of the now counter-revolutionary capitalism for the perpetuation of wage slavery. The Republican Party of today is nothing but the party of trusts, of finance capital, of the biggest business interests of the country.

The *Democratic Party* was in the early stages of its history the party of slavery, against Northern capitalism and in the interests of the Southern plantation owners. Today, though many times masked with phrases of liberalism, it stands for the perpetuation of the peonage of Negroes in the South and for the maintenance of wage slavery throughout the country.

There are no real political differences between the two big political parties. Both are parties of capitalism; both are the enemies of the working class. The very existence of the two-party system is the most reactionary factor in American politics, is one of the factors which are responsible for the lack of an independent mass political party of the working class. Both capitalist parties try to put up the semblance of being defenders of the farmers, vying with each other in putting forward fake "farm relief" measures. *The "struggle" between the Republican and Democratic Parties is a staged fight, a mock struggle. There are no political issues between these two parties.* On the question of tariff, prohibition, taxation, imperialist war, farm relief, League of Nations, and all other discussed political issues there is much more division *within* each party than *between* the two parties.

The main slogan of the Republican Party today is "Prosperity." But reality shows depression and unemployment. The main slogan of the Democratic Party is: "Honesty in Government." But reality shows at least as much corruption on the part of the Democrats as on that of the Republicans. Tammany Hall can successfully compete in corruption with Teapot Dome.

There are several classes combined in each of these parties. Both still mirror in many respects the old sectional and regional groupings of the country, but in both there is an outspoken, decisive dominance of finance capital. *Both are one on the basic issues: the oppression of the working class, the maintenance of the exploitation of the workers and working farmers, and the robber policies against the colonies and semi-colonies of American imperialism.*

The group of so-called *Progressives* is by no means better than the Republican "Old Guard" or the Democratic heroes of Tammany Hall and the "solid" South. In 1924, the bulk of the so-called progressive group supported the LaFollette movement, which betrayed the interests of the working class and the working farmers, dissipating the discontent of the masses and leading them back to the capitalist parties.

In 1928 the attitude of the so-called Progressives is still more cowardly. They have even deserted the idea of a third party, and have gone back meekly into the old capitalist parties. Senator Wheeler came out openly in support of Al Smith, who is the embodiment of the new Tammany Hall and the hero of the labor-smashing policies in the needle trades. Senators Borah and Norris and their Republican colleagues are equally untrustworthy. Borah's empty gesture of "outlawing" war serves only as a cover for Kellogg's imperialist wars and war preparations. Senator Shipstead, who still usurps the name of a Farmer-Laborite, is betraying the interests of the workers and exploited farmers in the most shameless way. He upholds the Nicaraguan war, and gives his support to the anti-labor injunction policies of the courts by introducing a fake anti-injunction bill. These "progressive" Senators and Congressmen are in many respects more dangerous enemies of the workers and working farmers than the official spokesmen of big business, because they hide their capitalist face and create illusions in the minds of the masses. *All these Progressives and semi-Progressives serve as a prop of the present capitalist society and must be combatted by all honest workers and farmers.*

The official leadership of the *American Federation of Labor* is today part and parcel of American imperialism. Under the leadership of the most corrupt trade-union bureaucracy in the world the A. F. of L. has become mainly an organization of the labor aristocracy, an instrument of class collaboration with the bosses instead of a means of struggle against big business. The capitalists are conducting the most murderous offensive of the open shop and wage cuts against the workers. The answer of the leaders of the A. F. of L. is a joint proposal with the American Bar Association for a Federal anti-strike law. *The trade-union bureaucrats are today the partners of the bosses.* They are trying to wrench the weapon of the strike from the hands of the workers. The whole infamous system of labor banks and trade-union insurance —trade-union capitalism—is nothing but the most elaborate system of class betrayal. The leadership of the A. F. of L. does not conduct any struggle against wage cuts or for higher wages and shorter hours. The trade-union bureaucracy sabotages the great task of organizing the unorganized. The worthy heirs of Gompers—Green, Woll and Co.— are the advocates of the *"Monroe Doctrine of Labor," are the spokesmen of a "labor imperialism."* They have come out openly for a policy of common exploitation of all Latin-American peoples by the capitalists and workers of the United States. The B. and O. plan, the Mitten plan, compulsory arbitration, the transformation of the trade unions into semi-Fascist and semi-company unions —is today the policy of the A. F. of L. These corrupt misleaders of labor are helping to keep the workers in the camp of the old capitalist parties by maintaining the sterile and treacherous policy of "reward your friends and punish your enemies" within the capitalist parties. There cannot be successful struggles of the working class against its exploiters without a systematic struggle against the whole edifice of the labor aristocracy and its corrupt bureaucratic leadership.

The *Socialist Party of America,* which still claims to be a working-class party, is in fact a party of the lower middle class. Its leadership has become part of the bureaucracy of the A. F. of L. Its whole ambition is to inherit the traditions of the LaFollette third-party movement. The militant spirit of Eugene Debs has been completely wiped out from the Socialist Party. In Wisconsin the Socialist Party is an official party of the capitalist administration. In New York the Socialist Party has substituted the red-white-and-blue flag of patriotism for the red flag of revolution. In Reading the city officials of the Socialist Party have pledged themselves to *"understand that their responsibilities will be those of capitalist officials rather than of Socialist Party members."* James H. Maurer, one of the councilmen elected by the Socialists in Reading and vice-Presidential candidate of the Socialist Party, declared: "We are going to give the workers a typical working-class government, but *if there is a strike in Reading while we are in power, the capitalist employer will have his property and life protected as he never had it before."* The presidential candidate of the Socialist Party, Norman Thomas, is the worst kind of

pacifist, a typical preacher, who performs the greatest service for American imperialism by creating illusions about the League of Nations, about the possibility of preventing wars by peaceful means. The Socialist Party today is an advocate of the League of Nations, and is a supporter of the hypocritical "peace offensive" of Secretary of State Kellogg. The Socialist Party is uttering some critical phrases about the war in Nicaragua not because it is an imperialist war in the interests of Wall Street but only because it is "unauthorized and unsanctioned by the people or Congress."

The Socialist Party of today is for the protection of capitalist law and order, is against revolution, is against the working-class government of Soviet Russia, and supports every measure of the A. F. of L. bureaucracy for class collaboration. The Socialist Party has transformed its party organization from a membership organization into a ward organization of voters. It has shifted its class basis from the working class entirely and definitely to the lower middle class. The last national convention of the Socialist Party in April, 1928, went so far as to drop the class struggle pledge that applicants for membership had to sign in the past.

The small sects, the *Socialist Labor Party* and the *Proletarian Party,* have become completely fossilized, and do not play any role in the political life of the country or in any of the struggles of the working class.

The Workers (Communist) Party is today the only genuine working-class party. It is the sole party which has a program for the workers and working farmers. It is the only party which conducts a relentless struggle against capitalism, against the old parties of the bosses and against the corrupt labor bureaucracy and the treacherous Socialist Party.

The Workers (Communist) Party is the party of the class struggle. It is the deadly enemy of class collaboration because it is the deadly enemy of capitalism. It is the revolutionary party of the working class. The Workers (Communist) Party is the champion of the interests of the working class and the working farmers. It is the advocate of the most exploited stratum of the working class, of the unskilled workers. It is the champion of the oppressed Negro race. It is the organizer of the struggle against imperialism, against imperialist wars.

The Workers (Communist) Party is the only

party which fights for the interests of the working class, working farmers, and the oppressed Negro race; and that is the very reason why *all the forces of the old capitalist parties, the bureaucrats of the A. F. of L and the leaders of the Socialist Party are united against the Communists.* The Republicans, Democrats, Socialists, and labor bureaucrats have a common platform. That platform is Red-baiting, anti-Communism.

In its 1928 election campaign the Workers (Communist) Party offers the *following program against trustified capital* and in the interests of the working class, working farmers, and oppressed Negro race:

II. The Curse of Unemployment

There is a heavy economic depression over the country with a very heavy unemployment in its wake. Bread-lines are long. Hypocritical "charity" is in its flower. Even conservative Senators estimate the number of unemployed at four million. *The curse of unemployment is the most terrible plight of the working class.* The cyclical crises of capitalist industry bring with them time and again the untold sufferings of mass unemployment. But there is unemployment not only at times of crises; it is here at all times. Unemployment on a mass scale is a *"normal"* phenomenon of this glorious capitalist society.

The very technical progress—the development of new machinery, the increased productivity of labor — becomes under capitalist conditions a source of growing unemployment. The introduction of new machines has decreased the number of workers. The opening up of new markets cannot keep pace with the speedy development of technique. The introduction of machinery makes the skill of the workers superfluous. Large masses of *unskilled* workers can take the place of the skilled. The time of apprenticeship is being greatly shortened. *Young workers* and even *children* can take the place of adults. A growing number of *women* are entering into industry.

The introduction of machinery creates the basis for mass production. Mass production with its murderous competition ruins the *lower middle class* and drives its members as workers into the industries. Monopoly capitalism ruins the *farmers* and forces them to sell their labor power as industrial workers in the cities. Mass production opens up hitherto backward agrarian regions industrially.

A large-scale industrialization of the South is taking place, and has driven hundreds of thousands of *Negroes* into the industries. Despite all prohibition of *immigration* there is an annual influx of hundreds of thousands of workers from other countries.

Under present capitalist conditions it is inevitable that there should be a constant industrial reserve army of jobless. Even in the best periods of prosperity the number of jobless is estimated at one and a half million. In 1927, the factories produced 26 per cent more than in 1919. During this same period the number of wage-earners employed in *manufacturing* decreased by not less than 980,000. Eleven per cent fewer wage-earners than in 1919 produced in manufacturing in 1927 26 per cent more products. In other words, each worker produced 42 per cent more. The same tendency manifests itself everywhere. The *railways* had in 1927 almost 200,000 less workers than in 1919. The number of *"superfluous"* miners is near to a quarter of a million. In manufacturing, mining and railroading, there were almost one and a half million fewer workers employed by the end of 1927 than in 1919. During the last few years there has been a continuous movement of population from the *farms* to the cities: in 1925, 834,000 in 1926, 1,020,000, in 1927, 604,-000 more persons left the farms for the cities than the cities for the farms. A large proportion of these bankrupt and ruined farmers became industrial workers or rather tried to become industrial workers. Even Secretary of Labor Davis has been forced to raise the question:

"Is automatic machinery driven by relentless power going to leave on our hands a state of chronic and increasing unemployment? Is the machinery that turns out our wealth also to create poverty? Is it giving us a permanent jobless class?"

A capitalist writer characterizes the present unemployment as a "technological unemployment, not cyclical—an unemployment developing gradually, almost unawares, *like creeping paralysis,* in the midst of unprecedented prosperity, the by-product of improved technological efficiency."

Unemployment is indeed the "creeping paralysis" of capitalist society. It represents the most vicious contradiction of the present economic order. The more machinery, the higher the productivity of labor, the more unemployed. Labor itself produces unemployment. Unemployment of one part produces overtime for the other part of the working class. The pressure of unemployment forces wage-earners to accept jobs at lower wages and longer hours. The fear of unemployment is the most powerful chain which binds the workers to wage slavery. The fear of unemployment increases competition among the workers. Unemployment lowers the power of resistance of the workers on the job. The working wage-earners are forced to accept overtime. Overtime again makes new masses of wage-earners super-fluous. *Unemployment creates overtime, and over-time creates unemployment.* The bigger the fac-tories, the more expensive the machinery, the greater is the tendency of the capitalists to lengthen the working times instead of increasing the number of workers. Hand in hand with the increasing accumulation of capital goes a relative and today even an absolute decrease in the number of workers.

The hypocritical advocates of capitalism lament about the existence of unemployment and call it the "greatest blot on our capitalist system" (Owen D. Young), but in fact the existence of a constant industrial reserve army is not a hindrance to capitalism. Quite the contrary. It is one of the basic conditions for the existence and maintenance of capitalism. Technical development, new in-ventions, the introduction of new labor-saving machinery will not cease. The opening up of new markets will not go on at the same speed as here-tofore. The industrialization of the colonies, the increasing competition with Europe, the existence of non-capitalistic Soviet Russia, and the revolt of the colonial peoples are the narrowing limita-tions.

The present depression is not an "accident." It has been brought about by prosperity itself. Disproportion between production and consump-tion, which is a part of the general anarchy of capitalist production, is responsible for cyclical crises. Saturation of the automobile and building construction markets, over-production of oil, the world coal crisis, the migration of the textile industry to the South, the limits of installment buying, the restriction of the farmers' market, the effects of American export of capital and of the stabilization of Europe, the increased competition with Europe—these are the basic features of the present economic depression. Neither the exist-ence of huge monopolies and trusts nor the "inter-ventions" of the Federal Reserve Bank are able to prevent the occurrence of economic crises.

There is no cure for unemployment under capitalism.

Shortening of the working day alone would not do away with unemployment. A general shortening of the working day would result in general part-time work, in perpetual overpro-duction, would bring about a crisis in permanence.

High wages alone cannot cure unemployment. It is futile to try to "convince" the capitalists to increase wages for the purpose of increasing the purchasing power of the workers. The capitalists will never sacrifice a portion of their profits, by transforming it into wages, for the purpose of broadening the home market. Just the opposite is the policy of imperialist capitalism. It is cutting wages everywhere, and trying to increase its exports for the foreign markets.

Neither can *public works alone* cure unemploy-ment. Public works would tend to increase the forces of production, and would in the long run tend to reproduce unemployment on a larger scale. Higher wages, shorter hours, and public works would not cure unemployment, but might bring about a certain limited and temporary re-lief.

An especially dangerous illusion is created in the minds of the workers by a whole string of efficiency experts and economists of capitalism who predict a so-called capitalist efficiency "social-ism." These capitalist engineers and experts try to make the workers believe that it is possible not only to cure unemployment but to liquidate capi-talism itself by social insurance, profit-sharing and employee stock-buying plans, by technical im-provements, by elimination of waste, increased mass production, or various forms of State capital-ism. This capitalist efficiency "socialism" is the more harmful because its real aim is not the liqui-dation of capitalism but the liquidation of the every-day struggles of the workers to improve their living and working conditions and the wiping out of all revolutionary movements of the working class.

Unemployment is a world phenomenon today. The constant industrial reserve army has always been in existence, but the present chronic unem-ployment has assumed such proportions that it is no longer a prop of capitalism but an *organic defect,* one of the basic sicknesses of post-war capitalism. Unemployment is a horrible curse upon the working class. It is the most powerful weapon in the hands of the bosses. It chains the worker to wage slavery. It brings tormenting uncertainty into the life of every wage-earner. It breaks up the family of the worker by driving the women and children into the factories. It brings about moral degradation, creates a slum proletariat. There follows in its wake a growing criminality. It is the foundation of prostitution. In other words, it embodies and sums up capitalism as a whole.

Demands

1. Unemployment insurance. A federal system of unemployment insurance should be established. A federal law must be enacted immediately by Congress providing for unemployment insurance for all wage-earners without any exceptions or disqualifications. The amount of compensation should be full wages for the entire period of unemployment, up to $30 per week. An unemployment insurance fund should be created, fifty per cent to be contributed by the employers and fifty per cent by the State. The amount contributed by the State should be raised by special taxes levied against inheritance, high incomes and corporation profits. The administration of unemployment insurance should be carried out by unemployment insurance commissions, composed of representatives of trade unions, organizations of the unemployed, and factory committees.

2. Immediate enactment of a federal law providing for a general 40-hour, 5-day week working time and forbidding all overtime.

3. A federal law should be enacted providing for immediate emergency help for all workers who have been unemployed two months or more, consisting of eight weeks' wages for each worker. The average wage received during the last four weeks of employment should serve as the basis.

4. Establishment of public kitchens by municipalities to provide free meals for all unemployed workers and their families.

5. Municipal provision for supplying free medical treatment, medicine and hospital care to all unemployed.

6. Public works. The federal, state and city governments should devise schemes for improving the roads and bridges of the country, improving the rivers, canals, docks and harbors, setting up electric power stations, reforestation, land drainage and land reclamation, extension and electrification of railways. On all public works trade union wages and conditions must be guaranteed by law.

7. Immediate abolition of all vagrancy laws. Protection of unemployed workers from arrest on charges of vagrancy.

III. THE OFFENSIVE OF THE BOSSES

The working class of this country is facing a great crisis. A general offensive of the bosses is being conducted against the workers, an offensive to smash the whole trade-union movement, to lower the standard of living of all workers.

The trustification of capital, the erection of huge monopolies, the all embracing rationalization have increased the power of the bosses tremendously.

The capitalists are using all methods of rationalization mercilessly. Wage-cuts everywhere —in the shoe, textile, automobile and rubber industries and in mining. A whole system of speed-up has been put in operation. The stopwatch, group piece work, bonus system, efficiency engineering, the conveyor or travelling-belt system increase mass production and intensify the exploitation of the workers. Concentration of industries, Fordization, technical innovations, and the wholesale introduction of new machinery is the order of the day. The lengthening of working hours is attempted everywhere, with especially disastrous results for the unskilled workers. An injunction mania raves against every movement of the workers to resist the effects of rationalization. All the forces of the Government—the police, the state constabulary, the coal and iron police, the most infamous spy system—are mobilized against the workers. The open-shop drive, the "American Plan," is today the official policy of the capitalist class on the whole front. Company unions are being set up by the bosses, and strenuous attempts are being made to company-unionize all existing trade unions. All the combined forces of the bosses and their government are concentrated to prevent the organization of the unorganized masses in the basic industries.

The trade union bureaucracy of the A. F. of L. has met the general offensive of the bosses—by a general surrender. There has never been in the history of labor such a shameful capitulation as the treachery of the A. F. of L. leadership and of the Socialist Party in the present grave situation of the American labor movement. Instead of fighting the harmful effects of capitalist rationalization, these misleaders try to cooperate in introducing speed-up systems and capitalist efficiency. They put forward the "union-management co-operation" policy. They babble about "industrial democracy." They have elaborated the "higher strategy of labor," the notorious theory of Matthew Woll about the three stages of the American labor movement: the stage of conflict, of collective bargaining, and of worker-employer cooperation. They proclaim the passing of *war* and *truce* and the coming of the age of *permanent peace* between the bosses and the workers. The trade union bureaucracy has dropped the last semblance of any resistance to company-unionizing the trade unions. They have come out openly for the Watson-Parker Bill and for a federal anti-strike law. They have dropped their previous petty-bourgeois trust-busting program and have become the high apostles of "efficient" trusts.

The result of the offensive of the bosses and the treachery of the trade union bureaucrats is *the growing crisis in the labor movement.* Trustified industry is out for a general open shop. The trade unions have been driven out from all basic industries. For the first time in the history of the A. F. of L. the number of organized workers has deceased even during a period of prosperity. The climax of the struggle was reached in the present fight of the United Mine Workers of America. This most powerful and most militant unit of the American labor movement has now been broken to pieces and delivered to the mercy of the operators.

The present depression has ruthlessly exposed the notorious formula of the trade union bureaucracy about "mass production, high wages and low prices" as the foundation of permanent prosperity. Millions of workers are jobless, desperately walking the streets. The crisis in the labor movement and the depression have exposed the true meaning of all class-collaboration plans. They show up the so-called profit-sharing, employee stock-buying, group insurance, B. and O. plan, Mitten scheme, and other systems of "union-management cooperation." The smash-up of the labor bank of the Brotherhood of Locomotive En-

gineers is beginning to open the eyes of the workers to the disastrous effects of trade-union capitalism.

Despite all the treachery of the labor bureaucrats, the workers are beginning to resist. The long struggle of the textile workers in Passaic, the Haverhill shoe strike, the battle of the Colorado miners, the firm and solid front of the needle trades workers in New York, the strike struggle of the textile workers in New Bedford and Fall River, and heroic struggle of the Pennsylvania and Ohio miners, who have already maintained their fight against the whole world for fourteen months, are the first powerful signs of the defensive struggle of the working class. Despite all the sabotage of the misleaders of labor, the vast masses of unorganized workers are beginning to organize themselves. The first attempts to organize the automobile workers have been made. The needle trades workers and the textile workers are being organized into new unions. *The mill committee movement of the textile workers, the shop chairman movement of the needle trades, the Save-the-Union movement of the miners, etc., constitute the basis and means for a consolidation of fighting unions in these industries and are the most promising signs of a militant future.*

The Workers (Communist) Party of America considers it its duty to mobilize the masses for a relentless struggle against all harmful effects of capitalist rationalization. The workers must understand that rationalization in a capitalist society, with the means of production in private hands, can only intensify the exploitation of the workers. Rationalization in the interests of the whole of society can be carried out only in a Communist society in which the means of production are the property of the whole nation.

Demands

1. Shorter hours of labor. A 5-day, 40-hour week. A minimum of 48 consecutive hours rest in seven days.

2. Fight for high wages. Strike against wage cuts.

3. Fight for the protection of the workers from the bad effects of capitalist rationalization, of the technical advances of mass production. Struggle against the speed-up system.

4. Organize the unorganized. Organize new unions in the unorganized industries. The Ameri-

can working class cannot successfully resist the power of the trusts without building up a powerful organization of the workers in the basic industries.

5. Destroy company unions. Abolish the B. and O. and Mitten plans. Eradicate trade-union capitalism.

6. Save the unions from the onslaught of the bosses and the treachery of the bureaucrats. Amalgamation of craft unions into industrial unions. Democratization of the trade unions. The present corrupt leadership must be driven out.

7. Trade-union methods alone cannot wage a successful fight. Trade-union struggle must be supplemented by political struggle.

IV. The Heroic Struggle of the Miners

There has never been a more heroic struggle than the present strike of the hundreds of thousands of miners. They are fighting against the whole capitalist world. They are not only up against the coal operators, who are in close alliance with the big railroad companies and banks and are backed by the government, but are also betrayed by their own leaders.

There is a deep-going crisis in the mining industry. The industry is unorganized. Production is in a chaotic state. Each of the 7,000 coal companies produces as much as it can. There is a murderous competition for markets. The mines are able to produce twice as much coal today as industry and consumers can absorb. The operators are closing down mine after mine, creating heavy unemployment. At the same time, new labor-saving machinery is being introduced, aggravating the unemployment situation everywhere. The miners are being forced to increase their daily output by speed-up and longer working hours, thus making themselves in growing numbers superfluous. *The operators say that the industry is faced with the problem: either it must get rid of its superfluous coal or its superfluous miners. They are driving out 250,000 miners from the industry.*

The government has exposed itself frankly as the instrument of the operators in the present struggle. It has mobilized everything against the miners. Courts, injunctions, the national guard, state constabulary, judges and sheriffs are at the service of the operators. Every miner must now clearly see that the government is but the organization of the bosses. *The operators them-selves sit in the government.* The Secretary of the Treasury, Mellon, a member of President Coolidge's cabinet, is one of the biggest shareholders of the most unscrupulous Pittsburgh Coal Company. The governor of Pennsylvania, Fisher, was a member of the Board of Directors of the Clearfield Coal Company. The officials of the government are either the bosses themselves or their paid agents. In the company towns the coal operators exercise directly State power in the form of coal and iron police and company gunmen. The coal operators there own everything—land, streets, buildings, stores. The local judges and sheriffs are paid by the operators, as has been proved by the Senate Investigating Committee. The Senate Investigating Committee itself is nothing but a smoke screen to deceive the workers, to create illusions in the minds of the miners. *The miners have no constitutional rights in the "freest" country in the world.* And there cannot be any real democracy and freedom in a society in which the few own everything and the masses do not own anything.

The scores of thousands of Pennsylvania and Ohio miners are engaged in a bitter, desperate strike struggle for higher wages, better conditions, and the right to organize. But to win their struggle—which will require a whole series of battles against the employers, the Government, and the Lewis bureaucracy, and which will be directed against the deadly effects of the rationalization drive of the capitalists and for higher wages and union conditions—they must completely defeat the Lewis bureaucracy and build up a new militant union in the mining industry. The Lewis machine is nothing but the agent of the bosses in the union. It sold out the struggle of the miners to the operators and to the government. The Lewis machine does not want to win the strike. Its whole history is but an uninterrupted betrayal of all the fights of the miners. It betrayed the miners in 1919, in 1922, in 1925, and it has betrayed them in the most shameless way in the present struggle.

District after district was lost for the United Mine Workers under the leadership of the Lewis machine. In 1919 the miners' strike tied up 70 per cent of production; the present strike only 20 per cent. Lewis and the operators have broken up the U. M. W. A. The Lewis machine criminally neglected the necessary preparations for the strike. It sabotaged the organization of the unorganized. It has signed up individual agreements. It has betrayed the cause of a national agreement. It has split the movement by ousting everybody from the union who wants a militant struggle. It is cutting off relief from every striking miner who dares to criticize it. It is trying to enforce a yellow dog pledge of starvation. The last vestiges of democracy have been eradicated from the union. Lewis stole the elections. *The Lewis machine is not a leadership set up by the rank and file, but a leadership set up with the aid of the bosses over the rank and file.* From June to December, 1927, while the striking miners were starving on a dollar or two a week relief, Lewis drew $11,093.66 in salary and personal expenses.

The mining industry is in a crisis. The issue is: Who shall pay the expenses of the crisis? Shall it be solved at the cost of the operators or of the miners? The miners, and with them the whole labor movement, must multiply their efforts to combat the onslaught of the operators. *The defeat of the miners would be a defeat for the whole labor movement.*

Demands

1. Lewis and the whole reactionary machine must go. The rank and file must take over the organization to build a new militant union in the industry, to organize the unorganized, to re-establish union conditions, to fight for a national agreement.

2. The unorganized miners must be organized. The big organization drive must be intensified and speeded up.

3. Support the Pennsylvania and Ohio strike. Fight against wage cuts and for the Jacksonville scale. Mass picketing and mass violation of injunctions against the workers. Mass resistance to evictions.

4. It is the duty of the whole labor movement to organize relief for the starving and struggling miners.

5. Railroad workers, don't haul scab coal!

V. Colonies and Imperialist War

Increasing rivalry with the other imperialist powers and brutal exploitation of the economically weaker, more backward peoples—these two features characterize the foreign policy of United States imperialism at present.

Wall Street's dollars and marines are extending their domination over ever greater sections of the world. Wherever there is a revolutionary upheaval United States imperialism is on hand and ready to crush it. United States imperialism is in a conspiracy with Great Britain against the Russian revolution. It cooperates with Japan and England in the interventions against China. *United States imperialism supported Great Britain in her infamous Nanking policies, and it now supports Japan in her ruthless intervention in Shantung.* All talk about the United States as the "friend of China" is mere babble in view of the fact that America supports Japan's domination over Manchuria in order to protect her own vast financial investments there. Japanese intervention in China today promotes the striving of the United States for financial hegemony in the Far East. American-British-Japanese cooperation in the dismemberment of China includes at the same time growing possibilities of a clash between the rival interests of these three leading imperialist powers on the Pacific. United States warships and thousands of marines are "pacifying" China, and Washington admits that Admiral Bristol is empowered to call out the whole Pacific fleet against China if United States imperialist policy requires it. The conquest of the tremendous Chinese market is in a growing degree one of the foremost aims of United States imperialism. United States imperialism goes hand in hand with Japanese imperialism in Shantung against the armies of Chiang Kai-Shek, but at the same time its representative, Admiral Bristol, cooperates with Chiang Kai-Shek in crushing Soviet Canton, suppressing all revolutionary movements of the Chinese workers and peasants.

The military dictatorship of United States imperialism is exercised more ruthlessly than ever before over the Philippines, Hawaii, Porto Rico, the Panama Canal Zone and the Virgin Islands. Cuba, Haiti, Panama and Liberia are today reduced to vassal states of United States imperialism. *The independence of all the Caribbean and Central American republics has become nothing more than a tragic farce in view of their increased bondage to Wall Street.* The Havana Conference, which was called in the name of Pan-Americanism, was only the instrument of United States imperialism. The Monroe Doctrine, which once served as a defense against European powers, is today the most aggressive means to conquer all America for the United States. The pressure of Wall Street forced Mexico to surrender her oil and land resources to dollar imperialism. The appointment of Morrow, the employee of Morgan, as United States Ambassador to Mexico exposes the whole Latin-American policy of the United States as the policy of finance capital and big business. The fake "good will" flights of Colonel Lindbergh tried to exploit the sentimental illusions of the North American masses for the conquest of Latin America. Large parts of Central and South America have already been reduced to a state of semi-colonies of United States imperialism, and Wall Street and its White House agency are trying to transform them into true colonies.

The most disgraceful action of United States imperialism is its robber war against Nicaragua. President Coolidge disclosed in his speech of the 10th of January, 1927, the true meaning of the Nicaraguan war: *"If the revolution in Nicaragua continues, American investments and business interests will be in danger."* The infamous, bloody crusade against Nicaragua is as naked an imperialist profit-war as any ever conducted.

United States imperialism cooperates with British imperialism against China, against Soviet Russia, against Nicaragua; but at the same time there is a murderous competition and increasing imperialist rivalry between the two robber powers. *There is hardly any part of the world in which there is no open or covert struggle between British and American imperialism.* United States imperialism is breaking up the British Empire by catering to Canada and Australia. United States imperialism has successfully challenged Great Britain's financial hegemony. There is a permanent rubber struggle and oil war going on between America and Great Britain. The fiasco of the Three-Power Naval Limitation Conference in Geneva and the American slogan for a "second to none" navy show the irreconcilable nature of this imperialist antagonism. *The present co-operation of the United States Government with Japan in China has in it the germs of future conflicts on the Pacific.*

The recent "peace offensive" of Secretary of State Kellogg under the slogan to "outlaw war" is nothing but an imperialist maneuver to counteract the genuine struggles for peace of the Soviet Union. United States imperialism aims through the Kellogg treaty to diminish the power of the League of Nations, which is the organization of the European big powers, and tries to render futile any attempt of the European powers to build a bloc against United States imperialism. At the same time the Kellogg treaty tries to unite all the capitalist powers, not under the leadership of the League of Nations, but under the leadership of United States imperialism against the Soviet Union. Despite all empty talk about "outlawing" war, imperialist antagonisms are steadily growing, and there is *increasing resistance* against the aggressive imperialist policies of the United States. The growing competition with Europe, the organization of European trusts and cartels, the tariff issues with Germany, Great Britain and France, the questions of the war debts and the Dawes Plan, the domination over the Pacific, the growing revolt of the Latin-American countries—all these conflicts are pregnant with future imperialistic wars.

The whole policy of United States imperialism is today a policy of preparedness for imperialist wars. The entire country is bristling with bayonets. The United States has never before had such a big army and navy. No other country in the world has spent as much for its navy as this country. In 1926-27 Japan spent $119,000,000, the British Empire $299,000,000 and the United States $334,000,000 for navy purposes. In 1928 the appropriation for the United States navy has already reached $363,000,000 and for the army $394,000,000, totalling $757,000,000. In his last message to Congress President Coolidge came out openly for the big navy program. On December 14, 1927, the big navy program was introduced in the House of Representatives, appropriating not less than $725,000,000. Federal government expenses for past and future wars amounted to 82 cents out of every dollar spent in 1927. *It is estimated that in 1928 Congress will directly or indirectly vote about two billion dollars for military purposes on land and sea and in the air.*

United States imperialism is making the most elaborate preparations for war. *The workers and working farmers must know that wars under capitalism are inevitable.* "Small" wars are going on all the time, even today, and the next big imperialist world war is already looming up. The next world war will be even more devastating than the first one. The whole life of the entire country will be subordinated to war purposes. The whole population will be mobilized. The whole country will be turned into a huge munition factory. The phrase about "outlawing war," the promise about preventing war by arbitration, and the babbling of the Socialist Party about democratizing the League of Nations of the European robber powers are only designed for one purpose—to distract the attention of the masses from the war danger, from the real revolutionary struggle against imperialistic wars. Disarmament is impossible under capitalism. Compulsory arbitration is a reactionary utopia and delusion. Only the proletarian revolution can be the way out from the present situation.

Demands

1. Not a man, not a gun, not a cent for the imperialist army and navy!

2. Down with the imperialist war against Nicaragua! Defeat Wall Street's war in Nicaragua! Marines sent to Nicaragua must refuse to fight against the National Liberation Army. American marines in Nicaragua and China, go over to the side of the Nicaraguan and Chinese revolutions!

3. Immediate withdrawal of all American troops from Latin America and from the colonies of the Pacific. Immediate withdrawal of United States warships and marines from China.

4. Complete and immediate independence for all American colonies and semi-colonies.

5. Hands off Mexico!

6. Abolition of the regimes of United States Customs control or "supervision" of finances in Latin America. Withdrawal of support from the puppet governments subsidized by United States imperialism, such as those of Gomez of Venezuela, Leguía of Peru, and Ibañez of Chile.

7. Abolition of all extra-territoriality privileges of the United States in Asia, Africa and Latin America.

8. Abolition of the present mercenary army and navy and State militia, and struggle for a toilers' militia. Election of officers by the soldiers and sailors. Full right to vote and hold office for the members of the military forces.

9. Fight for the abolition of the whole system of infamous imperialist "peace" treaties. Down with the Dawes Plan! Cancellation of all debts of the last imperialist world war. Immediate withdrawal from the World Court and refusal to enter into the League of Nations.

VI. Defense of the Soviet Union

The whole world is under capitalist domination. The Socialist Republic of the Soviet Union is the sole country in which there is a Workers' and Farmers' Government.

The very existence of the Soviet Union is the best proof that it is possible to overthrow capitalism and emancipate the working class. The example of Soviet Russia shows that socialism is not a dream. It is a fact—and a fact that looms big in the history of mankind—that under the leadership of the Russian workers, a nation of 150 million, not less than one-sixth of the earth, has been able to free itself from the yoke of capitalism and establish a workers' republic which has maintained power for over ten years in spite of all the capitalists of the world.

The capitalist countries are carrying out a ruthless rationalization at the expense of the workers. *Only the Soviet Union is carrying out a socialist rationalization for the benefit of the nation as a whole.* The proletarian dictatorship in the Soviet Union expropriated the capitalists and big landowners. The workers control the industries. The working farmers received the land of the big landowners. Soviet Russia is building socialism now, and is taking the first steps toward a higher, a collective type of agriculture. *There is the most complete system of labor protection and social insurance in Soviet Russia.* One of the first steps of the proletarian revolution was the introduction of the 8-hour day, and at the tenth anniversary of the existence of the Soviet Republic the Soviet Government established the 7-hour day. While the courts and the government of this country are smashing the unions in the name of the Constitution, the Code of Labor Laws, Paragraph 155, of the Soviet Union runs:

"In accordance with Statute 16 of the Constitution of the Soviet Union, all organs of the State must render to the industrial unions and their organizations every assistance, place at their disposal fully equipped premises to be used as Palaces of Labor and trade-union halls; charge reduced rates for public services, such as posts, telegraphs, telephones, railroad and shipping rates, etc."

There is a sinister conspiracy of all capitalist powers against the Socialist Soviet Union. Great Britain is the leader of the imperialist coalition, but the United States Government is actively participating in it. The United States Government refuses to recognize the Soviet Government, to recognize the very existence of one of the most powerful countries in the world, for the sole reason that the workers and not the capitalists run that country. The United States Government and its officials seize upon every opportunity to fight the Soviet Union. Ambassador Herrick's shameful statements in Paris, the American loans to finance the anti-Soviet policies of Poland and Finland, and the rejection of the gold bullion sent to the United States are convincing proofs of the hostile policy of United States imperialism toward Soviet Russia.

The Soviet Union is the only power which has reduced its military forces. It made the historic offer at the last international conference at Geneva for an immediate and complete disarmament of all countries. The capitalist governments refused to accept the proposal of the Soviet Union, because the very nature of capitalism is aggression, oppression, and war. All capitalist armies are deadly enemies of the working class, but the Red Army of workers and peasants of the Soviet Union is the defender of the working class of the whole world. *The solidarity of the working class of all countries must be with the only Workers' Republic in the world.*

Demands

1. Defend the Socialist Republic of the Soviet Union, the champion of the cause of the working class of all countries, against the conspiracies of the capitalist powers.

2. Immediate recognition of the Soviet Government by the United States Government.

3. Promotion of trade with the Union of Socialist Soviet Republics by the granting of sufficient credits by the Federal Government, as a means of stimulating American industry and absorbing the unemployed.

4. Establishment of direct connections between the American and Russian working class.

VII. CAPITALIST DEMOCRACY AND THE GOVERNMENT-STRIKEBREAKER

Many workers foster illusions as to the possibility of achieving their emancipation from the oppression and exploitation of capitalism through the election of a majority of the members of the legislative bodies and executive officials of the capitalist government. The American Federation of Labor and the Socialist Party help to maintain these dangerous and futile illusions. The national platform of the Socialist Party states: *"By intelligent use of the ballot, aided if need be by indus-*

trial action, all class divisions and class rule can be abolished." It is one of the foremost duties of the Communists to destroy such illusions and to expose all those yellow Socialist misleaders of the workers who help to create these illusions.

The present government is a government of the capitalists. It cannot be transformed into a government of the working class, and its sole purpose is to defend the interests of private property and oppress the workers, working farmers, the Negro masses, and the colonial peoples.

The Constitution of the United States was drawn up by the bankers, big landowners, and rich merchants of 1787, admittedly against the working masses. As Madison, the "Father of the Constitution," put it, the Government ought *"to protect the minority of the opulent against the majority."* It is an illusion to think that the *majority* of the people of the United States can change the Constitution. The vote of two-thirds of the members of the legislative bodies of three-fourths of the forty-eight States is required to initiate any movement for an amendment. On this basis one-fourth of the States, which may be the smallest ones and in which there may live only one-fourteenth of the population, can prevent any change of the so-called "democratic" Constitution.

The Constitution contains a whole series of notorious "checks and balances" for the sole purpose of making it impossible for a majority antagonistic to the ruling class to make its will effective. The members of the House of Representatives are elected every two years, the President every four years, and the members of the Senate every six years, so that a complete change of Government can be made only through elections spread over six years. The elections are not at the same time, because the Fathers of the Constitution wanted to give a chance for the "cooling off" of any mass discontent which might express itself in the elections. The Senate has a veto over the decisions of the House. A special joker of the Constitution is that a newly elected Congress cannot come into session until thirteen months after its election, thus giving a chance to the repudiated Congress to intrench its will by new legislation. The President can veto the actions of both houses of Congress, and over and above the House, the Senate, and the President stands the Supreme Court, which can nullify laws which all three have passed, declaring these laws unconstitutional.

Only a minority of the people entitled to vote participate in the elections, and large sections of the population of voting age are disfranchised. In the South the 5.7 million Negroes of voting age are today as much disfranchised as in the darkest days of chattel slavery. The 6.3 million foreign-born unnaturalized workers of voting age are disfranchised because they are "aliens." The disfranchised Negroes and foreign-born workers together constitute almost 20 per cent of the population of voting age. The youth between the ages of 18 and 21 is entirely disfranchised. The hundreds of thousands of migratory workers, who cannot comply with the residential qualifications, are likewise robbed of their elementary political rights.

The *two-party system,* which in the South is in reality only a one-party system, is also one of the props of American democracy, preventing the splitting-off of the bulk of the working class and working farmers from the parties of big business.

Elections are very expensive in this country. Campaign funds are huge; they run into millions, and big business is able to buy as many and as high offices as it likes. On the other hand, working-class parties, which rely only on the support of the exploited workers and farmers, are poor and are not able to compete with the rich capitalist parties.

Big business controls thousands of *newspapers.* Thirty million copies of poisonous capitalist propaganda every day fill the minds of the masses. *Big business has a monopoly of the schools, churches, moving picture theatres, radio, and the whole machinery of propaganda and agitation.*

And when, despite all obstacles and barriers, some representatives elected by the votes of the working class get into the legislative bodies, big business prevents their functioning by simply kicking them out. This was done in the case of the Socialist members of the Cleveland City Council because they protested against the imperialist war. The same procedure was repeated in the case of the Socialist Assemblymen of New York State.

Under such circumstances to prate about "democracy" is hypocrisy and conscious betrayal of the working class. *The present big business democracy of the United States is in reality nothing but a dictatorship of the capitalists.* The 1928 election platform of the Socialist Party, which accepts the present Constitution as a basis and demands only a "modernized Constitution," is thereby accepting the present capitalist State and the perpetuation of the oppression of the working class.

And if there is anything big business is unable to push through by "constitutional" means, it does it unscrupulously by *unconstitutioinal* means. *Corruption is inseparable from capitalist government.* There are very few countries in the world which show such a clear picture of governmental corruption. The Teapot Dome scandal, the Sinclair-Burns affair, the open purchases of elections by Vare and Smith, the Fall-Doheny affair, the dirty deals of Daugherty and the other members of the Harding-Coolidge cabinet, and the campaign funds of the Republican Hoover and the Democrat Al Smith are but a few examples of the venality of leading politicians. And if any of them are caught, there are still judges and fixed juries to save them. Few rich men are convicted in this country.

Democracy, corruption, and naked force and violence are the chief methods of capitalist dictatorship. Government by injunction, raids and deportations, penitentiaries for political prisoners, troops crushing strikes, frame-ups and lynchings— these are the realities of the unwritten Constitution. Today what George Washington, the first President of the United States, said is more true than ever before: "Government is not reason; it is not eloquence—it is force."

With imperialism the Government has grown into a mammoth monster of centralization. *The country has never had such a huge governmental apparatus.* In 1884 the number of Federal civil service employees was only 13,780; by 1912 it had mounted to 278,000; while today the figure (exclusive of army and navy forces) is not less than 559,138. The number of Government employees—Federal, State and local—in the whole country today mounts up to a total of three million. *This gigantic apparatus of bureaucracy is entirely in the hands of the capitalists.* There is a complete merger of trustified capital and government. The leaders of big business—Hoover, the efficiency expert; Mellon, one of the richest men in the country; Dawes, the banker; Morrow, the errand boy of Morgan; Hughes, of Standard Oil; Coolidge, the strikebreaker; Fall and Daugherty, the kept men of the oil magnates—have or had seats in the Government. Governmental power is being concentrated more and more in the hands of the executive and judicial departments at the expense of the elected legislative bodies. *The President, above all, has assumed almost unlimited power.* He has control over appropriations of funds, over tariff, runs the foreign policy of the country, and decides questions of war and peace. *The actual constitutional form of the "freest" democracy in the world is today that of an unconstitutional monarchy.*

The working class in its struggle for emancipation cannot reform or "take over" the present apparatus of government. The proletarian revolution will destroy this apparatus, and will build its own based on the factories as units of production and not on territorial congressional districts. The State form of the rule of the working class will be the councils of the workers, which will serve not as "talking shops" but as working bodies uniting legislative and executive power. This Soviet form of government constitutes the only real democracy for the overwhelming majority of the people, for the toiling masses.

Demands

1. Abrogation of government by injunction.
2. Prohibition of the use of guards, gunmen, deputy sheriffs, militia or Federal troops in labor struggles.
3. Unrestricted right to organize, to strike, and to picket. Unrestricted right of free speech, free press, and free assemblage for the working class.
4. Abolition of the Senate, of the Supreme Court, and of the veto power of the President.
5. Judges should not be appointed. They should be elected by the working people, and should be removable at any time. Legal aid should be gratis for all wage-earners.
6. Franchise for all foreign-born and migratory workers and for the youth between the ages of 18 and 21. Enforcement of the franchise for the Negroes.
7. Abolition of the anti-syndicalist laws and the Espionage Act.
8. Repeal of all industrial court laws.
9. Abolition of secret anti-labor organizations.
10. Abolition of censorship over moving pictures, theatres, radio.
11. Immediate release of all political prisoners.

VIII. A Labor Party

There are many strikes and labor struggles in this country, but there is no political *mass* party of the working class in the United States which can today rally *millions of wage-earners.* America is the only highly developed industrial country in the world in which the bulk of the working class is not yet politically independent.

It is a most vital necessity that the masses of workers should understand that the economic struggle must be supplemented by political struggle. Without economic fights, without building unions and conducting strikes, the workers would be unable to improve their living conditions, hours, and wages. But no permanent gain can be achieved by the weapon of a mere economic struggle. *The most powerful trade union can be paralyzed by the almighty Government of the bosses,* by its troops and injunctions. The workers may even be robbed of the results of a successful strike, because the *increasing cost of living* can nullify higher wages.

Mere economic struggle cannot free the workers from exploitation and oppression. Political struggle is also necessary. But it must be political struggle in the interests of the working class and carried on by political organizations of the working class. Many workers participate in political struggles but on the side of the bosses. Today the bulk of the workers—even those who economically, in their trade unions, by their strikes, fight the bosses—support the political parties of the same bosses, the Republican and Democratic parties. This is a fatal mistake, because it means that the workers themselves help the capitalists to hold their grip on the State power. *Those workers who still remain in the camps of the Republican and Democratic parties are helping the capitalists to be the bosses of the courts, to use injunctions and armed forces to crush the trade unions and to paralyze the strike movements of the workers.*

The workers have made several attempts to link up their trade unions and other labor organizations into a Labor Party. In certain places Farmer Labor parties are now in existence. The Workers (Communist) Party supports the formation of those labor parties which are based on trade unions and other organizations of the working class. It is willing to participate in the formation of such labor parties, because it considers this the *first decisive step toward independent political action* by the working class, the first step of the workers to break away from the parties of the bosses. At the same time the Communist Party considers it its duty to tell the workers frankly that a Labor Party has its limitations and that it will not be able to lead the workers in their final struggle for their emancipation. Only a Communist Party can do that. Only under the leadership of the Communist Party can the American working class emancipate itself from the double yoke of capitalist exploitation and oppression.

It is to the interest of the workers to participate in all election struggles. *It is necessary to fight for the election of workers to the various legislative bodies.* It is necessary to run workers' candidates for offices. *But it is a dangerous illusion to think that the workers can assume power by electing more and more members of Congress or executive officials.* The workers can never seize power by the mere means of the ballot. Only by revolution can the working class swing into power. The most important aim of participation in election campaigns is the mobilization of the working masses for the struggle against the bosses and for the political organization of the working class in preparation for the struggle for power. The chief usefulness of representatives in legislative bodies consists in securing a public tribune for the cause of the working class, from whence it is possible to expose the actions of the bosses and arouse the militancy of the masses. The workers must know that political struggle is much broader than mere election struggle. They must know that political struggle is in the interests of the working class only if it is conducted in the form of a politically independent working-class party. The notorious *"non-partisan" policy of the A. F. of L.,* which calls upon the workers "to reward their friends and punish their enemies" within the capitalist parties, amounts in fact to unqualified support of the capitalist parties and capitalism itself. The policy of the *Socialist Party,* which promises the workers that they can assume power, abolish classes, and control the industries by the "intelligent use of the ballot" is an equally base betrayal of the working class. The *I. W. W.,* which restricts itself to mere "industrial action" because it is afraid that through political activities it will lose its revolutionary integrity, has actually become a sectarian and reactionary organization.

Demands

1. Independent political action of the working class. Formation of a Labor Party on a national, state and local scale and an alliance between the Labor Party and the exploited farmers for a common political struggle against capitalism.

2. A genuine Labor Party must be based on trade unions and other labor organizations, and on factory, mill, and mine committees of the unorganized workers. A genuine Labor Party must exclude all politicians of big and small business, and must include as a true federated body all sections of the working class, without any discrimination, which accept the general principle of the class struggle and are willing to fight for the interests of the workers and exploited farmers.

3. We call upon every worker: Affiliate your trade union to the Labor Party and you yourself join the Workers (Communist) Party.

IX. SOCIAL LEGISLATION

There is hardly any labor protection and even less social insurance in this country. The aim of labor protection is the safeguarding of the workers from the harmful conditions of production. The aim of the United States government today is the safeguarding of the capitalist from the "harmful" effects of trade-union organization. There is no law setting a maximum to the working day or against overtime. No law guarantees a weekly rest for the workers. No legal yearly holiday is assured the wage-earners. Very few compulsory rules exist or are enforced for safety and sanitation. Labor inspection is ineffective.

America is the leading country of the world in the field of industrial accidents. In industry there occur annually 25,000 fatal accidents and 2½ million accidents causing temporary disability. In 1927 there were no less than 2,224 fatalities on the mining field of battle. New York State alone had in 1926-27 in structural iron work not less than 21,606 accident cases which required compensation. In the metal mines there were 2,865 accidents per 10,000 workers. In other words, one worker out of every four was the victim of an accident.

There is no social insurance deserving the name in the United States. No care is taken of the *unemployed,* of the *sick,* of the *old,* of *invalids* and *cripples.* No help is given to families of deceased workers. The A. F. of L., with its narrow craft attitude against any social legislation, and the Socialist Party, with its parliamentary idiocy, share with the capitalists the responsibility for this complete lack of social legislation. The workers must understand that social legislation can be brought about only as a by-product of revolutionary struggle.

As substitutes for social legislation there are only the voluntary organizations of fraternal societies. Some of the trade unions try to build up some insurance schemes. All these small-scale organizations are very limited in their effect and mean an additional burden for the workers. The group insurance of the employers means the enslavement of the workers to a certain corporation. The private insurance companies are fleecing the working masses. There is a general lack of security in the life of the working class of America. No worker grows old as fast as the American worker. Speed-up and lack of labor protection drive him to premature old age. Scores of poisons, extreme heat and dampness and dust, and lack of sanitary measures ruin the health of the toilers.

The lack of labor protection and social insurance in the United States, in the richest capitalist country in the world, is brought out in bold relief by *comparison with the Workers' Republic of the Soviet Union.* The Socialist Republic of Soviet Russia has the most complete system of labor protection and social insurance. Her social insurance provides the following benefits: temporary disability benefits; benefits for child-birth, infant nursing, burial of insured persons and members of their families; pensions for widows; permanent disability benefits; pensions to family in event of bread-winner's death; unemployed benefits; maintenance of rest homes, sanatoria, and health resorts for workers; free medical aid.

In Soviet Russia all forms of social insurance are under the management of the workers and are maintained at the expense of the State. Factory inspection and all State protection of labor organs are under the direct control of the trade unions. Compulsory yearly vacations on pay are assured. The 7-hour day is guaranteed by law. The law forbids systematic overtime. There is a legal weekly rest of 42 hours. Special protection of women and children in industry has been enacted. A large range of sanitation and safety measures in all factories has been instituted.

There is a world of difference between the lack of labor protection and social insurance in the United States of America and the complete system of labor protection and social insurance in the United States of Socialist Russia—*the difference between a capitalist and a socialist country.*

Demands

1. Federal law for social insurance in the case of sickness, accident, old age, and unemployment for all wage-earners. The administration of all social insurance measures should be in the hands of the workers. The expenses should be covered by the State and the employers.

2. Federal law for the enactment of the 40-hour, 5-day week, forbidding all overtime. The law to provide for a six-hour working day in especially dangerous industries. Immediate enactment of a federal law providing for 48 consecutive hours of weekly rest for all wage-earners.

3. Federal law for compulsory rules and technical measures for safety and sanitation.

4. Establishment of effective labor inspection; inspectors to be elected by the workers themselves.

5. Free medical treatment, medicine, and hospital care for all wage-earners.

X. Tariff and Taxation

The propaganda agencies of the bosses are spreading the fallacy that the workers do not pay taxes. *In reality the workers and working farmers are the classes of society which bear the burden of the bulk of all taxation.*

Direct and indirect taxation and tariff revenues weigh down upon the shoulders of the working masses. Taxes are the basis of public expenditures. Public expenditures, however, are nothing but the cost of maintenance of the state apparatus of big business. The collection of taxes from the masses is a method by which the exploited are forced to pay the expenses for the upkeep of the system of exploitation and oppression.

Both parties of big business have been vying with each other for years to lighten as much as possible the burden of taxation for the big capitalists, transferring the burden of taxation to the backs of the workers and exploited farmers. The various tax-reduction plans of the government have had only one single aim: to cut the taxes of the rich and to cut even more the taxes of the richest. Secretary of the Treasury Mellon, who himself is one of the richest men in the country, is brazenly following the policy of cutting down the super-tax on high incomes, and declares that he is against tax exemption of low incomes, on the ground that the payment of taxes creates for people with low incomes "a sense of part ownership in the government." The most outrageous privileges are enjoyed by the parasitic owners of federal, state and municipal securities. This *rentier* class, which is completely divorced from the process of production and whose only connection with industry is coupon-clipping, owns today no less than 16 billion dollars of such securities, which are wholly exempt from all taxation.

The most vicious form of indirect taxation is the tariff. The tariff raises the cost of living for the working class, and increases the price of industrial goods bought by the farmers. The United States has the highest tariffs in the world, despite the fact that the industries of this country are the most highly developed and enjoy the strongest position.

Trust monopoly and tariff go together in the United States. *The chief function of tariff is to secure unlimited monopoly to the trusts.* The tariff helps to exclude foreign competition. It makes it possible for the trusts to raise the prices of their products to the buyers of this country by an amount nearly equal to that of the tariff. At the same time it makes it possible for the trusts to sell their goods below cost price in foreign countries, thanks to the surplus profits they make in this country.

Trust monopoly and high tariff are the most dangerous factors working for new imperialist wars. The larger the territory "protected" by tariff, the greater the amount of super-profit. The trust monopolies, therefore, have a tendency to expand the territory of the United States, to occupy new regions. That can be done only by conquest, through threat of war, and war.

The high tariff wall around this country forces the other countries likewise to "protect" themselves by tariff walls. This hinders or even prevents the export of American products to other countries. But accumulation of capital is going on with increasing speed, and American big business, instead of exporting goods, is exporting capital on an ever greater scale. The next step is the "defense" of the investments of American bankers in foreign countries. A strong army and a "second to none" navy are necessary. War

threats, war danger, and wars are the order of the day. *The "protective," "defensive" tariff is in reality the most offensive weapon in the hands of big business.*

The tariff policy of both parties of big business exposes the emptiness of their so-called struggle against each other.

The Republican Party was originally the party of tariff, because it represented the growing manufacturing interests of the North. The Democratic Party was originally the party against tariff, because it expressed the interests of the large plantation owners of the South. But with the change in economic conditions both parties are altering their positions on tariff. The industrialization of the South has created a powerful capitalist section in that part of the country, too, and caused a portion of the Democrats to come out as advocates of high tariff. On the other hand, the international bankers of the North—who have invested billions in Europe and are afraid that Europe will not be able to pay her debts, if she cannot export industrial products to this country—are now in favor of the lowering or abolition of the tariff and are making their influence felt more and more in the high councils of the Republican Party which they dominate.

The interests of the working class are against high tariff. At the same time it would be an illusion to think that "free trade" would be a permanent relief for the toiling masses. Free trade under capitalist conditions is as much a capitalist institution as high tariff.

Demands

1. Abolition of all indirect taxes.

2. Exemption from all kinds of taxation for all wage-earners.

3. Tax-exemption for all working and exploited farmers.

4. Graduated income tax, starting with incomes above $5,000 and increasing gradually, so that all incomes over $25,000 per year are confiscated.

5. All tax exemptions on bonds, stocks and securities must be abolished.

6. Graduated inheritance and gift taxes on great fortunes must be introduced.

7. Tariff on all necessities of the working class and on all goods used by the farmers must be abolished.

XI. The Plight of the Farmers

For two decades the conditions of the farmers have been growing steadily worse. The working farmer is becoming poorer and poorer. Millions have been driven away from their farms. Other millions are bankrupt and are only nominally owners of their farms. Tenancy is growing. The standard of living for the farmer and his family is becoming lower and lower. Hardships, suffering and poverty are features of the life of the working farmer.

The working farmer is today in an increasing measure only nominally the owner of the land. The mortgages and other debts are an unbearable burden on the exploited farmer. The product of his labor no longer belongs to him but to his creditors. The total amount of debts of the farmers (mortgage, personal and commercial) is the stupendous sum of 15 billion dollars, which at 6 per cent means *an annual tribute of 900 million dollars to the bankers, merchants and other leeches of capitalism.* The number of exploiting absentee owners is steadily increasing. In 1880 tenant farmers were 25.6 per cent of all farmers; in 1925 they were 38.6 per cent. Farmers are forced into bankruptcy by hundreds of thousands. In the Middle West between 1920 and 1923 no less than 22.5 per cent of all farm owners and 35 per cent of all tenants lost their farms by bankruptcy, by foreclosure, or retained them only—as the Government expresses it—by the "leniency" of their creditors.

At least 40 per cent of the whole agricultural population, 4.2 million people, are neither owners nor tenant farmers but simply agricultural workers, who own nothing but their labor power. *The agricultural workers have the lowest standard of living, are forced to work the longest working day and under the worst conditions in the whole country.* Their wages are actually decreasing. The introduction of new machinery is replacing them by tens of thousands. They are unorganized, isolated, and completely at the mercy of their employers and the State power. The agricultural workers are part of the American working class and must be embraced by its economic and political organizations in the struggle against capitalism.

The working farmers are in the most disastrous condition, because they are up against trust monopoly. The farmers are forced to pay the highest percentage of taxation. *The taxes of the farmers have been increased in a most alarming fashion.* They amounted in 1913 to $624,000,000; today to $1,436,000,000. The general property tax is directed chiefly against the farmer rather than against other property owners. The local taxes increase the burden of the working farmer to an intolerable degree. Even Secretary of Agriculture Jardine was forced to admit that the *farmers spend not less than 30 per cent of their net income for taxes.*

Mechanization of agriculture is another reason for the ruin of the farmers. The number of tractors, which in 1920 was 229,000, by 1925 had grown to 506,000, and in 1927 amounted to 700,000. The use of combines is spreading, each of them displacing three harvest hands. The poor farmer is too poor to buy expensive machinery. His farm is too small to utilize machinery to its full extent.

Industry is trustified and by virtue of its monopoly is able to control the prices of machinery and all the other goods the farmer must buy. At the same time big business is able to dictate the prices of all products the farmer must sell. There is a whole series of special forms of exploitation to which the farmer is subjected. He is at the mercy of the powerful capitalist agencies of distribution of farm products, the railroads, meat packers, milk trusts, huge elevator combines, gamblers and cotton brokers, banks, and the government farm credit system.

The basic reason for the bankruptcy of the working farmers is trust monopoly, is capitalism.

All agricultural credit is in the hands of the banks. The cooperative organizations of the farmers are chained to capitalism by means of credit. Tariff, which is supposed to "protect" not only industrial products but agricultural products as well, operates only in the interests of the big trusts. All the promises of the Republican and Democratic parties have amounted only to betrayal of the farmers, and have only been in the interests of the bigger landowners and farm banks.

The big lesson the working and exploited farmers must learn from their own desperate situation is that they must break off their alliance with the bankers and other factors of big business and must form an alliance with the working class. The fate of the McNary-Haugen "farm relief" bill and the McFadden branch banking bill is the best proof of the futility of any alliance of the farmers with the bankers. The farm bloc in Congress—which speaks in the name of the working farmers, but is in fact the expression of the interests of the big landowners, farmer-capitalists, and farm bankers—made a bargain with the representatives of Wall Street to the end that both bills should pass jointly in Congress. Indeed, both bills passed. But President Coolidge, as the highest exponent of big business in the Government, signed only the McFadden banking bill and vetoed the McNary-Haugen "farm relief" bill. All the so-called friends of the farmers — banker Dawes, millionaire Lowden, the farm bloc, the "Progressives," such as LaFollette, Norris, Shipstead and their ilk—are only enemies of the exploited farmers in the disguise of friends.

The working and exploited farmers and the industrial and agricultural workers must fight shoulder to shoulder against their common enemies: against big business, against the trusts and against the government of capitalism.

Demands

1. A five-year moratorium on farm mortgage debts, including debts on chattels.

2. Protection of the working farmer against monopoly prices. Essential lowering of the prices of all trust products which the farmer uses.

3. Protection of the farmer against special exploitation by distributing agencies of production, by railroads, meat packers, milk trusts and grain elevator combines.

4. Federal law for the creation of a special farm relief fund of $1,000,000,000 to relieve the conditions of the tenant and mortgaged farmers, the fund to be administered by organizations of working farmers.

5. Federal law against forced farm foreclosures.

6. Abolition of all federal and local taxes on working and tenant farmers.

7. The land to belong to its users.

8. Complete freedom to organize and strike for the agricultural workers. Federal law to guarantee a seven-hour maximum working day and a 48-hour weekly rest for all agricultural workers. Yearly vacation with pay for all farm laborers. Extension to agricultural workers of all benefits of social insurance and labor protection legislation demanded for industrial workers.

XII. Oppression of the Negroes

American white imperialism oppresses in the most terrific way the ten million Negroes who constitute not less than one-tenth of the total population. White capitalist prejudice considers the Negroes a "lower race," the born servants of the lofty white masters. The *racial caste system* is a fundamental feature of the social, industrial and political organization of this country. The Communist Party declares that it considers itself not only the party of the working class generally but also the champion of the Negroes as an oppressed race, and especially the organizer of the Negro working-class elements. *The Communist Party is the party of the liberation of the Negro race from all white oppression.*

There is a "new Negro" in process of development. The social composition of the Negro race is changing. Formerly the Negro was the cotton farmer in the South and domestic help in the North. The industrialization of the South, the concentration of a new Negro working-class population in the big cities of the East and North, and the entrance of the Negroes into the basic industries on a mass scale have changed the whole social composition of the Negro race. *The appearance of a genuine Negro industrial proletariat creates an organizing force for the whole Negro race*, furnishes a new working-class leadership to all Negro race movements, and strengthens immensely the fighting possibilities for the emancipation of the race.

The Negro tenant farmers and share-croppers of the South are still, despite all the pompous phrases about freeing the slaves, in the status of virtual slavery. They have not the slightest prospect of ever acquiring possession of the land on which they work. By means of an usurious credit system they are chained to the plantation owners as securely as chattel slaves. Peonage and contract labor are the fate of the Negro cotton farmer. The landowners, who are at the same time the merchants and government of the South, rule over the Negroes with a merciless dictatorship.

There is the most dishonest and disgraceful "gentleman's agreement" between the two capitalist parties against the political rights of the Negroes. The famous Fourteenth and Fifteenth Amendments of the Constitution amount but to a scrap of paper. They were never carried out for a moment. The Supreme Court has upheld State laws which disfranchised the Negroes. Sheer force prevents the Negro from exercising his so-called political rights. The Federal Government has never made any attempt to reduce the representation of those Southern States which violate the Constitution, as Section Two of the Fourteenth Amendment of the Constitution provides. The Republican Party, the party of Lincoln, has sunk so low that it has provided for measures to segregate the Negro delegates in its 1928 Kansas City nominating convention. *Lynch law is the law over the Negroes. The terror of the Ku Klux Klan is the constitution for the Negroes.* They are burned alive, whipped to death, hunted to death with dogs in the name of white civilization.

There is a general segregation policy against the Negro race. Separate residential sections; Jim Crow cars; separate schools for Negro children; exclusion from "white" hotels, restaurants, theatres and railway waiting rooms; exclusion of Negroes from juries which try Negroes. Negro teachers cannot teach in most white schools. *The white masters try to reduce the Negroes to illiteracy.* According to the 1920 census, there were 4 per cent illiterates among the whites and 22.9 per cent among the Negroes. The Southern States spend hardly any money for the education of Negro children.

In the cotton States the Negro farmers are compelled to live in miserable shacks under conditions destructive of life and health. In the cities the Negroes do the unskilled, the most disagreeable, most hazardous work, and are crowded into the worst sections of the city. The death rate of the Negroes is much higher than that of the whites. In 1925 it was 11.8 per thousand for the whites and 18.2 for the Negroes.

The Southern plantation owners and their Government have tried to keep the Negro farmers and agricultural workers in the Southern cotton fields by force. But even their brutal terror has not been able to check the mighty migration from these cotton plantations to the industrial centers of the Northern and Eastern States. This migration is an "unarmed, Spartacan uprising" against slavery and oppression by a capitalist and feudal oligarchy.

The Negro fled from the South, but what has he found in the North? He has found in the company towns and industrial cities of the North and East a wage slavery virtually no better than the contract labor in the South. He has found crowded, unsanitary slums. He has exchanged the old segregation for a new segregation. He is doing the most dangerous, worst paid work in the steel, coal and packing industries. He has found the racial prejudices of a narrow, white labor aristocracy, which refuses to recognize the unskilled Negro worker as its equal. *He has found the treachery of the bureaucracy of the A. F. of L. which refuses to organize the Negroes into trade unions.* The lynchings of the South are replaced by the race riots of the East. The employing class deliberately arouses the racial hatred and prejudice of the white workers against the Negro workers with the sinister aim to split and divide the ranks of the working class, thereby maintaining the oppression and exploitation of white and Negro workers. What Marx said about the United States is still true: "Labor in a white skin cannot emancipate itself as long as labor in a dark skin is branded." The Negro worker must learn to utilize to the fullest extent the possibilities created by modern capitalism for organization and struggle against wage slavery in alliance with the workers of other races.

The Communist Party considers it as its historic duty to unite all workers regardless of their color against the common enemy, against the master class. The Negro race must understand that capitalism means racial oppression and Communism means social and racial equality.

Demands

1. Abolition of the whole system of race discrimination. Full racial, political, and social equality for the Negro race.

2. Abolition of all laws which result in segregation of Negroes. Abolition of all Jim Crow laws. The law shall forbid all discrimination against Negroes in selling or renting houses.

3. Abolition of all laws which disfranchise the Negroes.

4. Abolition of laws forbidding intermarriage of persons of different races.

5. Abolition of all laws and public administration measures which prohibit, or in practice prevent, Negro children or youth from attending general public schools or universities.

6. Full and equal admittance of Negroes to all railway station waiting rooms, restaurants, hotels, and theatres.

7. Federal law against lynching and the protection of the Negro masses in their right of self-defense.

8. Abolition of discriminatory practices in courts against Negroes. No discrimination in jury service.

9. Abolition of the convict lease system and of the chain gang.

10. Abolition of all Jim Crow distinctions in the army, navy, and civil service.

11. Immediate removal of all restrictions in all trade unions against the membership of Negro workers.

12. Equal opportunity for employment, wages, hours, and working conditions for Negro and white workers. Equal pay for equal work for Negro and white workers.

XIII. THE FOREIGN-BORN WORKERS

Next to the Negroes the foreign-born workers in the basic industries are the most exploited, most persecuted stratum of the toiling masses of this country. There are almost 14 million foreign-born in the United States. The overwhelming majority belong to the working class. *Nearly half of all the foreign-born are toiling in the manufacturing and mechanical industries. The majority of all industrial workers of America, not less than 58 per cent of the total employed in American industries, are foreign-born.* Steel, coal, textile, automobile—all these industries are based on the sweat of the foreign-born workers. Cut off by differences in language and customs, the foreign-born workers are an easy prey of the employing class. Their fate is the longest hours, the lowest wages, the worst housing, the poorest schooling. *Scores of state and federal laws discriminate against the foreign-born workers.* There is hardly a State in the United States which has no special laws discriminating against the foreign-born workers. According to the law of some States, the foreign-born person has no right to read newspapers or books not printed in English. He has no right to keep dogs or a gun or a rifle. He cannot teach in public schools. According to the laws of nine States, a foreign-born worker cannot be employed on public works. Some States do not allow public meetings to be conducted except in the English language.

But all this discrimination is not enough for 100 per cent Americanism. *The Coolidge administration is carrying out an offensive against the foreign-born workers as part of the open-shop drive of the bosses, is planning a whole series of vicious measures against them.* The foreign-born workers are to be registered. They are to be finger-printed and photographed like criminals. If naturalized, they are to have their citizenship papers taken from them if their conduct does not suit the bosses. They are to be deported if they participate in strikes or make speeches in strike meetings. The Chairman of the House Immigration Committee, Albert Johnson, during the powerful demonstrations demanding freedom for Sacco and Vanzetti, uttered the threat: "Aliens domiciled in America should remember that if they partake in anti-government demonstrations here they are liable to deportation under the 1919 Act."

There is a whole series of bills before Congress which are aimed against the foreign-born workers. The Brand Bill, the Hawes Bill, the Ashwell Bill, and other products of American Fascism try to reduce the foreign-born workers to modern industrial serfs. The Brand Bill would compel all foreign-born not only to register but "to report at such times and such places" when "in the judgment of the President the interests of the national defense so require." The same Act would decree that "whenever any alien is *temporarily* absent from the district in which he is registered, he shall report at such times and places and give such information in regard to his movements as may be required."

The *immigration laws* which restrict the freedom of movement of the foreign-born workers and discriminate against the peoples of Asia are part and parcel of the system of American imperialism. The newest demand of the bosses, as expressed in the notorious Brand Bill, is to give full authority to the President to regulate, restrict or enlarge the immigration quotas according to the actual needs of the different industries. The apostles of 100-percentism are not the enemies of the foreign-born workers, if they can use them as strikebreakers, as helpers "in industrial needs."

The labor aristocracy, under the leadership of the A. F. of L. bureaucracy, shares with big business the profits derived from high tariffs and restriction of immigration. High tariff is the material basis for the prohibition of immigration. The platform of the Socialist Party for 1928 shows the true colors of this renegade party in not demanding unrestricted freedom of immigration and the repeal of the infamous immigration laws, but calling only for the *"modification of the immigration laws to permit the reuniting of families."*

The Workers (Communist) Party of America is equally the party of the native-born, the foreign-born, and the Negro workers. It is the party of the whole working class. It fights the offensive of the bosses against the foreign-born workers. It fights against nationalist prejudices which divide the ranks of the workers. *Its slogan is: Workers of all languages and races in America unite!*

Demands

1. All workers must unite against the common enemy, the capitalist class, to prevent the enactment of new laws (to register, fingerprint, and photograph) against foreign-born workers and to abolish all existing laws of discrimination.

2. All workers must wage an active campaign to uproot the prejudices fostered by the employing class against the foreign-born workers and to draw the millions of foreign-born workers more and more into the political life of the country and the class struggle.

3. Immediate repeal of the immigration laws. Abolition of all restrictions on immigration.

4. Equal pay for equal work for native and foreign-born workers.

XIV. Working Women

The number of working women is steadily growing. There are today in this country 8½ million working women over the age of ten.

The capitalists are the apostles of the family, but they do not hesitate to break up the family life of the working class, if the needs of industry make it necessary. They cannot resist the call of profits. The number of adult and married women in industry is growing fast. It had reached in 1920 almost two million. Manufacturers prefer women, because they offer less resistance than male workers to capitalist oppression. Male workers are often replaced by women, because the introduction of new machinery makes the skill of male workers superfluous. *As a general rule, women work in less well-paid occupations and receive lower wages for identical work.* The logic of capitalism is that working women need more

protection, they are weaker than the male workers; therefore, *they get less protection and are subjected to greater exploitation than male workers.*

The Communist Party is by no means against women working in industry. It is of the opinion that in entering industry working women can become more effective participants in the struggle of the working class against capitalist exploitation. But it calls on the workers to fight the harmful effects of industrial work on women and to struggle for the adequate protection of working women. Only a Communist society can lift the double burden of housekeeping and factory work from the women of the working class.

Demands

1. Prohibition by law of night work, overtime and job work for working women.

2. The law shall provide for an allowance throughout the period of pregnancy and childbirth to the amount of full working wages.

3. Legal enactment of a special allowance for working women during the nursing period of nine months. Nursing mothers shall have a half hour's leave every three hours for child feeding in nurseries provided by employers at all working places.

4. The organization of working women into trade unions and elimination of all restrictions and discriminations against women in trade unions.

5. Equal pay for equal work for male and female workers.

XV. Youth, Child Labor and Education

Exploitation of children and young workers is one of the pillars of American capitalist society. Children's blood and young boys' and girls' sweat are a growing source of profit for big business. According to the 1920 census, which greatly underestimates the number of child laborers, there were over one million working children between the ages of 10 and 15. To increase the shame there were 378,000 toiling children between the ages of 10 and 13. There are no statistics on the work of children under the age of 10 —that is the sole reason why there is no report about the scores of thousands of the smallest children of the working class slaving to the glory of our dollar civilization.

There are almost four million young workers

and at least one million boys and girls in industry alone. Steel and iron, coal and textile factories are the chief "playgrounds" of our working-class youth. *Technical progress means progress of youth and child labor.* It is one of the biggest achievements of American "democracy" that the Supreme Court of the United States, that notorious guardian of American "liberties," declared any laws forbidding child labor unconstitutional.

The propaganda agencies of capitalism boast about the wonderful progress in education. They forget only that the sole aim of the education of the children of the working class is to implant in their minds as early as possible a feeling of awe towards capitalist society. *Education is class education in this country.* Higher education is too expensive for the children of the working class. Primary education is conducted in the spirit of jingoism and religious prejudice. According to official statistics, in 1920 only 73 per cent of the pupils reached the sixth and only 58 per cent the eighth grade. In other words, almost half of the children did not even graduate from the elementary school. The schools are overcrowded. Anti-evolution laws prevent the teaching of natural science in many States. In the South, Jim Crow education prevails. The famous "academic" freedom is only a legend.

Under capitalism education is a monopoly of the master class. Only a Communist society, which will combine the participation in production with vocational training and general education, will break this monopoly and will abolish the class character of education, transforming it into social education, making it compulsory, universal and equal.

Demands

1. Compulsory abolition by law of child labor under the age of 16, and State maintenance of all children at present employed. Abolition of underground work, night work, overtime, and work in dangerous occupations for all young workers. Six-hour working day and the five-day week for all young workers between the ages of 16 and 18.

2. A $20 minimum wage for young workers.

3. Establishment of work-schools in factories for the training of young workers in industry. These work-schools should be modeled on the work-schools in the Soviet Union, should be under the control of the young workers belonging to trade unions and workers' factory committees. Young workers to receive full wages while attending work-schools, and the hours attending school should be included in the general hours of work.

4. Immediate utilization of schools as feeding centers for children of unemployed workers, whether of school age or below it. These stations should be under labor-parent control. Free clothing and free medical treatment by the schools for the children of the unemployed.

5. Every young person 18 years of age or over must be given the right to vote. Old enough to work—old enough to vote.

6. In schools at present: (a) free and equal education from the elementary schools through the universities; (b) immediate relief from overcrowding by building new schools; (c) abolition of religious and jingoist instruction; abolition of anti-evolution laws; (d) abolition of Jim Crow education; (e) no discrimination against teachers on account of "subversive" political opinions; right of teachers and students to organize.

XVI. Housing

Nothing brings out into bolder relief "equality" under capitalist conditions than the matter of housing. The members of the master class dwell in the finest apartments, in the most luxurious palaces. They monopolize the clean, broad streets of the "respectable" residential sections. *The workers are segregated in the most disagreeable unsanitary sections of the crowded cities.*

Congested tenements, miserable slums are the main quarters for proletarian homes. Death has a bigger toll in the working-class sections, especially among the children. Rent is unbearably high for workers. On the average the worker is compelled to spend more than 25 per cent of his wages on rent. According to the law of social justice in capitalist society, the higher the income the lower relatively the rent.

The Government—federal, state and municipal governments alike—are doing nothing to relieve the housing shortage and to reduce the high rents. Building speculators do not construct homes for the workers, because the poorly-paid wage-earner is not able to pay the high rent demanded. Scores of thousands of workers are forced to live in lightless rooms without adequate plumbing and heating, with insufficient ventilation and water supply.

In striking contrast to the criminal attitude of the American capitalist Government toward the housing situation are the measures of the Workers' Government of the Soviet Union. The Workers' Government of the Soviet Union nationalized all dwellings of the employing class. It turned over all the palaces and villas of the capitalists to the workers. It lowered the rent for wage-earners so much that unskilled workers pay only a nominal rent. The building of homes for workers is an essential part of the whole constructive program of the Soviet Government, which spends millions yearly to erect houses for wage-earners.

Demands

1. Municipal fixing of low rents for workers. Rent for wage-earners should not amount to more than 10 per cent of their wages.

2. Municipally built houses should be rented to the workers without profit.

3. Immediate enactment of state laws providing for abolition of the right of eviction by landlords against wage-earner tenants.

4. Compulsory repair by the landlords of all working-class homes in bad condition.

5. Immediate establishment by municipalities of homes to shelter the unemployed.

6. Municipal aid to workers' building co-operatives.

XVII. Prohibition

Prohibition, as it is "enforced" and violated in this country, is one of the most outstanding examples of capitalist corruption and hypocrisy.

The Workers (Communist) Party takes the following stand on the prohibition issue:

Prohibition was introduced in the interests of the manufacturers. As the *Pennsylvania Manufacturers' Journal* put it: "We believe there is no question of greater importance to American manufacturers, the great employers of labor, than prohibition." The prohibition of the consumption of liquor decreases the needs of the worker, and thus tends to decrease the price of his labor power. *The introduction of prohibition was part and parcel of the big rationalization campaign of the employing class.* It makes the worker more efficient, more adaptable to the machinery. It is a link in the chain of the general speed-up. The enforcement of prohibition is a typical class meas-

ure. Rich people are exempt from its enforcement. Its whole burden falls upon the proletarian elements.

Prohibition embodies in the most classic manner the basic views of the employers toward the workers. The worker gives his life not only during the working hours but all day and all the time to the capitalist. Eating, drinking and sleeping, the worker serves only one purpose: the maintenance of his labor power for the capitalists. The very fact that the worker consumes the food which he buys for his wages forces him to sell his labor power again. It *does* concern the capitalist how the worker eats and drinks. If the worker spends his wages for liquor, if he gets drunk Sunday night, if he is not fit for work Monday morning—that concerns the capitalist not because it is a violation of the interests of the worker, not because it helps to destroy him physically and mentally, but because it constitutes high crime against capital, since it "defrauds" the capitalist of the labor power which belongs to him.

These are the views of the capitalists concerning the "private" life of the workers. Prohibition is nothing but the realization of these views.

On the other hand, the driving force behind the movement against the enforcement of prohibition, for the repeal of the Eighteenth Amendment and the Volstead Act, is the *powerful alcohol capital* which still has tremendous vested interests in the liquor industry.

The "enforcement" of prohibition has created a *huge governmental machine* of prosecutors, spies, provocateurs and courts. This machine tends to increase the power of the capitalist government and is a virtual part of its strikebreaking apparatus.

The lack of enforcement of capitalist prohibition has created a *powerful bootlegging industry* with a capital of hundreds of millions of dollars. The hazards of this industry are compensated by extremely high profits. An elaborate system of an underground capitalist world is hiding itself under the surface of respectable capitalist society. It has its own spies, provocateurs and gunmen, who are often utilized against the labor movement, against striking workers. *The combination of the twin brothers, capitalist prohibition enforcement and capitalist bootlegging, has created an unheard-of amount of corruption, crime and hypocrisy.*

The stand of the Republican and Democratic parties on the prohibition issue is a model example of capitalist demagogy. It is not an issue between the two parties but rather one within both. Very often from wet throats issue dry voices. The playing up of prohibition as a major political issue serves only one purpose. It covers up the lack of any real difference between the capitalist parties, and distracts the attention of the workers from the real major class issues of the toiling masses.

Especially shameful is the position of the Socialist Party of America on the prohibition issue. Its platform is against the present prohibition enforcement, because "further persistence in this tragic farce threatens a complete breakdown of law and order." This exposes the Socialist Party in its true role as the upholder of capitalist law and order. Many members of the employing class also, who favor prohibition from the point of view of capitalist efficiency, are against strict enforcement, because they realize its impossibility under present conditions and likewise are concerned lest the faith of the masses in "law and order" be shaken.

Alcoholism is one of the most terrible social diseases of capitalist society. Alcoholism is caused by capitalism itself. Insecurity of life, the monotony of standardized factory work, the low cultural level of the masses and desperate poverty are the reasons for this social disease. Only a Communist society can cure alcoholism by elevating the cultural level of the masses, by diversifying labor, by putting an end to insecurity of life, and by eradicating poverty. The struggle against alcoholism, which must be conducted by the Communists in the most energetic fashion, is a part of the general struggle against capitalism. *Only the overthrow of capitalism will sweep away the despicable bootlegging industry and the equally despicable, corrupt, hypocritical capitalist prohibition enforcement.*

Demands

1. The Workers (Communist) Party favors the repeal of the Volstead Act and the Eighteenth Amendment.

2. Dissolution of the federal and state prohibition enforcement apparatus.

3. Energetic propaganda against alcoholism as one of the most malignant social diseases under capitalism.

XVIII. FORWARD TO A WORKERS AND FARMERS GOVERNMENT

This is the platform of the class struggle. These are the demands the Workers (Communist) Party puts forward in the present Presidential election campaign. But none of these demands, and not even the total of demands, exhausts the program of the Communist Party. We call upon the workers to rally around the Communist Party in a relentless struggle for these demands which, realized, would protect the toiling masses against the most harmful effects of trustified capitalism. But even the realization of all these demands would not liberate the working class from the double yoke of capitalist exploitation and oppression. Only the full realization of the entire program of the Communist Party can bring about the emancipation of the working class. The Communist Party has the following aims:

The formation of the proletariat into a class; its separation from other classes; the development of its consciousness, organization, and fighting capacity;

The organization of a mass Communist Party to lead the struggles of the working class against all capitalist parties;

The representation of the most general international interests of the working class as a whole as expressed in the principles and practice of the Communist International;

The overthrow of capitalist rule;

The conquest of political power by the working class and the establishment of the Dictatorship of the Proletariat.

American imperialism is very powerful. Capitalism in this country is still on its upward grade, but it is becoming more and more part and parcel of world capitalism, which on the whole has entered into the last declining stage of its development.

United States imperialism will not be able to bribe broad sections of the working class for many more years. It is not the sole workshop in the world as Great Britain was for decades. There are other mighty imperialist powers limiting the expansion of United States imperialism, competing with it on every front. The menace of new imperialist wars is looming up ever bigger on the horizon.

The very existence of the Socialist Republic of the Soviet Union, which freed one-sixth of the earth from capitalist influence and expansion, is a limitation to the growth of United States imperialism. *The forces of the proletarian revolution are gathering in other countries, too.* The more than three million votes of the Communist Party of Germany, the over one million votes of the Communist Party of France, the election victories of the Communist Party of Poland, which, though driven underground, was able to rally the majority of the Polish working class—are so many indices of the growth of the legions of the working-class revolution.

The struggle for liberation of the oppressed peoples of Asia and the growing resistance of the suffering peoples of Latin America constitute another limitation to the upward development of United States imperialism. There are *inherent contradictions within American imperialism* which work with irresistible force to break up the whole system. The anarchy created by the private ownership of the means of production results inevitably in murderous competition, crises and wars. The class character of American capitalist society must lead without fail to class wars. The sharpening contradictions within American capitalism will arouse gigantic forces which will be strong enough to overthrow it. The alliance of the 17 million industrial workers, the 4 million agricultural workers, the 10 million Negroes, and the millions of exploited tenant farmers will constitute a powerful bloc which will be able to crush the present dictatorship of the bosses.

These exploited and oppressed masses will rise up and establish a workers' and farmers' govern-ment, will organize their own State apparatus in the form of workers' councils, and will break the monopoly of the capitalists over the means of production.

A genuine Workers' and Farmers' Government of the United States will expropriate all large-scale industries, railroads, super-power plants, meat-packing plants, grain elevator combines. It will nationalize all large land estates; it will establish huge collective State farms, and will satisfy the land needs of the mortgaged and tenant farmers. It will nationalize all banks and commercial institutions. A Workers' and Farmers' Government of the United States will free all American colonies immediately, will grant the right of full self-determination to all Latin-American peoples, will realize full social equality for Negroes. It will disarm the master class and will arm the working masses.

Forward to a Workers' and Farmers' Government! Forward by means of relentless class struggle! The Workers (Communist) Party is the party of the class struggle. It is the deadly enemy of capitalist society. It fights for the complete unity of the working class, for the united struggle of native-born, foreign-born, and Negro workers against the common enemy: trustified capital.

The Workers (Communist) Party calls upon all workers and exploited farmers to leave the old capitalist parties.

Workers and exploited farmers, vote for and join the Workers (Communist) Party!

Rally around the platform of the class struggle!

Down with capitalist rule!

Forward to a Workers' and Farmers' Government!

THE END.

CAMPAIGN OF 1932

In 1932, in the depths of the Depression, the Republicans at their convention in Chicago renominated the incumbent president, Herbert Hoover, on the first ballot; and, although he received some serious opposition, Charles Curtis was again chosen for the vice-presidency after one ballot.

The Democrats, also meeting in Chicago, nominated Franklin Delano Roosevelt of New York on the fourth ballot after a spirited floor fight with two other rivals—one of whom, House of Representatives Speaker John Nance Garner of Texas, emerged as Roosevelt's running mate.

The Socialist Party selected the same ticket as in 1928—Norman Thomas of New York for president and James Maurer of Pennsylvania for vice-president. The Communist Party again nominated William Z. Foster of Illinois, together with James W. Ford of New York. The Prohibitionists were represented by William Upshaw of Georgia and Frank S. Regan of Illinois. The Socialist Labor Party's candidates were Verne L. Reynolds of New York and John W. Aiken of Massachusetts. The Farmer-Labor Party offered Jacob S. Coxey of Ohio for president and Julius J. Reiter of Minnesota for vice-president.

The election in November produced an overwhelming victory for the Democrats. They received 22,825,016 popular votes to 15,758,397 for the Republicans. The Socialists polled 883,990 votes, 2.22 percent of the total. The Communists received 102,221 votes; the Prohibitionists, 81,916; the Socialist Labor Party, 34,028; and the Farmer-Laborites, 7,431 votes. In the electoral vote, Roosevelt received 472 votes to 59 for Hoover.

The Communist Party Platform

The Communist party is the political party of the oppressed masses of the people—the industrial workers, the persecuted Negroes, the toiling farmers.

The Communist party enters this election campaign explicitly to rally the toilers of city and country, Negro and white, in a united struggle for jobs and bread, for the fight against imperialist war.

The Communist party calls upon all workers to resist the attacks of the bosses and to fight to maintain and improve their living standards.

The Communist party calls upon the oppressed masses to rally under Communist leadership in the revolutionary struggle to overthrow capitalism and to establish a government in the United States of workers and farmers.

CAPITALISM CANNOT FEED THE PEOPLE

Capitalism has shown its inability to feed the people. The political parties of capitalism which rule the country—Republican and Democratic—have exposed their complete bankruptcy in this period of severe crisis.

Fifteen million workers, ready and anxious to work, and capable of producing the food, clothing and other goods so urgently needed by the people, are suffering enforced idleness.

Those workers who still desperately cling to their jobs have been forced to accept one drastic wage cut after another, until in some cases their wages are now 50 per cent below their former income.

Hoover's "stagger plan" has brought almost universal part-time work with great reductions in the weekly earnings of the workers. Only 15 per cent of the employed workers now have full time jobs. Eighty-five per cent of these workers are only working a few days per week.

The ruthless robbery of the farmers by the big banks, railroads and manufacturers, which has been going on for the past fifteen years, has during the crisis increased a hundredfold. Farmers, like the workers, are starving; they are being evicted from their homes; their farms are being grabbed by the parasite bankers.

Unemployment, part-time work and wage cuts have resulted in a lowering of the living standards of the entire working class by more than 50 per cent, bringing the American workers down to the level of the poorly-paid European workers.

PROMISES, BUT NO FOOD

The frequent promises of Hoover and his Republican and Democratic supporters about "returning prosperity" are being completely refuted by these undeniable facts. Instead of "returning prosperity," we find only that the suffering of the workers and farmers and of their wives and children becomes steadily worse.

What have the capitalist politicians—Republicans and Democrats—done about it? Warehouses are bursting with unused food and clothing. Hundreds of thousands of houses are standing empty. Idle factories are capable of producing all the goods the people need and more. Yet have these politicians taken any steps to start the factories going again, to open up the empty houses for the evicted workers, or to distribute the food and clothing now stacked up in the warehouses among the starving? Not a step!

Starvation in the midst of plenty. This is what is presented to the workers and toiling farmers of the United States by the ruling class, by the bankers, manufacturers, lawyers, publicists, politicians and their political parties.

The Capitalist Way Out of the Crisis

The capitalists and their political henchmen remain coldly unconcerned about the suffering of the masses. They think only about the profits of the rich. Their way out of the crisis is a way that will bring permanent poverty and misery to the workers and poor farmers, while the few rich bankers and manufacturers who control the country become still richer and still more powerful.

Their way out of the crisis—the capitalist way out—firstly, means direct help, not to the poor, but to the rich.

Under the guise of "economy" they categorically refuse unemployment insurance at the expense of the State and the employers. They refuse to appropriate money for a far-reaching public works program. They refuse to appropriate money for immediate relief for the starving workers and farmers. They refuse to pay the bonus to the ex-servicemen of the last war, most of whom are now unemployed or working only part-time.

In their opinion, the slop from the restaurants and hotels and the miserable charity system is good enough for the hungry masses. The employed workers, themselves suffering from part-time work and wage cuts, are being forced to pay for even the charity system. The abominable "block-aid," "community chest," and "family-help-family" systems, by means of forced collections in the factories and neighborhoods, are placing the burdens of charity also on the hungry masses and taking it off the rich who alone can afford to pay.

Yet the Republicans and Democrats, who control the National and State governments, despite their "economy" talk where the masses are concerned, have plenty of funds to aid the bankers and manufacturers and to provide huge amounts for graft and corruption.

The last session of Congress, the Democratic control of the House and with the approval of Hoover, appropriated billions of dollars for direct aid to the rich. Hoover's "Reconstruction Corporation" alone made $2,000,000,000 available for the big bankers. Changes in the banking, tariff and taxation laws, not only placed the burden of the huge government deficit on the middle class and chiefly on the broad masses, but paved the way for further trustification of industry, more firm control of industries and railroads by the Wall Street banks, and for still greater profits by the biggest and most powerful capitalists.

The capitalist way out of the crisis—secondly—embodies a further direct and brutal attack on the living standards of the toilers.

Workers' wages are being even more drastically slashed. The speed-up in the factories and mines is daily increased. More factories are being shut down; more workers are thrown into the streets to join the ranks of the unemployed. The miserable charity rations are being further reduced and the burdens of the charity system are being placed on the already breaking backs of the toilers. In this way the capitalists try to escape from the crisis—to maintain their bloated profits, while the workers are being forced nearer and nearer to the starvation level and even below.

Murderous Police Attacks

When the workers, by strikes and demonstrations, fight to maintain their living standards and to resist these attacks of the bosses, they meet the sharpest terror. Their political rights guaranteed by the Constitution are denied them. Meetings, demonstrations and picket lines are ruthlessly smashed. Foreign-born workers are torn from their families and callously deported. The attack on the foreign-born is directed against the entire working class with the aim of dividing native and foreign-born workers. Workers are clubbed and gassed by the police on the instruction of the capitalists and their political hirelings. The Negro masses are Jim-Crowed and lynched. Workers are shot down and killed.

This terror is not the monopoly of one capitalist, one politician or one party. The Republican, Hoover, orders the gassing and brutal clubbing of the workers in Washington. The "liberal" Republican, Pinchot, orders the clubbing and murder of the Pennsylvania coal strikers. The Democratic Mayor Cermak orders the beating, gassing and killing of Negro workers on Chicago's South Side. Ford and his "progressive" henchman, Murphy, carries through the murder of four Detroit workers at Dearborn. The Socialist Mayor Hoan, backed by the progressive Republican LaFollette, orders the same attacks on the Milwaukee workers.

All the capitalists and all their parties are determined to force through the lowering of the workers' living standard and the maintenance of their own profits by an unprecedented and growing terror.

The capitalist way out of the crisis—thirdly— provides for intense preparation for and the immediate launching of a new imperialist war in which the workers and farmers will be called upon to serve as cannon fodder.

In their greedy desire for greater profits the capitalists set out to wrest new markets from their imperialist rivals by armed force, and to further oppress the people of Latin America, of China, of the Philippines, etc., and rob them of their territory and natural resources.

In preparation for this war the terror against the workers is being carried through to crush all militancy among the workers' organizations; billions of dollars are spent for naval and military armaments, while the people starve.

Efforts are being made to herd the masses— workers, farmers, students — into military and auxiliary organizations in an effort to make them the cannon fodder to be ruthlessly slaughtered on the battlefields. All this is done behind the screen of fake peace talk and fake disarmament proposals.

War in the Far East

The imperialist war has already started in the East, on the borders of the Soviet Union, with the robber attacks of Japanese imperialism on the Chinese people in Manchuria and Shanghai, with actual warfare against the Soviet Union daily threatened.

The Hoover-Stimson tools of Wall Street are openly preparing to throw the American workers into this war, and in the first place, into a war against the Soviet Union. The battle fleet has been concentrated in the Pacific Ocean where the most gigantic and demonstrative maneuvers are being carried out.

The call to war has already been sounded in the Far East. War in the interests of Wall Street and the imperialist master class threatens to engulf the workers of America and other countries. Increased hunger and misery for the masses, terror and war—this is the capitalist way out of the crisis. The election programs of Republicans, Democrats and Socialists, no matter how skilfully concealed, reflect only the differences between these parties on how to carry through this capitalist way out, how to get the masses to accept hunger, terror and war.

Persecution of Negroes

The Negro people, always hounded, persecuted, disfranchised and discriminated against in capitalist America, are, during this period of crisis, oppressed as never before. They are the first to be fired when lay-offs take place. They are discriminated against when charity rations are handed out to the unemployed. They are cheated and robbed by the Southern white landlords and evicted from their land and homes when their miserable income does not enable them to pay rent. When they protest against this unbearable oppression and persecution they are singled out for police attacks in the North and for lynch victims in the South. Over 150 Negroes have been barbarously lynched at the instigation of the white ruling class since the crisis began. The Negro reformist misleaders are shamelessly aiding the white master class in these vicious attacks.

Every day of the crisis, every new effort of the bosses to find a capitalist way out of the crisis, brings new misery and new acts of terror to confront the oppressed Negro people.

Workers Must Militantly Resist Bosses' Attacks

Against these attacks of the employers, against these efforts of the capitalists to enrich themselves at the expense of the toilers, the workers, the farmers, Negro and white, must fight. They must rally all their forces for the most uncompromising class struggle against every effort of the capitalists to terrorize them into accepting worsened conditions, or to force them into another world imperialist slaughter.

The capitalists will never voluntarily yield an inch to the workers. They will continue ever more ruthlessly to maintain and increase their own profits and wealth by forcing the workers and farmers into greater misery. They will never voluntarily relax their pressure on the masses, nor will they cease for one moment their war preparations, particularly for a bloody war to crush the Soviet Union.

There is only one way out of the crisis for the workers. That is the way of mass struggles. A militant mass struggle can force concessions from the parasite ruling class. Such a struggle will lead to the final liberation from the horrors of capitalism.

In order to carry out this struggle, the workers and poor farmers, Negro and white, must organize. They must build powerful, fighting trade unions and unemployed councils and strong organizations of poor farmers. Under the leadership of the Communist party, the workers in such class organizations can defend their interests to-day, while fighting for the revolutionary way out of the crisis, for the overthrow of capitalism.

The most relentless struggle, now and through the election campaign, for the following demands —the demands of the Communist party—alone offers to the workers the means of defending their interests against the bosses' attack.

1. *Unemployment and social insurance at the expense of the state and employers.*

2. Against Hoover's wage-cutting policy.

3. Emergency relief for the impoverished farmers without restrictions by the government and banks; exemption of impoverished farmers from taxes, and no forced collection of rents or debts.

4. Equal rights for the Negroes and self-determination for the Black Belt.

5. Against capitalist terror; against all forms of suppression of the political rights of the workers.

6. Against imperialist war; for the defense of the Chinese people and of the Soviet Union.

Workers' and Farmers' Government Will End Misery

The Communist party calls upon the millions of workers and farmers, Negro and white, and particularly those rank and file workers who are now misled by the leaders of the Socialist party and the American Federation of Labor, to rally to fight for these demands. The mass fight for the demands can alone develop effective resistance to the starvation and war program of the capitalists.

The fight for these demands, as proposed by the Communist party, means even more. It is the starting point for the struggle for final victory of the toilers, for the establishment of the workers' and farmers' government in the United States. This is the workers' way out—the revolutionary way out of the crisis.

The Communist party proposes an organized mass struggle for the above immediate demands of the workers, as the first step toward the establishment of a *workers' and farmers' government.*

Such a *revolutionary government* alone can fully free the masses from misery and slavery, by taking over and operating the big industries, trusts, railroads and banks. Only such a government will open up every idle factory, mill and mine, and put the workers on their jobs again producing the goods which are needed for a hungry, starving population. Such a government will immediately seize and distribute to the hungry masses enormous stores of foodstuffs now kept locked up in the warehouses, thus caring for the masses and creating a demand for new production. It will open the millions of houses, now held empty by greedy private landlords, and provide comfortable housing for the million now living in the cellars, sewers, disgraceful public lodging houses and the terrible "Hoover cities" of the homeless unemployed. *It will immediately feed, clothe and house all the workers and put them busily at work reproducing all things necessary.*

There is plenty and to spare for all.

It is held away from the toilers by the capitalists and their private property and for their private profit. Only a revolutionary workers' and farmers' government can break through this paralysis of the capitalist crisis and start economic activity going full speed for the benefit of the masses of workers and farmers.

Moreover, such a revolutionary workers' and farmers' government alone can enforce full and complete equality for the oppressed Negro masses and grant unconditional independence to Hawaii, the Philippines and other colonial peoples now enslaved by Wall Street.

This is proven by the experiences of the Soviet Union. There the workers seized power in the revolution of 1917. With the government in their hands the last remnant of capitalism is being uprooted, Socialism is being built. The first Five-Year Plan is now being successfully completed; unemployment has been completely eliminated; wages are being steadily raised; the material and cultural level of the masses is being raised; no crisis such as in capitalist countries has affected their progress; the second Five-Year Plan is about to begin.

The Soviet Union stands out as proof that the workers can rule, not only in their own interests, but in the interests of all those who are oppressed by capitalism.

Old Parties Serve Capitalists

The capitalist parties—Republican, Democratic and Socialist—together with their American Federation of Labor henchmen—will each appear in this election campaign in different garb; each will pretend to offer a way out of the crisis beneficial to the masses; each will freely promise jobs and plenty to workers when elected.

But behind all their false promises and all of their apparent differences, the workers must see their reactionary actions while in office, their brutal attacks on the workers and their protection of the rich. The workers must see that these parties have been and are now the defenders of the capitalists and the bitter enemies of the workers.

Leading the attack against the workers is the Hoover government, with its bi-partisan coalition of Republican-Democratic parties, composed of rapacious profit-seekers, loyal agents of Wall Street, corporation promoters, and the biggest capitalists themselves, as Mellon, Hoover, Smith, Raskob, and Young.

In order to trick those workers and farmers who are no longer fooled by two-party fakery— new demagogy and promises are being indulged in to make the masses choose "Progressives" and "Reactionaries" within the two old capitalist parties.

The difference between progressive and reactionary is merely on the surface, for the purpose of demagogy, to hide the same basic program of the capitalist way out of the crisis.

Openly supporting the Hoover program, is the officialdom of the American Federation of Labor.

It fights against the workers and for the capitalists on every essential point. It fights against unemployment insurance, against the bonus for the ex-soldiers. It tries to stifle strikes and carries on strike-breaking where the workers take up the fight against the bosses' offensive. It fights for huge grants of money to the corporations and taxation of the masses; it supports new laws to help build greater monopolies, it helps prepare imperialist war, especially war against the Soviet Union. Through its deceitful "nonpartisan" policy of "reward friends and punish enemies," it delivers the workers gagged and bound to the Republicans and Democrats, "Progressives" and "Reactionaries," in order to further confuse and divide the working class. It decks itself out in "victories" like the so-called anti-injunction law which fastens injunctions and "yellow dog contracts" ever more firmly upon the workers than ever before.

The reactionary officialdom of the American Federation of Labor is an agency of capitalism among the workers for putting over the capitalist way out of the crisis.

The Socialist Party—The Agent of the Bosses

The Socialist party, together with its self-styled "left-wing"—the Muste group—is the little brother of the American Federation of Labor. Its special task is to cover up the same program with the mask of Socialist phrases, and thus to prevent the awakening workers from organizing for a really effective struggle. It supports capitalistic monopoly and trustification under the hypocritical slogans of "nationalization of banks, railroads and mines" through the capitalist "nation." It covers the worst capitalist robberies as "steps toward socialism." It fights against the Workers' Unemployment Insurance Bill, and puts forth its own demagogical emasculated proposals to keep the workers from fighting for their own bill. Its leaders in trade unions help sign wage-cutting agreements, and break the strikes of workers who resist.

The Socialist party and the Farmer-Labor party of Minnesota carry through the same policies in America, as their brother party, the Labor party in England, which launched the wage-cutting campaign, cut down the unemployed insurance, raised high tariffs and taxes on the masses, and carried through inflation. They support and operate on the same principle as their brother party in Germany, the Social Democracy, which is in coalition with the monarchist Hindenburg and supports his emergency decrees which cut wages, destroyed social services, halved unemployment relief, and threw the burden of taxation upon the masses, carrying through the Fascist suppression of the working class and preparation for the open Fascist government.

The Socialist party in Milwaukee and in Reading, when it is in power, carries out the capitalist program of hunger and terror as their big brothers of the Republican and Democratic parties.

They support the pacifist swindle of the League of Nations and especially help prepare war on the Soviet Union, one of their principle occupations being daily slander against the workers' republic.

Rally Against Starvation and War

Against all these parties which openly or hiddenly attempt to force through the capitalist way out of the crisis, the Communist party calls upon the workers and farmers of America, white and Negro, to rally for the struggle against starvation and war, for the immediate demands stated above, for the revolutionary way out of the crisis.

These measures represent what a large majority of workers and farmers *wish to have now*. These things can only be gotten by fighting for them. They cut across the capitalist way [sic] of the crisis, because they do not take into account capitalist profits, for which the capitalists and their lieutenants will fight to the death.

It was the Communist party alone which forewarned the workers of the approaching crisis long before the crisis began; it was the Communist party which alone raised the banner of mass struggle against unemployment, lynching, police terror, wage cuts and imperialist war.

The great hunger marches and demonstration of the unemployed in hundreds of cities; the strikes of the miners in Western Pennsylvania, Eastern Ohio, West Virginia and Kentucky; the textile strikes in Paterson, Lawrence and many other cities; the mass mobilization against terror in Chicago, Detroit, Harlan, etc.; the strong fight against lynching, for the defense of the Scottsboro boys; all these struggles of the masses, in which the Communist party played the leading role, are the best proof that the Communist party alone deserves the confidence of the workers.

The Socialist party and its "left" ally, the Muste

group, especially has tried in the past and tries now to break up the workers' fight for the program put forward by the Commuists, by bringing forward its own substitute of "something just as good," by making its fake program look as much as possible "like the Communists," by talking "revolutionary," by arguing for a choice of "the lesser evil," by putting themselves forth as "the same thing only more practical."

But all their demagogic claims are given the lie by the capitalist class itself, which takes the Socialist party and its leaders, especially its darlings, Norman Thomas, the respectable churchman, and Morris Hillquit, millionaire lawyer, to its heart.

The Socialist party is openly recognized by the capitalist press as the third capitalist party, which more and more becomes equally respectable in capitalist society with the other parties, as the capitalists more and more need it to fool and trick the awakening workers. Even to force concessions *now* from the three capitalist parties, there is no weapon so powerful as a militant daily struggle against the capitalist enemies and a strong vote for the Communist party.

For a United States of Soviet America

In the election campaign of the Communist party, there is room for the organized participation and support of every worker in America, man and woman, white and Negro, without regard to whether he is a member of the Communist party or not.

Every worker and workers' organization which is ready to fight for the *immediate demands* is invited to be represented in the *Communist Campaign Committees* which will organize and conduct this campaign.

Support the Communist Election Campaign! Rally behind its platform and candidates! Make this the starting point of a gigantic mass movement against starvation, terror and war! Resist with all your energy and strength the brutal attacks of the capitalists! Fight for unemployment insurance against wage cuts, for relief for the farmers, for equality for the Negroes, against the murderous capitalist terror and against the plans for a new bloody imperialist war. Resist the carrying through of the capitalist way out of the crisis! Fight for the workers' way—for the revolutionary way out of the crisis—for the United States of Soviet America! Vote for the workers' candidates—the Communist candidates! Vote Communist!

Democratic Platform for 1932

In this time of unprecedented economic and social distress the Democratic Party declares its conviction that the chief causes of this condition were the disastrous policies pursued by our government since the World War, of economic isolation, fostering the merger of competitive businesses into monopolies and encouraging the indefensible expansion and contraction of credit for private profit at the expense of the public.

Those who were responsible for these policies have abandoned the ideals on which the war was won and thrown away the fruits of victory, thus rejecting the greatest opportunity in history to bring peace, prosperity, and happiness to our people and to the world.

They have ruined our foreign trade; destroyed the values of our commodities and products, crippled our banking system, robbed millions of our people of their life savings, and thrown millions more out of work, produced wide-spread poverty and brought the government to a state of financial distress unprecedented in time of peace.

The only hope for improving present conditions, restoring employment, affording permanent relief to the people, and bringing the nation back to the proud position of domestic happiness and of financial, industrial, agricultural and commercial leadership in the world lies in a drastic change in economic governmental policies.

We believe that a party platform is a covenant with the people to have *[sic]* faithfully kept by the party when entrusted with power, and that the people are entitled to know in plain words the terms of the contract to which they are asked to subscribe. We hereby declare this to be the platform of the Democratic Party:

The Democratic Party solemnly promises by appropriate action to put into effect the principles, policies, and reforms herein advocated, and to eradicate the policies, methods, and practices herein condemned. We advocate an immediate and drastic reduction of governmental expenditures by abolishing useless commissions and offices, consolidating departments and bureaus, and

eliminating extravagance to accomplish a saving of not less than twenty-five per cent in the cost of the Federal Government. And we call upon the Democratic Party in the states to make a zealous effort to achieve a proportionate result.

We favor maintenance of the national credit by a federal budget annually balanced on the basis of accurate executive estimates within revenues, raised by a system of taxation levied on the principle of ability to pay.

We advocate a sound currency to be preserved at all hazards and an international monetary conference called on the invitation of our government to consider the rehabilitation of silver and related questions.

We advocate a competitive tariff for revenue with a fact-finding tariff commission free from executive interference, reciprocal tariff agreements with other nations, and an international economic conference designed to restore international trade and facilitate exchange.

We advocate the extension of federal credit to the states to provide unemployment relief wherever the diminishing resources of the states makes it impossible for them to provide for the needy; expansion of the federal program of necessary and useful construction effected *[sic]* with a public interest, such as adequate flood control and waterways.

We advocate the spread of employment by a substantial reduction in the hours of labor, the encouragement of the shorter week by applying that principle in government service; we advocate advance planning of public works.

We advocate unemployment and old-age insurance under state laws.

We favor the restoration of agriculture, the nation's basic industry; better financing of farm mortgages through recognized farm bank agencies at low rates of interest on an amortization plan, giving preference to credits for the redemption of farms and homes sold under foreclosure.

Extension and development of the Farm Co-operative movement and effective control of crop surpluses so that our farmers may have the full benefit of the domestic market.

The enactment of every constitutional measure that will aid the farmers to receive for their basic farm commodities prices in excess of cost.

We advocate a Navy and an Army adequate for national defense, based on a survey of all facts affecting the existing establishments, that the people in time of peace may not be burdened by an expenditure fast approaching a billion dollars annually.

We advocate strengthening and impartial enforcement of the anti-trust laws, to prevent monopoly and unfair trade practices, and revision thereof for the better protection of labor and the small producer and distributor.

The conservation, development, and use of the nation's water power in the public interest.

The removal of government from all fields of private enterprise except where necessary to develop public works and natural resources in the common interest.

We advocate protection of the investing public by requiring to be filed with the government and carried in advertisements of all offerings of foreign and domestic stocks and bonds true information as to bonuses, commissions, principal invested, and interests of the sellers.

Regulation to the full extent of federal power, of

(a) Holding companies which sell securities in interstate commerce;

(b) Rates of utilities companies operating across State lines;

(c) Exchanges in securities and commodities.

We advocate quicker methods of realizing on assets for the relief of depositors of suspended banks, and a more rigid supervision of national banks for the protection of depositors and the prevention of the use of their moneys in speculation to the detriment of local credits.

The severance of affiliated security companies from, and the divorce of the investment banking business from, commercial banks, and further restriction of federal reserve banks in permitting the use of federal reserve facilities for speculative purposes.

We advocate the full measure of justice and generosity for all war veterans who have suffered disability or disease caused by or resulting from actual service in time of war and for their dependents.

We advocate a firm foreign policy, including peace with all the world and the settlement of international disputes by arbitration; no interference in the internal affairs of other nations; and sanctity of treaties and the maintenance of good faith and of good will in financial obligations;

adherence to the World Court with appending reservations; the Pact of Paris abolishing war as an instrument of national policy, to be made effective by provisions for consultation and conference in case of threatened violations of treaties.

International agreements for reduction of armaments and cooperation with nations of the Western Hemisphere to maintain the spirit of the Monroe Doctrine.

We oppose cancelation of the debts owing to the United States by foreign nations.

Independence for the Philippines; ultimate statehood for Porto Rico.

The employment of American citizens in the operation of the Panama Canal.

Simplification of legal procedure and reorganization of the judicial system to make the attainment of justice speedy, certain, and at less cost.

Continuous publicity of political contributions and expenditures; strengthening of the Corrupt Practices Act and severe penalties for misappropriation of campaign funds.

We advocate the repeal of the Eighteenth Amendment. To effect such repeal we demand that the Congress immediately propose a Constitutional Amendment to truly represent [sic] the conventions in the states called to act solely on that proposal; we urge the enactment of such measures by the several states as will actually promote temperance, effectively prevent the return of the saloon, and bring the liquor traffic into the open under complete supervision and control by the states.

We demand that the Federal Government effectively exercise its power to enable the states to protect themselves against importation of intoxicating liquors in violation of their laws.

Pending repeal, we favor immediate modification of the Volstead Act; to legalize the manufacture and sale of beer and other beverages of such alcoholic content as is permissable under the Constitution and to provide therefrom a proper and needed revenue.

We condemn the improper and excessive use of money in political activities.

We condemn paid lobbies of special interests to influence members of Congress and other public servants by personal contact.

We condemn action and utterances of high public officials designed to influence stock exchange prices.

We condemn the open and covert resistance of

administrative officials to every effort made by Congressional Committees to curtail the extravagant expenditures of the Government and to revoke improvident subsidies granted to favorite interests.

We condemn the extravagance of the Farm Board, its disastrous action which made the Government a speculator in farm products, and the unsound policy of restricting agricultural products to the demands of domestic markets.

We condemn the usurpation of power by the State Department in assuming to pass upon foreign securities offered by international bankers as a result of which billions of dollars in questionable bonds have been sold to the public upon the implied approval of the Federal Government.[1]

And in conclusion, to accomplish these purposes and to recover economic liberty, we pledge the nominees of this convention the best efforts of a great Party whose founder announced the doctrine which guides us now in the hour of our country's need: equal rights to all; special privilege to none.

The Farmer-Labor Party Platform

BANKING, CURRENCY, GOLD STANDARD AND ECONOMIC BALANCE

The fifth clause of Section 8 of Article I of the United States Constitution provides:

"The Congress shall have power to coin money, regulate the value thereof, and of foreign coin, and fix the standard of weights and measures."

"To coin money" means to print money for the use of the Nation, States, counties, townships, cities, towns, villages, school districts, and for the people, at cost of printing and service.

"Regulate the value thereof" means the Congress gives by an act, authority and debt-paying power to foreign coin (money) coming into the United States, the same as that which it authorizes to be coined or printed.

---

[1] Inadvertently omitted from the reading of the platform, and later included, was the following statement:

"We condemn the Hawley-Smoot Tariff Law, the prohibitive rates of which have resulted in retaliatory action by more than forty countries, created international economic hostilities, destroyed international trade, driven our factories into foreign countries, robbed the American farmer of his foreign markets, and increased the cost of production."

The United States Supreme Court decided:

"Congress is authorized to establish a national currency either in coin or in paper and to make that currency lawful money for all purposes as regards the National government of private individuals."

Organized Banking and Currency System

(a) We demand legislation to abolish the Federal Reserve Banking System (Fiscal Agent of the United States), private ownership of the United States Banking and Currency System, by repealing the present unconstitutional banking laws on that subject, and then placing them in the hands of the Communities, i.e., the Federal, State, and local governmental bodies, so that the profits, if any, shall accrue to the people's governments, thereby preventing panics, depressions and crises, and private control of money.

Postal Savings Banks

(b) As a step to that goal, we demand a law to authorize Postal Savings Banks in each post-office to accept deposits and permit checking accounts without limit in amount, make loans at uniform interest rate of 2 per cent per annum.

Currency and Free Coinage of Silver

(c) We demand laws providing for the issuance of sound money, full legal tender currency, by the Federal government. And we favor the opening of the mints to the free coinage of silver produced in the United States at its present weight and fineness, but only as coordinate money with that sound money currency, and not as redeemable money. All such money to be redeemable in service rendered by the government, and said money and credit based on same to be properly regulated as to volume in circulation.

Payment of International Debts

(d) Germany should print 11½ billions of full legal tender currency, pay it to discharge the reparations due foreign nations that are indebted in like amount to the United States, each nation making it full legal tender and to tender such money in the United States in full payment of their debts; the United States Congress shall then make it full legal tender in the United States, and authorize the Secretary of the Treasury to accept it in full payment of such foreign nation's debts, place it in the Treasury and use it to pay, as they mature, bonds, compensation certificates in full, Treasury deficits and other indebtedness of the government. Additional issues of international currency can be created by international governmental agreement, free from control by or dictation from the international bankers.

Guarantee to Farmers

(e) (1) We favor a Federal and State government guarantee to the farmers of such prices for their products as will return to them the average cost of production plus a reasonable profit, which will give them a proper return upon their investment as well as a reasonable living. As a step to that goal, we favor the immediate enactment of a law based on the principles of the Bill H.R. 7797, now before Congress, the title of which reads: "*A Bill to abolish the Federal Farm Board. To secure to the farmer a price for agricultural products, at least equal to the cost of production thereof, and for other purposes.*"

Refinancing of Mortgages

(e) (2) For the benefit of farmers and other real estate owners, we favor the immediate enactment of a law based on the principles of the Bill S.F. 1197, now before Congress, the title of which reads: "*A bill to liquidate and refinance agricultural indebtedness,* and to encourage and promote agriculture, commerce, and industry, by establishing an efficient credit system, through which unjust and unequal burdens placed upon agriculture, during the period of price fixing and deflation, may be lightened by providing for the liquidating and refinancing of farm mortgages, . . . and creating a Board of Agriculture to supervise same."

(f) We demand Federal and State government guarantees to the laborers of an opportunity to work at a living wage, or failing, which they shall be paid unemployment insurance benefits by a Federal and State Unemployment Insurance Plan.

Limit Speculation

(g) We favor effective legislation to prohibit gambling in securities or commodities.

Public Works Measures

(h) (1) We favor a three billion dollar annual appropriation by the Federal government for a period of five years if necessary, for the employment of labor on public works over the entire United States, the money to be issued by the government and paid for services rendered, but not to bear interest, namely modern homes for workers, bridge and highway construction, waterways, farm-to-market roads, abolition of toll gates, grade crossings, reforestation, rural school buildings, public grain elevators, water power development, public buildings, recreation facilities, including public parks, etc.

Local Improvements

(h) (2) That can be partially accomplished by the communities depositing with the Federal government their non-interest-bearing 25-year bonds as security for an equal amount of legal tender Federal government money which can be paid by such communities to employ millions of the unemployed on public works and improvements, to be redeemed through taxation, 4 per cent of the principal annually in accordance with H.R. 5857.

Redemption of Bonds

(i) Liberty bonds and all other Federal government bond issues to be redeemed by the Federal government legal tender currency within a period of five years in equal annual proportions and further Federal bond issues to be prohibited by law.

UNEMPLOYMENT, VETERANS' BONUS, DEBTORS AND OTHER RELIEF

We favor measures to accomplish the following:

(a) Temporary immediate aid to unemployed by Federal and State appropriations until—

Unemployment Insurance

(b) An intermediate system of the Unemployment Insurance is set in operation with funds to be provided by (1) Federal government, (2) State government, (3) Employers, and (4) Employees, based on percentages of the pay rolls, which system will remain in operation for ten to twenty years or until permanent relief is attained by other means.

Cash Soldier Bonus

(c) The Federal government to issue two and one-half billion dollars full legal tender Treasury

Notes, good for all debts, public and private, to pay the veterans their unpaid balance of compensation already voted to them.

Old-Age Pensions

(d) A Federal and State system of indigent, accident, sickness, maternity and old-age pensions for the needy.

Moratorium

(e) A five-year moratorium on the foreclosure of real estate mortgages, so worded that the debtor who claims inability to pay will have his property rights properly protected. Federal land banks to refinance such small interest-bearing debts as are required for the necessities of life of the creditor.

Flood Relief, Etc.

(f) A Federal commission to be created and funds appropriated by Congress in advance, to take care of sufferers from floods and other catastrophies, so that immediate relief can be given without calling Congress to meet in special session.

Exclusion of Immigrants

(g) Total exclusion of all immigrants until the period of unemployment has terminated.

PUBLIC AND PRIVATE OWNERSHIP

Government Ownership

We demand public ownership of all monopolies.

(a) The community to gradually assume ownership and operation of:

(I) Railroads and other means of transportation, telegraph, telephone and cable lines, all by the Federal government.

(II) Other public utilities, including power, light, heat and water, by local or State authorities, or where necessary by the Federal government.

Provide Means to Distribute Profits and Surplus

(b) All other producing, distributing and retailing business to be privately owned and operated, but to pay all profits in excess of a certain percentage, to be fixed by Congress, on invested capital, to the government as taxes.

Patents

(c) The life of patents to be limited to ten years.

Compensation

(d) We favor the payment of a reasonable compensation for all property taken by the government bodies.

LABOR

We favor measures to accomplish the following:

Public Works and Six-Hour Day-Minimum Wage

(a) On public works establish a six-hour day, and a minimum wage of one dollar per hour for common labor, to be paid in full legal tender money issued by Congress.

Construct Mississippi River Waterway

(b) In order to control the overflow of the Mississippi River and to furnish work for unemployed, we favor the issuance of two billion dollars of full legal tender money to be issued to construct a one mile wide Mississippi channel from Cairo, Illinois, to the Gulf of Mexico, with concrete highways the full length of the 600-mile course on both sides of the waterway.

Reduce Working Hours

(c) Establish a reduced number of working hours per day in private industry in order to reduce unemployment.

Convict Labor

(d) Abolish exploitation of convict labor.

Stop Yellow-Dog Contracts

(e) No yellow-dog contract shall be enforceable in the courts, Federal or State.

(f) Prohibit by law injunctions in labor disputes.

TAXATION

We favor measures to accomplish the following:

Higher Income Tax

(a) Increase income taxes on incomes over $10,000.

(b) Reduce all taxes. Balance the budget by

paying all interest-bearing debts with full legal tender currency. This will abolish 50 per cent of our present burdensome taxation. Repeal the Garner-Hoover Sales Tax.

Higher Inheritance Tax

(c) Increase inheritance taxes in higher brackets.

Abolish Tax Exemptions

(d) Abolish all tax exemptions on property except homesteads up to the amount of $3,000.00, and personal property up to the amount of $1,000.00.

(e) Prohibit the tax on labor to pay debts and support war.

AMENDMENTS TO CONSTITUTION

We favor the calling of a Constitutional Convention to act on amendments as follows:

Lame Duck Congress

(a) Norris Act, abolishing lame duck sessions of Congress, and President to take office in January following election.

Election by Direct Vote

(b) Abolish the electoral college and decide presidential elections by popular vote.

Elect Federal Judges

(c) All Federal judges to be elected by popular vote for six years, on non-partisan ballot, provide for recall.

Exclude Aliens

(d) The exclusion of all aliens in the determination of the representation in Congress.

Child Labor

(e) Complete abolition of labor by child wage earners.

Initiative, Referendum and Recall

(f) Provide for a National Initiative and Referendum and Recall, on any subject, including prohibition and the Eighteenth Amendment.

(g) The establishment of a one-house legislative body in order to fix responsibility of government.

THE TARIFF—FOREIGN AFFAIRS AND NATIONAL DEFENSE

In view of the present improbability of getting International Agreement for several years to come, we favor the following principles until International Agreements are reached, or compelled by other circumstances, to abolish the tariffs and to adopt a sound economic system, and to preserve peace on earth.

The Tariff

(a) (1) The gradual reduction of all tariffs by International Agreement, except temporarily on those selected commodities the United States prices of which will be controlled and standardized as the result of the provisions of Plank No. 1 (e).

(a) (2) Until such International Agreement is reached we favor the maintenance of the present tariff rates until January 1, 1937, except those which are now or may before that date be fostering exorbitant profits.

(a) (3) If no International Agreement is reached before January 1, 1937, we favor thereafter the reduction of the United States tariff rates then existing by 10 per cent per annum until January 1, 1944.

Tariff on Oil

(a) (4) We favor an immediate tariff duty on oil and such other products as may be necessary to protect our independent producers in the meantime.

Disarmament, Foreign Affairs and National Defense

(b) (1) General disarmament by International Agreement.

League of Nations

(b) (2) United States shall not enter League of Nations or World Court, nor shall it voluntarily cancel the foreign inter-governmental debts.

Philippine Islands

(b) (3) Independence of the Philippine Islands, to be accomplished within a period of ten years.

Air, Army and Navy

(b) (4) A Department of National Defense

under one head with three Assistant Secretaries: of Air, Army, and Navy.

(b) (5) Build up the Navy to the treaty limits immediately and provide an adequate Army.

PEOPLE'S RIGHTS

"We demand equality before the law, political and religious freedom, and restore the economic rights of labor."

Workmen's Compensation Act

(a) Repeal the Federal Employer's Liability Act provision which now disfranchises the rights of railroad men by compelling them to prove negligence where, under State Workmen's Acts, negligence is presumed.

Contempt of Court

(b) Permit trial by jury in all contempt cases with right to change of venue in all courts, State or Federal.

Free Speech

(c) The full observance by Courts, police and other government officers of the constitutional rights of free speech, in schools and other public places, free press, freedom of assembly, and impartial access to the use of movies and radio by minority groups.

Abolish Third Degree

(d) The Courts should be prohibited from receiving evidence unlawfully obtained whether by "third degree" or unlawful search and seizure, or otherwise, or by tapping of wires or other means of communication.

Outlaw Holding Companies

(e) Prohibit by law trust companies, holding companies, corporation farms and chain stores. Strict enforcement of the anti-trust law.

Abolish Bureaucracy

(f) The abolition of Government Bureaus, Commissions, Committees, exercising legislative or judicial powers of either Federal, State or local governments.

Prisoners' Compensation

(g) All prisoners should be compensated for their labor.

Treatment of Patients

(h) All United States hospitals shall permit the patients the kind of treatment and the practitioners the patients desire, whether they be allopathic, homeopathic, osteopathic, Christian Science, chiropractic, or any other practitioners.

Women's Equal Rights

We demand the repeal of all laws, that deny to women equal rights and liberty to earn a living, freedom of occupation, with the same opportunities for economic advancement as offered to men; that marriage or sex shall not exclude or discriminate against women in any occupation, profession or employment; or likewise in the rates of pay, hours of labor or working conditions, and that women shall enjoy equal protection of the law.

OATH TO SUPPORT PLATFORM

Candidates' Oaths

All candidates for National Office, standing on this platform and party, shall be sworn to before a Notary Public in the presence of two members of the party, to support this platform in every respect.

Prohibition Party Platform of 1932

PREAMBLE

We, the representatives of the National Prohibition Party in National Convention assembled at Indianapolis, July 6, 1932, devoutly recognize the supreme authority and just government of Almighty God in the affairs of men and nations and declare that, only by obedience to the principles enunciated by the Prince of Peace, can our Country hope for deliverance from the tribulations now upon us as a people. Upon this basis we make the following declarations:

PROHIBITION

The liquor traffic never willingly obeyed any restrictive measures before prohibition, has not obeyed the law under prohibition, nor can it be expected to obey any restrictive measures should the Eighteenth Amendment be repealed or modified. The difficulty of enforcing any such restrictive measures would be greater than that now experienced.

We unequivocally oppose the repeal or weakening of the Eighteenth Amendment or of the laws enacted thereunder, and insist upon the strengthening of such laws. Being unanimously agreed upon the principle, having within our ranks no voter opposed thereto, this party if placed in power by voters of like mind, can and will co-ordinate all the powers of government, Federal, State and local, strictly to enforce, by adequate and unescapable punishment of all violators, this wise and beneficent law. Concurrently with such enforcement activities a constructive and comprehensive educational campaign will be conducted, stressing the evil effects of alcoholic beverages.

We indict and condemn the Republican and Democratic parties for the continued nullification of the Eighteenth Amendment and their present determination to repeal that amendment on the excuse that it cannot be enforced, and reiterate that adequate enforcement cannot be had from a party dependent on pro-liquor votes for success at the polls.

Economic Relief

The country finds itself in the depths of the most severe depression in its history. As a result of unemployment, the orgy of gambling on the stock exchanges, bank failures and consequent loss of confidence, millions of dollars have been withdrawn from banks and hoarded. The banks, in their turn are hoarding untold millions in their vaults, refusing to lend even on prime security. Thus a severe contraction of the currency actually in circulation, and of credit based thereon, has taken place with the consequent fall in prices and general business stagnation usually following such contraction. To stop this contraction, now constantly growing greater, and to restore the amount of money in actual circulation to normal proportions, with consequent expansion of credit, we advocate the purchase by the government of legally issued bonds of States and subdivisions thereof, now unable to market same through banks and bank-controlled agencies, to an amount sufficient to accomplish this purpose, paying therefor by the issue of legal-tender treasury notes, directly to the people through such States and subdivisions without the intermediary of the banking system, such bonds to be gradually retired by repayment to the government.

Would Set Up Council

To further restore and maintain normal prosperity, an economic council will be created to be composed of the best and most sincere leaders in the fields of economics, agriculture, labor, finance, commerce, and industry, for the consideration and development of further measures such as:

1. Regulation of stock exchange and boards of trade;
2. Rehabilitation of wage schedules and hours of labor;
3. Revision of tariff schedules;
4. Revision of the banking system to assure safety of deposits;
5. Development of a comprehensive economic plan to stabilize industry;
6. Relief of the destitute and unfortunate;
7. Governmental unemployment and other insurance;
8. The revaluation of all utilities, transportation systems and basic industries in order to disclose actual values so that earnings may be freed to pay a just schedule of wages and increase employment;
9. Any other related measures designed to assure economic security.

Taxation

We pledge an economical administration of government. Waste, extravagance, duplication in public office, unnecessary commissions and bureaus, padded payrolls and graft cost more than the amount required to pay the soldiers' bonus and feed the poor. We condemn the plan of the old political parties to raise revenue on beer, wine and whisky as being a scheme to tax the poor and exempt the rich. Vast increase in revenue can be obtained by compelling the payment of taxes of huge amounts of property now escaping taxation.

Agriculture

To aid agriculture, we favor the principle of the equalization fee, or such other measure as may be agreed upon by the leading farm organizations of the United States.

Conservation

We condemn the prodigal waste and criminal exploitation of the nation's coal, timber, oil, water power and other natural resources by private interests. All such remaining resources should be utilized and developed under government control for the benefit of all the people.

REFORM OF JUDICIAL PROCEDURE

We pledge a comprehensive reform in judicial procedure to eliminate legal technicalities and to secure speedy and substantial justice, and the abolition of unjust injunctions.

FOREIGN REPRESENTATIVES

All representatives of the United States Government in foreign nations should be required to observe the principles of the Eighteenth Amendment, and we condemn the negligence of the present administration in not requiring such observance. We also demand that representatives of foreign nations in this country shall not be permitted liquor concessions denied to American citizens.

MOTION PICTURES

We favor Federal control at the source of the output of the motion picture industry to prevent the degrading influence of immoral pictures and insidious propaganda connected therewith.

UNJUST BALLOT LAWS

We denounce the enactment by the Republican and Democratic parties in many States of unjust and discriminatory election laws that make it almost impossible for minor parties to retain their place on the official ballot, or for new parties to be formed.

PEACE

We declare our abhorrence of war and favor continued efforts for peaceful settlement of international differences, the reduction of military armaments and the entrance of our country into the World Court.

ALIEN REPRESENTATION

Representation in State and Federal legislative bodies should be based on citizenship and not on population.

FREE INSTITUTIONS

We reiterate our position in favor of free speech and a free press.

CHILD LABOR

We favor the abolition of all child labor in mills, factories, and other industries, that their places may be taken by adult laborers.

PUBLIC UTILITIES

We favor the governmental ownership of all public utilities which can be owned and operated by the Federal government, all proceeds above the cost of operation to be applied to the support of the Federal government.

CONCLUSION

On these principles the national Prohibition party invites all those who favor suppression of the liquor traffic, the enforcement of law, honesty and efficiency in administration, and the building of a better citizenship to join with us in a new political alignment to achieve these great objectives.

Republican Platform of 1932

We, the representatives of the Republican Party, in convention assembled, renew our pledge to the principles and traditions of our party and dedicate it anew to the service of the nation.

We meet in a period of widespread distress and of an economic depression that has swept the world. The emergency is second only to that of a great war. The human suffering occasioned may well exceed that of a period of actual conflict.

The supremely important problem that challenges our citizens and government alike is to break the back of the depression, to restore the economic life of the nation and to bring encouragement and relief to the thousands of American families that are sorely afflicted.

The people themselves, by their own courage, their own patient and resolute effort in the readjustments of their own affairs, can and will work out the cure. It is our task as a party, by leadership and a wise determination of policy, to assist that recovery.

To that task we pledge all that our party possesses in capacity, leadership, resourcefulness and ability. Republicans, collectively and individually, in nation and State, hereby enlist in a war which will not end until the promise of American life is once more fulfilled.

LEADERSHIP

For nearly three years the world has endured an economic depression of unparalleled extent and severity. The patience and courage of our people have been severely tested, but their faith in themselves, in their institutions and in their future remains unshaken. When victory comes, as it will, this generation will hand on to the next a great heritage unimpaired.

This will be due in large measure to the quality of the leadership that this country has had during this crisis. We have had in the White House a leader—wise, courageous, patient, understanding, resourceful, ever present at his post of duty, tireless in his efforts and unswervingly faithful to American principles and ideals.

At the outset of the depression, when no man could foresee its depth and extent, the President succeeded in averting much distress by securing agreement between industry and labor to maintain wages and by stimulating programs of private and governmental construction. Throughout the depression unemployment has been limited by the systematic use of part-time employment as a substitute for the general discharge of employees. Wage scales have not been reduced except under compelling necessity. As a result there have been fewer strikes and less social disturbance than during any similar period of hard times.

The suffering and want occasioned by the great drought of 1930 were mitigated by the prompt mobilization of the resources of the Red Cross and of the government. During the trying winters of 1930-31 and 1931-32 a nation-wide organization to relieve distress was brought into being under the leadership of the President. By the Spring of 1931 the possibility of a business upturn in the United States was clearly discernible when, suddenly, a train of events was set in motion in Central Europe which moved forward with extraordinary rapidity and violence, threatening the credit structure of the world and eventually dealing a serious blow to this country.

The President foresaw the danger. He sought to avert it by proposing a suspension of intergovernmental debt payments for one year, with the purpose of relieving the pressure at the point of greatest intensity. But the credit machinery of the nations of Central Europe could not withstand the strain, and the forces of disintegration continued to gain momentum until in September Great Britain was forced to depart from the gold standard. This momentous event, followed by a tremendous raid on the dollar, resulted in a series of bank suspensions in this country, and the hoarding of currency on a large scale.

Again the President acted. Under his leadership the National Credit Association came into being. It mobilized our banking resources, saved scores of banks from failure, helped restore confidence and proved of inestimable value in strengthening the credit structure.

By the time the Congress met the character of our problems was clearer than ever. In his message to Congress the President outlined a constructive and definite program which in the main has been carried out; other portions may yet be carried out.

The Railroad Credit Corporation was created. The capital of the Federal Land Banks was increased. The Reconstruction Finance Corporation came into being and brought protection to millions of depositors, policy holders and others.

Legislation was enacted enlarging the discount facilities of the Federal Reserve System, and, without reducing the legal reserves of the Federal Reserve Banks, releasing a billion dollars of gold, a formidable protection against raids on the dollar and a greatly enlarged basis for an expansion of credit.

An earlier distribution to depositors in closed banks has been brought about through the action of the Reconstruction Finance Corporation. Above all, the national credit has been placed in an impregnable position by provision for adequate revenue and a program of drastic curtailment of expenditures. All of these measures were designed to lay a foundation for the resumption of business and increased employment.

But delay and the constant introduction and consideration of new and unsound measures has kept the country in a state of uncertainty and fear, and offset much of the good otherwise accomplished.

The President has recently supplemented his original program to provide for distress, to stimulate the revival of business and employment, and to improve the agricultural situation, he recommended extending the authority of the Reconstruction Finance Corporation to enable it:

(a) To make loans to political subdivisions

of public bodies or private corporations for the purpose of starting construction of income-producing or self-liquidating projects which will at once increase employment;

(b) To make loans upon security of agricultural commodities so as to insure the carrying of normal stocks of those commodities, and thus stabilize their loan value and price levels:

(c) To make loans to the Federal Farm Board to enable extension of loans to farm cooperatives and loans for export of agricultural commodities to quarters unable to purchase them;

(d) To loan up to $300,000,000 to such States as are unable to meet the calls made on them by their citizens for distress relief.

The President's program contemplates an attack on a broad front, with far-reaching objectives, but entailing no danger to the budget. The Democratic program, on the other hand, contemplates a heavy expenditure of public funds, a budget unbalanced on a large scale, with a doubtful attainment of at best a strictly limited objective.

We strongly endorse the President's program.

UNEMPLOYMENT AND RELIEF

True to American traditions and principles of government, the administration has regarded the relief problem as one of State and local responsibility. The work of local agencies, public and private has been coordinated and enlarged on a nation-wide scale under the leadership of the President.

Sudden and unforeseen emergencies such as the drought have been met by the Red Cross and the Government. The United States Public Health Service has been of inestimable benefit to stricken areas.

There has been magnificent response and action to relieve distress by citizens, organizations and agencies, public and private throughout the country.

PUBLIC ECONOMY

Constructive plans for financial stabilization cannot be completely organized until our national, State and municipal governments not only balance their budgets but curtail their current expenses as well to a level which can be steadily and economically maintained for some years to come.

We urge prompt and drastic reduction of public expenditure and resistance to every appropriation not demonstrably necessary to the performance of government, national or local.

The Republican Party established and will continue to uphold the gold standard and will oppose any measure which will undermine the government's credit or impair the integrity of our national currency. Relief by currency inflation is unsound in principle and dishonest in results. The dollar is impregnable in the marts of the world today and must remain so. An ailing body cannot be cured by quack remedies. This is no time to experiment upon the body politic or financial.

BANKS AND THE BANKING SYSTEM

The efficient functioning of our economic machinery depends in no small measure on the aid rendered to trade and industry by our banking system. There is need of revising the banking laws so as to place our banking structure on a sounder basis generally for all concerned, and for the better protection of the depositing public there should be more stringent supervision and broader powers vested in the supervising authorities. We advocate such a revision.

One of the serious problems affecting our banking system has arisen from the practice of organizing separate corporations by the same interests as banks, but participating in operations which the banks themselves are not permitted legally to undertake. We favor requiring reports of and subjecting to thorough and periodic examination all such affiliates of member banks until adequate information has been acquired on the basis of which this problem may definitely be solved in a permanent manner.

INTERNATIONAL CONFERENCE

We favor the participation by the United States in an international conference to consider matters relating to monetary questions, including the position of silver, exchange problems, and commodity prices, and possible cooperative action concerning them.

HOME LOAN DISCOUNT BANK SYSTEM

The present Republican administration has initiated legislation for the creation of a system of Federally supervised home loan discount banks, designed to serve the home owners of all parts of the country and to encourage home ownership by making possible long term credits for homes on more stable and more favorable terms.

There has arisen in the last few years a disturbing trend away from home ownership. We believe that everything should be done by Governmental agencies, national State and local, to reverse this tendency; to aid home owners by encouraging better methods of home financing; and to relieve the present inequitable tax burden on the home. In the field of national legislation we pledge that the measures creating a home loan discount system will be pressed in Congress until adopted.

Agriculture

Farm distress in America has its root in the enormous expansion of agricultural production during the war, the deflation of 1919, 1920 and the dislocation of markets after the war. There followed, under Republican Administrations, a long record of legislation in aid of the cooperative organization of farmers and in providing farm credit. The position of agriculture was gradually improved. In 1928 the Republican Party pledged further measures in aid of agriculture, principally tariff protection for agricultural products and the creation of a Federal Farm Board "clothed with the necessary power to promote the establishment of a farm marketing system of farmer-owned and controlled stabilization corporations."

Almost the first official act of President Hoover was the calling of a special session of Congress to redeem these party pledges. They have been redeemed.

The 1930 tariff act increased the rates on agricultural products by 30 per cent, upon industrial products only 12 per cent. That act equalized, so far as legislation can do so, the protection afforded the farmer with the protection afforded industry, and prevented a vast flood of cheap wool, grain, livestock, dairy and other products from entering the American market.

By the Agricultural Marketing Act, the Federal Farm Board was created and armed with broad powers and ample funds. The object of that act, as stated in its preamble, was:

"To promote the effective merchandising of agricultural commodities in interstate and foreign commerce so that * * * agriculture will be placed on the basis of economic equality with other industries * * * By encouraging the organization of producers into effective association for their own

control * * * and by promoting the establishment of a farm marketing system of producer-owned and producer-controlled cooperative associations."

The Federal Farm Board, created by the agricultural marketing act, has been compelled to conduct its operations during a period in which all commodity prices, industrial as well as agricultural, have fallen to disastrous levels. A period of decreasing demand and of national calamities such as drought and flood has intensified the problem of agriculture.

Nevertheless, after only a little more than two years' efforts, the Federal Farm Board has many achievements of merit to its credit. It has increased the membership of the cooperative farms marketing associations to coordinate efforts of the local associations. By cooperation with other Federal agencies, it has made available to farm marketing associations a large value of credit, which, in the emergency, would not have otherwise been available. Larger quantities of farm products have been handled cooperatively than ever before in the history of the cooperative movement. Grain crops have been sold by the farmer through his association directly upon the world market.

Due to the 1930 tariff act and the agricultural marketing act, it can truthfully be stated that the prices received by the American farmer for his wheat, corn, rye, barley, oats, flaxseed, cattle, butter and many other products, cruelly low though they are, are higher than the prices received by the farmers of any competing nation for the same products.

The Republican Party has also aided the American farmer by relief of the sufferers in the drought-stricken areas, through loans for rehabilitation and through road building to provide employment, by the development of the inland waterway system, by the perishable product act, by the strengthening of the extension system, and by the appropriation of $125,000,000 to recapitalize the Federal land banks and enable them to extend time to worthy borrowers.

The Republican Party pledges itself to the principle of assistance to cooperative marketing associations, owned and controlled by the farmers themselves, through the provisions of the agricultural marketing act, which will be promptly amended or modified as experience shows to be necessary to accomplish the objects set forth in the preamble of that act.

TARIFF AND THE MARKETING ACT

The party pledges itself to make such revision of tariff schedules as economic changes require to maintain the parity of protection to agriculture with other industry.

The American farmer is entitled not only to tariff schedules on his products but to protection from substitutes therefor.

We will support any plan which will help to balance production against demand, and thereby raise agricultural prices, provided it is economically sound and administratively workable without burdensome bureaucracy.

The burden of taxation borne by the owners of farm land constitutes one of the major problems of agriculture.

President Hoover has aptly and truly said, "Taxes upon real property are easiest to enforce and are the least flexible of all taxes. The tendency under pressure of need is to continue these taxes unchanged in times of depression, despite the decrease in the owner's income. Decreasing price and decreasing income results in an increasing burden upon property owners ° ° ° which is now becoming almost unbearable. The tax burden upon real estate is wholly out of proportion to that upon other forms of property and income. There is no farm relief more needed today than tax relief."

The time has come for a reconsideration of our tax systems, Federal, State and local, with a view to developing a better coordination, reducing duplication and relieving unjust burdens. The Republican Party pledges itself to this end.

More than all else, we point to the fact that, in the administration of executive departments, and in every plan of the President for the coordination of national effort and for strengthening our financial structure, for expanding credit, for rebuilding the rural credit system and laying the foundations for better prices, the President has insisted upon the interest of the American farmer.

The fundamental problem of American agriculture is the control of production to such volume as will balance supply with demand. In the solution of this problem the cooperative organization of farmers to plan production, and the tariff, to hold the home market for American farmers,

are vital elements. A third element equally as vital is the control of the acreage of land under cultivation, as an aid to the efforts of the farmer to balance production.

We favor a national policy of land utilization which looks to national needs, such as the administration has already begun to formulate. Such a policy must foster reorganization of taxing units in areas beset by tax delinquency and divert lands that are submarginal for crop production to other uses. The national welfare plainly can be served by the acquisition of submarginal lands for watershed protection, grazing, forestry, public parks and game preserves. We favor such acquisition.

THE TARIFF

The Republican Party has always been the staunch supporter of the American system of a protective tariff. It believes that the home market, built up under that policy, the greatest and richest market in the world, belongs first to American agriculture, industry and labor. No pretext can justify the surrender of that market to such competition as would destroy our farms, mines and factories, and lower the standard of living which we have established for our workers.

Because many foreign countries have recently abandoned the gold standard, as a result of which the costs of many commodities produced in such countries have, at least for the time being, fallen materially in terms of American currency, adequate tariff protection is today particularly essential to the welfare of the American people.

The Tariff Commission should promptly investigate individual commodities so affected by currency depreciation and report to the President any increase in duties found necessary to equalize domestic with foreign costs of production.

To fix the duties on some thousands of commodities, subject to highly complex conditions, is necessarily a difficult technical task. It is unavoidable that some of the rates established by legislation should, even at the time of their enactment, to be too low or too high. Moreover, a subsequent change in costs or other conditions may render obsolete a rate that was before appropriate. The Republican Party has, therefore, long supported the policy of a flexible tariff, giving power to the President, after investigation by an impartial commission and in accordance with prescribed principles, to modify the rates named by the Congress.

We commend the President's veto of the measure, sponsored by Democratic Congressmen, which would have transferred from the President to Congress the authority to put into effect the findings of the Tariff Commission. Approval of the measure would have returned tariff making to politics and destroyed the progress made during ten years of effort to lift it out of log-rolling methods. We pledge the Republican Party to a policy which will retain the gains made and enlarge the present scope of greater progress.

We favor the extension of the general Republican principle of tariff protection to our natural resource industries, including the products of our farms, forests, mines and oil wells, with compensatory duties on the manufactured and refined products thereof.

VETERANS

Our country is honored whenever it bestows relief on those who have faithfully served its flag. The Republican Party, appreciative of this solemn obligation and honor, has made its sentiments evident in Congress.

Increased hospital facilities have been provided, payments in compensation have more than doubled and in the matter of rehabilitations, pensions and insurance, generous provision has been made.

The administration of laws dealing with the relief of the veterans and their dependents has been a difficult task, but every effort has been made to carry service to the veterans and bring about not only a better and generous interpretation of the law but a sympathetic consideration of the many problems of the veteran.

We believe that every veteran incapacitated in any degree by reason of illness should be cared for and compensated, so far as compensation is possible, by a grateful nation, and that the dependents of those who lost their lives in war or whose death since the war in which service was rendered is traceable to service causes, should be provided for adequately. Legislation should be in accord with this principle.

Disability from causes subsequent and not attributable to war and the support of dependents of deceased veterans whose death is unconnected with war have been to some measure accepted

obligations of the nation as a part of the debt due.

A careful study should be made of existing veterans' legislation with a view to elimination of inequalities and injustices and effecting all possible economies, but without departing from our purpose to provide on a sound basis full and adequate relief for our service disabled men, their widows and orphans.

FOREIGN AFFAIRS

Our relations with foreign nations have been carried on by President Hoover with consistency and firmness, but with mutual understanding and peace with all nations. The world has been overwhelmed with economic strain which has provoked extreme nationalism in every quarter, has overturned many governments, stirred the springs of suspicion and distrust and tried the spirit of international cooperation, but we have held to our own course steadily and successfully.

The party will continue to maintain its attitude of protecting our national interests and policies wherever threatened but at the same time promoting common understanding of the varying needs and aspirations of other nations and going forward in harmony with other peoples without alliances or foreign partnerships.

The facilitation of world intercourse, the freeing of commerce from unnecessary impediments, the settlement of international difficulties by conciliation and the methods of law and the elimination of war as a resort of national policy have been and will be our party program.

FRIENDSHIP AND COMMERCE

We believe in and look forward to the steady enlargement of the principles of equality of treatment between nations great and small, the concessions of sovereignty and self-administration to every nation which is capable of carrying on stable government and conducting sound orderly relationships with other peoples, and the cultivation of trade and intercourse on the basis of uniformity of opportunity of all nations.

In pursuance of these principles, which have steadily gained favor in the world, the administration has asked no special favors in commerce, has protested discriminations whenever they arose, and has steadily cemented this procedure by reciprocal treaties guaranteeing equality for trade and residence.

The historic American plan known as the most-favored-nation principle has been our guiding program, and we believe that policy to be the only one consistent with a full development of international trade, the only one suitable for a country having as wide and diverse a commerce as America, and the one most appropriate for us in view of the great variety of our industrial, agricultural and mineral products and the traditions of our people.

Any other plan involves bargains and partnerships with foreign nations, and as a permanent policy is unsuited to America's position.

Conditions on the Pacific

Events in the Far East, involving the employment of arms on a large scale in a controversy between Japan and China, have caused worldwide concern in the past year and sorely tried the bulwarks erected to insure peace and pacific means for the settlement of international disputes.

The controversy has not only threatened the security of the nations bordering the Pacific but has challenged the maintenance of the policy of the open door in China and the administrative and political integrity of that people, programs which upon American initiation were adopted more than a generation ago and secured by international treaty.

The President and his Secretary of State have maintained throughout the controversy a just balance between Japan and China, taking always a firm position to avoid entanglements in the dispute, but consistently upholding the established international policies and the treaty rights and interests of the United States, and never condoning developments that endangered the obligation of treaties or the peace of the world.

Throughout the controversy our government has acted in harmony with the governments represented in the League of Nations, always making it clear that American policy would be determined at home, but always lending a hand in the common interest of peace and order.

In the application of the principles of the Kellogg pact the American Government has taken the lead, following the principle that a breach of the pact or a threat of infringement thereof was a matter of international concern wherever and however brought about.

As a further step the Secretary of State, upon the instruction of the President, adopted the principle later enlarged upon in his letter to the chairman of the Committee on Foreign Relations of the Senate that this government would not recognize any situation, treaty or agreement brought about between Japan and China by force and in defiance of the covenants of the Kellogg pact.

This principle, associated as it is with the name of President Hoover, was later adopted by the Assembly of the League of Nations at Geneva as a rule for the conduct of all those governments. The principle remains today as an important contribution to international law and a significant moral and material barrier to prevent a nation obtaining the fruits of aggressive warfare. It thus opens a new pathway to peace and order.

We favor enactment by Congress of a measure that will authorize our government to call or participate in an international conference in case of any threat of non-fulfillment of Article 2 of the Treaty of Paris (Kellogg-Briand pact).

Latin-America

The policy of the administration has proved to our neighbors of Latin-America that we have no imperialistic ambitions, but that we wish only to promote the welfare and common interest of the independent nations in the western hemisphere.

We have aided Nicaragua in the solution of its troubles and our country, in greatly reduced numbers, at the request of the Nicaraguan Government only to supervise the coming election. After that they will all be returned to the United States.

In Haiti, in accord with the recommendations of the Forbes commission, appointed by the President, the various services of supervision are being rapidly withdrawn, and only those will be retained which are mandatory under the treaties.

Throughout Latin America the policy of the government of the United States has been and will, under Republican leadership, continue to be one of frank and friendly understanding.

World Court

The acceptance by America of membership in the World Court has been approved by three successive Republican Presidents and we commend this attitude of supporting in this form the settlement of international disputes by the rule of law. America should join its influence and gain a voice in this institution, which would offer us a safer, more judicial and expeditious instrument for the constantly recurring questions between us and other nations than is now available by arbitration.

REDUCTION OF ARMAMENT

Conscious that the limitation of armament will contribute to security against war, and that the financial burdens of military preparation have been shamefully increased throughout the world, the Administration under President Hoover has made steady efforts and marked progress in the direction of proportional reduction of arms by agreement with other nations.

Upon his initiative a treaty between the chief naval powers at London in 1930, following the path marked by the Washington Conference of 1922, established a limitation of all types of fighting ships on a proportionate basis as between the three great naval powers. For the first time, a general limitation of a most costly branch of armament was successfully accomplished.

In the Geneva disarmament conference, now in progress, America is an active participant and a representative delegation of our citizens is laboring for progress in a cause to which this country has been an earnest contributor. This policy will be pursued.

Meanwhile maintenance of our navy on the basis of parity with any nation is a fundamental policy to which the Republican Party is committed. While in the interest of necessary government retrenchment, humanity and relief of the taxpayer we shall continue to exert our full influence upon the nations of the world in the cause of reduction of arms, we do not propose to reduce our navy defenses below that of any other nation.

NATIONAL DEFENSE

Armaments are relative and, therefore, flexible and subject to changes as necessity demands. We believe that in time of war every material resource in the nation should bear its proportionate share of the burdens occasioned by the public need and that it is a duty of government to perfect plans in time of peace whereby this objective may be attained in war.

We support the essential principles of the National Defense Act as amended in 1920 and by the Air Corps Act of 1926, and believe that the army of the United States has, through successive reductions accomplished in the last twelve years, reached an irreducible minimum consistent with the self-reliance, self-respect and security of this country.

WAGES AND WORK

We believe in the principle of high wages.

We favor the principle of the shorter working week and shorter work day with its application to government as well as to private employment, as rapidly and as constructively as conditions will warrant.

We favor legislation designed to stimulate, encourage and assist in home building.

IMMIGRATION

The restriction of immigration is a Republican policy. Our party formulated and enacted into law the quota system, which for the first time has made possible an adequate control of foreign immigration.

Rigid examination of applicants in foreign countries prevented the coming of criminals and other undesirable classes, while other provisions of the law have enabled the President to suspend immigration of foreign wage-earners who otherwise, directly or indirectly, would have increased unemployment among native-born and legally resident foreign-born wage-earners in this country. As a result, immigration is now less than at any time during the past one hundred years.

We favor the continuance and strict enforcement of our present laws upon this subject.

DEPARTMENT OF LABOR

We commend the constructive work of the United States Department of Labor.

LABOR

Collective bargaining by responsible representatives of employers and employes of their own choice, without the interference of any one, is recognized and approved.

Legislation, such as laws, prohibiting alien contract labor, peonage labor and the shanghaiing of sailors; the eight-hour law on government contracts and in government employment; provision for railroad safety devices, of methods of conciliation, mediation and arbitration in industrial labor disputes, including the adjustment of railroad disputes; the providing of compensation for injury to government employes (the forerunner of Federal workers' compensation acts), and other laws to aid and protect labor are of Republican origin, and have had and will continue to have the unswerving support of the party.

EMPLOYMENT

We commend the constructive work of the United States Employment Service in the Department of Labor. This service was enlarged and its activities extended through an appropriation made possible by the President with the cooperation of the Congress. It has done high service for the unemployed in the ranks of civil life and in the ranks of the former soldiers of the World War.

FREEDOM OF SPEECH

Freedom of speech, press and assemblages are fundamental principles upon which our form of government rests. These vital principles should be preserved and protected.

PUBLIC UTILITIES

Supervision, regulation and control of interstate public utilities in the interest of the public is an established policy of the Republican Party, to the credit of which stands the creation of the Interstate Commerce Commission, with its authority to assure reasonable transportation rates, sound railway finance and adequate service.

As proof of the progress made by the Republican Party in government control of public utilities, we cite the reorganization under this administration of the Federal Power Commission, with authority to administer the Federal water power act. We urge legislation to authorize this commission to regulate the charges for electric current when transmitted across State lines.

TRANSPORTATION

The promotion of agriculture, commerce and industry requires coordination of transportation by rail, highway, air and water. All should be subjected to appropriate and constructive regulation.

The public will, of course, select the form of transportation best fitted to its particular service, but the terms of competition fixed by public authority should operate without discrimination, so that all common carriers by rail, highway, air and water shall operate under conditions of equality.

INLAND WATERWAYS

The Republican Party recognizes that low cost transportation for bulk commodities will enable industry to develop in the midst of agriculture in the Mississippi Valley, thereby creating a home market for farm products in that section. With a view to aiding agriculture in the middle west the present administration has pushed forward as rapidly as possible the improvement of the Mississippi waterway system, and we favor the continued vigorous prosecution of these works to the end that agriculture and industry in that great area may enjoy the benefits of these improvements at the earliest possible date.

The railroads constitute the backbone of our transportation system and perform an essential service for the country. The railroad industry is our largest employer of labor and the greatest consumer of goods. The restoration of their credit and the maintenance of their ability to render adequate service are of paramount importance to the public, to their many thousands of employes and to savings banks, insurance companies and other similar institutions, to which the savings of the people have been entrusted.

We should continue to encourage the further development of the merchant marine under American registry and ownership.

Under the present administration the American merchant fleet has been enlarged and strengthened until it now occupies second place among the merchant marines of the world.

By the gradual retirement of the government from the field of ship operations and marked economies in costs, the United States Shipping Board will require no appropriation for the fiscal year 1933 for ship operations.

ST. LAWRENCE SEAWAY

The Republican Party stands committed to the development of the Great Lakes-St. Lawrence seaway. Under the direction of President Hoover negotiation of a treaty with Canada for this development is now at a favorable point. Recognizing the inestimable benefits which will accrue to the nation from placing the ports of the Great Lakes on an ocean base, the party reaffirms allegiance to this great project and pledges its best efforts to secure its early completion.

HIGHWAYS

The Federal policy to cooperate with the States in the building of roads was thoroughly established when the Federal highway act of 1921 was adopted under a Republican Congress. Each year since that time appropriations have been made which have greatly increased the economic value of highway transportation and helped to raise the standards and opportunities of rural life.

We pledge our support to the continuation of this policy in accordance with our needs and resources.

CRIME

We favor the enactment of rigid penal laws that will aid the States in stamping out the activities of gangsters, racketeers and kidnappers. We commend the intensive and effective drive made upon these public enemies by President Hoover and pledge our party to further efforts to the same purpose.

NARCOTICS

The Republican Party pledges itself to continue the present relentless warfare against the illicit narcotic traffic and the spread of the curse of drug addiction among our people. This administration has by treaty greatly strengthened our power to deal with this traffic.

CIVIL SERVICE

The merit system has been amply justified since the organization of the Civil Service by the Republican Party. As a part of our governmental system it is now unassailable. We believe it should remain so.

THE EIGHTEENTH AMENDMENT

The Republican Party has always stood and stands today for obedience to and enforcement of the law as the very foundation of orderly government and civilization. There can be no national security otherwise. The duty of the President of the United States and the officers of the law is clear. The law must be enforced as they find it enacted by the people. To these courses of action we pledge our nominees.

The Republican Party is and always has been the party of the Constitution. Nullification by non-observance by individuals or State action threatens the stability of government.

While the Constitution makers sought a high degree of permanence, they foresaw the need of changes and provided for them. Article V limits the proposals of amendments to two methods: (1) Two-thirds of both houses of Congress may propose amendments or (2) on application of the Legislatures of two-thirds of the States a national convention shall be called by Congress to propose amendments. Thereafter ratification must be had in one of two ways: (1) By the Legislatures of three-fourths of the several States or (2) by conventions held in three-fourths of the several States. Congress is given power to determine the mode of ratification.

Referendums without constitutional sanction cannot furnish a decisive answer. Those who propose them innocently are deluded by false hopes; those who propose them knowingly are deceiving the people.

A nation-wide controversy over the Eighteenth Amendment now distracts attention from the constructive solution of many pressing national problems. The principle of national prohibition as embodied in the amendment was supported and opposed by members of both great political parties. It was submitted to the States by members of Congress of different political faith and ratified by State Legislatures of different political majorities. It was not then and is not now a partisan political question.

Members of the Republican Party hold different opinions with respect to it and no public official or member of the party should be pledged or forced to choose between his party affiliations and his honest convictions upon this question.

We do not favor a submission limited to the issue of retention or repeal, for the American nation never in its history has gone backward, and in this case the progress which has been thus far made must be preserved, while the evils must be eliminated.

We therefore believe that the people should have an opportunity to pass upon a proposed amendment the provision of which, while retaining in the Federal Government power to preserve the gains already made in dealing with the evils inherent in the liquor traffic, shall allow the States to deal with the problem as their citizens may determine, but subject always to the power of the Federal Government to protect those States where prohibition may exist and safeguard our citizens everywhere from the return of the saloon and attendant abuses.

Such an amendment should be promptly submitted to the States by Congress, to be acted upon by State conventions called for that sole purpose in accordance with the provisions of Article V of the Constitution and adequately safeguarded so as to be truly representative.

CONSERVATION

The wise use of all natural resources freed from monopolistic control is a Republican policy, initiated by Theodore Roosevelt. The Roosevelt, Coolidge and Hoover reclamation projects bear witness to the continuation of that policy. Forestry and all other conservation activities have been supported and enlarged.

The conservation of oil is a major problem to the industry and the nation. The administration has sought to bring coordination of effort through the States, the producers and the Federal Government. Progress has been made and the effort will continue.

THE NEGRO

For seventy years the Republican Party has been the friend of the American Negro. Vindication of the rights of the Negro citizen to enjoy the full benefits of life, liberty and the pursuit of happiness is traditional in the Republican Party, and our party stands pledged to maintain equal opportunity and rights for Negro citizens. We do not propose to depart from that tradition nor to alter the spirit or letter of that pledge.

HAWAII

We believe that the existing status of self-government which for many years has been enjoyed by the citizens of the Territory of Hawaii should be maintained, and that officials appointed to administer the government should be bona-fide residents of the Territory.

PUERTO RICO

Puerto Rico being a part of the United States and its inhabitants American citizens, we believe that they are entitled to a good-faith recognition of the spirit and purposes of their organic act.

We, therefore, favor the inclusion of the island in all legislative and administrative measures enacted or adopted by Congress or otherwise for the economic benefit of their fellow-citizens of the mainland.

We also believe that, in so far as possible, all officials appointed to administer the affairs of the island government should be qualified by at least five years of bona-fide residence therein.

ALASKA

We favor the policy of giving to the people of Alaska the widest possible territorial self-government and the selection so far as possible of bona-fide residents for positions in that Territory and the placing of its citizens on an equality with those in the several States.

WELFARE WORK AND CHILDREN

The children of our nation, our future citizens, have had the most solicitous thought of our President. Child welfare and protection has been a major effort of this administration. The organization of the White House Conference on Child Health and Protection is regarded as one of the outstanding accomplishments of this administration.

Welfare work in all its phases has had the support of the President and aid of the administration. The work of organized agencies—local, State and Federal—has been advanced and an increased impetus given by that recognition and help. We approve and pledge a continuation of that policy.

INDIANS

We favor the fullest protection of the property rights of the American Indians and the provision for them of adequate educational facilities.

REORGANIZATION OF GOVERNMENT BUREAUS

Efficiency and economy demand reorganization of government bureaus. The problem is nonpartisan and must be so treated if it is to be solved. As a result of years of study and personal contact with conflicting activities and wasteful duplication of effort, the President is particularly fitted to direct measures to correct the situation. We favor legislation by Congress which will give him the required authority.

DEMOCRATIC FAILURE

The vagaries of the present Democratic House of Representatives offer characteristic and appalling proof of the existing incapacity of that party for leadership in a national crisis. Individualism running amuck has displaced party discipline and has trampled under foot party leadership. A bewildered electorate has viewed the spectacle with profound dismay and deep misgivings.

Goaded to desperation by their confessed failure, the party leaders have resorted to "pork barrel" legislation to obtain a unity of action which could not otherwise be achieved. A Republican President stands resolutely between the helpless citizen and the disaster threatened by such measures; and the people, regardless of party, will demand his continued service.

Many times during his useful life has Herbert Hoover responded to such a call, and his response has never disappointed. He will not disappoint us now.

PARTY GOVERNMENT

The delays and differences which recently hampered efforts to obtain legislation imperatively demanded by prevailing critical conditions strikingly illustrate the menace to self-government brought about by the weakening of party ties and party fealty.

Experience has demonstrated that coherent political parties are indispensable agencies for the prompt and effective operation of the functions of our government under the Constitution.

Only by united party action can consistent, well-planned and wholesome legislative programs be enacted. We believe that the majority of the Congressmen elected in the name of a party have the right and duty to determine the general policies of that party requiring Congressional action, and that Congressmen belonging to that party are, in general, bound to adhere to such policies. Any other course inevitably makes of Congress a body of detached delegates which, instead of representing the collective wisdom of our people, become the confused voices of a heterogeneous group of unrelated local prejudices.

We believe that the time has come when Senators and Representatives of the United States should be impressed with the inflexible truth that their first concern should be the welfare of the United States and the well-being of all of its people, and that stubborn pride of individual opinion is not a virtue, but an obstacle to the orderly and successful achievement of the objects of representative government.

Only by cooperation can self-government succeed. Without it election under a party aegis becomes a false pretense.

We earnestly request that Republicans throughout the Union demand that their representatives in the Congress pledge themselves to these principles, to the end that the insidious influences of party disintegration may not undermine the very foundations of the Republic.

CONCLUSION

In contrast with the Republican policies and record, we contrast those of the democratic as evidenced by the action of the House of Representatives under Democratic leadership and control, which includes:

1. The issuance of fiat currency.

2. Instructions to the Federal Reserve Board and the Secretary of the Treasury to attempt to manipulate commodity prices.

3. The guarantee of bank deposits.

4. The squandering of the public resources and the unbalancing of the budget through pork-barrel appropriations which bear little relation to distress and would tend through delayed business revival to decrease rather than increase employment.

Generally on economic matters we pledge the Republican Party:

1. To maintain unimpaired the national credit.

2. To defend and preserve a sound currency and an honest dollar.

3. To stand steadfastly by the principle of a balanced budget.

4. To devote ourselves fearlessly and unremittingly to the task of eliminating abuses and extravagance and of drastically cutting the cost of government so as to reduce the heavy burden of taxation.

5. To use all available means consistent with sound financial and economic principles to promote an expansion of credit to stimulate business and relieve unemployment.

6. To make a thorough study of the conditions which permitted the credit and the credit machinery of the country to be made available, with-

out adequate check, for wholesale speculation in securities, resulting in ruinous consequences to millions of our citizens and to the national economy, and to correct those conditions so that they shall not recur.

Recognizing that real relief to unemployment must come through a revival of industrial activity and agriculture, to the promotion of which our every effort must be directed, our party in State and nation undertakes to do all in its power that is humanly possible to see that distress is fully relieved in accordance with American principles and traditions.

No successful solution of the problems before the country today can be expected from a Congress and a President separated by partisan lines or opposed in purposes and principles. Responsibility cannot be placed unless a clear mandate is given by returning to Washington a Congress and a Chief Executive united in principles and program.

The return to power of the Republican Party with that mandate is the duty of every voter who believes in the doctrines of the party and its program as herein stated. Nothing else, we believe, will insure the orderly recovery of the country and that return to prosperous days which every American so ardently desires.

The Republican Party faces the future unafraid!

With courage and confidence in ultimate success, we will strive against the forces that strike at our social and economic ideals, our political institutions.

Socialist Party Platform of 1932

"The Socialist party calls upon the nation's workers and all progressive citizens to unite with it in a mighty movement in behalf of justice, peace and freedom."

We are facing a breakdown of the capitalist system. This situation the Socialist Party has long predicted. In the last campaign it warned the people of the increasing insecurity in American life and urged a program of action which, if adopted, would have saved millions from their present tragic plight.

To-day in every city of the United States jobless men and women by the thousands are fighting the grim battle against want and starvation while factories stand idle and food rots on the ground. Millions of wage earners and salaried workers are hunting in vain for jobs while other millions are only partly employed.

Unemployment and poverty are inevitable products of the present system. Under capitalism the few own our industries. The many do the work. The wage earners and farmers are compelled to give a large part of the product of their labor to the few. The many in the factories, mines, shops, offices, and on the farms obtain but a scanty income and are able to buy back only a part of the goods that can be produced in such abundance by our mass industries.

Goods pile up. Factories close. Men and women are discharged. The Nation is thrown into a panic. In a country with natural resources, machinery, and trained labor sufficient to provide security and plenty for all, masses of people are destitute.

Capitalism spells not only widespread economic disaster but class strife. It likewise carries with it an ever-present threat of international war. The struggle of the capitalist class to find world markets and investment areas for their surplus goods and capital was a prime cause of the World War. It is to-day fostering those policies of militarism and imperialism which, if unchecked, will lead to another world conflict.

From the poverty, insecurity, unemployment, the economic collapse, the wastes, and the wars of our present capitalistic order, only the united efforts of workers and farmers, organized in unions and cooperatives, and above all in a political party of their own, can save the nation.

The Republican and Democratic Parties, both controlled by the great industrialists and financiers, have no plan or program to rescue us from the present collapse. In this crisis their chief purpose and desire has been to help the railroads, banks, insurance companies, and other capitalist interests.

The Socialist Party is to-day the one democratic party of the workers whose program would remove the causes of class struggles, class antagonisms, and social evils inherent in the capitalist system.

It proposes to transfer the principal industries of the country from private ownership and autocratic, cruelly inefficient management to social ownership and democratic control. Only by these means will it be possible to organize our industrial life on a basis of planned and steady operation, without periodic breakdowns and disastrous crises.

It proposes the following measures:

UNEMPLOYMENT AND LABOR LEGISLATION

1. A Federal appropriation of $5,000,000,000 for immediate relief for those in need to supplement State and local appropriations.

2. A Federal appropriation of $5,000,000,000 for public works and roads, reforestation, slum clearance, and decent homes for the workers, by Federal Government, States and cities.

3. Legislation providing for the acquisition of land, buildings, and equipment necessary to put the unemployed to work producing food, fuel, and clothing and for the erection of houses for their own use.

4. The 6-hour day and the 5-day week without reduction of wages.

5. A comprehensive and efficient system of free public employment agencies.

6. A compulsory system of unemployment compensation with adequate benefits, based on contributions by the Government and by employers.

7. Old-age pensions for men and women 60 years of age and over.

8. Health and maternity insurance.

9. Improved system of workmen's compensation and accident insurance.

10. The abolition of child labor.

11. Government aid to farmers and small home-owners to protect them against mortgage foreclosures and moratorium on sales for non-payment of taxes by destitute farmers and unemployed workers.

12. Adequate minimum wage laws.

SOCIAL OWNERSHIP

1. Public ownership and democratic control of mines, forests, oil, and power resources; public utilities dealing with light and power, transportation and communication, and of all other basic industries.

2. The operation of these publicly owned industries by boards of administration on which the wageworker, the consumer, and the technician are adequately represented; the recog-

nition in each industry of the principles of collective bargaining and civil service.

BANKING

1. Socialization of our credit and currency system and the establishment of a unified banking system, beginning with the complete governmental acquisition of the Federal reserve banks and the extension of the services of postal savings banks to cover all departments of the banking business and the transference of this department of the post office to a Government-owned banking corporation.

TAXATION

1. Steeply increased inheritance taxes and income taxes on the higher incomes and estates of both corporations and individuals.

2. A constitutional amendment authorizing the taxation of all government securities.

AGRICULTURE

Many of the foregoing measures for socializing the power, banking, and other industries, for raising living standards among the city workers, etc., would greatly benefit the farming population.

As special measures for agricultural upbuilding, we propose:

1. The reduction of tax burdens, by a shift from taxes on farm property to taxes on incomes, inheritance, excess profits, and other similar forms of taxation.

2. Increased Federal and State subsidies to road building and education and social services for rural communities.

3. The creation of a Federal marketing agency for the purchase and marketing of agricultural products.

4. The acquisition by bona fide cooperative societies and by governmental agencies of grain elevators, stockyards, packing houses, and warehouses and the conduct of these services on a nonprofit basis. The encouragement of farmers' cooperative societies and of the consumers' cooperatives in the cities, with a view of eliminating the middleman.

5. The socialization of Federal land banks and the extension by these banks of long-term credit to farmers at low rates of interest.

6. Social insurance against losses due to adverse weather conditions.

7. The creation of national, regional, and State land utilization boards for the purpose of discovering the best uses of the farming land of the country, in view of the joint needs of agriculture, industry, recreation, water supply, reforestation, etc., and to prepare the way for agricultural planning on a national and, ultimately, on a world scale.

Constitutional Changes

1. Proportional representation.
2. Direct election of the President and Vice President.
3. The initiative and referendum.
4. An amendment to the Constitution to make constitutional amendments less cumbersome.
5. Abolition of the power of the Supreme Court to pass upon the constitutionality of legislation enacted by Congress.
6. The passage of the Socialist Party's proposed Worker's rights amendment to the Constitution empowering Congress to establish national systems of unemployment, health and accident insurance and old age pensions, to abolish child labor, establish and take over enterprises in manufacture, commerce, transportation, banking, public utilities, and other business and industries to be owned and operated by the Government, and generally, for the social and economic welfare of the workers of the United States.
7. Repeal the 18th amendment and take over the liquor industry under government ownership and control with the right of local option for each state to maintain prohibition within its borders.

Civil Liberties

1. Federal legislation to enforce the first amendment to the Constitution so as to guarantee freedom of speech, press, and assembly, and to penalize officials who interfere with the civil rights of citizens.
2. The abolition of injunctions in labor disputes, the outlawing of "yellow-dog" contracts and the passing of laws enforcing the rights of workers to organize into unions.
3. The immediate repeal of the espionage law and other repressive legislation, and the restoration of civil and political rights to those unjustly convicted under wartime laws.
4. Legislation protecting aliens from being excluded from this country or from citizenship or from being deported on account of their political, social, or economic beliefs, or on account of activities engaged in by them which are not illegal for citizens.
5. Modification of the immigration laws to permit the reuniting of families and to offer a refuge to those fleeing from political or religious persecution.

The Negro

The enforcement of constitutional guarantees of economic, political, and legal equality for the Negro.

The enactment and enforcement of drastic antilynching laws.

International Relations

While the Socialist Party is opposed to all wars, it believes that there can be no permanent peace until Socialism is established internationally. In the meanwhile, we will support all measures that promise to promote good will and friendship among the nations of the world, including:

1. The reduction of armaments, leading to the goal of total disarmament by international agreement, if possible; but, if that is not possible, by setting an example ourselves. Soldiers, sailors, and workers unemployed by reason of disarmament to be absorbed, where desired, in a program of public works, to be financed in part by the savings due to disarmament. The abolition of conscription, of military training camps, and the Reserve Officers' Training Corps.
2. The recognition of the Soviet Union and the encouragement of trade and industrial relations with that country.
3. The cancellation of war debts due from the allied governments as part of a program for wiping out war debts and reparations, provided that such cancellation does not release money for armaments, but promotes disarmament.
4. The entrance of the United States into the World Court.
5. The entrance of the United States into the League of Nations under conditions which will make it an effective instrument for world peace and renewed cooperation with the working-class parties abroad to the end that the League may be transformed from a league of imperialist powers to a democratic assemblage representative of the aspirations of the common people of the world.

6. The creation of international economic organizations on which labor is adequately represented, to deal with problems of raw material, investments, money, credit, tariffs, and living standards from the viewpoint of the welfare of the masses throughout the world.

7. The abandonment of every degree of military intervention by the United States in the affairs of other countries. The immediate withdrawal of military forces from Haiti and Nicaragua.

8. The withdrawal of United States military and naval forces from China and the relinquishment of American extraterritorial privileges.

9. The complete independence of the Philippines and the negotiation of treaties with other nations safeguarding the sovereignty of these islands.

10. Prohibition of the sales of munitions to foreign powers.

Committed to this constructive program, the Socialist Party calls upon the Nation's workers and upon all fair-minded and progressive citizens to unite with it in a mighty movement against the present drift into social disaster and in behalf of sanity, justice, peace, and freedom.

Platform of the Socialist Labor Party

Social systems and their corresponding forms of government come into being as results of social forces making for social progress. The purpose of governments is ostensibly to insure life, liberty and the pursuit of happiness of the useful members of society.

Whenever a society fails in or becomes destructive of these ends, it has self-evidently outlived its usefulness, rendering it imperative for the exploited and oppressed class to organize its forces to put an end to the outworn social system.

Such a crucial period of history is facing humanity today, and in view of this the Socialist Labor Party in National Convention assembled, May 1, 1932, reaffirms its former platform declarations and in accord with the international Socialist principles declares:

The history of mankind has been a struggle for progress, taking the form of struggles for power between contending classes. Whenever a ruling class had fulfilled its mission, and its interests ceased to be in harmony with social interests, it was supplanted by the class below, which, by increasing economic and political powers, attained its revolutionary goal. This class, in turn, became a carrier of social progress until it had outlived its usefulness and, becoming reactionary and a stumbling block in the path of humanity, had to give way before the combined forces of social progress and a new revolutionary class.

With capitalism there remain in society just two contending classes, the capitalist class and the working class—the capitalist class, the owner of the means of production, which ownership today is wholly destructive of the life, liberty and happiness of the mass of the people; and the working class whose interests demand the abolition of private ownership in the means of life.

The interests of the working class demand the institution of collective ownership and control, guaranteeing to all the right to work, and by securing to all the full fruits of their labor, ending for all time the destructive class wars which have up to now torn humanity asunder.

For forty years the Socialist Labor Party has been moving upward toward this historic moment.

The capitalist system is now creaking and breaking in every joint and cranny. It is no more "on trial" than a horse-drawn vehicle is on trial beside a powerful motor van. Capitalism is outworn, obsolete, ready for the museum of social history. A mere glance at the world situation should suffice to convince even the dullest of this forceful fact.

Economic bonds have snapped; social bonds are dissolving. As a result, factories are closing down, machinery stands idle and rusts, until from ten to twelve million working men and women of this country are idle and they and their dependents stand bereft of food, clothing and shelter. The million mass of the people, the world over, are starving and dying, surrounded by tremendous wealth created by their own labor. Workers are unable to find work, to secure the necessities of life.

The Socialist Labor Party has ceaselessly pointed out the inevitable doom of the capitalist system of production and distribution:

has pointed to the fact that "free" competition—one of the beatitudes of the system—was inevitably leading to the elimination of the small, and gradually not so small either, business men and manufactures;

has shown that the cumulative effect of the gigantic machines of production in fewer and fewer hands would be so tremendous as to get beyond the possibility of control by the few industries;

has demonstrated beyond doubt that the capitalist profit system was built and could exist only on the exploitation of labor;

that this exploitation with the aid of the machines was becoming so tremendous that it would eventually become absolutely impossible for the capitalist expropriators to dispose of this surplus in either domestic or foreign markets;

that this "stolen goods" would eventually accumulate and lie like an incubus on the chest of humanity, preventing it from breathing and living while a multi-million army of unemployed would tramp the streets and highways unable to find the wherewithal to live.

This state of social dissolution is now upon us.

When a social system has reached the point of utter dissolution, when the bonds that held it together are snapping, ruling class interests eagerly offer palliatives and reforms to stave off the impending doom of the system. It is so with capitalism. In various disguises, but moved with one purpose, various agents of capitalism appear, holding out alluring promises of reform ostensibly to bring relief to the workers. But there can be no relief to a revolutionary class within a social system that is doomed.

Where a social revolution is pending and, for whatever reason, is not accomplished, reaction is the alternative. Every reform granted by capi-talism is a concealed measure of reaction. He who says reform says preservation, and he who says that reforms under capitalism are possible and worth while thereby declares that a continuation of capitalism is possible and worth while. But capitalism has grown into an all-destroying and all-devouring monster that must be destroyed if humanity is to live.

At this crucial moment the Socialist Labor Party calls upon the working class of America, more deliberately serious than ever before, to rally at the polls under the Party's banner.

The Socialist Labor Party also calls upon all other intelligent citizens to place themselves squarely upon the ground of working class interests, and join us in this mighty and noble work of human emancipation, so that we may put summary end to the existing barbarous class conflict and insane contradictions between unlimited wealth and wealth production, and the poverty and wretchedness suffered by those whose labor created all this wealth.

We call upon them to place the land and all the means of production, transportation and distribution in the hands of the useful producers as an organized industrial body, under a national industrial administration to take the place of the present outworn political or territorial government. And we further call upon the workers to hasten this work of social and human regeneration to the end that a speedy termination may be put to the present state of planless production, industrial war and social disorder, substituting for it the Socialist or Industrial Commonwealth of Emancipated Labor—a commonwealth in which every worker shall have the free exercise and full benefit of his faculties, multiplied by all the factors of modern civilization.

CAMPAIGN OF 1936

In 1936 President Franklin Roosevelt and Vice-President Garner were renominated by acclamation at the party's convention in Philadelphia in June. The Republicans, in Cleveland, nominated Alfred M. Landon, the governor of Kansas who had survived the Democratic tide that had swept through most of the states. Frank Knox, publisher of the *Chicago Daily News*, was selected as his running mate.

A new party, the Union Party, was headed by Representative William Lemke, a Republican from North Dakota, and Thomas O'Brien, a union lawyer from Boston. The party was supported by Father Charles E. Coughlin's National Union for Social Justice, as well as by Francis E. Townsend, leader of old-age pensioners.

The other minor parties also nominated candidates. Norman Thomas again ran as the Socialist Party nominee, this time with George Nelson of Wisconsin. Earl Browder of Kansas made his first bid for the presidency as the Communist Party candidate; James W. Ford of New York was the vice-presidential choice again. The Prohibitionists chose David L. Colvin of New York and a famous soldier of World War I, Alvin York of Tennessee, as their candidates. On the Socialist Labor Party ticket, John W. Aiken of Massachusetts was the presidential candidate and Emil F. Teichert of New York was his running mate.

In the November canvas the Democrats scored a landslide—carrying all but two states. The Democratic Party popular vote was 27,747,636 ballots; the Republicans received 16,679,543 votes—carrying Maine and Vermont. The new Union Party polled a surprising 892,492 votes, nearly 2 percent of the total. The Socialists obtained 187,785 votes; the Communists, 79,211; the Prohibitionists, 37,668; and the Socialist Labor candidates, 12,790 votes. President Roosevelt received 523 electoral votes to 8 for Governor Landon.

The Election Platform of the Communist Party

The American people today face the greatest crisis since the Civil War. Extreme reaction threatens the country, driving toward Fascism and a new world war.

To meet this danger to our liberties and welfare, we must unite our ranks. In common action we must go forward to overcome this crisis in an American way, in the spirit of 1776, in the interests of our people and of our country.

The collapse of the Hoover-Republican prosperity destroyed our boasted American standards of living. The New Deal failed to protect and restore our living standards. American capitalism is unable to provide the American people with the simple necessities of life.

Over 12,000,000 able-bodied and willing workers are without jobs. For a majority of these there is no hope of jobs.

The income of the working people has been cut in half. Half our farmers have lost their land. They are being converted into a pauperized peasantry.

Millions of young people face a future without hope, with no prospect of ever being able to establish a home or rear a family.

The Negro people suffer doubly. Most exploited of working people, they are also victims of jim-crowism and lynching. They are denied the right to live as human beings.

Civil rights are being systematically attacked and curtailed. The Supreme Court has usurped the power of Congress. It is destroying all labor and social legislation.

Reactionary forces, roused and organized by Hearst and the Liberty League, are striving to seize the government fully. They want to saddle the entire burden of the crisis upon the people, to establish a fascist régime and move toward war on the side of Hitler, the butcher of the German people and the chief maker of war.

The peace, freedom, and security of the people are at stake. Democracy or Fascism, progress or reaction—this is the central issue of 1936.

At the head of the camp of reaction stands the Republican party—the party of Wall Street, the party of the banks and monopolies. Landon and Knox are supported by the barons of steel, oil, auto, and munitions; by Morgan, the du Ponts; and by that arch-enemy of all decency, William Randolph Hearst. They are the candidates of the Liberty League, the National Association of Manufacturers, the American Bankers' Association, the United States Chamber of Commerce, the Ku Klux Klan, and the Black Legion.

Roosevelt is bitterly attacked by the camp of reaction. But he does not fight back these attacks. Roosevelt compromises. He grants but small concessions to the working people, while making big concessions to Hearst, to Wall Street, to the reactionaries.

The working people must organize themselves *independently*, under their own banner, with their own leadership and program. They must organize a great Farmer-Labor Party to fight for and establish a people's government—a government of, for, and by the people. They must unite the forces of progress against the forces of reaction.

The secretly formed Union party of Lemke and Coughlin is not the new party for which the people are looking. It is the creature of Landon, Hearst, and the Liberty League. Under cover of radical sounding words, its program contains essentially the some proposals as the Republican platform. It is deceiving its followers. It is the tool of the reactionaries.

But a real people's party is arising. Organized by the workers and farmers themselves, the Farmer-Labor party is growing in the majority of states. Unable to put up a presidential ticket this year, it is organizing on a national scale. It fights for local, state and Congressional offices. It is the most hopeful sign in American political life. It is cooperating with the powerful trade unions in the new Labor's Non-Partisan League against the Republicans. It will undoubtedly be a major contender in the presidential elections of 1940. The Communist party unconditionally supports the building of the Farmer-Labor party. It pledges itself to work to bring the trade unions and all progressive forces into its ranks. The Socialist party, on a national scale, is withholding its cooperation with all other groups. It conducts a harmful policy of isolation. It gives little help to the people's struggle against reaction. We appeal to the Socialist party to change its course. We urge it to unite with us and the mass of the toilers against reaction.

In this situation the Communist party comes forward with its own presidential ticket and its own platform. It enters the campaign to defend and promote the unity of the working people. It pledges to fight for their interests, to defeat the reactionaries, to build the Farmer-Labor party, and, finally, to win the masses to the banner of socialism. The chief aim of the Communist party today is to defeat the Landon-Hearst-Liberty League reaction, to defeat the forces of Wall Street.

The Communist party and its candidates stand on the following platform, which expresses the immediate interests of the majority of the population of our country.

I. PUT AMERICA BACK TO WORK. PROVIDE JOBS AND A LIVING WAGE FOR ALL.

Open the closed factories—we need all that our industries can produce. If the private employers will not or cannot do so, then the government must open and operate the factories, mills and mines for the benefit of the people.

Industry and the productive powers of our nation must be used to give every working man and woman a real, American standard of living, with a minimum annual wage guaranteed by law.

We demand equal opportunity for women in industry and in all spheres of life. We favor legislative measures for the improvement of the wages and working conditions of women.

We demand a 30-hour week without reduction in earnings, at trade union rates and conditions, in private industry and on public works.

We oppose the present railroad consolidation policy which results in the discharge of hundreds of thousands of workers.

We demand higher wages and vacations with pay. We demand the abolition of the wage differential between the North and the South.

II. PROVIDE UNEMPLOYMENT INSURANCE, OLD AGE PENSIONS, AND SOCIAL SECURITY FOR ALL.

It is the obligation of the American government to establish an adequate system of social insurance for the unemployed, the aged, the disabled and the sick, as provided in the Frazier-Lundeen Bill. This bill provides compensation to all unemployed without exception, and pensions for the aged from 60 years, at rates equal to former earnings, but in no case less than $15 per week. Make the Frazier-Lundeen Bill the law of the land!

We favor a federal system of maternity and health insurance.

We stand for adequate relief standards for all unemployed. We demand a stop to all relief cuts. The federal government must continue and extend the W. P. A. We favor an extensive Federal Works Program, to provide housing at low rentals, schools, hospitals, health and recreational facilities, as provided for in the proposed six billion dollar appropriation of the Marcantonio Relief Standards Bill.

We support the demands of the veterans for uniform pension laws and for adequate hospitalization.

III. Save the Young Generation!

Our country can and must provide opportunity, education, and work for the youth of America. These demands of the young people as embodied in the American Youth Act—the Benson-Amlie Bill—must be enacted into law.

This bill provides for jobs, educational opportunities, and vocational training for all young people between the ages of 16 and 25.

The National Youth Administration budget must be maintained and enlarged.

Military training in the C. C. C. and schools must be abolished.

Free education and financial assistance to the youth and the children must be guaranteed by both federal and state appropriations.

Child labor must once and for all be abolished and made unconstitutional.

IV. Free the Farmers From Debts, Unbearable Tax Burdens and Foreclosures. Guarantee the Land to Those Who Till the Soil.

We declare that the American government is obligated to save the American farmers from distress and ruin, to guarantee the farmers and tenants their inalienable rights to possession of their land, their homes and their chattels. We demand for this purpose the immediate refinancing of the farmers' debts with government loans at nominal interest.

We demand a halt to evictions and foreclosures, a long-term moratorium on all needy farmers' debts, and the adoption of measures to provide land for the landless farmers.

We favor immediate relief to the drought-stricken farmers by the government. We favor a graduated land tax to prevent the accumulation of large land holdings in the hands of the insurance companies, private and government banks, and other absentee owners.

We favor exemption from taxation of small operating farmers and farm cooperatives.

We are unalterably opposed to the policy of crop destruction and curtailment.

We support government regulation of farm prices with the aim of guaranteeing to the farmer his cost of production. We urge scientific soil conservation under supervision of the elected representatives of farmers' organizations, with compensation to farmer-owners and tenants for loss of income.

V. The Rich Hold the Wealth of Our Country; Make the Rich Pay.

We demand that social and labor legislation shall be financed and the budget balanced by taxation of the rich. We are opposed to sales taxes in any form, including processing taxes, and call for their immediate repeal. The main source of government finance must be a system of sharply graduated taxation upon incomes of over $5,000 a year, upon corporate profits and surpluses, as well as taxation upon the present tax-exempt securities and large gifts and inheritances. The people of small income, small property, and home owners must be protected against foreclosures and seizures and from burdensome taxes and high interest rates.

We are unconditionally opposed to inflationary policies which bring catastrophe and ruin to the workers, farmers, and middle classes, and enrich the speculators.

We favor nationalization of the entire banking system.

VI. Defend and Extend Democratic Rights and Civil Liberties! Curb the Supreme Court!

We support a Constitutional Amendment to put an end to the dictatorial and usurped powers of the Supreme Court. We demand further that Congress immediately reassert its Constitutional powers to enact social and labor legislation and to curb the Supreme Court usurpation.

We champion the unrestricted freedom of speech, press, radio and assembly and the right to organize and strike. We call upon the people to safeguard these traditional liberties.

We stand for federal legislation which will establish labor's full right to collective bargaining, which will outlaw the company unions, the spy and stool pigeon systems, and all other coercion by employers.

We demand heavy penalties and imprisonment for employers guilty of discharging workers for union or political activities.

We demand the abolition of poll taxes and all other limitations on the right to vote.

We demand the release of political prisoners, among whom Tom Mooney, Angelo Herndon, and the Scottsboro Boys are but the outstanding examples.

The infamous policy of deportation of foreign-born workers must be stopped. The traditional American right of asylum for political refugees must be reestablished. Anti-Semitic propaganda must be prohibited by law.

VII. Full Rights for the Negro People

We demand that the Negro people be guaranteed complete equality, equal rights to jobs, equal pay for equal work, the full right to organize, vote, serve on juries, and hold public office. Segregation and discrimination against Negroes must be declared a crime. Heavy penalties must be established against mob rule, floggers, and kidnappers, with the *death penalty for lynchers*. We demand the enforcement of the Thirteenth, Fourteenth and Fifteenth Amendments to the Constitution.

VIII. Keep America Out of War by Keeping War Out of the World!

We declare that peace must be maintained and defended at all costs. We declare in favor of strengthening all measures for collective security. We favor effective financial and economic measures to this end by the League of Nations, against Hitler Germany, Italian Fascism and Japanese imperialism. These measures should be supported by the United States government.

We consider the expenditure of billions for armaments and war preparations unnecessary and provocative, contributing to the danger of a new world war.

Instead of ever greater armaments, we believe that the United States should develop an American Peace Policy in close collaboration with the Soviet Union, based on complete prohibition of the sale or delivery of goods, or the granting of loans to nations engaged in a foreign war contrary to the provisions of the Kellogg Peace Pact. The huge funds now spent for armament should be turned to the support of the suffering people.

We demand the nationalization of the entire munitions industry.

We demand an end to American intervention in the internal affairs of the Latin-American countries and the Philippines.

We demand the strict non-recognition of the Japanese conquests in Manchuria and China, and the Italian conquest of Ethiopia.

We support the Puerto Rican demand for independence.

We support the complete independence and self-determination of all oppressed nations.

This platform represents the life needs of the majority of workers, farmers, and middle classes today. These demands can be won even under the present capitalist system. This is being conclusively proved by the victories of the People's Front in France. We appeal to all members of the American Federation of Labor and farm organizations, to our comrades in the Socialist party, to all who toil with hand or brain, Negro and white, to unite in a determined fight to achieve the demands of the people and to beat back the sinister forces of reaction.

The fight for those demands will organize and strengthen the people. It will give them deeper political experience and understanding. It will prepare them for the great decisions to come when it will be necessary to move forward to socialism.

Today the immediate issue is Democracy or Fascism. But the consistent fight for Democracy in the conditions of declining capitalism will finally bring us to the necessary choice of the socialist path.

Our land is the richest in the world. It has the largest and most skilled working class. Everything is present to provide a rich and cultured life for the whole population. Yet millions starve. The whole nation suffers, because capitalism is breaking down, because profits are the first law and are put above human needs—and the capitalist rulers are turning to Fascism and war.

The Communist party prepares the people to bring an end to this crucifixion of humanity. Our economy must be taken from the incompetent and greedy hands of Wall Street. It must be made the common property of the whole people. It must be operated fully for the benefit of all who work. This will be socialism. Only when socialism will be established, as today in the Soviet Union, will there be no crisis, no poverty, no unemployment—but abundance and security for all, with the gates of progress open to humanity.

Reactionaries of all shades cry out against socialism. They say it is revolutionary. True, the change to socialism will be revolutionary; but since when is revolution un-American? On the contrary, revolution is the proudest tradition of our people who have always been among the most revolutionary peoples of the world.

Communism is Twentieth-century Americanism. The Communist party continues the traditions of 1776, of the birth of our country, of the revolutionary Lincoln, who led the historic struggle that preserved our nation. In the greater crisis of today only the Communist party shows a way to a better life now, and to the future of peace, freedom, and security for all.

By supporting, working with, and voting for the Communist party in the November elections; by organizing the mass-production industries into powerful industrial unions, in a united American Federation of Labor, by independent political action and by building the American people's front—the Farmer-Labor party—the toilers of America can best fight for the realization of their aims in 1936.

Forward to a progressive, free, prosperous, and happy America.

VOTE COMMUNIST!

Democratic Platform of 1936

We hold this truth to be self-evident—that the test of a representative government is its ability to promote the safety and happiness of the people.

We hold this truth to be self-evident—that 12 years of Republican leadership left our Nation sorely stricken in body, mind, and spirit; and that three years of Democratic leadership have put it back on the road to restored health and prosperity.

We hold this truth to be self-evident—that 12 years of Republican surrender to the dictatorship of a privileged few have been supplanted by a Democratic leadership which has returned the people themselves to the places of authority, and has revived in them new faith and restored the hope which they had almost lost.

We hold this truth to be self-evident—that this three-year recovery in all the basic values of life and the reestablishment of the American way of living has been brought about by humanizing the policies of the Federal Government as they affect the personal, financial, industrial, and agricultural well-being of the American people.

We hold this truth to be self-evident—that government in a modern civilization has certain inescapable obligations to its citizens, among which are:

(1) Protection of the family and the home.

(2) Establishment of a democracy of opportunity for all the people.

(3) Aid to those overtaken by disaster.

These obligations, neglected through 12 years of the old leadership, have once more been recognized by American Government. Under the new leadership they will never be neglected.

For the Protection of the Family and the Home

(1) We have begun and shall continue the successful drive to rid our land of kidnappers and bandits. We shall continue to use the powers of government to end the activities of the malefactors of great wealth who defraud and exploit the people.

Savings and Investment

(2) We have safeguarded the thrift of our citizens by restraining those who would gamble with other peoples savings, by requiring truth in the sale of securities; by putting the brakes upon the use of credit for speculation; by outlawing the manipulation of prices in stock and commodity markets; by curbing the overweening power and unholy practices of utility holding companies; by insuring fifty million bank accounts.

Old Age and Social Security

(3) We have built foundations for the security of those who are faced with the hazards of unemployment and old age; for the orphaned, the crippled, and the blind. On the foundation of the Social Security Act we are determined to erect a structure of economic security for all our people, making sure that this benefit shall keep step with the ever-increasing capacity of America to provide a high standard of living for all its citizens.

Consumer

(4) We will act to secure to the consumer fair value, honest sales and a decreased spread between the price he pays and the price the producer receives.

Rural Electrification

(5) This administration has fostered power rate yardsticks in the Tennessee Valley and in several other parts of the Nation. As a result, electricity has been made available to the people at a lower rate. We will continue to promote plans for rural electrification and for cheap power by means of the yardstick method.

Housing

(6) We maintain that our people are entitled to decent, adequate housing at a price which they can afford. In the last three years, the Federal Government, having saved more than two million homes from foreclosure, has taken the first steps in our history to provide decent housing for people of meagre incomes. We believe every encouragement should be given to the building of new homes by private enterprise; and that the Government should steadily extend its housing program toward the goal of adequate housing for those forced through economic necessities to live in unhealthy and slum conditions.

Veterans

(7) We shall continue just treatment of our war veterans and their dependents.

FOR THE ESTABLISHMENT OF A DEMOCRACY OF OPPORTUNITY

Agriculture

We have taken the farmers off the road to ruin.

We have kept our pledge to agriculture to use all available means to raise farm income toward its pre-war purchasing power. The farmer is no longer suffering from 15-cent corn, 3-cent hogs, 2½-cent beef at the farm, 5-cent wool, 30-cent wheat, 5-cent cotton, and 3-cent sugar.

By Federal legislation, we have reduced the farmer's indebtedness and doubled his net income. In cooperation with the States and through the farmers' own committees, we are restoring the fertility of his land and checking the erosion of his soil. We are bringing electricity and good roads to his home.

We will continue to improve the soil conservation and domestic allotment program with payments to farmers.

We will continue a fair-minded administration of agricultural laws, quick to recognize and meet new problems and conditions. We recognize the gravity of the evils of farm tenancy, and we pledge the full cooperation of the Government in the refinancing of farm indebtedness at the lowest possible rates of interest and over a long term of years.

We favor the production of all the market will absorb, both at home and abroad, plus a reserve supply sufficient to insure fair prices to consumers; we favor judicious commodity loans on seasonal surpluses; and we favor assistance within Federal authority to enable farmers to adjust and balance production with demand, at a fair profit to the farmers.

We favor encouragement of sound, practical farm cooperatives.

By the purchase and retirement of ten million acres of sub-marginal land, and assistance to those attempting to eke out an existence upon it, we have made a good beginning toward proper land use and rural rehabilitation.

The farmer has been returned to the road to freedom and prosperity. We will keep him on that road.

Labor

We have given the army of America's industrial workers something more substantial than the Republicans' dinner pail full of promises. We have increased the worker's pay and shortened his hours; we have undertaken to put an end to the sweated labor of his wife and children; we have written into the law of the land his right to collective bargaining and self-organization free from the interference of employers; we have provided Federal machinery for the peaceful settlement of labor disputes.

We will continue to protect the worker and we will guard his rights, both as wage-earner and consumer, in the production and consumption of all commodities, including coal and water power and other natural resource products.

The worker has been returned to the road to

freedom and prosperity. We will keep him on that road.

Business

We have taken the American business man out of the red. We have saved his bank and given it a sounder foundation; we have extended credit; we have lowered interest rates; we have undertaken to free him from the ravages of cutthroat competition.

The American business man has been returned to the road to freedom and prosperity. We will keep him on that road.

Youth

We have aided youth to stay in school; given them constructive occupation; opened the door to opportunity which 12 years of Republican neglect had closed.

Our youth have been returned to the road to freedom and prosperity. We will keep them on that road.

MONOPOLY AND CONCENTRATION OF ECONOMIC POWER

Monopolies and the concentration of economic power, the creation of Republican rule and privilege, continue to be the master of the producer, the exploiter of the consumer, and the enemy of the independent operator. This is a problem challenging the unceasing effort of untrammeled public officials in every branch of the Government. We pledge vigorously and fearlessly to enforce the criminal and civil provisions of the existing anti-trust laws, and to the extent that their effectiveness has been weakened by new corporate devices or judicial construction, we propose by law to restore their efficacy in stamping out monopolistic practices and the concentration of economic power.

AID TO THOSE OVERTAKEN BY DISASTER

We have aided and will continue to aid those who have been visited by widespread drought and floods, and have adopted a Nation-wide flood-control policy.

Unemployment

We believe that unemployment is a national problem, and that it is an inescapable obligation of our Government to meet it in a national way.

Due to our stimulation of private business, more than five million people have been reemployed; and we shall continue to maintain that the first objective of a program of economic security is maximum employment in private industry at adequate wages. Where business fails to supply such employment, we believe that work at prevailing wages should be provided in cooperation with State and local governments on useful public projects, to the end that the national wealth may be increased, the skill and energy of the worker may be utilized, his morale maintained, and the unemployed assured the opportunity to earn the necessities of life.

The Constitution

The Republican platform proposes to meet many pressing national problems solely by action of the separate States. We know that drought, dust storms, floods, minimum wages, maximum hours, child labor, and working conditions in industry, monopolistic and unfair business practices cannot be adequately handled exclusively by 48 separate State legislatures, 48 separate State administrations, and 48 separate State courts. Transactions and activities which inevitably overflow State boundaries call for both State and Federal treatment.

We have sought and will continue to seek to meet these problems through legislation within the Constitution.

If these problems cannot be effectively solved by legislation within the Constitution, we shall seek such clarifying amendment as will assure to the legislatures of the several States and to the Congress of the United States, each within its proper jurisdiction, the power to enact those laws which the State and Federal legislatures, within their respective spheres, shall find necessary, in order adequately to regulate commerce, protect public health and safety and safeguard economic security. Thus we propose to maintain the letter and spirit of the Constitution.

THE MERIT SYSTEM IN GOVERNMENT

For the protection of government itself and promotion of its efficiency, we pledge the immediate extension of the merit system through the classified civil service—which was first established and fostered under Democratic auspices—to all non-policy-making positions in the Federal service.

We shall subject to the civil service law all continuing positions which, because of the emergency, have been exempt from its operation.

CIVIL LIBERTIES

We shall continue to guard the freedom of speech, press, radio, religion and assembly which our Constitution guarantees; with equal rights to all and special privileges to none.

GOVERNMENT FINANCE

The Administration has stopped deflation, restored values and enabled business to go ahead with confidence.

When national income shrinks, government income is imperilled. In reviving national income, we have fortified government finance. We have raised the public credit to a position of unsurpassed security. The interest rate on Government bonds has been reduced to the lowest point in twenty-eight years. The same Government bonds which in 1932 sold under 83 are now selling over 104.

We approve the objective of a permanently sound currency so stabilized as to prevent the former wide fluctuations in value which injured in turn producers, debtors, and property owners on the one hand, and wage-earners and creditors on the other, a currency which will permit full utilization of the country's resources. We assert that today we have the soundest currency in the world.

We are determined to reduce the expenses of government. We are being aided therein by the recession in unemployment. As the requirements of relief decline and national income advances, an increasing percentage of Federal expenditures can and will be met from current revenues, secured from taxes levied in accordance with ability to pay. Our retrenchment, tax and recovery programs thus reflect our firm determination to achieve a balanced budget and the reduction of the national debt at the earliest possible moment.

FOREIGN POLICY

In our relationship with other nations, this Government will continue to extend the policy of the Good Neighbor. We reaffirm our opposition to war as an instrument of national policy, and declare that disputes between nations should be settled by peaceful means. We shall continue to observe a true neutrality in the disputes of others; to be prepared, resolutely to resist aggression against ourselves; to work for peace and to take the profits out of war; to guard against being drawn, by political commitments, international banking or private trading, into any war which may develop anywhere.

We shall continue to foster the increase in our foreign trade which has been achieved by this administration; to seek by mutual agreement the lowering of those tariff barriers, quotas and embargoes which have been raised against our exports of agricultural and industrial products; but continue as in the past to give adequate protection to our farmers and manufacturers against unfair competition or the dumping on our shores of commodities and goods produced abroad by cheap labor or subsidized by foreign governments.

THE ISSUE

The issue in this election is plain. The American people are called upon to choose between a Republican administration that has and would again regiment them in the service of privileged groups and a Democratic administration dedicated to the establishment of equal economic opportunity for all our people.

We have faith in the destiny of our nation. We are sufficiently endowed with natural resources and with productive capacity to provide for all a quality of life that meets the standards of real Americanism.

Dedicated to a government of liberal American principles, we are determined to oppose equally, the despotism of Communism and the menace of concealed Fascism.

We hold this final truth to be self-evident— that the interests, the security and the happiness of the people of the United States of America can be perpetuated only under democratic government as conceived by the founders of our nation.

Prohibition Party Platform of 1936

PREAMBLE

After three and a half years of Republican administration, and three and a half years of Democratic administration since the depression, we find our gravest problems unsolved, the morals of the people greatly undermined and the national morals broken down to an incredible extent.

It is plain that the crass materialism of our dominant parties; their abandonment of moral precepts; their flouting of the majesty of the law; their double dealing; their supreme self interest must be replaced by a return to the early American principles of dependence upon Almighty God as the source of all just government and to a following of the principles of the Prince of Peace.

The conclusion is inevitable that the prosperity and progress of the nation can come only through the spiritual and moral regeneration of the people manifested in government.

PROHIBITION

We denounce the bipartisan conspiracy by which the Eighteenth Amendment was removed from the Constitution and the nation reopened to the exploitation of the people by a legalized liquor traffic.

Respect for this great moral provision of our Constitution had been weakened by the maladministration to which it was subjected by the two old parties. Both parties are organically incapable of effective enforcement by reason of the two-sided "wet-dry" character of each party and their dominant leadership.

Eighty years' history of non-partisan prohibition in three great prohibition waves has demonstrated that the great obstacles to the maintenance and effectiveness of prohibition has been the lack of a united party behind it.

We seek to unite the opponents of the liquor traffic and then marshal all the powers of government for the complete suppression of that traffic.

We present a sane, liberal and comprehensive program on the great problems of our time.

WORLD PEACE

We pledge ourselves to use every possible means to promote world peace and the settlement of international misunderstandings by arbitration.

TAXES

Must be reduced. Unnecessary governmental functions must be curtailed and the multitude of political jobs abolished. Taxes should be levied in accordance with ability to pay.

Assessments should be uniform and without favor. There should be no tax exemptions.

CRIME

We seek to diminish crime, first by suppressing the traffics in alcoholics and other narcotics, which pervert the brains of the people; second, by bringing about a re-alignment of politics which shall unite the anti-crime voters and overcome the alliance of the underworld with the political machines; third, by effective enforcement of the law, and fourth, by the reform and modernization of antiquated and outmoded system of judicial procedure.

OLD AGE PENSIONS

Our party was the first party to declare for old age pensions. We acknowledge the responsibility of government to adequately care for those handicapped by advanced age or other disabilities.

UNEMPLOYMENT

We must continue to accept responsibility for taking care of the unemployed until such time as industry is able to re-employ them.

DISTRIBUTION

We seek a better distribution of economic goods so that the increased consumption of the products of factory and farm may produce complete employment of labor without interruption.

CURRENCY

The privately owned Federal Reserve Banks should no longer have the special privilege of issuing the currency of the United States and of profiting financially thereby. Congress should resume the exercise of its constitutional right to coin money and fix the value thereof.

We favor a sound legal tender currency, issued directly by the United States government to the people, through the several States and subdivisions thereof, in exchange for an equal amount of legally issued bonds of such States and subdivisions, the funds thus obtained to be used partially for the construction of necessary public works, but chiefly in retiring present tax exempt bonds, as soon as the same shall become due and callable. To prevent undue expansion of bank credit based on such increased emission of currency, we favor a proportionate increase in the cash reserve requirements behind such credit. No further tax exempt securities whatever should be issued, and all those now outstanding whether

Federal, State or local, should be retired and cancelled as soon as practicable.

Thus we would substitute for the present irredeemable paper money a sound currency redeemable dollar for dollar in good and valid bonds, the interest on which would furnish the Treasury most, if not all, the revenues needed for the ordinary expenses of government, economically administered. This would greatly lessen the burden of Federal taxation. Furthermore, because the holders of present tax exempt securities would have to seek some other way to earn an income from their capital, this would contribute in large measure to increased employment and business recovery.

MOVIE CENSORSHIP

We stand for federal supervision of the creation of motion picture films at the source of production so that the public effect may be beneficial and uplifting.

GAMBLING

We are opposed to the legalization of lotteries, gambling and all other forms of exploitation of the people.

CONSTITUTION

We stand for loyalty to the principles of the Constitution and for the preservation of our system of government against the assaults of communism and of fascism, and the subversive influences exerted by the alliance of the old parties with predatory wealth, organized crime and the liquor power.

We invite the support of all patriotic Americans to help build a political party united in its loyalty to the best interests of the nation.

RESOLUTION

Adopted by the National Prohibition Convention. We appeal to the youth of the land with their idealism and enthusiasm to meet the challenge of the hour, and join with us in the solving of the great problems involving the preservation and integrity of American institutions.

Republican Platform for 1936

America is in peril. The welfare of American men and women and the future of our youth are at stake. We dedicate ourselves to the preservation of their political liberty, their individual opportunity and their character as free citizens, which today for the first time are threatened by Government itself.

For three long years the New Deal Administration has dishonored American traditions and flagrantly betrayed the pledges upon which the Democratic Party sought and received public support.

The powers of Congress have been usurped by the President.

The integrity and authority of the Supreme Court have been flouted.

The rights and liberties of American citizens have been violated.

Regulated monopoly has displaced free enterprise.

The New Deal Administration constantly seeks to usurp the rights reserved to the States and to the people.

It has insisted on the passage of laws contrary to the Constitution.

It has intimidated witnesses and interfered with the right of petition.

It has dishonored our country by repudiating its most sacred obligations.

It has been guilty of frightful waste and extravagance, using public funds for partisan political purposes.

It has promoted investigations to harass and intimidate American citizens, at the same time denying investigations into its own improper expenditures.

It has created a vast multitude of new offices, filled them with its favorites, set up a centralized bureaucracy, and sent out swarms of inspectors to harass our people.

It has bred fear and hesitation in commerce and industry, thus discouraging new enterprises, preventing employment and prolonging the depression.

It secretly has made tariff agreements with our foreign competitors, flooding our markets with foreign commodities.

It has coerced and intimidated voters by withholding relief to those opposing its tyrannical policies.

It has destroyed the morale of our people and made them dependent upon government.

Appeals to passion and class prejudice have replaced reason and tolerance.

To a free people, these actions are insufferable. This campaign cannot be waged on the traditional differences between the Republican and Democratic parties. The responsibility of this election transcends all previous political divisions. We invite all Americans, irrespective of party, to join us in defense of American institutions.

CONSTITUTIONAL GOVERNMENT AND FREE ENTERPRISE

We pledge ourselves:

1. To maintain the American system of Constitutional and local self government, and to resist all attempts to impair the authority of the Supreme Court of the United States, the final protector of the rights of our citizens against the arbitrary encroachments of the legislative and executive branches of government. There can be no individual liberty without an independent judiciary.

2. To preserve the American system of free enterprise, private competition, and equality of opportunity, and to seek its constant betterment in the interests of all.

REEMPLOYMENT

The only permanent solution of the unemployment problem is the absorption of the unemployed by industry and agriculture. To that end, we advocate:

Removal of restrictions on production.

Abandonment of all New Deal policies that raise production costs, increase the cost of living, and thereby restrict buying, reduce volume and prevent reemployment.

Encouragement instead of hindrance to legitimate business.

Withdrawal of government from competition with private payrolls.

Elimination of unnecessary and hampering regulations.

Adoption of such other policies as will furnish a chance for individual enterprise, industrial expansion, and the restoration of jobs.

RELIEF

The necessities of life must be provided for the needy, and hope must be restored pending recovery. The administration of relief is a major

failing of the New Deal. It has been faithless to those who must deserve our sympathy. To end confusion, partisanship, waste and incompetence, we pledge:

1. The return of responsibility for relief administration to non-political local agencies familiar with community problems.

2. Federal grants-in-aid to the States and territories while the need exists, upon compliance with these conditions: (a) a fair proportion of the total relief burden to be provided from the revenues of States and local governments; (b) all engaged in relief administration to be selected on the basis of merit and fitness; (c) adequate provision to be made for the encouragement of those persons who are trying to become self-supporting.

3. Undertaking of Federal public works only on their merits and separate from the administration of relief.

4. A prompt determination of the facts concerning relief and unemployment.

SECURITY

Real security will be possible only when our productive capacity is sufficient to furnish a decent standard of living for all American families and to provide a surplus for future needs and contingencies. For the attainment of that ultimate objective, we look to the energy, self-reliance and character of our people, and to our system of free enterprise.

Society has an obligation to promote the security of the people, by affording some measure of protection against involuntary unemployment and dependency in old age. The New Deal policies, while purporting to provide social security, have, in fact, endangered it.

We propose a system of old age security, based upon the following principles:

1. We approve a pay-as-you-go policy, which requires of each generation the support of the aged and the determination of what is just and adequate.

2. Every American citizen over sixty-five should receive the supplementary payment necessary to provide a minimum income sufficient to protect him or her from want.

3. Each state and territory, upon complying with simple and general minimum standards, should receive from the federal government a

graduated contribution in proportion to its own, up to a fixed maximum.

4. To make this program consistent with sound fiscal policy the Federal revenues for this purpose must be provided from the proceeds of a direct tax widely distributed. All will be benefited and all should contribute.

We propose to encourage adoption by the states and territories of honest and practical measures for meeting the problems of unemployment insurance.

The unemployment insurance and old age annuity sections of the present Social Security Act are unworkable and deny benefits to about two-thirds of our adult population, including professional men and women and all those engaged in agriculture and domestic service, and the self employed while imposing heavy tax burdens upon all. The so-called reserve fund estimated at forty-seven billion dollars for old age insurance is no reserve at all, because the fund will contain nothing but the Government's promise to pay, while the taxes collected in the guise of premiums will be wasted by the Government in reckless and extravagant political schemes.

LABOR

The welfare of labor rests upon increased production and the prevention of exploitation. We pledge ourselves to:

Protect the right of labor to organize and to bargain collectively through representatives of its own choosing without interference from any source.

Prevent governmental job holders from exercising autocratic powers over labor.

Support the adoption of state laws and interstate compacts to abolish sweatshops and child labor, and to protect women and children with respect to maximum hours, minimum wages and working conditions. We believe that this can be done within the Constitution as it now stands.

AGRICULTURE

The farm problem is an economic and social, not a partisan problem, and we propose to treat it accordingly. Following the wreck of the restrictive and coercive A.A.A., the New Deal Administration has taken to itself the principles of the Republican Policy of soil conservation and land retirement. This action opens the way for a non-political and permanent solution. Such a solution cannot be had under a New Deal Administration which misuses the program to serve partisan ends, to promote scarcity and to limit by coercive methods the farmer's control over his own farm.

Our paramount object is to protect and foster the family type of farm, traditional in American life, and to promote policies which will bring about an adjustment of agriculture to meet the needs of domestic and foreign markets. As an emergency measure, during the agricultural depression, federal benefits payments or grants-in-aid when administered within the means of the Federal government are consistent with a balanced budget.

We propose:

1. To facilitate economical production and increased consumption on a basis of abundance instead of scarcity.

2. A national land-use program, including the acquisition of abandoned and non-productive farm lands by voluntary sale or lease, subject to approval of the legislative and executive branches of the States concerned, and the devotion of such land to appropriate public use, such as watershed protection and flood prevention, reforestation, recreation, and conservation of wild life.

3. That an agricultural policy be pursued for the protection and restoration of the land resources, designed to bring about such a balance between soil-building and soil-depleting crops as will permanently insure productivity, with reasonable benefits to cooperating farmers on family-type farms, but so regulated as to eliminate the New Deal's destructive policy towards the dairy and live-stock industries.

4. To extend experimental aid to farmers developing new crops suited to our soil and climate.

5. To promote the industrial use of farm products by applied science.

6. To protect the American farmer against the importation of all live stock, dairy, and agricultural products, substitutes thereof, and derivatives therefrom, which will depress American farm prices.

7. To provide effective quarantine against imported live-stock, dairy and other farm products from countries which do not impose health and sanitary regulations fully equal to those required of our own producers.

8. To provide for ample farm credit at rates as low as those enjoyed by other industries, including commodity and live-stock loans, and preference in land loans to the farmer acquiring or refinancing a farm as a home.

9. To provide for decentralized, non-partisan control of the Farm Credit Administration and the election by National Farm Loan Associations of at least one-half of each Board of Directors of the Federal Land Banks, and thereby remove these institutions from politics.

10. To provide in the case of agricultural products of which there are exportable surpluses, the payment of reasonable benefits upon the domestically consumed portion of such crops in order to make the tariff effective. These payments are to be limited to the production level of the family type farm.

11. To encourage and further develop co-operative marketing.

12. To furnish Government assistance in disposing of surpluses in foreign trade by bargaining for foreign markets selectively by countries both as to exports and imports. We strenuously oppose so-called reciprocal treaties which trade off the American farmer.

13. To give every reasonable assistance to producers in areas suffering from temporary disaster, so that they may regain and maintain a self-supporting status.

Tariff

Nearly sixty percent of all imports into the United States are now free of duty. The other forty percent of imports compete directly with the product of our industry. We would keep on the free list all products not grown or produced in the United States in commercial quantities. As to all commodities that commercially compete with our farms, our forests, our mines, our fisheries, our oil wells, our labor and our industries, sufficient protection should be maintained at all times to defend the American farmer and the American wage earner from the destructive competition emanating from the subsidies of foreign governments and the imports from low-wage and depreciated-currency countries.

We will repeal the present Reciprocal Trade Agreement Law. It is futile and dangerous. Its effect on agriculture and industry has been de-structive. Its continuation would work to the detriment of the wage earner and the farmer.

We will restore the principle of the flexible tariff in order to meet changing economic conditions here and abroad and broaden by careful definition the powers of the Tariff Commission in order to extend this policy along non-partisan lines.

We will adjust tariffs with a view to promoting international trade, the stabilization of currencies, and the attainment of a proper balance between agriculture and industry.

We condemn the secret negotiations of reciprocal trade treaties without public hearing or legislative approval.

Monopolies

A private monopoly is indefensible and intolerable. It menaces and, if continued, will utterly destroy constitutional government and the liberty of the citizen.

We favor the vigorous enforcement of the criminal laws, as well as the civil laws, against monopolies and trusts and their officials, and we demand the enactment of such additional legislation as is necessary to make it impossible for private monopoly to exist in the United States.

We will employ the full powers of the government to the end that monopoly shall be eliminated and that free enterprise shall be fully restored and maintained.

Regulation of Business

We recognize the existence of a field within which governmental regulation is desirable and salutary. The authority to regulate should be vested in an independent tribunal acting under clear and specific laws establishing definite standards. Their determinations on law and facts should be subject to review by the Courts. We favor Federal regulation, within the Constitution, of the marketing of securities to protect investors. We favor also Federal regulation of the interstate activities of public utilities.

Civil Service

Under the New Deal, official authority has been given to inexperienced and incompetent persons. The Civil Service has been sacrificed to create a national political machine. As a result the Federal

Government has never presented such a picture of confusion and inefficiency.

We pledge ourselves to the merit system, virtually destroyed by New Deal spoilsmen. It should be restored, improved and extended.

We will provide such conditions as offer an attractive permanent career in government service to young men and women of ability, irrespective of party affiliations.

Government Finance

The New Deal Administration has been characterized by shameful waste, and general financial irresponsibility. It has piled deficit upon deficit. It threatens national bankruptcy and the destruction through inflation of insurance policies and savings bank deposits.

We pledge ourselves to:

Stop the folly of uncontrolled spending.

Balance the budget—not by increasing taxes but by cutting expenditures, drastically and immediately.

Revise the federal tax system and coordinate it with state and local tax systems.

Use the taxing power for raising revenue and not for punitive or political purposes.

Money and Banking

We advocate a sound currency to be preserved at all hazards.

The first requisite to a sound and stable currency is a balanced budget.

We oppose further devaluation of the dollar.

We will restore to the Congress the authority lodged with it by the Constitution to coin money and regulate the value thereof by repealing all the laws delegating this authority to the Executive.

We will cooperate with other countries toward stabilization of currencies as soon as we can do so with due regard for our National interests and as soon as other nations have sufficient stability to justify such action.

Foreign Affairs

We pledge ourselves to promote and maintain peace by all honorable means not leading to foreign alliances or political commitments.

Obedient to the traditional foreign policy of America and to the repeatedly expressed will of the American people, we pledge that America

shall not become a member of the League of Nations nor of the World Court nor shall America take on any entangling alliances in foreign affairs.

We shall promote, as the best means of securing and maintaining peace by the pacific settlement of disputes, the great cause of international arbitration through the establishment of free, independent tribunals, which shall determine such disputes in accordance with law, equity and justice.

National Defense

We favor an army and navy, including air forces, adequate for our National Defense.

We will cooperate with other nations in the limitation of armaments and control of traffic in arms.

Bill of Rights

We pledge ourselves to preserve, protect and defend, against all intimidation and threat, freedom of religion, speech, press and radio; and the right of assembly and petition and immunity from unreasonable searches and seizures.

We offer the abiding security of a government of laws as against the autocratic perils of a government of men.

Furthermore

1. We favor the construction by the Federal Government of head-water storage basins to prevent floods, subject to the approval of the legislative and executive branches of the government of the States whose lands are concerned.

2. We favor equal opportunity for our colored citizens. We pledge our protection of their economic status and personal safety. We will do our best to further their employment in the gainfully occupied life of America, particularly in private industry, agriculture, emergency agencies and the Civil Service.

We condemn the present New Deal policies which would regiment and ultimately eliminate the colored citizen from the country's productive life, and make him solely a ward of the federal government.

3. To our Indian population we pledge every effort on the part of the national government to ameliorate living conditions for them.

4. We pledge continuation of the Republican

policy of adequate compensation and care for veterans disabled in the service of our country and for their widows, orphans and dependents.

5. We shall use every effort to collect the war debt due us from foreign countries, amounting to $12,000,000—one-third of our national debt. No effort has been made by the present administration even to reopen negotiations.

6. We are opposed to legislation which discriminates against women in Federal and State employment.

CONCLUSION

We assume the obligations and duties imposed upon Government by modern conditions. We affirm our unalterable conviction that, in the future as in the past, the fate of the nation will depend, not so much on the wisdom and power of government, as on the character and virtue, self-reliance, industry and thrift of the people and on their willingness to meet the responsibilities essential to the preservation of a free society.

Finally, as our party affirmed in its first Platform in 1856: "Believing that the spirit of our institutions as well as the Constitution of our country guarantees liberty of conscience and equality of rights among our citizens we oppose all legislation tending to impair them," and "we invite the affiliation and cooperation of the men of all parties, however differing from us in other respects, in support of the principles herein declared."

The acceptance of the nomination tendered by the Convention carries with it, as a matter of private honor and public faith, an undertaking by each candidate to be true to the principles and program herein set forth.

Socialist Party Platform Adopted in Cleveland, Ohio, on May 26, 1936

The Socialist Party of the United States pledges itself anew to the task of building a society under which the industries of the country shall be socially owned and democratically managed for the common good; a society under which security, plenty, peace, and freedom shall be the heritage of all.

THE OLD DEAL FAILS

Eight years ago the people of this country voted to continue the capitalist Old Deal. The purpose of this deal was to preserve the rights of the few who own most of the Nation's wealth. Under the Old Deal the economic machine was plunged into the worst depression in our history.

THE NEW DEAL FAILS

Four years ago the voters of the United States threw their support to the New Deal. They elected to office Franklin D. Roosevelt and the Democratic Party. The New Deal, like the Old Deal, has utterly failed. Under it big business was given almost unheard-of powers. Untold wealth was destroyed. Prices rose. Profits advanced. Wages lagged. Twelve million men and women are still jobless, and hunger and destitution exist throughout the land.

Under the New Deal attacks have been made on our civil liberties more vicious than at any period since the days immediately following the World War. Gag and loyalty bills have been rushed through our legislatures. Labor organizers have been seized, kidnapped, maltreated, killed.

The militia has been used to crush attempts of labor to organize. Lynching, race discrimination, and the development of Fascist trends have continued unabated. Against these infringements of human rights the Democratic administration has kept an ominous silence.

Under the New Deal we are now spending on our Army and Navy three times as much as before the World War.

CAPITALISM MEANS INSECURITY

Under the capitalist Old Deal and the capitalist New Deal America has drifted increasingly toward insecurity, suppression, and war.

Insecurity is but the logical result of the workings of capitalism. For under capitalism, new and old, the many work for the owners of the machines and land. The owners will not employ the workers unless they expect to extract a profit. Labor is forced to divide up its earning with the owning group.

With their scanty wages, the workers are able to buy only a part of the goods which they create. Goods pile up. Factories close. Workers are discharged. The country finds itself face to face with another depression.

In the past after a period of hard times we could depend upon the settlement of the West, the development of new foreign markets, and the rapid expansion of our population to revive industry. These forces can no longer be depended upon, as formerly, to keep the system going while our gross and unjust inequality of wealth, our monopoly prices, and our growing debt structure are sowing the seeds of more tragic depressions in the days ahead.

Capitalism Sows Seeds of Dictatorship

Our capitalist system is also sowing the seeds of dictatorship. As unemployment increases under capitalism the masses, to save themselves from starvation, are compelled to make even greater demands on the Government for relief and for public jobs. These demands are resisted by the propertied classes, fearful of higher taxes. Restlessness grows.

Demand for greater appropriations increase. The struggle between the House of Have and the House of Want becomes ever more intense. Big business seeks to deny the masses their constitutional rights. Fascist trends develop, trends that only a powerful and militant labor movement on the economic and political fields can successfully stay.

Capitalism Brings War

Militarism, likewise, under a declining capitalism, becomes an ever greater menace. As unrest increases, the masters of industry seek to use the military forces as the bulwark of reaction at home. They support higher military budgets. They look toward imperialist adventures abroad as a means of diverting attention from the unrest at home, and of gaining new markets, new investment areas, new sources of raw material.

A race begins that can have but one ending— an international war. The Japanese seizure of Manchuria and Italy's invasion of Ethiopia are but examples of the forces at work under capitalism. These adventures may well be the forerunners of another world conflict.

Socialism Provides Only Solution

In socialism and in socialism alone will we find the solution of our problem. Under socialism the socially necessary industries would be socially owned and democratically administered by workers, consumers, and technicians. The farmer working his own farm would be secure in its possession. The workers would no longer be forced to pay tribute to private owners. They would be able to buy back the goods they created.

Socialism and the Good Life

Industry, finding a market for these goods, would run to capacity without periodic breakdowns. Unemployment and the wastes of unplanned industry would cease. Our national income would double or treble. Every useful worker would be assured of high living standards, short hours, freedom of thought and action, and a chance to live the good life. The young would be guaranteed an opportunity for a well-rounded education. The old, the sick, the invalided would be assured the necessaries of life. Industrial autocracy and war would pass. An economy of scarcity would give way to an economy of abundance.

Such a society cannot be obtained without a mighty struggle. That struggle must be made both by workers and farmers, organized on the economic and political fields and dedicated to the creation of a cooperative commonwealth.

In their fight for power and socialism the workers and farmer must gain new strength and unity by their daily struggle against poverty and exploitation. To improve the conditions of life and labor and thereby to weld together the strength and solidarity of the masses, the Socialist Party pledges itself to fight for a number of immediate proposals in legislative halls and side by side with labor in field and factory and office.

1. Constitutional changes

We propose the adaptation of the Constitution to the needs of the times through the farmers' and workers' rights amendment, ending the usurped power of the Supreme Court to declare social legislation unconstitutional and reaffirming the right of Congress to acquire and operate industries. We also propose to change the Constitution so as to make future amendments less difficult and pledge our continued support of the child-labor amendment.

2. Social ownership

We propose the social ownership and democratic control of mines, railroads, the power industry, and other key industries and the recognition of public industries of the right of collective bargaining.

3. Relief, insurance, jobs

We propose an immediate appropriation by Congress of $6,000,000,000 to continue Federal relief to the unemployed for the coming year; the continuance of W. P. A. projects at union wages; the inauguration of a public-housing program for the elimination of the Nation's slums and the building of modern homes for the workers at rents they can afford to pay; a Federal system of unemployment insurance and of old-age pensions for persons 60 years of age and over, with contributions for such social-insurance systems to be raised from taxes on incomes and inheritances, as provided in the Frazier-Lundeen bill; and adequate medical care of the sick and injured as a social duty, not as a private or public charity. Such services should be financed by taxation and should be democratically administered.

4. Youth

We propose the passage of the American Youth Act to meet the immediate educational and economic needs of young people; adequate Federal appropriations for public schools and free city colleges with a view to making possible a full education for all young people; and the abolition of the C. C. C., the National Youth Administration and other governmental agencies dealing with the youth problem which threaten the wage and the living standards of organized labor.

5. Taxation

We propose a drastic increase of income and inheritance taxes on the higher income levels and of excess-profits taxes and wide experimentation in land-value taxation.

6. Labor legislation

We propose the establishment of the 30-hour week; the abolition of injunctions in labor disputes; the prohibition of company unions, company spying, and private guards and gunmen; and the prohibition of the use of police, deputy sheriffs, and militia and Federal troops in labor disputes.

7. Agriculture

We propose the abolition of tenant and corporation farming and the substitution of the use-and-occupancy title for family-sized farms and the conversion of plantations and corporation farms into cooperative farms. We propose that the marketing, processing, and distribution of farm products be taken over by bona-fide cooperatives and other agencies to be created for this purpose. We propose that farm prices be stabilized at cost of production to the working farmer, such stabilization to be made by representatives of organized working farmers and consumers.

While these changes are taking place we urge:

a. That immediate relief be provided for debt-laden working farmers by advancing Government credit on such terms as do not threaten the farmer with the loss of his farm.

b. That social insurance be provided against crop failures.

8. Civil liberties

We urge the abolition of all laws that interfere with the right of free speech, free press, free assembly, and the peaceful activities of labor in its struggle for organization and power; the enforcement of constitutional guaranties of economic, political, legal, and social equality for the Negro and all other oppressed minorities; and the enactment and enforcement of a Federal antilynching law.

9. Militarism and war

Not a penny, not a man to the military arms of the Government. We reaffirm our opposition to any war engaged in by the American Government. We propose the elimination of military training from our schools; the abandonment of imperialistic adventures of a military or economic nature abroad; the maintenance of friendly relations with Soviet Russia; and the strengthening of neutrality laws, to the end that we may ward off immediate wars while fighting for the attainment of a social order which will eliminate the chief causes of war.

10. Cooperation

We recognize the importance of the consumers' cooperative movement, though realizing that it alone cannot be depended upon to achieve a Socialist cooperative commonwealth. We urge the Socialist and the organized-labor movement to give their support to consumers' cooperatives to the end that it may become a valuable auxiliary to labor on the economic and political fields, and that it may help lay the foundation for a new economic order. We urge the encouragement by the Federal Government by every legitimate means of genuine consumers' cooperation.

The Socialist Party calls upon the workers, farmers, and all advocates of social justice to join with it in its struggle to widen the channels through which may be made peaceful, orderly, and democratic progress; to resist all trends toward insecurity, fascism, and war; to strengthen labor in its battles for better conditions, and for increasing power; to refuse to support the parties of capitalism, or any of their candidates, and to unite with it in its historic struggle toward a cooperative world.

Platform of the Socialist Labor Party

The capitalist system has outlived its usefulness. If progress is to be the order of society in the future as in the past, this outworn system MUST give way to a new social order. Social development points in but one direction—to an Industrial Union Government, an administration of things in place of a political rule over men.

The avowed purpose of governments is to insure life, liberty, and the pursuit of happiness to the useful members of society. Whenever a given social system, and its corresponding government, fails in or becomes destructive of these ends, it has outlived its usefulness, rendering it imperative for the exploited and oppressed class to organize its forces to put an end to the outworn economic and political system. This historic duty and necessity now confront the working class of America.

Social systems and their corresponding forms of government come into being as results of social and economic forces. The history of mankind has been the history of class struggles, with Progress ever as the aim. Ancient autocracies fell before ancient republics, the slave labor systems gave way to feudalism, feudalism broke down before the onslaught of capitalism. Capitalism, with its concomitant—wage slavery—is the world system which has been the vanguard of progress through the eighteenth and nineteenth centuries. In the United States of America capitalism has reached the highest point of development; here also may be traced the most rapid decay.

When a ruling class can no longer live and exploit as previously, and the exploited class can no longer be fed and cared for while rendering useful social service, *the hour of Social Revolution has struck.*

At this crucial period, accordingly, the Socialist Labor Party, in National Convention assembled, April 27, 1936, reaffirms its former platform pronouncements and, in accord with international Socialist principles, declares:

For close to a decade now, millions of the working class have had to be fed by the exploiting masters, instead of, as heretofore, feeding and keeping the masters in luxury. The richest country in the world, with the highest degree of productivity in the world, has been turned into a gigantic poorhouse, with vast numbers of its useful and able workers turned into mendicants, suppliants for a handout to keep body and soul together. History's pages record no greater disgrace than this.

A decaying system creates nothing so surely as its own gravediggers. The germs of destruction are active within American capitalism. Competition is the very life of capitalism; markets constitute the indispensable condition for its continued existence.

The early termination of capitalism was clearly indicated when the fact was revealed that a few giant corporations virtually control the entire production and distribution machinery of the nation. "Rugged individualism" has gone by the board. There is no possibility for the "average man" to become a capitalist. The small farmer, the small manufacturer, and the business man with small capital who still hangs on, are perpetually on the verge of bankruptcy. In most cases the farmer is but a tenant farmer or a "sharecropper" working for some banking house; the small business man is but a repair man or an agent of some large corporation.

The markets, foreign and domestic, are becoming extinct. A social system will flourish only while there is room within it for expansion. The possibilities for expansion in the United States of America seemed unlimited during its first 150 years. Ships, canals, railroads, bridges, roads, farms, machinery of all sorts were the crying need of expanding and progressing capitalism. This called for millions of workers, skilled and unskilled, in mines, mills, factories, on railroads, on the land, in shops, stores, offices and the technical trades. This, in turn, opened a tremendous market for other commodities — houses, furniture, clothing, food, and the so-called public service industries. "Prosperity" ruled; capitalism was in its full flower.

With the beginning of the twentieth century reaction had already set in. The frontier had gone; internal improvements were approaching a limit and commenced to slacken; American capitalism for a decade had been on a sharp look-out for foreign markets. The era of imperialism was at hand.

In the world market America encountered Great Britain, a formidable rival, the erstwhile "workshop of the world." Germany, France, Japan were stepping up, with Italy and Russia in the offing. The World War brought the rivals together with a clash. World expansion turned into a battle of "survival of the fittest," with every one struggling with the view of destruction of all rivals. The *progress* of capitalism had stopped; decay and degeneration had definitely set in.

There was one avenue, however, where progress under capitalism DID NOT STOP, for that avenue and that alone leads to the future, viz., the invention and perfection of machinery. The World War gave this a tremendous impetus which has not relaxed since. As a result, production is keyed up tremendously. The increased productive capacity of the system demands more markets, and when no markets are forthcoming, the abundance of products results in social degeneration and decay.

To bolster up market prices by creating artificial scarcity, millions of dollars' worth of products have been destroyed—plowed under, or allowed to rot, or burnt or dumped in the ocean—and this was done while millions of workers were poorly housed, underfed and insufficiently clothed. Decay and degeneration of a social system cannot go further than that.

Ever more and better machinery is the demand of capitalism. As the machines go into a factory, the workers go out. Millions of those who are unemployed today will never again under capitalism have regular, useful employment.

The Socialist Revolutionary hour in America is at hand. For forty-five years the Socialist Labor Party has been moving upward to this historic opportunity. The working class of America cannot afford to, must not, at the peril of its own existence, and that of future generations, allow to slip by this moment of opportunity to free the world from wage slavery.

Where a social revolution is pending and, for whatever reason, is not accomplished, reaction is the alternative. Every reform granted by capitalism is a concealed measure of reaction, exemplified by the NRA, AAA, TVA, CCC, WPA, etc.

He who says reform says preservation, and he who says that reforms under capitalism are possible and worth while thereby declares that a continuation of capitalism is possible and worth while. But capitalism has grown into an all-destroying and all-devouring monster that must itself be destroyed if humanity is to live. Fascism, Nazism, Absolutism in government — in short, Industrial Feudalism—are but means in the attempts to preserve capitalism.

American capitalism, along with capitalism in the rest of the world today, is trembling in the balance between decay or progress, reaction or revolution. THIS IS THE HISTORIC HOUR OF THE AMERICAN WORKING CLASS.

The class struggle, which rages today, is destined to be the last. There is no exploited or enslaved class below that of the exploited working class. When the workers take possession of the government and the social means of production, they are bound to do so in the name of society as a whole. That means the abolition of all classes, the abolition of private property and the inauguration of a Socialist Industrial Republic, where the means of production will be the collective property of society, operated by all able workers, for the benefit of all. Social or collective ownership—administered by an Industrial Union Government of, by and for the workers—of the already socially operated means of production will be the fulfillment of the promise implicit in social evolution throughout the ages!

At this crucial moment in history, the Socialist Labor Party of America, earnestly and deliberately, calls upon the working class of America to rally at the polls under the banner of the Socialist Labor Party, the only Party with a program that meets the needs of the hour, i.e., a progressive and revolutionary program.

The Socialist Labor Party also calls upon all other intelligent citizens to place themselves squarely upon the ground of working class interests, and join in this mighty and noble work of human emancipation, so that we may put summary end to the existing barbarous class conflict and insane contradictions between unlimited wealth and wealth production, and the poverty and wretchedness suffered by those whose labor created all this wealth.

We, therefore, call upon the workers of America to organize into Socialist Revolutionary Industrial Unions in shop, mine, mill and factory, and on the land, to provide a lever to place the land and the means of production and distribution in the hands of the useful producers as a body organized into a national Industrial Union Administration to take the place of the present outworn political or territorial government.

So shall come into being the Socialist Industrial Commonwealth of Emancipated Labor—a commonwealth in which every worker shall have the free exercise and full benefit of his faculties, multiplied by all the factors of modern civilization.

Union Party Platform of 1936

1. America shall be self-contained and self-sustained—no foreign entanglements, be they political, economic, financial or military.

2. Congress and Congress alone shall coin and issue the currency and regulate the value of all money and credit in the United States through a central bank of issue.

3. Immediately following the establishment of the central bank of issue Congress shall provide for the retirement of all tax-exempt, interest-bearing bonds and certificates of indebtedness of the Federal Government and shall refinance all the present agricultural mortgage indebtedness for the farmer and all the home mortgage indebtedness for the farmer and all the home mortgage indebtedness for the city owner by the use of its money and credit which it now gives to the private bankers.

4. Congress shall legislate that there will be an assurance of a living annual wage for all laborers capable of working and willing to work.

5. Congress shall legislate that there will be an assurance of production at a profit for the farmer.

6. Congress shall legislate that there will be assurance of reasonable and decent security for the aged, who, through no fault of their own, have been victimized and exploited by an unjust economic system which has so concentrated wealth in the hands of a few that it has impoverished great masses of our people.

7. Congress shall legislate that American agricultural, industrial, and commercial markets will be protected from manipulation of foreign moneys and from all raw material and processed goods produced abroad at less than a living wage.

8. Congress shall establish an adequate and perfect defense for our country from foreign aggression either by air, by land, or by sea, but with the understanding that our naval, air, and military forces must not be used under any consideration in foreign fields or in foreign waters either alone or in conjunction with any foreign power. If there must be conscription, there shall be a conscription of wealth as well as a conscription of men.

9. Congress shall so legislate that all Federal offices and positions of every nature shall be distributed through civil-service qualifications and not through a system of party spoils and corrupt patronage.

10. Congress shall restore representative government to the people of the United States to preserve the sovereignty of the individual States of the United States by the ruthless eradication of bureaucracies.

11. Congress shall organize and institute Federal works for the conservation of public lands, waters, and forests, thereby creating billions of dollars of wealth, millions of jobs at the prevailing wage, and thousands of homes.

12. Congress shall protect small industry and private enterprise by controlling and decentralizing the economic domination of monopolies to the end that these small industries and enterprises may not only survive and prosper but that they may be multiplied.

13. Congress shall protect private property from confiscation through unnecessary taxation with the understanding that the human rights of the masses take precedence over the financial rights of the classes.

14. Congress shall set a limitation upon the net income of any individual in any one year and a limitation of the amount that such an individual may receive as a gift or as an inheritance, which limitation shall be executed through taxation.

15. Congress shall reestablish conditions so that the youths of the Nation, as they emerge from schools and colleges, will have the opportunity to earn a decent living while in the process of perfecting and establishing themselves in a trade or profession.

CAMPAIGN OF 1940

In 1940, after World War II had begun in Europe, leaders of the major parties in the United States took some distinctive actions at their conventions. The Democrats, in Chicago, nominated President Roosevelt for a third term on the very first ballot and, at the president's insistence, selected a new vice-presidential candidate, Henry A. Wallace, the secretary of agriculture from Iowa. Earlier, in Philadelphia, the Republicans had named a utility president who had never before run for public office, Wendell Lewis Willkie of New York, as their presidential candidate. Until 1938, Willkie had been a registered Democrat, and he had not competed in a single presidential primary election. He was chosen on the fifth ballot over ten other aspirants. Senator Charles McNary of Oregon was nominated for the vice-presidency.

Norman Thomas, with Maynard C. Krueger of Illinois as his running mate, ran for president on the Socialist Party ticket for the fourth time. Earl Browder and James W. Ford again were Communist or Workers Party candidates. Roger W. Babson of Massachusetts and Edgar V. Moorman of Illinois were candidates on the Prohibition Party ballot, and John W. Aiken of Massachusetts, running with Aaron M. Orange of New York, again represented the Socialist Labor Party.

In the November election, the Democrats polled 27,263,448 popular votes to 22,336,260 votes for the Republicans—the largest number of votes the G.O.P. had attracted up to that time. The Socialists garnered 116,827 votes; the Prohibitionists, 58,685; the Communists, 48,548; and the Socialist Laborites, 14,883. In the electoral college, Roosevelt received 449 votes, and Willkie carried ten states with 82 electoral votes.

Communist Platform of 1940

The life, liberty and the pursuit of happiness of the American people are now endangered as never before since our revolutionary forefathers one hundred and sixty-four years ago proclaimed these rights to be inalienable for all mankind.

For the flower of American youth, the right to life itself is challenged by those who claim the privilege to conscript them and to throw them into reactionary wars for the benfit of the propertied classes.

For the American people as a whole, their liberty is challenged by projects of conscription of even the civilian population, of tens of millions of workers of factories and farms—ostensibly for the security of the country, but really for the purpose of setting aside the sacred guarantees of our Bill of Rights and placing the civilian population under military law, to free the hands of ruling financiers for military adventures and conquest abroad.

For our country, as for the peoples of all the world, the pursuit of happiness can be realized only with work, with security against unemployment, against poverty in old age, with guaranteed education for the youth—and with a genuine policy of peace. But with 11,000,000 Americans unemployed, the Democratic Party Administration is sacrificing all social legislation, unemployment relief, unemployment and old-age insurance, and educational guarantees for the youth, in order to pour all resources of the nation as well as the blood of our people into the scramble of monopoly capital for domination of the world.

WALL STREET WANTS WAR

The predatory war unleashed by the imperialist ruling classes of Berlin, London, Paris, Rome and Tokyo is a worldwide struggle for the division of the world among imperialist bandits—a struggle for the right of capitalist imperialist exploitation of the world by sacrificing the freedom of all peoples and the national independence of all nations.

Therefore the richest and most predatory of international bankers and trust heads of the whole world—those of Wall Street—are determined to enter into this worldwide, military contest in order to claim for themselves a share in proportion to their gigantic wealth. While their war profits pile high they deliberately seek to prolong the war and feverishly prepare to enter it. They have already transformed our country into an arsenal for one side of the predatory European conflict, and into a chief source of war materials for the Japanese adventures in Asia — thus making the United States, while still a non-belligerent, nevertheless a participant in the worldwide military conflict.

The warmongers of Wall Street are feverishly

preparing to establish through military might the exclusive role of American finance capital over the two American continents at the sacrifice of the independence of twenty republics of Latin America. They are striving to strengthen their imperialist positions in China and aim toward control of the Dutch East Indies (Indonesia) in struggle for mastery of the Pacific.

Aspiring for world domination, the American finance capitalists strive to drag the American people into the European war on the side of Great Britain. They work for a continuation and extension of that war and share guilt for the fate of those countries already conquered in Europe, Asia and Africa. But the same American imperialists have not closed the door to possible temporary agreements with the German and Japanese conquerors for establishment of the "new orders" in Europe and Asia, if only the terms be advantageous to the bankers of Wall Street.

Just as the American imperialists applauded and supported the betrayal of the democracy of Europe in the Pact of Munich, so are they ready now, on the promise of a gain to themselves, to betray the people of the United States, the peoples of the twenty Latin American republics, and those of Asia and of all of Europe and Africa to new imperialist agreements—if only they can secure their monopolist domination through the suppression of American democracy under blanket conscription and M-Day laws.

The Democratic and Republican parties—twin parties of the financiers of Wall Street—are seeking in this election to goad the people into a war hysteria, into panic and confusion, and to induce the people to agree to a surrender of constitutional democracy to a virtual military dictatorship in time of peace. All war plans are dressed in the disguise of peace plans. All plans for dangerous military adventures are given the gentle name of "national security." All projects for military aggression are entitled "national defense plans." All imperialist ventures for subjecting the Latin American republics are entitled "protecting the Western Hemisphere." Every prospective imperialist venture and "Munich" arrangement designed to throw the American people into war and to sacrifice the independence of Latin American peoples are brought forward under slogans of "peace" and "democracy" as was the treaty of Munich.

THE PEOPLE WANT PEACE

All domestic policies defended or proposed in this election by the Democratic and Republican parties are domestic policies subordinated to and completely dominated by the common purpose of American finance capital, the economic royalists, to plunge this country into a worldwide military struggle for conquest. This fundamental and decisive agreement between the Sixty Families of Wall Street that control both the Democratic and Republican parties, on a foreign policy of aggressive and militaristic imperialism, has brought the Democratic and the Republican parties to strangely harmonious positions on domestic policies. Both have common class interests and objectives. The differences between the two parties arise from specific secondary rivalries and conflicts among great financial interests, as to division of the spoils, as well as from the traditional rivalry between the Ins and the Outs, and from partisan bureaucratic interests incidental to the two-party system of American capitalism.

The bogus Socialist Party and other Social-Democratic groups and leaders, like their counterparts in Europe, Blum, Citrine and Tanner, play the role of treacherous agents of the warmongers in labor's ranks. They beat the drums for war and strive to paralyze labor toward this goal, they lead the reactionary pack for a "holy crusade" against the land of socialism and peace, the Soviet Union. They perform a special task for reaction in its assault upon the democratic rights of our people.

The top leadership of the A. F. of L., the Hillman wing of the C. I. O. leadership and the leadership of the Railroad Brotherhoods have committed themselves to the "defense" program of the Roosevelt Administration and are attempting to subordinate the labor movement to Wall Street's war program.

All these parties are in opposition to the will of the majority of the American people. The overwhelming majority of our people are opposed to the entrance of our country into this predatory war. The overwhelming majority stand for the preservation and enlarging of social and progressive legislation, for unemployment insurance, old-age pensions, public works, farmer and youth aid, and for full civil liberties.

Only the Communist Party, among the political parties participating in the 1940 elections, fights on the side of and in harmony with the deepest desires of the majority of the people. The Communist Party alone of all political parties fights against the imperialist war, combats its prolongation and spread, and seeks to bring an end to the war.

Only the Communist Party opposes the imperialist policies of the economic royalists, their government and parties. The Communist Party is for a people's peace, and opposed to an imperialist peace based upon terror, annexations and oppression.

We want to keep our country out of the imperialist war. We want to ensure jobs and social security for all. We want to protect the Bill of Rights. We are opposed to imperialist ventures abroad, against M-Day plans and the militarization of our country.

The economic royalists once again have full domination over the Republican and Democratic parties.

In the name of "national unity" and "national defense" the Roosevelt Democrats have surrendered to the economic royalists. The ruling class is attempting to suppress the people's opposition to its war program through terror, attacks upon organized labor and with vicious alien and sedition laws.

The Roosevelt Democrats make every effort to retain support of the people on grounds of progressive labor and social legislation enacted in the past seven years, but the Roosevelt Administration has thrown overboard even the meager popular gains of the New Deal and has embraced the program of the Liberty League which was roundly rejected by the people in the 1936 election. This has been done on the ground that all national resources must be poured into war preparations, and in order to put through this unpopular war they find it necessary to fight the people's demands.

While playing for popular support with ambiguous phrases about differences, the Willkie-Hoover Republicans have joined hands with the reactionary Democratic Party leadership in championing the pro-war foreign policy and undemocratic domestic measures of the Roosevelt Administration. Republican advocacy of the interests of Wall Street may be more open and outspoken, but it is not more effective than that of the Roosevelt Democrats.

The gains which labor and the American people won by organization and struggle during the New Deal period are now under a concerted attack.

After eight years of New Deal "liberalism," just as in 1933 after twelve years of Republican "rugged individualism," the misery and poverty of the working people under capitalism is growing.

Eleven million Americans are denied the right to work. A huge armaments program for imperialist conquest and war has been substituted for the former meager work and relief program.

Millions of small farmers, sharecroppers and tenant farmers are impoverished, and are being driven from their land by banks and insurance companies, and by the Federal and state governments.

Big business strives to crush the labor and anti-war movements by F. B. I. and Dies Committee persecutions, by attacks upon the National Labor Relations Act, the Wages and Hours Law and through a renewed open-shop offensive.

The youth of America, deprived of a decent education and the right to work, face conscription and being turned into cannon fodder by the merchants of death.

The Negro people, most exploited of the toilers, suffering from lynching and Jim Crowism, robbed of their constitutional rights, are being prepared to fight another war for "democracy" in order to further enslave them.

Millions of innocent and industrious foreign-born immigrants, who have given their all to the development of America, are being harassed and persecuted with fingerprinting and registration as if common criminals.

Wall Street girds for war by striving to destroy the Bill of Rights, by attacking the civil rights of Communists and other anti-war fighters, by promoting red-baiting, labor disunity and religious prejudices, by smearing as "fifth columnists" and "foreign agents" all who love peace, liberty and democracy.

This is the plight of the common people under the rule of the Sixty Families. This is the type of "democracy" represented by the Democratic and Republican parties.

A PEOPLE'S PROGRAM

In this grave hour of crisis, the Communist Party calls upon the working class and toilers to close ranks, organize and unite around a common program of action to protect and advance the peace, liberties and welfare of our people, to defend the interests of our nation, the interests of the American people.

The Communist Party calls upon all opponents of imperialist war and capitalist reaction to establish unity of action, under labor's leadership, around a people's program to defend our country, for peace, jobs, security and civil liberties. Towards this end the Communist Party enters the election campaign with the following program of action:

KEEP AMERICA OUT OF THE IMPERIALIST WAR!

HALT THE WAR PREPARATIONS AND IMPERIALIST ADVENTURES OF WALL STREET AND THE GOVERNMENT!

AGAINST THE MILITARIZATION OF THE NATION!

FOR A PEOPLE'S PEACE!

1. Combat the imperialist policies and acts of the President, the State Department, Congress, the Democratic and Republican parties to spread the war and involve the United States in it. No aid to the imperialist war-makers in London, Berlin, Tokyo, Rome or to their satellites. Oppose all war loans and credits to the warring imperialist powers. Stop the sale and shipment of munitions and armaments to the imperialist belligerents.

2. Defeat Wall Street's imperialist policy of economic and political domination, and miltary adventures in Latin America, China, and the Dutch East Indies (Indonesia). Full solidarity with the anti-imperialist struggles of the peoples of Mexico, Cuba, and all other Latin American countries. For the immediate and complete national independence of the Philippines and Puerto Rico. Maximum support for the great Chinese people in their heroic struggle for national liberation. Halt the anti-Soviet policies and incitements of the government and Wall Street. For friendship and collaboration for peace between the two great peoples of the United States and the Soviet Union.

3. No armaments or American soldiers for imperialist wars or adventures. Democratize the armed forces. Protect the freedom and independence of the trade unions. Make the rich pay the costs of the war preparations and the economic crisis for which they are responsible. Fight against war profiteering.

4. Against a peace of "appeasement." Against an imperialist peace of violence and oppression. For solidarity with and support to the peoples in the warring nations in their struggle for a democratic people's peace.

PROTECT AND EXTEND CIVIL LIBERTIES!

FULL RIGHTS FOR THE NEGRO PEOPLE!

1. For the unrestricted freedom of speech, press, radio, assembly and worship, and the full right to organize, strike and picket. Defeat the anti-labor drive under the Sherman anti-trust law. Pass the La-Follette-Thomas Oppressive Labor Practices Bill without reactionary amendments. Stop the attacks upon labor by the F. B. I. and the Department of Justice.

2. Pass the Geyer Anti-Poll Tax Bill to give the vote to the Negro and white masses in the South. For full civil rights and the right to vote for all men in the armed services, migratory workers and seafaring men.

3. Guarantee the Negro people complete equality, equal rights to jobs, equal pay for equal work, the full right to organize, serve on juries and hold public office. Pass the Anti-Lynching Bill. Demand the death penalty for lynchers. Enforce the 13th, 14th and 15th Amendments to the United States Constitution.

4. End the dictatorial powers of the Dies and other Congressional anti-labor investigating committees. Repeal the vicious anti-alien and sedition laws that are a blot on the statute books of a free people. Put an end to anti-Semitism. Guarantee the traditional American right of asylum to all victims of imperialist war and oppression, especially to the refugees from Franco Spain.

5. Guarantee the civil rights and freedom of action of labor, including the Communists, and all other anti-war, anti-imperialist organizations. Against all reactionary measures requiring the registration, incorporation or Federal control of working class political organizations, trade unions and other popular organizations. For the freedom of all working class political prisoners now languishing in Federal and state prisons. Defend the Bill of Rights against the reactionaries and warmakers.

JOBS, SECURITY AND AN AMERICAN STANDARD OF LIVING FOR ALL TOILERS!

PROTECT THE FARMERS FROM WALL STREET!

PROTECT THE RIGHTS AND INTERESTS OF THE AMERICAN YOUTH!

CURB THE MONOPOLISTS!

1. For the organization of the unorganized. For higher wages and the thirty-hour week without reduction in pay. For equal rights for Negro workers, the foreign born, women and youth labor. Abolish the wage differential between North and South. Abolish child labor. Cancel all government orders to those employers who fail to comply with labor legislation.

2. For a Federal housing program providing for building a minimum of a million homes annually for the low-income groups. Expand W. P. A. to provide work for all unemployed with a minimum of 3,000,000 jobs to be provided immediately on socially beneficial projects, at union wage rates. Increase the present wage scale by 30 percent and make as minimum payment for any classification $70 monthly. Extend unemployment insurance to cover domestic, agricultural and all wage earners not now covered by the law. Increase minimum benefit payments to $10 weekly. Increase maximum payments from one-half to two-thirds of wages earned. Extend the period of unemployment compensation payments from the present maximum of thirteen weeks to twenty-six weeks.

3. Establish an *old-age pension* system providing $60 monthly for all over sixty. Enact an adequate Federal health program and a system of maternity insurance. Guarantee free education to all youth and children, Negro and white, by extending Federal and state appropriations.

4. Guarantee to all farmers their land, equipment, and livestock free from seizure. Free the working farmers and sharecroppers from debt, tax burdens and foreclosures. Provide a high homestead tax-exemption and heavier taxes on large farms. For a Homestead Act for Today to return all lands confiscated by the Federal, state, and local governments, by the banks and insurance companies to all small farmers, tenants and sharecroppers dispossessed from the land and who wish to engage in farming. Develop an adequate program of tenant rehabilitation, soil conservation and drought relief. Guarantee the cost of production to the family-sized farm. Provide Federal funds for direct farm relief so that no farm family shall lack the necessities of life. Establish a ten-year debt moratorium for the small-income farmers.

5. Extend the N. Y. A. and the C. C. C. under civilian control and on civilian projects at trade union standards. Adopt the American Youth Act.

6. Prosecute the trusts and monopolies for profiteering, monopoly practices, nullifying labor legislation, evading taxes and violating the laws of the land. Establish a heavy excess profits tax and a steeply graduated income tax on the higher brackets. Abolish tax-exempt securities. Confiscate all war profits. Repeal the provisions of the new tax laws hitting the low-income groups. Abolish all direct and indirect taxes on articles of mass consumption.

FOR A NATIONAL FARMER-LABOR PARTY

This is an anti-imperialist program of struggle for peace, real national defense, and social security. It can be realized by labor and the toiling people through organization and united struggle, by building and strengthening the trade unions and other progressive organizations of labor, and by promoting independent political action of labor and the common people, leading towards the building up of a united mass party—a national Farmer-Labor Party, an anti-imperialist third party of the people.

The struggle for such a united people's party for peace, security and civil liberties can be actively promoted in the November elections by voting for and supporting the Communist Party. It can be effectively developed by establishing unity of action by the workers in all unions and industries in defense of their immediate economic and political demands. It can be strengthened by supporting tested anti-war and labor candidates for Congress and state legislatures.

Capitalism has brought our people only tyranny, hunger, degradation and war. Capitalism has given us an ever-deepening crisis, with millions permanently unemployed. Capitalism is destroying the cultural achievements and constitutional guarantees of freedom provided in the Bill of Rights. Under capitalism the people face a hopeless future. Only when capitalism is abolished, when socialism is established, as today in the U. S. S. R., will there be no wars, no unemployment, no social retrogression. Under socialism there will be abundance and security for the toiling people. To make our country really free, united and prosperous—to make it possible for all the people to benefit from the tremendous resources of our country—demands a new social order in which the national economy will belong to the people—a socialist society. Only in a nation free from its monopoly and financial overlords and freed of bondage to the few who have seized its wealth and oppress its people can our people live and flourish.

The Communist Party fights for the immediate interests of the working class, as well as its socialist future. We pledge to continue our struggle for our socialist aim, the common goal of all progressive mankind, already triumphant over one-sixth of the earth.

VOTE COMMUNIST!

Workers! Toilers! The Democratic Party is the party of the Roosevelts and Dies, of the Garners and Woodrums, of the du Ponts and Cromwells, of the Boss Hagues and Kelleys, of Tammany and K. K. K. It is the party of "liberal" promises and reactionary deeds.

The Republican Party is the party of the Willkies and Hoovers, the Vandenbergs and Fords, of the Insulls, Weirs and Girdlers. It is the party of the Associated Farmers and the open shoppers.

The Morgans, Rockefellers and du Ponts are the Interlocking Directorate and Holding Company of both the Democratic and Republican parties. That is why *both* parties are war parties, M-Day parties, parties of imperialism, reaction and hunger.

This is why labor and the people cannot and must not vote for nor support the Democratic or the Republican parties, or their little brother, the Socialist Party.

This is why the working class and toilers should vote for and support the Communist Party.

A vote for the Communist Party is a vote against the imperialist war, against Wall Street's imperialist adventures and war preparations, for safeguarding the peace of America and defending the national interests of the American people.

A vote for the Communist Party is a vote for peace, freedom and socialism. Vote Communist! Vote for Browder and Ford!

Democratic Platform of 1940

PREAMBLE

The world is undergoing violent change. Humanity, uneasy in this machine age, is demanding a sense of security and dignity based on human values.

No democratic government which fails to recognize this trend—and take appropriate action—can survive.

That is why the Government of this nation has moved to keep ahead of this trend; has moved with speed incomprehensible to those who do not see this trend.

Outside the Americas, established institutions are being overthrown and democratic philosophies are being repudiated by those whose creed recognizes no power higher than military force, no values other than a false efficiency.

What the founding fathers realized upon this continent was a daring dream, that men could have not only physical security, not only efficiency, but something else in addition that men had never had before—the security of the heart that comes with freedom, the peace of mind that comes from a sense of justice.

To this generation of Americans it is given to defend this democratic faith as it is challenged by social maladjustment within and totalitarian greed without. The world revolution against which we prepare our defense is so threatening that not until it has burned itself out in the last corner of the earth will our democracy be able to relax its guard.

In this world crisis, the purpose of the Democratic Party is to defend against external attack and justify by internal progress the system of government and way of life from which the Democratic Party takes its name.

FULFILLING AMERICAN IDEAL

Toward the modern fulfillment of the American ideal, the Democratic Party, during the last seven years, has labored successfully:

1. *To strengthen democracy by defensive preparedness against aggression, whether by open attack or secret infiltration;*

2. *To strengthen democracy by increasing our economic efficiency; and*

3. *To strengthen democracy by improving the welfare of the people.*

These three objectives are one and inseparable. No nation can be strong by armaments alone. It must possess and use all the necessary resources for producing goods plentifully and distributing them effectively. It must add to these factors of material strength the unconquerable spirit and energy of a contented people, convinced that there are no boundaries to human progress and happiness in a land of liberty.

Our faith that these objectives can be attained is made unshakable by what has already been done by the present Administration—in stopping the waste and exploitation of our human and natural resources, in restoring to the average man and woman a stake in the preservation of our democracy, in enlarging our national armaments, and in achieving national unity.

We shall hold fast to these gains. We are proud of our record. Therefore the Party in convention assembled endorses wholeheartedly the brilliant and courageous leadership of President Franklin D. Roosevelt and his statesmanship and that of the Congress for the past seven trying years. And to our President and great leader we send our cordial greetings.

We Must Strengthen Democracy Against Aggression

The American people are determined that war, raging in Europe, Asia and Africa, shall not come to America.

We will not participate in foreign wars, and we will not send our army, naval or air forces to fight in foreign lands outside of the Americas, except in case of attack. We favor and shall rigorously enforce and defend the Monroe Doctrine.

The direction and aim of our foreign policy has been, and will continue to be, the security and defense of our own land and the maintenance of its peace.

For years our President has warned the nation that organized assaults against religion, democracy and international good faith threatened our own peace and security. Men blinded by partisanship brushed aside these warnings as war-mongering and officious intermeddling. The fall of twelve nations was necessary to bring their belated approval of legislative and executive action that the President had urged and undertaken with the full support of the people. It is a tribute to the President's foresight and action that our defense forces are today at the peak of their peacetime effectiveness.

Weakness and unpreparedness invite aggression. We must be so strong that no possible combination of powers would dare to attack us. We propose to provide America with an invincible air force, a navy strong enough to protect all our seacoasts and our national interests, and a fully-equipped and mechanized army. We shall continue to coordinate these implements of defense with the necessary expansion of industrial productive capacity and with the training of appropriate personnel. Outstanding leaders of industry and labor have already been enlisted by the Government to harness our mighty economic forces for national defense.

Experience of other nations gives warning that total defense is necessary to repel attack, and that partial defense is no defense.

We have seen the downfall of nations accomplished through internal dissension provoked from without. We denounce and will do all in our power to destroy the treasonable activities of disguised anti-democratic and un-American agencies which would sap our strength, paralyze our will to defend ourselves, and destroy our unity by inciting race against race, class against class, religion against religion and the people against their free institutions.

To make America strong, and to keep America free, every American must give of his talents and treasure in accordance with his ability and his country's needs. We must have democracy of sacrifice as well as democracy of opportunity.

To insure that our armaments shall be implements of peace rather than war, we shall continue our traditional policies of the good neighbor; observe and advocate international respect for the rights of others and for treaty obligations; cultivate foreign trade through desirable trade agreements; and foster economic collaboration with the Republics of the Western Hemisphere.

In self-defense and in good conscience, the world's greatest democracy cannot afford heartlessly or in a spirit of appeasement to ignore the peace-loving and liberty-loving peoples wantonly attacked by ruthless aggressors. We pledge to extend to these peoples all the material aid at our command, consistent with law and not inconsistent with the interests of our own national self-defense —all to the end that peace and international good faith may yet emerge triumphant.

We do not regard the need for preparedness a warrant for infringement upon our civil liberties, but on the contrary we shall continue to protect them, in the keen realization that the vivid contrast between the freedom we enjoy and the dark repression which prevails in the lands where liberty is dead, affords warning and example to our people to confirm their faith in democracy.

WE MUST STRENGTHEN DEMOCRACY BY INCREASING OUR ECONOMIC EFFICIENCY

The well-being of the land and those who work upon it is basic to the real defense and security of America.

The Republican Party gives its promises to the farmer and its allegiance to those who exploit him.

Since 1932 farm income has been doubled; *six million* farmers, representing more than 80 per cent of all farm families, have participated in an effective soil conservation program; the farm debt and the interest rate on farm debt have been reduced, and farm foreclosures have been drastically curtailed; rural highways and farm-to-market roads have been vastly improved and extended; the surpluses on the farms have been used to feed the needy; low cost electricity has been brought to five million farm people as a result of the rural electrification program; thousands of impoverished farm families have been rehabilitated; and steps have been taken to stop the alarming growth of farm tenancy, to increase land ownership, and to mitigate the hardships of migratory farm labor.

The Land and the Farmer

We pledge ourselves

To make parity as well as soil conservation payments until such time as the goal of parity income for agriculture is realized.

To extend and enlarge the tenant-purchase program until every deserving tenant farmer has a real opportunity to have a farm of his own.

To refinance existing farm debts at lower interest rates and on longer and more flexible terms.

To continue to provide for adjustment of production through democratic processes to the extent that excess surpluses are capable of control.

To continue the program of rehabilitation of farmers who need and merit aid.

To preserve and strengthen the ever-normal granary on behalf of the national defense, the consumer at home and abroad, and the American farmer.

To continue to make commodity loans to maintain the ever-normal granary and to prevent destructively low prices.

To expand the domestic consumption of our surpluses by the food and cotton stamp plan, the free school lunch, low-cost milk and other plans for bringing surplus farm commodities to needy consumers.

To continue our substantially increased appropriations for research and extension work through the land-grant colleges, and for research laboratories established to develop new outlets for farm products.

To conserve the soil and water resources for the benefit of farmers and the nation. In such conservation programs we shall, so far as practicable, bring about that development in forests and other permanent crops as will not unduly expand livestock and dairy production.

To safeguard the farmer's foreign markets and expand his domestic market for all domestic crops.

To enlarge the rural electrification [sic].

To encourage farmer-owned and controlled cooperatives.

To continue the broad program launched by this Administration for the coordinated development of our river basins through reclamation and irrigation, flood control, reforestation and soil conservation, stream purification, recreation, fish and game protection, low-cost power, and rural industry.

To encourage marketing agreements in aid of producers of dairy products, vegetables, fruits and specialty crops for the purpose of orderly marketing and the avoidance of unfair and wasteful practices.

To extend crop insurance from wheat to other crops as rapidly as experience justifies such extension.

To safeguard the family-sized farm in all our programs.

To finance these programs adequately in order that they may be effective.

In settling new lands reclaimed from desert by projects like Grand Coulee, we shall give priority to homeless families who have lost their farms. As these new lands are brought into use, we shall continue by Federal purchase to retire from the plow submarginal lands so that an increased percentage of our farmers may be able to live and work on good land.

These programs will continue to be in the hands of locally-elected farmer committees to the largest extent possible. In this truly democratic way, we will continue to bring economic security to the farmer and his family, while recognizing the dignity and freedom of American farm life.

Industry and the Worker

Under Democratic auspices, more has been done in the last seven years to foster the essential freedom, dignity and opportunity of the American worker than in any other administration in the nation's history. In consequence, labor is today taking its rightful place as a partner of management in the common cause of higher earnings, industrial efficiency, national unity and national defense.

A far-flung system of employment exchanges has brought together millions of idle workers and available jobs. The workers' right to organize and bargain collectively through representatives of their own choosing is being enforced. We have enlarged the Federal machinery for the mediation of labor disputes. We have enacted an effective wage and hour law. Child labor in factories has been outlawed. Prevailing wages to workers employed on Government contracts have been assured.

We pledge to continue to enforce fair labor standards; to maintain the principles of the National Labor Relations Act; to expand employment training and opportunity for our youth, older workers, and workers displaced by technological changes; to strengthen the orderly processes of collective bargaining and peaceful settlement of labor disputes; and to work always for a just distribution of our national income among those who labor.

We will continue our efforts to achieve equality of opportunity for men and women without impairing the social legislation which promotes true equality by safeguarding the health, safety and economic welfare of women workers. The right to work for compensation in both public and private employment is an inalienable privilege of

women as well as men, without distinction as to marital status.

The production of coal is one of our most important basic industries. Stability of production, employment, distribution and price are indispensable to the public welfare. We pledge continuation of the Federal Bituminous Coal Stabilization Act, and sympathetic consideration of the application of similar legislation to the anthracite coal industry, in order to provide additional protection for the owners, miners and consumers of hard coal.

We shall continue to emphasize the human element in industry and strive toward increasingly wholehearted cooperation between labor and industrial management.

Capital and the Business Man

To make democracy strong, our system of business enterprise and individual initiative must be free to gear its tremendous productive capacity to serve the greatest good of the greatest number.

We have defended and will continue to defend all legitimate business.

We have attacked and will continue to attack unbridled concentration of economic power and the exploitation of the consumer and the investor.

We have attacked the kind of banking which treated America as a colonial empire to exploit; the kind of securities business which regarded the Stock Exchange as a private gambling club for wagering other people's money; the kind of public utility holding companies which used consumers' and investors' money to suborn a free press, bludgeon legislatures and political conventions, and control elections against the interest of their customers and their security holders.

We have attacked the kind of business which levied tribute on all the rest of American business by the extortionate methods of monopoly.

We did not stop with attack—we followed through with the remedy. The American people found in themselves, through the democratic process, ability to meet the economic problems of the average American business where concentrated power had failed.

We found a broken and prostrate banking and financial system. We restored it to health by strengthening banks, insurance companies and other financial institutions. We have insured 62 million bank accounts, and protected millions of small investors in the security and commodity markets. We have thus revived confidence, safeguarded thrift, and opened the road to all honorable business.

We have made credit at low interest rates available to small-business men, thus unfastening the oppressive yoke of a money monopoly, and giving the ordinary citizen a chance to go into business and stay in business.

We recognize the importance of small business concerns and new enterprises in our national economy, and favor the enactment of constructive legislation to safeguard the welfare of small business. Independent small-scale enterprise, no less than big business, should be adequately represented on appropriate governmental boards and commissions, and its interests should be examined and fostered by a continuous research program.

We have provided an important outlet for private capital by stimulating home building and low-rent housing projects. More new homes were built throughout the nation last year than in any year since 1929.

We have fostered a well-balanced American merchant marine and the world's finest system of civil aeronautics, to promote our commerce and our national defense.

We have steered a steady course between a bankruptcy-producing deflation and a thrift-destroying inflation, so that today the dollar is the most stable and sought-after currency in the world —a factor of immeasurable benefit in our foreign and domestic commerce.

We shall continue to oppose barriers which impede trade among the several states. We pledge our best efforts in strengthening our home markets, and to this end we favor the adjustment of freight rates so that no section or state will have undue advantage over any other.

To encourage investment in productive enterprise, the tax-exempt privileges of future Federal, state and local bonds should be removed.

We have enforced the anti-trust laws more vigorously than at any time in our history, thus affording the maximum protection to the competitive system.

We favor strict supervision of all forms of the insurance business by the several states for the protection of policyholders and the public.

The full force of our policies, by raising the national income by thirty billion dollars from the low of 1932, by encouraging vast reemployment, and by elevating the level of consumer demand, has quickened the flow of buying and selling through every artery of industry and trade.

With mass purchasing power restored and many abuses eliminated, American business stands at the threshold of a great new era, richer in promise than any we have witnessed—an era of pioneering and progress beyond the present frontiers of economic activity—in transportation, in housing, in industrial expansion, and in the new utilization of the products of the farm and the factory.

We shall aid business in redeeming America's promise.

Electric Power

During the past seven years the Democratic Party has won the first major victories for the people of the nation in their generation-old contest with the power monopoly.

These victories have resulted in the recognition of certain self-evident principles and the realization of vast benefits by the people. These principles, long opposed by the Republican Party, are:

That the power of falling water is a gift from God, and consequently belongs not to a privileged few, but to all the people, who are entitled to enjoy its benefits;

That the people have the right through their government to develop their own power sites and bring low-cost electricity to their homes, farms and factories;

That public utility holding companies must not be permitted to serve as the means by which a few men can pyramid stocks upon stocks for the sole purpose of controlling vast power empires.

We condemn the Republican policies which permitted the victimizing of investors in the securities of private power corporations, and the exploitation of the people by unnecessarily high utility costs.

We condemn the opposition of utility power interests which delayed for years the development of national defense projects in the Tennessee Valley, and which obstructed river basin improvements and other public projects bringing low-cost electric power to the people. The successful power developments in the Tennessee and Columbia River basins show the wisdom of the Democratic Party in establishing government-owned and operated hydro-electric plants in the interests of power and light consumers.

Through these Democratic victories, whole regions have been revived and restored to prosperous habitation. Production costs have been reduced. Industries have been established which employ men and capital. Cheaper electricity has brought vast economic benefits to thousands of homes and communities.

These victories of the people must be safeguarded. They will be turned to defeat if the Republican Party should be returned to power. We pledge our Party militantly to oppose every effort to encroach upon the inherent right of our people to be provided with this primary essential of life at the lowest possible cost.

The nomination of a utility executive by the Republican Party as its presidential candidate raises squarely the issue, whether the nation's water power shall be used for all the people or for the selfish interests of a few. We accept that issue.

Developments of Western Resources

We take satisfaction in pointing out the incomparable development of the public land states under the wise and constructive legislation of this Administration. Mining has been revived, agriculture fostered, reclamation extended and natural resources developed as never before in a similar period. We pledge the continuance of such policies, based primarily on the expansion of opportunity for the people, as will encourage the full development, free from financial exploitation, of the great resources—mineral, agricultural, livestock, fishing and lumber—which the West affords.

Radio

Radio has become an integral part of the democratically accepted doctrine of freedom of speech, press, assembly and religion. We urge such legislative steps as may be required to afford the same protection from censorship that is now afforded the press under the Constitution of the United States.

WE MUST STRENGTHEN DEMOCRACY BY IMPROVING THE WELFARE OF THE PEOPLE

We place human resources first among the assets of a democratic society.

Unemployment

The Democratic Party wages war on unemployment, one of the gravest problems of our times, inherited at its worst from the last Republican administration. Since we assumed office, nine million additional persons have gained regular employment in normal private enterprise. All our policies—financial, industrial and agricultural—will continue to accelerate the rate of this progress.

By public action, where necessary to supplement private reemployment, we have rescued millions from idleness that breeds weakness, and given them a real stake in their country's well being. We shall continue to recognize the obligation of Government to provide work for deserving workers who cannot be absorbed by private industry.

We are opposed to vesting in the states and local authorities the control of Federally-financed work relief. We believe that this Republican proposal is a thinly disguised plan to put the unemployed back on the dole.

We will continue energetically to direct our efforts toward the employment in private industry of all those willing to work, as well as the fullest employment of money and machines. This we pledge as our primary objective. To further implement this objective, we favor calling, under the direction of the President, a national unemployment conference of leaders of government, industry, labor and farm groups.

There is work in our factories, mines, fields, forests and river basins, on our coasts, highways, railroads and inland waterways. There are houses to be built to shelter our people. Building a better America means work and a higher standard of living for every family, and a richer and more secure heritage for every American.

Social Security

The Democratic Party, which established social security for the nation, is dedicated to its extension. We pledge to make the Social Security Act increasingly effective, by covering millions of persons not now protected under its terms; by strengthening our unemployment insurance system and establishing more adequate and uniform benefits, through the Federal equalization fund principle; by progressively extending and increasing the benefits of the old-age and survivors insurance system, including protection of the permanently disabled; and by the early realization of a minimum pension for all who have reached the age of retirement and are not gainfully employed.

Health

Good health for all the people is a prime requisite of national preparedness in its broadest sense. We have advanced public health, industrial hygiene, and maternal and child care. We are coordinating the health functions of the Federal Government. We pledge to expand these efforts, and to provide more hospitals and health centers and better health protection wherever the need exists, in rural and urban areas, all through the cooperative efforts of the Federal, state and local governments, the medical, dental, nursing and other scientific professions, and the voluntary agencies.

Youth and Education

Today, when the youth of other lands is being sacrificed in war, this nation recognizes the full value of the sound youth program established by the Administration. The National Youth Administration and Civilian Conservation Corps have enabled our youth to complete their education, have maintained their health, trained them for useful citizenship, and aided them to secure employment.

Our public works have modernized and greatly expanded the nation's schools. We have increased Federal aid for vocational education and rehabilitation, and undertaken a comprehensive program of defense-industry training. We shall continue to bring to millions of children, youths and adults, the educational and economic opportunities otherwise beyond their reach.

Slum-Clearance and Low-Rent Housing

We have launched a soundly conceived plan of loans and contributions to rid America of overcrowded slum dwellings that breed disease and crime, and to replace them by low-cost housing projects within the means of low-income families. We will extend and accelerate this plan not only in the congested city districts, but also in the small towns and farm areas, and we will make it a powerful arm of national defense by supplying housing for the families of enlisted personnel and

for workers in areas where industry is expanding to meet defense needs.

Consumers

We are taking effective steps to insure that, in this period of stress, the cost of living shall not be increased by speculation and unjustified price rises.

Negroes

Our Negro citizens have participated actively in the economic and social advances launched by this Administration, including fair labor standards, social security benefits, health protection, work relief projects, decent housing, aid to education, and the rehabilitation of low-income farm families. We have aided more than half a million Negro youths in vocational training, education and employment. We shall continue to strive for complete legislative safeguards against discrimination in government service and benefits, and in the national defense forces. We pledge to uphold due process and the equal protection of the laws for every citizen, regardless of race, creed or color.

Veterans

We pledge to continue our policy of fair treatment of America's war veterans and their dependents, in just tribute to their sacrifices and their devotion to the cause of liberty.

Indians

We favor and pledge the enactment of legislation creating an Indian Claims Commission for the special purpose of entertaining and investigating claims presented by Indian groups, bands and tribes, in order that our Indian citizens may have their claims against the Government considered, adjusted, and finally settled at the earliest possible date.

Civil Service

We pledge the immediate extension of a genuine system of merit to all positions in the executive branch of the Federal Government except actual bona fide policy-making positions. The competitive method of selecting employes shall be improved until experience and qualification shall be the sole test in determining fitness for employment in the Federal service. Promotion and tenure in Federal service shall likewise depend upon fitness, experience and qualification. Arbitrary and unreasonable rules as to academic training shall be abolished, all to the end that a genuine system of efficiency and merit shall prevail throughout the entire Federal service.

Territories and District of Columbia

We favor a larger measure of self-government leading to statehood, for Alaska, Hawaii and Puerto Rico. We favor the appointment of residents to office, and equal treatment of the citizens of each of these three territories. We favor the prompt determination and payment of any just claims by Indian and Eskimo citizens of Alaska against the United States.

We also favor the extension of the right of suffrage to the people of the District of Columbia.

True First Line of Defense

We pledge to continue to stand guard on our true first line of defense—the security and welfare of the men, women and children of America.

Our Democratic Faith

Democracy is more than a political system for the government of a people. It is the expression of a people's faith in themselves as human beings. If this faith is permitted to die, human progress will die with it. We believe that a mechanized existence, lacking the spiritual quality of democracy, is intolerable to the free people of this country.

We therefore pledge ourselves to fight, as our fathers fought, for the right of every American to enjoy freedom of religion, speech, press, assembly, petition, and security in his home.

It is America's destiny, in these days of rampant despotism, to be the guardian of the world heritage of liberty and to hold aloft and aflame the torch of Western civilization.

The Democratic Party rededicates itself to this faith in democracy, to the defense of the American system of government, the only system under which men are masters of their own souls, the only system under which the American people, composed of many races and creeds, can live and work, play and worship in peace, security and freedom.

Firmly relying upon a continuation of the blessings of Divine Providence upon all our righteous endeavors to preserve forever the priceless heritage of American liberty and peace, we appeal to all the liberal-minded men and women of the nation to approve this platform and to go forward with us by wholeheartedly supporting the candidates who subscribe to the principles which it proclaims.

Prohibition Party Platform of 1940

We, the representatives of the National Prohibition Party, in convention assembled at Chicago, May 9, 1940, recognizing Almighty God as the source of all good government, make the following declaration of principles and purposes:

Moral Issues

We realize the permanent progress does not come merely by prohibiting certain things, but that prohibition of that which is evil must go hand in hand with the promotion of that which is good. Since all evils which are undermining character stand in the way of such promotion they should be prohibited. Among these evils we name specifically the liquor traffic, harmful narcotics, commercialized gambling, indecent publications, debasing moving pictures and the block booking thereof, deceptive radio broadcasting, political graft, and injustices of all kinds. We commend the work of those combating these and other evils.

Economic and Other Issues

We are vitally interested in, and pledge ourselves to enact measures for the purpose of purifying government, reducing debt and taxation, conserving natural resources both human and material, aiding farmers who occupy and till the soil, encouraging employers engaged in honest and useful business, assuring workers and consumers a fair share of industry's profits and products, preventing unfit persons or unfair goods entering this country, but applying to all nations equitable immigration and tariff policies, avoiding war by maintaining friendly relations and providing adequate defense, providing proper aid to the worthy youth and aged, and of securing tolerance to all, while insisting that governmental changes be made only in accordance with existing constitutional methods.

Need of Spiritual Awakening

We believe that to accomplish these and other worthy ends there must be a change in the purposes, motives and lives of our people. Such a spiritual awakening requires both encouraging churches and freeing schools and other forces of education from politics. The development of character—integrity, industry, self-control, initiative, a desire to be of service and a willingness to make sacrifices—must be the first aim of parents and teachers. Such a change in the hearts of employers, wage workers and consumers would so develop confidence as to restore real estate values, eliminate unemployment, and assure equal opportunities to all. We therefore, especially pledge ourselves to better and more useful public schools, and the teaching therein of fundamental moral precepts.

A COALITION PARTY

While both of the major political parties are performing useful service in emphasizing different needs, entangling alliances with corrupt interests, necessary to their success, make it impossible for these parties to take a definite stand on moral issues, even though these issues today are fundamental in solving our nation's problems. Therefore, there must be a union of church people and others who stand first for righteousness, into a Third Party. The NEW Prohibition Party serves such a purpose.

CONCLUSION

We, the members of this Party, are the one political group which has learned from sad experience that legislation alone—whether Old Deal or New Deal—is insufficient. We know that the solution of all problems—from liquor to unemployment—depends upon character, and the election to power of a political party committed to these principles. To this end we invite the co-operation and the votes of like minded men and women.

Republican Platform for 1940

INTRODUCTION

The Republican party, in representative Convention assembled, submits to the people of the United States the following declaration of its principles and purposes:

We state our general objectives in the simple and comprehensive words of the Preamble to the Constitution of the United States.

Those objectives as there stated are these:

"To form a more perfect Union; establish justice; insure domestic tranquility; provide for the common defense, promote the general welfare and secure the blessings of liberty to ourselves and our posterity."

Meeting within the shadow of Independence Hall where those words were written we solemnly reaffirm them as a perfect statement of the ends for which we as a party propose to plan and to labor.

The record of the Roosevelt Administration is a record of failure to attain any one of those essential objectives.

Instead of leading us into More Perfect Union the Administration has deliberately fanned the flames of class hatred.

Instead of the Establishment of Justice the Administration has sought the subjection of the Judiciary to Executive discipline and domination.

Instead of insuring Domestic Tranquility the Administration has made impossible the normal friendly relation between employers and employees and has even succeeded in alienating both the great divisions of Organized Labor.

Instead of Providing for the Common Defense the Administration, notwithstanding the expenditure of billions of our dollars, has left the Nation unprepared to resist foreign attack.

Instead of promoting the General Welfare the Administration has Domesticated the Deficit, Doubled the Debt, Imposed Taxes where they do the greatest economic harm, and used public money for partisan political advantage.

Instead of the Blessings of Liberty the Administration has imposed upon us a Regime of Regimentation which has deprived the individual of his freedom and has made of America a shackled giant.

Wholly ignoring these great objectives, as solemnly declared by the people of the United States, the New Deal Administration has for seven long years whirled in a turmoil of shifting, contradictory and overlapping administrations and policies. Confusion has reigned supreme. The only steady undeviating characteristic has been the relentless expansion of the power of the Federal government over the everyday life of the farmer, the industrial worker and the business man. The emergency demands organization—not confusion. It demands free and intelligent cooperation—not incompetent domination. It demands a change.

The New Deal Administration has failed America.

It has failed by seducing our people to become continuously dependent upon government, thus weakening their morale and quenching the traditional American spirit.

It has failed by viciously attacking our industrial system and sapping its strength and vigor.

It has failed by attempting to send our Congress home during the world's most tragic hour, so that we might be eased into the war by word of deed during the absence of our elected representatives from Washington.

It has failed by disclosing military details of our equipment to foreign powers over protests by the heads of our armed defense.

It has failed by ignoring the lessons of fact concerning modern, mechanized, armed defense.

In these and countless other ways the New Deal Administration has either deliberately deceived the American people or proved itself incompetent longer to handle the affairs of our government.

The zero hour is here. America must prepare at once to defend our shores, our homes, our lives and our most cherished ideals.

To establish a first line of defense we must place in official positions men of faith who put America first and who are determined that her governmental and economic system be kept unimpaired.

Our national defense must be so strong that no unfriendly power shall ever set foot on American soil. To assure this strength our national economy, the true basis of America's defense, must be free of unwarranted government interference.

Only a strong and sufficiently prepared America can speak words of reassurance and hope to the liberty-loving peoples of the world.

National Defense

The Republican Party is firmly opposed to involving this Nation in foreign war.

We are still suffering from the ill effects of the last World War: a war which cost us a twenty-four billion dollar increase in our national debt, billions of uncollectible foreign debts, and the complete upset of our economic system, in addition to the loss of human life and irreparable damage to the health of thousands of our boys.

The present National Administration has already spent for all purposes more than fifty-four billion dollars;—has boosted the national debt and current federal taxes to an all-time high; and yet by the President's own admission we are still wholly unprepared to defend our country, its institutions and our individual liberties in a war that threatens to engulf the whole world; and this in spite of the fact that foreign wars have been in progress for two years or more and that military information concerning these wars and the rearmament programs of the warring nations has been at all times available to the National Administration through its diplomatic and other channels.

The Republican Party stands for Americanism, preparedness and peace. We accordingly fasten upon the New Deal full responsibility for our unpreparedness and for the consequent danger of involvement in war.

We declare for the prompt, orderly and realistic building of our national defense to the point at which we shall be able not only to defend the United States, its possessions, and essential outposts from foreign attack, but also efficiently to uphold in war the Monroe Doctrine. To this task the Republican party pledges itself when entrusted with national authority. In the meantime we shall support all necessary and proper defense measures proposed by the Administration in its belated effort to make up for lost time; but we deplore explosive utterances by the President directed at other governments which serve to imperil our peace; and we condemn all executive acts and proceedings which might lead to war without the authorization of the Congress of the United States.

Our sympathies have been profoundly stirred by invasion of unoffending countries and by disaster to nations whole ideals most closely resemble our own. We favor the extension to all peoples fighting for liberty, or whose liberty is threatened, of such aid as shall not be in violation of international law or inconsistent with the requirements of our own national defense.

We believe that the spirit which should animate our entire defensive policy is determination to preserve not our material interests merely, but those liberties which are the priceless heritage of America.

Re-employment

The New Deal's failure to solve the problem of unemployment and revive opportunity for our youth presents a major challenge to representative government and free enterprise. We propose to recreate opportunity for the youth of America and put our idle millions back to work in private industry, business, and agriculture. We propose to eliminate needless administrative restrictions, thus restoring lost motion to the wheels of individual enterprise.

RELIEF

We shall remove waste, discrimination, and politics from relief—through administration by the States with federal grants-in-aid on a fair and non-political basis, thus giving the man and woman on relief a larger share of the funds appropriated.

SOCIAL SECURITY

We favor the extension of necessary old age benefits on an ear-marked pay-as-you-go basis to the extent that the revenues raised for this purpose will permit. We favor the extension of the unemployment compensation provisions of the Social Security Act, wherever practicable, to those groups and classes not now included. For such groups as may thus be covered we favor a system of unemployment compensation with experience rating provisions, aimed at protecting the worker in the regularity of his employment and providing adequate compensation for reasonable periods when that regularity of employment is interrupted. The administration should be left with the States with a minimum of Federal control.

LABOR RELATIONS

The Republican party has always protected the American worker.

We shall maintain labor's right of free organization and collective bargaining.

We believe that peace and prosperity at home require harmony, teamwork, and understanding in all relations between worker and employer. When differences arise, they should be settled directly and voluntarily across the table.

Recent disclosures respecting the administration of the National Labor Relations Act require that this Act be amended in fairness to employers and all groups of employees so as to provide true freedom for, and orderliness in self-organization and collective bargaining.

AGRICULTURE

A prosperous and stable agriculture is the foundation of our economic structure. Its preservation is a national and non-political social problem not yet solved, despite many attempts. The farmer is entitled to a profit-price for his products. The Republican party will put into effect such governmental policies, temporary and permanent, as will establish and maintain an equitable balance between labor, industry, and agriculture by expanding industrial and business activity, eliminating unemployment, lowering production costs, thereby creating increased consumer buying power for agricultural products.

Until this balance has been attained, we propose to provide benefit payments, based upon a widely-applied, constructive soil conservation program free from government-dominated production control, but administered, as far as practicable, by farmers themselves; to restrict the major benefits of these payments to operators of family-type farms; to continue all present benefit payments until our program becomes operative; and to eliminate the present extensive and costly bureaucratic interference.

We shall provide incentive payments, when necessary, to encourage increased production of agricultural commodities, adaptable to our soil and climate, not now produced in sufficient quantities for our home markets, and will stimulate the use and processing of all farm products in industry as raw materials.

We shall promote a cooperative system of adequate farm credit, at lowest interest rates commensurate with the cost of money, supervised by an independent governmental agency, with ultimate farmer ownership and control; farm commodity loans to facilitate orderly marketing and stabilize farm income; the expansion of sound, farmer-owned and farmer-controlled cooperative associations; and the support of educational and extension programs to achieve more efficient production and marketing.

We shall foster Government refinancing, where necessary, of the heavy Federal farm debt load through an agency segregated from cooperative credit.

We shall promote a national land use program for Federal acquisition, without dislocation of local tax returns, of non-productive farm lands by voluntary sale or lease subject to approval of the States concerned; and the disposition of such lands to appropriate public uses including watershed protection and flood prevention, reforestation, recreation, erosion control, and the conservation of wild life.

We advocate a foreign trade policy which will end one-man tariff making, afford effective protection to farm products, regain our export markets, and assure an American price level for the domestically consumed portion of our export crops.

We favor effective quarantine against imported livestock, dairy, and other farm products from countries which do not impose health and sanitary standards equal to our own domestic standards.

We approve the orderly development of reclamation and irrigation, project by project and as conditions justify.

We promise adequate asistance to rural communities suffering disasters from flood, drought, and other natural causes.

We shall promote stabilization of agricultural income through intelligent management of accumulated surpluses, and through the development of outlets by supplying those in need at home and abroad.

Tariff and Reciprocal Trade

We are threatened by unfair competition in world markets and by the invasion of our home markets, especially by the products of state-controlled foreign economies.

We believe in tariff protection for Agriculture, Labor, and Industry, as essential to our American standard of living. The measure of the protection shall be determined by scientific methods with due regard to the interest of the consumer.

We shall explore every possibility of reopening the channels of international trade through negotiations so conducted as to produce genuine reciprocity and expand our exports.

We condemn the manner in which the so-called reciprocal trade agreements of the New Deal have been put into effect without adequate hearings, with undue haste, without proper consideration of our domestic producers, and without Congressional approval. These defects we shall correct.

Money

The Congress should reclaim its constitutional powers over money, and withdraw the President's arbitrary authority to manipulate the currency, establish bimetallism, issue irredeemable paper money, and debase the gold and silver coinage. We shall repeal the Thomas Inflation Amendment of 1933 and the (foreign) Silver Purchase Act of 1934, and take all possible steps to preserve the value of the Government's huge holdings of gold and re-introduce gold into circulation.

Jobs and Idle Money

Believing it possible to keep the securities market clean without paralyzing it, we endorse the principle of truth in securities in the Securities Act. To get billions of idle dollars and a multitude of idle men back to work and to promote national defense, these acts should be revised and the policies of the Commission changed to encourage the flow of private capital into industry.

Taxation

Public spending has trebled under the New Deal, while tax burdens have doubled. Huge taxes are necessary to pay for New Deal waste and for neglected national defense. We shall revise the tax system and remove those practices which impede recovery and shall apply policies which stimulate enterprise. We shall not use the taxing power as an instrument of punishment or to secure objectives not otherwise obtainable under existing law.

Public Credit

With urgent need for adequate defense, the people are burdened by a direct and contingent debt exceeding fifty billion dollars. Twenty-nine billion of this debt has been created by New Deal borrowings during the past seven years. We pledge ourselves to conserve the public credit for all essential purposes by levying taxation sufficient to cover necessary civil expenditure, a substantial part of the defense cost, and the interest and retirement of the national debt.

Public Spending

Millions of men and women still out of work after seven years of excessive spending refute the New Deal theory that "deficit spending" is the way to prosperity and jobs. Our American system of private enterprise, if permitted to go to work, can rapidly increase the wealth, income, and standard of living of all the people. We solemnly pledge that public expenditures, other than those required for full national defense and relief, shall be cut to levels necessary for the essential services of government.

EQUAL RIGHTS

We favor submission by Congress to the States of an amendment to the Constitution providing for equal rights for men and women.

NEGRO

We pledge that our American citizens of Negro descent shall be given a square deal in the economic and political life of this nation. Discrimination in the civil service, the army, navy, and all other branches of the Government must cease. To enjoy the full benefits of life, liberty and pursuit of happiness universal suffrage must be made effective for the Negro citizen. Mob violence shocks the conscience of the nation and legislation to curb this evil should be enacted.

UN-AMERICAN ACTIVITIES

We vigorously condemn the New Deal encouragement of various groups that seek to change the American form of government by means outside the Constitution. We condemn the appointment of members of such un-American groups to high positions of trust in the national Government. The development of the treacherous so-called Fifth Column, as it has operated in war-stricken countries, should be a solemn warning to America. We pledge the Republican Party to get rid of such borers from within.

IMMIGRATION

We favor the strict enforcement of all laws controlling the entry of aliens. The activities of undesirable aliens should be investigated and those who seek to change by force and violence the American form of government should be deported.

VETERANS

We pledge adequate compensation and care for veterans disabled in the service of our country, and for their widows, orphans, and dependents.

INDIANS

We pledge an immediate and final settlement of all Indian claims between the government and the Indian citizenship of the nation.

HAWAII

Hawaii, sharing the nation's obligations equally with the several States, is entitled to the fullest measure of home rule; and to equality with the several States in the rights of her citizens and in the application of our national laws.

PUERTO RICO

Statehood is a logical aspiration of the people of Puerto Rico who were made citizens of the United States by Congress in 1917; legislation affecting Puerto Rico, in so far as feasible, should be in harmony with the realization of that aspiration.

GOVERNMENT AND BUSINESS

We shall encourage a healthy, confident, and growing private enterprise, confine Government activity to essential public services, and regulate business only so as to protect consumer, employee, and investor and without restricting the production of more and better goods at lower prices.

MONOPOLY

Since the passage of the Sherman Anti-trust Act by the Republican party we have consistently fought to preserve free competition with regulation to prevent abuse. New Deal policy fosters Government monopoly, restricts production, and fixes prices. We shall enforce anti-trust legislation without prejudice or discrimination. We condemn the use or threatened use of criminal indictments to obtain through consent decrees objectives not contemplated by law.

GOVERNMENT COMPETITION

We promise to reduce to the minimum Federal competition with business. We pledge ourselves to establish honest accounting and reporting by every agency of the Federal Government and to continue only those enterprises whose maintenance is clearly in the public interest.

FREE SPEECH

The principles of a free press and free speech, as established by the Constitution, should apply to the radio. Federal regulation of radio is necessary in view of the natural limitations of wave lengths, but this gives no excuse for censorship. We oppose the use of licensing to establish arbitrary controls. Licenses should be revocable only when, after public hearings, due cause for cancellation is shown.

SMALL BUSINESS

The New Deal policy of interference and arbitrary regulation has injured all business, but especially small business. We promise to encourage the small business man by removing unnecessary bureaucratic regulation and interference.

STOCK AND COMMODITY EXCHANGES

We favor regulation of stock and commodity exchanges. They should be accorded the fullest measure of self-control consistent with the discharge of their public trust and the prevention of abuse.

INSURANCE

We condemn the New Deal attempts to destroy the confidence of our people in private insurance institutions. We favor continuance of regulation of insurance by the several States.

GOVERNMENT REORGANIZATION

We shall reestablish in the Federal Civil Service a real merit system on a truly competitive basis and extend it to all non-policy-forming positions.

We pledge ourselves to enact legislation standardizing and simplifying quasi-judicial and administrative agencies to insure adequate notice and hearing, impartiality, adherence to the rules of evidence and full judicial review of all questions of law and fact.

Our greatest protection against totalitarian government is the American system of checks and balances. The constitutional distribution of legislative, executive, and judicial functions is essential to the preservation of this system. We pledge ourselves to make it the basis of all our policies affecting the organization and operation of our Republican form of Government.

THIRD TERM

To insure against the overthrow of our American system of government we favor an amendment to the Constitution providing that no person shall be President of the United States for more than two terms.

A PLEDGE OF GOOD FAITH

The acceptance of the nominations made by this Convention carries with it, as a matter of private honor and public faith, an undertaking by each candidate to be true to the principles and program herein set forth.

We earnestly urge all patriotic men and women, regardless of former affiliations, to unite with us in the support of our declaration of principles to the end that "government of the people, by the people and for the people shall not perish from this earth."

Socialist Platform of 1940

WE TAKE OUR STAND!

Every American knows that we have the resources and the machinery, the workers and the skill to conquer poverty. Every American knows that poverty and insecurity, the more unendurable because they are unnecessary, curse this most fortunate of lands.

That the situation has not already led to worse suffering and graver menace to our imperfect democracy is due to social legislation originating in Socialist immediate demands. The best of what goes by the New Deal name; social insurance, minimum wage laws, guarantees of the right to collective bargaining, public power projects were first demanded by the Socialist Party.

But these things, for reasons that Socialists have always proclaimed, have not averted the multiplying ills of a dying private capitalism nor given any assurance that out of its failure we shall not get the slavery of state capitalism under a fascist or totalitarian government.

Today more than 20 per cent of our people have no place in the social economic order; for ten years we have had an army of 10,000,000 unemployed. Two out of three American families must live on less than $1,500 a year.

Why? Because our private capitalism by its very nature exploits the mass of workers with hand and brain, in town and country, to provide profits for the few. And these profits are dependent on relative scarcity from which the whole community suffers. What planning there is, is not primarily for use, but for the profits of an owning class.

Neither old party offers any adequate remedy.

The Republicans want a qualified, and impossible, return to the system which brought us to ruin at the end of 1929. The Democrats as a party have never accepted the New Deal and the New Deal administration itself has turned from its failure to conquer poverty at home to armament economics and the hope of war-time profits.

Under these circumstances democratic Socialism becomes an immediate demand; the one road to plenty, peace and freedom. For the producing and consuming masses of America to recognize this fact and turn their faces while there is yet time to a deliberate harnessing of our machinery to peace, not war, abundance for all, not profit for the few is the one chance of our escape from fascism and war.

This means socialization. Socialization is social ownership and democratic control of industry, substituting the principle of public service or social usefulness for the system of private profit, preserving workers' free choice of occupation, consumers' free choice of goods and freedom of association for all functional groups.

Socialism Is Necessary

Wherever private exploitation of a limited natural resource is highly wasteful, as in the oil, coal and timber industries, there socialization is required in the interest of this as well as of future generations.

Wherever concentration of financial power leads to the restriction of the expansive forces of our economy, as in insurance and investment banking, we propose socialization.

Wherever private monopoly, in the drive for monopoly profit, restricts production to less than is justified by the social usefulness of the product, as in the steel and cement industries, the principle of socialization should be applied.

Wherever concentration of economic power creates a political interest which is too powerful for a democracy to tolerate in private hands, we should put this power in public hands.

Wherever natural monopoly has consumers at its mercy, as in the aluminum industry, socialization is both practical and necessary.

Wherever, as in the railroads, private operation cannot or will not undertake socially-needed investment, socialization becomes the order of the day.

Wherever, as in many large-scale corporations, ownership has lost its management function and the business is managed by hired men, these managers should be working for the public instead of for private owners.

Wherever one or more of these conditions exist it means that the private profit principle is destroying the very basis of living; that business must be taken over by the public.

This is a program of immediate socialization. It is the program of the Socialist Party. It is the only program capable of solving the economic plight of America, of putting men and machines to work, of giving abundance and plenty to all.

This is a program which is the only valid alternative to armament economics and war. Hysterical concern for the kind of defense which seems a threat to our neighbors is the first escape for a government and a system which cannot end unemployment.

War and Totalitarianism

To furnish supplies for other people's wars is, to the profit seekers, a welcome alternative to supplying our own people with their daily bread. But the search for war profits and armament economics leads straight to war. War and frantic preparation for war mean the totalitarian state, not Socialist freedom.

To the whole world let America say:

"We will not share in the collective suicide of your wars. We will, to the best of our ability, aid the victims of war and oppression. We will cooperate in disarmament and in all economic arrangements which will lessen the strain of insecurity and exploitation upon the peoples of all the world."

Other Campaign Issues

In its platform the Socialist Party presents a carefully considered, all-embracing program to build a free, secure and warless America. In this supplementary material, we present our stand on other issues of this campaign.

Socialism and Democracy mean the same thing. "Government of the people, by the people and for the people" cannot exist so long as we have government of industry by the bosses for the profits of an owning class.

The Socialist Party opposes dictatorship and the concept of party-state, either Fascist or Communist. The tragedy of Russia has shown that political and industrial democracy are inseparable, and without such democracy, economic collectivism becomes a new form of slavery.

Socialism means freedom. A Socialist state must serve the common good of the individual. Under true Socialism, our civil liberties will not only be preserved but extended.

UNEMPLOYMENT AND SOCIAL SECURITY

Under the Roosevelt administration, public works and housing have too often become a political football. Projects have been proposed for political prestige and then abandoned through false economy. The Socialist Party proposes reduction of the administration's huge and planless armament-building program and use of armament funds for a public works program which would provide low-rent housing, organized on a cooperative basis wherever possible, for millions of American families in rural and city slums.

We favor expansion of the WPA, NYA, and CCC. The unemployed are society's responsibility so long as we tolerate an economic system which denies them the right to work. We oppose any conspiracy to place the CCC, either partially or wholly, under military control. We advocate the provision by the government of useful jobs for young people at prevailing wages.

The Socialist Party proposes federal old-age pensions supplemented by a voluntary annuity system. We would extend unemployment benefits to all workers now unprotected, particularly agricultural, domestic and maritime workers, and provide more liberal benefits and shorter waiting periods. We propose a complete health and disability insurance program.

We favor a broad federal program for aid to education. For the first time in our history, children in many districts are receiving less schooling than their parents. Such federal aid must be given on terms which eliminate discrimination against Negroes and other minority groups. In all our educational programs, academic freedom, democratic control with teacher representation, and the principle of separation of church and state must be upheld.

AGRICULTURE

Half of the farmer's problem is in the city. If every American had what the U. S. Bureau of Home Economics calls a "decent diet," we should need more rather than less of every important farm product except wheat. We have no genuine farm surpluses—merely market surpluses resulting from the inability of the people to buy what they sorely need. The Socialist program of economic expansion will bring industrial production up to the level of farm production instead of dragging farm production down to the level of restricted industry.

But while industry is catching up with agriculture, the farmers must not be penalized for being able to feed the people better than the people can afford. Direct and large-scale government action is required to maintain farmers' income. We must continue and extend the government program to buy up the so-called farm surpluses for the people who need them.

The soil conservation program must be continued with long range planning, keyed to an expanding standard of living. In the local planning of the farm program, low-income farmers and tenants, Negroes as well as Whites, must take part.

We are utterly opposed to the present practice of using government subsidies to preserve the plantation peonage system. No benefit payments should be made to plantation owners unless there are rigorous provisions to prevent the diversion of those payments from tenants and sharecroppers. Plantation and ranch owners employing day and migratory labor on a large scale must be required to accept federal minimum wage standards as the basis for receiving benefit payments.

For the increasing number of migratory families, a wide program of camp relief and resettlement must be carried out by the federal government.

The Socialist Party is opposed to the brutal regimentation of agriculture employed by Stalin in Russia. We believe that no single type of farm organization is applicable to the whole country, and that the farmers themselves in democratic fashion should reach decisions on agricultural practice.

Clearly, however, the absentee ownership of farm lands conflicts with the interest of the public in general and of the farmers in particular. Therefore, the Socialist Party favors the use of land taxation and, where necessary, public purchase to abolish absentee landlordship.

In some cases the solution for sharecropping

and "factories in the field" will be cooperative collective farms. In other cases the answer to absentee land-owning will be by settling farm families on their own land under conditions which will establish the principle that their title rests upon occupancy and use.

Dwellers in farm areas as well as in towns and cities should receive the benefits of all social security legislation.

LABOR LEGISLATION

The Socialist Party is steadfastly opposed to any effort to weaken or destroy protection for collective bargaining either through the vicious Smith amendments or the underhanded slashing of the already meager appropriations for the proper enforcement of the law. We propose immediate extension of the Wages and Hours law to all lines of employment and the raising of the minimum wage level. Technological progress makes possible steady reduction of hours as a necessary safeguard against technological unemployment. Civil service employees must be allowed full economic and civil rights, including adequate machinery for dealing with grievance and dismissals.

As a political party which fights side by side with labor, we call upon the unions to end the civil war in labor's ranks. This conflict not only endangers the progress made by labor during the past half-century but threatens to block further advancement.

Socialists condemn as anti-democratic and anti-social the administration's use of anti-trust legislation against the unions. If labor is to prevent government intervention, however, it must eliminate bureaucratic and racketeering trends in its ranks. Democracy in public life must have, as a basic example, democracy in the ranks of labor.

TAXATION, TARIFFS AND THE FISCAL SYSTEM

In federal, state and local taxation, now chaotic and mismanaged, we favor simplification and co-ordination.

We condemn all taxes on consumption and especially general sales and payroll taxes, which bear most heavily on those with the lowest income and thus restrict production and employment by reducing the demand for goods.

Primarily, reliance must be placed on graduated income and inheritance taxes as a source of federal and state revenue. The application of this principle requires tax increases, especially on incomes from $5,000 up which now escape their fair share of taxation. Tax-exempt securities must be abolished. Undistributed corporate income which is not reinvested in productive equipment should be subject to surtax.

Taxation on unimproved real estate should be increased to discourage land speculation. In most cities, drastic revision of real estate taxes is a necessary aid to any housing program. Slum land appraisals must be written down. We oppose any increase of taxes on farms and homes.

We renew our endorsement of a scientifically graduated capital levy for reduction of the national debt and as an aid toward socialization.

We condemn action of states under various pretexts in levying imports duties, taxes or license fees which restrict free trade within the United States.

We favor encouragement of trade with peaceful peoples but not in materials of war.

Our present fiscal system, particularly in respect to gold and silver purchases, imposes a tax—disguised but enormous—upon the people, gives foreign nations, including Japan, a gigantic subsidy for their wars, and lays a basis for inflation of astronomical proportions. The gold purchase policy is particularly dangerous and should be abandoned as fast as possible without panic. In general, it is the Socialist Party's purpose to achieve a fiscal system protected against the evils both of inflation and deflation, and a system from which neither a small class of private bankers nor of gold and silver owners shall derive huge profits at public expense.

CIVIL LIBERTIES AND POLITICAL RIGHTS

We renew our pledge for the maintenance and increase of civil liberty for all groups, regardless of race, color or creed. We support everywhere the fight against poll taxes, undemocratic laws, and all limitations of suffrage.

Citizens of the District of Columbia should have the same right to local self-government and the same voice in national elections as other citizens.

Discrimination against Negroes must be abolished. Anti-Semitism or any form of racial, religious or group intolerance must be rigorously combatted as paving the road to fascism.

We oppose alien and sedition legislation as directed toward the abridgment of civil liberty.

We commend the methods and aim of the La-Follette Committee which has been investigating civil liberty and condemn, by contrast, the methods employed by the Dies Committee and particularly by its chairman.

We condemn the use of immigration laws to return, directly or indirectly, refugees to the tyranny of totalitarian states and favor a more generous treatment of them. America must be kept the land of political asylum.

INTERNATIONAL FRIENDSHIP

The Socialist Party favors active cooperation with all forces, particularly labor, farm and cooperative organizations in other lands which seek freedom, peace and justice. We pledge unstinted aid to the heroic underground movement in Germany and other totalitarian countries.

In order to establish an honest fraternal relationship between the nations of the western hemisphere, we demand withdrawal of economic dictation by the United States over Latin-American countries. We pledge full support to all forces in Latin-America which seek the establishment of working democracies.

SOCIALISTS, LABOR UNIONS AND COOPERATIVES

The Socialist Party calls upon its members and friends to be active in labor unions of their industry and trade, to seek democratically within them to advance an understanding and acceptance of the principles of Socialism, but not to seek control over them by power politics. We seek organization of the unorganized and of the unemployed.

The Socialist Party renews its endorsement of the cooperative movement. We rejoice in the sound progress made by this movement in recent years and note with especial approval the formation of farmer-labor cooperative councils in such an important farm state as Wisconsin.

We urge young people to seek a solution to their pressing economic problems in alliance with labor, farmers, unemployed and cooperatives.

Throughout its existence, the Socialist Party has endorsed and participated in genuine farmer-labor political parties and leagues. In 1940, however, Socialists see no sign whatever of any possibility of building a genuine farmer-labor party on a national scale. It will be too late for effective and constructive action by protesting groups which wait until after the old party conventions. Believers in a farmer-labor party will advance their cause by supporting the Socialist ticket.

WAR

Summary of Resolution Adopted by Socialist National Convention, Washington, D. C., April 7, 1940.

The present European war presents to the American workers a challenge that can be met only by hard thinking and great emotional self-control. Vast armies are being hurled at each other across devastated lands. Shall Americans plunge into the abyss?

The cause for which Hitler has hurled the German masses into war is one of ruthless brutality. Its record has horrified all decent men and women. But that does not mean that the Allied war itself will produce the kind of democratic world in which peace and security will be assured. Indeed, the very existence of the Hitler regime is based on the kind of peace that the Allies effected at the close of the World War.

Like war, fascism has its origin in capitalism. Both war and fascism spring from the failure of the capitalist economy to solve domestic problems and provide security for the masses of the people. Fascism has its roots in the breakdown of the national economy, the desperate turning of the frustrated people to a messiah who promises all. Like capitalism, it uses war in the competition among nations for the control of the world market, as dictated by the need for expansion. But war has its own dynamics, accelerates economic breakdown and itself leads to the further entrenchment of reaction and fascism.

Defeat of Hitler will be welcomed by all anti-fascists. But defeat of Hitler will mean the defeat of Hitlerism and a victory for democracy only if the roots of fascism and the war system are destroyed. The United States cannot contribute toward that end nor vindicate real democracy if it loses itself in the processes of war.

If America enters the war, we shall be subjected to military dictatorship, the regimentation of labor and ultimate economic collapse that must follow war. In an effort to "save democracy," we shall have destroyed its only remaining citadel.

The first demand of the American people must

now be: Keep America Out of War! That means a refusal to take any of those "steps short of war"—which by very definition are steps in the direction of war. The alternatives are few. Economic participation, by every test of past experience, must lead to military participation. However hard the decision, the American people must resolutely determine to avoid all roads to war and pursue only the paths of peace.

To drive war out of the world, we must first keep America out of war!

THE SOCIALIST CANDIDATES

In its candidate for President, the Socialist Party presents a distinguished American whose entire life has been devoted to the cause of the oppressed. As a thinker and writer, as a man of action, a fighter for civil liberties and against every manifestation of class, racial and religious prejudice, he has won the respect and admiration of all progressive forces throughout the nation.

Norman Thomas was born in Marion, Ohio, and lives in New York City, but he is at home wherever labor's cause and democracy in general are threatened—in Indiana, where he defied McNutt's martial law, in Florida where he fought and exposed the Ku Klux Klan, in Arkansas where he faced planter mobs in behalf of the share-croppers, in New Jersey where he fought and licked Boss Hague on the issue of free speech.

Norman Thomas joined the Socialist Party in 1917, when less courageous men were leaving it and when it was the only political force in the country actively opposing our participation in the first World War. Today, when we are threatened with participation in the second World War, he is America's leader in the fight against militarism, the fight to keep America out of war and to build a genuine democracy in this country. Alone, of all presidential candidates, he has taken an uncompromising stand against American participation, economic or military, in the European conflict.

Maynard C. Krueger, the Socialist candidate for Vice-President, is one of a rising school of American economists which is challenging our present economic and social order. Born 35 years ago on a Missouri farm, he completed his high school course at the age of 15 and entered the University of Missouri. He has since risen rapidly in academic circles and is now teaching at the University of Chicago.

Mr. Krueger is known to millions of radio listeners as a participant in the University of Chicago Round Table Sunday Afternoon Discussions where he has at all times upheld social progress for America. His fellow-teachers have thrice honored him by electing him vice-president of the American Federation of Teachers, A. F. of L.

His work among the coal miners of Illinois and West Virginia, among the unemployed and the farmers of the Mid-West has given him an intimate understanding of the problems of America. Representative of a new generation, Maynard C. Krueger is an ideal choice as running mate for Norman Thomas.

VOTE SOCIALIST!

Platform of the Socialist Labor Party

Socialism or Capitalism—that is the crucial issue confronting the workers of America!

Shall we institute a society of collective property, production for use, plenty for all and international peace, or shall we allow predatory capitalism to drag society back into a new dark ages?

The Socialist Labor Party of America, at its 20th National Convention in the City of New York, April 29, 1940, reiterates that capitalism cannot be amended, but must be ended. Indisputable evidence of hopeless social decay is apparent nationally in the concentration of wealth and power, on the one hand, and perpetual mass unemployment, and insecurity among the workers, on the other. Internationally the breakdown of capitalism reveals itself in world chaos—a desperate death struggle between capitalist nations over the world's markets and spheres of influence.

We hold that the existing contradiction between the theory of democratic government and the fact of a despotic economic system—the private ownership of the natural and social opportunities— divides the nation into two classes: the non-producing, but owning, Capitalist Class, and the producing but propertiless Working Class; throws society into the convulsions of the Class Struggle; and invariably perverts government to the uses and benefit of the Capitalist Class.

The incompetence of the Capitalist Class and its unfitness to rule any longer stand conspicuously demonstrated. Capitalist Class rule has created slums in the cities faster than it has torn them down. It has thrown millions of workers on the industrial scrap-heap barely to exist on the degrading pittance of relief. Its minimum wage has placed the stamp of approval on a starvation wage and in great industrial areas the "minimum wage" has become the *maximum* wage. In its insane efforts to raise prices and create scarcity, it has hailed drouths as blessings and bumper crops as a curse. Through its executive committee, the Political State, it has wantonly destroyed the surplus while millions were ill fed.

Capitalist political henchmen have placated the workers with sops and relief and the promise of jobs with the restoration of production. But when production soared above the 1929 peak, in December, 1939, its staunchest apologists admitted that higher production had been effected without reducing unemployment. In spite of billions spent for relief and additional billions spent to "prime the pump," in spite of scores of reforms acclaimed as "victories" for the workers, in spite of prodigious programs for rehousing, reclamation, resettlement, and work relief—unemployment and insecurity among the workers are as rampant as ever.

To swell its profits, the capitalist class seeks in the laboratory still newer means of cheapening commodities, new methods of eliminating workers, thus consigning them to permanent unemployment.

Private ownership stands as a solid wall between the useful producers and the product of their labor. The Socialist Labor Party declares that this wall shall be battered down and the wealth of the nation be made available to all who perform useful labor. Under Socialism, machines, collectively owned and operated for the benefit of society, can be made to fulfill the promise of the age and bring an end to unemployment and poverty. Instead of eliminating workers, socially owned and constantly improved machinery will eliminate hours from the working day, giving leisure and affluence to all.

Unable to solve the problems at home, the capitalist class diverts attention from its failures to the anarchy abroad. The long anticipated war is now an irrevocable fact. Capitalist democracy is perishing in its flames. The belligerents which boasted the broadest liberties have scrapped the conquests of centuries of struggle for freedom over night. Perceptibly America is being drawn into the bloody vortex. Its exports have shifted from grain, fruit and plows to war-planes, guns and munitions. On this grim traffic is its "prosperity" based. War feeds on commerce; commerce feeds on war. Under the pretext of "national defense" and to a chorus of declarations for peace, its statesmen, New Deal, old deal, liberal and conservative alike, gird the nation for its fateful role. Punchinello-like, the political henchmen of the capitalist class move as their masters pull the strings.

War referendums, pacifism and anti-war resolutions are futile, childish gestures. We hold that, given the capitalist system with its mutual antagonisms and relentless struggle for markets, American involvement in the European war is inescapable. Capitalism means war; one plank of capitalism means the whole of capitalism. To oppose one plank only is to leave all others standing and thus render abortive all seeming success against the monster. It is the capitalist system itself which must be destroyed!

Against this insane social system the Socialist Labor Party raises the banner of revolution and calls upon the working class to organize politically and industrially for the conquest of power.

POLITICAL ORGANIZATION

The Constitution of the United States provides for its own amendment. The Constitution thereby recognizes and legalizes revolution. Our people hold the government in the hollow of their hand. We propose, therefore, that the revolutionary change be effected by the peaceful and civilized means of the ballot.

In presenting the issue—Socialism or Capitalism —and a program for its solution, the Socialist Labor Party stands alone. All other parties, whether Republican, Democratic, "Socialist," "Labor," "Progressive," or "Communist," propose reforms which tend to preserve capitalism but fail to improve the lot of the workers. Therefore, we call upon the toilers of America, in order to implement their hope for life, liberty and the pursuit of happiness, to cast their ballot for the Socialist

Labor Party, for the abolition of the capitalist system.

ECONOMIC ORGANIZATION

Recognizing the simple truth that RIGHT without the MIGHT to support it is useless and meaningless, we call upon the workers of America to organize themselves into integral Socialist Industrial Unions to enforce the demand for collective ownership proclaimed through the ballot. But we at the same time caution the workers that such unions *must be organized,* for none now exist. The C.I.O., A.F. of L., and similar organizations are agencies of capitalism for the reason that they are pledged to maintain the system of private property, and structurally they lend themselves preeminently to the furthering of capitalist interests.

Organized *as a class,* along industrial lines, the workers can act instantaneously, and with such momentum that no power on earth can stop them. Only the thoroughly integrated Socialist Industrial Unions can block a brutal reaction, should the outvoted, expropriated capitalists rebel against the explicit decision of the majority.

SOCIALIST ADMINISTRATION

More than an invincible force behind Labor's ballot, the Socialist Industrial Union organizes the workers intelligently *to carry on production,* thus avoiding a chaotic period of transition. Finally, the Socialist Industrial Union becomes *the Government of the Socialist Republic,* supplanting the outworn, reactionary and inefficient capitalist Political State. *Democratically elected representatives* of the industrial constituencies will form an Industrial Union Congress, the duties of which will be the simple ones of directing, coordinating and supervising production for the benefit of all.

Workers of America! The issue of our age can no longer be postponed! Vote for the Socialist Republic! Organize the Socialist Industrial Union NOW to put a speedy end to barbarous capitalism. Unite under the banner of the Socialist Labor Party NOW to demand—

THE WORKSHOPS TO THE WORKERS!
THE PRODUCT TO THE PRODUCERS!
ALL POWER TO THE SOCIALIST
INDUSTRIAL UNION!

CAMPAIGN OF 1944

In 1944, during World War II, the Democratic incumbent, Franklin D. Roosevelt, was easily nominated by his party for the fourth time. His choice for his running mate was Senator Harry S. Truman of Missouri, who was chosen after the second ballot over the vice-president, Henry Wallace, and ten other hopefuls. The Republicans, meeting in Chicago, nominated (with only one dissenting vote) Governor Thomas E. Dewey of New York. His unanimously selected vice-presidential candidate was Governor John W. Bricker of Ohio.

Norman Thomas again ran for president as the Socialist Party candidate with Darlington Hoopes of Pennsylvania as the vice-presidential candidate. On the Prohibition Party ticket were Claude A. Watson of California and Andrew Johnson of Kentucky. Edward A. Teichert of Pennsylvania and Arla A. Albaugh of Ohio were the candidates of the Socialist Labor Party. In May of 1944, the Communist Party dissolved and its place was taken by a "Communist Political Association," which did not nominate a presidential candidate.

At the polls in November, the Democrats received 25,611,939 popular votes to 22,013,372 for the Republicans. The Socialists garnered 79,000 votes; the Prohibitionists, 74,733. The Socialist Labor Party ticket attracted 45,179 voters. Franklin Roosevelt was reelected president with 432 electoral votes; Governor Dewey received 99— from twelve states.

Democratic Platform of 1944

The Democratic Party stands on its record in peace and in war.

To speed victory, establish and maintain peace, guarantee full employment and provide prosperity —this is its platform.

We do not here detail scores of planks. We cite action.

Beginning March, 1933, the Democratic Administration took a series of actions which saved our system of free enterprise.

It brought that system out of collapse and thereafter eliminated abuses which had imperiled it.

It used the powers of government to provide employment in industry and to save agriculture.

It wrote a new Magna Carta for labor.

It provided social security, including old age pensions, unemployment insurance, security for crippled and dependent children and the blind. It established employment offices. It provided federal bank deposit insurance, flood prevention, soil conservation, and prevented abuses in the security markets. It saved farms and homes from foreclosure, and secured profitable prices for farm products.

It adopted an effective program of reclamation, hydro-electric power, and mineral development.

It found the road to prosperity through production and employment.

We pledge the continuance and improvement of these programs.

Before war came, the Democratic Administration awakened the Nation, in time, to the dangers that threatened its very existence.

It succeeded in building, in time, the best-trained and equipped army in the world, the most powerful navy in the world, the greatest air force in the world, and the largest merchant marine in the world.

It gained for our country, and it saved for our country, powerful allies.

When war came, it succeeded in working out with those allies an effective grand strategy against the enemy.

It set that strategy in motion, and the tide of battle was turned.

It held the line against wartime inflation.

It ensured a fair share-and-share-alike distribution of food and other essentials.

It is leading our country to certain victory.

The primary and imperative duty of the United States is to wage the war with every resource available to final triumph over our enemies, and we pledge that we will continue to fight side by side with the United Nations until this supreme objective shall have been attained and thereafter to secure a just and lasting peace.

That the world may not again be drenched in blood by international outlaws and criminals, we pledge:

To join with the other United Nations in the establishment of an international organization based on the principle of the sovereign equality of all peace-loving states, open to membership by all such states, large and small, for the prevention of aggression and the maintenance of international peace and security.

To make all necessary and effective agreements and arrangements through which the nations would maintain adequate forces to meet the needs of preventing war and of making impossible the preparation for war and which would have such forces available for joint action when necessary.

Such organization must be endowed with power to employ armed forces when necessary to prevent aggression and preserve peace.

We favor the maintenance of an international court of justice of which the United States shall be a member and the employment of diplomacy, conciliation, arbitration and other like methods where appropriate in the settlement of international disputes.

World peace is of transcendent importance. Our gallant sons are dying on land, on sea, and in the air. They do not die as Republicans. They do not die as Democrats. They die as Americans. We pledge that their blood shall not have been shed in vain. America has the opportunity to lead the world in this great service to mankind. The United States must meet the challenge. Under Divine Providence, she must move forward to her high destiny.

We pledge our support to the Atlantic Charter and the Four Freedoms and the application of the principles enunciated therein to the United Nations and other peace-loving nations, large and small.

We shall uphold the good-neighbor policy, and extend the trade policies initiated by the present administration.

We favor the opening of Palestine to unrestricted Jewish immigration and colonization, and such a policy as to result in the establishment there of a free and democratic Jewish commonwealth.

We favor legislation assuring equal pay for equal work, regardless of sex.

We recommend to Congress the submission of a Constitutional amendment on equal rights for women.

We favor Federal aid to education administered by the states without interference by the Federal Government.

We favor Federal legislation to assure stability of products, employment, distribution and prices in the bituminous coal industry, to create a proper balance between consumer, producer and mine worker.

We endorse the President's statement recognizing the importance of the use of water in arid land states for domestic and irrigation purposes.

We favor non-discriminatory transportation charges and declare for the early correction of inequalities in such charges.

We favor enactment of legislation granting the fullest measure of self-government for Alaska, Hawaii and Puerto Rico, and eventual statehood for Alaska and Hawaii.

We favor the extension of the right of suffrage to the people of the District of Columbia.

We offer these postwar programs:

A continuation of our policy of full benefits for ex-servicemen and women with special consideration for the disabled. We make it our first duty to assure employment and economic security to all who have served in the defense of our country.

Price guarantees and crop insurance to farmers with all practical steps:

To keep agriculture on a parity with industry and labor.

To foster the success of the small independent farmer.

To aid the home ownership of family-sized farms.

To extend rural electrification and develop broader domestic and foreign markets for agricultural products.

Adequate compensation for workers during demobilization.

The enactment of such additional humanitarian, labor, social and farm legislation as time and experience may require, including the amendment or repeal of any law enacted in recent years which has failed to accomplish its purpose.

Promotion of the success of small business.

Earliest possible release of wartime controls.

Adaptation of tax laws to an expanding peacetime economy, with simplified structure and wartime taxes reduced or repealed as soon as possible.

Encouragement of risk capital, new enterprise, development of natural resources in the West and other parts of the country, and the immediate reopening of the gold and silver mines of the West as soon as manpower is available.

We reassert our faith in competitive private enterprise, free from control by monopolies, cartels, or any arbitrary private or public authority.

We assert that mankind believes in the Four Freedoms.

We believe that the country which has the greatest measure of social justice is capable of the greatest achievements.

We believe that racial and religious minorities have the right to live, develop and vote equally with all citizens and share the rights that are guaranteed by our Constitution. Congress should exert its full constitutional powers to protect those rights.

We believe that without loss of sovereignty, world development and lasting peace are within humanity's grasp. They will come with the greater enjoyment of those freedoms by the peoples of the world, and with the freer flow among them of ideas and goods.

We believe in the world right of all men to write, send and publish news at uniform communication rates and without interference by governmental or private monopoly and that right should be protected by treaty.

To these beliefs the Democratic Party subscribes.

These principles the Democratic Party pledges itself in solemn sincerity to maintain.

Finally, this Convention sends its affectionate greetings to our beloved and matchless leader and President, Franklin Delano Roosevelt.

He stands before the nation and the world, the champion of human liberty and dignity. He has rescued our people from the ravages of economic disaster. His rare foresight and magnificent courage have saved our nation from the assault of international brigands and dictators. Fulfilling the ardent hope of his life, he has already laid the foundation of enduring peace for a troubled world and the well being of our nation. All mankind is his debtor. His life and services have been a great blessing to humanity.

That God may keep him strong in body and in spirit to carry on his yet unfinished work is our hope and our prayer.

Prohibition Party Platform of 1944

PREAMBLE

We, the representatives of the Prohibition Party in National Convention at Indianapolis, Indiana, November 10, 11, 12, 1943, recognizing Almighty God as the source of all just Government and with faith in the teachings of the Prince of Peace, do solemnly promise that if chosen to administer the affairs of the nation, we will use all the power placed in our hands to serve the people of the United States, and that we will hold their interests above those of ourselves and our party. To do this requires the effective carrying out of the following program of Government.

A CONSTITUTIONAL PARTY

Pledge of Loyalty:

In this time of our national crises we pledge our loyalty to the Constitutional Government of the United States, to our flag and to the Republic for which it stands. We have supreme confidence in this basic law of the United States to meet ever-changing national and world conditions. Believing this, we are utterly opposed to the violation of the Bill of Rights, and to the rapidly growing tendency toward totalitarian Government in the United States.

State Rights:

We will confine the power of the executive department of the Government within the limits provided by the Constitution, will decentralize the national administration and restore to the several states their constitutional place in Government.

The support of state government in all its constitutional rights is the current bulwark against tyranny and dictatorship. We condemn the present administration for its extreme concentration in Washington of control over minor affairs.

Abolition of Bureaucracy:

We will do away with all bureaucratic devices with overlapping functions which are causing enormous waste of public funds and manpower, and will conduct Government by means of constitutional methods.

No administrative board or agency should be at the same time accuser, jury, judge and hangman. Departmental decisions ought not to be final. All decisions of administrative boards or agencies should be reviewable by our courts to preserve our liberties.

Law Enforcement:

We will maintain the integrity of democracy by enforcing the laws enacted by elected representatives of the people or by popular vote.

Money:

We believe that the Constitutional provision for the issuance of money and determination of the value thereof is a sound and feasible monetary policy.

Taxes and Government Economy:

We pledge a reduction in taxes. We condemn most vigorously the administration's extravagance and maladministration of Government funds since long before the War. We stand for radical reduction in Government expenditures. In the States we favor the effort to limit the tax rate to one percent of full value of property, in order to prevent foreclosure and confiscation, and assist the home owner, farmer, real estate owner, and others to preserve their property. But there can be no reduction in taxes unless we abolish the present increasingly expensive paternalistic bureaucracy.

Ballot Law Reform:

We demand the repeal of the many state ballot laws which have been enacted to make the two-party system impregnable, and which now deny to independent voters and minority groups the fundamental right of free political expression.

Moral Issues Supreme:

Moral and spiritual considerations, as well as economic should determine national policies. Therefore, we pledge to give them first place. To this end we will strengthen and enforce laws against gambling, narcotics, and commercialized vice now so openly violated and nullified by inaction of the parties in power.

Prevent Juvenile Delinquency:

In the interests of the moral well-being of children, youth, and the public, we urge the necessity of higher standards of decency in the enactment and enforcement of laws concerning the radio, moving pictures, literature and the stage. Since the motion pictures and the radio

have become such powerful factors in the character formation of our youth, we pledge that all public officials concerned will enforce adequate laws to prevent obscenity, profanity and education tending to crime as now current in movie and radio. As a fundamental protection for youth, we will strengthen the teaching of moral precepts in the public schools and will establish and effectively enforce in the public school system scientific education on alcohol and other narcotics.

A Party of Service, Not Spoils:

The two dominant parties are committed to the spoils system and when in office have prostituted governmental power to serve their own selfish party interests instead of the whole people. That system has led to excessive government expenditures, higher taxes, and a scandalous alliance of crime with politics. We pledge ourselves to an honest, efficient and economical administration.

Social Security and Old Age Pensions:

We will extend the Social Security Act so as not to exclude any groups from its provisions, and will include a system of insurance for all aged persons, and administer it so as to preserve the incentives of initiative and thrift.

Co-operatives:

Co-operative and profit sharing enterprises are a natural outgrowth of democracy. Government under our administration will encourage such enterprises.

Labor and Capital:

We commend organized labor for its constructive contributions to the general welfare, but steps should be taken to protect labor unions from invasion and exploitation by racketeers. We would require unions to keep their records open to members and to government inspection and to file periodic financial reports, the same as corporations.

Because we stand for Industrial Peace and National Security, we believe the time has come for the Government to assume responsibility for the protection of itself and the public against the waste and terror of industrial warfare, and to that end we will enact and enforce legislation granting and defining the rights of labor to bargain individually or collectively, to negotiate, arbitrate and to establish courts of industrial relations as the final tribunal for all industrial disputes, which will seek for both labor and employing capital equal justice, and to the nation and the general public protection against the paralysis of industry due to their warfare.

Presidential Term:

American traditions will best be served by limiting the presidential office to a single term of six years.

Church and State:

The Constitutional separation of Church and State must be maintained. We will not tax church or religious activities. This, however, should not exempt individuals engaged in religious work who, as citizens, are subject to taxation.

Crime:

We seek to diminish crime, first by suppressing the traffic in alcoholic beverages and other narcotics which pervert the people; second, by bringing about a realignment of politics which shall unite the moral-minded citizens and overcome the alliance of the underworld with the political machines; third, by effective enforcement of the law; and, fourth, by the general adoption of those systems of judicial procedure which have proved most efficient and progressive.

Monopoly:

Monopolies have not ceased to exist but have become an increasing public evil. Government under our administration, in order to safeguard the rights of the common citizen, will be alert to prevent combinations of trade or of wealth which would monopolize any branch of industry or our natural resources.

No Racial Discrimination:

Recognizing that "God created of one blood all nations to dwell upon the face of the earth," we declare in favor of full justice and equal opportunity for all people, whatever their religion; racial or national origin.

Agriculture:

Believing that more people should be attracted to agriculture we favor an equitable, stable price structure for farm products. We will develop a sound program for the maintenance of individual ownership of farms.

Marriage and Divorce:

To maintain the sanctity of the home we favor the enactment of uniform marriage and divorce laws.

Freedom in Fact:

It is falsely said we should not criticize the administration in time of War. "We do not need less criticism in time of War, but more. It is to be hoped such criticism will be constructive, but better unfair attack than autocratic repression. HONESTY AND COMPETENCE REQUIRE NO SHIELD OF SECRECY," nor need fear criticism, dishonesty and fraud. Those who would usurp our rights while paying lip service to our ideals should not be shielded from it.

Domestic Post-War Problems:

The nation must accept responsibility for an adequate national program to provide opportunity for employment in suitable and satisfactory occupations not only for all men and women in the military service but also those civilians who have been employed in discontinued war industries. This program should provide special training for the disabled and unskilled. We pledge ourselves to utilize the services of public-spirited men and women representing labor, industry, and the general public, to join in a thorough-going honest effort to work out a solution of this complex problem.

World Co-operation:

Recognizing the supreme challenge and opportunity which confronts America to help secure a more just and permanent peace following this War, we insist upon preparation for that responsibility by setting up righteous standards which will guarantee to all people more equal opportunities and the rights to life, liberty, and the pursuit of happiness. To this end we advocate constructive co-operation and collaboration with all nations in some form of world organization but military alliance with none.

True Use of the Ballot:

We pledge our support to the original purpose of the ballot, which is to register the individual voter's conviction on principle, and not merely to elect persons to office. We recognize church leaders, pastors, church officials, members and editors of Christian literature as very influential on behalf of higher standards of political action, and we urge them to recognize and teach the true use of the ballot for principle. We urge them to unite in this party, which upholds righteousness as implied in the Ten Great Commandments and the Golden Rule.

The Liquor Problem:

Right thinking people are alarmed at the rapidly growing peril of the liquor power as now manifested:

1. Inflicting the alcoholic appetite upon millions of girls and women.
2. In multiplying juvenile delinquency.
3. In increasing gambling, vice and all kinds of crime.
4. In combating the efforts of the church and other moral forces.
5. In dominating our great organs of public opinion.
6. In subjecting political leaders and parties to its control.
7. In delaying, if not endangering, the success of our war effort.

The re-legalizing of the liquor traffic has brought about the worst moral reaction of modern times. Present conditions are due directly to the action of Government in restoring the liquor power through repeal of the Eighteenth Amendment, and repeal was due directly to the platform pledges of both the old parties in the 1932 presidential campaign.

Of all the wrongs committed by Government none has been worse than the authorizing of the liquor traffic to degenerate our own citizenship.

There is no higher duty of Government than to overcome the forces of evil. This cannot be done by political parties who are subservient to liquor votes. Parties dependent upon wet support are incapable of furnishing a solution.

We urge the realignment of voters and the union of good citizens in a political party not dependent upon the liquor traffic for votes. The Prohibition Party is that party.

A political party committed to prohibition (as a party principle) is the only adequate method for marshalling the agencies of Government to overcome the liquor power.

We urge all good citizens who believe in these principles, to cast their votes for them by supporting with their ballots this progressive program of government.

Republican Platform for 1944

INTRODUCTION

The tragedy of the war is upon our country as we meet to consider the problems of government and our people. We take this opportunity to render homage and enduring gratitude to those brave members of our armed forces who have already made the supreme sacrifice, and to those who stand ready to make the same sacrifice that the American course of life may be secure.

Mindful of this solemn hour and humbly conscious of our heavy responsibilities, the Republican Party in convention assembled presents herewith its principles and makes these covenants with the people of our Nation.

THE WAR AND THE PEACE

We pledge prosecution of the war to total victory against our enemies in full cooperation with the United Nations and all-out support of our Armies and the maintenance of our Navy under the competent and trained direction of our General Staff and Office of Naval Operations without civilian interference and with every civilian resource. At the earliest possible time after the cessation of hostilities we will bring home all members of our armed forces who do not have unexpired enlistments and who do not volunteer for further overseas duty.

We declare our relentless aim to win the war against all our enemies: (1) for our own American security and welfare; (2) to make and keep the Axis powers impotent to renew tyranny and attack; (3) for the attainment of peace and freedom based on justice and security.

We shall seek to achieve such aims through organized international cooperation and not by joining a World State.

We favor responsible participation by the United States in post-war cooperative organization among sovereign nations to prevent military aggression and to attain permanent peace with organized justice in a free world.

Such organization should develop effective cooperative means to direct peace forces to prevent or repel military aggression. Pending this, we pledge continuing collaboration with the United Nations to assure these ultimate objectives.

We believe, however, that peace and security do not depend upon the sanction of force alone, but should prevail by virtue of reciprocal interests and spiritual values recognized in these security agreements. The treaties of peace should be just; the nations which are the victims of aggression should be restored to sovereignty and self-government; and the organized cooperation of the nations should concern itself with basic causes of world disorder. It should promote a world opinion to influence the nations to right conduct, develop international law and maintain an international tribunal to deal with justiciable disputes.

We shall seek, in our relations with other nations, conditions calculated to promote world-wide economic stability, not only for the sake of the world, but also to the end that our own people may enjoy a high level of employment in an increasingly prosperous world.

We shall keep the American people informed concerning all agreements with foreign nations. In all of these undertakings we favor the widest consultation of the gallant men and women in our armed forces who have a special right to speak with authority in behalf of the security and liberty for which they fight. We shall sustain the Constitution of the United States in the attainment of our international aims; and pursuant to the Constitution of the United States any treaty or agreement to attain such aims made on behalf of the United States with any other nation or any association of nations, shall be made only by and with the advice and consent of the Senate of the United States provided two-thirds of the Senators present concur.

We shall at all times protect the essential interests and resources of the United States.

Western Hemisphere Relations

We shall develop Pan-American solidarity. The citizens of our neighboring nations in the Western Hemisphere are, like ourselves, Americans. Cooperation with them shall be achieved through mutual agreement and without interference in the internal affairs of any nation. Our policy should be a genuine Good Neighbor policy, commanding their respect, and not one based on the reckless squandering of American funds by overlapping agencies.

Postwar Preparedness

We favor the maintenance of postwar military forces and establishments of ample strength for the successful defense and the safety of the United States, its possessions and outposts, for the maintenance of the Monroe Doctrine, and for meeting any military commitments determined by Congress. We favor the peacetime maintenance and strengthening of the National Guards under State control with the Federal training and equipment as now provided in the National Defense Act.

Domestic Policy

We shall devote ourselves to re-establishing liberty at home.

We shall adopt a program to put men to work in peace industry as promptly as possible and with special attention to those who have made sacrifice by serving in the armed forces. We shall take government out of competition with private industry and terminate rationing, price fixing and all other emergency powers. We shall promote the fullest stable employment through private enterprise.

The measures we propose shall avoid federalization of government activities, to the end that our States, schools and cities shall be freed; shall avoid delegation of legislative and judicial power to administrative agencies, to the end that the people's representatives in Congress shall be independent and in full control of legislative policy; and shall avoid, subject to war necessities, detailed regulation of farmers, workers, businessmen and consumers, to the end that the individual shall be free. The remedies we propose shall be based on intelligent cooperation between the Federal Government, the States and local government and the initiative of civic groups—not on the panacea of Federal cash.

Four more years of New Deal policy would centralize all power in the President, and would daily subject every act of every citizen to regulation by his henchmen; and this country could remain a Republic only in name. No problem exists which cannot be solved by American methods. We have no need of either the communistic or the fascist technique.

Security

Our goal is to prevent hardship and poverty in America. That goal is attainable by reason of the productive ability of free American labor, industry and agriculture, if supplemented by a system of social security on sound principles.

We pledge our support of the following:

1. Extension of the existing old-age insurance and unemployment insurance systems to all employees not already covered.

2. The return of the public employment-office system to the States at the earliest possible time, financed as before Pearl Harbor.

3. A careful study of Federal-State programs for maternal and child health, dependent children, and assistance to the blind, with a view to strengthening these programs.

4. The continuation of these and other programs relating to health, and the stimulation by Federal aid of State plans to make medical and hospital service available to those in need without disturbing doctor-patient relationships or socializing medicine.

5. The stimulation of State and local plans to provide decent low-cost housing properly financed by the Federal Housing Administration, or otherwise, when such housing cannot be supplied or financed by private sources.

LABOR

The Republican Party is the historical champion of free labor. Under Republican administrations American manufacturing developed, and American workers attained the most progressive standards of living of any workers in the world. Now the Nation owes those workers a debt of gratitude for their magnificent productive effort in support of the war.

Regardless of the professed friendship of the New Deal for the workingman, the fact remains that under the New Deal American economic life is being destroyed.

The New Deal has usurped selfish and partisan control over the functions of Government agencies where labor relationships are concerned. The continued perversion of the Wagner Act by the New Deal menaces the purposes of the law and threatens to destroy collective bargaining completely and permanently.

The long series of Executive orders and bureaucratic decrees reveal a deliberate purpose to substitute for contractual agreements of employers and employees the political edicts of a New Deal bureaucracy. Labor would thus remain organized only for the convenience of the New Deal in enforcing its orders and inflicting its whims upon labor and industry.

We condemn the conversion of administrative boards, ostensibly set up to settle industrial disputes, into instruments for putting into effect the financial and economic theories of the New Deal.

We condemn the freezing of wage rates at arbitrary levels and the binding of men to their jobs as destructive to the advancement of a free people. We condemn the repeal by Executive order of the laws secured by the Republican party to abolish "contract labor" and peonage. We condemn the gradual but effective creation of a Labor Front as but one of the New Deal's steps toward a totalitarian state.

We pledge an end to political trickery in the administration of labor laws and the handling of labor disputes; and equal benefits on the basis of equality to all labor in the administration of labor controls and laws, regardless of political affiliation.

The Department of Labor has been emasculated by the New Deal. Labor bureaus, agencies and committees are scattered far and wide, in Washington and throughout the country, and have no semblance of systematic or responsible organization. All governmental labor activities must be placed under the direct authority and responsibility of the Secretary of Labor. Such labor bureaus as are not performing a substantial and definite service in the interest of labor must be abolished.

The Secretary of Labor should be a representative of labor. The office of the Secretary of Labor was created under a Republican President, William Howard Taft. It was intended that a representative of labor should occupy this Cabinet office. The present administration is the first to disregard this intention.

The Republican Party accepts the purposes of the National Labor Relations Act, the Wage and Hour Act, the Social Security Act and all other Federal statutes designed to promote and protect the welfare of American working men and women, and we promise a fair and just administration of these laws.

American well-being is indivisible. Any national program which injures the national economy inevitably injures the wage-earner. The American labor movement and the Republican Party, while continuously striving for the betterment of labor's status, reject the communistic and New Deal concept that a single group can benefit while the general economy suffers.

AGRICULTURE

We commend the American farmers, their wives and families for their magnificent job of wartime production and their contribution to the war effort, without which victory could not be assured. They have accomplished this in spite of labor shortages, a bungled and inexcusable machinery program and confused, unreliable, impractical price and production administration.

Abundant production is the best security against inflation. Governmental policies in war and in peace must be practical and efficient with freedom from regimentation by an impractical Washington bureaucracy in order to assure independence of operation and bountiful production, fair and equitable market prices for farm products, and a sound program for conservation and use of our soil and natural resources. Educational progress and the social and economic stability and well-being of the farm family must be a prime national purpose.

For the establishment of such a program we propose the following:

1. A Department of Agriculture under practical and experienced administration, free from regimentation and confusing government manipulation and control of farm programs.

2. An American market price to the American farmer and the protection of such price by means of support prices, commodity loans, or a combination thereof, together with such other economic means as will assure an income to agriculture that is fair and equitable in comparison with labor, business and industry. We oppose subsidies as a substitute for fair markets.

3. Disposition of surplus war commodities in an orderly manner without destroying markets or continued production and without benefit to speculative profiteers.

4. The control and disposition of future surpluses by means of (a) new uses developed through constant research, (b) vigorous development of foreign markets, (c) efficient domestic distribution to meet all domestic requirements, and (d) arrangements which will enable farmers to make necessary adjustments in production of any given basic crop only if domestic surpluses should become abnormal and exceed manageable proportions.

5. Intensified research to discover new crops, and new and profitable uses for existing crops.

6. Support of the principle of bona fide farmer-owned and farmer-operated cooperatives.

7. Consolidation of all government farm credit under a non-partisan board.

8. To make life more attractive on the family type farm through development of rural roads, sound extension of rural electrification service to the farm and elimination of basic evils of tenancy wherever they exist.

9. Serious study of and search for a sound program of crop insurance with emphasis upon establishing a self-supporting program.

10. A comprehensive program of soil, forest, water and wildlife conservation and development, and sound irrigation projects, administered as far as possible at State and regional levels.

BUSINESS AND INDUSTRY

We give assurance now to restore peacetime industry at the earliest possible time, using every care to avoid discrimination between different sections of the country, (a) by prompt settlement of war contracts with early payment of government obligations and disposal of surplus inventories, and (b) by disposal of surplus government plants, equipment, and supplies, with due consideration to small buyers and with care to prevent monopoly and injury to existing agriculture and industry.

Small business is the basis of American enterprise. It must be preserved. If protected against discrimination and afforded equality of opportunity throughout the Nation, it will become the most potent factor in providing employment. It must also be aided by changes in taxation, by eliminating excessive and repressive regulation and government competition, by the enforcement of laws against monopoly and unfair competition, and by providing simpler and cheaper methods for obtaining venture capital necessary for growth and expansion.

For the protection of the public, and for the security of millions of holders of policies of insurance in mutual and private companies, we insist upon strict and exclusive regulation and supervision of the business of insurance by the several States where local conditions are best known and where local needs can best be met.

We favor the re-establishment and maintenance, as early as military considerations will permit, of a sound and adequate American Merchant Marine under private ownership and management.

The Republican Party pledges itself to foster the development of such strong privately owned air transportation systems and communications systems as will best serve the interests of the American people.

The Federal Government should plan a program for flood control, inland waterways and other economically justifiable public works, and prepare the necessary plans in advance so that construction may proceed rapidly in emergency and in times of reduced employment. We urge that States and local governments pursue the same policy with reference to highways and other public works within their jurisdiction.

TAXATION AND FINANCE

As soon as the war ends the present rates of taxation on individual incomes, on corporations, and on consumption should be reduced as far as is consistent with the payment of the normal expenditures of government in the postwar period. We reject the theory of restoring prosperity through government spending and deficit financing.

We shall eliminate from the budget all wasteful and unnecessary expenditures and exercise the most rigid economy.

It is essential that Federal and State tax structures be more effectively coordinated to the end that State tax sources be not unduly impaired.

We shall maintain the value of the American dollar and regard the payment of government debt as an obligation of honor which prohibits any policy leading to the depreciation of the currency. We shall reduce that debt as soon as economic conditions make such reduction possible.

Control of the currency must be restored to Congress by repeal of existing legislation which gives the President unnecessary powers over our currency.

FOREIGN TRADE

We assure American farmers, livestock producers, workers and industry that we will establish and maintain a fair protective tariff on competitive products so that the standards of living of our people shall not be impaired through the importation of commodities produced abroad by labor or producers functioning upon lower standards than our own.

If the postwar world is to be properly organized, a great extension of world trade will be necessary to repair the wastes of war and build an enduring peace. The Republican Party, always remembering that its primary obligation, which must be fulfilled, is to our own workers, our own farmers and our own industry, pledges that it will join with others in leadership in every cooperative effort to remove unnecessary and destructive barriers to international trade. We will always bear in mind that the domestic market is America's greatest market and that tariffs which protect it against foreign competition should be modified only by reciprocal bilateral trade agreements approved by Congress.

RELIEF AND REHABILITATION

We favor the prompt extension of relief and emergency assistance to the peoples of the liberated countries without duplication and conflict between government agencies.

We favor immediate feeding of the starving children of our Allies and friends in the Nazi-dominated countries and we condemn the New Deal administration for its failure, in the face of humanitarian demands, to make any effort to do this.

We favor assistance by direct credits in reasonable amounts to liberated countries to enable them to buy from this country the goods necessary to revive their economic systems.

BUREAUCRACY

The National Administration has become a sprawling, overlapping bureaucracy. It is undermined by executive abuse of power, confused lines of authority, duplication of effort, inadequate fiscal controls, loose personnel practices and an attitude of arrogance previously unknown in our history.

The times cry out for the restoration of harmony in government, for a balance of legislative and executive responsibility, for efficiency and economy, for pruning and abolishing unnecessary agencies and personnel, for effective fiscal and personnel controls, and for an entirely new spirit in our Federal Government.

We pledge an administration wherein the President, acting in harmony with Congress, will effect these necessary reforms and raise the Federal

412   NATIONAL PARTY PLATFORMS

service to a high level of efficiency and competence.

We insist that limitations must be placed upon spending by government corporations of vast sums never appropriated by Congress but made available by directives, and that their accounts should be subject to audit by the General Accounting Office.

Two-Term Limit for President

We favor an amendment to the Constitution providing that no person shall be President of the United States for more than two terms of four years each.

Equal Rights

We favor submission by Congress to the States of an amendment to the Constitution providing for equal rights for men and women. We favor job opportunities in the postwar world open to men and women alike without discrimination in rate of pay because of sex.

Veterans

The Republican Party has always supported suitable measures to reflect the Nation's gratitude and to discharge its duty toward the veterans of all wars.

We approve, have supported and have aided in the enactment of laws which provide for re-employment of veterans of this war in their old positions, for mustering-out-pay, for pensions for widows and orphans of such veterans killed or disabled, for rehabilitation of disabled veterans, for temporary unemployment benefits, for education and vocational training, and for assisting veterans in acquiring homes and farms and in establishing themselves in business.

We shall be diligent in remedying defects in veterans' legislation and shall insist upon efficient administration of all measures for the veteran's benefit.

Racial and Religious Intolerance

We unreservedly condemn the injection into American life of appeals to racial or religious prejudice.

We pledge an immediate Congressional inquiry to ascertain the extent to which mistreatment, segregation and discrimination against Negroes who are in our armed forces are impairing morale

and efficiency, and the adoption of corrective legislation.

We pledge the establishment by Federal legislation of a permanent Fair Employment Practice Commission.

Anti-Poll Tax

The payment of any poll tax should not be a condition of voting in Federal elections and we favor immediate submission of a Constitutional amendment for its abolition.

Anti-Lynching

We favor legislation against lynching and pledge our sincere efforts in behalf of its early enactment.

Indians

We pledge an immediate, just and final settlement of all Indian claims between the Government and the Indian citizenship of the Nation. We will take politics out of the administration of Indian affairs.

Problems of the West

We favor a comprehensive program of reclamation projects for our arid and semi-arid States, with recognition and full protection of the rights and interests of those States in the use and control of water for present and future irrigation and other beneficial consumptive uses.

We favor (a) exclusion from this country of livestock and fresh and chilled meat from countries harboring foot and mouth disease or Rinderpest; (b) full protection of our fisheries whether by domestic regulation or treaties; (c) consistent with military needs, the prompt return to private ownership of lands acquired for war purposes; (d) withdrawal or acquisition of lands for establishment of national parks, monuments, and wildlife refuges, only after due regard to local problems and under closer controls to be established by the Congress; (e) restoration of the long established public land policy which provides opportunity of ownership by citizens to promote the highest land use; (f) full development of our forests on the basis of cropping and sustained yield; cooperation with private owners for conservation and fire protection; (g) the prompt reopening of mines which can be operated by miners and workers not subject to military service and which have been closed by bureaucratic denial of labor or material; (h) adequate stockpiling of war minerals and metals for possible future emergencies; (i) continuance, for tax purposes, of adequate depletion allowances on oil, gas and minerals; (j) administration of laws relating to oil and gas on the public domain to encourage exploratory operations to meet the public need; (k) continuance of present Federal laws on mining claims on the public domain, good faith administration thereof, and we state our opposition to the plans of the Secretary of the Interior to substitute a leasing system; and (l) larger representation in the Federal Government of men and women especially familiar with Western problems.

HAWAII

Hawaii, which shares the Nation's obligations equally with the several States, is entitled to the fullest measure of home rule looking toward statehood; and to equality with the several States in the rights of her citizens and in the application of all our national laws.

ALASKA

Alaska is entitled to the fullest measure of home rule looking toward statehood.

PUERTO RICO

Statehood is a logical aspiration of the people of Puerto Rico who were made citizens of the United States by Congress in 1917; legislation affecting Puerto Rico, in so far as feasible, should be in harmony with the realization of that aspiration.

PALESTINE

In order to give refuge to millions of distressed Jewish men, women and children driven from their homes by tyranny, we call for the opening of Palestine to their unrestricted immigration and land ownership, so that in accordance with the full intent and purpose of the Balfour Declaration of 1917 and the Resolution of a Republican Congress in 1922, Palestine may be constituted as a free and democratic Commonwealth. We condemn the failure of the President to insist that the mandatory of Palestine carry out the provision of the Balfour Declaration and of the mandate while he pretends to support them.

FREE PRESS AND RADIO

In times like these, when whole peoples have found themselves shackled by governments which denied the truth, or, worse, dealt in half-truths or withheld the facts from the public, it is imperative to the maintenance of a free America that the press and radio be free and that full and complete information be available to Americans. There must be no censorship except to the extent required by war necessity.

We insistently condemn any tendency to regard the press or the radio as instruments of the Administration and the use of government publicity agencies for partisan ends. We need a new radio law which will define, in clear and unmistakable language, the role of the Federal Communications Commission.

All channels of news must be kept open with equality of access to information at the source. If agreement can be achieved with foreign nations to establish the same principles, it will be a valuable contribution to future peace.

Vital facts must not be withheld.

We want no more Pearl Harbor reports.

GOOD FAITH

The acceptance of the nominations made by this Convention carries with it, as a matter of private honor and public faith, an undertaking by each candidate to be true to the principles and program herein set forth.

CONCLUSION

The essential question at trial in this nation is whether men can organize together in a highly industrialized society, succeed, and still be free. That is the essential question at trial throughout the world today.

In this time of confusion and strife, when moral values are being crushed on every side, we pledge ourselves to uphold with all our strength the Bill of Rights, the Constitution and the law of the land. We so pledge ourselves that the American tradition may stand forever as the beacon light of civilization.

Socialist Platform of 1944

FREEDOM FOR ALL

In their struggle for freedom, peace and plenty,

the American people face four paramount and closely interrelated issues: (1) the winning of the earliest possible peace that will last; (2) the provision of economic security for every American, with the preservation and increase of liberty; (3) the establishment of fraternity among all races, with equality of rights and obligations; (4) the improvement of the techniques of democratic political action.

On this platform for dealing with these issues, the Socialist Party, confident that the development of a strong party with mass support is essential to the struggle against fascism and the winning of the kind of world we want, seeks the support of the American people.

1. WINNING OF THE PEACE

The winning of the peace cannot be the result of appeasement of Nazism or of any other aggressive imperialisms.

Neither can it be the consequence of the "unconditional surrender" of the Germans and Japanese to the rulers of the USSR, Great Britain and the United States of America. Shouting that slogan the Roosevelt administration is prolonging this war and inviting the next by underwriting with the lives of our sons the restoration and maintenance of the British, Dutch and French empires in the Far East, and the Balkanization of Europe between Moscow and London.

Averting New Wars

New war will not be averted by a triple alliance of the major powers—with China as a "poor relation"—even though such an alliance with its already obvious rivalries may be masked behind a plan for a vague association of nations. Yet this is the pattern for the future which most Republican as well as Democratic leaders accept.

The alternative to an uneasy and impermanent triple alliance for policing and exploiting the world is not an America first or isolationist imperialism equally dangerous to democracy and peace. But toward one or the other of these forms of imperialism and the fascism which accompanies it the policies of both old parties inexorably lead us.

Against so dire a fate, we summon the American people and the people of our allies to demand an immediate political peace offensive based on the offer of an armistice to the people of the Axis nations on the following conditions:

Conditions for Peace

1. The peace should be organized on the acceptance of two fundamental principles: (a) the equal rights of all peoples of every race to order their lives without subjection to any race or nation; (b) the necessity that self-determination be accompanied by organized co-operation, from which no people, enemy, neutral or colonial, shall be excluded, and the establishment of political and economic arrangements for removing the causes of war, settling disputes, guaranteeing security and conquering poverty.

2. As a guarantee of good faith and a condition of armistice, the German and Japanese people must: (a) replace governments guilty of gross deceit and cruel aggression by governments in whose good faith reasonable confidence may be reposed; (b) withdraw their military forces from all occupied territory and rapidly disarm; and (c) wherever possible, restore loot and give refugees a new economic start.

3. The United Nations, on their part, must pledge themselves specifically (a) to free the European nations overrun by Germany; (b) to help them guarantee their independence through a United States of Europe or strong regional federations to supplement a world federation; (c) to refrain from interference in the internal affairs of nations thus freed; (d) to extend material aid for immediate relief and reconstruction of devastated countries without using such aid as a weapon for political domination; (e) to reject all demands for Axis slave labor in the postwar world; (f) to decide boundary questions which do not yield to negotiation by plebiscite under international authority; (g) to turn away from imperialism by guaranteeing speedy self-government, not only to lands now occupied by Japan, but to colonial territories under white rule. Where guidance to such independence is necessary, it shall be under international authority.

4. As a guarantee of good faith and a condition of the success of any federation, the United Nations must pledge themselves after the establishment of peace to follow the disarmament of the enemy countries by ending their own competitive armaments and military conscription and working out international guarantees of mutual security.

These points together comprise a peace offensive capable of inspiring revolt against the Axis dictators, winning the confidence of their victims and saving thousands of American lives.

2. ECONOMIC SECURITY WITH LIBERTY

The people of America fear the joblessness and depression which they think that the great boon of peace will bring. They remember that on the eve of the war boom, 23% of them were dependent on made work or relief and 40% lived just on, or below, the level of proper subsistence in respect to food.

In spite of this fear, what can be done in war can be better and more democratically done in peace, but only if we will plan for plenty for all as we have planned to meet the insatiable appetites of the god of war.

Poverty and joblessness cannot be conquered by private capitalism under the false alias of "free enterprise," which is extolled today, ignorantly or hypocritically, by such diverse groups as the Republicans, the Democrats, the Communists, Wall Street monopolists, little business, farmers—and even labor leaders.

Planning for plenty is wholly incompatible with a return of the control over our great productive machinery to private owners—very largely absentee owners—while the government commits itself to overcome the periodic crisis of a scarcity economy by maintaining the unemployed at subsistence levels. This has been and is the economic program of the New Deal.

Socialists pioneered in the advocacy of social insurance. We favor its extension and improvement. We endorse all possible help to returning veterans. We demand that the new public domain —the war plants now owned by the government— be used in the struggle against unemployment and not handed over to big business.

But that is not enough. Only profound social and economic reorganization will enable men to use our marvelous technological resources for the complete conquest of poverty.

Democracy—Not Bureaucracy

The commanding heights of our economic order; our system of money, banking and credit; our natural resources; our public utilities and all monopolies, semi-monopolies, and other exploitive industries, must be socially controlled. To be effective that requires social ownership, but not autocratic administration by agents of a bureaucratic state. We do not need to exchange "government of the workers, by the bosses, for the profits of absentee owners" for "government of the workers, by the bureaucrats, for the glory and power of the military state."

Two forms of administration of socialized enterprise will go far to protect us against this danger: (1) public corporations operated for the people's benefit through directors representing consumers and the various categories of workers with hand and brain in each such industry; and (2) growth of consumers' co-operatives on the Rochdale Plan.

The democratic state can further play its part by the proper control of the fiscal system and by taxation based on the two principles of the ability to pay and the encouragement of production, both of which exclude the sales tax. A postwar tax program must not be used to support the big business system and hinder the growth of social enterprise. Taxes on the rental value of land should be used to end absentee landlordism; sharply graduated inheritance taxes should prevent the perpetuation of vast estates and a carefully proportioned capital levy tax should aid socialization. Such taxation will also be found necessary to prevent enormous and growing national debt from leading us into financial disaster.

As against exploitation by private owners or the state, the right of workers to organize and to bargain collectively must be restored and protected. We oppose in war or peace the conscription of labor and the outlawry of the right to strike. Free labor is essential to a free America.

There is no more essential function of labor than the raising of food and fibre. We pledge our support to all measures looking to the conservation of our soil and the production of abundance with adequate reward to American farmers. We pledge our aid to the working farmers against exploitation by absentee landlords, bankers and middlemen. We recognize the principle of occupancy and use as the only rightful title to farm land.

Where family farming has already been replaced by great plantations and company farms, or where modern technology forces large scale farming, we demand the social ownership and co-operative operation of such land plus the use of the most modern techniques and tools. Where conditions favor family farming we encourage the security of such farmers through cooperative credit, purchasing and marketing. We reject the compulsory collectivization of family farms along Russian lines.

We advocate the extension of social insurance to farm workers and provision of social security for farmers and farm workers displaced by age or technological changes. We advocate planning for full and balanced production of food and fibre in a hungry world. We advocate the further development of government agencies essential to carrying out these proposals, including the upbuilding of a Bureau of Cooperatives in the Department of Agriculture. We oppose the subversion—often the illegal subversion—of government agencies, especially the extension service of the Department of Agriculture, and agricultural colleges, to promote the profit and power of special interest groups now so dominant in the farm bloc.

3. Equality and Fraternity of Races

Democracy requires the application of the principle that each person is to be accorded social, political and economic equality, and judged solely on the basis of his own deeds, rather than by his race, religion, or national origin.

Specifically, we pledge ourselves to work for American hospitality to war refugees and the end of the exclusion of certain Asiatic peoples. The law applying to the Chinese the general provisions concerning immigration and admitting them to citizenship, should be extended to all Asiatic countries.

We demand the complete restoration of their rights as citizens to the 70,000 Americans of Japanese origin on the West Coast who were evacuated en masse, without trial or even hearing, and confined in centers which, however humanely run, are concentration camps.

We condemn anti-Semitism, Jim-Crowism, and every form of race discrimination and segregation in the armed forces as well as civil life. We urge the passage of anti-lynching and anti-poll tax laws and the prompt enactment of legislation to set up a permanent federal Fair Employment Practice Committee.

We reaffirm our historic opposition to any doctrine or practice of a master or favored race, not only in the realm of law, but in such labor unions —fortunately a minority—churches, political parties, and other basic social organizations as today countenance it. One of the conditions that will help make permanent the end of racial prejudice is the maintenance of full employment.

4. Democratic Political Action

Year after year, by law and custom, the two old parties tighten their monopoly of the ballot. They are divided by no principles, but only by tradition and desire for office. Their platforms consist of generalities which are designed to prevent intelligent discussion and clear decision of issues. In consequence, pressure groups are the principal effective agencies in legislation and a situation is created which will aid the rise of a fascist demagogue in a period of postwar reaction.

The situation cries aloud for a democratic socialist party with mass support, such as our Canadian neighbors have developed in their Cooperative Commonwealth Federation.

Labor in the United States must establish its independence of current governmental control if it is to bargain freely with employers and government. The interests of a free labor movement are going to be better served as it severs its connections with the old parties, and unites with farm and consumer groups and minority groups seeking justice, to build a new kind of political party.

The issues here discussed are basic; they affect the lives of us all and the destiny of America. They cannot be solved separately.

An America disgraced by racial tensions which occasionally find expression in lynchings and race riots cannot lead the way to a peace which depends upon worldwide reconciliation of races on the basis of equality of right.

An America which cannot or will not provide useful jobs for its own people will easily be led into militarism, imperialism, and new war itself as palliatives for unemployment.

An America which cannot or will not perfect the tools of democracy will be relatively defenseless against a rising fascism.

Platform of the Socialist Labor Party

Our society stands where the road forks. The signs are plainly marked.

One points to a continuation of capitalism. It leads to a postwar world of chronic economic crisis, of idle factories and idle men, of spreading anti-Semitism and racism, of fascist controls and Statism, and of perpetual struggle and war.

The other points to Socialism—a world of social ownership, democratic management of the industries, jobs and plenty for all, human brotherhood, and enduring peace.

The Socialist Labor Party of America, at its 21st National Convention in the City of New York, May 1, 1944, in placing its program for a Socialist reconstruction of society before the American workers, declares this to be the issue that confronts them: Either society moves onward and upward to peace and plenty via collective ownership of the industries, or it continues under the economic despotism of private property to a new dark age. There is no middle way.

The present global war—the greatest crisis ever to face civilized man—grew out of the prewar struggle among the capitalist powers for the markets and resources of the world. The chaos it has wrought is evidence of the breakdown of the capitalist system, of its inability to manage for the benefit of society the immensely productive machinery created under it.

Capitalism could not solve the problems besetting society before the war began; it cannot solve the immensely greater problems which will arise when the war ends.

For more than a decade prior to the outbreak of World War II the factories stood idle or operated part-time, while the army of unemployed workers numbered millions. The reason is self-evident. The capitalists, owning the instruments of production and using them to exploit the propertiless workers, could not find markets for labor's product. Only one "market" could absorb the abundant output of our fields and factories. That market is war.

What the New Deal failed to do—after spending billions of dollars in a vain attempt to prime the pump of business—war did. Production has soared to unprecedented heights. But note this: We *could* have produced just as much for peace in 1939 as we produce for war in 1944. We *could* have built new factories then, factories that would turn out just as many kitchen gadgets, automobiles, refrigerators, etc., as the shells, warplanes and guns our new plants are turning out today. We did not do this because the capitalists who own the factories and decide what shall be

produced, or shall not be produced, could not find markets for more than a fraction of labor's actual or potential product.

The capitalists could not find a market for labor's product before the war began; how can they sell the immensely greater product when the war ends? The capitalists themselves stand appalled before the magnitude of this problem. Their desperation is reflected in their preoccupation, in the very midst of war, with *postwar* markets and the *postwar* struggle for markets. The war has intensified and multiplied the problems confronting the capitalist class—it has, therefore, merely delayed, it has not averted, the collapse of capitalism.

The capitalist class turns more and more to the State as an agency to prolong its existence as the ruling class. Internationally the American capitalist State has become a huge cartel which utilizes the nation's military and economic might to the furtherance of capitalist aims. Domestically the State is called upon to control the forces unleashed by competitive capitalism—for the benefit of the capitalist proprietors. If private property remains the basis of society, and the capitalists are left in control of affairs, we may expect them to do precisely what the capitalists of Germany and Italy did when their rule was threatened—attempt to preserve dominion over the workers by putting totalitarian shackles upon them.

Signs of the capitalist reaction abound. The policy of dealing with fascists abroad is paralleled at home by the demand for fascist-pioneered controls over the workers—conscription of labor, for example, in open contempt of the Constitutional ban on involuntary servitude. Hardly less ominous are the demands to continue wartime controls into the postwar era, the establishment of permanent military conscription, the anti-strike laws, the creation of a huge State bureaucracy, and the spread of anti-Semitism and racism.

Anticipating unprecedented postwar unemployment and social unrest, the capitalist class and its reformer henchmen advance numerous schemes to appease the workers. Foremost among these are a vast postwar public works program and the extension of "social security"—a patent misnomer under a system which, by its very nature, dictates insecurity for the useful producers. From these proposals it is abundantly clear that what the capitalists envision is a condition of servility wherein the unemployed are held in reserve by the State in a huge public works reservoir.

Against this insane social system of capitalism, the Socialist Labor Party raises its voice in emphatic protest and unqualified condemnation, and calls upon the working class to organize politically and industrially to put an end to capitalism, and to establish the Socialist Industrial Commonwealth of Labor.

Socialism and Socialism alone is the hope of humanity! If the vast potentialities of this technological age are to be realized, capitalism must be destroyed. The industries and the land of the nation must become the collective property of society. Thus only can an end be put to unemployment, poverty, the scourge of racism and anti-Semitism, and the barbarity of war.

The Constitution of the United States provides for its own amendment. The Constitution thereby recognizes and legalizes revolution. The working class, the majority, holds the government in the hollow of its hand. We propose, accordingly, that the revolutionary change be effected by the peaceful and civilized means of the ballot.

In presenting the issue—the *only* issue, Socialism or Capitalism—and a program for its solution, the Socialist Labor Party stands alone. All other parties, whatever their names or claims, propose to reform and to preserve the criminal, and crime-breeding, capitalist system. Recognizing the simple truth that RIGHT without MIGHT to support it is useless and meaningless, we call upon the workers of America to organize themselves into integral Socialist Industrial Unions to enforce the demand for collective ownership proclaimed through the ballot. Such unions must be organized, for none now exist adequate to the great task, the existing unions—A. F. of L., C.I.O. and kindred bodies—being avowed supporters and agencies of the capitalist class and their despotic social system.

Organized along Socialist industrial lines, the working class can act instantaneously, and with such momentum that no power on earth can stop it. Only the thoroughly integrated Socialist Industrial Unions could block a brutal reaction should the outvoted, expropriated capitalists rebel against the ballot-box decision of the majority.

More than an invincible force behind Labor's ballot, the Socialist Industrial Union organizes the workers intelligently *to carry on production*, thus averting chaos. Finally, the Socialist Industrial Union becomes the *Government of the Socialist Republic*, supplanting the outworn and reactionary capitalist political State. *Democratically elected* representatives of the industrial constituencies will form an Industrial Union Congress, the duties of which will be the simple ones of directing and coordinating production for the benefit of all.

Workers of America! Repudiate the barbarous social system that exploits the mass of useful producers for the benefit of the few who merely own! Repudiate the political representatives of capitalism, be they Republican, Democratic, so-called "Socialist" or "Communist" or "Labor," who preach the criminal falsity that capitalism can be reformed and that it is worth reforming. Vote for the candidates of the Socialist Labor Party! Unite with us to demand the termination of the social system which dooms us to a lifelong tenure of wage slavery, with unemployment, poverty and wars as inseparable and ever recurrent features. Unite with us to establish the Socialist Brotherhood of Man, the Republic of Peace, Plenty and International Fraternity.

CAMPAIGN OF 1948

In 1948, a divided Democratic Party met in Philadelphia in July and, after much debate over civil rights and states rights, renominated the incumbent, Harry S. Truman. Alben W. Barkley, United States senator from Kentucky, was selected as his running mate. Many southern delegates at the convention refused to support Truman because of his civil rights program, and three days after the close of the Democratic convention a group of southern Democrats met in Birmingham, Alabama, to nominate candidates who would reflect their positions more accurately than the national ticket. This convention nominated Governor J. Strom Thurmond of South Carolina for president and Governor Fielding Wright of Mississippi for vice-president. This group, known as the States' Rights or "Dixiecrat" Party, lasted only one election.

The Republicans had met previously in Philadelphia and on the third ballot again nominated the 1944 standard-bearer, Governor Thomas E. Dewey of New York, over six competitors. Earl Warren, governor of California, accepted second place on the ticket.

A former vice-president, Henry A. Wallace of Iowa, ran for president on the Progressive Party ticket. Senator Glen Taylor of Idaho was his vice-presidential candidate. In addition, Norman Thomas of New York and Tucker P. Smith of Michigan ran as candidates for the Socialist Party; Claude Watson of California and Dale Learn of Pennsylvania made up the National Prohibition Party ticket; Farrell Dobbs of New York and Grace Carlson of Minnesota were Socialist Workers Party candidates; and Edward A. Teichert of Pennsylvania and Stephen Emery of New York ran on the Socialist Labor Party platform. 1948 was also the year in which Gerald L. K. Smith of Missouri made his first bid for the presidency as head of the Christian Nationalist Party. Henry A. Romer of Ohio was his running mate. The Communist Party issued a platform, but it did not nominate candidates.

In November, the Democrats obtained 24,105,587 popular votes—49.5 percent of the total—to 21,970,017 for the Republicans. The States' Rights or Dixiecrat Party polled 1,169,134 votes and the Progressives cast 1,157,057 for their candidate. The Socialists received 138,973; the Prohibitionists, 103,489; the Socialist Labor Party, 29,038; and the Socialist Workers, 13,614. Gerald L. K. Smith received 42 votes in California.

President Truman received 303 electoral votes to 189 for Governor Dewey. Governor Thurmond carried Alabama, Louisiana, and Mississippi, and received 1 electoral vote in Tennessee, for a total of 39.

The Platform of the Christian Nationalist Party, 1948

1. CHRISTIANITY

As a political party, we recognize the fact that only Christianity embraces the principle, the ethics and the spiritual dynamic fundamental to the establishment of a party equal to the present crisis.

We reassert the belief of our Founding Fathers that at all times the organic substance of the church and the organic substance of the state must be separate and distinct entities, but we hold the conviction that the righteousness of Christianity must characterize our social and political leadership if America is to survive.

All questions of dogma and doctrine are the responsibility of the organized church, but we boldly assert that the United States of America was founded as a Christian nation, dedicated to Christian principle. We believe that it is our duty to re-instate militant Christianity as a positive factor in the political, economic and national life of our country. We call all members of the Christian clergy to a realization of the fact that the same forces which crucified our Lord Jesus Christ are now attempting to crucify the civilization that grew from His teachings.

We believe that the Cross of Christ should stand beside the Stars and Stripes in the legislative halls, the schools and the courts of the land —"Lift high the Cross, unfurl the Flag; may they forever stand united in our hearts and hopes, God and our native land."

2. COMMUNISM

The Christian Nationalist Party recognizes the fog of materialism that is descending upon mankind as the greatest threat to continued existence of American liberty and American security. We further recognize the Internationalist Communist movement as one of the prime manifestations of satanic materialism. Having full knowledge that the aim of the Communist movement is to destroy Christianity and overrun America, we pledge ourselves to unending warfare against every phase and facet of atheistic Communism and dictatorial Marxism. It is our ambition to finally obliterate Communism from the face of the world.

It is well known that Communist forces first infiltrate, then weaken, that which they wish to destroy. They have infiltrated the "old" political parties and government offices of the United States. They have weakened the United States Government by instituting an economic program of state socialism; by a program of Communist appeasement in our foreign relations; by continuing to allow Communists to organize politically inside the United States. For the safeguarding of our country we demand that all members of the Communist Party, all members of Communist-front organizations, all supporters of Communism be removed from the Federal payrolls and from all positions in Government service.

J. Edgar Hoover, Director of the F. B. I., has stated that the backbone of the Communist Party in America is composed of aliens and foreign born. We, therefore, demand the immediate deportation of every alien who is a member of the Communist Party, a member of a Communist-front organization, or supporters of Communism.

Further, we believe that all persons naturalized within the past 15 years should have their citizenship applications re-examined for the purpose of deporting those persons who are members of the Communist Party, members of Communist-front organizations, or supporters of Communism.

For the purpose of declaring to the world our opposition to Communism; for the purpose of alerting the citizens of our country to the evil inherent in Communism; for the purpose of protecting the United States from the insidious destructiveness of Communism we demand the arrest of all members of the Communist Party as agents of a foreign power and the outlawing of the Communist Party in America as a conspiracy to overthrow the Constitution and the government of the United States.

3. THE JEW

The power of the Jew has become America's problem. His influence, brought about by the manipulation of minority votes, international and domestic finance, has created an intolerable situation in America. He has coerced and intimidated the old parties and all political parties to the point where no existing American political party dares challenge his authority. This circumstance is one of the chief fundamentals which make necessary the formation of the Christian Nationalist Party.

The Jew now exercises this authority and power in numerous ways contrary to natural sentiment, public good, Christian principle and American tradition.

Our indictment of the organized Jew grows out of numerous situations that have recently developed in our national life, including the following:

Political Zionism

An overwhelming majority of all Jews in America are obviously committed to political Zionism which calls for the establishment of a Jewish state. This commitment involves dual citizenship. We hold that these Jews cannot be loyal Americans and political Zionists at the same time. We believe that anyone claiming to be an American citizen and holding allegiance to a foreign state should be deported. Therefore, we call for the immediate deportation of all supporters of the political Zionist movement. We demand that this international political machine and all its activity be outlawed in the United States. We take this position in order that we may defend ourselves from an obvious plot to make the United States subservient to a Jewish state with international headquarters in Jerusalem.

Jewish Gestapo Organizations

The Jewish international state would destroy the independence of our nation. At the same time, the Jewish gestapo tends to destroy the peace and happiness and the liberty of the individual Christian American citizen. Jewish-operated, Jewish-controlled and Jewish-financed gestapo organizations now exist in America for the purpose of controlling, intimidating, coercing, punishing, boycotting and abusing in general individuals who hold the express frank and accurate opinions concerning the Jew.

Even beyond this, we find these organizations operating with unlimited sums of money in an attempt to discredit all men who are out-spoken in their defense of Christianity, of Nationalism and American tradition.

We call for the dissolution of such organizations as the so-called Anti-Defamation League, the American Jewish Congress, the so-called Non-Sectarian Anti-Nazi League, the self-styled Friends of Democracy and all other organizations that spy on, threaten, coerce and smear American citizens. These organizations are un-American in spirit and criminal in practice.

The Jew and Communism

We assert, and eventually all intelligent American citizens must admit, that behind Communism stands the organized Jew. It now becomes increasingly obvious that the power and support of the International Jewish cabal has been given to the various forms of Communism growing out of the teachings of the Jew, Karl Marx.

These powers of support have exercised themselves in numerous ways, including the following: Their journals have been used to make Communism seem good to our people. Their power in the realm of the radio and motion picture has been definitely exerted in support of the atheistic, Christ-hating philosophies of Marx and his disciples. Their financial, political and organizational power has brought Communism into the American home and American school and even into certain of the American churches. This power, exerted in defense of civilization's worst enemy, must be broken and it can only be broken by putting Christian Nationalists in control of the Government of the United States.

4. IMMIGRATION

All immigration of Asiatics, including Jews, and members of the colored races must be stopped by law.

We favor a program of constructive immigration which would include the Christian peoples of Europe, such as the Scandinavians, the Anglo-Saxons and the Germanic groups. These people and their types almost without exception become constructive citizens in the development of a Christian community and a Christian nation.

Millions of undesirables now reside within the borders of the United States who have entered this country illegally or have been admitted because of loosely-drawn and loosely-enforced immigration laws. These individuals furnish most of the membership of Marxist organizations and supply most of the destructive agitation now menacing our Nation. We advocate the deportation of these undesirables.

5. THE NEGRO

The enemies of America are missing no opportunity to organize and exploit the American Negro. This exploitation takes on three forms of abuse. The Communists would make the Negro a revolutionary backlog for an era of bloodshed and slaughter. The organized Jew is attempting to use the American Negro to break down the influence and power of the white man's leadership. Numerous Jewish pressure groups encourage intermarriage, mongrelization and social intermixture. The political demagogue is using the Negro vote in doubtful states as a pawn in his greed for power.

The Negro, without his knowledge, is being used to destroy the Nation that exposed him to Christian civilization. We condemn the original enslavement of the Negro. We brand it as a crime of which Northern and Southern interests were equally guilty. We must atone for that crime but not by the destruction of our Nation.

Therefore, the Christian Nationalist Party supports the Abraham Lincoln Plan for the Negro—a homeland in Africa. We believe that this homeland should be opened to all American Negroes and that $5,000 per family should be set aside for Negroes willing to migrate to this homeland where all public officials shall be Negroes and where only Negroes shall be eligible for office. We accept the philosophy of Abraham Lincoln expressed in his address to the free Negroes of Washington when he said: "You and we are a different race. We have between us a broader difference than exists between almost any other two races. It is better for us both, therefore, to be separated."

Segregation

In the light of the historic fact that the intermarriage of the black and white races invariably spells the destruction of a civilization, we Christian Nationals shall support an amendment to the Constitution of the United States which would require the segregation of the black and white races and which would outlaw intermarriage and make of same a Federal crime. Pending such a time as the American people can atone for the crime of slavery by the establishment of a Negro homeland, immediate steps must be taken to prevent the destruction of our Nation by mongrelization.

6. RELATIONSHIP TO OTHER NATIONS

We shall support constructive Nationalism wherever it exists. We shall support the doctrine of self-determination, intelligent self-interest and national pride wherever it exists. Our intercourse with these nations would rest upon the philosophy expounded by the father of our country, George Washington, who said: "Friendship with all nations; trade with all nations; entangling alliances with none."

The United Nations

The United Nations is a Jewish-Communist instrument for the destruction of the sovereignty of all nations. America should withdraw from it and lend its influence to its complete destruction. Steps must be taken to remove this embryonic superstate and its agencies from American soil.

Secret Commitment

We denounce, and demand the publication and repudiation of, all secret promises and agreements entered into by the late Franklin D. Roosevelt, Josef Stalin, their cohorts and advisors.

Bi-Partisan Plan

This is a betrayal of the American people. It is a conspiracy to end intelligent discussion and open debate on all matters pertaining to our relationship to other nations. This conspiracy of agreement made it possible for Internationalists to put over the Marshall Plan, UNRRA and the Truman doctrine without exposing the electorate to intelligent discussion and debate.

Marshall Plan

We favor a policy of encouraging the anti-Communist forces of the various European countries, and we favor extending humanitarian aid to all starving people. We condemn, however, the appeasement of the Socialist politicians who are thriving on the fear and hunger of Europe; we condemn the rank hypocrisy and graft of the "Marshall Plan"—whereby we are spending millions of dollars for liquor and tobacco, millions of dollars to repay Mussolini's debts to international financiers, millions of dollars to American newspapers and magazines—we condemn the treason that allowed export of American materials to the Communist dominated states of Europe. Money-wasting enterprises such as the Marshall Plan, designed to fatten the purses and the financial empires of international bankers must be ended.

Spain

We recognize the fact that Stalin, the International Jew and all Marxist forces have attempted to destroy the present Spanish Government. We recognize further that it has proved to be an uncompromising bulwark against Communist aggression. We advocate a development of friendly relations with this courageous people.

Germany

We favor the immediate and absolute end of the satanic Morgenthau policy of starving and enslaving the innocent women and children of Germany merely to satisfy the blood-lust of certain power-mad, sadistic, Christ-hating International Jews. We challenge the clergy and the Christian leadership of the world to help build a strong Christian Germany to help us contain the Communist beast, to prevent the invasion of Western Europe by the Red Army of Josef Stalin.

Russia

We recognize the fact that Russia is ruled by savages. It has no moral capacity to complete agreements or to fulfill treaties. It has fattened and become powerful through the exploitation of secret and pro-Russian commitments made by Franklin D. Roosevelt. We advocate that all diplomatic relations with the present Russian government be broken and that ways and means be devised for encouraging white Russians all over the world and anti-Communist Russians within Russia to rise and rebuild a Christian nation.

Palestine

The political Zionists in cooperation with the forces of Russia as well as by the favor and consent of President Truman, Thomas E. Dewey and others have driven 300,000 Arabs out of their homes and away from their own land where they now starve on the desert. We oppose this abortive state which the Jews named "the New Israel." We refuse to endorse this savage policy in its attempt to exploit the Christian's faith in the destiny of Jerusalem. We deny that it is in harmony with Christian teaching to steal land and slaughter innocents. This the Jews have done. We oppose the partition of Palestine. It is our conviction that it is a political Zionist plot for establishing headquarters for world control.

China

The Nationalists of China should be encouraged. We recognize the fact that were it not for the Nationalists of China, now led by General Chiang Kai-shek, Stalin could mobilize 400 million Chinese against the Christian world. We strongly urge the encouragement of Chiang Kai-shek on the sound basis of intelligent self-interest and constructive American Nationalism.

Japan, Korea, and Kindred Communities

Postwar policy in Japan should encourage all anti-communist forces and should be alert to all attempts being made by materialistic elements to exploit our victory to the disadvantage of Christianity and the best interests of America.

7. War Criminals

It is a matter of common knowledge that prior to and during World War II men high in office, including the late Franklin D. Roosevelt, committed crimes against our people which tax the imagination of even the most enlightened. The Pearl Harbor attack was precipitated. The Pearl Harbor investigation was a hypocritical whitewash. The Morgenthau Plan was a sadistic plot to liquidate 100 million Christians. Certain high officials, including the war-time President, actually plotted the continuation of the war unnecessarily. The American armies were actually ordered to withdraw from Berlin in favor of the Russian forces. It is our belief that a thorough investigation by a Congressional Committee would reveal scores of high crimes which would call for the punishment of the culprits who precipitated such crimes.

8. Atomic Energy

Control of the atom bomb and atomic energy must be removed immediately from the hands of the Lilienthal committee and returned to the control of the military. All who know the secret of atomic energy should be kept under surveillance by the FBI, the Military Intelligency and the Secret Service for the remainder of their lives. Inasmuch as it is the belief of certain students of world affairs that important information concerning atomic energy has been taken from America to Russia and others, those guilty of this act should be brought to justice immediately and double safeguards should be thrown around all atomic energy information from this moment forward.

9. National Defense

We believe that citizenship carries with it the responsibility to defend the Nation whenever invasion threatens or the menace of international revolution appears. The military power of the nation at all times must be sufficiently strong to guarantee the preservation of our national self-respect and to support pronounced policies of a true Nationalist state. It is our belief that a wage scale for a peace-time army comparable to the wage scale of American industry would supply the necessary peace-time personnel.

10. Economic Stability

We believe that the constant alternating between periods of perilous depression and wild inflation (with the slaughtering of livestock and plowing under of foodstuffs on the one hand, and the siphoning off of our production to maintain a world-wide WPA on the other) is a planned program to keep the American people in a state of economic insecurity. By removing the control of our monetary system from private banking houses and returning it to Congress, by instituting an economy of abundance and full-production we can free our citizens from the threat of economic slavery and provide security through the abolition of speculation and usury.

11. Price Control

We denounce all price controls and all forms of rationing as forms of bureaucratic regimentation. Such practices menace the system of private enterprise and fatten the purses of the Jewish black marketeers who grew fat during the recent war. We believe in an economy of abundance. The available supply of necessities would be greatly increased and prices greatly reduced if American production could be reserved for Americans first. If Marshall Plan waste could be checked, if mysteriously accumulated American currency now flooding this country in the hands of refugees could be recalled, the purchase power of the American housewife would be greatly enhanced.

12. HOUSING

We recognize the shortage of houses. We propose the solution of this problem by certain direct and simple steps.

a. Vacate and make available to veterans and citizens all housing units now occupied by illegal immigrants and non-citizens.

b. Declare vacant and make available to American citizens all housing units now occupied by non-citizens.

c. Destroy the power of the labor racketeer who refuses to permit the introduction of assembly-line science and labor-saving methods necessary to effect inexpensive and speedy housing construction. It is now a matter of common knowledge that houses could be constructed twice as rapidly and for one-half the cost if the above mentioned practices could be introduced.

d. Bureaucratic controls over construction and rentals should be abolished and avoided in order that private enterprise may be given the maxium encouragement in solving our housing problem.

e. As these aliens vacate American houses to be made available for American people, they should be extended humanitarian treatment and provided with temporary shelter in quickly constructed public camps during the time they are being screened for deportation as undesirables. Following the screening, desirable aliens will then be free to qualify for citizenship.

13. THE AGED AND THE INFIRM

Improvement in our mode of living has extended the age of the American citizen ten years in the past generation. Labor saving devices will continue to retire the average man from productive labor at an increasingly younger age. Our senior citizens must be made the benefactors of this progress, not the victims. A simple but effective system must be provided whereby the children of one generation can provide well for those of the passing generation. We favor a pension that will guarantee a self-respecting and in-

dependent standard of living for all regardless of their economic standing, just as veterans compensations are paid to all regardless of economic standing. Monetary reforms which will remove our money system from the hands of the money changers and establish Constitutional controls will go a long way toward solving this important problem. To specify an amount for a pension is demagoguery unless our economy stabilizes the purchase power of the amount paid.

14. CITIZENSHIP

Our plan for naturalizing citizens should be reexamined and requirements should be made more stringent. In light of the fact that a phenomenal number of aliens have entered this country illegally, the time has come for us to demand that a roster of all citizens be made available to every community and be open to inspection in every county court house. Non-citizens who have dwelt within the borders of the USA for some time without attempting to become citizens should be viewed with suspicion.

15. PRIVATE ENTERPRISE

Private enterprise has made America the richest nation on earth. It has developed a strong middle class which has kept our people relatively free from regimentation and monopoly. The two greatest enemies of private enterprise are: regimentation and monopoly control. As long as private enterprise is permitted to operate in an atmosphere of health and freedom, the humblest plough-hand and the son of the most obscure worker has the opportunity to become a citizen of prominence and abundance.

16. LABOR

The Christian Nationalist Party is determined that American citizens who perform common and skilled labor shall be freed from the exploitation of the revolutionist and labor racketeer and the feudal lord. The men and women who perform the necessary task in the field of skilled and unskilled labor must be freed from bureaucratic interference to the end that they may establish a free, unhampered relationship between themselves and their employers. Incentive systems must be encouraged and all constructive steps must be taken necessary to create a situation where the laborer shall be paid in proportion to the labor he performs. The Marxist system of levelling all workers under a uniform, union scale where the competent and efficient are paid no more than the lazy and inefficient, must be discouraged and wherever possible abolished.

17. AGRICULTURE

The prices of farm crops must be stabilized in such a way as to guarantee the cost of production, plus a reasonable profit. Upon these stable prices freed from tyranny and uncertainty of speculation and money-changing tactics, the farmer will be rewarded for abundance, not scarcity; for the ingenuity of production and not the ingenuity of destruction. Wealth under a Nationalist administration would be determined by the production of the soil and not the arbitrary price of an ounce of metal subject to the whims of the money changers. Under all circumstances, the great American market must be reserved exclusively for the American farmer.

18. VETERANS

The two world wars were fought by citizen armies which drew on the youth of the Nation. The recent war took 13 million men. We hold that the following fundamental principles must be observed in relation to the veterans of all wars.

    a. Totally disabled men must be guaranteed a self-respecting and generous livelihood for themselves and their families.

    b. Impaired men suffering from wounds and sickness due to war must have every modern facility necessary to the maximum amount of comfort, and their compensation must be generous and consistent with their impairment.

    c. Able-bodied men who returned in sound health will naturally share in the abundance and opportunity which will be guaranteed to all citizens in a regime of Christian Nationalism.

    d. Veterans of all wars should be given priority in jobs and houses over non-citizens. Whenever unemployment appears, non-citizens should surrender their jobs and make them available to veterans. In the same manner houses occupied by aliens should be vacated and made available to veterans.

CONCLUSION

We who have framed and adopted this platform are realistic. We are conscious of the fact that evil and materialistic forces will oppose the fulfillment of this Platform with every power at their command. It is our conviction that deep in the hearts of millions of American citizens—Yes, more than a majority of our citizens—is a pronounced hunger for the moral courage and the Christian statesmanship necessary to enforce the ideals expressed in this Platform. The summary of the whole matter is: Shall the lovers of Jesus Christ or the enemies of Jesus Christ determine the destiny of America. The time has come for all citizens of our Nation to take their stand. There is no middle ground. Believing that the teaching and the spirit of Jesus Christ constitute the dynamic with which this party must be built, we recognize the fact that only through the help of Divine Power can the maximum victory be accomplished.

It is agreed by this Convention assembled that this Platform be reproduced in print and made available to all members of the Party and interested friends and observers.

Communist Party Platform, 1948

In this crucial 1948 election the American people have a fateful decision to make: Shall America follow the path of peace or war, democracy or fascism?

Our boys returned from World War II with the hope that their wartime sacrifices had not been in vain.

Remember the promises:

    Fascism would be wiped out.

    The great-power unity that brought war victory would bring enduring peace.

    An economic bill of rights would provide every American with security.

These promises have been broken.

Instead of peace, there is war—in Greece, in China, in Israel.

Instead of peace, we witness feverish preparations for a new world war.

Instead of peace, American boys are being regimented for war with the enactment of the peacetime draft.

Instead of security and abundance, we have sky-rocketing prices, lowered living standards and the shadow of an impending economic crash with mass unemployment. Farmers fear the inevitable collapse of farm prices. After three years our veterans are still denied housing. Our youth face a future of insecurity and new wars.

Instead of greater democracy, we have lynch law, mounting Jim-Crowism and anti-Semitism, and a conspiracy to undermine our sacred democratic heritage. We have anti-Communist witch-hunts, the arrest and conviction of anti-fascist leaders, the harassment and intimidation of writers, artists and intellectuals. We have phony spy scares, the hounding of government employees and former Roosevelt associates, the persecution of foreign-born workers, and the adoption of anti-labor legislation, attempts to outlaw the Communist Party through Mundt-Nixon Bills, and now the indictment of the twelve Communist leaders on the trumped-up charge of "force and violence." These are the methods by which the American people are step by step being driven down the road to a police state and fascism.

These are the chief issues of the 1948 elections.

America is a great and beautiful land, endowed with immense natural resources and a people skilled in producing abundance. Why then the fear of insecurity?

We are today threatened by no outside force. We are in no danger of attack from any nation. Why then the war hysteria?

The answer lies in this simple fact—250 giant corporations, operating through a handful of banks, control the economic life of the United States. These in turn are largely owned by a few plutocratic families—Morgan, Rockefeller, Mellon, du Pont and Ford.

The nation's industries are not operated for the public welfare, but for the private gain and power of the multi-millionaire ruling class. Prices continue to rise because of vast military expenditures and because the monopolies, through price-fixing agreements and other devious devices, extract exorbitant profits.

They make huge profits from war and from armaments. They extract super-profits abroad by forcing other nations into economic dependence upon Wall Street. This drive for foreign markets, for Wall Street domination of the world, is at the bottom of the war hysteria and war preparations. Big Business strives to crush the growth and advance of democracy and socialism throughout the world, in order to protect and swell its profits.

Big Business seeks to re-establish the old Nazi cartels and to use Germany and Japan as military bases for new aggression. But the failures of the bipartisan policy to achieve its main aim of world conquest have increased the frenzy with which Wall Street seeks to plunge the nation into fascism and World War III.

WAR AND PEACE . . .

Neither the American people nor the Soviet Union is responsible for the sharpening tension in international relations. The responsibility rests squarely on Wall Street and the bipartisan Truman-Dewey atomic diplomacy. Only the capitalists trusts want war. The Soviet Union is a socialist country. It has no trusts, no I. G. Farben or du Pont cartels to profit from wars. That is why the Soviet Union is the most powerful force for peace in the world.

The Communist Party calls upon the labor movement and all progressive, peace-loving Americans to struggle for the realization of the following peace program:

End the "cold war," the draft, and the huge military budget.

Restore American-Soviet friendship, the key to world peace and the fulfillment of the people's hope in the United Nations.

Conclude a peace settlement for a united, democratic Germany and Japan based on the Yalta and Potsdam agreements. Guarantee the complete democratization and demilitarization of these Countries.

Stop military aid and intervention in China, Korea and Greece.

Break diplomatic and economic ties with Franco Spain.

Scrap the Marshall Plan and the Truman Doctrine. Furnish large-scale economic assistance to the war-ravaged victims of fascist attack. Give this aid through the United Nations without political strings.

Lift the embargo on, and extend full recognition to Israel.

Give immediate, unconditional independence to Puerto Rico.

Aid the economic development of the colonial and semi-colonial countries of Asia, Africa and Latin America on the basis of full support to their fight for their national independence. De-

feat the Truman Arms Standardization Plan.

Abandon economic, political and military pressures on the countries of Latin America.

The Attack on Labor and Our Living Standards

The trusts have inflated prices and battered down the real wages of American workers to 16 per cent below 1944.

Huge war expenditures amount to 15 billion dollars this year—one-third of the entire national budget. The American people are already paying dearly for this "cold war economy," through a heavy tax burden, speed-up and reduction in real wages. We will pay still more heavily as the inflationary boom speeds the day of the oncoming economic bust.

Big Business has decreed that labor's hands be tied and its rights destroyed. The Taft-Hartley Law and strike-breaking injunctions are weapons against the people's resistance to the monopoly drive towards war and fascism.

To defend the labor movement and the vital economic interests of the overwhelming majority of the American people, labor and all progressives should unite in stubborn and militant struggle for the following demands:

Repeal the Taft-Hartley Law and end strike-breaking injunctions. Adopt a code of Federal labor legislation including the best features of the Wagner Act and the Norris-LaGuardia Anti-Injunction Law.

Restore price control and roll back prices, without any wage freeze.

Enact an extensive program for Federally-financed low-rent public housing, minimum wage legislation, old-age pensions, adequate health insurance, and increased aid to education.

Provide increased security for the working farmers through up-to-date parity price and income guarantees, based on unlimited farm production. Such income guarantees require farm subsidies, effective crop insurance and sharp curbs on the giant food trusts and their marketing agencies. Carry out a program of planned conservation and River Valley projects. Extend the Federal minimum wage and social security laws to agricultural workers, including seasonal and migratory labor.

We call for heavier taxation on high incomes and excess profits, with increased exemption for the low brackets. We demand a capital levy on big fortunes and corporations to finance essential social legislation.

We support all steps to curb the power of the trusts, the source of reaction, fascism and war. The American people can make gains, even under capitalism, by mass resistance to the monopolies.

We support measures to nationalize the basic industries, banks and insurance companies, but point out that such measures can only be useful as part of the fight to realize a people's democratic government in the United States. Democratic nationalization of trustified industries requires guarantees of democratic controls and the right of labor to organize, bargain collectively and strike. This can only be accomplished by a people's government dedicated to curbing the power of the trusts.

We point out that capitalism cannot become "progressive" even by curbing the excesses of the monopolies. The basic causes of unemployment, economic crisis, fascism and war can only be removed by the establishment of Socialism through the democratic will of the majority of the American people.

Civil Rights . . .

The destruction of the rights of the Communists is the classical first step down the road to fascism. The tragedy of Germany and Italy proves this. Therefore, it is incumbent upon the working class and all Americans who hate fascism to defend the rights of the Communists, and to help explode the myth that Communists are foreign agents or advocate force and violence.

We Communists are no more foreign agents than was Jefferson who was also accused of being a foreign agent by the Tories of his day. We follow in the best traditions of the spokesmen of labor, science and culture whose contributions to human progress knew no national boundaries. We follow in the tradition of Abraham Lincoln, who said: "The strongest bond of human sympathy, outside of the family relation, should be one uniting all working people, of all nations and tongues, and kindreds."

It is the monopolists who advocate and practice force and violence, not the Communists. Reaction has always resorted to force and violence to thwart the democratic aspirations of the people.

In 1776, force and violence were the weapons of King George against the American colonists seeking national independence. In 1861, force and violence were used by the Southern slave owners in an attempt to overthrow the democratic republic headed by Lincoln. Today the people suffer the violence of the K.K.K., the lynch mobs, the fascist hoodlum gangs and police brutality.

We are Marxists, not adventurers or conspirators. We condemn and reject the policy and practice of terror and assassination and repudiate the advocates of force and violence. We Communists insist upon our right to compete freely in the battle of ideas. We Communists insist upon our right to organize and bring our program to the people. Let the people judge our views and activities on their merits.

We call upon the American people to fight with all their strength against the danger of fascism to resist every fascist measure, to defend every democratic right.

End the witch-hunts, loyalty orders and phony spy scares.

Abolish the Un-American Committee. Withdraw the indictments against the twelve Communist leaders and the contempt citations against the anti-fascist victims of Congressional inquisitions.

Stop the campaign of terror and intimidation against labor leaders, intellectuals and people of the professions.

End persecution and deportation of the foreign born and lift the undemocratic bars to citizenship.

Outlaw all forms of anti-Semitism, anti-Catholicism, and every other expression of racial and religious bigotry.

End all discrimination against the Mexican-American people in the Southwest.

The Communist party calls for an end to any and all political, social, and economic inequalities practiced against women and demands the maintenance and extension of existing protective legislation.

Extend the suffrage. Remove the bars directed against minority parties. Lower the voting age to 18 years in every state.

NEGRO RIGHTS . . .

The hypocrisy of the democratic pretensions of Wall Street and the Administration are shattered by the reality of the Jim-Crow system in America. The most shameful aspect of American life is the Jim-Crowism, the terror and violence imposed upon the Negro people, especially in the South. Discrimination in employment, only slightly relaxed during the war, is once again widespread.

The Communist Party, which has pioneered in fighting for full political, economic and social equality for the Negro people, calls for an end to the policies of the Federal and state governments which give official sanction to the Jim-Crow system in the United States.

We call upon all progressives, especially white progressives, to carry on an unceasing day-to-day struggle to outlaw the poll tax, lynchings, segregation, job discrimination and all other forms of Jim-Crowism, official and unofficial, and to give their full support to the rising national liberation movement of the Negro people. This is vital to the Negro people, to the white workers, and to the whole fight for democracy in America.

We demand a national F.E.P.C. law, to be vigorously and fully enforced.

We demand that the Ingram family be freed and adequately compensated for the ordeals to which they have been subjected.

We demand that the Ku Klux Klan and all other hate-and-terror organizations be outlawed.

We condemn President Truman's cynical evasion of the issue of segregation in the armed forces. We demand that he immediately issue an Executive Order ending every form of segregation and discrimination in the armed forces and the government services.

We defend the right of the Negro people to full representation in government, and demand Federal enforcement of the 13th, 14th, and 15th Amendments, so that the Negro people, North and South, may participate freely and fully in the 1948 elections and all elections thereafter.

We call for a democratic agricultural program which will give land and other forms of assistance to millions of Negro and white tenants and sharecroppers in the South, and thereby help put an end to the semi-feudal plantation system.

Such reforms will help provide the material basis for the Negro people's advance towards full liberation from their national oppression, towards their full political, economic and social equality.

THE TWO-PARTY SYSTEM . . .

Millions of American working people have come to realize the futility of any further support for the bankrupt two-party system of Big Business. Both major parties are committed to the bipartisan war program, reflected in both the Truman Doctrine and its New Look version, the Marshall Plan. Both major parties are united in this program of fattening the billionaires and bleeding the people.

Both major parties are responsible for runaway inflation. Both the Democratic Administration and the Republican Congress have done nothing to curb the powers of the trusts to hoard food, rig markets, boost prices and gouge consumers.

Both major parties are responsible for the atrocities committed against the Bill of Rights. Both helped pass the Taft-Hartley Law. Both the Democratic Congressional leaders and the cynical Dewey-Warren-Taft Republican leadership are responsible for the failure to enact civil rights legislation. Neither the Democratic platform nor President Truman's demagogy will fool any enlightened American. The President's deeds belie his words. He has refused to end segregation in the armed forces and the government and fire from his cabinet those who maintain it.

Both major parties are responsible for the Hitler-like hysteria expressed in spy scares, loyalty probes, government witch-hunts and the arrest and indictment of Americans whose "crime" it is to oppose the Wall Street war plans. The Democratic-controlled Department of Justice and the Republican-controlled Un-American Committee are equally guilty of subverting the Bill of Rights.

Chief allies of the twin parties of Big Business in the ranks of labor and the progressive organizations of the people are those who pretend to criticize the corruption and decay of the two old parties while, in fact, keeping the people tied hand and foot to the two-party system. These include the top officialdom of the A.F.L., C.I.O. and R.R. Brotherhoods and groups like the Americans for Democratic Action and such Social-Democrats as Norman Thomas and David Dubinsky.

THE NEW PARTY . . .

Millions of Americans, disillusioned with the two-party system, have joined to found a new people's party.

The new Progressive Party is an inescapable historic necessity for millions who want a real choice now between peace and war, democracy and fascism, security and poverty.

The Communists, who support every popular progressive movement, naturally welcome this new people's party. We supported the progressive features of Roosevelt's policies, domestic and foreign. We helped organize the C.I.O. in the 1930's. We have supported every democratic movement since the Communists of Lincoln's generation fought in the Union cause during the Civil War.

On most immediate questions before the people of the country the Progressive Party has offered detailed platform planks around which all forward-looking people can unite. Our support of the Progressive Party policies and campaign does not alter the fact that we have fundamental as well as some tactical differences with Henry Wallace and related third-party forces.

The Communist Party is not nominating a Presidential ticket in the 1948 elections. In 1944 we Communists supported Roosevelt to help win the anti-Axis war. Similarly, in 1948 we Communists join with millions of other Americans to support the Progressive Party ticket to help win the peace. The Communist Party will enter its own candidates only in those districts where the people are offered no progressive alternatives to the twin parties of Wall Street.

The Progressive Party is by its very nature a great coalition of labor, farmers, the Negro people, youth, and professional and small business people. It is anti-monopoly, anti-fascist, anti-war. By its very nature it is not an anti-capitalist party. It is not a Socialist or a Communist Party and we are not seeking to make it one. It is and should develop as a united front, broad, mass people's party.

There is only one Marxist Party in America, one party dedicated to replacing the capitalist system with Socialism—and that is the Communist Party.

Our firm conviction that only a Socialist reorganization of society will bring permanent peace, security and prosperity is no barrier to cooperation with all other progressive Americans, in helping create a great new coalition in order to save our people from the twin horrors of war and fascism.

We seek no special position in this movement and will, of course, oppose any attempt to discriminate against us because of our Socialist aims.

We Communists are dedicated to the proposition that the great American dream of life, liberty and pursuit of happiness, will be realized only under Socialism, a society in which the means of production will be collectively owned and operated under a government led by the working class. Only such a society can forever banish war, poverty and race hatred. Only in such a society can there be the full realization of the dignity of man and the full development of the individual. Only such a society can permanently protect the integrity of the home and family. Only a Socialist society can realize in life the vision of the brotherhood of man.

Fellow Americans:

We live in times of great danger.

Fascism and war now threaten our country.

But the common people of America, and in the first place the working people, can defeat these dangers. They can turn our country to the path of democracy and peace, to the path of social progress.

The 1948 elections will help decide which way America will go.

Your united action in this election, your determined defense of your rights, can become powerful forces for peace and progress. The future of our country is in your hands.

Democratic Party Platform 1948

The Democratic Party adopts this platform in the conviction that the destiny of the United States is to provide leadership in the world toward a realization of the Four Freedoms.

We chart our future course as we charted our course under the leadership of Franklin D. Roosevelt and Harry S. Truman in the abiding belief that democracy—when dedicated to the service of all and not to a privileged few—proves its superiority over all other forms of government.

Our party record of the past is assurance of its policies and performance in the future.

Ours is the party which was entrusted with responsibility when twelve years of Republican neglect had blighted the hopes of mankind, had squandered the fruits of prosperity and had plunged us into the depths of depression and despair.

Ours is the party which rebuilt a shattered economy, rescued our banking system, revived our agriculture, reinvigorated our industry, gave labor strength and security, and led the American people to the broadest prosperity in our history.

Ours is the party which introduced the spirit of humanity into our law, as we outlawed child labor and the sweatshop, insured bank deposits, protected millions of home-owners and farmers from foreclosure, and established national social security.

Ours is the party under which this nation before Pearl Harbor gave aid and strength to those countries which were holding back the Nazi and Fascist tide.

Ours is the party which stood at the helm and led the nation to victory in the war.

Ours is the party which, during the war, prepared for peace so well that when peace came reconversion promptly led to the greatest production and employment in this nation's life.

Ours is the party under whose leadership farm owners' income in this nation increased from less than $2.5 billions in 1933 to more than $18 billions in 1947; independent business and professional income increased from less than $3 billions in 1933 to more than $22 billions in 1947; employees' earnings increased from $29 billions in 1933 to more than 128 billions in 1947; and employment grew from 39 million jobs in 1933 to a record of 60 million jobs in 1947.

Ours is the party under which the framework of the world organization for peace and justice was formulated and created.

Ours is the party under which were conceived the instruments for resisting Communist aggression and for rebuilding the economic strength of the democratic countries of Europe and Asia— the Truman Doctrine and the Marshall Plan. They are the materials with which we must build the peace.

Ours is the party which first proclaimed that the actions and policies of this nation in the foreign field are matters of national and not just party concern. We shall go forward on the course charted by President Roosevelt and President Truman and the other leaders of Democracy.

We reject the principle—which we have always rejected, but which the Republican 80th Congress enthusiastically accepted—that government exists for the benefit of the privileged few.

To serve the interests of all and not the few; to assure a world in which peace and justice can prevail; to achieve security, full production, and full employment—this is our platform.

Our Foreign Policy

We declared in 1944 that the imperative duty of the United States was to wage the war to final triumph and to join with the other United Nations in the establishment of an international organization for the prevention of aggression and the maintenance of international peace and security.

Under Democratic leadership, those pledges were gloriously redeemed.

When the United States was treacherously and savagely attacked, our great Democratic President, Franklin D. Roosevelt, and a Democratic Congress preserved the nation's honor, and with high courage and with the invincible might of the American people, the challenge was accepted. Under his inspiring leadership, the nation created the greatest army that ever assembled under the flag, the mightiest air force, the most powerful navy on the globe, and the largest merchant marine in the world.

The nation's gallant sons on land, on sea, and in the air, ended the war in complete and overwhelming triumph. Armed aggression against peaceful peoples was resisted and crushed. Arrogant and powerful war lords were vanquished and forced to unconditional surrender.

Before the end of the war the Democratic administration turned to the task of establishing measures for peace and the prevention of aggression and the threat of another war. Under the leadership of a Democratic President and his Secretary of State, the United Nations was organized at San Francisco. The charter was ratified by an overwhelming vote of the Senate. We support the United Nations fully and we pledge our whole-hearted aid toward its growth and development. We will continue to lead the way toward curtailment of the use of the veto. We shall favor such amendments and modifications of the charter as experience may justify. We will continue our efforts toward the establishment of an international armed force to aid its authority. We advocate the grant of a loan to the United Nations recommended by the President, but denied by the Republican Congress, for the construction of the United Nations headquarters in this country.

We pledge our best endeavors to conclude treaties of peace with our former enemies. Already treaties have been made with Italy, Hungary, Bulgaria and Rumania. We shall strive to conclude treaties with the remaining enemy states, based on justice and with guarantees against the revival of aggression, and for the preservation of peace.

We advocate the maintance of an adequate Army, Navy and Air Force to protect the nation's vital interests and to assure our security against aggression.

We advocate the effective international control of weapons of mass destruction, including the atomic bomb, and we approve continued and vigorous efforts within the United Nations to bring about the successful consummation of the proposals which our Government has advanced.

The adoption of these proposals would be a vital and most important step toward safe and effective world disarmament and world peace under a strengthened United Nations which would then truly constitute a more effective parliament of the world's peoples.

Under the leadership of a Democratic President, the United States has demonstrated its friendship for other peace-loving nations and its support of their freedom and independence. Under the Truman doctrine vital aid has been extended to China, to Greece, and to Turkey. Under the Marshall Plan generous sums have been provided for the relief and rehabilitation of European nations striving to rebuild their economy and to secure and strengthen their safety and freedom. The Republican leadership in the House of Representatives, by its votes in the 80th Congress, has shown its reluctance to provide funds to support this program, the greatest move for peace and recovery made since the end of World War II.

We pledge a sound, humanitarian administration of the Marshall Plan.

We pledge support not only for these principles—we pledge further that we will not withhold necessary funds by which these principles can be achieved. Therefore, we pledge that we will implement with appropriations the commitments which are made in this nation's foreign program.

We pledge ourselves to restore the Reciprocal Trade Agreements program formulated in 1934 by Secretary of State Cordell Hull and operated successfully for 14 years—until crippled by the Republican 80th Congress. Further, we strongly endorse our country's adherence to the International Trade Organization.

A great Democratic President established the Good Neighbor Policy toward the nations of the Western Hemisphere. The Act of Chapultepec was negotiated at Mexico City under Democratic leadership. It was carried forward in the Western Hemisphere defense pact concluded at Rio de Janeiro, which implemented the Monroe Doctrine and united the Western Hemisphere in behalf of peace.

We pledge continued economic cooperation with the countries of the Western Hemisphere. We pledge continued support of regional arrangements within the United Nations Charter, such as the Inter-American Regional Pact and the developing Western European Union.

President Truman, by granting immediate recognition to Israel, led the world in extending friendship and welcome to a people who have long sought and justly deserve freedom and independence.

We pledge full recognition to the State of Israel. We affirm our pride that the United States under the leadership of President Truman played a leading role in the adoption of the resolution of November 29, 1947, by the United Nations General Assembly for the creation of a Jewish State.

We approve the claims of the State of Israel to the boundaries set forth in the United Nations resolution of November 29th and consider that modifications thereof should be made only if fully acceptable to the State of Israel.

We look forward to the admission of the State of Israel to the United Nations and its full participation in the international community of nations. We pledge appropriate aid to the State of Israel in developing its economy and resources.

We favor the revision of the arms embargo to accord to the State of Israel the right of self-defense. We pledge ourselves to work for the modification of any resolution of the United Nations to the extent that it may prevent any such revision.

We continue to support, within the framework of the United Nations, the internationalization of Jerusalem and the protection of the Holy Places in Palestine.

The United States has traditionally been in sympathy with the efforts of subjugated countries to attain their independence, and to establish a democratic form of government. Poland is an outstanding example. After a century and a half of subjugation, it was resurrected after the first World War by our great Democratic President, Woodrow Wilson. We look forward to development of these countries as prosperous, free, and democratic fellow members of the United Nations.

OUR DOMESTIC POLICIES

The Republican 80th Congress is directly responsible for the existing and ever increasing high cost of living. It cannot dodge that responsibility. Unless the Republican candidates are defeated in the approaching elections, their mistaken policies will impose greater hardships and suffering on large numbers of the American people. Adequate food, clothing and shelter—the bare necessities of life—are becoming too expensive for the average wage earner and the prospects are more frightening each day. The Republican 80th Congress has lacked the courage to face this vital problem.

We shall curb the Republican inflation. We shall put a halt to the disastrous price rises which have come as a result of the failure of the Republican 80th Congress to take effective action on President Truman's recommendations, setting forth a comprehensive program to control the high cost of living.

We shall enact comprehensive housing legislation, including provisions for slum clearance and low-rent housing projects initiated by local agencies. This nation is shamed by the failure of the Republican 80th Congress to pass the vitally needed general housing legislation as recommended by the President. Adequate housing will end the need for rent control. Until then, it must be continued.

We pledge the continued maintenance of those sound fiscal policies which under Democratic leadership have brought about a balanced budget and reduction of the public debt by $28 billion since the close of the war.

We favor the reduction of taxes, whenever it is possible to do so without unbalancing the nation's economy, by giving a full measure of relief to those millions of low-income families on whom the wartime burden of taxation fell most heavily. The form of tax reduction adopted by the Republican 80th Congress gave relief to those who need it least and ignored those who need it most.

We shall endeavor to remove tax inequities and to continue to reduce the public debt.

We are opposed to the imposition of a general federal sales tax.

We advocate the repeal of the Taft-Hartley Act. It was enacted by the Republican 80th Congress over the President's veto. That act was proposed with the promise that it would secure "the legitimate rights of both employees and employers in their relations affecting commerce." It has failed. The number of labor-management disputes has increased. The number of cases before the National Labor Relations Board has more than doubled since the Act was passed, and efficient and prompt administration is becoming more and more difficult. It has encouraged litigation in labor disputes and undermined the established American policy of collective bargaining. Recent decisions by the courts prove that the Act was so poorly drawn that its application is uncertain, and that it is probably, in some provisions, unconstitutional.

We advocate such legislation as is desirable to establish a just body of rules to assure free and effective collective bargaining, to determine, in the public interest, the rights of employees and employers, to reduce to a minimum their conflict of interests, and to enable unions to keep their membership free from communistic influences.

We urge that the Department of Labor be rebuilt and strengthened, restoring to it the units, including the Federal Mediation and Conciliation Service and the United States Employment Service, which properly belong to it, and which the Republican 80th Congress stripped from it over the veto of President Truman. We urge that the Department's facilities for collecting and disseminating economic information be expanded, and that a Labor Education Extension Service be established in the Department of Labor.

We favor the extension of the coverage of the Fair Labor Standards Act as recommended by President Truman, and the adoption of a minimum wage of at least 75 cents an hour in place of the present obsolete and inadequate minimum of 40 cents an hour.

We favor legislation assuring that the workers of our nation receive equal pay for equal work, regardless of sex.

We favor the extension of the Social Security program established under Democratic leadership, to provide additional protection against the hazards of old age, disability, disease or death. We believe that this program should include:

Increases in old-age and survivors' insurance benefits by at least 50 percent, and reduction of the eligibility age for women from 65 to 60 years; extension of old-age and survivors' and unemployment insurance to all workers not now covered; insurance against loss of earnings on account of illness or disability; improved public assistance for the needy.

We favor the enactment of a national health program for expanded medical research, medical education, and hospitals and clinics.

We will continue our efforts to aid the blind and other handicapped persons to become self-supporting.

We will continue our efforts to expand maternal care, improve the health of the nation's children, and reduce juvenile delinquency.

We approve the purposes of the Mental Health Act and we favor such appropriations as may be necessary to make it effective.

We advocate federal aid for education administered by and under the control of the states. We vigorously support the authorization, which was so shockingly ignored by the Republican 80th Congress, for the appropriation of $300 million as a beginning of Federal aid to the states to assist them in meeting the present educational needs. We insist upon the right of every American child to obtain a good education.

The nation can never discharge its debt to its millions of war veterans. We pledge ourselves to the continuance and improvement of our national program of benefits for veterans and their families.

We are proud of the sound and comprehensive program conceived, developed and administered under Democratic leadership, including the GI Bill of Rights, which has proved beneficial to many millions.

The level of veterans' benefits must be constantly re-examined in the light of the decline in the purchasing power of the dollar brought about by inflation.

Employment and economic security must be

afforded all veterans. We pledge a program of housing for veterans at prices they can afford to pay.

The disabled veteran must be provided with medical care and hospitalization of the highest possible standard.

We pledge our efforts to maintain continued farm prosperity, improvement of the standard of living and the working conditions of the farmer, and to preserve the family-size farm.

Specifically, we favor a permanent system of flexible price supports for agricultural products, to maintain farm income on a parity with farm operating costs; an intensified soil conservation program; an extended crop insurance program; improvement of methods of distributing agricultural products; development and maintenance of stable export markets; adequate financing for the school lunch program; the use of agricultural surpluses to improve the diet of low-income families in case of need; continued expansion of the rural electrification program; strengthening of all agricultural credit programs; intensified research to improve agricultural practices, and to find new uses for farm products.

We strongly urge the continuance of maximum farmer participation in all these programs.

We favor the repeal of the discriminatory taxes on the manufacture and sale of oleomargarine.

We will encourage farm cooperatives and oppose any revision of federal law designed to curtail their most effective functioning as a means of achieving economy, stability and security for American agriculture.

We favor provisions under which our fishery resources and industry will be afforded the benefits that will result from more scientific research and exploration.

We recognize the importance of small business in a sound American economy. It must be protected against unfair discrimination and monopoly, and be given equal opportunities with competing enterprises to expand its capital structure.

We favor non-discriminatory transportation charges and declare for the early correction of inequalities in such charges.

We pledge the continued full and unified regional development of the water, mineral, and other natural resources of the nation, recognizing that the progress already achieved under the initiative of the Democratic Party in the arid and semi-arid states of the West, as well as in the Tennessee Valley, is only an indication of still greater results which can be accomplished. Our natural resources are the heritage of all our people and must not be permitted to become the private preserves of monopoly.

The irrigation of arid land, the establishment of new, independent, competitive business and the stimulation of new industrial opportunities for all of our people depends upon the development and transmission of electric energy in accordance with the program and the projects so successfully launched under Democratic auspices during the past sixteen years.

We favor acceleration of the Federal Reclamation Program, the maximum beneficial use of water in the several states for irrigation and domestic supply. In this connection, we propose the establishment and maintenance of new family-size farms for veterans and others seeking settlement opportunities, the development of hydroelectric power and its widespread distribution over publicly owned transmission lines to assure benefits to the water users in financing irrigation projects, and to the power users for domestic and industrial purposes, with preference to public agencies and R.E.A. cooperatives.

These are the aims of the Democratic Party which in the future, as in the past, will place the interest of the people as individual citizens first.

We will continue to improve the navigable waterways and harbors of the nation.

We pledge to continue the policy initiated by the Democratic Party of adequate appropriations for flood control for the protection of life and property.

In addition to practicing false economy on flood control, the Republican-controlled 80th Congress was so cruel as even to deny emergency federal funds for the relief of individuals and municipalities victimized by recent great floods, tornadoes and other disasters.

We shall expand our programs for forestation, for the improvement of grazing lands, public and private, for the stockpiling of strategic minerals and the encouragement of a sound domestic mining industry. We shall carry forward experiments for the broader utilization of mineral resources in the highly beneficial manner already demonstrated in the program for the manufacture of synthetic liquid fuel from our vast deposits of coal and oil shale and from our agricultural resources.

We pledge an intensive enforcement of the anti-trust laws, with adequate appropriations.

We advocate the strengthening of existing anti-trust laws by closing the gaps which experience has shown have been used to promote concentration of economic power.

We pledge a positive program to promote competitive business and to foster the development of independent trade and commerce.

We support the right of free enterprise and the right of all persons to work together in cooperatives and other democratic associations for the purpose of carrying out any proper business operations free from any arbitrary and discriminatory restrictions.

The Democratic Party is responsible for the great civil rights gains made in recent years in eliminating unfair and illegal discrimination based on race, creed or color.

The Democratic Party commits itself to continuing its efforts to eradicate all racial, religious and economic discrimination.

We again state our belief that racial and religious minorities must have the right to live, the right to work, the right to vote, the full and equal protection of the laws, on a basis of equality with all citizens as guaranteed by the Constitution.

We highly commend President Harry S. Truman for his courageous stand on the issue of civil rights.

We call upon the Congress to support our President in guaranteeing these basic and fundamental American Principles: (1) the right of full and equal political participation; (2) the right to equal opportunity of employment; (3) the right of security of person; (4) and the right of equal treatment in the service and defense of our nation.[1]

We pledge ourselves to legislation to admit a minimum of 400,000 displaced persons found eligible for United States citizenship without discrimination as to race or religion. We condemn the undemocratic action of the Republican 80th

[1] When this platform was presented to the Convention, this section stated: "We again call upon the Congress to exert its full authority to the limit of its constitutional powers to assure and protect these rights." The last two paragraphs in the text above were inserted as an amendment to the platform by a vote of 651½ to 582½.

Congress in passing an inadequate and bigoted bill for this purpose, which law imposes un-American restrictions based on race and religion upon such admissions.

We urge immediate statehood for Hawaii and Alaska; immediate determination by the people of Puerto Rico as to their form of government and their ultimate status with respect to the United States; and the maximum degree of local self-government for the Virgin Islands, Guam and Samoa.

We recommend to Congress the submission of a constitutional amendment on equal rights for women.

We favor the extension of the right of suffrage to the people of the District of Columbia.

We pledge adherence to the principle of non-partisan civilian administration of atomic energy, and the development of atomic energy for peaceful purposes through free scientific inquiry for the benefit of all the people.

We urge the vigorous promotion of world-wide freedom in the gathering and dissemination of news by press, radio, motion pictures, newsreels and television, with complete confidence that an informed people will determine wisely the course of domestic and foreign policy.

We believe the primary step toward the achievement of world-wide freedom is access by all peoples to the facts and the truth. To that end, we will encourage the greatest possible vigor on the part of the United Nations Commission on Human Rights and the United Nations Economic and Social Council to establish the foundations on which freedom can exist in every nation.

We deplore the repeated attempts of Republicans in the 80th Congress to impose thought control upon the American people and to encroach on the freedom of speech and press.

We pledge the early establishment of a national science foundation under principles which will guarantee the most effective utilization of public and private research facilities.

We will continue our efforts to improve and strengthen our federal civil service, and provide adequate compensation.

We will continue to maintain an adequate American merchant marine.

We condemn Communism and other forms of totalitarianism and their destructive activity overseas and at home. We shall continue to build firm defenses against Communism by strengthening the economic and social structure of our own democracy. We reiterate our pledge to expose and prosecute treasonable activities of anti-democratic and un-American organizations which would sap our strength, paralyze our will to defend ourselves, and destroy our unity, inciting race against race, class against class, and the people against free institutions.

We shall continue vigorously to enforce the laws against subversive activities, observing at all times the constitutional guarantees which protect free speech, the free press and honest political activity. We shall strengthen our laws against subversion to the full extent necessary, protecting at all times our traditional individual freedoms.

We recognize that the United States has become the principal protector of the free world. The free peoples of the world look to us for support in maintaining their freedoms. If we falter in our leadership, we may endanger the peace of the world—and we shall surely endanger the welfare of our own nation. For these reasons it is imperative that we maintain our military strength until world peace with justice is secure. Under the leadership of President Truman, our military departments have been united and our Government organization for the national defense greatly strengthened. We pledge to maintain adequate military strength, based on these improvements, sufficient to fulfill our responsibilities in occupation zones, defend our national interests, and to bolster those free nations resisting Communist aggression.

This is our platform. These are our principles. They form a political and economic policy which has guided our party and our nation.

The American people know these principles well. Under them, we have enjoyed greater security, greater prosperity, and more effective world leadership than ever before.

Under them and with the guidance of Divine Providence we can proceed to higher levels of prosperity and security; we can advance to a better life at home; we can continue our leadership in the world with ever-growing prospects for lasting peace.

Progressive Party Platform, 1948

PREAMBLE

Three years after the end of the second world war, the drums are beating for a third. Civil liberties are being destroyed. Millions cry out for relief from unbearably high prices. The American way of life is in danger.

The root cause of this crisis is Big Business control of our economy and government.

With toil and enterprise the American people have created from their rich resources the world's greatest productive machine. This machine no longer belongs to the people. Its ownership is concentrated in the hands of a few and its product used for their enrichment.

Never before have so few owned so much at the expense of so many.

Ten years ago Franklin Delano Roosevelt warned: "The liberty of a democracy is not safe if the people tolerate the growth of private power to a point where it becomes stronger than their democratic state. That, in its essence, is fascism."

Today that private power has constituted itself an invisible government which pulls the strings of its puppet Republican and Democratic parties. Two sets of candidates compete for votes under the outworn emblems of the old parties. But both represent a single program—a program of monopoly profits through war preparations, lower living standards, and suppression of dissent.

For generations the common man of America has resisted this concentration of economic and political power in the hands of a few. The greatest of America's political leaders have led the people into battle against the money power, the railroads, the trusts, the economic royalists.

We of the Progressive Party are the present-day descendants of these people's movements and fighting leaders. We are the political heirs of Jefferson, Jackson and Lincoln — of Frederick Douglass, Altgeld and Debs—of "Fighting Bob" LaFollette, George Norris, and Franklin Roosevelt.

Throughout our history new parties have arisen when the old parties have betrayed the people. As Jefferson headed a new party to defeat the reactionaries of his day, and as Lincoln led a new party to victory over the slave-owners, so today the people, inspired and led by Henry Wallace, have created a new party to secure peace, freedom, and abundance.

With the firm conviction that the principles of the Declaration of Independence and of the Constitution of the United States set forth all fundamental freedoms for all people and secure the safety and well being of our country, the Progressive Party pledges itself to safeguard these principles to the American people.

Betrayal by the Old Parties

The American people want peace. But the old parties, obedient to the dictates of monopoly and the military, prepare for war in the name of peace.

They refuse to negotiate a settlement of differences with the Soviet Union.

They reject the United Nations as an instrument for promoting world peace and reconstruction.

They use the Marshall Plan to rebuild Nazi Germany as a war base and to subjugate the economies of other European countries to American Big Business.

They finance and arm corrupt, fascist governments in China, Greece, Turkey, and elsewhere, through the Truman Doctrine, wasting billions in American resources and squandering America's heritage as the enemy of despotism.

They encircle the globe with military bases which other peoples cannot but view as threats to their freedom and security.

They protect the war-making industrial and financial barons of Nazi Germany and imperial Japan, and restore them to power.

They stockpile atomic bombs.

They pass legislation to admit displaced persons, discriminating against Catholics, Jews, and other victims of Hitler.

They impose a peacetime draft and move toward Universal Military Training.

They fill policy-making positions in government with generals and Wall Street bankers.

Peace cannot be won—but profits can—by spending ever-increasing billions of the people's money in war preparations.

Yet these are the policies of the two old parties —policies profaning the name of peace.

The American people cherish freedom.

But the old parties, acting for the forces of special privilege, conspire to destroy traditional American freedoms.

They deny the Negro people the rights of citizenship. They impose a universal policy of Jim Crow and enforce it with every weapon of terror. They refuse to outlaw its most bestial expression—the crime of lynching.

They refuse to abolish the poll tax, and year after year they deny the right to vote to Negroes and millions of white people in the South.

They aim to reduce nationality groups to a position of social, economic, and political inferiority.

They connive to bar the Progressive Party from the ballot.

They move to outlaw the Communist Party as a decisive step in their assault on the democratic rights of labor, of national, racial, and political minorities, and of all those who oppose their drive to war. In this they repeat the history of Nazi Germany, Fascist Italy, and Franco Spain.

They support the House Committee on Un-American Activities in its vilification and persecution of citizens in total disregard of the Bill of Rights.

They build the Federal Bureau of Investigation into a political police with secret dossiers on millions of Americans.

They seek to regiment the thinking of the American people and to suppress political dissent.

They strive to enact such measures as the Mundt-Nixon Bill which are as destructive of democracy as were the Alien and Sedition Laws against which Jefferson fought.

They concoct a spurious "loyalty" program to create an atmosphere of fear and hysteria in government and industry.

They shackle American labor with the Taft-Hartley Act at the express command of Big Business, while encouraging exorbitant profits through uncontrolled inflation.

They restore the labor injunction as a weapon for breaking strikes and smashing unions.

This is the record of the two old parties—a record profaning the American ideal of freedom.

The American people want abundance.

But the old parties refuse to enact effective price and rent controls, making the people victims of a disastrous inflation which dissipates the savings of millions of families and depresses their living standards.

They ignore the housing problem, although more than half the nation's families, including millions of veterans, are homeless or living in rural and urban slums.

They refuse social security protection to millions and allow only meagre benefits to the rest.

They block national health legislation even

though millions of men, women, and children are without adequate medical care.

They foster the concentration of private economic power.

They replace progressive government officials, the supporters of Franklin Roosevelt, with spokesmen of Big Business.

They pass tax legislation for the greedy, giving only insignificant reductions to the needy.

These are the acts of the old parties—acts profaning the American dream of abundance.

No glittering party platforms or election promises of the Democratic and Republican parties can hide their betrayal of the needs of the American people.

Nor can they act otherwise. For both parties, as the record of the 80th Congress makes clear, are the champions of Big Business.

The Republican platform admits it.

The Democratic platform attempts to conceal it.

But the very composition of the Democratic leadership exposes the demogogy of its platform. It is a party of machine politicians and Southern Bourbons who veto in Congress the liberal planks "won" in convention.

Such platforms, conceived in hypocrisy and lack of principle, deserve nothing but contempt.

PRINCIPLES OF THE PROGRESSIVE PARTY

The Progressive Party is born in the deep conviction that the national wealth and natural resources of our country belong to the people who inhabit it and must be employed in their behalf; that freedom and opportunity must be secured equally to all; that the brotherhood of man can be achieved and scourge of war ended.

The Progressive Party holds that basic to the organization of world peace is a return to the purpose of Franklin Roosevelt to seek areas of international agreement rather than disagreement. It was his conviction that within the framework of the United Nations different social and economic systems can and must live together. If peace is to be achieved capitalist United States and communist Russia must establish good relations and work together.

The Progressive Party holds that it is the first duty of a just government to secure for all the people, regardless of race, creed, color, sex, na-

tional background, political belief, or station in life, the inalienable rights proclaimed in the Declaration of Independence and guaranteed by the Bill of Rights. The government must actively protect these rights against the encroachments of public and private agencies.

The Progressive Party holds that a just government must use its powers to promote an abundant life for its people. This is the basic idea of Franklin Roosevelt's Economic Bill of Rights. Heretofore every attempt to give effect to this principle has failed because Big Business dominates the key sectors of the economy. Anti-trust laws and government regulation cannot break this domination. Therefore the people, through their democratically elected representatives, must take control of the main levers of the economic system. Public ownership of these levers will enable the people to plan the use of their productive resources so as to develop the limitless potential of modern technology and to create a true American-Commonwealth free from poverty and insecurity.

The Progressive Party believes that only through peaceful understanding can the world make progress toward reconstruction and higher standards of living; that peace is the essential condition for safe-guarding and extending our traditional freedoms; that only by preserving liberty and by planning an abundant life for all can we eliminate the sources of world conflict. Peace, freedom, and abundance—the goals of the Progressive Party—are indivisible.

Only the Progressive Party can destroy the power of private monopoly and restore the government to the American people. For ours is a party uncorrupted by privilege, committed to no special interests, free from machine control, and open to all Americans of all races, colors, and creeds.

The Progressive Party is a party of action. We seek through the democratic process and through day-by-day activity to lead the American people toward the fulfillment of these principles.

We ask support for the following program:

PEACE

American-Soviet Agreement

Henry Wallace in his open letter suggested, and Premier Stalin in his reply accepted, a basis for sincere peace discussions. The exchange showed that specific areas of agreement can be found if the principles of non-interference in the internal affairs of other nations and acceptance of the right of peoples to choose their own form of government and economic system are mutually respected.

The Progressive Party therefore demands negotiation and discussion with the Soviet Union to find areas of agreement to win the peace.

The Progressive Party believes that enduring peace among the peoples of the world community is possible only through world law. Continued anarchy among nations in the atomic age threatens our civilization and humanity itself with annihilation. The only ultimate alternative to war is the abandonment of the principle of the coercion of sovereignties by sovereignties and the adoption of the principle of the just enforcement upon individuals of world federal law, enacted by a world federal legislature with limited but adequate powers to safeguard the common defense and the general welfare of all mankind.

Such a structure of peace through government can be evolved by making of the United Nations an effective agency of cooperation among nations. This can be done by restoring the unity of the Great Powers as they work together for common purposes. Since the death of Franklin Roosevelt, this principle has been betrayed to a degree which not only paralyzes the United Nations but threatens the world with another war in which there can be no victors and few survivors.

Beyond an effective United Nations lies the further possibility of genuine world government. Responsibility for ending the tragic prospect of war is a joint responsibility of the Soviet Union and the United States. We hope for more political liberty and economic democracy throughout the world. We believe that war between East and West will mean fascism and death for all. We insist that peace is the prerequisite of survival.

We believe with Henry Wallace that "there is no misunderstanding or difficulty between the USA and USSR which can be settled by force or fear and there is no difference which cannot be settled by peaceful, hopeful negotiation. There is no American principle of public interest, and there is no Russian principle of public interest, which would have to be sacrificed to end the cold war and open up the Century of Peace which the Century of the Common Man demands."

We denounce anti-Soviet hysteria as a mask for monopoly, militarism, and reaction. We demand that a new leadership of the peace-seeking people of our nation—which has vastly greater responsibility for peace than Russia because it has vastly greater power for war—undertake in good faith and carry to an honorable conclusion, without appeasement or sabre-rattling on either side, a determined effort to settle current controversies and enable men and women everywhere to look forward with confidence to the common task of building a creative and lasting peace for all the world.

End the Drive to War

The Progressive Party calls for the repeal of the peacetime draft and the rejection of Universal Military Training.

We call for the immediate cessation of the piling up of armament expenditures beyond reasonable peacetime requirements for national defense.

We demand the repudiation of the Truman Doctrine and an end to military and economic intervention in support of reactionary and fascist regimes in China, Greece, Turkey, the Middle East, and Latin America. We demand that the United States completely sever diplomatic and economic relations with Franco Spain.

We call for the abandonment of military bases designed to encircle and intimidate other nations.

We demand the repeal of the provisions of the National Security Act which are mobilizing the nation for war, preparing a labor draft, and organizing a monopoly-militarist dictatorship.

These measures will express the American people's determination to avoid provocation and aggression. They will be our contribution to the reduction of mistrust and the creation of a general atmosphere in which peace can be established.

United Nations

The Progressive Party will work to realize Franklin Roosevelt's ideal of the United Nations as a world family of nations, by defending its Charter and seeking to prevent its transformation into the diplomatic or military instrument of any one power or group of powers.

We call for the establishment of a United Nations Reconstruction and Development Fund to promote international recovery by providing assistance to the needy nations of Europe, Africa and Asia, without political conditions and with priorities to those peoples that suffered most from Axis aggression.

We call for the repudiation of the Marshall Plan.

We urge the full use of the Economic and Social Council and other agencies of the United Nations to wipe out disease and starvation, to promote the development of culture and science, and to develop the peaceful application of atomic energy.

We demand that the United States delegation to the United Nations stop protecting fascist Spain and press for effective economic and diplomatic sanctions against Franco's dictatorship.

Disarmament

The Progressive Party will work through the United Nations for a world disarmament agreement to outlaw the atomic bomb, bacteriological warfare, and all other instruments of mass destruction; to destroy existing stockpiles of atomic bombs and to establish United Nations controls, including inspection, over the production of atomic energy; and to reduce conventional armaments drastically in accordance with resolutions already passed by the United Nations General Assembly.

Germany and Japan

The Progressive Party calls for cooperation with our wartime allies to conclude peace treaties promptly with a unified Germany and with Japan. The essentials for a German settlement are denazification and democratization, punishment of war criminals, land reform, decartelization, nationalization of heavy industry, Big-Four control of the Ruhr, reparations to the victims of Nazi aggression, and definitive recognition of the Oder-Neisse line as the Western boundary of Poland. On this basis, we advocate the speedy conclusion of a peace treaty and a simultaneous withdrawal of all occupation troops.

Similar principles should govern a settlement with Japan.

State of Israel

The Progressive Party demands the immediate de jure recognition of the State of Israel.

We call for admission of Israel to the United Nations.

We call for a Presidential proclamation lifting the arms embargo in favor of the State of Israel.

We pledge our support for and call upon the Government of the United States to safeguard the sovereignty, autonomy, political independence, and territorial integrity of the State of Israel in accordance with the boundaries laid down by the Resolution of the General Assembly of the United Nations of November 29, 1947.

We support the prompt extension to Israel of generous financial assistance without political conditions.

We oppose any attempt to interfere with Israel in its sovereign right to control its own immigration policy.

We call upon the United States Government to provide immediate shipping and other facilities for the transportation of Jewish displaced persons in Europe who desire to emigrate to Israel.

We support, within the framework of the United Nations, the internationalization of Jerusalem and the protection of the Holy Places.

We appeal to the Arab workers, farmers and small merchants to accept the United Nations decision for a Jewish and Arab state as being in their best interest. We urge them not to permit themselves to be used as tools in a war against Israel on behalf of British and American monopolies, for the latter are the enemies of both Arabs and Jews.

The Far East

The Progressive Party supports the struggle of the peoples of Asia to achieve independence and to move from feudalism into the modern era. We condemn the bipartisan policy of military and economic intervention to crush these people's movements. World peace and prosperity cannot be attained unless the people of China, Indonesia, Indo-China, Malaya and Asian lands win their struggle for independence and take their place as equals in the family of nations.

We call for the immediate withdrawal of American troops and abandonment of bases in China.

We demand cessation of financial and military aid to the Chiang Kai-shek dictatorship.

We follow the policy of Franklin Roosevelt in encouraging the creation of a democratic coalition government in China. We urge support for and the granting of large scale economic assistance to such a government.

We support the efforts of the people of Korea to establish national unity and the kind of government they desire. We demand an early joint withdrawal of occupation troops.

Colonial and Dependent Peoples

We believe that people everywhere in the world have the right to self-determination. The people of Puerto Rico have the right to independence. The people of the United States have an obligation toward the people of Puerto Rico to see that they are started on the road toward economic security and prosperity.

We demand the repeal of the Bell Trade Act relating to the Philippines and the abrogation of other unequal trade treaties with economically weaker peoples.

We urge action by the people of the United States and cooperation with other countries in the United Nations to abolish the colonial system in all its forms and to realize the principle of self-determination for the peoples of Africa, Asia, the West Indies, and other colonial areas.

We support the aspirations for unified homelands, of traditionally oppressed and dispersed people such as the Irish and Armenians.

Latin America

The Progressive Party urges a return to, and the strengthening of, Franklin Roosevelt's good-neighbor policy in our relations with republics to the South.

We demand the abandonment of the inter-American military program.

We call for economic assistance without political conditions to further the independent economic development of the Latin American and Caribbean countries.

Displaced Persons

The Progressive Party calls for the repeal of the anti-Catholic, anti-semitic Displaced Persons Act of 1948 which permits the entry into the United States of fascists and collaborators. We call for the enactment of legislation to open our doors in the true American tradition to the victims of fascist persecution.

FREEDOM

End Discrimination

The Progressive Party condemns segregation and discrimination in all its forms and in all places.

We demand full equality for the Negro people, the Jewish people, Spanish-speaking Americans, Italian Americans, Japanese Americans, and all other nationality groups.

We call for a Presidential proclamation ending segregation and all forms of discrimination in the armed services and Federal employment.

We demand Federal anti-lynch, anti-discrimination, and fair-employment-practices legislation, and legislation abolishing segregation in interstate travel.

We call for immediate passage of anti-poll tax legislation, enactment of a universal suffrage law to permit all citizens to vote in Federal elections, and the full use of Federal enforcement powers to assure free exercise of the right to franchise.

We call for a Civil Rights Act for the District of Columbia to eliminate racial segregation and discrimination in the nation's capital.

We demand the ending of segregation and discrimination in the Panama Canal Zone and all territories, possessions and trusteeships.

We demand that Indians, the earliest Americans, be given full citizenship rights without loss of reservation rights and be permitted to administer their own affairs.

We will develop special programs to raise the low standards of health, housing, and educational facilities for Negroes, Indians and nationality groups, and will deny Federal funds to any state or local authority which withholds opportunities or benefits for reasons of race, creed, color, sex or national origin.

We will initiate a Federal program of education, in cooperation with state, local, and private agencies to combat racial and religious prejudice.

We support the enactment of legislation making it a Federal crime to disseminate anti-Semitic, anti-Negro, and all racist propaganda by mail, radio, motion picture or other means of communication.

We call for a Constitutional amendment which will effectively prohibit every form of discrimination against women—economic, educational, legal, and political.

We pledge to respect the freedom of conscience

of sincere conscientious objectors to war. We demand amnesty for conscientious objectors imprisoned in World War II.

The Right of Political Association and Expression

The Progressive Party will fight for the constitutional rights of Communists and all other political groups to express their views as the first line in the defense of the liberties of a democratic people.

We oppose the use of violence or intimidation, under cover of law or otherwise, by any individual or group, including the violence and intimidation now being committed by those who are attempting to suppress political dissent.

We pledge an all-out fight against the Mundt-Nixon Bill and all similar legislation designed to impose thought control, restrict freedom of opinion, and establish a police state in America.

We demand the abolition of the House Un-American Activities Committee and similar State Committees, and we mean to right the wrongs which these committees have perpetrated upon thousands of loyal Americans working for the realization of democratic ideals.

We pledge to eliminate the current "Loyalty" purge program and to reestablish standards for government service that respect the rights of Federal employees to freedom of association and opinion and to engage in political activity.

We demand the full right of teachers and students to participate freely and fully in the social, civic and political life of the nation and of the local community.

We demand that the Federal Bureau of Investigation and other Government agencies desist from investigating, or interfering with, the political beliefs and lawful activities of Americans.

We demand an end to the present practices of Congressional Committees — such as the House Labor Committee — in persecuting trade unionists and political leaders at the behest of Big Business.

We demand an end to the present campaign of deportation against foreign-born trade unionists and political leaders, and will actively protect the civil rights of naturalized citizens and the foreign born.

Nationality Groups

The Progressive Party recognizes the varied contributions of all nationality groups to American cultural, economic, and social life, and considers them a source of strength for the democratic development of our country.

We advocate the right of the foreign born to obtain citizenship without discrimination.

We advocate the repeal of discriminatory immigration laws based upon race, national origin, religion, or political belief.

We recognize the just claims of the Japanese Americans for indemnity for the losses suffered during their wartime internment, which was an outrageous violation of our fundamental concepts of justice.

We support legislation facilitating naturalization of Filipinos, Koreans, Japanese, Chinese, and other national groups now discriminated against by law.

We support legislation facilitating naturalization of merchant seamen with a record of war service.

Democracy in the Armed Forces

The Progressive Party demands abolition of Jim Crow in the armed forces.

We demand abolition of social inequalities between officers and enlisted personnel.

We call for basic revision in the procedure of military justice, including the more adequate participation of enlisted men in courts-martial.

We urge that admission to West Point and Annapolis be based on the candidates' qualifications, determined by open competitive examinations, and that an increasing percentage of young men admitted be drawn from the ranks.

Representative Government

The Progressive Party proposes a constitutional amendment providing for the direct election of the President and Vice President by popular vote.

We call for Home Rule and the granting of full suffrage to the disfranchised citizens of the District of Columbia.

We favor the immediate admission of Hawaii and Alaska as the 49th and 50th states of the Union.

We urge that all general and primary election days be declared holidays to enable all citizens to vote.

Separation of Church and State

The Progressive Party intends to maintain the traditional American separation of church and state and protect the freedom of secular education.

ABUNDANCE

High Cost of Living

The living standards of the American people are under bipartisan attack through uncontrolled inflation. The only effective method of combating inflation is to take the profits out of inflation.

The Progressive Party calls for legislation which will impose controls that will reduce and keep down the prices of food, shelter, clothing, other essentials of life, and basic materials. Such controls should squeeze out excessive profits, provide for the payment of subsidies to farmers wherever necessary to maintain fair agricultural prices, and allocate materials and goods in short supply.

We call for removal by the President of the Housing Expediter who is administering rent control in the interests of the real estate lobby.

We call for strengthening rent control, providing protection against evictions, and eliminating the present "hardship" regulations which are a bonanza for the large realty interests.

Economic Planning

The Progressive Party believes in the principle of democratic economic planning and rejects the boom-and-bust philosophy of the old parties.

We mean to establish a Council of Economic Planning to develop plans for assuring high production, full employment, and a rising standard of living.

We mean to develop, on the TVA pattern, regional planning authorities in the major river-valleys the country over to achieve cheap power, rural electrification, soil conservation, flood control and reforestation, and to accelerate the growth of undeveloped areas, particularly in the South and West.

We mean to promote, through public ownership and long-range planning, the peaceful use of atomic energy to realize its great potential as a source of power and as a tool in science, medicine, and technology.

Only through the planned development of all our resources will the full benefit of the nation's wealth and productivity be secured for the people.

Breaking the Grip of Monopoly

Monopoly's grip on the economy must be broken if democracy is to survive and economic planning become possible. Experience has shown that anti-trust laws and government regulation are not by themselves sufficient to halt the growth of monopoly. The only solution is public ownership of key areas of the economy.

The Progressive Party will initiate such measures of public ownership as may be necessary to put into the hands of the people's representatives the levers of control essential to the operation of an economy of abundance. As a first step, the largest banks, the railroads, the merchant marine, the electric power and gas industry, and industries primarily dependent on government funds or government purchases such as the aircraft, the synthetic rubber and synthetic oil industries must be placed under public ownership.

We mean to strengthen and vigorously enforce the anti-trust laws to curb monopoly in the rest of the economy.

We call for the immediate abolition of discriminatory freight rates, which help to keep the South and West in bondage to Wall Street.

Tideland oil resources belong to the people, and we fight the efforts of the oil companies to steal them. We support Federal control of such resources.

We demand the repeal of the Bulwinkle law which exempts railroads from anti-trust prosecution.

We call for the repeal of the Miller-Tydings legislation which eliminated retail competition in branded goods, excluding these from the coverage of the Anti-trust laws.

Labor

The Progressive Party recognizes that from the earliest period of its history the organized labor movement has taken leadership in the struggle for democratic and humanitarian objectives. Organized labor remains the mainspring of America's democratic striving, and the just needs of labor are of special concern to the Progressive Party.

We hold that every American who works for a living has an inalienable right to an income sufficient to provide him and his family with a high standard of living. Unless the rights of labor to organize, to bargain collectively, and to strike are secure, a rising standard of living cannot be realized.

We demand the immediate repeal of the Taft-Hartley Act and the reinstatement of the principles of the Wagner and Norris-LaGuardia acts. These last measures are essential to restore labor's equality in collective bargaining and to prevent business from using government to establish a dictatorship over labor by injunction.

We will demand the right for employees in publicly owned industries to organize, to bargain collectively, and to strike.

We call for the establishment of collective bargaining machinery for Federal employees.

We support the legitimate demands of all wage and salary earners, including Federal employees, for wage and salary increases and improved working conditions. We demand the enactment of a minimum wage of $1 an hour, extension of the Fair Labor Standards Act to cover all workers, enforcement of equal pay for equal work regardless of age or sex, and the elimination of any regional wage differential.

We oppose governmental strike-breaking through seizure of struck industries under the pretext of Federal operation, while profits continue to go to private employers.

We urge the enactment and stringent enforcement of Federal and State laws establishing adequate safety and health standards for miners, longshoremen, railroad workers, merchant seamen, and all other workers in hazardous industries.

We pledge drastic amendment of the Railway Labor Act to make certain that the railroad workers enjoy genuine collective bargaining and the right to strike. We call for amendment of the Railroad Retirement Act to grant railroad workers pensions of $100 minimum after 30 years' service or when they become 60 years old.

We call for Federal legislation to improve railroad working conditions by establishing a 40-hour, 5-day week for non-operating and terminal employees, and a six-hour day for roadmen, and train limit and full crew provisions.

We actively support measures to repair and improve the living standards of the 12 million white collar and professional employees, who have suffered particularly under the inflation.

We call for an end to the second-class citizenship of our nation's two and a half million agricultural wage workers, and the thousands of food-processing workers who are excluded from the protection of social and labor legislation. We stand for legislation to protect the right of agricultural workers to bargain collectively. We call for extension of social security and fair labor standards coverage to all agricultural and food-processing workers.

We demand an immediate end to the arbitrary security orders issued by the Department of National Defense which blacklist employees in private industries under government contracts.

Agriculture

The Progressive Party recognizes that the welfare of farmers is closely tied to the living standards of consumers. We reject the "eat-less" policy of the old parties and proclaim our intention to develop within the framework of an economy of planned abundance, a long-range program of full agricultural production, combined with necessary safeguards for the security of farmers and for the conservation of our natural resources.

We stand for the family-type farm as the basic unit of American agriculture. The Farmer's Home Administration, (formerly, Farm Security Administration) must be expanded to provide ample low-cost credit to assist tenants, sharecroppers, and returned veterans to become farm-owners. Marginal farmers must be assisted to become efficient producers. Where farming is incapable of yielding an adequate family income, supplementary employment on needed conservation and public works projects must be provided.

We propose as a major goal of Federal farm programs that all farm families be enabled to earn an income of not less than $3000 a year. We repudiate the program of Big Business which would eliminate as many as two-thirds of the nation's farmers.

We call for a 5-year program of price-supports for all major crops at not less than 90 percent of parity—parity to be calculated according to an up-to-date formula. Dairy products and certain specialties should be supported at higher rates than 90 percent.

We demand that all essential crops be insured against hazards which are beyond the control of the individual farmer.

We support the principle of direct payments to farmers for soil conservation practices, crop adjustment, and rodent control.

We favor the principle of compensating payments and production subsidies when needed to encourage a high level of consumption without jeopardizing farm income. We also call for assistance to low-income consumers through such programs as the food stamp plan and the school hot-lunch program.

We favor international commodity agreements

and a World Food Board under the United Nations Food and Agriculture Organization to stabilize world markets and to move farm surpluses to deficient areas.

We call for a long-range national land policy designed to discourage the growth of corporation farms and absentee ownership. This policy is especially important in the South to promote the proper development of its resources and to provide land for the landless. Priority in the purchase of land made available by river-valley projects must be given to tenants, sharecroppers, and small farmers.

We regard it as of utmost importance that programs of conservation, production, marketing, and price-support be administered by democratically-elected farmer committeemen, as in the Triple-A program.

We stand for the principle of a graduated land tax and for the 160-acre limitation in the use of public irrigation.

We support farmer and consumer cooperatives as a highly important answer to the problem of monopoly control over markets and supplies. We oppose the tax drive being staged by Big Business against cooperatives.

We favor immediate flood control projects and universal electrification of all farms. REA lines and generating facilities should be rapidly expanded, and river-valley projects for power and irrigation should be undertaken as promptly as possible.

Independent Business

The Progressive Party believes that independent businessmen can survive only in an economy free from monopoly domination, where workers and farmers receive incomes sufficient to permit them to purchase the goods they need.

We propose to encourage and safeguard independent business by providing adequate working capital and development loans at low interest rates, granting tax relief, and giving independent and small business a fair share of government contracts. We propose to make available to independent business, through an expanded government research program, the know-how essential to efficient operation.

Housing

The Progressive Party charges that private enterprise, under monopoly control, has failed to house the American people. It is the responsibility of democratic government to guarantee the right of every family to a decent home at a price it can afford to pay.

We demand a Federal emergency housing program to build within the next two years four million low-rent and low-cost dwellings for homeless and doubled-up families, with priority to veterans.

We recognize that to accomplish this objective it will be necessary to curb non-essential construction, to allocate scarce materials, and to reduce the cost of land, money, and building materials.

We pledge an attack on the chronic housing shortage and the slums through a long-range program to build 25 million new homes during the next ten years. This program will include public subsidized housing for low-income families.

We pledge that as a part of our general program of economic planning the building industry will be reorganized and rationalized, capacity to produce presently scarce materials will be expanded, and year-round employment will be guaranteed to workers in the building trades.

Government—Federal, state and local—has the responsibility to insure that communities are well-planned, with homes conveniently located near places of employment and with adequate provision for health, education, recreation, and culture.

We pledge the abolition of discrimination and segregation in housing.

Security and Health

The Progressive Party demands the extension of social security protection to every man, woman and child in the United States.

We recognize the service which the Townsend Plan has performed in bringing to national attention the tragic plight of the senior citizens of America, and we condemn the bipartisan conspiracy in Congress over the past ten years against providing adequate old-age pensions.

We pledge our active support for a national old-age pension of $100 a month to all persons at 60 years of age, based on right and not on a pauperizing need basis.

We call for a Federal program of adequate disability and sickness benefits and increased unemployment benefits, protecting all workers and their standards of living.

We call for maternity benefits for working mothers for thirteen weeks, including the period before and after childbirth, and the granting of children's allowances to families with children under 18.

We favor adequate public assistance for all persons in need, with Federal grants-in-aid proportionate to the needs and financial ability of the states, pending the enactment of a comprehensive Federal Social Security program.

We support the right of every American to good health through a national system of health insurance, giving freedom of choice to patient and practitioner, and providing adequate medical and dental care for all.

We favor the expenditure of Federal funds in support of an effective program for public health and preventive medicine and a program of dental care.

We favor the expenditure of Federal funds for the promotion of medical and dental education and research.

We look forward to the eventual transfer of the entire cost of the security and health program to the government as an essential public service.

Women

The Progressive Party proposes to secure the rights of women and children and to guarantee the security of the American family as a happy and democratic unit and as the mainstay of our nation.

We propose to raise women to first-class citizens by removing all restrictions—social, economic, and political without jeopardizing the existing protective legislation vital to women as mothers or future mothers.

We propose to extend fair labor standards for women, to guarantee them healthful working conditions, equal job security with men, and their jobs back after the birth of children.

We propose to guarantee medical care for mother and child prior to, during and after birth, through a national system of health insurance.

We propose a program of Federal assistance for the establishment of day care centers for all children.

Young People

The Progressive Party believes young people are the nation's most valuable asset; their full potentialities can be realized only by implementing our complete program for peace, freedom and abundance. We challenge the failure of the old parties to meet the special problems of youth.

We call for the right to vote at eighteen.

We call for the enforcement and extension of child labor laws.

We call for Federal and state expenditures for recreational facilities, particularly in needy rural communities.

Veterans

The Progressive Party recognizes the veterans' special sacrifices and contributions in the nation's most critical period.

We demand priority for veterans in obtaining homes.

We call for a Federal bonus to veterans based on length of service.

We demand the expansion of the Veterans Administration program and increased G. I. benefits and allowances and the elimination of discrimination.

We demand that the coverage of the GI Bill of Rights and other servicemen's benefits be extended to war widows and to merchant seamen with war service.

We call for the prompt refund of the overcharges collected from veterans by National Service Life Insurance.

We demand that the government enforce the right of Negro veterans in the South to file terminal leave applications and to collect their benefits.

We call for increased benefits for disabled veterans and a program to guarantee them jobs at decent wages.

Taxation

The Progressive Party demands the overhaul of the tax structure according to the democratic principle of ability to pay. We propose to employ taxation as a flexible instrument to promote full employment and economic stability.

We propose to exempt from personal income taxes all families and individuals whose income falls below the minimum required for a decent standard of living. We propose that income from capital gains, be taxed at the same graduated rate as ordinary income.

We propose to enact effective excess profits and undistributed profits taxation.

We propose to curb tax-dodging by closing existing loopholes.

We propose to work towards the progressive elimination of Federal excise taxes on the basic necessities of life.

We oppose all state and local sales taxes.

We propose to close existing loopholes in estate and gift taxes and establish an integrated system of estate and gift taxation.

Education

The Progressive Party proposes to guarantee, free from segregation and discrimination, the inalienable right to a good education to every man, woman, and child in America. Essential to good education are the recognized principles of academic freedom—in particular, the principle of free inquiry into and discussion of controversial issues by teachers and students.

We call for the establishment of an integrated Federal grant-in-aid program to build new schools, libraries, raise teachers' and librarians' salaries, improve primary and secondary schools, and assist municipalities and states to establish free colleges.

We call for a system of Federal scholarships, fellowships, and cost-of-living grants, free from limitations or quotas based on race, creed, color, sex or national origin, in order to enable all those with necessary qualifications but without adequate means of support to obtain higher education in institutions of their own choice.

We call for a national program of adult education in cooperation with state and local authorities.

We oppose segregation in education and support legal action on behalf of Negro students and other minorities aimed at securing their admission to state-supported graduate and professional schools which now exclude them by law.

We call for a Department of Education with a Secretary of Cabinet rank.

Culture

The Progressive Party recognizes culture as a potentially powerful force in the moral and spiritual life of a people and through the people, in the growth of democracy and the preservation of peace, and realizes that the culture of a democracy must, like its government, be of, by, and for the people.

We pledge ourselves to establish a department of government that shall be known as the Department of Culture, whose function shall be the promotion of all the arts as an expression of the spirit of the American people, and toward the enrichment of the people's lives, to make the arts available to all.

Promotion of Science

The Progressive Party calls for the enactment of legislation to promote science, including human and social sciences, so that scientific knowledge may be enlarged and used for the benefit of all people.

We condemn the militarization of science and the imposition of military control over scientific expression and communication.

We support measures for public control of patents and licensing provisions to insure that new inventions will be used for the benefit of the people.

The Progressive Party has taken root as the party of the common man. It has arisen in response to, and draws growing strength from, the demand of millions of men and women for the simple democratic right to vote for candidates and a program which satisfy their needs. It gives voters a real choice.

Purposeful and deeply meant, the program of the Progressive Party carries forward the policies of Franklin Roosevelt and the aspirations of Wendell Willkie and holds forth the promise of a reborn democracy ready to play its part in one world. The American people want such a program. They will support it.

Under the leadership of Henry A. Wallace and Glen H. Taylor, a great new people's movement is on the march. Under the guidance of Divine Providence, the Progressive Party, with strong and active faith, moves forward to peace, freedom and abundance.

1948 Platform of the Prohibition Party

PREAMBLE

We, the representatives of the Prohibition Party, assembled in national convention at Winona Lake, Indiana, June 26, 27, 28, 1947, recognizing Almighty God as the source of all just government and with faith in the teachings of the Prince of Peace, do solemnly promise that, if our party is chosen to administer the affairs of this nation, we will use all the power of our administration to serve the people of the United States.

World Peace and Order

We believe in World peace, and universal brotherhood.

Having united with other national groups to restore world order and preserve world peace, our nation should lead them all in submerging selfish interests for the common good of all.

This is a severe test for American statesmen and the men to be intrusted with the task should be men whose dependence is upon a Higher Power for wisdom and guidance.

Atomic Energy

We favor the development of a constructive plan for the international control of atomic energy, involving a system of international inspection of the manufacture of atomic energy and punishment for violation of regulations.

Universal Military Training

Believing that peacetime military training in our country does not represent a safeguard for world peace, that it is contrary in principle to our American way of life, that it places an unnecessary burden upon our peacetime economy, that it could lead only to military dictatorship, and that it would, under existing conditions, lead to the moral and spiritual deterioration of our youth, we declare our opposition to any program of peacetime military conscription.

Constitutional Government

We renew our loyalty to the Constitution of the United States and have supreme confidence in this form of government to meet ever-changing national and world conditions.

We are opposed to Nazism, Communism and Fascism and all other forms of totalitarianism. We are convinced that the best and only safeguard against these dangerous doctrines is to protect the rights and guard the welfare of our citizens.

War spending has set an extravagant example of wasteful government operation. The time is here for rigid curtailment. We believe that for any government to take nearly one-third of its citizen's income to pay the expenses of government is a most unjust, immoral act. We believe the only way to materially reduce the cost of government is to reduce the number of functions performed by government. Hence, in accordance with the principle which we believe to be the basis of all sound government—namely, that government ought not to do what the people, without government intervention, can do. We promise, if elected to power, to reorganize the federal government in accordance with this principle, discarding all departments, bureaus or other unnecessary personnel that cannot qualify as legitimate when measured by this principle.

Taxes

With proper economy, government will cost less and thus make it possible to steadily reduce the public debt and gradually lift the tax load from the average citizen.

In the states we favor the effort to limit the tax rate whenever possible to one percent of full value of property, in order to prevent foreclosure and confiscation, and assist the home owner, farmer, and others to preserve their property.

Enforcement of Law

We are opposed to nullification of law by non-enforcement, and will maintain the integrity of democracy by enforcing the Constitution and the laws enacted under it by elected representatives of the people or by popular vote.

Ballot Law Reform

We demand the repeal of the many state ballot laws which have been enacted to make the two-party system a bi-partisan political monopoly and which now deny to independent voters and minority groups the fundamental right of free political expression as guaranteed by the Constitution.

Church and State

The Constitutional separation of Church and State must be maintained. We will not tax church or religious activities, except those operated for profit. We are opposed to the appropriation of public money for any sectarian purposes.

Monopoly

Because monopolies, whether by capital, labor or any other group or individual are harmful in result, wrong in principle and tend to dictatorship, we shall enact and enforce laws to break them up and prevent their operations.

Public Morality

Moral and spiritual considerations should be primary factors in determining national policies. We will strengthen and enforce laws against gambling, narcotics and commercialized vice now so openly violated and nullified by the inaction of the parties in power, and thus prevent further disintegration of the public morals.

Money

The Constitution provides for the issuance of money and the determination of the value thereof by Congress. This is a sound and feasible monetary policy, which we shall enforce.

No Racial Discrimination

Recognizing that "God created of one blood all nations to dwell upon the face of the earth," we declare in favor of full justice and equal opportunity for all people, whatever their religion, or racial or national origin.

Marriage and Divorce

To maintain the sanctity of the home we favor the enactment of uniform marriage and divorce laws.

Labor and Industry

Labor organizations are entitled to great credit for improving the status of the workers, and for their constructive contributions to the general welfare. It is our purpose to give the public good paramount consideration. Neither capital nor labor can be permitted to dominate at the expense of the other or the public welfare.

Social Security and Old Age Pensions

We will extend the Social Security Act so as to include all employed groups in its provisions. We will also develop a system of annuity insurance for aged persons and so administer it as to preserve the incentives of initiative and thrift.

Home Ownership

We greatly deprecate the fact that so many ex-service men are without sufficient housing facilities for themselves and families.

It should be possible for every American family that desires to do so to own its own house. We favor such legislation as may facilitate the realization of this objective.

Co-operatives

Co-operatives and profit sharing enterprises are a natural outgrowth of democracy. Government under our administration will encourage such enterprises.

A Party of Service, Not Spoils

The two dominant parties are committed to the spoils system and when in office have prostituted government to serve their own selfish party interests instead of serving the whole people. That policy has led to excessive government expenditures, and higher taxes. We pledge ourselves to an honest, efficient and economical administration.

Prohibition

No self governing nation can survive the mass alcoholization of its voters and the mass perversion of the judgments of its citizens.

As the result of the repeal of the 18th Amendment our government has authorized and empowered the liquor traffic to derange the minds and pervert the judgment of a multitude of American citizens both young and old.

No political issue confronting our citizens compares in magnitude with the necessity for suppressing the alcohol beverage traffic.

The present liquor conditions, which are far worse than ever before, are due directly to the joint action of the two major parties when they adopted platform planks to destroy the 18th Amendment.

The moral forces have to contend with the liquor power which is highly capitalized, strongly organized, and is promoting liquor sales by every possible means to create an ever growing appetite in youth, men and women. This power dominates our politics and government. It controls large numbers of voters. Every saloon is a center for mobilizing and controlling votes. Both parties are subservient to the liquor power. So long as good citizens continue to give their votes to liquor parties, so long as they continue to be yoked by party membership with the liquor interests and the underworld, so long will they be incapable of making moral principles prevail.

What is needed is a re-alignment of voters and the union of good citizens in a party unitedly committed to the principles of Prohibition—a party not dependent upon votes wielded and delivered by the liquor power. American government is party government. There are constitutional reasons why this is so. To overcome the liquor power it is necessary to employ the agency of a political party unitedly committed to Prohibition.

We summon the voters of America to help elect the Prohibition party to power. We will then marshal the resources of the government, legislative, executive and judicial, to overcome the liquor power.

Republican Party Platform of 1948

I

DECLARATION OF PRINCIPLES

To establish and maintain peace, to build a country in which every citizen can earn a good living with the promise of real progress for himself and his family, and to uphold as a beacon light for mankind everywhere, the inspiring American tradition of liberty, opportunity and justice for all—that is the Republican platform.

To this end we propose as a guide to definite action the following principles:

Maximum voluntary cooperation between citizens and minimum dependence on law; never, however, declining courageous recourse to law if necessary.

Our competitive system furnishes vital opportunity for youth and for all enterprising citizens; it makes possible the productive power which is the unique weapon of our national defense; and is the mainspring of material well-being and political freedom.

Government, as the servant of such a system, should take all needed steps to strengthen and develop public health, to promote scientific research, to provide security for the aged, and to promote a stable economy so that men and women need not fear the loss of their jobs or the threat of economic hardships through no fault of their own.

The rights and obligations of workers are commensurate with the rights and obligations of employers and they are interdependent; these rights should be protected against coercion and exploitation from whatever quarter and with due regard for the general welfare of all.

The soil as our basic natural resource must be conserved with increased effectiveness; and farm prices should be supported on a just basis.

Development of the priceless national heritage which is in our West is vital to our nation.

Administration of government must be economical and effective.

Faulty governmental policies share an important responsibility for the present cruelly high cost of living. We pledge prompt action to correct these policies. There must be decent living at decent wages.

Our common defense must be strengthened and unified.

Our foreign policy is dedicated to preserving a free America in a free world of free men. This calls for strengthening the United Nations and primary recognition of America's self-interest in the liberty of other peoples. Prudently conserving our own resources, we shall cooperate on a self-help basis with other peace-loving nations.

Constant and effective insistence on the personal dignity of the individual, and his right to complete justice without regard to race, creed or color, is a fundamental American principle.

We aim always to unite and to strengthen; never to weaken or divide. In such a brotherhood will we Americans get results. Thus we will overcome all obstacles.

II

In the past eighteen months, the Republican Congress, in the face of frequent obstruction from the Executive Branch, made a record of solid achievement. Here are some of the accomplishments of this Republican Congress:

The long trend of extravagant and ill-advised Executive action reversed;

the budget balanced;

taxes reduced;

limitation of Presidential tenure to two terms passed;

assistance to veterans, their widows and orphans provided;

assistance to agriculture and business enacted;

elimination of the poll tax as a requisite to soldier voting;

a sensible reform of the labor law, protecting all rights of Labor while safeguarding the entire community against those breakdowns in essential industries which endanger the health and livelihood of all;

a long-range farm program enacted;

unification of the armed services launched;

a military manpower law enacted;

the United Nations fostered;

a haven for displaced persons provided;

the most far-reaching measures in history adopted to aid the recovery of the free world on a basis of self-help and with prudent regard for our own resources;

and, finally, the development of intelligent plans and party teamwork for the day when the American people entrust the Executive as well as the Legislative branch of our National Government to the Republican Party.

We shall waste few words on the tragic lack of foresight and general inadequacy of those now in charge of the Executive Branch of the National Government; they have lost the confidence of citizens of all parties.

III

Present cruelly high prices are due in large part to the fact that the government has not effectively used the powers it possesses to combat inflation, but has deliberately encouraged higher prices.

We pledge an attack upon the basic causes of inflation, including the following measures:

progressive reduction of the cost of government through elimination of waste;

stimulation of production as the surest way to lower prices;

fiscal policies to provide increased incentives for production and thrift;

a sound currency;

reduction of the public debt.

We pledge further, that in the management of our National Government, we shall achieve the abolition of overlapping, duplication, extravagance, and excessive centralization;

the more efficient assignment of functions within the government;

and the rooting out of Communism wherever found.

These things are fundamental.

IV

We must, however, do more.

The Constitution gives us the affirmative mandate "to establish justice."

In Lincoln's words: The dogmas of the quiet past are inadequate to the stormy present. The occasion is piled high with difficulty and we must rise with the occasion. As our case is new, so we must think anew and act anew.

The tragic experience of Europe tells us that popular government disappears when it is ineffective and no longer can translate into action the aims and the aspirations of the people.

Therefore, in domestic affairs, we propose:

The maintenance of armed services for air, land and sea, to a degree which will insure our national security; and the achievement of effective unity in the Department of National Defense so as to insure maximum economy in money and manpower, and maximum effectiveness in case of war. We favor sustained effective action to procure sufficient manpower for the services, recognizing the American principle that every citizen has an obligation of service to his country.

An adequate privately operated merchant marine, the continued development of our harbors and waterways, and the expansion of privately operated air transportation and communication systems.

The maintenance of Federal finances in a healthy condition and continuation of the efforts so well started by the Republican Congress to reduce the enormous burden of taxation in order to provide incentives for the creation of new industries and new jobs, and to bring relief from inflation. We favor intelligent integration of Federal-State taxing and spending policies designed to eliminate wasteful duplication, and in order that the State and local governments may be able to assume their separate responsibilities, the Federal government shall as soon as practicable withdraw or reduce those taxes which can be best administered by local governments, with particular consideration of excise and inheritance taxes; and we favor restoring to America a working federalism.

Small business, the bulwark of American enterprise, must be encouraged through aggressive anti-monopoly action, elimination of unnecessary controls, protection against discrimination, correction of tax abuses, and limitation of competition by governmental organizations.

Collective bargaining is an obligation as well as a right, applying equally to workers and employers; and the fundamental right to strike is subordinate only to paramount considerations of public health and safety. Government's chief function in this field is to promote good will, encourage cooperation, and where resort is had to intervention, to be impartial, preventing violence and requiring obedience to all law by all parties involved. We pledge continuing study to improve labor-management legislation in the light of experience and changing conditions.

There must be a long-term program in the interest of agriculture and the consumer which should include: An accelerated program of sounder soil conservation; effective protection of reasonable market prices through flexible support prices, commodity loans, marketing agreements, together with such other means as may be necessary, and the development of sound farm credit; encouragement of family-size farms; intensified research to discover new crops, new uses for existing crops, and control of hoof and mouth and other animal diseases and crop pests; support of the principle of bona fide farmer-owned and farmer-operated cooperatives, and sound rural electrification.

We favor progressive development of the Nation's water resources for navigation, flood control and power, with immediate action in critical areas.

We favor conservation of all our natural resources and believe that conservation and stockpiling of strategic and critical raw materials is indespensable to the security of the United States.

We urge the full development of our forests on the basis of cropping and sustained yield with cooperation of States and private owners for conservation and fire protection.

We favor a comprehensive reclamation program for arid and semi-arid areas with full protection of the rights and interests of the States in the use and control of water for irrigation, power development incidental thereto and other beneficial uses; withdrawal or acquisition of lands for public purposes only by Act of Congress and after due consideration of local problems; development of processes for the extraction of oil and other substances from oil shale and coal; adequate representation of the West in the National Administration.

Recognizing the Nation's solemn obligation to all veterans, we propose a realistic and adequate adjustment of benefits on a cost-of-living basis for service-connected disabled veterans and their dependents, and for the widows, orphans and dependents of veterans who died in the service of their country. All disabled veterans should have ample opportunity for suitable, self-sustaining employment. We demand good-faith compliance with veterans preference in Federal service with simplification and codification of the hundreds of piecemeal Federal laws affecting veterans, and efficient and businesslike management of the Veterans Administration. We pledge the highest possible standards of medical care and hospitalization.

Housing can best be supplied and financed by private enterprise; but government can and should encourage the building of better homes at less cost. We recommend Federal aid to the States for local slum clearance and low-rental housing programs only where there is a need that cannot be met either by private enterprise or by the States and localities.

Consistent with the vigorous existence of our competitive economy, we urge: extension of the Federal Old Age and Survivors' Insurance program and increase of the benefits to a more realistic level; strengthening of Federal-State programs designed to provide more adequate hospital facilities, too improve methods of treatment for the mentally ill, to advance maternal and child health and generally to foster a healthy America.

Lynching or any other form of mob violence anywhere is a disgrace to any civilized state, and we favor the prompt enactment of legislation to end this infamy.

One of the basic principles of this Republic is the equality of all individuals in their right to life, liberty, and the pursuit of happiness. This principle is enunciated in the Declaration of Independence and embodied in the Constitution of the United States; it was vindicated on the field of battle and became the cornerstone of this Republic. This right of equal opportunity to work and to advance in life should never be limited in any individual because of race, religion, color, or country of origin. We favor the enactment and just enforcement of such Federal legislation as may be necessary to maintain this right at all times in every part of this Republic.

We favor the abolition of the poll tax as a requisite to voting.

We are opposed to the idea of racial segregation in the armed services of the United States.

V

We pledge a vigorous enforcement of existing laws against Communists and enactment of such new legislation as may be necessary to expose the treasonable activities of Communists and defeat their objective of establishing here a godless dictatorship controlled from abroad.

We favor a revision of the procedure for the election of the President and Vice President which will more exactly reflect the popular vote.

We recommend to Congress the submission of a constitutional amendment providing equal rights for women.

We favor equal pay for equal work regardless of sex.

We propose a well-paid and efficient Federal career service.

We favor the elimination of unnecessary Federal bureaus and of the duplication of the functions of necessary governmental agencies.

We favor equality of educational opportunity for all and the promotion of education and educational facilities.

We favor restoration to the States of their historic rights to the tide and submerged lands, tributary waters, lakes, and streams.

We favor eventual statehood for Hawaii, Alaska and Puerto Rico. We urge development of Alaskan land communications and natural resources.

We favor self-government for the residents of the nation's capital.

VI

We dedicate our foreign policy to the preservation of a free America in a free world of free men. With neither malice nor desire for conquest, we shall strive for a just peace with all nations.

America is deeply interested in the stability, security and liberty of other independent peoples. Within the prudent limits of our own economic welfare, we shall cooperate, on a basis of self-help and mutual aid, to assist other peace-loving nations to restore their economic independence and the human rights and fundamental freedoms for which we fought two wars and upon which dependable peace must build. We shall insist on

businesslike and efficient administration of all foreign aid.

We welcome and encourage the sturdy progress toward unity in Western Europe.

We shall erect our foreign policy on the basis of friendly firmness which welcomes cooperation but spurns appeasement. We shall pursue a consistent foreign policy which invites steadiness and reliance and which thus avoids the misunderstandings from which wars result. We shall protect the future against the errors of the Democrat Administration, which has too often lacked clarity, competence or consistency in our vital international relationships and has too often abandoned justice.

We believe in collective security against aggression and in behalf of justice and freedom. We shall support the United Nations as the world's best hope in this direction, striving to strengthen it and promote its effective evolution and use. The United Nations should progressively establish international law, be freed of any veto in the peaceful settlement of international disputes, and be provided with the armed forces contemplated by the Charter. We particularly commend the value of regional arrangements as prescribed by the Charter; and we cite the Western Hemispheric Defense Pact as a useful model.

We shall nourish these Pan-American agreements in the new spirit of cooperation which implements the Monroe Doctrine.

We welcome Israel into the family of nations and take pride in the fact that the Republican Party was the first to call for the establishment of a free and independent Jewish Commonwealth. The vacillation of the Democrat Administration on this question has undermined the prestige of the United Nations. Subject to the letter and spirit of the United Nations Charter, we pledge to Israel full recognition, with its boundaries as sanctioned by the United Nations and aid in developing its economy.

We will foster and cherish our historic policy of friendship with China and assert our deep interest in the maintenance of its integrity and freedom.

We shall seek to restore autonomy and self-sufficiency as rapidly as possible in our post-war occupied areas, guarding always against any rebirth of aggression.

We shall relentlessly pursue our aims for the

universal limitation and control of arms and implements of war on a basis of reliable disciplines against bad faith.

At all times safeguarding our own industry and agriculture, and under efficient administrative procedures for the legitimate consideration of domestic needs, we shall support the system of reciprocal trade and encourage international commerce.

We pledge that under a Republican Administration all foreign commitments shall be made public and subject to constitutional ratification. We shall say what we mean and mean what we say. In all of these things we shall primarily consult the national security and welfare of our own United States. In all of these things we shall welcome the world's cooperation. But in none of these things shall we surrender our ideals or our free institutions.

We are proud of the part that Republicans have taken in those limited areas of foreign policy in which they have been permitted to participate. We shall invite the Minority Party to join us under the next Republican Administration in stopping partisan politics at the water's edge.

We faithfully dedicate ourselves to peace with justice.

VII

Guided by these principles, with continuing faith in Almighty God; united in the spirit of brotherhood; and using to the full the skills, resources and blessings of liberty with which we are endowed; we, the American people, will courageously advance to meet the challenge of the future.

Socialist Party Platform—1948

PREAMBLE

Mankind is haunted by new fears. In the crowded metropolis and on the distant farm, men ask themselves whether, under freedom, depression can be avoided, poverty vanquished and war uprooted.

Starvation stalks much of the world, and in our own land men dread the insecurity that tomorrow may bring. While millions go in rags, the world's looms are again knitting the uniforms that will shroud new victims to be offered on the altars of nationalism, imperialism and tyranny.

In 1948, we face the elemental question of survival. The atomic revolution has burst upon the world and a new unity has been forged among the human race: men who have refused to be brothers one of another may now become children of a common doom.

. . . Unless we learn to reorganize our society for survival and not for mutual extinction;

. . . Unless we learn new techniques of cooperation to replace the old policies of competition;

. . . Unless we move rapidly toward socialization by which alone the individual can be preserved in the inter-dependent world of the turbine, the plane, the steel mill and the uranium pile;

. . . Unless we move rapidly to a world order without greed, profit and hate.

The American people, because of the accidents of geography, will make the decision for mankind. Our mines and factories were not devastated by the physical havoc of the last war. For America, and consequently the world, it is not too late.

Three forces today are competing for the loyalty of men. And in this race, the stakes are the survival of mankind.

On the one hand, an economic system calling itself "free enterprise" asserts that it can lead to the salvation of humanity. It has brought us repeatedly to depressions and wars, yet its spokesmen in the Democratic and Republican Parties still pretend they have solutions.

They have, in fact, betrayed the promises with which they woo the American people every four years. They offered prosperity and delivered depression. They pledged peace and delivered war. They promised to increase our standard of living and are now raising the cost of living. They promised freedom to organized labor and hobbled it with new bonds.

They have sought partisan advantage and jeopardized national welfare. The dominant wings in their parties have combined to destroy price control and give us inflation, to undermine restraints on greed and give us shortage, to favor the rich and deny the poor, to cut the taxes of the wealthy and insult the common man with a crumb.

There is a second force in the world—which promises security and speaks of freedom but delivers only economic bondage and dictatorship. It is the force of totalitarianism. Yesterday its most sinister front was Fascism; today it is Communism.

In the United States, it marches under masked

banners. It calls itself a "new party" and has pushed into the forefront well-meaning liberals who do not know the purposes of their Communist allies. And this alliance, though speaking for civil liberties at home, defends the most powerful tyranny in the modern world. It speaks of peace but is blind to the most aggressive imperialism of the present day. It speaks of one world but works for two spheres of influence. It urges the brotherhood of man but sanctifies the divisive principle of national sovereignty.

As against these forces, the Socialist Party of the United States speaks for the Third Force—democratic socialism, the principles of democratic planning and international order. This socialist program for the United States today includes these major goals:

BASIC SOCIALIST DEMANDS

1. The natural resources of the nation—minerals, oil, electric and atomic power—are the property of the people. Their preservation for future generations and their management by the people for social purposes can be achieved democratically under socialism.

2. The basic industries, public utilities, banking and credit institutions—all the economic facilities needed for the satisfaction of the fundamental requirements of the people—must be socially owned and democratically managed.

3. Socialism will democratize the economic life of the nation by the joint representation of workers, the working management and the consuming public, in the management of socialized enterprises; by the guarantee of popular control of enterprise through the maximum decentralization economically feasible and the use of various types of organization, particularly the public corporation and the voluntary cooperative; and by the preservation of the freedom of labor organization and of consumer choice.

With such control we can have democratic planning. The lessons of the last war have taught that only by planning, by large-scale government investment, by decisive national action, can production be increased to meet the goals set by the nation. In place of the destructive ends sought in wartime, the nation must now fix its peacetime goals—food for the ill-fed, clothing for the ill-clothed, homes for the ill-housed.

A nation that could fill the skies with planes and the oceans with warships can fill its streets and avenues with homes, schools and hospitals; swell its granaries and storehouses; bring joy to its people and the world. In the light of this Socialist program for democratic planning, we offer this platform to the American people in the 1948 elections. It can be achieved.

DOMESTIC PROGRAM

1. *Raise the Standard of Living*

It must be the constant task of the nation to raise the standard of living of its people. This can be effected only by a continually rising trend in production and wage levels, the stabilization of prices, and the immediate elimination of profits as the determining factor in production. In a period of inflation wage increases without price controls are delusions.

2. *Expand the Productive Facilities of the Nation*

The American standard of living and the needs of world economic rehabilitation make it essential that our national production be rapidly expanded. An economy based on profit will not expand so long as scarcity is profitable and inflation an easy road to gain.

The Socialist Party calls for government action to assure investment in new plant capacity through the establishment of public corporations for the production of ever-mounting quantities of steel, oil and other raw materials, and the utilization of the nation's water resources for the development of cheaper and more abundant electric power. A far-flung program of Tennessee Valley Administrations, Missouri Valley Administrations and Rural Electrification Administration cooperatives can effect the electrification of whole areas that are lagging far behind their agricultural and industrial potential. Only by planned growth in our national output of civilian goods can we end the menace of inflation, which is now dangerously increased by our enormous expenditures on arms.

3. *Expand Social Legislation*

The intricacies of twentieth century living and the potentialities of modern technology have at last made it possible to guarantee a national minimum standard of living for the population. The Socialist Party advocates:

a. Expansion of unemployment insurance and social security. Millions of workers are as yet uncovered by the unemployment and social security provisions. The present law discriminates against farm labor, domestic servants and other working groups despite the constitutional guarantee of the "equal protection of the laws." Even so, the Democratic-Republican coalition in Congress has been whittling down the number of workers protected by the existing law at a time when extension of coverage should be the order of the day.

The age at which workers become eligible for old age pensions should be promptly reduced to 60, and the system should be financed by net progressive income taxation rather than by the regressive payroll tax. The benefits—now drastically cut by the current inflation—should be raised.

The Social Security law should be amended to include family allowances. The proper care of children is at least as important as the care of the aged.

b. Minimum Wage. The present legal minimum wage under the Wage-Hour Law should be immediately raised to the 75 cents an hour demanded by organized labor, with progressive increases to occur periodically.

The number of employees protected by the Act must be increased by a redefinition of coverage; and the present reactionary drive to reduce the coverage must be defeated.

c. Health services. Legislation for comprehensive medical and hospital care, financed by a national contributory system of health insurance, must be enacted by Congress. The Democratic-Republican coalition has successfully blocked the health insurance bill. In contrast, the Taft health bill will not provide comprehensive medical care nor remove the economic barriers now depriving millions of proper medical service.

Only a national health insurance program can guarantee free access to medical care, freedom of doctors' choice and freedom for the medical profession within a framework of public responsibility.

Neither a fee-for-service system nor voluntary prepayment plans can bring the benefits of modern medical science to all the people, regardless of race, color, creed, geography or economic condition.

Federal tax funds should be used to supplement an insurance program in creating a fully rounded national health service.

Public health services must be increased; the construction of new hospitals and clinics must be pushed. Federal action must be taken to stimulate research and public preventive medicine in cancer, heart diseases, mental illness, alcoholism and other ailments, as was done in the field of atomic fission. The maternal and child services provided by the Social Security Act must be extended.

d. Education. It is a national disgrace that the richest nation in the world does not have the best possible educational program from the nursery school to the university. America has subjected its children and youth to a shameful chronic emergency in this field. Higher standards of teacher training, enlarged and improved facilities, curricula better designed to meet pupil needs, adequate salaries, attractive conditions for superior professional work—all require that Federal contributions to public education be vastly multiplied without reducing local community initiative and existing State responsibilities.

At the same time, legislative efforts to divert public funds to private sectarian schools must be defeated. The principle of separation of church and state must be consistently applied in the use of public educational funds.

We propose passage of State and Federal laws aimed at eliminating racial, cultural and religious discrimination and segregation in education.

e. Veterans. Because of the special hardships war worked upon the veterans and conscientious objectors, we favor legislation to provide them substantial and adequate benefits in the form of education, medical care and loans; and full care for the families of those who did not return. We demand immediate steps to end the vicious discrimination and outright fraud now being practiced against Negro, Nisei, Spanish- or Mexican-American veterans by prejudiced local employees of the Veterans Administration, particularly in the South and Southwest.

4. Expand the Nation's Housing Facilities

Private enterprise has failed dismally to meet the challenge of housing the American people. Its boast that the lifting of controls on new construction would stimulate large-scale building has proved hollow. The lower income groups most desperately in need of housing, the young people —particularly our veterans—and the inhabitants of our ever-growing slums, are not in a position to buy or rent the facilities that private contractors are willing or able to erect.

The Taft-Ellender-Wagner Bill should be passed —but only as the merest fraction of a beginning, precisely because its major reliance is on the private construction industry.

The Socialist Party proposes the creation of a Home Loan Bank to finance the purchase of homes, a Public Supply and Fabricating Corporation to set up factory units needed to produce materials and to develop large-scale prefabricated housing; the expansion of public housing activities in the field of low-income multiple dwellings; the expansion of publicly built, cooperative tenant-operated housing; the integration of national and local housing plans, including revision of municipal building codes; the development of a government program of bona fide collective bargaining with the building and construction unions, providing for a guaranteed annual wage to remove one of the worst evils of the building industry and for the development of apprentice-training programs.

We favor the extension and strengthening of rent control for the duration of the housing emergency. The people of America must call to account those legislators who are destroying rent controls, permitting eviction of tenants by subterfuge and so contributing to disastrous inflation in the field of housing.

5. Protect the Nation's Title to Atomic Energy Pending Internationalization

The United States has made a good beginning in reserving to the nation, rather than ceding to business, the ownership of atomic energy. But this principle is already being undermined by cost-plus contracts, granted to private corporations to exploit this new storehouse of power for profit as coal, oil and other resources have been in the past. Nuclear fission was not the product of private enterprise. It was financed by the nation and was achieved by cooperative scientific effort operating in complete disregard of the profit motive. As the peace-time uses of atomic energy begin to emerge, it becomes increasingly important that the constructive applications of atomic power be utilized only through non-profit public corporations.

6. Strengthen Civil and Political Liberties

Civil and political liberties are in serious danger today. The Socialist Party calls for greater vigilance and specifically demands:

a. Repeal of the Taft-Hartley Act which undermines the right to strike, the right to organize, the right to sign contracts guaranteeing union security and furthering the economic interests of organized workers; and which permits the power of the state to be used in behalf of employers and against workers with just grievances. The Socialist Party pledges its full support to organized labor in its effort to repeal the Taft-Hartley Act and similar state laws.

b. Elimination of the Committee on Un-American Activities which has pursued the dishonest tradition of the Dies Committee. The Committee has abused the legitimate democratic function of Congress to investigate and collect data on matters of national importance.

c. Defeat of any legislation that would force the Communist Party further underground and that would appear to give moral justification to its conspiratorial policies. The right to free expression of political views must not be impaired. But the existing laws against overt acts should be vigorously enforced.

d. Elimination of poll taxes and opening of the ballot to citizens regardless of income.

e. Full amnesty and restoration of civil rights for war objectors, several hundred of whom are still in prison and thousands of whom have lost citizenship.

7. Establish Racial Equality

Democracy cannot tolerate two classes of citizenship. Complete political economic and social equality, regardless of race, religion or national origin must be established.

a. Segregation must be abolished in the armed forces, in all public institutions and in housing.

b. Legislation for a Fair Employment Practices Committee, long overdue, should be passed.

c. Anti-lynching legislation must be enacted to wipe out the worst blot on the American scene.

d. Naturalization rights should be granted to Japanese immigrants who have demonstrated their loyalty, and indemnification should be given to Japanese immigrants and their American descendants who suffered property losses because of government policy during World War II.

e. All forms of discriminating barriers against immigration on grounds of race, color or national origin must be abolished.

f. Guarantee the right to vote to many citizens now robbed of suffrage. The 14th Amendment of the Constitution, depriving states of representation in Congress in proportion to the number of citizens deprived of the right to vote by virtue of race, color, or previous condition of servitude, should be promptly enforced.

8. Safeguard American Agriculture

The Socialist Party opposes the absentee ownership of farms and its attendant tenancy in America. We reaffirm our position that occupancy and use should be the only rightful title to farmland. Where conditions favor family farming, the security of such farmers should be strengthened through cooperative credit purchasing and marketing, aided by government financing. Where modern techniques and specialization require large-scale farm enterprises, we call for social ownership and cooperative operation to replace the corporation farm which threatens both the security and freedom of farm workers.

We disapprove of the New Deal idea of agricultural scarcity, aimed at keeping prices up by limiting production. Our domestic needs and those of the world require an agricultural program based on maximum production.

We urge the continuation and expansion of the present conservation program to check destruction by floods, erosion of topsoil and depletion of farm fertility. Our obligation to our grandchildren demands a greater concern with the heritage we leave in productive farmland.

The proper distribution and marketing of food and fiber does not require gambling. Our present Board of Trade pricing of farm produce, with its poker game practices of buying on futures, must be ended.

9. Establish a Progressive Tax System

The Tax Law of 1948 is legislation for the direct and immediate benefit of the wealthiest group in the country. Their taxes have been drastically lowered without any real assurance that corresponding economic benefits in the form of additional equity capital for new production will result. The tax reduction for those in the lower income brackets is petty, and will disappear altogether after November if a Democratic or Republican Congress is elected.

We Propose:

a. Raising the present exemption levels to equal the amounts necessary to sustain minimum standards of living.

b. Restoring the earned Income Credit in such form that it grants a tax benefit (with an appropriate maximum) to income from wages and salary in contrast to income from investment.

c. Tightening of the provisions of the Estate Tax section of the Internal Revenue Code by increasing the rates, lowering the exemption and plugging the loop-holes by which inherited wealth can be passed on for two and sometimes more generations, by means of trusts, without paying succession taxes. Corresponding changes must be made in the Gift Tax section.

d. Modification of the Internal Revenue Code's favored treatment of speculative and gambling profits, and encouragement of new equity capital for production by revision of the treatment of Capital Assets.

e. Financing of extraordinary government expenses through a capital levy, especially on the increase in private capital since 1939, so that those who benefited directly from World War II will bear the burden of the nation's war deficit.

f. We condemn the fraudulent joint-return provision of the new tax law as a device which enables the wealthy to minimize their share of the tax burden.

10. Financing the Socialist Program

The American people will be told that it is impossible to finance this program for economic security. The cost of World War II to the American people was some 350 billion dollars. It is fantastic to assert that we cannot afford to devote a fraction of that sum to the peace and happiness of the nation. On the basis of the program submitted to Congress by the Armed Forces, it is apparent that our military budget alone in 1952 will equal the present total national budget. The path to plenty lies in expanding our production and in reallocating our budget in the service of life and peace.

Foreign Policy

Victory by the U. S. and its allies in two world wars has not established justice or peace. A third world war fought with atom bombs and bacteria will complete the ruin of mankind.

The major, but by no means the only threat of war, lies in the aggression of the Soviet empire and the international communist movement. That aggression has been invited and encouraged by the blunders of American policy from the Cairo and Teheran through the Yalta and Potsdam conferences. Disregard for those principles of peace which the Socialist Party has steadily urged since the campaign of 1944 has contributed directly to the present crisis. The problem of peace cannot be solved by any attainable superiority of American military might. The bi-partisan effort in Washington to achieve such superiority and the hysteria which accompanies it make war more likely, and threaten our internal democracy with a dangerous American militarism.

The road to peace lies neither through the policy of appeasement laid down at Yalta and now supported by Henry Wallace, nor through the confused military commitments of the Truman doctrine. Neither of these contradictory policies can defeat international communism or the conditions that breed it.

A far better approach is the European Economic Recovery Program. It is a significant recognition that cooperative economic action must be taken if the European continent is not to pass into chaos and so into communist hands. But the helpful economic cooperation necessary to peace cannot be confined to Western Europe. In Europe itself vigilance is necessary lest the Recovery Program be subverted into an attempt to re-establish capitalist reaction or fascism, or to promote an American economic imperialism.

In addition to the proper conduct of the ERP a policy looking to the winning of lasting peace must include the following proposals:

1. Conscription

The representatives of the United States should immediately propose to the United Nations that peacetime conscription be outlawed by all nations. We are opposed to all forms of peacetime conscription in the U. S. Conscription contributed greatly to the growth of totalitarianism in Europe and has been sharply criticized as unnecessary even from the military standpoint.

2. Disarmament

The United States should propose the rigid limitation and international control of all armaments, to be followed by universal—not unilateral —disarmament; all such measures to be accompanied by the unlimited right of inspection through an authorized agency of the United Nations. The principle of unlimited international inspection must be recognized as a fundamental safeguard of world security.

3. World Government

The achievement of true democratic federal world government is the ultimate structure of peace. The U. N. as we have repeatedly pointed out is not by its nature such a government. Yet in the critical years before us it may serve a great interim usefulness if its constructive agencies are strengthened and if it is given power to deal with aggression by abolition of the veto in the Security Council. To the rapid achievement of these ends the Socialist Party pledges itself.

4. Atomic Control

The United States should renew its efforts for United Nations adoption of the Majority Plan, based on the Baruch proposals; a campaign of unceasing world education on the contents of the plan should be launched immediately; and meanwhile production of atomic bombs should be halted.

5. Raw Materials

All peoples of the world must be assured access to the raw materials now controlled by international, private, and state monopolies. For this, the area of operation of the world Food and Agriculture Organization, in cooperation with the International Trade Organization where necessary, must be extended. At the same time, world planning is necessary to allocate materials in short supply on the basis of need. World production must be planned to meet the needs of world, not national, markets.

6. International Waterways

The United States should offer to join in the internationalization and demilitarization of the strategic waterways of the world, e.g. Panama, Suez, the Danube, the Dardanelles, Gibraltar, the Baltic, the Black Sea, the Arctic, etc., as part of the general program of world disarmament.

7. Police Force

The organization of world peace requires the existence of an international police or security force. Along with the principle of unlimited international inspection, an international police force is indispensable for the solution of such problems as Palestine, Kashmir, and other crises which may arise.

8. Colonialism

The United States should urge immediate action to begin the permanent liquidation of all colonialism—whether resting on military might, economic domination or political infiltration. The United Nations should establish commissions to supervise an early transition to self-government.

9. Trade Barriers

The United States should support all efforts to establish customs unions as a first step in the direction of a world-wide outlawry of trade barriers.

10. Refugees

The United States, whose greatness has been built by the creativity of generations of immigrants from all parts of the world, must open its doors to those displaced persons who have no home. At the very least, 400,000 such persons can be admitted under unused immigration quotas from the war years. Full support for the International Refugee Organization is essential as long as the present emergency exists, but the goal must be the free and unrestricted movement of peoples, according to their own choice, throughout the world.

11. Palestine

The present disastrous situation has been precipitated by the monstrous Nazi terror, conflicting promises to Jews and Arabs, and repeated betrayal of a pledged word. It is now the duty of the United Nations, with the wholehearted support of the United States, to establish order, to guarantee to the Jewish community in Palestine full self-government, and to protect the right of immigration since it has not reached a saturation point. Whether the political structure necessary to establish these rights is partition or a federation of cantons somewhat on the Swiss model, the civil rights of minorities must be preserved within each district. In no event can immigration into Palestine be considered a complete and adequate answer to the problem of anti-semitism. Every country must be made a desirable homeland for those who live in it, regardless of race, creed or color.

12. Occupied Countries

Military occupation of conquered peoples is by nature inimical to democracy. American armies are now in occupation in Germany, Japan, Korea and various island outposts. Any attempts to use such occupation for economic advantage to American businessmen or for strategic military moves and counter-moves must be defeated. The encouragement of democratic self-government and functioning economies controlled by the people is the responsibility of occupying government, and as soon as this is done it must withdraw. Plans for fifty-year occupations have been mentioned; they must be defeated and dates for withdrawal set.

13. Economic Rehabilitation

The American government must increase its economic aid in the rehabilitation or development of all countries accepting the principles of political freedom, irrespective of the economic direction they choose for themselves in a free expression at the ballot box. Not only Europe but Asia, Africa and Latin America are in need of U. S. assistance.

INTERNATIONAL ORGANIZATION

Above all, it is essential that the United States use its great resources to hasten the world on the road to democratic international organization. Even if any other power rejects the concept of a world sovereignty and continues to assert the outmoded principle of individual national sovereignty, the United States must continue to press toward the goal. It should invite all nations that agree with the program described here to join in a close and effective organization, leaving the door open to the others to participate at a later date.

In 1948, the American people will decide their course. A spirit of defeatism now will result only in defeat. A willingness to vote for your convictions and hopes can start America and the world on the road to peace, to freedom and to plenty.

Socialist Labor Party Platform 1948

The crucial issue of our age is written in gigantic letters across the social sky.

It is: *Capitalist Despotism* or *Socialist Freedom.*

The Socialist Labor Party of America, at its last National Convention in the City of New York, in placing its program for a Socialist reconstruction of society before the American workers, declares this to be the issue that confronts them:

Either the working class takes control of affairs out of the hands of the capitalist class, ends the system of capitalist private ownership, and rebuilds our society on the basis of social ownership of the means of production, democratic management and production for use;

Or, as surely as night follows day, the capitalist system will lead us down the road to a third world war, totalitarian dictatorship and imperialist barbarism.

The Socialist Labor Party earnestly asks you to consider the facts of the present situation:

With the invention of atomic bombs and guided missiles, and the development of germ warfare, war at last looms as the potential destroyer of the human race. Despite this portentous fact and its frightful implications, the plutocratic masters of this country are preparing for another global war.

Through the press, radio and motion pictures, they are conditioning the country psychologically for a war with America's imperialist rival, Soviet Russia.

They have launched a huge rearmament program that will divert the energies of millions of workers from the tasks of peace.

Flouting America's traditional hostility to militarism, they are scheming to enact a system of permanent military conscription.

By means of fabulous subsidies voted by Congress for military research, they are reducing science and education to mere tools of an exalted military machine.

They have drafted plans for total war and the regimentation of industry.

They have brazenly acknowledged their intention to flout the Constitution. In plain violation of the Thirteenth Amendment they are scheming to conscript industrial manpower, and thus to reduce the workers to involuntary servitude.

Their politicians and spokesmen say this huge militarization program is for peace, but everyone in his senses knows that it is for war, and that if matters are allowed to drift, sooner or later there will be war.

Why is the plutocracy taking this desperate and suicidal course?

The Socialist Labor Party declares that the capitalists who guide America's policies are acting in response to their material and class interests, and that the real cause of war is not "bad men," but an outmoded, predatory social system. The logic of this is easily explained:

The international rivalries that erupt in war are a direct result of the system of wage labor—of the fact that the workers receive in wages only a fraction of the value of their product, hence can buy back only a fraction. Of the surplus, a part is consumed by the capitalist class in extravagant living, a part is wasted, a part is employed in expanding industry, and another part goes down the huge drain of the bureaucratic political State.

All of this represents wealth of which labor is robbed, and which in no manner or sense accrues to the benefit of the producing workers or contributes to social progress. That which remains after these deductions must be sold in foreign markets to relieve the glut at home. It is competition for these markets and for spheres of economic influence and sources of raw materials that makes the recurrence of war inevitable as long as the capitalist principle prevails as the basis of society.

It follows that attempts to insure peace via the United Nations are doomed to fail. Sooner or later, every world-organization edifice that is built on the foundation of capitalist dry rot must collapse.

Socialism alone supplies a sound foundation for peace and for the free cultural and material intercourse among the peoples of the world. Socialism does this by destroying the parent evil —the exploitation of wage labor—and thereby ending the problem of "unsold surpluses." Capitalism has everything standing on its head. Under capitalism surpluses are a curse. Under Socialism, which puts things right side up, there will be *production for use* instead of *production for sale and profit*, and surpluses, should they occur, will be a blessing. There can be no lasting peace without Socialism!

War is one consequence of prolonging the outmoded capitalist system; another is the scrapping of the Bill of Rights and the Statification of society.

In recent years the capitalists have turned more

and more to the State as an agency to break the back of working class resistance to increased exploitation, and to prolong their existence as a ruling, privileged class.

Signs of the capitalist reaction abound.

One is the enactment by a pliant capitalist Congress of the labor-shackling Taft-Hartley Law and the revival of the medieval weapon of the court injunction.

Another is the attempt, typical of the police State, to intimidate the workers and break their spirit by launching a Gestapo-like "disloyalty" witch hunt among them.

Still another is the ominous spread of police brutality and officially condoned mob violence and terrorism, and the alarming growth of race prejudice.

Finally, and most conspicuous of all, is the rapid militarization of the country and the corresponding rise in the influence and power of the anti-democratic military caste.

The Socialist Labor Party holds this reaction to be but a manifestation of an irreconcilable class struggle that rages in capitalist society.

One aim of the capitalist class is to hold wages down during the period of brisk demand for labor, to intensify exploitation, and thus to insure higher profits for itself.

A second aim is to reduce labor to the status of unresisting industrial serfs, thus evolving a labor-shackling system that corresponds to the needs of the present huge concentrations of feudalistic corporate capital.

The Socialist Labor Party warns the American workers that they are unprepared, ideologically and organizationally, to block this reaction or to prevent its success. Their present unions (A. F. of L., C.I.O. and kindred bodies), by reason of their pro-capitalist philosophy, treacherous labor-faker leadership and job-trust character, are, like the German trade unions (which were taken over by the Nazis and converted into the Labor Front), preeminently capitalist weapons to bridle the working class.

To remove the menace of fascism and industrial feudalism, the American workers must scrap the unions that accept capitalism as a finality. They must build a new union based on their class interests, and one that will consciously fight for the Socialist goal. They must organize the all-embracing Socialist Industrial Union—the workers' power!

The Socialist Labor Party appeals to you to accept the logic of these facts: WAR, FASCISM AND POVERTY AMIDST PLENTY ARE THE EVIL BROOD OF CAPITALISM. No worker who reaches this conclusion can, without consciously aligning himself with the forces of reaction, support the parties that have as their aim the preservation of capitalism. In this category, besides the Republicans and Democrats, we include the "Third Party Progressives" (who acclaim "progressive capitalism"), and the "Liberal," "Labor," "Socialist" and "Communist" reformers. To speak of "progressive capitalism" today is as nonsensical as it would have been to speak of "progressive slavery" in 1860. And to propose capitalist reforms is to help prolong the capitalist cause of war and fascism. The logic of this is inescapable.

The Socialist Labor Party, therefore, calls upon the American workers, and all other enlightened citizens, to repudiate the parties of capitalism, and to support its program for a Socialist reconstruction of society.

The goal of the Socialist Labor Party is an Industrial Republic of Labor—a system based on collective ownership by the people of the land and all the instruments of wealth production, and one in which the workers will manage industry democratically through socially integrated Socialist Industrial Union Councils.

To bring to birth this society of peace, abundance and boundless human happiness, the Socialist Labor Party appeals to the working class, and to all other enlightened citizens, to support the principles of the Socialist Labor Party, and prepare now to help build the Socialist Industrial Union to back up the Socialist ballot. Unite with us to end the social system that dooms us to a lifelong tenure of wage slavery, with unemployment, poverty and wars as inseparable and ever recurrent features. Unite with us to establish the free Socialist Republic of Peace, Plenty and International Brotherhood!

Socialist Workers Party Platform—1948

Our vast natural resources and productive plant, the unexampled skill and energy of our workers, farmers and technicians, are the essential elements for abolishing poverty and creating a rational and harmonious society.

At the same time, never have the American people viewed the future with so much uncertainty and fear. For our generation, war and depression are the outstanding memories of the past and the imminent perspectives of the future.

The price of a loaf of bread or a pound of meat, the right to speak freely without persecution, questions of war and peace, every aspect of life presents the mass of our people with perpetual insecurity and unending crisis.

What are the reasons our rulers give for this ruinous condition? Since 1914 Democrats and Republicans alike have been reduced to diverting the people's wrath to a foreign enemy, the Kaiser and German militarism, Hitler and German fascism, and now Stalin and the "Iron Curtain."

This explanation is repeated by politicians and the government, by the press, the pulpit and the radio, taught in schools and universities, hammered into the heads of the population by every technical resource at the command of our capitalist masters. It can no longer deceive the people.

Gone are the days when individuals could carve out wealth for themselves and at the same time develop the country's economy. Today huge monopolies choke our splendid industrial resources.

But capitalism has not only created these monstrous monopolies. It has also brought into being the working class comprising tens of millions of people, with a high standard of education, great technical skills and long traditions of democracy and social equality.

Shaken by the collapse of 1929, this working class has already shown its tremendous capabilities by its organization of the CIO and the rapid growth of industrial unionism.

The workers are becoming increasingly aware of capitalist inefficiency in the use of resources. They are beginning to see through the warmongering of the imperialists. They resent the capitalist cheating of the people by inflation. They know that the Sixty Richest Families of the United States, like their counterparts abroad, will abandon democracy for fascism at any serious threat to their profits, privileges and power.

The irrepressible conflict between the monopolists and the workers shakes America with evergrowing convulsions and inexorably extends into a battle for rulership of the country.

The middle classes, the great mass of agricultural workers and small farmers, are ravaged by the anarchy of the profit system.

Millions of women bear the burden of a double oppression. Exploited and abused like all workers, they are also discriminated against and often denied jobs in industry, as well as having upon them the burden of the home.

The generations of the youth face the prospect of serving in permanent conscript armies and providing the fodder for a new war. Capitalist corruption bears down with increasing force upon the high ideals of the professions of medicine, journalism, education and upon the workers in the arts, sciences and engineering.

Far from seeing any end to segregation, the Negro people have seen the Federal Government of Roosevelt and Henry Wallace carry the infamy of a Jim Crow Army to every quarter of the globe.

Tormented by these conditions, the oppressed classes and groups are looking for a way out. There is no way out for them except to follow the leadership of organized labor. On the day when the working class can assure them of its determination to end capitalist anarchy and chaos, the rule of the capitalists is doomed.

The capitalists know this. That is why they concentrate all their power and energy to crush the growing challenge of the working class. The Taft-Hartley Act, the Mundt Bill, the Committee on un-American Activities, the preparation for transforming the FBI into a Gestapo, militarization of the country, the strangling of liberties traditional in the United States since the beginning of the Republic—this long train of abuses and usurpations reveals that their aim is to subject the working class to an absolute despotism, the sole guarantee of capitalist rule in its period of decay.

Twice our people have faced a similar threat. Twice they have known how to meet it.

In 1776 the farmers, mechanics and artisans, led by revolutionists such as Sam Adams, Jefferson and Washington, destroyed the power of the British ruling class who sought to crush the birth of a new nation.

In 1860 William Lloyd Garrison and Wendell Phillips, John Brown and Frederick Douglass, Abraham Lincoln and Thaddeus Stevens, personified the forces which waged merciless war against the slaveowners' attempt to perpetuate their outmoded system, halt the expansion of our economy and destroy the liberties of our people.

The Socialist Workers Party, in these years of

decision, comes forward as the continuator of these revolutionary traditions. The socialist revolution is even more imperative for the salvation of the U.S. than was the Civil War and the War for Independence.

The Socialist Workers Party warns the people that the present struggle is so deeply rooted in a bankrupt economic system that it must end either in the complete destruction of civilization or in the socialist reconstruction of society under the leadership of the working class.

Let him who dares, face the workers and farmers and tell them that they do not possess the knowledge, the will, the physical and intellectual resources, and the political capacity to pull this country back from the brink of the abyss to which monopoly capitalism has led it. The Socialist Workers Party bases itself upon its supreme confidence in the creative capacities of the working people.

The Socialist Workers Party presents itself under the banner of Marx and Engels, Lenin and Trotsky, Debs and Haywood. Their banner is our banner. These great leaders of international socialism were animated by the conviction that unless the tremendous powers of modern industry were taken over by the workers of the world, society would collapse into barbarism. The state of the world today is proof of how correct they were.

Genuine labor politics, however, can have nothing in common with the politics of the Democratic and Republican parties. Against the background of national and international crisis, increasing numbers of the American people view their antics with indignation and disgust. These parties are bi-partisan in foreign policy, bi-partisan in their devotion to capitalism, bi-partisan in their incapacity to cure its evils, bi-partisan in their assault upon the working class and the civil liberties of the American people. The only difference between them is the dispute over who can best secure the privileges and the pilfering which fall to those who administer the capitalist government.

These two parties would long ago have been repudiated and abandoned by the working men and women except for the treacherous and opportunist practices of the top union leaders, who are tied to the apron strings of the capitalist politicians and act as apologists, recruiters and vote-solicitors for them in the ranks of the workers.

The party of Henry Wallace represents nothing but an attempt to exploit the disgust of the people with the Democrats and the Republicans. The Wallace party is the unashamed champion of decaying capitalism. Claiming support as an anti-war party, its leader, Wallace, has betrayed the struggle in advance by declaring his readiness to support the projected war when it breaks out. Wallace's stock-in-trade is a recitation of evils without one single concrete proposal to mobilize labor's strength against monopoly capitalism, the source of all the evils he criticizes.

The Communist Party (Stalinists), which is supporting the Wallace party in this year's election, is interested in the class struggle only insofar as it can be exploited to advance the interests of the arch reactionary Stalinist bureaucracy in the Kremlin. When it serves Stalin's purposes, as it did during the period of the Stalin-Hitler Pact, the American Stalinists talk class struggle, support strikes, pay lip-service to the need for socialism, etc. And similarly, when it serves Stalin's purposes, as it did during the wartime period of the Washington-Moscow alliance, the American Stalinists advocate class collaboration, "national unity," cessation of labor and Negro struggles, strike-breaking, etc. In their case they remain instruments of Stalin's reactionary foreign policy and must be seen as enemies of the workers' true class interests and revolutionary socialism.

The Socialist Party of Norman Thomas pretends that war can be stopped by the United Nations just as it pretended that the war could be stopped by the League of Nations. While denouncing war in general it is no less ready to support World War III than it was to support World War II. It seeks to reform and not to abolish capitalism.

The Socialist Workers Party alone consistently and unconditionally champions the interests of the workers in their struggles against capitalism, and works to organize them for its abolition. This goal is expressed and concretized in the Socialist Workers Party's fundamental objective in the 1948 campaign—the mobilization of the masses for a Workers and Farmers Government.

Such a government, based on direct representation from democratically elected councils of workers, farmers, housewives, soldiers and minority groups, will initiate the reign of real and complete democracy in every sphere of life. It will take over the means of production, expand and coordinate them in a planned economy, and create the conditions for permanent prosperity. It will end the rule of coupon-clippers and put the former capitalists to work at honest toil. Its victory will bring peace and harmony to the United States by doing away with the material cause of class divisions and therefore of class conflicts. The victory of socialism in the most powerful country will serve as an inspiring example to be quickly followed by the rest of the world.

Only a Workers and Farmers Government can reorganize our crumbling society on a rational basis and bring that new birth of freedom and prosperity which is socialism.

Only a Workers and Farmers Government, pledged to irreconcilable opposition to every vestige of monopoly capitalism, can prevent a Third World War.

The program, the platform, the policies and the methods which we advocate will be realized through the formation of a great independent party, led and organized by the working class, including all those tens of millions whose basic hostility to capitalism needs only this leadership to achieve full consciousness and resolute action. Such a party, embracing the productive, social and political activity of the vast majority of the nation, is today the guarantee of democracy. By its mere existence it will be an invincible safeguard against totalitarianism in any form.

The platform of the Socialist Workers Party is not designed to patch up the dying capitalist system, but to protect the interests of the toilers against the brutal aggressions of their capitalist enemies. It is an election platform, to be supported by the ballot on election day, but it is more than that—it is also a program of action to unite and guide the struggles of the workers on a year-round basis. Its effectiveness depends not only on the support it receives in Congress and other legislative bodies, but even more on the extent to which it receives support from the masses in their daily struggles in the factories, in the unions, etc. Its aim is to organize and mobilize the working people for the part they are destined to play in the march to a better world.

In line with these fundamental objectives, the Socialist Workers Party advocates this platform:

1. FOREIGN POLICY

Take the war-making powers out of the hands of Congress! Let the people vote through nationwide referendum on the question of war or peace!

No secret diplomacy! Withdraw all troops from foreign soil! For the complete independence of the colonial peoples! No confidence whatever in the United Nations, dominated by despots of every variety and designed to spread the illusion that peace is possible under capitalism! Full solidarity with the revolutionary struggles of workers and farmers in all lands—those dominated by American imperialism as well as those dominated by reactionary Stalinism! For the Socialist United States of the World!

2. LABOR'S STANDARD OF LIVING

For the inclusion in all union contracts of an escalator clause (also known as the sliding scale of wages or automatic cost-of-living bonus) to meet the rising cost of living, with the safeguard that wages shall not fall below the basic rates established in the contract! For the application of this principle to wages of all government employes, veterans' allotments, old-age allowances, old-age pensions and social security. For the establishment of price control, to be regulated and enforced by mass consumers committees of housewives, unionists, working farmers and small shopkeepers! For the 6-hour day, 30-hour week, with no reduction in pay! For unemployment insurance equal to trade union wages!

3. LABOR AND CIVIL RIGHTS

Repeal the Taft-Hartley Act! No government interference in union affairs! No restrictions on the right to organize, strike and picket! No compulsory arbitration! Repeal all anti-labor laws! Down with government by injunction!

An end to red-baiting, witch hunts and political persecution! Withdraw the "subversive" blacklists used for political persecution of government and other employees! Abolish the House Committee on un-American Activities! Defeat the Mundt Bill and all other measures to totalitarianize American politics! Liberalize the election laws which discriminate against minority parties through excessive petition requirements and subject them to arbitrary exclusion from the ballot! Old enough to be drafted, old enough to vote! Safeguard and extend the Bill of Rights!

4. RIGHTS OF MINORITY GROUPS

Smash the Jim Crow system! Full economic, political and social equality for the Negro people and other minorities! Pass and enforce legislation to punish lynching, abolish the poll tax, establish a Fair Employment Practices Committee with power to root out discriminatory practices, eliminate segregation wherever it exists! Combat anti-Semitism in all its forms! Wipe out discriminatory immigration policies and open the doors of the U.S. to refugees! Unite the workers of all races for the common struggle against their exploiters!

5. FARM POLICY

Establish a federal farm program to guarantee the cost of production to working farmers and to be operated under the control of their own representatives! Expand rural electrification! No limitation on crops! A federal program for soil conservation and flood control! No taxes on savings of cooperatives! A federal ban on all speculation in farm commodities! Abolish sharecropping and landlordism! The land to those who work it!

6. MILITARY POLICY

Against a permanent conscript army! It is necessary to establish a system of military training, financed and equipped by the government, but operating under the control and discipline of the trade union movement! Abolish the officer caste system in the armed forces! Full democratic rights for the ranks in all the services, including their right to participate in politics and public life, to elect their own officers, to organize along union lines and engage in collective bargaining! Abolish race segregation in the armed forces! Trade union wages for the servicemen!

7. HOUSING

The Federal government must be forced to declare a state of national housing emergency and to initiate a program to erect 25 million permanent low-cost, low-rent housing units! Nationalize and operate under workers' control all feeder industries which provide building materials! Operate this housing program through a government planning board of outstanding architects, engineers and representatives of the workers in the building trades! Finance the program with the billions now spent for war preparations! Homes, not atom bombs! Clear the slums! Restore rent control, under supervision of tenants committees!

8. TAXATION

Repeal all payroll taxes! Abolish all sales taxes! No taxes on incomes under $5,000 a year! A 100% tax on incomes over $25,000 a year! Tax the rich, not the poor!

9. GOVERNMENT OWNERSHIP OF INDUSTRY

Nationalize the basic industries, all war plants, all natural resources, and operate them in the interests of the producers and consumers by democratically-elected committees of workers and technicians! Nationalize the banks! Institute a planned economy of abundance, based on production for use, not for profit!

10. INDEPENDENT POLITICAL ACTION

Labor must break all ties with the capitalist parties—Democratic, Republican, Wallaceite! For an Independent Labor Party based on the trade unions and embracing the working farmers, Negroes and veterans! For a United Labor Conference, with representation from all unions, to launch labor's own party and run labor's own candidates for office!

For a Workers and Farmers Government!

States' Rights Platform of 1948

We affirm that a political party is an instrumentality for effectuating the principles upon which the party is founded; that a platform of principles is a solemn covenant with the people and with the members of the party; that no leader of the party, in temporary power, has the right or privilege to proceed contrary to the fundamental principles of the party, or the letter or spirit of the Constitution of the United States; that to act contrary to these principles is a breach of faith, a usurpation of power, and a forfeiture of the party name and party leadership.

We believe that the protection of the American people against the onward march of totalitarian government requires a faithful observance of Article X of the American Bill of Rights which provides that: "The powers not delegated to the United States by the Constitution, nor prohibited by it to the states, are reserved to the states respectively, or to the people."

THE PRINCIPLE OF STATES' RIGHTS

We direct attention to the fact that the first platform of the Democratic Party, adopted in 1840, resolved that: "Congress has no power under the Constitution to interfere with or control the domestic institutions of the several states, and that such states are the sole and proper judges of everything appertaining to their own affairs not prohibited by the Constitution."

Such pronouncement is the cornerstone of the Democratic Party. A long train of abuses and usurpations of power by unfaithful leaders who are alien to the Democratic parties of the states here represented has become intolerable to those who believe in the preservation of constitutional government and individual liberty in America.

The Executive Department of the government is promoting the gradual but certain growth of a totalitarian state by domination and control of a politically minded Supreme Court. As examples of the threat to our form of government, the Executive Department, with the aid of the Supreme Court, has asserted national dominion and control of submerged oil-bearing lands in California, schools in Oklahoma and Missouri, primary elections in Texas, South Carolina and Louisiana, restrictive covenants in New York and the District of Columbia, and other jurisdictions, as well as religious instruction in Illinois.

PERIL TO BASIC RIGHTS

By asserting paramount Federal rights in these instances, a totalitarian concept has been promulgated which threatens the integrity of the states and the basic rights of their citizens.

We have repeatedly remonstrated with the leaders of the national organization of our party but our petitions, entreaties and warnings have been treated with contempt. The latest response to our entreaties was a Democratic convention in Philadelphia rigged to embarrass and humiliate the South.

This alleged Democratic assembly called for a civil-rights law that would eliminate segregation of every kind from all American life, prohibit all forms of discrimination in private employment, in public and private instruction and administration and treatment of students; in the operation of public and private health facilities; in all transportation, and require equal access to all places of public accommodation for persons of all races, colors, creeds and national origin.

PROPOSED FBI POWERS

This infamous and iniquitous program calls for the reorganization of the civil rights section of the Department of Justice with a substantial increase in a bureaucratic staff to be devoted exclusively to the enforcement of the civil rights program; the establishment within the FBI of a special unit of investigators and a police state in a totalitarian, centralized, bureaucratic government.

This convention hypocritically denounced totalitarianism abroad but unblushingly proposed and approved it at home. This convention would strengthen the grip of a police state upon a liberty-loving people by the imposition of penalties upon local public officers who failed or refused to act in accordance with its ideas in suppressing mob violence.

We point out that if a foreign power undertook to force upon the people of the United States the measures advocated by the Democratic convention in Philadelphia, with respect to civil rights, it would mean war and the entire nation would resist such effort.

The convention that insulted the South in the party platform advocated giving the Virgin Islands and other dependencies of the United States "the maximum degree of local self-government."

When an effort was made to amend this part of the platform so as to make it read that the party favored giving the Virgin Islands and the several states the maximum degree of local self-government, the amendment adding the words "these several states" was stricken out and the sovereign states were denied the rights that the party favors giving the Virgin Islands.

PAST LOYALTY

We point out that the South, with clock-like regularity, has furnished the Democratic Party approximately 50 per cent of the votes necessary to nominate a President every four years for nearly a century. In 1920 the only states in the union that went Democratic were the eleven Southern states.

Notwithstanding this rugged loyalty to the party, the masters of political intrigue now allow Republican states in which there is scarcely a Democratic office holder to dominate and control the party and fashion its policies.

NEW POLICY

As Democrats who are irrevocably committed to democracy as defined and expounded by Thomas Jefferson, Andrew Jackson and Woodrow

Wilson, and who believe that all necessary steps must be taken for its preservation, we declare to the people of the United States as follows:

1. We believe that the Constitution of the United States is the greatest charter of human liberty ever conceived by the mind of man.

2. We oppose all efforts to invade or destroy the rights vouchsafed by it to every citizen of this republic.

3. We stand for social and economic justice, which we believe can be vouchsafed to all citizens only by a strict adherence to our Constitution and the avoidance of any invasion or destruction of the constitutional rights of the states and individuals. We oppose the totalitarian, centralized, bureaucratic government and the police state called for by the platforms adopted by the Democratic and Republican conventions.

4. We stand for the segregation of the races and the racial integrity of each race; the constitutional right to choose one's associates; to accept private employment without governmental interference, and to earn one's living in any lawful way. We oppose the elimination of segregation employment by Federal bureaucrats called for by the misnamed civil rights program. We favor home rule, local self-government and a minimum interference with individual rights.

5. We oppose and condemn the action of the Democratic convention in sponsoring a civil rights program calling for the elimination of segregation, social equality by Federal fiat, regulation of private employment practices, voting and local law enforcement.

6. We affirm that the effective enforcement of such a program would be utterly destructive of the social, economic and political life of the Southern people, and of other localities in which there may be differences in race, creed or national origin in appreciable numbers.

7. We stand for the checks and balances provided by the three departments of our Government. We oppose the usurpation of legislative functions by the executive and judicial departments. We unreservedly condemn the effort to establish nation-wide a police state in this republic that would destroy the last vestige of liberty enjoyed by a citizen.

8. We demand that there be returned to the people, to whom of right they belong, those powers needed for the preservation of human rights and the discharge of our responsibility as Democrats for human welfare. We oppose a denial of those rights by political parties, a barter or sale of those rights by a political convention, as well as any invasion or violation of those rights by the Federal Government.

We call upon all Democrats and upon all other loyal Americans who are opposed to totalitarianism at home and abroad to unite with us in ignominiously defeating Harry S. Truman and Thomas E. Dewey, and every other candidate for public office who would establish a police state in the United States of America.

CAMPAIGN OF 1952

In 1952, the incumbent but divided Democrats met in Chicago and nominated a genuinely reluctant candidate, Governor Adlai E. Stevenson of Illinois, for the presidency on the third ballot and over ten other aspirants for the nomination. To balance the ticket, Senator John Sparkman of Alabama was selected by acclamation for vice-president. The Republicans held a bitter convention in 1952. Out of it, however, came one of the most popular candidates in history, General Dwight D. Eisenhower, a relative newcomer to G.O.P. politics, who was nominated after the first ballot over veteran Senator Robert Taft of Ohio. Senator Richard M. Nixon was the general's choice for the vice-presidency.

The States' Rights Party had dissolved shortly after the 1948 election, and the Progressive Party, less prominent in 1952 than it had been four years previously, nominated Vincent Hallinan of California and Charlotta Bass of New York as its presidential and vice-presidential candidates. The Prohibition Party members nominated Stuart Hamblen of California and Enoch Arden Holtwick of Illinois. Eric Hass and Stephen Emery, both of New York, were the Socialist Labor Party candidates, and Darlington Hoopes of Pennsylvania and Samuel H. Friedman of New York made up the Socialist Party ticket. Farrell Dobbs, running this time with Myra Tanner Weiss of New York, again represented the Socialist Workers Party. General Douglas MacArthur was the Christian Nationalist candidate on the ballots of twenty or more states.

In the November election, the candidates of the two major parties received the highest popular votes in the history of presidential elections in the United States. The Republicans polled 33,936,137 votes to 27,314,649 votes for the Democrats. The Progressives obtained 140,416 votes, and the Prohibitionists attracted 73,413. The Socialist Labor ticket got 30,250 votes; the Socialist candidates, 20,065 votes; and the Socialist Workers, 10,312. In the electoral college Eisenhower received 442 votes to 89 for Stevenson.

Christian Nationalist Party

1952 PLATFORM

This is an era characterized by a universal sentiment of nationalism.

In this day of gathering storms, as the moral deterioration of political power spreads its growing infection, it is essential that every spiritual force be mobilized to defend and preserve the religious base upon which this nation was founded. For it is that base which has been the motivating impulse to our moral and national growth. History fails to record a single precedent in which nations subject to moral decay have not passed into political and economic decline. There has been either a spiritual reawakening to overcome the moral lapse, or a progressive deterioration leading to ultimate national disaster.

Our people are desperate for a plan which will revive hope and restore faith as they feel the oppressive burden of the tax levy upon every source of revenue and upon every property transaction; as they see the astronomically rising public debt heavily mortgaging the industry, the well-being and the opportunity of our children and our children's children; as they observe the rising costs of the necessities of life impairing the effectiveness of pensions, insurance and other fixed incomes and reducing the aged and infirm to appalling circumstances.

They look to their leaders, but their protests are silenced by the grim warnings of the disaster of a possible total war. They see no sign of concern, hear no words of encouragement, find no basis for easing fear. Their every expression of hope for reduction in the tax burden is met by the angry rejoinder that taxes must go even higher. There is no plan to transform extravagance into frugality, no desire to regain economic and fiscal stability, no prospect of return to the rugged idealism and collective tranquility of our fathers.

Perhaps it is unnecessary here to indict the present administration for all of its tragic blunders. For that indictment has already found full expression in the resentments which have poured from the hearts of the American people from north to south, from east to west. Many who thus register their resentments do not fully comprehend the nature and degree of the policy misdirection which has brought us to fiscal instability, political insecurity and military weakness.

The issues which today confront the nation are clearly defined and so fundamental as to directly involve the very survival of the Republic.

Are we going to preserve the religious base to our origin, our growth and our progress or yield to the devious assaults of atheistic or other anti-religious forces?

Are we going to maintain our present course toward State Socialism with Communism just beyond or reverse the present trend and regain our hold upon our heritage of liberty and freedom?

Are we going to squander our limited resources to the point of our own inevitable exhaustion or adopt commonsense policies of frugality which will insure financial stability in our time and a worth-while heritage in that of our progeny?

Are we going to continue to yield personal liberties and community autonomy to the steady and inexorable centralization of all political power or restore the Republic to constitutional direction, regain our personal liberties and reassume the individual State's primary responsibility and authority in the conduct of local affairs?

Are we going to permit a continuing decline in public and private morality or re-establish a high ethical standard as the means of regaining a diminishing faith in the integrity of our public and private institutions?

Are we going to continue to permit the pressure of alien doctrines to strongly influence the orientation of foreign and domestic policy or regain trust in our own traditions, experience and free institutions and the wisdom of our own people?

Other issues which deeply stir the conscience of the American people are many and varied, but all stem from irresponsibility in leadership. Domestic policy is largely dictated by the political expediencies of the moment. Foreign policy is as shifting as the sands before the winds and tides. Spendthriftness and waste have lost us our heritage of stability; weakness and vacillation, the moral leadership of the world.

In short, is American life of the future to be characterized by freedom or by servitude, strength or weakness. The answer must be clear and unequivocal if we are to avoid the pitfalls toward which we are now heading with such certainty.

DOMESTIC POLICY

Our government now differs substantially from the design of our forefathers as laid down in the Constitution. In this march away from our traditional standards, few of our former liberties have been left unimpaired. Rights and powers specifically reserved to State, community and individual by constitutional mandate have been ruthlessly suppressed by Federal authority. Our economic stature built under the incentives of free enterprise is imperiled by our drift through the back door of confiscatory taxation toward State Socialism. We find ourselves already past the point where higher taxes might be expected to produce higher revenue.

Expenditure upon expenditure, extravagance upon extravagance have so burdened our people with taxation and fed the forces of infiltration that our traditionally high standard of life has become largely fictitious and illusory.

As always, it is the great masses of the people, not the rich or prosperous, but the farmer, the laborer, and the average office worker who suffer the most.

Some of these penalties are now obscured by the reckless extravagance of government spending which creates a false sense of security, but the day of reckoning is inevitable.

The great bulwark of the Republic, individual and collective self-reliance, is under constant threat through a carefully designed paternalism which renders both community and individual increasingly dependent upon the support of the Federal Government. In all areas of private welfare, the Socialist planners seek to inject the Federal hand to produce a progressive weakening of the structure of individual character.

This process is sapping the initiative and energies of the people and leaves little incentive for the assumption of those risks which are inherent and unescapable in the forging of progress under the system of free enterprise. Worst of all, it is throwing its tentacles around the low income bracket sector of our society from whom is now exacted the major share of the cost of government.

The so-called "forgotten man" of the early thirties now is indeed no longer forgotten as the government levies upon his income as the main remaining source to defray reckless spendthrift policies.

More and more we work not for ourselves but for the State. In time, if permitted to continue, this trend cannot fail to be destructive. For no nation may survive in freedom once its people become the servants of the State, a condition to which we are now pointed with dreadful certainty. Labor, as always, will be the first to feel its frightful consequence.

But our failures in domestic policy can be overcome, for government takes its tone, its character, even its general efficiency from its leadership. Sound leadership can restore integrity to the public service; can economize in the public administration; can eliminate disloyal elements from public authority; can purge our educational system of subversive and immoral influence; can restore to youth its rightful heritage; can strengthen the fabric of our free economy; can raise the dollar to its true value; can reduce the tax burden on individual and industry; can regain the course of constitutional direction; can recapture personal liberties now impaired; can correct social inequities; can strengthen the position of both worker and owner in private industry, even while protecting the public interest; can fortify the initiative, energy and enterprise of the farmer so as to insure the adequacy of the production of food in lean years and its distribution in those of plenty, without being crippled by the unwarranted interference and domination of government; and can rearm the nation without undue burden upon the people. The correction of domestic evils and lapses would not be too difficult provided the will to do so firmly exists.

Foreign Policy

Foreign policy has been as tragically in error as has domestic policy. We practically invited Soviet dominance over the free peoples of Eastern Europe through strategic dispositions of Soviet force at the close of the European war; we deliberately withdrew our armies from thousands of square miles of hard-won territory, permitting the advance of Soviet forces to the west to plant the Red flag of Communism on the ramparts of Berlin, Vienna and Prague, capitals of western civilization; we recklessly yielded effective control over areas of vast uranium deposits without which the Soviet might never have developed the threat of atomic power.

We foolishly permitted the encirclement of Berlin by Soviet forces, rendering almost inevitable the tragically high cost we have had to pay to secure open lines of supply and communication between our zones of occupation there and in West Germany; we authored, sponsored or approved policies under which the German industrial plant was subjected to major postwar dismantling and destruction; we turned over to the Soviet for slave labor hundreds of thousands of German prisoners of war in violation of every humanitarian concept and tradition; we failed to protest the murder by the Soviet of the flower of the Polish nation, and, even after victory had been achieved, we continued to supply the Soviet with quantities of war material, despite the clear and inescapable warnings of the Soviet threat to future peace.

In the East we gave over to Soviet control the industrial resources of Manchuria, the area of North Korea, and the sword pointed at the heart of the Japanese home islands. We condemned our faithful wartime ally, the Chinese people, to the subjugation of Communist tyranny. And, in the course of these moves we proceeded with precipitate haste to divest ourselves of our own military strength. Despite the threat to our security then clearly apparent, our executive flaunted and ignored the judgment and will of the Congress which appropriated funds for the expansion of our air arm which he arbitrarily refused to expend for such purpose.

Then, suddenly, with our military strength standing at possibly the lowest relativity in history—our divisions in Japan reduced from three to two regiments, our regiments from three to two battalions, our battalions from three to two companies—without protection withdrawn from South Korea as a militarily indefensible peninsula, we there and then plunged our forces into war to defend it.

We defeated the North Korean armies; but, when the Communist armies of China struck, our leaders lacked the courage to fight to a military decision, even though victory was then readily within our grasp—a victory which would not only have discharged our commitment to the Korean people but which in the long run might well have saved continental Asia from Red domination. And, after discarding victory as the military objective and thereby condemning our forces to a stale-mated struggle of attrition and the Korean nation and people to progressive obliteration, we again yielded to Communist intrigue and entered into protracted armistice negotiations even though every lesson of experience had clearly shown such negotiations to be but the means whereby such an enemy gains time to reinforce his military capabilities.

We have yielded to selfish pressures both at home and abroad and, in so doing, have unduly directed the distribution of our wealth into privileged channels, have taken sides in international disputes which were fundamentally none of our affair, and have endeavored to impose our will on other nations' purely domestic problems in an imperialistic manner. We have ignored traditional friends while showering our favors on others, and we have lost that sense of judicial fairness which formerly characterized our relations abroad.

In our preoccupation with Europe, we have tended to discard from our concern, those great people of Asia and the Middle East who historically have sought not our wealth, but our friendship and understanding. Our "good neighbor" policy with respect to the people of Central and South America—of greater strategic concern than all others—has been largely subordinated. Through the paternalistic attitude which has dominated our material asistance abroad, we have promoted as much weakness as strength, as much resentment as friendship.

PRESERVATION OF OUR REPUBLIC

It is not of any external threat that we chiefly concern ourselves but rather of insidious forces working from within which have already so drastically altered the character of our free institutions—those institutions which formerly we hailed as beyond question or challenge.

Foremost of these forces is the scourge of Communism—but they have many allies, who, blind to reality, ardently support the Communist aims while denying violently that they do so. They have infiltrated into positions of public trust and responsibility—into journalism, the press, the radio and the schools. They seek to pervert the truth, impair respect for moral values, suppress human freedom and representative government.

They first make traitors among those of high degree and through them seek to destroy nations and bend peoples to its malevolent will. Their plan is to abolish private property and free enterprise in order to secure that degree of power over material things necessary to render absolute their power to suppress the spiritual things.

This evil force, with neither spiritual base nor moral standard, rallies the abnormal and subnormal elements among our citizenry and applies internal pressure against all things we hold decent and all things that we hold right—the type of pressure which has caused many Christian Nations abroad to fall.

Our need for patriotic fervor and religious devotion was never more impelling. There can be no compromise with atheistic Communism. Any complacent tolerance of this destructive force of evil should be replaced by an implacable and uncompromising determination to resist its every threat to basic and traditional ideals.

As a counter-balance to those forces is the deep spiritual urge in the hearts of our people—a spiritual urge capable of arousing and directing a decisive and impelling public opinion. This, indeed, is the greatest safeguard and resource of America. It is an infallible reminder that our greatest hope and faith rests upon two mighty symbols—the Cross and the Flag; the one based upon those immutable teachings which provide the spiritual strength to persevere along the course which is just and right—the other based upon the invincible will that human freedom shall not perish from the earth.

We must unite in the high purpose that the liberties etched upon the design of our lives be unimpaired and that we maintain the moral courage and spiritual leadership to preserve inviolate that mighty bulwark of all freedom, our Christian faith.

CONCLUSION

We stand today at a critical moment of history —at a vital crossroad. In one direction is the path of courageous patriots seeking in humility but the opportunity to serve their country; the other that of those selfishly seeking to entrench autocratic power. The one group stands for implacable resistance against Communism; the other for compromising with Communism. The one stands for our traditional system of government and freedom; the other for a Socialist State and slavery. The one boldly speaks the truth; the other spreads propaganda, fear and deception. The one denounces excessive taxation, bureaucratic government and corruption; the other seeks more taxes, more bureaucratic power and shields corruption.

Our leaders must throw off the complacent belief that the only threat to our survival is from without. All freedoms lost since war's end have been the result of internal pressures rather than external assault.

To free ourselves from the greatest internal menace, we must end invisible government based upon propaganda and restore truly representative government based upon truth.

Despite failures in leadership, they have it in their power to rise to that stature which befits their lofty heritage of spiritual and material strength; to reject the Socialist policies covertly and by devious means being forced upon us; to stamp out Communist influence which has played so ill-famed a part in the past misdirection of our public administration; to reorganize our government under a leadership invincibly obedient to our Constitutional mandates. To re-enforce existing safeguards to our economy of free-enterprises; to reassert full protection for freedom of speech and expression and those other freedoms now threatened; to regain State and community autonomy; to renounce undue alien interference in the shaping of American public policy; and to re-establish our governmental process upon a foundation of faith in our American institutions, American traditions, and the time-tested adequacy of American vision.

Many pessimistic voices are being raised today throughout the land. But the times are full of hope, if the vision and courage and faith of the early pioneer continue to animate the American people in the discharge of their sovereign responsibilities.

The people have it in their hands to restore morality, wisdom and vision to the direction of our foreign and domestic affairs and regain the religious base which in times past assured general integrity in public and private life.

Not for a moment do we doubt the decision or that it will guide the nation to a new and fuller greatness.

In this unusual assignment we feel a deep consciousness of the nature and gravity of the crusade upon which we now embark—a crusade to which all sound and patriotic Americans, irrespective of party, may well dedicate their hearts and minds and fullest effort. Only thus can our beloved country restore its spiritual and temporal strength and regain once again the universal respect.

Democratic Party Platform of 1952

PREAMBLE

Our nation has entered into an age in which Divine Providence has permitted the genius of man to unlock the secret of the atom.

No system of government can survive the challenge of an atomic era unless its administration is committed to the stewardship of a trustee imbued with a democratic faith, a buoyant hope for the future, the charity of brotherhood, and the vision to translate these ideals into the realities of human government. The Government of the United States, administered by the Democratic Party, is today so entrusted.

The free choice of the Democratic Party by the people of America as the instrument to achieve that purpose will mean world peace with honor, national security based on collective pacts with other free nations, and a high level of human dignity. National survival demands that these goals be attained, and the endowments of the Democratic Party alone can assure their attainment.

For twenty years, under the dedicated guidance of Franklin Delano Roosevelt and Harry S. Truman, our country has moved steadily along the road which has led the United States of America to world leadership in the cause of freedom.

We will not retreat one inch along that road. Rather, it is our prayerful hope that the people, whom we have so faithfully served, will renew the mandate to continue our service and that Almighty God may grant us the wisdom to succeed.

TWENTY YEARS OF PROGRESS

Achieving Prosperity

An objective appraisal of the past record clearly demonstrates that the Democratic Party has been the chosen American instrument to achieve prosperity, build a stronger democracy, erect the structure of world peace, and continue on the path of progress.

Democratic Party policies and programs rescued American business from total collapse—from the fatal economic consequences of watered stock, unsound banks, useless and greedy holding companies, high tariff barriers, and predatory business practices, all of which prevailed under the last Republican administrations. Democratic policies have enabled the Federal Government to help all business, small and large, to achieve the highest rate of productivity, the widest domestic and world markets, and the largest profits in the history of the Nation.

The simple fact is that today there are more than four million operating business enterprises in this country, over one million more than existed in 1932. Corporate losses in that fateful year were over three billion dollars; in 1951, corporate profits, after taxes, reached the staggering total of eighteen billion.

Democratic policies and programs rescued American agriculture from the economic consequences of blight, drought, flood and storm, from oppressive and indiscriminate foreclosures, and from the ruinous conditions brought about by the bungling incompetence and neglect of the preceding twelve years of Republican maladministration. Economic stability, soil conservation, rural electrification, farm dwelling improvement, increased production and efficiency and more than sevenfold increase in cash income have been the return to farmers for their faith in the Democratic Party.

Democratic labor policies have rescued the wage earners in this country from mass unemployment and from sweatshop slavery at starvation wages. Under our Democratic administrations, decent hours, decent wages, and decent working conditions have become the rule rather than the exception.

Self organizations of labor unions and collective bargaining, both of which are the keystone to labor management, peace and prosperity, must be encouraged, for the good of all.

Unemployment is now less than 3 per cent of the labor force, compared with almost 25 per cent in 1932. Trade union membership has reached a total of 16 million, which is more than five times the total of 1932.

The welfare of all economic and social groups in our society has been promoted by the sound, progressive and humane policies of the Democratic Party.

Strengthening Democracy

We are convinced that lasting prosperity must be founded upon a healthy democratic society respectful of the rights of all people.

Under Democratic Party leadership more has been done in the past twenty years to enhance the sanctity of individual rights than ever before in our history. Racial and religious minorities have progressed further toward real equality than during the preceding 150 years.

Governmental services, Democratically administered, have been improved and extended. The efficiency, economy, and integration of Federal operations have been advocated and effectuated through sound programs and policies. Through cooperative programs of Federal aid, State and local governments have been encouraged and enabled to provide many more services.

The Democratic Party has been alert to the corroding and demoralizing effects of dishonesty and disloyalty in the public service. It has exposed and punished those who would corrupt the integrity of the public service, and it has always championed honesty and morality in government. The loyalty program of President Truman has served effectively to prevent infiltration by subversive elements and to protect honest and loyal public servants against unfounded and malicious attacks.

We commend the relentless and fearless actions of Congressional Committees which, under vigorous Democratic leadership, have exposed dereliction in public service, and we pledge our support to a continuance of such actions as conditions require them.

The administration of our government by the Democratic Party has been based upon principles of justice and equity, and upon the American tradition of fair play. Men who are elected to high political office are entrusted with high responsibilities. Slander, defamation of character, deception and dishonesty are as truly transgressions of God's commandments, when resorted to by men in public life, as they are for all other men.

Building Peace with Honor

The Democratic Party has worked constantly for peace—lasting peace, peace with honor, freedom, justice and security for all nations.

The return of the Democratic Party to power in 1933 marked the end of a tragic era of isolationism fostered by Republican Administrations which had deliberately and callously rejected the golden opportunity created by Woodrow Wilson for collective action to secure the peace.

This folly contributed to the second World War. Victory in that war has presented the nations of the world a new opportunity which the Democratic Party is determined shall not be lost.

We have helped establish the instrumentalities through which the hope of mankind for universal world peace can be realized. Under Democratic leadership, our Nation has moved promptly and effectively to meet and repel the menace to world peace by Soviet imperialism.

Progress in the New Era

The Democratic Party believes that past progress is but a prelude to the human aspirations which may be realized in the future.

Under Democratic Party leadership, America has accepted each new challenge of history and has found practical solutions to meet and overcome them. This we have done without departing from the principles of our basic philosophy, that is, the destiny of man to achieve his earthly ends in the spirit of brotherhood.

A great Democrat—Franklin Delano Roosevelt—devised the programs of the New Deal to meet the pressing problems of the 1930s. Another great Democrat—Harry S. Truman—devised the programs of the Fair Deal to meet the complex problems of America in the 1940s. The Democratic Party is ready to face and solve the challenging problems of the 1950s. We dedicate ourselves to the magnificent work of these great Presidents and to mould and adapt their democratic principles to the new problems of the years ahead.

In this spirit we adopt and pledge ourselves to this, the Democratic platform for 1952:

OUR GOAL IS PEACE WITH HONOR

Peace with honor is the greatest of all our goals.

We pledge our unremitting efforts to avert another world war. We are determined that the people shall be spared that frightful agony.

We are convinced that peace and security can be safeguarded if America does not deviate from the practical and successful policies developed under Democratic leadership since the close of World War II. We will resolutely move ahead with the constructive task of promoting peace.

THE DEMOCRATIC PROGRAM FOR PEACE AND NATIONAL SECURITY

Supporting the United Nations

Under Democratic leadership, this country sponsored and helped create the United Nations and became a charter member and staunchly supports its aims.

We will continue our efforts to strengthen the United Nations, improve its institutions as experience requires, and foster its growth and development.

The Communist aggressor has been hurled back from South Korea. Thus, Korea has proved, once and for all, that the United Nations will resist aggression. We urge continued effort, by every honorable means, to bring about a fair and effective peace settlement in Korea in accordance with the principles of the United Nations' charter.

Strong National Defense

Our Nation has strengthened its national defenses against the menace of Soviet aggression.

The Democratic Party will continue to stand unequivocally for the strong, balanced defense forces for this country—land, sea and air. We will continue to support the expansion and maintenance of the military and civil defense forces required for our national security. We reject the defeatist view of those who say we cannot afford the expense and effort necessary to defend ourselves. We express our full confidence in the Joint Chiefs of Staff. We voice complete faith in the ability and valor of our armed forces, and pride in their accomplishments.

COLLECTIVE STRENGTH FOR THE FREE WORLD

We reject the ridiculous notions of those who would have the United States face the aggressors alone. That would be the most expensive—and the most dangerous—method of seeking security. This nation needs strong allies, around the world, making their maximum contribution to the common defense. They add their strength to ours in the defense of freedom.

The Truman Doctrine in 1947, the organization of hemisphere defense at Rio de Janeiro that same year, the Marshall Plan in 1948, the North Atlantic Treaty in 1949, the Point IV program, the resistance to Communist aggression in Korea, the Pacific Security pacts in 1951, and the Mutual Security programs now under way—all stand as landmarks of America's progress in mobilizing the strength of the free world to keep the peace.

Encouraging European Unity

We encourage the economic and political unity of free Europe and the increasing solidarity of the nations of the North Atlantic Community.

We hail the Schuman Plan to pool the basic resources of industrial Western Europe, and the European Defense Community. We are proud of America's part in carrying these great projects forward, and we pledge our continuing support until they are established.

Support for Free Germany

We welcome the German Federal Republic into the company of free nations. We are determined that Germany shall remain free and continue as a good neighbor in the European community. We sympathize with the German people's wish for unity and will continue to do everything we can by peaceful means to overcome the Kremlin's obstruction of that rightful aim.

Support for the Victims of Soviet Imperialism

We will not abandon the once-free peoples of Central and Eastern Europe who suffer now under the Kremlin's tyranny in violation of the Soviet Union's most solemn pledges at Tehran, Yalta, and Potsdam. The United States should join other nations in formally declaring genocide to be an international crime in time of peace as well as war. This crime was exposed once more by the shocking revelations of Soviet guilt as disclosed in the report filed in Congress by the special committee investigating the Katyn Forest massacre. We look forward to the day when the liberties of Poland and the other oppressed Soviet satellites, including Czechoslovakia, Hungary, Rumania, Bulgaria, Albania, Lithuania, Estonia and Latvia and other nations in Asia under Soviet domination, will be restored to them and they can again take their rightful place in the community of free nations. We will carry forward and expand the vital and effective program of the "Voice of America" for penetration of the "Iron Curtain," bringing truth and hope to all the people subjugated by the Soviet Empire.

Support for the Nations of the Middle East

We seek to enlist the people of the Middle East to work with us and with each other in the de-velopment of the region, the lifting of health and living standards, and the attainment of peace. We favor the development of integrated security arrangements for the Middle East and other assistance to help safeguard the independence of the countries in the area.

We pledge continued assistance to Israel so that she may fulfill her humanitarian mission of providing shelter and sanctuary for her homeless Jewish refugees while strengthening her economic development.

We will continue to support the tripartite declaration of May 1950, to encourage Israel and the Arab States to settle their differences by direct negotiation, to maintain and protect the sanctity of the Holy Places and to permit free access to them.

We pledge aid to the Arab States to enable them to develop their economic resources and raise the living standards of their people. We support measures for the relief and reintegration of the Palestine refugees, and we pledge continued assistance to the reintegration program voted by the General Assembly of the United Nations in January 1952.

South Asia: A Testing Ground for Democracy

In the subcontinent of South Asia, we pledge continuing support for the great new countries of India and Pakistan in their efforts to create a better life for their people and build strong democratic governments to stand as bastions of liberty in Asia, secure against the threat of Communist subversion.

Collective Security in the Pacific

We welcome free Japan as a friendly neighbor and an ally in seeking security and progress for the whole Pacific area. America's security pacts with Japan and with the Philippines, Australia, and New Zealand are indispensable steps toward comprehensive mutual security arrangements in that area. Our military and economic assistance to the Nationalist Government of China on Formosa has strengthened that vital outpost of the free world, and will be continued.

Strengthening the Americas

In the Western Hemisphere, we pledge ourselves to continue the policy of the good neighbor. We will strive constantly to strengthen the bonds of friendship and cooperation with our Latin

American allies who are joined with us in the defense of the Americas.

Disarmament Remains the Goal

The free world is rearming to secure the peace. Under Democratic leadership, America always stands prepared to join in a workable system for foolproof inspection and limitation of all armaments, including atomic weapons. This Nation has taken the leadership in proposing concrete, practical plans for such a system. We are determined to carry on the effort for real, effective disarmament.

We look forward to the day when a great share of the resources now devoted to the armaments program can be diverted into the channels of peaceful production to speed the progress of America and of the underdeveloped regions of the world.

Helping Other People to Help Themselves

Even though we cannot now disarm, we will go forward as rapidly as possible in developing the imaginative and farsighted concept of President Truman embodied in the Point IV program.

We will continue to encourage use of American skills and capital in helping the people of underdeveloped lands to combat disease, raise living standards, improve land tenure and develop industry and trade. The continuance of ever stronger and more vigorous Point IV programs—sponsored both by this country and by the United Nations—is an indispensable element in creating a peaceful world.

Upholding the Principle of Self-Determination

In an era when the "satellite state" symbolizes both the tyranny of the aggressor nations and the extinction of liberty in small nations, the Democratic Party reasserts and reaffirms the Wilsonian principle of the right of national self-determination. It is part of the policy of the Democratic Party, therefore, to encourage and assist small nations and all peoples in the peaceful and orderly achievement of their legitimate aspirations toward political, geographical and ethnic integrity so that they may dwell in the family of sovereign nations with freedom and dignity.

Expanding World Trade

The Democratic Party has always stood for expanding trade among free nations. We reassert that stand today. We vigorously oppose any restrictive policies which would weaken the highly successful reciprocal trade program fathered by Cordell Hull.

Since 1934, the United States has taken the lead in fostering the expansion and liberalization of world trade.

Our own economy requires expanded export markets for our manufactured and agricultural products and a greater supply of essential imported raw materials. At the same time, our friends throughout the world will have opportunity to earn their own way to higher living standards with lessened dependence on our aid.

Progressive Immigration Policies

Solution of the problem of refugees from communism and over-population has become a permanent part of the foreign policy program of the Democratic Party. We pledge continued cooperation with other free nations to solve it.

We pledge continued aid to refugees from communism and the enactment of President Truman's proposals for legislation in this field. In this way we can give hope and courage to the victims of Soviet brutality and can carry on the humanitarian tradition of the Displaced Persons Act.

Subversive elements must be screened out and prevented from entering our land, but the gates must be left open for practical numbers of desirable persons from abroad whose immigration to this country provides an invigorating infusion into the stream of American life, as well as a significant contribution to the solution of the world refugee and over-population problems.

We pledge continuing revision of our immigration and naturalization laws to do away with any unjust and unfair practices against national groups which have contributed some of our best citizens. We will eliminate distinctions between nativeborn and naturalized citizens. We want no "second-class" citizens in free America.

Our Domestic Policy

Economic Opportunity and Growth

The United States is today a land of boundless opportunity. Never before has it offered such a large measure of prosperity, security and hope for all its people.

Horizons of even greater abundance and opportunity lie before us under a Democratic Administration responsive to the will of the people.

The Democratic Administration has had a guiding principle since taking office 20 years ago: that the prosperity and growth of this Nation are indivisible. Every step we have taken to help the farmers has also helped the workers and business. Every improvement in the status of the worker has helped both farmers and business. Every expansion of business has provided more jobs for workers and greater demand for farm products.

A STABILIZED ECONOMY

Combatting Inflation

The Democratic Administration early recognized that defense production would limit the amount of goods in civilian markets, and subject our economy to heavy inflationary pressure. To prevent this from resulting in ruinous inflation, the Administration proposed pay-as-we-go taxation to keep the national debt as low as possible and to prevent excess money pressure on scarce goods and services.

Direct controls were also proposed to channel scarce materials into highly essential defense production, and to keep prices down.

In 1951 and 1952 Republican Congressmen demonstrated their attitude toward these necessary measures when they sponsored amendments which would have destroyed all controls.

Prices

We shall strive to redress the injury done to the American people—especially to white collar workers and fixed-income families—by the weakening amendments which the Republicans in Congress have forced into our anti-inflation laws.

We pledge continuance of workable controls so long as the emergency requires them. We pledge fair and impartial enforcement of controls and their removal as quickly as economic conditions allow.

Rents

We strongly urge continued federal rent control in critical defense areas and in the many other localities still suffering from a substantial shortage of adequate housing at reasonable prices.

Full Employment

The Democratic Administration prudently passed the Employment Act of 1946 declaring it to be national policy never again to permit large-scale unemployment to stalk the land. We will assure the transition from defense production to peace-time production without the ravages of unemployment. We pledge ourselves at all times to the maintenance of maximum employment, production, and purchasing power in the American economy.

Integrity in Government Finances

We solemnly pledge the preservation of the financial strength of the Government. We have demonstrated our ability to maintain and enhance the nation's financial strength. In the six full fiscal years since V-J Day, our fiscal policy has produced a $4 billion budget surplus. We have reduced the public debt $17 billion from the postwar peak.

We have demonstrated our ability to make fiscal policy contribute in a positive way to economic growth and the maintenance of high-level employment. The policies which have been followed have given us the greatest prosperity in our history. Sustained economic expansion has provided the funds necessary to finance our defense and has still left our people with record high consumer incomes and business with a record volume of investment. Employment and personal incomes are at record levels. Never have Americans enjoyed a higher standard of living and saved more for contingencies and old age.

Federal Taxes

We believe in fair and equitable taxation. We oppose a Federal general sales tax. We adhere to the principle of ability to pay. We have enacted an emergency excess profits tax to prevent profiteering from the defense program and have vigorously attacked special tax privileges.

Tax Reductions

In the future, as in the past, we will hold firm to policies consistent with sound financing and continuing economic progress. As rapidly as defense requirements permit, we favor reducing taxes, especially for people with lower incomes. But we will not imperil our Nation's security by making reckless promises to reduce taxes. We deplore irresponsible assertions that national security can be achieved without paying for it.

Closing Tax Loopholes

Justice requires the elimination of tax loopholes

which favor special groups. We pledge continued efforts to the elimination of remaining loopholes.

Government Expenditures

We believe in keeping government expenditures to the lowest practicable level. The great bulk of our national budget consists of obligations incurred for defense purposes. We pledge ourselves to a vigilant review of our expenditures in order to reduce them as much as possible.

THE AMERICAN FARMER AND AGRICULTURE

We know that national prosperity depends upon a vigorous, productive and expanding agriculture.

We take great pride in our Party's record of performance and in the impressive gains made by American agriculture in the last two decades. Under programs of Democratic Administrations the net agricultural income has increased from less than two billion dollars to almost fifteen billion dollars. These programs must be continued and improved.

Resource Conservation

The soil resources of our country have been conserved and strengthened through the Soil Conservation Service, the Agricultural Conservation Program, the Forestry and the Research programs, with their incentives to increased production through sound conservation farming. These programs have revolutionized American agriculture and must be continued and expanded. We will accelerate programs of upstream flood prevention, watershed protection, and soil, forest and water conservation in all parts of the country. These conservation measures are a national necessity; they are invaluable to our farmers, and add greatly to the welfare of all Americans and of generations yet unborn.

Grass Roots Administration

We will continue the widest possible farmer participation through referenda, farmer-elected committees, local soil conservation districts, and self-governing agencies in the conduct and administration of these truly democratic programs, initiated and developed under Democratic adminstrations.

Price Supports

Under the present farm program, our farmers have performed magnificently and have achieved unprecedented production. We applaud the recent Congressional action in setting aside the "sliding scale" for price support through 1954, and we will continue to protect the producers of basic agricultural commodities under the terms of a mandatory price support program at not less than ninety percent of parity. We continue to advocate practical methods for extending price supports to other storables and to the producers of perishable commodities, which account for three-fourths of all farm income.

Abundant Production

We will continue to assist farmers in providing abundant and stable supplies of agricultural commodities for the consumers at reasonable prices, and in assuring the farmer the opportunity to earn a fair return commensurate with that enjoyed by other segments of the American economy.

The agricultural adjustment programs encourage the production of abundant supplies while enabling producers to keep supply in line with consumer demand, preventing wide fluctuations and bringing stability to the agricultural income of the Nation. We pledge retention of such programs.

We pledge continued efforts to provide adequate storage facilities for grain and other farm products with sufficient capacity for needed reserves for defense, and other emergency requirements, in order to protect the integrity of the farm price support programs.

Research

We are justly proud of the outstanding achievements of our agricultural research. We favor a greatly expanded research and education program for American agriculture in order that both production and distribution may more effectively serve consumers and producers alike, and thus meet the needs of the modern world. We favor especial emphasis on the development of new crops and varieties, on crop and livestock disease and pest control, and on agricultural statistics and marketing services.

Marketing

We must find profitable markets for the products of our farms, and we should produce all that these markets will absorb. To this end we will continue our efforts to reduce trade barriers, both at home and abroad, to provide better marketing and inspection facilities, and to find new uses and outlets for our foods and fibers both in domestic and foreign markets.

Farm Credit

We have provided credit facilities for all agriculture, including means by which young men, veterans of military service, and farm tenants have been encouraged to become farmers and farm home-owners, and through which low-income farmers have been assisted in establishing self-sustaining and fully productive farm units. We will not waver in our efforts to provide such incentives.

Crop Insurance

Crop insurance to protect farmers against loss from destruction of their crops by natural causes has been created and developed under Democratic Administrations into a sound business operation. This program should be expanded as rapidly as experience justifies, in order that its benefits may be made available to every farmer.

Rural Electrification

Democratic Administrations have established the great Rural Electrification Program, which has brought light and power to the rural homes of our Nation. In 1935, only 10% of the farm homes of America had the benefits of electricity. Today 85% of our rural homes enjoy the benefits of electric light and power. We will continue to fight to make electricity available to all rural homes, with adequate facilities for the generation and transmission of power. Through the Rural Telephone Program, inaugurated by the Democratic 81st Congress, we will provide the opportunity for every farm home to have this modern essential service. We pledge support of these self-liquidating farm programs.

Cooperatives

We will continue to support the sound development and growth of bona fide farm cooperatives and to protect them from punitive taxation.

Defense Needs

We will continue to recognize agriculture as an essential defense industry, and to assist in providing all the necessary tools, machinery, fertilizer, and manpower needed by farmers in meeting production goals.

Family Farming

The family farm is the keystone of American agriculture. We will strive unceasingly to make the farm homes of our country healthier and happier places in which to live. We must see that our youth continues to find attractive opportunity in the field of agriculture.

The Republican Party platform is loud in its criticism of our great farm programs. We challenge Republicans and other enemies of farm progress to justify their opposition to the program now in operation, to oppose the improvements here proposed, or to advocate repeal of a single vital part of our program.

A FAIR DEAL FOR WORKERS

Good Incomes

There can be no national prosperity unless our working men and women continue to prosper and enjoy rising living standards. The rising productivity of American workers is a key to our unparalleled industrial progress. Good incomes for our workers are the secret of our great and growing consumer markets.

Labor-Management Relations

Good labor-management relations are essential to good incomes for wage earners and rising output from our factories. We believe that to the widest possible extent consistent with the public interest, management and labor should determine wage rates and conditions of employment through free collective bargaining.

Taft-Hartley Act

We strongly advocate the repeal of the Taft-Hartley Act.

The Taft-Hartley Act has been proved to be inadequate, unworkable, and unfair. It interferes in an arbitrary manner with collective bargaining, tipping the scales in favor of management against labor.

The Taft-Hartley Act has revived the injunction as a weapon against labor in industrial relations. The Act has arbitrarily forbidden traditional hiring practices which are desired by both management and labor in many industries. The Act has forced workers to act as strikebreakers against their fellow unionists. The Act has served to interfere with one of the most fundamental rights of American workers—the right to organize in unions of their own choosing.

We deplore the fact that the Taft-Hartley Act provides an inadequate and unfair means of meeting with national emergency situations. We advocate legislation that will enable the President to deal fairly and effectively with cases where a breakdown in collective bargaining seriously threatens the national safety or welfare.

In keeping with the progress of the times, and based on past experiences, a new legislative approach toward the entire labor management problem should be explored.

Fair Labor Standards

We pledge to continue our efforts so that government programs designed to establish improved fair labor standards shall prove a means of assuring minimum wages, hours and protection to workers, consistent with present-day progress.

Equal Pay for Equal Work

We believe in equal pay for equal work, regardless of sex, and we urge legislation to make that principle effective.

The Physically-Handicapped

We promise to further the program to afford employment opportunities both in government and in private industry for physically handicapped persons.

Migratory Workers

We advocate prompt improvement of employment conditions of migratory workers and increased protection of their safety and health.

STRENGTHENING FREE ENTERPRISE

The free enterprise system has flourished and prospered in America during these last twenty years as never before. This has been made possible by the purchasing power of all our people and we are determined that the broad base of our prosperity shall be maintained.

Small and Independent Business

Small and independent business is the backbone of American free enterprise. Upon its health depends the growth of the economic system whose competitive spirit has built this Nation's industrial strength and provided its workers and consumers with an incomparably high standard of living.

Independent business is the best offset to monopoly practices. The Government's role is to insure that independent business receives equally fair treatment with its competitors.

Congress has established the permanent Small Business Committee of the Senate and the Special Small Business Committee of the House, which have continued to render great service to this important segment of our economy. We favor continuance of both these committees with all the powers to investigate and report conditions, correct discriminations, and propose needed legislation.

We pledge ourselves to increased efforts to assure that small business be given equal opportunity to participate in Government contracts, and that a suitable proportion of the dollar volume of defense contracts be channeled into independent small business. The Small Defense Plants Administration, which our Party caused to be established, should retain its independent status and be made a continuing agency, equipped with sufficient lending powers to assist qualified small business in securing defense contracts.

We urge the enactment of such laws as will provide favorable incentives to the establishment and survival of independent businesses, especially in the provision of tax incentives and access to equity or risk capital.

Enforcement of Anti-Trust Laws

Free competitive enterprise must remain free and competitive if the productive forces of this Nation are to remain strong. We are alarmed over the increasing concentration of economic power in the hands of a few.

We reaffirm our belief in the necessity of vigorous enforcement of the laws against trusts, combinations, and restraints of trade, which laws are vital to the safeguarding of the public interest and of small competitive business men against predatory monopolies. We will seek adequate appropriations for the Department of Justice and the Federal Trade Commission for vigorous investigation and for enforcement of the anti-trust laws. We support the right of all persons to work together in cooperatives and other democratic associations for the purpose of carrying out any proper business operations free from any arbitrary and discriminatory restrictions.

Protection of Investors and Consumers

We must avoid unnecessary business controls. But we cannot close our eyes to the special problems which require Government surveillance. The Government must continue its efforts to stop unfair selling practices which deceive investors, and unfair trade practices which deceive consumers.

Transportation

In the furtherance of national defense and commerce, we pledge continued Government support, on a sound financial basis, for further development of the Nation's transportation systems, land, sea and air. We endorse a policy of fostering the safest and most reliable air transportation system of the world. We favor fair, nondiscriminatory freight rates to encourage economic growth in all parts of the country.

Highways

In cooperation with State and local governmental units, we will continue to plan, coordinate, finance, and encourage the expansion of our road and highway network, including access roads, for the dual purposes of national defense and efficient motor transportation. We support expansion of farm-to-market roads.

Rivers and Harbors

We pledge continued development of our harbors and waterways.

Merchant Marine

We will continue to encourage and support an adequate Merchant Marine.

Our Natural Resources

The United States has been blessed with the richest natural resources of any nation on earth.

Yet, unless we redouble our conservation efforts we will become a "have-not" nation in some of the most important raw materials upon which

depend our industries, agriculture, employment and high standard of living. This can be prevented by a well rounded and nation-wide conservation effort.

Land and Water Resources

We favor sound, progressive development of the Nation's land and water resources for flood control, navigation, irrigation, power, drainage, soil conservation and creation of new, small family-sized farms, with immediate action in critical areas.

We favor the acceleration of all such projects, including construction of transmission facilities to load centers for wider and more equitable distribution of electric energy at the lowest cost to the consumer with continuing preference to public agencies and REA Cooperatives.

The Democratic Party denounces all obstructionist devices designed to prevent or retard utilization of the Nation's power and water resources for the benefit of the people, their enterprises and interests.

The wise policy of the Democratic Party in encouraging multipurpose projects throughout the country is responsible for America's productive superiority over any nation in the world and is one of the greatest single factors leading toward the accomplishment of world peace. Without these projects our atomic weapons program could never have been achieved, and without additional such projects it cannot be expanded.

The Democratic Party is dedicated to a continuation of the natural resources development policy inaugurated and carried out under the administrations of Presidents Roosevelt and Truman, and to the extension of that policy to all parts of the Nation—North, South, East, Midwest, West and the territories to the end that the Nation and its people receive maximum benefits from these resources to which they have an inherent right.

The Democratic Party further pledges itself to protect these resources from destructive monopoly and exploitation.

River Basin Development

We pledge the continued full and unified regional development of the water, mineral and other natural resources of the nation, recognizing that the progress already achieved under the initiative of the Democratic Party in the arid and semi-arid States of the West, as well as in the Tennessee Valley, is only an indication of still greater results which can be accomplished.

Fertilizer Development

Great farming areas, particularly of the Midwest and West, are in acute need of low-cost commercial fertilizers. To meet this demand, we favor the opening of the Nation's phosphate rock deposits in the West, through prompt provision of sufficient low-cost hydro-electric power to develop this great resource.

Forests and Public Lands

We seek to establish and demonstrate such successful policies of forest and land management on Federal property as will materially assist State and private owners in their conservation efforts. Conservation of forest and range lands is vital to the strength and welfare of the Nation. Our forest and range lands must be protected and used wisely in order to produce a continuing supply of basic raw materials for industry; to reduce damaging floods; and to preserve the sources of priceless water. With adequate appropriations to carry out feasible projects, we pledge a program of forest protection, reforestation projects and sound practices of production and harvesting which will promote sustained yields of forest crops.

We propose to increase forest access roads in order to improve cutting practices on both public and private lands.

On the public land ranges we pledge continuance of effective conservation and use programs, including the extension of water pond construction and restoration of forage cover.

Arid Areas

In many areas of the Nation assistance is needed to provide water for irrigation, domestic and industrial purposes. We pledge that in working out programs for rational distribution of water from Federal sources we will aid in delivering this essential of life cheaply and abundantly.

Minerals and Fuels

The Nation's minerals and fuels are essential to the national defense and development of our country. We pledge the adoption of policies which will further encourage the exploration and development of additional reserves of our mineral resources. We subscribe to the principles of the Stockpiling Act and will lend our efforts to strengthening and expanding its provisions and those of the Defense Production Act to meet our military and civilian needs. Additional access roads should be constructed with Government aid. Our synthetic fuels, including monetary metals, research program should go forward. Laws to aid and assist these objectives will be advocated.

Domestic Fisheries

We favor increased research and exploration for conserving and better utilizing fishery resources; expanded research and education to promote new fishery products and uses and new markets; promotion of world trade in fish products; a public works and water policy providing adequate protection for domestic fishery resources; and treaties with other nations for conservation and better utilization of international fisheries.

Wildlife Recreations

In our highly complex civilization, outdoor recreation has become essential to the health and happiness of our people.

The Democratic Party has devoted its efforts to the preservation, restoration and increase of the bird, animal and fish life which abound in this Nation. State, local and private agencies have cooperated in this worthy endeavor. We have extended and vastly improved the parks, forests, beaches, streams, preserves and wilderness areas across the land.

To the 28,000,000 of our citizens who annually purchase fishing and hunting licenses, we pledge continued efforts to improve all recreational areas.

Atomic Energy

In the field of atomic energy, we pledge ourselves:

(1) to maintain vigorous and non-partisan civilian administrations, with adequate security safeguards;

(2) to promote the development of nuclear energy for peaceful purposes in the interests of America and mankind;

(3) to build all the atomic and hydrogen firepower needed to defend our country, deter aggression, and promote world peace;

(4) To exert every effort to bring about bona

fide international control and inspection of all atomic weapons.

Social Security

Our national system of social security, conceived and developed by the Democratic Party, needs to be extended and improved.

Old Age and Survivors Insurance

We favor further strengthening of old age and survivors insurance, through such improvements as increasing benefits, extending them to more people and lowering the retirement age for women.

We favor the complete elimination of the work clause for the reason that those contributing to the Social Security program should be permitted to draw benefits, upon reaching the age of eligibility, and still continue to work.

Unemployment Insurance

We favor a stronger system of unemployment insurance, with broader coverage and substantially increased benefits, including an allowance for dependents.

Public Assistance

We favor further improvements in public assistance programs for the blind, the disabled, the aged and children in order to help our less fortunate citizens meet the needs of daily living.

Private Plans

We favor and encourage the private endeavors of social agencies, mutual associations, insurance companies, industry-labor groups, and cooperative societies to provide against the basic hazards of life through mutually agreed upon benefit plans designed to complement our present social security program.

Needs of Our Aging Citizens

Our older citizens constitute an immense reservoir of skilled, mature judgment and ripened experience. We pledge ourselves to give full recognition to the right of our older citizens to lead a proud, productive and independent life throughout their years.

In addition to the fundamental improvements in Old Age and Survivors Insurance, which are outlined above, we pledge ourselves, in cooperation with the States and private industry, to encourage the employment of older workers. We commend the 82nd Congress for eliminating the age restriction on employment in the Federal Government.

Health

We will continue to work for better health for every American, especially our children. We pledge continued and wholehearted support for the campaign that modern medicine is waging against mental illness, cancer, heart disease and other diseases.

Research

We favor continued and vigorous support, from private and public sources, of research into the causes, prevention and cure of disease.

Medical Education

We advocate Federal aid for medical education to help overcome the growing shortages of doctors, nurses, and other trained health personnel.

Hospitals and Health Centers

We pledge continued support for Federal aid to hospital construction. We pledge increased Federal aid to promote public health through preventive programs and health services, especially in rural areas.

Cost of Medical Care

We also advocate a resolute attack on the heavy financial hazard of serious illness. We recognize that the costs of modern medical care have grown to be prohibitive for many millions of people. We commend President Truman for establishing the non-partisan Commission on the Health Needs of the Nation to seek an acceptable solution of this urgent problem.

Housing

We pledge ourselves to the fulfillment of the programs of private housing, public low-rent housing, slum clearance, urban redevelopment, farm housing and housing research as authorized by the Housing Act of 1949.

We deplore the efforts of special interests groups, which themselves have prospered through Government guarantees of housing mortgages, to destroy those programs adopted to assist families of low-income.

Additional Legislation

We pledge ourselves to enact additional legislation to promote housing required for defense workers, middle income families, aged persons and migratory farm laborers.

Veterans' Housing

We pledge ourselves to provide special housing aids to veterans and their families.

EDUCATION

Every American child, irrespective of color, national origin, economic status or place of residence should have every educational opportunity to develop his potentialities.

Local, State and Federal governments have shared responsibility to contribute appropriately to the pressing needs of our educational system. We urge that Federal contributions be made available to State and local units which adhere to basic minimum standards.

The Federal Government should not dictate nor control educational policy.

We pledge immediate consideration for those school systems which need further legislation to provide Federal aid for new school construction, teachers' salaries and school maintenance and repair.

We urge the adoption by appropriate legislative action of the proposals advocated by the President's Commission on Higher Education, including Federal scholarships.

We will continue to encourage the further development of vocational training which helps people acquire skills and technical knowledge so essential to production techniques.

Child Welfare

The future of America depends on adequate provision by Government for the needs of those of our children who cannot be cared for by their parents or private social agencies.

Maternity, Child Health and Welfare Services

The established national policy of aiding States and localities, through the Children's Bureau and other agencies, to insure needed maternity, child health and welfare services should be maintained and extended. Especially important are the detection and treatment of physical defects and diseases which, if untreated, are reflected in adult life in draft rejections and as handicapped workers. The Nation, as a whole, should provide maternity and health care for the wives, babies and pre-school children of those who serve in our armed forces.

School Lunches

We will enlarge the school lunch program which has done so much for millions of American school children and charitable institutions while at the same time benefiting producers.

Day Care Facilities

Since several million mothers must now be away from their children during the day, because they are engaged in defense work, facilities for adequate day care of these children should be provided and adequately financed.

Children of Migratory Workers

The Nation, as a whole, has a responsibility to support health, educational, and welfare services for the children of agricultural migratory workers who are now almost entirely without such services while their parents are engaged in producing essential crops.

Veterans

The Democratic Party is determined to advance the welfare of all the men and women who have seen service in the armed forces. We pledge ourselves to continue and improve our national program of benefits for veterans and their families, to provide the best possible medical care and hospitalization for the disabled veteran, and to help provide every veteran an opportunity to be a productive and responsible citizen with an assured place in the civilian community.

STRENGTHENING DEMOCRATIC GOVERNMENT

Streamlining the Federal Government

The public welfare demands that our government be efficiently and economically operated and that it be reorganized to meet changing needs. During the present Democratic Administration, more reorganization has been accomplished than by all its predecessors. We pledge our support to continuing reorganization wherever improvements can be made. Only constant effort by the Executive, the Congress, and the public will enable our Government to render the splendid service to which our citizens are entitled.

Improving the Postal Service

We pledge a continuing increase in the services of the United States Postal Service. Through efficient handling of mail, improved working conditions for postal employees, and more frequent services, the Democratic Party promises its efforts to provide the greatest communication system in the world for the American people.

Strengthening the Civil Service

Good government requires a Civil Service high in quality and prestige. We deplore and condemn smear attacks upon the character and reputations of our Federal workers. We will continue our fight against partisan political efforts to discredit the Federal service and undermine American principles of justice and fair play.

Under President Truman's leadership, the Federal Civil Service has been extended to include a greater proportion of positions than ever before. He has promoted a record number of career appointees to top level policy positions. We will continue to be guided by these enlightened policies, and we will continue our efforts to provide Federal service with adequate pay, sound retirement provisions, good working conditions, and an opportunity for advancement.

We will use every proper means to eliminate pressure by private interests seeking undeserved favors from the Government. We advocate the strongest penalties against those who try to exert improper influence, and against any who may yield to it.

Democracy in Federal Elections

We advocate new legislation to provide effective regulation and full disclosure of campaign expenditures in elections to Federal office, including political advertising from any source.

We recommend that Congress provide for a non-partisan study of possible improvements in the methods of nominating and electing Presidents and in the laws relating to Presidential succession. Special attention should be given to the problem of assuring the widest possible public participation in Presidential nominations.

Strengthening Basic Freedoms

We will continue to press strongly for worldwide freedom in the gathering and dissemination of news and for support to the work of the United Nations Commission on Human Rights in furthering this and other freedoms.

Equal Rights Amendment

We recommend and endorse for submission to the Congress a constitutional amendment providing equal rights for women.

Puerto Rico

Under Democratic Party leadership, a new status has been developed for Puerto Rico. This new status is based on mutual consent and common devotion to the United States, formalized in a new Puerto Rican Constitution. We welcome the dignity of the new Puerto Rican Commonwealth and pledge our support of the Commonwealth, its continued development and growth.

Alaska and Hawaii

By virtue of their strategic geographical locations, Alaska and Hawaii are vital bastions in the Pacific. These two territories have contributed greatly to the welfare and economic development **of our country and have become integrated into** our economic and social life. We, therefore, urge immediate statehood for these two territories.

Other Territories and Possessions

We favor increased self-government for the Virgin Islands and other outlying territories and the trust territory of the Pacific.

District of Columbia

We favor immediate home rule and ultimate national representation for the District of Columbia.

American Indians

We shall continue to use the powers of the Federal Government to advance the health, education and economic well-being of our American Indian citizens, without impairing their cultural traditions. We pledge our support to the cause of fair and equitable treatment in all matters essential to and desirable for their individual and tribal welfare.

The American Indian should be completely integrated into the social, economic and political life of the nation. To that end we shall move to secure the prompt final settlement of Indian claims and to remove restrictions on the rights of Indians individually and through their tribal councils to handle their own fiscal affairs.

We favor the repeal of all acts or regulations that deny to Indians rights or privileges held by citizens generally.

Constitutional Government

The Democratic Party has demonstrated its belief in the Constitution as a charter of individual freedom and an effective instrument for human progress. Democratic Administrations have placed upon the statute books during the last twenty years a multitude of measures which testify to our belief in the Jeffersonian principle of local control, even in general legislation involving nation-wide programs. Selective service, Social Security, Agricultural Adjustment, Low Rent Housing, Hospital, and many other legislative programs have placed major responsibilities in States and counties and provide fine examples of how benefits can be extended through Federal-State cooperation.

In the present world crisis with new requirements of Federal action for national security, and accompanying provision for public services and individual rights related to defense, constitutional principles must and will be closely followed. Our record and our clear commitments, in this platform, measure our strong faith in the ability of constitutional government to meet the needs of our times.

Improving Congressional Procedures

In order that the will of the American people may be expressed upon all legislative proposals, we urge that action be taken at the beginning of the 83rd Congress to improve Congressional procedures so that majority rule prevails and decisions can be made after reasonable debate without being blocked by a minority in either House.

Civil Rights

The Democratic Party is committed to support and advance the individual rights and liberties of all Americans.

Our country is founded on the proposition that all men are created equal. This means that all citizens are equal before the law and should enjoy equal political rights. They should have equal opportunities for education, for economic advancement, and for decent living conditions.

We will continue our efforts to eradicate discrimination based on race, religion or national origin.

We know this task requires action, not just in one section of the Nation, but in all sections. It requires the cooperative efforts of individual citizens and action by State and local governments. It also requires Federal action. The Federal Government must live up to the ideals of the Declaration of Independence and must exercise the powers vested in it by the Constitution.

We are proud of the progress that has been made in securing equality of treatment and opportunity in the Nation's armed forces and the civil service and all areas under Federal jurisdiction. The Department of Justice has taken an important part in successfully arguing in the courts for the elimination of many illegal discriminations, including those involving rights to own and use real property, to engage in gainful occupations and to enroll in publicly supported higher educational institutions. We are determined that the Federal Government shall continue such policies.

At the same time, we favor Federal legislation effectively to secure these rights to everyone: (1) the right to equal opportunity for employment; (2) the right to security of persons; (3) the right to full and equal participation in the Nation's political life, free from arbitrary restraints. We also favor legislation to perfect existing Federal civil rights statutes and to strengthen the administrative machinery for the protection of civil rights.

Conclusion

Under the guidance, protection, and help of Almighty God we shall succeed in bringing to the people of this Nation a better and more rewarding life and to the peoples of the entire world, new hope and a lasting, honorable peace.

Progressive Party Platform

Preamble

Cease Fire in Korea at Once—No Ifs,
Ands or Buts

The American people want peace.

In recognition of this universal desire, each

political party will claim to be the peace party in 1952.

There is one touchstone by which every voter can test the sincerity of these claims: Does the party have a program for ending the fighting in Korea? Has it any proposal to stop a useless and senseless war which has already cost over 110,000 American casualties and untold suffering to the Korean people, and under cover of which the people are being robbed of their freedom and their substance?

Judged by this acid test, the professions of peace made by the Democratic and Republican candidates are a fraud and a pretense. They may differ on how the war in Korea should be fought and vie with each other in reckless acts and proposals that threaten to spread it beyond Korea's borders, engulfing the world. But neither old party and none of its candidates—be they generals, bankers or politicians—has any realistic plan for ending it.

Only the Progressive Party opposed the Korean War from its outset. Only the Progressive Party has a program for its immediate termination.

The Progressive Party is the only genuine party of peace.

For more than two years before the fighting started in Korea the Progressive Party warned that the Truman-Dulles cold war would inevitably lead to a shooting war. It has consistently opposed each cold war step taken by the two old parties: Truman Doctrine, Marshall Plan, North Atlantic Pact, the huge arms program at home, the arming of Western Germany and Japan, alliances with Franco and Chiang Kai-shek, the support of reaction, renascent fascism and dying colonialism in Europe, Asia, Africa and Latin America.

Even if the fighting were to end in Korea tomorrow, there are other Koreas in the making, in areas of international tension, particularly in a divided Germany. These must be averted before they result in the catastrophe of total war. Civilized negotiations among the powers can avert them.

We recognize the integral link between the bi-partisan war drive and the racist violence which seeks to suppress by napalm bombs and other atrocities the mighty upsurge of the peoples of Korea, South Africa, Indo-China, Malaya, the Philippines, India and Japan in the assertion of their inherent right to determine their own destinies.

The Progressive Party has steadfastly demanded a return to the Roosevelt-Willkie policy of One World that proved itself in the victory over fascism and held out the promise of an enduring peace.

That glorious promise can still be redeemed by the American people. The Progressive Party enters the 1952 election campaign dedicated to its redemption.

Defend the Rights of Labor; Protect the Living Standards of the American People

The Democratic and Republican parties offer no end to the war in Korea because that war, and the billions spent in preparation for an even bigger war, have been profitable business for the giant corporations which these parties serve, netting them 150 billion dollars in profits and tax-free new plants in the past four years.

These fabulous profits have been extracted from the people.

Expenditures for war are taxing away one-third of the average worker's income and have cut the purchasing power of the farmer by one-third. The cost of living stands at the highest point in our history. Yet, in the name of a so-called national emergency, the right of the trade unions to secure just wage increases is being wrecked. Even as they scuttle price controls and clamp a tighter freeze on wages, the bi-partisans are legislating out of existence the right to bargain and to strike.

The promise of prosperity through a war economy is fading before the harsh reality of growing layoffs and unemployment in the automobile and other industries geared for war as well as in textiles and consumer industries. At the same time, a rigid cold-war embargo shuts off the limitless peace-time markets of China, the Soviet Union and Eastern Europe to the products of American workers and farmers.

The need for housing, schools and playgrounds, the protection of the people's health, for harnessing our river valleys and conserving our soil resources, for assuring our senior citizens a decent income on retirement, for providing our young people with education and peace-time jobs, are all sacrificed in the race for bigger and deadlier weapons. This year the bi-partisans propose to spend 65 billion dollars for arms while less than one-tenth of that amount has been appropriated for the people's welfare.

FULL AND EQUAL RIGHTS FOR THE NEGRO PEOPLE—NOW

The war program of the bi-partisans has been accompanied by the intensification of racist acts and practices against the Negro people, the Mexican-American people, the Puerto Rican people and the Jewish people.

In Korea, American bombs are wiping out the villages and snuffing out the lives of a colored people. Here at home, the terror-weapon of the bomb is turned upon the Negro people in an attempt to stem the rising militancy of their struggle for full equality and freedom. But bombs, violence and terror will not halt the Negro people in their march to full liberation. Nor will they be put off by the pious repetition of platform promises by the two old parties which have shamelessly betrayed their pledges of anti-lynch and anti-poll tax legislation and an F.E.P.C. The magnificent struggle of the Negro people for equality and full representation at every level of government is making a vital contribution to the fight for the peace and freedom of all Americans.

RESTORE THE BILL OF RIGHTS FOR ALL AMERICANS

Under the pretense of the so-called national emergency, American democratic liberties are being destroyed. Free speech and assembly, the right to counsel, to bail, to a fair hearing—the Bill of Rights itself are nullified by Taft-Hartley, Smith and McCarran Acts, McCarthyism and McCarranism, with the support of both old parties, and the participation of every arm of government, executive, legislative and judicial. The example of the Federal government has been followed by a rash of similar legislation in almost every state.

Workers, teachers, authors, actors, government employees, small business men and professional people, are hounded, harassed, denied passports, driven from their jobs, terrorized and blacklisted for daring to express political criticism. Men and women are victimized and jailed on the unsupported testimony of stool-pigeons and paid informers or on the charges of nameless accusers brought by the FBI.

Foreign born non-citizens are deported or jailed indefinitely. Naturalized Americans are having their citizenship revoked for their political opinions.

This nullification of constitutional freedom was at first ostensibly directed against the Communists alone. Now, inevitably, all Americans—and organized labor foremost—are the victims. The so-called "emergency" used to justify the conviction of Communists under the Smith Act is invoked to destroy labor's basic right to bargain collectively through the use of injunctions, governmental seizures and the wage freeze. Not content with these measures, the bi-partisans are now pushing further legislation in Congress, sponsored by the author of the Smith Act itself, which would completely outlaw the right to strike.

The events of the past four years have fully confirmed our platform statement in 1948 that defense of the constitutional rights of Communists and all other political groups to express their views is the first line in the defense of the liberties of a democratic people.

THE BIGGEST GRAFT OF ALL: THE WAR-RACKET

The only liberty guaranteed by both old parties is the liberty to pilfer the public purse. The tax graft, the police graft, the mink coat scandals have revolted all honest Americans. But these are penny-ante games compared to the big racket—the war racket. Billions are made in the deals arrived at in the Pentagon and in the very halls of Congress. Tideland oil, natural gas, pipelines, extravagant ship subsidies, control over railroad ratemaking, control of the air waves, rapid tax write-offs, tax loopholes—these mean billions to the profit-mad backers of the two old parties.

It is clear that in 1952, neither Democrats nor Republicans can offer the people anything but more war in Korea, more spending for war, and the consequences of war spending: a tighter belt on the living standards and liberties of our people. Neither party offers any alternative. Both disclaim responsibility for this grim outlook. They blame Soviet aggression. Yet, the generals and politicians have themselves punctured the carefully nurtured myth of aggressive Soviet intentions by stating in unguarded moments that they don't believe the USSR will start a war now or at any time. As the Chicago Tribune—no friend of Communism—observed, if Soviet Russia did not exist, it would be necessary for the war spenders to invent her.

THE KEY TO PEACE: AMERICAN-SOVIET UNDERSTANDING AND CO-OPERATION

American-Soviet understanding and cooperation still remain the key to peace. Despite the differences in political and economic viewpoints between the United States and the Soviet Union, whatever mistakes each may have made, whatever the shortcomings of each great country may be, they can and must work together on the basis of mutual self-interest and the dictates of survival, for world peace, far-reaching disarmament and normal international trade.

The Progressive Party asserts that the real threat to American security comes, not from without, but from within: from the policies of the bipartisans themselves. Those policies have not protected our national security but undermined it. They have debased the living standards and are destroying the freedoms of the American people, on which our national security rests.

The tremendous armaments program that the Truman Administration has forced upon Western Europe, together with its disruption of East-West trade, have steadily lowered living standards in England, France and Italy; and are bringing those countries to the brink of economic disaster. America's get-tough policy is also tough on the hard-pressed peoples of Western Europe. It is tough, too, on the people of Turkey and Greece who suffer under a fascist government and a decaying monarchy, supported by American dollars.

The devastation our weapons have wrought in Korea and the repression of the colonial liberation movements in Asia and Africa have earned us the enmity of the colored peoples. The rearming of Germany and Japan is not only a gross violation of our war-time agreements, but is alienating the freedom-loving people of the world who fought beside us to extirpate the scourge of fascism.

The reservoir of good will for America, filled to overflowing under Franklin Roosevelt, has run dry. We stand today without firm friends or stable allies anywhere.

THE AMERICAN PEOPLE ARE FIGHTING BACK

The American people have not remained silent. They are voicing a powerful mandate for a cease-fire in Korea at once; labor is standing up in aroused strength against the wage-freeze, injunctions, and anti-union shackles. A militant Negro people is splendidly asserting its right to full citizenship and all mankind. Such an America—and only such an America—can be a secure America.

To restore such an America, we offer the following platform:

In offering it, we reaffirm our belief in the validity of the democratic process. "Freedom is the right to choose." We dedicate ourselves to the preservation and extension of that basic right. So long as that right is secured to the American people, we are confident that the program for which we stand can be obtained through the exercise of the processes guaranteed by the Constitution, and we will vigorously oppose any group that would subvert the democratic process and seek its objectives by any other means.

Our platform and our candidates give to every voter, whatever his political affiliation, the opportunity to use his precious ballot as part of a people's referendum for peace, security and freedom.

I. PEACE: THE MANDATE OF THE PEOPLE

The Progressive Party was founded in the belief that the way to peace is through negotiation of differences among nations.

The events of the past four years now cry out clearly and urgently that this is the only alternative to world destruction.

The Progressive Party rejects the idea that war is inevitable.

We reaffirm that peaceful co-existence of the Soviet Union and the United States is both possible and essential, without the sacrifice of a single interest of the American people, based upon peaceful competition between the two systems in the service of humanity.

We reject the idea of the stockpiling of A-bombs and H-bombs and the militarization of our country is needed to defend America. We reaffirm that the best defense of America is peaceful understanding and peaceful relations with all the nations of the world.

The conference table for peace must replace the battlefields of war.

Toward these ends, the Progressive Party submits the following program:

1. Agree to a cease-fire in Korea today, without any ifs, ands or buts. Propose an immediate

armistice at the agreed upon demarcation line; all disputed questions, including the exchange of war prisoners, to be settled by civilian representatives of all nations involved in the war after the fighting stops.

2. Stop the rearmament and renazification of a disunited Germany. We must work out an agreement at the conference table with England, France and the Soviet Union to make Germany a united and disarmed neutral. We also oppose the rearming of Japan and call for a conference of all the former belligerents against Japan for the renegotiation of a peace treaty.

3. Negotiate an international agreement outlawing the use of the A-bomb, and the H-bomb, with effective control and inspection of atomic stockpiles and installations. Ratify the Geneva Protocol outlawing the use of germ warfare. Take action in the UN for progressive universal disarmament, starting with an immediate and substantial reduction in the arms of all nations.

4. Contribute to a United Nations fund of $50 billion for working with the peoples of the underprivileged areas of the world in the development by them of their own resources and the improvement of their own living standards, without any political or economic interference.

5. Provide full representation in the United Nations by admitting all present applicant nations, including the People's Republic of China. Recognize the People's Republic of China; and withdraw recognition from fascist Spain.

6. Defeat any bill for Universal Military Training. Repeal the Draft Law.

7. Abolish the trade barriers to peaceful trade between America and the Soviet Union, China and Eastern Europe.

8. Support the demands for independence and freedom of colonial peoples all over the world. Stop support for fascist and racist regimes such as the Malan government in South Africa and all other imperialisms which hold African and Asian peoples in colonial bondage. Support democratic movements in Latin America and reverse the present policy of support to South American dictatorships. Repeal all laws imposing restrictions on the economic and political independence of the Philippines.

9. Grant the Puerto Rican people the right to full and immediate independence, and extend them economic assistance.

10. Extend full statehood to the territories of Alaska and Hawaii.

11. Proceed to hold a conference of the five great powers, as the only peaceful means for securing an over-all settlement of differences.

II. Jobs and Security for America

A prompt return to a peacetime economy is the only real guarantee of economic security for the American people. The old parties offer war and a war economy as the only way to have prosperity and stave off a depression.

The fact is that production for war has meant soaring prices, crushing taxes, frozen wages, mounting unemployment and sharply reduced living standards.

Production for peace would mean millions of lasting new jobs, decent wages, lower prices, lower taxes, improved social security and higher living standards.

In the midst of a so-called war boom, 5½ million Americans are on relief, some 40 million Americans try to make ends meet on incomes of less than $2,000.00 a year and one out of every four American children live in want and bitter poverty. The overwhelming majority of our people are unable to meet the costs of sickness and a third of the illnesses of the low-income groups goes without medical care. We lack almost 1,000,000 hospital beds. More than one-half the nation's families live in rural or urban slums which blight our country. Not a city or county in our country has sufficient teachers, schools, facilities or books. Not only do we waste and endanger our basic resources, the health and welfare of our people, but we waste and endanger our natural resources as well. We suffer periodic disasters and floods which are entirely within our power to prevent.

The richest nation in the world, we have the resources to assure all Americans against want, to build all the houses, schools, hospitals we need. A fraction of what we waste on insane war preparations could provide an adequate social welfare program.

Only through the planned development of all our resources will the full benefit of the Nation's wealth and productivity be secured for all of the people. Farmer and laborer, housewife and shopkeeper, all remember and urgently seek the Economic Bill of Rights first put forth by Franklin Delano Roosevelt.

The Progressive Party urges the following program to make that Economic Bill of Rights a reality today:

1. Strict Federal dollar and cents price ceilings and restoration of Federal Rent Control at pre-Korea levels.

2. End of wage-freeze. Return to free collective bargaining.

3. Repeal the Taft-Hartley Act and re-enact the Wagner Act. Defeat the Smith Anti-labor bill.

4. Launch a national housing program to provide 2.5 million low-rent homes a year, with public subsidies to make low rents possible. Wipe out the slums and provide all Americans with decent homes, without descrimination or segregation.

5. Tax exemption for families of four whose income is below $4000 and individuals whose income is below $2000. Allow tax deductions to working mothers for the cost of child care. Raise corporation taxes. Defeat the proposed Federal sales tax. Repeal the excise tax on necessities. Provide tax relief for small business.

6. A comprehensive Federal system of old-age, unemployment and disability compensation, guaranteeing to every American, without discrimination, benefits equal to a minimum decent standard of living. For the aged, not less than $150 monthly; for the unemployed or disabled, not less than $40 weekly, with additional dependency allowances. Extend the Social Security Act to all workers and all who are self-employed, including the farmer.

7. Provide family allowance of $3 weekly per child. Virtually every industrial nation, except ours, pays a weekly or monthly grant to the parent of every child, to assure a basic minimum standard of living for children.

8. A system of national health insurance, guaranteeing to all Americans as a matter of right, and not as charity, and without discrimination, adequate dental and medical care, together with a hospital and health center construction program and an expanded program of medical education and research. Provide dependency benefits to working mothers equal to the unemployment compensation. We are now the only industrial Nation in the world without a system of health insurance.

9. Enact a comprehensive farm program, providing that the prices to be paid farmers will be agreed upon and set well in advance of the production season. So long as necessary, the market place returns to farmers should be supplemented by production payments at national expense—and with no nonsense about basic and non-basic farm commodities and with all working farmers receiving equal and equitable treatment. The total return to farmers for their products should be such as to enable them to adopt and enjoy living standards on a parity with the rest of the population and, in addition, to finance soil conservation practices and the restoration of soil fertility. Participation should be voluntary, conditioned upon performance, and limited to family type farmers with corporate and large scale operations excluded as a matter of public policy. Only through such a program can the long standing inequities between agriculture on the one hand and industry and commerce on the other be corrected, scarcity abolished, abundance assured, and the agricultural threat to our national survival removed. To that end, we call for the following:

(1) 100 per cent parity prices for all farm commodities on the basis of a revised and modernized parity formula. We condemn the shameful betrayal of the Brannan Plan by the Truman Administration, which lifted this program from the Progressive Party's program of 1948, and reaffirm our support for these principles, without dilution or demagogy.

(2) Halt the draft of our farm youth.

(3) Use production payments to encourage food production and reduce farm-to-market price spreads. Provide government credit at low rates to working farmers and enact a farm debt moratorium law.

(4) Provide federal development and conservatism of soil, water and power resources on an integrated basin-wide scale, including the St. Lawrence seaway, to provide publicly owned low-cost power and irrigation water and protect against the ravages of flood and drought. Develop and conserve harbors and fisheries.

(5) Reduce taxes on working farmers and eliminate federal income taxes on farm cooperatives.

(6) Recognize the elementary right of agricultural workers and sharecroppers to organize and bargain collectively and end sharecropper peonage in the South. Enact a tenant purchase program. Provide full coverage of agricultural workers under Workmen's Compensation, Unemployment Insurance, and Social Security legislation. Establish minimum federal standards for

the protection of agricultural workers, including all who come from Mexico, Puerto Rico, and the British West Indies.

10. Appropriate ten billion dollars for a 10 year program of federally financed school construction; immediate appropriation of one billion dollars for federal aid for public schools to raise teachers' salaries, employ additional needed teachers and provide essential materials and services for the children. Eliminate segregation and all forms of discrimination in education.

11. Increase to $1.25 the minimum hourly wage under the Fair Labor Standards Act, with overtime pay for work in excess of 30 hours in any work week.

12. Empower the Federal Bureau of Mines to fine or close down mines not conforming to Government standards of safety.

13. Provide and guarantee equal job opportunities and job training for Negroes, Mexican-Americans, Puerto Ricans and other minority groups.

14. Establish a system of nation-wide job training centers for youth; full social security protection for youth. Federal scholarships and cost-of-living grants, free from discrimination by reason of race, color, creed or national origin, to insure full educational opportunities. Grant the right to vote to 18 year olds.

15. We demand for all women all of the economic rights of first class citizens. We urge legislation forbidding discrimination against women, guaranteeing them equal pay and job security and removing all social and economic restrictions upon women, without jeopardizing existing protective legislation.

16. Enact a GI Bill of Rights for all veterans since World War II, providing all the benefits granted to World War II veterans. Increase all veterans' benefits in amounts which reflect the increased cost of living. Extend all veterans' benefits to merchant seamen with war service.

17. Establish a Federally subsidized arts and theatre program.

III. END AMERICA'S SHAME; GUARANTEE FULL CIVIL RIGHTS FOR THE NEGRO PEOPLE AND OTHER MINORITIES; END SEGREGATION

The deliberate official policy of government on all levels which denies full equality of rights to sixteen million Negro Americans is responsible for the evils of segregation, discrimination, police brutality, terror, lynching and second-class citizenship.

That policy has shortened the average life span of the Negro people in America to eight years less than the life span of whites. It sanctions violence and murder against Negroes solely because they are Negroes—and this violence is being wrought on so mounting a scale that it approaches what is defined as "genocide" under the United Nations Convention against genocide.

An aroused and determined Negro people properly insist on their protection, on their full status as American citizens, and on full representation in the political life of the nation.

In vigorous and uncompromising support of these aims and steps toward stamping out every form of discrimination against the Negro people, the Mexican-American people, the Puerto Rican people, the Jewish people and other minority groups, the Progressive Party calls for:

1. A Federal Fair Employment Practices Law with effective enforcement powers to guarantee equality in job opportunities and training for the Negro people, Puerto Ricans, Mexican-Americans and all other minorities.

2. A Federal anti-poll tax law together with Federal legislation to guarantee to the Negro people, Puerto Ricans, Mexican-Americans and other minorities the right to register and to vote in primary and general elections for Federal office. Revise Senate cloture rules to make filibusters impossible.

3. A Federal anti-lynch law to direct the full power of the Federal government against lynchers.

4. The immediate issuance of an Executive Order by the President to prohibit discrimination in employment, under any contract entered into by the Federal government or any of its agencies.

5. The immediate issuance of an Executive Order by the President for effective prosecution under the Federal civil rights statutes of the violation of the civil rights of Negro citizens and other minorities.

6. End segregation and discrimination in housing; replace Jim Crow ghettos with low-rent, unsegregated housing.

7. The immediate issuance of an Executive Order to end segregation and discrimination in the armed forces, in all Federal departments and agencies, and in the Panama Canal Zone.

8. Real Home Rule for the District of Colum-

bia and Congressional legislation to prohibit every form of segregation and discrimination in the nation's capital.

9. Full representation of the Negro and Puerto Rican and Mexican-American people in Congress, in State legislatures and all levels of public office, elective and appointive.

10. Provide that all Federal laws appropriating Federal monies for any public purpose contain a specific provision prohibiting the use of any such funds in a manner which discriminates against the Negro people, Puerto Ricans, Mexican-Americans or any other minorities.

11. Full citizenship for the American Indians and the right to administer their own affairs without loss of Reservation rights. Adequate compensation for loss of tribal land rights.

IV. RESTORE FREEDOM TO ALL AMERICANS

The right freely to petition, to speak, to think, to write, to travel, to assemble peacefully, to vote for candidates of one's own choice,—these are the bedrocks of American democracy. We support these freedoms of all individuals and groups in our American community, for those with whom we disagree as well as those with whom we agree. Only a nation which guarantees and implements these freedoms can find the path of social progress and develop science, art and other fields of creative endeavor in the peaceful service of the people.

The Progressive Party calls for a great national crusade to restore the full meaning of the Bill of Rights to all Americans.

1. Repeal the Smith, McCarran, and the new McCarran-Walter Acts. No concentration camps in America.

2. End all prosecution under the Smith Act, stop the proceedings under the McCarran Act, grant unconditional pardons and restore full civil rights to all persons convicted under the Smith Act.

3. Stop the persecution, deportation and imprisonment of native or foreign-born Americans because of their trade union of political activities or opinions.

4. Guarantee the freedom of advocacy for lawyers and the right of accused to counsel of their own choice. Free the lawyers who have courageously defended advocates of minority opinion and causes.

5. Abolish the House Committee on un-American Activities, and the McCarran Committees of the Senate on Internal Security. Establish fair and equitable procedures for all legislative investigating committees.

6. End the "loyalty" and "screening" programs and the Attorney-General's subversive list which affect millions of government workers, teachers, members of the arts and professions, and millions more in private industry. Repeal the Magnusson Act providing for the screening of maritime workers. Restore all those fired under these procedures to their jobs.

7. Maintain the traditional American principle of separation of church and state and protect the freedom of public education.

8. Provide compulsory public hearings on major legislation; end government by secret star chamber proceedings; insure public knowledge of the public business. End government by secrecy and censorship.

9. Ratify the UN Convention on Genocide and the UN Convention on Human Rights.

10. Stop attempts to impose thought control on teachers and pupils and the use of the public schools to promote war hysteria.

Prohibition Party—1952 Platform

PREAMBLE

We, the representatives of the Prohibition Party, assembled in national convention at Indianapolis, Indiana, November 13, 14, and 15, 1951, recognizing Almighty God as the source of all just government and with faith in the teachings of the Prince of Peace, do solemnly promise that, if our party is chosen to administer the affairs of this nation, we will use all the powers of our administration to serve the people of the United States.

We reaffirm our loyalty to the Constitution of the United States. We have supreme confidence in this form of Government to meet all changing national and world conditions.

CONSTITUTIONAL GOVERNMENT

We are strongly opposed to atheistic communism and every other form of totalitarianism. We deplore their infiltration throughout the nation. We challenge all loyal citizens to work against this menace to civilization. We are convinced that the best safeguard against these dangerous doctrines is to protect the rights of our citizens by enforcing the provisions of the Constitution and the Bill of Rights.

GOVERNMENTAL ECONOMY

Extravagant spending has set an example of wasteful governmental operation. We believe it is unjust for any government to take nearly one-third of the total income of its citizens to pay the expense of government. We believe that government ought not to do for the people what they can do for themselves. We promise to reorganize the federal government, abolishing all departments and bureaus that cannot qualify when measured by this principle.

TAXES

The constant increase in taxation is approaching the point of confiscation and economic bankruptcy. With proper economy, governmental costs will be lowered, making it possible to reduce the public debt and lighten the tax load for the average citizen.

WORLD PEACE AND ORDER

We believe in World Peace.

Having united with other nations to restore world order and preserve world peace, our nation should lead in subordinating selfish interests for the common good.

The leadership to be entrusted with this task should be men whose dependence for wisdom and guidance is upon Almighty God.

RELIGIOUS LIBERTY

We believe in religious liberty.

By religious liberty we mean the freedom of individual worship and fellowship and the right to evangelize, and educate, and establish religious institutions. When religious liberty is lost political liberty perishes with it.

UNIVERSAL MILITARY TRAINING

Believing that compulsory military training in peacetime in our country would not represent a safeguard for world peace, would be contrary in principle to our American way of life, would place an unnecessary burden upon our peacetime economy, would lead only to military dictatorship, and would, under existing conditions, lead to the moral and spiritual deterioration of our youth, we declare our opposition to any program of peacetime compulsory military training.

PUBLIC MORALITY AND LAW ENFORCEMENT

Moral and spiritual considerations should be primary factors in determining national policies. We will strengthen and enforce laws against gambling, narcotics, and commercialized vice, now so openly violated and nullified by the inaction of the parties in power, and thus prevent further disintigration of the public morals.

We oppose the present nullification of law by non-enforcement and will maintain the integrity of democracy by enforcing the Constitution and the laws enacted under it.

HONESTY IN GOVERNMENT

There is a law of cause and effect which rules in the affairs of men. With the repeal of the Eighteenth Amendment there has been a rapid decline in the moral standards of the nation, culminating in such revelations as those made by the Senate Crime Investigating Committee. We pledge ourselves to break this unholy alliance between organized crime and those in positions of trust in the government at all levels.

FREE ENTERPRISE

We deplore the current trend toward a socialistic state, with its increasing emphasis upon governmental restraint of free enterprise, regulation of our economic life, and federal interference with individual freedom. We declare ourselves in favor of freedom of opportunity, private industry financed within the structure of the present anti-trust laws, and an economic program based upon sound business practice.

LABOR AND INDUSTRY

Labor organizations are entitled to great credit for improving the status of the workers and for their constructive contributions to the general welfare. It is our purpose to give the public welfare paramount consideration. Neither capital nor labor can be permitted to dominate at the expense of the other or of the common good. We favor the compulsory arbitration of labor disputes.

SOCIAL SECURITY AND OLD AGE PENSIONS

We endorse the general principle of social security, including all employed groups. We deplore, however, the widespread current abuses of its privileges and the maladministration of its provisions for political ends, and pledge ourselves to correct these evils.

MONEY

The Constitution provides that Congress shall have the power to "coin money" and "regulate the value thereof." This is a sound and feasible monetary policy which we promise to re-establish and enforce.

NO RACIAL DISCRIMINATION

Recognizing that "God created of one blood all nations to dwell upon the face of the earth," we declare in favor of full justice and equal opportunity for all people, regardless of race, creed, or national origin.

MARRIAGE AND DIVORCE

We favor the enactment of uniform marriage and divorce laws as a help toward maintaining the sanctity of the home.

SEPARATION OF CHURCH AND STATE

The American principle of separation of Church and State must be maintained. We are opposed to the appropriation of public money for any sectarian purpose.

BALLOT LAW REFORM

We demand the repeal of the many state ballot laws which have been enacted to make the two-party system a bipartisan political monopoly by keeping minor parties off the ballot, thus denying to independent voters and minority groups the fundamental right of free political expression.

PROHIBITION

As the result of the repeal of the Eighteenth Amendment the government now endorses an industry whose product deranges the mind of the user and whose propaganda perverts the judgment of its citizens.

We do not believe that our nation can long survive if this trend continues.

No other political issue confronting our citizens compares in magnitude with the necessity for suppressing the alcohol beverage traffic.

The present liquor conditions, which are far worse than ever before, are due in large measure to the action of the two major parties when they adopted platform planks designed to destroy the Eighteenth Amendment.

The moral forces have to contend with the liquor power which is well financed, competently organized, and is creating an ever-growing appetite for its products among youth and adults through its promotion of the sale of alcoholic beverages. This power dominates our politics and government. It controls large numbers of voters. Every saloon or tavern is a center for mobilizing and controlling votes. Both parties are subservient to the liquor power. As long as good citizens continue to give their votes to the liquor parties, as long as they continue to be yoked by party membership with the liquor interests and the underworld, they will be incapable of making moral principles prevail.

What is needed is a re-alignment of voters and the union of good citizens in a party unitedly committed to prohibition.

We summon the voters of America to help elect the Prohibition Party to power. We will then marshal the resources of the government—executive, legislative and judicial—to overthrow the liquor traffic and usher in a new day for America.

1952 Republican Platform

PREAMBLE

We maintain that man was not born to be ruled, but that he consented to be governed; and that the reasons that moved him thereto are few and simple. He has voluntarily submitted to government because, only by the establishment of just laws, and the power to enforce those laws, can an orderly life be maintained, full and equal opportunity for all be established, and the blessings of liberty be perpetuated.

We hold that government, and those entrusted with government, should set a high example of honesty, of justice, and unselfish devotion to the public good; that they should labor to maintain tranquillity at home and peace and friendship with all the nations of the earth.

We assert that during the last twenty years, leaders of the Government of the United States under successive Democrat Administrations, and especially under this present Administration, have failed to perform these several basic duties; but, on the contrary, that they have evaded them, flouted them, and by a long succession of vicious acts, so undermined the foundations of our Republic as to threaten its existence.

We charge that they have arrogantly deprived our citizens of precious liberties by seizing powers never granted.

We charge that they work unceasingly to achieve their goal of national socialism.

We charge that they have disrupted internal tranquillity by fostering class strife for venal political purposes.

We charge that they have choked opportunity and hampered progress by unnecessary and crushing taxation.

They claim prosperity but the appearance of economic health is created by war expenditures, waste and extravagance, planned emergencies, and war crises. They have debauched our money by cutting in half the purchasing power of our dollar.

We charge that they have weakened local self-government which is the cornerstone of the freedom of men.

We charge that they have shielded traitors to the Nation in high places, and that they have created enemies abroad where we should have friends.

We charge that they have violated our liberties by turning loose upon the country a swarm of arrogant bureaucrats and their agents who meddle intolerably in the lives and occupations of our citizens.

We charge that there has been corruption in high places, and that examples of dishonesty and dishonor have shamed the moral standards of the American people.

We charge that they have plunged us into war in Korea without the consent of our citizens through their authorized representatives in the Congress, and have carried on that war without will to victory.

FOREIGN POLICY

The present Administration, in seven years, has squandered the unprecedented power and prestige which were ours at the close of World War II.

In that time, more than 500 million non-Russian people of fifteen different countries have been absorbed into the power sphere of Communist Russia, which proceeds confidently with its plan for world conquest.

We charge that the leaders of the Administra-

tion in power lost the peace so dearly earned by World War II.

The moral incentives and hopes for a better world which sustained us through World War II were betrayed, and this has given Communist Russia a military and propaganda initiative which, if unstayed, will destroy us.

They abandoned friendly nations such as Latvia, Lithuania, Estonia, Poland and Czechoslovakia to fend for themselves against the Communist aggression which soon swallowed them.

They required the National Government of China to surrender Manchuria with its strategic ports and railroads to the control of Communist Russia. They urged that Communists be taken into the Chinese Government and its military forces. And finally they denied the military aid that had been authorized by Congress and which was crucially needed if China were to be saved. Thus they substituted on our Pacific flank a murderous enemy for an ally and friend.

In all these respects they flouted our peace-assuring pledges such as the Atlantic Charter, and did so in favor of despots, who, it was well-known, consider that murder, terror, slavery, concentration camps and the ruthless and brutal denial of human rights are legitimate means to their desired ends.

Tehran, Yalta and Potsdam were the scenes of those tragic blunders with others to follow. The leaders of the Administration in power acted without the knowledge or consent of Congress or of the American people. They traded our overwhelming victory for a new enemy and for new oppressions and new wars which were quick to come.

In South Korea, they withdrew our occupation troops in the face of the aggressive, poised for action, Communist military strength on its northern border. They publicly announced that Korea was of no concern to us. Then when the Communist forces acted to take what seemed to have been invited, they committed this nation to fight back under the most unfavorable conditions. Already the tragic cost is over 110,000 American casualties.

With foresight, the Korean War would never have happened.

In going back into Korea, they evoked the patriotic and sacrificial support of the American people. But by their hampering orders they produced stalemates and ignominious bartering with our enemies, and they offer no hope of victory.

They have effectively ignored many vital areas in the face of a global threat requiring balanced handling.

The people of the other American Republics are resentful of our neglect of their legitimate aspirations and cooperative friendship.

The Middle East and much of Africa seethe with anti-American sentiment.

The peoples of the Far East who are not under Communist control find it difficult to sustain their morale as they contrast Russia's "Asia First" policy with the "Asia Last" policy of those in control of the Administration now in power.

Here at home they have exhibited corruption, incompetence, and disloyalty in public office to such an extent that the very concept of free representative government has been tarnished and has lost its idealistic appeal to those elsewhere who are confronted with the propaganda of Communism.

They profess to be following a defensive policy of "containment" of Russian Communism which has not contained it.

Those in control of the Party in power have, in reality, no foreign policy. They swing erratically from timid appeasement to reckless bluster.

The good in our foreign policies has been accomplished with Republican cooperation, such as the organization of the United Nations, the establishment of the trusteeship principle for dependent peoples, the making of peace with Japan and Germany, and the building of more solid security in Europe. But in the main the Republican Party has been ignored and its participation has not been invited.

The American people must now decide whether to continue in office the party which has presided over this disastrous reversal of our fortunes and the loss of our hopes for a peaceful world.

The Republican Party offers, in contrast to the performances of those now running our foreign affairs, policies and actions based on enlightened self-interest and animated by courage, self-respect, steadfastness, vision, purpose, competence and spiritual faith.

The supreme goal of our foreign policy will be an honorable and just peace. We dedicate ourselves to wage peace and to win it.

We shall eliminate from the State Department and from every Federal office, all, wherever they may be found, who share responsibility for the needless predicaments and perils in which we find ourselves. We shall also sever from the public payroll the hordes of loafers, incompetents and unnecessary employees who clutter the administration of our foreign affairs. The confusions, overlappings, and extravagance of our agencies abroad hold us up to the ridicule of peoples whose friendship we seek.

We shall substitute a compact and efficient organization where men of proven loyalty and ability shall have responsibility for reaching our objectives. They will reflect a dynamic initiative. Thus we can win the support and confidence which go only to those who demonstrate a capacity to define and get results.

We shall have positive peace-building objectives wherever this will serve the enlightened self-interest of our Nation and help to frustrate the enemy's designs against us.

In Western Europe we shall use our friendly influence, without meddling or imperialistic attitudes, for ending the political and economic divisions which alone prevent that vital area from being strong on its own right.

We shall encourage and aid the development of collective security forces there, as elsewhere, so as to end the Soviet power to intimidate directly or by satellites, and so that the free governments will be sturdy to resist Communist inroads.

In the balanced consideration of our problems, we shall end neglect of the Far East which Stalin has long identified as the road to victory over the West. We shall make it clear that we have no intention to sacrifice the East to gain time for the West.

The Republican Party has consistently advocated a national home for the Jewish people since a Republican Congress declared its support of that objective thirty years ago.

In providing a sanctuary for Jewish people rendered homeless by persecution, the State of Israel appeals to our deepest humanitarian instincts. We shall continue our friendly interest in this constructive and inspiring undertaking.

We shall put our influence at the service of peace between Israel and the Arab States, and we shall cooperate to bring economic and social stability to that area.

Our ties with the sister Republics of the Americas will be strengthened.

The Government of the United States, under Republican leadership, will repudiate all commitments contained in secret understandings such as those of Yalta which aid Communist enslavements. It will be made clear, on the highest authority of the President and the Congress, that United States policy, as one of its peaceful purposes, looks happily forward to the genuine independence of those captive peoples.

We shall again make liberty into a beacon light of hope that will penetrate the dark places. That program will give the Voice of America a real function. It will mark the end of the negative, futile and immoral policy of "containment" which abandons countless human beings to a despotism and godless terrorism, which in turn enables the rulers to forge the captives into a weapon for our destruction.

We shall support the United Nations and loyally help it to become what it was designed to be, a place where differences would be harmonized by honest discussion and a means for collective security under agreed concepts of justice. We shall seek real meaning and value for our regional security treaties, which implies that all parties shall contribute their loyal support and fair shares.

We shall see to it that no treaty or agreement with other countries deprives our citizens of the rights guaranteed them by the Federal Constitution.

We shall always measure our foreign commitments so that they can be borne without endangering the economic health or sound finances of the United States. Stalin said that "the moment for the decisive blow" would be when the free nations were isolated and were in a state of "practical bankruptcy." We shall not allow ourselves to be isolated and economically strangled, and we shall not let ourselves go bankrupt.

Sums available by this test, if competently used, will be more effective than vastly larger sums incompetently spent for vague and endless purposes. We shall not try to buy good will. We shall earn it by sound, constructive, self-respecting policies and actions.

We favor international exchange of students and of agricultural and industrial techniques, and programs for improvement of public health.

We favor the expansion of mutually-advanta-geous world trade. To further this objective we shall press for the elimination of discriminatory practices against our exports, such as preferential tariffs, monetary license restrictions, and other arbitrary devices. Our reciprocal trade agreements will be entered into and maintained on a basis of true reciprocity, and to safeguard our domestic enterprises and the payrolls of our workers against unfair import competition.

The policies we espouse will revive the contagious, liberating influences which are inherent in freedom. They will inevitably set up strains and stresses within the captive world which will make the rulers impotent to continue in their monstrous ways and mark the beginning of their end.

Our nation will become again the dynamic, moral and spiritual force which was the despair of despots and the hope of the oppressed. As we resume this historic role, we ourselves will come to enjoy again the reality of peace, security and solvency, not the shabby and fleeting counterfeit which is the gift of the Administration in power.

NATIONAL DEFENSE

On the prudent assumption that Communist Russia may not accommodate our own disgracefully-lagging program for preparedness, we should develop with utmost speed a force-in-being, as distinguished from paper plans, of such power as to deter sudden attack or promptly and decisively defeat it. This defense against sudden attack requires the quickest possible development of appropriate and completely-adequate air power and the simultaneous readiness of coordinated air, land, and sea forces, with all necessary installations, bases, supplies and munitions, including atomic energy weapons in abundance.

Generally, we shall see to it that our military services are adequately supported in all ways required, including manpower, to perform their appropriate tasks in relation to the defense of this country and to meet our treaty obligations.

We shall coordinate our miltary policy with our foreign policy, always seeking universal limitation and control of armaments on a dependable basis.

We shall review our entire preparedness program and we shall strip it clean of waste, lack of coordination, inertia, and conflict between the services. We shall see that our fighting men in Korea, or wherever they may be, shall not lack the best of weapons or other supplies or services needed for their welfare.

COMMUNISM

By the Administration's appeasement of Communism at home and abroad it has permitted Communists and their fellow travelers to serve in many key agencies and to infiltrate our American life. When such infiltrations became notorious through the revelations of Republicans in Congress, the Executive Department stubbornly refused to deal with it openly and vigorously. It raised the false cry of "red herring" and took other measures to block and discredit investigations. It denied files and information to Congress. It set up boards of its own to keep information secret and to deal lightly with security risks and persons of doubtful loyalty. It only undertook prosecution of the most notorious Communists after public opinion forced action.

The result of these policies is the needless sacrifice of American lives, a crushing cost in dollars for defense, possession by Russia of the atomic bomb, the lowering of the Iron Curtain, and the present threats to world peace. Our people have been mired in fear and distrust and employees of integrity in the Government service have been cruelly maligned by the Administration's tolerance of people of doubtful loyalty.

There are no Communists in the Republican Party. We have always recognized Communism to be a world conspiracy against freedom and religion. We never compromised with Communism and we have fought to expose it and to eliminate it in government and American life.

A Republican President will appoint only persons of unquestioned loyalty. We will overhaul loyalty and security programs. In achieving these purposes a Republican President will cooperate with Congress. We pledge close coordination of our intelligence services for protecting our security. We pledge fair but vigorous enforcement of laws to safeguard our country from subversion and disloyalty. By such policies we will keep the country secure and restore the confidence of the American people in the integrity of our Government.

SMALL BUSINESS IN A FREE ECONOMY

For twenty years the Administration has praised free enterprise while actually wrecking it. Here a little, there a little, year by year, it has sought to curb, regulate, harass, restrain and punish. There is scarcely a phase of our economic and social life today in which Government does not attempt to interfere.

Such hostility deadens initiative, discourages invention and experiment, and weakens the self-reliance indispensable to the Nation's vitality. Merciless taxation, the senseless use of controls and ceaseless effort to enter business on its own account, have led the present Government to unrestrained waste and extravagance in spending, irresponsibility in decision and corruption in administration.

The anti-monopoly laws have been employed, not to preserve and foster competition, but to further the political ambitions of the men in power. Wage and price controls have been utilized, not to maintain economic stability, but to reward the friends and punish the enemies of leaders of the Party in power.

Neither small nor large business can flourish in such an atmosphere. The Republican Party will end this hostility to initiative and enterprise.

We will aid small business in every practicable way. We shall remove tax abuses and injurious price and wage controls. Efforts to plan and regulate every phase of small business activity will cease. We will maintain special committees in Congress whose chief function will be to study and review continuously the problems of small business and recommend legislation for their relief. We shall always be mindful of the importance of keeping open the channels of opportunity for young men and women.

We will follow principles of equal enforcement of the anti-monopoly and unfair-competition statutes and will simplify their administration to assist the businessman who, in good faith, seeks to remain in compliance. At the same time, we shall relentlessly protect our free enterprise system against monopolistic and unfair trade practices.

We will oppose Federal rent control except in those areas where the expansion of defense production has been accompanied by critical housing shortages. With local cooperation we shall aid slum clearance.

Our goal is a balanced budget, a reduced national debt, an economical administration and a cut in taxes. We believe in combating inflation by encouraging full production of goods and food, and not through a program of restrictions.

TAXATION AND MONETARY POLICY

Only with a sound economy can we properly carry out both the domestic and foreign policies which we advocate. The wanton extravagance and inflationary policies of the Administration in power have cut the value of the dollar in half and imposed the most confiscatory taxes in our history. These policies have made the effective control of Government expenditures impossible. If this Administration is left in power, it will further cheapen the dollar, rob the wage earner, impoverish the farmer and reduce the true value of the savings, pensions, insurance and investments of millions of our people. Further inflation must be and can be prevented. Sound tax and monetary policies are essential to this end. We advocate the following tax policies:

1. Reduction of expenditures by the elimination of waste and extravagance so that the budget will be balanced and a general tax reduction can be made.

2. An immediate study directed toward reallocation of fields of taxation between the Federal, State, and municipal governments so as to allow greater fiscal freedom to the States and municipalities, thus minimizing double taxation and enabling the various divisions of government to meet their obligations more efficiently.

3. A thorough revision and codification of the present hodge-podge of internal revenue laws.

4. Administration of the tax laws free from politics, favoritism and corruption.

We advocate the following monetary policies:

1. A Federal Reserve System exercising its functions in the money and credit system without pressure for political purposes from the Treasury or the White House.

2. To restore a domestic economy, and to use our influence for a world economy, of such stability as will permit the realization of our aim of a dollar on a fully-convertible gold basis.

AGRICULTURE

The good earth is the food storehouse for future generations. The tending of the soil is a sacred responsibility. Development of a sound farm program is a high national duty. Any program that will benefit farmers must serve the national welfare. A prosperous agriculture with free and independent farmers is fundamental to the national interest.

We charge the present Administration with seeking to destroy the farmers' freedom. We denounce the Administration's use of tax money and a multitude of Federal agencies to put agriculture under partisan political dictation and to make the farmer dependent upon government. We condemn the Brannan plan which aims to control the farmer and to socialize agriculture. We brand as unscrupulous the Administration's manipulation of grain markets during the 1948 election campaign to drive down farm prices, and its deliberate misrepresentation of laws passed by the Republican 80th Congress, which authorized a long-range farm price support program and provided for adequate grain storage.

We condemn as a fraud on both the farmer and the consumer the Brannan plan scheme to pay direct subsidies from the Federal Treasury in lieu of prices to producers.

We favor a farm program aimed at full parity prices for all farm products in the market place. Our program includes commodity loans on non-perishable products, "on-the-farm" storage, sufficient farm credit, and voluntary self-supporting crop insurance. Where government action on perishable commodities is desirable, we recommend locally-controlled marketing agreements and other voluntary methods.

Our program should include commodity loans on all non-perishable products supported at the level necessary to maintain a balanced production. We do not believe in restrictions on the American farmers' ability to produce.

We favor a bi-partisan Federal Agricultural Commission with power to review the policies and administration of our farm programs and to make recommendations.

We support a constructive and expanded soil conservation program administered through locally-controlled local districts, and which shall emphasize that payments shall be made for practices and improvements of a permanent nature.

Flood control programs should include the application of sound land use, reforestation and water-management practices on each watershed. These, so far as feasible, should be decentralized and locally-controlled to insure economy and effective soil conservation.

We recommend expanded agricultural research and education to promote new crops and uses, new markets, both foreign and domestic, more trustworthy crop and market estimates, a realistic trade program for agriculture aimed at restoring foreign markets and developing new outlets at home. Promotion of world trade must be on a basis of fair competition.

We support the principle of bona fide farmer-owned, farmer-operated co-operatives and urge the further development of rural electrification and communication, with federally-assisted production of power and facilities for distribution when these are not adequately available through private enterprise at fair rates.

We insist that an adequate supply of manpower on the farm is necessary to our national welfare and security and shall do those things required to assure this result.

The Republican Party will create conditions providing for farm prosperity and stability, safeguarding the farmers' independence and opening opportunities for young people in rural communities. We will do those things necessary to simplify and make efficient the operation of the Department of Agriculture, prevent that Department from assuming powers neither intended nor delegated by Congress, and to place the administration of farm programs as closely as possible to State and local levels.

Labor

The Republican Party believes that regular and adequate income for the employee together with uninterrupted production of goods and services, through the medium of private enterprise, are essential to a sound national economy. This can only be obtained in an era of industrial peace.

With the above in mind, we favor the retention of the Taft-Hartley Act, which guarantees:

To the Working Man:—

The right to quit his job at any time.

The right to take part in legal union activities.

The right to remain in his union so long as he pays his dues.

The right to protection against unfair practices by either employer or union officials.

The right to political activity of his own choice and freedom to contribute thereto.

The right to a job without first joining a union.

The right to a secret ballot in any election concerned with his livelihood.

The right to protection from personal financial responsibility in damage cases against his union.

To the Labor Unions:

The right to establish "union shop" contracts by agreement with management.

The right to strike.

The right to free collective bargaining.

The right to protection from rival unions during the life of union contracts.

The right to assurance from employers that they will bargain only with certified unions as a protection against unfair labor practices.

We urge the adoption of such amendments to the Taft-Hartley Act as time and experience show to be desirable, and which further protect the rights of labor, management and the public.

We condemn the President's seizure of plants and industries to force the settlement of labor disputes by claims of inherent Constitutional powers.

Natural Resources

We vigorously advocate a full and orderly program for the development and conservation of our natural resources.

We deplore the policies of the present Administration which allow special premiums to foreign producers of minerals available in the United States. We favor reasonable depletion allowances, defense procurement policies, synthetic fuels research, and public land policies, including good-faith administration of our mining laws, which will encourage exploration and development of our mineral resources consistent with our growing industrial and defense needs.

We favor stockpiling of strategic and critical raw materials and special premium incentives for their domestic exploration and development.

We favor restoration to the States of their rights to all lands and resources beneath navigable inland and offshore waters within their historic boundaries.

We favor protection of our fisheries by domestic

regulation and treaties, including safeguards against unfair foreign competition.

Public Works and Water Policy

The Federal Government and State and local governments should continuously plan programs of economically justifiable public works.

We favor continuous and comprehensive investigations of our water resources and orderly execution of programs approved by the Congress. Authorized water projects should go forward progressively with immediate priority for those with defense significance, those in critical flood and water-shortage areas, and those substantially completed.

We favor greater local participation in the operation and control, and eventual local ownership, of federally-sponsored, reimbursable water projects.

We vigorously oppose the efforts of this national Administration, in California and elsewhere, to undermine state control over water use, to acquire paramount water rights without just compensation, and to establish all-powerful federal socialistic valley authorities.

Public Lands

We favor restoration of the traditional Republican public land policy, which provided opportunity for ownership by citizens to promote the highest land use. We favor an impartial study of tax-free Federal lands and their uses to determine their effects on the economic and fiscal structures of our States and local communities.

In the management of public lands and forests we pledge the elimination of arbitrary bureaucratic practices. To this end we favor legislation to define the rights and privileges of grazers and other cooperators and users, to provide the protection of independent judicial review against administrative invasions of those rights and privileges, and to protect the public against corrupt or monopolistic exploitation and bureaucratic favoritism.

Veterans

We believe that active duty in the Armed Forces of the United States of America during a state of war or national emergency constitutes a special service to our Nation, and entitles those who have so served to aid and compensation in return for this service.

Consequently we propose:

That the aid and compensation given to veterans of previous wars be extended to veterans of the Korean conflict;

That compensation be fairly and adequately adjusted to meet changes in the cost of living;

That aid be given to veterans, particularly disabled veterans, to obtain suitable employment, by providing training and education, and through strict compliance with veterans' preference laws in Federal service;

That the Veterans' Administration be maintained as a single, independent agency in full charge of all veterans' affairs, and that the Veterans' Administration manage veterans' affairs in an efficient, prompt and uniform manner;

That the Veterans' Administration should be equipped to provide and maintain medical and hospital care of the highest possible standard for all eligible veterans.

Social Security

Inflation has already cut in half the purchasing power of the retirement and other benefits under the Federal Old Age and Survivors Insurance system. Sixty million persons are covered under the system and four and one-half million are now receiving benefits.

The best assurance of preserving the benefits for which the worker has paid is to stop the inflation which causes the tragic loss of purchasing power, and that we propose to do.

We favor amendment of the Old Age and Survivors Insurance system to provide coverage for those justly entitled to it but who are now excluded.

We shall work to achieve a simple, more effective and more economical method of administration.

We shall make a thorough study of universal pay-as-we-go pension plans.

Health

We recognize that the health of our people as well as their proper medical care cannot be maintained if subject to Federal bureaucratic dictation. There should be a division of responsibility between government, the physician, the voluntary hospital, and voluntary health insurance. We are opposed to Federal compulsory health insurance with its crushing cost, wasteful inefficiency, bureaucratic dead weight, and debased standards of medical care. We shall support those health activities by government which stimulate the development of adequate hospital services without Federal interference in local administration. We favor support of scientific research. We pledge our continuous encouragement of improved methods of assuring health protection.

EDUCATION

The tradition of popular education, tax-supported and free to all, is strong with our people. The responsibility for sustaining this system of popular education has always rested upon the local communities and the States. We subscribe fully to this principle.

CIVIL RIGHTS

We condemn bigots who inject class, racial and religious prejudice into public and political matters. Bigotry is un-American and a danger to the Republic.

We deplore the duplicity and insincerity of the Party in power in racial and religious matters. Although they have been in office as a Majority Party for many years, they have not kept nor do they intend to keep their promises.

The Republican Party will not mislead, exploit or attempt to confuse minority groups for political purposes. All American citizens are entitled to full, impartial enforcement of Federal laws relating to their civil rights.

We believe that it is the primary responsibility of each State to order and control its own domestic institutions, and this power, reserved to the states, is essential to the maintenance of our Federal Republic. However, we believe that the Federal Government should take supplemental action within its constitutional jurisdiction to oppose discrimination against race, religion or national origin.

We will prove our good faith by:

Appointing qualified persons, without distinction of race, religion or national origin, to responsible positions in the Government.

Federal action toward the elimination of lynching.

Federal action toward the elimination of poll taxes as a prerequisite to voting.

Appropriate action to end segregation in the District of Columbia.

Enacting Federal legislation to further just and equitable treatment in the area of discriminatory employment practices. Federal action should not duplicate state efforts to end such practices; should not set up another huge bureaucracy.

CENSORSHIP

We pledge not to infringe by censorship or gag-order the right of a free people to know what their Government is doing.

EQUAL RIGHTS

We recommend to Congress the submission of a Constitutional Amendment providing equal rights for men and women.

We favor legislation assuring equal pay for equal work regardless of sex.

STATEHOOD

We favor immediate statehood for Hawaii.

We favor statehood for Alaska under an equitable enabling act.

We favor eventual statehood for Puerto Rico.

DISTRICT OF COLUMBIA

We favor self-government and national suffrage for the residents of the Nation's Capital.

INDIAN AFFAIRS

All Indians are citizens of the United States and no longer should be denied full enjoyment of their rights of citizenship.

We shall eliminate the existing shameful waste by the Bureau of Indian Affairs which has obstructed the accomplishment of our national responsibility for improving the condition of our Indian friends. We pledge to undertake programs to provide the Indians with equal opportunities for education, health protection and economic development.

The next Republican Administration will welcome the advice and counsel of Indian leaders in selecting the Indian Commissioner.

CIVIL SERVICE

We condemn the flagrant violations of the Civil Service merit system by the Party in power.

We favor a personnel program for the Federal career service comparable to the best practices of progressive private employers. Federal employees shall be selected under a strengthened and extended merit system. Civil servants of ability and integrity shall receive proper recognition, with merit the sole test for promotion.

Delivery of Mail

We pledge a more efficient and frequent mail delivery service.

Government Reorganization

We pledge a thorough reorganization of the Federal Government in accordance with the principles set forth in the report of the Hoover Commission which was established by the Republican 80th Congress.

We denounce the duplicity in submitting to Congress for approval, reorganization plans which were represented as being in accordance with the principles of the Hoover Commission recommendations, but which in fact were actually intended to further partisan political purposes of the Administration in power.

Corruption

The present Administration's sordid record of corruption has shocked and sickened the American people. Its leaders have forfeited any right to public faith by the way they transact the Federal Government's business.

Fraud, bribery, graft, favoritism and influence-peddling have come to light. Immorality and unethical behavior have been found to exist among some who were entrusted with high policy-making positions, and there have been disclosures of close alliances between the present Government and underworld characters.

Republicans exposed cases of questionable and criminal conduct and relentlessly pressed for full investigations into the cancer-like spread of corruption in the Administration. These investigations uncovered a double standard in Federal tax law enforcement—lenient treatment to political favorites including even some gangsters and crooks, but harassment and threats of prosecution for many honest taxpayers over minor discrepancies.

Besides tax fixes and scandals in the Internal Revenue Bureau, investigations have disclosed links between high officials and crime, favoritism and influence in the RFC, profiteering in grain, sale of postmasterships, tanker-ship deals in the Maritime Commission, ballot-box stuffing and thievery, and bribes and pay-offs in contract awards by officials in agencies exercising extraordinary powers and disbursing billions of dollars.

Under public pressure, the Administration took reluctant steps to clean house. But it was so eager to cover up and block more revelations that its clean-up drive launched with much fanfare ended in a farce.

The Republican Party pledges to put an end to corruption, to oust the crooks and grafters, to administer tax laws fairly and impartially, and to restore honest government to the people.

Republican 80th Congress

The Republican Party does not rest its case upon promises alone. We have a record of performance which was grossly defamed by the Party in power. The Republican 80th Congress launched the program to stop Communism; unified the armed services; authorized a 70-group Air Force which the President blocked; enacted a national service law; balanced the budget; accumulated an eight-billion-dollar surplus; reduced taxes, with 70 per cent of the tax savings to those with incomes under $5,000; freed 7,400,000 wage earners in the lower brackets from having to pay any further income tax at all, allowed married couples to divide their incomes for tax purposes, and granted an additional $600 exemption to those over 65 years of age and to the blind; enacted the Taft-Hartley law for equitable labor-management relations; passed the first long-range agriculture program; increased social security benefits; and carried out every single pledge they made to the voters in the 1946 election.

Conclusion

Upon this statement of truths and this pledge of performance, the Republican Party stands confident that it expresses the hopes of the citizens of America and certain that it points out with integrity a road upon which free men may march into a new day—a new and better day—in which shall be fulfilled the decent aspirations of our people for peace, for solvency and for the fulfillment of our best welfare, under the guidance of Divine Providence.

Socialist Party—1952 Platform

PREAMBLE

Socialism has been catapulted into a major political issue in the United States today by the action of its enemies. The press, the radio, the halls of Congress, are filled with the hate and hysteria of the diehards of American capitalism who fear that they may no longer be able to dictate the economic life of the country for private profit. All the propaganda that their great fortunes can buy is unleashed in a vicious anti-socialist campaign.

What is this Socialism that the American people are asked to fear and to reject? It is any form of enterprise where public service cuts out private profit.

Public housing is under attack by the real estate lobby. Socialists were first to propose it, and they would expand it until there are decent homes for all our people.

Public power is denounced by utility monopolies. It can bring the comfort of the electric age to gladden the life of the farmer, and provide life-giving irrigation to redeem land that we need. Socialists believe that the power resources of America should serve the people, not the monopolies.

Public education, the basis of an informed citizenry and a functioning democracy, is starved out. The people's faith in our schools is constantly undermined by repeated smear attacks on teachers and text-books. Socialists insist that the wealth of the United States is great enough to provide equal educational opportunity for every child.

Public health suffers while private profit dominates medicine. Socialists demand that the people's health be protected from the inordinate greed of the drug and insurance monopolies and of the AMA.

Socialism and Liberty

Socialism, it is claimed, will destroy democracy. Nothing could be further from the truth. Socialism and democracy are one and inseparable. Socialists are in the forefront of the fight for civil liberties: freedom of speech, freedom of religion, freedom of the press, freedom to organize and vote for candidates of one's own choice. Socialism also stands for the economic freedoms of the people: the right to a job; the right to a fair wage; the right of workers to organize and strike; the right to security in old age, sickness or unemployment, and for widows and orphans.

Reaction tears down traditional civil liberties and stoops even to terror in an attack to delay progress towards racial equality. Only the great strength of organized labor has prevented the destruction of the trade union movement. An alarming trend on the domestic scene is one that the present administration has started. The witch-hunts against progressive thought are not the monopoly of the McCarthies. They are equally the responsibility of the "Fair Deal" Administration's loyalty program, and its concern with convincing the American people of its opposition to communism, which has been enlarged lately to include all non-conformist thought.

And reaction at home seeks reaction abroad as its mate. A foreign policy increasingly based on military expediency and American dominance is in the making, a policy that would embrace fascism in the name of anti-fascism.

A democratic offensive is overdue, and only Socialism can give democracy the drive it needs to win.

The industrial society that performed miracles to deepen the destructiveness of war must perform miracles to achieve abundance for all and the peace in which it can be enjoyed.

The American people, who pioneered in political democracy, must complete their democracy by taking control of their economic life.

Socialism will democratize the economic life of the nation by the joint representation of workers, the working management, and the consuming public, in the operation of socialized enterprises; by the guarantee of popular control of enterprises through the maximum decentralization economically feasible and the use of various types of organization, particularly the public corporation and the voluntary cooperative, and by the preservation of the freedom of labor organization and of consumer choice.

The basic industries, public utilities, banking and credit institutions—all the economic facilities needed for the satisfaction of the primary wants of the people—must be socially owned and democratically managed.

The natural resources of the nation—minerals, oil, atomic and electric power—are the property of the people. Their preservation for future generations and their management by the people for social purposes can be achieved democratically only under Socialism.

Planned production for use, and not for profit, in the United States will not only enrich the life of the American people. It alone can make possible the full use of American facilities, without exploitation, to raise the standard of living in underdeveloped areas and ease the economic strains that break out in war. Against the false promise of a machiavellian communism and the bankrupt incapacity of an outworn capitalism, it provides hope for a disillusioned world.

Security with liberty and peace in freedom is the goal of international Socialism, and of American Socialism. The Socialist Party urges all Americans who share this goal to join us in 1952; vote your hopes and not your fears.

Vote Socialist.

Join the Socialist Party and do your part to win this goal.

The World

The road to peace which the world's peoples desperately seek is barred by four tremendous obstacles. The greatest obstacle to enduring peace today is the aggressive imperialism of the Soviet Union, which has absorbed hundreds of millions of people into the totalitarian vise since the end of World War II. The second great obstacle to achieving peace has developed in reaction to the Communist offensive but has now become an obstacle in itself. This is the militarization of the western democracies which has resulted from the devastating arms race and the division of the world into armed camps under such tension that incidents may create war. Worse yet is the taking over of their economies for military objectives and the dictation of their foreign policy by military expediency which prevents taking constructive action for peace.

The third great obstacle to world peace and a basic cause of conflict which must be removed before we can hope to have permanent peace is the unwillingness of the privileged nations to deal fairly with the peoples of the have-not nations. The western democracies must recognize that, although colonialism has been largely overthrown, millions live at a starvation level and are oppressed by reason of color or status. They demand and deserve livelihood and liberty.

A fourth and basic obstacle to peace is capitalism, which by its nature is centered on profit, rather than on human welfare. In its international dealings, capitalism results in exploitation and injustice to the weak in every country. Aggressive totalitarianisms represent a threat to peace which must be dealt with. But Hitlers and Stalins may come and go, and—until we replace it—capitalism will still breed insecurity and resentment, new totalitarianisms and new threats of war. In the long view, the greatest single contribution the American people can make to peace is to replace an economic system dealing with the world on the basis of selfishness and conflict with a cooperative economy which can build a basic structure of economic interdependence and mutuality among ourselves and the people of the world.

The threat that Soviet aggression has hurled against the world is tragic. But just as tragic is the inability of the present government of our nation to understand its nature and to prepare to meet it with any degree of success. If we are to have permanent peace, there are some basic things that must be understood. The most important of these is that capitalism is a root cause of war and that capitalism keeps its creaking economy going through preparation for and participation in war. Therefore, the very existence of capitalism constantly threatens the world with war.

In the quest for peace, the United States under a bi-partisan foreign policy has played an equivocal role. Its war-time demand for unconditional surrender, the appeasement of the Soviet Union at Yalta, Teheran, and Potsdam, and the introduction of atomic warfare laid a foundation for permanent conflict rather than permanent peace. Yet in the early post-war period the United States pioneered generously in the rebuilding of war-devastated countries, planned expansion of aid for building up undeveloped areas, and led in the organization of a United Nations.

On the other hand, at no time did it offer the sanctuary for the dispossessed refugees of war or religious strife or to political exiles that its tradition and resources demanded of it. And recently, the rigid control of entrance into the United States has begun to approach the totalitarian pattern.

At first, the United States amazed the world by offering to subject its uniquely possessed atomic bomb to international control. Increasingly, it has placed its faith in armaments to curb Communist expansion. It is burdening our people with inflation and higher taxes. Throughout the world, in order to contain the Soviet Union, it has too often bolstered reactionary regimes that have denied the aspirations of the common people. In addition, these military efforts have also burdened the already strained economies of the democratic nations of western Europe. These increased efforts have resulted in part in the development of enmity against the United States and thus have played into the hands of Communist propagandists. Our capitalist government has failed to win the support of the peoples of the world and has sought alliances with dictators and reactionary regimes as well as with democratic governments. Both old parties share responsibility for American failure to take leadership for the crusade that might have achieved peace. And the bitterest failure is that, seven years after V-J Day, war continues.

Military influence in the American government has grown rather than declined. Military conscription continues year after year, and the pattern of the military mind grows stronger among the people. A continuing arms economy can only result in bankruptcy for our nation and the western world. In the chaos that follows, either fascism or communism is almost certain to take over. Democratic Socialism is our only hope of preserving freedom, human dignity, and justice. The gathering of people of this persuasion into a single, mighty, and organized force will furnish the strength that can overwhelm totalitarianism throughout the world, prevent a third world war, and bring peace and freedom.

A Socialist government in the United States can and will meet the threat of Soviet expansion with a foreign policy that is in keeping with the facts of political life. In this course lies the only hope that the American people have for peace, genuine prosperity, and democracy. A Socialist policy for peace, although flexible to meet changing situations, will develop from these ideas:

Internationalism

Our interdependent world, with its complex communications and transportation network supporting a vast industrial machine, has no room for isolation or economic nationalism. We are affected by developments in the far corners of the earth, as they are affected by us. The world that trans-portation, communication, and habit have bound together cannot be separated by political differences or national boundaries. Self-preservation lies in the world-wide cooperative commonwealth of free men.

STRENGTHEN THE UNITED NATIONS

There is now only the beginning of an imperfect world organization. The present defects of the United Nations stem from the fact that the United States and the Soviet Union dominate their respective blocs in the U.N. The fact that the United States is currently able to muster the larger bloc should not blind us to the need to democratize the United Nations, as well as strengthen it to deal with aggression, by eliminating the unilateral veto in the Security Council. This should make possible the inclusion of all nations who adhere to the Charter of the United Nations.

Socialists would eliminate points of possible conflict by giving the United Nations power to handle them before trouble starts by . . . initiating a movement for controlled and supervised disarmament, and international control and inspection of all armaments including atomic developments, as the beginning of the end of national militarism, and organizing an international police force so that the U.N. can be truly international in dealing with any disputes that may then arise.

. . . internationalizing and demilitarizing strategic waterways.

. . . ensuring access to food and raw materials to all peoples at prices fair to both producers and consumers. World planning through international agencies such as the Food and Agriculture Organization could be used to allocate materials in short supply on the basis of need, as well as to encourage expanded production where needed. Countries producing or monopolizing strategic materials, such as oil or tungsten, should be encouraged to dispose of their entire surplus, above domestic requirements, through international agencies.

. . . reducing trade barriers gradually, leading to free trade, with programs of retraining for workers in industries that are no longer protected; urging the principle of free travel, so that men as well as goods have equal access to the world.

. . . establishing a Peace Council not dominated

by the five major powers which could use good offices in tension situations (Iran or Indo-China) or act to alleviate war-breeding potentials (population pressures, racism).

. . . encouraging regional federation, which may break down artificial economic barriers and promote ideals broader than national sovereignty.

. . . insisting on international control and formulation of policy on Korea and the Korean peace.

We favor the development of the United Nations into a federal world government with careful provision to respect the rights of all countries, including the right to socialize their economies. We favor a partial world government if certain countries refuse to join the world government.

STRENGTHEN THE SOCIALIST INTERNATIONAL

Organizations of governments alone will not bring peace; and our desire for world federation does not mean that we favor the creation of the leviathan state. The unity of peoples for common goals irrespective of national boundaries can be a powerful force in developing that kinship of feeling which must be the basis of a world society. Democratic Socialism, which aims at liberating all men from every form of economic, spiritual, and political bondage, holds as primary purpose the strengthening of international democracy.

Anti-Militarism

The present arms race must be halted before it produces war by accident or subverts democracy so that war itself becomes a goal. A Socialist government would provide active American leadership to secure universal disarmament under enforceable controls, with recognition of the principle of unlimited international inspection.

Actions speak louder than words to guarantee the will to peace. A Socialist government would lead in proposing immediate outlawry of conscription by all nations, renewing the proposal for international control of atomic weapons, and taking advantage of any national offer for negotiation on disarmament to achieve that goal. It would end conscription in the United States.

The remilitarization of any other country or its participation in military pacts should not be made the condition for economic aid or other treaty arrangements. Pressure for remilitarization of Japan should be halted, and the policy of a united, demilitarized Germany advocated in Europe.

Commitments of the present foreign policy to foreign people make immediate withdrawal of American troops from abroad impossible; but the speediest withdrawal consistent with the security of the people involved should be arranged and announced as national policy.

The growing control of the military over civilian decisions in the United States must be halted. Militarization of education and the threat of permanent military training programs indoctrinate American youth to accept war as the solution to the world's problems. Military demands are wasting irreplaceable natural resources, making impossible adequate aid to less fortunate areas of the world, and threatening our standard of living. The military have overruled the state department in the demand for aid to fascist Spain and are strengthening the alliance with Chiang Kai-shek and forces of reaction the world over.

Solidarity

WORLD DEVELOPMENT

The United States, possessing so much of the industrial resources of the world, must be foremost in aid to underdeveloped areas. But this effort to build up economies, to raise the standard of living, the education and technical skills of the people, to provide the economic basis for democracy, is not a unilateral task. It should be organized through the United Nations, with a pooling of resources by all nations, and the United States contributing its fair share. Thus can the danger of exploitation, either of nation over nation or of private profiteers over underdeveloped areas, be avoided. A peace tax in the form of an income tax upon all peoples, contributed through the United Nations, would widen the basis of responsibility and participation still further.

WORLD BROTHERHOOD

The shame of racial discrimination still disfigures whole countries and oppresses millions. As we insist on the achievement of racial equality in the United States, so we also insist that the United States participate in the world-wide struggle to achieve it; that world opinion and world organization protest situations as vicious as that growing in South Africa, and stop its extension. Nor is race the only point of discrimination. Again after centuries, religious difference has become a major reason for persecution of men in millions.

And political opinion is a crime in vast areas of the world, while political asylum is too often denied. Protection for minority rights is a vital part of the Socialist recognition of the common humanity that unites us irrespective of race, creed, or color.

WORLD FREEDOM

Conscious of the failings of our own democracy, we nevertheless retain the freedom to work for its perfection and to aid democratic forces in less fortunate areas of the world. Our faith in the spirit of man insists to us that, regardless of the rigor of oppression, forces for freedom will arise and will need to be heard and to be helped throughout the world. In their natural alignment with the forces of freedom in opposition to the forces of tyranny, Socialists insist that the alternatives before the world are not simply war or communist domination; the hope of the world lies in escaping the war which would doom all people alike, and pressing the fight for freedom by methods consistent with the goal.

We recognize the enslaved peoples of the Iron Curtain countries as our friends and not our enemies. Our endeavor is: to tear down the curtain, establishing contact by radio and every means at our disposal; to pledge refuge to all those who escape; to demand no extension of slavery; to offer friendship and support to any democratic freedom movement that may develop and seek it.

Totalitarianism, though the worst, is not the only form of tyranny. Relics of colonial empire still oppress millions; to gain national freedom and the chance for individual betterment, they may take help where they find it. Time and time again, the failure of western democracies to practice democracy in Asia and Africa drives nationalist movements into the hands of communism. The victory of Stalinism in much of the world has been possible because Stalinists have been able to subvert the spirit of revolt of colonial and oppressed people where there has been no democratic alternative. Wherever there has been a strong Socialist movement, the Communists have been unable to win unless they were in a position to bring overwhelming force to bear. It is because the Stalinists have falsely identified themselves with the strivings of the people for economic advancement and political independence that they have become strong. A mighty international democratic Socialist movement is our only hope for conquering Stalinism in the political field.

Democratic Socialism rejects every form of imperialism and supports every struggle for freedom. Our one world must be a free world. The world community and the lasting peace we seek must be achieved in freedom, as it will find its fruition in fellowship.

THE NATION

American capitalism never recovered from the great collapse of the thirties when millions went hungry and homeless although the basic wealth of the country was great and unavailable for their use only because of the despotism of the private profit system. There was no recovery in the sense of devotion of the economy to human needs. Superficial prosperity returned with a war economy and the brutal and wanton destructiveness of war.

Twenty years later, the real floor under the American economy is still military expenditures. 85 per cent of 1952 federal expenditures (over 61 billion dollars) are ear-marked for past, present, and future wars. By the end of 1952, 20 per cent of the total national output will be diverted to military and related production—not comparable to the 45 per cent of World War II, but with a cumulative impact on the economy that includes the previous total-war strain. At the pre-Korea spending rate, we had enough copper for only 15 years or enough high-grade iron for 30. Similarly, our other resources drain away. The only thing military expenditure can add to is the profit which private individuals manufacture out of the nation's misfortune. Capitalism has no economic equivalent for war.

Between them, the goal of profit and the acceptance of war are ruining the American economy. One-fourth of presently tillable land is in critical condition and another fourth suffering from erosion. The present annual use of timber is many times the growth. Drought in farmland and water famine in large cities have revealed dramatically a frightening condition of our watershed. The animal-carrying capacity of western grassland has been reduced by one-half (while the cattle lobby moves in on our last reserves of public land) and fishing beds are damaged by pollution.

Conservation of American resources, essential

to the life of the nation, has been neglected. But this is not all.

To the needs of the nation for flood control soil conservation, reforestation, preservation of water resources, we can add the needs of the states for development of power resources, highways and turnpikes, institutional buildings such as hospitals; and to this again, innumerable needs of local areas for improvements that local budgets can no longer afford.

The Socialist Party can and does offer a substitute for war as a motivating factor behind production. It is our internal development program framed to meet the needs of the nation.

Education

The present shortage of classrooms is 200,000. It will reach 500,000 by 1960. They can be provided at an annual expense of $1.35 billion—a little more than 2 per cent of 1952 military expenditures. Additional schools needed will take two billion dollars more. An expanded teacher-training program and adequate salary standards can change the present situation in which we graduate only one-fifth the number of qualified teachers required by our schools. An expanded scholarship program is needed to equalize educational opportunities for young people.

Health

Federal assistance in social security, health, welfare, and education costs us $4.60 per American per year. The support of one man in the armed services costs us $5,600. We can afford a national health program that will

Establish an all-inclusive health insurance plan;

Train more doctors, dentists, nurses, and other needed personnel;

Advance medical research and expand hospital building services;

Increase state maternal, child health, and crippled children's services;

Expand public health services.

Natural Resources

One year's expenditures for the cold war (estimated at $85 billion after 1952) would supply

Nine regional development projects each providing at the end of seven years

. . . irrigated land for 18,000 new family sized farms.

. . . supplemented irrigation for 53,000 farms.

. . . 3.2 million KW of new generating capacity.

An investment of three billion dollars a year for thirty years would save our land and our water and would return wealth endlessly to the people.

The Socialist Party would make this investment in America. Our resources are the basis of our strength and the first line of any defense.

Housing

The real estate lobby, which leads the national campaign against aid to people in desperate need of homes which private enterprise has failed to supply, itself accepts subsidy and makes tremendous profit out of the present FHA legislation. Recent votes in Congress to limit the low-rent public housing program to 45,000 units a year, against a national housing need for 500,000 (and an administration plan for 75,000) to prevent further deterioration of the already bad housing situation, expose the unfitness of Congressmen of both major parties.

Private industry has never been able to house the American people adequately. Public and cooperative enterprise can do so. A national budget of two billion dollars a year is not excessive. (The budget was $2.2 billion for aircraft alone in 1951, and the plan for 1952 is $6.8 billion.)

The Socialist Party would create a Home Loan Bank to finance the purchase of homes at low interest rates; a Public Supply Corporation to set up factory units needed to produce materials and develop large-scale housing; integration of national and local building plans including revision of municipal building codes; and development of a program of collective bargaining with the building and construction unions, providing a guaranteed annual wage, and the development of apprentice-training programs. For the duration of the housing emergency, rent control must be retained or restored.

Our Standard of Living

INFLATION AND DEFLATION

The standard of living of the American people is constantly threatened either by inflationary or deflationary tendencies in the economy. Either the struggle is to push up wages to the level of prices, or to maintain the level of employment at wages at or above the level of prices.

The sources of economic instability are no longer among the great mysteries of life, however. The principal lesson of the Employment Act of 1946 is that it is possible to know what is going on in the economy. The failure of this and other enactments of a similar nature is that they either make no provision or inadequate provision for meeting the problems whose existence is revealed or forecast by the agencies set up under their provisions.

The effect of the present inflation on living standards should be alleviated by price controls on essential items, but this is treating a symptom, not a disease. Taxation policy and the expansion of production can do better.

TAXATION

In the past six years, the idea of taxation according to ability to pay has been reversed in practice. The tax burden has been shifted increasingly from the rich to the poor as more and more taxes have been needed to finance the government and the armaments program. Inflation has raised costs and thus increased the load still further, unnecessarily. Low- and fixed-income groups have lost most. Merchants and speculators have profited.

The nearer we come to a pay-as-you-go tax policy, the less the ultimate cost to the people. Socialists say: pay as you go.

The more loop-holes for privileged groups can be removed, the more equally the tax burden will be shared. Socialists would abolish preferential treatment for capital gains, state and municipal bonds, percentage depletion allowances on oil and natural gas wells and other mining.

Excise taxes have two purposes. They can both raise revenue, and discourage non-essential and luxury spending. They can be increased without hurting low-income groups. We vigorously oppose sales taxes which, under the guise of equality, hit the low-income groups the hardest.

Individual-income taxation, based on ability to pay, is the fairest way to raise taxes and one of the most important. A reactionary campaign to limit taxation of high incomes (the millionaire's amendment) must be exposed and defeated.

SOCIAL SECURITY

Increases to begin to catch up with inflation are needed in social security benefits for the old and unfortunate who need this aid.

Coverage should be expanded to end discrimination against any group of workers.

The age of eligibility for old-age pensions should be reduced to 60.

Family allowances, so that the young are protected as well as the old, must be added. Four and a half million children in the United States live in families with total incomes of less than $20.00 a week.

NATIONAL INCOME

The top one-fifth of the population receive 47 per cent of the national income. Socialization would restore most of that wealth to the nation.

The bottom one-fifth of the people receive only 3 per cent of the national income. Their standard of living must be raised in many ways—through organization in trade unions; through cooperatives; through public social services. A small beginning on the part of government would be to raise the minimum wage from 75¢ to $1, and to call for progressive increases as the productivity level of the nation rises.

AGRICULTURE

The Socialist Party would halt the growing trend to absentee ownership of farms and the increase of farm tenancy. Occupancy and use should give the only rightful title to farmland. The security of family farms should be strengthened through cooperative credit purchasing and marketing, aided by government financing. Reactionary attempts to destroy rural electrification and to tax cooperatives out of existence must be defeated. Proper distribution and marketing of agricultural products does not require gambling. The present Board of Trade pricing of farm produce, with its poker-game practices of buying on futures, must be ended.

Where modern techniques and specialization require large-scale farm enterprises, we call for social ownership and cooperative operation to replace the corporation farm which threatens both the security and freedom of farm workers.

Security for all the people, and a rising standard of living, can be guaranteed by the vast resources and productive facilities of this nation. A Socialist administration will make this its first concern.

Defense of Democracy

Socialists strive to build a new society in freedom and by democratic means. We would expand the political democracy which the United States possesses to include industrial democracy and full racial equality. But the first urgent task today is to halt the destruction of political democracy which the last four years have witnessed. In the guise of defense against communist totalitarianism, the foundations of an American totalitarianism are rising.

THE RIGHT TO WORK

The Socialist Party recognizes the necessity of screening where employment of persons belonging to totalitarian organizations might endanger the security of our nation. But because civil liberties do not include the right of any person to any job without proper qualifications for fitness which may include loyalty provisions, care must be taken not to deprive individuals of the right to work at non-sensitive positions for which training and experience fit them.

DEMOCRATIC PROCEDURES

The right to hear and answer charges which may affect the livelihood, liberty, or citizenship of the individual must be protected. We ask elimination of the Committee on Un-American Activities which has abused the Congressional right of investigation. We ask the right to hear and answer charges in all security screening cases, and the inclusion of labor representation on hearing boards. We ask the elimination of loyalty oaths that totalitarians would not hesitate to swear falsely, but that discriminate against honest citizens in an increasing number of occupations. We ask recognition of the right of the individual to change his political opinions, and protest retroactive retribution for commitments made in previous years.

THE FREE BALLOT

Discrimination against minority parties through excessive requirements for gaining ballot status must be changed. The poll tax which deprives citizens of the right to vote because of income must be repealed. The growing number of states that have added to technical requirements a legal discrimination against the Communist Party—often worded with dangerous vagueness—are only driving that Party underground into illegal channels, making it more dangerous than if its ideas were exposed to the light.

FREEDOM OF OPINION

Conviction of Communist leadership under the Smith Act, which the Socialist Party has opposed from its inception, followed by the rounding up of successive layers of Communist Party leadership, is a denial of political freedom more worthy of a totalitarian nation than of a democracy. Where illegal acts have taken place—such as spying—legislation on the books, applying equally to Communist and non-Communist alike, has been successfully used in prosecution. Where overt acts take place, democracy has the ability and the duty to defend itself against the totalitarian foe from within. But persecution based on political belief and expression of political opinion must be stopped.

FREEDOM OF EDUCATION

Unwarranted censorship and pressure on teachers' opinions and of textbooks threatens free inquiry and access to full information in our schools and universities. This attacks the very basis of democratic education and scientific progress, as the exchange of ideas is impeded. Part of this pressure stems from a justifiable concern to protect children against indoctrination by Communists and fascists. Much of it comes from reactionaries such as the National Council on American Education who would turn back the clock to the economic and social practices of the last century. In some communities the pressure of organized religion imposes an unwarranted censorship. These combined efforts must be resisted on every level. Teaching must be made an attractive, not a persecuted, profession. Students must learn to discriminate among ideas through free experience with them. Adequate funds must be made available to provide equal educational opportunities for all children.

FREEDOM FOR LABOR

The Socialist Party seeks repeal of Taft-Hartley and similar state laws which undermine the right to strike, the right to organize, the right to sign contracts guaranteeing union security and furthering the economic interests of organized workers. But as we insist on freedom of action for unions on behalf of their members, so we fight for internal democracy within the union, regular and free election of officers, protection of minority rights, and racial equality.

CONSCIENTIOUS OBJECTION

We urge full amnesty and restoration of civil rights for war objectors, thousands of whom have lost voting and other citizenship rights. We ask complete exemption for absolutist objectors to war and conscription. We protest the narrowness of the present Selective Service Act which excludes many sincere conscientious objectors. We oppose re-institution of the CPS system of forced labor without pay. Any alternative service should be recompensed by accepted wage standards for the occupation and area.

RACIAL EQUALITY

Complete political, economic, and social equality, regardless of race, religion, or national origin, must be established. Equality can be achieved only after the ending of segregation practices.

Segregation must be abolished in all public or public-supported institutions, in housing, in the armed services. We shall work on a community level for abolition of segregation which cannot be handled by legislation.

Fair Employment Practices legislation must be passed nationally, and adopted on a state-wide basis in states that do not yet have it.

Anti-lynching legislation must be enacted. The Civil Rights Section of the Justice Department must move to safeguard the lives of citizens in states where "legal lynching" is protected by the state machinery.

Discriminating barriers against immigration on grounds of race, color, national origin, or political opinion, must be removed.

The right to vote must be guaranteed to all citizens. The 14th Amendment, depriving states of representation in Congress in proportion to the number of citizens deprived of the right to vote by virtue of race, color, or previous condition of servitude, should be enforced.

FULL CITIZENSHIP

The District of Columbia should be given self-government, and its citizens full citizenship rights. Statehood should be granted to Alaska and Hawaii, and to Puerto Rico if the people so desire.

THE COMMUNITY

Democratic Socialism aims at extending individual freedom on the basis of economic and social security and an increasing prosperity. While the guiding principle of capitalism is private profit, and that of totalitarianism is complete subservience of the individual to the dictatorship, the purpose of Socialism is the democratic satisfaction of human needs to liberate the full creativity of the human personality.

Socialism is thus a community as well as a world endeavor. It stresses voluntary and cooperative action in the achievement of its goal. The independent organizations of the people—unions, cooperatives, cultural and social groupings—will retain full freedom under Socialism and will guarantee the maintenance of a free society. Where social objectives are too broad for realization by individuals or private organizations, they must be undertaken by the people through government.

The forms of public ownership are not an end in themselves. Government ownership, cooperative ownership, public-authority ownership, will exist. Control is more important than ownership. It must include workers. It must include working management. It must include public or consumer representation. Under democratic control, production can be for purposes decided by the people. Under decentralized control—which Socialism will use wherever possible—bureaucracy can be limited and watched. With free consumer choice, an important economic power remains in the hands of the people.

The choice between the democratic and the authoritarian state is clarified at the local level. Civil liberties exist where men are free in their own communities. Racial justice is achieved where people live together in equality. Economic security is made real when the fear of age, of illness, of hunger, is removed from the family circle. Peace will come as the boundaries of the democratic community are extended until abundance and freedom are the property of all men.

Your vote for Socialism in this election may influence the direction of the United States. Your voice in the community in organization for a new society will bring closer the day when American policy is shaped by the Socialist objective: Humanity First.

JOIN THE SOCIALIST PARTY!
VOTE SOCIALIST IN 1952!

Socialist Labor Party—1952 Platform

The Socialist Labor Party of the United States of America, in National Convention assembled on this 4th day of May, 1952, reaffirms its previous platform pronouncements and declares:

The crisis that shakes the world today is a revolutionary crisis. It is one of those crucial turning points of history when an outmoded system is in a state of impending collapse, and a new order is waiting to be born.

The capitalist system rose on the ruins of feudalism—in this country on the transplanted feudal power of the British Crown. It had a mission to perform, the mission of establishing mass production and of organizing the workers in industry in keeping with that purpose. Its mission has been fulfilled: Abundance is now possible for all without arduous toil. But in fulfilling its historic mission the capitalist class has rendered itself useless—nay worse, it has become an encumbrance on the productive process, an incubus on society as a whole, and its continued presence as a useless class has become a menace to our very civilization.

Accordingly, the downfall of the capitalist system is certain. It is foredoomed by contradictions resulting from the division of society into classes and the exploitation of wage labor. Its economy is kept going today by rearmament and the waging of war. Without this huge, war-inciting multi-billion-dollar war-preparations program, capitalism would quickly sink in a quagmire of economic depression.

This is a permanent condition. The plutocratic rulers are committed to a permanent arms economy. In order to stave off the threatened economic breakdown, they are compelled to build and amass ever more military weapons and supplies, thereby accelerating the forces, *inherent in capitalist rivalry for world trade,* that are leading fatedly to a third world war.

Thus, decadent capitalism has brought society to the brink of catastrophe and ruin. The question now is: *Shall this doomed system be allowed to drag humanity down into the abyss? Or will the working class, in whose hands the future lies, wake up in time, organize its immense latent power, and put society on the road to safety and freedom?*

The Socialist Labor Party declares that such is the crucial nature of the crisis that grips our civilization.

The plutocratic capitalists are confused, intellectually bankrupt and divided among themselves. Although they still pay lip-service to the American tradition of civilian government, in practice they have renounced this tradition and have given professional military men a dominant role in formulating foreign and domestic policy.

The Korean war, a senseless war to all but the capitalists and Russian imperialist interests that profit from it, is a tragic consequence of ruling-class confusion and the military approach in international relations.

The frequent demands by high military leaders, and even by Cabinet members, that the United States abandon its moral scruples against "striking the first (sneak attack) blow," and that the country become the aggressor in a "preventive war" with Russia, are frightening evidence of the panic that is overtaking the American ruling class.

The Socialist Labor Party asserts that the ferocious conflict that divides the world and threatens to hurl mankind into the fiery furnace of global war is an imperialist conflict. It is basically a struggle between the plutocratic masters of the United States and the bureaucratic masters of Soviet Russia for control of the world's economic resources. Both these ruling groups must share the guilt for the appalling danger of extinction today threatening the human race.

Let no one underestimate the danger. A third world war would be an atomic war, a war of universal desolation. The Socialist Labor Party holds that peace today hangs only by a thread of fear. For the moment both imperialist rivals are deterred by the atomic bomb—the knowledge that if either attacks the other, retaliation will be swift and terrible.

In this revolutionary crisis the class struggle is becoming more intense.

The plutocratic capitalists sit uneasily on their mountains of stolen wealth. To secure their class privileges and to weaken the workers' resistance to increased exploitation, they have enacted the labor-shackling Taft-Hartley Law and revived the medieval weapon of the court injunction.

It is an incontestable fact that the workers are steadily falling behind in the race with living costs, which means, in effect, that their real wages, hence their standards of living, are being steadily reduced. By means of a wage freeze, restrictions on the right to strike and the regimentation of the workers that is accomplished through the faker-controlled, job-trust unions, the American worker is being reduced to the status of an unresisting industrial serf. Thus a new form of slavery is evolving, more in keeping with the despotic needs of the present huge concentrations of corporate capital.

By means of falsehoods and smears, whipped-up hysteria, witch-hunts and loyalty oaths, the capitalist plutocrats are attacking the very heart of American political democracy. They are imposing a "black silence of fear" on millions of once proudly independent and fearlessly outspoken Americans.

The Socialist Labor Party declares that the real target of this un-American attack is not the Communists, but the fundamental rights and civil liberties of the American people. The Communists are merely a convenient and vulnerable target. It has been said, not without logic, that if there were no Communist party in America, the capitalist reaction would organize one.

The assault on liberty and the attempted Prussianization of the country via permanent compulsory military training are, we assert, desperate efforts to prolong an outmoded and foredoomed social system.

The Socialist Labor Party appeals to you to accept the logic of these facts:

WAR, FASCISM, EXPLOITATION, AND POVERTY AMIDST PLENTY ARE THE EVIL BROOD OF CAPITALISM. No person who reaches this conclusion can, without consciously aligning himself with the forces of reaction, support candidates and parties that have as their aim the reform or preservation of capitalism. In this category, besides the Republicans and Democrats, we include all other parties, whatever their designation. For one and all they follow principles of capitalism or of State despotism. One and all they preach reforms and promise improvement of conditions that are past improving. To propose reform when a fundamental social change is called for is to help prolong the capitalist cause of war, fascism and working-class exploitation. "To reform is to preserve."

The Socialist Labor Party, therefore, calls upon the American workers of brain and brawn, and all other enlightened citizens, to repudiate the parties of capitalism and to support its program for a peaceful and orderly Socialist reconstruction of society.

The Socialist Labor Party program, in line with social evolution, demands the abolition of the political State with all its organs of class coercion. Political government (based on geographic constituencies), which was suited to an age of agriculture and primitive production, has been rendered obsolete by the growth of modern industry. The goal of the Socialist Labor Party is a democratic Socialist industrial government—a society based on collective ownership of the land and all the instruments of wealth production, with the management of industry completely in the hands of the workers through socially integrated Socialist Industrial Union Councils.

To bring to birth this society of peace, abundance and freedom, the Socialist Labor Party appeals to the working class of America, and all other enlightened and social-minded citizens, to support its principles at the polls by voting for Socialist Labor Party candidates. And we call upon the workers to repudiate the present unions, which accept capitalism as a finality and are faker-controlled, and to build a new union based squarely on their working class interests and with Socialism as its goal. Build the integral Socialist Industrial Union, as the only union capable of enforcing the Socialist ballot and of assuming the administration of social production.

This program repudiates the kind of bureaucratic despotism masquerading as "Marxist" in Soviet Russia, and the reformist outfits, such as the British Labor party, falsely claiming to be "Socialist."

What Abraham Lincoln said ninety years ago, in the midst of another revolutionary crisis, applies with even greater force today. He said: "The dogmas of the quiet past are inadequate for the stormy present. . . . As our case is new, so must we think anew and act anew. We must disenthrall ourselves, and then we shall save our country."

Unite with us to save society from catastrophe —and to set an example in free, industrial self-government for all mankind! Unite with us to establish the Socialist Republic of Peace, Plenty and International Brotherhood!

Socialist Workers Party—1952 Election Platform

We are told every day that Americans live in a special "paradise-on-earth," the richest, the most peaceful, the most stable country in the world.

But the truth is we face disaster.

We stand on the brink of the most destructive of all wars. Half the peoples of the world will be ranged against us. It is doubtful that we can win such a war. But whether our generals win or lose, we, the American people, will be the losers. Millions of our sons, brothers and husbands will lose their lives on foreign battle fronts in the remotest corners of the world. Our cities will be pounded by bombs, turned into rubble as were Coventry and London, Berlin and Hamburg, Hiroshima and Nagasaki in the last war.

The military machine will devour our great national wealth and resources. Our standard of living will be driven down to the European level. Our cherished rights and liberties will be trampled underfoot by a military dictatorship. Labor will be regimented and dissenters locked up in concentration camps.

This is the tomorrow our rulers are planning for us and our children. And it is later than most of us think. In the midst of our present seeming well-being such a prospect looks like sheer madness. But it is not the common people who have lost their reason, it is not they who are plotting national suicide. It is the capitalist system under which we live, the giant banks and monopolies which dominate it and the politicians of the two major parties who serve their interest. These are the real betrayers of our country. They are the enemy within the gates.

Nothing is so frightening to them as the word "peace." There is cold calculation behind their fears.

The present prosperity is an unhealthy one. Its chief beneficiaries have been the kings of finance and industry. They have made fabulous profits running into astronomical sums.

The mass of working people have received only the crumbs of this prosperity. Every slight improvement has been undermined by higher taxes and rising prices.

Meanwhile our industrial plant has been enlarged and speeded up. We produce twice as much as we did 15 years ago. The people earn too little to consume this vast output. Each year labor gets a smaller share of the national wealth. While productivity of labor rises and profits skyrocket, wages are held back by government controls, inflation and the tax bite.

This unequal distribution of wealth has resulted in accumulation of billions upon billions of dollars by the rich, who cannot invest them at a high enough rate of profit. And there are too few dollars in the hands of the working people to purchase the goods and services of the nation's industries. These conditions caused the 10-year depression that began in 1929.

The Second World War pulled us out of that depression. Now preparations for World War III are keeping us out of a new depression. Big Business likes this war profiteering. It prefers to have the nation's wealth invested in the means of destruction instead of in a system of social insurance to provide medical care and security for everyone. It finds it more profitable to build the engines of death—atom bombs, rockets and jet planes—than to build low-cost homes within the reach of millions of slum-dwellers. It has no competitors in this business of armaments; it extorts the prices it wants from the government, which gives it free plants and tax exemptions running into billions of dollars.

To keep this boom going requires war "scares" and wars, small ones as in Korea, or a bigger war later against China, the Soviet Union and the countries of Eastern Europe. That is the reason why it has been so difficult to arrange even a truce in Korea; that is why the State Department is pushing through the rearmament of Western Germany and Japan under the old Nazi officers and war-lords, against the resistance of most of the peoples of Europe and Asia.

A war machine has a logic of its own; once set in motion it is hard to stop. In the end it must touch off the powder kegs of World War III.

There is one condition on which our monopoly-banker rulers will consider peace. It is that the people of the world permit them to establish a "dollar" empire where French, British and Dutch imperialism ruled before.

But peace is impossible on that condition. The world of imperialism is finished.

The millions of brown, yellow and black-skinned people—who constitute the majority of the human race—have thrown off the yoke of centuries of exploitation by the masters from the Old World; they will not willingly accept the new would-be master from Wall Street.

The peoples of the Soviet Union and Eastern Europe have eliminated capitalist rule and have begun the difficult climb to a planned socialist system. Despite the oppression of their dictatorial rulers, they will not willingly permit a return of the speculators, landlords and profiteers.

If they have not rid themselves of the Kremlin over-lords and the Stalinist bureaucrats, it is because they fear the threat of economic strangulation and military intervention from our financial-military oligarchy. They have in effect been told by the State Department that it plans to supplant the Stalinist dictatorship with dictatorships of the Old Regime. It plans to add foreign subjugation and economic exploitation to political tyranny. Its hue and cry against "Stalinism" is only a camouflage for the return of private profit and corporation property in areas where it has been eliminated.

We socialists are the only genuine opponents of Stalinist rule. We have fought it from the beginning as a treacherous leadership within the camp of the workers—as an aid not a foe of capitalist reaction. But we know that only the elimination of world capitalism—only a system of production for use, of economic equality between nations—will spell the doom for Stalinist dictatorship.

It is not "communism" which threatens America. It is Wall Street and the Pentagon, in their hunger for profits, investments and empire, which threatens one-third of the peoples of the world. Our so-called Atlantic "community" is a fraud. Our "allies" are a few plutocrats bought with dollars. But the people of England and the continent who are hungrier and poorer than ever, have come to hate the name of America. They don't want Washington's anti-communist crusade. They won't fight Wall Street's war. They don't believe we are fighting for "democracy" against dictatorship and totalitarianism. And they are right. They know that the only real friends of the State Department are the capitalist despots: Syngman Rhee, Chiang Kai-shek, the Greek King, the Nazi generals and the Japanese militarists.

Are we threatened by military assault from the so-called "Soviet Empire"?

The Russian army is not within 200 miles of the American border. But an American force of half a million men is within 200 miles of the Manchurian and Siberian borders.

The Russians and Chinese do not have troops and air bases in 55 foreign countries scattered around the globe. But the United States does.

The Russians and Chinese are not encircling America; but the United States, heading the greatest military alliance in history, is forging an iron ring around the borders of the Soviet Union.

It is not "communism" from afar, but reaction directed from Washington that threatens the precious liberties of the American people at home.

The Constitution and the Bill of Rights are being supplanted with a "dangerous thoughts" code.

Trial and imprisonment on accusation of advocating the 100-year old ideas of Marxism is now an everyday occurrence.

Charges of guilt by association, contrary to Anglo-Saxon law, is a customary procedure in Congress and in State Legislatures.

A sinister political police, called the FBI, conducts vast operations of prying, snooping into personal lives, making informers out of honest people, intimidating, purging workers from government jobs and even private employment.

Teachers are forbidden the right to political association outside the two major parties. Students are taught the ideological goose-step instead of being encouraged to inquire into new ideas.

The McCarran immigration law bolts the doors on racial and political grounds, against those who would come to our shores. We are not allowed to travel abroad without first being "screened" for our political views.

The Bi-Partisan Gang

The same gang that dreams of invading New China and restoring capitalism to the USSR put over the Taft-Hartley slave labor act at home, and is planning new curbs for the unions.

The same gang that has burned and bombed Korea to a wasteland is responsible for the disfranchisement and segregation of the Negro people, and the mob-and-bomb law against their most courageous leaders.

Open shop, race terror and fascism at home are the natural inclinations of the would-be masters of

China, Russia and the world. The enemy of the peoples of the world is also our enemy—and that enemy is at home.

Who are the war-makers and the witch hunters? The Democrats and Republicans are both for war. It will make little difference whether Eisenhower or Stevenson is elected; both are for the war program of Big Business.

Republicans and Democrats are also united on the witch hunt. The Democratic administration under Truman is the real inspirer of Republican witch-hunter McCarthy. Truman initiated and gave official sanction to the government "loyalty" purge, restricting and violating the democratic rights of millions.

The Democrats decreed "loyalty" oaths, and the "subversive" lists. The Republicans applauded. The Democrats object to McCarthy's character assassination only when it affects the administration itself. The truth is the Democrats have put into effect most of McCarthy's vigilante proposals.

Both old parties have aided the growing military domination of government. The Pentagon is virtually a state within a state. The military brass are in league with Big Business; together they are wasting our national resources, devouring our wealth, plundering the public treasury and plotting war on a world scale.

The Democrats brought this Brass Hat–Big Business gang into positions of power. A Republican victory would put a general in the White House and perpetuate and extend their control.

One obstacle stands on this road that leads to military dictatorship, war and catastrophe: The working people! They are the majority in the country. Through their powerful union organizations they possess tremendous strength. They don't want imperialist war or foreign conquest.

They don't want to dictate to other countries. They are not interested in the profits of the billionaire bankers and corporations, or in the glories of generals.

They want to live at peace with the peoples of the world.

They want to see the great wealth of our country and the products of its industry distributed in such a manner as to guarantee a decent standard of living to those who work, without depression or war. Only the subservience of the official union leadership, who back the war policy of the State Department, keeps the American working people politically powerless.

WE NEED A LABOR PARTY

This force of the American working people has yet to be organized in its own political party—the party of labor and the Negro people. Such a labor party could stay the hand of the war-makers; it could break the power of the race-haters; it could remove the threat of depression amid plenty; it could knit together bonds of solidarity with the peoples of the world fighting for national liberation and a better life, in keeping with our own traditions of the Revolution for Independence and the war against slavery.

The Socialist Workers Party fights for the creation of a Labor Party. It is confident it will come into being and change the whole course of American life and history.

The working people have a voice and a program in the 1952 elections—the Socialist Workers Party and its banner bearers: Farrell Dobbs for President and Myra Tanner Weiss for Vice President.

The great issue before the human race today is capitalism or socialism. Shall America join the march of history, or will it go down in ruins and poverty in a disastrous war to save the outlived dying system of capitalism? That is the burning question of our times.

The Socialist Workers Party takes its stand on the side of progress, on the side of the peoples who have taken the first step in the direction of a new society. The peoples of this new world hate their present despotic Stalinist rulers, but they hate capitalism more. The American people can aid them against oppressive Stalinist political rule and save themselves from catastrophic war only by joining the world march to socialism.

ONLY ROAD TO PEACE

The SWP urges the American people to reorganize the wealth of our country on a socialist basis, to rid ourselves of minority government of the parasites and plutocrats and to establish genuine democracy—the rule of the workers and poor farmers. That is the only road to lasting peace.

The Progressive Party fears to face this decisive issue. It cultivates the vain illusion that capitalism can be reformed into a system of peace instead of war, that the irreconcilable differences between socialism and capitalism can be compromised out of existence. Such a program cannot effectively organize the struggle against the impending counter-revolutionary war. It can only demoralize the ranks of the anti-war fighters and in the end lead to new defeats and to the victory of reaction.

The Socialist Workers Party warns the American people of the terrible future the Wall Street–Brass Hat rulers are preparing for them. We urge resistance against the threatening catastrophe, to save our vanishing democratic rights. We enter this campaign to blaze the trail for a real government of the people, a government of the majority —a Workers and Farmers Government.

The Democratic and Republican parties are war parties of the rich; the Socialist Workers Party is the party of labor, of equality for all races, of peace and a prosperous life for all under the rational human system of socialism.

Your choice is clear. Resist the imperialist war! Resist the witch hunt!

Vote the SWP ticket! Vote for Dobbs and Weiss!

1. FOREIGN POLICY

The Socialist Workers Party proposes a foreign policy of peace, friendship and assistance to the peoples of the world. Instead of military bases, we advocate the building of factories, homes, schools, dams, parks and hospitals. We propose sending men abroad with tools, knowledge and skill instead of men with guns; we propose genuine aid to the people of less favored nations without making them satellites of our Big Business oligarchy. Above all we stand for the right of all peoples to establish governments of their own choice. We propose to stop the war drive and direct our foreign policy toward building a socialist world of peace and plenty.

Withdraw all U. S. troops from foreign soil. Get out of Korea. Recognize the new Chinese government.

Let the American people vote on war or peace. Give the vote to 18-year-olds. Old enough to fight —old enough to vote.

2. DEMOCRATIC RIGHTS

The bi-partisan war bloc wants to muzzle any-one who opposes the war drive. Roosevelt started the witch hunt with the Minneapolis prosecution against the 18 leaders of the Socialist Workers Party and Teamsters Local 544. Truman continued it with the purge of government workers, prosecutions against the Communist Party under the Smith Act, and loyalty oaths and "subversive" lists. The states picked up this campaign and extended it on a local basis. The Republican party, supporting all these measures, criticizes Truman for not going far enough. Any ideas which do not conform to the official policy of Washington are in effect being outlawed.

Stop the prosecution of political minorities for mere expression of opinion. Repeal the Smith Act. Amnesty for all victims of Smith Act prosecutions.

Rescind the "loyalty" program and the "subversive" list.

Repeal the McCarran "Concentration Camp" Law. Repeal the McCarran-Walters "Race-Hate" Immigration Law. Preserve the Bill of Rights for all.

3. EQUAL RIGHTS FOR ALL

The Negro people and other minority groups were promised an effective FEPC law by Truman in 1948. This promise has been betrayed. Intimidation of minorities has assumed new and even more terrible forms. Negro families are bombed in their homes. Leaders of the Negro people, like Harry T. Moore and his wife, are murdered. Police brutality against Negroes, Mexicans and Puerto Ricans has taken scores of victims. The federal government has done nothing to stop this. Those who defend minority rights are smeared and terrorized by the witch hunters.

Full social, political and economic equality for the Negro people. Smash the Jim Crow system. Wipe out the poll tax. Enact an FEPC Law with teeth. Abolish restrictive covenants in housing. Stop segregation wherever it exists. Enact a Federal Anti-Lynch Law.

Unite workers of all races for the common struggle against their exploiters.

4. WOMEN'S RIGHTS

The war economy is effecting a revolution in the character of the American family. The improvement in living standards of sections of the working class has occurred only through its greater exploitation. Inflation and taxes have increasingly necessitated the employment of two or more members of the family.

The startling fact that 20 million women are wage earners, constituting 20% of the employed population, reveals the extent of this trend. Of these working women, almost one-fourth are mothers with children under 18 years of age.

The especially oppressed position of women is graphically illustrated by this double exploitation, with the women responsible for the family at home and at the same time working to support the family.

The Socialist Workers Party champions the struggle of women for an end to discrimination of the job. We demand:

Equal pay for equal work. Adequate Federal nursery care and Federally supported summer camps for children of working mothers.

5. Organized Labor

The two party-coalition against labor has already dealt heavy blows to unionism. The Taft-Hartley law has hamstrung the campaign to organize the unorganized. Truman has broken more strikes than any other president. The Wage Stabilization Board machinery has effectively stalled union demands in hearings dominated by Big Business. The witch-hunt has victimized union militants.

The Socialist Workers Party stands for the repeal of all laws both federal and state, restricting labor's rights. We are for the abolition of injunctions and all forms of compulsory arbitration. We are for laws guaranteeing labor's right to organize and strike without government interference.

Repeal the Taft-Hartley Law. Repeal all state anti-labor laws.

6. Inflation

Inflation is one of the major enemies of the workers' standard of living. Chief cause of this disguised wage cutting is the huge war budget, and government-sponsored profiteering. Price increases, such as the boost in steel prices, are allowed by Big Business, while wages are curbed.

Abolish the wage freeze. Produce for peace, not for war.

For committees of unionists, housewives and small merchants authorized to stop profiteering and control prices and rents.

For a compulsory cost-of-living clause covering all wages, pensions and unemployment compensation, based upon a labor-controlled cost-of-living index which would include Federal, state and local taxes in computing living costs.

7. Taxes

The government's tax policy shifts the burden of war costs to the workers and low income groups. The billionaires are allowed to continue their record-breaking profits. Workers' wages are taxed in many forms, direct and indirect. Taxation is rapidly becoming the biggest menace to the standard of living won by American workers through years of struggle. What is won on the picket line is taken away by Washington.

Tax the rich and not the poor.

Abolish all taxes on incomes below $7,500 a year. Abolish all sales taxes. Stop the war profiteers by a 100% tax on all war-goods profits.

8. Security and Welfare

The so-called "Fair Deal" welfare program promised by Truman in 1948 has been put in moth balls. It was only a campaign promise. Now it is being taken out of storage for the 1952 campaign. The Republicans and Democrats will never enact a genuine public welfare program. Their program is billions for war, not for the social benefit of the people. The Socialist Workers Party proposes to use this country's great wealth to benefit the social welfare of the majority.

For the building of 20,000,000 low-cost housing units. For a national health service to provide free medical attention and hospitalization for all. For an adequate old age pension. For a Federal education program to guarantee a college education for all youth.

9. Militarism

Militarism more and more dominates our country. The Pentagon drains the nation of its wealth and its youth. The U.S. is dragged toward war by the two-party bloc and the brass hats. We are being transformed into a garrison state.

Stop the draft. Abolish the officer caste. For full democratic rights for the ranks in all the services. No troops to be sent abroad without a referendum of the people. Union wages for all service men.

For the right of unions to investigate conditions in the armed services and to protest against all undemocratic and oppressive actions of the officers.

10. FARM POLICY

Establish a federal farm program to guarantee the cost of production to working farmers and to be operated under the control of their own representatives. Expand rural electrification. No limitation on crops. A federal program for soil conservation and flood control. No taxes on savings of co-operatives. A federal ban on all speculation in farm commodities. Abolish sharecropping and landlordism. The land to those who work it!

11. GOVERNMENT OWNERSHIP OF INDUSTRY

Today the big trusts own and control the basic wealth of America. They run the government and decide the fate of our country.

Nationalize the basic industries, all war plants, all natural resources, and operate them in the interests of the producers and consumers by democratically-elected committees of workers and technicians.

Nationalize the banks. Institute a planned economy of abundance, based on production for use, not for profit.

12. WORKERS AND FARMERS GOVERNMENT

Labor has no representation in Washington. The Socialist Workers Party fights for the creation of a Labor Party which can unite the working people, farmers and professional people, and put a government in power which represents the majority.

The Socialist Workers Party alone consistently and unconditionally champions the interests of the workers in their struggles against capitalism and works for its abolition. This goal is concretely expressed in the Socialist Workers Party's fundamental objective in the 1952 campaign, the mobilization of the masses for a Workers and Farmers Government.

Only a Workers and Farmers Government can reorganize our society on a rational basis, and utilize the tremendous potential wealth and strength of our country for the benefit of humanity.

For a Workers and Farmers Government that will stop the drive toward World War III and reorganize America on a socialist basis!

CAMPAIGN OF 1956

In August, 1956, the Democrats renominated their titular leader, Adlai E. Stevenson of Illinois, for the presidency on the first ballot. Senator Estes Kefauver of Tennessee was chosen as the vice-presidential candidate in a distinctive open contest—on the second ballot and over twelve other candidates including Senator John F. Kennedy of Massachusetts. Later in the month the Republicans also renominated their 1952 candidates, incumbent President Dwight D. Eisenhower and Vice-President Richard M. Nixon.

The principal third parties in 1956 were the Prohibition Party, represented by Enoch Arden Holtwick of Illinois and Edward M. Cooper of California; the Socialist Party, for which Darlington Hoopes and Samuel H. Friedman again were the candidates; and the Socialist Labor Party, with Eric Hass again the presidential candidate and Georgia Cozzini of Wisconsin the vice-presidential candidate. Farrell Dobbs and Myra Tanner Weiss again made up the Socialist Workers Party ticket. In mid-September, 317 delegates from several splinter groups representing voters in approximately half of the states gathered in Memphis, Tennessee, to form a "National Conservative Movement." Although the delegates supported the independent candidacy of T. Coleman Andrews of Virginia for president and Thomas H. Werdel of California for vice-president, they voted against the formation of a third party and published only a declaration of principles instead of a platform. The Progressive Party of 1948 and 1952 did not offer a candidate in 1956, but some minor parties were established in individual states.

In the election, Eisenhower increased his majority by nearly 3 million votes over his 1952 figure. The Republicans polled 35,585,245 votes to 26,030,172 for the Democrats. T. Coleman Andrews received 108,055 votes, and the Socialist Labor Party got 44,300. The Prohibition Party attracted 41,937 votes, and the Socialist Workers obtained 7,797. Darlington Hoopes, for the Socialists, had 2,044 votes cast for him.

President Eisenhower received 457 electoral votes to 73 for Governor Stevenson and 1 for Walter Jones, an Alabama judge.

Democratic Platform 1956

PREAMBLE

In the brief space of three and one-half years, the people of the United States have come to realize, with tragic consequences, that our National Government cannot be trusted to the hands of political amateurs, dominated by representatives of special privilege.

Four years ago they were beguiled, by empty promises and pledges, to elect as President a recent convert to Republicanism. Our people have now learned that the party of Lincoln has been made captive to big businessmen with small minds. They have found that they are now ruled by a Government which they did not elect, and to which they have not given their consent. Their awareness of this fact was demonstrated in 1954 when they returned control of the legislative machinery of the Federal Government to the 84th Democratic Congress.

From the wreckage of American world leadership under a Republican Administration, this great Democratic Congress has salvaged a portion of the world prestige our Nation enjoyed under the brilliant Administrations of Franklin Delano Roosevelt and Harry S. Truman.

Our Democratic 84th Congress made one of the greatest legislative records in the history of our country. It enacted an active program of progressive, humane legislation, which has repudiated the efforts of reactionary Republicanism to stall America's progress. When we return to the halls of Congress next January, and with a Democratic President in the White House, it will be the plan and purpose of our Party to complete restoration and rehabilitation of American leadership in world affairs. We pledge return of our National Government to its rightful owners, the people of the United States.

On the threshold of an atomic age, in mid-Twentieth Century, our beloved Nation needs the vision, vigor and vitality which can be infused into it only by a government under the Democratic Party.

We approach the forthcoming election with

a firm purpose of effecting such infusion; and with the help and assistance of Divine Providence we shall endeavor to accomplish it. To the end that the people it has served so well may know our program for the return of America to the highway of progress, the Democratic Party herewith submits its platform for 1956.

I. Foreign Policy and National Defense

The Democratic Party affirms that world peace is a primary objective of human society. Peace is more than a suspension of shooting while frenzied and fearful nations stockpile armaments of annihilation.

Achievement of world peace requires political statesmanship and economic wisdom, international understanding and dynamic leadership. True peace is the tranquillity of ordered justice on a global scale. It may be destroyed without a shot being fired. It can be fostered and preserved only by the solid unity and common brotherhood of the peoples of the world in the cause of freedom.

The hopes and aspirations of the peoples of all nations for justice and peace depend largely upon the courageous and enlightened administration of the foreign and defense policies of the United States. We deplore the fact that the administration of both policies since 1953 has confused timidity with courage, and blindness with enlightenment.

The Republican Record of Confusion and Complacency Is the President's Responsibility. The world's hopes for lasting peace depend upon the conduct of our foreign policy, a function which the Constitution vests in the President of the United States and one which has not been effectively exercised by President Eisenhower. Since 1953, responsibility for foreign affairs has been President Eisenhower's, his alone, and his in full.

In the past three years, his conduct of our policies has moved us into realms where we risk grave danger. He has failed to seek peace with determination, for his disarmament policy has failed to strike hard at the institution of war. His handling of the day-by-day problems of international affairs has unnecessarily and dangerously subjected the American people to the risk of atomic world war.

Our Government Lacks Leadership. We need bold leadership, yet in the three years since Stalin's death, in the full year since President Eisenhower's meeting at the "summit," the Republican Administration has not offered a single concrete new idea to meet the new-style political and economic offensive of the Soviets, which represents, potentially, an even graver challenge than Stalin's use of force. President Eisenhower and his Secretary of State talk at cross-purposes, praising neutralism one day, condemning it the next. The Republicans seem unable either to make up their minds or to give us leadership, while the unity of the free world rapidly disintegrates.

We in America need to make our peaceful purpose clear beyond dispute in every corner of the world—yet Secretary Dulles brags of "brinks of war." We need a foreign policy which rises above jockeying for partisan position or advantage—yet, not in memory has there been so little bipartisanship in the administration of our policies, so little candor in their presentation to our people, so much pretending that things are better than they are.

The Republican Bluster and Bluff. Four years ago the Republican Party boasted of being able to produce a foreign policy which was to free the Communist satellites, unleash Chiang Kai-shek, repudiate the wartime agreements, and reverse the policy of containing Communist expansion.

Since 1953 they have done just the opposite, standing silent when the peoples rise in East Germany and Poland, and thereby weakening the positive Democratic policy of halting Communist expansion.

Our Friends Lose Faith In Us. Our friends abroad now doubt our sincerity. They have seen the solid assurance of collective security under a Democratic Administration give place to the uncertainties of personal diplomacy. They have seen the ties of our international alliances and friendship weakened by inept Republican maneuvering.

They have seen traditional action and boldness in foreign affairs evaporate into Republican complacency, retrenchment and empty posturing.

The Failure Abroad. Blustering without dynamic action will not alter the fact that the unity and strength of the free world have been drastically impaired. Witness the decline of NATO, the bitter tragedy of Cyprus, the withdrawal of French forces to North Africa, the uncertainty and dangers in the Middle East, an uncertain and insecure Germany, and resentment rising against United States leadership everywhere.

In Asia—in Burma, Ceylon, Indonesia, India—anti-Americanism grows apace, aggravated by the clumsy actions of our Government, and fanned by the inept utterances of our "statesmen."

In the Middle East, the Eisenhower Administration has dawdled and drifted. The results have been disastrous, and worse threatens. Only the good offices of the United Nations in maintaining peace between Israel and her neighbors conceal the diplomatic incapacities of the Republican Administration. The current crisis over Suez is a consequence of inept and vacillating Republican policy. Our Government's mistakes have placed us in a position in the Middle East which threatens the free world with a loss of power and prestige, potentially more dangerous than any we have suffered in the past decade.

The Failure at Home. Political considerations of budget balancing and tax reduction now come before the wants of our national security and the needs of our Allies. The Republicans have slashed our own armed strength, weakened our capacity to deal with military threats, stifled our air force, starved our army and weakened our capacity to deal with aggression of any sort save by retreat or by the alternatives, "massive retaliation" and global atomic war. Yet, while our troubles mount, they tell us our prestige was never higher, they tell us we were never more secure.

The Challenge Is For Democracy to Meet. The Democratic Party believes that "waging peace" is a monumental task to be performed honestly, forthrightly, with dedication and consistent effort.

The way to lasting peace is to forego bluster and bluff, to regain steadiness of purpose, to join again in faithful concert with the community of free nations, to look realistically at the challenging circumstances which confront us, to face them candidly and imaginatively, and to return to the Democratic policy of peace through strength.

This is a task for Democrats. This facing of new problems, this rising to new challenges, has been our Party's mission and its glory for three generations past. President Truman met and mastered Stalin's challenge a decade ago, with boldness, courage and imagination, and so will we turn to the challenge before us now, pressing the search for real and lasting peace. TO THIS WE PLEDGE:

Support for the United Nations. The United Nations is indispensable for the maintenance of world peace and for the settlement of contro-versies between nations small and large. We pledge our every effort to strengthen its usefulness and expand its role as guide and guardian of international security and peace. We deplore the Republicans' tendency to use the United Nations only when it suits them, ignoring or by passing it whenever they please.

We pledge determined opposition to the admission of the Communist Chinese into the United Nations. They have proven their complete hostility to the purposes of this organization. We pledge continued support to Nationalist China.

Release of American Prisoners. We urge a continuing effort to effect the release of all Americans detained by Communist China.

Support for Effective Disarmament. In this atomic age, war threatens the very survival of civilization. To eliminate the danger of atomic war, a universal, effective and enforced disarmament system must be the goal of responsible men and women everywhere. So long as we lack enforceable international control of weapons, we must maintain armed strength to avoid war. But technological advances in the field of nuclear weapons make disarmament an ever more urgent problem. Time and distance can never again protect any nation of the world. The Eisenhower Administration, despite its highly publicized proposals for aerial inspection, has made no progress toward this great objective. We pledge the Democratic Party to pursue vigorously this great goal of enforced disarmament in full awareness that irreparable injury, even total destruction, now threatens the human race.

Adequate Defense Forces. We reject the false Republican notion that this country can afford only a second-best defense. We stand for strong defense forces so clearly superior in modern weapons to those of any possible enemy that our armed strength will make an attack upon the free world unthinkable, and thus be a major force for world peace. The Republican Administration stands indicted for failing to recognize the necessity of proper living standards for the men and women of our armed forces and their families. We pledge ourselves to the betterment of the living conditions of the members of our armed services, and to a needed increase in the so-called "fringe benefits."

Training for Defense. The Democratic Party pledges itself to a bold and imaginative program devised to utilize fully the brain power of America's youth, including its talent in the scientific and technical fields.

Scholarships and loan assistance and such other steps as may be determined desirable must be employed to secure this objective. This is solely in the interest of necessary and adequate national defense.

Strengthening Civil Defense. We believe that a strong, effective civil defense is a necessary part of national defense. Advances in nuclear weapons have made existing civil defense legislation and practices obsolete.

We pledge ourselves to establish a real program for protecting the civilian population and industry of our Nation in place of the present weak and ineffective program. We believe that this is essentially a Federal responsibility.

Collective Security Arrangements. The Democratic Party inaugurated and we strongly favor collective defense arrangements, such as NATO and the Organization of American States, within the framework of the United Nations. We realize, as the Republicans have not, that mutually recognized common interests can be flexibly adapted to the varied needs and aspirations of all countries concerned.

Winning the Productivity Race. The Republican Party has not grasped one of the dominant facts of mid-century—that the growth of productive power of the Communist states presents a challenge which cannot be evaded. The Democratic Party is confident that, through the freedom we enjoy, a vast increase in productive power of our Nation and our Allies will be achieved, and by their combined capacity they will surmount any challenge.

Economic Development Abroad. We believe that, in the cause of peace, America must support the efforts of underdeveloped countries on a cooperative basis to organize their own resources and to increase their own economic productivity, so that they may enjoy the higher living standards which science and modern industry make possible. We will give renewed strength to programs of economic and technical assistance. We support a multilateral approach to these programs, wherever possible, so that burdens are shared and resources pooled among all the economically developed countries with the capital and skills to help in this great task.

Further, while recognizing the relation of our national security to the role of the United States in international affairs, the Democratic Party believes the time has come for a realistic reappraisal of the American foreign aid program, particularly as to its extent and the conditions under which it should be continued. This reappraisal will determine the standards by which further aid shall be granted, keeping in mind America's prime objective of securing world peace.

Bringing the Truth to the World. The tools of truth and candor are even more important than economic tools. The Democratic Party believes that once our Government is purged of the confusion and complacency fostered by the Republican Administration a new image of America will emerge in the world: the image of a confident America dedicated to its traditional principles, eager to work with other peoples, honest in its pronouncements, and consistent in its policies.

Freedom for Captive Nations. We condemn the Republican Administration for its heartless record of broken promises to the unfortunate victims of Communism. Candidate Eisenhower's 1952 pledges to "liberate" the captive peoples have been disavowed and dishonored.

We declare our deepest concern for the plight of the freedom-loving peoples of Central and Eastern Europe and of Asia, now under the yoke of Soviet dictatorship. The United States, under Democratic leaders, has never recognized the forcible annexation of Lithuania, Latvia, and Estonia, or condoned the extension of the Kremlin's tyranny over Poland, Bulgaria, Rumania, Czechoslovakia, Hungary, Albania and other countries.

We look forward to the day when the liberties of all captive nations will be restored to them and they can again take their rightful place in the community of free nations.

We shall press before the United Nations the principle that Soviet Russia withdraw its troops from the captive countries, so as to permit free, fair and unfettered elections in the subjugated areas, in compliance with the Atlantic Charter and other binding commitments.

Upholding the Principle of Self-Determination. We rededicate ourselves to the high principle of national self-determination, as enunciated by Woodrow Wilson, whose leadership brought freedom and independence to uncounted millions.

It is the policy of the Democratic Party, therefore, to encourage and assist small nations and all peoples, behind the Iron Curtain and outside, in the peaceful and orderly achievement of their legitimate aspirations toward political, geographical, and ethnic integrity, so that they may dwell in the family of sovereign nations with freedom and dignity. We are opposed to colonialism and Communist imperialism.

We shall endeavor to apply this principle to the desires of all peoples for self-determination.

Reciprocal Trade Among the Nations. The Democratic Party has always worked for expanding trade among free nations. Expanding world trade is necessary not only for our friends, but for ourselves; it is the way to meet America's growing need for industrial raw materials. We shall continue to support vigorously the Hull Reciprocal Trade Program.

Under Democratic Administrations, the operation of this Act was conducted in a manner that recognized equities for agriculture, industry and labor. Under the present Republican Administration, there has been a most flagrant disregard of these important segments of our economy resulting in serious economic injury to hundreds of thousands of Americans engaged in these pursuits. We pledge correction of these conditions.

Encouraging European Unity. Through the Marshall Plan, the European Economic Organization and NATO, the Democratic Party encouraged and supported efforts to achieve greater economic and political unity among the free nations of Europe, and to increase the solidarity of the nations of the North Atlantic community. We will continue those efforts, taking into account the viewpoints and aspirations of different sectors of the European community, particularly in regard to practical proposals for the unification of Germany.

Peace and Justice in the Middle East. The Democratic Party stands for the maintenance of peace in the Middle East, which is essential to the well-being and progress of all its peoples.

We will urge Israel and the Arab States to settle their differences by peaceful means, and to maintain the sanctity of the Holy Places in the Holy Land and permit free access to them.

We will assist Israel to build a sound and viable economy for her people, so that she may fulfill her humanitarian mission of providing shelter and sanctuary for her homeless Jewish refugees while strengthening her national development.

We will assist the Arab States to develop their economic resources and raise the living standards of their people. The plight of the Arab refugees commands our continuing sympathy and concern. We will assist in carrying out large-scale projects for their resettlement in countries where there is room and opportunity for them.

We support the principle of free access to the Suez Canal under suitable international auspices. The present policies of the Eisenhower Administration in the Middle East are unnecessarily increasing the risk that war will break out in this area. To prevent war, to assure peace, we will faithfully carry out our country's pledge under the Tripartite Declaration of 1950 to oppose the use or threat of force and to take such action as may be necessary in the interest of peace, both within and outside the United Nations, to prevent any violation of the frontiers of any armistice lines.

The Democratic Party will act to redress the dangerous imbalance of arms in the area resulting from the shipment of Communist arms to Egypt, by selling or supplying defensive weapons to Israel, and will take such steps, including security guarantees, as may be required to deter aggression and war in the area.

We oppose, as contrary to American principles, the practice of any government which discriminates against American citizens on grounds of race or religion. We will not countenance any arrangement or treaty with any government which by its terms or in its practical application would sanction such practices.

Support for Free Asia. The people of Asia seek a new and freer life and they are in a commendable hurry to get it. They struggle against poverty, ill health and illiteracy. In the aftermath of war, China became a victim of Communist tyranny. But many new free nations have arisen in South and Southeast Asia. South Korea remains free, and the new Japan has abandoned her former imperial and aggressive ways. America's task and interest in Asia is to help the governments of free peoples demonstrate that they have improved living standards without yielding to Communist tyranny or domination by anyone. That task will be carried out under Democratic leadership.

Support of Our Good Neighbors to the South. In the Western Hemisphere the Democratic Party will restore the policy of the "good neighbor" which has been alternately neglected and abused by the Republican Administration. We pledge ourselves to fortify the defenses of the Americas. In this respect, we will intensify our cooperation with our neighboring republics to help them strengthen their economies, improve educational opportunities, and combat disease. We will strive to make the Western Hemisphere an inspiring example of what free peoples working together can accomplish.

Progressive Immigration Policies. America's long tradition of hospitality and asylum for those seeking freedom, opportunity, and escape from oppression, has been besmirched by the delays, failures and broken promises of the Republican Administration. The Democratic Party favors prompt revision of the immigration and nationality laws to eliminate unfair provisions under which admissions to this country depend upon quotas based upon the accident of national origin. Proper safeguards against subversive elements should be provided. Our immigration procedures must reflect the principles of our Bill of Rights.

We favor eliminating the provisions of law which charge displaced persons admitted to our shores against quotas for future years. Through such "mortgages" of future quotas, thousands of qualified persons are being forced to wait long years before they can hope for admission.

We also favor more liberal admission of relatives to eliminate the unnecessary tragedies of broken families.

We favor elimination of unnecessary distinctions between native-born and naturalized citizens. There should be no "second class" citizenship in the United States.

The administration of the Refugee Relief Act of 1953 has been a disgrace to our country. Rescue has been denied to innocent, defenseless and suffering people, the victims of war and the aftermath of wars. The purpose of the Act has been defeated by Republican mismanagement.

Victims of Communist Oppression. We will continue to support programs providing succor for escapees from behind the Iron Curtain, and bringing help to the victims of war and Communist oppression.

The Challenge of the Next Four Years. Today new challenges call for new ideas and new methods.

In the coming years, our great necessity will be to pull together as a people, with true non-partisanship in foreign affairs under leaders informed, courageous and responsible.

We shall need to work closely with each other as Americans. If we here indict the Republican record, we acknowledge gratefully the efforts of individual Republicans to achieve true bipartisanship. In this spirit an affirmative, cooperative policy can be developed. We shall need to work closely, also, with others all around the world. For there is much to do—to create once more the will and the power to transform the principles of the United Nations into a living reality; to awaken ourselves and others to the effort and sacrifice which alone can win justice and peace.

II. The Domestic Policy—The Republican Reaction to 20 Years of Progress

The Democratic Bequest. Twenty years of vivid Democratic accomplishments revived and reinforced our economic system, and wrote humanity upon the statute books. All this, the current Republican Administration inherited.

The Republican Brand of Prosperity. Substituting deceptive slogans and dismal deeds for the Democratic program, the Republicans have been telling the American people that "we are now more prosperous than ever before in peacetime." For the American farmer, the small businessman and the low-income worker, the old people living on a pittance, the young people seeking an American standard of education, and the minority groups seeking full employment opportunity at adequate wages, this tall tale of Republican prosperity has been an illusion.

The evil is slowly but surely infiltrating the entire economic system. Its fever signs are evidenced by soaring monopoly profits, while wages lag, farm income collapses, and small-business failures multiply at an alarming rate.

The first time-bomb of the Republican crusade against full prosperity for all was the hard-money policy. This has increased the debt burden on depressed farms, saddled heavier costs on small business, foisted higher interest charges on millions of homeowners (including veterans), pushed up unnecessarily the cost of consumer credit, and swelled the inordinate profits of a few lenders of money. It has wrought havoc with the bond market, with resulting financial loss to the ordinary owners of Government bonds.

The Republican tax policy has joined hands in an unholy alliance with the hard-money policy.

Fantastic misrepresentation of the Government's budgetary position has been used to deny tax relief to low- and middle-income families, while tax concessions and handouts have been generously sprinkled among potential campaign contributors to Republican coffers. The disastrously reactionary farm program, the hardhearted resistance to adequate expansion of Social Security and other programs for human well-being, and favoritism in the award of Government contracts, all have watered the economic tree at the top and neglected its roots.

The Stunting of Our Economic Progress. The Republicans say that employment and production are "higher" than ever before. The fact is that our over-all rate of growth has been crippled and stunted in contrast to its faster increase during the Democratic years from 1947 to 1953, after World War II.

With production lagging behind full capacity, unemployment has grown.

The Republican claim that this stunted prosperity is the price of peace is a distortion. National-security outlays have averaged a higher part of our total production during these Republican years than during 1947-53, and yet the annual growth in total production during these Republican years has been only about 60 percent as fast as in the preceding Democratic years. The progress of low-income families toward an American standard of living, rapid during the Democratic years, has ground to a stop under the Republicans.

Federal budgetary outlays for education and health, old-age assistance and child care, slum clearance and resource development, and all the other great needs of our people have been mercilessly slashed from an annual rate of more than $57 per capita under the Democrats to $33 per capita under the Republicans, a cut of 42 percent.

The Failure of the Republican Budget-Balancers. During the Republican fiscal years 1954-1957 as a whole, the deficits have averaged larger, and the surpluses smaller, than during the Democratic fiscal years 1947-1953, financial manipulation to the contrary notwithstanding.

Democratic Principles for Full Prosperity for All:

(1) We repudiate the Republican stunting of our economic growth, and we reassert the principles of the Full Employment Act of 1946;

(2) We pledge ourselves to achieve an honest and realistic balance of the Federal Budget in a just and fully prosperous American economy;

(3) We pledge ourselves to equitable tax revisions and monetary policies designed to combine economic progress with economic justice. We condemn the Republican use of our revenue and money systems to benefit the few at the expense of the vast majority of our people;

(4) We pledge ourselves to work toward the reduction and elimination of poverty in America;

(5) We pledge ourselves to full parity of income and living standards for agriculture; to strike off the shackles which the Taft-Hartley law has unjustly imposed on labor; and to foster the more rapid growth of legitimate business enterprise by founding this growth upon the expanding consuming power of the people; and

(6) We pledge ourselves to expand world trade and to enlarge international economic cooperation, all toward the end of a more prosperous and more peaceful world.

Democratic Goals To Be Achieved During Four Years of Progress. By adhering to these principles, we shall strive to attain by 1960 the following full prosperity objectives for all American families:

(1) A 500 billion dollar national economy in real terms;

(2) An increase of 20 percent or better in the average standard of living;

(3) An increase in the annual income of American families, with special emphasis on those whose incomes are below $2000;

(4) A determined drive toward parity of incomes and living standards for those engaged in the vital pursuit of agriculture;

(5) The addition of all necessary classrooms for our primary and secondary schools; the construction of needed new homes, with a proper proportion devoted to the rehousing of low- and middle-income families in urban and rural areas; the increase of benefits under the Old Age Assistance and Old Age Survivors Insurance Programs; a substantial expansion in hospital facilities and medical research; and a doubling of our programs for resource development and conservation; and

(6) National defense outlays based upon our national needs, not permitting false economy to jeopardize our very survival.

This country of ours, in the factory, in business

and on the farm, is blessed with ever-increasing productive power. The Republicans have not permitted this potential abundance to be released for the mutual benefit of all. We reject this stunted Republican concept of America. We pledge ourselves to release the springs of abundance, to bring this abundance to all, and thus to fulfill the full promise of America.

These are our Democratic goals for the next four years. We set them forth in vivid contrast to Republican lip-service protestations that they, too, are for these goals. Their little deeds belie their large and hollow slogans. Our performance in the past gives validity to our goals for the future.

Our victory in 1956 will make way for the commencement of these four years of progress.

III. FREE ENTERPRISE

"Equal rights for all and special privileges for none," the tested Jeffersonian principle, remains today the only philosophy by which human rights can be preserved by government.

It is a sad fact in the history of the Republican Party that, under its control, our Government has always become an instrument of special privilege; not a government of the people, by the people, and for the people. We have had, instead, under Harding, Coolidge and Hoover, and now under Eisenhower, government of the many, by the few, and for the few.

We recognize monopolies and monopolistic practices as the real barriers between the people and their economic and political freedom. Monopolies act to stifle equality of opportunity and prevent the infusion of fresh blood into the lifestream of our economy. The Republican Administration has allowed giant corporate entities to dominate our economy. For example, forty thousand automobile dealers now know they were incapable of coping with these giants. They were, as the Democratic 84th Congress found, subjected to abuse and threatened with extinction. The result was passage of the O'Mahoney-Celler bill giving the automobile dealers of America economic freedom. We enacted this law, and we pledge that it shall be retained upon the statute books as a monument to the Democratic Party's concern for small business.

We pledge ourselves to the restoration of truly competitive conditions in American industry. Affirmative action within the framework of American tradition will be taken to curb corporate mergers that would contribute to the growth of economic concentration.

Small and Independent Business. In contrast to the maladministration by the Republican Party of the Federal program to assist small and independent business, we pledge ourselves—

(1) To the strict and impartial enforcement of the laws originally fostered and strengthened by the Democratic Party and designed to prevent monopolies and other concentrations of economic and financial power; and to enact legislation to close loopholes in the laws prohibiting price discrimination;

(2) To tax relief for all small and independent businesses by fair and equitable adjustments in Federal taxation which will encourage business expansion, and to the realistic application of the principle of graduated taxation to such corporate income. An option should be provided to spread Federal estate taxes over a period of years when an estate consists principally of the equity capital of a closely held small business;

(3) To adoption of all practical means of making long- and short-term credit available to small and independent businessmen at reasonable rates;

(4) To the award of a substantially higher proportion of Government contracts to independent small businesses, and to the award of a far larger percentage of military procurement, by value, after competitive bids rather than by negotiation behind closed doors. We severely condemn Republican discrimination against small and independent business;

(5) To replacement of the weak and ineffective Republican conduct of the Small Business Administration, and its reconstitution as a vigorous, independent agency which will advocate the cause of small and independent businessmen, and render genuine assistance in fulfilling their needs and solving their problems. We condemn the Republican Administration for its failure to serve this important segment of our economy.

Law Enforcement. We pledge ourselves to the fair and impartial administration of justice. The Republican Administration has degraded the great powers of law enforcement. It has not used them in the service of equal justice under law, but for concealment, coercion, persecution, political advantage and special interests.

Merchant Marine. In the interest of our national security, and of the maintenance of American standards of wages and living, and in order that our waterborne overseas commerce shall not be unfairly discriminated against by low-cost foreign competition, we pledge our continued encouragement and support of a strong and adequate American Merchant Marine.

Transportation. The public and national defense interests require the development and maintenance, under the competitive free enterprise system, of a strong, efficient and financially sound system of common-carrier transportation by water, highway, rail, and air, with each mode enabled, through sound and intelligent exercise of regulatory powers, to realize its inherent economic advantages and to reflect its full competitive capabilities. Public interest also requires, under reasonable standards, the admission of new licensees, where public convenience may be served, into the transport fields. We deplore the lack of enforcement of safety regulations for protection of life and property under the present Republican Administration, and pledge strict enforcement of such regulations.

Highways. We commend the foresight of the Democratic 84th Congress for its enactment of the greatest program in history for expansion of our highway network, and we congratulate it upon its rejection of the unsound, unworkable, inadequate and unfair roads bill proposed by the present Republican Administration. In cooperation with state and local governments, we will continue the programs developed and fostered under prior Democratic Administrations for planning, coordinating, financing and encouraging the expansion of our national road and highway network so vital to defense and transportation in the motor age. We support expansion of farm-to-market roads.

Rivers and Harbors. We pledge continued development of harbors and waterways as a vital segment of our transportation system. We denounce as capricious and arbitrary the Eisenhower pocket veto of the 1956 Rivers and Harbors bill, which heartlessly deprived the people in many sections of our country of vitally needed public works projects.

IV. A MAGNA CHARTA FOR LABOR

Labor-Management Relations. Harmonious labor-management relations are productive of good incomes for wage earners and conducive to rising output from our factories. We believe that, to the widest possible extent consistent with the public interest, management and labor should determine wage rates and conditions of employment through free collective bargaining.

The Taft-Hartley Act passed by the Republican-dominated 80th Congress seriously impaired this relationship as established in the Wagner National Labor Relations Act, enacted under the Roosevelt Administration. The Wagner Act protected, encouraged and guaranteed the rights of workers to organize, to join unions of their own choice, and to bargain collectively through these unions without coercion.

The vicious anti-union character of the Taft-Hartley Act was expressly recognized by Candidate Eisenhower during the 1952 election campaign.

At that time, he made a solemn promise to eliminate its unjust provisions and to enact a fair law. President Eisenhower and his Administration have failed utterly, however, to display any executive initiative or forcefulness toward keeping this pledge to the workers. He was further responsible for administratively amending Taft-Hartley into a more intensely anti-labor weapon by stacking the National Labor Relations Board with biased pro-management personnel who, by administrative decision, transformed the Act into a management weapon. One such decision removed millions of workers from the jurisdiction of the NLRB, which in many cases left them without protection of either State or Federal legislation.

We unequivocally advocate repeal of the Taft-Hartley Act. The Act must be repealed because State "right-to-work" laws have their genesis in its discriminatory anti-labor provisions.

It must be repealed because its restrictive provisions deny the principle that national legislation based on the commerce clause of the Constitution normally overrides conflicting State laws.

The Taft-Hartley Act has been proven to be inadequate, unworkable and unfair. It interferes in an arbitrary manner with collective bargaining, causing imbalance in the relationship between management and labor.

Upon return of our National Government to the Democratic Party, a new legislative approach toward the entire labor-management problem will be adopted, based on past experience and the principles of the Wagner National Labor Relations Act and the Norris-La Guardia Anti-Injunction Law.

Fair Labor Standards. We commend the action of the Democratic 84th Congress which raised the minimum wage from 75 cents to $1.00 an hour despite the strenuous objection of President Eisenhower and the Republicans in Congress. However, the inadequacies of the minimum wage become apparent as the cost of living increases, and we feel it imperative to raise the minimum wage to at least $1.25 an hour, in order to approximate present-day needs more closely.

We further pledge as a matter of priority to extend full protection of the Fair Labor Standards Act to all workers in industry engaged in, or affecting, interstate commerce.

Walsh-Healey Contracts Act. We pledge revision and honest administration of the Walsh-Healey Act, to restore its effectiveness and usefulness as an instrument for maintaining fair standards of wages and hours for American workers.

Equal Pay for Equal Work. We advocate legislation to provide equal pay for equal work, regardless of sex.

The Physically Handicapped. The Democratic Party has always supported legislation to benefit the disabled worker. The physically handicapped have proved their value to Government and industry. We pledge our continued support of legislation to improve employment opportunities of physically handicapped persons.

Migratory Workers. We shall support legislation providing for the protection and improvement of the general welfare of migratory workers.

Jobs for Depressed Areas. We pledge our Party to support legislation providing for an effective program to promote industry and create jobs in depressed industrial and rural areas so that such areas may be restored to economic stability.

V. AGRICULTURE

Sustained national prosperity is dependent upon a vigorous agricultural economy.

We condemn the defeatist attitude of the Eisenhower Administration in refusing to take effective action to assure the well-being of farm families. We condemn its fear of abundance, its lack of initiative in developing domestic markets, and its dismal failure to obtain for the American farmer his traditional and deserved share of the world market. Its extravagant ex-

penditure of money intended for agricultural benefit, without either direction or results, is a national calamity.

The Eisenhower Administration has failed utterly to develop any programs to meet the desperate needs of farmers in the face of fantastic promises, and it has sabotaged the progressive programs inherited from prior Democratic Administrations by failing to administer them properly in the interest either of farmers or of the Nation as a whole.

Specifically, we denounce President Eisenhower's veto of the constructive legislation proposed and passed by the Democratic 84th Congress to reverse the alarming fall of farm prices and restore farmers to a position of first-class economic citizenship in the sharing of benefits from American productive ability.

We also condemn the Republican Administration for its abandonment of the true principles of soil conservation and for its destruction of the Soil Conservation Service. We pledge to support continued improvements in the soil bank program passed by the Democratic 84th Congress and originally opposed by President Eisenhower and Secretary Ezra Taft Benson. We deplore the diversion of this conservation program into a direct vote-buying scheme.

Farmers have had to struggle for three and one-half years while their net farm income has fallen more than one billion dollars a year. Their parity ratio, which under Democratic Administrations had been 100 percent or more during the eleven years prior to 1953, dropped to as low as 80 percent during the Eisenhower Administration, and the farmers' share of the consumers' food dollar shrank from 47 cents in 1952 to as low as only 38 cents. One stark fact stands out clearly for all to see—disastrously low farm prices and record high consumer prices vie with each other for the attention of responsible government. In a reduction of this incongruous spread lies the answer to some of the most vexing problems of agricultural economics.

In their courageous fight to save their homes and land, American farmers have gone deeper and deeper into debt. Last year farmers' mortgage indebtedness increased more than in any year in history with the exception of the year 1923.

The Democratic Party met similar situations forthrightly in the past with concrete remedial action. It takes legitimate pride in its consistent record of initiating and developing every constructive program designed to protect and conserve the human and natural resources so vital to our rural economy. These programs enabled consumers to obtain more abundant supplies of high-quality food and fiber at reasonable prices while maintaining adequate income for farmers and improving the level of family living in rural areas.

In order to regain the ground lost during the Eisenhower Administration, and in order better to serve both consumers and producers, the Democratic Party pledges continuous and vigorous support to the following policies:

Sponsor a positive and comprehensive program to conserve our soil, water and forest resources for future generations;

Promote programs which will protect and preserve the family-type farm as a bulwark of American life, and encourage farm-home ownership, including additional assistance to family farmers and young farmers in the form of specially designed credit and price-support programs, technical aid, and enlarged soil conservation allowances.

Maintain adequate reserves of agricultural commodities strategically situated, for national security purposes. Such stockpiles should be handled as necessary strategic reserves, so that farmers will not be penalized by depressed prices for their efficiency and diligence in producing abundance;

Promote international exchange of commodities by creating an International Food Reserve, fostering commodity agreements, and vigorously administering the Foreign Agricultural Trade Development and Assistance Act;

Undertake immediately by appropriate action to endeavor to regain the full 100 percent of parity the farmers received under the Democratic Administrations. We will achieve this by means of supports on basic commodities at 90 percent of parity and by means of commodity loans, direct purchases, direct payments to producers, marketing agreements and orders, production adjustments, or a combination of these, including legislation, to bring order and stability into the relationship between the producer, the processor and the consumer;

Develop practical measures for extending price supports to feed grains and other nonbasic storables and to the producers of perishable commodities such as meat, poultry, dairy products and the like;

Inaugurate a food-stamp or other supplemental food program administered by appropriate State or local agencies to insure that no needy family shall be denied an adequate and wholesome diet because of low income;

Continue and expand school lunch and special milk programs to meet the dietary needs of all school children;

Increase the distribution of food to public institutions and organizations and qualified private charitable agencies, and increase the distribution of food and fiber to needy people in other nations through recognized charitable and religious channels;

Devise and employ effective means to reduce the spread between producers' prices and consumers' costs, and improve market facilities and marketing practices;

Expand the program of agricultural research and education for better distribution, preservation and marketing of farm products to serve both producers and consumers, and promote increased industrial use of farm surpluses;

Provide for an increased reservoir of farm credit at lower rates, designed particularly to accommodate operators of small family-type farms, and extend crop insurance to maximum coverage and protection;

Return the administration of farm programs to farmer-elected committeemen, eliminate the deplorable political abuses in Federal employment in many agricultural counties as practiced by the Eisenhower Administration, and restore leadership to the administration of soil conservation districts;

Insure reliable and low-cost rural electric and telephone service;

Exercise authority in existing law relating to imports of price-supported agricultural commodities in raw, manufactured or processed form as part of our national policy to minimize damage to our domestic economy;

Encourage bona fide farm cooperatives which help farmers reduce the cost-price squeeze, and protect such cooperatives against punitive taxation;

Expand farm forestry marketing research and price reporting on timber products, and provide adequate credit designed to meet the needs of timber farmers; and

Enact a comprehensive farm program which, under intelligent and sympathetic Democratic administration, will make the rural homes of America better and healthier places in which to live.

VI. General Welfare

The Democratic Party believes that America can and must adopt measures to assure every citizen an opportunity for a full, healthy and happy life. To this end, we pledge ourselves to the expansion and improvement of the great social welfare programs inaugurated under Democratic Administrations.

Social Security. By lowering the retirement age for women and for disabled persons, the Democratic 84th Congress pioneered two great advances in Social Security, over the bitter opposition of the Eisenhower Administration. We shall continue our efforts to broaden and strengthen this program by increasing benefits to keep pace with improving standards of living; by raising the wage base upon which benefits depend; and by increasing benefits for each year of covered employment.

Unemployment Insurance. We shall continue to work for a stronger unemployment insurance system, with broader coverage and increased benefits consistent with rising earnings. We shall also work for the establishment of a floor to assure minimum level and duration of benefits, and fair eligibility rules.

Wage Losses Due to Illness. In 1946, a Democratic Congress enacted an insurance program to protect railroad workers against temporary wage losses due to short-term illnesses. Because this program has worked so effectively, we favor extending similar protection to other workers.

Public Assistance. We pledge improvements in the public assistance program even beyond those enacted by the Democratic 84th Congress, through increased aid for the aged, the blind, dependent children, the disabled and other needy persons who are not adequately protected by our contributory insurance programs.

Additional Needs of Our Senior Citizens. To meet the needs of the 14 million Americans aged 65 or over, we pledge ourselves to seek means of assuring these citizens greater income through expanded opportunities for employment, vocational retraining and adult education; better housing and health services for the aged; rehabilitation of the physically and mentally disabled to restore them to independent, productive lives; and intensified medical and other research aimed both at lengthening life and making the longer life more truly livable.

Health and Medical Care. The strength of our Nation depends on the health of our people. The shortage of trained medical and health personnel and facilities has impaired American health standards and has increased the cost of hospital care beyond the financial capacities of most American families.

We pledge ourselves to initiate programs of Federal financial aid, without Federal controls, for medical education.

We pledge continuing and increased support for hospital construction programs, as well as increased Federal aid to public health services, particularly in rural areas.

Medical research. Mindful of the dramatic progress made by medical research in recent years, we shall continue to support vigorously all efforts, both public and private, to wage relentless war on diseases which afflict the bodies and minds of men. We commend the Democratic Party for its leadership in obtaining greater Congressional authorizations in this field.

Housing. We pledge our Party to immediate revival of the basic housing program enacted by the Democratic Congress in 1949, to expansion of this program as our population and resources grow, and to additional legislation to provide housing for middle-income families and aged persons. Aware of the financial burdens which press upon most American communities and prevent them from taking full advantage of Federal urban redevelopment and renewal programs, we favor increasing the Federal share of the cost of these programs.

We reaffirm the goal expressed by a Democratic Congress in 1949 that every American family is entitled to a "decent home and a suitable living environment." The Republican Administration has sabotaged that goal by reducing the public housing program to a fraction of the Nation's need.

We pledge that the housing insurance and mortgage guarantee programs will be redirected in the interest of the home owner, and that the availability of low-interest housing credit will be kept consistent with the expanding housing needs of the Nation.

We favor providing aid to urban and suburban communities in better planning for their future development and redevelopment.

Education. Every American child, irrespective of race or national origin, economic status or place of residence, has full right under the law and the Constitution, without discrimination, to every educational opportunity for developing his potentialities.

We are now faced with shortages of educational facilities that threaten national security, economic prosperity and human well-being. The resources of our States and localities are already strained to the limit. Federal aid and action should be provided, within the traditional framework of State and local control.

We pledge the Democratic Party to the following:

(1) Legislation providing Federal financing to assist States and local communities to build schools, and to provide essential health and safety services for all school children;

(2) Better educational, health and welfare opportunities for children of migratory workers;

(3) Assistance to programs for training teachers of exceptional children;

(4) Programs providing for the training of teachers to meet the critical shortage in technical and scientific fields; and

(5) Expansion of the program of student, teacher and cultural exchange with other nations.

Vocational Education. We commend the 84th Congress for voting the maximum authorized funds for vocational education under the Smith-Hughes Act for the first time in the history of the Act. We pledge continuing and increased support of vocational training for youth and adults, including aid to the States and localities for area technical-vocational schools.

Child Welfare. To keep pace with the growing need for child care and welfare, we pledge an expanded program of grants to the States. We pledge continued support of adequate day care centers to care for the children of the millions of American mothers who work to help support their families.

Aid to the Physically Handicapped. There are today several million physically handicapped citizens, many of whom could become self-supporting if given the opportunity and training for rehabilitation. We pledge support to a vastly expanded rehabilitation program for these physically handicapped, including increased aid to the States, in contrast to the grossly inadequate action of the Republican Administration.

VII. FINANCIAL POLICY

Tax Adjustment. A fully expanding economy can yield enough tax revenues to meet the inescapable obligations of government, balance the Federal Budget, and lighten the tax burden. The immediate need is to correct the inequities in the tax structure which reflect the Republican determination to favor the few at the expense of the many. We favor realistic tax adjustments, giving first consideration to small independent business and the small individual taxpayer. Lower-income families need tax relief; only a Democratic victory will assure this. We favor an increase in the present personal tax exemption of $600 to a minimum of at least $800.

Debt Management. The Republican debt management policy of higher interest rates serves only to benefit a few to the detriment of the general taxpayer, the small borrower, and the small and middle-class investor in Government bonds. We pledge ourselves to a vigilant review of our debt management policy in order to reduce interest rates in the service of our common welfare.

Protection of Investors. Effective administration of the Federal securities laws has been undermined by Republican appointees with conflicting interests. Millions of investors who have bought securities with their savings are today without adequate protection. We favor vigorous administration and revision of the laws to provide investor safeguards for securities extensively traded in the over-the-counter market, for foreign securities distributed in the United States, and against proxy contest abuses.

VIII. GOVERNMENT OPERATIONS

The Democratic Party pledges that it will return the administration of our National Government to a sound, efficient, and honest basis.

Civil Service and Federal Employee Relations. The Eisenhower Administration has failed either to understand or trust the Federal employee. Its record in personnel management constitutes a grave indictment of policies reflecting prejudices and excessive partisanship to the detriment of employee morale.

Intelligent and sympathetic programs must be immediately undertaken to insure the re-establishment of the high morale and efficiency which were characteristic of the Federal worker during 20 years of Democratic Administrations.

To accomplish these objectives, we propose:

(1) Protection and extension of the merit system through the enactment of laws to specify the rights and responsibilities of workers;

(2) A more independent Civil Service Commission in order that it may provide the intelligent leadership essential in perfecting a proper Civil Service System;

(3) Promotion within the Federal Service under laws assuring advancement on merit and proven ability;

(4) Salary increases of a nature that will insure a truly competitive scale at all levels of employment;

(5) Recognition by law of the right of employee organizations to represent their members and to participate in the formulation and improvement of personnel policies and practices; and

(6) A fair and non-political loyalty program, by law, which will protect the Nation against subversion and the employee against unjust and un-American treatment.

Restoring the Efficiency of the Postal Service. The bungling policies of the Republican Administration have crippled and impaired the morale, efficiency and reputation of the U. S. Postal Service. Mail carriers and clerks and other Postal employees are compelled to work under intolerable conditions. Communication by mail and service by parcel post have been delayed and retarded with resulting hardships, business losses and inconveniences. A false concept of economy has impaired seriously the efficiency of the best communication system in the world.

We pledge ourselves to programs which will:

(1) Restore the principle that the Postal Service is a public service to be operated in the interest of improved business economy and better communication, as well as an aid to the dissemination of information and intelligence;

(2) Restore Postal employee morale through

the strengthening of the merit system, with promotions by law rather than caprice or partisan politics, and payment of realistic salaries reflecting the benefits of an expanded economy;

(3) Establish a program of research and development on a scale adequate to insure the most modern and efficient handling of the mails; and

(4) Undertake modernization and construction of desperately needed Postal facilities designed to insure the finest Postal system in the world.

Conflict of Interests. Maladministration and selfish manipulation have characterized Federal Administration during the Eisenhower years. Taxpayers, paying billions of dollars each year to their Government, demand and must have the highest standards of honesty, integrity and efficiency as a minimum requirement of Federal Executive conduct. We pledge a strong merit system as a substitute for cynical policies of spoils and special favor which are now the rule of the day. We seek the constant improvement of the Federal Government apparatus to accomplish these ends.

Under certain conditions, we recognize the need for the employment of personnel without compensation in the Executive Branch of the Government. But the privileges extended these dollar-a-year men have resulted in grave abuses of power. Some of these representatives of large corporations have assumed a dual loyalty to the Government and to the corporations that pay them. These abuses under the Republican Administration have been scandalous. The Democratic Party proposes that any necessary use of non-compensated employees shall be made only after the most careful scrutiny and under the most rigidly prescribed safeguards to prevent any conflict of interests.

Freedom of Information. During recent years there has developed a practice on the part of Federal agencies to delay and withhold information which is needed by Congress and the general public to make important decisions affecting their lives and destinies. We believe that this trend toward secrecy in Government should be reversed and that the Federal Government should return to its basic tradition of exchanging and promoting the freest flow of information possible in those unclassified areas where secrets involving weapons development and bona fide national security are not involved. We condemn the Eisenhower Administration for the excesses practiced in this vital area, and pledge the Democratic Party to reverse this tendency, substituting a rule of law for that of broad claims of executive privilege.

We reaffirm our position of 1952 "to press strongly for world-wide freedom in the gathering and dissemination of news." We shall press for free access to information throughout the world for our journalists and scholars.

Clean Elections. The shocking disclosures in the last Congress of attempts by selfish interests to exert improper influence on members of Congress have resulted in a Congressional investigation now under way. The Democratic Party pledges itself to provide effective regulation and full disclosure of campaign expenditures and contributions in elections to Federal offices.

Equal Rights Amendment. We of the Democratic Party recommend and indorse for submission to the Congress a Constitutional amendment providing equal rights for women.

Veterans Administration. We are spending approximately 4¾ billion dollars per year on veterans' benefits. There are more than 22 million veterans in civil life today and approximately 4 million veterans or dependents of deceased veterans drawing direct cash benefits from the Veterans Administration. It is clear that a matter of such magnitude demands more prominence in the affairs of Government. We pledge that we will elevate the Veterans Administration to a place of dignity commensurate with its importance in national affairs.

We charge the present Administration with open hostility toward the veterans' hospital program as disclosed by its efforts to restrict severely that program in fiscal year 1954. We further charge the Administration with incompetence and gross neglect in the handling of veterans' benefits in the following particulars:

(1) The refusal to allow service connection for disabilities incurred in or aggravated by military service, and the unwarranted reduction of disability evaluations in cases where service connection has been allowed; and

(2) The failure to give proper protection to veterans purchasing homes under the VA home loan program both by inadequate supervision of the program and, in some instances, by active

cooperation with unscrupulous builders, lenders and real estate brokers.

In recognition of the valiant efforts of those who served their Nation in its gravest hours, we pledge:

(1) Continuance of the Veterans Administration as an independent Federal agency handling veterans programs;

(2) Continued recognition of war veterans, with adequate compensation for the service-connected disabled and for the survivors of those who have passed away in service or from service-incurred disabilities; and with pensions for disabled and distressed veterans, and for the dependents of those who have passed on, where they are in need or unable to provide for themselves;

(3) Maintenance of the Veterans Administration hospital system, with no impairment in the high quality of medical and hospital service;

(4) Priority of hospitalization for the service-connected disabled, and the privilege of hospital care when beds are available for the non-service-connected illness of veterans who are sick and without funds or unable to procure private hospitalization;

(5) Fair administration of veterans preference laws, and employment opportunities for handicapped and disabled veterans;

(6) Full hearings for war veterans filing valid applications with the review, corrective and settlement boards of the Federal Government; and

(7) Support for legislation to obtain an extension of the current law to enable veterans to obtain homes and farms through the continuance of the GI Loan Program.

Statehood for Alaska and Hawaii. We condemn the Republican Administration for its utter disregard of the rights to statehood of both Alaska and Hawaii. These territories have contributed greatly to our national economic and cultural life and are vital to our defense. They are part of America and should be recognized as such. We of the Democratic Party, therefore, pledge immediate Statehood for these two territories. We commend these territories for the action their people have taken in the adoption of constitutions which will become effective forthwith when they are admitted into the Union.

Puerto Rico. The Democratic Party views with satisfaction the progress and growth achieved by

Puerto Rico since its political organization as a Commonwealth under Democratic Party leadership. We pledge, once again, our continued support of the Commonwealth and its development and growth along lines of increasing responsibility and authority, keeping as functions of the Federal Government only such as are essential to the existence of the compact of association adopted by the Congress of the United States and the people of Puerto Rico.

The progress of Puerto Rico under Commonwealth status has been notable proof of the great benefits which flow from self-government and the good neighbor policy which under Democratic leadership this country has always followed.

Virgin Islands. We favor increased self-government for the Virgin Islands to provide for an elected Governor and a Resident Commissioner in the Congress of the United States. We denounce the scandalous administration of the first Eisenhower-appointed Governor of the Virgin Islands.

Other Territories and Possessions. We favor increased self-government for Guam, other outlying territories and the Trust Territory of the Pacific.

District of Columbia. We favor immediate home rule and ultimate national representation for the District of Columbia.

American Indians. Recognizing that all American Indians are citizens of the United States and of the States in which they reside, and acknowledging that the Federal Government has a unique legal and moral responsibility for Indians which is imposed by the Constitution and spelled out in treaties, statutes and court decisions, we pledge:

Prompt adoption of a Federal program to assist Indian tribes in the full development of their human and natural resources, and to advance the health, education and economic well-being of Indian citizens, preserving their traditions without impairing their cultural heritage;

No alteration of any treaty or other Federal-Indian contractual relationships without the free consent of the Indian tribes concerned; reversal of the present policies which are tending toward erosion of Indian rights, reduction of their economic base through alienation of their lands, and repudiation of Federal responsibility;

Prompt and expeditious settlement of Indian claims against the United States, with full recognition of the rights of both parties; and

Elimination of all impediments to full citizenship for American Indians.

Governmental Balance. The Democratic Party has upheld its belief in the Constitution as a charter of individual rights, an effective instrument for human progress. Democratic Administrations placed upon the statute books during their last 20 years a multitude of measures which testify to our belief in the Jeffersonian principle of local control even in general legislation involving Nation-wide programs. Selective Service, Social Security, agricultural adjustment, low-rent housing, hospital, and many other legislative programs have placed major responsibilities in States and counties, and provide fine examples of how benefits can be extended through Federal-State cooperation.

While we recognize the existence of honest differences of opinion as to the true location of the Constitutional line of demarcation between the Federal Government and the States, the Democratic Party expressly recognizes the vital importance of the respective States in our Federal Union. The Party of Jefferson and Jackson pledges itself to continued support of those sound principles of local government which will best serve the welfare of our people and the safety of our democratic rights.

Improving Congressional Procedures. In order that the will of the American people may be expressed upon all legislative proposals, we urge that action be taken at the beginning of the 85th Congress to improve Congressional procedures so that majority rule prevails and decisions can be made after reasonable debate without being blocked by a minority in either House.

IX. NATURAL RESOURCES

Our national economic strength and welfare depend primarily upon the development of our land, water, mineral and energy resources, with which this Nation has been abundantly blessed.

We pledge unstinting support to a full and integrated program of development, protection, management and conservation of all of our natural resources for all of the people.

The framework of time-tested conservation and mining policy is fixed in laws under which America has developed its natural resources for the general welfare.

The Democratic 84th Congress has remained steadfast to this traditional policy. It has built upon the tremendous conservation and development achievements of the Roosevelt and Truman Administrations by undertaking the greatest program of natural resources development ever assumed by any Congress in our Nation's history.

This constructive Democratic record, embracing all resources of land, water, energy and minerals, is in sharp contrast to the faithless performance of the Eisenhower Administration which has despoiled future generations of their heritage by utter failure to safeguard natural resources. Our people will long remember this betrayal of their heritage as symbolized by the infamous Dixon-Yates contract; the Al Sarena timber scheme; the low-level Hells Canyon Dams; and for its unreasonable resistance to authorizing the Niagara Project which would benefit so many millions in the State of New York and adjacent areas.

We condemn, and will continue to decry, this pillaging of our dwindling natural resource wealth through political manipulation and administrative subversion by the Eisenhower Administration. We pledge ourselves to halt this betrayal of the people's trust.

We shall devise for the American people a dynamic, far-reaching and progressive conservation program.

The Democratic Party proposes, and will strive to secure, this comprehensive resources program for America's future.

Land. Our land will be preserved and improved for the present and future needs of our people, and not wastefully exploited to benefit special-interest groups.

Soil Conservation. In contrast to the wasteful neglect of the present Administration, soil conservation practices will be stimulated and intensified to reduce land deterioration under the vital Soil Conservation Service assistance program conceived and fostered by the Democratic Party.

National Parks, Recreation and Wildlife. We pledge adoption of an immediate and broad policy to mobilize the efforts of private and public agencies for protection of existing recreational areas, provision of new ones, and improvement of inadequate facilities. Slum conditions fostered by Republican neglect are intolerable to the tens of millions of Americans using our national parks and forests. Democratic Administration will end this shocking situation.

Fish and game habitats will be guarded against encroachment for commercial purposes. All river basin development plans will take into full consideration their effect upon fish, wildlife, national park and wilderness areas. The Fish and Wildlife Service must and will be returned to the career status from which it was removed by the political patronage policy of the present Administration.

Recreational facilities for the millions of field and stream sportsmen of America will be conserved and expanded.

Forest and Grazing Lands. Timber on Federal commercial forest lands will be harvested and managed on a sustained-yield basis.

We propose to increase forest access roads in order to improve cutting practices on both public and private lands.

Private owners of farm, forest and range lands need and must have financial and technical assistance so that all lands will be utilized to contribute more fully to the national welfare by production of food and fiber and protection of our watersheds. Any effort to transform grazing permits from a revocable license to a vested right will be rejected.

We will vigorously advocate Federally-financed forestation, upstream erosion control and flood control programs on our public range, timber lands and small drainage basins to protect our watersheds and double the rate of forage and commercial timber growth. We will promote cooperative programs with Government assistance to reduce timber losses from fire, insects, and disease.

Prospecting and mining on unreserved Federal lands will be encouraged, but surface areas not needed in mining will be safeguarded by appropriate legislation.

Water. We pledge the resumption of rapid and orderly multiple-purpose river basin development throughout the country. This program will bring into reality the full potential benefits of flood control, irrigation and our domestic and municipal water supply from surface and underground waters. It will also materially aid low-cost power, navigation, recreation, fish and wildlife propagation and mineral development. We pledge our aid to the growing requirements of the semiarid Western States for an adequate water supply to meet the vital domestic, irrigation and industrial needs of the rapidly growing urban centers. Enhanced regional economies will strengthen the economy of the Nation as a whole.

We will take appropriate and vigorous steps to prevent comprehensive drainage basin development plans from being fragmented by single-purpose projects. The conservation of water is essential to the life of the Nation. The Democratic Party pledges itself to conservation of water in the public interest.

The Democratic 84th Congress has taken a long step toward reducing the pollution of our rivers and streams. We pledge continuation and expansion of this program, vital to every citizen.

The program of obtaining a large new source of fresh water supply from salt water was begun by the Democratic Party, but has been allowed to lapse by the Eisenhower Republican Administration. It will be resumed and accelerated.

Energy. We pledge ourselves to carry forward, under national policy, aggressive programs to provide abundant supplies of low-cost energy, including continued research for the development of synthetic liquid fuel from coal, shale and agricultural products. These we must have to feed our insatiable industrial economy, to enable our workers to develop their skills and increase their productivity, to provide more jobs at higher wages, to meet the ever-mounting demands for domestic and farm uses, including the production of lower-cost farm fertilizers and lower-cost power to consumers.

We will carry forward increased and full production of hydroelectric power on our rivers and of steam generation for the Tennessee Valley Authority to meet its peacetime and defense requirements. Such self-liquidating projects must go forward in a rapid and orderly manner, with appropriate financing plans. Integrated regional transmission systems will enhance exchange of power and encourage diversified industrial development.

We shall once more rigorously enforce the anti-monopoly and public body preference clauses, including the Holding Company Act, administratively circumvented by the Eisenhower Republican Administration. We shall preserve and strengthen the public power competitive yard-stick in power developments under TVA, REA, Bureau of Reclamation, Bonneville, Southeast and Southwest Power Administrations and other future projects, including atomic power plants, under a policy of the widest possible use of electric energy at the lowest possible cost.

Minerals. The Republican Administration has seriously neglected and ignored one of the Nation's basic industries, metal mining. We recognize that a healthy mining industry is essential to the economy of the Nation, and therefore pledge immediate efforts toward the establishment of a realistic, long-range minerals policy. The Nation's minerals and fuels are essential to the safety, security and development of our country. We pledge the adoption of policies which will further encourage the exploration and development of additional reserves of our mineral resources.

Domestic Fisheries. We will undertake comprehensive scientific and economic research programs for the conservation and better utilization of, and new markets for, fishery products. We favor and will encourage reciprocal world trade in fish products.

We pledge ourselves to a public works and water policy providing adequate protection for domestic fishery resources.

We favor treaties with other nations for conservation and better utilization of international fisheries.

Scenic Resources. To the end that the scenic beauty of our land may be preserved and maintained for this and future generations to enjoy, we pledge accelerated support of educational programs to stimulate individual responsibility and pride in clean, attractive surroundings—from big cities to rural areas.

X. Atomic Energy

The atomic era came into being and was developed under Democratic Administrations.

The genius of American scientists, engineers and workmen, supported by the vision and courage of Franklin D. Roosevelt, made possible the splitting of the atom and the development of the first atomic bomb in time to end World War II.

With the ending of the war, the supremacy of America in atomic weapons was maintained under the leadership of President Truman, and the United States pushed ahead vigorously toward utilizing this new form of energy in peaceful pursuits, particularly in the fields of medicine, agriculture and industry. By the end of the Truman Administration, the pre-eminence of the United States in the nuclear field was clearly established, and we were on the threshold of large-scale development of industrial nuclear energy at home and as an instrument of world peace.

The Eisenhower Administration promptly reversed the field and plunged the previously independent and nonpartisan Atomic Energy Commission into partisan politics. For example, President Eisenhower ordered the Commission to sign the scandalous Dixon-Yates contract. He was later forced to repudiate the same contract, after the exposure of the illegal activities of one of his own consultants with a secret office in the Bureau of the Budget.

The Republican Administration has followed the same pattern in the field of atomic energy that it has pursued in its treatment of other natural resources—lofty words, little action, but steady service to selfish interests. While the AEC and the special private interests consult and confer, the United States is lagging instead of leading in the world race for nuclear power, international prestige and world markets.

The Democrats in Congress believed that the national interest thus became imperiled, and they moved to meet the challenge both at home and abroad. They established a nonpartisan panel of eminent Americans to study the impact of the peaceful atom.

Following the comprehensive report of this panel, the Joint Congressional Committee on Atomic Energy held extensive hearings on bills to accelerate the atomic reactor demonstration program. Though the bills were reported unanimously from committee, the Republican members of Congress, under heavy pressure from the White House, insured the final defeat of this legislation in the Congress.

But the fight to bring nuclear power to the people has only begun. As the United States was first in the development of the atom as a weapon, so the United States must lead in bringing the blessings of the peaceful uses of nuclear energy to mankind.

Hence, the Democratic Party pledges itself:

(1) To restore nonpartisan administration of the vital atomic energy program and to expand and accelerate nuclear development by vigorous action:

(2) To accelerate the domestic civilian atomic power program by the construction of a variety of demonstration prototype reactors;

(3) To give reality—life and meaning—to the "Atoms for Peace" program. We will substitute deeds for words;

(4) To increase the production of fissionable material for use in a stockpile for peacetime commitments at home and abroad, and for an ever-present reserve for weapons to guarantee freedom in the world;

(5) To conduct a comprehensive survey of radiation hazards from bomb tests and reactor operations, in order to determine what additional measures are required to protect existing and future generations from these invisible dangers; and

(6) To make the maximum contribution to the defense of our Nation and the free world through the development of a balanced and flexible stockpile of nuclear weapons, containing a sufficient number and variety to support our armed services in any contingency.

XI. CIVIL RIGHTS

The Democratic Party is committed to support and advance the individual rights and liberties of all Americans. Our country is founded on the proposition that all men are created equal. This means that all citizens are equal before the law and should enjoy all political rights. They should have equal opportunities for education, for economic advancement, and for decent living conditions.

We will continue our efforts to eradicate discrimination based on race, religion or national origin. We know this task requires action, not just in one section of the Nation, but in all sections. It requires the cooperative efforts of individual citizens, and action by State and local governments. It also requires Federal action. The Federal Government must live up to the ideals of the Declaration of Independence and must exercise the powers vested in it by the Constitution.

We are proud of the record of the Democratic Party in securing equality of treatment and opportunity in the nation's armed forces, the Civil

Service, and in all areas under Federal jurisdiction. The Democratic Party pledges itself to continue its efforts to eliminate illegal discriminations of all kinds, in relation to (1) full rights to vote, (2) full rights to engage in gainful occupations, (3) full rights to enjoy security of the person, and (4) full rights to education in all publicly supported institutions.

Recent decisions of the Supreme Court of the United States relating to segregation in publicly supported schools and elsewhere have brought consequences of vast importance to our Nation as a whole and especially to communities directly affected. We reject all proposals for the use of force to interfere with the orderly determination of these matters by the courts.

The Democratic Party emphatically reaffirms its support of the historic principle that ours is a government of laws and not of men; it recognizes the Supreme Court of the United States as one of the three Constitutional and coordinate branches of the Federal Government, superior to and separate from any political party, the decisions of which are part of the law of the land. We condemn the efforts of the Republican Party to make it appear that this tribunal is a part of the Republican Party.

We condemn the Republican Administration's violation of the rights of Government employees by a heartless and unjustified confusing of "security" and "loyalty" for the sole purpose of political gain and regardless of consequences to individual victims and to the good name of the United States. We condemn the Republican Administration's misrepresentation of facts and violation of individual rights in a wicked and unprincipled attempt to degrade and destroy the Democratic Party, and to make political capital for the Republican Party.

Prohibition Party Platform for 1956

PREAMBLE

We, the representatives of the Prohibition Party, assembled in National Convention at Camp Mack, Milford, Indiana, September 4, 5, and 6, 1955, recognizing Almighty God as the source of all just government and with faith in the teachings of the Prince of Peace, do solemnly promise that, if our party is chosen to administer the affairs of the nation, we will carefully use all the powers of our administration to preserve the rights, privileges and basic freedoms of the people of the United States.

CONSTITUTIONAL GOVERNMENT

We solemnly affirm our loyalty to the Constitution of the United States, to the principles of liberty enunciated in our Declaration of Independence and in the Preamble and Bill of Rights of our Constitution, our deep confidence in our form of government, and our earnest desire to serve our people with a constructive program based upon the principles of righteousness and democracy.

We are unalterably opposed to any form of totalitarianism. We challenge all loyal citizens to work against this menace to civilization. We believe that the best safeguard against these dangerous doctrines is to preserve the rights of our citizens by enforcing the provisions of the Constitution and the Bill of Rights.

We deplore the actions of any administration in exceeding its authority, through executive agreements, thereby violating the Constitutional prerogatives of our legislative bodies.

WORLD PEACE

We, in this age of atomic and hydrogen bombs (capable of destroying civilization) pledge ourselves to search for peaceful solutions of international conflicts, under an international "good neighbor" policy, call for an immediate outlawing of all weapons of annihilation, propose a progressive multi-lateral limitation of armaments and their ultimate abolition, leading to world peace and the brotherhood of man.

MILITARISM

We are opposed to the militarization of our youth, through universal military training, universal conscription, or universal reserve service.

ECONOMIC AID

Our government should give much greater emphasis to relief, rehabilitation and economic aid, especially for technical assistance, to help the people raise their own standard of living in the underdeveloped areas where widespread hunger and human misery now prepare the soil for communist propaganda.

Economy of Abundance

We pledge ourselves as opposed to the continuation of the wastage of God-given abundance, created through science, technology and the genius and labors of our people, and declare our purpose to search for means to distribute justly such abundance, as provided under our Constitution, "to promote the general welfare."

Governmental Economy

Extravagant spending has set an example of wasteful government operations. We believe it is unjust for any government to take nearly one-third of the total income of its citizens to pay the expense of government. We believe that government ought not to do for our people what they can do for themselves. We promise to reorganize the federal government, abolishing all departments and bureaus that cannot qualify when measured by this principle.

Taxes

The constant increase in taxation is approaching the point of confiscation and economic bankruptcy. With proper economy, governmental costs will be lowered, making it possible to reduce the public debt and lighten the tax load for the average citizen.

Economic Freedom

We oppose any trend toward excessive concentration of power over our economic life, whether it takes the form of unnecessary regulation by government or monopolistic control by private industry.

Co-operatives

Co-operatives and profit-sharing enterprises are a natural outgrowth of democracy. Government under our administration will encourage such enterprises.

Labor and Industry

Labor organizations are entitled to great credit for improving the status of the workers and for their constructive contributions to the general welfare. It is our purpose to give the public welfare paramount consideration. Neither capital nor labor can be permitted to dominate at the expense of the other or of the common good. We favor the compulsory arbitration of labor disputes where the public welfare is endangered.

Agriculture

We vehemently protest against the immoral policy of creating artificial scarcity by wasting or destroying farm products amid widespread hunger and want. We believe that this policy can and should be replaced by a plan which will assure every working farmer and his family an adequate income while maintaining abundant production and making it available to meet the world's needs.

Social Security and Old Age Pensions

We endorse the principle of social security, old age pensions, and unemployment compensation, including all employed groups. We deplore the abuse of its privileges, the maladministration of its provisions for political ends, and pledge ourselves to correct these evils. We propose to administer these programs in such a way as to preserve the incentives of initiative and thrift.

Money

The Constitution provides that Congress shall have the power to "coin money" and "regulate the value thereof." This is a sound and feasible monetary policy which we promise to re-establish and enforce.

Religious Liberty

We believe in religious liberty. By religious liberty we mean the freedom of individual worship and fellowship, and the right to evangelize, educate, and establish religious institutions. When religious liberty is lost political liberty perishes with it.

Separation of Church and State

We reaffirm our loyalty to the Constitutional principle of separation of Church and State, and will expose, and resist vigorously, any attempt from whatever source to weaken or subvert this fundamental principle.

Public Morality and Law Enforcement

Moral and spiritual considerations must be primary factors in determining national policies. We will strengthen and enforce laws against gambling, narcotics, and commercialized vice, now so widely violated and nullified by the political parties in power, and thus prevent further disintegration of the public morals.

We oppose the present nullification of law by non-enforcement and will maintain the integrity of democracy by enforcing the Constitution and the laws enacted under it.

Honesty in Government

There is a law of cause and effect which rules in the affairs of men. With the repeal of the Eighteenth Amendment there has come a rapid decline in the moral standards of the nation, culminating in shocking revelations of crime and political corruption. We pledge ourselves to break this unholy alliance between organized crime and those in positions of trust in the government at all levels.

No Racial Discrimination

Recognizing that "God hath created of one blood all nations to dwell upon the face of the earth," we declare in favor of full justice and equal opportunity for all people, regardless of race, creed, or national origin.

Marriage and Divorce

We favor the enactment of uniform marriage and divorce laws as a help toward maintaining the sanctity of the home.

Ballot Law Reform

We demand the repeal of the many state ballot laws which have been enacted to make the two-party system a bipartisan political monopoly by keeping minor parties off the ballot, thus denying to independent voters and minority groups the fundamental right of free political expression.

Extension of Democracy

To help perfect our political democracy and extend it to all who live under our flag we urge:

(1) The submission to the people of an amendment to the Constitution to provide for the election of the President and Vice-President directly by the people;

(2) Immediate home rule and the franchise and representation in Congress for the District of Columbia;

(3) Immediate statehood for Alaska and Hawaii;

(4) Encouraging Puerto Rico, the Virgin Islands, Guam and Samoa to advance as rapidly as possible to complete internal self-government.

(5) We recognize the right of all Indians to full citizenship.

The Alcohol Problem

The widespread and increasing use of alcoholic beverages since Repeal is one of the major causes of accidents, insanity, wasted manpower, poverty, broken homes, juvenile delinquency, vice, crime and political corruption.

The highly capitalized, strongly organized and socially irresponsible liquor industry out of its enormous profits, spends huge sums in promoting liquor sales by every possible means, to create a growing habitual use by youth and adults.

Both through its financial and organizational connections and through the effects of its product in weakening moral resistance, the liquor power is linked with, and supports, a nation-wide network of organized gambling, vice and crime. This power dominates our politics and government. Through its advertising it has corrupted large sections of the nation's press, and it is increasingly extending its control to radio and television.

All these social effects of the liquor industry make the beverage alcohol problem one which concerns the whole nation, and requires immediate action looking toward a solution.

Our program includes removing the cause for drinking by:

(1) Raising the economic standards of the country as outlined in this platform;

(2) Increasing psychiatric aid to treat alcoholics and help others in need of counselling;

(3) Developing community recreational programs to provide a wholesome alternative to the tavern;

(4) Publicizing scientific facts about beverage alcohol through the press, motion pictures, radio, television, the public schools and other media; and

(5) A program of publicity, education, legislation and administration leading to the elimination of the alcoholic beverage industry.

The Prohibition Party demands the repeal of all laws that legalize the liquor traffic and the enactment and enforcement of new laws which prohibit the manufacture, distribution and sale of alcoholic beverages.

An administration pledged to the above program is essential for effective steps toward solving this important problem.

CONCLUSION

What is needed is a re-alignment of voters and the union of good citizens in a party which will support only candidates of unquestioned integrity and competence, who will faithfully serve the commonwealth and set a good example of public and private morality, and who are committed to the principles of this platform.

We urge all who believe in these principles to vote their convictions and help us achieve a clean, honest and humane government "of the people, by the people, and for the people," under God.

Republican Platform 1956

DECLARATION OF FAITH

America's trust is in the merciful providence of God, in whose image every man is created . . . the source of every man's dignity and freedom.

In this trust our Republic was founded. We give devoted homage to the Founding Fathers. They not only proclaimed that the freedom and rights of men came from the Creator and not from the State, but they provided safeguards to those freedoms.

Our Government was created by the people for all the people, and it must serve no less a purpose.

The Republican Party was formed 100 years ago to preserve the Nation's devotion to these ideals.

On its Centennial, the Republican Party again calls to the minds of all Americans the great truth first spoken by Abraham Lincoln: "The legitimate object of Government is to do for a community of people whatever they need to have done but cannot do at all, or cannot so well do, for themselves in their separate and individual capacities. But in all that people can individually do as well for themselves, Government ought not to interfere."

Our great President Dwight D. Eisenhower has counseled us further: "In all those things which deal with people, be liberal, be human. In all those things which deal with people's money, or their economy, or their form of government, be conservative."

While jealously guarding the free institutions and preserving the principles upon which our Republic was founded and has flourished, the purpose of the Republican Party is to establish and maintain a peaceful world and build at home a dynamic prosperity in which every citizen fairly shares.

We shall ever build anew, that our children and their children, without distinction because of race, creed or color, may know the blessings of our free land.

We believe that basic to governmental integrity are unimpeachable ethical standards and irreproachable personal conduct by all people in government. We shall continue our insistence on honesty as an indispensable requirement of public service. We shall continue to root out corruption whenever and wherever it appears.

We are proud of and shall continue our far-reaching and sound advances in matters of basic human needs — expansion of social security — broadened coverage in unemployment insurance —improved housing—and better health protection for all our people. We are determined that our government remain warmly responsive to the urgent social and economic problems of our people.

To these beliefs we commit ourselves as we present this record and declare our goals for the future.

Nearly four years ago when the people of this Nation entrusted their Government to President Eisenhower and the Republican Party, we were locked in a costly and stalemated war. Now we have an honorable peace, which has stopped the bitter toll in casualties and resources, ended depressing wartime restraints, curbed the runaway inflation and unleashed the boundless energy of our people to forge forward on the road to progress.

In four years we have achieved the highest economic level with the most widely shared benefits that the world has ever seen. We of the Republican Party have fostered this prosperity and are dedicated to its expansion and to the preservation of the climate in which it has thrived.

We are proud of our part in bringing into a position of unique authority in the world one who symbolizes, as can no other man, the hopes of all peoples for peace, liberty and justice. One leader in the world today towers above all others and inspires the trust, admiration, confidence and good will of all the peoples of every nation— Dwight D. Eisenhower. Under his leadership, the Republican Administration has carried out foreign policies which have enabled our people to enjoy in peace the blessings of liberty. We shall continue to work unceasingly for a just and enduring peace in a world freed of tyranny.

Every honorable means at our command has been exercised to alleviate the grievances and causes of armed conflict among nations. The advance of Communism and its enslavement of people has been checked, and, at key points, thrown back. Austria, Iran and Guatemala have been liberated from Kremlin control. Forces of freedom are at work in the nations still enslaved by Communist imperialism.

We firmly believe in the right of peoples everywhere to determine their form of government, their leaders, their destiny, in peace. Where needed, in order to promote peace and freedom throughout the world, we shall within the prudent limits of our resources, assist friendly countries in their determined efforts to strengthen their economies.

We hold high hopes for useful service to mankind in the power of the atom. We shall generously assist the International Atomic Energy Agency, now evolving from President Eisenhower's "Atoms for Peace" proposal, in an effort to find ways to dedicate man's genius not to his death, but to his life.

We maintain that no treaty or international agreement can deprive any of our citizens of Constitutional rights. We shall see to it that no treaty or agreement with other countries attempts to deprive our citizens of the rights guaranteed them by the Federal Constitution.

President Eisenhower has given the world bold proposals for mutual arms reduction and protection against aggression through flying sentinels in an "open sky."

We support this and his further offer of United States participation in an international fund for economic development financed from the savings brought by true disarmament. We approve his determined resistance to disarmament without effective inspection.

We work and pray for the day when the domination of any people from any source will have ended, and when there will be liberation and true freedom for the hundreds of millions of individuals now held in subjugation. We shall continue to dedicate our best efforts to this lofty purpose.

We shall continue vigorously to support the United Nations.

We shall continue to oppose the seating of Communist China in the United Nations.

We shall maintain our powerful military strength as a deterrent to aggression and as a guardian of the peace. We shall maintain it ready, balanced and technologically advanced for these objectives only.

Good times in America have reached a breadth and depth never before known by any nation. Moreover, it is a prosperity of a nation at peace, not at war. We shall continue to encourage the good business and sound employee relationships which have made possible for the first time in our history a productive capacity of more than $400 billion a year. Nearly 67 million people have full-time jobs, with real wages and personal income at record highs.

The farmers of America are at last able to look to the future with a confidence based on expanding peacetime markets instead of on politically contrived formulas foredoomed to fail except in a wartime economy. The objective is to insure that agriculture shares fairly and fully in our record prosperity without needless Federal meddlings and domination.

Restoration of integrity in government has been an essential element to the achievement of our unparalleled good times. We will faithfully preserve the sound financial management which already has reduced annual spending $14 billion below the budgets planned by our Democratic predecessors and made possible in 1954 a $7.4-billion tax cut, the largest one-year tax reduction in history.

We will ever fight the demoralizing influence of inflation as a national way of life. We are proud to have fulfilled our 1952 pledge to halt the skyrocketing cost of living that in the previous 13 years had cut the value of the dollar by half, and robbed millions of the full value of their wages, savings, insurance, pensions and social security.

We have balanced the budget. We believe

and will continue to prove that thrift, prudence and a sensible respect for living within income applies as surely to the management of our Government's budget as it does to the family budget.

We hold that the major world issue today is whether Government shall be the servant or the master of men. We hold that the Bill of Rights is the sacred foundation of personal liberty. That men are created equal needs no affirmation, but they must have equality of opportunity and protection of their civil rights under the law.

We hold that the strict division of powers and the primary responsibility of State and local governments must be maintained, and that the centralization of powers in the national Government leads to expansion of the mastery of our lives.

We hold that the protection of the freedom of men requires that budgets be balanced, waste in government eliminated, and taxes reduced.

In these and all other areas of proper Government concern, we pledge our best thought and whole energy to a continuation of our prized peace, prosperity and progress.

For our guidance in fulfilling this responsibility, President Eisenhower has given us a statement of principles that is neither partisan nor prejudiced, but warmly American:

The individual is of supreme importance.

The spirit of our people is the strength of our nation.

America does not prosper unless all Americans prosper.

Government must have a heart as well as a head.

Courage in principle, cooperation in practice make freedom positive.

To stay free, we must stay strong.

Under God, we espouse the cause of freedom and justice and peace for all peoples.

Embracing these guides to positive, constructive action, and in their rich spirit, we ask the support of the American people for the election of a Republican Congress and the re-election of the Nation's devoted and dedicated leader — Dwight D. Eisenhower.

DECLARATION OF DETERMINATION

In the interest of complete public understanding, elaboration of Republican aspirations and achievements is desirable in the areas of broadest public concern.

DYNAMIC ECONOMY—FREE LABOR

TAXATION AND FISCAL POLICY

The Republican Party takes pride in calling attention to the outstanding fiscal achievements of the Eisenhower Administration, several of which are mentioned in the foreword to these resolutions.

In order to progress further in correcting the unfortunate results of unwise financial management during 20 years of Democrat Administrations, we pledge to pursue the following objectives:

Further reductions in Government spending as recommended in the Hoover Commission Report, without weakening the support of a superior defense program or depreciating the quality of essential services of government to our people.

Continued balancing of the budget, to assure the financial strength of the country which is so vital to the struggle of the free world in its battle against Communism; and to maintain the purchasing power of a sound dollar, and the value of savings, pensions and insurance.

Gradual reduction of the national debt.

Then, insofar as consistent with a balanced budget, we pledge to work toward these additional objectives:

Further reductions in taxes with particular consideration for low and middle income families.

Initiation of a sound policy of tax reductions which will encourage small independent businesses to modernize and progress.

Continual study of additional ways to correct inequities in the effect of various taxes.

Consistent with the Republican Administration's accomplishment in stemming the inflation —which under five Democrat Administrations had cut the value of the dollar in half, and so had robbed the wage earner and millions of thrifty citizens who had savings, pensions and insurance—we endorse the present policy of freedom for the Federal Reserve System to combat both inflation and deflation by wise fiscal policy.

The Republican Party believes that sound money, which retains its buying power, is an essential foundation for new jobs, a higher standard of living, protection of savings, a secure national defense, and the general economic growth of the country.

BUSINESS AND ECONOMIC POLICY

The Republican Party has as a primary concern the continued advancement of the well-being of the individual. This can be attained only in an economy that, as today, is sound, free and creative, ever building new wealth and new jobs for all the people.

We believe in good business for all business—small, medium and large. We believe that competition in a free economy opens unrivaled opportunity and brings the greatest good to the greatest number.

The sound economic policies of the Eisenhower Administration have created an atmosphere of confidence in which good businesses flourish and can plan for growth to create new job opportunities for our expanding population.

We have eliminated a host of needless controls.

To meet the immense demands of our expanding economy, we have initiated the largest highway, air and maritime programs in history, each soundly financed.

We shall continue to advocate the maintenance and expansion of a strong, efficient, privately-owned and operated and soundly financed system of transportation that will serve all of the needs of our Nation under Federal regulatory policies that will enable each carrier to realize its inherent economic advantages and its full competitive capabilities.

We recognize the United States' world leadership in aviation, and we shall continue to encourage its technical development and vigorous expansion. Our goal is to support and sponsor air services and to make available to our citizens the safest and most comprehensive air transportation. We favor adequate funds and expeditious action in improving air safety, and highest efficiency in the control of air traffic.

We stand for forward-looking programs, created to replace our war-built merchant fleet with the most advanced types in design, with increased speed. Adaptation of new propulsion power units, including nuclear, must be sponsored and achieved.

We should proceed with the prompt construction of the Atomic Powered Peace Ship in order that we may demonstrate to the world, in this as in other fields, the peaceful uses of the atom.

Our steadily rising prosperity is constantly reflecting the confidence of our citizens in the policies of our Republican Administration.

SMALL BUSINESS

We pledge the continuation and improvement of our drive to aid small business. Every constructive potential avenue of improvement—both legislative and executive—has been explored in our search for ways in which to widen opportunities for this important segment of America's economy.

Beginning with our creation of the very successful Small Business Administration, and continuing through the recently completed studies and recommendations of the Cabinet Committee on Small Business, which we strongly endorse, we have focused our attention on positive measures to help small businesses get started and grow.

Small Business can look forward to expanded participation in federal procurement—valuable financing and technical aids—a continuously vigorous enforcement of anti-trust laws—important cuts in the burdens of paper work, and certain tax reductions as budgetary requirements permit.

Small business now is receiving approximately one-third, dollarwise, of all Defense contracts. We recommend a further review of procurement procedures for all defense departments and agencies with a view to facilitating and extending such participation for the further benefit of Small Business.

We favor loans at reasonable rates of interest to small businesses which have records of permanency but who are in temporary need and which are unable to obtain credit in commercial channels. We recommend an extension at the earliest opportunity of the Small Business Administration which is now scheduled to expire in mid 1957.

We also propose:

Additional technical research in problems of development and distribution for the benefit of small business;

Legislation to enable closer Federal scrutiny of mergers which have a significant or potential monopolistic connotations;

Procedural changes in the antitrust laws to facilitate their enforcement;

Simplification of wage reporting by employers for purposes of social security records and income tax withholding;

Continuance of the vigorous SEC policies which are providing maximum protection to the investor and maximum opportunity for the financing of small business without costly red tape.

LABOR

Under the Republican Administration, as our country has prospered, so have its people. This is as it should be, for as President Eisenhower said: "Labor is the United States. The men and women, who with their minds, their hearts and hands, create the wealth that is shared in this country—they are America."

The Eisenhower Administration has brought to our people the highest employment, the highest wages and the highest standard of living ever enjoyed by any nation. Today there are nearly 67 million men and women at work in the United States, 4 million more than in 1952. Wages have increased substantially over the past 3½ years; but, more important, the American wage earner today can buy more than ever before for himself and his family because his pay check has not been eaten away by rising taxes and soaring prices.

The record of performance of the Republican Administration on behalf of our working men and women goes still further. The Federal minimum wage has been raised for more than 2 million workers. Social Security has been extended to an additional 10 million workers and the benefits raised for 6½ million. The protection of unemployment insurance has been brought to 4 million additional workers. There have been increased workmen's compensation benefits for longshoremen and harbor workers, increased retirement benefits for railroad employees, and wage increases and improved welfare and pension plans for federal employees.

In addition, the Eisenhower Administration has enforced more vigorously and effectively than ever before, the laws which protect the working standards of our people.

Workers have benefited by the progress which has been made in carrying out the programs and principles set forth in the 1952 Republican plat-

form. All workers have gained and unions have grown in strength and responsibility, and have increased their membership by 2 millions.

Furthermore, the process of free collective bargaining has been strengthened by the insistence of this Administration that labor and management settle their differences at the bargaining table without the intervention of the Government. This policy has brought to our country an unprecedented period of labor-management peace and understanding.

We applaud the effective, unhindered, collective bargaining which brought an early end to the 1956 steel strike, in contrast to the six months' upheaval, Presidential seizure of the steel industry and ultimate Supreme Court intervention under the last Democrat Administration.

The Eisenhower Administration will continue to fight for dynamic and progressive programs which, among other things, will:

Stimulate improved job safety of our workers, through assistance to the States, employees and employers;

Continue and further perfect its programs of assistance to the millions of workers with special employment problems, such as older workers, handicapped workers, members of minority groups, and migratory workers;

Strengthen and improve the Federal-State Employment Service and improve the effectiveness of the unemployment insurance system;

Protect by law, the assets of employee welfare and benefit plans so that workers who are the beneficiaries can be assured of their rightful benefits;

Assure equal pay for equal work regardless of sex;

Clarify and strengthen the eight-hour laws for the benefit of workers who are subject to federal wage standards on Federal and Federally-assisted construction, and maintain and continue the vigorous administration of the Federal prevailing minimum wage law for public supply contracts;

Extend the protection of the Federal minimum wage laws to as many more workers as is possible and practicable;

Continue to fight for the elimination of discrimination in employment because of race, creed, color, national origin, ancestry or sex;

Provide assistance to improve the economic

conditions of areas faced with persistent and substantial unemployment;

Revise and improve the Taft-Hartley Act so as to protect more effectively the rights of labor unions, management, the individual worker, and the public. The protection of the right of workers to organize into unions and to bargain collectively is the firm and permanent policy of the Eisenhower Administration. In 1954, 1955 and again in 1956, President Eisenhower recommended constructive amendments to this Act. The Democrats in Congress have consistently blocked these needed changes by parliamentary maneuvers. The Republican Party pledges itself to overhaul and improve the Taft-Hartley Act along the lines of these recommendations.

HUMAN WELFARE AND ADVANCEMENT

HEALTH, EDUCATION AND WELFARE

The Republican Party believes that the physical, mental, and spiritual well-being of the people is as important as their economic health. It will continue to support this conviction with vigorous action.

Republican action created the Department of Health, Education and Welfare as the first new Federal department in 40 years, to raise the continuing consideration of these problems for the first time to the highest council of Government, the President's Cabinet.

Through the White House Conference on Education, our Republican Administration initiated the most comprehensive Community-State-Federal attempt ever made to solve the pressing problems of primary and secondary education.

Four thousand communities, studying their school populations and their physical and financial resources, encouraged our Republican Administration to urge a five-year program of Federal assistance in building schools to relieve a critical classroom shortage.

The Republican Party will renew its efforts to enact a program based on sound principles of need and designed to encourage increased state and local efforts to build more classrooms.

Our Administration also proposed for the first time in history, a thorough nation-wide analysis of rapidly growing problems in education beyond the high schools.

The Republican Party is determined to press all such actions that will help insure that every child has the educational opportunity to advance to his own greatest capacity.

We have fully resolved to continue our steady gains in man's unending struggle against disease and disability.

We have supported the distribution of free vaccine to protect millions of children against dreaded polio.

Republican leadership has enlarged Federal assistance for construction of hospitals, emphasizing low-cost care of chronic diseases and the special problems of older persons, and increased Federal aid for medical care of the needy.

We have asked the largest increase in research funds ever sought in one year to intensify attacks on cancer, mental illness, heart disease and other dread diseases.

We demand once again, despite the reluctance of the Democrat 84th Congress, Federal assistance to help build facilities to train more physicians and scientists.

We have encouraged a notable expansion and improvement of voluntary health insurance, and urge that reinsurance and pooling arrangements be authorized to speed this progress.

We have strengthened the Food and Drug Administration, and we have increased the vocational rehabilitation program to enable a larger number of the disabled to return to satisfying activity.

We have supported measures that have made more housing available than ever before in history, reduced urban slums in local-federal partnership, stimulated record home ownership, and authorized additional low-rent public housing.

We initiated the first flood insurance program in history under Government sponsorship in cooperation with private enterprise.

We shall continue to seek extension and perfection of a sound social security system.

We pledge close cooperation with State, local and private agencies to reduce the ghastly toll of fatalities on the Nation's highways.

RURAL AMERICA'S RECOVERY—AGRICULTURE

The men and women operating the farms and ranches of America have confidence in President Eisenhower and the Republican farm program. Our farmers have earned the respect and appreciation of our entire nation for their energy, resourcefulness, efficiency, and ability.

Agriculture, our basic industry, must remain free and prosperous. The Republican Party will continue to move boldly to help the farmer obtain his full share of the rewards of good business and good Government. It is committed to a program for agriculture which creates the widest possible markets and highest attainable income for our farm and ranch families. This program must be versatile and flexible to meet effectively the impact of rapidly changing conditions. It does not envision making farmers dependent upon direct governmental payments for their incomes. Our objective is markets which return full parity to our farm and ranch people when they sell their products. There is no simple, easy answer to farm problems. Our approach as ever is a many-sided, versatile and positive program to help all farmers and ranchers.

Farm legislation, developed under the Democrat Administration to stimulate production in wartime, carried a built-in mechanism for the accumulation of price-depressing surpluses in peacetime. Under laws sponsored by the Republican Administration, almost $7 billion in price-depressing surplus farm products have been moved into use, and the rate of movement is being accelerated.

Agriculture is successfully making the transition from wartime to peacetime markets, with less disruption than at any time after a great war. We are gratified by the improvement this year in farm prices and income as a result of our policies.

Our Republican Administration fostered a constructive Soil Bank Program further to reduce surpluses and to permit improvement of our soil, water and timber resources. The Democrat Party tactics of obstruction and delay have prevented our farm families from receiving the full benefits of this program in 1956.

However, by aggressive action, we now have the Soil Bank in operation, and in 3 months, half a million farmers have contracted to shift more than 10 million acres from producing more surpluses to a soil reserve for the future. For this they already have earned $225 million.

This program is a sound aid to removing the burdens of surpluses which Democrat programs placed on farmers. It is now moving into full operation.

Benefits of Social Security have been extended to farm families. Programs of loans and grants for farm families hit by flood and drought have been made operative.

Tax laws were improved to help farmers with respect to livestock, farm equipment, and conservation practices. We initiated action to refund to the farmers $60 million annually in taxes on gasoline used in machinery on the farm.

Cooperation between the U. S. Department of Agriculture, the State Departments of Agriculture and land grant colleges and universities is at an all-time high. This Republican Administration has increased support for agricultural research and education to the highest level in history. New records of assistance to farm and ranch families in soil and water conservation were attained in every year of this Republican Administration.

Convinced that the Government should ever be the farmer's helper, never his master, the Republican Party is pledged:

To establish an effective, new research program, fully and completely implemented to find and vigorously promote new uses for farm crops;

To move our agriculture commodities into use at home and abroad, and to use every appropriate and effective means to improve marketing, so that farmers can produce and sell their products to increase their income and enjoy an improving level of living;

To encourage the improvement of quality in farm products through agricultural research, education and price support differentials, thus increasing market acceptance both at home and abroad;

To further help and cooperate with the several States as co-equals with the federal government to provide needed research, education, service and regulatory programs;

To develop farm programs that are fair to all farmers;

To work toward full freedom instead of toward more regimentation, developing voluntary rather than oppressive farm programs;

To encourage agricultural producers in their efforts to seek solutions to their own production and price problems;

To provide price supports as in the Agricultural Act of 1954 that protect farmers, rather than price their products out of the market;

To continue our commodity loan and marketing agreement programs as effective marketing tools;

To make every effort to develop a more accurate measurement of farm parity;

To safeguard our precious soil and water resources for generations yet unborn;

To encourage voluntary self-supporting federal crop insurance;

To bring sympathetic and understanding relief promptly to farm and ranch families hard hit with problems of drought, flood or other natural disaster, or economic disaster, and to maintain the integrity of these programs by terminating them when the emergency is over;

To assist the young people of American farms and ranches in their development as future farmers and homemakers;

To continue and expand the Republican-sponsored school milk program, to encourage further use of the school lunch program now benefiting 11 million children, and to foster improved nutritional levels;

To provide constructive assistance by effective purchase and donation to ease temporary market surpluses, especially for the producers of perishable farm products;

To give full support to farmer-owned and farmer-operated co-operatives;

To encourage and assist adequate private and cooperative sources of credit, to provide supplemental credit through the Farmers Home Administration where needed, with an understanding of both the human and economic problems of farmers and ranchers;

To expand rural electrification through REA loans for generation and transmission, and to expand rural communication facilities;

To continue the improvement of rural mail delivery to farm families;

To promote fully the Republican-sponsored Rural-Development Program to broaden the operation and increase the income of low income farm families and help tenant farmers;

To work with farmers, ranchers and others to carry forward the Great Plains program to achieve wise use of lands in the area subject to wind erosion, so that the people of this region can enjoy a higher standard of living; and in summation:

To keep agriculture strong, free, attuned to peace and not war, to stand ready with a reserve capacity at all times as a part of our defense, based on sound agricultural economy.

We are an expanding nation. Our needs for farm products will continue to grow. Farm prices are improving and farm income is climbing.

Our farm and ranch people are confident of the future, despite efforts to frighten them into accepting economic nostrums and political panaceas. Record numbers of farms are owned by those who operate them.

The Republican Party is pledged to work for improved farm prices and farm income. We will seek that improvement boldly, in ways that protect the family farm. Our objective is a prosperous, expanding and free agriculture. We are dedicated to creating the opportunity for farmers to earn a high per-family income in a world at peace.

FEDERAL GOVERNMENT INTEGRITY

The Republican Party is wholeheartedly committed to maintaining a Federal Government that is clean, honorable and increasingly efficient. It proudly affirms that it has achieved this kind of Government and dedicated it to the service of all the people.

Our many economic and social advances of the past four years are the result of our faithful adherence to our 1952 pledge to reverse a 20-year Democratic philosophy calling for more and more power in Washington.

We have left no stone unturned to remove from Government the irresponsible and those whose employment was not clearly consistent with national security.

We believe that working for the Government is not a right but a privilege. Based on that principle we will continue a security program to make certain that all people employed by our Government are of unquestioned loyalty and trustworthiness. The Republican Party will, realistically and in conformity with constitutional safeguards for the individual, continue to protect our national security by enforcing our laws fairly, vigorously, and with certainty. We will act through the new division established to this end in the Department of Justice, and by close coordination among the intelligence services.

We promise unwavering vigilance against corruption and waste, and shall continue so to manage the public business as to warrant our people's full confidence in the integrity of their Government.

We condemn illegal lobbying for any cause and improper use of money in political activities, including the use of funds collected by compulsion for political purposes contrary to the personal desires of the individual.

Efficiency and Economy in Government. We pledge to continue our far reaching program for improving the efficiency and the effectiveness of the Federal Government in accordance with the principles set forth in the report of the Hoover Commission.

We are unalterably opposed to unwarranted growth of centralized Federal power. We shall carry forward the worthy effort of the Kestnbaum Commission on Intergovernmental Affairs to clarify Federal relationships and strengthen State and local government.

We shall continue to dispense with Federal activities wrongfully competing with private enterprise, and take other sound measures to reduce the cost of Government.

GOVERNMENTAL AFFAIRS

Postal Service. In the last four years, under direction from President Eisenhower to improve the postal service and reduce costs, we have modernized and revitalized the postal establishment from top to bottom, inside and out. We have undertaken and substantially completed the largest reorganization ever to take place in any unit of business or government:

We have provided more than 1200 badly-needed new post office buildings, and are adding two more every day. We are using the very latest types of industrial equipment where practicable; and, through a program of research and engineering, we are inventing new mechanical and electronic devices to speed the movement of mail by eliminating tedious old-fashioned methods.

We have improved service across the country in hundreds of ways. We have extended city carrier service to millions of new homes in thousands of urban and suburban communities which have grown and spread under the favorable economic conditions brought about by the Eisenhower Administration.

We have re-inspired the morale of our half-million employees through new programs of promotion based on ability, job training and safety,

and through our sponsorship of increased pay and fringe benefits.

We have adopted the most modern methods of transportation, accounting and cost control, and other operating procedures; through them we have saved many millions of dollars a year for the taxpayers while advancing the delivery of billions of letters by a day or more—all this while reducing the enormous deficit of the Department from its all time high of almost three-quarters of a billion dollars in 1952 to less than half that amount in 1955.

We pledge to continue our efforts, blocked by the Democratic leadership of the 84th Congress, for a financially sound, more nearly self-sustaining postal service—with the users of the mails paying a greater share of the costs instead of the taxpayers bearing the burden of huge postal deficits.

We pledge to continue and to complete this vitally needed program of modernization of buildings, equipment, methods and service, so that the American people will receive the kind of mail delivery they deserve—the speediest and best that American ingenuity, technology and modern business management can provide.

Civil Service. We will vigorously promote, as we have in the past, a non-political career service under the merit system which will attract and retain able servants of the people. Many gains in this field, notably pay increases and a host of new benefits, have been achieved in their behalf in less than four years.

The Republican Party will continue to fight for eagerly desired new advances for Government employees, and realistic reappraisement and adjustment of benefits for our retired civil service personnel.

Statehood for Alaska and Hawaii. We pledge immediate statehood for Alaska, recognizing the fact that adequate provision for defense requirements must be made.

We pledge immediate statehood for Hawaii.

Puerto Rico. We shall continue to encourage the Commonwealth of Puerto Rico in its political growth and economic development in accordance with the wishes of its people and the fundamental principle of self-determination.

Indian Affairs. We shall continue to pursue our enlightened policies which are now producing exceptional advances in the long struggle to help the American Indian gain the material and social advantages of his birthright and citizenship, while maintaining to the fullest extent the cultural integrity of the various tribal groups.

We commend the present administration for its progressive programs which have achieved such striking progress in preparing our Indian citizens for participation in normal community life. Health, educational and employment opportunities for Indians have been greatly expanded beyond any previous level, and we favor still further extensions of these programs.

We favor most sympathetic and constructive execution of the Federal trusteeship over Indian affairs, always in full consultation with Indians in the management of their interests and the expansion of their rights of self-government in local and tribal affairs.

We urge the prompt adjudication or settlement of pending Indian claims.

District of Columbia. We favor self-government, national suffrage and representation in the Congress of the United States for residents of the District of Columbia.

Equal Rights. We recommend to Congress the submission of a constitutional amendment providing equal rights for men and women.

EQUAL OPPORTUNITY AND JUSTICE

CIVIL RIGHTS

The Republican Party points to an impressive record of accomplishment in the field of civil rights and commits itself anew to advancing the rights of all our people regardless of race, creed, color or national origin.

In the area of exclusive Federal jurisdiction, more progress has been made in this field under the present Republican Administration than in any similar period in the last 80 years.

The many Negroes who have been appointed to high public positions have played a significant part in the progress of this Administration.

Segregation has been ended in the District of Columbia Government and in the District public facilities including public schools, restaurants, theaters and playgrounds. The Eisenhower Administration has eliminated discrimination in all federal employment.

Great progress has been made in eliminating employment discrimination on the part of those who do business with the Federal Government and secure Federal contracts. This Administration has impartially enforced Federal civil rights statutes, and we pledge that we will continue to do so. We support the enactment of the civil rights program already presented by the President to the Second Session of the 84th Congress.

The regulatory agencies under this Administration have moved vigorously to end discrimination in interstate commerce. Segregation in the active Armed Forces of the United States has been ended. For the first time in our history there is no segregation in veterans' hospitals and among civilians on naval bases. This is an impressive record. We pledge ourselves to continued progress in this field.

The Republican Party has unequivocally recognized that the supreme law of the land is embodied in the Constitution, which guarantees to all people the blessings of liberty, due process and equal protection of the laws. It confers upon all native-born and naturalized citizens not only citizenship in the State where the individual resides but citizenship of the United States as well. This is an unqualified right, regardless of race, creed or color.

The Republican Party accepts the decision of the U. S. Supreme Court that racial discrimination in publicly supported schools must be progressively eliminated. We concur in the conclusion of the Supreme Court that its decision directing school desegregation should be accomplished with "all deliberate speed" locally through Federal District Courts. The implementation order of the Supreme Court recognizes the complex and acutely emotional problems created by its decision in certain sections of our country where racial patterns have been developed in accordance with prior and longstanding decisions of the same tribunal.

We believe that true progress can be attained through intelligent study, understanding, education and good will. Use of force or violence by any group or agency will tend only to worsen the many problems inherent in the situation. This progress must be encouraged and the work of the courts supported in every legal manner by all branches of the Federal Government to the end that the constitutional ideal of equality before the law, regardless of race, creed or color, will be steadily achieved.

IMMIGRATION

The Republican Party supports an immigration policy which is in keeping with the traditions of America in providing a haven for oppressed peoples, and which is based on equality of treatment, freedom from implications of discrimination between racial, nationality and religious groups, and flexible enough to conform to changing needs and conditions.

We believe that such a policy serves our self-interest, reflects our responsibility for world leadership and develops maximum cooperation with other nations in resolving problems in this area.

We support the President's program submitted to the 84th Congress to carry out needed modifications in existing law and to take such further steps as may be necessary to carry out our traditional policy.

In that concept, this Republican Administration sponsored the Refugee Relief Act to provide asylum for thousands of refugees, expellees and displaced persons, and undertook in the face of Democrat opposition to correct the inequities in existing law and to bring our immigration policies in line with the dynamic needs of the country and principles of equity and justice.

We believe also that the Congress should consider the extension of the Refugee Relief Act of 1953 in resolving this difficult refugee problem which resulted from world conflict. To all this we give our wholehearted support.

HUMAN FREEDOM AND PEACE

Under the leadership of President Eisenhower, the United States has advanced foreign policies which enable our people to enjoy the blessings of liberty and peace.

The changes in the international scene have been so great that it is easy to forget the conditions we inherited in 1953.

Peace, so hardly won in 1945, had again been lost. The Korean War, with its tragic toll of more than an eighth of a million American casualties, seemed destined to go on indefinitely. Its material costs and accompanying inflation were undermining our economy.

Freedom was under assault, and despotism was on the march. Armed conflict continued in the Far East, and tensions mounted elsewhere.

The threat of global war increased daily.

International Communism which, in 1945, ruled the 200 million people in the Soviet Union and Baltic States, was conquering so that, by 1952, it dominated more than 700 million people in 15 once-independent nations.

Today. Now, we are at peace. The Korean War has been ended. The Communist aggressors have been denied their goals.

The threat of global war has receded.

The advance of Communism has been checked, and, at key points, thrown back. The once-monolithic structure of International Communism, denied the stimulant of successive conquests, has shown hesitancy both internally and abroad.

The Far East. The Korean War was brought to a close when the Communist rulers were made to realize that they could not win.

The United States has made a Collective Defense Treaty with the Republic of Korea which will exclude, for the future, the Communist miscalculation as to announced American interests and intentions which led to the original aggression.

The United States has made a security Treaty with the Republic of China covering Formosa and the Pescadores; and the Congress, by virtually unanimous action, has authorized the President to employ the armed forces of the United States to defend this area. As a result, the Chinese Communists have not attempted to implement their announced intention to take Formosa by force.

In Indochina, the Republics of Vietnam and Cambodia and Laos are now free and independent nations. The Republic of Vietnam, with the United States assistance, has denied the Communists the gains which they expected from the withdrawal of French forces.

The security of Southeast Asia has now been bolstered by the collective-defense system of SEATO, and its peoples encouraged by the declarations in the Pacific Charter of the principles of equal rights and self-determination of peoples.

The Middle East and Southeast Asia. The Middle East has been strengthened by the defensive unity of the four "northern tier" countries —Turkey, Iraq, Iran and Pakistan—which hold gateways to the vast oil resources upon which depend the industry and military strength of the free world. This was made possible by the liberation of Iran from the grip of the Communist Tudeh Party. Iran has again made its oil reserves available to the world under an equitable settlement negotiated by the United States.

We have maintained, and will maintain, friendly relations with all nations in this vital area, seeking to mediate differences among them, and encouraging their legitimate national aspirations.

Europe. In Western Europe, the scene has been transformed. The Federal Republic of Germany, which until 1953 was denied sovereignty and the opportunity to join the North Atlantic Treaty Organization, has now had full sovereignty restored by the Treaties of 1954, and has become a member of NATO despite the intense opposition of the Soviet Union.

NATO itself has been strengthened by developing reliance upon new weapons and retaliatory power, thus assisting the NATO countries increasingly to attain both economic welfare and adequate military defense.

On our initiative, the political aspects of NATO are being developed. Instead of being merely a military alliance, NATO will provide a means for coordinating the policies of the member states on vital matters, such as the reunification of Germany, the liberation of the satellites, and general policies in relation to the Soviet Union.

Austria has been liberated. The freedom treaty, blocked since 1947 by the Soviet Union, was signed in 1955. For the first time since the end of World War II, Red Army forces in Europe evacuated occupied lands.

The emotion charged dispute between Italy and Yugoslavia about Trieste was settled with the active participation of the United States. The City of Trieste was restored to Italian sovereignty, and United States and British forces withdrawn.

The Spanish base negotiations, which had long languished, were successfully concluded, and close working relations in this important respect established between the United States and Spain.

The Americas. Our good neighbor policy continues to prove its wisdom.

The American Republics have taken effective steps against the cancer of Communism. At the Caracas Conference of March, 1954, they agreed that if International Communism gained control of the political institutions of any American republic, this would endanger them all, and would call for collective measures to remove the danger. This new Doctrine, first proposed by the United States, extends into modern times the principles of the Monroe Doctrine.

A first fruit of the Caracas Doctrine was the expulsion of the Communist regime ruling Guatemala. Today, Guatemala is liberated from Kremlin control. The Organization of American States has grown in vigor. It has acted promptly and effectively to settle hemispheric disputes. In Costa Rica, for the first time in history, international aerial inspection was employed to maintain peace. The Panama Conference was probably the most successful in the long history of the Organization of American States in its promotion of good will, understanding and friendship.

Relations with Soviet Russia. Far-reaching steps have been taken to eliminate the danger of a third world war. President Eisenhower led the way at Geneva. There he impressed the Soviet leaders and the world with the dedication of the United States to peace, but also with its determination not to purchase peace at the price of freedom.

That Summit Conference set new forces into motion. The Soviet rulers professed to renounce the use of violence, which Stalin had made basic in the Communist doctrine. Then followed a repudiation of Stalin, the growth of doctrinal disputes within the Communist Party, and a discrediting of Party authority and its evil power. Forces of liberalism within the Soviet Bloc challenge the brutal and atheistic doctrines of Soviet Communism. For the first time, we see positive evidence that forces of freedom and liberation will inevitably prevail if the free nations maintain their strength, unity and resolution.

The future. We re-dedicate ourselves to the pursuit of a just peace and the defense of human liberty and national independence.

We shall continue vigorously to support the United Nations.

We shall continue our cooperation with our sister states of the Americas for the strengthening of our security, economic and social ties with them.

We shall continue to support the collective-security system begun in 1947 and steadily developed on a bipartisan basis. That system has joined the United States with 42 other nations in common defense of freedom. It has created a deterrent to war which cannot be nullified by Soviet veto.

Where needed, we shall help friendly countries maintain such local forces and economic strength as provide a first bulwark against Communist aggression or subversion. We shall reinforce that defense by a military capacity which, operating in accordance with the United Nations Charter, could so punish aggression that it ceases to be a profitable pursuit.

We will continue efforts with friends and allies to assist the underdeveloped areas of the free world in their efforts to attain greater freedom, independence and self-determination, and to raise their standards of living.

We recognize the existence of a major threat to international peace in the Near East. We support a policy of impartial friendship for the peoples of the Arab states and Israel to promote a peaceful settlement of the causes of tension in that area, including the human problem of the Palestine-Arab refugees.

Progress toward a just settlement of the tragic conflict between the Jewish State and the Arab nations in Palestine was upset by the Soviet Bloc sale of arms to Arab countries. But prospects of peace have now been reinforced by the mission to Palestine of the United Nations Secretary General upon the initiative of the United States.

We regard the preservation of Israel as an important tenet of American foreign policy. We are determined that the integrity of an independent Jewish State shall be maintained. We shall support the independence of Israel against armed aggression. The best hope for peace in the Middle East lies in the United Nations. We pledge our continued efforts to eliminate the obstacles to a lasting peace in this area.

We shall continue to seek the reunification of Germany in freedom, and the liberation of the satellite states—Poland, Czechoslovakia, Hungary, Rumania, Bulgaria, Latvia, Lithuania, Estonia and other, once-free countries now behind the Iron Curtain. The Republican Party stands firmly with the peoples of these countries in their just quest for freedom. We are confident that our peaceful policies, resolutely pursued, will finally restore freedom and national independence to oppressed peoples and nations.

We continue to oppose the seating of Communist China in the United Nations, thus up-holding international morality. To seat a Communist China which defies, by word and deed, the principles of the United Nations Charter would be to betray the letter, violate the spirit and subvert the purposes of that charter. It would betray our friend and ally, the Republic of China. We will continue our determined efforts to free the remaining Americans held prisoner by Communist China.

Recognizing economic health as an indispensable basis of military strength and world peace, we shall strive to foster abroad and to practice at home, policies to encourage productivity and profitable trade.

Barriers which impede international trade and the flow of capital should be reduced on a gradual, selective and reciprocal basis, with full recognition of the necessity to safeguard domestic enterprises, agriculture and labor against unfair import competition. We proudly point out that the Republican Party was primarily responsible for initiating the escape clause and peril point provisions of law to make effective the necessary safeguards for American agriculture, labor and business. We pledge faithful and expeditious administration of these provisions.

We are against any trade with the Communist world that would threaten the security of the United States and our allies.

We recognize that no single nation can alone defend the liberty of all nations threatened by Communist aggression or subversion. Mutual security means effective mutual cooperation. Poverty and unrest in less developed countries make them the target for international communism. We must help them achieve the economic growth and stability necessary to attain and preserve their independence.

Technical and economic assistance programs are effective countermeasures to Soviet economic offensives and propaganda. They provide the best way to create the political and social stability essential to lasting peace.

We will strive to bring about conditions that will end the injustices of nations divided against their will, of nations held subject to foreign domination, of peoples deprived of the right of self-government.

We reaffirm the principle of freedom for all peoples, and look forward to the eventual end of colonialism.

We will overlook no opportunity that, with prudence, can be taken to bring about a progressive elimination of the barriers that interfere with the free flow of news, information and ideas, and the exchange of persons between the free peoples and the captive peoples of the world. We favor the continuance and development of the "exchange-of-persons" programs between free nations.

We approve appropriate action to oppose the imposition by foreign governments of discrimination against United States citizens, based on their religion or race.

We shall continue the bipartisan development of foreign policies. We hold this necessary if those policies are to have continuity, and be regarded by other free nations as dependable.

The Republican Party pledges itself to continue the dynamic, courageous, sound and patriotic policies which have protected and promoted the interests of the United States during the past four years.

In a world fraught with peril, peace can be won and preserved only by vigilance and inspired leadership. In such a world, we believe it is essential that the vast experience of our proven leader, President Dwight D. Eisenhower, continues to guide our country in the achievement and maintenance of a just, honorable and durable peace.

BULWARK FOR THE FREE WORLD—OUR NATIONAL DEFENSE

The military strength of the United States has been a key factor in the preservation of world peace during the past four years. We are determined to maintain that strength so long as our security and the peace of the world require it.

This Administration, within six months after President Eisenhower's inauguration, ended the war in Korea by concluding an honorable armistice. The lesson of that war and our lack of preparedness which brought it about will not be forgotten. Such mistakes must not be repeated.

As we maintain and strengthen the security of this Nation, we shall, consistent with this Administration's dedication to peace, strive for the acceptance of realistic proposals for disarmament and the humanitarian control of weapons of mass destruction.

Our country's defense posture is today a visible and powerful deterrent against attack by any enemy, from any quarter, at any time.

We *have* the strongest striking force in the world—in the air—on the sea—and a magnificent supporting land force in our Army and Marine Corps. Such visible and powerful deterrents must continue to include:

A) A jet-powered, long-range strategic air force, and a tactical air force of the fastest and very latest type aircraft, with a striking capability superior to any other;

B) The most effective guided and ballistic missiles;

C) A modern navy, with a powerful naval aircraft arm prepared to keep the sea lanes open to meet any assignment;

D) An army whose mobility and unit firepower are without equal;

E) Bases, strategically dispersed at home and around the world, essential to all these operations.

We will maintain and improve the effective strength and state of readiness of all these armed forces.

To achieve this objective, we must depend upon attracting to, and retaining in our military services vigorous and well-trained manpower, and upon continuously maintaining in reserve, an enthusiastic and well-informed group of men and women. This will require incentives that will make armed service careers attractive and rewarding. A substantial start has been made toward bolstering the rewards and benefits that accompany a military career. We must continue to provide them.

In order that American youth in our armed services shall be provided with the most modern weapons, we have supported and will continue to support an effective and well-directed program of research and development, staffed by men of the highest caliber and ability in this field. There is no substitute for the best where the lives of our men and the defense of our Nation are concerned.

We fully appreciate the importance of scientific knowledge and its application particularly in the military field.

We pledge ourselves to stimulate and encourage the education of our young people in the sciences with a determination to maintain our technological leadership.

In this age of weapons of inconceivable destructiveness, we must not neglect the protection of the civilian population by all known means, while, at the same time, preparing our armed forces for every eventuality.

We wholeheartedly agree with President Eisenhower that our military defense must be backed by a strong civil defense, and that an effective civil defense is an important deterrent against attack upon our country, and an indispensable reliance should our nation ever be attacked.

We support his proposals for strengthening civil defense, mindful that it has become an effective Government arm to deal with natural disasters.

We shall continue to carry forward, vigorously and effectively, the valued services of the Federal Bureau of Investigation, as well as all other Government intelligence agencies, so as to insure that we are protected at all times against subversive activities. We will never relax our determined efforts to keep our Government, and our people, safely guarded against all enemies from within.

We agree and assert that civilian authority and control over our defense structure and program must be maintained at all times. We believe, without qualification, that in our present Commander-in-Chief, Dwight D. Eisenhower, this Nation possesses a leader equipped by training, temperament, and experience in war and in peace, for both that personal example and that direction of our national defense in which the American people will continue to have confidence, and in which the peoples of all the free world will find an increasing sense of security and of an opportunity for peace.

Veterans

We believe that active duty in the Armed Forces during a state of war or national emergency is the highest call of citizenship constituting a special service to our nation and entitles those who have served to positive assistance to alleviate the injuries, hardships and handicaps imposed by their service.

In recognizing this principle under previous Republican Administrations we established the Veterans Administration. This Republican Administration increased compensation and pension benefits for veterans and survivors to provide more adequate levels and to off-set cost of living

increases that occurred during the most recent Democratic Administration.

We have also improved quality of hospital service and have established a long-range program for continued improvement of such service. We have strengthened and extended survivors' benefits, thus affording greater security for all veterans in the interest of equity and justice.

In advancing this Republican program we pledge:

That compensation for injuries and disease arising out of service be fairly and generously provided for all disabled veterans and for their dependents or survivors;

That a pension program for disabled war veterans in need and for their widows and orphans in need be maintained as long as necessary to assure them adequate income;

That all veterans be given equal and adequate opportunity for readjustment following service, including unemployment compensation when needed, but placing emphasis on obtaining suitable employment for veterans, particularly those disabled, by using appropriate facilities of government and by assuring that Federal employment preference and re-employment rights, to which the veteran is entitled, are received;

That the Veterans Administration be continued as a single independent agency providing veterans services;

That the service-disabled continue to receive first-priority medical services of the highest standard and that non-service disabled war veterans in need receive hospital care to the extent that beds are available.

Guarding and Improving Our Resources

One of the brightest areas of achievement and progress under the Eisenhower Administration has been in resource conservation and development and in sound, long-range public works programing.

Policies of sound conservation and wise development—originally advanced half a century ago under that pre-eminent Republican conservation team of President Theodore Roosevelt and Gifford Pinchot and amplified by succeeding Republican Administrations—have been pursued by the Eisenhower Administration. While meeting the essential development needs of the people, this Administration has conserved and safeguarded our natural resources for the greatest good of all, now and in the future.

Our national parks, national forests and wildlife refuges are now more adequately financed, better protected and more extensive than ever before. Long-range improvement programs, such as Mission 66 for the National Parks system, are now under way, and studies are nearing completion for a comparable program for the National Forests. These forward-looking programs will be aggressively continued.

Our Republican Administration has modernized and vitalized our mining laws by the first major revision in more than 30 years.

Recreation, parks and wildlife. ACHIEVEMENTS: Reversed the 15-year trend of neglect of our National Parks by launching the 10-year, $785 million Mission 66 parks improvement program. Has nearly completed field surveys for a comparable forest improvement program. Obtained passage of the so-called "Week-end Miner Bill." Added more than 400,000 acres to our National Park system, and 90,000 acres to wildlife refuges. Has undertaken well-conceived measures to protect reserved areas of all types and to provide increased staffs and operating funds for public recreation agencies.

We favor full recognition of recreation as an important public use of our national forests and public domain lands.

We favor a comprehensive study of the effect upon wildlife of the drainage of our wetlands.

We favor recognition, by the States, of wildlife and recreation management and conservation as a beneficial use of water.

We subscribe to the general objectives of groups seeking to guard the beauty of our land and to promote clean, attractive surroundings throughout America.

We recognize the need for maintaining isolated wilderness areas to provide opportunity for future generations to experience some of the wilderness living through which the traditional American spirit of hardihood was developed.

Public land and forest resources. ACHIEVEMENTS: Approved conservation programs of many types, including improvement of western grazing lands through reseeding programs, water-spreading systems, and encouragement of soil- and moisture-conservation practices by range users. Returned to the States their submerged

lands and resources of their coasts, out to their historical boundaries—an area comprising about one tenth of the area off the Continental Shelf and about 17 per cent of the mineral resources. Initiated leasing of the Federally owned 83 per cent of the Continental Shelf which is expected ultimately to bring from 6 to 8 billion dollars into the Treasury and already has brought in over 250 million dollars. Enacted new legislation to encourage multiple use of the public domain.

We commend the Eisenhower Administration for its administration of our public lands and for elimination of bureaucratic abuses. We recommend continuing study and evaluation of the advisability of returning unused or inadequately used public lands.

We commend the Administration for expanding forest research and access road construction.

We shall continue to improve timber conservation practices, recreational facilities, grazing management, and watershed protection of our national forests and our public domain.

Minerals. Recognizing that a vigorous and efficient mineral industry is essential to the long-term development of the United States, and to its defense, we believe the Federal Government should foster a long-term policy for the development and prudent use of domestic mineral resources, and to assure access to necessary sources abroad, without dangerously weakening the market for domestic production of defense-essential materials.

We favor reasonable depletion allowances. We favor freedom of mineral producers from unnecessary governmental regulation; expansion of government minerals exploration and research, and establishment of minerals stockpile objectives which will reduce, and, where possible, eliminate foreseeable wartime shortages.

ACHIEVEMENTS: St. Lawrence Seaway and power projects, Colorado River Storage Project, Great Lakes connecting channels, small watershed protection and flood prevention under local control, Mississippi Gulf level canal, extension of water-pollution control program, survey of power potential of Passamaquoddy Bay tides, expansion of small project development for flood control, navigation and reclamation; extension to all 48 States of water facilities act, accelerated research on saline water conversion, authorized planning surveys and construction of more than 200 navigation, flood-control, beach erosion, rivers and harbors, reclamation, and watershed projects throughout the nation, advanced partnership water resource developments in a number of states.

Water resources. Water resource development legislation enacted under the Eisenhower Administration already has ushered in one of the greatest water resource development programs this Nation has ever seen, a soundly-conceived construction program that will continue throughout this Century and beyond.

We recognize that the burgeoning growth of our Nation requires a combination of Federal, State and local water and power development— a real partnership of effort by all interested parties. In no other way can the nation meet the huge and accelerated demands for increasing generating capacity and uses of water, both by urban and agricultural areas. We also are aware that water demands have been accentuated by the ravages of drought, creating emergency conditions in many sections of our country. We commend the Eisenhower Administration for encouraging state and local governments, public agencies, and regulated private enterprise, to participate actively in comprehensive water and power development. In such partnership we are leading the way with great Federal developments such as the Upper Colorado Project and with partnership projects of great importance, some of which have been shelved by the Democratic 84th Congress.

In the marketing of federally produced power we support preference to public bodies and cooperatives under the historic policy of the Congress.

We will continue to press for co-operative solution of all problems of water supply and distribution, reclamation, pollution, flood control, and saline-water conversion.

We pledge legislative support to the arid and semi-arid states in preserving the integrity of their water laws and customs as developed out of the necessities of these regions. We affirm the historic policy of Congress recognizing State water rights, as repeatedly expressed in Federal law over the past 90 years.

We pledge an expansion in research and planning of water resource development programs, looking to the future when it may be necessary to re-distribute water from water-surplus areas to water-deficient areas.

Fisheries. ACHIEVEMENTS: Accelerated research and administrative action to rehabilitate our long-neglected fishing industry. Approval of measures for additional conservation and propagation of fish. Development of the comprehensive program for fisheries management and assistance adopted by the Congress.

We favor continuation of the Eisenhower program to rehabilitate our long-neglected domestic fishing industry.

We advocate protective treaties insuring the United States commercial-fisheries industry against unfair foreign competition.

The Republican Party is acutely aware that a foundation stone of the nation's strength is its wealth of natural resources and the high development of its physical assets. They are the basis of our great progress in 180 years of freedom and of our nation's military and economic might.

We pledge that we will continue the policies of sound conservation and wise development instituted by this Administration to insure that our resources are managed as a beneficial trust for all the people.

For a Brighter Tomorrow

Atomic Energy. The Republican Party pledges continuous, vigorous development of Atomic Energy:

for the defense of our own country and to deter aggression, and

for the promotion of world peace and the enhancement of our knowledge of basic science and its application to industry, agriculture and the healing arts.

From the passage of the first Atomic Energy Act in 1946 to the beginning of this Republican Administration, a stalemate had existed, and only an arms race with the prospect of eventual catastrophe faced the nations of the world.

President Eisenhower has inaugurated and led a strong program for developing the peaceful atom—a program which has captured the imagination of men and women everywhere with its widespread, positive achievements.

The Government and private enterprise are working together on a number of large-scale projects designed to develop substantial quantities of electric power from atomic sources. The first power reactor will be completed next year. More and more private funds are being invested as the Government monopoly is relaxed.

In relaxing its monopoly, Government can stimulate private enterprise to go ahead by taking recognition of the tremendous risks involved and the complexity of the many technical problems that will arise, and assist in those ways that will make advances possible.

The Atomic Energy Commission also is encouraging a vigorous rural electrification program by cooperatives.

Every day, radioactive isotopes are brought more and more into use on farms, in clinics and hospitals, and in industry. The use of isotopes already has resulted in annual savings of hundreds of millions of dollars and the nuclear age has only begun.

It is to the benefit of the United States, as well as to all nations everywhere, that the uses of atomic energy be explored and shared. The Republican Party pledges that it will continue this imaginative, world-embracing program. We shall continue to chart our course so as to fortify the security of the free nations and to further the prosperity and progress of all people everywhere.

DECLARATION OF DEDICATION

With utmost confidence in the future and with justifiable pride in our achievements, the Republican Party warmly greets the dawn of our second century of service in the cause of unity and progress in the Nation.

As the Party of the Young and in glowing appreciation of his dynamic leadership and inspiration, we respectfully dedicate this Platform of the Party of the Future to our distinguished President Dwight D. Eisenhower, and to the Youth of America.

Socialist Party Platform: 1956

The Socialist Party is pledged to building a new, more democratic society in the United States; a society in which human rights come before property rights; a nation which can take its place in a World Federation of Cooperative Commonwealths which will eliminate war, racial antagonism, hunger, disease, poverty and oppression.

The Socialist Party is pledged to building and

to maintaining this new society by democratic means, for without freedom there can be no true socialism and without socialism there can be no enduring freedom.

Socialism is the social ownership and democratic control of the means of production. Social ownership, which includes cooperatives, is not usually government ownership. Democratic control is not administration by the central government but control by the people most directly affected and in the interest of all the people rather than for profit. The American people have already adopted many socialist measures to serve their needs when capitalism, with its profit motive, failed them.

In a big business economy, the claim that "free enterprise" and liberty go hand-in-hand is arrant nonsense. The power of monopoly is a threat to the democratic process. The right of the few to rob the many is a flagrant denial of freedom. Not until the robbery is ended can we have liberty, equality and fraternity.

The Socialist Party is committed to a policy of forthright, deliberate, planned introduction of socialism. Creeping into socialism when capitalism fails does not promote the welfare of the people or preserve democracy and freedom.

The Socialist Party of the United States is dedicated to building socialism in this stronghold of capitalism because, even at its greatest, capitalism fails to satisfy the finest aspirations of its people. For war, it achieved great heights of productivity; for peace, it is incapable of equal performance. The development of the highest living standard in the world cannot excuse the inequality in division of wealth, which means that one family in ten receives an annual income of less than $1,000 and more than two families in ten have less than $2,000 per year. In fact, the lower half of our population receives a smaller share of the total money income of the United States now than it did early in this century.

Our program is international as well as domestic. The American people do not share fairly in the wealth they themselves create; still less have the people of the underdeveloped areas been helped to pull themselves up to the level of decency which alone can provide the stability for enduring peace. The basic purpose of socialist foreign policy is to prevent another world war. The first step is to abolish every form of colonialism, racism and imperialism, wherever it appears, and no matter upon whose toes we tread. The second step is the encouragement of the developing democratic socialism in Asia and the movements for racial justice in Africa.

These policies will have far greater appeal to the hungry and oppressed millions of Asia, Africa, Eastern Europe and Latin America than will military aid and defensive pacts which threaten to involve them in nuclear war. It will provide them with greater benefits than totalitarian Communism can offer, without any of its ugly evils. The democratic challenge to totalitarianism can be made successful only through rejecting imperialism and adopting democratic socialism, thus winning the minds and hearts of the downtrodden and oppressed everywhere. But most important of all we advocate these policies because they are morally right.

In this struggle, American Socialists find their allies around the world in the Socialist International and the Asian Socialist Conference and they look for the strengthening of the United Nations as a step in the development toward federal world government.

American foreign policy must be based on an imaginative campaign for universal disarmament, including the ending of the production of fission and thermo-nuclear weapons, under effective international supervision and control. This is absolutely essential if the living standards of the under-privileged half of the world are to be raised. As long as we spend billions for armaments there is little likelihood that large scale economic aid to underdeveloped nations will be forthcoming. The ending of thermo-nuclear tests is one way in which the United States could demonstrate its sincerity in seeking disarmament. Another way is by the abolition of peacetime military conscription.

The new society for which the Socialist Party strives would organize the American economy to produce for the welfare of the many at home and abroad rather than the profits of the favored few.

Capitalism fails to guarantee basic security to the people. We would establish social insurance with adequate provision for unemployment compensation, old-age pensions and death benefits, and provide for medical care, family allotments and sickness insurance.

Private enterprise threatens the future of the country by the waste or destruction of our irreplaceable natural resources. We would conserve these resources by the most carefully planned use under organizations like the TVA.

Private enterprise inevitably develops giant business and monopolies which threaten the economic or political welfare of the people. Socialists would step in and operate public utilities, basic industry, banks and insurance companies either by genuine cooperatives or by publicly owned and democratically managed corporations. Private enterprise inevitably encourages the recurring collapse of individual capitalist enterprises thus threatening the livelihood of the workers involved. Sectional unemployment—whether by locality or by industry—cannot be tolerated, regardless of how high the general economic level may remain. Partial measures like adequate insurance, retraining for workers, financing movement to new work, may suffice in some situations. But where private enterprise ceased to offer opportunities for productive work, social enterprise must take over and provide them. The right to a job is a basic right which should be guaranteed to all people.

In seeking greater social controls over the American economy, Socialists would guard against the substitution of irresponsible state bureaucracy for irresponsible state bureaucracy. To achieve this we propose that:

Wherever possible, the public enterprise should be at least one step removed from government control, not the patronage-run post office but the TVA is a better form.

Wherever efficient management is possible on a decentralized basis, Socialists prefer this to operation on a national basis.

Wherever the people themselves can organize the needed institution, popular participation should be given preference. Cooperatives should be aided and encouraged to expand.

Wherever a public form of enterprise is set up, various categories of workers in the industry and of consumers must be represented in its control. At all times preservation of freedom of labor organization and of consumer choice is the safeguard of liberty. Social control must extend democracy and not create a new managerial hierarchy.

. . . .

While working towards these Socialist goals, Socialists are acutely aware of other pressing immediate problems which the American people must face in this presidential year.

The first of these is the achievement of full equality for all Americans, regardless of race, sex, creed, color or national origin. We applaud the Supreme Court decisions that separate but equal facilities do not provide the same opportunity for all citizens, whether in regard to education, or elsewhere. We call for the protection of the law for all citizens in exercise of their constitutional liberties, particularly the right to vote.

We oppose any action by Congress which will surrender to the individual states the right to legislate on matters which by their nature should be under the direction of the Federal Government. This includes laws on sedition, as well as legislation affecting interstate commerce.

The second is the protection and improvement of the American standard of living. The growing threat of unemployment, both from automation and from other forces, must be met primarily by increasing workers' wages but also by expanded insurance coverage and by increasing governmental action to influence investment and production. Community needs, such as schools, slum clearance, flood controls, etc., provide a wide area for useful work and stimulus to renewed productivity; we need a Point Five for America.

Taxation policies must be revised to get back to the idea of taxation in accordance with ability to pay.

We favor the establishment of government agencies or cooperatives to assist in the expansion of domestic and export consumption of farm products, to strengthen the family type farm, and to facilitate the shift from farm work to non-farm employment. But we oppose unequivocally any plan to limit the production of food or its destruction in order to keep up prices. In today's hungry world we advocate the production of more, rather than less, food.

While planning to achieve equity for the farmer, we do not forget the farm laborer or the plight of the migrant farm worker. It is essential that they be provided with steady employment, minimum wage standards, maximum hours and working conditions comparable with those of other workers and that they be provided with adequate housing and equal and identical schooling for their children.

The decline of American democracy is attested by the fact that minority parties—old or future— are being driven from the ballot by restrictive legislation; from access to the people by the incredible expense of television and new advertising techniques; and out of public favor by a manufactured conformity which stifles creative statesmanship in majority as well as minority political life.

Trade unions, too, are under attack. We continue to call for repeal of the Taft-Hartley act. So-called "right-to-work" laws passed and pending in various states, pretend to safeguard the rights of the individual to work while actually depriving him of his only real protection on the job—his union shop.

The right to work has another aspect. Where employment of persons might endanger the security of the nation, screening is a natural part of qualification for the position—and most jobs have qualifications attached. But this necessity has been distorted almost beyond recognition. Individuals must not be deprived of the right to work at non-sensitive positions for which training and experience fit them.

The right to hear and answer charges which may affect the livelihood, liberty or citizenship of the individual must be protected by law. We ask elimination of the Committee on Un-American Activities which has abused the Congressional right of investigation. We oppose any congressional investigations into areas of personal belief.

We demand repeal of the Smith Act, which we protested long before its provisions were applied to the Communist Party and when that Party supported its use against other minorities.

. . . . .

Such, in brief, is the platform of the Socialist Party. This program is based on the highest ideals of human brotherhood. It will bring peace instead of war. It will replace fear and hate with goodwill and love. Death and despair will give way to life and hope.

We urge you to join with us in a call for a democratic Socialist economy with production for use, social planning for the benefit of all, equality of opportunity and full recognition of the dignity of every human being.

Socialist Labor Platform for 1956

The Socialist Labor Party of America, in National Convention assembled on the 6th day of May, 1956, reaffirms its previous platform pronouncements and declares:

Humanity stands today on the threshold of a new social order. The old order—capitalism—is doomed; it is an outmoded system shot through with fatal contradictions. For the time being, the capitalist economy is prevented from collapsing by two major props. One is the bubble of consumer credit. The other is government spending for arms—a multi-billion dollar military boondoggling program.

Sooner or later the credit bubble will burst and set in motion the forces leading to economic paralysis. Society then will be confronted by an economic crisis of the first magnitude. In this crisis the warehouses will groan with unsold surpluses while the mass of the people suffer increasing want. Unemployment among the useful producers—the working class—will be on a scale that will make the depression of the 'thirties seem mild by comparison. And business failures will spread like a plague among the petty capitalists, while the capitalist giants, the great corporate empires, concentrate even more economic power in their power-greedy hands.

H-Bomb Stalemate v. Ruling-Class Desperation

A world war that quickly consumed the piled-up surpluses enabled capitalism to extricate itself from the depression of the 'thirties. And war remains today the only real alternative the capitalists have to ultimate economic collapse. But war in 1956 means an H-bomb war, a war of annihilation and therefore a war that is suicidal not only to capitalism, but to civilization and to much, if not all, of the human race. Practically, capitalism today can postpone economic breakdown only by plunging the whole world into a veritable hell of hydrogen-bomb destructiveness and deadly radioactivity.

At the Geneva conference the political heads of the two rival imperialisms—Soviet Russia and the United States—solemnly agreed that war in these circumstances is unthinkable. Their agreement underscored the fact of atomic stalemate. But atomic stalemate, however, is no protection against a catastrophic third World War. Ruling classes, faced with the breakdown of their system and the consequent loss of their property and class privileges, become desperate. And desperate men do desperate things. It is cause for the most sober reflection that today a few hundred top capitalists, and their military and political pawns —or their imperialist adversaries, the Russian despots—can, when their material interests so demand, set in motion fateful forces that could destroy the world.

Socialism Abolishes Bureaucracy

The Socialist Labor Party declares that the only alternative to social ruin and possible atomic war is the abolition of capitalism and all forms of class rule and the establishment of Socialism. We must add that bona fide Socialism has nothing in common with the bureaucratic despotism which, despite the "collective leadership" that has replaced Stalin's one-man rule, masquerades as "Socialism" in Soviet Russia. Nor does Socialism mean "making the politician the boss." Socialism, as Karl Marx conceived it, as Daniel De Leon, the great American Marxist, developed it, and as advocated by the Socialist Labor Party, is a society of industrial democracy in which the factories, mills, mines, railroads and land, etc., are owned collectively by all the people, where production is carried on for use instead of for sale and profit, and where the industries are operated and administered democratically by the workers themselves, organized in Socialist Industrial Unions.

In the "Iron Curtain" countries the bureaucrat is the master. In the West, too, the bureaucrat is tending to replace the capitalist as the overlord of modern society. The Socialist Industrial Union Government, as proposed by the Socialist Labor Party, is in reality the only form of social and industrial administration that eliminates both capitalists and bureaucrats and gives the workers of brain and brawn a collective mastery of their tools and products.

Socialism Will Cleanse Society!

Socialism is the answer to all social problems. Socialism is the cure for every evil spawned by the capitalist class rule:

It is the cure for recurring war because it eliminates the competition for markets and raw materials that is the basic cause of war and brings universal economic cooperation, thus creating a foundation for a durable peace.

It is the cure for recurring depression because it replaces capitalist production for sale with production for human needs, thus freeing social production from the anarchy and restrictions of private ownership and a capricious market.

It is the answer to the threat of technological unemployment—a threat underscored by the rapid spread of automation—because democratic Socialist control of industry insures that, instead of kicking workers out of their jobs, new machines will kick hours out of the working day.

It is the cure for social strife and the class struggle because Socialism terminates exploitation of man by man and creates the economic basis of collective interests essential to social harmony.

It is the cure for race prejudice because it cleanses society of the sordid material interests that profit from fomenting racism and creates the cooperative climate for human brotherhood.

Socialism is the answer to crime and juvenile delinquency, too, and to the alarming spread of mental illness, alcoholism, dope addiction, and other similar manifestations of capitalist insanity, for it will replace irrational, inhuman relationships with rational, human ones.

For a Better World!

To bring to birth this sane society of peace, abundance and freedom, the Socialist Labor Party appeals to the working class of America, and to all other enlightened and social-minded citizens, to support its principles at the polls by voting for the candidates of the Socialist Labor Party. It appeals to all enlightened elements of our population to repudiate the Republican and Democratic parties, which are the Siamese twins of capitalism. It appeals to them to repudiate the self-styled "radicals" and "liberals" whose platforms consist of reform demands, measures that are meant to sweetscent capitalist rule, and that, when granted by decadent capitalism, are in fact concealed measures of reaction.

Finally, the Socialist Labor Party appeals to the working class to repudiate the present unions. All of them accept capitalism as a finality, and are under the domination and control of labor

lieutenants of the capitalist class. It calls upon the workers to build a new union based squarely on working-class interests, one which has Socialism as its goal. And it calls upon them to build the integral Socialist Industrial Union as the only power capable of enforcing the Socialist ballot and of assuming the administration of social production.

This is the peaceful and civilized way to accomplish the Socialist revolution in America.

The issue in this campaign—the burning issue confronting mankind—is Socialism v. capitalism. Until it is resolved mankind's aspirations for the abundant life, in liberty and happiness, are doomed to frustration.

Unite with us to save society from catastrophe —and to set an example in free industrial self-government for all mankind! Unite with us to establish the democratic Socialist Republic of Peace, Plenty and International Brotherhood!

Socialist Workers Party 1956 Election Platform

Mankind stands at the threshold of an era in which human culture can rise to unprecedented heights. Giant leaps in technology, ranging from the mechanization of agriculture to the control of atomic energy, have today made it possible to produce enough to meet all the needs of all the people. Now within reach are the means to eliminate human want in food, housing, health care, to satisfy all the necessities of life.

Across this brilliant prospect lies the dark shadow of a parallel leap in militarism. Nearly one-quarter of the national income is taken in taxes, mainly to create a vast war machine. Natural resources and manpower are diverted from useful production and wasted on instruments of destruction. Living standards and democratic rights stand in peril before the despotism of war. And in every mind lurks a terrible fear of the death-dealing horrors of the hydrogen bomb.

The role of militarism as the fundamental feature of American foreign policy is determined by the world conflict of rival social systems. The capitalist class wants to use America's power to prevent the birth of a world socialist order. The issue is posed: Shall capitalist exploitation of natural resources and productive labor remain dominant? Or shall mankind throw off the fetters of outlived capitalism and advance to a system of planned economy capable of eliminating human want?

Colonial Independence Struggle

A universal demand for industrialization has arisen throughout the world. People everywhere seek the benefit of technological progress to improve their living standards and raise their cultural level. The main obstacle to progress in the underdeveloped countries has been the direct or indirect domination of foreign capitalist powers. Revolutionary struggles for independence, stemming from this imperialist domination, have erupted in country after country.

The indomitable determination of the colonial and semi-colonial peoples to win their independence is today typified by the heroic struggles of the people of Cyprus and Algeria. Egypt's fight for the right to nationalize the Suez Canal and to build the Aswan dam symbolizes the aspirations of the underdeveloped countries to lay new foundations for economic and social progress.

The colonial revolution can be successful only through fusion with the working class struggle against capitalism. It must gravitate toward the socialist forms of nationalized property and planned economy which open the way to rapid development of the productive forces. This tendency of the colonial revolution to become transformed into a socialist revolution has reached its highest manifestation in the case of China. Starting as an independence struggle against imperialism, the third Chinese revolution has transformed the country into an anti-capitalist world power and its rise, together with the extension of Soviet property forms to Eastern Europe, has already abolished capitalism on one-third of the globe.

Targets of Imperialism

At the same time the Soviet Union has rapidly risen to the status of a great industrial power, second only to the United States. Within it exists a working class almost 50 million strong, a mighty force now gaining in self-confidence and asserting its own rights against the usurping bureaucracy. The repudiation of the hated dictator Stalin and the crisis now shaking the world Stalinist movement mark the beginning of a political revolution to establish workers democracy in the Soviet sphere. With that political transformation the way will be opened for a new upsurge in the world socialist revolution.

The anti-capitalist struggles, stemming from a fundamental drive for ever-higher living standards, for freedom and national independence, are the targets against which American foreign policy is aimed. The imperialists are arming to turn back the revolutionary tide and reconquer the world for capitalist exploitation. The bipartisan gang of Republicans and Democrats are forming military pacts with hated dictators and colonial despots. They are forging a chain of American military bases throughout the world. Never before has there been such a vast peacetime military expansion.

Puppets of Wall Street

Every alliance formed by the American capitalist government is aimed directly at the revolutionary masses abroad. In Iran the government backed by the people was forcefully overthrown with imperialist aid in order to block nationalization of the oil reserves and perpetuate exploitation of these natural resources by the capitalist oil cartel. The dictatorial Armas regime in Guatemala received thinly-veiled American support to overthrow the constitutional government by force when mass pressures began to threaten the super-profits of the United Fruit Company, an American corporation.

In country after country similarly discredited governments are imposed on the people and propped up as direct or indirect agencies of American imperialism. In return they are expected to guarantee special privileges for United States capital investments in these lands in violation of the interests of the masses. As a result the same old colonialism against which the peoples are in revolt is continued in open or concealed form. Where camouflaged forms of imperialist domination fail, resort must be had to naked force. A current example is the threat to overturn nationalization of the Suez Canal through armed intervention.

Truman's use of the United Nations as a cover in the Korean invasion revealed its true role as a front organization for imperialism and exploded the myth that the UN can serve as an instrument for peace. No less illusory is the hope that the hydrogen bomb by its very destructiveness will outlaw war.

Revolt Against Status Quo

The war drive has been slowed down primarily by the revolutionary gains abroad. World capitalism has been dealt a series of setbacks and defeats weakening its power in relation to the anticapitalist forces. Revolutionary China has emerged as a factor of great weight in world politics. These reverses have compelled the imperialists to mask their war aims through hypocritical peace maneuvers but militarism remains the ultimate instrument of capitalist rule. In the attempt to achieve world domination American imperialism won't hesitate to risk atomic war at whatever cost to humanity.

The Kremlin bureaucrats, although forced to repudiate Stalin, nevertheless continue his basic policy. They advocate "peaceful coexistence" as the answer to war. Their aim is to preserve the status quo. But the status quo is what the masses the world over are rebelling against. They are in revolt against capitalist exploitation and oppression, as well as against the authoritarian bureaucracy in the Soviet orbit. The struggle for socialism is a continuous, uninterrupted struggle against the status quo.

In the hope of making a diplomatic deal with imperialism the Soviet rulers undertake to derail revolutions in the capitalist sphere, substituting capitalist reform policies for revolutionary socialism. Stalin's heirs seek coexistence with imperialism in order to retain their bureaucratic privileges and the power to repress the struggle for workers democracy in the Soviet sphere. Using the Communist Parties to disarm the masses politically in the struggle against capitalism, they undermine the revolutionary process which stands as the only effective obstacle to imperialist war.

SWP Fights War Program

The Socialist Workers Party opposes the war program of American imperialism. It combats the Stalinist policy of curbing the anti-capitalist struggle in an effort to appease imperialism. The foreign policy of the SWP aims to align the United States with the world social transformations now in process, mobilizing our country's full power in support of the advance to a world system of planned economy.

Such a foreign policy requires in the first instance a basic change in the United States itself. Class-collaboration with the capitalist parties must give way to independent working class political action through labor's own party. The capitalist government must be replaced by a workers and farmers government. To serve these needs the vanguard of the working class must advance a principled socialist program flowing from the economic and political realities on the world arena and within this country.

The American economy is based primarily on arms expenditures. Boom conditions have prevailed consistently in industries central to war production but mere preparations for war have not been enough to sustain capitalist production as a whole. Despite the military build-up in the cold war a serious economic decline began in 1949. Overcome temporarily by American entry into the Korean war, the slump reappeared in 1953-54 after the fighting in Korea ended.

Danger of Economic Crisis

The country has for the time being been pulled out of the slump by creating record consumer debts through installment and mortgage buying. So great is the expansion that the overall consumer debt has climbed above total personal savings and the rate of continued increase is outstripping the rise in personal income. As the workers thus go deeper into debt, the monopoly corporations are coining record profits in what for them is genuine prosperity.

War spending and credit expansion tend to increase inflationary pressures. The consumers price index stands at the highest level on record and shows every sign of a continued climb. At the same time a chronic decline has hit industries like coal, textiles and shipbuilding. Periodic slumps impair employment in such industries as auto. A sag in the farm equipment field reflects the fundamental decline in agriculture. Inflationary pressures and the threat of unemployment thus appear side by side, spelling out the danger of economic crisis as the alternative to war under capitalism.

Subcurrents of Discontent

For the present, boom conditions still predominate. A high level of employment exists despite the serious trouble spots. Most workers accept capitalism and continue to rely on the capitalist politicians in government but with anxieties as to the future. The workers fear war, yet they also fear unemployment and feel the need of war production to assure them jobs. They see their economic security being destroyed by automation, decentralization of industries, corporation mergers, runaway plants and the periodic production slumps. On the job anger is generated by the speedup.

The subcurrents of discontent within the prevailing conservative mood come to the fore when the workers are forced on strike by the corporations. Unusual militancy is shown, especially among younger workers, Negroes and other minorities and women workers who are in the least secure position, who generally have the most grievances. Some of the most determined struggles have been waged by the Southern workers who want to win union protection and end the wage differential. Industrialization of the South is having a strong economic and political impact on white and Negro workers alike. Their common class interests, sharply revealed in struggle against the corporations, will tend to cut across color lines as happened in the rise of the CIO. Foreshadowed in this process is the stormy rise of unionism below the Mason-Dixon line.

Negro Struggle for Equality

Also from the South has come a sharp leap in the Negro struggle for equality. The Montgomery bus boycott has produced a powerful new weapon for mass action by the Negro people in support of their democratic demands. The Montgomery freedom fighters have shown unbreakable solidarity, a grim fighting mood and tremendous staying power. Their long battle has inspired the Negro masses nationally and is producing a more militant type of leadership. Inspired by the independence struggles of the colored peoples in the colonial countries, the Negro people of America are now fighting with determination to win economic, political and social equality.

The White Citizens Councils organized to combat the Negro movement are actually the tool of the bankers, industrialists and big planters. Their white supremacist program involves more than the anti-democratic denial of Negro equality. The WCC is deliberately intensifying racial antagonisms in order to split the white and Negro workers to block unionization of the South. Taking advantage of the AFL-CIO failure to get a union drive going, the WCC uses all forms of pressure to recruit white workers in the open shop plants and indoctrinate them against giving Negroes union rights. Where unions now exist the WCC campaigns for a separate all-white Southern Federation.

The white workers of the nation therefore have a direct stake in the fight of the Negro people to win their rights, just as the Negroes need labor's aid to achieve their aims. Unionization of the South, an open-shop haven for runaway plants, is vital to labor nationally but it cannot be accomplished without the support of the Negro workers who justly demand full equality. A need therefore arises to smash the Southern political system of white supremacy and the open shop not only to win Negro equality but also for the workers to advance economically and politically. This need leads directly toward a political alliance of labor and the Negro people.

Yet another labor ally is appearing on the land. Mechanization of agriculture is putting a squeeze on the small farmers. They are caught between a rise in capital investment for mechanization and a decline in farm commodity prices due to the capitalist crisis of overproduction. The small farmer is gradually going under, farm units are getting bigger and fewer, the monopolists are expanding their holdings.

In trying to survive mechanization the small farmers feel themselves much in the same position as the industrial workers trying to hold their jobs in the face of automation. To protect themselves they seek government assistance to assure the cost of production plus a fair rate of annual income. The government has offered little more than token aid to the small farmer, solving few of his problems. For the big capitalist farmer, however, the same program provides a neat profit since his unit costs are lower because he operates on a larger scale. Government policy has veered more and more in the direction of the big operator's needs with less and less regard for the plight of the little man.

As a result the small farmers are beginning to modify their political outlook. They are breaking with the old-time farm organizations dominated by the big operators and forming new setups designed to press for a government policy meeting their own needs. They are also moving toward collaboration with organized labor and would constitute potential allies of an independent labor party.

Migratory Workers Need Help

The growth of monopoly on the land has uprooted large numbers of people who have become migratory farm workers. They travel from area to area working as seasonal help on the corporation farms. Paid only a starvation wage, whole families are compelled to labor in the fields, mother and children alongside the father. Seasonal gaps in employment reduce their average earnings below $1,000 a year. Yet they are generally denied the benefits of existing social legislation.

These migratory workers badly need the help of organized labor to build the unions they have started in an effort to improve their lot. Especially they need the benefit of a labor party to compel government action for correction of the social wrongs they now suffer.

Meaning of Witch Hunt

The capitalist politicians are fully aware that the industrial working class, the strongest social force in the nation, would be unbeatable in a political alliance with the Negro people, agricultural labor and small farmers. They also know that for labor to break with capitalist politics would mean the doom of capitalism. To ward off this danger and maintain the capitalist monopoly in politics and in government, they have launched a witch hunt against radicalism. A political blacklist of "subversives" has been maintained to weed out anti-capitalist tendencies in the mass movement. "Loyalty" purges have been conducted as a terror device to compel mass conformity with capitalist policies. Starting against federal employees, the attack has spread to all spheres of national life.

Mounting public opposition to the witch hunt and several limited legal victories against it have slowed down the attack to a certain degree. But the laws and executive orders on which the assault is based remain in effect. Persecution of organizations and individuals continues. A new law has been enacted to undermine the Fifth Amendment. Penalties under the thought-control Smith Act have been stiffened. Passage in 1954 of the Humphrey-Butler law was intended to do more than outlaw the Communist Party. This wholly anti-democratic law, proscribing a political party for the first time in American history, also set the stage for attacks on the unions themselves as "subversive." Such strikebreaking, union-busting smears have already been hurled at two unions, the United Electrical Workers and the Mine, Mill and Smelter Workers.

Need for Political Action

Basic to the war program are ultimate cuts in real wages and reductions in social benefits which are bound to provoke mass resistance. The capitalists are therefore moving in stages to weaken the unions through governmental attacks and direct corporation assaults. The Taft-Hartley Act restricts the economic power of the unions. Enactment of "Right to Work" laws in the states intensifies the government pressures against labor. Corporation-provoked strikes in industry, often lockouts in affect, result from rejection of moderate union demands and from corporation counter-demands intended to impair wages and conditions, weaken union job control and sharpen the speedup.

When this combined assault by the corporations and the capitalist government is intensified labor will no longer be able to defend itself through union action alone. Realizing they will have to fight on the political field, the union officials engineered the AFL-CIO merger primarily to strengthen labor politically. Then they showed their fatal weakness as working class leaders by keeping the union power tied to the Democratic Party, hoping thereby to secure a return to the New Deal days.

Role of Labor Bureaucracy

The union officials base their expectations on the prospects of a permanent war economy. They count on war production to prevent a deep unemployment crisis. In return for their support of the war program they expect capitalist concessions to appease the union membership. With this outlook, stemming from their social position as a privileged bureaucracy, the union officials spread capitalist ideology in labor's ranks. They retard the development of class consciousness among the workers and oppose class struggle policies in the unions.

Although most workers instinctively distrust the

Republicans as the party of Big Business, general illusions remain that they can solve their problems through the Democratic Party. Alongside these illusions, doubts about the Democratic Party are appearing as shown by a trend toward class polarization in political action.

A growing tendency has arisen among the workers to choose between the capitalist politicians as a class and to intervene in capitalist politics as a labor faction. This trend reflects an awakening political consciousness of the greatest significance. The workers realize their economic security can be guaranteed and their social welfare advanced mainly by action at the government level. They are also coming to understand their own social power if they act together politically as a class and to understand the need for them to use their power to secure government action.

For Independent Labor Party

As against the workers needs and aspirations, the Democratic Party serves the basic interests of the capitalist class. Its New Deal reputation was forced upon it in the first place out of necessity to ward off the mass radicalization following the 1929 market crash. Since the New Deal became transformed into a War Deal during the latter part of the Thirties not one major social reform has been introduced. The Democrats have broken their repeated promises to repeal the Taft-Hartley Act and pass civil rights legislation. The 1956 Democratic convention voted down a proposed pledge to enforce the Supreme Court decision against segregation. In fact the Democrats have shown real action only in their efforts to out-bid the Republicans on military appropriations for the bipartisan war program and in their support of the bi-partisan witch hunt.

Already implicit in the Democratic Party policy are the conditions leading to a union break with capitalist politics. The assault on labor has been deepening ever since the beginning of the cold war. The workers' determination to defend their living standards was dramatically revealed by the strike actions during the Korean war, conducted in defiance of the Truman administration. The conflict between capital and labor has become more and more political in character. In every showdown both the Democrats and Republicans have stood on the side of capital, their policies differing only in degree, not in basic content.

Under these conditions a class struggle program backed up by militant leadership could soon prepare the way for an advance to independent labor political action.

Communist Party Betrayal

The Communist Party policy of playing Democratic Party politics cuts squarely across this objective process. It helps tie the workers politically to the class enemy and serves to hold the Negro people in a coalition with the white supremacists. Mass demands remain limited to a capitalist reform program and the monopoly capitalists are permitted to retain unchallenged control of the government. This policy has nothing whatever in common with Leninist principles of class struggle. It violates the basic interest of the workers, Negro people and small farmers in a transparent effort to serve the Kremlin's foreign policy of "co-existence."

To enter Democratic Party politics on the pretext of helping to organize a labor faction in a capitalist party only feeds mass illusions that capitalism can be reformed and retards the break with capitalist politics. The resulting mis-education delays the fusion of the socialist program with the mass power of organized labor in an independent political party fighting for socialism.

SWP Tells the Truth

It is the duty of socialists to tell the class truth. The workers can defend their interests only outside the framework of the capitalist political parties and in class struggle against them. The toilers of America have nothing in common with the capitalist class but they have everything in common with the revolutionary masses of the world against whom capitalism is preparing a war of conquest.

To be combatted are the union bureaucracy, the conservative Negro leaders and all other elements within the mass movement who support the foreign policy of the capitalist government. To be combatted are the policies of the Communist Party seeking to preserve the status quo, thus giving outlived capitalism a new lease on life. Only those political tendencies aligning themselves against capitalism through a policy of independent working class political action are progressive and deserving of support.

In the 1956 elections only the Socialist Workers

Party presents a principle, realistic vehicle for anti-capitalist political action through support of its national ticket—Farrell Dobbs for president and Myra Tanner Weiss for vice-president—and through support of its local candidates. In line with the fundamental objectives toward which the labor and socialist movement must strive the SWP candidates are running on this platform:

1. FOREIGN POLICY

Take the war-making powers out of the hands of Congress and the President. Let the people vote through a nation-wide referendum on the question of war or peace. Withdraw all troops from foreign soil. Halt all nuclear weapons tests.

No secret diplomacy. Abolish all military alliances. Recognize the government of revolutionary China. End all trade restrictions against anti-imperialist countries. Hands off Egypt.

Support the right of all peoples to a government of their own choice, including the right to abolish capitalism and replace it with a system of planned economy.

Solidarity with all colonial and socialist revolutions against imperialism and with the struggles of the workers in the Soviet sphere for the establishment of workers democracy.

2. ECONOMIC SECURITY AND SOCIAL WELFARE

For the 30 hour week. Reduce the hours of work with no reduction in take-home pay. Jobless benefits at full union rates for the entire period of unemployment. Government operation under workers control of all production facilities made idle by mergers, decentralization, runaways and production cutbacks. Abolish the speedup through union control of production speeds by majority vote of the workers involved.

Guarantee women workers equal pay for equal work; the right to a job and full seniority rights in upgrading; maternity care and federally-financed day nurseries and summer camps for children.

Adequate old-age pensions. Free medical care and hospitalization. Full disability benefits. A government-guaranteed college education for all youth.

An escalator clause on all wages, unemployment compensation, pensions and other benefits, with taxes to be included in computing living costs.

3. DEMOCRATIC RIGHTS

Repeal the Taft-Hartley and Humphrey-Butler Acts, the "Right to Work" laws and all other federal, state and city anti-labor laws. No restrictions on the right to organize, strike and picket. No government interference in the unions.

Abolish the "subversive" list. Repeal the McCarran Internal Security and Immigration laws. Halt all deportations. Repeal the Smith Act and grant amnesty to all victims of this thought-control law. Abolish the "loyalty" oaths and "loyalty" purges. Repeal the law abridging the Fifth Amendment. Abolish the House un-American Committee and the Senate Internal Security Committee. Halt all political prosecutions for contempt and perjury based on the testimony of stool-pigeons. No political tampering with pensions or other social benefits.

Liberalize the election laws.

4. RIGHTS OF MINORITIES

Full economic, political and social equality to the Negro people and to all other minority peoples. Solidarity with all mass actions of the embattled Negro freedom fighters. For the immediate enforcement and implementation of the Supreme Court decision against segregation.

Enact and enforce legislation to abolish lynching, the poll tax and all forms of segregation. Create an FEPC with full powers of enforcement. Put a stop to police brutality.

Combat all forms of anti-Semitism.

5. FARM POLICY

Establish a federal farm program to guarantee the cost of production on all farm commodities to working farmers to be operated under the control of their own representatives. Limit government price supports to small farmers only. Set up a federal all-risk crop insurance program with the premiums to be figured in the cost-of-production program. No limitation on crops so long as a single person remains hungry. Government food subsidies for families living on sub-standard diets.

Low cost, long term government credits to small farmers for modernization of production facilities. A moratorium on repayment of distress loans until the farm problem is solved. Expand rural electrification. A federal program for soil conservation and flood control. No taxes on sav-

ings of cooperatives. A federal ban on all speculation in farm commodities.

Abolish sharecropping and landlordism; the
land to those who work it.

6. Housing and Public Works

Declare a national housing emergency and
initiate a program to erect 20 million low-rent
housing units. Rigid rent controls under the
supervision of tenants committees. Build schools,
hospitals and other public needs in adequate
supply. Finance all public works from funds now
allocated for arms expenditures.

7. Taxation

Tax the rich, not the poor. Repeal all payroll
and sales taxes. Abolish all forms of hidden taxes.
No tax on incomes under $7,500 a year. A 100%
tax on all incomes over $25,000 a year. A 100%
tax on all profits on war goods.

8. Military Policy

Stop the draft. Abolish the officers caste. Full
democratic rights to the ranks, including election
of their own officers and collective bargaining
in defense of their interests. Union wages for all
servicemen.

9. Government Ownership of Industry

Nationalize the banks, basic industries, food
trusts and all natural resources, including nuclear
power. Operate all these facilities in the interests
of the producers and consumers through democratically-elected committees of workers and technicians. Institute a system of planned economy.

10. Independent Political Action

Break all ties with capitalist politics. Form an
independent labor party based on the unions and
embracing the Negro people and working farmers.
Create a Workers and Farmers government to reorganize America on a socialist basis.

Key to Political Parties

AKN	American (Know Nothing) (1856) (1888)		NS	National Silver (1896)
AM	Anti-Monopoly (1884)		P	Prohibition (1872–1956)
APN	American Prohibition National (1884)		PA	Progressive Political Action (1924)
C	Workers (Communist) (1928–1940) (1948)		PF	People's (Fusion Faction) (1900)
CN	Christian Nationalists (1948–1952)		PP	People's (Populists) (1892–1908)
CU	Constitutional Union (1860)		PR	Progressive (1912) (1948–1952)
D	Democratic (1840–1956)		R	Republican (1856–1956)
DB	Democratic (Breckenridge Faction) (1860)		S	Socialist (1904–1956)
FD	Free Democratic (1852)		SD	Social Democratic (1900)
FL	Farmer-Labor (1920) (1928)		SL	Socialist Labor (1892–1956)
FS	Free Soil (1848)		SOD	Democratic (Straight-Out) (1872)
G	Greenback (1876–1884)		SR	Silver Republican (1900)
I	Independence (1908)		SRT	States' Rights (1948)
L	Liberty (1844)		SW	Socialist Workers (1948–1956)
LF	La Follette (1924)		U	Union (1936)
LR	Labor Reform (1872)		UNL	Union Labor (1888)
LRP	Liberal Republican (1872)		UTL	United Labor (1888)
N	National (1896)		W	Whig (1844–1856)
ND	National Democratic (1896)			

Subject Index

Index of Names